Employment Law

James Holland LLB, PhD, Barrister

Professor of Employment Law, Head of the Law School, University of the West of England, Bristol

and

Stuart Burnett MA, LLM, Barrister

Formerly Director of Operations, EEF Western, Visiting Lecturer, University of the West of England, Bristol

OXFORD
UNIVERSITY PRESS

OXFORD

UNIVERSITY PRESS

Great Clarendon Street, Oxford ox2 6DP

Oxford University Press is a department of the University of Oxford.
It furthers the University's objective of excellence in research, scholarship,
and education by publishing worldwide in

Oxford New York

Auckland Cape Town Dar es Salaam Hong Kong Karachi
Kuala Lumpur Madrid Melbourne Mexico City Nairobi
New Delhi Shanghai Taipei Toronto

With offices in

Argentina Austria Brazil Chile Czech Republic France Greece
Guatemala Hungary Italy Japan Poland Portugal Singapore
South Korea Switzerland Thailand Turkey Ukraine Vietnam

Oxford is a registered trademark of Oxford University Press
in the UK and in certain other countries

Published in the United States
by Oxford University Press Inc., New York

British Library Cataloguing in Publication Data

Data available

Typeset by Laserwords Private Limited, Chennai, India
Printed in Great Britain
on acid-free paper by
Ashford Colour Press Limited, Gosport, Hampshire

978–0–19–956127–8

1 3 5 7 9 10 8 6 4 2

Employment Law

OUTLINE CONTENTS

DETAILED CONTENTS

PREFACE

This book is designed for use on the various Legal Practice Courses offered throughout the country. In writing the book we have tried to take into account the comments received from colleagues in other institutions concerning the particular needs of their courses as well as practitioners who also use the text, so that we hope we have at least pleased some of the people for some of the time. Each chapter deals with a specific area of employment law, but we have attempted throughout the text to show the overlap that exists between the common law and statutory rights and which pervades the subject so as to recreate the concerns that have to be foremost in a solicitor's mind when advising a client.

The book concentrates on what is usually termed 'individual employment law', touching on trade union matters only where they relate directly to this theme. Individual employment law nevertheless covers an extensive range of activities, so that we have sought to weight the chapters according to two main criteria: first, the need to address the concerns of both corporate and private clients; secondly, according to the workload of the courts and tribunals. Further, we have tried to identify the areas which cause students most concern and provide practical guidance on how these problems may be resolved.

We have had to make a key decision in this edition (breaking our own rules of only dealing with changes to the law which are operative on 1 October). At the time of writing, the latest Employment Bill is making its way through Parliament. It will not contain large-scale reforms of employment law, but it will do away with the ill-conceived 2004 Dispute Resolution Regulations. These overly-complicated rules were condemned by practitioners, personnel officers, academics and employment judges alike. Their removal was recommended in the Gibbons Report in 2007 and they are due to disappear in April 2009 when the Employment Act becomes law. Knowing this, and thinking of the timing of most LPC courses, we have removed the rules from this edition and provided as much information as we can on the proposed new rules. If something unexpected happens so that these unwanted guests stay on a little longer we will publish updating material through the Online Resource Centre. One significant element with all this is the re-appearance of the 'flared trousers' theory of law whereby everything comes back into fashion at some stage: practitioners and lecturers will welcome back (perhaps) the old *Polkey* rules on deciding fairness (dealt with in Chapter 10).

In 1998 industrial tribunals were renamed employment tribunals and now, since the last edition, tribunal chairmen have become employment judges. This is long overdue and we look forward to the next re-naming—possibly with imperial connotations.

We would like to offer our thanks to the many people who have helped us with this and previous editions. At UWE, Bristol: to Tim Angell and Carol Crowdy for their help in ploughing through various drafts, and to our past students on the LPC. At the EEF: to practitioners and former colleagues for all their assistance and suggestions. We would also like to acknowledge the comments received from our colleagues in other LPC-provider institutions. We hope that we have incorporated the points raised.

We would also like to express our gratitude to all the firms who have participated in the various surveys we have conducted over the years, many of which went well beyond merely supplying us with examples of their drafting practice.

Our thanks as usual to the publishers for their patience and encouragement and, specifically, to Helen Davis for all her work on this edition. Finally, we would also like to recognise the work of Alistair MacQueen, former Managing Director of Blackstone Press—who originally published this work. Sadly, Alistair died in September 2008. It is not an exaggeration to say he changed the world of legal publishing. He was a gregarious and generous man who will be missed by all who knew him.

The law is stated as at 1 October 2008.

James Holland
Stuart Burnett
Bristol

Personal note: Stuart has decided to step down from co-writing this text so this edition sees his last contribution (after some 16 years). I would like to record my appreciation for all his contributions in making this book the success it has been. We have worked together in various organisations and on many cases, industrial disputes and employment projects, on and off, for 30 years and I will miss working with him. The joys of tackling the intricacies of discrimination law and redundancy provisions were clearly outweighed by the prospect of lazing on some sunlight beach. I cannot think why.

James Holland

ABBREVIATIONS

ACAS	Advisory, Conciliation and Arbitration Service
art.	Article
Convention	European Convention on Human Rights
CRE	Commission for Racial Equality
DDA	Disability Discrimination Act 1995
DPA	Data Protection Act 1998
DRC	Disability Rights Commission
DTI	Department of Trade and Industry
EAT	Employment Appeal Tribunal
EC	European Community
ECJ	European Court of Justice
EDT	effective date of termination
EOC	Equal Opportunities Commission
EPA	Equal Pay Act 1970
EPCA	Employment Protection (Consolidation) Act 1978
ERA 1996	Employment Rights Act 1996
ERA 1999	Employment Relations Act 1999
ERDRA	Employment Rights (Dispute Resolution) Act 1998
ETA	Employment Tribunals Act 1996
ET Regs	Employment Tribunals (Constitution and Rules of Procedure) Regulations 2001
ET Rules	Employment Tribunals Rules of Procedure 2001
GMD	genuine material difference
GMF	genuine material factor
HRA 1998	Human Rights Act 1998
HSE	Health and Safety Executive
NDC	National Disability Council
NMWA 1998	National Minimum Wage Act 1998
para.	paragraph
PHI	permanent health insurance
PHR	pre-hearing review
PIDA	Public Interest Disclosure Act 1998
PTW Regs 2000	Part-time Workers (Prevention of Less Favourable Treatment) Regulations 2000
r.	rule
reg.	regulation
RRA	Race Relations Act 1976
s.	section
sch.	schedule

SDA	Sex Discrimination Act 1975
TULRCA	Trade Union and Labour Relations (Consolidation) Act 1992
TUPE	Transfer of Undertakings (Protection of Employment) Regulations 1981
TURERA	Trade Union Reform and Employment Rights Act 1993
UCTA 1977	Unfair Contract Terms Act 1977
WT Regs 1998	Working Time Regulations 1998

TABLE OF CASES

TABLE OF STATUTES

TABLE OF RULES AND REGULATIONS

Overview of employment law

1.1 Introduction

Employment law, on the whole, is not a conceptually difficult subject and a good dollop of analytical common sense can often work wonders. But instinct will not provide all the answers or the best advice. Employment law can be extremely detailed at times and a solicitor needs to grasp both the detail and the overall implications in order to give proper guidance to his or her client. The interrelationship between matters such as breach of contract and unfair dismissal, for instance, can cause some confusion to those new to the subject. Nevertheless, at its best employment law is logical, dynamic, interesting, and real. At its worst it resembles the M25: it all seems to have been built at the wrong time and in the wrong place, it grinds to a halt periodically for no apparent reason, it is frequently being dug up and expanded, and sometimes seems to go round in circles.

1.2 The topics covered in the book

These can be seen from the chapter headings. They centre on the substantive law, practice and procedure relating to the formation, operation, and termination of the contract of employment.

Collective employment law (i.e., the law concerning the rights, duties, and operations of trade unions) is not covered in this book except where it is necessary to explain the matters affecting individual rights.

1.3 The mixture of statutory and contractual rights

Modern employment law emerged out of a jumble of the Poor Laws, the history of Craftsmen's Guilds and Trade Unions, family law as applied to the behaviour of domestic servants and agricultural workers and, in the nineteenth century, the law of contract. By the 1960s one would find most employment texts set alongside contract textbooks, but, from the middle of that decade onwards, UK and European legislation has been the major driving force in the creation of employment rights and obligations.

Any questions raised in employment law may now involve: pure common law principles (mainly contractual); pure statutory principles; a combination of European Union and UK legislation and concepts; or a mixture of all the above. The lawyer who dabbles in employment law tends not to appreciate the detail (and often the conflict) involved in this mixture, so one of the recurrent themes in this book is to indicate the overlap between all these areas of law, but especially the key one of common law and statutory rules.

By way of a simple example, imagine that an employer has asked an employee to work at their Birmingham factory instead of the Coventry site (these are about 20 miles apart) but she objects. Clearly, this problem centres on what the contract of employment says or means and one would hope that the dispute might be resolved by examining the contract to see whether there is a clause detailing when the employee can be required to work at different sites—a 'mobility' clause. If the contract is silent on the point, one would have to look at whether there are any implied terms which cover the situation and, in employment law, arguments on the use and range of 'implied terms' have kept many a lawyer's family from starving.

The contractual analysis does not reveal the whole picture, however. For instance, hidden in this simple order to move site may lurk questions of discrimination based on sex, race or disability, all involving a range of UK statutes and/or European Directives. And the position may become even more complicated if a dismissal results from the refusal of the employee to move to Birmingham.

Once dismissal has occurred (and even some resignations are deemed to amount to dismissals) the employee may have claims at common law and under statute. The most obvious common law claim is that of *wrongful dismissal,* which arises when a person is dismissed without notice or with inadequate notice and the employer had no contractually justifiable reasons for that action. The most obvious statutory claim is for *unfair dismissal* which is essentially based on two questions: (a) did the employer have a fair reason to dismiss; and (b) was that reason handled fairly (e.g., by use of proper procedures)? Many reports in newspapers or on television confuse wrongful and unfair dismissal, but they are quite different animals.

Thus the lawyer who thinks solely in terms of either common law or statutory rights may not cover all the potential claims (and there are other possibilities beyond those noted above). Equally, one needs to know where the issues will be determined. The main forum for employment disputes is that of the employment tribunals (known as industrial tribunals until August 1998), and they would have jurisdiction to determine nearly all the points raised in our example, though in contract-based matters they can only award a maximum of £25,000 and they would only have jurisdiction in the example above if a dismissal had occurred as they generally cannot entertain arguments about the operation of the contract while the employment relationship is still running. The ordinary courts, however, have some overlapping jurisdiction, so all the contractual claims could be decided there, but they could not hear any discrimination claims, nor the unfair dismissal action.

Figure 1.1 below sets out in diagrammatic form the various jurisdictions of the courts and tribunals. Employment tribunal practice and procedure is dealt with in **Chapter 13**.

1.4 A skeleton outline of the topics covered

1.4.1 Definition of 'employee'

Most of the rights and obligations dealt with in this book concern employers and employees; rights such as unfair dismissal, for instance, do not extend to independent contractors. The distinction is the same as you encountered at your academic stage of

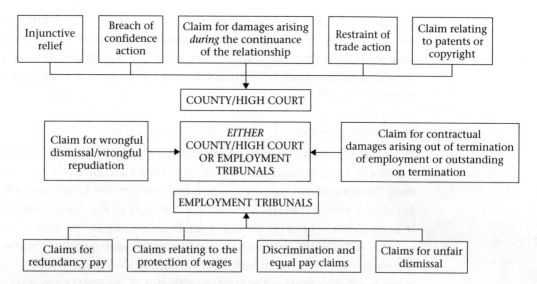

Figure 1.1 Jurisdictions of the courts and employment tribunals.

training in the law of torts (or obligations). Unfortunately, the term 'employee' has no workable statutory definition, so the analysis rests on a number of common law tests which explore the level of control a *company* has over an individual's work pattern, the extent to which the individual's work is *integrated* into the main work of the company, whether there are *mutual obligations* present between the parties such as the payment of sick pay and the provision of personal service, and whether the individual in all the circumstances can be said to be *in business on their own account*.

However, modern work patterns have fudged the line between employees and independent contractors, e.g., one large company we know of has more people on site who are hired through employment agencies than it has full-time employees. Further, a great deal of EU-derived legislation does not make such a clear distinction between employees and other categories so that recent legislation has tended to define rights and obligations by reference to the more expansive term 'worker'. The question of who qualifies for employment rights (dealt with in **Chapter 2**) is therefore an important one but will not concern most people as they will fall easily within the classification of 'employee'. When such problems do arise, however, they tend to centre on 'peripheral' workers such as those supplied by employment agencies and can often be extremely complicated matters.

1.4.2 The contract of employment

1.4.2.1 The form of the contract

We will deal in detail with the formation, contents, and operation of the contract in **Chapters 3** to **5**. Here we can say that a contract of employment is created like any other contract and may be made orally or in writing (or in any combination) and will be found in a mixture of express and implied terms. There is no standard format for such contracts and a solicitor should be wary of relying on general precedents that do not fit the circumstances of the case. There is a tolerated myth in employment law that each contract is negotiated on an individual basis with each employee. The reality is that most employees were simply given no option as to the contents of the contract, that many have never seen a written contract, that some think they have no contract (this applies to employers too), and that, if there are recognised trades unions in the company, they negotiated the terms of the contract (including those of non-members).

With this level of confusion over such a basic matter, it is hardly surprising, as we noted in passing above, that the employment contract is also riddled with *implied terms*. Very often these shape the contract; sometimes in a surprising way. Some, such as the duty of fidelity, cannot be excluded; others will stand unless express terms state the contrary.

1.4.2.2 Statutory intervention

There was a time when there was little statutory control over the *contents* of the contract. The first real intervention came in the 1960s with a document known as the *written statement*. The form of this statement is now prescribed by the Employment Rights Act 1996, s. 1 (ERA 1996). It is meant to provide a summary of the main contractual provisions. If an employer has not provided a contract containing all the matters which are meant to be included in the written statement he or she must provide a written statement to the employee within two months of their starting work. This is not the contract, though it can stand as very strong *prima facie* evidence of the contract and disputes regarding its alleged inaccuracies or its non-production can be referred to employment tribunals. Unfortunately, many employees have never seen one of these either.

More intervention has occurred recently covering matters such as the regulation of: the national minimum wage, maximum working hours, unauthorised deductions from wages, and the so-called 'family friendly' provisions. These are dealt with in **Chapter 4**.

1.4.2.3 The operation of the contract

Leaving aside questions of dismissal, the major concern of employees centres on how the contract is performed on a day-to-day basis. Problems will generally arise here relating to:

(a) what the terms are (a question of evidence); or

(b) what do those terms mean (a question of interpretation); or

(c) when can the employer change the terms (a question of law)?

As with our simple example above on mobility clauses, it is at this point that one first notices the real interplay between common law matters such as breach of contract and the other statutory rights and remedies. As we will explore in **Chapter 5** in particular, it is often best to approach this area by considering what the employee's response could be to any proposed interpretation or variation of the contractual terms. At one end the employee may simply put up with the employer's views, but there is a range of legal remedies which can be pursued such as seeking an injunction, suing for breach of contract or resigning and claiming wrongful and/or unfair dismissal.

1.4.3 Discrimination and equal pay

This topic is dealt with in **Chapter 6**.

Issues of sex, gender, disability, race, religious belief, age or trade union membership discrimination may arise during recruitment, or in the operation of the contract or at termination.

The various forms of prohibited discrimination are described in **Chapter 6** and mentioned throughout the text. Discrimination may come in different forms: *direct* and *indirect* discrimination. Direct sex discrimination comes from an obvious act of treating the woman (usually) less favourably than a man. Indirect discrimination arises where the proportion of women (or a racial group) who can comply with a particular requirement or condition is considerably smaller than the proportion of men (or other racial groups) and it is to the person's detriment.

There are exceptions and defences to these general rules, e.g., that there is a genuine occupational qualification required (e.g., decency or authenticity points).

Enforcement is by means of application to an employment tribunal, which may make an order declaring the applicant's rights and award compensation.

1.4.4 Termination of the contract

The rights and remedies regarding termination at common law are dealt with in **Chapter 9** of this book; the statutory consequences are covered in **Chapters 10** and **11**. The central feature of **Chapter 9** is the concept of wrongful dismissal; **Chapter 10** deals with the most well-known aspect of employment law *viz* unfair dismissal; and **Chapter 11** deals with redundancy. We have hinted at how these topics interrelate in the text above.

A contract of employment can come to an end in a number of different ways:

(a) by agreement;

(b) by completion of a specific task;

(c) by expiry of a fixed-term;

(d) by automatic termination, e.g., frustration of the contract;

(e) by dismissal;

(f) by resignation.

1.4.4.1 Common law remedies

Dismissal and resignation are the most common forms of termination. In most cases either party may terminate the contract by giving adequate notice and, at common law, an employer can dismiss an employee for any reason. The only thing that matters to the common law is whether adequate notice was given. Notice periods are determined by the contract, subject to statutory minima which vary according to the length of service.

If the employer dismisses without giving adequate notice or payment in lieu of that notice, he or she may be in breach of contract. The claim is for what is termed a 'wrongful dismissal'. The employer is entitled to dismiss without notice (called a 'summary dismissal') only if the employee has committed a serious breach of the contract. Hence it is in both parties' interests to have the express terms clearly defined so that they know exactly where they stand on any given issue.

The amount of damages an employee will obtain is limited to what would have been earned during the notice period and is subject to the normal contractual rules—for example, the duty to mitigate loss.

If, on the other hand, the *employer* commits a serious breach of contract (e.g., the employer does not pay the employee) this will amount to a repudiation which the employee may accept as terminating the contract and resign. This is termed a 'wrongful repudiation' by the employer and means that the employee will be held to have been effectively dismissed. Damages are calculated in the same way as with a wrongful dismissal. The employee who does not resign and continues in employment may of course sue the employer for damages relating to any breach.

In limited cases one of the parties may obtain an injunction to prevent a breach of contract, e.g., to prevent a dismissal taking effect until contractual procedures have been followed. An order for specific performance will not be granted, however. The real importance of injunctions lies in actions for breach of confidence and restraint of trade.

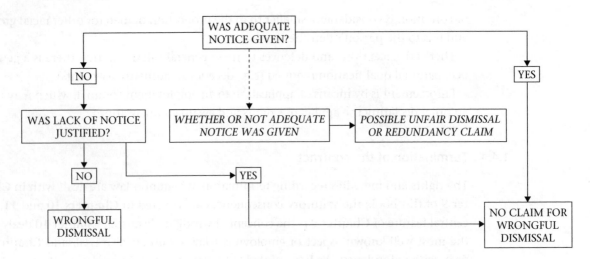

Figure 1.2   Dismissal with or without notice.

In **Figure 1.2** you can see that where dismissal is with adequate notice there are no further common law consequences. Where dismissal is without notice (and that lack of notice cannot be justified) the employee will be entitled to damages for wrongful dismissal. *Note, however, that in either case there may be statutory consequences such as a claim for unfair dismissal.*

1.4.4.2   Statutory remedies: unfair dismissal

'Unfair dismissal' is a technical term which has its own peculiar set of rules and procedures. Cases are heard exclusively in employment tribunals. Any claim must be presented within three months of what is termed the 'effective date of termination' (e.g., the end of the notice period).

Every employee is said to have the right not to be unfairly dismissed, but there are certain preliminary conditions to be met. First, the employee must qualify for the right. For instance, the right generally applies only to employees who have at least one year's continuous employment.

The employee must prove that he or she has been dismissed but, as with common law rights, a resignation may be deemed a dismissal if the employee resigned in the face of a serious breach by the employer. This is the same thing as wrongful repudiation but is called a 'constructive dismissal' in this setting.

'Fairness' is determined by a three-stage process. First, if there is any dispute on the matter an employee will have to prove they were, in law, dismissed, e.g., where there has been a resignation. Secondly, the burden is on the employer to show that the dismissal was for a 'fair reason'.

There are only six acceptable fair reasons: capability or qualifications; conduct; retirement; redundancy; statutory illegality; and 'some other substantial reason'. Dismissal for any other reason is unfair.

The third stage is to assess whether the fair reason was implemented fairly. The burden of proof here is neutral. Fairness is determined by three main factors:

- the definition contained in ERA 1996, s. 98(4) ('whether the dismissal is fair or unfair . . . (a) depends on whether in the circumstances (including the size and administrative resources of the employer's undertaking) the employer acted reasonably or unreasonably in treating . . . [the fair reason] . . . as a sufficient reason for dismissing the employee, and (b) shall be determined in accordance with equity and the substantial merits of the case');

- a vast amount of case law explaining the application of this definition in the setting of the tribunal's sense of industrial reality; and

- whether a fair procedure has been followed by the employer.

The primary remedies for unfair dismissal are reinstatement in the same job and re-engagement in a similar job. These are seldom ordered so that the main practical remedy is that of compensation.

Compensation is made up of two main elements—the basic and compensatory awards. They are assessed on different grounds *and the maximum figures are reviewed annually,* usually changing in February. The basic award is a fixed calculation, determined by reference to the age, length of service and earnings of the employee. The maximum basic award at the time of writing is £9,900. The compensatory award is based on what is just and equitable. It is calculated on nett payments. The maximum award is currently £63,000.

Both the basic award and the compensatory award may be subject to a number of deductions, e.g., in relation to contributory fault, *ex gratia* payments made, or failure to mitigate loss.

1.4.4.3 Statutory remedies: redundancy

Redundancy is a dismissal for a particular reason. That reason is that:

(a) the business has closed down; *or*

(b) the employee's particular place of work has closed down (even though other sites may still continue); *or*

(c) the requirement for employees to do that employee's particular work has ceased or diminished.

In effect, a redundancy arises where (without necessarily any fault on the employee's part) there is a surplus of labour. Where an employee is dismissed for redundancy there may be an entitlement to a statutory redundancy payment. This is calculated in the same way as the basic award for an unfair dismissal, i.e., according to age, length of service, and pay (again, to a maximum of £9,900). The contract may also entitle the employee to a contractual redundancy payment.

Redundancy is a fair *reason* for dismissal but, as with any other dismissal, if it is handled badly by the employer it may still constitute an unfair dismissal.

We can now consider an overview of the possible consequences of dismissal. You can see in **Figure 1.3** that, whatever the reason for dismissal, and whether adequate notice was given or not, the dismissal may yet be an unfair dismissal.

The solicitor *must* be aware of this overview when giving advice to an employer. This applies at any stage: during the contract when the employer is issuing orders or varying terms of the contract, and also where a decision has been made to dismiss the employee. We have not included every possible consequence in the diagram, so matters such as discrimination must also be noted (there is no maximum figure for compensation in discrimination claims).

1.4.5 Takeovers and transfer of undertakings

This topic considers what happens to the employee's rights and duties when the ownership of the business changes (it is dealt with in **Chapter 12**). In many cases the transfer of ownership will be by share acquisition and this has no effect on the employee at all. However, where a business is transferred by other means (e.g., the business or part

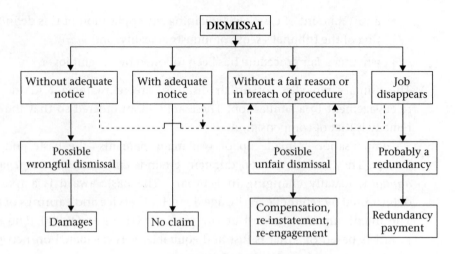

Figure 1.3   Possible consequences of dismissal.

of it is sold), the position is that all the contractual and statutory rights concerning employees (except for pensions) will be automatically transferred as well. This will apply only where the transfer is a *'relevant transfer'*, i.e., one in which:

(a) business activity passes from one legal person to another;

(b) the transfer is of an economic entity which retains its identity.

Employees will maintain their contractual and statutory rights and obligations only if they are 'employed [by the transferor] immediately before the transfer', but the term 'immediately before' is now given a loose interpretation. In essence, therefore, employees employed as part of a transferred business can regard the transferee as having been their employer all along. Thus an employee who is dismissed at any time by the transferee can bring any contractual or statutory claims against the transferee.

1.4.6   Employment tribunal procedure

Chapter 13 examines employment tribunal procedure and the special rules that apply to actions for unfair dismissal and redundancy in particular. Employment tribunals operate in much the same way as the ordinary courts but there are peculiarities that can catch the unwary. They are presided over by employment judges and are not as informal as is commonly believed. The settlement of cases before they reach the tribunal is quite common practice.

1.4.7   Protecting the employer's interests

Chapters 7 and **8** concentrate on topics which do not fall within the jurisdiction of employment tribunals, *viz*, confidentiality and restraint of trade. These are technically complicated areas which require special attention. At one time employment lawyers very often did not deal with these topics at all, leaving them to Chancery specialists; but in the modern employment law context this is no longer the case as the advice given in relation to, say, a dismissal may have major repercussions on the efficacy of restraint or confidentiality clauses.

1.4.7.1   Confidentiality

During employment an employee owes his employer a fairly strict duty to maintain the secrecy of the employer's confidential information. Once the relationship has ended, however, only certain types of highly confidential information continue to receive protection. In **Chapter 7** we will see that a difficult balance has to be struck between the employer's trade secrets (which can be protected) and the employee's know-how (which cannot). The arguments (as with restraint of trade below) are usually set in the world of interim injunctions.

1.4.7.2 Restraint of trade

Employers are often anxious to guard against direct competition once employees have left the organisation. As well as seeking to protect their confidential information, employers may also wish to ensure that an ex-employee does not have the opportunity to exert influence over the employer's hard-earned trade connexions. Restraint clauses are used by all manner of businesses, from the small high-street hairdresser who wants to prevent the ex-stylist 'stealing' his clients, to the solicitor's firm which wishes to do the same as against the partner or assistant solicitor who has moved elsewhere, through to multi-national enterprises. In all cases the restraint is presumed to be void unless it passes a test of reasonableness as between the parties in terms of the time covered by the restraint, the area affected, and the market in which the business operates.

Restraint clauses take three main forms: *non-competition* restraints which prevent the ex-employee working in that industry or at least working for named competitors; *non-dealing* restraints which prevent ex-employees accepting business from, or conducting business with, former clients; and *non-solicitation* restraints which prevent ex-employees actually initiating contact with former clients. In all cases enforcement will be granted to the minimum level needed to protect the employer's legitimate interests. The aim is to protect against *unfair* competition, not competition *per se*.

1.5 The institutions

There are three main arenas in which employment law issues are settled:

(a) *At the workplace between employers and employees, or their trade unions*

This always gets extensive publicity in the media and the image is usually one of constant warfare. The reality is that, in general, major battle-lines are not drawn here on a day-to-day basis.

(b) *In the ordinary courts*

It is a key point that we will be dealing with *contracts* of employment, and thus the normal law of contract plays a vital role in our considerations. Anything which centres on breach of contract is primarily, and often exclusively, the province of the county court or High Court and not that of employment tribunals, e.g., restraint of trade.

(c) *In employment tribunals*

These bodies were set up to deal with employment law problems and their jurisdiction is immense. Most commonly they will hear unfair dismissal, redundancy, and discrimination cases. An appeal from the decision of an employment tribunal lies with the Employment Appeal Tribunal (almost exclusively on a point of law only) and from there to the Court of Appeal (which, strictly speaking, reviews the decision of the ET, not the EAT).

In addition to all this there are other institutions which are relevant to this book and need to be noted specifically here.

1.5.1 ACAS

The Advisory, Conciliation and Arbitration Service (ACAS) seeks to promote improvements in industrial relations, e.g.:

(a) as regards collective matters in relation to the settlement of trade disputes, e.g., by arranging arbitration;

(b) to give employers, employers' associations, workers and trade unions advice on matters of industrial relations;

(c) to provide Codes of Practice (e.g., relating to disciplinary procedures) which are not legally binding on parties but are admissible as evidence of good industrial practice so that failure to adhere to these codes may go to show that an employer acted unfairly or, if not that, can result in extra (or reduced) compensation being paid; and

(d) to promote the settlement of any complaint presented to employment tribunals, e.g., for unfair dismissal.

ACAS may now charge for its services.

ACAS now has a new function as regards unfair dismissal complaints: that of offering litigants the option of arbitration instead of going to an employment tribunal (see **10.12.2** below).

1.5.2 The Equality and Human Rights Commission

As from October 2007 the Equality and Human Rights Commission became the new single body covering equal opportunities, racial and sexual equality, disability and human rights. As well as promoting equality etc. and issuing guidance to this effect the Commission's predecessors have been held to have sufficient locus to bring judicial review actions.

1.6 European influences

Employment law has been one of the most active areas of European legislation. Thus matters such as free movement of workers, rights to receive particulars of employment, equal pay, transfers of undertakings and redundancy consultations have all been the subject of Treaties, Regulations or Directives of the EU.

The effect of all this is three-fold:

(a) Some legislation is directly enforceable by individuals against the state or other individuals, i.e., they can enforce rights such as equal pay under art. 141, EC Treaty, by reference to the EC legislation itself. The EC legislation may therefore be cited and relied upon in any action (having direct applicability and direct effect).

(b) Other forms of EC legislation do not have direct applicability; though in limited cases they may have *direct effect,* which will amount to much the same thing. In the case of *Faccini Dori* v *Recreb srl* [1995] ECR I-3325, the full court of the ECJ addressed the issue of the *horizontal* direct effect of Directives, i.e., the applicability of Directives, outside any enacting national legislation, to legal persons (individuals and companies) suing other legal persons. The *Faccini Dori* case made it quite clear that Directives did not have direct horizontal effect. So, all employees in the *private sector* who seek to sue their employer must rely either on the wording of the

UK legislation *simpliciter* or sue the UK Government under the *Francovich* principles (*Francovich* v *Italian Republic* [1995] ICR 722). Most Directives, however, do have *vertical direct effect,* so if the employee is employed by the State he or she may be able to rely on the wording of the Directive itself. It is therefore quite possible to have different rights ascribed to different groups of employees by reason only of who they work for.

(c) Where UK legislation has been implemented to comply with EC legislation it may be interpreted in a very purposive manner. That is, the statutory interpretation techniques used by the courts and their willingness to read the UK legislation so as to comply with the spirit of the EC enactment means that a purely literal approach to such UK legislation is unsafe even when the words are unambiguous in themselves. This is known as giving the Directive *indirect effect* and may be applied to both private and public sector employees.

1.7 The Human Rights Act 1998 and employment law

In the general part of the LPC you will already have dealt with the key issues of incorporation of the European Convention on Human Rights via the 1998 Act. You will have seen that:

(a) All legislation, whenever enacted, must be interpreted in such a way as to comply with the rights granted under the Convention: HRA 1998, s. 3(1).

(b) But, in all cases, unless the UK legislation can be interpreted so as to comply with Convention rights, an Act of Parliament still takes precedence over Convention rights. This means that the *validity* of primary legislation is beyond judicial control. The same will be true of secondary legislation. However, even before the introduction of the HRA 1998, secondary legislation which was *ultra vires* its parent Act could be struck down by the normal process of judicial review. That principle can also be applied when human rights issues are involved unless the primary legislation prevents removal of the incompatibility between the legislation and human rights principles: s. 3(2)(c) and s. 6(2)(b), i.e., the incompatibility lies in the primary legislation itself. For these purposes primary legislation includes commencement orders and orders which amend primary legislation: HRA 1998, s. 21(1).

(c) All courts and tribunals must take into account the jurisprudence of the Convention, which means the decisions of the European Court of Human Rights, whenever a Convention right arises (HRA 1998, s. 2). However, UK courts are not bound to apply the decisions of the European Court. Equally, the doctrine of *stare decisis* is modified in that domestic binding precedents which are now found to conflict with Convention rights may be ignored.

(d) Certain courts (but not employment tribunals or the EAT) have the right to declare primary and secondary legislation incompatible with Convention Rights: HRA 1998, s. 4. A declaration of incompatibility only allows judges to scrutinise legislation. Such a declaration does not affect the validity of primary legislation, nor does it affect secondary legislation (subject to our comments above in (b)). Neither is the declaration directed at the litigants, so the case in hand is not affected by the declaration; it has no legal effect and is simply a 'warning shot' aimed at Parliament.

(e) There is no system of sending references (akin to art. 234, EC Treaty) to the European Court of Human Rights so that there is a possibility of conflict between the UK courts' interpretation of the Convention and that of the European Court of Human Rights (to which a 'victim' can still apply after exhausting the UK system).

(f) All public authorities must act in a way which is compatible with Convention rights: HRA 1998, s. 6. 'Public authority' includes 'any person certain of whose functions are functions of a public nature'; s. 6(3) (b). This includes courts and tribunals.

(g) Certain rights have not been incorporated e.g., art. 13 of the Convention.

(h) The areas which are likely to impact on employment law are detailed below.

1.7.1 Which employers are affected?

Action may be taken directly against a 'public authority' under the HRA 1998, s. 6 claiming a breach of Convention rights; with ordinary employers an employee would have to persuade a court that, in analysing a cause of action, existing legislation or judicial precedents should be read in the light of Convention rights. Thus there is a distinction between 'vertical' and 'horizontal' effect akin to the application of Directives in EU Law.

The term 'public authority' has not been defined in the Act but will obviously include bodies such as local authorities. This still begs the question whether all activities undertaken by a public authority are caught by s. 6 or only those which are clearly a 'public function'. It was confirmed in parliamentary debates that the definition of 'public authority' in s. 6 was intended to apply to public bodies even when acting as employers (which is not a public function *per se*). Following *Pepper* v *Hart* [1993] AC 593 on the use of Hansard this may well settle any argument on s. 6 for employment purposes so that employees of public bodies will have a direct cause of action against their employers, whereas employees of private organisations will have to take the more circuitous route.

However, the Act does recognise that there will be hybrid bodies (e.g., privatised utilities, the BBC, and professional bodies) who exercise both private and public functions. In relation to hybrid bodies s. 6(5) states that, ' . . . a person is not a public authority by virtue of subsection (3)(b) if the nature of the act is private'.

At the time of writing, there is still a debate as to whether employment matters should be classified as public or private functions. It may well be that some such activities (e.g., health and safety matters) are classified as public whilst general employment matters are private.

1.7.1.1 Victim

A person can only rely on Convention rights against a public authority where they fall within the definition of 'victim' (HRA 1998, s. 7(7)). This generally means that the claimant must be a person who is directly affected by the alleged breach and prevents representative actions (e.g., by trade unions) except for very limited situations.

Proceedings against public authorities must be brought within one year of the act complained of.

1.7.2 Rights directly relevant to employment

1.7.2.1 Forced/compulsory labour, under art. 4 of the Convention

No forced labour claim has succeeded in Strasbourg to date, and speculations that working conditions, long hours and compulsory overtime amount to such a breach are not convincing. The employment relationship is a contractual one which both parties can terminate and, even within the relationship, existing legislation on working time, harassment etc. cover these areas adequately.

1.7.2.2   Freedom to join or not to join trade unions, under art. 11 of the Convention

Article 11 establishes the right to peaceful assembly and to freedom of association with others, including the right to form and join a trade union. Domestic law on this topic is already well-developed and this article is unlikely to have a major impact on employment law.

1.7.3   Other rights (indirectly) relevant to employment

1.7.3.1   Fair and public hearing, under art. 6 of the Convention

This is the most frequently-invoked article of the Convention. It states that ' . . . everyone is entitled to a fair and public hearing within a reasonable time by an independent and impartial tribunal established by law'. Clearly this exists in the procedures adopted by the courts and employment tribunals. Some arguments have been raised that internal disciplinary proceedings are caught by this provision but these appear to be speculation for its own sake as any such decision can be 'reviewed' in a tribunal or court.

What is not so clear-cut is whether the lack of legal help/representation in tribunals might breach this article (see for instance *Airey* v *Ireland* (1979) 2 EHRR 305) or even the fact that some rights (e.g., unfair dismissal and redundancy) require qualification periods. As regards the latter point Convention jurisprudence shows (e.g., in cases dealing with limitation periods such as *Stubbings* v *United Kingdom* (1996) 23 EHRR 213) that the argument will centre on whether the qualification period is part of the substantive right to claim, say, unfair dismissal (in which case interference is unlikely) or whether it is a procedural 'add on'. ERA 1996, s. 94(1) states that an employee has the right not to be unfairly dismissed which looks like a bare declaration of the right with any qualifying period being an add on, but s. 94(2) makes subsection (1) subject to a range of sections including s. 108 which sets out the qualification. The point is therefore quite well-balanced.

The question of tribunals hearing cases involving their paymasters and what constitutes a public hearing have already caused some consternation and brought about changes in procedure. And on the commercial side, Part 25 of the Civil Procedure Rules was clearly drafted with art. 6 in mind, but the question of how interim injunctions and search orders operate may still occupy the attention of the courts. Whether the proposed ACAS arbitration scheme may breach art. 6 (in that the participating parties must waive their rights to a trial) is one of those issues still under debate. We would suggest that, as the new scheme is a voluntary one, it is unlikely that art. 6 would be breached.

1.7.3.2   Respect for private and family life, home and correspondence, under art. 8 of the Convention

This does raise the thorny problem of employers monitoring staff by use of devices such as CCTV, drug testing, interceptions of e-mails, and the keeping of personnel records. There exists plenty of case law and legislation covering matters such as access to medical information and data protection, but less on monitoring employees (though see *Halford* v *United Kingdom* [1997] IRLR 471 on telephone interceptions). We can reasonably expect developments in this area (see for example, **7.8.4** on monitoring communications).

The Privy Council was recently faced with an interesting problem on the question of art. 8 in *Whitefield* v *General Medical Council* [2002] UKPC 62, [2003] IRLR 39, where a doctor with a serious history of alcohol problems was required by the General Medical Council to abstain absolutely from alcohol, to submit to random breath, blood, and urine tests, and to attend Alcoholics Anonymous. The doctor argued that together or individually these amounted to a breach of art. 8 as the conditions interfered with the right to respect for his private life. His argument was rejected on the basis that there was no authority to support the proposition that a ban on the consumption of alcohol is, *per se*, a breach of art. 8 and that he could still socialise without consuming alcohol. Further, even if these actions were a breach of art. 8(1) the conditions were lawfully imposed in the circumstances under art. 8(2) which allows for the interference in private life in limited circumstances such as the protection of health or morals. This also applied to the compulsory medical tests, which have been held to be in breach of art. 8 in other jurisdictions and circumstances.

On the facts, one has little difficulty with the analysis in *Whitefield*. Whether it gives birth to a whole range of arguments determining just how far bans by (public authority) employers on employees' 'out of work' activities will be held acceptable without breaching art. 8 (e.g., bans on smoking or taking part in dangerous sports) is more debatable.

The impact of the Human Rights Act 1998 on unfair dismissal was considered by the Court of Appeal in *xvy* [2004] EWCA Civ 662 concerning the activities of an employee in a public toilet, and by the EAT in *McGowan* v *Scottish Water* [2005] IRLR 167 relating to covert surveillance of an employee (see **10.9.1** below).

1.7.3.3   Freedom of thought, conscience and religion, under art. 9 of the Convention

The UK has specific legislation covering religious activities, e.g., Race Relations Act 1976, the Religion or Belief Regulations 2003, the Equality Act 2006 and aspects relating to working on Sundays in the ERA 1996 so that references to art. 9 for these purposes are now less relevant.

1.7.3.4   Freedom of expression, under art. 10 of the Convention

This article includes the right to receive and impart information and ideas without interference, subject to restrictions which are necessary in a democratic society. Matters such as the law of defamation, the Public Interest Disclosure Act 1998 and the duty of confidentiality already cover many aspects raised here (see **Chapters 7** and **8** below). The extent to which 'expression' extends to matters like dress codes has been the subject of speculation, though there is nothing in the Convention case law to support this.

1.7.3.5   Non-discrimination, under art. 14 of the Convention

This is not a free-standing right but relates to the provisions of the Convention itself *viz* it only prohibits discrimination in the enjoyment of one or other of the rights guaranteed by the Convention. The new Protocol 12 modifies this position.

1.8   The internet and other sources

There are numerous sites on the internet that now give access to a wide range of information on employment law. We cannot list all of those here, but a useful starting point is: www.emplaw.co.uk which is a portal to a whole host of relevant sites; **www.employment-appeals.gov.uk** for the EAT; **www.berr.gov.uk** for the Department for

Business, Enterprise and Regulatory Reform (formerly the Department of Trade and Industry); **www.acas.org.uk** for ACAS; **www.opsi.gov.uk/acts.htm** for recent statutes and www.opsi.gov.uk/stat.htm for statutory instruments. Equality issues can be investigated at www.equalityhumanrights.com

The best practitioners' text is *Harvey on Industrial Relations and Employment Law* (London: Butterworths) and, amongst the many journals in this field, the *IDS Brief* (Income Data Services Ltd) stands out as being informative and up to date.

Definition of 'employee'

2.1 Introduction

This chapter examines how the presence of an employment relationship is determined, what factors should be considered in making that determination, and what are the possible consequences of the classification.

The relevance of these questions is that they will determine:

(a) who is *responsible* for matters such as liability for tax and National Insurance contributions, injury in the workplace and damage caused to others;

(b) what contractual *rights* the company has in controlling the activities of the worker;

(c) what specific *statutory rights* the worker has acquired, such as unfair dismissal compensation, redundancy pay, maternity rights and so on.

Thus the first, and most basic, problem confronting anyone dealing with employment law is: 'How does one determine whether a worker is an employee or self-employed (i.e., an independent contractor)?' Few of the statutes covering the working environment relate to the self-employed. Legislation relating to discrimination together with health and safety matters has general application, but most of the statutory rights refer only to employees. As will be seen, the mere fact that the parties reach agreement on their respective status is not the determining feature.

This chapter will adopt the following structure:

(a) The tests for an employment relationship.

(b) The benefits and pitfalls of each type of relationship.

(c) Types of employee.

(d) Vicarious liability.

(e) The statutory meaning of 'Worker'.

To most employment lawyers this area has usually been of general background relevance only. However, the basic questions raised here have begun to surface more frequently.

Some employers, recognising the increased protection the law now gives to 'permanent' or 'core' employees (whether full-time or part-time), have sought to create a second tier of temporary or 'peripheral' workers with fewer rights. Sometimes this involves an attempt to categorise them as independent contractors and not employees at all, or to devise fictions such as 'zero hours' contracts. These tests of employment status are therefore currently a very live issue. It is also the case, however, that both EU and Government policy is moving towards doing away with the distinction between employees and independent contractors. It is increasingly common to find the term 'worker' appearing in Directives and statutes concerned with employment rights. Indeed, ERA 1999, s. 23 specifically confers upon the Secretary of State by order the power to extend statutory employment rights to workers other than employees.

We will therefore first examine the practicalities of the classic distinctions of employees and independent contractors and then look at the effect of the new classification of 'worker' used in modern legislation.

2.2 The tests for an employment relationship

Various tests have been developed over the years to answer what appears to be a very simple question—how to define the term 'employee'. There is a statutory definition contained in ERA 1996, s. 230(1) but it has been deliberately left vague. It states that an 'employee' means an individual who has entered into or works under a contract of employment—which in turn is defined as a contract of service or of apprenticeship. This is less than helpful but sums up the approach of the courts *viz*, if it looks like a duck and quacks like a duck, it is a duck. Other (more legal) tests exist, as described below.

Note: to avoid confusion between the noun 'worker' and the legally-defined, statute-protected 'Worker' we have used the inelegant term 'workman' to describe the non-statutory kind. For brevity, the term also applies to women.

2.2.1 The control test

The problems associated with defining the term 'employee' or, in older terminology, 'servant' have been with us for centuries, arising long before the application of contract terminology to the employment relationship. The assessment of the presence and extent of responsibilities closely followed the analytical line as to whether the putative employer had 'control' over what the individual did and the manner in which it was done. This seemed a natural path to take. The greater the degree of control, the more likely it was that there was a contract *of* service rather than a contract *for* services; that the person was a servant rather than an independent contractor or agent. The employee sells his labour; the contractor sells a product.

The courts are concerned here to find who it is that determines the operation of the contract; who exercises the discretion? This is achieved by what may be termed a *'Who, what, where, when and how' test.* That is to say:

(a) *Who*

To what extent does the 'employer' control who does the work? The contract of employment is a contract of *personal* service, so if the workman can delegate the task or send replacements this essential element of personal service will be missing. This point was strongly emphasised in *Ready Mixed Concrete (South East) Ltd v Minister of Pensions and National Insurance* [1968] 2 QB 497, which held that a lorry driver (who had to obey a wide range of company rules) was nevertheless an independent contractor because, *inter alia*, he could, with the company's consent, arrange for a substitute driver to do his job instead. This analysis was affirmed in another 'driver' case (*Express and Echo Publications Ltd v Tanton* [1999] ICR 693), where the Court of Appeal went further in stating that it was established on the authorities that where a person who works for another is not required to perform his service personally, then *as a matter of law* the relationship between the worker and the person for whom he works is not that of employer and employee. But case law since then has shown that this is a starting point only: a limited power of delegation may not be inconsistent with employee status, e.g., where the individual is allowed to delegate because of illness (see *Staffordshire Sentinel Newspapers* v *Potter* [2004] IRLR 752, EAT). *A general* power to delegate remains inconsistent with a contract of employment unless that power is inserted by the employer deliberately as a sham to avoid setting up an employment relationship. The fact that the clause is not utilised does not matter: its presence will prevent the contract being an employment contract unless the employer is acting 'fraudulently': *Real Time Civil Engineering Ltd* v *Callaghan* (unreported, UKEAT/515/05).

(b) *What*

Does the 'employer' control what work is done, e.g., the order in which jobs are undertaken?

(c) *Where*

What control does the 'employer' have over the place of work? If work is done at home or on the workman's own business premises, this will point away from an employment relationship.

(d) *When*

A similar point to 'where' which relates to the hours worked.

(e) *How*

Can the 'employer' control how the work is to be performed? With skilled workmen it becomes unrealistic to suppose that control can be exercised here. In truth, though, the courts have approached this by asking, does the 'employer' have the *right* to control activities, rather than asking whether control is *physically* exercised.

The control test is still used widely today, though usually in combination with other tests.

2.2.2 The integration test

The integration test developed to cope with the problems of controlling *how* a job is to be done. 'Integration' was never accurately defined and the test only ever really applied to fringe occupations. The formula applied was: If the workman was fully integrated into—'a part and parcel of'—the enterprise then there was likely to be a contract of service. This meant investigating whether the workman took part in administrative duties, management decisions or undertook other tasks. If some degree of mutuality was present, with the 'employer' providing benefits such as holiday pay, this would tend to indicate a contract *of* service. However, where a person performed only a single task, usually for only a short time, this raised the presumption of a contract *for* services.

2.2.3 Economic reality test

The control test and the integration test tend now to be subsumed into a more general balancing exercise which goes by various names—the economic reality test, the mixed test, and the multiple test. The question of who is or is not an employee is generally one of fact, not law (except in the interpretation of written contracts).

This economic reality test recognises that it is the *combination and balance* of features and the degree of emphasis that matters more than one simple checklist. So the modern approach demands that all the factors for and against the presence of an employment relationship are put into balance. Two key questions are then posed. These are:

(a) *Are these workmen in business on their own account?*

Here one looks to the financial risk and input of capital as regards equipment and varying profits. Any company, when set against an individual, will obviously have injected more capital and have taken more sizeable financial risks, so the emphasis has to be on the level provided by the workman: Is it higher than one would normally expect from an employee? This entrepreneurial aspect of the test was emphasised in one of the key cases in this area, *viz Ready Mixed Concrete* v *Minister of Pensions* (see **2.2.1**) as regards lorry drivers. If a workman is in business on his or her own account not only will he or she have some chance of increasing his or her profits (a pieceworker could claim the same), but he or she will also be at some *risk* of losing money.

(b) *Is there a mutual obligation to provide work and perform tasks as directed?*

Here one looks to matters such as: is there a 'wage-work bargain', i.e., *some* obligation to provide work and *some* obligation to do that work; does the putative employer provide sick pay or holiday pay; are there set hours; and does the workman do the same tasks as ordinary employees? This last aspect of mutuality was emphasised in *Nethermere of St Neots* v *Gardiner and Taverna* [1984] ICR 612, where homeworkers, who largely regulated their own workload, were nevertheless found to be employees on the basis that in many respects they were treated the same (and did the same type of work) as their full-time equivalents.

The tests above are the guiding forms of analysis adopted by the courts, but in the end the exercise is one of balancing these features. As the Court of Appeal has stated in *Hall (Inspector of Taxes)* v *Lorimer* [1992] ICR 739, although one needs to compile a detailed checklist the court must evaluate the overall effect of that detail.

2.2.4 Labels and descriptions

It may be thought that, in a contractual setting such as this, what the parties call themselves would be determinative. However, the history of this area is littered with cases where one or other party attempts to avoid liability with the use of such devices, and so the relationship is analysed under an objective test: the label is just one factor to take into account. For instance, in *Young and Woods* v *West* [1980] IRLR 201, West opted to be called self-employed although doing the same work as ordinary employees. The Inland Revenue treated him as self-employed, and all would have been well, but the company declared redundancies and, as a self-employed worker, West was not entitled to any compensation. He therefore claimed that, in reality, he was an employee all along. The Court of Appeal eventually agreed (though they also referred the matter to the Inland Revenue as regards past tax bills).

Mere labels therefore do not carry much weight, but how the contract is expressed—the written terms defining duties, etc.—is a factor which is being used more widely to determine the workman's status. Thus, in *Express and Echo Publications Ltd* v *Tanton* (above), the Court of Appeal noted that one should look first at the terms of the agreement and then consider whether any of those terms are inherently inconsistent with the existence of a contract of employment. If there is an inherently inconsistent term, such as clear arrangements for the provision of substitute workers on a commercial footing (i.e., a clause showing personal service is not important), the term is more likely to mean that this is not an employment relationship; if there is no inconsistency one must still look at the balance of all the terms. More recently, the EAT has stated that one should presume the description on the express terms is accurate unless there is some sham present: *Autoclenz v Belcher* (UKEAT/0160/08/DA). The contractual documents may well determine status, especially if it can be shown that they were intended to be an exclusive record of the agreement, but in most cases one will need to look at factors such as oral exchanges and subsequent conduct in order to determine the individual's position.

It should also be stressed that the mere fact that an external body, such as the Inland Revenue, classes a workman as one thing or another, is only marginally important for employment law purposes.

2.2.5 Irreducible minima?

You may gather from all this (and the point is reinforced below when we look at *types of employees*) that this area is in something of a mess. The courts are constantly trying to find some overriding factors which can be used to determine all situations—often referred to as the *irreducible minima* which go to make an employment relationship—but it is the search for the Holy Grail. As the practitioners' 'bible' in this area (*Harvey*) concludes: 'If the obligation is merely to get the job done, then the individual is an independent contractor and not an employee; if the obligation is to do the job himself, then he could be either.' Nevertheless, the main modern contenders are as follows:

(a) The question of who exercises *control* in terms *of procedures*, e.g., the *right* to control as seen in *Ready Mixed Concrete* (above); or the presence or absence of grievance and disciplinary procedures, which was the central point in *Montgomery v Johnson Underwood Ltd* [2001] EWCA Civ 318; [2001] IRLR 269.

(b) The question of *who* exercises *control* in terms of the requirement of *personal service/the right to delegate*.

(c) The question of whether there is *mutuality of obligation* in terms of:

    (i) commitment, as evidenced in the presence of sick pay schemes, holiday arrangements, etc.—*Nethermere* (above, and at **2.4.5** below);

    (ii) some form of continuing consideration, as with the use of a retainer—*Clark v Oxfordshire Health Authority* [1998] IRLR 125 (see below at **2.4.6**); or

    (iii) some binding commitment, or express or implied guarantee of work and guarantee of service: see *Carmichael v National Power plc* [2000] IRLR 43, HL (below at **2.4.6**) and *McMeechan v Secretary of State for Employment* [1997] ICR 549 (below at **2.4.7.1**).

(d) As noted in **2.2.4** above, what the parties actually *agree*. Although not determinative, if the parties expressly negative mutuality of obligation, e.g., they agree that there is no obligation to provide work or to accept any work offered, and that the relationship is *ad hoc* and casual, then, short of finding this to be a sham, the courts will have the devil's own job to say that a casual worker (even a regular one) was employed on some form of global contract: *Stevedoring & Haulage Services Ltd v Fuller* [2001] EWCA Civ 651, [2001] IRLR 627. Further, if the *purpose* of the agreement is to oust the jurisdiction of the tribunal (e.g., by stating that the workman is not an employee and so cannot claim employee-related statutory rights such as unfair dismissal) then it will be struck down by the anti-avoidance provisions in s. 203 ERA 1996 (see **10.3.5** below).

2.2.6 Noting the basis of the question

The decisions in this area are not always consistent, but it is often useful to ask *why* the court had to make its judgment. If the matter is a simple question of money, e.g., tax liability, the court tends to take a very detached and analytical stance. If, however, the question is one of responsibility for safety as was the case in *Lane* v *Shire Roofing Co. (Oxford) Ltd* [1995] IRLR 493, one may find the Court of Appeal stretching definitions to their limit to prise the workman into the category of 'employee'. The grey area arises when the question of establishing status relates to the acquisition of rights (e.g., unfair dismissal); and, as noted above, perhaps this is the very area most likely to give rise to problems in the future.

The arguments on tax liability relate, of course, to the advantages gained by being self-employed in terms of deductions, etc. that can be made in assessing a person's yearly income. Most people are employees and so subject to the PAYE scheme, which allows for little or no leeway in the calculation of tax liability. The rules on National Insurance contributions differ according to status as well. The most recent controversy on 'employee' status and tax liability has arisen in the area of 'service providers', i.e., a person who operates a business or is engaged through an agency but works so regularly (often exclusively) for one company (e.g., providing IT services) that he or she looks to all the world like an employee. A new Inland Revenue scheme, commonly referred to as IR35, now creates a presumption that, under certain conditions, such people are deemed to be employees rather than self-employed.

2.3 The benefits and pitfalls of each type of relationship

Advantages to a company of hiring independent contractors

(a) That the company will not have to take on the administrative difficulties of tax, National Insurance, including the costs of the employer's contributions, or statutory sick pay.

(b) That the company is unlikely to be vicariously liable for the actions of the workmen (see **2.5** below).

(c) That a notionally lower duty as to safety is owed to independent contractors at common law under the tort of negligence if not under the Health and Safety at Work etc. Act 1974.

(d) That the company does not have to issue written statements of terms and conditions (under ERA 1996, s. 1—see **Chapter 3**).

(e) That the company is not responsible for the provision of training or the payment of training levies.

(f) That the company owes no duty to deal with trade unions as regards collective bargaining, redundancy consultation, or the provision of office facilities or time off.

Advantages to workmen of being independent contractors

(a) The workman will be able to register under Schedule D for tax purposes, gaining benefits of claiming expenses, etc.

(b) The workman will be free to undertake work from other sources without gaining permission from the 'employer'.

(c) The workman can determine his or her own pattern of work to fit in with personal commitments or other jobs.

(d) The workman may hire others to undertake the work.

(e) The workman is often free to choose where the work will be done.

(f) The workman may be able to negotiate better contractual terms than the equivalent employee.

(g) Work completed ahead of time will mean that the workman may move on to other tasks or even obtain a completion bonus.

(g) That the company will be dealing with commercial operators and so the contracts formed, the terms and conditions, will be viewed by courts in that setting. The company can thus hire groups of employees for specific tasks for short periods of time only.

(h) That the company cannot be liable for unfair dismissal or redundancy.

Advantages to a company of hiring employees

(a) The contract of employment requires *personal* service. The employer has made the judgment as to the make-up of its workmen.

(b) The employer maintains a higher level of control over employees, particularly where the company wishes the workmen to perform tasks on the periphery of the 'job description'.

(c) This control can be emphasised by the use of disciplinary procedures and sanctions.

(d) The contract is viewed as containing a much higher degree of loyalty and good faith via the device of implied terms (see **Chapter 5**).

(e) Unfair dismissal actions etc. on the whole will cost less than the termination of a commercial contract. Furthermore, actions short of dismissal can be taken more easily under a contract of employment's disciplinary procedures.

(f) The company does not have to pay VAT.

Advantages to workmen of being classed as employees

(a) Minimal financial input and risk.

(b) Fringe benefits, e.g., company cars and accommodation.

(c) Membership of company sick pay and pension schemes.

(d) The payment of holiday pay.

(e) Greater job security in terms of increased potential for capital investment.

(f) Greater job security in terms of statutory rights, e.g., unfair dismissal.

(g) The ability to demand more money for the performance of additional tasks not defined in the contract through trade union negotiation.

(h) The employer must indemnify the employee for expenses and liabilities occasioned in the course of employment.

2.4 Types of employee

Although the position of most workmen will never lead to litigation, specific occupations still cause problems. The questions raised above have grown in importance with the advent of different patterns of work, the move towards establishing small businesses and the massive increase in the numbers of women joining the workforce, mainly through a variety of forms of part-time jobs (e.g., temporary work, casual work, job-share schemes, and homeworking). It is fast becoming the norm to encounter employment relationships which do not fit the standard full-time pattern.

2.4.1 Crown servants

Crown servants are those individuals employed under or for a Government department or any body exercising Crown functions, e.g., civil servants. Traditionally, Crown servants have not been classed as 'employees' but have had protection against unfair dismissal. Under TULRCA 1992, s. 273, Crown servants have now gained 'employee status, and even those employed in the armed services have acquired certain employment rights under the ERA 1996, s. 192 and sch. 2, para. 16.

2.4.2   Directors and shareholders

Directors will not be classed as employees unless there is a contract of employment to that effect. In many cases, however, a director's duty as a fiduciary will create a greater burden of responsibility and accountability than if there were a contract of employment. The appointment of directors as employees is subject to various statutory controls. There is, however, no rule of law which prevents even a controlling shareholder from being held to be an employee too—it is a question of fact and public policy: *Secretary of State for Trade and Industry* v *Bottrill* [1999] IRLR 326 – and extensive guidelines have now been laid down by the EAT in *Clark* v *Clark Construction Initiatives Ltd* [2008] IRLR 364.

2.4.3   Consultants

Consultants may be classed as employees if they become sufficiently integrated into the business—and note the IR35 scheme above.

2.4.4   Part-timers

Under common law no real distinction has ever been made between full-time and part-time employees. Part-time employees will, for instance, owe duties of fidelity and confidentiality and will be covered by the law on intellectual property rights (e.g., patents). And although the courts have become increasingly aware that the standard expected of part-time employees (especially where restrictions are imposed on their activities) must inevitably be less than that expected of full-timers, the residual elements of the duties will nevertheless be present.

Neither does the epithet of 'part-time' affect a person's statutory rights (see below at **10.3.2**). As the amount of work taken diminishes, however, there may be problems as to status—as with those who work at home or who are casual workers.

The Part-time Workers (Prevention of Less Favourable Treatment) Regulations 2000 (SI 2000/1551), and are dealt with in **Chapter 6**.

2.4.5   Homeworkers

Once a workman is removed from the normal workplace, he or she gains some measure of independence as to 'control'. The more the workman can exercise discretion as to workload, timing and organisation of work, the more he or she is likely to be an independent contractor. However, as was seen in *Nethermere of St Neots* v *Gardiner and Taverna* [1984] ICR 612, if these workmen are treated in much the same way as full-time employees and gain benefits as to holiday entitlements, sick pay, etc., they are more likely to be employees. There are over three million people working wholly or mainly from home—some as a result of exercising their 'flexible working' rights (see **4.7** and **4.8** below).

In *Nethermere* the company manufactured boys' trousers. They employed full-time staff in their factory and a number of homeworkers. The applicants were part-time homeworkers. Taverna had previously worked in the factory as an employee. Both had worked with the company since the late 1970s. They sewed trouser flaps and pockets using machines provided by the company. There were no fixed hours of work; but they usually worked four to five hours a day. They were paid weekly by piece-rate. They filled out time sheets and received daily deliveries. They were not obliged to accept any particular quantity of work. There arose a dispute over holiday payments, as a consequence of which the arrangement came to an end. The workmen claimed they were unfairly dismissed. The company argued they were self-employed. The Court of Appeal held that there was sufficient mutuality of obligations for the relationship to constitute a contract of employment. Although the traditional use of homeworkers has now declined, the points raised here will take on a greater significance as more and more people work from home utilising information technology as the means of performing their jobs.

2.4.6   Casuals

Presently, the two most litigated areas on the definition of 'employee' relate to casuals and 'temps'.

In certain industries, e.g., catering or agriculture, it is quite common for staff to be employed casually or seasonally. Some are employed on a regular basis, others from time to time according to demand. The more regular the 'employment', the more the workers look like employees: but what does it take before an employment relationship is triggered by this regular contact? In one of the major cases in this area (*O'Kelly* v *Trust-house Forte* [1983] ICR 728) the Court of Appeal held that some staff who worked exclusively for the hotel chain for an average of 31 hours per week, were paid weekly and received holiday pay and incentive bonuses, were still not employees because they were not compelled to take work if it was offered to them and did not receive sick pay or belong to the company pension scheme. They were deemed to be in business on their own account.

O'Kelly highlights the problem: it may well be the case that on each occasion when the workman is hired by the company there is a contract of employment for a day, a week, a month or even longer, but such intermittent periods would be unlikely to form such a cohesive whole that there could be said to be an overall employment relationship continuing during the off-periods. Without such continuity of employment the workman would not gain access to many statutory employment rights, such as redundancy payments. The rights could be present only if one could find some form of 'global' contract, spanning the gap between the periods of engagement; and to establish that one needs to find that there is sufficient mutuality of obligation between company and workman during that slack time so as to override any view that these putative employees are simply people in business on their own account.

How can such mutuality be found? One needs to find some express or implied term that work would be provided and performed when reasonably required. Thus, in *Clark* v *Oxfordshire Health Authority* [1998] IRLR 125, bank nurses were found to be employees on the basis that they were paid a retainer during the off-period; on the other hand, in *Carmichael* v *National Power plc* [2000] IRLR 43, the House of Lords held that power station tour guides who worked as much as 25 hours per week, were paid an hourly rate, given training and wore company uniforms, were not employees because their letters of appointment stated that they worked on an 'as required basis' and they were not paid between engagements.

These cases are, however, far from satisfactory in providing practical solutions which a solicitor can put in place for his or her client. First, it should be noted that on each occasion the putative employee provides his or her service, the primary tests used above (control etc.) determine whether *that particular contract* is a contract of employment or not. If it is, and that employment goes on for long enough, the employee will gain various statutory employment rights anyway (e.g., generally a year for unfair dismissal). Secondly, even if the contractual periods are for short bursts, that does not mean there *cannot* be an employment relationship. The cases have not properly explored whether these contract periods could be melded together under the rules on establishing continuity of employment so that, even with a number of short-duration contracts, statutory rights might be acquired (see below at **5.3** for the rules on continuity). Thus, we would suggest that the focus should be on whether the established rules of continuity apply and not on the nebulous problem of whether there is a 'global contract' covering the off-periods. We would submit that the existence of any global contract can be determined by the purely contractual analysis of whether there is continuing consideration during those off-periods (as in *Clark*). One should not need to go beyond that contractual analysis and explore the vague topic of 'mutuality'.

2.4.7   Temp agency workers

Employment Businesses exist to supply workmen to client companies as temporary workers—or 'temps' as they are often called. The Employment Businesses enter into contracts with both the workman and the client company. These organisations are colloquially known as 'employment agencies', though this tag has a particular meaning in law, referring to recruitment consultants ('headhunters'). The difference is that 'headhunters' are forbidden from paying the workman; their money is made from finders' fees. As our interest lies with the status of 'temps' we shall concentrate on Employment Businesses (but note that older cases refer to these same organisations as 'employment agencies').

For many years, temps were not regarded as employees of either the employment business or their clients. Their position was said to be *sui generis: Ironmonger* v *Movefield Ltd* [1988] IRLR 461. But in the late 1990s the courts began to find contracts of employment, even where the contract itself specified that none existed. This did not happen on every occasion and the tide has begun to turn again. The problem lies in the fact that there is a tripartite agreement here: the Employment Business 'takes on' the temp, the temp is then sent to a client company, the temp works under the general rules of the client company (perhaps receiving benefits such as sick pay), the client company pays the Employment Business an agreed rate, the Employment Business pays the temp as per *their* agreement. There are plenty of contracts floating around, but are any of them contracts of employment? The problem is illustrated in **Figure 2.1**. Effectively, there are three possible outcomes: an employment contract exists between the Employment Business and the temp; or one exists between the temp and the client company (sometimes referred to as the 'end user'); or no employment contract exists.

2.4.7.1   Contract with the employment business?

In *McMeechan* v *Secretary of State for Employment* [1997] ICR 549 the Court of Appeal decided that there could (if the facts were right) be two contracts between a temp and an Employment Business: (i) an 'umbrella contract'—more often referred to as 'being on the books'; and (ii) separate contracts for each assignment given to the temp, even if the umbrella contract described the temp as 'self-employed'. However, *McMeechan* also made it clear that if a contract of employment did exist it was likely to be a contract regarding each specific assignment in question rather than any umbrella contract. In *Bunce* v *Postworth Ltd t/a Skyblue* [2005] EWCA Civ 490, [2005] IRLR 557 the Court of Appeal made it clear that it would be rare for a temp to have *any* form of employment contract with the Employment Business and that in those rare cases day-to-day control over the temp's activities would normally have to be present. It was thought by many that this sounded the death-knell for such claims but the Court of Appeal did remit such a case (involving the hiring of Polish temporary workers in the hotel industry) to a different tribunal for a re-hearing in *Consistent Group Ltd* v *Kalwak* [2008] EWCA Civ 430, [2008] IRLR 505 where all the classic conditions of personal service and control were present.

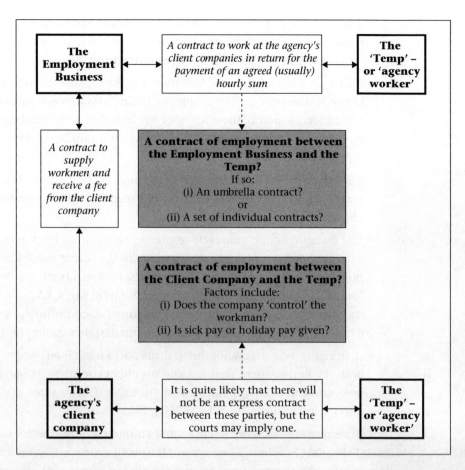

Figure 2.1 The possible inter-relationship of the parties.

2.4.7.2 Contract of employment with the client company (the 'end-user')?

Motorola Ltd v *Davidson and Melville Craig Group* [2001] IRLR 4 set out the view that, given sufficient control by the client company, there could be a contract of employment between the temp and that company. The same was seen in *Franks* v *Reuters Ltd* [2003] EWCA Civ 417, [2003] IRLR 423, where the Court of Appeal emphasised the need to examine the facts (uninterrupted service with the client company for six years and high degree of control) rather than rest the whole analysis on mutuality of obligations (e.g., the presence or absence of sick pay etc.).

In *Dacas* v *Brook Street Bureau (UK) Ltd* [2004] EWCA Civ 217, [2004] ICR 1437 the Court of Appeal confirmed (*obiter*) that a temp could become an employee of the client company in the right circumstances, again despite a clause to the contrary in the agreement, but the Court of Appeal have now clearly established in *James* v *London Borough of Greenwich* [2008] EWCA Civ 35, [2008] IRLR 302 that an employment contract between the temp and the client company will only be implied where it is *necessary* to give the arrangement business efficacy.

2.4.7.3 General guidance

- Until the next twist in the case law occurs it is a relatively safe presumption that a temp is employed by no one.

- It is highly unlikely (but just legally possible) that there will be an 'umbrella' agreement between the Employment Business and the temp which amounts to a contract of employment (see *McMeechan* and comments in *Bunce*). The more detailed the provisions in the contract as to what is to happen with each particular assignment the less likely such a contract can arise *(Bunce)*.

- Although *McMeechan* stated that there may be separate contracts of employment between the temp and the Employment Business for each particular assignment one still has to add all these together (with the breaks amounting only to 'temporary' cessations of employment) to get the right number of days to gain statutory rights.

- Though there is case authority that a temp may be employed by the client company such an occurrence will require exceptional facts (see *James v Greenwich LBC*).

- The documentation can exclude the inference of an employment relationship (e.g., an 'entire agreement' clause) but, to do this it should be very clear and not contain contradictory or conflicting statements (such conflict arose in *Royal National Lifeboat Institution* v *Bushaway* [2005] IRLR 674, EAT so that where a temp was made permanent in the client company her continuity of employment was dated from her original start date as a temp despite wording to the contrary).

- In bringing a claim (say, for unfair dismissal) a temp is advised to proceed against both the Employment Business and the client company. Tribunals also have the power to join a party: Employment Tribunals (Constitution and Rules of Procedure) Regulations, r. 10(2)(k), SI 2004/1861.

The Conduct of Employment Agencies and Employment Businesses Regulations 2003, SI 2003/3319 affect how both Employment Businesses and employment agencies operate and there are separate regulations covering workmen who operate as limited companies and the specialist Nursing Agencies. 'Temps' are now known as 'work-seekers'—but not by most people. The Regulations lay out detailed rules on the provision of contractual documents as between all parties, including statements on whether the work-seeker is to be an employee of the Employment Business or is working under a contract for services. The details of these documents are outside the scope of this text but the key question as to the determination of status is not clarified in the Regulations.

2.4.8 Employees on limited-term contracts

Employers sometimes use the device of a limited-term to define the length of an acknowledged employment contract. There is nothing untoward here and the term may be short (e.g., months) or long (years) or even relate to a specific task. When the time expires or the task is completed there are no further consequences at common law, though (as will be seen in **Chapter 6** and **Chapter 10**) the non-renewal of a limited-term contract will constitute a dismissal for statutory purposes such as unfair dismissal. Whether the non-renewal *actually is* an unfair dismissal is a separate question.

2.4.9 Apprentices

Apprentices are a *sui generis* category of employees. The purpose of an apprenticeship is primarily that of training so that, although most of the normal rules will cover them, there are some key differences from ordinary contracts, e.g., there are restrictions on how the contract can be terminated and damages may be awarded for loss of training and status. The so-called 'Modern Apprenticeship Agreement' is another of the tri-partite schemes (between the individual, the 'employer', and the local training organisation). The latest pronouncement by the Court of Appeal on the status of these modern apprentices is that they can be apprentices as we know them (which means they gain extra damages for loss of training): *Flett* v *Matheson* [2006] EWCA Civ 53, [2006] ICR 673.

2.4.10   Employees of unincorporated associations

The issue here is simply: 'Whom do such employees sue?' The answer has been provided by the EAT in *Affleck* v *Newcastle MIND* [1999] IRLR 405: one member of the committee should be named as respondent, in his own right and on behalf of all the other members of the committee. Any compensation should be awarded against all those on the committee at the relevant time.

2.4.11   Posted workers

The Posting of Workers Directive (96/71/EC), implemented by the ERA 1999, s. 32, covers the situations where: (a) workers temporarily work in Great Britain; and (b) workers temporarily work abroad.. This requires that where a Member State has certain minimum terms and conditions of employment (see **3.4.3.1** below), these must apply to workers posted temporarily by their employer to work in that state. The contract may allow for greater benefits. It does not matter for these purposes whether the organisation posting the worker is from a Member State or not. Unfortunately, this is just the tip of the iceberg when dealing with employees working abroad and one needs to look at a whole raft of specialist legislative measures and House of Lords' decisions in the context of each type of claim before giving advice on this area.

2.4.12   Voluntary workers

Many people work on a voluntary basis (e.g., for charities); this does not make them employees. In *South East Sheffield Citizens Advice Bureau* v *Grayson* [2004] IRLR 353 the EAT held that an unpaid CAB volunteer was not an employee (for the purposes of Discrimination legislation), even when paid expenses and even where the CAB would be liable to indemnify the person against negligence claims, as there was no mutuality present. The same analysis has now been applied to unfair dismissal in *Melhuish* v *Redbridge Citizens Advice Bureau* [2005] IRLR 419.

2.4.13   Seconded employees

There are instances where one company hires an employee's services from another company. When this arrangement becomes long term awkward questions arise as to who now employs that person. The test is essentially a factual one: where does the mutuality of obligation and element of control lie? Thus, in *Fitton* v *City of Edinburgh Council* (2008 UKEATS/0010/07/MT) the fact that the employee, seconded on an open-ended basis, opted to work under the terms and conditions of the seconding employer and held no substantive job title with her old employer (although there was a fairly loose arrangement for her to return to her old job if the secondment came to an end) led to the conclusion that she no longer worked for her original employer (when she resigned her post and claimed unfair dismissal).

2.5 Vicarious liability

An employer may be vicariously liable for the actions of employees where those actions were undertaken by the employee 'in the course of employment' and not, in the magical phrase 'on a frolic of his own'. The traditional test has been that if the employee is performing a task which falls within the general expectations of the contract but is performing it in an unauthorised manner, the employer is still likely to be held vicariously liable. Obviously, the employer is liable for any wrongful acts which have been authorised. In *Lister* v *Helsey Hall Ltd* [2001] UKHL 22, [2001] IRLR 472, however, the House of Lords adopted a broader test: were the employee's acts and the nature of his duties closely connected? Using this test (which is similar to that used in discrimination cases, see below at **6.5.3**), their Lordships held that an employer (operating a children's residential school) was vicariously liable for the sexual assaults on boys in the school committed by an employee-warden.

If this test is satisfied, the employer will be liable for any personal injury or other damage caused by the employee. This principle can even apply where the injured person is another employee.

The position becomes more complicated when the employee in question is a seconded employee: who bears the vicarious liability - the hiring company or the hirer? The leading House of Lords' case of *Mersey Docks and Harbour Board* v *Coggins and Griffith (Liverpool) Ltd* [1947] AC 1 established that this depended on who exercised control over how the job was done. It was thought at that time that this would usually be the permanent employer, but in *Hawley* v *Luminar Leisure plc* [2006] EWCA Civ 18, [2006] IRLR 817 the Court of Appeal held that where a doorman injured a customer the real control rested with the nightclub rather than the permanent employer for the purposes of vicarious liability so that the doorman was a 'temporary deemed employee' of the nightclub (a decision possibly influenced by the severity of the injuries caused by the doorman and the insolvency of the permanent employer). This idea of attaching legal liability to the 'user company' fits in with previous Court of Appeal authorities which had held that in some instances *both* the permanent and temporary employers could be vicariously liable for the employee's actions if the employee is 'so much a part of the work . . . of both employers that it is just to make both employers answer for his negligence'—i.e., where both 'employers' are controlling the employee's actions: *Viasystems (Tyneside) Ltd* v *Thermal Transfer (Northern) Ltd* [2005] EWCA Civ 1151, [2006] ICR 327.

2.6 The statutory meaning of 'worker'

At one time all that had to be asked was, 'Is this person an employee or an independent contractor?' If the former then all the employment rights we will cover in this book came into play; if, not, then they did not. Now, however, as we noted above, some employment rights extend to 'workers' as well as employees. The genuinely self-employed will still not fall within this definition, but 'worker' covers a wider range of people than 'employee'. For instance, the definition to be found in the Working Time Regulations 1998 (dealing with the regulation of hours of work, holidays, etc., see **Chapter 4**) and the Part-time Workers (Prevention of Less Favourable Treatment) Regulations 2000 is the same (see **Chapter 6**). The definition includes anyone who has entered into, or works under, a contract of employment and any other contract 'whereby the individual undertakes to do or perform personally any work or services for another party to the contract whose status is not by virtue of the contract that of a client or customer of any profession or business undertaking carried on by the individual', e.g., agency workers and homeworkers.

In *Edmonds* v *Lawson, Pardoe & Del Fabro* [2000] IRLR 391, the Court of Appeal held that a pupil barrister was not a 'worker' for the purpose of the National Minimum Wage Act 1998. The Northern Ireland Court of Appeal, however, extended equal pay protection (under EU law) to employment tribunal chairmen (who are statutory office-holders), classifying them as 'workers' by reference to EU legislation on equal pay and freedom of movement: *Perceval-Price* v *Department of Economic Development* [2000] IRLR 380. The EAT have also held that 'labour-only subcontractors' in the building industry who worked exclusively for one employer and undertook to provide personal service were not 'in business on their own account' and were 'workers' for the purpose of the Working Time Regulations (and so entitled to holiday pay): *Byrne Brothers (Farmwork) Ltd* v *Baird* [2002] IRLR 96. On the other hand, sub-postmasters (who were not employees even under pre-WTRegs case law) are apparently neither employees nor workers: *Commissioners of Inland Revenue* v *Post Office Ltd* [2003] IRLR 199. Bricklayers have received special attention in 2004 from the Court of Appeal where a group of subcontractors was classified as 'workers' for the purposes of the Working Time Regulations in *Redrow Homes (Yorkshire) Ltd* v *Wright* [2004] EWCA Civ 469, [2004] IRLR 720, largely because the contract involved an obligation to carry out work personally. This decision follows similar reasoning seen in the EAT recently as regards joiners and (another group of) bricklayers.

In an attempt to bring some order to this topic the President of the EAT set out guidelines on 'spotting the worker' in *James* v *Redcats (Brands) Ltd* [2007] IRLR 296 (a case concerning the status of a courier). Here, the. two key factors he identified were: (i) is there mutuality of obligations during the time the worker undertakes work for the organization?; and (ii) is the personal service involved the dominant purpose of the contract?—if it is then the individual is more likely to be a 'worker'.

2.7 Summary

- Most employment rights depend upon the claimant fitting the description of 'employee', though 'workers' have been given rights under specific statutory provisions.

- The definition of 'employee' rests on utilising a series of tests which focus on control, mutuality of obligations, and the economic reality of the relationship.

- The label given to the relationship is not the determining feature.

- Most problems arise with non-standard relationships such as homeworkers and 'temps'. Although each case turns very much on its facts, the courts take a pragmatic approach to such situations and tend to compare the putative employee's relationship with the employer to that of more obvious 'employees'. Recent case law has made it much more difficult for temps to argue that they have a contract of employment with anyone.

Formation of the contract

3.1 Introduction

The role played by the contract of employment is central to understanding all aspects of employment law. For many years contractual principles were the sole determinant of all issues within the employment relationship. Today, many features of that relationship are determined by statutory provisions, e.g., rights to claim unfair dismissal and redundancy. However, these features have not supplanted contractual theories but have been annexed to the basic contractual points, so that many issues discussed in this book require an understanding of both contractual and statutory matters.

The next two chapters describe briefly where a solicitor may discover the contractual terms. **Chapter 5** will then examine what may be done with those terms. In dealing with any employment question the first port of call has to be the contract itself as made up from the express and implied terms. It is nevertheless an unfortunate feature of employment law practice that, whereas a solicitor may regard the contract as the first port of call, the employer-client tends to regard it as 'any port in a storm', often arguing *ex post facto,* and without evidence, that the contract justifies the action taken.

We can start with the fact that the ordinary rules of contract apply to contracts of employment. All the classic offer and acceptance points, the need for consideration, etc., can be seen at work here. However, there are also specially-formulated rules which apply only to employment contracts, e.g., principles of fidelity and rules of procedure. These rules have arisen for three main reasons:

(a) Employers and employees have traditionally shown complete indifference to recording accurately, or even understanding, the terms of their agreements so that *someone* has had to iron out the basic requirements (i.e., the courts and tribunals).

(b) Employment contracts generally last for an indefinite term and therefore rules have had to be created to allow the contract to change and develop with time.

(c) Employment contracts were born out of feudal and criminal law concerns. The feudal notions stretch back to legislation in the fourteenth century (1348) which set limits on the movement of labourers and on wage increases. And it was not until late in the nineteenth century that actions such as disobedience to lawful orders on the part of an employee ceased to be criminal offences. When judges had to analyse the structure of the contract of employment it was hardly surprising, then, to find that they drew upon many of the old and established feudal notions of service. This history still influences the judicial view of the employment relationship, especially as regards notions of loyalty and commitment to the enterprise.

These three factors have meant that the strict rules of contract have often had to be bent a little in order to make sense in the employment setting. This 'bending' can cause problems because it leaves some uncertainty as to when distortion can occur. One of the aims of this chapter and, in particular, **Chapter 5** will be to give some structure to this uncertainty.

Some commonly used concepts will inevitably be vague, and much of this can be seen in the extensive use of *implied terms* to determine the scope and intentions of the contract of employment, e.g., the requirement that the parties owe each other a duty of mutual trust and confidence. The device of implying a term is used in the same way as with ordinary commercial contracts (e.g., 'officious bystander' test), but the range of questions posed—from whether sick pay is due to the extent that an employee is expected to perform work outside the strict terms of the contract—means that a great deal of judicial inventiveness is evident, and has been necessary, over the years.

This chapter will adopt the following structure:

(a) The needs of the client.

(b) Types of contract.

(c) Sources of terms.

(d) Written statements of terms and conditions.

(e) The process of incorporation of terms.

(f) The role of trade unions in the employment relationship.

3.2 The needs of the client

The most obvious need is to obtain the best terms possible. The employee will look primarily at remuneration and benefits; the employer's concerns may be wider, stretching to matters of protecting confidentiality, rights to inventions, flexibility of operations, etc. As with any contract there is a bargain to be struck. However, this tends to give the impression of detailed haggling over terms when the reality for the vast majority of employees is quite different.

When drafting or analysing a contract of employment you will need to consider the size and resources of the administration, the requirements of the business and the market in which it operates, the types of employees involved, and the resulting industrial relations consequences of any action.

3.2.1 Needs of the employee-client

Many contracts will be the subject of long-standing agreements with trade unions so that the individual has no say in the basic format of the contract. And even when the individual does negotiate a specific contract, or negotiates certain aspects of it, e.g., pay or holiday rights, employers still effectively dictate the *form* of the contract. Thus, if involved at all, solicitors will most likely be asked to advise employees or trade unions on the structure and content of the contract, on any legal requirements, and on any pitfalls to the proposals.

If the individual employee does seek advice at the formation stage, his or her concerns will tend to centre on the *meaning and scope* of stated or unstated obligations and take the form of the following types of questions:

(a) How is pay calculated, especially regarding things such as commission rates?

(b) How are other benefits (perks) calculated?

(c) What, if any, are the requirements to be moved to other sites?

(d) What, if any, are the requirements as to overtime?

(e) What are the notice requirements?

(f) What are the pension and sickness benefit rights?

(g) What happens if I leave? Can I take a job elsewhere in the same line of business?

All these points are addressed in **Chapters 4, 5,** and **9**.

3.2.2   Needs of the employer-client

Employers will tend to be more concerned with establishing to their satisfaction matters such as the employee's duties, flexibility of operations, and rights to vary the contract. But even here, many employers rely on their personnel departments or on antiquated standard forms which have not been altered in years (but should have been). A further problem is that the contract may be made orally or in writing (or in any combination). Many employees in this country have never seen written evidence of their contract. Thus the scope for imprecision and misunderstanding is great.

Consequently, the more control that can be exercised by the solicitor at these early stages the better; from the wording of any advertisement through to the final offer letter. If such control is possible, the solicitor should be briefed clearly on points such as:

(a) Does the employer wish to hire an employee, or would an independent contractor be better suited to the needs of the business? (see **Chapter 2**)

(b) If an employee is needed, what is to be the job description and what degree of flexibility do you want from the post?

(c) Is the advertisement, appointment or promotion in any way discriminatory? (see **Chapter 6**)

(d) What are the needs of the business in terms of working patterns, e.g., shift work, job-sharing, overtime, mobility clauses? (see **Chapter 5** in particular)

(e) Is there a special need to protect business secrets, e.g., by use of confidentiality or restraint of trade clauses? (see **Chapters 7** and **8**)

(f) What does the client want in terms of disciplinary and dismissal procedures? (see **Chapters 9** and **10** in particular)

(g) The need, if any, for any special requirements such as compulsory medical examinations or outlawing the introduction of computer disks to the workplace (this sort of term appears in an increasing number of contracts, e.g., on oil-rig platforms, where the presence of computer viruses could prove disastrous or even fatal).

3.3   Types of contract

Chapter 2 dealt with problems as to *status* (e.g., whether casual workers can be classed as employees). In this chapter we are concerned only with proven employees and the *contractual terms* themselves. Thus when we talk of 'types' of contract here we are referring to the variations in drafting styles necessary to meet specific organisational needs. The structure of employment contracts can vary tremendously, from the kind whose complexity could justify inclusion in a Tolkien novel to the rather prosaic 'I said he could start work on Monday'.

Where an employer wishes to employ workers who do not fall within the traditional definition of full-time permanent workers each *type* of worker will require special attention in the drafting of contractual terms. Issues as to formation of contract do not vary as between these different types of workers but any standard contractual terms will obviously have to be modified to take account of the employee's status in the organisation. If the employer requires distinctive provisions or working arrangements for these employees then the contract needs to reflect this explicitly.

3.3.1 Limited-term contracts

Most employment contracts are open-ended (i.e., for an indefinite term). They are usually terminated by one or other party giving notice (see **Chapter 9** for more detail). However, contracts may be made to last for a fixed term (say, six months) or for the completion of a particular task. Employees may be employed on a seasonal basis or to cover work for a short period (e.g., agricultural workers or shop assistants working specifically for the Christmas period). Employees may also be employed to cover for maternity or sick leave or for a specific project, e.g., setting up a new database. The arrival of the agreed date, or the completion of the task, terminates the contract automatically and there are no further consequences at common law (though the position is different as regards statutory remedies such as unfair dismissal). These forms of contract are collectively known as *limited-term contracts,* the most common of which is the *fixed-term* contract. Both expressions appear in the legislation, though *limited-term* is wider and includes both fixed-term and specific-task contracts (see sch. 2, para. 3(18) of Fixed-term Employees (Prevention of Less Favourable Treatment) Regulations 2002, SI 2002/2034, inserting new ERA 1996, s. 235 (2A) and (2B)).

The certainty that a limited-term contract possesses also brings with it a degree of inflexibility. Therefore most limited-term contracts will contain a clause permitting the contract to be terminated before expiry in the case of, for example, gross misconduct by the employee. It is also possible, strange as it sounds, to have a limited-term contract which allows for termination by either party giving notice *for any reason* to take effect before the set finish date.

3.4 Sources of terms

Employment contracts are frequently a nightmare in practice. Except in the larger and better organised companies, the discovery of the precise up-to-date terms would tax even the skills of Indiana Jones on a good day.

Terms of employment are derived from a number of sources. The most obvious is that of a written contract. Unfortunately many employees have never seen a written contract and, even if they have, it was probably issued when they started, no one can find a copy, and there is no firm evidence that it has been changed in the intervening years. Your client, employer or employee, will tell you that it has been altered several times, but proving this fact tends to be somewhat perplexing. Your employer-client will also justify his understanding of the terms with phrases such as: 'We've always done it that way'; 'They (the employees) all knew about it'; 'We definitely agreed that with the union sometime'; 'I would have said that in the interview'; 'I didn't think to ask—it's obvious isn't it?'; and, from the heart, 'I haven't got time for legal technicalities—I've a business to run'.

You may therefore be faced with two equally unpalatable situations—a total lack of evidence or a wealth of jumbled evidence. You must be prepared to accept, in even the best organised companies, that many 'rules' will still not appear in writing and that relevant dates of changes in practice are lost in the mists of time.

The range of source material can be extensive. You must be aware of the possible existence of:

(a) written terms;

(b) orally agreed terms;

(c) written statements (under ERA 1996, s. 1: see **3.5** below);

(d) itemised pay statements;

(e) collective agreements reached with trade unions;

(f) national and local agreements of the industry concluded between employers' associations and trade unions;

(g) works' rules and staff handbooks;

(h) custom and practice;

(i) job descriptions;

(j) job advertisements;

(k) related documents, e.g., disciplinary arrangements, grievance procedures, health and safety policies, pension booklets;

(l) a vast range of implied terms derived from the facts of the relationship, from the common law and from statute; and

(m) EC legislation, e.g., Treaties and Directives.

We shall examine these sources below. One 'source' deserves a special mention at this point: the written statement, under ERA 1996, s. 1. This is something of a sheep in wolf's clothing. As we shall see in **3.5**, written statements must be given to every employee (including agency workers) within two months of starting work; they act as summaries of the contractual terms. These documents are not, strictly, a source of contractual terms but they are nevertheless important enough to warrant particular attention.

3.4.1   The parties

In many, if not most, cases there will be three parties involved in setting the contractual terms: the employer, the employee, and trade unions. The law works on the basis that each employee has an individual contract with the employer, but most contracts have been the subject of a collective agreement between an employer and trade union, the terms of the agreement then being translated into individuals' contracts (which may have been varied from time to time, as with an annual pay rise—see **3.6** below). Not all terms of an employer-trade union agreement are capable of being applied to individual workers; they may relate only to how the employer and trade union conduct themselves. In such cases (such as union recognition agreements) the terms do not translate into the employee's contract.

3.4.2   The express terms

As may have been gathered, employment contracts are treated with far less respect by the parties than are other contracts; many only exist as oral agreements. To quote Sam Goldwyn, the result is that, when it comes to a dispute, these oral contracts are often not worth the paper they are written on.

Express terms may be found in oral statements and in a variety of documents. Thus the most reliable source would be a written contract. There you would expect to find a wide range of terms which we shall explore in **Chapter 5**, e.g., payment, hours of work, and notice requirements.

There may be many other different terms, e.g., as to the maintenance of confidentiality. Equally, the contract does not have to detail every aspect of the contract so that (as with pension scheme details) reference may be made to other documents. These documents should have been given to the employee, or at least have been available for inspection at, say, the personnel department.

3.4.2.1   Works' rules, employment policy statements, and staff handbooks

These documents can present particular difficulties. They usually take the form of booklets, or notices posted on boards, containing rules of practice or behaviour in the workplace. Intranet sites can also count as 'handbooks': *Harlow* v *Artemis International Corporation Ltd* [2008] EWHC 1126 (QB), [2008] IRLR 629. However, most of these various types of document tend to be nothing more than codes of conduct and are significant only because their breach might *indicate* incompetence or misconduct. They are not strictly terms of the contract. But if these rules are expressly or impliedly incorporated in the contract, or can be used to make sense of a bald statement in the contract, they may have become as much a term as any other statement, despite the fact that they probably have been imposed unilaterally.

Where an employee has signed a document which acknowledges the binding effect of the works' rules then the rules will become a term of the contract. But even without a signature, if the employer has given reasonable notice of the rules and their importance they are most likely to be classed as terms. Much will depend on the availability of the rules (e.g., handed out or displayed in a prominent place) and whether they were treated by the employer as important. The trick lies in distinguishing on the facts between a mere *policy* and an obligatory term: see *Grant* v *South West Trains Ltd* (C-249/96) [1998] IRLR 188 (equal opportunities policy not incorporated) and *Deadman* v *Bristol City Council* [2007] EWCA Civ 822, [2007] IRLR 888 (policy statement to treat harassment claims 'sensitively' too vague to be incorporated but policy on the make-up of the panel for hearing the grievance was clear and incorporated); and is really a question of intention to create legal relations.

The arguments in this area are therefore purely contractual, but the question of incorporation is not always straightforward and even tribunal judges can approach the topic from quite different presumptions as to what is required to incorporate 'rules' which are not clearly stated as express contractual terms (see the problems relating to disciplinary procedures raised in **Chapters 9** and **10**, for instance). Certainly, the more precise the policy's terms and the more it ties in with obvious contractual terms, the more likely incorporation has been effected. Indeed, somewhat against expectations, in *Keeley* v *Fosroc International Ltd* [2006] EWCA Civ 1277, [2006] IRLR 961 the Court of Appeal held that a clause in a staff handbook which dealt with enhanced redundancy payments was a contractual term.

3.4.2.2 Orally agreed terms

Oral statements have the same status as written documents. Their disadvantage is one of proof. Where there is a conflict between written and oral evidence clearly the document will have the edge. But statements made at interview, for instance, have been allowed to stand in the face of apparently contradictory written evidence. Thus, say two site engineers have been instructed to transfer from the company's Bristol plant to Coventry. Both have refused, claiming this to be outside their contractual obligations. They tell you that when they commenced work in 1998 they were given a written contract of employment which stated they would be required to work on any site in the UK 'at the discretion of Grime Ltd'. However, before agreeing to sign the contract they were assured by the personnel director that their work would be limited to the Bristol area.

The written contract will be taken as binding unless evidence can be adduced to prove otherwise. The oral assurance will suffice if it can be proven, either as a collateral contract or as an overriding oral undertaking (this was so in the case on which this example is based: *Hawker Siddeley Power Engineering Ltd* v *Rump* [1979] IRLR 425). You can imagine that the question of proof could be an obstacle but, if proven, the contract would be that the employees are not required to move. With these sorts of cases in mind some employers now make use of 'entire agreement' clauses which specify that no other material or representations except those contained in the contract may amount to a contractual term: see *White* v *Bristol Rugby Club* [2002] IRLR 204 for such an example.

3.4.2.3 Custom and practice

Terms may be found by reference to established custom, though this has always been a debatable area and its use is not common today. To have effect the custom cannot be inconsistent with express terms or statutory rights. But, if a custom is reasonable, certain (i.e., can be stated precisely) and well known in the company and has been treated *consistently* as a term in the past (see *Quinn* v *Calder Industrial Materials Ltd* [1996] IRLR 126), it may be classed as a term of the contract. The employee's ignorance of the custom is not a valid point if 'everyone else' in the company or industry knew about it.

3.4.2.4 Proof of terms

You will have gathered from the above that this is not always a simple exercise, and often there is conflicting evidence. Further, in interpreting the contract the general rule, of course, is that the use of evidence as to what the parties said or did *after* the contract was made is not permitted. In reality, however, tribunals have tended to take such evidence where nothing else is available. In *Dunlop Tyres Ltd* v *Blows* [2001] EWCA Civ 1032, [2001] IRLR 629, the Court of Appeal effectively acknowledged this practice when faced with a very ambiguous agreement on the level of pay to be made for working on bank holidays. Their Lordships admitted evidence of the position before and after the date of the relevant agreement, on the basis that 'the absence of any change of practice would be a clear indication that the parties . . . intended no change in the contractual terms'. It should be stressed, however, that this case rested on a very ambiguous agreement reached some 30 years before the case itself.

3.4.3 Implied terms

A word of caution is needed regarding implied terms: in the employment setting the courts frequently operate from a set of long-established presumptions. Many of these presumptions can look rather strange because they are feudal in their origin. But the basic rules for implying terms will normally apply. Thus, in keeping with general contractual theory, terms will only be implied where they are *necessary* for the business efficacy of the contract, not simply because it would be *reasonable* so to imply them (*Liverpool* v *Irwin* [1977] AC 239). However, once a term has been found to be necessary to the contract the court will then determine the limits of that term within reasonable parameters. The idea is to make the contract workable, no more than that; and the courts will certainly avoid *writing* the contract for the parties.

A full discussion of the importance of implied terms in contracts of employment will take place in **Chapters 4** and **5**. An implied term has the same force as an express term and may even be used to resolve conflicts between express terms. However, implied terms will give way to any inconsistent express statement. The range of terms is not fixed. Implied terms will include the following:

The duties incumbent on the employer	*The duties incumbent on the employee*
The duty to pay.	A duty to act in good faith.
A limited duty to provide work.	The duty to obey lawful orders.
Duties relating to the health and safety of employees.	A duty to provide personal service.
A duty of mutual trust and confidence.	The duty to exercise reasonable skill and care.
A duty to provide proper information to employees.	The duty to take care of the employer's property.

3.4.3.1   Terms implied by law

Terms may be implied by law. For instance, the courts have created a term that employers and employees must show the other party mutual trust and confidence. Such terms are often called 'legal incidents' of the relationship and do not depend upon the intentions of the parties. Many are a matter of common sense, e.g.:

(a) a duty to act honestly;

(b) a duty on the employee's part to cooperate and obey lawful orders;

(c) a duty on the employee's part to provide faithful service, e.g., not to disclose the employer's confidential information;

(d) a duty on the employee's part not to take bribes or make secret profits from the position;

(e) a reciprocal duty of mutual trust and confidence (which is something of a minefield to define precisely—see **Chapter 5**);

(f) a duty on the employer's part not to act capriciously in operating express terms (e.g., disciplinary rules);

(g) a duty on the employee's part to be adaptable as the contract changes over time.

Others have been worked out over the years to deal with more specific situations, e.g.:

(h) that there is no *presumption* whether contractual sick pay will or will not be payable;

(i) that there is no rule that the parties will act *reasonably* towards each other;

(j) that the employer will ensure the reasonable safety of the employee at work;

(k) that the employer is usually under no duty to provide references.

Equally, statutes have created similar irrebuttable points. Thus, for example, non-discrimination clauses relating to sex and race are automatically deemed to be part of the contract, whatever the terms may say. Clauses which seek to oust the jurisdiction of the court will be void. And the duties may take a more positive form in requiring compulsory insurance for employees or in the creation of employers' liability for the provision of defective equipment.

3.4.3.2 Terms implied in fact

Terms may also be implied from the particular conduct of the parties and by examining the parties' presumed intentions. Custom and practice is one example; documents not expressly included in the contract but used frequently by the parties may be another.

The two devices used by the courts (which will be familiar from studies of contract law) are those of the 'business efficacy test' and the 'officious bystander'. Conduct subsequent to the original agreement should be treated with caution unless it shows some form of estoppel varying the original terms. It can be useful to show what the parties *seem* to have left unstated at the outset. So, with our example above (at **3.4.2.2**) regarding the transfer of employees from Bristol to Coventry there would be scope for arguing that an implied term, arising from the *nature* of their work (they were site engineers) or custom and working practice over the last few years might exist requiring the men to move.

Of course, all this fails if there is a clear, express term to the contrary; though, even here, there is the possibility of arguing for a move under the duty to cooperate if the distance is, say, within reasonable commuting distance.

The key rule therefore has to be: would the parties have agreed to such a term if the problem had been posed to them at the outset of the contract, and is such a term necessary to make the contract work?

3.5 Statements of terms and conditions

3.5.1 The right

Most employees have the right, under ERA 1996, s. 1, to receive from their employer a statement of initial employment particulars (usually called a *written statement* of their terms and conditions). These particulars must be issued not later than *two months* after the beginning of employment. The necessary contents are detailed below. This s. 1 statement largely complies with the Proof of Employment Directive 91/533.

It needs to be stressed, however, that this written statement is *not* the contract. Rather it is very strong *prima facie* evidence of the terms. It is like an MOT certificate: it tells you what the contract/vehicle looks like at a particular moment—it is no guarantee of the real condition of the contract/vehicle or its 'roadworthiness'. Employment tribunals and courts will accept such evidence only if there is nothing in the contract proper to contradict it. Thus written or oral evidence of agreed terms, express or implied, will all prevail over a written statement. For example, in *Robertson v British Gas Corporation* [1983] ICR 351, the employee's letter of appointment gave details of an incentive bonus agreed with the union. The employers subsequently withdrew from the agreement with the union and ceased paying the bonus. The employee sued for the arrears of pay. The mere withdrawal from the agreement with the union did not alter the employee's contract and a written statement permitting withdrawal from the agreement as a contractual right was held to be ineffective in altering the terms of the original agreement.

Nor does this fundamental point alter simply because the employee has signed the written statement as a receipt (as in *System Floors (UK) Ltd* v *Daniel* [1982] ICR 54) or has continued in employment after it has been issued without objection. Signing a written statement *as a contract of employment,* however, will bind the employee.

Nevertheless, a written statement may be the only documentary evidence and an employee may have a hard job convincing a court or tribunal that a document, issued by the employer, does not accurately reflect the contractual agreement.

The qualifying period for this right is one month (ERA 1996, s. 198) and a qualifying employee is entitled to the statement even where the employment ends before the period of two months in case they need to make a claim against the employer and need to refer to the statement in evidence. Also, in keeping with logic, those employees who have received a document containing express terms detailing the particulars required under ERA 1996, s. 1, do not have to be given a s. 1 statement (ERA 1996, s. 7A).

Written statements are a useful way of informing employees of the general terms of the contract. They are no substitute for a properly drafted contract. Despite all this, many employees have never seen a written statement of terms (or a written contract).

3.5.2 The contents

Under ERA 1996, ss. 1–7 the written statement must contain:

(a) the names of the employer and employee;

(b) the date when the employment began;

(c) the date on which the employee's period of continuous employment began (usually the same as the start date, but work with another employer might be included);

(d) the scale, rate, and method of calculating remuneration;

(e) the pay intervals (e.g., weekly);

(f) terms and conditions of hours of work;

(g) holiday entitlements;

(h) sickness and incapacity details and entitlements;

(i) pension scheme details;

(j) notice entitlement;

(k) job title or brief description of the work;

(l) if the job is not permanent, the period for which it is meant to last, including any fixed term;

(m) the expected place of work and address of the employer;

(n) any collective agreements affecting the employment, including things such as national agreements;

(o) details of any work abroad lasting more than one month;

(p) a note specifying any grievance and disciplinary rules applicable to the employee.

If there are no details to enter under any of these heads, e.g., there is no sick pay payable, this must be so stated (s. 2).

The statement may be given in instalments but certain matters must be given in a *single document,* namely: names of the parties; start date and dating of continuous employment; method of calculating payment and pay intervals; hours of work; holiday entitlement; job title; and place of work. The statement may, exceptionally, refer to other documents to which the employee has reasonable access in respect of terms relating to sickness, incapacity, notice periods, collective agreements, disciplinary rules and procedures, and pensions.

Where a change occurs to any of the provisions mentioned above then, under s. 4, the employer must notify the employee of such changes at the earliest opportunity (and not later than a month after the change).

3.5.3 Enforcement

Should the employer fail to comply with the requirements of ERA 1996, ss. 1 to 7, ss. 11 and 12 allow reference to be made to an employment tribunal. Where no particulars have been issued concerning any matter falling within s. 1, or the particulars are said to be inaccurate, the tribunal may determine what the parties have actually agreed and so what should have appeared in the statement.

However, this is almost a right without a remedy because the tribunal will not make the contract for the parties, it will not insert a term; it will simply *record* what the evidence reveals had been agreed by the parties. The tribunal will look first for evidence of express terms and then implied terms, and will also look at how the contract has actually been performed. Thus, in *Mears* v *Safecar Security Ltd* [1982] IRLR 183, the fact that employees asking for details on sick pay had not previously been paid any sick pay was damning to the question posed under s. 11.

There is uncertainty as to what is the correct approach when there is no evidence of the terms whatsoever. Should the tribunal then invent something? In *Mears* it was suggested, *obiter,* that this would be acceptable. But the Court of Appeal in *Eagland* v *British Telecommunications plc* [1992] IRLR 323 reaffirmed the rule that the tribunal should not make the contract. Thus, if the relevant term *should* have appeared in the statement then the tribunal may have to make some form of ruling; if the term in question is not one specifically covered by the s. 1 statement the tribunal should leave well alone.

Under EA 2002, s. 38 tribunals have acquired additional powers. If an employee:

- makes a claim under one of the jurisdictions set out in sch. 5 to the Act (an extensive list including an unfair dismissal claim, a redundancy payments claim, an action for breach of contract, a discrimination claim, and a minimum wages claim); and

- the tribunal finds in favour of the employee in respect of that claim; and

- the tribunal finds that the employer was also in breach of ERA 1996, s. 1 or s. 4(1) at the time the claim was made,

then the tribunal must make an award to reflect this unless there are exceptional circumstances which would make this unjust or inequitable. If the tribunal has made no award regarding the triggering claim it must award the employee two weeks' pay and may award four weeks' pay. If the tribunal has made an award regarding the triggering claim the tribunal must increase that award by two weeks' pay and may increase it by four weeks' pay. A **'week's pay' is statutorily defined in Chapter 2 of Part 14 ERA 1996 and is increased annually in February**. At the time of writing it is £330 per week (or lower if the employee is not paid this much).

3.5.4 Written statements on Sunday working

The classic written statement has a sibling. Under ERA 1996, s. 42(1), where a person becomes a shop or betting worker he or she must receive (within two months of starting) a written statement in a prescribed form detailing rights to 'opt out' of Sunday working by giving three months' notice to do so. If the employer fails to provide this statement the employee need only give one month's notice of opting out.

This right applies to new and existing shop and betting workers, but does not apply to those employed only to work on Sunday.

3.6 The process of incorporation of terms

From the text above it will have become clear that there is rarely *one single* document constituting the contract of employment. It should also be clear that the contract of employment is not immutable; that because it deals with a continuing relationship it is subject to express and implied change.

Many terms are *incorporated in the contract by reference*. Such incorporation may occur through notification or working practice but the best insurance is that of the written contract. Equally, sometimes it might be better to leave things such as 'works' rules' on the level of non-contractual conditions.

The most common problem of incorporation, however, relates to collective agreements. An agreement between an employer and a trade union does not in itself form part of an employee's contract. If the terms are vague (e.g., that both parties will seek to promote industrial harmony), or if the terms can relate only to collective matters (i.e., how disputes are to be settled between employers and trade unions) they *cannot* form part of an individual's contract. Thus even clauses which guarantee 'no compulsory redundancies' have been held to have no contractual force: *Kaur* v *MG Rover Group* [2004] EWCA Civ 1507, [2005] ICR 625. The test is whether the term itself is appropriate for incorporation. If a guarantee of no compulsory redundancies cannot meet this test one can see that very few terms could.

Incorporation is not an automatic process. Even if there are parts of the agreement which are capable of being applied to the individual, unless they are specifically incorporated into the employee's contract neither the employer nor the individual employee is bound by them.

Membership or non-membership of the trade union is not the issue here. All employees' contracts *may* be determined by collective agreements. The most common method by which this will happen is by express incorporation, e.g., a clause that states the employee's contract is 'subject to the collective agreements for the time being in force between' the employer and trade union. The second method is by *custom*, where the practice is so well established that it has clearly become part of each employee's contract (what has been termed 'tacitly embodied' in the contract—see **3.4.2.3** above). The third method is by implication in fact. A fourth, but less common, method is by arguing that the union had ostensible or implied authority to bind the members. We would only comment that reliance on anything other than express incorporation is a dangerous game, though if the idea of *custom* is accompanied by general acquiescence on the part of the employees (as was seen in *Henry* v *London General Transport Services Ltd* [2002] IRLR 472 (CA)) then employees will have great difficulty saying at a later date (here, two years after the agreement was reached) that the collective agreement was not incorporated.

3.7 The role of trade unions in the employment relationship

Collective agreements may adopt different guises. The most obvious form of collective agreement is that conducted between an employer and the trade union in the company. But there may also be local-level agreements relating to a group of companies or an industry, and there may be national agreements along the same lines, e.g., as between employers' federations and trade union groups. In such negotiations it is common to find agreements on minimum levels of conditions (e.g., as to holiday entitlements) which would apply to the member companies or trade unions.

Agreements between trade unions and employers are not legally binding even as between these parties unless they are in writing and expressly state that they are legally binding: TULRCA 1992, s. 179.

The role and impact of trade unions, however, goes much wider than this. Although many matters concerning trade unions are outside the scope of this book it is worth noting the following:

(a) trade union rights depend largely on the trade union being 'independent' (i.e., not within an employer's control) and, more importantly, 'recognised' for bargaining purposes by the employer;

(b) those rights will include such matters as being consulted when redundancies are being made and being consulted when a business is being transferred.

These matters will be discussed further in **Chapters 11** and **12**. Furthermore:

(a) trade unions may be sued in respect of tortious actions, usually those arising out of industrial disputes;

(b) trade unions may be joined in actions brought by employees against employers, e.g., in unfair dismissal claims where the union has brought industrial pressure to dismiss the employee (for instance, where the employee has refused to join the union);

(c) union members have specific rights concerning exclusion from trade union membership.

When considering employment law issues it would be short-sighted to think only in legal terms. The industrial relations consequences need to be accounted for too. Thus, as you will see, it may be lawful to dismiss striking employees (sometimes without any legal repercussions), but few solicitors would advocate such action apart from in extreme circumstances. An employment contract is not a one-off event like a commercial contract; the participants usually have to continue working with each other when the dispute is over and businesses normally work best when there is cooperation rather than confrontation.

3.8 Summary

- Most employment contracts are open-ended, with no fixed date for completion. These can be terminated by either party giving adequate notice.

- Other types of contract are permissible, e.g., contracts for specific periods or for the completion of specific tasks. These are known as 'limited-term' contracts. During their currency they are no different from 'permanent' contracts. The exception lies in the fact that the arrival of the fixed date or the completion of the task terminates the contract at common law and no notice is needed. There may, however, still be statutory consequences (e.g., unfair dismissal) when such contracts are not renewed.

- Terms are derived from a very wide range of sources, and employment contracts are notoriously loose in both drafting and evidence of terms. Both express and implied terms must be taken into account.

- To help overcome this employers are required to issue written statements of terms and conditions or issue contracts which cover the same prescribed headings. Many employers do neither.

- The failure to issue a written statement has limited consequences but employees may seek clarification from tribunals or use the non-issue to gain extra compensation when suing for other matters such as unfair dismissal.

- Many terms and conditions emanate from employer-trade union agreements and affect non-union members as well as unionists.

- The validity of terms may be affected by statutory obligations and rules. These are dealt with in **Chapters 4** and **5** below.

Statutory controls on the contents of the contract

4.1 Introduction

At the start of this book we commented on the often haphazard growth of employment law. Most of it grew out of the law of contract, itself mostly developed during the nineteenth century to reflect the preoccupation of the age with *laissez-faire* and the freedom of the parties to agree whatever terms they liked.

Much of the law that fills this book reflects a recognition by the courts of the practical reality that employer and employee are not equal partners. Most job-seekers have the stark choice of accepting the job as the employer offers it or looking elsewhere, and therefore need some protection in an unequal bargaining position. This explains the ever-growing list of common-law implied terms that we shall examine in **Chapter 5**.

Statute law used to confine itself generally to termination of the contract of employment (unfair dismissal in **Chapter 10**; redundancy in **Chapter 11**; takeovers in **Chapter 12**), and to certain specific areas which cover employment as one among several areas of human activity (discrimination in **Chapter 6**; health and safety, which is outside the scope of this book).

That position has now changed dramatically. In the National Minimum Wage Act 1998 (in this chapter, NMWA 1998) and the Working Time Regulations 1998 (WTRegs 1998), we have for the first time (except for war-time and in specific occupations) a statutory control of the two most basic elements of the contract of employment: how much employees are paid and how long they can be required to work in return. This chapter therefore examines the limitations that statute now imposes on the freedom of employer and employee to decide the terms of the contract. As well as NMWA 1998 and WTRegs 1998, we shall consider briefly some other topics, especially the 'family-friendly' measures introduced by the Employment Relations Act 1999 (ERA 1999) and the Employment Act 2002 (EA 2002). Solicitors need to know that these rights exist, but the complicated rules governing them and the detailed statutory instruments lie outside the scope of this book. The matters to be looked at are:

- National minimum wage.
- Working time.
- The protection of wages.
- Work on Sundays.
- Maternity rights.
- Paternity and adoption leave.
- Parental leave.

- Time off for dependants.
- Flexible working.

Perhaps we should note before we start on the detail that this is not a comprehensive list of statutory controls on the content of the contract of employment. There are quite a few other matters that space will not permit us to discuss—including tax and social security, statutory sick pay, and also the complex subject of pensions, despite the existence now of the European Occupational Pensions Directive 2003/41/EC.

The first three of those rights are matters about which employees have been required since 2004 to use the statutory grievance procedures (SGPs) before starting tribunal proceedings. Otherwise a tribunal claim will not normally be accepted. The 'family friendly' rights do not appear on the list. As we stated at the start of this book, SGPs are due to be abolished in April 2009, and we have not therefore covered them at all. As we go to press an ACAS code about disciplinary and grievance procedures is in an advanced stage of preparation and it will probably urge claimants to exhaust other means of redress before starting tribunal proceedings. There will be no formal rule that requires tribunals not to accept claims where other means have not been used, but at the least we imagine that tribunals will expect the code to be followed. Furthermore, failure to use voluntary means risks losing 25 per cent of any compensation awarded. Solicitors will continue to wish to advise individual clients accordingly.

4.2 The national minimum wage

The national minimum wage (NMW) stands at £5.73 per hour from 1 October 2008. The basis of the law is set out in NMWA 1998, but this is then expanded by several sets of regulations, the most important of which are the National Minimum Wage Regulations 1999 (NMWRegs 1999). While the basic principles of NMW are quite simple, the special rules to govern exceptional cases are complex and a guidance booklet published by the Department of Trade and Industry runs to some 112 pages including some worked examples. We shall therefore examine in brief outline:

- who is entitled to NMW;
- how the entitlement is calculated;
- administration of NMW and the remedy for infringements.

4.2.1 The scope of NMW

Under NMWA 1998, s. 54(3), the entitlement to the NMW belongs to *workers*, a broader term than merely *employees*, and the definition reproduces that used in WTRegs 1998. This seems to reflect the general approach of the present Government of widening the scope of employment protection to include many who would previously have been regarded as self-employed. Workers are both those working under a contract of employment (i.e., employees) and also those working under some other contract to perform personal work or services except for those who are genuinely clients or customers of professions or businesses. The decision of the EAT in *James v Redcats (Brands) Ltd* [2007] ICR 1006 stresses the statutory burden of proof: it is for the employer to prove that anyone claiming to be covered by NMW is *not* a worker under this definition. The fact that the claimant was permitted to substitute someone else if she was unable to deliver packages (but by implication only if *unable* to do it, and not merely because *choosing* not to) meant that she was a worker, and not within a non-personal business relationship. The result is a broader coverage than under some of the classical tests of employee status that we discussed in **Chapter 2**. There have also been cases about this definition in relation to other statutes where it appears—see, e.g., **6.11.1.1** below.

The broad scope of the statutory definition is then restricted by NMWRegs, reg. 12. Apprentices under the age of 19 are excluded, as are apprentices under the age of 26 during the first year of their apprenticeship. There are two lower rates for workers under 22: £3.53 per hour for those aged 16 and 17; £4.77 per hour for those aged 18 to 21. The latter rate also applies to those over 21 during the first six months of their employment if they are undergoing defined training.

There is no exclusion of those over retirement age, and both agency workers and homeworkers are included. The only significant exclusions are those working outside the United Kingdom (NMWA 1998, s. 1(2)), certain workers in family businesses (reg. 2(2) and (3)) and those undergoing work experience as trainees on certain Government schemes or as a compulsory element in undergraduate courses (reg. 12(5) and (8)).

4.2.2 Calculation of the entitlement

For most people, most of the time, the calculation of their NMW entitlement is straight-forward: the number of hours worked × £5.73 or the lower figure where it applies. The time that qualifies for NMW has been interpreted broadly. Time that a night watchman spent on the employer's premises counted as working time, although he was permitted to sleep, according to the Court of Session in *Scottbridge Construction Ltd* v *Wright* [2003] IRLR 21. Time spent training or travelling on the employer's business counts too, as does time spent at home waiting to answer the telephone on the employer's night-time service—*British Nursing Association* v *Inland Revenue* [2002] EWCA Civ 494, [2003] ICR 19.

There is a more complex case where the worker is not paid by the hour but by reference to output and the employer does not control the length of working time. An example is traditional 'piecework', although this is now much less common in industry than was the case a generation or two ago. The rules here are set out in the National Minimum Wage Regulations 1999 (Amendment) Regulations 2004, which require the employer to test workers to determine the 'mean hourly output rate' and to pay workers 120 per cent of that rate. For factory-based employment this is now quite rare and these cases are relatively few, but payment by the piece is still normal for most home-work.

There is another set of rules governing the case of workers paid an annual salary in return for annual hours. The practical problem here is that some such people may be paid a standard amount at regular weekly or monthly intervals, but if their hours of work during those periods vary they may receive less than NMW per hour actually worked in some reference periods and more in others. However, most salaried employees (including manual workers on annualised hours arrangements) are probably paid sufficiently more than NMW that this will also be a relatively rare problem. See regs 21–23 for the detail.

The next question is how to decide whether the worker is actually being paid the NMW, and which payments can be offset against the employer's liability.

Most money payments made by the employer count. Payments in kind do not (reg. 9) and neither do payments not in the nature of wages (reg. 8). There are some more detailed rules in regs 30–35. Thus, for example, by reg. 31(1)(e), tips in a restaurant given by customers but passed on by the employer count against the employer's liability only if paid through the payroll; payments not through the payroll are additional to NMW and any payments made direct by customers to staff are not payments *by the employer*. See *Revenue and Customs Commissioners v Annabels (Berkeley Square) Ltd* [2008] ICR 1076 for confirmation that tips paid into a 'tronc' are not payments by the employer and therefore cannot count towards the employer's obligation to pay NMW. The Government announced in the summer of 2008 that it intends to change the law so that tips become additional to NMW in all circumstances, but no amendments have yet been introduced. By reg. 31(1)(c), premium payments made to workers in return for working unsocial hours do not count if identifiable as additional payments. Thus it seems that the employer who simply pays people £6.00 an hour for work on a Saturday has met NMW; but another employer whose conditions of employment specify time-and-a-half for Saturdays has not met NMW if paying the same cash amount, because the balance when premium is excluded is less than £5.73.

4.2.3 Administration and enforcement

The sole administrative obligation on employers is to keep records 'sufficient to establish' that a worker is receiving NMW, and the record for each employee must consist of a single document which is retained for three years. For employees paid substantially more than NMW, this requires very little. Workers are entitled to inspect the employer's record concerning themselves.

The fundamental point about enforcement of NMW is that it is made a contractual right of every worker: NMWA 1998, s. 17. All the usual civil remedies for breach of contract then apply (see **5.8** below), and it becomes the minimum for other statutory rights—see **10.13.2**.

There is provision under NMWA 1998 for the appointment of 'officers' to ensure enforcement of NMW. Generally this means Revenue & Customs, but powers also belong to the agricultural wages inspectors. It is an offence for an employer to pay less than NMW or to fail to keep adequate records, and the officers are entitled to bring prosecutions.

Any employee who takes steps to secure payment of NMW is protected against suffering any detriment for doing so—NMWA 1998, s. 23. Furthermore NMWA 1998, s. 25 adds a new s. 104A to ERA 1996, so that two new sets of circumstances are added to the list where dismissal is automatically unfair. First, it is automatically unfair to dismiss an employee for seeking to be paid NMW (whether or not in the event that attempt succeeds) or as a consequence of a prosecution of the employer. Secondly, it is automatically unfair to dismiss an employee as a means of avoiding paying NMW.

4.3 The Working Time Regulations 1998

4.3.1 The origin of the regulations

The WTRegs 1998 are the implementation in Great Britain of the European Working Time Directive 93/104/EC of 23 November 1993. The Directive was adopted under art. 138 of the Treaty of Rome, as amended by the Amsterdam Treaty (previously art. 118a), the article that permits qualified majority voting on matters concerned with the health and safety of workers.

The original form of WTRegs 1998 was amended by regulations in 1999, which removed many of the uncertainties. There have been other amendments since. There are several instances of 'copy-out' of Eurospeak and some scope for uncertainty still exists.

In *Gibson* v *East Riding of Yorkshire Council* [2000] ICR 890, the Court of Appeal held that art. 7 of the Directive (dealing with annual leave as in WTRegs, reg. 13—see **4.3.9** below) was insufficiently precise to be capable of direct enforcement against an emanation of the state.

There has been much discussion of revision of the current Directive ever since WTRegs were first introduced in this country. The provisions in the UK for opt-out from the 48-hour week that we shall discuss at **4.3.4** below have been very unpopular in much of the rest of Europe. In July 2008 an agreement was reached at the European Council for revision of the Directive and we therefore expect some legislative change soon.

4.3.2 The form of the regulations

For anyone involved in categorising legal materials, WTRegs 1998 represent something of a novelty. Previously employment law and the law about health and safety were largely separate topics, and practitioners were able to claim expertise in one while admitting to massive ignorance of the other. In particular, individual remedies in the employment tribunals and enforcement by the Health and Safety Executive (HSE) have had little overlap.

That distinction is blurred in WTRegs 1998. As we shall see there are six substantive rules. The first two are limits: the 48-hour week and restrictions on nightshift. Subject to the precise rules we shall consider shortly, employers must not exceed them, and any who are found by HSE inspectors to have done so risk prosecution. By contrast the remaining four (daily and weekly rest, rest breaks, and annual leave) are entitlements. Individuals denied them can bring a complaint in the employment tribunal; but where employees forgo the entitlement and choose not to complain, the employer has done nothing wrong.

4.3.3 Scope of the regulations and some definitions

As we noted at **4.2.1** above, both NMWA 1998 and WTRegs give rights to *workers*, a broader term than merely *employees*. In relation to WTRegs, this reproduces the wording of the Directive, but also seems to reflect the trend to include in employment protection many who would previously have been regarded as self-employed. The definition in reg. 2 provides that workers are both those working under a contract of employment (i.e., employees) and also those working under some other contract to perform personal work or services except for those who are genuinely clients or customers of professions or businesses. Thus in *Redrow Homes (Yorkshire) Ltd* v *Wright* [2004] EWCA Civ 469, [2004] IRLR 720 it was held that bricklayers engaged as sub-contractors qualified as workers under this rule because they were obliged to perform work personally.

Most of the rules apply to workers of all ages, but there are a few stricter rules that apply only to those over minimum school leaving age but under 18, described in some guidance issued by the Department of Trade and Industry as 'adolescent workers'. The rules do not apply to children: so a paper-boy was not entitled to paid annual leave—*Addison* v *Ashby* [2003] ICR 667.

Various parts of the Regulations are subject to specific exceptions, often picking up derogations available in the Directive. In addition it is possible for employers and trade unions or other employee representatives to agree to *modify or exclude* many of the Regulations, subject to certain restrictions in some cases. The original general exclusions have largely been removed by subsequent amendments, especially the Working Time (Amendment) Regulations 2003. Mobile transport workers are now generally covered by regulations specific to particular modes of transport as too are doctors in training. The only remaining general exception is the armed services, the police and some civil protection services under reg. 18.

'Working time' is defined so as to include expressly most kinds of work experience, but more generally as time which meets the following three tests:

(a) the worker is working;

(b) the worker is at the employer's disposal; and

(c) the worker is carrying out his activity or duties.

There is some scope for speculation here. We had assumed from a classical British approach to the interpretation of a statute that *all three* elements of the definition must be satisfied for time to count as working time. Thus time while the worker is on standby would generally not count, as (a) and (c) are not satisfied, even if (b) is satisfied. The ECJ, construing the wording of the Directive in *Sindicato de Médicos de Asistencia Pública (SIMAP)* v *Conselleriá de Sanidad y Consumo de la Generalidad Valenciana* (Case C-303/98) [2001] ICR 1116, took a more purposive approach. Working time and rest periods are mutually exclusive within the scheme of the Directive, the objective of which is to grant workers minimum periods of rest. Thus doctors on call are at work if required to be present and available at the workplace, but not if they are merely required to be contactable at all times but not necessarily at the health centre.

Application of the same principle to the other main area of doubt, time when the worker is travelling on the employer's business, might suggest that the critical question will be whether the mode of travel allows the worker to rest or not. There is obviously much opportunity for argument, e.g., about the difficulty of sleeping given the restricted leg-room provided by airline economy class! One of the items included in the July 2008 agreement that we mentioned at the end of **4.3.1** will involve the introduction of a distinction between 'active' and 'inactive' working time.

4.3.4 The 48-hour week

By reg. 4, workers must not work on average more than 48 hours a week. The average is normally calculated over a period of 17 weeks, which can be a fixed period if so agreed between employer and worker, but by default is the last 17 weeks. In certain defined cases it can be longer—up to 26 weeks—and up to a year if some justification exists and the employer so agrees with employee representatives.

Workers who agree to work more than 48 hours may continue to do so. The original rules about formalities of such agreements were deleted by the 1999 amendments to WTRegs, except that notice to terminate the agreement cannot exceed three months.

Employees have the choice whether to sign the opt-out. In *Barber* v *RJB Mining (UK) Ltd* [1999] ICR 679, the EAT held that reg. 4(1) had the effect of prohibiting employers from requiring employees to work more than 48 hours.

Managing executives and others *with autonomous decision-taking powers*, family workers and clergy are excluded from the 48-hour rule under reg. 20 on the basis that their working time is not measured or predetermined or can be fixed by the worker concerned. The terms we have emphasised are undefined.

4.3.5 Nightshift

There is a complicated definition in reg. 2(1) of night work and, by reference to it, of what constitutes a night worker. On the face of the definitions, it might seem that a worker is only a night worker if working at least three hours a day during night time on a *majority* of the days of work, i.e., presumably more than half. This ignores the crucial element in the regulation, 'without prejudice to the generality' of the expression, 'as a normal course'. Thus in *R* v *Attorney-General for Northern Ireland, ex parte Burns* [1999] IRLR 315, the High Court in Northern Ireland held that three hours of night work per shift had only to be a *regular feature* of the worker's pattern of working time.

Workers who fall within the statutory definition of a night worker must not work more than eight hours on average per 24-hour period (reg. 6(1)). Again there is a 17-week reference period subject to some possibilities of variation. In the case of those whose work involves *special hazards or heavy physical or mental strain* (terms that are simply copied out of the Directive), the eight-hour limit applies under reg. 6(7) to each nightshift and not to an average. The only definition supplied by the Regulations for the crucial terms is that they are to be understood by reference to an agreement between employer and worker representatives or to the risk assessment the employer carries out as part of normal health and safety management.

Those undertaking night work must be given the opportunity under reg. 7 of a free health assessment before doing so and at intervals thereafter. The form of the health assessment is not specified but it does not seem to extend necessarily to a medical examination by a doctor. Slightly more stringent requirements exist in the case of adolescent workers. The employer's obligation appears to be limited to ensuring that workers have the opportunity of a health assessment and not that they avail themselves of it.

4.3.6   Daily rest

In principle, adult workers are entitled to 11 consecutive hours rest in each 24-hour period, and adolescent workers to 12 hours (reg. 10). There are various flexibilities about the operation of the rules for adults (mostly under regs 21 and 22) but the exceptional cases are precisely defined. In *Gallagher* v *Alpha Catering Services Ltd* [2004] EWCA Civ 1559, [2005] ICR 673, airline catering workers were found to fall outside reg. 21 (c). Although the *employers' activities* involved the need for continuity of service, there was no evidence that the *workers' activities* involved any such need, and that was the correct test under WTRegs 1998. The broad principle is that workers whose daily rest is not strictly in accordance with reg. 10 should have some *compensatory rest* instead (reg. 24). This term is undefined, but it seems that a commonsense approach is taken.

4.3.7   Weekly rest

Adult workers are entitled to one day off each week under reg. 11 and adolescent workers to two days off. Again there is some flexibility about the way weekly rest is arranged for adults, subject to the same principle of compensatory rest as for daily rest. In addition there is specific provision under reg. 11(2) enabling an employer to provide two days a fortnight as an alternative arrangement for adults.

The 24-hour weekly rest under reg. 11 and the 11-hour daily rest under reg. 10 are separate and additional to each other. However, despite some suggestions to the contrary, it does not seem that they must necessarily be consecutive so as to provide an obligatory 35-hour break for every shift rota.

4.3.8   Rest breaks

Adult workers are entitled under reg. 12 to a rest break of at least 20 minutes if their daily working time exceeds six hours. There is no requirement for the break to be paid. Flexibility about the rule again depends on compensatory rest.

The rule about adolescent workers is stricter. Their break is a minimum of 30 minutes if daily working time exceeds four and a half hours. There is much less flexibility. Furthermore, if the adolescent has more than one job, daily working time must be aggregated across the jobs to determine entitlement to a break. There is no explanation of how employers are to obtain the information to operate this rule.

4.3.9   Annual leave

Workers are entitled under reg. 13 to 4.8 weeks' paid leave annually. There is no service qualification—as a result of the Working time (Amendment) Regulations 2001. Employers may not require a worker to accept pay in lieu. The entitlement in days is obtained by multiplying the number of days in a worker's normal week by 5.6 and rounding up—never down—to the nearest half-day.

The slightly odd figure of 5.6 weeks is a result of recent history. Until the Working Time (Amendment) Regulations 2007, the entitlement was to four weeks' leave. It was a regular complaint of the trade unions that elsewhere in Europe annual leave was regarded as additional to the public or bank holidays; here, while most large employers in fact gave employees the customary eight bank holidays in addition to the four weeks of annual leave, they were not obliged to do so. It proved too difficult to introduce a concept of compulsory days of public holiday into English law, and so the 2007 regulations simply raised the entitlement in two stages, with the 5.6 weeks (four weeks plus eight days for most five-day a week workers) taking effect on 1 October 2008.

There are rules in reg. 16 about the calculation of payment for annual leave, which are broadly the same as for all other statutory purposes (see ERA 1996, ss. 220–229). There are also rules in reg. 15 about the notices employer and worker can serve on each other as to when leave can and cannot be taken. Some of these rules may cause practical difficulties in that they conflict with established practices in many workplaces.

There has been rather more litigation about this aspect of WTRegs 1998 than about the rest. One question that has arisen from the cases was whether a worker, away from work on long-term sickness, could elect to take annual leave and to claim payment, even if prevented by the sickness from being at work and possibly not otherwise due any payment, having exhausted any entitlement to sick pay. The Court of Appeal held in *Inland Revenue Commissioners* v *Ainsworth* [2005] EWCA Civ 441, [2005] ICR 1149 that the worker could not do so. The decision rested on a purposive interpretation of WTRegs 1998: if not required to be at work the worker could not be said to be taking 'leave' from work. It criticised an earlier contrary EAT decision for having concentrated too much on the status of the worker and having missed the underlying purpose of reg. 13 and the Directive. There has been another long-running debate whether it is possible for the employer to pay a 'rolled-up' rate of pay inclusive of holiday pay and then not to pay separately for holidays. It has finally been resolved by the ECJ in *Robinson-Steele* v *RD Retail Services Ltd* (C-131/04), [2006] ICR 932, where the practice was held to be contrary to the purposes of the Directive.

4.3.10   Enforcement and remedies

We noted at **4.3.2** above that the first two of the items we have just been discussing are limits enforced by inspection by HSE and possible criminal prosecution, while the remaining four are entitlements enforceable by individual claim in the employment tribunal.

HSE inspectors do not enforce the limits by any rigorous policing of employers. Indeed *The Health and Safety Practitioner* of September 1998 quotes HSE as saying it lacks the resources to enforce the Regulations effectively. In *Sayers* v *Cambridgeshire County Council* [2006] EWHC 2029, [2007] IRLR 29, the claimant claimed that her psychiatric injury resulted in part from excessively long hours. Ramsey J held that the 48-hour week limit under WTRegs did not provide her with a right of action for breach of statutory duty, but instead created only criminal liability. The apparently complete exclusion of any civil liability is perhaps surprising, given the connexion of the Directive with health and safety of workers, and we suspect that the point may be tested again.

As regards the four entitlements, reg. 30 sets out the procedure for a worker to complain to an employment tribunal. The claim must be presented within three months of the alleged denial of the right concerned. If the tribunal finds the claim well founded it must make a declaration to that effect and may make an award of compensation of an amount to reflect both the degree of the employer's fault and the amount of the worker's loss. In *Miles* v *Linkage Community Trust Ltd* [2008] IRLR 602, the EAT approved a pragmatic and practical assessment by the employment tribunal of the employer's default, which led to the making of a declaration but no award of compensation.

4.4 Protection of wages

Subject to the minimum set under NMWA 1998, it is for the parties to set the level of pay under the contract. Nevertheless, whatever level they set, Part II of the ERA 1996 provides that employers may not make deductions from workers' wages other than those required by statute and those that meet specified conditions. The rules, still often referred to as from the Wages Act 1986, although that is now consolidated into ERA 1996, are (broadly speaking) that either workers must expressly authorise the deduction or they must be subject to the deduction under some term of the contract which the employer has confirmed in writing. We shall see in **5.8** that there is sometimes an overlap between this rule and that giving workers a remedy in the employment tribunals for breaches of contract.

4.4.1 The meaning of 'wages'

Wages are defined in s. 27 of ERA 1996. Under s. 27(1), the term includes any fee, bonus, commission, holiday pay or other emolument referable to the employment, whether payable under the contract or otherwise. It also includes various payments made as a result of employment tribunal orders, statutory guarantee payments, statutory sick pay, and statutory maternity pay.

By s. 27(2), the following are *excluded* from the definition:

(a) advances of wages as a loan;

(b) expenses payments (even where the employee makes a profit from the expenses: *London Borough of Southwark* v *O'Brien* [1996] IRLR 420);

(c) pensions or other retirement provisions;

(d) redundancy payments;

(e) payments made to the worker in another capacity.

By s. 27(5), benefits in kind are also excluded except where they consist of vouchers or the equivalent with a fixed monetary value.

The inclusion by s. 27(1) of certain non-contractual matters is enlarged in s. 27(3) by specific reference to non-contractual bonuses. The test seems to be that discretionary commission or similar payments may be included if it is the reasonable expectation of the parties that they will be paid: *Kent Management Service* v *Butterfield* [1992] ICR 272.

The breadth of this definition is obvious. It includes almost any payment made by the employer to the worker *qua* worker. Thus, tips paid to waiters by customers in cash are never the property of the employer and therefore do not count as remuneration; tips paid by cheque or credit card, initially to the employer, become the employer's property and therefore *are* remuneration from the employer: *Nerva* v *R. L. & G. Ltd* [1997] ICR 11. About the only item that has been held to fall outside the definition is *pay in lieu of notice*, which of course has been regarded by the law as liquidated damages for breach of contract rather than as a payment referable to the employment. However, it took a decision of the House of Lords (*Delaney* v *Staples* [1992] ICR 483) finally to exclude payments in lieu of notice, by holding that payments in lieu relate to termination of the employment and not to the provision of services under the employment.

4.4.2 Permitted deductions

Sections 13 and 14 ERA 1996 start from the premise that an employer cannot make a deduction from wages except in defined circumstances. These can be quite detailed, but the broad categories where deductions will be permitted are:

(a) *Deductions authorised or required by statute.* Examples might be the collection of income tax or maintenance payments under a court order.

(b) *Deductions provided for by a term of the worker's contract of employment* where either that term is already recorded in writing to the worker, or the employer has previously notified the worker of it in writing. The deduction must also be justified on its facts, however.

(c) *Deductions expressly authorised in writing by the worker.* Examples might be payments to a pension scheme or a savings plan, or recovery in instalments of the cost of initial purchase of working clothes.

(d) *Deductions in retail employment* for the recovery of cash shortages or stock deficiencies, subject to specific controls including a limit to the deduction of 10 per cent of gross pay: see ERA 1996, ss. 17 to 22.

(e) *Deductions to recover an overpayment by the employer.* This, though, is merely an exception to the general ban on deductions and does not give the employer a right to recover overpayments where no such right exists otherwise, and this is often a problem for employers when the employee has in good faith spent the money. In *Murray* v *Strathclyde Regional Council* [1992] IRLR 396, the EAT limited the scope of the exception to deductions relating to the same pay period as the overpayments.

(f) *Deductions made because the worker is taking part in a strike or other industrial action.*

Sections 15 and 16 deal with the situation where an employee is required to make payments to the employer and the provisions mirror those of ss. 13 and 14 (thereby preventing the employer from circumventing ss. 13 and 14 by demanding reimbursement rather than making a deduction).

4.4.3 Remedies for unlawful deductions from wages

If the worker has suffered an unauthorised deduction from wages, the remedy provided by ERA 1996, s. 23 is by way of a claim in an employment tribunal. The claim must be presented within three months of the making of the deduction complained of, or (where there has been a series of similar deductions) within three months of the most recent deduction. In this instance there seems to be no limit on the retrospective period the employment tribunal may examine: *Reid v Camphill Engravers* [1990] ICR 435.

The employment tribunal is given little discretion as to its award if it finds the claim well-founded. It is bound to make a declaration to that effect, and also to order the employer to reimburse the money improperly deducted or received, subject only to a possible reduction of the full amount if there has been a partial authorisation or repayment: ss. 24 and 25.

4.4.4 Practical uses of the remedy in the employment tribunals

This topic may seem an obscure possibility. It is not. In practice, almost a sixth of all claims recently brought to the employment tribunals fall under this jurisdiction and we shall discuss it further at **5.7.5** below.

The point is that there is no jurisdiction for the employment tribunals to deal with alleged breaches of contract concerning current employees. The only such jurisdiction concerns people whose employment has ended. So if an employee wishes to complain about an alleged breach of contract the case must be brought in the courts, with consequently higher costs than are incurred in the tribunals. If the same claim can be presented as an alleged deduction from wages, the tribunal has jurisdiction and this possibility may be attractive to the employee.

An example may help. Suppose the issue is a dispute about the calculation of a bonus. Maybe a group of people in a sales office are paid a bonus based on sales of the company's products. When the company starts export sales the employer bases calculation of the bonus on home sales (which is all there has been until now), but the sales staff argue that it has always been based on total sales. Both sides argue that their case is a continuation of past practice and there is logic behind both contentions, depending whether the bonus was originally intended to reward the effort of the staff concerned or to reflect the success of the enterprise. The legal issue is one of construction of the rules of the bonus scheme, wherever they are to be found, whether in writing or not. An employment tribunal cannot entertain a case of construction of the contract of employment in respect of current employees, but the amount at stake for a small group of people does not seem to warrant litigation in the courts. So the employees, through their trade union perhaps, present their case to the tribunal as an alleged unlawful deduction from wages. Their bonus, they argue, should properly be based on the total sales of the company and the employer has unlawfully *deducted* the part which represents export sales. Now, when it is presented in this way, the tribunal acquires jurisdiction to adjudicate on the issue, which is legally precisely the same as it would have been in the court—construction of the contract of employment.

With a little ingenuity many contractual issues can be presented in an alternative form like this. As we shall see at **5.6** there are other ways of dealing with such issues; the relative merits of this against the others are considered at **5.7**.

4.5 Sunday working for shop and betting workers

4.5.1 The right

Under ERA 1996, Part IV, special statutory rights have been created covering employees who may be asked to work on Sundays. The legislation is somewhat convoluted but, in essence, seeks to provide shop and betting workers with the right not to work on Sundays if they so wish. The following points may be noted by way of summary:

(a) The definition of 'shop worker' in s. 232 extends beyond sales assistants to cover employees such as clerical workers, security staff, and cleaners. The definition of 'betting worker' in s. 233 covers work 'which consists of or includes dealing with betting transactions' at a track and 'work in a licensed betting office . . . open for use for the effecting of betting transactions'.

(b) Employees employed to work only on Sundays are not covered by the Act.

(c) Those who were shop workers at 25 August 1994 or betting workers at 2 January 1995 are covered provided their contracts do not, and may not, require them to work on Sundays—these are termed 'protected workers'.

(d) Any shop or betting worker who is or may be required under the contract to work on Sunday may give three months' written notice of 'opting-out' (hence 'opted-out employees'). During that notice period he or she may be required to work on Sunday.

(e) Employees may also give 'opting-in' notice, expressly agreeing to work Sundays or a particular Sunday—and, indeed, may opt in or out as the whim takes them.

(f) Questions of age, length of service or hours worked are irrelevant for qualification for these rights.

(g) An attempt by a worker in another kind of employment, a quarry, to obtain the right not to work on Sundays by arguing under HRA 1998 that a requirement to work on Sundays infringed his right to practise his religion under art. 9 of the European Convention of Human Rights failed in *Copsey* v *WWB Devon Clays Ltd* [2005] EWCA Civ 932, [2005] ICR 1789.

4.5.2 Written statements

As we noted at **3.5.4** above, new shop and betting workers are entitled to receive a written statement in a prescribed form summarising their right to opt out of Sunday work.

4.5.3 Remedies

Both protected and opted-out workers (in the meanings defined above) have the right to complain to an employment tribunal if they suffer any detriment by reason of refusing to work on Sundays or a particular Sunday (ERA 1996, s. 45). We shall note below that they have a similar protection against dismissal or selection for redundancy for the same reason.

4.6 Maternity rights

There has been much recent attention by the legislators on the balance between work and family life. Thus ERA 1999 established several 'Family-Friendly Policies,' as they had been described in an earlier White Paper. Two of them were new, derived from the Parental Leave Directive 96/34/EC and are discussed in detail in **4.8** and **4.9** below. Then EA 2002 introduced several more rights by further amendment to ERA 1996, and we shall consider them in **4.7** and **4.10**. Some employers go beyond the statutory requirements, e.g., by providing work-based crèche facilities. By contrast, provisions relating to pregnancy and childbirth are of much longer standing, dating back originally to the Employment Protection Act 1975, although now much amended—including amendments from ERA 1999, EA 2002 and the Work and Families Act 2006, and associated statutory instruments. There are four matters to consider:

(a) time off with pay for antenatal care;

(b) protection against dismissal because of pregnancy;

(c) maternity leave; and

(d) maternity pay.

The fourth of those rights is found in the Social Security Act 1986; the remaining three in ERA 1996, as amended. The main impact of the amendments is on maternity leave, where the old law has extensively been simplified. We shall also note in **Chapter 6** that any detriment suffered by a woman because of her pregnancy constitutes unlawful sex discrimination and this point is of particular importance in relation to protection against dismissal. The employer also has special responsibilities for the health and safety of pregnant women, especially in relation to risk assessment, but such matters lie outside the scope of this book.

Most of the changes under the Work and Families Act 2006 and associated regulations took effect on 1 October 2006. It was expected that other changes, including the extension of leave to a year, would take effect in April 2009, but we understand that that change has now been delayed to April 2010 at the earliest.

4.6.1 Time off with pay for antenatal care

By s. 55 of ERA 1996, every pregnant employee is entitled to time off with pay for antenatal appointments she is medically advised to attend. There is no qualifying service and no limit to the time off.

4.6.2 Protection against dismissal because of pregnancy

By s. 99 of ERA 1996, almost any dismissal because of pregnancy or childbirth is automatically unfair and there is no service qualification. The employer is not permitted to dismiss an employee even if her pregnancy makes her incapable of doing her usual job. Indeed, if her incapability is because of some statutory restriction relating to pregnancy, childbirth or breastfeeding or some similar recommendation of a code of practice, she is to be treated under ERA 1996, s. 66 as suspended from work and she is entitled to be paid. In an unusual exception the EAT held in *Ramdoolar* v *Bycity Ltd* [2005] ICR 368 that the dismissal of a pregnant woman for poor work performance was not unfair, because the employer did not know of her pregnancy. However the EAT added that an employer who detects the symptoms of pregnancy and dismisses the employee before his suspicions can be proved may well find the dismissal automatically unfair.

The scope of the statutory protection afforded to pregnant women is now very wide, mostly because women have successfully argued that any detriment suffered because of pregnancy or childbirth is unlawful discrimination on grounds of sex. As we shall note at 6.5.6 below, that rule from the cases acquired statutory force on 1 October 2005.

4.6.3 Maternity leave

Until the amendments under ERA 1999, the rules on maternity leave had become very complicated. We now find in sch. 4 of ERA 1999 a complete replacement of Part VIII of ERA 1996, and in particular new ss. 71 to 75 setting out the structure of maternity leave. In addition we need to take account of the Maternity and Parental Leave etc. Regulations 1999 (MPL Regs 1999) as amended in 2002 and 2006 which enlarge on the statutory framework. There are three kinds of maternity leave:

(a) ordinary maternity leave;

(b) compulsory maternity leave; and

(c) additional maternity leave.

We shall examine each of them in turn and then consider the right not to suffer detriment on account of exercising any of them.

4.6.3.1 Ordinary maternity leave

Ordinary maternity leave is covered by ERA 1996, s. 71 as amended. All pregnant employees, regardless of length of service, are entitled to a 26-week period of leave. The contract of employment subsists throughout this absence and the employee continues to benefit from her terms and conditions of employment except for remuneration. MPL Regs, reg. 9 defines remuneration for this purpose as wages or salary. Some advice to employers has interpreted wages and salary very narrowly, so that occasional bonuses are not covered and the woman on ordinary maternity leave is entitled to receive them. That advice now seems to be wrong, according to the decision of the EAT in *Hoyland* v *Asda Stores Ltd* [2005] ICR 1235. The employer was entitled to pay a woman a reduced bonus, pro rata to time actually spent at work, including two weeks compulsory maternity leave, but excluding ordinary maternity leave. The definition, however, means that the employee is entitled to all fringe benefits during the leave period, a position that was generally thought to exist before but was never clearly set out.

The start of the ordinary maternity leave period is a matter over which the employee has some choice but it cannot start earlier than the beginning of the eleventh week before the EWC. If childbirth occurs early, ordinary leave starts at once. Childbirth includes a live birth and a stillbirth or miscarriage after 24 weeks of pregnancy.

The employee returns to work after ordinary maternity leave with that whole period of absence counting for seniority and pension purposes. The right to return is to the job in which she was employed before her absence on terms and conditions not less favourable than those which would have applied if she had not been absent. There are special provisions in MPL Regs, reg. 10 covering the position if the employee becomes redundant during maternity leave, ordinary or additional.

No later than the 15th week before EWC, or as soon as reasonably practicable, she must tell the employer that she is pregnant, what her EWC is (by means of a medical certificate if the employee so requests) and when she wishes to start her leave (in writing if her employer so requests). Under the 2002 amendments the employer must respond, notifying her of the date when her maternity leave will end.

A woman returning to work after ordinary maternity leave does not need to give notice of her return unless she wishes to return early, in which case she must give her employer eight weeks' notice of her intended return date. Failure to do so will allow the employer to postpone her return.

4.6.3.2 Compulsory maternity leave

Under ERA 1996, s. 72 as amended, the employer is not permitted to allow the employee to work during the compulsory maternity leave period which is the two weeks following the baby's birth. This provision implements the health and safety requirement in the Pregnant Workers Directive.

4.6.3.3 Additional maternity leave

Under ERA 1996, s. 73, employees qualifying for ordinary maternity leave are also entitled to additional maternity leave, the right to return up to 26 weeks after the birth. The rule restricting this right to those with a certain length of service was removed on 1 October 2006. The two kinds of leave remain distinct, despite the common qualification. Additional maternity leave follows on after ordinary maternity leave.

The employee's contract of employment continues to subsist throughout the period of additional maternity leave as during ordinary leave. Until recently the rights and duties of the parties during additional maternity leave were much reduced, but that has now changed under the Sex Discrimination Act (1975) Amendment Regulations 2008. During her additional leave the woman is now entitled to all benefits under the contract excluding pay, but including fringe benefits, exactly as during ordinary leave.

The one significant remaining difference between ordinary and additional leave concerns the right to return to work. As we have noted, the right to return after ordinary leave is straightforwardly to the same job, whereas under MPL Regs, reg. 18, the employee is entitled to return after additional leave to the same job or, if it is not reasonably practicable for the employer to permit her to do that, to a job which is both *suitable* for her and *appropriate for her to do in the circumstances*. The words we have emphasised are undefined and so we await clarification from cases. In any event, however, her terms and conditions of employment are to be the same as would have applied to her if she had not been absent.

Under the 2008 regulations the period of additional leave counts towards continuity of service, exactly as ordinary leave. Prior to April 2008 (or strictly for any EWC starting before 5 October 2008), this was not the position for non-statutory purposes. However, if at some point in the future you find yourself pursuing some service-based, contractual right for a client where additional leave prior to that date is important, it may still be possible to base an argument on the Equal Treatment Directive 76/207 as interpreted in *Sarkatzis Herrero* v *Instituto Madrileño de la Salud* (C-294/04) [2006] IRLR 297.

The employee is required to give no notice of her intention to return if she returns at the end of the 26-week period but must give eight weeks' notice of an intention to return early (reg. 11). A statement of her intention to return at all can be required by the employer in a prescribed written form, in which event the woman must reply in writing (reg. 12).

4.6.3.4   The right not to suffer detriment

Under s. 47C, which ERA 1999 inserts into ERA 1996, an employee who is subjected by her employer to any detriment because of pregnancy, childbirth or maternity, or because she exercised her right to maternity leave, can bring a claim to the employment tribunal. If she succeeds, the tribunal can award compensation of an amount it considers just and equitable in the circumstances having regard to the employee's loss.

4.6.3.5   'Keeping in touch' days

Under the 2006 amendments, employees on statutory maternity leave (ordinary or additional) may, by agreement with the employer, return to work for up to ten days without bringing the leave to an end.

4.6.4   Maternity pay

Statutory maternity pay is payable for a nine-month period. For the first six weeks it is at the rate of 90 per cent of normal weekly earnings. For the remaining 33 weeks it is either 90 per cent of normal weekly earnings or a prescribed rate which is reviewed annually and has stood since April 2008 at £117.18 per week, whichever of those is lower. It is usually a straightforward administrative matter that causes few problems, although a woman is entitled in the calculation to the benefit of pay rises taking effect during the period prior to the leave that is used for the calculation of maternity pay, even if the rise is decided subsequently and takes effect retrospectively, as in *Alabaster* v *Barclays Bank Ltd (No 2)* [2005] EWCA Civ 508, [2005] ICR 1246. In *Gillespie* v *Northern Health Board* [1996] ICR 498, the ECJ rejected the argument that full pay was due during maternity leave.

4.7   Paternity and adoption leave

Both these rights arise under EA 2002 which amends ERA 1996 by adding new sections that we shall identify shortly. In both cases the statutory provision acts as little more than an enabling measure for delegated legislation and both are governed by the Paternity and Adoption Leave Regulations 2002 (PALRegs 2002). There are also other more detailed sets of regulations, mostly dealing with pay. We shall give only an outline. The government plans further increases in these rights, possibly from April 2009, and also a link in which additional paternity leave becomes (wholly or partially) an alternative to additional maternity leave.

4.7.1   Paternity leave

The statutory basis of this right is ss. 80A and 80B of ERA 1996. For an employee to be eligible for paternity leave, three tests must be satisfied.

(a) The employee must have at least 26 weeks' service at the start of the 14th week before EWC, or in the case of an adoption at the end of the week in which the adopter is matched with the child.

(b) The employee must be the father of the child or married to or the partner (of either sex) of the child's mother or adopter. (So women may be eligible for paternity leave.)

(c) The employee must have or expect to have responsibility for the upbringing of the child.

Employees can take either one or two consecutive weeks of paternity leave. It can be taken at any time from the birth or placement up to 56 days later (or up to 56 days from EWC in the case of a premature birth). They must give the employer notice of the intention to take paternity leave by the 15th week before EWC in the case of a birth or no later than seven days after being told of being matched in the case of adoption. If it is not reasonably practical to give that amount of notice, they must give notice as soon as reasonably practical.

The rate of statutory paternity pay is the same as the later rate (after the first six weeks) of statutory maternity pay—see **4.6.4** above.

4.7.2 Adoption leave

The statutory basis of this right is ss. 75A and 75B of ERA 1996. The rules in many ways mirror those for maternity leave. Where a couple adopts, either but not both can take adoption leave. The other may be able to take paternity leave. Where there is a single adopter, it is that person who may take adoption leave and the partner may be able to take paternity leave.

In order to be eligible for adoption leave, the employee must have at least 26 weeks service at the end of the week of notification of being matched with the child. The employee must notify the employer of the intention to take adoption leave within seven days of that notification, or as soon as is reasonably practicable if that is not reasonably practicable. The employer must respond, informing the employee of the date adoption leave will end. Ordinary adoption leave lasts for 26 weeks and additional adoption leave for a further 26 weeks.

The employee must give eight weeks notice of an intention to return early from additional adoption leave.

Statutory adoption pay is payable for nine months and its rate is the same as the later rate (after the first six weeks) of statutory maternity pay—see **4.6.4** above.

4.8 Parental leave

The next 'family friendly' right we need to consider derives from Directive 96/34/EC and is provided for in ERA 1996, s. 76, as amended by ERA 1999, sch. 4. It gives both parents a right to unpaid time off during the first five years of a child's life, or the first five years after adoption.

4.8.1 The form of the Directive

The Parental Leave Directive 96/34/EC was one of the measures agreed by the other Member States of the EU at a time when the United Kingdom remained outside the 'Social Chapter' of the Maastricht Treaty. After the Labour Government decided to abandon the 'opt-out' there was a further Directive 97/75/EC which simply extended the 1996 Directive to the United Kingdom.

The 1996 Directive was the means of giving statutory force to an agreement reached between European trade unions and employers' organisations (the 'social partners') through the process of negotiation known as social dialogue. It is much more common elsewhere in Europe than in the United Kingdom for collective agreements to be given some sort of legal force so that they then apply to more employees and employers than just the original signatories. In this case the Directive expressly encouraged the social partners at local level to agree voluntary arrangements which could become an alternative to the law in defined workplaces. Such a process is virtually unknown in this country, and there is no legal basis for it to be built upon. However, MPL Regs provide in reg. 16 for voluntary arrangements to be agreed as an alternative to the detailed default provisions in sch. 2. The difficulty of any such arrangement is the provision in reg. 21 that employees may not treat statutory and contractual rights as cumulative, but may choose whichever is better in any particular regard. We do not yet know whether this rule might enable an employee, in a case where a voluntary arrangement exists, to argue that some particular provision in the voluntary arrangement fails to satisfy the minimum terms of the Directive, and that sch. 2 is therefore still relevant. Few employers will want to become test cases. Furthermore the first addition to the default provisions that any employee representative will seek is some kind of payment for parental leave, and most employers will wish to resist that. In practice, therefore, voluntary arrangements are unlikely to become common for the time being. For the remainder of this section we shall concentrate on the default provisions.

4.8.2   Qualification for the right

The right to take parental leave applies to all employees with service of one year or more if they have responsibility for a child. Parental responsibility is defined by reference either to the provisions of the Children Act 1989, or to registration as a child's father.

Under ERA 1996, s. 76(5) (inserted by ERA 1999, sch. 4), the regulations implementing parental leave may specify things that are to be taken as done for the purpose of caring for a child. Such rules would limit the circumstances in which parental leave can be taken. There is no such provision in MPL Regs 1999. Consequently employees do not have to justify a request to take parental leave by reference to the circumstances.

4.8.3   The right

Each qualifying employee may take parental leave up to a total of 13 weeks for each child. Thus each parent of twins may take up to 26 weeks. Under the default provisions the leave cannot be taken in blocks shorter than a week, as confirmed in *New Southern Railway Ltd* v *Rodway* [2005] EWCA Civ 443, [2005] ICR 1162, nor for more than four weeks in any year (sch. 2, paras 7 and 8).

The right normally expires on the child's fifth birthday. Where the child is adopted it expires on the fifth anniversary of the adoption, or the child's 18th birthday, whichever is earlier. If the child is disabled (defined by reference to entitlement to a disability living allowance), the maximum leave is 18 weeks instead of 13, the right expires on the child's 18th birthday, and in this instance the default provisions do not apply the rule about minimum blocks of a week; the minimum is a day.

The employee's rights during parental leave are exactly the same as those concerning additional maternity leave—see **4.6.3.3** above. The right to return at the end of it is to the same job if the leave is four weeks or less. If leave exceeds four weeks, or it is added on to additional maternity leave, the right to return is the same as after additional maternity leave.

4.8.4   Notices and administration

Under the default provisions, the employee is normally required to give the employer 21 days' notice of an intention to take parental leave. The employer may delay the leave for up to six months if the business would unduly be disrupted and an alternative time is offered. The expiry of the right that we discussed above will be delayed to cover this postponement if necessary. The employer is entitled to ask for evidence of the employee's entitlement, but not of course for any explanation of the circumstances of the particular request.

Fathers wanting to take parental leave at the time of a birth are required to give 21 days' notice of the expected week of childbirth and of the required length of leave. They are then entitled to take the leave whenever the birth actually occurs and the employer cannot postpone it. There is a similar provision covering both parents in relation to an expected adoption.

The employee's right is to a *total* of 13 weeks' leave in relation to each child. Thus an employee who changes jobs after taking eight weeks of leave in the first two years of a child's life enjoys no entitlement during the next year, having not yet achieved the necessary service in the new job, but thereafter has a right to five more weeks in the period up to the child's fifth birthday. There is no obligation on the first employer to pass any records to the second, and monitoring of this rule may therefore cause problems.

4.8.5 Remedies

The right not to suffer any detriment and to present a claim to an employment tribunal under s. 47C of ERA 1996 (considered in relation to maternity rights at **4.6.3.4** above) also applies to parental leave. Under ERA 1996, s. 80, claims can also be presented of unreasonable postponement of parental leave.

4.9 Time off for dependants

The third of the 'family friendly' provisions that we are considering is also a result of the Parental Leave Directive 96/34/EC. Unlike parental leave, it is not subject to regulations but is set out in detail in ERA 1999, which inserts a new s. 57A into ERA 1996. The requirement in the Directive is *for time off work for urgent family reasons*; in the UK version this has become *time off for dependants*, which is probably significantly broader in its scope. The time off is unpaid.

4.9.1 Circumstances when the right arises

There are two aspects to the statutory definition of the circumstances when employees have a right to time off for dependants. First, there is the question of who is a dependant; and, secondly, there is the question of when the right arises in relation to those dependants.

A dependant is defined in s. 57A(3), (4) and (5) as:

(a) a spouse;

(b) a child;

(c) a parent;

(d) anyone else living in the same household except as employee, tenant etc.;

(e) *for certain purposes only*, anyone else who 'reasonably relies on the employee' for that help.

The circumstances are defined in precise terms in s. 57A(1). In outline, the employee must need the time off to take action related to any of the following events concerning a dependant:

(a) where any of the above dependants falls ill or is injured or assaulted, or where a dependant in categories (a) to (d) above gives birth;

(b) arranging care in relation to illness or injury—all dependants;

(c) death—(a) to (d) only;

(d) unexpected disruption or termination of arrangements for care—all dependants;

(e) unexpected incidents at school, only in relation to a child—(b).

The circumstances are thus quite tightly defined. For example, the right relates to making arrangements for the provision of care, but not to provision of care by employees themselves. In *Forster* v *Cartwright Black* [2004] ICR 1728 the EAT did not permit a claimant whose mother had recently died to use s. 57A to obtain additional bereavement leave when no need to 'take action' existed.

4.9.2   Time off

The statutory right is to unpaid time off. There is no stated limit to the amount of time, beyond the reference to *a reasonable amount* of time off in ERA 1996, s. 57A. In *Qua* v *John Ford Morrison* [2003] ICR 482, the EAT held that time off was permitted for urgent reasons such as dealing with a child who has fallen ill unexpectedly, but not regular relapses from a known underlying condition. Reasonableness related to the employee's needs and her compliance with conditions about notification to the employer; not disruption or inconvenience caused to the employer's business. In many employments, there is already a contractual right to paid time off in defined circumstances like bereavement or childbirth, but the duration is usually defined. There is no statutory reference to the interrelationship of two such rights and they therefore exist independently.

4.9.3   Notices and administration

The whole purpose of these provisions is to enable employees to deal with emergencies. There can therefore be no requirement on employees to give advance notice. They are, however, required to tell the employer the reason for the absence as soon as reasonably practicable and, unless the explanation is only being given on return to work, to state how long the absence is expected to last.

Despite the strict statutory definition of the circumstances in which the right arises, there is nothing in s. 57A to give the employer any right to demand evidence of the employee's entitlement. In *Truelove* v *Safeway Stores Ltd* [2005] ICR 589 the EAT accepted that the employee cannot be expected to communicate the need for time off in the language of the statute. A more general statement indicating the disruption of a stable arrangement was enough to indicate to the employer that an emergency had arisen so as to give rise to the right to time off. That decision, coupled with the lack of any right to evidence, seems to make it very difficult for an employer safely to refuse a request and it may be that some future case will give guidance to employers on what they may require.

4.9.4   Remedies

Under ERA 1996, s. 57B (inserted by ERA 1999), an employee can present a claim to an employment tribunal of being refused time off for a dependant and the tribunal may award compensation.

Perhaps of greater practical significance is the addition of this right to the list of those in connexion with which dismissal is automatically unfair under ERA 1999, s. 99 (see **10.8.7** below). This could cause employers a lot of difficulty in dealing with absenteeism. Employees with a poor attendance record are sometimes warned and are told that further unauthorised absence will lead to dismissal. If further absence occurs, but is in fact covered by s. 57A, it will automatically be unfair for the employer to dismiss.

4.10 Flexible working

The last of the 'family friendly' rights we need to consider is the right of the employee to ask the employer for a variation of the contract of employment in order to care for young or disabled children or (since April 2007) certain adults. It exists as s. 80F of ERA 1996, inserted by EA 2002, and is supplemented by two sets of regulations issued in 2002 and an amendment in 2006. Permitted requests are for changes in hours of work, place of work, or time of work.

To be eligible to make such a request employees must satisfy the following criteria:

(a) They must have 26 weeks service when making the request.

(b) The child must not be more than six years old, 18 if disabled, two weeks after the request is made.

(c) The employee must have or expect to have responsibility for the child's upbringing.

(d) The request must be to enable the employee to care for the child.

(e) The employee must be the mother, father, guardian, adopter or foster parent of the child, or alternatively married to or the partner of such a person. From 6 April 2007 carers are included.

(f) An employee may also make a request for flexible working if caring or expecting to be caring for a person who is over the age of 18 and in need of care, and who is married to or the partner or civil partner of the employee, or a relative of the employee, or living at the same address as the employee.

(g) The employee must not have made another application to work flexibly within the preceding 12 months.

The application must be made in writing and the employer must consider it seriously. The grounds on which it may be refused are set out in detail—to summarise, they are grounds of cost, detrimental consequences, effect on other staff, or planned structural changes. In *Commotion Ltd* v *Rutty* [2006] ICR 290 the EAT confirmed that the employer is not required to produce objective justification for refusal, but the grounds must be made out. In that case the employment tribunal was entitled to find that the employer had made an outdated, 'off the cuff' response without research and that was not good enough.

An employee who is refused unreasonably or whose employer does not properly consider the request can present a claim to the employment tribunal. The tribunal can order the employer to reconsider the request and can award compensation up to a maximum of eight weeks' pay, subject to the usual statutory maximum of £330 per week. In *Shaw* v *CCL Ltd* [2008] IRLR 284 the EAT found on the facts in the case that the employer's flat rejection of the claimant's request for flexible working undermined the necessary trust and confidence between the parties and was in fundamental breach of her contract of employment, so that she succeeded in a claim of unfair constructive dismissal (see **Chapter 10**).

4.11 Summary

- All workers are entitled to the national minimum wage (£5.73, per hour for adults) for all hours worked.
- All workers are entitled to a limit on their weekly hours, to further limits on night shift, and to daily rest, weekly rest, rest breaks, and paid annual leave.
- Employers may not make deductions from wages without express authority and employees can often bring their contractual disputes about the amount they are paid within this rule.
- Shop workers and betting workers have the right not to be required to work on Sundays.
- Qualifying employees have 'family friendly' rights—to maternity pay and leave, to paternity and adoption leave, to time off for dependants, and to ask for flexible working.

4.12 Self-test questions

1. A 19-year-old student friend had been earning some extra money by working in a bar on Friday evenings from 7.30 to about 11.45. He has just started an additional job working in a shop on Saturday mornings from 8.00 to 1.00 pm. He gets no break and is paid £30 for five hours' work. Your friend tells you that he understands that other people get time-and-a-half for Saturdays. The shop manager told him that as a part-time worker he is not entitled to holidays.

Your friend is fed up with feeling tired when he goes to play football on Saturday afternoon, feels he is being exploited for a poor rate of pay, and wonders if there is anything you can do to help. Do you think the shop has broken any of the rules set out in this chapter?

2. An employer has until now paid at the rate of time-and-a-half for Saturday overtime. Recently the employer announced that such additional costs made the company uncompetitive compared with others overseas and gave three months' notice that weekend overtime would henceforth be paid at time-and-a-quarter. The trade union objected on behalf of the employees but the employer was adamant that the change was necessary and the trade union responded that its members would not work overtime on that basis. In fact, the employer did not require any overtime for several weeks after the expiry of the three months, but then a request was made and several people agreed to work on a Saturday. There is some suggestion that one or two expressly asked their supervisor about payment and he replied evasively, saying that payment would be sorted out later. They were in fact paid at time-and-a-quarter. Their trade union now asks whether that payment can be challenged in the tribunals. Could you use the 'deductions from wages' jurisdiction?

Operation of the contract

5.1 Introduction

This chapter Examines how the contract of employment operates on a day-to-day basis. The sort of questions asked by employers and employees alike tend to be:

- Which terms usually appear in a contract?
- Does the law place limitations on how those terms can be used by either party?
- How may those terms be varied over the course of time?
- What are the legal rules for resolving disputes as to the content or implementation of those terms?
- What are the rights and duties regarding the payment of wages?

In attempting to answer these points this chapter will concentrate on the common law position and will adopt the following structure:

(a) The usual terms (express and implied) and how they are used.

(b) Qualifying for employment rights.

(c) Management decisions and employees' responses.

(d) Methods of resolving disputes, short of termination of contract.

(e) Breach: summary of sanctions and enforcement.

(f) Civil remedies for breach of contract.

(g) Deductions versus breach of contract.

(h) Example of an employment contract.

5.2 The usual terms and how they are used

We saw in **Chapters 3** and **4** that the contract is made up of express, implied, and statutory terms. We have set out below the *most commonly occurring express terms* you would find in a contract, together with commentary on their purpose, scope, and operation. Some additional terms encountered in contracts will also be noted. Many of the express terms listed below correlate to the information that must be provided under the written statement detailed in **Chapter 3.**

Having looked at express terms, we will then consider the implied terms, arising from common law and from statute. There is no fixed list of implied terms and some will be more applicable to a particular contract than others.

STANDARD EXPRESS TERMS	IMPLIED TERMS
(a) The names of the parties.	*The duties incumbent on the employer*
(b) Job title.	(a) The duty to pay.
(c) Commencement date.	(b) A limited duty to provide work.
(d) The expiry date of a fixed-term contract.	(c) Duties relating to health and safety.
(e) Pay.	(d) The duty of mutual trust and confidence.
(f) Hours of work.	(e) A duty to provide proper information to
(g) Place of work.	employees.
(h) The sick pay scheme, if any.	
(i) Holiday entitlement.	*The duties incumbent on the employee*
(j) Pension scheme.	(a) A duty to act in good faith.
(k) Notice requirements.	(b) The duty to obey lawful orders.
(l) Dedication to enterprise clause.	(c) A duty to provide personal service.
(m) Disciplinary/grievance procedures.	(d) The duty to exercise reasonable skill
(n) Confidentiality clause.	and care.
(o) Intellectual property protection.	(e) The duty to take care of the employer's
(p) Restraint of trade clause.	property.
(q) Details of other benefits.	
(r) Any 'contracting out' clause.	

Figure 5.1   Common terms of the contract.

5.2.1 Express terms

The extent of such terms, reached orally or in writing, will vary a great deal. The style of drafting is also quite variable, especially with the more complicated terms such as confidentiality and restraint of trade clauses. Therefore we have not provided 'model' clauses because these will change with the needs of the client and, more importantly, this is a matter for your course rather than this book. We have attached an example of a working contract taken from practice. We had considered using a contract which we considered to be an example of good practice, but in the end decided that a faulty contract might provide more help (and realism). This appears at the end of the chapter together with commentary so that you can see some of the clauses in situ. The common terms will be:

(a) The *names* of the parties.

(b) *Job title* and general statement of duties.

   The wider this is drafted the more built-in flexibility there is for the employer (e.g., 'clerk/typist and receptionist' allows for mobility between tasks). However, if there is ever a dispute as to performance of duties, or if the employer needs to declare the employee redundant, then an expansive list of duties may prove problematic (e.g., the job of clerk/typist might have disappeared but not that of receptionist).

(c) When the *commencement date* occurred.

   This is important in establishing the employee's continuity of employment, the timing of which may affect rights to claim, *inter alia,* unfair dismissal compensation, redundancy payments, and pension rights (for details see **5.2** below).

(d) The *expiry date* of a fixed-term contract.

   We noted these and other forms of limited-term contracts above in **Chapter 3.**

(e) *Pay.*

   Always an essential ingredient and an apparently simple point, but if payment is determined by piece-work, commission, or is variable according to the shift pattern worked then these points need to be spelled out clearly. The application of minimum pay levels under the National Minimum Wage Act 1998 was dealt with at **4.2** above.

Included in the general description of 'pay' one might also find other benefits—'perks' and bonuses—such as company cars, accommodation, 'golden handshakes', share option agreements, private health insurance schemes, and discretionary performance-related payments. The range is extensive and, especially in relation to senior employees, quite inventive.

(f) *Hours of work,* including a statement as to the status of overtime, i.e., is overtime compulsory or merely voluntary and how is payment calculated? The number of hours worked by employees together with patterns of working (e.g., shift systems, part-time, flexitime, 'annualised hours') vary enormously but working patterns for many workers are now subject to specific constraints (see above at **4.3**).

(g) *Place of work.*

The employer's business may have more than one site. If the employer wishes to be able to move the employee from place to place it is advisable to spell this out. Equally, the employer may wish to show that the employee is only expected to work in Southampton even though there are sites in London and Plymouth (see **Chapter 11** on how this relates to redundancies in a particular place of work).

(h) *The sick pay scheme,* if any.

The employer is under no duty to provide company sick pay and many employees only receive statutory sick pay. These entitlements will be administered by the employer but they are usually much more limited than a company sick pay scheme (e.g., nothing is payable for the first three days' illness and payment is limited to 28 weeks at a fixed rate)., Even where company schemes do exist there is often a sliding scale of payments, e.g., no sick pay until the employee has worked for one year, one month's entitlement for service between one and three years, and so on and it is not uncommon for employers to exclude certain types of illness from the sick pay scheme: e.g., those relating to the employee's own misconduct or generated by some activities outside work.

Some employers go beyond this and offer their employees membership of permanent health insurance (PHI) schemes (i.e., schemes drawn up by health insurance companies and offered at preferential rates to companies). Unfortunately, the wording of the sick pay scheme and that of the PHI scheme sometimes do not correlate. For instance, the PHI scheme may provide generous terms and payments (e.g., long-term incapacity payments continuing until retirement), whereas the contractual scheme will usually be framed more narrowly and allow for dismissal of incapacitated employees after (say) six months' absence. In such cases the courts may adjudge, on the wording of the various documents or by implication of terms, that the employer's contractual scheme has to give way to these more beneficial insurance provisions.

One important consequence of these cases is that, as Staughton LJ states *obiter* in *Brompton* v *AOC International Ltd and UNUM Ltd* [1997] IRLR 639, there was 'a good deal to be said for' the idea that in these circumstances a term should be implied to the effect that the employer would not terminate the contract so as to deny the employee of his or her rights under the PHI scheme (at least not without having inserted some power to do so in the PHI agreement or having to pay a great deal in damages). A dismissal for good cause or a genuine redundancy, however, will not be covered by this implied term: *Hill v General Accident Fire & Life Assurance Corporation plc* [1998] IRLR 641 (see further at **10.9.6.3**).

(i) *Holiday entitlement.*

This area has traditionally been the domain of pure contract law. However, the Working Time Regulations now lay down established patterns of holiday entitlement for many workers. For those workers not covered by the Regulations, this area is still governed by the express and implied terms of the contract.

(j) *Pension scheme* arrangements, if any.

Such details will relate to any schemes operating outside the state provisions. An employer is not bound to operate a company pension scheme and an employee is not bound to join it. There are a number of different schemes available, e.g., final salary schemes and money-purchase schemes. Details are outside the scope of this book.

(k) *Notice* requirements.

This will detail what length of notice to terminate the contract is due from each party. The amount will often vary according to length of service, though there are certain *statutory minima* required under ERA 1996, s. 86 (see **5.2.3** below and **Chapter 9**). Employers may also wish to insert a term that *payment in lieu of notice* may be given by the employer. Payment in lieu simply means that the employer makes a money payment equivalent to the sum the employee would have earned during the notice period. If calculated correctly the sum equates to any damages the employee might have been awarded for the failure actually to give notice. The employer can choose to do this even if there is no clause in the contract allowing for such action. However, although no further damages will fall due, giving a payment in lieu when there is no term to that effect is technically a breach of contract and, as will be seen, this may negate any restraint of trade clause in the contract (see **8.9**). The disadvantage to having such a clause is that it becomes an agreed contractual liability and so tax will certainly be deducted.

Notice clauses can take a variety of forms. The notice due from one party does not have to be the same as from the other, and there is no standard term which one could expect to occur in every industry. Moreover, with senior employees a whole host of ingenious devices may be found, often designed to minimise tax liabilities. One increasingly common term is the 'garden leave' clause—a mechanism whereby the employer is given notice but allowed not to work but to stay at home in the garden. This device attempts to use notice provisions to overcome some of the problems of restraint of trade clauses (see **8.10** for details).

Some employers use a clause which requires an employee to forfeit part of their final salary or holiday pay if the employee fails to give adequate notice. In *Giraud v Smith* [2000] IRLR 763, Kay J held that such clauses would have to constitute a genuine pre-estimate of loss in order to stand—otherwise they amounted to penalty clauses. Oddly enough, the Working Time Regulations (see **Chapter 4**) do permit such deductions provided *some* payment is still made: *Witley & District Men's Club v Mackay* [2001] IRLR 595, EAT, so different analyses apply depending on how the claim is framed.

(l) *Dedication to enterprise clause,* sometimes called a 'whole time and attention clause'. This clause states the limitations under which an employee can undertake other work for a different employer, either during or after working hours. The clause, especially with senior employees, may also impose a duty to inform on colleagues' misdeeds.

(m) *Disciplinary/grievance procedures.*

Procedures have always been very important in employment law disputes. For instance, an employer's conduct in, say, an unfair dismissal action will be judged against his own published disciplinary procedure (or lack of one) in determining the fairness of any dismissal. Until the implementation of EA 2002, ss. 31 to 40 by the Employment Act 2002 (Dispute Resolution) Regulations SI 2004/752, employers were relatively free to devise their own procedures. These regulations introduced overly-complex mandatory statutory procedures. However, as we commented in the **Preface**, by the time you are studying this subject these procedures will have been repealed (due date April 2009) and will have been replaced by simpler procedures. Consequently, we shall not deal with the Regulations here (we shall outline the anticipated new procedures in **Chapter 10**).

The following terms will occur more frequently, though not exclusively, in contracts for senior employees, sales people, and research and development staff:

(n) *Confidentiality clause.*

During the currency of the contract an employer's 'secrets' will be protected by the implied terms relating to confidentiality and fidelity (see below at **5.2.2** and **Chapter 7**). However, an express term can serve to detail the nature of the confidential information and also serve as a warning to employees. Without such a clause there may be circumstances where junior employees who come into contact with confidential information are not bound by any duty of confidence because this was not made obvious to them.

Confidentiality clauses are also frequently drafted to protect against the use or disclosure of information once the relationship has terminated. It is a matter of some debate whether such clauses are effective and we will deal with this point extensively in **Chapter 7**. For the moment we can say that it is advisable to insert properly drafted clauses of this nature in the contract; certainly as regards employees who are likely to handle confidential information.

(o) *Intellectual property clause.*

This clause seeks to detail ownership of copyright, designs and inventions made by the employee during the working relationship. Such clauses cannot overturn certain statutory definitions.

(p) *Restraint of trade clause.*

Such clauses endeavour to prevent an employee working in a particular job or industry for a set time, and usually within a defined area, after the contract has ended. The effect of restraint clauses is therefore far more dramatic than any confidentiality clause. Many employers seek to rely on both types of clause in order to protect against disclosure of secrets and/or to prevent the former employee poaching the employer's trade connexions.

The presumption with restraint of trade clauses is that they are void unless:

(i)   they seek to protect a *legitimate interest;* and

(ii) they are shown to be *reasonable* by reference to time, area and the market setting. See **Chapter 8** for details.

The following terms, which may apply to all staff, occur occasionally but are useful:

(q) *A right to search employees.*

Companies wishing to protect against the removal of confidential documents or, more generally, against the removal of stock, are advised to insert such a clause.

There will be no general implied term to this effect and there may well now be human rights implications under art. 8 of the European Convention on Human Rights. We would suggest that the same degree of caution should be applied to searching employees' offices and desks, even though, technically, these are the employer's property.

(r) *A right to demand employees undergo medical examinations on request.*

As will be seen in **Chapter 7**, a term will not be implied which forces an employee to submit to a medical examination. An express term is necessary and often very useful. Indeed, it has become common practice in some industries (e.g., oil exploration) for the employer to have the contractual right to demand that employees undertake regular drug tests. This is defended on the grounds of health and safety; but many employers would like to see this sort of term extended to all kinds of employees. Again, art. 8 of the European Convention on Human Rights needs to be considered here (see *Whitefield* v *General Medical Council* at **1.7.3.2** above).

(s) *Suspension clause.*

This gives the employer the right to suspend an employee (i) with pay, or (ii) without pay as part of disciplinary proceedings or sanctions. It should occur in the disciplinary details (see (m) above). There will be no right for an employer to suspend without pay in the absence of such a clause, and any prolonged suspension *with* pay may be a breach of contract even with such powers in the contract as it may strike at the mutual trust of the relationship. Employees may seek to prevent long-term suspensions through applications for injunctive relief.

(t) *Lay-off and guarantee clauses.*

If an employer 'lays off ' the employee (i.e., sends him or her home without pay because there is a shortage of work) this will constitute a breach of contract and may eventually be deemed a redundancy. Many industries therefore have specific rates of pay relating to short-time working, termed 'guarantee payments'. There are statutory guarantee payments as well which will operate as a minimum (at the time of writing, £20.40 per day to a maximum of five days in any three-month period).

(u) *Variation clause.*

As we will see below, although the unilateral variation of a contract by the employer is not unknown, there may be complex legal consequences (see **5.4.2.1**). Some employers therefore incorporate an express term allowing for the power to vary the contract (usually in stated circumstances). Such clauses are viewed with great suspicion by the courts and tribunals.

(v) *Maternity leave.*

Some employers offer maternity rights which are more beneficial to the employee than the bare statutory rights (see **Chapter 4** above).

5.2.2   Terms and age discrimination

Pay and benefits which depend on age or length of service may be indirectly discriminatory under the Employment Equality (Age) Regulations 2006, SI 2006/1031 because older employees are more likely to benefit than younger ones. Thus, terms and conditions noted above which vary according to service (such as notice periods or sick pay entitlement) may fall foul of the new regulations. Equally, in the past older employees have been excluded from certain benefits such as private medical insurance—because of the cost in maintaining membership—or from sick pay schemes or occupational pension schemes for a whole host of organisational reasons. Any such exclusions will now have to be justified. Cost, in itself, will not be justification, but cost that might break the scheme and so disadvantage all other employees might be. Pension schemes are given specific treatment in sch. 2 to the 2006 regulations.

The regulations came into effect on 1 October 2006 and have already been referred to the European Court of Justice on whether the mandatory retirement age of 65 is permissible (decision expected early 2009). For the moment we make the following points.

5.2.2.1   General rules

- Regulation 27 of the 2006 regulations provides that any act done in order to comply with a statutory requirement is not unlawful.

- Variations in pay and benefits where the service required is five years or less are exempted under reg. 32. So, for instance, having different holiday entitlements for new employees as opposed to those with, say, four years' service is justifiable but once an employee has worked for five years they must be treated the same as any longer-standing employee.

- Regulation 32 also allows employers to put forward objective justifications for having terms which depend on length of service.

- 'Positive action' is permitted in limited circumstances under reg. 29 in redressing imbalances in matters such as affording access to training.

- A defence of 'genuine occupational requirement' is available under reg. 8: which could apply, e.g., in acting roles (see **Chapter 6**).

- Enhanced contractual redundancy pay schemes are exempted if they follow the rules set out in reg. 33.

5.2.2.2   The 'less than five years' exemption

Terms which allow for increases in benefits after, say, two years' service (e.g., admission to the sick pay scheme or gaining extra holiday entitlement) are lawful because they do not require five years' service.

5.2.2.3   Objective justification

Where the service required to gain a benefit is longer than five years the term will not be discriminatory if the employer can demonstrate that the term 'fulfils a business need of his undertaking (for example, by encouraging the loyalty or motivation, or rewarding the experience, of some or all of his workers'—reg. 32(2)). Regulation 32(3) then sets out a prescribed method of calculating 'length of service' which the employer must adhere to in order to gain protection. We have not set these out here but they essentially follow the normal rules for calculating continuity of service covered in **5.3** below.

5.2.2.4 Benefits based on age

It is very rare to find benefits calculated according to age rather than length of service. One example would the National Minimum Wage, but this and others often receive specific exemption or fall within the exemption of statutory authority. An employer must, however, adhere to the strict rules attached to the operation of such potentially discriminatory terms in order to gain protection.

5.2.2.5 Employees aged over 65

The 'default age' for compulsory retirement is set at 65 but workers may work beyond this and gain or maintain certain rights when they do so (e.g., on unfair dismissal). This 'default age' has been challenged and a preliminary reference has been made to the ECJ. The Advocate-General's opinion (dated 23 September 2008) favours the UK's arguments on the legality of the default age.

5.2.3 Implied terms

Employment contracts are rarely thought out by the parties. The exact terms of contracts are often difficult to locate or are silent on many aspects. There is therefore great scope for implying terms; for instance, 'Is sick pay payable?', 'Is there a limit on overtime hours that may be worked?', 'Can the employee be asked to work at different sites?'.

The various methods of implying terms were noted in **Chapter 3** (by law, under the 'officious bystander' test, by custom and by statute). In line with general contractual theory, terms will be implied only where they are *necessary* for the business efficacy of the contract, not simply because it would be *reasonable* so to imply them. However, once a term has been found to be necessary to the contract the court will then determine the limits of that term within reasonable parameters. Thus it may be found reasonable to imply a term that an employee will work at a variety of sites operated by the employer; it may, however, be unreasonable to include the Birmingham site when the employee normally works in Oxford.

The courts and tribunals are not afraid of implying terms, either to give a purposive interpretation to the contract or on the basis of *general* employment practice rather than by detailed analysis of the negotiations, etc. entered into by the specific parties. These general points, however, centre on how the parties would be expected to behave, e.g., to act in good faith; the courts and tribunals are more wary of accepting arguments of 'common practice' or 'general working practice' within a company without firm evidence of the fact. The generally established implied terms as to duties owed are set out below.

5.2.3.1 The duties incumbent on the employer

(a) The duty to *pay* the employee the agreed remuneration for being ready and willing to work. There is no general duty actually to supply work, though there are exceptional cases here (see (b) below).

The major statutory controls on pay are the Employment Rights Act 1996, Part II, Protection of Wages (which concerns the right for employers to make deductions from pay) and the National Minimum Wage Act 1998. Various other pieces of legislation also outlaw discriminatory pay schemes (e.g., the Equal Pay Act 1970).

Particular problems have nevertheless arisen over:

(i) *Sick pay.*

If there is no written or oral evidence of a contractual sick pay scheme, can such a right be implied? The Court of Appeal has stated that there is no presumption either way: *Mears* v *Safecar Security Ltd* [1982] ICR 626 (sick pay not due on the facts). One would thus have to look at all factors such as custom and practice within the company and even the seniority of the employee. If there is a term as to sick pay its duration is limited to that stated in the contract or for a reasonable period: *Howman* v *Blyth* [1983] ICR 416.

(ii) *Share purchase option schemes.*

The problem here is: what happens to the option to purchase when the contract is terminated? In *Levett* v *Biotrace International plc* [1999] IRLR 375, the contract included an option for the employee to purchase shares in the company. The right lapsed in the event of the employee being dismissed following disciplinary procedure (it is quite common to find such terms in contracts of employment, whereby the option lapses on termination). Here, however, the employee had been summarily dismissed in breach of the disciplinary procedure. The Court of Appeal held that he was still entitled to exercise his option; the employers were not entitled to deprive the employee of his rights by relying on their own breach of contract.

Equally, wording the scheme so that employers have an 'absolute discretion' on dismissal to reduce any share option has been held not to entitle the employer to reduce it to nil: *Mallone* v *BPB Industries plc* [2002] EWCA Civ 126, [2002] ICR 1045. This is particularly interesting because, as we will see when we come to consider how each party reacts to demands made by the other (see **5.3** below), this was the first real acknowledgement by the Court of Appeal of a power to limit managerial discretion based not merely on the technicalities of 'collateral' contracts or on the presence of dishonesty, bad faith or perversity but rather on 'irrationality'.

(b) A limited duty to *provide work*. Traditionally, only in exceptional cases will there be a duty to provide work. The most significant example occurs where the lack of work leads to an effective wage reduction, as where pay is related to commission or piece-work. A time when this is likely to be an issue is when the employee has been given notice of dismissal and not provided with work (or pay in lieu) during that time: see *Devonald* v *Rosser* [1906] KB 728. Where lack of work might have a damaging effect on reputation (e.g., in the case of actors, television personalities, or perhaps even senior business executives) there is the possibility of arguing breach of contract. And where the employer deliberately refuses to allow the employee to work for no good contractual reason, the possibility of arguing a repudiatory breach of contract becomes stronger: *Breach* v *Epsylon Industries* [1976] ICR 316. Although the above propositions have been established law for some time, the Court of Appeal decision in *William Hill Organisation Ltd* v *Tucker* [1998] IRLR 313 has confirmed that there will be cases where a right to work exists (and changing social attitudes may mean the list is wider than previously thought). The case is detailed at **8.12** below and concerned the doctrine of restraint of trade. The key point here is that their Lordships, on the facts, held that the employee, a senior dealer in the fixed odds compiling department, had not just a right to receive wages but also a right to perform his work. As in many a bad Dracula film, it seems this area was not dead, only undead, and consequently may yet be revived (darkness permitting).

(c) A duty to *indemnify* the employee regarding expenses necessarily incurred in the course of employment. Obviously this extends to expenses such as hotel and travel costs; it may also extend to covering the employee's legal costs, but only to those relating to actions undertaken during employment.

(d) Duties relating to *safety*. In *Wilsons and Clyde Coal* v *English* [1938] AC 57, these duties were said to relate to the provision of safe fellow employees, equipment, premises, and the system of work. There are also statutory duties relating to defective equipment and compulsory insurance in addition to the responsibilities created by the Health and Safety at Work etc. Act 1974 which impose criminal liabilities in this field. There is a vast body of case law and statutory authority on duties of health and safety. More recent developments, however, have caused employers concern. The Management of Health and Safety Regulations 1992 require employers to carry out risk assessments for both physical and mental hazards at work. To this has been added case law developing the implied terms relating to psychological damage arising out of stress at work. In *Walker* v *Northumberland County Council* [1995] ICR 702 the employer's duty of care was extended to cover lack of attention in dealing with the workload of an (already distressed) employee (for more detail see **9.10.1.4** below).

(e) The duty of *mutual trust and confidence*. This is a rather nebulous duty and much of the case law has arisen in the context of unfair dismissal claims based on constructive dismissals (see **Chapter 10**). Just as employees have found that duties of obedience and loyalty can be vastly extended beyond the perceived agreement by implied terms, so too is an employer bound by an element of reciprocity. Thus there will be a serious breach of the duty of mutual trust (and so of the contract) if the employer victimises the employee, acts capriciously towards the employee, fails to allow *some* employees (e.g., part-timers) access to benefits, maliciously undermines an employee's authority in front of subordinates, harasses the employee, and so on. The list is open-ended and the use of this duty as a sort of 'default rule' in the governing of employment relationships has been endorsed by the House of Lords in *Malik and Mahmud* v *Bank of Credit and Commerce International SA (in compulsory liquidation)* [1997] ICR 606. In *French* v *Barclays Bank plc* [1998] IRLR 646, the Court of Appeal applied such principles to the case where an employee had been directed to move across country within the organisation and had been granted a discretionary relocation bridging loan by his employer which was then withdrawn when the employee had difficulty selling his house. The employee was forced to sell his house at a lower value than anticipated and so sued for breach of contract in respect of the shortfall. He succeeded on the grounds that the bank had breached the duty of mutual trust by seeking to change the arrangement once the employee had relied upon it.

We shall see more of this in operation in **Chapter 10**; we should stress, however, that this is not a duty to act reasonably, only a duty to give fair treatment under the terms of the contract. What the courts are looking for is to establish a breach of contract which makes further continuance of the relationship impossible. This will not always be the same as a finding of unreasonableness; especially if express terms allow the employer to take that particular action. Indeed, in *Johnson* v *Unysis Ltd* [2001] UKHL 13, [2001] ICR 480 (dealt with at **9.10.1.6** below), the House of Lords did not see the duty of mutual trust as an overarching legal principle which might be used to control the wording of express contractual provisions (at least in relation to cases on termination of the contract). Thus it may seem unreasonable to move employees across the country every two or three years, but it is less likely to constitute a breach if a mobility clause has been incorporated in the contract. Matters such as a right to harass or discriminate cannot of course form part of an express term.

The issue of an employer's (bad faith) motives, what constitutes a lawful order, and the boundaries of mutual trust and confidence was explored in *Macari* v *Celtic Football and Athletic Club Ltd* [1999] IRLR 787. Macari claimed the employers had acted in bad faith in dismissing him. The Court of Session, Inner House (equivalent to the Court of Appeal) held that the issue of bad faith motive was irrelevant provided the orders themselves were lawful, i.e., within the terms of the contract, even if such conduct had been proven (which, on the facts, it had not).

What is clear from all this is that the area of bad faith and the ambit of the duty of mutual trust and confidence is still open to a wide range of arguments and applications and that the 'pure contract' approach seen above is at some variance with the analysis of the same topic employed in unfair dismissal cases (see **Chapter 10** below).

(f) A limited duty to *provide proper information* to employees regarding matters affecting rights under the contract. This implied term arises out of the decision of the House of Lords in *Scally v Southern Health and Social Services Board* [1991] ICR 771, where new employees were not informed of their rights to enhance their years of pension entitlement. This case effectively gave legal force to what is good practice anyway; but it did not create a universal rule regarding the provision of information. In *University of Nottingham* v *Eyett and the Pensions Ombudsman* [1999] IRLR 87, for instance, the High Court did not find as an implied term a duty for an employer to inform an employee taking voluntary early retirement that if he had waited a month he would have received a higher pension owing to the operation of the annual pay rise. The employer had not set out to mislead the employee but had merely implemented its general policy of offering no advice to employees on retirement provisions (see also *Outram v Academy Plastics Ltd* [2000] IRLR 499 (CA) to the same effect). In *Scally*, Lord Bridge had stated that a positive term of this nature would only be implied when the contract had not been negotiated with the individual employee, the particular term required the employee to take some action to avail him of the right and the employee could not reasonably be expected to be aware of the term without notice.

Further limitations have now been put on the term by the Court of Appeal. In *Lennon v Commissioner of Police of the Metropolis* [2004] EWCA Civ 130, [2004] IRLR 385 the Court acknowledged the existence of liability where the employer voluntarily assumed responsibility for providing information (and negligently misstated it) but distinguished this from implying a term that the employer owed any *positive* duty to provide information. Thus, *Scally* is looking more and more like a flash in the pan.

(g) One may also imply a term of *affording employees a reasonable opportunity to obtain redress of grievances:* see *W. A. Goold (Pearmak) Ltd* v *McConnell* [1995] IRLR 516.

5.2.3.2   The duties incumbent on the employee

(a) A duty to act in *good faith*. This is a wide and undefined duty which relates to the loyalty and fidelity that can be expected of an employee. This duty has had a major bearing on matters such as confidentiality, spare-time working and employees competing with their employer. Its operation can be seen in the following examples:

(i)   A duty *not to disrupt* the employer's business interests: *Secretary of State for Employment v ASLEF* [1972] 2 QB 455. This case concerned workers observing their contracts to the letter under a 'work-to-rule'. The disruption that followed was held to be a breach of contract. It appears therefore that the employees were held to be in breach of contract because they had observed the terms of the contract to the letter. Why this should be so is explained at **5.4.3** below.

(ii) A duty of *honesty*. This incorporates actions beyond simple theft or fraud. In *Sinclair* v *Neighbour* [1967] 2 QB 279, a betting shop manager habitually left IOUs in the till, though he always repaid them. He was expressly forbidden to do this, but he continued. The summary dismissal was held to be justified. It was said that a breach occurred where further continuance of the relationship would prove impossible. That was the case here. Again, in *Denco Ltd* v *Joinson* [1991] ICR 172, the use of an unauthorised password to gain access to a computer was found to constitute gross misconduct, analogous to dishonesty.

(iii) A duty to *account for secret profits: Boston Deep Sea Fishing and Ice Co.* v *Ansell* (1888) 39 ChD 339. Most cases involve high-ranking employees taking bribes, or who have undisclosed interests which affect the employment relationship. Strictly speaking, however, this duty extends to such things as the gift from a client of a bottle of whisky at Christmas time.

Note: Points (i) to (iii) do not mean that the employment relationship is a fiduciary relationship (except in the case of certain employees such as directors). As was noted in *Nottingham University* v *Fishel* [2000] IRLR 471, an employee's duty of fidelity requires the employee to take the employer's interests into account; it does not require the employee to act in the employer's interests. In *Fishel* this meant that the head of the university's infertility unit was not under a fiduciary duty in respect of the work he did abroad (and the money earned), but he was liable to account for the money earned from work done by other university employees.

(iv) A duty to *disclose misdeeds*. There is no obligation to incriminate oneself: *Bell* v *Lever Bros* [1932] AC 161. When asked direct questions, however, there is a duty not to mislead. An intermediate area exists here under the provisions of the Rehabilitation of Offenders Act 1974. In general, this Act allows certain criminal convictions to be 'spent' after an appropriate length of time so that they do not have to be declared. What has also developed recently is the idea that there is a duty, at least incumbent on senior management whose responsibilities are affected by the actions, to notify the employer of serious breaches by fellow employees even when that involves self-incrimination: *Sybron Corp.* v *Rochem Ltd* [1983] ICR 801. This 'duty to rat' may often be made explicit or extended by the express terms. Thus in *Fishel*, although it was held that there was no *implied* term requiring the employee to inform the employer of his extra-university activities, there was a valid *express* clause to this effect. The High Court decision of *Item Software (UK) Ltd* v *Fassihi* [2003] EWHC 3116, [2003] IRLR 769 added two interesting points to this discussion: first, that a senior employee involved in negotiations on behalf of his employer owed a duty to the employer to disclose factors which could affect the negotiations (including his own attempts to sabotage those negotiations!); secondly, that the activities in *Bell* v *Lever Bros* were held not to be fraudulent, and where fraud was present (as here) the *Bell* v *Lever Bros* principle could not apply, so there was a duty to self-incriminate (when the case went to the Court of Appeal the matter was decided only on the point of directors' duties and the employment angle was ignored: [2004] EWCA Civ 1244, [2004] IRLR 928).

This is in keeping with other High Court decisions (e.g., *Horcal* v *Gatland* [1983] IRLR 459—with *obiter* agreement in the Court of Appeal—and more recently (again *obiter*) *Tesco Stores* v *Pook* [2004] IRLR 618) that senior employees may well owe a duty to incriminate themselves, their positions being treated as akin to fiduciaries.

(v)   A duty not to disclose *confidential information*: *Thomas Marshall (Exporters) Ltd* v *Guinle* [1978] ICR 905. This duty arises during the course of the relationship and, in some cases, will continue to operate after its termination: *Faccenda Chicken* v *Fowler* [1986] ICR 297 (see **Chapter 7**).

(vi) A duty to surrender *inventions*. Sections 39 to 43 of the Patents Act 1977 deal with this point extensively. As regards most employees any invention arising out of the employee's *normal duties* will belong to the employer: *Harris's Patent* [1985] RPC 19.

(vii) A duty *not to compete* with the employer: *Hivac Ltd* v *Park Royal Scientific Instruments Ltd* [1946] Ch 169. This duty relates to actions during the currency of the contract and corresponds with 'whole time and attention' express terms. Competition cannot be prevented once the contract has been determined, subject to a valid restraint of trade clause.

(b)   The duty to *obey lawful orders*. This is an essential element in the relationship. The nomenclature begs the question as to what is a lawful order. 'Lawful' in the employment context means 'contractually justified'; such orders do not necessarily have to be reasonable as well (see, for instance, *Cresswell* v *Board of Inland Revenue* [1984] ICR 508 and **5.4.1** below).

(c)   A duty to provide *personal service* and to be ready and willing to work. Things such as taking part in a strike or other industrial action will generally amount to a breach. This will allow the employer either to withhold some or all of the wages due, or even to accept the employee's repudiation by dismissing him (see **5.4.4.6**). Illness is not a breach of this duty and, once the employee has recovered, the employer will be in breach if (subject to any express term in the contract) he insists on the employee delaying the return to work in order to undergo an examination by the company doctor and not paying the employee during that period: *Beveridge* v *KLM UK Ltd* [2000] IRLR 765.

(d)   The duty to exercise *reasonable skill and care*: *Janata Bank* v *Ahmed* [1981] ICR 791.

(e)   The duty to *take care* of the employer's property. Negligence in allowing property in the employee's care to be stolen has fallen within this heading. There are obvious limits: losing the company cat has been held to be an insufficient ground to justify dismissal.

Interestingly, there is no corresponding duty placed on the employer to safeguard the employee's property.

5.2.4   Automatically imposed terms

As we saw in **Chapter 4**, terms may also be imposed by statute. For example, terms relating to sex discrimination and equal pay will automatically become part of the contract and cannot be evaded even by express agreement (see **Chapter 6**). The most important of these terms, for present purposes, relates to notice periods. There are requirements for the provision of minimum periods of notice laid down in ERA 1996, s. 86. *The contractual periods may be longer, but not shorter.* They operate on a sliding scale; the greater the length of service, the greater the minimum notice entitlement. The maximum statutory minimum allowed under s. 86 is 12 weeks' notice (see **Chapter 9** for a fuller explanation).

5.3 Qualifying for employment rights

Employment rights do not necessarily apply automatically to all employees. For example:

(a) unfair dismissal and redundancy rights do not usually accrue until the employee has acquired some 'continuity of employment' with that employer (see **10.3** below);

(b) the right to claim the statutory minimum period of notice on dismissal usually requires one month's continuous employment.

The detailed rules governing continuity are found in ERA 1996 ss. 210– 219 and in the Employment Protection (Continuity of Employment) Regulations 1996, SI 1996/3147 and whereas employers and employees can agree *contractual* variations to the rules, these agreements cannot affect the *statutory* rights: *Secretary of State for Employment* v *Globe Elastic Thread Co. Ltd* [1979] ICR 706 HL, and *Collison* v *British Broadcasting Corporation* [1998] IRLR 238, EAT.

It is unfortunately not uncommon for solicitors to advise on the merits of, say, an unfair dismissal case, without determining the basic qualification rights first. Thus solicitors need to establish:

(a) What rights are being claimed and whether the worker actually is an 'employee' or, in some cases such as under the Working Time Regulations, a qualifying 'worker';

(b) exactly when the employment began;

(c) exactly when it ended;

(d) any breaks in that employment; and

(e) especially if there has been a dismissal, whether the reason falls under the continuity exceptions so that no time qualification is required.

Some of the basic questions in computing continuity are:

(a) *Who must prove continuity?* Continuity of employment and the calculation of lengths of continuous employment are rebuttable presumptions. The basic presumption of continuity is set out in s. 210(5) of the ERA 1996: 'A person's employment during any period shall, unless the contrary is shown, be presumed to have been continuous.' In *Nicoll* v *Nocorrode Ltd* [1981] ICR 348, the EAT held that if it is unclear whether the employee had worked the necessary number of qualifying weeks, the employee need only show some weeks count and then the burden shifts to the employer to disprove continuity.

(b) *When does continuity start and finish?* Sections 211– 213 detail the start and finish dates for calculating continuity as beginning on the day on which the employee starts work, and ending with the 'effective date of termination' for unfair dismissal purposes (called the 'relevant date' in redundancies).

(c) *Which weeks count towards continuity?* Under s. 212(1), any week during the whole or part of which an employee's relations with his employer are governed by a contract of employment counts in computing the employee's period of employment, e.g., in *Colley* v *Corkindale* [1995] ICR 965 the employee only worked for five-and-a-half hours every alternate Friday; she nevertheless qualified to bring an unfair dismissal claim because the court found that there was one contract governing the intervening periods between actual work. However, this must be distinguished from the case of regular but *separate* contracts: see *Hellyer Bros* v *McLeod* [1987] ICR 526, where trawlermen employed for separate sea voyages did not gain continuity of employment.

(d) *What happens with maternity leave?* The basic rules of statutory continuity apply in such situations but the rules are more complicated when it comes to pure contractual rights: see **4.6.3.1** and **4.6.3.3** above.

(e) *What happens when there is no contract?* The basic rule is that if there is no contract then continuity is broken. A good illustration of this is *Booth* v *United States of America* [1999] IRLR 16, where the US Government deliberately dismissed employees in the UK just short of the qualifying period for unfair dismissal (then, two years) but gave them the option to reapply for their old jobs. This dismissal and re-engagement broke the continuity of employment.

(f) *Can continuity be preserved even when there is no contract?* In limited circumstances, yes. The position is governed by s. 212(3), which states that certain weeks *will* count in computing the employee's period of employment even though the employee appears not to have a contract with the employer. These are very odd and highly technical provisions which occasionally cause problems in practice. The weeks which count are those weeks during the whole or part of which an employee is:

(i) incapable of work in consequence of sickness or injury. Note here that if the employee has not been dismissed the contract will have continued as normal. The point of this provision is that if an employee has been absent because of illness, has been dismissed and then is re-employed at a future date, those weeks during which he was not employed may still count towards continuity provided the gap between dismissal and re-engagement was no more than 26 weeks;

(ii) absent from work on account of a temporary cessation of work. There is no definition of 'temporary'—it is a question of fact. How both parties regarded the absence would be cogent evidence, but, if necessary, one must use hindsight rather than intent to establish just how temporary it was. In *Ford* v *Warwickshire County Council* [1982] ICR 520 (a case concerning continuity of employment for part-time teachers employed only during each term and not for the school holidays), 'temporary' was said to mean 'transient'—which might exclude seasonal workers. In that case Lord Diplock also favoured a strictly mathematical approach in calculating length of service, though the Court of Appeal, in *Flack* v *Kodak Ltd* [1986] ICR 775, preferred a 'broad brush' approach, i.e., was the absence 'short' in relation to the overall employment relationship. Taking a job in the interim is not fatal to a claim of continuity (*Thompson* v *Bristol Channel Ship Repairers and Engineers Ltd* (1970) 5 ITR 85, CA) but is unlikely to cover the situation where an employee moves to a new employer, fails to settle, and quickly moves back to his old job. A 'cessation' has been defined in *Fitzgerald* v *Hall Russell & Co. Ltd* [1970] AC 984, HL: it refers to a cessation of the employee's work (not the employer's business). Thus, there was no temporary cessation in *Booth* v *USA* (above) because the work still remained;

(iii) absent from work in circumstances such that, by arrangement or custom, he is regarded as continuing in the employment of his employer for any purpose. The custom must exist when the absence begins: *Todd* v *Sun Ventilating Co. Ltd* [1976] IRLR 4; an arrangement does not have to: *London Probation Board* v *Kirkpatrick* [2005] ICR 965, EAT. Equally, the mere fact that the parties might have discussed terms and conditions on which the employee might return did not amount to an implied arrangement: *McEwen* v *Brentwood & Ongar Conservative Association* (EAT 399/96, unreported). The reason for the absence appears immaterial (e.g., personal reasons, employee on 'reserve list' to be called on when necessary: *Puttick* v *John Wright & Sons (Blackwell) Ltd* [1972] ICR 457).

This area has re-emerged from the shadows over the question of 'career breaks'. In *Curr* v *Marks & Spencer plc* [2002] EWCA Civ 1852, [2003] ICR 443 the Court of Appeal held that an agreed career break (here, a 'child break scheme') did not preserve continuity on the facts because there was no evidence of mutual agreement *regarding the issue of continuity*. In other words, the agreement to take the break was not enough; one needed direct evidence on the matter of continuity, e.g., an express agreement or perhaps the continuation of contractual benefits such as pension scheme arrangements.

(g) *Can some weeks which do not count still not break continuity?* The most common example arises in the case of industrial disputes. Under s. 212, if during the week, or any part of the week, the employee takes part in a strike action then the week cannot count towards calculating the total period of continuous employment but this does not break continuity.

(h) *What happens if an employee is made redundant and then re-employed at a later date?* Section 214 states that the continuity of a period of employment is broken and then re-starts afresh as regards redundancy pay entitlements only where a redundancy payment has previously been paid to the employee.

(i) *What happens when there is a change of employer?* If the employee leaves to join another company then continuity is generally broken unless that company is an associated company, or the absence and return can be classed as a temporary cessation. Where the employer changes identity the likelihood is that continuity will be maintained with the new employer (see **Chapter 12** below).

As you will see in later chapters, some rights arise immediately on employment so that no qualification period is necessary, e.g., the rights relating to discrimination on grounds of sex, race, disability, or trade union membership, 'protective awards' in redundancies, and time off for antenatal care.

5.4   Management decisions and employees' responses

I't is quite common for an employee to ask for legal advice along the lines of, 'They've told me I have to take on a different job. Can they do that?'; the context being perhaps an order to change shifts, take a pay cut, change duties, move to another site, and so on. The pragmatic advice might be unpalatable: 'No, but are you prepared to fight?'

The corresponding question from the employer might be, 'We need to cut costs: can we change the system of working?'. There is a practical angle here too: what will the employer do in the face of individual or collective resistance? Is the employer willing to venture into brinkmanship, e.g., threatening to dismiss in the face of refusal to cooperate? It is therefore vital to know what the contract allows, whether that is legally permissible in itself, and how the terms might be open to both expansion and alteration.

In deciding on the balance between these two views you need to keep in mind all the points detailed above on express and implied terms.

5.4.1 What management can demand: lawful orders

A 'lawful order' is one which is permitted under the contract, derived from the express terms, the implied terms or a mixture of both. Should the employee fail to obey this order he or she will be in breach of contract. If the breach is serious the employer will be entitled to dismiss the employee without notice. Equally, employers can only demand that lawful orders be obeyed. An employee is free to disregard anything which falls outside the scope of contract.

As with ordinary contracts, therefore, the courts *could* have adopted the view that the parties are restricted to the originally-agreed express terms (with limited help from implied terms) and bound by nothing else. But this view does not hold true for three main reasons:

(a) Most employment contracts are for an indefinite period, terminable by notice. They may therefore last a considerable length of time and the nature of the work changes.

(b) Employment contracts are made up from a variety of sources, many of them not reduced to writing, so that certainty and proof is always a problem.

(c) The employment contract stands in the wider setting of the *employment relationship* so that the range of implied terms is more extensive than with most contracts and includes matters such as loyalty and mutual trust.

5.4.2 The employer's handling of the contract

The employer generally has the economic bargaining power to insert terms which best serve the employer's interests. Further, it is the employer who issues orders under the contract. Both these points engender a high level of managerial prerogative. What curbs are placed on managerial prerogative?

5.4.2.1 Curbs on managerial prerogative: the legitimacy of terms

There are now *statutory limitations* which make certain terms in contracts of employment illegal or ineffective. For example, those terms that:

(a) seek to license various forms of discrimination; or

(b) offend against the principle of equal pay; or

(c) attempt to diminish employee–inventors' rights; or

(d) seek generally to contract out of statutory rights (such as unfair dismissal or redundancy); or

(e) seek to exclude liability for negligence which causes death or personal injury; or

(f) offend against safety legislation; or

(g) are illegal in themselves, such as instructions to undertake criminal activities.

Away from these statutory concerns, however, there are few cases which have addressed the issue as to the *type* of terms acceptable in an employment contract. Thus, *prima facie,* employers are free to insert any terms they wish and the parties can construct any form of reasonable or unreasonable contract (restraint of trade clauses providing the rare example of common law interference: see **Chapter 8**). And express terms generally take precedence over implied terms. We use the word 'generally' because it is not clear whether terms 'implied by law' (sometimes referred to as legal incidents of the relationship), e.g., the duty of mutual trust and confidence, can be expunged by express terms. In *Johnstone* v *Bloomsbury Health Authority* [1991] IRLR 118, for instance, the Court of Appeal held that an express term requiring health workers to be 'available' for 48 hours over and above their normal 40-hour week could not stand in the face of the implied term to protect the employees' health and safety (see **5.2.2.1(d)** above). However, to do this the court had to find that the express term did not create an absolute duty (only a discretionary one as to requests for overtime), and because the term was equivocal the implied term had not been overridden. If the term had created an absolute duty of absurd overtime hours the court would have faced a more difficult question. In contrast to this problem of 'basic obligations', terms implied in fact (i.e., under the officious bystander test) cannot stand against contradictory express terms.

Judicial moderation of all this has had little focus. The concept of public policy might be invoked to overcome express terms, or the uncertainty of the term or, more recently, the implying of a term that contractual rights must be implemented on reasonable grounds.

PROBLEM

An employer encounters financial difficulties. The written contract is a complicated document, laden with detailed clauses, which sets out a very generous sick pay scheme. The employer decides to reduce the benefits substantially. The union objects o'n behalf of its members. The employer points to page 5 of the contract, where the final clause reads: 'The employer reserves the power to alter, amend, withdraw, terminate or revoke any term in this contract for any reason by giving one calendar month's notice.' The union has come to you for advice on the legality of this action.

ANSWER

The arguments available to you are multiple. You may seek to challenge the drafting of the term. For instance, you could argue that it is uncertain because of its width or seek to rely on *contra proferentem* interpretations (which is becoming a favoured method: see *Bainbridge* v *Circuit Foil UK Ltd* [1997] ICR 541). You could argue that such a clause permits only minor changes to be made (a point conceded by counsel and accepted by the EAT in *United Association for the Protection of Trade* v *Kilburn* (LEXIS transcript, EAT 787/84). You might seek to argue that such a clause can only be implemented in good faith and inherently requires renegotiation rather than mere unilateral change. Arguing from basic contractual principles you could claim that the court should try to avoid a construction which effectively destroys the aim of the contract or which produces absurd consequences. Similarly you might argue that reliance on this term *in this particular way* constitutes a breach of mutual trust and confidence; that such a term can be exercised only where it is reasonable in all the circumstances so as not to damage the employment relationship irrevocably. In all these cases, however, you are on uncertain ground; the express terms clearly outflank you so that on a literal reading of the contract the odds are against your client on the strict wording.

Cases in this area are now becoming more common. In *Airlie* v *City of Edinburgh District Council* [1996] IRLR 516, a majority of the EAT held that a bonus scheme payable under a collective agreement (which had been incorporated into the individual contracts) *was* open to variation by the employers on the proper construction of its wording (here, 'the scheme . . . may be altered at the request of either side after consultation . . . '). The employers had consulted, failed to reach an agreement, and acted accordingly. In *Candler* v *ICL System Services* (1996, unreported), based on the then Wages Act 1986 (now ERA 1996, Part II), the EAT held against the employer on the wording of the clause, but did not question the efficacy of the clause itself. The employer lost again in *Glendale Managed Services Ltd v Graham* [2003] EWCA Civ 773, [2003] IRLR 465 when they decided not to adhere to a nationally agreed pay rise. The employers argued that this national agreement was stated to be 'normally paid' to the employees but they had the power to withdraw it as the contract said the rate of pay would be the national rate 'as adopted by the Authority from time to time'; they had chosen not to adopt it. True, said the Court of Appeal, but only with sufficient notice so as not to breach mutual trust.

The employer will therefore argue that the clause is valid because: (i) it is an express term; and (ii) it simply reflects managerial prerogatives. The employee's arguments are more nebulous but the main ones must be: (i) to attack the wording itself on a *contra proferentem* basis; (ii) to argue that such a clause changes the nature of the contract itself and is therefore void.

We have also seen that in the cases concerning PHI schemes and share option agreements (**5.2.3.1** above) the courts have become more inventive in limiting the use of discretionary powers in the contract. A further step in this direction was taken in *Jenvey v Australian Broadcasting Corporation* [2002] EWHC 927, [2002] IRLR 520. Here, an employee fell into dispute with his employer over his contractual terms. He was dismissed shortly afterwards. The employment tribunal found that there was a redundancy situation on the facts, but that the actual reason for dismissal was the 'assertion of a statutory right' and therefore automatically unfair (see **10.8.8.2** below for details). They had to make an award based on this reason and, at the time of the hearing, an unfair dismissal award was subject to a cap of £12,000. This would have been fine except that the employee's contract incorporated a contractual redundancy scheme, which meant that if he had been dismissed for redundancy, he would have had a contractual claim of £58,000. By the tribunal's justified finding of an automatically unfair reason for dismissal the employee had effectively been deprived of the contractual redundancy package.

The employee had wisely reserved his right to bring a breach of contract claim in the High Court. He was estopped from claiming that the reason for his dismissal was redundancy and so brought a claim that there was a breach of the implied term on use of discretion in that the employer had decided to dismiss for redundancy and could not then be allowed (without good cause as noted above) to dismiss for some other or no reason, even though notice had been given. Elias J agreed with this and awarded damages for the contractual redundancy package.

Judicial interference is therefore still somewhat unpredictable and has tended to focus more on the *use* of terms rather than their innate legitimacy. This is illustrated by the *obiter* comments of Lord Woolf MR in *Wandsworth LBC v D'Silva* [1998] IRLR 193 that with such terms:

(a) clear language is required to reserve to one party an unusual power of this sort;

(b) the court is unlikely to favour an interpretation which does more than enable the employer to vary contractual provisions with which the employer is required to comply (i.e., the outlawing of major changes to substantive rights);

(c) the courts should avoid constructions which produce unreasonable results.

It is certainly the case that arguments based on *implying* a power of unilateral variation are, to use the words of Fraser in *Dad's Army*, doomed: *Hayes v Securities and Facilities Division* [2001] IRLR 81, CA.

5.4.2.2   Curbs on managerial prerogative: reasonable use of terms

At the beginning of the nineteenth century employers held a position of feudal dominance over their employees (servants). Practically *any* order given by an employer was lawful. Slowly, judgments began to place limitations on the employer's discretionary powers. However, it is still a well-established axiom that an employer does not have to act *fairly: Western Excavating (ECC) Ltd v Sharp* [1978] ICR 221. The fact that your client works for (or is) the worst employer in the city does not, in itself, matter in law.

Nevertheless, despite the avowed intentions of the EAT and the Court of Appeal that fairness is not a matter for contractual relationships, the rudiments of managerial prerogative constraints can be detected. As with so many of the recent developments of contractual theory, most of the examples have arisen in unfair dismissal cases, especially those centring round the concept of constructive dismissal. In *Cawley v South Wales Electricity Board* [1985] IRLR 89, for instance, the employer utilised the disciplinary procedure (technically within the contractual bounds) to demote an employee. The EAT decided nevertheless that this was an *excessive* use of the contractual power and found a breach of contract. Again, in *Woods v WM Service (Peterborough) Ltd* [1981] ICR 666, it was stated that 'employers will not, without reasonable and proper cause, conduct themselves in a manner calculated or likely to destroy or seriously damage the relationship of confidence and trust between employer and employee'.

There is thus a 'scale of reasonableness'. The *reasonable* use of legitimate terms (including ones that the employee does not like) carries with it no potential for breach. Neither does the *unreasonable* use of terms in itself constitute a breach. A court might concur with your employee-client's refusal to obey these orders, but you could not be certain of this (and see **5.4.3** on 'employee adaptability' below). The employer's action needs to lie somewhere over the halfway line of the reasonableness scale, heading towards the capricious use of power and the extreme end of unreasonableness, before a breach will have occurred and your client, in law at least, can legitimately choose to refuse to obey the order. The further over the halfway line, the more serious (repudiatory) the breach and, as you will see, the more the employee may have to decide whether to accept the repudiation, resign, and claim damages—or simply put up with it.

To challenge the legitimacy of the clearly expressed terms, therefore, one must find unconscionability rather than mere unreasonableness. Thus, the Court of Appeal permitted an employer's unilateral reduction of pay (here, a car allowance) on the basis that proper notice had been given and the power was not exercised 'for an improper purpose, capriciously or arbitrarily, or in any way in which no reasonable employer, acting reasonably, would exercise it': *Wetherill v Birmingham City Council* [2007] EWCA Civ 599, [2007] IRLR 781. A wise employer will also note, however, that even if the contractual terms are fulfilled there is always the possibility that the exercise of such terms may amount to indirect discrimination (see **5.4.2.3** below).

A word of caution is needed here. What constitutes a lawful order falls to be decided in two quite different arenas. As a pure contractual matter (where a declaration, injunction, or damages are sought) that arena is the county court or High Court. There is a tradition for tying the rules of contracts of employment to ordinary contracts here and so things like the employee's individual needs tend to be put to one side.

But matters of contract can arise in the setting of employment tribunals; both as separate issues and as adjuncts of unfair dismissal actions, redundancy claims, etc. (see **5.7**). With one eye on contractual principles, the tribunals and the EAT are not averse to implying terms which look far more like imposing a standard of reasonableness. Interestingly, in a pure contractual setting, we saw above (at **5.2.2.1(a)(ii)**) that the Court of Appeal appears to be moving more towards an analysis based on irrationality/unreasonableness too: see *Mallone v BPB Industries plc*.

Students often raise the question whether legislation relating to exclusion clauses and 'unfair terms' is relevant here. The answer is: only in extremely rare circumstances, where the employee can somehow be classed as a 'consumer' or operating under the employer's 'written standards of business': *Commerzbank AG* v *Keen* [2006] EWCA Civ 1536, [2007] ICR 623.

5.4.2.3 Curbs on managerial prerogative: discriminatory clauses

The Court of Appeal decision in *Meade-Hill and National Union of Civil and Public Servants* v *British Council* [1995] IRLR 478 brought into play the question of discrimination and the use of mobility (and similar) clauses. Here, an express mobility clause was held to be indirectly discriminatory unless the employer could justify the clause in relation to the position held by the employee, irrespective of her sex.

The appraisal of all contractual provisions against 'non-discrimination' criteria has become increasingly important, and the sophistication of the analysis involved can easily trap the unwary. Employers need to be able to justify imposing changes in working patterns such as moving employees from part-time to full-time employment. In *London Underground Ltd* v *Edwards (No. 2)* [1998] IRLR 364, CA, for instance, the contractual issue focused on a change in shift patterns for train operators. The change was agreed with the relevant unions and, out of an affected workforce of 2,044, Ms Edwards was the only person unable to comply with the new system. Her problem centred on childcare provisions as a single parent. The change in contractual terms was found by the EAT to constitute indirect discrimination. The problem lay in deciding whether a 'considerably smaller' proportion of women than men could comply with the change. Ms Edwards may have been the only person affected, so that statistically this reasoning looks weak, but there were only 21 female train operators—a figure which makes comparison statistically unreliable. The EAT thus found that: 'The disproportionate impact of the condition may be assessed by looking both at the picture as it was at the time, and as it may be, had the small pool of women been larger and statistically significant'. Further, on the facts, the employer could not justify the change in the light of its business arrangements as set against Ms Edwards' personal circumstances. The Court of Appeal agreed with the EAT's approach.

Such clauses, or variations on the general theme, appear in many contracts. Employers need to show objective reasons why such clauses are necessary rather than merely relying on the fact that the clause was lifted from a precedent book and looked useful.

5.4.2.4 Curbs on managerial prerogative: discretionary payment clauses

As we noted at **5.2.1(e)** above, pay is often built up from a range of different elements: basic salary, commission payments, piece-rate, and 'bonus schemes'. If the bonus can be calculated on a mathematical basis it is no different from commission or piece-rate; but sometimes there is an element of discretion built in to preserve management powers or in the hope of avoiding tax. Here, both the wording of the discretionary payment clause and the exercise of that discretion are open to argument. Employers tend to believe that the use of the word 'discretion' means absolute freedom; the case law shows otherwise.

In *Horkulak* v *Cantor Fitzgerald International* [2004] EWCA Civ 1287, [2004] IRLR 942, the Court of Appeal examined the cases on the exercise of discretion, e.g., *Clark* v *BET* [1997] IRLR 348 (payment to be at the 'absolute discretion' of the board still subject to good faith application). It then reviewed *Laverack* v *Woods* [1967] 1 QB 278 (CA) (which established that an employer is entitled to discharge his obligations under a contract in the most beneficial way possible) and *Reda* v *Flag* [2002] IRLR 747 (where the Privy Council refused to allow an implied term of good faith to overturn an express provision, see **5.4.2.1** above) and concluded that it is still possible to construe an unrestricted discretion as being subject to an implied term that it will be exercised in good faith and rationally, even in the face of express provisions (confining *Reda* to its facts). The same analysis applies to cases involving discretionary share options (see *Mallone* v *BPB Industries plc* above at **5.2.2.1(a)(ii)**).

Again, in *Brand* v *Compro Computer Services Ltd* [2004] EWCA Civ 204, [2005] IRLR 196—decided before *Horkulak* and not mentioned in that decision—it was held that, unless the contract makes it very clear that accrued commission on work done is not payable after termination then it is recoverable (the phrase here that payment was made if the employee remained 'in full-time employment at all times' was not specific enough to exclude the right). There is still a problem here, though. If the contract is very specific about how commission etc. is earned or accrued (thereby excluding discretion as such) then the question is one of interpretation rather than implying terms such as good faith application. Thus, in *Peninsula Business Services Ltd* v *Sweeney* [2004] IRLR 49, the EAT refused to award accrued commission in the face of a term which clearly stated that the employee only became entitled to it if in employment at the relevant date of calculation (this case was not dealt with in *Horkulak* or *Brand*).

5.4.3 Stretching the contract—employee adaptability

If the employer must adhere to an honest use of the contract, the same is certainly true for the employee. This will mean that as well as observing instructions given under the express terms of the contract, the employee is expected to be flexible in the observance of those terms. At its very basic level, this is a duty to observe the contract reasonably, or at least not to disrupt the enterprise; it has also been described as a more positive duty of cooperation. The most famous example of this arose in *Secretary of State for Employment* v *ASLEF* [1972] 2 QB 455. As part of an industrial dispute the employees decided to 'work-to-rule', i.e., to observe the absolute letter of the contract. This meant that extensive safety checks were undertaken, no leeway was allowed on manning levels, etc., and disruption to the rail network followed. The question was: could the strict observance of the contract constitute a breach of that contract? The Court of Appeal decided that it could because the purpose behind the strict observance was to cause disruption. There was an implied duty not to cause disruption. The duty was also described as the more burdensome 'duty to promote the commercial interests of the employer'. In *British Telecommunications plc* v *Ticehurst* [1992] ICR 383, the Court of Appeal further classified the withdrawal of goodwill (as part of industrial action) as a breach of contract (see also *Sim* v *Rotherham Metropolitan Borough Council* [1986] IRLR 391 on the level of duties owed by professional employees (here, schoolteachers)).

Much of the development in this area relates yet again to claims of constructive dismissal. Perhaps the clearest statement of 'employee adaptability' came in *Cresswell* v *Board of Inland Revenue* [1984] ICR 508. The employers sought to change the method of working by the introduction of computers. The employees objected, at least on the grounds that the acquisition of new skills should bring with it extra pay. The issue was whether the alteration in how the job was done could be enforced as a lawful order, or whether this was beyond the scope of the contract. It was held that employees are expected to be adaptable in performing their duties. If the change is merely as to *how* the job was done, rather than a change to the job content itself, modern employees are expected to respond favourably. Certainly, if the change is temporary an employee is expected to cooperate provided the work is suitable and the employee will suffer no disadvantage in contractual benefits or status.

Many cases have centred on employee mobility. In *White* v *Reflecting Roadstuds Ltd* [1991] ICR 733, an *express term* reserved to the employer the power to transfer employees to alternative work on grounds of business efficiency. White was not the best of employees and his performance affected the work of others in his team. He was transferred to a lower-paid job. This was held not to be in breach. One key factor was that the transfer correlated to the aims stated in the contract, i.e., it was for business efficiency. But there is no general requirement for any transfer to be made on reasonable operational grounds.

Subject to the possibility of arguing indirect discrimination, express mobility clauses therefore tend to be left alone by the courts provided they are clear and unambiguous. But if a mobility term is not clear, or is missing, there is still room for implication. Thus, if the job is of the kind where mobility might be expected (i.e., it is quite common for employees to move around in the industry, such as construction workers), or the individual employee has moved during employment, a term will be implied easily. In any other case a term might still be implied (see the constructive dismissal case of *United Bank Ltd v Akhtar* [1989] IRLR 507—junior employee told to move from Leeds to Birmingham at six days' notice) provided:

(a) the transfer is not actuated by malice;

(b) reasonable notice is given; and

(c) the employer does not effectively frustrate the employee's attempt to perform the contract.

But even then, the transfer is commonly limited to within commuting distance: *Courtaulds Northern Spinning Ltd v Sibson* [1988] ICR 451 (a heavy goods driver whose place of work was really only a starting and finishing point).

There are limits to adaptability. First, the contract may be stretched, but there comes a breaking point—usually some abuse of discretion. Secondly, *pay* has nearly always been sacrosanct: see *Burdett-Coutts v Hertfordshire County Council* [1984] IRLR 91 and *Rigby v Ferodo* [1988] ICR 29; it takes a clear term permitting a cut in wages (as in *White v Reflecting Roadstuds*) and no apparent abuse of that right to overcome this. There are, however, conflicting decisions of the EAT on whether the use of an express term to alter working patterns, which has an indirect adverse affect on wages or hours worked (e.g., because of changes in shift patterns), constitutes a breach of contract. In view of the comments and caveats in *White v Reflecting Roadstuds* and *United Bank v Akhtar*, it is respectfully submitted that such indirect effects should not be deemed a breach of contract. Lastly, the court or tribunal may also choose to interpret a wide clause quite narrowly, almost using the *contra proferentem* idea. For instance, in *Haden v Cowen* [1982] IRLR 314, the Court of Appeal took a common phrase 'the employee is required to undertake, at the discretion of the company, any and all duties which reasonably fall within the scope of his capabilities' and restricted the range of additional duties to those which would normally fall within the employee's job as a quantity surveyor. Certainly, 'adaptability' or 'flexibility' clauses do not allow an employer *carte blanche* authority to change an employee's work or conditions if these changes are unreasonable in themselves: *Land Securities Trillium Ltd v Thornley* [2005] IRLR 765 (EAT).

5.4.4 Variation of contract and reorganisations

Under strict contract theory a contract cannot be varied unilaterally. It can be varied by agreement, either by individual agreement or through the use of collective agreements, notably where a contract is subject to 'alteration from time to time agreed with XYZ union'. The most familiar example is the annual pay increase. Consideration should also be present, although courts have paid little genuine attention to this (though see *Lee v GEC Plessey Telecommunications* [1993] IRLR 383 in holding that continuing to work for a company constituted consideration for an enhanced redundancy payments scheme).

Thus, if an employer seeks to change the rate of pay or the place of work, or to insert a new restraint of trade clause, the employee is not bound in law to accept such an alteration unless the instruction is lawful, i.e., contractually justified.

Business reorganisation is the area where the real question of employee adaptability arises. The employer either clearly seeks to change the terms of the contract, or argues that the proposed changes in working practice fall within the general ambit of the contract anyway. These situations may come about in a number of ways:

(a) The employer argues that the contract is clear. In this case any opposing argument must rest on the legitimacy of the terms themselves.

(b) The employer argues that, although the express terms do not sanction the change, the implied terms (derived from adaptability or custom and practice) allow for the change: see *ASLEF*.

(c) The employer argues that there is still no real change to the job, only a change in *how* the job is done: see *Cresswell* v *BIR*.

(d) The employer simply imposes the terms, offering no argument apart from economic necessity: see *Rigby* v *Ferodo,* below.

(e) The employer accepts that there is a breach but presents the argument of 'accept the change or be sacked'.

(f) The employer formally terminates the contract and offers new contracts with different terms (see below, **5.4.4.5**).

To consider the full impact of all this, it is best to look to the possible actions that **employees** may take in response and their consequences. This is because the power to do things lies with the employer and it is of no use to ask whether an employer can, say, cut wages, unless you know how the employee intends to respond. If, for instance, the employee does not want to make waves then the employer will succeed even if the action is not strictly legitimate. The overall position can be seen in **Figure 5.2**. Although in this chapter

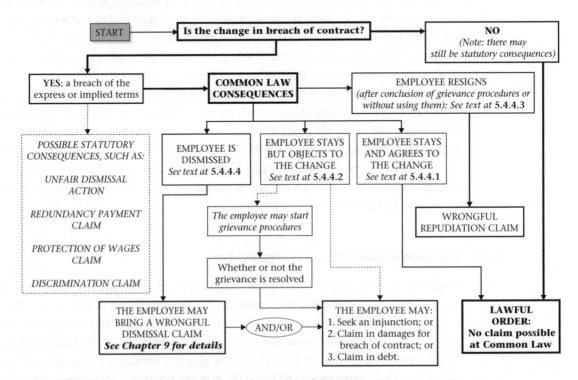

Figure 5.2   Possible consequences of variation of the contract.

we are dealing only with *contractual* rights and remedies, it is worth noting here that a serious breach of contract (such as a unilateral reduction in pay) will not always amount to an unfair dismissal if the employee is dismissed for refusing to accept the change (see **Chapter 10** on the topic of business reorganisations constituting 'some other substantial reason' as a fair reason for dismissal).

Figure 5.2 looks daunting at first sight but shows that out of one simple question there are numerous factors to consider. Do not therefore be put off by the complexity; in the following text we will break this diagram down and examine each particular consequence. The overall picture will then make more sense.

Note that **Figure 5.2** takes into account both the common law claims (wrongful dismissal, wrongful repudiation, injunctions, and damages) and also notes the statutory claim of unfair dismissal. Changes in contractual terms may well lead to resignation or dismissal and such occurrences carry statutory consequences as well as contractual ones. As we are concerned in this chapter only with the common law position, we can simplify the discussion for the moment by ignoring the statutory consequences noted on the left of the diagrams. **In discussing the various consequences we will repeat the whole diagram but highlight only the parts relevant to the particular issues.**

5.4.4.1   The employee stays in the job and agrees to the change

Most employees cannot afford to lose their job (whether on principle or by default), so it may well be that they are effectively forced to continue in their employment. They may simply have to put up with the change.

If the employee specifically agrees to, or acquiesces in, the alteration it will be deemed a legitimate change in the terms of the contract. It is the employee's responsibility to object or be deemed to have affirmed the breach. However, where a change in terms *does not have immediate effect* on a particular employee, e.g., as to retirement ages or the right to move employees from one site to another, silence on the employee's part may not constitute acquiescence or agreement. In *Jones* v *Associated Tunnelling Co. Ltd* [1981]

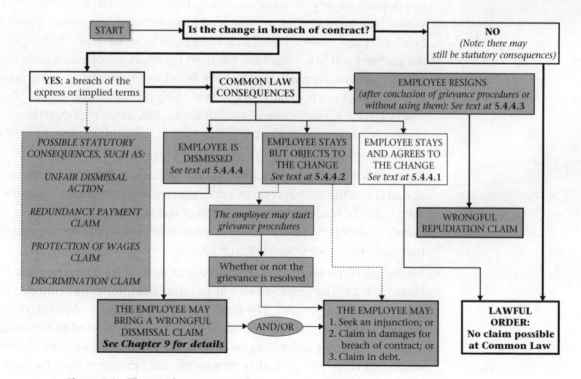

Figure 5.3   The employee stays and agrees to the change.

IRLR 477, the EAT stated that mere failure to object to a matter which had no immediate practical effect did not imply assent. The matter may lie dormant for a number of years only to emerge long after the change was thought to have been implemented. Thus an employer may well have to decide whether to risk this course or take the equally risky alternative of terminating the contracts and re-engaging the employees on the modified terms. The second course brings with it clarity at the cost of possible wrongful and unfair dismissal claims (see **5.4.4.5** below).

5.4.4.2 The employee stays in the job and objects to the change

It is difficult for employees to take this course of action where they are not supported by a trade union. Nevertheless, it is possible for an employee to continue to work for an employer whilst arguing that the change is unlawful.

In the face of more immediate changes, and certainly if they relate to pay, however, the employees would have to do something to demonstrate their opposition; their objections would have to take on substance or be deemed acquiescence. There are four basic routes here:

(a) The employee may simply to refuse to comply with the new terms. Obviously this has to relate to changes in things such as duties (pay, for instance, would be beyond the employee's control). This action brings matters to a head and the employer may simply respond by dismissing the employee for not obeying (what he sees) to be a lawful order. This option can therefore be a dangerous one for the employee to pursue.

(b) A second option is for the employee to continue working (under the newly-imposed terms) but voice objections to the change through devices such as the grievance procedures—a much safer option and one to be preferred to (a) above.

(c) The employee may seek a *declaration or an injunction* to prevent any unlawful variation. This does not happen frequently as more than a simple breach is required to obtain an injunction (however serious the breach) because damages would be an adequate remedy. Normally, to obtain injunctive relief the courts need to convinced that there is still trust and confidence between the parties: *Powell v Brent London Borough Council* [1988] ICR 176—some cases have posed the question: is the contract still 'workable'? So, the most common use of injunctions here is to seek to restrain dismissals which have fallen down purely on some procedural defect such as their not complying with binding contractual procedures: *Dietmann v Brent London Borough Council* [1988] ICR 842. But, as the remedy is discretionary, there is no guarantee of effectiveness and a dismissed employee will not be able to obtain an order for *specific performance* to regain employment.

An application can be under Part 24, Civil Procedure Rules to determine a question of law or the construction of a document. A final determination of the whole action may be made provided questions of fact are not at issue: see *Jones v Gwent County Council* [1992] IRLR 521. *This option is not included in the diagrams* (for further explanation see **Chapter 9**, at **9.10.6.3**).

(d) Finally, an employee may object and sue in debt or for damages: *Rigby v Ferodo* [1988] ICR 29. The employer sought to implement, for good economic reasons, a wage cut of five per cent. The employees not unnaturally objected; their union did not accept the change. Eventually the employer imposed the wage cut. The employees did not resign, nor were they dismissed. Instead, they continued to voice their objections and, after six months, sued their employer for the lost five per cent. The House of Lords held that they were entitled to recover the lost money as the employer's unilateral variation of the contract constituted a repudiation which the employees had neither affirmed in continuing to work nor accepted as repudiatory by resigning.

One would not argue with the principle of this case. However, four points deserve attention:

- The employers did not contend that Rigby had accepted the change, because Rigby's objections were made obvious.

- The employers did not argue that the change was lawful; their argument was the more technical one that the contract had been effectively automatically terminated by their announcement and that the employees could not therefore recover any more than their contractual notice period by way of damages (12 weeks here).

- The employers were sloppy in their response to the objections. They might have dismissed the employees and offered them re-engagement on new terms.

- The level of damages was easy to assess on the facts. If the change in terms centred on working practice, as in our example about hours of work, damages would be more difficult to assess (e.g., loss of commission); there might not even be a quantifiable loss.

The full range of options open to an employee who stays on but objects to the change can be seen in **Figure 5.4** below. One key feature of taking this 'stay but sue' course was, however, highlighted by the EAT in *Robinson* v *Tescom Corporation* [2008] IRLR 408: once the employee opts for staying on and arguing his point he *must* work under the new terms whilst the issue is being resolved. If the employee refuses to accept the new terms he must either resign or take his chances on how the employer responds. These outcomes are explored in **5.4.4.3** and **5.4.4.4** below.

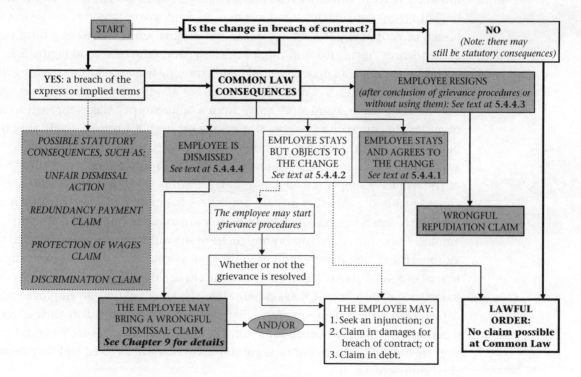

Figure 5.4   The employee stays but objects to the change.

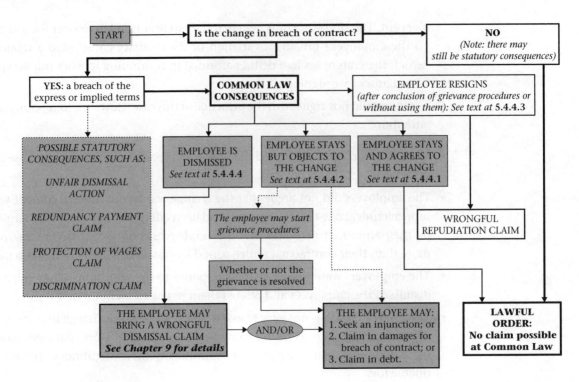

Figure 5.5   The employee resigns.

5.4.4.3   The employee refuses to accept the new terms and resigns

If the employer's actions constitute a *repudiation* of the contract the employee can lawfully accept the repudiation by resigning and sue for damages. This action is strictly termed a *wrongful repudiation* claim but is sometimes referred to as 'constructive dismissal'. The term 'constructive dismissal' really belongs to claims for unfair dismissal but both terms describe the situation where an employee resigns in response to a serious breach of contract by the employer and this resignation is classed as a dismissal. The consequences flowing from an employee's resignation can be seen in **Figure 5.5.**

There is common analytical ground in determining what constitutes a wrongful repudiation and a constructive dismissal. The sorts of acts (there is an extensive range) that may be classified as repudiatory range from a failure to pay wages through to a series of minor but cumulative breaches (for a fuller list see **9.8.2** below). In all cases the employer must have committed a **serious** breach of the contract so the employee (or you as his solicitor) has to make a judgment call on this. If the employee gets this wrong, he or she will have simply resigned and, indeed, will be in breach himself for not giving contractual notice. Another mistake employees frequently make in this area is to wait too long before resigning (often because they are trying to find another job first). If the employee does not act promptly enough, he or she will at some stage be deemed to have affirmed the change in terms and be in the same position as if they had expressly agreed to it as in **5.4.4.1** above. Having affirmed the change the employee is no longer entitled to resign and, by doing so, is again in breach. The length of time an employee may wait depends upon the seriousness of the change in terms, how immediate their effect is and whether he or she maintained some form of objection. Damages for wrongful repudiation are limited to the amount the employee would have received had they been given their contractual notice.

5.4.4.4 The employee is dismissed

As we noted above, the employer might simply dismiss the 'non-cooperative' employee. If the dismissal is with adequate notice or payment in lieu of notice the employee has no further contractual claim. If the dismissal is without adequate notice there will be a potential claim for wrongful dismissal.

But remember that, at common law, the courts are only concerned with the *contractual right* to dismiss summarily, so that the employer's business reasons for the change are irrelevant here. The question is whether the employee has seriously breached the contract by not giving adequate notice. Note, in **Figure 5.6**, that we have included the possibility of a dismissed employee claiming damages/debt or seeking an injunction. The damages/debt aspect here will relate to any outstanding claims that the employee may have (e.g., for past failures to pay wages).

Whether or not the employee is given notice, he or she might also claim unfair dismissal. In such a case, the employer is likely to argue business reorganisation or misconduct (here, disobedience to a lawful order) as a defence to this action (see **Chapter 10**).

5.4.4.5 The employee is dismissed and then re-engaged

When contemplating large-scale changes to the contract some employers believe it is easier to terminate all the contracts and re-engage immediately but on the new terms. The points noted in **5.4.4.4** on the giving of notice apply here. The notice must be unequivocal, so merely announcing the change (as in *Rigby* v *Ferodo*), will not be sufficient to amount to a termination and re-engagement. But if the termination is clear the employee will then be deemed to have accepted the new contract by continuing to work after the set date.

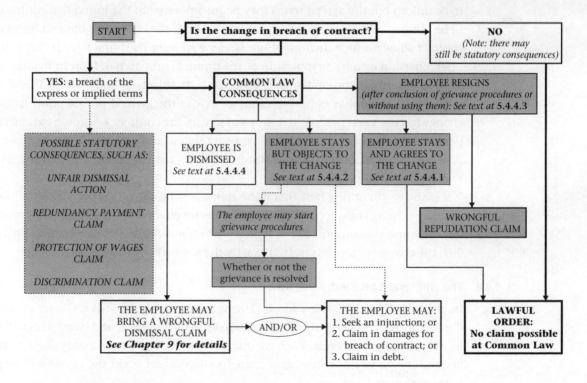

Figure 5.6   The employee is dismissed.

Contractually speaking, the employer gains an advantage with this option. But from an industrial relations angle this may prove disastrous; the loss of goodwill may rebound at a later stage on the employer. Equally, employees working out a notice period will most likely feel disaffected and work poorly; the alternative of paying in lieu of notice being an expensive tactic.

Employees dismissed in these circumstances may also have a claim for unfair dismissal even if they are re-engaged immediately.

5.4.4.6 Duty to consult with trade unions

You will see below in **Chapter 11** at **11.4.2** that where dismissals arise by reason of re-dundancy the employer has both a duty to consult with the individual employee and, where 20 or more employees are being made redundant, a separate duty of collective consultation with employee representatives. In *GMB* v *Man Truck & Bus Ltd* [2000] IRLR 636 and *Scottish Premier Meat Ltd* v *Burns* [2000] IRLR 639, the EAT held that this duty of collective consultation applied not only to standard redundancies but also to dismissals arising out of restructuring. In *GMB* the employer sought to impose a change in terms by dismissing the employees and immediately re-engaging them on less favourable terms. The employer argued that the duty to consult under the TULRCA 1992, s. 188 did not apply to such 'technical' dismissals, but the EAT disagreed. This imposes quite a differ-ent burden on employers who seek to 'strong arm' the imposition of new terms (though note that the duty only kicks in where there are 20 or more affected employees).

5.4.4.7 The employee objects but the trade union agrees

Although the law regards contracts of employment as being made between employer and the individual employee, the reality for about 70 per cent of employees is that the terms are negotiated by the employer and trade unions (known as collective agree-ments). Collective agreements are virtually never enforceable between employers and trade unions but the agreed terms may be incorporated in the individual contracts and so be binding as between *employer and employee*—if the express or implied terms of the contract allow for such incorporation: *Marley* v *Forward Trust Group Ltd* [1986] ICR 891.

Membership or non-membership of the union is immaterial. If an individual whose contract already incorporates such an agreement objects to the change, therefore, he or she must make that objection clear; otherwise the general presumption is that the change has been accepted. And if the right to vary the contract according to terms incor-porated by collective agreements is expressly stated in the contract, the employee will have no option (subject to such considerations as arguing indirect discrimination) but to accept the change.

It is also worth noting here that if the employer or trade union unilaterally withdraws from an existing collective agreement this has no effect upon the employee's terms un-less the employee consents to the change: *Robertson* v *British Gas Corporation* [1983] IRLR 302; the change of terms is treated exactly the same as with any other variation.

5.4.4.8 The employees take industrial action

Industrial action takes many forms. The most obvious is the strike. Others exist: work-ing to rule, go-slows, overtime bans, and so on. The employer and employees will there-fore be in a power struggle. We have not included this in our summary diagram simply because the variety of consequences are too dependent upon the employer's response to the action.

In response to industrial action the employer may:

(a) dismiss the employees, with or without notice;

(b) refuse to accept the deficient performance and send the employees home, withholding pay;

(c) accept their partial performance but withhold wages equivalent to the time lost (see below);

(d) sue the employees for damages. Here the employee is liable only for the loss for which he or she is responsible.

The response of withholding pay is often used where the industrial action is sporadic or set for one day every week, or aimed at fulfilling only the non-contentious part of the contract: see *British Telecommunications plc* v *Ticehurst* [1992] ICR 383. Here, a longstanding dispute had developed into a 'rolling campaign of strategic strikes'. The employees refused to sign an undertaking to work normally and were told to leave the premises. Their claim for wages during this period was based on the fact that they were prepared to work, though not to comply with all the terms. The Court of Appeal held that the employer could legitimately refuse to pay for this partial performance.

It should also be noted that *an employee dismissed whilst taking part in industrial action may also lose any right to claim unfair dismissal* (see **Chapter 10**).

5.5 Methods of resolving disputes, short of termination of contract

If at all possible, both parties should seek to resolve differences before any termination occurs. The most obvious method is by consultation and negotiation, leading eventually to agreement.

If *employers* wish, for instance, to instigate changes they are advised to consider the practical consequences as well as the legal ones. Thus:

(a) consider the effect on the individuals in terms of future loyalty and performance;

(b) consider the effect on any relationship with trade unions;

(c) consider whether this change, if challenged, would lead to an injunction being granted or to claims for wrongful or unfair dismissal;

(d) take into account the possibility that the change may be indirectly discriminatory. Look at the effect on employees, consider whether alternatives or additional facilities are possible and be prepared to justify the change;

(e) get any agreement in writing with effect from the proposed date of change. Consider the effect of 'sleepers' in the organisation. Do not presume that simply because a change has been implemented it is legally effective;

(f) do not forget disciplinary procedures;

(g) if the change is necessary to the business it is probably worth paying for—make the change part of the annual pay negotiations thus avoiding all the problems of unilateral variation.

From the *employee's perspective* any action tends to be in response to proposed changes. Again, however, the practical and legal consequences need to be considered:

(a) consider whether the change is worth fighting in terms of job security, promotion prospects, and so on;

(b) do not resign hastily;

(c) make use of the grievance procedure;

(d) do not assume that silence equals valid opposition;

(e) consider applying for declarations or injunctions;

(f) make use of any trade union representation.

5.6   Breach: summary of sanctions and enforcement

Most of the substantive content of the following points has been made in the text at various stages. We have added this section merely to recap.

The employer is in breach	The employee is in breach
In response to a breach by the employer the employee may:	In response to a breach by the employee the employer may:
(a) accept the order or change as being lawful;	(a) discipline the employee (e.g., downgrading, refusal to promote, or provision of a warning);
(b) instigate grievance procedures;	(b) dismiss the employee with notice;
(c) seek a declaration as to the meaning of the contract;	(c) dismiss the employee without notice (though this is justifiable only in the face of a serious breach);
(d) seek an injunction to prevent a breach;	(d) sue the employee for any loss attributable to his or her actions (though quantifying the amount can be difficult);
(e) remain in employment but claim damages for any loss sustained;	(e) seek an injunction to prevent disclosure of confidential information or to enforce a restraint of trade clause (as regards ex-employees).
(f) resign and claim for wrongful repudiation (though this will only prove successful if the employer's breach was serious);	
(g) claim damages for wrongful dismissal, if dismissed without adequate notice;	
(h) claim in a debt action;	
(i) claim that the change constitutes indirect discrimination.	

5.7   Civil remedies for breach of contract

If the employee alleges a breach of contract there are several (potentially overlapping) possible courses of action.

5.7.1   In the civil courts

Most obviously, a breach of the contract of employment can be pursued like any other breach in the courts, either the High Court or a county court. Perhaps, for example, the employee understood at interview that a greater bonus was to be paid than has in fact been received. However, the sum involved may be unlikely to justify the expense of litigation, especially where the chance of success is poor because of the evidential difficulty of showing a clear promise. Furthermore, such litigation by an individual will not be conducive to good future working relationships. So such a remedy is really only feasible if a trade union takes the case on behalf of a number of employees in the same position, e.g., *Burdett-Coutts* v *Hertfordshire County Council* [1984] IRLR 91. The same analysis applies if the action is framed as a debt.

5.7.2   In the employment tribunal by claiming a constructive dismissal

It is open to an employee who is faced with a serious breach of the contract of employment to resign, argue constructive dismissal and to present a complaint of unfair dismissal to the employment tribunal. The employee must usually have one year's continuous employment with the employer in order to qualify to bring such an action. For instance, any substantial underpayment by the employer may well give good grounds for resignation, provided of course that the underpayment was in breach of contract, though a failure to give a pay increase at an annual review is unlikely to constitute a breach: *Murco Petroleum* v *Forge* [1987] ICR 282. However, reinstatement of the employee is not guaranteed even if the complaint succeeds; and the employee consequently runs a real risk of losing everything—the sum not paid and also the job. This mechanism for bringing such an issue within employment tribunal jurisdiction is dangerous territory.

5.7.3   In the employment tribunal by arguing discrimination

If the employee is able to show, for instance, that another employee of the opposite sex or of a different racial background received some benefit denied to him or her, this may be a means of bringing a claim for discrimination within the employment tribunal jurisdiction. For the purposes of the claim it may be sufficient to imagine a 'notional other employee' rather than an actual example: see **Chapter 6**.

5.7.4   In the employment tribunal for action short of dismissal

Related to a discrimination action is the position where an employer subjects an employee to a detriment after the employee has sought to enforce some statutory right, e.g., where the employee has sought to enforce some of the rights noted in **Chapter 4** or has made a 'protected disclosure' against the employer in the light of the employer's unlawful behaviour. The range of actions which receive special protection is given in **10.11** below. The relevance here is that if the employee's actions fall within this list and the employer responds by, e.g., demoting him, then, as well as any of the remedies noted in this chapter, there may be further remedies under Part V of the ERA 1996.

5.7.5   In the employment tribunal for breach of contract

The Employment Tribunals Extension of Jurisdiction Order 1994 restricts the tribunal jurisdiction to a claim which **'arises or is outstanding on the termination of the employee's employment'**. It cannot therefore be used, for example, by current employees wishing to challenge the amount of wages paid to them, nor for claiming a breach of a compromise agreement concluded after termination: see *Miller Bros* v *Johnston* [2002] ICR 744. The maximum that can be claimed in the employment tribunal is £25,000 and matters such as personal injury claims and intellectual property rights cannot be brought before a tribunal. The phrase 'arises or is outstanding on the termination . . . ' means that an actual date has to be fixed, not a process (*Capek* v *Lincolnshire CC* [2000] ICR 878). Thus, a settlement procedure begun before termination but not concluded until afterwards was not 'outstanding' on termination, nor is it enough that an employee had a claim before termination if this was not started before that date (see *Hendricks* v *Lewden Metal Products Ltd* (1996, unreported, EAT) where an employee had not been paid sick pay for some four years but had taken no action during that time to recover it; when she raised the matter on termination it was held this did not fall within the scope of the 1994 Order).

The tribunal has no jurisdiction on misrepresentation claims: *Lakin* v *British Steel Engineering Ltd* (2000, EAT 183/99, unreported), though an argument based on a collateral contract is within the tribunal's general jurisdiction.

A novel aspect for tribunal claims is that an employer is permitted to counterclaim against the employee for breach of contract, subject to the same restrictions noted above, but only if the employee has first brought a claim *under this jurisdiction*. Employees vulnerable to counterclaims may therefore prefer to bring their claims by a different method. For example, an employee not paid outstanding holiday pay on dismissal for alleged theft will be better advised to bring a protection of wages claim than to risk an employer's counterclaim for the proceeds of the alleged theft.

The time limit for presenting the claim is three months from the Effective Date of Termination or last date worked.

5.7.6 In the employment tribunal by arguing unlawful deduction from wages

Part II of ERA 1996 forbids employers making deductions from employees' wages except in the defined circumstances set out **4.4** above. Wages are defined quite broadly but the sum involved must be quantifiable (i.e., a right to receive a 'bonus' is not covered though

Protection of wages	Breach of contract
Unlawful deductions brought under ERA 1996, s. 23.	Under the Employment Tribunals Extension of Jurisdiction Order 1994, and ETA 1996, s. 3.
(a) Available to current employees.	(a) Only available on termination of employment.
(b) No counterclaim permitted—except that the employer may make deductions in retail employment for cash shortages and stock deficiencies.	(b) An employer's counterclaim is possible and is a self-contained cause of action which can survive the failure, withdrawal or settlement of the employee's initial claim: *Patel* v *RCMS Ltd* [1999] IRLR 161.
(c) No limit to amount of claim.	(c) Claim limited to a maximum of £25,000.
(d) Claims for payment in lieu of notice excluded.	(d) Claims for payment in lieu of notice included.
(e) Statutory exceptions exist, e.g., loans, expenses, compensation for loss of office.	(e) A narrower set of statutory exceptions exist, e.g., those claims relating to intellectual property rights.
(f) Errors of computation are excluded (though 'errors' are narrowly construed: *Morgan* v *West Glamorgan CC* [1995] IRLR 68);	(f) The test is the factual one of whether a breach has occurred and the employer's intentions are irrelevant.
(g) The amount must be quantifiable.	

Note: None of the above affects an employee's right to bring a claim *in a county or High Court* for breach of contract or debt during the term of the contract or on, or after, termination.

an obligation to pay a percentage of future profits would be: *Coors Brewers Ltd* v *Adcock* [2007] EWCA Civ 19; [2007] ICR 983.

5.7.7 Choosing between an unlawful deduction claim and breach of contract

It is clearly important that a solicitor realises, as a matter of tactics and law, which forum is best-suited to the breach of contract claim. The most problematic area centres on pay, for here the claimant will have to choose between a common law action in the county court, a breach of contract action in the employment tribunal, and a claim for unlawful deduction of wages, again in the employment tribunal. The problems with an ordinary civil action are noted above at **5.7.1**. The advantages and disadvantages of the tribunal actions are listed below.

5.8 Summary

- Terms can be found in a wide range of documents and oral statements.

- Jurisdiction for dealing with contract-based disputes lies with the ordinary courts for disputes occurring during employment.

- The exception to this arises where the claim is for an unlawful deduction from wages under s. 23 ERA 1996: this can be heard only in the employment tribunals.

- Contractual disputes arising on or after termination can be heard in the employment tribunals as well as the courts.

- Other than the statutory controls dealt with in **Chapter 4**, the parties are generally free to set their own terms. However, one of the key areas of constraints which will affect a contract is that of discrimination.

- There is always the possibility that the enforcement of any term or the variation of an existing term may be discriminatory even if this was not intended by the employer (see **Chapter 6** for the consequences). No clause which is discriminatory will be allowed to stand. Direct discrimination may be easy to identify but employers need to take great care in drafting clauses which may be indirectly discriminatory, especially as regards points which do not appear obvious such as age discrimination.

- Because the employment contract is generally for an indefinite period (rather than a one-off commercial agreement) the courts and tribunals have been extremely inventive in creating implied terms, the most wide-sweeping of which is the duty of mutual trust and confidence.

- What matters most is not whether the terms in dispute are 'reasonable' but whether they are 'lawful' (contractually justified).

- The two most commonly-occurring problems with the contract of employment are: (i) trying to ascertain exactly what the contract states; (ii) dealing with situations where the employer wants to change the normal work pattern. These can overlap.

- Employees are expected to be reasonably adaptable: so 'sticking to the literal terms of the contract' is frowned upon by the courts and tribunals.

- In practical terms an employer can seek to impose or change any term: what matters in legal terms is how the employee reacts to this.

- Failure to follow disciplinary and grievance procedures (including ACAS codes and guidelines) may lead to extra compensation being payable (or the employee's claim being dismissed or reduced) in cases such as unfair dismissal claims.

5.9 Example of an employment contract

We noted at the start of this chapter that we intended to include an employment contract by way of example of industrial practice. We have chosen to include a contract that is deficient in a number of respects so that we can make some specific comments on it. Because each LPC will develop its own methods of examining drafting and interpretation, and because there is no such thing as a 'model contract' to cover all situations, we must emphasise that this contract is **not** an example of good practice. Our comments in **5.9.2** are placed after the text of the contract in order for you to determine, as you read the contract, what are its strengths and weaknesses.

We have chosen to use a modified version of a real contract originally drafted in 1992 which was still in use a few years ago. Only the names, as they say, have been changed to protect the innocent.

5.9.1 The contract of employment

AN AGREEMENT made on [4th October 1992]
BETWEEN [MONTANA AND MARINO LTD] WHOSE REGISTERED OFFICE IS
SITUATED AT [221B QUARTER BACK LANE, BRISTOL]
AND
[MS VICKY LOMBARDI] OF 113, ALLESLEY OLD ROAD, CLIFTON, BRISTOL
IN THE COUNTY OF AVON
WHEREBY IT IS MUTUALLY AGREED AS FOLLOWS

1. SAVE Where a contrary intention appears the following terms shall hereinafter have the following meanings:

   (a) 'the Company' shall mean [Montana and Marino Ltd]

   (b) the 'Employee' shall mean Ms Vicky Lombardi

2. The Company shall employ the Employee and the Employee shall serve the Company or any of its subsidiaries in the capacity as

Secretary, Grade A4

or in any other such capacity as the Company may reasonably require Upon the terms and conditions hereinafter appearing. For the purpose of this employment the Employee shall reside in such place in the United Kingdom as the Company may reasonably require. The Employee shall be entitled to receive payment towards the expenses resulting from any change in residence required by the Company as set out in scales of terms and conditions laid out in the document 'Removal expenses' which may be amended from time to time. A copy of this document is available from the personnel department.

3. The Company shall pay the Employee a salary of £10,000 per annum to be paid monthly in arrears together with such expenses or allowances as may be approved. The Company shall in each calendar year review the remuneration hereunder payable to the Employee and any increase in such remuneration shall be notified to the Employee in writing and shall be substituted for the sum specified above and shall be payable as from the date specified in such notification. It is also recognised that the Employee will from time to time be required to work beyond normal working hours. Where the Employee at the date hereof or at any date hereafter is classified by the Company as being below Job Grade 6 the Employee will be paid subject to the conditions in force at that time for any overtime worked. Where the Employee at the date hereof or at any date hereafter is classified by the Company as being in a Grade 6 Job or higher his salary is deemed to include a supplement in respect of overtime and no further entitlement is due.

4. This agreement shall be deemed to have commenced on the First day of November 1992 and unless previously determined in accordance with Clause 12 of this agreement or by mutual agreement shall continue until determined by either party giving to the other One month's notice in writing expiring at any time ALWAYS PROVIDED that the period of employment shall terminate in any event on the last day of the month during Which the Employee, if male, attains the age of 65 or, if female, attains the age of 60.

5. EMPLOYEES who wish to publish papers give addresses or lectures or engage in discussions on professional or technical subjects connected with their work must first seek and obtain the written consent of the Company.

6. DURING the period of his employment hereunder the Employee shall join and shall be entitled to the benefits of membership of such Pension Scheme as may be provided by the Company for the benefit of the Employee. The Employee shall contribute to such scheme in accordance with the scale of contributions from time to time in force and conform to and be bound by the rules and regulations thereof.

7. DURING his period of employment hereunder the Employee shall perform such duties and carry out such instructions and directions within the scope of his employment hereunder as from time to time may be given to him by the Company and shall obey and conform to all the general orders service regulations and notices from time to time issued by the Company and shall in all respects use his best endeavours to assist in carrying on the duties of the business of the Company in the most economical and profitable way and diligently and faithfully serve the Company and protect its interests in all things to the best of his ability and judgment.

8. DURING his period of employment hereunder the Employee shall devote the whole of his time and attention during ordinary business hours to his duties with the Company and shall not without the consent in writing of the Company previously obtained be in any way engaged in any other trade or business on his own account or with or on behalf of any other person.

9. THE Employee shall not whether during the continuance of his employment hereunder or at any time hereafter without the consent in writing of the Company previously obtained either directly or indirectly divulge or make known to any person any information relating to the business customers methods

processes or secrets of the Company which may have come to his knowledge at any time during his service with the Company. Information relating to the business customers methods processes or secrets of any third party possessed by the Company and information in respect of which the Company is under an obligation of confidence towards any third party shall be deemed to be a secret of the Company for this purpose. All instructions drawings notes and memoranda relating to the said business customers methods processes or secrets made by the Employee or coming into his possession during his said service shall be the exclusive property of the Company and the Employee shall use his best endeavours to prevent the publication or disclosure of any such information or documents.

10. THE Employee shall forthwith communicate to the Company every improvement, invention, discovery, design, Trade Mark or specification which he may devise during the continuance of his employment hereunder whether capable of legal protection or not and which might be used in connection with or relate to the business of the Company or any articles manufactured or dealt with in any of the processes or methods employed by the Company or any tools or machines or plant used by the Company. The Company will ensure that the Company and its professional advisers keep confidential all details of any invention which the Employee simultaneously claims belongs to him until either those details have entered the public domain, or it has been established that the invention belongs to the Company or the Employee releases the Company from its obligation to ensure the maintenance of confidentiality. Every such improvement, invention, discovery, design, Trade Mark or specification shall, except insofar as it may be deemed by statute to belong to the Employee, become the sole and absolute property of the Company. The Employee at any time whether during his period of employment hereunder or thereafter when required by the Company and at the Company's expense shall do and execute all acts deeds and things which may be required to enable the Company to obtain the fullest benefit and advantage from every such improvement, design, discovery, Trade Mark or specification (including the copyright in any design data in whatever form or specification) not deemed by statute to belong to the Employee.

11. THE Employee shall be entitled to such payments in respect of periods of service during which he is incapacitated due to illness or accident and to such holidays on such terms as are specified in instructions from time to time by the Company.

12. IF during his period of employment hereunder the Employee shall be guilty of any misconduct (including misconduct of a personal nature likely in any way to affect the carrying out of his duties hereunder) or of any breach or neglect of the terms of this Agreement or of the duties from time to time assigned to him the Company may without previous notice or payment in lieu of notice terminate his employment hereunder and in such circumstances he shall be paid the remuneration due to him hereunder down to the date of such termination and no more.

13. THE Employee shall not for one year after his employment hereunder ceases either on his own account or for any other person solicit or interfere with or endeavour to entice away from the Company any person who shall have been

a customer of the Company during the Employee's period of service provided that this restriction shall only apply:

(i) with respect of business of the type on which the Employee was employed

(ii) to customers other than those introduced to the Company by the Employee at the beginning of his said employment.

14. ALL notices and other documents required to be served or given pursuant to this Agreement shall be deemed:

(i) to be duly served upon the Employee if left for him or sent by prepaid registered post to him at his address last known to the Company

(ii) to be duly served upon or given to the Company if served or given to the Company at its registered office and all notices and other documents sent by post shall be deemed to have Been delivered and served at the time at which they would be delivered in the ordinary course of post.

AS WITNESS the hand of an authorised official of the Company and the hand of the Employee the day and year first above written

SIGNED

for and on behalf of the Company: ....

in the presence of: ....

SIGNED by the above named: ....

5.9.2 Comments

5.9.2.1 General comments on style

This document will not win any 'Good English' prizes. Presumably the draftsman had rushed headlong from an intensive course in conveyancing and probate gobbledygook. The purpose of this contract seems to be that it should sound legal; certainly most employees and employers would not understand half of it—though they might be suitably impressed by this and maybe this is what your client wants. There is the risk that the more legalistic the contract appears, the more a court or tribunal will interpret it accordingly, offering little leeway for the employer to argue that the real meaning of any clause 'was common knowledge'.

Apart from the language it is also difficult to see why this contract should be used for a secretary. The intellectual property clause (clause 10) and the restraint of trade clause (clause 13) are irrelevant to this position and clearly reflect the use of one general contract designed to meet the needs of all kinds of employees. Such blanket coverage is not desirable and may have adverse effects as we shall note below (or should it be hereunder?).

Punctuation also appears to be a variable theme. With one eye on nineteenth-century approaches there is generally no punctuation, but then in clause 10 it appears from nowhere. Why? Lastly, the agreement was drafted in 1992. It had not been updated and suffered from this both in style and detail. The agreement was reached in advance of starting work, which is fine, but the date 'deemed' to be the starting date is in fact a Sunday. Presumably a secretary would have no reason to start work on a Sunday and so this is likely to be mere carelessness. If the employee actually contractually started work before November that earlier date will in fact be the start date. The document also fails to meet the requirements of an ERA 1996, s. 1 written statement (even in the form required in 1992).

5.9.2.2 Some specific clauses

Clause 2 begins in a standard way with a job grading. In reality, the grading system for this company was changed in 1998 and there is documentary evidence to show regarding this. The phrase 'or in any other such capacity' is very wide; it was meant to mean 'in any other capacity at that grade' which would make more sense—especially if at some time the employer claims the job is redundant. But why a secretary must reside in a required place is puzzling. If this is a limitation on living within so many miles of the site then such terms usually only apply to employees who might be called upon urgently. If it is a disguised 'mobility' clause, again this is most odd for a secretary.

Clause 3 is simply convoluted. The grade A4 is below grade 6 so the secretary is entitled to overtime payments.

Clause 4 was generous in its notice period in 1992, but now falls short of ERA 1996, s. 86 requirements. The different ages of retirement for men and women are discriminatory. Even if the retirement age were the same (at 65) this would still be subject to the employer complying with the requirements now imposed as regards 'retirement dismissals' (see **Chapter 10**).

Clause 5 is irrelevant to this employee and again shows the use of a standard clause. Likewise *Clause 10* (intellectual property rights) is general waffle.

Clause 9 concerns confidentiality and may be relevant to a secretary (though we will see in **Chapter 7** that it may be ineffective anyway once employment has finished). *Clause 13* is a restraint of trade clause. It is totally inappropriate to the status of the employee and would fail.

Clause 12 concerns gross misconduct but never specifies what is meant by this.

Discrimination and equal pay

6.1 Introduction and sources

In this chapter we look at unlawful discrimination, by which we mean treating one person less favourably than another for one of the prohibited reasons. There are now seven prohibited heads of discrimination related to aspects of the individual person:

- race;
- sex;
- sexual orientation;
- religion;
- disability;
- age; and
- trade union membership.

There are two other heads of discrimination related to aspects of the job, sometimes called 'atypical work':

- part-time work; and
- fixed-term work.

Another description of this area of law is *equal opportunities*, but it is important to recognise that there is currently no generalised law of equal opportunities in this country. We shall speculate later that this is beginning to change and may change further in the future, but for the present we have a sequence of statutes and regulations forbidding certain defined heads of discrimination, and it is only discrimination falling within one of the definitions that is unlawful. There is no single, coherent structure to the sequence, although some of the measures contain useful common features. It is convenient to begin by listing the various statutes and regulations. As we have already examined maternity and other parental rights in some detail in **Chapter 4**, we shall not repeat the discussion here, but there is obviously some overlap.

6.1.1 Statutory sources

6.1.1.1 Race Relations Act 1976

Racial discrimination was the first category of discrimination to be outlawed in this country. The original statute of 1965 is now incorporated into the Race Relations Act (RRA) 1976. Our task in understanding discrimination is greatly simplified by the fact that RRA 1976 adopts exactly the same definitions of discrimination as the Sex Discrimination Act (SDA) 1975. The scope of RRA 1976 is much broader than employment alone but we shall be concerned with only that aspect.

6.1.1.2   Sex Discrimination Act 1975

This statute outlaws discrimination based on sex or married status. It was enacted in 1975 so as to be brought into effect at the same time as the final stage of phased implementation of the Equal Pay Act (EPA) 1970. The two statutes are therefore complementary: EPA 1970 deals with pay, while SDA 1975 deals with other matters, especially non-contractual ones. Both statutes are drafted in terms of a woman who is discriminated against in comparison with a man, but make it plain that the opposite comparison is equally valid. Like RRA 1976, SDA 1975 covers employment but also other possible areas of discrimination.

6.1.1.3   Equal Pay Act 1970

This statute requires that men and women receive the same pay and other heads of remuneration if doing similar or equivalent work. The original 1970 version was found to be inadequate to satisfy a European Directive and is now subject to the Equal Pay (Amendment) Regulations 1983. Unlike RRA 1976 and SDA 1975, EPA 1970 deals only with employment.

6.1.1.4   Employment Equality (Sexual Orientation) Regulations 2003

These regulations ('Sexual Orientation Regs 2003') took effect on 1 December 2003. They follow a similar structure to RRA 1976 and SDA 1975, and prohibit discrimination on the grounds of sexual orientation towards the same sex, the opposite sex or both sexes.

6.1.1.5   Employment Equality (Religion or Belief) Regulations 2003

These regulations ('Religion or Belief Regs 2003') took effect on 2 December 2003. Like the Sexual Orientation Regs 2003, their structure is similar to RRA 1976 and SDA 1975. Discrimination is forbidden on grounds of religion, religious or philosophical belief or, as a result of amendments under the Equality Act 2006, a lack of any of those.

6.1.1.6   Part-time Workers (Prevention of Less Favourable Treatment) Regulations 2000, SI 2000/1551

It is unlawful discrimination to treat part-time workers less favourably than those working full time under the above regulations, which we shall refer to as PTW Regs 2000. The regulations have themselves since been amended by the regulations covering fixed-term workers mentioned at **6.1.1.7** below. These regulations, like those we shall consider next, derive from European Directives concerned with 'atypical work'.

6.1.1.7   Fixed-Term Employees (Prevention of Less Favourable Treatment) Regulations 2002

These regulations ('Fixed-Term Regs 2002') make it unlawful to treat a fixed-term employee less favourably than a comparable permanent employee, unless the less favourable treatment can be justified objectively.

6.1.1.8   Disability Discrimination Act 1995

On 2 December 1996 another category of unlawful discrimination was added to the list: discrimination on grounds of a person's disability. Like RRA 1976 and SDA 1975, the scope of the Disability Discrimination Act (DDA) 1995 is wider than employment alone.

It also covers provision of goods and services, occupation of premises, education, and transport. We shall consider only the employment aspects.

There are some similarities between the approach of DDA 1995 and the common elements of RRA 1976 and SDA 1975, but also some important differences.

6.1.1.9 Employment Equality (Age) Regulations 2006

Another significant head of discrimination took effect under the above regulations ('Age Regs 2006') on 1 October 2006, and it is now unlawful to discriminate on grounds of age. The basic structure of the prohibition is similar to that under RRA 1976 and SDA 1975, but there are exemptions and exceptions unparalleled in the other heads of discrimination.

6.1.1.10 Trade Union and Labour Relations (Consolidation) Act 1992

It is generally unlawful for the employer to treat trade union members less favourably than non-members, or the reverse. It is also unlawful to penalise those who take part in trade union activities.

6.1.1.11 Human Rights Act 1998

As we noted at **1.7** above, the Human Rights Act 1998 (HRA 1998) came into force in England on 2 October 2000. It incorporates into UK law the European Declaration on Human Rights. There was some debate in the early days as to whether this would in fact have much impact, but that was before the terrorist attacks of 11 September 2001 in the United States, since when there has been much debate about the balance between detention of terrorist suspects and issues of individual liberty where HRA 1988 has become very relevant. However, nothing has happened to change our view expressed in the earlier chapter that the direct and immediate effect on employment law is limited, especially outside public authorities, and we therefore intend to say very little about it in the present chapter. It is worth noting, however, that some believe that the law on discrimination and that on human rights generally will become more intertwined.

6.1.1.12 The future

It seems that in almost every revision of this book we have either introduced at least one new head of discrimination or speculated that others might come soon. However, a year ago it seemed that the list was not about to be expanded further: age discrimination was relatively new and we were all still adjusting to its effect; business deregulation or the reduction of European red tape seemed a vogue concept; and at European level there appeared to be more interest in applying the existing rules to the newer Member States than in creating new rules. Wrong! Earlier this year there was an agreement at the European Council on new rules about temporary workers (something we understood it had been agreed to drop in 2005), and here in the UK there has been an agreement among government, employers and trade unions about protection of agency workers. So two new heads of prohibited discrimination against atypical workers will soon join the list.

A more interesting prospect is the long-discussed proposed rationalisation within the UK which would take the form of a Single Equality Act (SEA). Simplification of the rules and elimination of some of the inconsistencies that result from historical chance would be of great benefit to practitioners and law students alike. More importantly, perhaps, it would address the criticism of the present structure as 'complex and inaccessible' by the Equality and Diversity Forum, a group of national organisations including the statutory institutions who regard it as unequal to give different rights to some groups from others.

Certainly a SEA would make the law clearer for victims to understand. There are many lawyers and others who would like to grasp the opportunity presented by an extensive revision of discrimination law to strengthen the links between equality law and human rights. In those circumstances the impact of HRA 1998 on employment law could increase considerably.

We noted at the start of the chapter the present state of the law in forbidding certain kinds of *discrimination*, rather than promoting *equal opportunities*. Many had thought that a SEA would adopt a different approach. The Equality Act 2006 already paves the way. It amends SDA 1975 by adding s. 76A which lays on public authorities a general statutory duty both of eliminating unlawful discrimination and harassment and of promoting equality of opportunity between men and women. It also provides in s. 3 that the Commission for Equality and Human Rights (CEHR: see **6.1.3.2**) will have a general duty to encourage and promote a society 'not limited by prejudice or discrimination' and by s. 8 it must 'promote ... equality and diversity'. The latest information as we go to press is that a new Equality Bill will be introduced in the 2008–09 parliamentary session, and it appears from a Government statement in 2008 about consultation during 2007 that the comparative approach will be retained.

6.1.2   Evidence in particular cases

There has been a large increase recently in the number of cases brought to the employment tribunals alleging unlawful discrimination: from just over 4,000 in 1993–4 to more than 85,000 (including 44,000 equal pay claims, many of them concerning the National Health Service) in 2006–7. A few have been spectacularly successful for the applicants—for example, female army officers forced to resign when pregnant or policewomen subjected to sexual harassment—whether as a result of tribunal hearings or in out-of-tribunal settlements.

In practice only a small minority of cases are of this kind. A great many involve very little law, and a lot of difficulty with the evidence.

Suppose, for example, that a client comes to you complaining of having been discriminated against. Maybe the client is a woman who has been rejected in an application for promotion in favour of a man, or an Asian applicant for a job who knows that only whites were shortlisted for interview. You ask some preliminary questions and may well find that you are drawn to one of the following two views:

(a) The unfavourable treatment received sounds as if it was very possibly discriminatory on grounds of race or sex, although you may have reservations about the client's ability to prove it. The employer has perhaps already been challenged directly by the client and claims reasons that have nothing to do with race or sex. Sometimes you may establish that a junior member of management involved in making the choice has said something foolish that helps your case.

(b) Alternatively, it may seem to you that the client has all the marks of one of those people with an inflated idea of their own ability, who find it impossible to accept that an employer should find someone else a better candidate than they are, and the alleged discrimination is merely part of their denial of their own shortcomings.

Your hunch or 'gut feeling' may be important. While it is of course your role to represent one party and not to decide the case, and further you cannot really assess the weight of the evidence when you have only heard one side, your reaction to the story told by the client may be similar to the reaction of the tribunal if the case ever gets there. We suggested at the start of this book that a little common sense often works wonders in understanding employment law. Nowhere is that more so than in relation to discrimination. More cases in this subject rest on straightforward analysis of the facts and on the quality of the evidence than on complicated principles distilled from the cases, a view supported by the EAT in *Stewart* v *Cleveland Guest (Engineering) Ltd* [1996] ICR 535. We shall return to the evidential difficulties a little later in the chapter.

Inevitably, though, some cases become more complicated. From the point of view of those trying to understand the topic, it is perhaps unfortunate that the following factors get in the way of the simplicity we have mentioned.

6.1.3 Non-statutory sources

6.1.3.1 A European dimension

The principle of equal pay for men and women is contained in art. 141 of the Treaty of Rome, the treaty which established the European Community. It is directly enforceable in the courts of the UK. The elimination of discrimination, especially on grounds of sex, has since become one of the major strands of European social policy and the original Treaty provision is now supplemented by several Directives. The most important are:

- Equal Pay Directive 75/117/EEC;
- Equal Treatment Directives 76/207/EEC, 2000/78/EC and 2002/73/EC;
- Directive on Reversal of the Burden of Proof 97/80/EC; and
- Race Discrimination Directive 2000/43/EC.

As in so many other areas of the law, the Directives establish general principles that then have to be expanded in domestic legislation. Early versions of the UK statutes contained restrictions and limitations that did not appear in the Treaty or Directives. As we shall see shortly, in some cases these have been held by the ECJ to be a legitimate setting of procedural rules by the member state; in other cases they have been held not to comply with the relevant European requirement. Where an individual has a choice of bringing a case either under UK legislation or directly under European law (either because the Treaty provision is directly enforceable or because, e.g., a Directive may be directly enforceable against an emanation of the state), there has sometimes been an advantage in the latter route because it circumvents the restrictions. Many such restrictions have progressively been removed, often as we shall see by new UK regulations following ECJ decisions, and the difference is not as great as it used to be, but new possibilities for imaginative use of European law may of course still arise.

Seven Directives dealing with equal pay and sex discrimination were consolidated in August 2006 into Directive 2006/54/EC, although the consolidated Directives are not formally repealed until August 2009.

The second Equal Treatment Directive mentioned above, 2000/78/EC, led in 2003 to the Religion or Belief Regs and the Sexual Orientation Regs, and in 2006 to the Age Regs.

The third Equal Treatment Directive, 2002/73/EC, led to the Employment Equality (Sex Discrimination) Regulations 2005 which made amendments to SDA 1975 that took effect on 1 October 2005.

6.1.3.2 The institutions

When the statutes about discrimination on grounds of race, sex and disability were new, the implementation of each was supported by a statutory institution. Under the Equality Act 2006 the three bodies were replaced in October 2007 by a single Commission for Equality and Human Rights (CEHR) which also has responsibility for supervision of the newer heads of discrimination—religion or belief, sexual orientation and age. Like its predecessors, it can provide advice and help to individuals including assistance in litigation, it can issue codes of practice and it can take other steps it considers advance the cause of equality. Although the older three bodies no longer exist, codes of practice they have issued remain current and you therefore need to know that they were the Commission for Racial Equality (CRE), the Equal Opportunities Commission (EOC)—dealing with sex discrimination and equal pay—and the Disability Rights Commission (DRC).

6.1.3.3 Codes of practice

Both RRA 1976 and SDA 1975 are to be interpreted by the tribunals having regard to codes of practice. The code on racial discrimination was issued by the CRE and came into force in April 2006 and that about sex discrimination by the EOC in 1985. In 2003 a new code came into force on equal pay, issued by the EOC under SDA 1975. Both bodies had (and CEHR still has) a statutory authority to issue codes which can be used in the employment tribunals as evidence of good practice. All three codes recommend practices by employers that go well beyond anything contained in the statutes.

While RRA 1976 and SDA 1975 are each supported by one code of practice, DDA 1995 already has one code, one book of guidance issued under statutory authority and two statutory instruments. Much of this complexity arises from a basic problem. Whether an employee is male or female, or from a different ethnic group from a comparator is usually a straightforward matter of fact. Whether the same person ought to be protected as disabled is much more a matter of judgment, and the guidance, for example, is entirely concerned with this definition.

6.1.3.4 Maternity rights

Under ERA 1996, as we noted in **4.6** above, women enjoy certain rights in relation to maternity, especially a right to maternity pay, a right to maternity leave and a special protection against dismissal because of pregnancy. All these rights are precisely defined, but cases outside the statutory restrictions have sometimes been brought under SDA 1975 or under the European rules, on the basis that anything dealing with limiting women's rights in relation to maternity is inevitably discriminatory, since men do not (often!) become pregnant.

The interrelationship of maternity rights and sex discrimination law can become a complex topic. Men are not permitted to bring complaints of sex discrimination on the basis of provisions made for women about pregnancy or maternity (SDA 1975, s. 2(2)) but women can complain that any action taken against them because of pregnancy is by definition action that would not have been taken against a man, especially since the 2005 amendments.

6.1.4 The content of the chapter

Discrimination has become an important and very interesting part of employment law. Our aim in this book is to concentrate on the current law as practitioners have to work within it and we shall not therefore attempt to touch on some of the fascinating aspects of this subject that might feature in a more academically orientated book, like the political question of the proper role of the law in leading or reflecting public opinion, the effectiveness of some of the measures taken or the fortuitous but remarkable history of discrimination as a major feature of European social policy.

In practice, discrimination cases accounted for more than a third of claims in the employment tribunals in the last fiscal year. We also suspect, although there are no statistics to prove it, that it is a topic where employment lawyers are more likely to become involved than, for example, deductions from wages, because the much higher amounts of compensation available make clients more willing to incur the costs involved. Nevertheless, as we have already commented, it is an area of employment law where the outcome of a great many cases depends more on the facts and the quality of the evidence than on difficult points of law. We shall set out the chapter in the following sequence, which aims to group together those heads of discrimination with important common features.

- *RRA 1976 and SDA 1975*. The common features of the two long-established statutes will lead on naturally to two newer heads under Religion or Belief Regs 2003 and Sexual Orientation Regs 2003.
- *EPA 1970*. Although, as we have noted, EPA 1970 and SDA 1975 are designed to be complementary, there are some distinct features of equal pay law, including the direct enforceability of art. 141 of the Treaty of Rome.
- The atypical work regulations, *PTW Regs 2000 and Fixed-Term Regs 2002*.
- *DDA 1995*.
- *Age Regs 2006*.
- Trade union membership, activities and non-membership.

6.2   The meaning of discrimination under RRA 1976 and SDA 1975

Discrimination is defined by both RRA 1976 and SDA 1975 as taking four forms:

(a) direct discrimination;

(b) indirect discrimination;

(c) harassment;

(d) victimisation.

6.2.1   Direct discrimination

Direct discrimination consists of treating one person (in this context meaning either an employee or an applicant for a job) less favourably than another, and doing so because of the person's race or sex: RRA 1976, s. 1(1)(a); SDA 1975, ss. 1(2)(a) and 3(1)(a). Examples might be the following:

(a) When recruiting to fill a vacant job, the employer short-lists a white candidate for interview while a black candidate with equivalent qualifications is not called for interview.

(b) The employer promotes a man to a supervisory post when a woman is apparently better suited to the job.

The employer's intention is immaterial. The test is not the employer's motive but the objective fact of less favourable treatment, viewed from the perspective of the applicant's reasonable perception. Some early cases where the courts ignored minor differences in treatment on the basis of the maxim *de minimis non curat lex* are no longer reliable. Almost any less favourable treatment falls within the definition, provided that the applicant can show that some detriment resulted—see *Shamoon* v *Chief Constable of the Royal Ulster Constabulary* [2003] UKHL 11, [2003] ICR 337.

There is an important difference between direct discrimination and indirect discrimination. In the latter it is possible for the employer to defend an otherwise discriminatory act as a proportionate means of achieving a legitimate business aim. There is no such argument in relation to direct discrimination.

We must introduce at this point a particular kind of discrimination, *sexual harassment*. At one time it was treated as an example of direct discrimination, usually meaning unwanted sexual attention from one employee to another or occasionally from the employer. The equivalent of *racial harassment* includes taunts and other mistreatment because of a person's race. Both terms cover a very wide range of conduct from criminal assaults at one extreme to such verbal banter at the other as may seem jocular and inoffensive apart from an understanding of the victim's feelings in the circumstances in which it takes place. As a result of recent amendments to RRA 1976 and SDA 1975 to comply with European Directives there are now express provisions in both statutes dealing with harassment, including a precise definition, and we shall consider the topic at **6.2.3** below. However, it is not new. Harassment, rather more narrowly defined than under the new provisions, has long been regarded as a particular example of direct discrimination on the ground that it consists of less favourable treatment *because of* a person's sex or race. It is a serious matter, both because of the devastating effect it can have on a victim's life and also because of the very large amounts of compensation the tribunals and courts have consequently been prepared to award.

6.2.2   Indirect discrimination

The concept of indirect discrimination is not difficult, but unfortunately a sequence of statutory amendments has made the definition rather complicated. It may be best to start with a simple example.

EXAMPLE

Suppose the employers operate a system of 'flexitime,' where employees have some limited choice when they may start and finish work, provided they are at work during the 'core time' which these employers insist starts at 9.00 am. That rule is not directly discriminatory: it is neutral in the sense that it applies equally to everyone. However, in practice it puts women at a disadvantage compared with men because more women than men have the responsibility of getting children to school and cannot easily meet the requirement. It therefore appears to constitute indirect discrimination against any female employee who suffers a disadvantage, but it is not necessarily unlawful, as the employers may be able to defend it. Perhaps the main function of the department concerned is dealing with telephone and e-mail enquiries from continental Europe which need to be answered quickly and there is evidence that most of them arrive during the early morning, UK time. If the woman presents a complaint the tribunal will have to consider whether the employers' rule is a proportionate means of achieving that business objective. How much delay in starting time would the woman really need? Can the employers accommodate a small exception in her case, or is 9.00 am already perhaps a negotiated compromise when the main surge of calls is even earlier? Has the employer tried to find the woman a comparable alternative job where a later start would not matter, and what was the woman's reaction?

That, then, is an example of what is meant by indirect discrimination; we now need to think about a statutory definition to cover it. Originally, the definitions in s. 1(1)(b) of RRA 1976 and in both s. 1(1)(b) and s. 3 (1)(b) of SDA 1975 were identical. It was very convenient, as authorities under one statute could usually also be applied to the other. Then various European Directives required the original provisions to be amended. First there was the Burden of Proof Directive 97/80/EC, which required changes in the definition under SDA 1975 as far as rights in employment were concerned. But now a practical problem arose for the Government. Under the European Communities Act 1972, the Secretary of State can (in summary) amend any UK statute by statutory instrument if it is necessary to do so to comply with a European Directive. However, the power is limited to amendments that are strictly *necessary* to comply with the Directive, and does not allow the Secretary of State to 'gold-plate' or go beyond the terms of the Directive. Here, that meant that the change in definition had to be limited to employment issues—Part 2 of SDA 1975. So, from 12 October 2001, the Sex Discrimination (Indirect Discrimination and Burden of Proof) Regulations 2001 introduced a new definition of indirect discrimination in employment issues that is now found in s. 1(2), while leaving s. 1(1) unchanged for other issues. Even in employment issues the precise equivalence between RRA 1976 and SDA 1975 was lost and we could no longer assume that cases about one statute necessarily applied to the other.

Matters then got worse. The Race Discrimination Directive 2000/43/EC required amendments to the definition in RRA 1976. Again the parliamentary timetable did not permit primary legislation and the changes were to be made by regulations under the European Communities Act 1972. This time the practical problem was that the Directive related only to discrimination on grounds of race or ethnic or national origins, whereas RRA 1976 covered colour, race, nationality or ethnic or national origins. So the Race Relations Act 1976 (Amendment) Regulations 2003 amended the RRA 1976 definition from 19 July 2003 (by adding a new s. 1(1A), which is different both from the old s. 1(1) and also from the amended SDA 1975) in relation to the three heads of discrimination covered by the Directive, but left it unchanged in relation to the other two, colour and nationality, which appear only in RRA 1976. The consequence was that for a little over two years we had to contend with three different definitions of indirect discrimination. The authors decline to speculate about the parliamentary drafters' ability to organise a party in a brewery.

Now at last hope is on the horizon—well, at least in part. Under the Employment Equality (Sex Discrimination) Regulations 2005, the regulations that implement the third Equal Treatment Directive 2002/73/EC, a new definition of indirect discrimination has applied under SDA 1975 since 1 October 2005. It is substantially the same as that which exists under RRA 1976, s. 1(1A)(b) for the three heads of discrimination covered by the Directive. The other two heads, colour and nationality, are in practice unlikely to arise apart from the three and, although we shall return very briefly to mention them at the end of this section, we shall therefore concentrate on the common definition under SDA 1975 and most of RRA 1976. The final step in elimination of the previous complexity so as to have a single definition for all heads of discrimination under RRA 1976 seems unlikely to be taken until we have the unifying statute, SEA, that we predicted at **6.1.1.12**.

We must therefore now proceed on the basis found in RRA 1976 s. 1(1A)(b) or the amended s. 1(2)(b) and s. 3(1)(b) of SDA 1975 that an employer discriminates indirectly against a person if four elements are present (for simplicity, we shall express the rule as relating to indirect discrimination against a woman under SDA):

(a) the employer applies to her a provision, criterion or practice (PCP) which he applies or would apply equally to a man; but

(b) which puts or would put women at a particular disadvantage when compared with men;

(c) which puts her at that disadvantage; and

(d) which the employer cannot show to be a proportionate means of achieving a legitimate aim.

6.2.2.1 Provision, criterion or practice

This definition comes straight from the Directive and is obviously broader than the 're-quirement or condition' that existed previously. In *British Airways plc v Starmer* [2005] IRLR 862, a discretionary management decision to limit the option of part-time work for aircrew to 50 per cent or 75 per cent of full time was held to fall within the definition of a PCP: it was a provision, even if not a criterion or practice.

6.2.2.2 Disadvantage to the sex or racial group concerned

There is now a very simple requirement that a claimant must show a disadvantage to her sex or to the racial group concerned. In cases under the old law as it existed prior to October 2005 we shall find that a claimant was required to show that a considerably smaller proportion of those of one sex or race could comply than could others. Some statistical approach was implied, but now a claimant has a much broader opportunity to prove relative disadvantage. Statistics may still be a convenient means of doing so but are no longer essential.

Some of the earlier cases about the use of statistics seem to prove the old adage about lies, damned lies and statistics. The expression *considerably smaller* was not defined and often caused problems, especially when statistics could be presented in various ways. For an example of a case decided by the EAT under the new rules but drawing on some of the older authorities on the use of statistics see *Tyne and Wear Passenger Transport Executive v Best* [2007] ICR 523.

In *London Underground Ltd v Edwards* [1995] ICR 574, the employee was a female single parent employed as a train operator. She was unable to work a new duty roster because of her family responsibility. The employment tribunal had found indirect discrimination on the ground that amongst train operators a smaller proportion of female single parents could cope with the new roster than male single parents. The EAT held that this selective statistical analysis was not permitted: comparison had to be between all male train operators and all female train operators. However, the second employment tribunal found such small numbers of female train operators that simple statistical comparison was impossible. In deciding that indirect discrimination had occurred, they relied in part on the statistics and in part on 'common knowledge that females are more likely to be single parents and caring for a child than males'. In *London Underground Ltd v Edwards (No. 2)* [1998] IRLR 364, the Court of Appeal approved that reasoning and suggested that analysis of statistics needed to be flexible and not purely mechanistic. A difference of 4.8 per cent as in this case might often show a less than *considerably smaller* proportion, but there was a necessary 'area of flexibility (or margin of appreciation)'.

The flexible approach recommended by the Court of Appeal in *Edwards (No. 2)* was re-flected, albeit with no express reference, in guidance on the use of statistics set out by the EAT in *Harvest Town Circle Ltd v Rutherford* [2002] ICR 123. (The case was subsequently appealed to the Court of Appeal—[2004] EWCA Civ 1186, [2004] IRLR 892—which affirmed the decision of the EAT, apparently including this guidance). There were some cases where on the statistics a disparate impact was obvious. In less obvious cases, the tribunal would have to look at more than one form of comparison—numbers as well as proportions, both disadvantaged and non-disadvantaged groups, and even the respective proportions in the disadvantaged groups expressed as a ratio of each other.

The authorities we have just cited need now to be regarded with some care. Any tribunal or court that wished to distinguish them could easily do so on the ground that they relate to a different definition of indirect discrimination. However, as *Best* demonstrates, it may also be that the movement away from a mechanistic approach to statistics, which *Edwards (No. 2)* and *Rutherford* reflect, demonstrates the kind of flexibility permitted under the new rule, and the cases may still have some relevance. The difference is that other, non-statistical evidence, perhaps from some kind of expert, can now also be led in the tribunal to show that a PCP causes a particular disadvantage to women or to some specified racial group in comparison with others who are in the same, or not materially different circumstances. The case we mentioned earlier of *British Airways plc v Starmer* [2005] IRLR 862 provides a good example of the new test of disadvantage. Statistics were of some limited use, but additional evidence and 'common knowledge', as in *Edwards (No. 2)*, were in the end more compelling.

6.2.2.3 Actual disadvantage

The requirement that the claimant has suffered a *detriment* under the old definition has now been replaced with a requirement to have suffered a *disadvantage*, the wording of the Directive. We do not suppose, in the absence of any indication to the contrary, that the change in terminology will in practice have much effect. The more important aspect of the rule seems unlikely to change. The claimant must actually have suffered a disadvantage. It is not enough that the provision, criterion or practice is theoretically capable of being discriminatory—see *De Souza v Automobile Association* [1986] ICR 514, CA.

6.2.2.4 The employer's defence

Employers have a defence against a claim of indirect discrimination if they can show that the PCP or policy which causes a particular disadvantage

- was directed to a legitimate aim, and
- was a proportionate means of achieving it.

In practice the first element causes less difficulty than the second. It will usually be possible for employers to show that the PCP meets a legitimate business aim, like the speedy handling of European enquiries in the example we used earlier. The important point is that the burden of proof in this defence lies on the employer and the first step cannot be taken for granted: employers need to establish what aim they had in mind.

The concept of proportionality in the second element is of course familiar to those who have studied European law. It allows a broad assessment of the question whether the PCP is an appropriate and necessary means of achieving the aim, and the likelihood is that tribunals will want to examine all the surrounding circumstances—hence the various questions we asked in the example above, not only about the employer's policy, but also about the circumstances in which it was introduced and the feasibility of alternatives. The employer's defence under the rule prior to 2005 was much broader—that the equivalent of the PCP should be *justified*—and old cases should be used with care. However some later cases seem to reflect the underlying Directive. Thus in *Hardys and Hansons plc v Lax* [2005] EWCA Civ 846, [2005] IRLR 668, the Court of

Appeal was invited on behalf of the employers to adopt a 'band of reasonableness' test in assessing the employer's argument of justification, so that (as with unfair dismissal in **Chapter 10**) the employment tribunal would not merely make its own decision on what a reasonable employer would do, but rather would accept that different reasonable employers might take different actions. It would limit itself to deciding whether the action actually taken fell within that band or not. The Court refused and required the employment tribunal 'to make its own judgment, upon a fair and detailed analysis of the working practices and business considerations involved, as to whether the proposal is reasonably necessary'. In the particular case the employer's argument for rejecting the employee's request after maternity leave to 'job-share' had been rejected by the tribunal and the Court of Appeal dismissed the appeal. This is a robust interpretation of the old rules that takes account of earlier decisions in the ECJ under the underlying Directive and seems likely to remain important under the new rules, especially as it contains the express reasoning that the word 'reasonable' reflects the presence and applicability of proportionality.

6.2.2.5 Unintentional discrimination

Under SDA 1975, s. 66 as amended in 1996, the award of compensation by the tribunal is restricted (see **6.6.3** below) if the employer proves that the indirect discrimination was unintentional. However, in *London Underground Ltd* v *Edwards* (see above) it was held that this defence did not mean that the employer was only liable for the results of discrimination deliberately applied *against the applicant*. In that case the employment tribunal was entitled to infer that the new roster was introduced with knowledge of its unfavourable consequences for the applicant as a single parent and an intention to produce those consequences could be inferred. A similar provision exists in RRA 1976, s 57(3) and similar logic was applied in *J. H. Walker Ltd* v *Hussain* [1996] ICR 291. A rule about when holidays could be taken affected the religious observance of Muslim employees: compensation was awarded.

In the light of those cases it is not easy to think of examples of unintentional indirect discrimination that would fall within the rule. We expect that it may well be removed under the predicted unifying statute, the SEA, and perhaps it is surprising that it still exists. Recently issued Government advice to employers about the 1 October 2005 amendments, for example, suggests that indirect sex discrimination is often inadvertent and lists the following as possibly indirectly discriminatory:

(a) a change in working hours or location imposed by the employer;

(b) a requirement for employees to be mobile in their workplace;

(c) a provision that employees should be available to work their normal contractual hours without variation;

(d) a requirement to work overtime;

(e) a contractual obligation or a practice of undertaking long hours;

(f) a refusal to allow employees to work from home; and

(g) a requirement to work without set hours, but as and when required.

6.2.2.6 Colour and nationality

The comparisons we have made in the preceding paragraphs between the versions of RRA 1976 and SDA 1975 before and after they were subject to amendments resulting from the European Directives show that the changes are greatly to the benefit of claimants. As a claimant has the choice of how to present a claim, it is difficult to imagine why anyone would choose to complain about discrimination on grounds of colour or nationality (where the pre-July 2003 definition would apply) when the same complaint could probably equally well be expressed in terms of race or national origin (thereby gaining the benefit of the newer s. 1(1A)(b) definition). In that unlikely event, the above paragraphs identify the differences that would arise; if required, more detail can be found in an older edition of this book.

6.2.3 Harassment

The topic of harassment was introduced at **6.2.1** as an example of direct discrimination. The earliest examples of its recognition concerned *sexual harassment,* but *racial harassment* was soon recognised as the equivalent. At first there was almost always a sexual element and not merely discrimination based on sex: typically the male boss trying to exploit his position of authority to obtain sexual favours from a female subordinate. There was no statutory definition, and the judges were able to develop the concept more broadly. Then a definition was introduced into RRA 1976, by the Race Relations Act 1976 (Amendment) Regulations 2003 in order to comply with Directive 2000/43/EC. Harassment is defined in RRA, s. 3A as unwanted conduct on grounds of race or ethnic or national origins which has the purpose or effect of violating another person's dignity or creating an intimidating, hostile, degrading, humiliating or offensive environment for that person. There is no requirement for an intention to harass; if the conduct is unwanted and its effect is as described, it is unlawful. In practice the new statutory definition did not greatly differ from the established definition in *Wardman* v *Carpenter Farrar* [1993] IRLR 374, where the EAT borrowed from a European code of practice:

Sexual harassment means 'unwanted conduct of a sexual nature, or other conduct based on sex affecting the dignity of women and men at work.' This can include unwelcome physical, verbal or non-verbal conduct.

That definition was applied by the EAT in *British Telecommunications plc* v *Williams* [1997] IRLR 668 where they went on to note that the conduct which constitutes sexual harassment is itself gender-specific, so that there is no necessity to look for a male comparator. Some subsequent cases appeared to suggest that a comparator was often required, but in view of the 2005 amendments we shall consider next, they are now of historical interest only, and in any event comparators were not always required, as in *Moonsar* v *Fiveways Express Transport Ltd* [2005] IRLR 9, where the EAT accepted without requiring any comparator that the downloading of pornography from the internet could cause more offence to a woman than to a man.

Major amendments were made to SDA 1975 by the Employment Equality (Sex Discrimination) Regulations 2005 and by the Sex Discrimination Act 1975 (Amendment) Regulations 2008. The definition now includes both *sexual harassment* in the sense in which we have usually understood it from the cases, but also *harassment related to a person's sex* which is not necessarily sexual in nature. The statutory definition now provides that a person subjects a woman to harassment if:

(a) related to her sex or that of another person, he engages in unwanted conduct that has the purpose or effect of violating her dignity, or of creating an intimidating, hostile, degrading, humiliating or offensive environment for her; or

(b) he engages in any form of unwanted verbal, non-verbal or physical conduct of a sexual nature that has the purpose or effect of violating her dignity, or of creating an intimidating, hostile, degrading, humiliating or offensive environment for her; or

(c) on the ground of her rejection of or submission to unwanted conduct of the kind mentioned in (a) or (b), he treats her less favourably than he would treat her had she not rejected, or submitted to, the conduct.

Government advice on the new rules give an example of the sort of conduct that would fall into (a) above but that would not have been included before: putting essential equipment on a high shelf so as to make it difficult for women to reach it. Conduct like sexually explicit remarks will fall into (b) if sexual in nature even if not made *because of* a person's sex.

Authorities under SDA 1975 prior to the 2005 amendments, especially those where a claim of harassment was rejected, must now be used with some care. For example, the new definition approaches the matter very much from the claimant's perspective. This is different from some of the older cases like *Williams* mentioned above, where the EAT seemed to concentrate more on what a male interviewer may or may not have done than on the claimant's reaction. Government advice on the new rules, though, seems in keeping with the EAT decision in *Reed* v *Stedman* [1999] IRLR 299. If a victim had made it clear that she found conduct unwelcome, continuation of such conduct constituted harassment, even if some might regard her as being unduly sensitive. On the other hand, there were some kinds of conduct that, unless expressly invited, could generally be described as unwelcome.

There is no requirement for an intention to harass; conduct which has the effect of creating an intimidating, hostile, degrading, humiliating or offensive environment can be harassment, even if creating such an environment was not the intention behind it. Further, as a result of the 2008 amendments, the unwanted conduct no longer has to be *on the ground of* the victim's sex to fall within the definition, but only *related* to it, or indeed to the sex of someone else.

Many employers already have policies in place to prevent inappropriate behaviour among their workforce, and rules about harassment feature in the employment handbooks (or equivalent) of most large companies. Nevertheless the practical circumstances in which complaints of harassment arise often involve some complexity for managers and supervisors for reasons like the following:

(a) The term covers a very wide range of conduct, ranging from criminal acts, possibly as serious as rape, to seemingly trivial remarks, the sexual overtones of which can only be understood by the recipient concerned and in all the surrounding circumstances. The usual pattern of a man harassing a woman is not invariable. Like other kinds of misconduct, there is no one disciplinary sanction appropriate for all incidents of sexual harassment, regardless of seriousness.

(b) Those perpetrating sexual harassment rarely commit the outrageous or major offences. Typically they go just one small step beyond that which the victim will tolerate. So the employer will often be faced with the seemingly trivial.

(c) Victims are typically reluctant to complain, and put up with unwelcome attention for a long time. When it eventually becomes unbearable, they expect instant remedial action from the employer, so as to remove them from contact with the perpetrator.

(d) Perpetrators often claim to have believed that their attentions were welcomed. Sometimes such a claim is ludicrous; in other cases it is plausible. If the perpetrator was genuinely unaware that the victim found the attention objectionable, no disciplinary offence can be said to have been committed until the perpetrator is put on notice of that fact. This is a special kind of warning.

6.2.4 Victimisation

The fourth kind of discrimination is victimisation, which is defined as less favourable treatment of an employee by reason that the person has taken some kind of action under RRA 1976, or SDA 1975 or EPA 1970, or has been involved in such action.

The House of Lords redefined victimisation in *Nagarajan* v *London Regional Transport* [1999] ICR 877. The applicant was an Indian who had previously made several successful complaints of racial discrimination against the same (or a closely associated) employer, and now alleged that his latest rejection for two vacancies was victimisation. The employment tribunal found in his favour, mostly by inference: the interviewers had been 'consciously or unconsciously' influenced by their knowledge of the previous complaints. Both EAT and the Court of Appeal found that the process of inferring victimisation from unexplained events was insufficient to meet the necessary tests but the majority in the House of Lords disagreed. Motive was irrelevant and it was the objective fact that mattered, as with direct and indirect discrimination. In *Chief Constable of West Yorkshire* v *Khan* [2001] UKHL 48, [2001] ICR 1065, the House of Lords held that employers, acting honestly and reasonably, should be able to take steps to preserve their position in discrimination proceedings without laying themselves open to a charge of victimisation. Under that test the Chief Constable was entitled to decline to provide Sgt Khan with a reference while discrimination proceedings continued.

That 'honest and reasonable' test was confirmed by the House of Lords in *Derbyshire* v *St Helen's Metropolitan Borough Council* [2007] UKHL 16, [2007] ICR 841, although they felt that the emphasis in *Khan* on the statutory words 'by reason that' was uncomfortable. In the long-running *Derbyshire* case the employer, faced with claims of equal pay from employees in the schools meal service, wrote to the few who had refused to accept a settlement, warning them that a decision against the employer if the cases went to hearing could make school meals so expensive that the service was no longer viable, and redundancies could follow. Initially, the employment tribunal rejected the employees' claims of victimisation, but, after a successful appeal to the EAT, a different employment tribunal then upheld them, regarding the intimidation and detrimental treatment as going beyond acceptable protection of position by the employer. The EAT upheld that decision but the majority in the Court of Appeal did not, regarding the employer's actions as falling within the *Khan* test. The House of Lords has now allowed an appeal and restored the employment tribunal decision; there was nothing wrong with its conclusion after careful consideration that such letters would not have been sent by an honest and reasonable employer. The long saga of the appeal process perhaps demonstrates that this action in the particular circumstances of *Derbyshire* falls close to the margin. Where an employee tried to harass the employer into offering him a settlement by making unjustified claims of race discrimination in *HM Prison Service* v *Ibimidun* EAT 0408/07, the employer's dismissal of the employee was not victimisation.

Action protected under these rules is not limited to action concerning the claimant personally. In *National Probation Service for England and Wales (Cumbria area)* v *Kirby* [2006] IRLR 508 the complainant had merely given information in connexion with another employee's complaint of racial discrimination: the EAT held that she had been victimised contrary to s. 2(1)(c) of RRA 1976.

6.2.5 Employees and others

We have noted elsewhere in this book the growing tendency to extend employment rights to *workers*, a broader term than employees, and one which includes various people who are not employed under conventional contracts of employment. Thus, for example, the most recent extension of discrimination law gives rights to part-time workers and not only employees.

The older measures against discrimination use the term *employee*, but there are express provisions in SDA 1975, s. 9 and RRA 1976, s. 7 which perhaps anticipate the modern trend and prohibit discriminatory acts by principals against contract workers. In *MHC Consulting Services Ltd* v *Tansell* [2000] ICR 789, also reported as *Abbey Life Assurance Co. Ltd* v *Tansell* [2000] IRLR 387, the Court of Appeal interpreted a very similar rule under DDA 1995, s. 12. It included a relationship where there was no direct link between the principal and the contract worker, but only one through an intermediate contractor. The 2005 amendments to SDA 1975 extend its coverage by adding new sections dealing with office-holders and others.

6.2.6 Positive discrimination

A question that is often asked is whether an employer can discriminate positively, i.e., in favour of one sex or a particular racial group that may be under-represented at the workplace generally or in particular groups. Generally speaking, to discriminate *in favour* of one person is to discriminate *against* another, and the employer is given no protection against a complaint by the second. There are very limited exceptions to be found in RRA 1976, ss. 35 and 37–38, and in SDA 1975, ss. 47–48. Employers may discriminate positively to the extent of providing specialist training to remedy underrepresentation and of encouraging people in under-represented groups to apply for jobs, but no more.

The position has been different elsewhere in Europe. There has been a string of ECJ decisions, for example, about the validity under European law of German rules permitting positive discrimination. In *Marschall* v *Land Nordrhein-Westfalen* (C–409/95) [1998] IRLR 39, the ECJ permitted positive discrimination in favour of women if subject to a safeguard protecting the interests of an individual equally qualified male. Without such a safeguard, a rule of positive discrimination cannot be operated—*Abrahamsson* v *Fogelqvist* C–407/98 [2000] IRLR 732. In a Dutch case, *Lommers* v *Minister van Landbouw, Natuurbeheer en Visserij* (Case C–476/99) [2002] IRLR 430, the ECJ held that the Directive did not preclude a scheme giving women preferential access over men to subsidised nursery places for their children, provided that it gave special treatment to men who cared for children by themselves.

6.3 Scope of RRA 1976

The definition of 'racial grounds' is found in s. 3 of RRA 1976. Discrimination is unlawful if on grounds of:

(a) colour;

(b) race;

(c) nationality; or

(d) ethnic or national origins.

There are few cases in which that definition causes problems or uncertainty. 'National origins' has been held to refer to race rather than citizenship: *Tejani* v *Peterborough Superintendent Registrar* [1986] IRLR 502. An 'ethnic group' has been held to be broader than race alone and may include any community with a shared history and culture. Sikhs and Jews satisfy the definition; Rastafarians do not, because they are defined by religion alone: *Crown Suppliers* v *Dawkins* [1993] ICR 517. This point has of course lost its significance since the implementation of the regulations on religious discrimination mentioned at **6.1.1.5**. Language alone (e.g., restricting employment to speakers of Welsh) does not define an ethnic group: *Gwynedd County Council* v *Jones* [1986] ICR 833. As we noted earlier, the Race Directive 2000 43/EC covers only (b) and (d) above.

An interesting aspect of the scope of RRA 1976 came to be examined in *Serco Ltd* v *Redfearn* [2006] EWCA Civ 659. The employee, a driver for a bus company that served many Asian customers, was dismissed after being elected to the local authority as a member of the British National Party. He had insufficient service to complain of unfair dismissal and brought a complaint under RRA 1976. The employment tribunal rejected his complaint, finding that his dismissal was on grounds of health and safety, given the high proportion of Asians in the local community. The EAT noted that the expression 'on racial grounds' was not restricted to the *claimant's* race and found in his favour, but the Court of Appeal overturned the decision, regarding it as contrary to the purpose of race relations legislation.

The exceptions to RRA 1976 are set out in s. 5(2) and are very limited. They cover circumstances where being a member of a particular racial group is a genuine occupational qualification for a job in one of the following cases:

(a) actors/actresses or other entertainers;

(b) artists' and photographers' models;

(c) waiters/waitresses or other workers in public restaurants, etc. with a setting requiring a particular race for authenticity;

(d) those providing welfare services to a particular racial group.

There is also an exception under s. 35 to allow the employer to provide special services such as training or welfare to specific racial groups. Lessons in English would be a good example.

6.4 Scope of SDA 1975

6.4.1 Discrimination prohibited by SDA 1975

The SDA 1975 makes unlawful by s. 1 any discrimination on the basis of a person's sex, a relatively straightforward provision. The statutory rules are expressed in terms of a woman who is less favourably treated than a man, but s. 2(1) states that they apply equally the other way round.

An identical set of provisions in s. 3 makes unlawful any discrimination against married people in comparison with single people. In this case the reverse does not apply. It has been assumed that this permits employers to treat married employees more favourably, e.g., by giving them a better reimbursement of relocation expenses than single employees, but that interpretation is now open to some doubt. In some cases, e.g., if the better reimbursement is denied to same-sex couples, such a policy could breach the regulations prohibiting discrimination on grounds of sexual orientation that we shall discuss at **6.5.9**. Furthermore, under the Civil Partnership Act 2004 the protection of s. 3 has been extended to those who have concluded a civil partnership.

6.4.2 Exception from SDA 1975

There are limited exceptions, establishing circumstances in which acts that would otherwise constitute unlawful discrimination are permitted:

(a) where the essential nature of the job requires a person of one sex rather than the other, including dramatic performances, but excluding physical strength or stamina;

(b) where decency or privacy requires it, e.g., a changing room attendant; or if providing personal services like welfare or education;

(c) in domestic service involving close personal contact and in single-sex hospitals and prisons;

(d) if living accommodation is provided and cannot reasonably be equipped to provide separately for both sexes;

(e) if the job involves work in a country (e.g., Saudi Arabia) where the law or custom requires one sex rather than the other;

(f) in relation to any payment (which is covered by EPA 1970 instead);

(g) if consisting of provisions for death or retirement. This is a particularly complicated area which we shall consider as a separate matter at **6.4.3** below.

An exemption from SDA 1975 in respect of those employing five or fewer employees was repealed in 1986 and the Act applies to all employers regardless of number of employees.

6.4.3 Provisions for death or retirement

This topic is partly covered by SDA 1975 and partly by EPA 1970, but the difference is unimportant; if it is not one it is the other, and there is no middle ground excluded entirely.

By s. 6(4) of SDA 1975, provisions for death or retirement are excluded, but subject to such a wide exception that in practice the scope of the exclusion is small. In *Marshall* v *Southampton and South West Hampshire Area Health Authority (Teaching)* [1986] ICR 335, the ECJ held that it was contrary to a European Directive to require women to retire at an earlier age than men. The Sex Discrimination Act 1986 was introduced in consequence and amended s. 6 of SDA 1975.

The discriminatory provisions of many occupational pensions schemes were examined by the ECJ in *Barber* v *Guardian Royal Exchange Assurance Group* [1990] ICR 616. It was held that pension benefits were a part of pay under art. 119 (now art. 141) and therefore subject to a strict rule of equality, whatever exclusion appeared in the UK statute. The judgment was delivered on 17 May 1990 and provided that equality should run from that date.

The time limitation in the *Barber* decision was unclear. Did it refer to pensions paid from that date, or to service after it or to something else? The question was answered clearly by the ECJ (after having been covered in a Protocol attached to the Maastricht Treaty of the EC) in *Ten Oever* v *Stichting Bedrijfspensioenfonds* [1995] ICR 74 and some subsequent cases. It required equality in respect of *service* after 17 May 1990.

That case did not exhaust the questions raised by the underlying principle of the *Barber* decision that pensions were an element of pay subject to art. 141 and cases continue to arise, both in the UK and at the ECJ. For example, in *Quirk v Burton Hospitals NHS Trust* [2002] EWCA Civ 149, [2002] ICR 602, it was held that benefits on early retirement after 17 May 1990 had to be equal in respect of service after that date but could differentiate between the sexes in relation to earlier service. See also **6.9** below about the right of access to pension schemes for part-time workers.

6.5   The circumstances in which racial or sex discrimination may arise

6.5.1   Guidance from codes of practice

There are various stages in the employment relationship where discrimination may occur, and these are listed in the codes of practice, especially the EOC code on sex discrimination. The codes are primarily directed to employers with the intention of encouraging positive steps to eliminate discrimination, especially through the establishment of equal opportunity policies. They may, however, sometimes be of use to solicitors preparing a case for an individual client.

6.5.1.1   Advertisements for jobs

There is a specific prohibition of discriminatory advertising in s. 29 of RRA 1976 and s. 38 of SDA 1975. This is particularly a problem under SDA 1975, since words like 'waiter' or 'stewardess' as well as 'he' and 'she' are taken as indicating an intention to discriminate. However, only the CEHR can bring proceedings to enforce s. 38 of SDA 1975.

6.5.1.2   Recruitment

Both codes urge employers to adopt recruitment practices that will avoid unintentional discrimination. Close contacts between employers and single-sex schools, advertising in publications which some racial groups are unlikely to read, and recruitment by word of mouth from existing employees may all produce discriminatory results. However, breach of the codes does not provide a ground of complaint without evidence of such results—*Lord Chancellor v Coker* [2001] EWCA Civ 1756, [2002] ICR 321.

6.5.1.3   Selection methods

Whilst both codes refer to this matter, the code on race relations makes a particular point about language difficulties. Complicated application forms or aptitude tests that require a higher standard of English than is necessary for the job probably constitute unlawful indirect discrimination.

6.5.1.4   Opportunities in employment

There are references in the codes to opportunities for promotion, transfer, and training, and also to provision of benefits, facilities, and services. It is also suggested that grievance and disciplinary procedures can easily be operated in a discriminatory way, probably quite unintentionally.

6.5.1.5   Dismissal

There is no separate category of unfair dismissal to cover discriminatory reasons for dismissal, but (as we shall see in **Chapter 10**) such reasons can increase the amount of compensation that might otherwise be awarded. This includes discriminatory selection for redundancy, as mentioned in **Chapter 11**. See **6.5.6** below, however, for specific rules about pregnancy-related dismissals.

6.5.1.6 Post-dismissal

A long argument whether the employment provisions of RRA 1976 or SDA 1975 could still apply after employment was ended was resolved in *Rhys-Harper* v *Relaxion Group plc* [2003] UKHL 33, [2003] ICR 867. The rule from that case, that the provisions continued to apply, was then given statutory force from 19 July 2003 by a new s. 20A added to SDA 1975. Thus, e.g., a refusal by an employer on discriminatory grounds to supply a reference to a former employee would fall within the relevant statute.

6.5.2 Pressure to discriminate

There are specific provisions (in RRA 1976, ss. 30 and 31, and in SDA 1975, ss. 39 and 40) making it unlawful for anyone, including one employee, to instruct another to discriminate or to put pressure on another to discriminate. Only the CEHR may enforce these provisions.

6.5.3 Vicarious liability

It is expressly provided by s. 32 of RRA 1976 and by s. 41 of SDA 1975 that if a discriminatory act is done by an employee in the course of employment, *both* employer and employee may be liable. This is particularly of importance in relation to harassment: *Strathclyde Regional Council* v *Porcelli* [1986] ICR 564. In *Miles* v *Gilbank* [2006] EWCA 543, [2006] ICR 12 the Court of Appeal upheld a finding that a hairdressing company and its salon manager were jointly and severally liable for unlawful sex discrimination. The employment tribunal had found that the manager's behaviour went 'beyond malicious and amount(ed) to downright vicious'. It is a defence for the employer to have taken reasonable steps to prevent the discrimination, but this is not limited to steps that would have succeeded in achieving that result—*Canniffe* v *East Riding of Yorkshire Council* [2000] IRLR 555.

At one time, it seemed that the question of whether an act was done by an employee in the course of employment was to be answered using the standard test for vicarious liability from the law of tort that we encountered at **2.5** above. Thus, for example, in *Irving and Irving* v *Post Office* [1987] IRLR 289, a postman wrote a racially abusive remark ('Go back to Jamaica, Sambo') on the back of an envelope addressed to one of his neighbours. The Court of Appeal held that the misconduct formed no part of his duties and could not be classified as merely a means of performing them. Therefore, the employer was not liable for the racial harassment.

That approach to harassment of an employee was comprehensively rejected by the Court of Appeal, perhaps not before time, in *Jones* v *Tower Boot Co. Ltd* [1997] ICR 254. A 16-year-old mixed-race employee had been subjected to verbal abuse and to physical assault that extended to whipping and deliberate branding with a hot screwdriver. A majority of the EAT had felt bound by *Irving* to hold that these were independent wrongs, committed outside the course of employment and for which the fellow employees (but not the employer) were liable. Waite LJ suggested that the rules of vicarious liability might have been relevant in *Irving* (presumably because the injured party was not an employee), but could not be used to evade employer responsibility in a case like this. The words 'in the course of employment' must be given their ordinary meaning by the employment tribunal, acting as an industrial jury.

The extent to which activity outside work falls within the definition of 'in the course of employment' is a fine point, and the *Tower Boot* decision probably represents a watershed. The Court of Appeal held earlier in *Waters* v *Commissioner of Police of the Metropolis* [1997] ICR 1073 that the employer was not liable when a woman police constable was sexually assaulted by a male colleague while both were off duty but, more recently, in *Chief Constable of Lincolnshire Police* v *Stubbs* [1999] ICR 547, that incidents in a pub immediately after work fell within the definition. It is difficult to reconcile these two decisions, especially since the incidents in the first were rather more serious than the second, except on the basis of a changing attitude to employers' responsibilities. (Other parts of the Court of Appeal decision in *Waters* were subsequently overturned by the House of Lords—[2000] ICR 1064—but the complaint under SDA 1975 was not appealed.)

Despite the extension of the employer's liability for discrimination, there are still cases where the employer can use the defence of having taken reasonable steps and where the individual employee remains liable, e.g., *Yeboah* v *Crofton* [2002] EWCA Civ 794, [2002] IRLR 634.

6.5.3.1   Vicarious liability under the Protection from Harassment Act 1997

The previous section discussed the employer's vicarious liability for discriminatory acts, especially harassment, prohibited under RRA 1976, SDA 1975 or one of the other heads we have been considering, and committed by one employee against another. The employer's more general vicarious liability for tortious acts committed by employees may be related to employment, but is not part of employment law and we have not attempted to cover it in this book. However, harassment is not a problem that arises only in employment and we need to say something about another statute that has been used recently to try to establish vicarious liability.

The Protection from Harassment Act 1997 was enacted to deal with the problem of 'stalkers', and its criminal sanctions were generally regarded as of more importance than any civil aspect. It leaves the concept of harassment undefined (certainly not adopting the definition we discussed at **6.2.3**) and has in fact been used more broadly. So bullying and other oppressive treatment may fall within its scope even if there is no connexion with race, sex or any of the other prohibited grounds of discrimination. In *Majrowski* v *Guy's and St Thomas's NHS Trust* [2006] UKHL 34, [2006] ICR 1199, a gay man claimed that his departmental manager had bullied and intimated him because of homophobia. The House of Lords unanimously rejected the employer's contention that the statute was a response to the public order problem of stalking and was not aimed at the workplace; Parliament must have intended to create a new civil wrong that was subject to the usual rules of vicarious liability of employers—that the offending conduct was closely connected with acts the employee was authorised to do. Majrowski's contention had been rejected at first instance and had been accepted only by a majority of the Court of Appeal; so the clear decision of their Lordships is significant. However, its impact is subject to limits. In *Banks* v *Ablex Ltd* [2005] EWCA Civ 173, [2005] ICR 819 the Court of Appeal treated harassment under this statute as requiring evidence of persistence and it was therefore a narrower concept than the workplace harassment we have been discussing. They declined to find against the employer. Further, in *Sunderland City Council* v *Conn* [2007] EWCA Civ 1492, [2008] IRLR 324, they held that the 1997 Act requires conduct to be of such gravity that criminal sanctions are appropriate, and the conduct in that case was bad-tempered but fell well short of the necessary gravity.

Although, as we have said, employers' tortious liability for personal injury is outside our scope, it is worth noting the considerable potential of the 1997 Act. In *Green* v *DB*

Group Services (UK) Ltd [2006] EWHC 1898, [2006] IRLR 764, an employee was awarded just over £850,000 as a result of bullying that caused her psychiatric problems.

6.5.4 Employees working under illegal contracts

We shall see at **10.3.7.1** below that employees whose contracts are tainted by illegality, usually tax evasion, may have no right to complain of unfair dismissal. A less strict approach is taken under discrimination law. In *Leighton* v *Michael* [1995] ICR 1091, a woman worked in a fish and chip shop without paying tax or National Insurance contributions. The majority in the EAT acknowledged that she could not complain of unfair dismissal, a right that depended on the existence of a contract untainted by illegality, but held that her right to complain under SDA 1975 rested on a statutory protection independent of the contract. The EAT decision was approved by the Court of Appeal in *Hall* v *Woolston Hall Leisure Ltd* [2000] IRLR 578. A different result ensued when the Court of Appeal held that the conduct of the employee, an asylum seeker, was 'causative of the illegality' in *Vakante* v *Governing Body of Addey and Stanhope School (No. 2)* [2004] EWCA Civ 1065, [2005] ICR 231.

6.5.5 The employer's handling of cases of harassment

We have already discussed harassment, including sexual harassment and racial harassment, in some detail at **6.2.3**. We noted that it can be a serious matter for victims whose lives are sometimes made intolerable as a result. It can be serious too for employers, especially in the light of the considerations we have just been examining about vicarious liability for the actions of other employees, because very large awards of compensation have sometimes been made. Before we leave the topic we need to note that it can also be serious for individuals accused of harassment, especially if the accusation is unjust. Someone wrongly accused of sexual harassment may find there are serious consequences of trust from a partner or ostracism by other employees; someone in any sort of public job may find an unjustified accusation of racial harassment appears to damage career prospects. Employers very often face a daunting task in dealing with cases of alleged harassment where both alleged victim and alleged perpetrator are employees, and both have the right to be treated fairly. The authors have been involved in cases where an employer, anxious to protect a victim, has taken action against a perpetrator that has led to a claim of unfair dismissal that the employer has then lost.

Solicitors may find themselves asked to advise employers what to do in such difficult circumstances. Some recognition of the possible background may help, as we discussed at **6.2.3**. Authorities about fair treatment for those accused of harassment are limited to tribunal cases, but the authors offer the following suggestions:

(a) Encourage victims to complain informally and in confidence at an early stage. It was suggested in *Insitu Cleaning* v *Heads* [1995] IRLR 4 that this may best be done by means of a separate grievance procedure.

(b) Ensure that the confidence is respected, that support is given and that some action is seen to be taken, as the victim may otherwise have good grounds to resign and to claim constructive dismissal.

(c) Be careful about suspension of the alleged perpetrator, especially if the complaint of harassment appears ill-founded and/or if there are other temporary solutions like transfer to another department to avoid contact with the victim. In *Gogay* v *Hertfordshire County Council* [2000] IRLR 703, a care worker in a children's home was suspended following allegations of sexual abuse by a disturbed child and this led to clinical depression. The Court of Appeal held that the employers were in breach of the implied duty of trust and confidence.

(d) In any disciplinary proceedings, ensure that the perpetrator's rights are respected and that fair treatment results, recognising the need for some warning except when gross misconduct has occurred.

(e) Encourage complaints early enough that action can be taken before relationships have deteriorated to the point where victim and perpetrator cannot safely be left to work together.

(f) Ensure that employees generally are aware that sexual harassment will be viewed seriously.

6.5.6 Pregnancy-related dismissal

We noted at **4.6.2** above that by s. 99 of ERA 1996, dismissal of a woman because of pregnancy or childbirth is almost always unfair, so that the remedies we shall consider in **Chapter 10** are available. Such a dismissal is also likely to be direct sex discrimination, so that the woman also has rights under SDA 1975 and/or European law. The importance of this alternative right of action is that compensation for unfair dismissal is subject to a statutory maximum, while compensation for sex discrimination is unlimited. Furthermore, discrimination law covers forms of less favourable treatment other than dismissal as in *Busch* v *Klinikum Neustadt GmbH* C-320/01 [2003] IRLR 625.

The rule that discrimination law applies to unfavourable treatment on grounds of pregnancy or maternity leave has clearly been established by such cases, but the 2005 amendments to SDA 1975 now also give it a statutory basis. A new s. 3A in SDA 1975 provides that women (both employees and applicants for employment) are protected from discrimination first on the ground that they are pregnant and secondly in relation to their right to maternity leave. The second provision covers both ordinary maternity leave and additional maternity leave—see **4.6.3** above. Despite the new statutory provision, it is still worth looking at the development of these rules, especially from the European cases.

In *Webb* v *EMO Air Cargo (UK) Ltd* [1994] ICR 727, the ECJ ruled on questions referred by the House of Lords. A woman employee was recruited to fill a vacancy created when another employee was on maternity leave and then was herself found to be pregnant. The replacement was dismissed and had too little service to complain of unfair dismissal under the law as it then existed. She complained of sex discrimination on the ground that an equivalent man would not have been dismissed; the employer justified the dismissal on the ground that a man would indeed have been dismissed if he had for any reason become incapable of fulfilling the whole purpose of the contract—to remain at work during the maternity leave. In an important judgment the ECJ ruled that, because a male replacement could not have become incapable of fulfilling the contract in the same circumstances, the dismissal was by definition unlawful sex discrimination. This approach has now been confirmed by the House of Lords on the return of *Webb* from the ECJ (*Webb* v *EMO Air Cargo (UK) Ltd (No. 2)* [1995] ICR 1021).

During pregnancy and childbirth, women thus enjoy a very high level of protection, and there is an obvious question of how long it lasts. The ECJ laid down a rule in *Brown* v *Rentokil Ltd* [1998] ICR 790, which was followed by the Court of Appeal in *Halfpenny* v *IGE Systems Ltd* [1999] ICR 834. The House of Lords overruled the *Halfpenny* decision at [2001] ICR 73, but not on this point. There are two distinct phases. Dismissal (or indeed any other action) in relation to sickness that starts during pregnancy or maternity leave and results from pregnancy is sex discrimination and automatically unfair. Once the baby has been born and the woman has returned to work after her maternity leave, she must be treated like any other employee. Thus, for example, if her attendance record is unsatisfactory, she can fairly be dismissed for incapability (see **Chapter 10**) provided that a man with comparable absence would be treated similarly. This rule apparently includes conditions caused by pregnancy or childbirth, provided that sickness starts after the return to work. In *Caledonia Bureau Investment & Property* v *Caffrey* [1998] ICR 603, the applicant's postnatal depression started during her maternity leave. Her dismissal after she was due to return to work was therefore related to maternity and unfair.

The new statutory base of these rules makes clear that they apply to all kinds of less favourable treatment, so that it remains unlawful to demote a woman or to refuse her promotion or access to vocational training because she is pregnant or on maternity leave. Thus in *Fletcher* v *NHS Pensions Agency* [2005] ICR 1458 the EAT held that it was unlawful to deny a bursary to trainee midwives during absence because of pregnancy and maternity, although they were neither employees nor workers. Any less favourable treatment on such grounds is of itself discriminatory; the woman does not need to find a male comparator. In a slightly surprising Irish case the ECJ has held in *North Western Health Board* v *McKenna* (C-191/03) [2005] IRLR 895 that it is not contrary to European law for a woman on pregnancy-related sick leave during pregnancy to be paid like anyone else under the employer's sick pay scheme, although this involved a reduction after a period of absence to less than full pay. Both s. 3A (under the 2005 amendments) and the rule from *Brown* v *Rentokil* provide that the special protection ceases when the woman actually returns to work after maternity leave.

6.5.7 Transsexuals

Under the Sex Discrimination (Gender Reassignment) Regulations 1999, a new s. 2A was added to SDA 1975. This section created a new category of discrimination to cover any person undergoing gender reassignment, who is intending to do so or who has done so. This additional category is subject to the other provisions of SDA 1975 that we have been considering, including (in particular) the rules about harassment at **6.2.3** but not those about genuine occupational qualifications (see below).

The Government was forced to make those regulations by the decision of the ECJ in *P* v *S* [1996] ICR 795 that the Equal Treatment Directive applied to discrimination on the basis of gender reassignment as well as discrimination on the basis of sex alone. This cut across the conventional view of United Kingdom law that a person's sex is fixed at birth as recorded on the birth certificate and cannot be changed. A convenient distinction was drawn by the EAT in *Chessington World of Adventures* v *Reed* [1998] ICR 97 between *sex* which is unchangeable from birth and *gender* which is capable of *reassignment*. Later the European Court of Human Rights held in *Goodwin* v *United Kingdom* [2002] IRLR 664 that there was a breach of both art. 8 and art. 12 of the European Convention on Human Rights when a male to female transsexual was denied the opportunity to marry a man. In *KB* v *National Health Service Pensions Agency* (Case C-117/01) [2004] ICR 781 the ECJ held that art. 141 EC precluded domestic legislation which breached the rule from *Goodwin* by denying a female to male transsexual the opportunity to marry a woman and therefore denying him part of her pay, namely her pension. Those cases led to the Gender Recognition Act 2004, as a result of which the conventional approach in the UK was abandoned from 4 April 2005. Transsexuals can now gain legal recognition in their acquired gender, may marry in their new gender and can apply for a substitute birth certificate. From that date too the provisions of SDA 1975 about genuine occupational qualifications, listed at **6.4.2** above, no longer apply to those who have undergone gender reassignment.

The new statutory rule can perhaps be regarded as extending to non-employment issues the approach adopted by the House of Lords in their decision in *Chief Constable of the West Yorkshire Police* v *A* [2004] UKHL 21, [2004] ICR 806 that a post-operative male to female transsexual had unlawfully been discriminated against when (prior to the 1999 regulations) rejected for appointment as a police constable on the ground of a supposedly genuine occupational qualification—the requirement to undertake intimate personal searches of women. After the operation it was no longer possible in the context of employment to regard her as other than female.

In relation to a very practical matter the Court of Appeal took a more pragmatic view in *Croft* v *Royal Mail Group plc* [2003] EWCA Civ 1045, [2003] ICR 1425. It was necessary to be sensitive about the provision of toilet facilities before the operation, and the employment tribunal had not erred in accepting a compromise put forward by the employer.

6.5.8 Religion or belief

Under the Religion or Belief Regs 2003 it is unlawful for an employer to discriminate on grounds of religion or of religious or philosophical belief. As a result of an amendment under the Equality Act 2006, the protection also applies to the absence of such a belief, so that atheists now acquire protection too. The definition also extends to any *perception* of religion or belief, so that it does not have to be factually based.

The structure of the Religion or Belief Regs 2003 is very much based on that under RRA 1976 or SDA 1975. Unlawful discrimination consists of direct discrimination, indirect discrimination, victimisation and harassment, subject to similar definitions. There is a defence to indirect discrimination if the employer can show a proportionate response to a legitimate business aim, and there is an exception for genuine occupational requirement (GOR), which is doubtless of importance to churches and other religious or faith communities. However, in *Glasgow City Council* v *McNab* EAT 0037/06 the EAT upheld an employment tribunal finding that the employer had discriminated against an atheist teacher when refusing him interview for promotion in a Roman Catholic school to a post where it was considered an appointee had to be of that faith. The GOR exception was interpreted narrowly and the employer could not rely on it in this case.

The regulations have not produced a great many cases, but some have attracted much publicity, such as those dealing with the wearing of veils by Muslim women. In *Azmi* v *Kirklees Metropolitan Borough Council* [2007] ICR 1154, the EAT upheld the rejection by the employment tribunal of claims of direct discrimination, indirect discrimination, and harassment brought by a school support worker who was asked not to wear the veil while teaching children. (Her claim of victimisation was allowed and this was not appealed.) The employment tribunal was entitled to find that the provision, criterion or practice was a proportionate means of achieving a legitimate aim.

6.5.9 Sexual orientation

Until 2003 there was a long history of unsuccessful attempts by homosexuals to secure protection against discrimination by arguing that sexual orientation falls within a broad definition of sex under SDA 1975, especially when interpreted to accord with HRA 1998 or the Equal Treatment Directive. The cases about 'gays in the military' were some of the best known. The House of Lords confirmed in *Macdonald* v *Ministry of Defence* [2003]

UKHL 34, [2003] ICR 937, where a former officer in the Royal Air Force had been forced to resign in 1997 after admitting that he was homosexual, that such discrimination did not breach SDA 1975. The statute would apply only if less favourable treatment was accorded to a male homosexual than would have been accorded to a female homosexual. Such cases are now relevant only to allegedly discriminatory acts or omissions prior to 1 December 2003.

Since that date any such discrimination is made unlawful by the Sexual Orientation Regs 2003. Less favourable treatment is prohibited on the ground of a person's sexual orientation—whether towards the same sex, the opposite sex or both sexes. As with the Religion or Belief Regs 2003, the alleged discriminator's perception is included as an unlawful ground of discrimination.

Like the Religion or Belief Regs 2003, the structure of the Sexual Orientation Regs 2003 is similar to that under RRA 1976 or SDA 1975. Unlawful discrimination consists of direct discrimination, indirect discrimination, victimisation and harassment, subject to similar definitions. There is a defence to indirect discrimination if the employer can show a proportionate response to a legitimate business aim, and there is an exception for genuine occupational qualifications, which has been of relevance to religious organisations with a conscientious objection to homosexuality.

A few cases have arisen in the employment tribunals since the regulations came into force, but there have been very few significant decisions on appeal. In *R (Amicus) v Secretary of State for Trade and Industry* [2004] EWHC 860 (Admin), [2004] IRLR 430 a group of trade unions sought judicial review of the regulations on the ground that they were an inadequate transposition of the Directive, especially as regards the scope of the exception for 'genuine occupational requirements'. Richards J rejected the application. He accepted that the regulations had to strike a balance between the right of individuals not to suffer discrimination on the grounds of sexual orientation and the right of others to manifest their religious belief, and in doing so indicated that the meaning of the exception must be construed narrowly. In *English v Thomas Sanderson Blinds Ltd* [2008] ICR 607 the claimant suffered homophobic banter at work, but the employment tribunal found as a fact that his colleagues did not perceive him to be homosexual; the EAT held that he did not fall within the regulations.

6.6   Remedies in relation to discrimination under RRA 1976 or SDA 1975

A claim of unlawful discrimination in employment can be made only to the employment tribunals. Enforcement in other fields is generally to the county court. There are certain respects in which the procedure in these tribunal cases is slightly different from others. We have given references to RRA 1976 and SDA 1975, but this discussion applies also to cases under the Religion or Belief Regs 2003 and the Sexual Orientation Regs 2003.

6.6.1   Employment tribunal procedure

The claim in the tribunal must be presented within three months of the act complained of, although the tribunals have a discretion to extend this period if they think it just and equitable to do so: RRA 1976, ss. 54 and 68; SDA 1975, ss. 63 and 76. (See also **Chapter 13**.)

The CEHR is able to provide assistance to claimants in pursuing cases, especially if:

(a) the case raises a question of principle;

(b) it is unreasonable to expect the applicant to act alone;

(c) any other special consideration applies.

Applicants are also permitted, either before or after starting tribunal proceedings, to serve on the employer a questionnaire in a prescribed form, inviting the employer to comment on the applicant's version of events and asking specific questions. The employer is not obliged to reply, but any reply sent or the absence of a reply is admissible as evidence in the tribunal. An eight-week period is set for the employer to send the reply.

Those representing claimants often find the questionnaire procedure very useful in assembling evidence, especially where direct evidence of discrimination is lacking. It is possible, for example, to ask the employer to supply statistics about the proportions of people of one sex or racial group among the workforce, which can be compared with the local population, or among applicants for a job compared with those selected for interview or for appointment. Explanations can be required for particular treatment given to the client. Employers, on the other hand, often regard responding to these questionnaires as a time-consuming and unnecessary chore, and may if left on their own provide answers that are incomplete or less thoroughly researched or considered than they should be. Those representing respondents need to ensure that proper care is taken. A good example of the exploitation by a claimant of inconsistencies in the story told by the employer at different stages occurred in *Dattani* v *Chief Constable of West Mercia Police* [2005] IRLR 327.

Since October 2004 claimants have been required to use the statutory grievance procedure (unless there are exceptional circumstances) before a tribunal claim will be accepted but that rule is set to be abolished in April 2009. As we go to press we do not believe it will be replaced by any new formal rule requiring claimants to use voluntary means of resolving disputes before recourse to the tribunals, but it is obviously good practice to do so, and any who do not may find that they are in breach of the forthcoming ACAS code of practice. Furthermore, they risk losing 25 per cent of any compensation awarded.

Conciliation officers from ACAS automatically receive copies of tribunal paperwork and attempt to reach settlements. In most ACAS regions certain conciliation officers are designated as having special responsibility for discrimination cases.

6.6.2 The burden of proof

Proving discrimination is often a problem. Your client, perhaps an Asian woman, may have been turned down for a job for which she seemed well qualified but which was in fact given to a white male. When challenged, the employer says that the man had better personal qualities. Maybe there is an element of truth in the employer's statement; indeed some other white males may have been rejected. But you doubt it was the full story. Under the usual rule of law that 'those who assert must prove', where do you start with the difficult task of getting into the employer's mind to find the real reason for rejection? Was the true reason direct race or sex discrimination, or were the 'personal qualities' so closely related to traditional white culture as to be indirectly discriminatory?

As we shall see shortly the courts have long been sympathetic to the difficult task faced by a complainant in such circumstances, but it has been made simpler by an amendment under regulations of 2001 that inserts a new s. 63A into SDA 1975 so as to implement the Burden of Proof Directive. A similar addition of a new s. 54A has been made to RRA 1976 by 2003 regulations, at least in relation to complaints of discrimination on grounds of race or ethnic or national origins and complaints of harassment brought from 19 July 2003. It does not apply to complaints of victimisation—*Oyarce* v *Chester County Council* [2008] EWCA Civ 434, [2008] IRLR 653. Where the applicant proves facts from which the tribunal could conclude, in the absence of an adequate explanation, that the employer has committed an act of unlawful discrimination or harassment, it is then for the employer to prove otherwise.

The new rule was examined in *Barton* v *Investec Henderson Crosthwaite Securities Ltd* [2003] ICR 1205 where the EAT produced a 12-point list of steps for employment tribunals to consider. Then the approach in *Barton* was considered in *Igen Ltd* v *Wong* [2005] EWCA Civ 142, [2005] ICR 931, where the Court of Appeal approved the list in a slightly amended 13-point form. It was not essential for tribunals to go through the *Barton* guidance paragraph by paragraph; they must obtain their main guidance from the statutory language of s. 63A, which required a two-stage approach. Although the tribunal would generally hear all the evidence at once, their decision-making process must involve the two stages separately. In essence:

(a) Has the claimant proved facts from which, in the absence of an adequate explanation, the tribunal could conclude that the respondent had committed unlawful discrimination?

(b) If the claimant satisfies (a), but not otherwise, has the respondent proved that unlawful discrimination was not committed or was not to be treated as committed?

The Court of Appeal in *Igen Ltd* v *Wong* emphasised the importance of *could* in (a); it may mean making an assumption contrary to reality.

The amended *Barton* guidance recognises that it is unusual to find any direct evidence of discrimination. The applicant is to be required to produce evidence from which the tribunal *could* conclude that discrimination has occurred. This could include any evasive reply to a questionnaire and reference to a code of practice but the tribunal must establish there is prima facie evidence of a link between less favourable treatment and the difference of sex and not merely two unrelated events—*University of Huddersfield* v *Wolff* [2004] IRLR 534. In *Laing* v *Manchester City Council* [2006] ICR 1519, a manager treated everyone ineptly, and the EAT approved the finding of the employment tribunal that there had been no racial discrimination. The case was unusual in that the tribunal's process of reaching that conclusion under the first *Igen Ltd* v *Wong* stage included consideration of the employer's explanation under the second, a possibility approved by the Court of Appeal in *Madarassy* v *Nomura International plc* [2007] EWCA Civ 33, [2007] ICR 867. In most cases the tribunal considers the two stages in sequence and, if they find that the necessary link is established, the burden of proof then moves to the respondent who has to prove on the balance of probabilities that the treatment received was in no sense on the ground of sex (or race, as the case may be). The Court of Appeal had earlier adopted a very similar approach in the case that became the leading authority prior to the 2001 amendments, *King* v *Great Britain China Centre* [1992] ICR 516, although they disliked the idea of a shifting burden of proof.

Cases since the 2003 amendments and *Igen Ltd* v *Wong* have tended to discredit the *King* authority because the two-stage approach was then permitted but is now mandatory. Furthermore the *Igen Ltd* v *Wong* decision indicates that the proof required from the respondent under s. 63A that the explanation was indeed innocent and untainted by unlawful discrimination may go farther than that in *King*. It approved the requirement from *Barton* that the employer should prove on the balance of probabilities that the unfavourable treatment was *in no sense* on the ground of sex or race, etc. In *EB* v *BA* [2006]

EWCA Civ 132, [2006] IRLR 471 the Court of Appeal criticised the employment tribunal for not having required enough of the employer. In effect, the tribunal had looked to the claimant, a male-to-female transsexual who had been selected for redundancy because her billing level was low, to disprove merely plausible explanations by the employer, and this had denied her a fair trial.

Statistical evidence can be a very effective way of satisfying the first requirement: *West Midlands PTE* v *Singh* [1988] IRLR 186. If the case is about promotion, for example, evidence of a substantially different racial balance (or balance of the sexes) between the group from which selection is made and the group of those selected will require the employer to produce a detailed innocent justification. This is why the questions procedure can be so useful. If the employer is unable to supply statistical evidence, that itself may be evidence of having failed to meet the recommendation of the code of practice concerning ethnic monitoring.

The *Igen* tests were adopted by the EAT in a case under the Religion or Belief Regs 2003: *Mohmed* v *West Coast Trains Ltd* UKEAT/0682/05. Mr Mohmed was a Muslim who argued that the employer's instruction to all to keep beards trimmed and smart conflicted with his religious beliefs. The employment tribunal had found first that there was no evidence that the instruction had been issued to Mohmed on a date the regulations were in force, but also that there was no evidence he had been treated less favourably, since a Sikh complied with the employer's policy by keeping his beard tidy but not by cutting or trimming it. The EAT held that the tribunal was entitled to find that the first part of the *Igen* test had not been satisfied.

It is usually essential to have concrete evidence of less favourable treatment. Sometimes it is possible to produce a comparison with an actual person of the opposite sex or a different racial group, but in *Balamoody* v *United Kingdom Central Council for Nursing, Midwifery and Health Visiting* [2001] EWCA Civ 2097, [2002] ICR 646, the Court of Appeal accepted that it would often be impossible to do so and that a hypothetical comparator would suffice. It is essential that the employment tribunal draws its inferences from findings of primary fact and not just from evidence that is not taken to a conclusion, as the Court of Appeal emphasised in *Anya* v *University of Oxford* [2001] EWCA Civ 405, [2001] ICR 847. An employer may behave unreasonably or dismiss unfairly in circumstances that involve no unlawful discrimination.

An exception to the requirement for an actual comparison occurs if the treatment complained of was 'gender-specific' or race-specific, i.e., if it can be shown to have been meted out *because of* the complainant's sex or race. This exception was expressly approved, albeit *obiter*, by the Court of Appeal in *Sidhu* v *Aerospace Composite Technology Ltd* [2000] ICR 602.

6.6.3 Compensation to be awarded

Compensation to be awarded in the event of a successful claim of discrimination is to be calculated by the tribunal as an amount that is just and equitable to reflect the loss suffered by the applicant and there is no statutory limit. Under the Sex Discrimination and Equal Pay (Miscellaneous Amendments) Regulations 1996, compensation for indirect discrimination is restricted to cases where the tribunal considers it would not be just and equitable to grant one or both of the other possible remedies alone—a declaration or a recommendation of action by the employer. Otherwise the rules are the same as for awards of damages in the county court, and damages for injury to feelings are often awarded. There have been some large awards for injury to feelings, but the Court of Appeal has now held in *Vento* v *Chief Constable of West Yorkshire Police* [2002] EWCA

Civ 1871, [2003] ICR 318 that there should be three broad bands: between £15,000 and £25,000 for the most serious cases involving a lengthy campaign of discriminatory harassment; between £5,000 and £15,000 for serious cases not meriting an award in the highest band; and between £500 and £5,000 for less serious cases, such as an isolated or one-off act of discrimination. In *Sheriff* v *Klyne Tugs (Lowestoft)* [1999] ICR 1170 CA, it was held that psychiatric illness brought on by harassment was an additional head of damages beyond injury to feelings and in *Laing Ltd* v *Essa* [2004] EWCA Civ 2, [2004] ICR 746 it was confirmed that the test was one of causation rather than foreseeability. Where more than one form of discrimination is established, the tribunal must examine injury to feelings under each of them, although it may not be necessary to fix separate sums where there is overlap—*Al Jumard* v *Clwyd Leisure Ltd* [2008] IRLR 345.

6.7 Equal pay

The EPA 1970 establishes the principle that women should receive the same pay as men. Like SDA 1975, EPA 1970 states in s. 1(13) that the converse comparison is equally valid, but it is expressed throughout in terms of giving a woman equality of treatment with a man.

Under s. 1(1) of EPA 1970, every woman's contract of employment is deemed to include an equality clause, unless one already exists, and s. 1(2) explains what this means. The following is a simplification, although the layout of (a), (b), and (c) is as in the statute:

Each term of the woman's contract is to be no less favourable than a man's in the same employment if:

(a) she is employed on like work to his; or

(b) she is employed on work rated as equivalent to his under a job evaluation scheme; or

(c) (if neither (a) or (b) applies) her work is of equal value to his,

unless the difference can be justified on the basis of a genuine material factor other than the difference of sex.

The two paragraphs (a) and (b) above both derive from the original 1970 version of EPA; paragraph (c) was added by the Equal Pay (Amendment) Regulations 1983 in order that the 1970 statute was brought into compliance with the Equal Treatment Directive. There are some significant differences between the conditions attached to (a) and (b), and those attached to (c). It is therefore convenient to examine the detailed application of s. 1(2) in three parts:

(a) general remarks about all equality clauses;

(b) equal pay for like work and work rated as equivalent;

(c) equal pay for work of equal value.

Despite more than 30 years of operation of EPA 1970, national statistics on pay for women and men in a wide variety of occupations still show a substantial 'gender gap' and Government ministers have expressed determination to eradicate or at least to reduce it. The 2003 Code of Practice mentioned at **6.1.3.3** above is part of the process. Under the Employment Act 2002 the questionnaire procedure (as described in **6.6.1** above) is extended to equal pay claims.

6.7.1 General remarks about equality clauses

The mechanism by which equal pay is achieved is *contractual* and s. 1(2) allows for both the case where a term in a woman's contract is inferior to the equivalent term in a man's, and that where a term in the man's contract is wholly absent from the woman's. So, once the existence of an equality clause is established by any of the three comparisons, it can be enforced like any other contractual term. The parties may not contract out of the effect of EPA 1970: SDA 1975, s. 77(3).

The scope of s. 1(2) includes all contractual terms and not only pay or remuneration. The only significant exception is that preventing men from claiming any statutory restriction on the employment of women or any benefit related to pregnancy or childbirth: EPA 1970, s. 6(1). Non-contractual differences may of course fall within SDA 1975.

Every case must be brought on the basis of a specific *comparison*: it is not possible for a woman to use EPA 1970 to seek an assessment of a fair rate of pay apart from a comparison with a man: *Pointon* v *University of Sussex* [1979] IRLR 119. (We shall adopt the same practice as EPA 1970 of describing a case brought by a woman in comparison with a man; the reverse comparison could equally well be made, but it is not possible for any comparison to be brought with another employee of the same sex.)

The comparison must be made with a man *in the same employment*. This normally means a man employed by the same employer or by an associated employer at the same establishment. However, it also includes other establishments where common terms and conditions of employment are applied: EPA 1970, s. 1(6)—and 'common' does not only mean identical or the same, but also sufficiently similar for a fair comparison to be made—*British Coal Corporation* v *Smith* [1996] ICR 515, HL. The rule was broad enough to permit a comparison between two Scottish local authorities, although they acted independently of each other, in *South Ayrshire Council* v *Morton* [2002] ICR 956, Court of Session. However in *Robertson* v *Department for Environment, Food and Rural Affairs* [2005] EWCA Civ 138, [2005] ICR 750 it did not extend to two Government departments when pay was determined departmentally, and central pay bargaining had been abandoned.

It has been held that EPA 1970 requires a comparison with a man employed contemporaneously, but that art. 141 of the Treaty of Rome does not, so that EPA 1970 must be interpreted accordingly: *Macarthys* v *Smith* [1979] ICR 785, CA, [1980] ICR 672 on reference to ECJ; and [1980] ICR 672, CA, permitting the woman to compare herself with her *predecessor* in the job. A woman cannot compare herself with her successor in the job: *Walton Centre for Neurology and Neurosurgery NHS Trust* v *Bewley* [2008] ICR 1047.Often the employer has to pay more to recruit a new employee than was paid to a predecessor, irrespective of the sex of the two people.

The equality clause operates in relation to *each individual term* of the woman's contract. It is therefore no defence for the employer to argue that, taken overall, the woman is treated as favourably as the man, and that a benefit in one term must be offset against a detriment in another: *Hayward* v *Cammell Laird* [1988] ICR 464. By contrast, in *Degnan* v *Redcar and Cleveland Borough Council* [2005] EWCA Civ 726, [2005] IRLR 615, the Court of Appeal refused to interpret the *Hayward* principle as allowing a woman to make a string of comparisons, selecting different male comparators for different elements of the remuneration package, and thereby claiming a total hourly monetary rate higher than any single male comparator.

We shall consider shortly in **6.7.2** and **6.7.3** the slightly different defences of genuine material factors and genuine material differences available to employers under the provisions concerning like work, work rated as equivalent or work of equal value. Meanwhile there are some common features of the way the defences operate that are applicable to all those categories. In the Scottish case of *Glasgow City Council* v *Marshall* [2000] ICR 196, the House of Lords set out the key steps in a form not dissimilar to that concerning indirect sex discrimination as we discussed at **6.2.2**. A rebuttable presumption of sex discrimination arises once it is shown that a woman doing like work, work rated as equivalent or work of equal value to a man is being paid or treated less favourably. The variation in their contracts is presumed to be due to the difference of sex. The burden then passes to the employer to show that the explanation is not tainted with sex (sic), and this involves four points:

(a) the proffered explanation is *genuine* and not a sham or pretence;

(b) the less favourable treatment is due to this reason, i.e., that the reason is *material*;

(c) the reason is *not the difference of sex*; and

(d) the factor is or may be a *material difference* (the significance of those words will emerge as we get to **6.7.2** and **6.7.3**).

We have already noted at **6.2.2.2** that statistics can be used in many varied ways and that their interpretation is not straightforward. The same problems arise here, as confirmed in *Grundy* v *British Airways plc* [2007] EWCA Civ 1020, [2008] IRLR 74. The Court of Appeal held that the assessment of disparate impact is a matter of fact for the employment tribunal, and that there are few general rules about which statistical groups should be considered, provided that the groups examined are not so small as to make a reliable conclusion impossible. The Court of Appeal approved the analysis by the EAT in *Ministry of Defence* v *Armstrong* [2004] IRLR 672, where the EAT reviewed leading cases in the ECJ and concluded that the definition of indirect discrimination for purposes of EPA 1970 was broader than that under SDA 1975, although they of course based their comparison on the version of SDA current at the time which did not include the 2005 amendments. In *Armstrong* a difference in pay between two groups of retired army officers now serving in recruiting offices showed an obvious and recognisable form of sex discrimination in the pay structure. The choice of comparator is for the complainant to make, but a group comparison must not be with an arbitrary or artificial group, as the employment tribunal had wrongly allowed in *Cheshire & Wirral Partnership NHS Trust* v *Abbott* [2006] EWCA Civ 523, [2006] IRLR 546.

There is a partial exception in s. 6 of EPA 1970 in respect of *pensions*. However, in consequence of the recent cases on this aspect already discussed at **6.4.3** above, it seems that these provisions are largely inoperative, since European law circumvents most of the restrictions in UK law.

6.7.2 Equal pay for like work and work rated as equivalent

'Like work' is defined in s. 1(4) of EPA 1970. There are two steps:

(a) the man's and woman's work must be the same or broadly similar; and

(b) differences between their work must not be of practical importance.

The consideration whether the man and the woman are doing like work is a practical one, with the emphasis on what is actually done rather than what the contract might in theory require, e.g., *Shields* v *Coomes* [1978] IRLR 263.

'Work rated as equivalent' is defined in s. 1(5) of EPA 1970 to mean jobs that have been given an equal value as a result of an evaluation of those jobs under various headings. This is of course a reference to the technique usually referred to in business and industry as *job evaluation*, but not every such scheme is included. Examples are given of the kinds of headings envisaged: effort, skill, and decision. The statutory definition requires that the job evaluation should involve an *analytical process* and not merely a comparison of the whole job. Some schemes in use in business (e.g., 'paired comparisons') are of this latter type and do not satisfy the statutory definition: *Bromley* v *Quick* [1988] IRLR 249. Taking a purposive approach under the EU Directive (now 2006/54/EC) in *Redcar and Cleveland Borough Council* v *Bainbridge* [2007] EWCA Civ 929, [2008] ICR 238, the Court of Appeal held that 'rated as equivalent' must include male jobs rated lower than the woman's, if the woman was paid less than those comparators.

The scheme itself must be *non-discriminatory*. For example, there must not be excessive emphasis on the physical strength required.

Under either of these two possibilities of equal pay for like work or equal pay for work rated as equivalent, it is possible for the employer to escape the effect of the equality clause if it can be shown that a *genuine material difference* (GMD) exists between the woman's case and the man's. It must be other than the difference of sex.

Employers have a variety of reasons for paying one person differently from another, e.g., skill or experience, length of service, qualifications, grading. The problem arises when any such factor has a disproportionate effect on men and on women, because it will not fall within the definition of a GMD if it is tainted by indirect discrimination. The important tests are:

(a) the GMD must not be a reflection of the difference of sex; and

(b) it must actually exist in the two individual cases being compared.

A difficult question is whether the GMD needs *objective justification*. Is it enough that the employer genuinely applies some non-discriminatory reason to pay people differently, or should a tribunal look behind the reason? There is no requirement within SDA 1975 for the GMD to be objectively justified, and the House of Lords confirmed that position in *Glasgow City Council* v *Marshall* [2000] ICR 196. That case remains the authority as the Court of Appeal confirmed in *Armstrong* v *Newcastle-upon-Tyne NHS Hospital Trust* [2005] EWCA Civ 1608, [2006] IRLR 124. If the employer shows a reason for a difference in pay that is not tainted by sex, there is no requirement for objective justification. More recently the EAT seems to have struggled with that rule, especially in reconciling it with such ECJ authorities as *Brunnhofer* v *Bank der Österreichischen Postsparkasse AG* (C-381/99), [2001] IRLR 571. In *Middlesbrough Borough Council* v *Surtees* [2007] ICR 1644 the EAT said they were bound by *Armstrong* and declined to require objective justification. Leave to appeal was granted, but we are unaware that any appeal has been made in that case. In due course there will doubtless be further consideration by the Court of Appeal.

In *Grundy* v *British Airways plc* [2007] EWCA Civ 1020, [2008] IRLR 74 the Court of Appeal attached very little significance to the employer's argument that an otherwise discriminatory pay structure was justified by the fact that it had been agreed with a trade union through collective bargaining.

A good practical example of a widely-used GMD is length of service. Many employers operate pay structures that add pay increments depending on service. It is seen as a good reward for loyalty, but as more women than men tend to take career breaks it is capable of discriminatory results. We shall see shortly in **6.12.4.6** that there are specific rules about benefits that depend on length of service under the Age Regs 2006, but cases can still be brought under EPA 1970. In *Cadman* v *Health & Safety Executive* Case C-17/05 [2006] ICR 1623, the ECJ held that employers do not have to provide special justification for basing pay on length of service unless the worker produces evidence raising serious doubts about its inappropriateness in the particular circumstances. Service, they decided, goes hand-in-hand with experience and rewarding experience is generally a legitimate aim of pay policy.

A possible GMD that has caused difficulty occurs when the employer pays more in order to attract a particular person into employment than is paid to an existing employee. In *Rainey* v *Greater Glasgow Health Board* [1987] ICR 129, it was held that market forces could indeed be a GMD. However, market forces will not be a sufficient GMD if in truth they represent discrimination on historical grounds of sex: see *Ratcliffe* v *North Yorkshire County Council* [1995] IRLR 439.

One other example that has caused difficulty is the practice of 'red-circling' a particular employee's rate of pay when he is perhaps down-graded and is allowed to keep his old rate for some period of time. Is this a GMD to prevent a woman in the same job from claiming equal pay with the red-circled man? The answer from a string of cases is that it depends on the reason for the historical anomaly. If it was not the result of any past discrimination, a GMD probably exists: *Methven* v *Cow Industrial Polymers* [1980] ICR 463. If it is a method of perpetuating past discrimination, no GMD exists: *Snoxell and Davies* v *Vauxhall Motors* [1977] ICR 700.

6.7.3   Equal pay for work of equal value

The third possible comparison a woman can introduce is with a man who is not doing the same work and whose work has not been rated as equivalent, but who is claimed to be doing work of equal value. The fact that she is in a job where there are men doing the same job or work rated as equivalent does not prevent her from finding another man with whom to make this different comparison: *Pickstone* v *Freemans* [1988] ICR 697.

When the equal value amendments adding s. 1(2)(c) to EPA 1970 were first introduced in 1983 they were seen as likely to lead to a massive increase in claims to the employment tribunals for equal pay. The new rule opened up new possibilities for women in traditional 'female jobs' who were paid much less than men in traditional 'male jobs' but who were not doing the same work as any of those men and whose jobs were not included in the same job evaluation scheme as the men's. Now they could compare themselves with men in wholly different jobs.

Employers were understandably worried. In some cases women would be able to make comparisons that no one had really thought about before.

EXAMPLE 1

In an engineering factory, the factory nurse (almost always a woman) claimed she was doing work of equal value to that of the foreman (almost invariably male at that time) in a production department. Who could say whether she was right or not? Their two jobs had almost nothing in common. The outstanding features of his (much physical effort, uncongenial working conditions, long experience on the shop floor, extensive supervisory responsibility) were factors that tended to rate more highly in any system of job evaluation than those in hers (good manual dexterity, care for others). Depending on the weight given to any of those factors it was possible to produce any desired result from an evaluation. The real point in such cases was that such inequalities in pay were very much 'tainted with sex' as the House of Lords so delicately put it. The factors typically found in 'male jobs' tended to be weighted much more heavily—whether in any formal job evaluation or merely in other people's perception of 'felt fair' relativities in pay. To put it another way, the employer was obliged to pay a competitive wage to attract shop-floor workers in the market and then to pay supervisors a decent differential above that; by contrast there were plenty of trained women prepared to work as nurses (maybe on a part-time, job-sharing basis) at a much lower rate of pay. When the issue of equal value was referred to a tribunal, the tribunal (adopting a procedure we shall consider shortly) was obliged to answer the question whether the jobs were indeed of equal value. The answer had to be yes or no: there was no 'not proven' option on the ground that the question was too difficult or that the jobs were too different to compare properly. Thus, once an investigation started to look at issues like the training and qualifications required to do the two jobs, it was very likely the nurse's job would be found of at least equal value to the foreman's.

EXAMPLE 2

In a public authority, there were separate pay negotiations for different sections of the workforce represented by different trade unions. As a result there was a job-evaluated pay structure for technical staff and an entirely separate job-evaluated pay structure for clerical and administrative staff. In many instances, the negotiating power of the second union was less, or the market was more competitive for the first, or both, and rates of pay in the second structure were generally less, although it was impossible for anyone to make precise like-for-like comparisons, because they were not doing the same work. Now a woman, graded X under the second structure, could choose whichever man, graded Y under the first, best made her case and argue that her work was of equal value to his. The problem for the employer was that if a tribunal found that X = Y, that had enormous implications for everyone, male or female, graded under the second structure.

The enormous impact predicted in 1983 never happened; the actual number of early cases was remarkably small. Some employers took remedial action to remove the most blatant inequalities; many potential claimants were put off by the tortuous procedure that was provided in the original regulations.

More recently there has been renewed interest in pursuing equal value cases. In part this results from simplifications of the procedure, but also from greater public awareness of the issues of equal pay, assisted no doubt by publicity from CEHR and EOC. You may well find yourself in practice called upon to advise. Cases like the second example raise difficult practical issues for both employers and trade unions; several banks and public health authorities have recently found themselves exposed to very large costs in reconciling pay structures after losing such cases, and the disturbance of established pay relativities often causes great resentment among employees who do not benefit.

The operation of an equality clause established by this third possibility is subject to an escape clause rather wider than that in relation to cases brought under (a) or (b). Here a genuine material factor (GMF) *may* be the kind of closely restricted GMD we considered above: EPA 1970, s. 1(3)(b). There is still very limited guidance from the cases on what may be included in GMF that is excluded from GMD. In *Enderby* v *Frenchay Health Authority* [1994] ICR 112, doubt was expressed by ECJ as to whether market forces constituted a sufficient GMF under art. 141 of the Treaty of Rome to justify a difference in pay between speech therapists and pharmacists. In the early days of the equal value provisions, many cases involved women in jobs where most employees were women, comparing themselves with men in predominantly male jobs. A quarter of a century later such sex-stereotyping is much less common: there are frequently both men and women employed in the claimant's job and also in the comparator job, so that careful scrutiny of any suggested GMF becomes an important part of the tribunal's consideration of the case. A good recent example is *Cumbria County Council* v *Dow (No. 1)* [2008] IRLR 91, where the EAT applied its description of three categories of sex tainting from *Middlesbrough Borough Council* v *Surtees* [2007] ICR 1644, and stressed that the onus lies on the employer to refute prima facie evidence of sex tainting.

6.8 Remedies in relation to equal pay

An employee or former employee may present a claim to the employment tribunal that the equality clause in the contract of employment is being contravened: EPA 1970, s. 2(1). There is a little used provision in s. 2(1A) that enables an employer to seek clarification from the tribunal of the meaning of an equality clause: this is a rare example of the opportunity for an employer to initiate tribunal proceedings.

The ECJ and then the House of Lords considered whether the procedural rules in EPA 1970 complied with art. 141 EC Treaty in *Preston* v *Wolverhampton NHS Trust*, respectively (Case C-78/98) [2000] ICR 961 and (No 2) [2001] UKHL/5, [2002] ICR 217. The rule in s. 2(4) that requires an employee to bring a complaint while still employed or within six months of the ending of employment was held to comply with art. 141 in that it was for the member state to regulate such procedural matters. In the same case, a rule limiting the arrears of pay that could be claimed to two years was held to breach the principle of equivalence and consequently not to comply with art. 141. As a result, the Equal Pay Act 1970 (Amendment) Regulations 2003 were passed and the arrears recoverable are now limited to six years like any other action for breach of contract. However, retrospective claims for up to 20 years are permitted if the employer has concealed necessary information for the claim to be brought, and retrospective claims about pension schemes can go back to 8 April 1976, the date of the ECJ judgment in *Defrenne* v *Sabena* (Case 43/75) [1976] ICR 547.

The burden of proof rests with the applicant in cases brought under the provisions dealing with like work and work rated as equivalent, although there is a suggestion in the '*Danfoss*' case [1989] IRLR 532 that this may conflict with the Equal Pay Directive. However, as with sex discrimination, the evidential burden quickly shifts to the employer to explain if a *prima facie* case of unequal treatment is established.

The procedure in cases brought under the equal value provisions in paragraph (c) of EPA 1970, s. 1(2) was changed by the Equal Pay Act 1970 (Amendment) Regulations 2004 and the Employment Tribunals (Constitution and Rules of Procedure) (Amendment) Regulations 2004. Despite some simplification the procedure remains quite complicated. It is still not operated often, so that many established practitioners have no actual experience of it. We shall therefore deal with it only briefly.

The procedure operates in three stages. At the first stage a full tribunal (not an employment judge sitting alone) has three options:

(a) Where a job evaluation study has ascribed different values to the work of the claimant and the comparator, the tribunal *must* conclude that the work is *not of equal value* unless it has reasonable grounds for suspecting that the study was itself discriminatory or otherwise unreliable.

(b) The tribunal can choose to determine the question of equal value itself.

(c) The tribunal may appoint an independent expert from an ACAS-appointed panel to prepare a report.

If either of the last two options is adopted, the tribunal makes orders setting a timetable for the next stages of the case. There are extensive case management powers with the aim of speeding up equal value cases. If option (c) is adopted, a second stage hearing takes place, also before a full tribunal, to resolve facts in dispute, so as to simplify the task of the independent expert, who must now prepare a report within the time fixed by the tribunal. Finally there is a third stage hearing for the full tribunal to decide whether the claimant's and comparator's jobs are indeed of equal value. If the jobs are of equal value, it is at this stage that any argument from the employer of a GMF will be considered, and the tribunal will decide the outcome and award a remedy. As well as the rules requiring tribunals to set time limits, an indicative timetable for equal value cases is set out in an annex—a total of 37 weeks for cases involving a report from an independent expert and 25 weeks otherwise. These changes may have started to reduce the enormous costs these cases have generally involved until now, and solicitors will not find them such a rarity.

6.9 Part-time workers

Until 2000 part-time workers obtained some protection under SDA 1975 on the basis of the argument that there are significantly more women than men among the part-time workforce. Consequently any rule or practice that treats part-time employees less favourably than full-time employees (without justification—something very difficult to establish) is indirectly discriminatory on grounds of sex. The key case that established that rule in the ECJ was *Bilka Kaufhaus GmbH* v *Weber von Hartz* [1987] ICR 110. In this country it was followed by *R* v *Secretary of State for Employment, ex parte Equal Opportunities Commission* [1994] ICR 317, which extended the rule to statutory rights such as the right to complain of unfair dismissal.

Now the PTW Regs 2000 (see **6.1.1.6** above) have provided a statutory basis of protection. The regulations bring into force the Part-time Workers Directive (97/81/EC), which incorporates a 'framework agreement' between European trade unions and employers' associations.

Part-time workers have the right under PTW Regs 2000 not to be treated less favourably than their employer treats a comparable full-time worker. There thus needs to be a comparison with a full-time worker, defined generally as one who is employed by the same employer under the same type of contract, engaged in the same or broadly similar work and working or based at the same establishment as the part-time worker. This language is reminiscent of the kind of comparison involved in cases under EPA 1970 (see **6.7** above). In this case, conditions of employment have to be applied pro rata. The key point under PTWRegs as distinct from the previous position under SDA 1975 is that the comparison is between a part-time and a full-time worker; the sex of either is irrelevant. In *Matthews* v *Kent & Medway Towns Fire Authority* [2006] UKHL 8, [2006] ICR 365 the issue arose whether part-time ('retained') firefighters could use PTWRegs 2000 to claim parity of pension provision with full-time firefighters. It divided their Lordships three to two. The majority disagreed with the employment tribunal, the EAT and the Court of Appeal who had all held that they did not do the same or broadly similar work: it was necessary to examine similarities in the work the two groups did and not (as the lower courts had done) to concentrate on the differences. The question was remitted to the employment tribunal for reconsideration, and the case demonstrates how fine a point this can be.

There are circumstances where the pro rata principle laid down by reg. 5 (3) is not straightforward. In *McMenemy* v *Capita Business Services Ltd* [2007] CSIH 25, [2007] IRLR 400, a part-time employee who worked on Wednesdays, Thursdays, and Fridays claimed that he was disadvantaged because more bank holidays fall on Mondays than on any other day. The Court of Session approved the reasoning of he employment tribunal and the EAT that he had indeed suffered a disadvantage, but that it flowed from the fact that he did not work on Mondays, not from his part-time status, as a full-time employee who worked from Tuesday to Saturday would have been treated similarly. This basis of finding that there had been no unlawful discrimination is of course specific to the facts, as in many employments it would be impossible to find such full-time comparators. Many employers in fact approach such issues on the 'gain-on-the-swings, lose-on-the-roundabouts' principle of overall fairness and the decision does not consider whether that is acceptable. In *Sharma* v *Manchester City Council* [2008] ICR 623, the EAT accepted that the employment tribunal had only to be satisfied that part-time status was the 'real reason' for less favourable treatment for a claimant to succeed; there was no requirement for the claimant to prove that it was the sole reason, despite the wording of the Directive.

Workers can complain to an employment tribunal if the employer treats them less favourably, or dismisses them or subjects them to a detriment for a reason related to the exercise of rights under the regulations. There is a defence available to the employer if the unfavourable treatment can be justified on objective grounds. Compensation can be awarded but does not include injury to feelings. Workers are entitled to a written statement of reasons for less favourable treatment.

The initial surge of over 10,500 complaints to the employment tribunals during 2000–01 after the Regulations came into force, most of them about the pensions rights of part-timers, has not been maintained since. While ERA 1999, s. 20 made provision for the issue of codes of practice about part-time work, none has yet been produced.

6.10 Fixed-term workers

The Fixed-Term Regs 2002 (see **6.1.1.7**) are also the result of a European Directive, in this case the Fixed Term Work Directive 99/70/EC, and follow a very similar pattern to PTWRegs 2000. It is unlawful to treat a fixed-term employee less favourably than a comparable permanent employee. The pro rata principle applies again. Less favourable treatment may be justified objectively and there is express provision that it may be justified for one condition of employment to be less favourable, if, taken overall, conditions of the fixed-term worker are as good as those of the permanent person—reg. 4. Fixed-term workers are entitled to a written statement of the reasons why they are less favourably treated, and they also have the right to be informed by the employer of available permanent vacancies.

When the employer failed to renew a fixed term contract in *Department of Work and Pensions* v *Webley* [2004] EWCA Civ 1745, [2005] ICR 577, that omission was held not to be less favourable treatment within the meaning of these regulations.

The fact that a fixed-term contract contains a provision allowing it to be terminated earlier by notice does not deny the worker the protection of the regulations—*Allen* v *National Australia Group Europe Ltd* [2004] IRLR 847.

People who have been employed for four years or more under successive fixed-term contracts have the right under reg. 8 to be treated as permanent employees unless the employer can justify objectively the continued use of fixed-term contracts. Such objective justification requires specific factors—*Adeneler* v *Ellinikos Organismos Galaktos* (Case C-212/04) [2006] IRLR 716.

6.11   Disability discrimination

As we noted at the start of the chapter, DDA 1995 adds an additional category of unlawful discrimination. The decided cases show that we must have regard not only to the provisions of the statute, but also to the code, the guidance and the statutory regulations.

There are some significant differences between the framework of DDA 1995 and that of RRA 1976 or SDA 1975. The aspects we shall need to cover are these:

(a) the scope of DDA 1995;

(b) the meaning of discrimination under DDA 1995;

(c) the employer's duty to make 'reasonable adjustments';

(d) remedies.

It seemed to take a long while after the employment aspects of DDA 1995 were brought into effect for many significant cases to reach the EAT and the higher courts, so that we were forced to rely on the statutory provisions alone. Now, however, there are quite a few decided cases, several of them taking the trouble to set out a sequence of questions that need to be addressed in interpreting the statutory language.

Some readers may find it helpful to have the key issues under DDA 1995, incorporating the 2004 amendments, set out in the form of **Figure 6.1** (overleaf). Inevitably it summarises very briefly the material in the text, and it may be useful to keep one finger in this page to refer to the diagram while considering the detail in the sections that follow, especially the five kinds of discrimination set out in **6.11.2**.

6.11.1   The scope of DDA 1995

6.11.1.1   Differences between the scope of DDA 1995 and the other rules

Since we have already considered the scope of RRA 1976 and SDA 1975, a convenient starting point in defining the scope of DDA 1995 is to note some main points of difference. We shall then move on to look at the statutory definition of disability.

(a) While both RRA 1976 and SDA 1975 apply to all employers irrespective of the number employed, there was a specific exclusion under DDA 1995 for those employing fewer than 15 but it was removed from 1 October 2004 by the Disability Discrimination Act 1995 (Amendment) Regulations 2003.

(b) Subject to the point we mentioned at **6.2.5** above, both RRA 1976 and SDA 1975 apply (in relation to the aspects that concern us) only to job applicants and to employees. By contrast, the definition in 3.68(1) of DDA 1995 expressly includes anyone subject to a contract personally to do any work. It therefore covers the self-employed and other sub-contractors—see *Burton* v *Higham* [2003] IRLR 257, but not ex-employees—*Jones* v *3M Healthcare Ltd* [2002] ICR 341. Further, there is provision in s. 4B, s. 4C, s. 6A and s. 7A to extend the rules to contract workers, office holders, partners, and barristers respectively.

(c) We noted that SDA 1975 speaks of a comparison brought by a woman with a man, but applies equally to one brought by a man with a woman. There is a similarly reciprocal approach in RRA 1976: a member of any racial group could complain of discrimination compared with a member of any other group. The comparison under DDA 1995 is in one direction only: a disabled person can complain of being discriminated against, but a non-disabled person cannot. So the employer is permitted to discriminate 'positively'—i.e., in favour of disabled people.

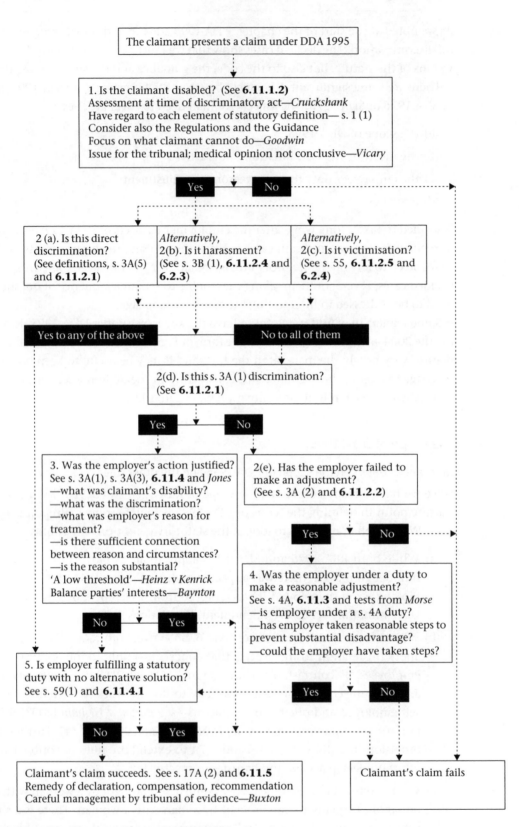

Figure 6.1 Key questions under DDA 1995.

(d) We noted certain exceptions under RRA 1976 and SDA 1975 where the nature of the job required a particular kind of person. There are no equivalent exceptions under DDA 1995. The only exception remaining after 1 October 2004 is the armed forces.

6.11.1.2   The meaning of 'disabled'

Under s. 1 of DDA 1995 a person is defined as disabled who

has a physical or mental impairment which has a substantial and long-term adverse effect on his ability to carry out normal day-to-day activities.

Each element of that definition merits closer attention.

(a) The impairment may be *physical or mental*. The conventional view of disability probably emphasises physical disability, but DDA 1995 also protects those with mental illnesses and those with learning difficulties. From December 2005 the requirement for mental illness to be 'clinically well recognised' was removed under DDA 2005, but some kind of medical evidence is usually still required. There is no requirement for medical evidence about learning difficulties; other evidence will suffice as in *Dunham* v *Ashford Windows* [2005] IRLR 608. Where the effects of the disability are plain, medical diagnosis of the cause may not be necessary, as in *Millar* v *Inland Revenue Commissioners* [2005] IRLR 112.

(b) The effect must be *substantial*. This term is further defined in the guidance issued under s. 2 as meaning more than minor or trivial. That is undoubtedly a lower threshold than might have been expected from the use of the term 'substantial' on its own. In *Kapadia* v *London Borough of Lambeth* [2000] IRLR 699 the Court of Appeal held that uncontested medical evidence on the degree of effect is generally conclusive. In *Woodrup* v *London Borough of Southwark* [2002] EWCA Civ 1716, [2003] IRLR 111, the applicant claimed she was disabled under the rule in para. 6(1) of sch. 1 that requires a condition to be assessed as if medical treatment were not being given. The Court of Appeal supported the rejection by the employment tribunal of that contention on the ground that she had produced no medical evidence in support. However, the EAT, in *Vicary* v *British Telecommunications plc* [1999] IRLR 680 and in *Abadeh* v *British Telecommunications plc* [2001] ICR 156, has emphasised that it is a matter of fact for the employment tribunal to decide, and medical evidence must not usurp the tribunal's function.

(c) The effect must be *long-term*. This is also further defined in the guidance as meaning likely to last for 12 months or more, or for the rest of the person's life. Furthermore, past disability also brings the person within the definition. So, those once qualifying as disabled remain protected by DDA 1995 for the rest of their lives.

(d) The effect must be on *normal day-to-day activities*. A person is not regarded as disabled if suffering an impairment which merely limits exceptionally strenuous activities or only specific kinds of job. However, this does not exclude impairments such as an asthmatic response which may be aggravated by specialist work—*Cruickshank* as above.

(e) Anyone with cancer, HIV infection or multiple sclerosis is deemed to be disabled, irrespective of the usual tests above of the extent of the effect on normal day-to-day activities. The Secretary of State has the power to make an order to exclude prescribed cancers, but has not done so yet. There has been speculation that he may exclude certain relatively straightforwardly treated skin cancers.

(f) The Disability Discrimination (Meaning of Disability) Regulations 1996 list some *specific exclusions*. Not many statutory instruments manage to link kleptomania, hayfever, and body piercing. Pub quiz enthusiasts might take note! However, the exclusions are interpreted narrowly: thus addiction to alcohol is excluded, but depression is not, even if there is a causal link with alcoholism—*Power* v *Panasonic Ltd* [2003] IRLR 151. In *Edmund Nuttall Ltd* v *Butterfield* [2005] IRLR 751 the claimant had indecently exposed himself, but it was argued that his exhibitionism (one of the exclusions) was the consequence of depression. The EAT laid down the rule that the material issue was the actual reason for the offending behaviour, whether the excluded condition or the legitimate impairment.

An issue that has caused some controversy is the question when an employment tribunal must assess whether a claimant met that statutory definition of disability: is it on facts known at the time of the alleged discriminatory act, or is it at the date of a tribunal hearing? Those who preferred the latter often relied on an 1891 authority dealing with the assessment of damages, but this led to the absurd result that the employer (and therefore any solicitor providing advice) could not know at the relevant time whether the claimant was indeed disabled or not. The uncertainty was resolved in *Richmond Adult Community College* v *McDougall* [2008] EWCA Civ 4, [2008] ICR 431. The tribunal must base its conclusion on evidence available at the time the employer decided on taking the action that is now alleged to be discriminatory.

The combined effect of those elements of the definition has been to include many more people than most practitioners would probably have expected. In particular, the tribunals have taken a broad approach to depression and other mental illnesses, so that many employers have found themselves defending complaints of unfair dismissal against applicants they had never regarded as disabled. In *Goodwin* v *The Patent Office* [1999] ICR 302, the applicant was a paranoid schizophrenic but managed to care for himself, largely satisfactorily, at home. The employment tribunal had held that the effect of his impairment was not substantial and he was consequently not disabled. The EAT disagreed and in doing so gave lengthy and detailed guidance for the tribunals on how to approach the question of whether an applicant is disabled. The proper approach was to focus on things G could not do or could only do with difficulty and not merely on things he could do, an approach also adopted in *Leonard* v *Southern Derbyshire Chamber of Commerce* [2001] IRLR 19.

In *Coleman* v *Attridge Law* (Case C-303/06) [2008] IRLR 722 the ECJ decided that the Directive required an employee who was not disabled but who was the carer for her disabled child to have a remedy when she suffered direct discrimination or harassment.

6.11.2 The meaning of discrimination

The definitions of discrimination under DDA 1995 were substantially amended by the Disability Discrimination Act 1995 (Amendment) Regulations 2003 with effect from 1 October 2004, implementing Directive 2000/78. As a result we now have five kinds of discrimination under DDA 1995:

(a) the 'standard' case under s. 3A (1);

(b) failure under s. 3A (2) to take steps to prevent disadvantage;

(c) direct discrimination under s. 3A(5);

(d) harassment under s. 3B (1); and

(e) victimisation under s. 55.

We shall discover more about the significance of the distinctions as we look at the five categories in more detail. We shall restrict our consideration to the most common case of an employee or job applicant—hence the reference in (a) above to s. 3A (1). We have already noted at **6.9.1.1** (b) above that there are separate, largely equivalent, provisions to cover contract workers, office holders, partners in a partnership, and barristers, but those special cases lie outside the scope of this book.

6.11.2.1 Discrimination under s. 3A(1)

This first kind of discrimination is unchanged by the 2004 amendments and earlier authorities can therefore be regarded as still of relevance. It is in this sense that we referred to it above as standard. Under s. 3A(1) an employer discriminates against a disabled person if, for a reason which relates to the person's disability, he treats that person less favourably than he treats or would treat others to whom the reason does not apply. There is then a defence for the employer who can show that the treatment in question was justified, as we shall discuss at **6.11.4** below.

We have already noted when discussing a comparable provision at **6.2.1** that the employer's intention is irrelevant under RRA 1976 and SDA 1975: it is the objective fact of less favourable treatment that matters. In relation to DDA 1995 a connected issue arises in a different form. Can the employer be said to treat a disabled person less favourably *for a reason which relates to the person's disability* if the evidence is that the employer did not know the person was disabled?

In examining that question the courts have had their attention drawn to the absence of any reference to the employer's knowledge in s. 3A(1), an omission that contrasts with the specific provision under s. 4A that an employer is not under a duty to make adjustments in relation to a disability that is not known. In an early case, *O'Neill* v *Symm & Co. Ltd* [1998] ICR 481, the EAT ignored that omission and held that the employers' dismissal of Miss O'Neill was not unlawful discrimination under DDA 1995. The employers knew only that she suffered from a viral illness and not (as subsequently emerged) that it was more serious, so that she was in fact disabled. In *H. J. Heinz Co. Ltd* v *Kenrick* [2000] ICR 491 the EAT reviewed that decision in the light of the judgment of the Court of Appeal in *Clark* v *Novacold* [1999] ICR 951 and effectively decided it was wrong: the test was objective and not subjective. The employer dismissed Mr Kenrick for excessive absence and therefore clearly knew of his symptoms; it was immaterial that a medical diagnosis of chronic fatigue syndrome only came later.

Another area of difficulty is the proper comparison. In *Clark* v *Novacold* [1999] ICR 951, Mr Clark was dismissed for long-term sickness absence and his incapability resulted from a disability. Should he be compared with a non-disabled person with comparable absence (someone it would actually be very difficult to find) or with someone who because not disabled had not been absent? The EAT took the first of those options, but the case was then appealed. The Court of Appeal contrasted the language of DDA 1995 with RRA 1976 and SDA 1975 and concluded that it did not require the same like-for-like comparison, a conclusion later approved by the House of Lords in *Archibald* v *Fife Country Council* [2004] UKHL 32, [2004] IRLR 651—see below. Others without C's disability would not have been absent to the same extent and would not have been dismissed. So his treatment was less favourable.

The *Clark* v *Novacold* rule, under which the test is one of causation and a comparative approach is not required, has now been applied consistently for some years and many practitioners were surprised recently to see it overturned by the House of Lords in a case not related to employment, *London Borough of Lewisham* v *Malcolm* [2008] UKHL 43, [2008] IRLR 700. Malcolm was a schizophrenic who sublet a council flat in breach of his tenancy agreement and went to live elsewhere, and he claimed that he did so because of his disability as he had not been taking his medication at the relevant time. The council served notice to quit. Their Lordships (Baroness Hale dissenting) decided that the right comparator in deciding whether his treatment was less favourable and therefore discriminatory was a non-disabled tenant who had similarly breached the tenancy agreement and who would have been evicted too, and not (as the *Clark* v *Novacold* rule would require) a non-disabled tenant who did not therefore have the same reason to breach the agreement and in fact was not in breach. The council's appeal succeeded and their Lordships held that *Clark* v *Novacold* had been wrongly decided. The decision may arguably be in some conflict with *Archibald*, but the overruling of *Clark* v *Novacold* is likely to have a considerable effect on the operation of DDA 1995, which, as we go to press, it is difficult to gauge. Further legislation is a possibility.

6.11.2.2   Failure to take steps to prevent disadvantage

As we shall see shortly at **6.11.3**, the employer is under a duty to take reasonable steps to prevent a disabled person from being placed at a substantial disadvantage in defined circumstances. The side-head in the statute, both now and prior to the 2004 amendments, refers to the employer's duty to make adjustments, and despite some possible broadening as a result of the amendments the duty is still widely referred to as a duty to make reasonable adjustments. Where such a duty exists and the employer has failed to make reasonable adjustments, that omission itself constitutes unlawful disability discrimination under s. 3A(2). This is a concept of discrimination without parallel in RRA 1976 or SDA 1975.

Until the 2004 amendments, the defence of justification applied here as well as to the category of discrimination we have just been discussing at **6.11.2.1**. It led to some logical nonsense: if the tribunal concluded that in all the circumstances the employer was reasonably under a duty to make adjustments, how could it then find that the employer was also justified in failing to comply with the duty? The illogicality has been removed and under the 2004 amendments the defence no longer applies to this form of discrimination. Some of the older cases must be read in the light of this change, as we shall see at **6.11.4**.

6.11.2.3   Direct discrimination

The concept of direct discrimination under DDA 1995, s. 3A(5) is introduced for the first time by the 2004 amendments. It does not simply mean all discrimination that is not indirect in the sense we have encountered at **6.2.2** under RRA 1976 or SDA 1975. Rather it is narrowly defined as arising when the employer, on the grounds of a person's disability, treats that person less favourably than he would treat someone without the particular disability, whose relevant circumstances including their abilities are the same as, or not materially different from, the disabled person's. The narrow definition *on the grounds of* must be contrasted with the broader *which relates to* under the first case above, **6.11.2.1**. This definition includes some element of the employer's reasoning or motive, even if not always deliberate intention. The significance of this separate category is that it is not subject to the defence of justification that we shall encounter at **6.11.4** below. A disabled claimant who can prove to a tribunal direct discrimination under this definition will have a successful ground of complaint, whatever justification the employer argues.

In fact there have been very few cases where claimants have successfully claimed direct discrimination. We know of one employment tribunal case that has attracted some attention—*Tudor* v *Spen Corner Veterinary Centre Ltd*, Manchester employment tribunal, Case 2404211/05. The employee was a veterinary nursing assistant and receptionist who suffered a stroke which left her blind, and it was not known whether her sight would recover. The employer dismissed her and declined to hear a grievance she raised under the statutory procedure until she completed a questionnaire. The employment tribunal found that she had been treated less favourably than a hypothetical comparator employee with a broken leg and that this was *on the ground of* her disability. Among other claims she made to the tribunal she therefore succeeded in one of direct discrimination. By contrast in *High Quality Lifestyles Ltd* v *Watts*, [2006] IRLR 850 the EAT found that the dismissal on health and safety grounds of an HIV-positive care worker, working with people with learning disabilities where scratching and biting sometimes happened, was *related to his disability* but not *on the grounds of* disability. Someone with another serious and infectious condition might also have been dismissed; he was dismissed because of the risk and not because he was HIV-positive. So there was discrimination under s. 3A (1), but not direct discrimination.

6.11.2.4   Harassment

The concept of harassment under the amended DDA 1995 is defined similarly to that under RRA 1976, s. 3A, and under the 2005 amendments to SDA 1975. We can expect similar results, as discussed at **6.2.3** above.

6.11.2.5   Victimisation

Victimisation is a long-standing concept under DDA 1995, s. 55 and is unaffected by the 2005 amendments. It is defined in similar terms to those in RRA 1976, s. 2 and SDA 1975, s. 4. While we know of no significant cases under DDA 1995, the authorities we discussed at **6.2.4** above probably apply here too.

6.11.3   **The employer's duty to make reasonable adjustments**

This duty arises under s. 4A where a disabled person (an employee or an applicant for a job) is placed at a substantial disadvantage compared with non-disabled people because of some provision, criterion or practice (PCP) applied by the employer or because of any physical feature of the premises. The employer is under a duty to take such steps as it is reasonable to take in all the circumstances to prevent that effect.

Further explanation of the kinds of steps that are envisaged is provided. In s. 18B(2) there is a list of examples which includes making adjustments to premises, altering working hours, providing an interpreter and much else. In s. 18B(1) there is a list of factors that may be taken into account in deciding whether a particular step is reasonable. Both lists are then subject to much further expansion in the code of practice.

Some of the authorities on the approach an employment tribunal must adopt in deciding whether an employer has met the duty under s. 4A predate the 2004 amendments and must now be viewed with some care. In *Environment Agency* v *Rowan* [2008] ICR 218 the EAT laid down under the current law that the proper sequence of matters to be identified is this:

(a) the PCP applied by or on behalf of an employer; or

(b) the physical feature of premises occupied by the employer;

(c) the identity of non-disabled comparators (where appropriate); and

(d) the nature and extent of the substantial disadvantage suffered by the claimant—looking at the overall picture.

Without going through that process, according to the EAT, an employment tribunal cannot properly make findings of fact that an employer has failed to comply with s. 3A (2).

Just as the meaning of 'disabled' under DDA 1995 is much wider than the conventional view of physical disability, so it is important not to think of adjustments as limited to physical steps such as providing wheelchair access. In *Archibald* v *Fife County Council* [2004] UKHL 32, [2004] ICR 954 the applicant was left almost unable to walk by complications from minor surgery and could not carry out her duties as a roadsweeper. The House of Lords held that the duty to make adjustments was triggered when the employee was put at a substantial disadvantage because her disability made it impossible for her to perform the main or essential function of her job, and she was therefore at risk of dismissal, a risk that would not have arisen for a non-disabled employee. The employer had investigated transferring her to a different job (which the code of practice requires), but their Lordships felt it was insufficient for this to be on the basis of merely giving her the opportunity to participate in competitive interviews. Applying those principles in *Southampton City College* v *Randall* [2006] IRLR 18, the EAT held that the employer's duty extended to devising a new job for the complainant lecturer whose voice had been damaged by the need to shout above the noise of a machine shop.

An example where a practical limit was placed on the employer's duty is *O'Hanlon* v *Commissioners for HM Revenue & Customs* [2007] EWCA Civ 283, [2007] ICR 1359: it would be very rare for the duty to extend to providing longer periods of sick pay to a disabled employee than to one who was not disabled.

The employer is not required to make adjustments in connexion with any disability he did not know about and could not reasonably be expected to know about—s. 4A(3). The scope of that exception was examined by the EAT in *Ridout* v *TC Group* [1998] IRLR 628. Morison J held that the employer was not put under any duty to undertake extensive enquiries of a job applicant about the suitability of an interview room, merely because of the mention on an application form of a rare form of epilepsy that in fact made her sensitive to bright light. This is very much a decision on the particular facts and the EAT upheld the employment tribunal. It may be dangerous for employers to assume that they do not need to react to more obvious indications of disability or to investigate further.

The duty to take steps to prevent disadvantage applies to job-related matters. In *Kenny* v *Hampshire Constabulary* [1999] ICR 27 the applicant needed personal help to use the toilet and this was held to fall outside the duty.

Some of the cases we have just mentioned relate to the pre-2004 wording of the equivalent of the current s. 4A, relating to *arrangements made* by the employer rather than (as now) to a *PCP* but we believe the principles they establish still apply. However, as *Environment Agency* v *Rowan* (above) makes plain, it is important when basing advice on any of the older cases to check whether the difference in wording matters in the particular circumstances.

6.11.4   Justification by the employer

An act that would otherwise constitute discrimination under s. 3A(1) ceases to do so if the employer can show that it is *justified*. This term is defined in DDA 1995 as meaning a reason that is both *material to the circumstances of the particular case* and *substantial*. The code of practice gives some examples. Failure to appoint a person with a disfiguring skin condition to a job that involves modelling cosmetics, for example, is said to satisfy both parts of the definition of 'justified'. Not to appoint the same person to a clerical post because other employees or customers might feel uncomfortable is unlikely to be a substantial reason.

In the early days of DDA 1995, tribunals seemed reluctant to accept employers' arguments of justification. However, as the more recent cases we have discussed make it relatively easier for workers to establish that they are disabled, or that treatment they have received is discriminatory, so the balance seems to have shifted in the employer's favour about what constitutes justification. In *H. J. Heinz Co. Ltd* v *Kenrick* [2000] ICR 491, Lindsay J described the statutory test as a very low threshold. The Court of Appeal quoted his comment without disapproval in *Post Office* v *Jones* [2001] EWCA Civ 558; [2001] ICR 805. Here the employee was a delivery driver who became diabetic, and the justification depended on medical evidence of the risks presented by an insulin-requiring driver. The Court of Appeal ruled that the function of the employment tribunal was merely to assess the employer's reasoning against the statutory definition and not to substitute their own view, even if presented with conflicting medical evidence. Arden LJ set out the sequence of questions that were summarised in box 3 of the diagram at **Figure 6.1** above:

- What was the claimant's disability?
- What was the nature of the discrimination?
- What was the employer's reason for treating the claimant in this way?
- Is there sufficient connexion between the reason and the circumstances?
- Is the reason substantial?

The process of answering those questions may involve the presentation at the tribunal hearing of expert evidence not available to the employer at the time—see *Surrey Police* v *Marshall* [2002] IRLR 843.

In *Baynton* v *Saurus General Engineers Ltd* [2000] ICR 375, the EAT suggested justification required a 'balancing exercise' between the interests of the employer and the disabled employee. In the particular case, the fact that the disabled employee was unable to do his job was insufficient, as the employers had not warned him of the risk of dismissal or found out the up-to-date medical position before dismissing him.

6.11.4.1   Conflict with any statutory duty

In addition to the general defence for the employer of justification under s. 3A(1) and s. 3A(3), which applies only to the category of discrimination under s. 3A(1), there is a more specific defence which applies to all categories of discrimination and which exists under s. 59 of DDA 1995. This rule states simply that nothing in DDA 1995 makes unlawful anything done in pursuance of an enactment, a statutory instrument, or any requirement under one of them, or anything done in pursuance of national security. The circumstance in which the rule is most likely to arise in the employment relationship is in connexion with requirements of health and safety. The Health and Safety at Work etc. Act 1974, and the many sets of regulations made under it impose many obligations on employers, and s. 59(1) means that those requirements take precedence over DDA 1995.

The rule came to be explored by the EAT in *Lane Group plc* v *Farmiloe* [2004] PIQR 324, where an employee with a skin condition, psoriasis, was unable to wear protective footwear provided by the employer. The local authority responsible for enforcing safety regulations insisted that the employee wore the protective footwear; the employee said he could not do so and, after the employer unsuccessfully went to some lengths to find an alternative solution, he was dismissed. He argued before the tribunal that the employer was under a duty to make an adjustment, and to approach the enforcing authority to make an exception in his case. The EAT accepted that the employer was obliged to seek suitable protection for this employee and (if it could not be found) to seek alternative employment for him but if neither was possible, so that dismissal was the only option, the employer was protected by s. 59(1). In accepting that s. 59 required that health and safety legislation takes precedence over disability discrimination, the EAT imposed the proviso that employers must take all reasonable steps to accommodate the individual worker. In many cases this requires an individual risk assessment.

6.11.5   Remedies under DDA 1995

The remedy for any infringement of the employment provisions of DDA 1995 is by way of a claim in the employment tribunal, which must be brought within three months of the act complained of. If the tribunal finds the complaint well founded, it must use such of the following remedies as it considers just and equitable:

(a) a declaration of the rights of the claimant and the employer;

(b) an award of compensation, with no statutory limit, and including an award for injury to feelings; and

(c) a recommendation of action the employer should take to alleviate the claimant's problem.

According to the EAT in *Buxton* v *Equinox Design Ltd* [1999] ICR 269, the assessment of compensation in disability discrimination cases may require careful management by the tribunal and medical evidence of the applicant's prognosis. If the tribunal issues a recommendation and the employer fails without justification to comply, the amount of compensation may be increased.

The overlap with dismissal actions is dealt with in **Chapter 10** (particularly at **10.9.6.4**).

6.12   Age discrimination

We must now consider the newest head of discrimination which (as we noted at **6.1.1.9**) took effect under the Age Regs 2006 on 1 October 2006. The impact of the new regulations is broad: they affect many other aspects of employment law, so that a rule denying those over the age of 65 the right to complain of unfair dismissal has been removed, as we shall see in **Chapter 10**, and the rules regarding statutory redundancy payments have had to be changed, as discussed in **Chapter 11**. The regulations also impinge on many employment practices: employers have often favoured younger recruits when a job requires expensive training, and many companies provided benefits like additional holidays that depended on length of service, indirectly favouring older workers. Provisions for retirement from most jobs have required some revision or at least reconsideration. There are also some complicated rules about the inter-relationship between these regulations and the rules of pension schemes, but they lie outside the scope of this book.

We shall find that much of the structure of the Age Regs 2006 looks very like that of RRA 1976 or SDA 1975, but their wide impact has required very different rules about exemptions and exceptions.

6.12.1   Scope of the Age Regs 2006

Under reg. 7 the regulations prohibit discrimination against 'persons' who may in fact be employees or job applicants, but 'employee' is defined as in DDA 1995 to include anyone subject to a contract to do any work. So the regulations cover many self-employed people and sub-contractors. In addition there are specific regulations as in DDA 1995 to cover the cases of contract workers, office-holders and other special kinds of employment. In respect of the exceptions dealing with service-related benefits and life assurance, they refer to 'workers' but the distinction seems unimportant in view of the broad definition given to employee.

6.12.2   The meaning of 'discrimination' under Age Regs 2006

The regulations reproduce definitions of discrimination very similar to those under RRA 1976 and SDA 1975, although the presentation may look slightly different.

Direct discrimination is defined in reg. 3(1)(a) as occurring when person 'A' (i.e., the employer in most circumstances) treats another person 'B' less favourably on grounds of age (or apparent age) than other people are treated or would be treated.

Indirect discrimination is defined in reg. 3(1)(b) as occurring when A applies to B a provision, criterion or practice (PCP), which is applied to people of a different age group from B, which puts or would put B's age group at a particular disadvantage compared with them, and which actually puts B at that disadvantage.

In both cases B's circumstances must be the same as the comparator's, or the cases must not be materially different. Unlike RRA 1976 and SDA 1975, these regulations permit a defence of justification to *both* kinds of discrimination, but, as in the other statutes, the defence requires the employer to show the treatment or the PCP was a *proportionate means* of achieving a *legitimate aim*. We shall return to the topic at **6.12.4.1** when we consider defences and exceptions more generally.

Discrimination by way of victimisation and harassment are included with similar definitions to RRA 1976 and SDA 1975. There is also a similar provision to the other statutes making it a discriminatory act to treat someone less favourably because that person has failed to carry out an instruction to discriminate unlawfully.

6.12.3   The circumstances of unlawful age discrimination

Discrimination in employment and training is mainly covered in reg. 7. Regulation 7(1) covers the recruitment process—the 'arrangements' for deciding whom to appoint, the terms of any job offer and the failure to offer a job to a particular person. Regulation 7(2) covers treatment during employment—in terms and conditions of employment, in promotion, transfer or training, or in dismissal or subjecting the person to some other detriment. Subject to the exceptions, discriminatory treatment in any of those circumstances is unlawful if on grounds of age.

6.12.4   Defences and exceptions to age discrimination

The extensive list of possible defences or exceptions to the regulations seem likely to make this one of the most interesting practical aspects of their operation.

6.12.4.1   Justification

We noted at **6.12.2** that Age Regs 2006 permit a defence of justification to both direct and indirect discrimination, if the employer can show that less favourable treatment or the application of a PCP was a *proportionate means* of achieving a *legitimate aim*. That formula is of course familiar from RRA 1976 and SDA 1975, although it only applies to indirect discrimination under those statutes. Experience suggests that the employment tribunals have been reluctant to accept cost-saving as a sufficient aim on its own, and we expect the same approach to be adopted here. Thus, for example, the employer who wants to argue that there is a better prospect of a return from the investment in training if a 22-year-old is appointed to a vacancy than a 52-year-old will probably find that the tribunal does not regard this as proportionate. Indeed, there is a strong argument that any other finding undermines the whole purpose of legislation about age discrimination. It might be different if the employer could show a particular or exceptional need to contain cost, and the disadvantaged applicant had a much shorter period left before a normal retirement age of 65.

6.12.4.2 Genuine occupational qualification

Under reg. 8 there is an exception, as in the other statutes, if a characteristic related to age is a genuine and proportionate requirement of the job. We imagine this will arise only rarely.

6.12.4.3 Statutory authority

Under reg. 27 there is an exception if an act that would otherwise be unlawful discrimination is done to comply with some statutory provision. The equivalent provision of DDA 1995 has been used where the statutory requirement related to health and safety at work; it is possible the same issue could arise here, but it is difficult to imagine how, save in very exceptional circumstances. We must await some cases.

There is a separate rule in reg. 31 that provides an exception where the employer pays the appropriate different levels of the national minimum wage to people of different ages.

6.12.4.4 Retirement

While these regulations were under discussion before a final form was produced, one of the most difficult aspects was the treatment of retirement. The compromise that emerged from the consultations permits employers to continue to operate a normal retirement age of 65 or more but does not allow them to force anyone to retire any younger than 65—reg. 30 (2).

The compromise has not satisfied everyone and a challenge is being referred to the ECJ in *R (on the application of Incorporated Trustee of the National Council for Ageing)* v *Secretary of State for Trade and Industry* [2006] EWHC 3723 (Admin), (Case C-388/07), widely known as the *Heyday* case. The broad rule is said to lack objective justification and to be in breach of the Directive. A hearing took place in the ECJ on 2 July 2008 and the Advocate General gave his opinion on 23 September 2008, finding in favour of the UK government. A final decision is not expected until 2009. In *Palacios de la Villa* v *Cortefiel Servicios SA* (Case C-411/05), [2007] IRLR 989 the ECJ held that a Spanish law permitting compulsory retirement was not in breach of the Directive. Although the circumstances are not identical it looks likely that the UK default age will remain in place.

Employers are permitted not to recruit people over the age of 65, or normal retirement age if it is greater, without the candidate rejected having any right to claim unlawful discrimination—reg.7 (4).

Under Sch. 6, employers must operate a procedure for anyone they wish to retire. The steps are as follows:

- Between 6 and 12 months before employees are due to retire the employer must send a notification informing them of the fact and notifying them of their right to request to continue working.

- The employee may make such a request.
- The employer must consider the request at a meeting.
- If the request is refused, the employee may appeal.
- The employee has the right to be accompanied at both meeting and appeal.
- The employer may refuse the request, and the employee has no redress provided the procedure has been complied with.
- If the procedure is not complied with, the employee may complain to an employment tribunal, which (if they uphold the complaint) may award compensation of up to eight weeks' pay.

6.12.4.5   Positive action

With the exception of DDA 1995, which gives rights to disabled people but does not permit others to draw comparisons with those who are disabled, we have already noted that positive action is generally not permitted under the other heads of discrimination, especially RRA 1976 and SDA 1975. Preferential treatment of one sex or one racial group is always unlawful discrimination against the other sex or another racial group. Under reg. 29 the employer is expressly permitted to provide training or some encouragement to people of a particular age or age group if they seem to be at a disadvantage compared with others.

6.12.4.6   Length of service

It is at least arguable that differential treatment based on length of service is capable of being justified on the basis we have already discussed. So the fact the regulations list this as a separate exception indicates that it is intended to have some special status.

Under reg. 32 there is no separate need for an employer to justify a difference of treatment as a result of a difference in length of service between two workers if the disadvantaged worker has service of five years or less. The difference can relate to any benefit other than one relating to the termination of employment, and length of service can be measured in terms of total service (under the usual statutory formula) or service at a particular level.

Where the disadvantaged worker's service exceeds five years, it must reasonably appear to the employer that the use of length of service in this way fulfils a business need of the undertaking, e.g., encouraging loyalty or motivation or rewarding experience—reg. 32(2). This formula suggests that it is the belief of the employer that is paramount, rather than any objective test of the business need, but the employer's view must be reasonably based.

There has still been relatively little guidance from the courts on the tests employment tribunals should apply in assessing employers' arguments of justification. In both *MacCulloch* v *Imperial Chemical Industries plc* EAT 0119/08 and *Loxley* v *BAE Systems Land Systems (Munitions and Ordnance) Ltd* EAT 0156/08 the EAT had to examine findings by employment tribunals that age-related differences in contractual redundancy terms were justified. (See also **11.4.8.2**.) In the first case the tribunal had been entitled to conclude that the differences related to a legitimate aim, but the tribunal had failed properly to consider the other important question—whether the means was proportionate. In the second case, which dealt with pension arrangements in circumstances of redundancy, the tribunal had focussed on pension issues and not enough on the redundancy. The requirement for detailed examination of proportionality in *MacCulloch* suggests that some employers may have difficulty in justifying differential holiday arrangements that sometimes reward employees for lengths of service very much in excess of the five-year period.

6.12.4.7   Redundancy payments

We shall mention at **11.4.8.1** the changes the regulations make to the scheme of statutory redundancy payments and at **11.4.8.2** the rule from reg. 33 that permits employers to operate their own age-dependent schemes if they are based on the statutory scheme.

6.12.5   The remedy for unlawful age discrimination

The remedy for anyone claiming to have been discriminated against in breach of the Age Regs 2006 is to present a complaint to the employment tribunal—reg. 36. Under reg. 42(1) it must be presented within three months of the act complained of, with the tribunal having a discretion to extend time if it is just and equitable to do so.

In Sch. 3 to the regulations there is a questionnaire that an aggrieved person may serve on the employer to obtain information.

6.13   Trade union membership and activities

The last of the nine heads of unlawful discrimination we identified at the start of the chapter is that on the basis of trade union membership or activities. This is on the fringe of the topics covered in this book, since it consists of individual rights related to collective employment law. The following is therefore only a very brief outline of the relevant statutory provisions, all of them taken from TULRCA 1992.

By s. 137 of the Act, it is unlawful to discriminate in making offers of employment on the basis of:

- trade union membership or non-membership; or
- willingness to become a trade union member.

By s. 144, it is unlawful to take any action short of dismissal against an individual employee for the purpose of:

- stopping the employee from being a trade union member;
- stopping the employee from taking part in trade union activities;
- forcing the employee to join some trade union; or
- forcing the employee to join a particular trade union.

The scope of this section is much narrower than the definition of discrimination at **6.2** above under RRA 1976 or SDA 1975, or even that at **6.11.2** under DDA 1995. It clearly includes the employer's intention. The action must be direct and must be for the *purpose* of deterring or forcing. Action for some other purpose which happens to affect unionists and non-unionists in a discriminatory way is not included, and neither is action taken against the union rather than against the individual.

By s. 152, any dismissal where the main reason is the employee's trade union membership, non-membership or participation in activities is automatically unfair. (See **Chapter 10** for a fuller explanation.) Particularly heavy penalties follow for the employer. Furthermore, it is possible for the employee apparently dismissed for such reasons to seek an order continuing the employment until a tribunal hearing can be held about the fairness of dismissal—see s. 161, 'interim relief'.

By s. 153, it is unfair to select an employee for dismissal for redundancy on the basis of trade union membership, non-membership or activities. See **Chapter 11**.

Claims about all these matters must be presented to the employment tribunal within three months of the allegedly discriminatory act or of the dismissal. The tribunal may only prolong that period if satisfied that it was 'not reasonably practicable' for the claim to be presented in time. See **Chapter 13**.

6.14 Summary

We noted at the start of the chapter that in total there are nine prohibited heads of discrimination. For our purposes, the most important six are those within the ambit of the CEHR:

- race;
- sex;
- sexual orientation;
- religion or belief;
- disability; and
- age.

Discrimination is generally defined as taking any of four forms:

- direct (although DDA 1995 uses this term in a different sense from the other heads);
- indirect: applying a *provision, criterion or practice* which cannot be justified as a *proportionate means* of achieving a *legitimate aim*;
- victimisation; and
- harassment.

In relation to disability discrimination, the unique features are the definition of disability and the employer's duty to make a reasonable adjustment. Failure to make an adjustment constitutes unlawful discrimination.

In relation to age discrimination, the special feature is the extent of the exceptions, and the rules are so recently introduced that there are as yet no cases to explore them.

While the Equal Pay Act 1970 was intended to complement exactly SDA 1975, the special position of this topic under European law (art. 141 being directly enforceable in the member states as a treaty obligation) gives it greater stringency.

6.15 Self-test questions

1. The Department for Work and Pensions has a dress code under which all staff are required to dress 'in a professional and businesslike way'. Men are required to wear a collar and tie but women merely 'to dress appropriately and to a similar standard'. The

code goes on to ban denim clothing, lycra leggings, shorts, cropped tops, trainers, and baseball caps. Matthew Thompson, an administrative assistant whose work does not bring him face-to-face with the public, objects to the rule about collar and tie and brings to the employment tribunal a claim of direct sex discrimination. What factors should decide whether he succeeds?

2.   What are the key elements that define whether someone is disabled under DDA 1995?

Protecting business secrets

7.1 Introduction

7.1.1 Scope of Chapters 7 and 8

The next two chapters deal with the complex topics of confidentiality and restraint of trade. Questions of protecting *confidential information* can arise both during the employment relationship and afterwards; the *restraint of trade doctrine* applies only to ex-employees. The remedy for an alleged breach (of either type of duty) is by way of a claim for damages in the ordinary courts, usually accompanied by an application for injunctive relief. **Employment tribunals have no jurisdiction over confidentiality or restraint matters**.

For reasons of space, neither **Chapter 7** nor **8** will deal with intellectual property rights such as patents, copyright, trademarks, or design rights, though all these areas may be relevant to higher-ranking employees and researchers.

7.1.2 Introductory comments on confidentiality

This chapter deals with the protection of information. Every business, from the small backstreet engineering company to the large multinational, will generate business secrets of some nature. These may take the simple form of customer lists, discount concessions, or manufacturing know-how. Equally, the information may take the form of formulae, inventions, secret recipes, or technical data and drawings. All these items are at least *capable* of attracting the protection of the law. The size and importance of the company is not the determining feature; nor will the perceived value of the information be conclusive of any classification of secrecy. The problems of protecting confidential information are quite real. Recent research has shown that over 65 per cent of professionals have admitted to having stolen commercially sensitive information, and departing employees often take with them e-mail lists, customer lists, and technical specifications. Computer misuse is a particular problem.

Anyone claiming that another has breached their confidence must show three things:

(a) the law would class the information as possessing the necessary quality of confidence about it; and

(b) the information was imparted in circumstances which conveyed an obligation of confidence; and

(c) there was unauthorised use of that information.

The information does not have to be contained in a document but it must have an identifiable source.

7.2   How will a duty of confidentiality arise?

Mere receipt of information is not enough to generate a duty of confidentiality. The recipient of the information must accept or realise that the information is to be treated as confidential before any duty will be imputed to him or her. This is tested objectively. Employees will acquire a duty of confidentiality by way of express or implied terms. Third parties (e.g., the companies that employees move to) may also be caught by the duty of confidentiality.

7.2.1   Express terms of the contract

Employers use two key express terms to protect confidential information: *confidentiality clauses* and *restraint of trade clause*. A confidentiality clause only seeks to prevent the use or disclosure of information. Here is a fairly standard draft:

- 'The employee shall not either during his appointment or at any time for two years after its termination: disclose to any person(s) (except those authorised by the Company to know or as otherwise authorised by law); use for his own purposes or for any purposes other than those of the Company any information of a confidential or secret nature which may be made known to the employee by the Company or any customer or supplier of the Company or which may be learned by the employee during his employment, including, in particular, information which relates to: (a) research and development; (b) technical programmes, technical data and operations; (c) manufacturing formulae, processes and techniques; (d) customers' details and specific requirements. Saving that, in all cases, this list of confidential items is not to be treated as closed or exhaustive of the employee's duties.'

We will deal with restraint clause in **Chapter 8**. These clauses seek to close off the opportunities available to an employee to disclose information by prohibiting the employee working (in some capacity) for another employer. For the moment, here is an example:

- *'Non-Dealing with Clients:* For a period of 12 months after termination of the Employment, the Employee shall not directly or indirectly (and whether on his own account or for any other person, firm, company, or organisation) deal with any person, firm company, or organisation who or which at any time during the preceding 12 months shall have been a client customer of, or a person or company in the habit of dealing with, or any person or company who has been in negotiations with, the Company, and with whom or which the Employee has had direct dealings or personal contact as part of the Employment so as to harm the goodwill of the Company or any other Group company or so as to compete with the Company or any other Group Company.'

Employers should set out in clear terms what the responsibilities of the employee are as regards information gained in the course of employment, otherwise, as in *United Indigo Chemical Co. Ltd* v *Robinson* (1932) 49 RPC 178, an injunction to restrain a former employee from using 'secret processes' learned during employment may be refused on the grounds that access to the information was freely available within the company and the employee had never been told that what he had learned was to be regarded as confidential.

Although the law will usually imply obligations necessary for the protection of confidential information the inclusion of an express clause is recommended as an additional precaution. Certainly one would expect such clauses to appear in contracts with scientific, research, technical and other skilled or professional employees. The advantages of the inclusion of an express term are:

(a) it makes obvious to a court the employer's 'subjective' assessment regarding the importance of confidentiality;

(b) in borderline situations it may be that a clear policy will convince a court that certain information deserves to be labelled 'confidential';

(c) such clauses serve as a warning to employees;

(d) a negative formulation of the duty (i.e., that disclosure will constitute a breach) may serve as the basis for an injunction.

7.2.2   Implied terms of the contract

The existence of a duty of confidentiality is treated as axiomatic in the employment relationship because a violation of confidence is a breach of the duty of fidelity or good faith which is an intrinsic part of every employee's contract. Indeed, the courts treat this so seriously that even the *possibility* of a breach of confidence may prevent employees being permitted to work for others in their spare time: *Hivac Ltd* v *Park Royal Scientific Instruments Ltd* [1946] Ch 169.

The implied duty is usually expressed as a *negative* responsibility, i.e., a duty not to use or disclose confidential information acquired during the course of employment (*Thomas Marshall (Exporters) Ltd* v *Guinle* [1978] ICR 905), not to make unauthorised copies of documents (*Robb* v *Green* [1895] 2 QB 315), nor deliberately to memorise documents for further use after the relationship has ended (*Johnson & Bloy* v *Wolstenholme Rink plc and Fallon* [1987] IRLR 499). The duty covers all levels of employees who come into contact with confidential information.

The duty of confidentiality owed by an employee whilst the contract subsists is now different in nature from that owed by former employees. In *Faccenda Chicken* v *Fowler* [1986] ICR 297, it was said that the only implied term which continues after the contract has ended is that the employee must still respect the employer's *trade secrets* to the same extent as when the contract subsisted; the employee is free to make use of all other information. We will return to this below in **7.6**.

7.3   What makes information confidential?

Anyone seeking an injunction to restrain the use or disclosure of confidential information will be called upon to specify the secrecy element; to give clear particulars of the information. It will not suffice for an employer merely to say that there is *some* confidential information in need of protection. In *Thomas Marshall* v *Guinle* (**7.2.2** above), Megarry V-C laid out the basic requirements:

(a) the information must not be in the public domain already;

(b) the employer must believe that the information is of a kind whereby disclosure would harm the business;

(c) those beliefs must be reasonable. For instance, what has the employer done to protect the secrecy of the information? How widely is the information disseminated within the organisation?

(d) the information must be judged in the light of the usage and practices of the particular industry or trade;

(e) the maintenance of secrecy must not offend the public interest.

7.3.1   What kind of information is capable of attracting protection?

The range is extensive. The list would include chemical formulae; customer lists; sales figures; drawings; industrial designs; fashion designs; details of an invention currently under development; information contained in computer programs; computer access codes; an e-mail contacts' list; discount concessions given to customers; delivery route plans; research papers; financial and other reports; and, of course, state official secrets. All of these items and more are *capable* of being classed as confidential. The information may be of a technical, commercial or even personal nature, but it should have what has been termed a 'basic quality of inaccessibility' about it. The mere fact that other companies are willing to pay for the information in question does not, however, mean the information is confidential: *Potters-Ballotini* v *Weston-Baker* [1977] RPC 202. Equally, confidential information does not have to be *novel* to draw protection. It is the *security* of secrets that matters, not inventiveness.

Whilst the employment relationship continues, the employer can rely heavily on the duty of fidelity to ensure that secrets are protected. The grade of that information (trade secret or merely confidential) does not really matter.

7.3.2   What is expected of the employer?

Employers are well-advised not to rely on the implied terms alone but also to ensure that employees are: informed as to their duty in respect of confidential information and told of any changes in company policy, or to the status or responsibility of the employee, or to changes in access to information. Employers should restrict access to confidential information and detail in writing any information which might not normally be classified as confidential in that industry but which the employer has special reason to regard as such. As regards the ability of employers to monitor employees' communications as part of a security policy, see **7.8.4** below.

7.3.3   Information in the public domain

Although information in the public domain it is no longer confidential, how that product was developed may still be protectable. For instance, just because an item has been constructed from *materials* which themselves are in the public domain does not mean the *preparatory information* fails the confidentiality test, for the ingenuity in constructing the finished item may be the confidential information, not the final product *per se*. The fact that competitors or others might eventually ascertain how and why the information was used to produce an item, e.g., the basis for combining certain features, does not destroy confidentiality—at least in the meantime: see *Weir Pumps Ltd* v *CML Pumps Ltd* [1984] FSR 33.

7.3.4   The springboard doctrine

Inextricably tied in with the 'public domain' point is the 'springboard doctrine'. The doctrine was the brainchild of Roxburgh J in *Terrapin Ltd* v *Builders' Supply Co (Hayes) Ltd* [1960] RPC 128. The springboard doctrine is used by the courts in two ways:

(a) 'Theft': here an individual is making use of information which he or she has taken (effectively stolen) from the former employer, such as customer lists: *Roger Bullivant* v *Ellis* [1987] ICR 464. The basis for the claim is the breach of confidence (not merely any breach of contract) by the employee during the currency of the contract. This breach is deemed to continue to have an effect even after termination and can therefore form the basis of a claim for damages and injunctive relief. The 'springboard advantage' is that the employee has gained an unfair competitive edge by stealing the information rather than compiling it himself.

(b) 'Competitive edge from insider knowledge': this arises when the information has entered the public domain but the *background knowledge* of the product or process gives the employee an advantage or headstart over those who also have access to that publicised information. Here the employee will not be allowed to take advantage of such an edge to take the appropriate short cuts in development of the product. He will have to wait until the market has been deemed to 'catch up'. This is a difficult one to apply in practice.

A 'springboard injunction' can thus operate even if there is no express contractual clause preventing use or disclosure, particularly as regards (a) above. Thus, in *Crowson Fabrics Ltd* v *Rider* [2008] IRLR 288 the copying of the employer's 'Supplier Bible' amounted to a springboard advantage even though the contract was silent on this point. This sort of injunction can be very useful in practice because the information does not have to be of a highly confidential nature for it is the unfair advantage gained by the ex-employee that is the key feature.

7.3.5 The maintenance of secrecy must not offend the public interest

7.3.5.1 What is the public interest?

In *Gartside* v *Outram* (1857) 26 LJ Ch 113 at p. 114, Sir Wiliam Page Wood V-C declared that: 'There is no confidence as to the disclosure of iniquity'. Under the common law, therefore, an employee was not acting in breach of confidence by disclosing the employer's wrongdoings: *Lion Laboratories Ltd* v *Evans* [1984] 2 All ER 417. The case law shows that disclosure had to be made to the appropriate bodies, usually the police, regulatory and professional bodies or even Royal Commissions (newspapers have been occasionally accepted but with criticism: *Initial Services Ltd* v *Putterill* [1968] 1 QB 396). Criminal behaviour is not a prerequisite. The defence has, however, not extended to the 'public good', e.g., disclosing the employer's suppression of the apocryphal everlasting lightbulb.

7.3.5.2 Public Interest Disclosure Act 1998

This Act affords special protection for 'whistle-blowers' in defined circumstances. The Act is convoluted at best, but its aim is to give protection to workers (not just employees, but also independent contractors and third-party contractors) who disclose specified forms of information using the procedures laid out in the Act. That protection focuses on providing rights to workers in cases of action short of dismissal being taken against them as well as dismissal itself following their disclosure of information. We will return to the dismissal aspect more fully in **Chapter 10**.

Our concern here is to note the types of information that fall within the Act and the procedures to be utilised in order to gain protection.

The information disclosed

The Public Interest Disclosure Act (PIDA) 1998 created a new s. 43B to the ERA 1996. Section 43B provides that for a worker to gain protection:

(a) the disclosure in question must be a 'qualifying disclosure';

(b) the worker must have followed the correct procedure on disclosure; and

(c) the worker must have suffered a detriment or have been dismissed as a result of all this.

A 'qualifying disclosure' means one that, in the reasonable belief of the worker, tends to show one or more of the following (occurring anywhere in the world):

(a) a criminal offence has been committed or is likely to be so;

(b) a person has failed, is failing or is likely to fail to comply with any *legal obligation* to which he or she is subject. *Parkins* v *Sodexho Ltd* [2002] IRLR 109 EAT, held (with some doubt) that the idea of a 'legal obligation' was not limited to statutory obligations and could encompass complaints made by the employee that the contract had been breached;

(c) a miscarriage of justice has occurred or is likely to occur;

(d) the health or safety of any individual has been, is being or is likely to be endangered;

(e) the environment has been, is being or is likely to be damaged;

(f) information tending to show any matter falling within any of the above has been, is being or is likely to be deliberately concealed.

Note that the standard is the *reasonable belief* of the worker, but the protection does not apply where the worker commits a criminal offence in making the disclosure. Equally, 'illegal' activities prior to disclosure, such as hacking into the employer's computers to show that the employer was not complying with data protection rules, are not protected: *Bolton School* v *Evans* [2006] EWCA Civ 1653, [2007] IRLR 140. This appears to limit an employee's opportunity to demonstrate the employer's questionable activity where all the information lies with the employer. However, other decisions have shown that the standard of 'reasonable belief' is not that high an obstacle. This is because reasonable belief is judged against the standards of good faith, so an employee can be mistaken but still act in good faith (what the Americans call the 'pure heart but empty head test'): see *Babula* v *Waltham Forest College* [2007] EWCA Civ 174, [2007] IRLR 347. However, where there is a predominant ulterior motive for making the disclosure this may destroy the element of good faith: *Street* v *Derbyshire Unemployed Workers Centre* [2004] EWCA Civ 964, [2005] ICR 97 (e.g., personal antagonism).

The procedures

The Act sets out the ways in which a disclosure may be made in order to gain protection. These are:

(a) disclosures to the worker's employer or other responsible person: s. 43C, ERA 1996;

(b) disclosures made in the course of obtaining legal advice: s. 43D;

(c) disclosures to a Minister of the Crown, under s. 43E, where the worker's employer is an individual appointed under any enactment by a Minister of the Crown;

(d) disclosures to a 'prescribed person': s. 43F. The list of prescribed persons is set out in the Public Interest Disclosure (Prescribed Persons) Order 1999, SI 1999/1549 and includes people such as the Information Commissioner, the Civil Aviation Authority, the Environment Agency and the Health and Safety Executive.

Additionally, where the worker cannot follow the above procedural lines of communication, disclosures which are made in good faith and without personal gain (except as provided for under an enactment) will be permitted to other people:

(a) in 'other cases' which fall within the guidelines laid out in s. 43G. Essentially these are instances where the worker reasonably believes that the employer will subject them to a detriment if they follow the procedure noted in s. 43C; or where there is no 'prescribed person' and the worker reasonably believes that evidence may be concealed or destroyed; or where disclosures have been made to the relevant people before. The reasonableness of the worker's actions are decided by reference to matters such as the seriousness of the relevant failure, whether the disclosure is made in breach of the duty of confidentiality, etc.

(b) in cases of 'exceptionally serious' breaches: s. 43H. The bypassing of the noted procedures is again allowed where the worker acts in good faith and without personal gain. In determining the reasonableness of the worker's actions, it is specifically provided that regard must be had to the identity of the person to whom the disclosure was made, i.e., as with the common law before, merely running to the press without thought is frowned upon.

Once a whistle-blowing worker has complied with the above requirements, he or she will gain protection from a dismissal related to the disclosure etc., as set out in **10.8.8.3** below. Any term in the worker's contract which purports to prevent any worker from making a protected disclosure (i.e., a gagging clause) will be void.

7.4 The duty owed by employees

As we have seen, the identification of the employee's duties is a fairly straightforward exercise: an employee will be forbidden from competing with the employer during the currency of the contract if harm is likely to be occasioned. So, how is the employee's duty formulated? We shall explore the following:

(a) What level of information is protected.

(b) The role of honesty.

(c) The positive duty to disclose details about oneself and others.

7.4.1 What level of information is protected?

Can trivia be the subject of a duty of confidentiality? One would think not; though defining trivia might prove difficult. So the fact that the company chairman has a cat called Henry is hardly deserving of protection. However, information need not be complex in order to attract protection. As was noted in *Coco v Clark (A. N.) (Engineers) Ltd* [1969] RPC 41, the simpler the idea the more likely it is to require protection. In the same case, however, Megarry J also noted that 'equity ought not to be invoked to protect trivial tittle-tattle, however confidential'.

However, in different contexts information may be trivial or important. What biscuits the chairman has with his tea strikes a chord of irrelevancy, unless the information reveals that the company produces biscuits and these are either 'test' biscuits or biscuits from another manufacturer. And when pieces of information are put together the sum might be greatly more significant than the parts—the individual pieces of the jigsaw might now reveal a discernible picture. The safest presumption to make, therefore, is that during the currency of the contract any doubt is likely to be decided in favour of the employer.

7.4.2 The role of honesty

An employee is expected to act with honesty. With regard to confidentiality the most obvious example of this is that the employee will not be permitted to copy or memorise confidential documents for use after the contract ends (see 'springboard doctrine' at **7.3.4** above). Companies often include such a term demanding 'delivery up' of such items as books, records, computer software, memoranda, lists and other documents relating to the business of the company on termination of the contract.

Thus, copying and deliberately memorising lists (see *Roger Bullivant* v *Ellis* at **7.3.4**) have been held to be actions which restrict the employee's use of that information. The same with copying an e-mail list of contacts: *Pennwell Publishing (UK) Ltd* v Ornstein [2007] IRLR 700. And in the area of unfair dismissal the EAT has held accessing computer files using another employee's identity code and password can amount to gross misconduct: *Denco Ltd* v *Joinson* [1991] ICR 172.

7.4.3 The extent to which the duty requires positive action by the employee

As well as the duty *not to disclose* confidential information, an employee (at least a senior employee) also owes a positive duty to surrender information relevant to the relationship, e.g., where an employee detects patterns in the market which might have an adverse or beneficial effect on the employer's business: see *Sanders* v *Parry* [1967] 1 WLR 753, *Industrial Development Consultants* v *Cooley* [1972] 1 WLR 443 and *General Nutritions Ltd* v *Yates*, *The Times*, 5 June 1981. In *MacMillan Inc.* v *Bishopsgate Investment Trust plc* [1993] 1 WLR 1372, however, the Court of Appeal limited this general duty was limited to information obtained *in the course of employment*.

There is no common pattern of practice in this area. Some precedents do indeed include an express duty to surrender information gained in the course of employment, but most contracts (if dealing with positive duties at all) focus on a term requiring the employee to do all that is reasonable to *prevent* disclosures. This clause is, of course, aimed mainly at those in managerial positions.

But the idea of positive duties becomes more problematic when it involves self-incrimination. In the absence of fraud there is no duty to volunteer information regarding the employee's own misconduct: *Bell* v *Lever Brothers* [1932] AC 161. However, in *Swain* v *West (Butchers) Ltd* [1936] 3 All ER 261, it was held that employees were under a duty to notify their employer of the misconduct of their fellow employees. When these two principles were combined in the case of *Sybron Corp.* v *Rochem* [1983] ICR 801, the finding was that there is a duty, at least incumbent on senior management whose responsibilities are affected by the actions, to notify the employer of serious breaches by fellow employees even when that involves self-incrimination (as was the case here).

In this context one should also note the limited effects of the Rehabilitation of Offenders Act 1974 regarding statements of 'spent' convictions and the fact that for some occupations employers have to conduct checks with the Criminal Records Bureau.

7.5   The duty owed by former employees

Most disclosures or use of information are likely to occur once the employee has left the company. It is here that the real battle lines are drawn and the courts are wary of imposing the same level of duty on former employees as they place on existing employees. Partly, this is because once the employee has left then any fetters placed on the exercise of that person's skill, expertise, technical competence or general ability to earn a living could be disastrous to the employee (see also **Chapter 8**).

This is an area which demands that the practitioner makes a number of judgment calls, often based on commercial or scientific practices. Many LPC students find that 'flow charts' can at least help to reduce some of the problems and so we have tried in **Figure 7.1** to map out the basic analytical structures employed by practitioners. This diagram shows you the overall pattern of analysis, but we shall repeat the diagram with highlighted sections to accompany the relevant text.

The key questions we need to address are:

- Does it matter how the contract came to an end?

- What sort of information is protectable? In particular, can an employer prevent an employee making use of the employee's own skill and knowledge acquired during his employment?

- If the information is protectable, does this mean that all confidential information gains protection or are there further limitations?

- What is the protection offered by the law (i.e., what are the remedies for breach of confidence)?

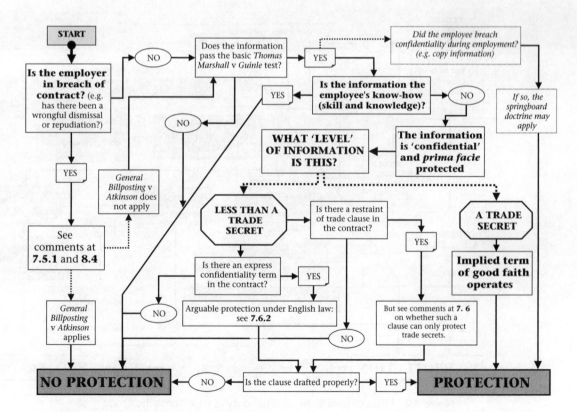

Figure 7.1   Diagrammatic summary.

7.5.1   The importance of how the contract came to an end

Figure 7.2 highlights the fact that, in some instances, ex-employees may be relieved of any post-termination duties owed to their former employer. So the first question addressed in the flow chart is: has the employer committed a breach of contract by **wrongfully dismissing** the employee or **wrongfully repudiating** the contract of employment? Wrongful dismissal will be covered in depth in **Chapter 9**. For the moment, we can say that a wrongful dismissal occurs where the employer terminates the contract without giving the employee due notice; a wrongful repudiation occurs where the employer breaches the contract and the employee resigns as a consequence. In 1909 the House of Lords held that a wrongful dismissal or repudiation destroyed the efficacy of a restraint of trade clause.

However, there has been no direct authority on whether a wrongful dismissal or wrongful repudiation affects the validity of either the implied term or any express term of *confidentiality,* and practitioners have been divided on this one. The only case to comment on the topic of confidentiality has been *Campbell* v *Frisbee* [2002] EWCA Civ 1374, [2003] ICR 141, where, on an appeal based on an application for summary judgment, Lightman J had to decide whether an express confidentiality term survived a repudiatory breach (here, an alleged assault by the model, Naomi Campbell on her ex-personal assistant). Their relationship, however, was one of a contract *for* services so any comments on the position of employees had to be *obiter*. Lightman J held: (a) that Ms Campbell's confidentiality regarding her private life was a form of property and this could not be destroyed by a repudiatory breach; (b) (*obiter*) the same would apply to employment relationships had this been one (an observation itself based on more *obiter* statements in a Court of Appeal case on restraint of trade, *Rock Refrigeration*

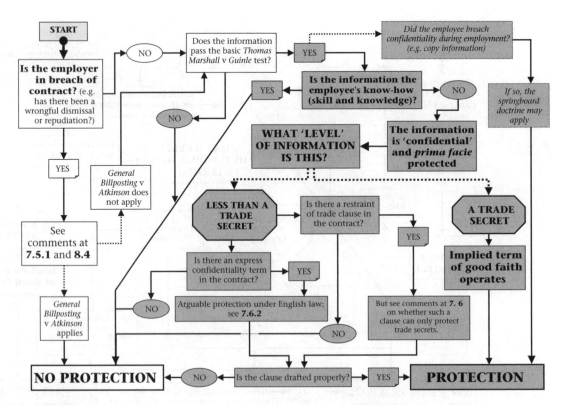

Figure 7.2   Effect of termination on the duty of confidentiality.

Ltd v *Jones* [1997] ICR 938). Ms Frisbee's appeal from this decision to the Court of Appeal was successful, but only on the ground that the issue of law involved was not suitable for summary determination under Part 24 CPR. Lord Phillips MR did, however, comment (again *obiter*) at [22] that,

> We do not believe that the effect on duties of confidence assumed under contract when the contract in question is wrongfully repudiated is clearly established. While we do not consider that it is likely that Miss Frisbee will establish that Lightman J erred in his conclusions in a manner detrimental to her case, it cannot be said that she has no reasonable prospect of success on the issue.

This comment indicates that a wrongful dimissal or repudiation may not now destroy the duty of confidentiality—but nothing has been decided on this since.

The highlighted boxes in **Figure 7.2** illustrate the place of this argument in the overall structure. The dotted lines denote the different consequences. You can see that if there has been no breach or the case law makes the breach irrelevant, the next step in the analysis is to apply the *Thomas Marshall* v *Guinle* test noted above at **7.2.2**.

7.5.2   Information: the basic protection

The *Thomas Marshall* v *Guinle* test is essentially a simple one, requiring us to determine whether or not the employer has done something which shows the information is confidential and that it is not already in the public domain. **Figure 7.3** then takes us down that simple analysis, but then leads us to the very vexed question of whether the information is in reality the employee's 'know-how'. Again, the highlighted boxes illustrate the place of this argument in the overall structure.

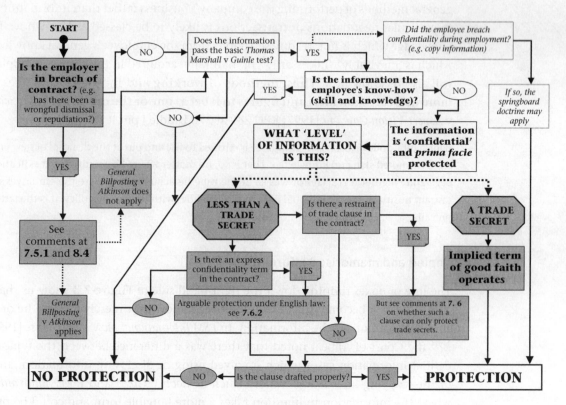

Figure 7.3   What sort of information is protectable?

7.5.3   Information: distinguishing employees' know-how

The information may have survived any possible argument of wrongful repudiation; it may have survived the *Thomas Marshall* test, but it may still not belong to the employer if it amounts to the employee's 'know-how'. Exactly what information will constitute an employee's know-how (otherwise referred to as the employee's 'skill and knowledge'), as opposed to the employer's confidential information, is a difficult judgment call even for experienced practitioners. We would suggest that, in essence, *technical information* is likely to belong to the employer whereas *the technique* of performing the job belongs to the employee.

In *FSS Travel and Leisure Systems Ltd* v *Johnson* [1998] IRLR 382 (a restraint of trade case based on the protection of confidential information), for instance, the Court of Appeal again confirmed that the exercise of an employee's skill, experience, know-how and general knowledge cannot be controlled by a former employer. This will apply whether that employer is claiming the information is a trade secret or under an express confidentiality clause. Indeed, the *FSS Travel* case shows how difficult the line between know-how and confidential information can be to draw sometimes. Here the company was seeking to show that, as the ex-employee programmer knew that a program could be run to produce a certain effect (e.g., to obtain credit card bookings), the knowledge of this *design solution* could be applied in competitors' systems so that mere disclosure of the solution could be damaging to the company. Thus, it was not the detailed knowledge of the 2,852 programs that was at issue but the knowledge of what the programs could achieve by way of problem-solving. The company's claim failed; this was skill and knowledge.

Although the cases cannot be said to describe clear tests, certain features can be discovered in order to identify employees' know-how. Anything which relates to general methods of performing the company's business rather than information related to particular negotiations or transactions is likely to be classed as know-how. Equally, knowledge which is not 'readily separable' from the employee's general knowledge and which is 'inevitably', 'necessarily', or 'naturally' acquired in the course of employment will also be know-how. **Thus, methods of working and industrial practices will be more difficult than facts and figures to label as one or the other.** In *Ocular Science Ltd* v *Aspect Vision Care Ltd* [1997] RPC 289 at 370 Laddie J put it this way:

[F]or public policy reasons, an employee is entitled to use and put at the disposal of new employers all his acquired skill and knowledge. That is so, no matter where he acquired that skill and knowledge and whether it is secret or was so at the time he acquired it. Where the employer's right to restrain misuse of his confidential information collides with the public policy, it is the latter which prevails.

7.5.4   Copied and memorised information

The line of boxes running down the right-hand side of **Figure 7.3** show us that something does not become part of the employee's know-how merely because he or she has copied or memorised the information. In *PSM International plc* v *Whitehouse* [1992] IRLR 279 the Court of Appeal noted that there was a difference between the typical confidential information cases which involved using or disclosing information, and those of the 'copying and taking' variety (such as *Robb* v *Green* and *Roger Bullivant* v *Ellis*) where the information in question takes a more tangible form and could be protected under the springboard doctrine. It was suggested that the 'springboard doctrine' we saw above could be used as *an alternative method* of protecting information which did not qualify as a trade secret. In line with this the Court of Appeal has confirmed that information which is carried away in the employee's head does not automatically belong to the employee (*Johnson & Bloy* v *Wolstenholme Rink plc and Fallon* [1987] IRLR 499). Nor does ownership of the information depend on whether the information was or was not learned with the deliberate intent to misuse. Even where the employee has memorised information without any thought of misuse, it is an objective test whether that information belongs to the employer or not: *SBJ Stephenson* v *Mandy* [2000] IRLR 233.

You can see from **Figure 7.3** above that, if the information can be classed as something other than the employee's know-how and is not covered by the springboard doctrine the next stage is to ask: what *level* of information is it? For even if the information is 'confidential', not all types of confidential information will be protected.

7.5.5   Levels of information: defining trade secrets

One would be forgiven for believing that the employer had jumped all the necessary hurdles by now but **Figure 7.4** tells us otherwise. An employer does not gain protection for every piece of information in his possession: the information must be either a *trade secret eo nomine* (by that name) or *information akin to a trade secret.* That protection arises from the continuing nature of the implied duty of good faith/fidelity which is present in all employment relationships and which is deemed to run on even after the contract has been terminated.

Until the case of *Faccenda Chicken* v *Fowler* [1986] ICR 297 the term 'trade secret' simply meant anything that was not the employee's know-how. Use of this 'know-how' could not—and still cannot—restrict the activities of former employees; but anything which was not part of an employee's know-how was referred to as the employer's 'trade secret' and *prima facie* could be protected. That was the traditional distinction. However,

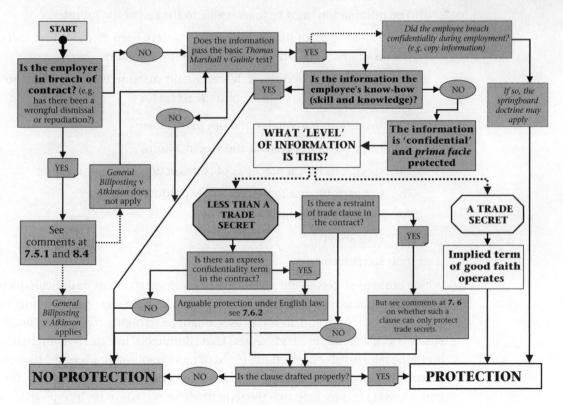

Figure 7.4   Trade secrets and the implied term of good faith.

in *Faccenda Chicken* Neill LJ created a further distinction, dividing an employer's confidential information into two categories: (a) trade secrets, which could be protected by the implied term of good faith; and (b) information which, though confidential, was not important enough to be classed as a trade secret and so not protected by the implied term.

Neill LJ sought to identify what would make information a 'trade secret'. He listed the following points as a general guide:

(a) *The nature of the employment*—where 'confidential' material is habitually handled by the employee this may impose a high obligation of confidentiality.

(b) *The nature of the information itself*—a limited circulation list for the information may indicate a higher level of secrecy.

(c) *Whether the employer impressed on the employee the confidentiality of the information.*

(d) *Whether the relevant information can be easily isolated from other information which the employee is free to use or disclose.*

The courts have obviously become wary of making the criteria too restrictive in deciding what information should be classed as a trade secret. Equally, the mere designation of information as either 'confidential' or as a 'trade secret' does not determine the matter; though in borderline cases it may be persuasive. The information must also have passed the *Thomas Marshall* v *Guinle* [1978] ICR 905 basic test (see **7.3**).

As Neill LJ noted, it is impossible to provide a definitive list of trade secrets or their equivalent. Secret processes of manufacture provide obvious examples, but innumerable other pieces of information are *capable* of being trade secrets. With a heavy defensive *caveat* our suggestions for classification are:

(a) The information must provide a competitive edge so that disclosure would cause significant harm to the employer.

(b) The information must be inaccessible to the rest of the industry.

(c) There must be proof that serious attempts have been made to limit and safeguard the dissemination of the material within the company.

(d) The 'pure and applied research' cases tend to cause fewer problems so that it is reasonably safe to give the tag of trade secret to:

    (i)   inventions (patentable and not patentable);

    (ii)   technical or design data and specifications;

    (iii) specific technical processes of construction and manufacture;

    (iv) test performance figures for a new product;

    (v)   chemical and other formulae;

    (vi) craft secrets;

    (vii) secret recipes.

Which business secrets are the equivalent of trade secrets is a more difficult question. The names and commercial preferences of customers, for instance, can obviously amount to sensitive information and, in some cases, might be so highly confidential and useful to a business as to amount to a trade secret. That commercial information might be as deserving of the same level of protection offered to more traditional 'scientific' trade secrets was a principle recognised in *Lansing Linde Ltd* v *Kerr* [1991] 1 All ER 418. There, for instance, Butler-Sloss LJ commented that the term 'trade secret' has to be 'interpreted in the wider context of highly confidential information of a non-technical or non-scientific nature'.

With that in mind, we offer the following points as to what business secrets may amount to trade secrets:

(a) manufacturer's 'know-how' (as distinct from the employee's know-how). By this we mean the *particular applications* of technology unique to that company and which are not part of public knowledge. This might extend to things such as specific and detailed 'quality control' procedures developed by the company;

(b) customer lists when connected to things such as discount or purchasing policies and which are not otherwise available. Although customer pricing lists were not protected in *Faccenda,* this should not be taken as a rule of universal application because (as was noted by Staughton LJ's in *Lansing Linde* v *Kerr* and again in *Frayling Furniture Ltd* v *Premier Upholstery Ltd* (1998, unreported, ChD) and in *SBJ Stephenson* v *Mandy* the importance of these lists and their relative secrecy may matter a great deal to particular companies' business;

(c) operative tenders and quotations which have not been published;

(d) detailed plans for expansion and market projections;

(e) computer software containing novel features;

(f) access codes for computers and secure areas.

7.5.6 Levels of information: other confidential information

Neill LJ's guidelines for determining whether information meets the test of being a trade secret are used widely; but there was a more controversial aspect to his Lordship's judgment. Neill LJ also decided that information which ranked lower than a trade secret not only failed to gain the protection of the implied term but also could not be protected by the use of an express confidentiality clause. This was a surprise to practitioners. His Lordship then speculated that such information might be protectable by means of a restraint of trade clause. There was no express confidentiality term in *Faccenda Chicken* so, strictly, the comments as regards express terms are *obiter.* Nevertheless, as you will see, this aspect of the case has caused problems.

The question of how to deal with information which is confidential but less than a trade secret is a complicated one, but it lies at the heart of how practitioners deal with matters of confidentiality, both from a litigation and drafting perspective. To best explain this, therefore, instead of going straight to the next diagram we have laid out the text in section **7.6** in the following order:

- Description of *Faccenda Chicken* v *Fowler.*
- The case law since *Faccenda Chicken.*
- The practical effects.

The relevant diagrams (**Figures 7.5** and **7.6**) appear at the end of **7.6.3** below.

7.6 Faccenda Chicken v Fowler

Fowler was employed as a sales manager for the company. He established a system of selling fresh chickens from refrigerated vans and subsequently resigned from Faccenda Chicken to set up a similar competing business. He took a number of Faccenda's employees with him. It was alleged that Fowler and the others had used and disclosed information, derived from Faccenda's operations, in their new business. The information related to delivery routes, customers' addresses, delivery times, and pricing policy. Faccenda sought an injunction to prevent the use and disclosure of this information. The contract did not contain a restraint of trade clause, or a confidentiality clause so protection could only be gained through the continuing implied term of good faith/fidelity.

7.6.1   The decision

In the Court of Appeal, Neill LJ gave the only judgment. His Lordship generally confirmed the decision of Goulding J in the High Court and reiterated that the duty of confidentiality owed in employment relationships is based purely on contractual, not equitable, principles—thus focusing on express and implied terms in the contract. His Lordship identified **two** categories of information:

(a) *trade secrets*, which are protected by the implied term of good faith; and

(b) *everything else*, ranging from trivia through skill and knowledge and onto the borders of trade secrets.

On the facts, the information was not classed as a trade secret. Further, as there was no express clause in the contract the information was not protected by any other means so Fowler et al. could do with it what they wanted.

7.6.2   The unresolved practical issue

So far so good, but then came the *obiter* observations from both Goulding J and Neill LJ as to what would have been the position *had there been* an express confidentiality clause or a restraint of trade clause in the contract. Goulding J indicated that 'express terms' or 'restraint of trade clauses' could be used to protect information which was not a trade secret. Neill LJ said the same but used the phrase 'restrictive covenants'. These asides have caused some practical difficulties:

- We do not know whether the phrases 'express terms', 'restrictive covenants', and the like are meant to mean that **both** express confidentiality clauses and restraint of trade clauses can provide protection, or whether only restraint clauses can so operate.

- If the phrases mean that both restraint and express confidentiality clauses can be used to protect information which is lower than a trade secret then this helps employers greatly, as information not protected by the implied term can be covered by a well-drafted express term. This is the way practitioners viewed the law before *Faccenda* but it is probably not what Neill LJ, in particular, meant.

- More likely, Neill LJ meant that lower-level information could only be protected by using a restraint clause. Unfortunately, Neill LJ indicated that 'it was clear' from the case law that a restraint of trade clause seeking to protect against the disclosure of confidential information would only be enforceable if the information was a trade secret or its equivalent. But, as we have noted, if the information is already of such a high level, the implied term of good faith will protect it anyway.

- All this means that Neill LJ was saying (*obiter*) that an express confidentiality clause could not add any further protection to the implied term already there but that a restraint clause *could* if the information was akin to a trade secret (which, he seemed to forget, was already protected by the implied term of good faith anyway, so this point just goes around in a circle).

- Perhaps the key point here is the very practical one that it is very difficult to police a confidentiality clause (when do you know what was said to whom?) but a restraint clause, which stops someone working for a competitor, is more obvious in its observance and breach.

Had both the High Court and the Court of Appeal avoided making such *obiter* comments, the decision in *Faccenda* would have been a useful illustration of the categorisation of types of information according to the industry in which they arise. The *obiter* points have caused problems since their utterance (and it should also be noted in passing that the two principal cases cited by Neill LJ do not support his conclusions anyway: see *Printers & Finishers Ltd* v *Holloway* [1965] 1 WLR 1 and *Worsley (E.) & Co. Ltd* v *Cooper* [1939] 1 All ER 290).

7.6.3   The case law since *Faccenda Chicken*

Faccenda has been accepted as the leading authority on this area by all levels of court (though the *obiter dicta* on express confidentiality clauses have not been reviewed directly by the House of Lords).

Most LPC courses do not deal in depth with this area anymore so we shall simply list the key cases here for your reference: *Balston Ltd* v *Headline Filters Ltd* [1987] FSR 330; *Roger Bullivant* v *Ellis* [1987] ICR 464 (CA); *Poly Lina Ltd* v *Finch* [1995] FSR 751; *Lancashire Fires Ltd* v *S. A. Lyons & Co. Ltd* [1996] FSR 629 (CA); *Poeton Industries Ltd* v *Horton* [2000] ICR 1208 (CA). These cases have not had to tackle the issue directly. They do, however, recognise that some form of protection can be gained by express terms, and Scott J (as he then was) recognised in *Balston* that it is pointless allowing for an express term to protect trade secrets as they are already protected.

We really should not be in this position where we do not know whether an express confidentiality clause or a restraint of trade clause can or cannot protect information once the employment contract has ended. In effect, the courts have sidestepped the problem and concentrated instead on extending the boundaries of what is meant by 'trade secret' to bring more commercial information within the protection of the implied term of good faith. Perhaps this is more pragmatic.

If we look at all this in diagrammatic form, **Figures 7.5** and **7.6** overleaf demonstrate the analytical pathways. You will see that, whether you are dealing with have an express confidentiality clause or a restraint of trade clause based on the preservation of confidence (or both), and even if it is accepted that these clauses can protect information lower than a trade secret, you must still look to the actual drafting of the clauses (especially in the case of restraint terms) to see whether they do in fact provide the protection sought.

7.6.4   The practical effects of *Faccenda Chicken* and drafting strategies

7.6.4.1   Practical effects

There are probably no fewer than *six* ways of classifying information:

(a) *trade secrets,* which will gain automatic protection by the continuing effect of the implied term;

(b) *high-level confidential information;* so high-level that it is equivalent to a trade secret and protected by the implied term;

(c) *confidential information,* falling short of such protection but which may be the subject of a reasonable restrictive covenant (either a confidentiality clause or restraint of trade clause);

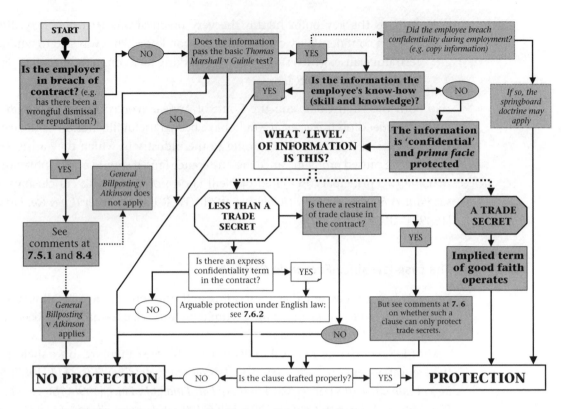

Figure 7.5 Protecting lower-level information by use of an express term.

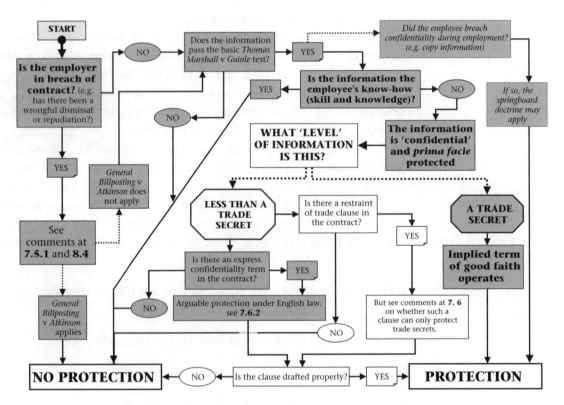

Figure 7.6 Protecting lower-level information by use of a restraint clause.

(d) *copied or memorised information* which will be protected by the springboard doctrine because it involves a breach of fidelity occurring *during* the relationship;

(e) *skill and knowledge,* which inevitably becomes part of the employee's experience and cannot be protected;

(f) *trivia,* which, except in rare cases, cannot be protected.

The *level of protection* afforded to each type of information can be seen in **Figure 7.7**.

Information clearly protected under Faccenda Trade secrets. High-level confidential information.		*Information possibly protected under Faccenda* Lower-level confidential information, by means of an effective restraint of trade clause.
Information protected under other cases Copied or memorised information.	*Information arguably protected* Lower-level confidential information, by means of an express confidentiality clause.	*Information never protected* Skill and knowledge. Trivia.

Figure 7.7   Levels of protection afforded to information.

7.6.4.2   Drafting practice

The decision in *Faccenda Chicken* means that there is *prima facie* little value in inserting a clause in the contract which seeks to protect information once the relationship has ended. The implied term will protect trade secrets (or their equivalent) and nothing else can be covered. But an express clause might nevertheless achieve two things: first, it may help to determine whether particular information could be regarded by the courts as attaining the level of trade secrets; secondly, it may deter employees.

Alternatively, we would say that the inclusion of an express term is vital in order to give information which is not automatically protected by the implied term any chance of being safeguarded. Express terms may appear in two forms: (a) as part of the contract itself; and (b) as part of a termination agreement. We shall cover specific points relating to the latter in **Chapter 8**.

The key point as regards drafting practice, however, is that *even if Faccenda Chicken is correct* there is a great deal to gain and very little to lose by inserting such a clause. For, if *Faccenda Chicken* is right, the clause will be ignored; but if *Faccenda Chicken* is wrong and the draftsman has not inserted such a clause, then protection will be lost for all but 'trade secrets'. The full 'belt and braces' approach, of course, demands the use of a restraint of trade clause as well.

Thus, if your client asks whether a former employee can be stopped from disclosing some lower-level confidential information, your answer might have to be: 'Possibly not'. But turn the point around: if you wish to give your client any chance of protection in the future you will need to insert an express confidentiality clause and/or a restraint of trade clause. In a slightly different context the Court of Appeal has affirmed this approach. In *Brooks v Olyslager OMS (UK) Ltd* [1998] IRLR 590 the employer and employee reached a compromise agreement concerning the employee's resignation. The employee later told an investment banker a few 'home truths' about the management style and financial stability his former employer. The company heard about this and refused to pay the balance of the agreement, claiming there should be an implied term in the agreement that the employee would not disclose information of a sufficiently high degree of confidentiality as to amount to a trade secret. The Court of Appeal disagreed: the information did not fall into the category of trade secret, merely being information concerning the reason for the employee's resignation and matters which might be seen as detrimental to the company. An express term may still, on the facts, not have saved the day; but it would have provided a fighting chance.

The most secure line to take is that anything which is not clearly part of an employee's know-how should be included in an express confidentiality term. Materials such as general research data, details of drawings, costings, accounting information, customers' credit ratings, the contents of forthcoming catalogues, company-produced quality maintenance manuals (if not already a trade secret), restricted circulation memos and minutes of meetings, problems encountered in the development of a product or reasons why certain matters were rejected, and personnel records such as salary packages would therefore seem appropriate to this category. One might also include in this clause any item which may only be debatable as a trade secret (e.g., customer lists or sales strategies).

7.6.5   Precedents

Our surveys of practice have revealed a fair degree of commonality in the definitions of confidential information being protected. Most precedents include a general ban on the use or disclosure of trade secrets or other confidential information and then provide a (non-exhaustive) list of examples. In addition to the items mentioned above, common items were: customer requirements; trade arrangements; marketing strategies; mark-ups; the affairs of clients; expansion plans; the movements of senior employees; litigation in progress; potential customer lists; and various terms on computer information.

Most draft precedents also include a specific clause on the 'delivery up' of documents, papers, computer disks, etc. on the termination of employment. Some prohibit writing papers, giving lectures, etc. *during* employment without the express permission of management.

7.7   Remedies for breach of confidence

Any unauthorised disclosure of information during the currency of the contract is likely to amount to a breach of contract; a serious one if the effect is to cause harm to the enterprise (potential or actual). Disciplinary action may result. Realistically, however, these responses strike at the symptom and not the cause. What the employer wants is to prevent the use or disclosure of the information and to recover any lost profit.

Many judges have commented that the duty of confidentiality is of minimal value to an employer because of the difficulty of enforcement. The alternative sometimes suggested by the courts is for employers to rely more on the insertion of a restraint of trade clause which will prevent the employee from working in the industry. But while it is true that restraint clauses are generally a more effective means of impeding ex-employees, they are not a panacea because (i) it is likely that such clauses can only protect trade secrets anyway and (ii) they are far more likely to fail for lack of reasonableness than any confidentiality clause.

Thus the first 'remedy' is prevention: insert both confidentiality and restraint of trade clauses in order to protect confidential information. Failing prevention, the remedies available for breach of the duty will include:

Permanent remedies	*Interim remedies*
Injunction.	Interim injunction.
Delivery up or destruction of documents.	Order for delivery up of documents.
Damages.	Search order (formerly called
An account of profits.	an *Anton Piller order*).
Declaration as to confidentiality.	

To this list the Civil Procedure Rules have added: interim declarations (r. 25(1)(b)); preaction disclosures (r. 31.16); and summary judgments (under Part 24), now obtainable by both claimant and defendant.

Note: To avoid repetition, injunctions are discussed in **Chapter 8** regarding confidentiality and restraint of trade (at **8.11**) and more generally in **Chapter 9** (at **9.10**).

However, it is useful to note here the comments of Laddie J in the *Ocular Science* case on drafting statements of case (p. 359). These show that the claimant must be able to provide full and proper particulars of all the confidential information in question. The defendant must know what breach is being alleged; it is not enough to rely on a loose contention that a 'package' of information is confidential.

With this burden placed on the claimant it also follows that the claimant should not be obstructed in establishing the evidence. Thus, it is also possible for the claimant to obtain a disclosure order requiring the employee to give up the names and addresses of business contacts, irrespective of whether those contacts had been made before or after termination of employment. When it comes to lists of post-termination contacts, however, the defendant's own confidentiality is in need of *prima facie* protection. The best way to achieve this is by way of undertakings from the defendant's solicitor as to use of that information: *Intelec Systems Ltd* v *Grech-Cini* [1999] 4 All ER 11.

7.7.1 The parties

The employer may well join the new employer as a third party, but there are difficulties attached to this. First, this will inevitably slow things down. Secondly, one of the factors the court takes into account in awarding an injunction (see **8.11** below) is the ability of the defendant to pay any damages that might be awarded at trial; the joining of a company with all its resources is therefore disadvantageous to the applicant. Thirdly, there is the question of proving that the new employer received the information knowing of the breach or at least turning a blind eye to its potential. In *Thomas* v *Pearce* [2000] FSR 718 the Court of Appeal made it clear that the test is one of honesty not reasonableness.

7.7.2 Springboard injunctions

In some cases an employer may be able to obtain an injunction even where the information is not a trade secret: see above at **7.3.4**.

7.7.3 Database rights

Databases can take a lot of time and money to create. They are valuable pieces of information and they are open to abuse from copying. The EC Database Directive 96/9/EC addressed this issue. As well as extending copyright protection in this area this Directive also created a creature known as a 'database right'. In the UK this was implemented as a property right through the Copyrights and Rights in Databases Regulations 1997, SI 1997/3032. The right is infringed where all or substantial parts of the database are extracted or re-utilised (reg. 16) and employees who fall foul of this may be liable under the regulations through the application of breach of copyright remedies (reg. 23).

7.7.4 Defences to breach of confidentiality

Aside from arguing that the information is simply not confidential at all, the two main defences are: (a) publication; and (b) just cause. We touched on publication at **7.3.3** above regarding 'the public domain'. 'Just cause' was covered at **7.3.5** above in the discussions on public interest.

Some further points need to made on publication. Although publication destroys confidentiality, two points need to be noted:

(a) The case law shows (notably *Attorney-General* v *Guardian Newspapers Ltd (No. 2)* [1988] 3 All ER 545 (CA)—the *Spycatcher* case) that **partial** publication may not destroy confidentiality as long as the information retains the 'basic attributes of inaccessibility' i.e., it is not *generally* available to the public.

(b) Publication by the **defendant** may (strange as it sounds) destroy confidentiality. Although one would think the defendant should not profit from his or her own wrong (see *Speed Seal Products Ltd* v *Paddington* [1986] 1 All ER 91), Lord Goff in *Spycatcher* expressed the view that once disclosed, by whatever means, the information was no longer confidential. This would affect the calculation of damages aspect (i.e., dating the termination of the duty), though the defendant would still probably be bound by the springboard doctrine.

7.8 The employee's right to confidentiality

In addition to the human rights implications noted at **1.7** above, there are four main areas to note here:

(a) The Data Protection Act 1998.

(b) The Access to Medical Reports Act 1988.

(c) The provision of references.

(d) The interception of communications.

7.8.1 The Data Protection Act 1998

The aim of this Act is to allow employees access to data held on them by 'data controllers' (i.e., their employer). Employees have the right to challenge inaccuracies and claim compensation for any ensuing loss. The Office of the Information Commissioner has issued guidance notes and a draft Code of Practice: see the website at **www.ico.gov.uk** and, under the Criminal Justice and Immigration Act 2008, has powers to impose fines for unlawful processing of personal data.

7.8.1.1 Outline of the provisions

At the heart of the Data Protection Act (DPA) 1998 lie eight principles around which the Act is structured, enforced and interpreted (see sch. 1). There is an obligation on all data users to observe these principles, e.g., that the information shall be processed fairly and lawfully; that 'personal data' (a term which includes expressions of opinions) shall be accurate and, where necessary, kept up to date; that personal data shall not be kept for longer than is necessary; that unauthorised processing shall be guarded against; and that personal data should not be transferred outside the EC unless that recipient country has adequate levels of data protection. The Act confers on the Information Commissioner extensive powers of enforcement.

7.8.1.2 The meaning of 'data'

In addition to computer-based information the 1998 Act extended the meaning of 'data' to information which is 'recorded as part of a relevant filing system or with the intention that it should form part of a relevant filing system', e.g., personal files (s. 1(1)(c)). A 'relevant filing system' is defined at s. 1(1) as:

any set of information relating to individuals to the extent that, although the information is not processed by means of equipment operating automatically in response to instructions given for that purpose, the set is structured, whether by reference to individuals or by reference to criteria relating to individuals, in such a way that specific information relating to a particular individual is readily accessible.

In the case of *Durant* v *Financial Services Authority* [2003] EWCA Civ 1746, the Court of Appeal considered the meanings of 'data' and 'relevant filing system'.

(a) *Data*

'Data' will relate to an individual if they are: 'information that affects [a person's] privacy, whether in his personal or family life, business or professional capacity'. The Court held that this will include information which is biographical in a significant sense. The Information Commissioner's comment is that this means that, 'Simply because an individual's name appears on a document, the information contained in that document will not necessarily be personal data about the named individual.' The Information Commissioner gives examples of personal data: information about the medical history of an individual, an individual's salary details, information concerning an individual's tax liabilities, information comprising an individual's bank statements, and information about individuals' spending preferences: see also *Common Services Agency* v *Scottish Information Commissioner* [2008] UKHL 47, [2008] 1 WLR 1550 on the meaning of personal and sensitive data in relation to requests made to public authorities under the freedom of information legislation.

(b) *Relevant filing system*

The Court of Appeal gave a narrower meaning to 'relevant filing system' than many had thought to be the case. It is limited to a system:

'(i) in which the files forming part of it are structured or referenced in such a way as to clearly indicate at the outset of the search whether specific information capable of amounting to personal data of an individual requesting it under section 7 is held within the system and, if so, in which file or files it is held; and

(ii) which has, as part of its own structure or referencing mechanism, a sufficiently sophisticated and detailed means of readily indicating whether and
where in an individual file or files specific criteria or information about the
applicant can be readily located.'

This means that not all manual filing systems are covered by the Act: only manual filing
systems broadly equivalent to computerised systems in ready accessibility are within the
system of data protection. The Information Commissioner's website provides a number
of working examples.

7.8.1.3 Accessible records

The question of 'relevant filing systems' does not arise in relation to *accessible records,*
so that in such cases, rights of access are much wider. Section 68 defines this term as
covering health records, certain educational records (set out in sch. 11), and certain
public records (set out in sch. 12). A 'health record' is one which consists of information relating to the physical or mental health of an individual which has been made
by or on behalf of a 'health professional' (see s. 69) in connexion with the care of that
individual.

7.8.1.4 Sensitive personal data

This term covers racial or ethnic origin, political opinions, religious beliefs, trade union
membership, physical and mental health, the employee's sexual life, and the commission of an offence or proceedings relating to an offence (s. 2). There are specific *additional* restrictions placed on the processing of such information (see sch. 3). Problems
are beginning to surface here with regard to the standing of 'sickness absence' records
by employers.

7.8.1.5 Employees' rights

An employee, as a 'data subject', has certain rights under the Act (see generally ss. 715).
These can be broadly categorised as:

(a) the right to be informed, in response to a written request, that personal data about
him or her is being processed;

(b) the right of access (on payment of a fee) to personal data held by the employer.
This must be communicated in an 'intelligible form';

(c) the right to apply to a county court or to the High Court to have inaccurate data
corrected or deleted;

(d) the right, in certain cases, to be informed of the logic involved in computerised
decision-making;

(e) the right to compensation for damage caused by any breach of the Act as well as
in certain cases of distress;

(f) the right to complain to the Commissioner that the principles of the Act have
been broken.

Section 7 allows certain information or parts of it not to be disclosed if information relating to another individual would be revealed, and sch. 7 lays out the exemptions relating
to the general rights, e.g., in relation to references supplied by the employer, data processed in connexion with proposed redundancies, company takeovers, or negotiations
on pay increases.

7.8.1.6 Contractual and other obligations

Under s. 56 employers (or prospective employers in the case of recruitment) commit a criminal offence if they seek to require an employee or third party to supply them with certain records (i.e., emanating from certain data controllers (e.g., a chief officer of police) and relating mainly to criminal convictions) unless required by an enactment or by showing that, in the circumstances, this was justified as being in the public interest.

Under s. 57 any term or condition of a contract is void in so far as it requires an employee to supply any record which has been obtained by the employee under s. 7 and which consists of the information contained in any health record as defined by s. 68(2): see **7.8.1.3** above.

7.8.2 Access to Medical Reports Act 1988

Under the provisions of this Act a person may apply to gain access to medical reports relating to that person which are to be, or have been, supplied by a medical practitioner for employment or insurance purposes.

7.8.2.1 The basic right

An employer may request a medical report on physical or mental health matters (made after 1 January 1989) concerning an employee at any time. The medical report must be for 'employment purposes', but no distinction is drawn in the Act between existing and prospective employees; or for that matter with those undertaking a contract *for* services. The Act allows an employee or prospective employee to withhold consent to a medical report being sought. This will apply whatever the contract states. Further, under s. 3 the employer seeking a medical report *cannot* do so unless the employee has been notified of this right *and* the employee notifies the employer that consent is given.

The right to withhold consent is a fine theoretical right but, in the end, of less practical significance than it first appears because the employer will still have to make a decision (e.g., to employ or even to dismiss) on the evidence available. And what the Act does not permit is the suppression of *particular* items of information by the employee.

7.8.2.2 Outline of the Act's provision

- The 1988 Act concerns reports made by a 'medical practitioner' (as defined in the Medical Act 1983) who is or has been responsible for the clinical care of the individual. Thus, the Act seems to be aimed at the employee's general practitioner, consultant or psychiatrist who has treated the employee on a continuing basis. Company doctors appear to be exempt from the Act unless there is this element of continuity present in providing 'care'.

- The employee must also be notified of his or her right to withhold consent, a right of inspection, and a right to request that amendments be made before submission of the report. Equally, information may be withheld by the medical practitioner from the employee where disclosure would be likely to cause serious harm to that individual or others, or would be likely to reveal information about another person, or the identity of the supplier of the information. This last point does not apply where the affected individual has given consent or is a health professional involved in the care of the employee.

7.8.2.3 The effect on employers

Aside from the detailed administrative requirements, the 1988 Act did not effect changes to the law of confidentiality. Neither did the Act create extra rights of protection from dismissal, etc. Thus, although an individual may obtain an order securing compliance with the terms of the Act (s. 8), there is no separate right of damages.

7.8.2.4 Requesting medical examinations

Where the request relates to prospective employees there are few restraints placed on employers, save the practical one of deterring employees who might object to the examination. The reporting medical practitioner will owe a duty of care to the prospective employee to produce an accurate assessment. But as regards existing employees, express terms allowing an employer to demand a medical examination and report are necessary. Such a clause will still be subject to the provisions of the 1988 Act. It would seem extremely unlikely that a refusal by an employee to consent to the release of the report could be construed as misconduct which might justify a dismissal; although an employee's refusal to submit to *any* medical examination where there is justifiable concern, or a valid dispute, as to suitability to perform the job may be held to constitute misconduct.

There is, however, no implied duty to participate in medical examinations: *Bliss* v *South East Thames Regional Health Authority* [1987] ICR 700, though exceptions might occur where there is a justifiable need for a report, e.g., following an accident. Mandatory medical examinations may also, in some cases, be a breach of human rights (see **1.7** above).

7.8.2.5 Testing employees

It is estimated that about 8 per cent of the workforce in Britain are subject to some form of drug testing. On blood and urine, the ECHR has determined that individuals have the right not to be subjected to such testing but these cases did not arise in the employment context.

Two cases have considered the relevance of art. 8 ECHR to this analysis. In *O'Flynn* v *Airlinks The Airport Coach Co. Ltd* [2002] Emp LR 1217, the applicant was dismissed after testing positive for cannabis in a random drugs test. The dismissal took place before the Human Rights Act 1998 came into force, so art. 8 could not be relied on in any event. However, the EAT considered whether the Convention would have made any difference and concluded that it would not. They said that they had difficulty seeing how the zero-tolerance policy operated by the employer interfered with the employee's right to a private life, save to the extent that she could not report for duty with drugs in her system. In any event, they would have held any interference to have been justified under art. 8(2) for public safety reasons, given that she could be called upon to serve hot drinks on moving coaches.

The Privy Council has strengthened this approach with *Whitefield* v *General Medical Council* [2003] IRLR 39 where a general practitioner appealed against conditions imposed on his registration by the Health Committee of the General Medical Council. These conditions included complete abstention from alcohol at all times and submitting to random blood and breath tests. He argued that these restrictions were disproportionate to the object to be achieved and deprived him of the enjoyment of social drinking on family occasions contrary to his rights under art. 8(1). The Privy Council rejected his appeal and took the view that there was no authority supporting a view that an absolute ban on alcohol infringed a right to private family life and rather chastely reminded him that he was free to enjoy a social life with non-alcoholic drinks. They also held that any interference would have been permissible under art. 8(2) in any event, for public safety reasons.

7.8.2.6   Employee's declarations

Prospective employees do not owe a duty to volunteer information about themselves but do owe a duty not to misrepresent their position. This will include, in some cases, information concerning spent criminal convictions under the Rehabilitation of Offenders Act 1974. Where employees have been asked direct questions at an interview, on an application form, or during the course of their employment, they will come under a duty not to mislead or be fraudulent. Following this line, it is becoming quite common for companies to make use of questionnaires on health matters. Apart from questions which may be discriminatory (direct or indirect) there is no legal bar as such on this type of investigation, though again we may have to take account of human rights issues.

If an employee is taken on under false pretences this may well justify a later dismissal when the concealment is discovered. This principle applies to concealment of physical or mental illness, at least where such illness affects the job: *O'Brien* v *Prudential Assurance Co. Ltd* [1979] IRLR 140.

7.8.3   References

7.8.3.1   The common law position

At common law an employer is not obliged to provide references, though the specific rules of bodies created under statute (e.g., financial institutions) may mean that an employer is bound to do so and these rules may require the inclusion of specific information so that any failure may amount to a breach of contract between the employer and employee: *TSB Bank plc* v *Harris* [2000] IRLR 157. The general common law rule is also subject to the law on discrimination. Thus, the provision of defective references (or even the refusal to give references) because an employee has previously brought a sex discrimination claim against the employer may amount to discrimination under Equal Treatment Directive 76/207: *Coote* v *Granada Hospitality Ltd* (Case C-185/97) [1998] IRLR 656 (ECJ). And here, the EAT was prepared to stretch the words in the SDA 1975, s. 6(2) ('a woman employed by him') to include *ex-employees*.

Employers will owe the *recipient* of references a duty of care under the principles of negligent misstatement. It is quite common, and good practice, for a new employer to make any offer of employment subject to the receipt of satisfactory references; the meaning of 'satisfactory' is essentially a subjective one: *Wishart* v *National Association of Citizens Advice Bureaux* [1990] IRLR 393.

The *employee* will have an action against the employer who provides faulty references for defamation and malicious falsehood; though not for breach of confidentiality, if permission for full disclosure has been given. References are therefore subject to qualified privilege and the key point, in defamation or malicious falsehood, will be the presence or absence of malice.

An employee also has a cause of action in negligence against the employer for any failure to use reasonable skill and care in the provision of references: *Spring* v *Guardian Assurance plc* [1994] ICR 596. This House of Lords' decision has caused employers some consternation. The Court of Appeal has now added a gloss, and further problems, to this area. In *Bartholomew* v *London Borough of Hackney* [1999] IRLR 246 the Court dealt with the position where references were provided which detailed (beyond the information actually requested) that the employee had left Hackney after disciplinary action had been taken against him, this action only ceasing when the employee had agreed to voluntary severance. The reference did not give a full explanation of the position (e.g., that the employee had been counter-claiming race discrimination). Although finding against the employee on the facts, the Court indicated that the mere accuracy of a reference is not enough to provide protection to an employer; what is required is a broader test of 'fairness'—although the reference need not be comprehensive, it must not give an unfair overall impression of the employee.

One aspect of 'fairness' is that if employers provide negative information on employees they will be at risk if the employees have not had the opportunity to comment on these complaints. Thus, in *Cox v Sun Alliance Life Ltd* [2001] EWCA Civ 649, [2001] IRLR 448, an ex-employee succeeded in his claim against his former employer on facts very similar to *Bartholomew,* because whereas in *Bartholomew* it was held that the statements did not ultimately give a false impression, here the references were seriously inaccurate and the allegations cited had never been put to the ex-employee.

7.8.3.2   Effect of Data Protection Act 1998

Schedule 7 of the DPA 1998 (dealing with exemptions from the provisions of s. 7) lays out certain rules as regards access to references. References given in confidence by the data controller (the employer) relating to the employee are exempt from the provisions of s. 7 if given for the purposes of education and training, the appointment to any office, or the provision of services.

Employees may therefore gain access to references given by previous employers if held on their present employer's files, but as the author's identity would be revealed by such an investigation this access seems to fall within the exceptions to s. 7 so that the ex-employer's permission would most likely have to be gained first.

7.8.4   The interception of communications

Many employees now have access to computers as part of their work. The development of e-mails and the growth of the internet have begun to cause problems for employers in terms of monitoring their employees' communications. The issues involve abuse of company time and facilities, employees accessing pornographic internet sites, confidential information being disclosed through e-mails, etc., and (in this great age of constant quality-control) the need for employers to standardise or regulate telephone and written communications. The more employers intercept such communications, the more they open themselves to problems of infringement of privacy (see *Halford v United Kingdom* [1997] IRLR 471, regarding the tapping of telephone calls without prior warning).

7.8.4.1   Surveillance

It is estimated that about 80 per cent of all employees are subject to monitoring or surveillance of some form in the workplace. Surveillance may take many forms, given the wide availability and low cost of employee-monitoring technology. There is also some indication that disciplinary proceedings/dismissals for breaches of e-mail and internet policies now outnumber proceedings for breaches of health and safety regulations, dishonesty and theft. No distinction is made in the various pieces of legislation between systematic monitoring and occasional monitoring.

The starting point for any analysis of the legality of this now has to be art. 8(1) ECHR which states that: 'Everyone has the right to respect for his private and family life, his home and his correspondence.' Article 8 rights were extended to the workplace in

Niemietz v *Germany* (1992) 16 EHRR 97 (search of a lawyer's office), where the ECHR stated that the term 'private life' does not exclude professional and business activities.

Although (debatably) the Human Rights Act 1998 only applies cases involving 'public authorities', courts and tribunals are also public authorities within the Act so that, in reaching any decision, they must operate within the Convention (see **Chapter 1** above). Article 8 may therefore be used indirectly in relation to the acts of a private employer (or, debatably against a public authority undertaking a private act as per HRA 1998, s. 6(5)).

Halford v *United Kingdom* also established the idea of the 'reasonable expectation of privacy' at the workplace. American authorities would indicate that 'reasonable expectation' includes both a **subjective** expectation which is **objectively** reasonable. This leaves open the question whether an employer can remove the 'reasonable expectation of privacy'. In *Halford* this was not an issue as there was no waiver/warning, but the cases dealing with contracting-out regarding the related articles, 9 and 10 ECHR, strongly suggest that workers may 'opt-out' or be deemed to have opted-out of the protection of Convention rights in the employment context.

7.8.4.2 The statutory framework on accessing information

Interception of communications occurs when the contents of the communication can be read by a third party. The Regulation of Investigatory Powers Act 2000 (RIPA) governs the interception of communications over both public and private networks (if attached to a public system). It creates criminal liability and a civil tort of unlawful interception.

Under these regulations it is unlawful for a person, without authority, intentionally to intercept a communication in the course of its transmission by means of the postal service or public telecommunications system. The employer may **monitor** communications and **not be in breach where:**

- the employee and other sender/recipient have consented; or
- the employer has reasonable grounds to so believe; or
- the employer does other acts which comply with RIPA.

Monitoring of *traffic data* is not covered by RIPA. Instead, this is covered by the Telecommunications (Lawful Business Practice) (Interception of Communications) Regulations 2000 (LBP Regs). These regulations authorise monitoring and recording of all communications (telephone or e-mail) *without consent*:

- to ensure compliance with regulatory practices, e.g., Financial Services Authority requirements;
- to ensure standards of service are maintained, e.g., in call centres, to prevent or detect crime;
- to protect the communications system—this includes guarding against unauthorised use and potential viruses;
- to determine the relevance of the communication to the employer's business, i.e., picking up relevant messages when someone is away from work.

The monitoring should be limited to cases where it is necessary and relevant to the employer's business needs (thus *obviously* private communications do not fall within the permission to monitor, etc.). The LBP Regs require businesses to make all reasonable efforts to inform users of possible interception (there is no requirement to get consent). However, the LBP Regs also allow employers to monitor (but not record) for the purpose of determining whether the communications are relevant to the system controller's business (and thus open up employees' e-mail accounts).

The Information Commissioner's Code of Practice, *Monitoring at work: an employer's guide,* states that any monitoring of e-mails should only be undertaken where: the advantage to the business outweighs the intrusion into the workers' affairs; employers carry out an impact assessment of the risk they are trying to avert; workers are told they are being monitored; information discovered through monitoring is only used for the purpose for which the monitoring was carried out; the information discovered is kept secure; employers are careful when monitoring personal communications such as e-mails which are clearly personal; employers only undertake covert monitoring in the rarest circumstances where it is used for the prevention or detection of crime.

Further, the Information Commissioner's guidance indicates that the employer should only undertake acts such as monitoring where there is a clear problem which needs to be examined. The theme throughout the Codes is transparency. If monitoring takes place, then save in exceptional circumstances the employer should ensure that employees know what is being done, how it is being done, and the reasons for it.

The Information Commissioner has also issued a wide range of Codes covering matters such as the use of CCTV cameras in the workplace.

7.8.4.3 Storage of information

This is covered by the Data Protection Act 1998 as detailed above.

7.9 Summary

- The duty of confidentiality is concerned with protecting information which is central to the employer's business, the use or disclosure of which would cause harm to the employer.

- Once employment has been terminated the employer's confidential information may still be protected by the implied duty of fidelity which will continue even though the relationship has ended.

- But, confidential information will generally be protected only if it can be classified as a trade secret. There is no one common definition of 'trade secret' that can be applied to all organisations.

- What cannot be protected is the employee's 'know-how' acquired during employment and which he wishes to use in another employment.

- There is some debate as to whether an express term of confidentiality can extend protection to information which falls outside the definition of trade secret.

- An ex-employee may be prevented from using or disclosing his ex-employer's confidential information for a defined limited period, or forever, depending upon the nature of the information.

- The normal method of enforcement of a confidentiality term is by means of an injunction. Any application will be dealt with under the *American Cyanamid* principles.

- Employees also have rights of confidentiality. These centre mainly on the Data Protection Act 1998 and anti-surveillance legislation.

A combined 'self-test' question covering the topics raised in this chapter and the next will appear at the end of Chapter 8.

Restraint of trade

8.1 Introduction

Employers are often anxious to guard against direct competition from former employees. The only sure way to guarantee this is to remove them from the marketplace for a limited period of time, and the only way to do this is by means of a restraint of trade clause. Restraint of trade clauses seek to curtail the employee's opportunity to gain employment and are so subject to stringent analysis, justification resting solely on the prevention of *unfair* competition.

In this chapter we will examine the doctrine of restraint of trade under the following general headings:

(a) What constitutes a restraint of trade?

(b) Importance of how the contract was terminated.

(c) How reasonableness is determined: legitimate interests.

(d) How reasonableness is determined: reasonableness of drafting.

(e) Drafting and interpretation.

(f) Implied restraints.

(g) Restraints during employment.

(h) Preparatory actions.

(i) Garden leave.

(j) Injunctions.

8.2 What constitutes a restraint of trade?

8.2.1 Definition

A restraint clause is designed to stifle competition from ex-employees. When faced with such a clause the courts will presume the restraint to be *void* unless the employer can show it is reasonable. Reasonableness is assessed in two stages: (i) is there a 'legitimate interest' to protect? (ii) is the wording of the clause acceptable? We shall return to 'legitimate interest' at **8.5** below. As to the wording used, there are four headings to be considered in determining reasonableness:

(a) reasonableness in terms of the '*market*' in which the parties are operating and the appropriateness of the clause in relation to that employee;

(b) reasonableness in terms of *time*;

(c) reasonableness in terms of *area* covered;

(d) *public policy.*

A major caveat is necessary: each case turns very much on its facts. One cannot say that a one-year restraint, for instance, will always be reasonable or that a worldwide restraint is automatically unreasonable. Indeed, in *Dairy Crest Ltd* v *Pigott* [1989] ICR 92, the Court of Appeal made it clear that even authorities concerning the same trade (here a milkman) were not to be regarded as binding precedents. The basic rule is that an employer cannot be protected from competition *per se,* only from *unfair competition.*

Any practitioner in this area will tell you that merely relying on standard terms, without seeking to modify them according to the client's needs, is a particularly disastrous tactic. Thus it has been said that the client who demands to be given a standard clause is misguided and the solicitor who provides one is a fool.

8.2.2 Types of restraint

The most common types of restraint are:

(a) *Non-competition restraints* (i.e., preventing the employee working in that industry as a whole, or at least with named competitors). These are the most draconian clauses and are viewed with great suspicion by the courts.

(b) *Non-dealing restraints* (i.e., preventing employees accepting business from or conducting business with former clients or specifically named former clients). These are still treated carefully, especially as they may affect third party rights. For instance, even if a former customer prefers to take his business to the employee in the new job rather than continue dealing with the employer, any action by the employee may still constitute a breach of contract (see *John Michael Design plc* v *Cooke* [1987] ICR 445).

(c) *Non-solicitation restraints* (i.e., preventing employees actually initiating contact with former clients, though not barring the employee from dealing with such clients who transfer their business without solicitation). Non-solicitation clauses are usually less dramatic in their effect and, in many cases, procure a more sympathetic reception from the courts; though this does not necessarily ensure their success. We will deal with non-solicitation clauses later as a separate topic (see **8.8.5** below).

(d) *Non-poaching restraints* (i.e., preventing the employee from soliciting former colleagues to join him in the new venture).

8.2.2.1 Termination agreements

Although most restraint clauses arise under the ordinary terms of the contract, some will be found in termination agreements negotiated with departing employees (usually senior employees). Confidentiality agreements may appear here too. Obviously, the employer will have to pay for these, but the clauses themselves will be treated in the same way as those arising in the employment contract. If a covenant is introduced for the first time at this stage, or an existing one is varied, any monies paid may be subject to tax.

8.2.3 Which type of restraint to choose

Many employers will wish you to draft a clause that would make a pact with the devil look like an attractive alternative. For the most part, this should be resisted if only because a clause which seeks to restrain an employee more than is necessary will fail on this ground alone. Therefore, one should ask what level of protection is necessary to protect those interests, starting with non-solicitation clauses and moving on to non-dealing and then non-competition clauses. Tactics may also play a part here. Your client may insist upon a non-competition clause in order simply to scare off ex-employees. If so, you need (in writing) to advise that the clause is likely to fail. Equally, from the employee's perspective, one might accept the imposition of a draconian clause on the basis that it will never stand up in court so why worry about it! Whatever the ethical points here, both tactics carry dangers. These dangers may be summarised as follows:

8.2.3.1   From the employer's perspective

(a) Such a wide clause may well alienate an otherwise loyal employee.

(b) The opportunity to draft a potentially workable clause may be lost.

8.2.3.2   From the employee's perspective

(a) The court may find a way to 'blue-pencil' (i.e., edit) the clause so that a clause, assumed to be unlawful, becomes binding.

(b) The court may narrow the ambit of wide-ranging phrases (e.g., restrict the term 'business' to a particular aspect of the company's business) even though the strict meaning of the words might not allow for this and, in doing so, catch the unwary employee who has agreed to the clause believing it meant something else.

(c) Precedent, or at least *stare decisis,* is treated with caution in this area. Even the same clause (appearing in slightly different circumstances) may not be treated with consistency.

8.2.3.3   The basic approach

As with confidentiality in **Chapter 7** we have tried, in **Figure 8.1**, to map out the basic analytical structures employed by practitioners as regards restraint of trade. This diagram

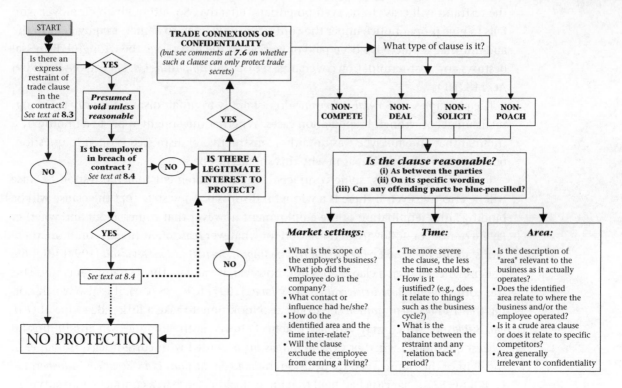

Figure 8.1 Diagrammatic summary.

shows you the overall pattern of analysis and the text below follows the pattern of the diagram.

8.3 Is there an express term?

The courts will not imply a restraint of trade to the employer's benefit. They will, however, interpret a term in the contract which seeks to restrain an employee's activities but which masquerades as an ordinary term of the contract as being in restraint of trade and strike it out. *Marshall v NM Financial Management Ltd* [1997] IRLR 449 is a good example of this. Here, the contract stipulated that commission should be payable to an employee after termination of the contract *only if* the employee did not enter into competition with the former employer. By another name this was a restraint clause.

The next point to note in the diagram is the presumption described above: even if there is an express restraint of trade clause, it will be presumed void unless reasonable. We will leave aside analysing 'reasonableness' for the moment and presume the clause in question passes this test.

8.4 The importance of how the contract was terminated

8.4.1 Wrongful dismissal

At common law an employer can terminate the contract for any reason provided the proper notice is given. In such a case, there is no breach of contract and the restraint clause will survive the termination of the relationship. However, if the dismissal constitutes a wrongful dismissal this will amount to a repudiation by the employer and the restraint will cease to be even potentially effective. So, although an employer who fails to give proper notice under the contract is only open to damages equivalent to the amount that should have been paid or worked in the first place, the wrongful dismissal destroys any post-termination covenants: see *General Billposting Co. Ltd v Atkinson* [1909] AC 118 (HL).

The principles of *General Billposting* do not apply to unfair dismissals; only to wrongful dismissal or wrongful repudiation cases. Whether they might apply to a finding by a tribunal that an employee was unfairly (constructively) dismissed is open to question, but there seems no good reason why this should not be so.

To guard against this, some contracts contain a statement that the restraint clause will be effective even if there is a wrongful dismissal. They state that the clause will be binding 'after termination of the employment however that comes about and whether lawful or not', or 'following termination for whatever reason'. Although common, these terms are ineffective: *Living Design (Home Improvements) Ltd v Davidson* [1994] IRLR 69. The presence of such a clause does not, however, invalidate the restraint generally. This was confirmed in *Rock Refrigeration Ltd v Jones* [1997] ICR 938 (CA). It is also worth noting that in *Rock Refrigeration* the Court also took time to take a little side-swipe at *General Billposting* which may yet have practical effects. Both Simon Brown and Philips LJJ (*obiter*) questioned whether *General Billposting* accorded with current legal principle in the light of the House of Lords' decision in *Photo Productions Ltd v Securicor Transport Ltd* [1980] AC 827. That case had held that an exclusion clause in a contract could survive a fundamental breach. Their Lordships' point was that if this is so then perhaps a restraint clause can survive a wrongful dismissal.

8.4.2   Justifiable dismissal

A dismissal without notice or with inadequate notice may still be a lawful dismissal if there is a contractually justifiable reason. In dismissing the employee the employer has accepted the repudiation of the contract by the employee. The employer is therefore still able to rely on the restraint covenants.

8.4.3   Resignation by the employee

If the employee resigns without giving notice, in the face of repudiatory conduct by the employer, he or she will have accepted the repudiation so that the restraint clause will cease to have any effect, as with a wrongful dismissal. If the employee gives notice, however, it seems that this will preserve the restraint clause: *Normalec* v *Britton* [1983] FSR 318.

8.4.4   Dismissal with payment in lieu of notice

Payment in lieu of notice is not a breach of contract if the contract so allows for it. If the contract does not allow for this then payment in lieu is a technical breach even though no damages would be due: *Rex Stewart Jeffries Parker Ginsberg Ltd* v *Parker* [1988] IRLR 483 (CA). The technical breach will invalidate the restraint clause.

8.4.5   Transfer of the business

As will be seen in **Chapter 12**, when a business is transferred existing employment rights are generally transferred as well. In *Morris Angel & Son Ltd* v *Hollande* [1993] IRLR 169, the question raised was whether a restraint of trade clause was subject to this rule. The Court of Appeal decided that a restraint clause entered into by the transferor company and the employee could be enforced by the transferee (purchaser) of the business. But in this case, the employee's contract was terminated very soon after the transfer so that the 'inherited restraint' related directly to contacts, etc. gained by the employee in the *transferor's* business. The position is unclear where there is a larger gap.

As will also be seen in **Chapter 12**, there is a general rule that any alteration to an employee's contractual rights following a relevant transfer is invalid if the reason for the alteration relates to the transfer of the business. In *Crédit Suisse First Boston (Europe) Ltd* v *Lister* [1998] IRLR 700, a business was taken over and new terms (some better than before, some worse) were introduced by the transferee. One disadvantageous change to the employee was the replacement of a 12-month non-solicitation clause with a three-month non-solicitation clause coupled with a three-month non-competition clause. The Court of Appeal held that, as these changes were detrimental to the employee and were as a result of the transfer, they were invalid (despite the fact that, on balance, the employee's position after all the changes, including monetary payments, was at least neutral).

8.5   Legitimate interests

As you can see from **Figure 8.1**, at the heart of all that follows is the first aspect of 'reasonableness', namely that the employer must be seeking to protect a legitimate proprietary (business) interest. The restraint must afford adequate, but no more than adequate, protection to the employer's interest. It is legitimate to:

(a) seek to prevent the potential disclosure of confidential information;

(b) seek to prevent the employee making use of the employer's trade connexions.

These are the standard touchstones, though a court can always recognise other legitimate interests.

8.5.1 Legitimate interest: preventing the potential disclosure of confidential information

We noted in **Chapter 7** that it is uncertain (following the *obiter* comments in *Faccenda Chicken* v *Fowler* [1986] ICR 297, CA) whether an express confidentiality clause can have any effect. Thus employers are often advised to insert a restraint of trade clause if they wish to protect confidential information which is important but not a trade secret. The advantage to a restraint clause is that a breach is more easily detectable and policed than the mere act of disclosing information. We have voiced the opinion that the use of a restraint clause is not justifiable simply to protect confidential information lower than a trade secret, but the 'belt and braces' practical thing to do is to insert both restraint and confidentiality clauses side by side.

8.5.2 Legitimate interest: preventing the employee making use of the employer's trade connexions

The debate flowing from *Faccenda Chicken* is not relevant to trade connexions: these are protectable legitimate interests.

8.5.2.1 Trade connexions: what are they?

There are a number of aspects hidden in the term 'trade connexions'. There are categories to which the term clearly applies, namely:

(a) the employer's customers and clients;

(b) the employer's suppliers.

There are categories where the application is likely to be made, namely:

(c) existing employees.

And there are categories where the application is more debatable, namely:

(d) the employee's previous client base;

(e) customers who no longer deal with the employer;

(f) future potential customers.

We shall examine these interests in turn.

8.5.2.2 Trade connexions: customers, clients, and suppliers

These categories—(a) and (b) in the list above—are sometimes referred to as the employer's 'goodwill' because they sum up the range of the employer's contacts and therefore the operational value of the business. Most cases will be concerned with these types of trade connexions. A solicitor's clients are treated no differently here from, say, a milkman's customers: the professional connexion with those clients does not carry with it some form of implied restraint of trade: *Wallace Bogan & Co.* v *Cove* [1997] IRLR 453.

8.5.2.3   Trade connexions: existing employees

The starting point for (c) is that recruiting another employer's employees is not unlawful provided those employees are not induced to breach their existing contracts. But can an employer set up a restraint of trade clause which prevents one of its own former employees from 'stealing away' (poaching) fellow employees when she leaves? Can the employer's own employees be regarded as 'legitimate interests'? In *Dawnay, Day & Co. Ltd* v *De Braconier D'Alphen* [1997] IRLR 442, the Court of Appeal reviewed what was becoming a long line of cases and decided that an employer did have a legitimate interest in maintaining a **stable workforce** within the limits of reasonableness, unhelpfully adding that 'it does not always follow that this will always be the case'. On this basis, it is suggested that any *non-poaching* clause can relate only to employees who were former colleagues, and probably only to those of senior status, though, like many 'rules' in this field, this is not a certainty (see, for instance, *SBJ Stephenson* v *Mandy* [2000] IRLR 233 where Bell J allowed a clause which protected against the poaching of all staff on the basis that the prime assets of the company—an insurance brokerage—were its staff).

Where solicitors' precedents contain such a clause, the majority of these do indeed refer to 'senior employees' or similar descriptions (e.g., 'skilled employees' as defined in the contract). Some extend this category to employees above a certain (defined) level of seniority or pay, or those who have to report to the Board, or those with whom the employee has had direct contact (or combinations of these), or to those who are also similarly covered by a restraint clause. A small percentage give more limited definitions of 'forbidden employees'; mainly those whose work involved the handling of confidential information or who had influence over customers.

8.5.2.4   Trade connexions: the employee's previous client base

The employee may have legitimately brought to the business useful connexions which he or she now wishes to carry forward to the next employment. To what extent have these connexions become the 'property' of the employer? In *M&S Drapers* v *Reynolds* [1956] 3 All ER 814 (concerning a salesman), the Court of Appeal viewed such contacts as still belonging to the employee. In contrast to this, in *Hanover Insurance Brokers Ltd* v *Schapiro* the former employee—a *senior* employee—was offered no such sympathy. It is likely that the longer an employee works for a particular employer, the more their 'property' in their previous contacts is eroded. The legitimacy of inserting an express clause in the contract to counter such possibilities, akin to partnership agreements, does not appear to have been reviewed by the courts.

8.5.2.5   Trade connexions: past and future customers

In *Hinton & Higgs (UK) Ltd* v *Murphy and Valentine* [1989] IRLR 519, a clause attempting to restrain contact with the employer's 'previous or present' connexions was declared unreasonable because of the width of the term 'previous clients'. The category needed to be defined and limited. Equally employers have not been able to guard against the exemployee dealing with the employer's potential **future** customers (*Konskiv Peet* [1915] 1 Ch 530) unless the departing employee has made some initial contact with the customer before leaving: *Rex Stewart Jeffries Parker Ginsberg Ltd* v *Parker* [1988] IRLR 483.

Sometimes an employee leaves just when the employer and a customer are at the stage of negotiating potential contracts. It is unlikely that any restraint could legitimately cover such potential contacts. An exception was seen in *International Consulting Services (UK) Ltd* v *Hart* [2000] IRLR 227 where the High Court held that, in principle, such trade connexions could be protected even where the employee's contact with the customer was unconnected with those negotiations and fell outside the 'relation back' period in the contract of 12 months, but here the employee had been in a central and influential position within the company during the negotiations.

8.6 What type of clause is it?

We outlined the four main types of restraint clauses in **8.2.2** above. The severest restraint is a non-competition clause. Courts take a lot of persuasion to enforce one of these unless the employer shows a very good reason, e.g., the time factor is very short and/or the area covered is small. The courts are more relaxed with, say, a non-solicitation clause as this only seeks to prevent the former employee approaching the employer's contacts for a set period or within a specified area.

You can see in **Figure 8.2** that the clause has to be reasonable as between the parties and reasonable on its specific wording. We shall now examine these ideas in **8.8** below, but first we should note the idea of 'blue-pencilling'.

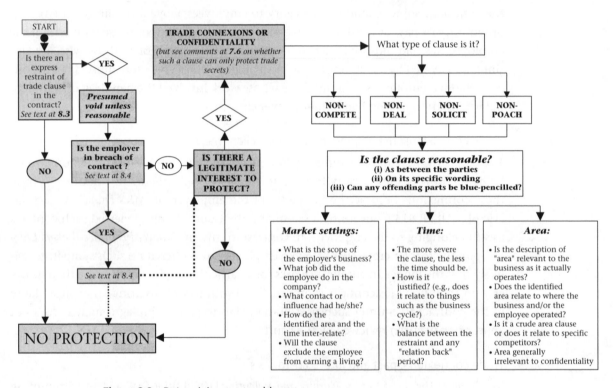

Figure 8.2 Determining reasonableness.

8.7 Severance and 'blue-pencilling'

'Blue-pencilling' means that the courts may, within limitations, remove words or sentences which are felt to make the clause unreasonable. The courts have no general power to rewrite a restraint to make it reasonable. They may give some interpretation to the wording, but it is not the courts' function to make contracts. What they have long accepted, however, is the idea of editing the clause—or applying the infamous blue pencil.

The remaining part of the clause is then allowed to stand and be effective. In *Sadler* v *Imperial Life Assurance of Canada* [1988] IRLR 388, three conditions were stated as necessary for severance (or 'blue-pencilling') to occur:

(a) the unenforceable provisions could be capable of being removed without the need to add to or modify the remaining part;

(b) the remaining terms continue to be supported by adequate consideration; and

(c) the removal of the words does not change the character of the clause, i.e., make the contract substantially different from that which was originally agreed.

In truth this will occur most often when there are separate clauses: one clause may be struck out leaving the other (narrower) clause operative. A final clause stating that 'each undertaking is a separate and distinct undertaking and the invalidity or unenforceability of any part of any of them shall not affect the validity or enforceability of the remainder' can prove useful and appears frequently in practice.

Asking a court to 'blue-pencil' is the equivalent of clutching at straws and what is never tolerated is a clause which states that the restraint will be effective 'so far as the law allows': *Davies* v *Davies* (1887) 36 ChD 359.

8.8 How is reasonableness determined?

The traditional dimensions to be measured in restraint cases have been those of *time and area*. Although the unreasonableness of either factor by itself may invalidate the restraint, the factors do overlap a great deal. Thus a restraint that is too wide in geographical terms will generally fail, but it may be saved if the time limitation is short. Likewise, a lengthy restraint may be valid especially where the geographical limitation is not extensive.

In the text below we have analysed the concept of 'reasonableness' in relation to the headings of:

(a) the market setting;

(b) time; and

(c) area.

We have created these headings merely as a device to help explain the courts' reasoning. They overlap and interreact; one affects the other.

8.8.1 When is reasonableness determined?

Reasonableness is determined by looking at the point the agreement was entered into (i.e., the date of the contract, any amendment or separate agreement). Promotions and changes in job titles, which effectively involve new contracts, can therefore have an effect on the reasonableness of any clause: what was reasonable for a salesperson with numerous contacts may not be suitable for an office-bound sales manager. It is common practice, therefore, to draft clauses which refer to events at the point of termination such as the prevention of the solicitation of customers 'who have been clients of the employer during the last 12 months prior to the termination of the contract'.

8.8.2   Width of the clause: reasonableness in terms of the 'market setting'

In every case the court has to relate the restraint to the market setting of the company and the individual in question: what is the scope of the employer's activities and what did the employee do? It is not reasonableness as an abstract concept that matters but rather reasonableness in relation to the *particular* contract of employment.

8.8.2.1   The scope of the employer's business

The first question to ask is: what sort of business are we dealing with? The effects (and therefore the reasonableness) of a standard clause will be different, for instance, when dealing with a butcher's business, a finance company, an estate agency, or a national frozen foods company. It may well be reasonable to have a 12-month restraint for an accountant because clients will probably visit the practice annually to submit their tax returns but the same period would be difficult to justify where a butcher leaves a shop and customers return weekly or monthly.

The next question is: where is the employer's business located? The type of restraint that is acceptable (reasonable) can often be affected by the company's location. Say, for instance, that you have a restraint of not competing within a two-mile radius of the business. Would it make a difference if the business was located in the centre of London as opposed to a provincial town such as Taunton? In both instances a two-mile restraint might, in the abstract, appear reasonable, but those two miles may well cover many more customers in the heart of London than in Taunton. Paradoxically, the whole market for the service might be wiped out in a small town whilst not being significantly affected in London. So, the key point is: what business are we trying to apply this to? A two-mile radius restraint for a hairdresser in Taunton probably cuts out most of Taunton. It cuts out a large slice of London too, but there are other areas where the employee might set up shop. So, one cannot say that, say, a two-mile radius restraint is automatically reasonable in every case: one has to look at the market in which the employer operates.

It is, of course, also true that location may be completely irrelevant. A person can be situated in London and still *deal* with customers in Bristol, for instance, by means of telephone, advertisement, fax, internet or letter as well as by personal proximity. Such was the position in *Office Angels Ltd* v *Rainer-Thomas and O'Connor,* regarding an employment agency. Here, a clause which sought to prevent the employee engaging in or undertaking the trade or business of an employment agency within an area of 1.2 square miles from the relevant branch looked reasonable but was held void. The clause was not over-demanding but, again, client contact was generally made by telephone. The actual siting of any rival office was largely irrelevant and the clause was meaningless.

Thus, a small radius restraint might be unreasonable and restraint extending to the whole of the UK European Union, or even worldwide ban could be reasonable, *depending on the market in which the business operates.* Most draft contracts we have seen, therefore, would only employ a ban on competition within a certain 'radius' from the employer's business in relation to small businesses such as hairdressers, butchers, etc. where the catchment area is defined by the siting of the business. The use of 'radius' is not applicable to many other types of business today though it was applied to solicitors in *Hollis* v *Stocks* [2000] IRLR 712, where the Court of Appeal upheld a one-year, ten-mile radius non-competition clause against an assistant solicitor which also forbade the solicitor representing any clients at specified police stations and a named Magistrates' Court. The Court of Appeal interpreted the phrase 'work within ten miles from the firm's office' to mean 'to work as a solicitor' and, looking at the geography of the East Midlands, the proximity of large towns not covered by the restraint, and the general work of the solicitor's practice, held that the clause was reasonable.

In summary, the employer must be able to show a functional correspondence between the activities prohibited under the restraint and the activities of the business. It may very well be the case, for instance, that a non-solicitation clause would be the highest level of protection acceptable and all others would fail.

8.8.2.2 The job done and the status of the employee

At its simplest level the employer needs to be able to justify the fact that the job done and the position held by the employee warrants the imposition of a restraint. For instance, area restraints may be appropriate for salesmen and confidentiality restraints may be justifiable for researchers, but having one standard restraint that applies to both plus, say, manual workers, is hard to justify. The case of *Marley Tile Co. Ltd* v *Johnson* [1982] IRLR 75 provides a good example of the sort of thing to be considered. Here, the clause in question sought to restrain the employee (a salesman) from soliciting, canvassing or dealing with customers of the employer in products made, sold or fixed by the company or in other similar products in any area in which he had been employed by the company for a period of one year after termination. The restraint covered *any area* in which the employee had worked during the year prior to leaving. In that year the employee had worked mainly in Devon, but several months before leaving he had also worked in Cornwall. This meant that the possible number of customers covered by the clause was in the region of 2,500 and the range of products was enormous. The restraint was held to be void—it could not legitimately apply to products the employee never dealt with (see also *Commercial Plastics Ltd* v *Vincent* [1965] 1 QB 623).

Junior employees may get more gentle treatment from the courts than their seniors. However, care should be taken when dealing with employees who have gained expertise in a particular field to the exclusion of all else. If the restraint effectively prevents them working within that field it is likely to fall foul of the test for reasonableness.

EXAMPLE

Your client is a salesman in the drapery trade. His contract contains a non-solicitation clause set to last for five years and is applicable to the employer's connexions who had been customers during the three years prior to termination. He wants to know whether he is likely to be restrained from working for a rival company.

This is based on the case of *M&S Drapers* v *Reynolds* [1956] 3 All ER 814. The Court of Appeal refused the restraint, partly on the grounds that the employee did not hold a position which warranted such a restriction. That was in 1956: today such a lengthy clause, even for a more senior employee, would be difficult to justify. Ask yourself: 'why does the employer need a five-year restraint covering customers from the last three years of the employee's employment?' What is the justification? One aspect of the justification might be that the employee has had extensive contact with these customers. The time still looks excessive but, as we shall see, this idea of 'contact' is much more important than status in assessing reasonableness.

8.8.2.3 The level of contact between the employee and the trade connexion

Here we ask:

(a) does the employee have to have had *contact* with the trade connexion before a restraint is valid; and, if so,

(b) what level of contact is necessary?

To answer question (a): the long-standing approach has been that contact is necessary. Usually this has meant *physical contact,* but repeated indirect contact can change this and those who procure business *without direct contact* have been held to fall within the ambit of restraint clauses. This is because frequency of contact coupled with some degree of attachment can generate reliance and influence. The closer the contact and the more reliant on the employee the customer/supplier becomes the more justifiable the restraint: *Scorer* v *Seymour Johns* [1966] 1 WLR 1419 and *Office Angels Ltd* v *Rainer-Thomas and O'Connor* [1991] IRLR 214. What is more debatable is whether an employee's *reputation* can be considered as a trade connexion (and therefore a legitimate interest) because it has long been established that mere personal attributes cannot be the subject of a restraint. In *Austin Knight (UK) Ltd* v *Hinds* [1994] FSR 52 Vinelott J noted that it was possible that influence might exist via *reputation* (at least in a business operating in a tightly knit market) although on the facts would not infer such influence. It is suggested that, if any form of restraint is permissible, it is most likely to be that of preventing solicitation of existing clients, rather than a general ban on acting within the general field of, say, financial services.

To answer question (b): on the whole it would be unwise for an employer to rely on merely proving *some form* of contact. The courts are really looking for the degree of *influence* that could be exerted by the employee over the customer or client: *Hinton & Higgs (UK) Ltd* v *Murphy and Valentine* [1989] IRLR 519. In analysing the degree of influence the court must set the 'employer's hold' over the customer against the type of contact the customer has with the employee (the level of reliance), the seniority of the employee, the nature of the goods or services, and the frequency of contact.

EXAMPLE

The owner of a hairdresser's business is tired of losing staff to rivals. She particularly values the work of the new stylist, and the receptionist who gets on very well with customers. She wants to know, in principle, whether she can impose a restraint of trade clause on either or both employees.

Receptionists will come into contact with all customers, but the degree of influence is infinitely less than is likely with the particular stylist and, though a restraint might prove to be effective, the argument favours the employee. But if we move to the stylist there is greater justification for the imposition of a restraint clause. So now, if that stylist sets up in business a short distance away it is arguable that some customers may well follow (see *Marion White Ltd* v *Francis* [1972] 3 All ER 857). However, this argument will only succeed where *influence* is shown—unless there are other factors present such as deceit: *East* v *Maurer* [1991] 1 WLR 461.

For some reason, hairdressers have long occupied the minds of judges in this area. In *Steiner (UK) Ltd* v *Spray* (1993, unreported, LEXIS transcript) the Court of Appeal was again concerned with this trade. Affirming the test of *influence* the court approved a *noncompetition* clause on the basis that a ban on solicitation was irrelevant in this business and that non-dealing was impossible to police. Their Lordships were, however, influenced by the fact that the clause covered an area of only three-eighths of a mile for six months.

8.8.2.4   Contact: relationship with employee's past dealings

In practice, both non-dealing and non-solicitation restraints tend to relate the restraint to contacts which the employee made during some period prior to termination. For instance, a clause which seeks to restrain an employee from dealing with customers or suppliers of the company for 12 months from termination will frequently contain a 'relation back' phrase such as:

who are at the date of termination of the employment and who shall have been at any time in the preceding 12 months a customer of . . . the Company and with whom the employee has had direct dealings or personal contact as part of that employment.

The 'relation back period' of prior dealings/contact tends to be either of six or 12 months. In assessing reasonableness the courts often balance the length of the restraint against the length of the 'relation back' period: see *Dentmaster (UK) Ltd v Kent* [1997] IRLR 636, CA.

8.8.3 Width of the clause: reasonableness in terms of time

The middle of the three 'reasonableness' boxes in **Figure 8.2** is 'time'.

8.8.3.1 Time in relation to confidential information

'Time' is the key element in relation to the protection of confidential information. The restraint can last no longer than the projected useful life of that information. An obvious difference lies in the considerations applied to ex-employees of organisations famed for their 'secret recipes' and those, say, in the fashion industry, where the secrecy of next season's designs has a limited lifespan. It may be reasonable in the former case to impose a lifetime ban; in the latter case, probably no more than a few months. Highly technical information will probably have a short lifespan, both because of the speed at which technology changes and also because an employee could not retain enough detail of the information for too long. So the vital question for a draftsman to ask the employer is: what is the lifespan of the information? The cynical practitioner then reduces this period by at least 25 per cent.

It must also be the case that different employees, or at least groups of employees, will have access to varying levels and types of confidential information. Thus, a restraint clause applied without variation to all employees is likely to fall foul of the reasonableness test because a one-year restraint, whilst reasonable in relation to the head of computer design, may be too great when applied even to a computer programmer or a technician.

8.8.3.2 Time in relation to trade connexions

A more relaxed attitude to lengthy or unlimited restraints has been taken by the courts in relation to trade connexions: *Fitch v Dewes* [1921] 2 AC 158—a solicitor's managing clerk who interviewed about half of the firm's clients was prevented from practising within seven miles of Tamworth Town Hall for an unlimited time. But this case does not set a general pattern. Before a restraint runs its course any advantage gained by the former employee will begin to fade. Knowledge of the market will become out of date and, more importantly, connexions will be lost. With this in mind, Jessel MR suggested a very workable test in *Middleton v Brown* (1878) 47 LJ Ch 411, at p. 413: that the duration of the restraint should be limited to the time it takes for a replacement employee to demonstrate his effectiveness to customers.

We would propose that any time limit must be justifiable both in relation to the 're-placement employee' idea coupled with an investigation into the *cycle* of the employer's business, i.e., how often contracts are renewed or repeat customer contact expected. We used the example of a firm of accountants being in contact with clients only every 12 months in **8.8.2.1** above as part of identifying the appropriateness of a restraint to what the nature of the employer's business: here we see how that assessment of 'market set-ting' can overlap with the assessment of acceptable time periods.

8.8.4   Width of the clause: reasonableness in terms of area covered

This is the final box in **Figure 8.2**. The key point here is that the size of the area is related more to density of population than mere acreage. It is thus an oversimplification to state that the wider the area the more likely it will be unreasonable; although it is a conven-ient rule of thumb.

Both UK and worldwide bans have succeeded. In *Littlewoods Organisation Ltd* v *Har-ris* [1976] ICR 516, a director concerned with mail order catalogues was restrained from employment within the UK for one year. *Under Water Welders and Repairers Ltd* v *Street and Longhorne* [1968] RPC 498, concerned a diver under a three-year worldwide restraint. With the increasing presence of national and multi-national companies in the marketplace, the problems as to which area is to be covered by the restraint will be everincreasing.

8.8.4.1   Area in relation to confidential information

Where the justification for a restraint rests on the protection of information, its geo-graphical ambit may have to be very wide. After all, information knows no real bounda-ries. Thus, the general 'market' in which the employer operates is a justifiable 'area'; and that area might these days be the UK, Europe, or even worldwide.

The restraint based on protecting confidential information is most likely to be aimed at preventing competitors from benefiting from the employee's expertise. It is a bet-ter tactic for an employer to limit a restraint to named competitors or competitors within a defined area: *Littlewoods Organisation Ltd* v *Harris* [1977] 1 WLR 1472. Here the restraint was for one year. The clause was drafted to prevent Harris working for Lit-tlewoods' major rival, Great Universal Stores (GUS). Harris left Littlewoods and went to work for GUS. The clause (which was effectively worldwide in its scope) was construed as applying only to the UK (because that was the only place where Littlewoods and GUS were rivals) and only to the type of business in which GUS competed with Lit-tlewoods. With these limitations (and debatable interpretations) the clause was held to be enforceable.

The *Littlewoods* case also illustrates the point that the courts are quite capable of adopting a generous interpretation where the overall package appears reasonable. For instance, in *Turner* v *Commonwealth & British Minerals Ltd* [2000] IRLR 114, the restraint was worded so as to apply to geographical areas which fell within the company's influ-ence but in which the employees had not worked. The clause might have failed on the same analysis as *Marley Tile Co. Ltd* v *Johnson* (see **8.8.2.2** above), but the Court of Appeal construed the clause as only applying to those areas in which the employees *had* worked, thereby saving the restraint.

8.8.4.2   Area in relation to trade connexions

The reasonableness of geographical restraints in relation to trade connexions is more problematic. Because non-dealing or non-competition clauses are crude devices the courts must do two things: first, they must survey the actual width of the employer's operations; secondly, they must determine whether the restriction effectively negates the former employee's potential *influence* over the company's connexions. On the first point, for instance, if a company operates only in Coventry, a restraint extending to Newcastle would go beyond what is necessary. This form of analysis works very well with localised businesses but note the comments on 'radius' restraints above.

When the employer's business is less localised the definition of a reasonable area has to rest on the factual point of understanding the employer's business and the appropriateness to the employee. It can no longer be the case that merely because the employer operates across the whole UK, the restraint should also cover such an area. The clause should relate to the siting of the employer's competitors and/or the employee's activities.

8.8.5   Non-solicitation covenants and trade connexions

The general rules described above apply equally to non-solicitation covenants as to non-dealing and non-competition clauses. We have separated out this area only because it brings with it some extra matters for consideration. Non-solicitation clauses relate to the protection of trade connexions only. The time qualification in the restraint will therefore be germane, though the question of the area covered is usually irrelevant. Oddly enough, there appears to be no case where a non-solicitation clause has been held void purely on the grounds of its duration; but this does not negate the need for the employer to show it is reasonable on the facts.

8.8.5.1   What constitutes solicitation?

Solicitation involves action by the employee: the enticing or active attraction of connexions away from the former employer. The terms 'soliciting' and 'enticing' have not, however, been defined authoritatively. We would suggest that anything which seems to carry an invitation to defect, rather than merely provide information, will amount to soliciting. Certainly, being approached by a former customer of the employer is not solicitation; and to prevent this activity the employer will need to have inserted a non-dealing clause.

Apart from the more obvious act of contacting connexions directly and overtly, it is also probable that *indirect* approaches such as advertising in newspapers and trade journals will constitute solicitation if they contain some form of inducement. Merely informing clients that one has left the old employer is not solicitation—the solicitation part would come with any 'I can now be contacted at. . .' statement.

If the solicitation clause has a geographical limit the issue of advertising material which spills over into the forbidden zone could present a problem. There appears to be no direct case law on this point, though in *Cullard* v *Taylor* (1887) 3 TLR 698, a solicitor restrained from operating within a particular area who sent letters to clients residing in the area was held to be in breach of the restraint; and New Zealand authority (*Sweeney* v *Astle* (1923) 42 NZLR 1198) indicates that advertising which spills over into the protected area so that customers become aware of the employee's position will be outlawed. If such is the position then the question of time constraint becomes particularly important if the clause is to be seen as reasonable rather than punitive.

8.8.5.2   Which connexions are covered?

These need to be capable of identification. The conclusive factor will then be whether the clause is protecting against influence being exerted by the former employee. Thus, in *Gledhow Autoparts* v *Delaney* [1965] 1 WLR 1366, the clause sought to restrict the activities of a salesman. The clause prohibited solicitation 'within the districts in which the traveller operated'. Many of the customers had no contact with the employee. The clause was therefore wider than necessary and void (see also *Marley Tile Co. Ltd v Johnson* [1982] IRLR 75).

The comments on prior contact noted above at **8.8.2.3** apply equally here and are not repeated.

We should also note again that if a clause is otherwise reasonable it will not be deemed unreasonable simply because the employer's connexions state they are unlikely to continue doing business with the employer anyway: see *John Michael Design plc v Cooke* [1987] ICR 445.

8.8.6   Public policy considerations

Strictly speaking, the whole doctrine of restraint of trade is based on the concept of public interest; the balancing of an individual's liberty with principles of freedom of contract. Courts can therefore 'fall back' on pronouncements of public interest or public policy in order to strike out clauses which, though reasonable perhaps as between the parties, offend some vague judgment as to what is acceptable.

One thing which is certain about public policy is that it is not immutable. As a starting point, however:

(a) If the restraint has passed the tests of legitimate interest as well as temporal and spatial reasonableness it will fall on the employee to prove that it is nevertheless contrary to public policy: *Herbert Morris v Saxelby*.

(b) It will not be contrary to public policy simply on the grounds that the employee's interests are more adversely affected than the employer's interests are protected. Except in the extreme cases where the employee is prevented from working at all the effect on the employee is not really a consideration addressed by the courts. The test is not based on the *balancing* of interests: *Allied Dunbar (Frank Weisenger) Ltd v Weisenger* [1988] IRLR 60.

(c) It was suggested in *Faccenda Chicken v Fowler* that the use to which an employee puts confidential information may have an effect on the court's approach to the protection sought, e.g., seeking to earn a living is viewed as potentially warranting protection but merely *selling* the information will lose the court's favour.

Other examples of courts invoking 'public policy' to strike out clauses include: *Bull v Pitney-Bowes* [1967] 1 WLR 273, where a pension scheme contained a clause stating that if a retired employee entered into any form of competition with the employer that employee's pension rights would be affected; and *Kores Manufacturing Co. Ltd v Kolok Manufacturing Co. Ltd* [1959] Ch 108 (a reciprocal agreement, made between two companies, restraining the employment of each other's former employees held to be contrary to public policy).

But public policy does not always damn restraint clauses. Thus in *Bridge v Deacons* [1984] AC 705 the Privy Council perceived the value of restraint clauses as providing a means whereby the young can replace the old. And in *Kerr v Morris* [1987] Ch 90 the Court of Appeal did not agree that doctors in general practice formed a special class which was exempt from the applications of restraint of trade clauses.

It would also appear that a defective restraint cannot be saved by the fact that during the time it should have applied the employee also received some post-termination payments: *TSC Europe (UK) Ltd v Massey* [1999] IRLR 22, ChD.

8.9 Drafting and interpretation

8.9.1 The problems in giving meaning to the clause

The basic premise is that an employer stands or falls by what is written in the restraint clause. Here is a typical restraint clause:

Non-competition
For a period of 6 months after termination of the Employment, the Employee shall not (whether directly or indirectly) be engaged or interested whether as principal, servant, agent, consultant or otherwise in any trade or business which by virtue of its location competes with any trade or business being carried on in the United Kingdom at the date of termination of the Employment by the Company and in which trade or business the Employee has been involved as part of his Employment.

It does not make for light reading, partly because the tradition of not using punctuation (which died out elsewhere in legal documents years ago) still rears its ugly head in this area. Further, the clause often makes no sense at all when actually applied to the employer and employee, because it has simply been lifted from a book of precedents. It is therefore advisable to make the meaning of any clause as clear as possible. Phrases such as 'engage', or 'undertake' or 'carry on a business' are somewhat flexible expressions which may bear a different meaning in a given context. A solicitor must make sure the context fits. If the contract is silent or ambiguous on a particular point it will most likely be construed against the employer.

As a matter of drafting practice, therefore, it is imperative that any restraint clause actually reflects both a legitimate interest *and* the relevance of that clause to the employee's work. The easiest clauses to draft are those which prohibit actions on a sweeping basis. They are equally the most dangerous clauses because they cannot hope to cover all eventualities. Even an immaculately worded contract which contains only one general clause intended to cover the entire workforce will probably be drafted too widely to cover specific situations or will not be appropriate to grades of employees.

8.9.1.1 Narrowly drafted clauses

Clauses which are very specific will generally not be read as protecting wider interests. The courts will not write words into a clause to make it effective. If an interest needs protecting the restraint clause must be drafted to achieve this. At its simplest, this will mean that a non-solicitation clause will fail to prevent employees dealing with customers *who contact them*.

8.9.1.2 Construing wide wording

Courts may choose to read wide wording in a restricted way so as to make it workable. Thus, sometimes the courts have limited the application of any restraint, however widely worded, to the employer's actual business interests. In *Business Seating (Renovations) Ltd v Broad* [1989] ICR 713 a non-solicitation clause failed to say what the *'business* of any customers or clients' actually was. The court interpreted the clause by reference to other clauses in the contract to define the business as that of the repair and renovation of office furniture; but the court could simply have struck out the clause for ambiguity. Indeed, this is exactly what happened in *Mont (J. A.) (UK) v Mills* [1993] IRLR 173. The clause was again too general and did not attempt to focus on the need to protect confidential information; its defects were not a 'mere want of accuracy of expression'. It is advisable to define the 'business' involved, especially in multi-product companies.

Recently, some level of unspoken disagreement has emerged in the Court of Appeal as to the most appropriate style of interpretation to be used. A literal (or *contra proferentem*) approach was seen in *Mont* v *Mills* (Glidewell, Beldam, and Simon Brown LJJ), *Ingham* v *ABC Contract Services* (unreported, 1993: per Russell and Leggatt LJJ) and the approach was specifically approved by Sedley and Simon Brown LJJ (perhaps not surprisingly) in *Wincanton* v *Cranny & SDM European Transport Ltd* [2000] IRLR 716. *In Hanover* v *Schapiro,* however, the Court had adopted a far more purposive approach (Dillon and Nolan LJJ) and in *Beckett Investment Management Group Ltd* v *Hall* [2007] EWCA Civ 613, [2007] IRLR 793 the Court permitted a clause, drafted in favour of a holding company which effectively dealt with no one, to be applied to the subsidiary companies on the basis of 'practical reality'. It is not surprising that their Lordships, in all cases, have expressed the need for a full hearing of a case to resolve what is a fundamental divergence of principle.

The draftsman's dilemma is this: where the restraint clause does not specifically state the interest which the covenant is intended to protect the court can look at the wording and the general circumstances to ascertain the parties' intentions, but it can also hold that the wording is simply too wide to protect anything. But where the covenant *does* state the interest the employer the court is likely to follow that wording and limit the scope of the protection. Thus spelling out the legitimate interest gains the advantage of definition and certainty, but runs the risk of limitation. What the courts will not tolerate from the ex-employee are 'colourable evasions'—minor and meaningless alterations of status on the behalf of the employee (e.g., a change in job title) made simply to avoid the exact wording of the restraint. An employee who argues that acting as an assistant to, say, an architect, is not in breach of a restraint which forbids him 'carrying on that profession', will see little sympathy from the courts. Setting up a limited company under which to continue in the same trade will also count as a colourable evasion: *Gilford Motors* v *Horne* [1933] Ch 935.

8.10   Restraints during employment

The doctrine of restraint applies to post-termination events. Cases that use the term to refer to restrictions during employment (see *Schroeder (A) Music Publishing Co. Ltd* v *Macaulay* [1974] 1 WLR 1308 and *Davis (Clifford) Management Ltd* v *WEA Records Ltd* [1975] 1 WLR 61) have not been concerned with employment law at all, but rather with commercial contracts (and most recently relating to exclusive contracts for 'exploited' songwriter-performers).

There are important analytical distinctions between the two types of term. First, courts are reluctant even today to upset express terms relating to the operation of the contract, e.g., terms relating to hours, pay, etc. At the same time, courts have always subjected restraint clauses to a detailed and rigorous analysis. Secondly, an express term relating to the currency of the contract is presumed **valid** unless shown otherwise; restraint clauses are presumed to be void. Thus both restraint of trade and servile incidents may be based upon the same *common rule* of preventing undue restrictions on personal liberty, but one should be clear as to which is being used.

8.10.1   Express terms

These usually appear in the form of 'whole time and attention'. Frequently they state as their justification the prevention of competition. An express term can indeed limit the activities of employees undertaken in their spare time. Any restriction the employer imposes on the employee will not deprive the employee of earning any livelihood and therefore will most likely be tolerated by the courts. At least this should hold true with full-time workers; contracts with part-time workers or consultants will be viewed more in the employee's favour.

8.10.2   Implied terms

In the absence of an express term the employee (at least senior employees) will still be bound under the duty of fidelity to use the employer's time for the employer's purposes, i.e., not to pursue other activities during working hours—at least if those activities are in competition with the employer, cause harm to the employer's interests, e.g., by divulging (or having the potential to divulge) confidential information (see *Hivac Ltd* v *Park Royal Scientific Instruments Ltd* [1946] Ch 169), or cause harm to the relationship (e.g., by undertaking work which adversely affects the proper fulfilment of the employment contract).

It follows that some low-ranking staff will have greater freedom as to the use of their spare time and cannot be so easily limited: *Nova Plastics Ltd* v *Froggatt* [1982] IRLR 146 (odd-job man not in breach when working for a competitor in his spare time). Proof of real or potential harm to the employer would be necessary for any restriction to have effect.

8.11   Employees' preparatory actions before termination

If an employee is planning to resign and set up in business, he or she will have made some preparations. Any business venture will need some planning. If the employee uses the employer's time and facilities to do this then this action will constitute a breach of contract: *Wessex Dairies Ltd* v *Smith* [1935] 2 KB 80, where the employee milkman (on his last day of employment) set about informing customers of his plans to set up in business on his own account.

Some latitude is given to enterprising employees. In *Laughton* v *Bapp Industrial Supplies* [1986] IRLR 245, the two employees wrote to their employer's clients informing them of their intention to set up in business on their own account and asking for product lists, price lists, and general terms. They were summarily dismissed when this was discovered by the employers. The EAT held that their actions did not amount to a breach of fidelity; their actions were *merely preparatory*. The position would have been different if they had used the employers' time and equipment (such an example would be seen in the later case of *Crowson Fabrics Ltd* v *Rider* [2008] IRLR 288 where employees 'overstepped the line' setting up e-mail accounts and actively soliciting customers); or even if there had been express terms forbidding such action. Again, in *Balston Ltd* v *Headline Filters Ltd* [1987] FSR 330, a director's *intentions* to set up in a competing business were held not to be a breach of fiduciary duty or breach of fidelity; neither were his actions which were undertaken during his notice period but at a time when he had been released from his duties. But in *Marshall* v *Industrial Systems & Control Ltd* [1992] IRLR 294, the employee was in breach when he formed concrete plans with a fellow employee to steal away the business of the employer's best client. And again, in *Adamson* v *B&L Cleaning Services Ltd* [1995] IRLR 193 the EAT found the dismissal of a foreman to be fair when he had sought to tender for a contract in competition with his employer. This was a breach of fidelity and distinguishable from *Laughton* v *Bapp*. The Court of Appeal has also noted that where an employee can be classed as a fiduciary (usually because he is a director as well as employee) preparatory acts are treated much less leniently: *Helmet Integrated Systems* v *Tunnard* [2007] IRLR 126. However, in this particular case the Court was keen to point out that it will not imply a term that an employee cannot prepare to compete and any express terms would be read *contra proferentem*.

These cases tended to focus on acts of preparation as distinct from substantive actions. What is not entirely clear, however, is whether potentially harmful acts such as soliciting customers, suppliers or even fellow employees, *pursued in the employee's own time,* will constitute a breach of fidelity. There are indications (see *Thomas Marshall* v *Guinle* [1978] ICR 905, at p. 925 and *Hivac Ltd* v *Park Royal Scientific Instruments Ltd* [1946] Ch 169, at p. 178) that the answer would be that a breach has occurred. Certainly this should be the case where the contract contains a 'whole time and attention' clause.

If the employee is simply planning to leave the company to join another (e.g., attending interviews), it follows from the above discussion that this will **not** constitute any breach of fidelity. Care must be taken here to distinguish preparatory acts, such as attending interviews, from acts such as copying confidential information or memorising data or diverting business opportunities. In *Sanders* v *Parry* [1967] 1 WLR 753, for instance, an assistant solicitor agreed with one of his principal's clients to resign and set up in business, in premises provided by the client, taking with him the client's business. Havers J commented that the employee was 'knowingly, deliberately and secretly acting, setting out to do something which would inevitably inflict great harm on his principal'. Thus, such actions will constitute a breach of contract and may render the employee subject to an injunction.

8.12 Garden leave

The rather graphic term 'garden leave' refers to attempts to hold the employee (who usually wishes to terminate the contract) to his or her notice period. The idea is that the employee will not be forced to work during that notice period but may stay at home (in the garden!) and still be paid. If successful, the effect of such a clause is that it operates as some form of indirect restraint as the employee cannot work for any competitor during this time because of the employee's continuing duty of fidelity. Contacts and confidential information thus become less and less useful. Injunctions have been granted to this effect. Such relief is discretionary.

The case law really began with *Evening Standard Co. Ltd* v *Henderson* [1987] ICR 588. Henderson sought to leave to work for a rival newspaper, giving only two months' notice instead of the 12 required. The company sought to put him on garden leave. An injunction was granted because the company was not seeking to compel Henderson to continue working as such, nor was the company refusing him the right to work, nor would it be seeking damages from him for not working. But an injunction was refused on similar facts in *Provident Financial Group plc* v *Hayward* [1989] ICR 160 because the Court of Appeal found that the employer's position would not be seriously affected by the employee's actions. In *GFI Group Inc* v *Eaglestone* [1994] IRLR 119 a 20-week notice period/garden leave was held to be arbitrary and the garden leave was reduced to 13 weeks.

It is advisable to have an express 'garden leave' provision in the contract, rather than merely rely on the notice provision covering this by implication: see *Eurobrokers Ltd* v *Rabey* [1995] IRLR 206. Here, the employee (a money broker) resigned and the employers sought to bind him to an express six-month garden leave clause. He declined to observe this and an injunction was granted enforcing the period. The court noted that the employer had expended a great deal of money in developing contacts for the employee and that this period represented a reasonable time for the employer to cement new relations with those customers.

William Hill Organisation Ltd v *Tucker* [1998] IRLR 313, saw the Court of Appeal again refuse to grant a 'garden leave' injunction where there was no express term allowing for this, holding that the employer was under an obligation to let this senior employee perform his job, not just receive his wages (which is a little odd given that the employee actually wanted to leave his job to work elsewhere). Therefore, on a 'belt and braces' approach it is advisable for an employer to include both a garden leave clause and a payment in lieu clause in the contract. The case did not end there. Morritt LJ went on to comment that in the case of a garden leave injunction being sought, 'it had to be justified on similar grounds to those necessary to the validity of the employee's restraint covenant in restraint of trade . . . '. The same point was made again by Morritt LJ in *Symbian Ltd* v *Christenson* [2001] IRLR 77. This case also contains the controversial view of Sir Richard Scott V-C that, during garden leave periods, an employee no longer owed a duty of good faith or fidelity to his employer.

Where an employer seeks to enforce both a garden leave clause and a restraint clause there is a persuasive argument that the overall effect might be unreasonable. Some contracts therefore specify that if the garden leave is enforced the restraint will be reduced accordingly. Following the Court of Appeal decision in *Crédit Suisse Asset Management Ltd* v *Armstrong* [1996] IRLR 450, however, we now know that (except in extreme cases) there is no juridical basis for such a set-off. The Court also confirmed its powers in deciding on the permissible length of garden leave clauses in any particular case.

It is also sometimes argued that a garden leave clause should be unenforceable where employees need to be allowed to work to preserve their particular skills. There is the basis for an argument here but the employees involved must come, so to speak, with clean hands. Where they have committed an act of serious misconduct that led to their being given notice, they will not get the sympathy of the court: *SG & R Valuation Services Co* v *Boudrais* [2008] IRLR 770. This case also demonstrated that whereas a court will usually look for an express garden leave term, in some instances an employer (as here) can rely on notice clauses alone through the device of implied terms.

8.13 Injunctions

Though a claimant may have a remedy of damages as of right there exists the additional or alternative discretionary remedy of an injunction. However, if damages will compensate the claimant fully an injunction will not be granted. Neither will the court grant an injunction which amounts to an order for specific performance.

8.13.1 Basic rules for injunctions

Injunctions come in two forms: interim (pending a full hearing of the issues) and final (granted at the conclusion of the full action). In either case they may be limited in duration or perpetual in their effect. The granting of injunctions is a discretionary remedy. The key section of the Civil Procedure Rules is Part 25.

As far as employment matters are concerned, interim injunctions have the greater prominence. Despite the fact that the interim injunction really does not decide the merits of the case at all, the granting of such injunctions can effectively determine the issue.

For instance, if the lifespan of a restraint of trade clause is one year it is unlikely that the full action will be heard before its expiry. Thus where an employer is faced with an employee or former employee who is about to divulge confidential information, breach copyright, destroy the novelty of a patentable invention and so forth, the effectiveness of an injunction can come into play. Even in advance of any breach it is possible to obtain a *quia timet* (because he fears) injunction.

Almost inevitably, where an interim injunction is granted the claimant will have to undertake to pay any damages due should the final action determine that the injunction was not justified. In some cases, the court will require proof that this undertaking can be honoured. It is also possible for a defendant to seek to avoid the full implications of an interim injunction by offering to the applicant or the court an undertaking in relation to some or all of the relief sought.

8.13.2   American Cyanamid v Ethicon

The decision of the House of Lords in the patent case of *American Cyanamid Co. v Ethicon Ltd* [1975] AC 396 established the position as regards *with notice* applications for prohibitory injunctions. In these cases evidence is normally given by witness statement, to the exclusion of cross-examination. The employer does not have to show a *prima facie* case to obtain an injunction preventing, for example, the breach of a restraint of trade or confidentiality clause. Rather, the test is whether:

(a) there is a serious issue to be tried at the full hearing. This is a low-level test. In *Arbuthnot Fund Managers Ltd* v *Rawlings* [2003] EWCA Civ 518, Chadwick LJ stated (at [30]) that the question at this interim stage is, '[W]hether it is plain and obvious that the restraint will fail after examination at a trial. If it is not plain and obvious—because the determination as to what is in the interests of the parties and in the interests of the public must await a trial—then the clauses must at this stage be regarded as having a reasonable prospect of being upheld'; and

(b) if there is, whether the 'balance of convenience' favours the granting of the injunction. This aspect has been described as a shorthand phrase for 'the balance of the risk of doing an injustice' or 'the balance of hardship'. The primary factor in deciding this question is whether damages at trial would be a sufficient remedy. If they would be, this negates the need for an injunction. However, damages are often not an adequate remedy in this area as (especially in confidentiality cases) once the 'cat is out of the bag' the injury caused may well be uncompensatable in monetary terms. Equally, if the defendant is unlikely to be able to pay any damages awarded this points towards an injunction being granted—and if the applicant cannot give a cross-undertaking on damages this makes the granting of an injunction less likely. The focus of 'balance of convenience' often amounts to gauging the cost to the employer of allowing the employee to use/disclose or continue to use/disclose the secret as against the possibility that the employee will be unable to work in the industry. The cases show that the employer's needs are usually seen to be paramount, though some notice was taken of the employee's (unopposed) claim of potential job loss in *Corporate Express Ltd* v *Lisa Day* [2004] EWHC 2943 where the remaining part of the restriction was quite short. A very good and straightforward application of this balancing act can be seen in *Steffen Hair Designs* v *Wright* [2004] EWHC 2995, where a 'half-mile radius' non- competition injunction was granted against a hair stylist working for a competitor some two hundred yards away, but this was limited in scope to cover only ex-clients of the stylist's previous employer (effectively turning it into a non-dealing clause—which is very practical but highly questionable as it involves rewriting the contract to turn a non-competition clause into one of non-dealing).

In *Lawrence David v Ashton* [1989] ICR 123, the Court of Appeal stated that the *American Cyanamid* principles will *normally* apply to restraint of trade and confidentiality cases. The court will then seek to make an order for a speedy trial of the full action, usually on the application of the defendant. If, however, a speedy trial is not possible the judge is placed in something of a dilemma: to tie down the employee for a lengthy period so that long-term employment prospects might be adversely and seriously affected; or to allow the employee to continue working for the competitor so that, even if the restraint is finally found to be valid, the employer's remedy is purely a Pyrrhic one. In such instances (as was noted specifically in *Lansing Linde Ltd v Kerr* [1991] ICR 428 by the Court of Appeal), the judge at the interim hearing may have to investigate the substantive merits of the case in order to decide whether or not to grant the injunction. Thus, if the full action cannot be tried before the period of the restraint has expired (or almost expired), the court's decision could for most practical purposes effectively determine the issue at the interim stage. Equally, there is little point in granting an interim injunction concerning confidential information where there can be no further material damage to the employer.

As a basic approach, therefore, if a speedy trial is not possible a judge will have to consider, in a limited way because of the availability of evidence, the actual merits of the case. Indeed, in *Series 5 Software Ltd v Philip Clarke* [1996] FSR 273 Laddie J made the point that assessing the merits of the case was not in itself contrary to the spirit or intentions of *American Cyanamid*. Laddie J reviewed the authorities in depth and concluded that Lord Diplock in *American Cyanamid* had not intended to exclude consideration of the strength of the parties' cases; what was intended was that the court should not at this stage attempt to resolve difficult issues of fact or law. Thus it is necessary that a clear view of the evidence adduced can be gained by the judge without great debate before the relative strengths can be considered. The application of the *American Cyanamid* principles, as modified by *Series 5*, remains the position as regards interim injunctions applications based on restraint of trade clauses relating to the protection of trade connexions. With applications relating to the protection of confidential information (based on the implied term, any operative express terms or any restraint justified by the protection of information) matters have taken a different route because of the impact of the Human Rights Act 1998.

8.13.3 Impact of the Human Rights Act 1998

Article 10 ECHR states:

1. Everyone has the right to freedom of expression. This right shall include freedom to hold opinions and to receive and impart information an ideas without interference by public authority . . .

2. The exercise of these freedoms, since it carries with it duties and responsibilities, may be subject to such formalities, conditions, restrictions or penalties as are prescribed by law and are necessary in a democratic society . . . for the protection of the reputation or the rights of others, *for preventing the disclosure of information received in confidence* . . . [emphasis added]

In cases involving the publication of material concerning others, therefore, this article (via the Human Rights Act) has to be considered. In terms of the granting of interim injunctions, the procedural method of dealing with this is set out in s. 12(3) HRA 1998 which states: 'No [relief affecting the exercise of a Convention right to freedom of expression] is to be granted so as to restrain publication before trial unless the court is satisfied that the applicant is likely to establish that publication should not be allowed.'

High-profile case law has sprung up in this area (sometimes involving the potential conflict between art. 10 and art. 8—respect for private and family life): see, for instance, *Douglas* v *Hello! Ltd* [2001] QB 967, on the infamous wedding photos of the Douglas's; *A* v *B (a company)* [2002] EWCA Civ 337, [2002] 3 WLR 542 on the sexual exploits of a footballer; *Venables* v *News Group Newspapers Ltd* [2001] Fam 430, on the identities of the killers of James Bulger and the more technically biased case of *Imutran Ltd* v *Uncaged Campaigns Ltd* [2001] 2 All ER 385, where a group campaigning for the cessation of animal experiments sought to publish confidential information belonging to a pharmaceutical company. These cases have generally been concerned with the freedom of the press or the protection of reputation. None of the cases had to consider, as part of the *ratio*, what was meant by the phrase in s. 12(3): 'the applicant is likely to establish that publication should not be allowed'. That problem fell to the Court of Appeal in *Cream Holdings Ltd* v *Banerjee* [2003] EWCA Civ 103, [2003] 2 All ER 318. As Sedley LJ puts it: how likely is 'likely'? The Court of Appeal held that the word 'likely' means *'a real prospect of success, convincingly established'*—a standard higher than that expected under *American Cyanamid* but lower than the notion of 'more probable than not'. 'Real prospect' here means 'not fanciful' rather than 'on the cards'.

As was noted in *Cream Holdings,* however, this test is just the first step; it is still open to the court to decide on the merits available to it whether to grant or refuse the injunction (indeed, in *Cream Holdings* itself the Court of Appeal was divided on the application issue). Simon Brown LJ put it this way: 'That is not, of course, to say that, whenever the [likely to succeed] test is satisfied, the court will grant interlocutory relief [sic] . . . . Often the court will not think it right to exercise that discretion in favour of prior restraint unless it is indeed satisfied that the claim will more probably than not succeed at trial' (at [61]). This is because, as Simon Brown LJ further commented (at [56]) on the move away from the original *American Cyanamid* principles, 'there will indeed be a number of claims for injunctive relief which will now fail when earlier they would have succeeded; they will fail because the court is required by s. 12(3) actually to consider the merits . . . '.

It is possible that human rights issues may arise in an employment context and trigger a s. 12(3) analysis but most employment-based cases will not centre on issues such as freedom of expression and privacy in the way these terms have so far been used in human rights' jurisprudence. Nevertheless, the potential is always there. *Cream Holdings* itself involved an ex-employee in-house accountant passing information about alleged company malpractices to a local newspaper. The employee was under a duty of confidentiality and was in breach of this by relating her stories to the newspaper. Much of the detail of this case is contained in a closed judgment owing to the nature of the information, but, since the court affirmed the granting of the injunction, we must conclude that the presence of the duty was enough to persuade the court to continue with the temporary stop to publication (together with the fact that the delay in publication would not destroy the newsworthiness of the article itself). Nor did the well-established principle that there can be no confidentiality in iniquity (i.e., the company's alleged misconduct) prove to be a major decisive factor (but contrast, for instance, Sedley LJ's comments at [87] with those of Arden LJ at [96]). The injunction did not, however, relate to disclosures made by the accountant to relevant professional and supervisory bodies under the Public Interest Disclosure Act 1998.

8.13.4   Summary of rules regarding interim applications

There are different standards to apply in justifying the granting of interim injunctions depending upon the basis for the claim.

(a) Where the issue is one of the protection of trade connexions *only* the normal *American Cyanamid* principles should apply.

(b) The merits of the case may nevertheless have to be examined where a speedy trial is not possible. This is a matter of discretion and the courts should rarely attempt to resolve complex issues of disputed fact or law: *Series 5*.

(c) Any case involving the disclosure of confidential information may bring with it human rights implications in the form of art. 10 ECHR and even, possibly, art. 8 rights. If so, the procedures described in s. 12(3) HRA 1998 must be adhered to. If not, one presumes that the *American Cyanamid/Series 5* principles continue unabated (though this is not clear and it seems safer to work on the basis that s. 12(3) is the guiding light).

(d) Although *American Cyanamid* was distinguished in *Cream Holdings,* and a different test used, in many practical ways the test under s. 12(3) is not that dissimilar to the one created by Laddie J in *Series 5* (though generated by different considerations).

8.13.5   Search orders (formerly *Anton Piller* orders)

The idea of search orders is derived from the case of *Anton Piller KG* v *Manufacturing Processes Ltd* [1976] RPC 719. They represent the final link in a chain of orders which seek to deal with physical evidence. Along with freezing orders (formerly *Mareva* injunctions) they have been described as the law's nuclear weapons. Search orders have now been placed on a statutory footing: Civil Procedure Act 1997, s. 7. They are dealt with in CPR, r. 25.1(1)(h) and by Practice Direction 25.

The effect of search orders (to varying degrees) is to allow the claimant immediate access to the defendant's premises to search for and seize documents and other evidence such as information stored on computer. The purpose behind such orders is to prevent dishonest defendants dealing with the evidence in a manner prejudicial to the case. Circumstances have to be exceptional for a search order to be made. There must be an extremely strong *prima facie* case, the extent of possible damage must be serious, there must be clear evidence that the other party is likely to disobey any court order, and the items to form the subject of the order must be clearly identifiable. An order might be made, for instance, where an employee is secretly making 'pirate' copies of the employer's copyright work and selling them abroad. An order will not be made where the claimant is simply on a 'fishing expedition'.

Care must also be taken where the right of inspection (and consequent search) might actually reveal the other side's trade secrets, etc. An undertaking for damages will be required and the court demands that the applicant comes with 'clean hands' so that all matters even remotely relevant to the case must be disclosed. The order must be served by an independent solicitor who must explain the effect of the order to the defendant and inform the defendant of the legal right to seek legal advice before complying with the order.

An application for a search order may be refused where there is the possibility of self-incrimination regarding criminal offences on the provision of the evidence by the defendant. This privilege does not, however, extend to the possibility of physical violence being meted out to the defendant by his associates should he comply with the order (*Coca-Cola Co. & Schweppes Ltd* v *Gilbey* [1996] FSR 23).

8.14 Summary

- A restraint of trade clause seeks to prevent unfair competition from ex-employees by restricting their activities after termination of the contract.
- Restraints of trade come in four main forms. Ranging from the severest to the mildest these are:

  a. *non-competition restraints* (i.e., preventing the employee working in that industry as a whole, or at least with named competitors);

  b. *non-dealing restraints* (i.e., preventing employees accepting business from or conducting business with former clients or specifically named former clients);

  c. *non-solicitation restraints* (i.e., preventing employees actually initiating contact with former clients, though not barring the employee from dealing with such clients who transfer their business without solicitation);

  d. *non-poaching restraints* (i.e., preventing the employee from soliciting former colleagues to join him in the new venture).

- Restraint clauses are presumed to be void unless they are reasonable. Reasonableness depends upon the employer showing that there was a 'legitimate interest' to protect (e.g., customer contacts) and that the wording of the clause is reasonable as between the parties in terms of the length of the restraint, area covered, the status of the employee, and the general market conditions.

- Restraint clauses are usually concerned with preventing the ex-employee making use of his customer contacts made when he was employed by the former employer, but such clauses can be used to prevent the dissemination of the employer's information by precluding the ex-employee from operating within the same field of business. It is therefore possible for a contract to contain an implied duty of fidelity relating to confidential information, an express term on the same subject, and have a restraint clause which seeks to do the same thing.

- Restraint clauses come in varying degrees of severity e.g., *non-competition clauses* seek to prevent the ex-employee working in a particular industry for a defined period, whereas *non-solicitation clauses* only seek to prevent the ex-employee approaching clients of the former employer. The more draconian the clause, the stricter the test of reasonableness applied by the courts.

- Enforcement is by way of injunction. Interim injunctions are governed by the rules emanating from *American Cyanamid* v *Ethicon*.

8.15 Self-test question on Chapters 7 and 8

Your client is Phoenix Guitars of Bristol. The company manufactures guitars and guitar parts and employs 26 employees. Your Principal wishes you to provide some preliminary guidance notes on a key question: if *Phoenix Guitars Ltd* go ahead and dismiss one of their employees (Mr Setters), will they still be able to enforce the confidentiality and restraint of trade clauses against him? The Personnel Director, Mr Burek, briefs you as follows:

1.   **The business:** *Phoenix Guitars Ltd* is a long-established company which makes and sells a range of standard handmade guitars and guitar parts to retail outlets, plus custom-made guitars for individual customers (ranging from ordinary guitar players to internationally renowned rock stars). It is located in Bristol. It has a network of sales across the UK to specialist guitar shops and general musical outlets but receives the custommade orders directly from the public through telephone, internet or personal contact. The company derives its raw materials (various kinds of hardwood, electrical fixtures, etc.) from across the world.

2.   **The work undertaken by Setters:** Mr Setters is the senior (of two) product designers. Mr Setters has been with the company for five years. His contractual notice period is two months. His work involves creating new designs for sale to the retail outlets together with designing the custom-made guitars we produce for individual customers. His work is mainly factory-centred, but involves some contact with those customers who get in touch with us directly as well as with the retail outlets that stock our goods. He reports directly to the managing director. Mr Setters has access to a wide range of information which the company regards as confidential, *viz:*

   (i)   Customers' (retail and personal) specific requirements, especially in the case of long-established relationships;

   (ii)   Future expansion plans;

   (iii) Details of contracts with suppliers around the world, including discounts obtained.

This information is held in electronic and paper form and Mr Setters is aware of the importance to the company of all this information. The establishment of customer contacts is very dependent on the reputation of employees.

3.   **Recent events:** A couple of weeks ago we held an investigation into Setters' conduct during a presentation team's visit to a potential client. At dinner one evening he informed the potential client that '*Phoenix* may be a market leader now but they are not investing enough in general research or advertising for the future'. The potential client immediately asked us to respond to this. We recalled Setters immediately and instigated disciplinary procedures. Setters has insisted that this was 'only general talk and taken out of context'. Nevertheless, we are considering dismissing him. However, we have received reliable information that Setters has already been in negotiations with a rival company (*Andrea Amati*) and that they are on the verge of offering him a contract of employment. It would also seem that Setters has been talking to his fellow designer about transferring with him to *Andrea Amati.*

4.   **Competitors:** We have two main competitors within the UK: *Le Strad Ltd* (whose headquarters are in Birmingham) and *Andrea Amati (Musical Instruments) Ltd* (in London). There are, of course, numerous American, Japanese, Korean, and Mexican companies operating worldwide, including within the UK, but these produce mass-market guitars and parts. Ours is a specialist operation and we do not compete directly with these the large-scale-production companies. Until now, *Andrea Amati* has concentrated on the European market (in which we have no interest). However, we have firm evidence that *Andrea Amati* is seeking to expand its share of the UK market in the near future and plans

to offer new designs centred on a very competitive pricing policy. Such a development could affect our market share adversely. We do not therefore want to lose any of our key employees to any of our competitors, especially *Andrea Amati*. We believe that Mr Setters is likely to use or disclose our trade secrets in these areas if he leaves or is dismissed.

5.   **Likelihood of damage to the company:** Should Setters leave and disclose our trade secrets he will cause us substantial harm in that the financial deals and design/production methods we use, together constitute business processes which provide us with a competitive edge over our rivals. *Andrea Amati Ltd* is a major rival who is seeking to mirror our activities and undercut our prices. Our new business strategy has emerged after intensive analysis and is near completion. The life-span for the information in Mr Setters' possession can be conservatively calculated as three years in terms of business strategy/redesigns.

Setters has good contacts with both customers and suppliers and would undoubtedly make use of these in any new business venture. It is a fickle market; some would transfer their allegiance from us and follow him, especially if his new employer were to undercut us.

Extracts from Setter's contract of employment relating to restraint and confidentiality terms

8.   CONFIDENTIALITY

8.1   The Employee acknowledges that during the course of his employment with the Company he will receive and have access to confidential information of the Company and he will also receive and have access to detailed client/customer lists and information relating to the operations and business requirements of those clients/customers.

8.2   The Employee shall not (other than in the proper performance of his duties or with the prior written consent of the Board or unless ordered by a court of competent jurisdiction) at any time either during the continuance of his employment or after its termination disclose or communicate to any person or use for his own benefit or the benefit of any person other than the Company or any Associated Company any confidential information which may come to his knowledge in the course of his employment and the Employee shall use his best endeavours to prevent the unauthorised publication or misuse of any confidential information provided that such restrictions shall cease to apply to any confidential information which may enter the public domain other than through the actions of the Employee.

8.3   For the avoidance of doubt and without prejudice to the generality of Clause 8.1 the following is a non-exhaustive list of matters which in relation to the Company are considered confidential and must be treated as such by the Employee:-

8.3.1   any secrets of the Company or any Associated Company:

8.3.2   marketing strategies and plans;

8.3.3   customer lists and details of contracts with or requirements of customers;

8.3.4   pricing strategies;

8.3.4   discount rates obtained from suppliers or given to customers and sales figures;

8.3.5   lists of suppliers;

8.3.6   any invention technical data know-how or other manufacturing or trade secrets of the Company or any Associated Company and their clients/ customers.

9.   RESTRICTIONS ON ACTIVITIES FOLLOWING TERMINATION

9.1   For a period of TWELVE MONTHS after termination of the Employment, the Employee shall not directly or indirectly (and whether on his own account or for any other person, firm, company, or organisation) deal with any person, firm, company or organisation who or which at any time during the preceding TWENTY FOUR MONTHS shall have been a customer of or in the habit of dealing with the Company, and with whom or which the Employee has had direct dealings or personal contact as part of the Employment so as to harm the goodwill of the Company or any Associated Company or so as to compete with the Company or any Associated Company.

9.2   For a period of SIX MONTHS after termination of the Employment, the Employee shall not canvass solicit or approach or cause to be canvassed, solicited or approached in relation to a business which may in any way be in competition with the Company, the custom of any person who at the date hereof or at any time during the period of TWENTY FOUR MONTHS prior to the Termination Date shall have been a client or customer of the Company or any Associated Company.

9.3   The covenants given by the Employee in sub-clauses 9.1 and to 9.2 inclusive above will not cease to apply in the event that the Employment is terminated by the Company in breach of contract.

Termination of the contract at common law

9.1 Introduction

A contract of employment can come to an end in a number of different ways:

(a) by agreement;

(b) by completion of a specific task;

(c) by expiry of a fixed term;

(d) by automatic termination, e.g., frustration of the contract;

(e) by dismissal;

(f) by resignation.

These forms of termination describe the basic layout of the chapter. However, we are also interested in the consequences of any termination, so that we will adopt the following additional headings:

(g) Justifiable and wrongful dismissals;

(h) Post-termination duties;

(i) Damages and other remedies;

(j) Outline of tax considerations.

Under every heading there may be statutory as well as common law consequences. We shall concentrate on the common law consequences in this chapter, but will make cross-references to certain statutory points where there is a substantial overlap.

The points raised in **Chapters 3, 4,** and **5** should also be noted regarding the structure and operation of the contract. We saw there, for instance, that where the employer makes unilateral changes to the contract there may be a number of consequences such as wrongful dismissal claims, wrongful repudiation claims, and the granting of injunctions (see **Chapter 5** at **5.4.4**). But clearly there does not have to be an attempt at altering the contract before resignations and dismissals may occur. A termination of the contract may occur for a variety of reasons, e.g., because of the employee's misconduct or incapability, or because there is a redundancy. Before examining these consequences we need to note the other, less common forms in which a termination may occur.

9.2 Termination by agreement

The parties are free to agree at any time that the contract may terminate on the happening of certain circumstances. They might also agree at any time that if the contract comes to an end in specific or general circumstances then an agreed sum (a 'golden handshake') will be payable. This will stand as liquidated damages (enforceable if a genuine pre-estimate of loss).

Agreements simply to end the contract are not common. Usually there will be a dismissal or resignation. As a consensual termination cannot by its very nature amount to a dismissal the courts are naturally suspicious of these arrangements because, without some form of a dismissal, statutory rights such as unfair dismissal will be nullified. Indeed, ERA 1996, s. 203 forbids any *exclusions* of statutory rights. Therefore the burden of proving the presence of a genuine agreement and absence of an exclusion of rights is an onerous one. Anything that smacks of duress, fraud, or general bad faith will find disfavour and so be classed as a dismissal. The areas that have caused most problems are:

(a) *Apparent resignation.*

The employer and employee may agree to termination without notice so that the employee can take another job more easily. This is genuine and unlikely to cause problems. But where a resignation has arisen from an employer's statement along the lines of 'resign or be sacked', the courts are reluctant to accept this as a valid agreement. We shall deal with this more fully at **9.8.1**.

(b) *Employees' concessions.*

In granting extended leave of absence employers have developed a practice of asking for a written undertaking that, should the employee fail to return by a set date, the parties agree that this will automatically terminate the contract. In *Igbo* v *Johnson Matthey Chemicals Ltd* [1986] ICR 505, the Court of Appeal outlawed such terms; to find otherwise, it was noted, could lead to every contract containing a clause whereby the employee 'agreed' that if late to work on Monday mornings this would automatically terminate the contract.

The most common *valid* consensual terminations therefore relate to contracts for the completion of specific tasks and non-renewal of fixed-term contracts.

9.3 Termination by completion of a specific task

A termination in these circumstances used not to count as a dismissal for common law or statutory purposes, but such contracts are now classed as 'limited-term' and subject to the rules noted below: see EA 2002, sch. 2, paras 3(7) and 13.

9.4 Expiry of limited-term contracts

Both contracts for the completion of a specific task and fixed-term contracts fall under the general description of 'limited-term'. 'Task' contracts will include things such as employees doing so-called 'seasonal' or 'casual' work who have contracts for a short period or task that ends when the period expires or the task is completed (e.g., agricultural workers or shop assistants working specifically for Christmas or another busy period). The most commonly-occurring limited-term contract, however, is the fixed-term one. We will generally use the phrase 'limited-term' below. Where we refer to 'fixed-term' this is simply because that is the best example, but the regulations still apply to both forms of contract.

A fixed-term contract usually has clear start and finish dates. The contract may last weeks, months or years. At common law the arrival of the agreed date terminates the contract automatically and no further consequences flow from this. The contract has terminated by effluxion of time and no advance notice by either party is necessary.

It should be noted, however, that the expiry *and non-renewal* of any limited-term contract *will constitute a dismissal for statutory purposes* and employees on 'limited-term' contracts have also gained protection from receiving less favourable treatment than other employees under the Fixed-Term Employees (Prevention of Less Favourable Treatment) Regulations 2002, SI 2002/2034 noted above at **6.1.1.7**.

9.4.1 Limited-term contracts and notice provisions

Odd though it sounds, it is possible to have limited-term contracts which expressly allow for termination (by either party giving notice) which will take effect at an earlier date than the set finish date: *Dixon* v *BBC* [1979] ICR 281. The reasons for this are again tied in with preserving statutory rights. Do not worry about the apparent illogicality of it all.

Some fixed-term contracts will delineate the stated period but permit indefinite continuance after the final date. A notice period applicable to this second stage will then be specified. In these circumstances the parties may give notice during the fixed term to terminate the contract at the end of the fixed term (and so before the extension has begun) or to take effect at some time during the extension: *Costigan* v *Gray Bovier Engines Ltd* (1925) 41 TLR 372.

If a limited-term contract is terminated prematurely the amount of damages will be either for the given notice period (if there is one) or else for the remainder of the term (see **9.10** below). There may also be an action for unfair dismissal or redundancy.

Where a limited-term contract is about to end employers often notify employees of this fact. There is no requirement to do so, but it does make for sound practice. However, employers should be wary of issuing any such letter in the form of 'giving notice'; such words may invite a tribunal to conclude that the dismissal occurred for reasons other than expiry of the term and this may revive arguments about unfair dismissal.

9.4.2 Waiver/contracting-out clauses

Such clauses state that an employee will not be able to claim *statutory* rights such as unfair dismissal and redundancy payments on the expiry and non-renewal of the contract. Although these clauses can still be found in a number of contracts, they are of decreasing validity (see **10.3.6** below).

9.4.3 Successive terms

It has been quite common for employers to use a succession of fixed-term contracts rather than create a contract of indefinite duration. The reason for this was to add on waiver clauses and thereby seek to avoid any liability for unfair dismissal or redundancy.

Under reg. 8 of the Fixed-Term Employees (Prevention of Less Favourable Treatment) Regulations 2002, SI 2002/2034, such employees are now regarded as ordinary employees (i.e., the contract will be regarded as having no temporal restrictions) if:

(a) the employee was employed on a fixed-term contract before the start of the present contract, or the current fixed-term contract has been renewed; *and*

(b) discounting any period before 10 July 2002, the employee's period of continuous employment is four years or more; *and*

(c) the employment of the employee under a fixed-term contract was not justified on objective grounds. That justification must be present either at the time of the last renewal or, where the contract has not been renewed, at the time it was entered into. This means that a burden is placed on the employer to justify the continuing use of fixed-term contracts. The term 'renewal' includes any extension.

Under reg. 9, an employee on a limited-term who believes they should be classed as a permanent employee may request a statement from the employer confirming or denying this, with reasons. If the employer does not respond, or denies permanency, an employee may also make an application to the tribunal for such a declaration (reg. 9(5)). These points may be modified by way of a collective agreement with a trade union or through a workforce agreement (see sch. 1).

9.4.4 Probationary periods

These are devices commonly used by employers when hiring or promoting employees. They purport to offer some form of 'trial period'. In fact they are generally meaningless. Unless the wording specifies such they are *not* fixed-term contracts of any nature and dismissal can occur during the course of the probationary period: *Dalgleish* v *Kew House Farm Ltd* [1982] IRLR 251. They are a traditional warning to employees, nothing more. New employees will generally only have a claim if the employer acts in breach of the contract, e.g., by not giving adequate notice of dismissal. This is because unfair dismissal rights generally do not accrue until there has been one years' service (although note **10.3.1** below). Existing employees who are promoted and put on a 'probationary' period maintain any existing rights they have to claim unfair dismissal.

9.5 Automatic termination

9.5.1 Frustration

Frustration of a contract occurs when unforeseen circumstances, which are beyond the control of either party, make it impossible to perform the objectives of the contract. The most common examples of the doctrine of frustration applying to employment contracts are illness, death, and imprisonment. A frustrating event terminates the contract automatically, except where the event relates to the employer and the claim is for redundancy; in this case the employee's rights are preserved.

If the 'frustrating event' has been *caused* by the fault of one party, that party cannot rely on it. The burden of proof lies with the party claiming frustration of the contract.

9.5.1.1 Frustration and sickness

The application of the doctrine of frustration to employment contracts, especially where illness is the issue, should be treated with great caution. Cases like *Condor* v *Barron Knights Ltd* [1966] 1 WLR 87, where a pop group drummer was unable to 'drum' for the seven nights per week required, are rare examples of frustrating events. Guidelines on when illness will frustrate a contract have been laid down: see, for instance, *Egg Stores (Stamford Hill) Ltd* v *Leibovici* [1977] ICR 260. Thus the following factors need to be considered:

(a) What is the nature of the illness?

(b) How long has the incapacity lasted?

(c) How long is it likely to continue?

(d) What are the terms of the contract, e.g., as to sick pay?

(e) How long was the employment set to last?

(f) What was the nature of the employment, e.g., was he or she a key employee?

(g) For how long has the employee been employed?

Questions of frustration tend to arise either when there is an accident or illness which will obviously have long-term effects, or where the position with a long-term illness employee has been allowed to drift. This may seem unlikely, but it happens, e.g., an employee is off work, the sick pay scheme becomes exhausted, the employers lose contact with the employee and then maybe a year or more later someone decides to 'tidy up the books'. They then discover the employee—or 25 such workers in one case dealt with by the authors.

On the other hand, the acceptance of medical certificates and retention of the P45 does not necessarily mean the frustration *has not occurred*. This is because the matter is beyond the control or the intentions of the parties—it has either happened or not happened: *Hart* v *Marshall & Sons (Bulwell) Ltd* [1977] ICR 539. The right to receive notice does not survive a frustrating event.

The key point is whether performance of the contract has now become impossible, or at least radically different from the original undertaking. The doctrine can also apply to contracts where a short period of notice is due (see *Notcutt* v *Universal Equipment Co. (London) Ltd* [1986] ICR 414); but whatever the type of contract, reliance on the doctrine is generally inadvisable—the employer would be wiser to decide whether or not to dismiss for incapacity. First, as will be seen in Chapter 10, the test for fairness in ill-health dismissals bears a remarkable similarity to the issues raised in frustration. Secondly, if there is the prospect of recovery then, unless there is an issue of 'key worker', this will usually mean there is no frustration.

9.5.1.2 Frustration and imprisonment

The second possibility of a frustrating event occurs when the employee is sent to prison. This makes turning up for work slightly difficult! In *Shepherd* v *Jerrom* [1986] ICR 802, the Court of Appeal decided that imprisonment is capable of frustrating the contract (here, an apprentice received a sentence of between six months' and two years' borstal training). The longer the sentence the more likely the frustration; though again one must relate this to the actual contract—status of the employee as a key worker, length of notice period, whether there is a fixed-term contract, etc. The same considerations will apply to restrictive bail conditions and being placed on custodial remand: see *Four Seasons Healthcare Ltd* v *Maughan* [2005] IRLR 324 (contract was not frustrated during the period where an employee was suspended from work whilst on bail awaiting trial).

9.5.2 Winding up of the company

The compulsory winding up of a company will operate as a notice of dismissal. A resolution for voluntary winding up will, in most cases, also constitute such notice; at least where the business is being discontinued. An employee may then have a claim for wrongful dismissal.

9.5.3 Appointment of a receiver

The appointment of a receiver by the court or as an agent for the creditors will again constitute an automatic termination of the contracts of employment. Not so, it appears, with an appointment by the debenture holders, at least for junior employees whose positions effectively remain intact.

9.5.4 Changes in a partnership

The retirement of a partner operates as a dismissal at law. Most employees will simply be re-engaged, however, and the employees' continuity of employment is preserved under ERA 1996, s. 218(5): *Stevens* v *Bower* [2004] EWCA Civ 496. The practical effects are therefore minimal. The dissolution of the partnership does, technically, bring about a termination. So, where re-engagement does not occur the employee may claim wrongful dismissal plus any statutory rights.

9.5.5 Transfer of the business

At common law, where the business is sold, this will operate as a termination; but the position now has to be read in the light of the Transfer of Undertakings (Protection of Employment) Regulations 2006, SI 2006/246, as discussed in **Chapter 12**, so that if there is a 'relevant transfer' under these Regulations it is most likely that the contracts of employment will simply be transferred along with the sale. Consequently there will be no dismissal and continuity of employment gained with the old employer will be deemed to have been with the new employer. The basic idea behind the Regulations is that nothing should really have changed simply because the business has been transferred.

9.6 The meaning of dismissal

The meaning of 'dismissal' is central to employment law. It ranges from 'being given the sack' through to resignations which are deemed dismissals. The area contains technicalities which can trap the unwary solicitor, and it is for the employee to prove dismissal if the employer challenges the claim (e.g., following a resignation). Employees may therefore find themselves 'dismissed' (as legally defined) for the purposes of common law and statutory claims in the following circumstances:

(a) where the employee is given the sack (see **9.6.1** below);

(b) where the employer uses language which amounts to dismissal (see **9.6.1**);

(c) where the employer intimates a future dismissal (see **9.8** below);

(d) where the employer says 'resign or be sacked' (see **9.8**);

    (e) where the employer repudiates the contract and the employee resigns (see **9.6.3** and **9.8**);

    (f) where a fixed-term contract is not renewed. This applies only to statutory claims such as unfair dismissal (see **9.4** above).

At common law the consequences of being dismissed are that if the employer has acted in breach of contract the employee will be able to sue for damages. This is known as a *wrongful dismissal action.* As we will see, the assessment of damages is governed by ordinary contractual principles. In employment contracts this generally means that an employee will be able to sue for the amount that he or she should have received as a notice of termination payment.

In **Chapters 10** and **11** we will see how a dismissal may lead to other *statutory* forms of compensation, i.e., unfair dismissal compensation and redundancy payments.

9.6.1 Being sacked

A dismissal will normally occur when the employer terminates the contract *with or without notice.* The decision to dismiss must be *communicated,* orally or in writing, to be effective. Where notice is given by post (which is not too clever when seen from an unfair dismissal angle) there is no debate as to 'postal rules' applying: the notice is communicated when the employee reads or could reasonably have been expected to read the letter (*Brown* v *Southall and Knight* [1980] ICR 617).

In most cases the act of dismissal will be obvious: 'you are dismissed'; 'you're sacked'; 'collect your P45 and get out'; 'I'm giving you four weeks' notice', and so on. The 'sack', by the way, comes from the days when a dismissed worker would be handed his bag of tools; the message was obvious.

Problems will arise when the words used are not clear, were meant merely as a censure or are said in anger (and perhaps regretted). The basic rule has to be: how would a reasonable person understand the words? If the reasonable man would perceive the words as amounting to a dismissal, they will constitute a dismissal; if the employee is wrong then he or she has resigned and is in breach of the contract. There is always the possibility, however, that the words (though not an overt dismissal) were such as to destroy the mutual trust and confidence in the relationship and so amount to a wrongful repudiation/constructive dismissal. Claims in the alternative are therefore advisable, i.e., the employee was dismissed on *x* date; alternatively, if the words did not amount to an overt dismissal they destroyed the mutual trust and confidence and so amounted to a repudiation.

Harsh words can therefore produce a 'dismissal' by a number of routes. A fascinating line of cases has developed on the meaning of language in industrial and commercial settings. Consider the following:

    (a) 'Go, get out, get out'—not a Victorian melodrama but the case of *Stern (J &J)* v *Simpson* [1983] IRLR 52;

    (b) 'You're finished with me'—*Tanner* v *Kean* [1978] IRLR 110;

    (c) 'If you do not like the job, fuck off'—*Futty* v *Brekkes (D & D) Ltd* [1974] IRLR 130.

None of these utterances amounted to a dismissal *in the circumstances.* This is a key point. In *Futty* v *Brekkes,* the employee was a fish filleter on Hull docks; and, strange though it seems, such language is not abnormal on Hull docks. The case stands out in the memory not because of the language used (there are many variations on this theme), but because of the attempt to define the term as: 'If you are complaining about the fish you are working on, or the quality of it, or if you do not like what, in fact, you are doing, then you can leave your work, clock off, and you will be paid up to the time when you do so. Then you can come back when you are disposed . . . '. And the same would not necessarily hold true if the characters were a bank manager and junior clerk—more so if said in front of customers.

Words spoken in anger can cause more problems. The act of dismissal can be clear but then regretted. In *Martin* v *Yeoman Aggregates Ltd* [1983] IRLR 49, a retraction within five minutes of an angry outburst was held sufficient to counter the dismissal even though the employee insisted he had been dismissed. This owes more to the promotion of good industrial relations practice than pure logic. It is a question of degree whether the words are withdrawn too late.

9.6.2   Intention

The courts have not been consistent on the status to be given to intention. If an employer intimates dismissal but does not intend this to be the case, should this make any difference?

We have seen that if the words are *ambiguous* the general test to be applied is what would reasonably be understood from the context. The same should hold true for *unambiguous* language, and this appears to be so following the Court of Appeal's decision in *Sovereign House Security Services Ltd* v *Savage* [1989] IRLR 115. However, as with words spoken in anger, an employee will be best advised to get confirmation of dismissal before taking any further action.

9.6.3   Resigning

A dismissal may also occur when the employer repudiates the contract (e.g., by some radical alteration of the terms) and the employee accepts this repudiation by resigning. Strictly this is known as *wrongful repudiation* by the employer; though when used nowadays in relation to unfair dismissal it is usually referred to as 'constructive dismissal'. Some people incorrectly refer to both common law and statutory claims under the heading of constructive dismissal; it's not the worst sin in the world.

This topic is discussed more fully in **9.8** below.

9.7   Justifiable and wrongful dismissals

The word 'justifiable' can cause some initial problems here. Remember that we are concerned only with common law rights in this chapter, so a dismissal is 'justifiable' when it is not in breach of contract. It is irrelevant for these purposes whether it was 'fair' in all the circumstances. So, if an employee is dismissed with proper notice the common law will not be bothered that the employee had been loyal to the company for 20 years and has been treated abysmally, or that the dismissal was really motivated by sex or race discrimination. These factors are irrelevancies as far as the common law is concerned.

EXAMPLE1

Anna is an employee who falls ill. She has worked for the company for five years and this is the first time she has been absent from work. Unfortunately the employer has suffered a bad spate of malingerers taking time off. This has caused immense organisational problems. The employer decides to make an example of someone and dismisses Anna. The employer gives proper notice under the contract.

It would be very unlikely that this constituted a wrongful dismissal, although one would need to see the exact terms of the contract to be sure, e.g., the contract may have a mandatory disciplinary procedure. The action does, however, seem very unfair to Anna. This is not the concern of the common law. The common law does not care whether the employer might have been a central character in a Dickens novel. If there is an 'unfair dismissal' here Anna will have to take that to an employment tribunal.

9.7.1 Justifiable dismissals: notice given

Since any contract of employment can be lawfully terminated by the giving of proper notice it is irrelevant *why* the employer decides to dismiss. The only exceptions to this general power to dismiss arise (rarely) when the contract specifies that dismissal can be only for certain defined reasons or that (even more rarely) the contract lasts for life: see respectively *McLelland* v *Northern Ireland General Health Service Board* [1957] 1 WLR 534 and *Ivory* v *Palmer* [1975] ICR 340. As we noted in **Chapter 5**, however, if the contract makes certain procedures mandatory before a dismissal can occur then an injunction may be obtained to prevent dismissal until the procedures have been completed (see **5.4.4.1**).

9.7.1.1 Proper notice

Proper notice is determined according to the terms of the contract. A payment in lieu of notice is an acceptable way of meeting the requirements. Both forms of giving notice are subject to the minima stated in ERA 1996, s. 86, which are as follows:

Length of service	*Minimum notice entitlement*
less than one month	no notice due
after one month	1 week
after 2 years' completed service	2 weeks
after 3 years' completed service	3 weeks
after 4 years' completed service	4 weeks
for each year of completed service	one additional week's notice
after 12 years' service	12 weeks
BUT:	
after 13 years' service	still only 12 weeks
after 20 years' service	still only 12 weeks

The statutory minimum period of notice therefore has a ceiling of 12 weeks. To determine an employee's notice entitlement, therefore, one should ask:

(a) What does the contract state? Usually this is solved by examining the express terms, though occasionally one may have to resort to devices such as custom and practice to determine the period.

(b) Is this equivalent to or greater than the s. 86 notice required?

(c) If not then apply s. 86 minimum notice.

Section 86 uses the term 'not less than *[x weeks]*': the courts and tribunals do not have to award only the minimum period. It is still open to the tribunal or court to award 'reasonable notice'. However, the idea that 'reasonable notice' may be awarded often gives the impression that courts and tribunals are quite creative in assessing notice entitlement. That idea should be discarded. Where courts have turned to reasonable notice either the contract has been unclear or the facts have been extreme, e.g., an employee of senior status with 25 years' service being awarded six months' notice.

EXAMPLE 2

An employee has been employed for eight and a half years. When new machines are introduced on to the production line he is dismissed as surplus to requirements. His contract stipulates that he is entitled to one month's notice; the employer duly pays wages in lieu of the employee working the notice.

The payment in lieu of notice is irrelevant here. However, on these facts the notice does not meet the s. 86 minimum, which should be eight weeks. Note that portions of years are not generally counted and that any questions of 'reasonable notice' will not be admitted on these facts.

Limited-term contracts are treated no differently, *provided there is a notice clause.*

Where notice is given the date of termination must be ascertainable. There is no dismissal if all that is given is a general warning of dismissal unless the warning is so specific that it amounts to an ultimatum and therefore an anticipatory breach: *Greenaway Harrison Ltd* v *Wiles* [1994] IRLR 381.

Sections 87–91, ERA 1996 deal with rights once notice has been given. For instance, subject to the technicalities of s. 87(4) (see *Scotts Company (UK) Ltd* v *Budd* [2003] IRLR 145), if the employee falls sick during the notice period he is entitled to be paid, even if not otherwise entitled to sick pay. But, under ss. 88(2) and 89(4), any payments made to the employee by the employer (e.g., statutory sick pay) go towards meeting the employer's liability under these sections.

9.7.1.2 Waiving rights to notice

The parties are free to agree to give shorter notice than would normally be required or even to waive notice. Provided such variations are genuine there will be no breach of contract and therefore no damages payable: *Baldwin* v *British Coal Corporation* [1995] IRLR 139.

9.7.1.3 Notice and age discrimination

As mentioned in earlier chapters, the idea of preventing age discrimination extends to terms and conditions of the contract. Thus, varying notice periods which depend on length of service (and therefore indirectly to age) may be seen as discriminatory—this time as against younger employees.

The s. 86 statutory notice periods probably fall within reg 27 of the Employment Equality (Age) Regulations 2006, SI 2006/1031 which provides that the Regulations will not 'render unlawful any act done in order to comply with a requirement of any statutory provision'. But this is not certain because s. 86 lays down *minimum* periods, not mandatory ones. Nevertheless, it is likely that an employer adhering to s. 86 notice periods will be safe.

Contractual notice periods based on length of service do not receive the reg. 27 protection but may be saved under reg. 32 (service-related benefits exceptions). Under this regulation contractual rights dependent on up to five years' service are exempted and anything over this can be justified if the employer shows the term fulfils a business need for the undertaking, e.g., by rewarding loyalty.

Payments in lieu of notice provide a further problem as they do not fit within reg. 32 and therefore will be discriminatory unless they are objectively justified as constituting a proportionate means of achieving a legitimate aim.

9.7.2 Justifiable dismissal: no notice given

When an employee is in serious breach of contract (e.g., commits an act of serious misconduct) the employer has a number of options available. These include:

(a) doing nothing;

(b) disciplining the employee;

(c) suing the employee for damages;

(d) dismissing the employee with notice;

(e) dismissing the employee without notice.

This is in line with ordinary contract principles that the innocent party may, in the face of a repudiation by the other party, affirm the contract as it stands or accept the repudiation. Thus a dismissal without notice (known as a *summary dismissal*) will be justified where the employee's actions show that further continuance of the relationship is impossible: *Sinclair* v *Neighbour* [1967] 2 QB 279 (here, dishonesty).

It follows, therefore, that the contract of employment itself is of vital importance in assessing whether the employee's conduct justifies dismissal without notice. The contract may define terms such as 'gross misconduct', or it may lay down specific procedures for dealing with any dismissal point, e.g., that no dismissal may occur until the employee has been given an opportunity to state a case. The more technical the contractual terms become the more likely it is that the employer will be in breach by not following them. Thus it might be that, even in the face of obvious misconduct, an employer will have to adhere to the procedures laid out in the contract *if the terms specifically set out what must happen before a dismissal can occur: Dietmann v Brent London Borough Council* [1988] ICR 842.

This does not establish a rule that a breach of disciplinary procedures will render a dismissal wrongful, though, because:

(a) if the dismissal is with proper notice (or payment in lieu) no further damages will be payable—though there is the possibility that the employee might obtain an injunction to prevent dismissal *until* the procedures have been complied with;

(b) most procedures are drafted more loosely than the *Dietmann* example. The issue is therefore one of construction of the particular contract. We should note, however, that some tribunal chairmen are becoming keener to hold that disciplinary rules set out in a variety of company documents do have contractual effects. Phrases such as 'the totality of documentation shows that the term was intended to be incorporated' are used to justify such inclusion (see discussion above at **3.4.2.1**).

If notice is *not given* the employer will have to justify this. If it is not justified the employee will recover damages for wrongful dismissal. Justification for dismissal without notice depends solely on the employer having a sound *contractual* reason for so dismissing. This will mean that the employee must have committed a serious breach of contract (see *Laws* v *London Chronicle (Indicator Newspapers) Ltd* [1959] 1 WLR 698). *The breach may be of express or implied terms.* Examples of serious breach by an employee will include:

(a) refusal to obey a lawful order;

(b) failure to cooperate;

(c) dishonesty (in its widest sense);

(d) assault;

(e) prolonged absenteeism;

(f) disclosing confidential information;

(g) failing to disclose the misdeeds of subordinates;

(h) gross negligence;

(i) drunkenness at work;

(j) most forms of industrial action.

However, it is usually stressed by judges that each case turns on its facts. Certainly this will be true when dealing with one-off incidents. Whereas the normal approach would be that a one-off incident is not a repudiation of the contract, that clearly cannot be a universal rule. A pilot bouncing the company jet, for instance, does not deserve a second chance. But should the pilot be dismissed with or without notice? Would you say that the same result would be reached with a salesman who crashed a company car? And an accumulation of petty incidents may also amount to a serious breach: *Pepper* v *Webb* [1969] 2 All ER 216.

The more serious the breach the more likely a summary dismissal will be justified.

9.7.2.1 Contractual term

Employers sometimes attempt to set out a right to dismiss without notice on the occurrence of certain events, other than gross misconduct. This is a questionable practice in itself; but, certainly, the wording of such clauses will be construed *contra proferentem*: *T&K Improvements Ltd* v *Skilton* [2000] IRLR 595, CA, where a clause allowing dismissal 'with immediate effect' on failing to reach sales targets was held not to permit dismissal without notice. A similar approach to contractual terms was seen in **9.7.1** above.

9.7.3 Wrongful dismissals

9.7.3.1 Definition

A dismissal *without notice or with inadequate notice* will constitute a wrongful dismissal unless the employer was acting in response to a serious breach of the contract by the employee.

Payment in lieu of notice, unless specifically allowed for in the contract, will also constitute a technical breach of contract. For the most part this is an irrelevancy, given that damages for wrongful dismissal would amount to the same sum, but classifying this as a technical breach may have an effect on matters such as the efficacy of restraint of trade clauses: see *Rex Stewart Jeffries Parker Ginsberg Ltd* v *Parker* [1988] IRLR 483, above at **8.4.4** and below at **9.9**.

Employers often refer to 'instant dismissal'. This is in fact a vague term and should not be taken at face value. Certainly, an employee might be 'instantly dismissed' when he or she is dismissed without notice; but the employee or the employer may also use the

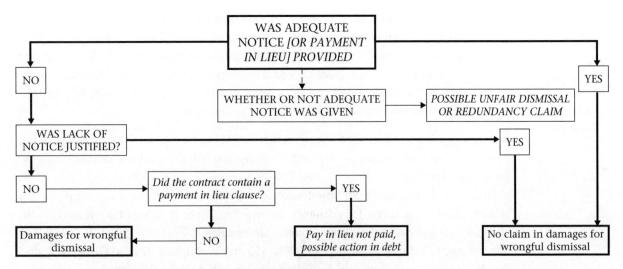

Figure 9.1   Dismissal with or without notice.

term 'instant dismissal' to describe a dismissal with payment in lieu or a dismissal with notice where the employee is not required to work out the notice. There can therefore be important differences between 'instant dismissals' and 'summary dismissals' and you need to be sure which you are talking about (a point missed by the employers in *Skilton* above).

Figure 9.1 illustrates the possible consequences of dismissing with or without adequate notice. The right-hand side of the diagram illustrates the fact that damages are unavailable at common law if the contract is terminated lawfully. The far left-hand side shows that the mere fact that notice has not been given does not conclude the analysis; the lack of notice may be justified. The section concerning payments in lieu of notice takes account of the decision in *Abrahams* v *Performing Rights Society* [1995] IRLR 486 and we will return to discuss the significance of this decision at **9.10.3** below.

The diagram also notes the possibilities of an unfair dismissal claim flowing from either type of dismissal. This point will be taken further in **Chapter 10** but highlights the fact that there may be a dismissal which is both unfair and wrongful, a fair but wrongful dismissal and even an unfair but lawful dismissal.

9.7.3.2   Relationship with repudiation

A wrongful dismissal is sometimes viewed as another form of repudiation of the contract. If this is so then, as in the ordinary law of contract, the repudiation does not automatically bring the contract to an end—it must be accepted by the innocent party. An unaccepted repudiation, it is said, is a thing writ in water. The innocent party has a choice whether or not to accept the repudiation. The argument is that when the employee is told to go (in breach of contract) he or she should be able to say, 'No. This is in breach and I do not accept the repudiation.' In practice, this simply shows us that law and reality do not always coincide. But there can be cases where this point matters.

We have already seen some spin-off practical points that have developed from the debate. Since a repudiation does not have to be accepted by the innocent party then a breach by the employer during the currency of the contract can be met with various tactics, e.g.:

(a) It is now well established that employees faced with a repudiation may object to the breach but remain in employment and sue for damages: *Rigby* v *Ferodo* [1988] ICR 29 (discussed in **Chapter 5**);

(b) We have also seen that, even when a dismissal is about to occur or has just occurred, an employee may be able to invoke the courts' help. Injunctions can be granted to restrain dismissals or declare dismissals invalid which do not comply with mandatory contractual procedures: *Dietmann* v *Brent London Borough Council* [1988] ICR 842, although this does not mean that the rules of natural justice will be imputed to contracts of employment generally.

But the question in relation to wrongful dismissal is more difficult. Assume that an employer has just told the employee that he is dismissed without notice. Does the employee have to accept this?

There has been a long-standing debate on whether an employee must simply accept this repudiation and sue for damages, or whether there is some other remedy available: see *Gunton* v *Richmond-upon-Thames London Borough Council* [1980] ICR 755, *London Transport Executive* v *Clarke* [1981] ICR 355 and comments by Lord Oliver in *Rigby* v *Ferodo*. In most cases, however, this debate is somewhat sterile since there is no practical benefit in having a right other than for damages. The employee may object but, given that specific performance will not be ordered, the objection may be futile. Thus, an employee may prevent a dismissal occurring or may have a dismissal nullified on the grounds noted above, but faced with a straightforward dismissal without notice there is nothing that most employees can do but accept the dismissal and sue for damages.

However, if the 'repudiation' argument is correct in relation to wrongful dismissal the practical effects are:

(a) the employee, by accepting the *de facto* position, will have in law accepted the wrongful repudiation by the employer. The employee will therefore, technically speaking, have resigned (see below) rather than have been overtly dismissed;

(b) there may be a difference in calculating the exact date of termination.

9.7.3.3 Proof of conduct

The employer will have to justify any dismissal *without notice*. Normally proof will relate to the facts known at the time of the dismissal. However, the employer is also entitled to rely on evidence *not known to him at the time of dismissal: Boston Deep Sea Fishing and Ice Co.* v *Ansell* (1888) 39 ChD 339. This is because the arguments are based on as whether or not there has been a breach of contract. The employer's knowledge or lack of it does not affect the materiality of the breach.

EXAMPLE 3

The employer summarily dismisses an employee for theft. The employer has no proof, only strong suspicions. Some weeks after the dismissal the employer discovers the proof. The employer may use this subsequently discovered information in order to prove the employee's breach of contract, thereby justifying the dismissal without notice. The same logic applies even if the employer had *no reason* to dismiss but later discovered one.

By way of advance warning, however, the rules regarding proof in an unfair dismissal action are different. There the employer can rely only on facts known *at the time of dismissal*. Thus out of one incident of dismissal there may be different rules of proof depending on whether one is claiming for wrongful or unfair dismissal.

9.8 Resignation

An employee may resign at any time by giving proper notice under the contract. The minimum s. 86 period is one week; and this does not alter with length of service. The contract may set any notice requirement.

If an employee leaves without serving proper notice then he or she is in breach of contract. The employee will be liable for damages, though specific performance will not be ordered. The employee may, however, still be subject to a restraint of trade clause. The fact that the employer has accepted the employee's repudiation of the contract is ignored because the employee will not be allowed to profit from his or her own breach.

Once a lawful resignation has been given it cannot be withdrawn except:

(a) with the employer's permission; or

(b) where the resignation came in the heat of the moment and is retracted quickly; or

(c) where the resignation was in breach of contract and the employer has not yet obviously accepted the repudiation.

However, an employee is entitled to resign, with or without serving notice, and claim damages where the employer has repudiated the contract (see 'wrongful repudiation' below).

The discussion on 'resignation' and its effect should be read in conjunction with the topic of 'constructive dismissal' in **Chapter 10**. When this is taken into account you will see that a resignation may amount to an unfair dismissal as well as to a wrongful repudiation at common law.

9.8.1 Meaning of 'resignation'

In most cases an employee will resign to take up another job elsewhere. If the employee gives proper notice (and there is no question of restraint of trade) no further problems will occur. There can be no claim for wrongful or unfair dismissal or for redundancy payments and the employer cannot force the employee to remain in employment. The employer may indeed waive all or some of the notice because an employee who is set to leave can prove disruptive (intentionally or otherwise).

We are concerned here with *apparent* resignations which might turn out to be *dismissals*:

(a) resignations in the heat of the moment;

(b) pressure from the employer;

(c) the employer's bad faith;

(d) voluntary redundancies and early retirement.

9.8.1.1 Resignations in the heat of the moment

Employees, like employers (see **9.6.1**), are allowed some leeway with heated outbursts. If the words spoken are ambiguous there is the preliminary point as to whether they constituted a resignation at all. If the words are unambiguous the employer is entitled to take these at their face value and the employee must live with the consequences. However, an employee is allowed to retract within a reasonable time if the words were spoken in anger: *Kwik-Fit (GB) Ltd* v *Lineham* [1992] ICR 183.

An employer who refuses to allow a reasonable retraction will have dismissed the employee from that point.

9.8.1.2   Resignations under pressure

Employees who resign following an invitation to 'resign or be dismissed' may still have a claim for wrongful or unfair dismissal—were they pushed or did they jump? But advance warning of dismissal at some future time does not constitute pressure and so is not a dismissal (nor is this enough to amount to a repudiatory breach by the employer). If the employer were to indicate that the future termination will be in breach of contract, however, then this will amount to an anticipatory breach which the employee may act upon immediately.

There may be a fine line between these two points. The key aspect is whether there is to be found in the employer's words an *ascertainable future date of dismissal;* if there is then any resignation may be treated as a dismissal.

EXAMPLE 4

A month ago the employer told the employee that the factory would be closed down by next September, i.e., in 11 months' time. The employee has just resigned and wishes to claim a redundancy payment on the basis that he has been dismissed.

Although there is a final date when the employee's contract will seemingly come to an end this is not enough. The employee might be dismissed before then, or the redundancy may never come about. The resignation is just that: there is no further claim based on a 'dismissal' (see *International Computers Ltd* v *Kennedy* [1981] IRLR 28).

The real cases of 'resign or be sacked' therefore arise when the employee is clearly going to face some form of disciplinary procedure and is 'given the honourable choice'—a sort of industrial hara-kiri option. This may indeed be honourable, but it is also possible that it is a dismissal. It is not a dismissal simply to instigate disciplinary procedures, nor even to offer the employee a way out of the proceedings. Such conversations become dismissal when the employer threatens dismissal by other words: when the conversation is effectively, 'We are going to dismiss you come what may, go now'. One recent example arose when an employer told the employee she had a choice of either moving from full-time to part-time work or taking redundancy. She chose the latter. The employment tribunal felt this was a termination by agreement but the EAT disagreed, holding that, as she had rejected the only alternative she had been faced with a compulsory redundancy. The case was remitted to the tribunal to be heard on its merits.

9.8.1.3   Resignation generated by the employer's bad faith

This bears a close resemblance to pressurised resignations. In *Caledonian Mining* v *Bassett and Steel* [1987] ICR 425, the employers had announced the proposed closure of the workplace. No date was actually given. The employers informed the employees that they could arrange transfers to another site some distance away. Alternatively, they said that they had reached agreement with the Coal Board so that the employees could change employers, stay in the area, but take a wage cut. The employees chose this option. They then claimed redundancy pay from Caledonian Mining, who replied that the employees had resigned and so were not entitled. It was held that the employers had acted in bad faith and had inveigled the employees into resigning in order to deprive them of their statutory rights. Therefore this constituted a dismissal.

9.8.1.4 Voluntary redundancies and early retirement

In many cases where redundancies are announced the employer will first ask for volunteers. Any subsequent termination could be classed as a resignation, a dismissal, or even a consensual termination. In order to claim a redundancy payment the employee must have been dismissed.

Early retirement usually takes a considerable amount of time to work out problems with dates, pension arrangements and so on. Such cases are therefore more likely to constitute mutual agreement (provided the agreement was genuine) rather than dismissal or resignation: *Birch* v *University of Liverpool* [1985] ICR 470. An employee could not claim redundancy pay in addition to the terms of the early retirement scheme.

9.8.2 Wrongful repudiation

What constitutes a *serious breach* of contract on the employer's part? Examples would include:

(a) a failure to pay wages;

(b) harassment (including harassment by other employees);

(c) victimisation by the employer or senior staff;

(d) unilaterally changing the employee's job content or status;

(e) humiliating employees in front of others including the use by a manager of foul and abusive language, whether or not the employer argues that that is part of the 'normal working environment': *Horkulak* v *Cantor Fitzgerald International* [2003] IRLR 756;

(f) unwarranted demotion or disciplinary sanctions;

(g) falsely accusing an employee of misconduct or incapability;

(h) unilateral variation in contract terms, e.g., a change in hours or pay;

(i) requiring a substantial transfer of location (certainly if without reasonable notice);

(j) suspension without pay where the contract does not allow for this—and even *with pay* if prolonged.

A series of breaches may also fall within the definition of repudiation, though this is always more difficult to substantiate unless the employee has kept careful records.

Many of these points tend to be classified as a breach of the implied term of *mutual trust and confidence* owed by the employer to the employee. Clearly the list is not closed.

It should also be remembered from **Chapter 5** (at **5.4.4**) that an employee does not have to resign in the face of a repudiatory breach. If the contract is still capable of being performed the employee may remain and seek other remedies, e.g., suing for breach, or may simply put up with the breach.

9.9 Post-termination duties

In **Chapters 7** and **8** we noted that a breach or even a technical breach may have the effect of invalidating post-termination terms such as restraint of trade clauses: see *Rex Stewart Jeffries Parker Ginsberg Ltd* v *Parker* [1988] IRLR 483. A wrongful dismissal will invalidate a restraint of trade clause: *General Billposting Co. Ltd* v *Atkinson* [1909] AC 118. Even a payment in lieu will invalidate a restraint clause *unless* the contract expressly allows for this form of termination.

9.10   Damages and other remedies

9.10.1 Damages

Employment contracts are no different from other contracts, in that the basis for award-ing damages is to fulfil the reasonable expectations of the parties; to put the injured party in the same position as if the contract had been performed properly: *Hadley* v *Baxendale* (1854) 9 Exch 341. Damages for wrongful dismissal are therefore based on the contemplation of the parties—which means payments that would have fallen due in the notice period. The limitation period is six years (three months if claiming in an employment tribunal).

Employment tribunals have jurisdiction to hear wrongful dismissal claims (and other contractual claims arising from or outstanding on termination). However, their juris-diction is limited to awarding £25,000 maximum. This should be borne in mind when deciding on the appropriate forum in which to make the claim and *Fraser* v *HLMAD Ltd* [2006] EWCA Civ 738 should be taken as a salutary lesson. Here the employment tribunal awarded the employee damages for wrongful dismissal but capped the award at £25,000. The Court of Appeal held that the employee was not entitled to bring proceed-ings in the High Court to recover the excess even though he had 'reserved his right' to do so. The practical advice is: (a) choose the forum carefully; and (b) if an error has been made as to forum, seek to withdraw that part of the claim from the tribunal and pursue the matter in the ordinary courts. Bear in mind, however, that under tribunal rules, with-drawn claims cannot be reactivated in the tribunal.

It is worth noting in this context that an employee may have a claim under the law of contract and under ERA 1996, Part II for any outstanding wages on termination. These are claims which are distinct from wrongful dismissal claims (see **4.4** and **5.8** above). Fur-ther, as noted above in **Chapter 5** and at **9.7.1.3**, there are arguments that service-related notice periods are discriminatory in that they favour older employees. We have no au-thority yet on this so we will work on the basis that discrimination is not a key factor.

9.10.1.1 Employees' damages

In the abstract one could argue that when the employee is wrongfully dismissed (espe-cially if jobs are scarce) the loss could be enormous. But at any given time and for any reason an employment contract may be lawfully terminated by one or other party giving the notice required under the contract. Thus, in assessing what has been lost one needs to know the maximum that could have been gained had the parties behaved properly in bringing the contract to an end. The maximum that could have been gained in the overwhelming majority of employment contracts is payment for the notice period. Thus damages are limited to the amount that would have been paid if notice had been prop-erly given, or any shortfall between the payment due and that which was made.

Where an employee has resigned and successfully claims *wrongful repudiation* of the contract, the amount of damages will be equivalent to a wrongful dismissal claim and the same rules as to calculation will apply.

To the basic figure of wages one needs to add (at least in some cases) other sums which could have been gained *during that notice period*. Thus, to the basic wages figure one might add:

(a) fringe benefits, e.g., a company car, medical insurance;

(b) tips, to which the employee was contractually entitled (usually given as estimated value);

(c) commission and bonus to which the employee was contractually entitled;

(d) share options and payments under profit-sharing schemes;

(e) pension loss—at its lowest level an amount representing the employee's contributions;

(f) backpay (including holiday entitlements);

(g) interest from date of dismissal to date of hearing.

As with so many of these lists, therefore, one needs to know the terms of the contract in order to determine quantum. These additional elements, however, are given *for the length of the notice period* and not as general, life-long sums. The loss of the company car will therefore be calculated according to its value to the employee for the eight-week (or other) period of notice. Reference is made here to tables such as those compiled by the AA to determine value.

9.10.1.2 Damages not related to the notice period

In some circumstances the damages for wrongful dismissal may actually be *greater* than the notice period. If, for instance, an employee has been dismissed without notice and in breach of contractually binding disciplinary rules (e.g., the procedure clearly laid down in the contract was not followed) the damages may be calculated in this way:

(a) take the date of dismissal and calculate how long it *would have taken* to comply with the contractual disciplinary scheme;

(b) add the notice due from the imaginary date of the disciplinary hearing properly conducted.

We will return to this at **9.10.6.2** below.

Occasionally you will find an employee who has been dismissed just before a key date in their employment relationship. For instance, they might have been dismissed just short of a year's service (which is the point where most employees gain the right to claim unfair dismissal), or maybe the dismissal occurs just short of an anniversary of their employment which, if they had passed this point, would have meant they gained a better pension payment. To what extent can an employee claim damages to take account of such 'lost opportunities'?

We start with a long-standing presumption derived from *Laverack Woods* [1967] 1 QB 278, CA: that an employer must be assumed to discharge his contractual responsibilities in the manner most favourable to him. So, if an employer dismisses an employee at a time which best suits the employer then there is nothing wrong with this and no damages will be awarded for lost opportunity. This may be a dangerous game in terms of brinkmanship and rules have been developed in the area of unfair dismissal which sometimes come as a shock to such employers (see **10.3.1.2** below) but the basic principle remains the same, as confirmed in *Harper v Virgin Net Ltd* [2004] EWCA Civ 271, [2004] IRLR 390.

Employers can get things wrong (sometimes innocently). In *Silvey* v *Pendragon plc* [2001] EWCA Civ 784, [2001] IRLR 6, for instance, an employee was dismissed with payment in lieu of notice. As we shall note below, the date of dismissal when payment in lieu of notice is given is deemed to be the date of the dismissal itself and not the date when notice would have expired had it been worked. This meant here that the employee lost out on an accrual to his pension which, if he had worked his notice, he would have acquired. The Court of Appeal found that the payment in lieu was not authorised in the contract and was therefore a technical breach (even though no damages could be paid as Silvey had received the proper sum). Having decided that, the Court found that Silvey could claim a sum to which he would have been entitled had it not been for this repudiatory breach.

One claim that has clearly been killed off in this area is the argument that there is an implied term in the contract not to be unfairly dismissed: *Fosca* v *Birkett* [1996] IRLR 325.

9.10.1.3   Injured feelings

Damages are not generally awarded for loss of future prospects or injured feelings: *Addis* v *Gramophone Co. Ltd* [1909] AC 488 and *Bliss* v *South East Thames Regional Health Authority* [1987] ICR 700. However, loss of reputation (stigma damages) has now been recognised as a head of damage by the House of Lords in *Malik and Mahmud* v *Bank of Credit and Commerce International SA (in compulsory liquidation)* [1997] ICR 606, emanating from breach of the implied term of mutual trust and confidence (specifically, not to run a corrupt and dishonest business so as to damage the employees' future employment prospects). This head of damages has so far been given a narrow application, so the fact that an unjustifiable, even capricious, dismissal diminishes future job prospects does not trigger *Malik* damages.

Although injury to feelings may be excluded, we noted above at **5.2.3(d)** that an employer owes a duty of care not to injure an employee. This has been a growth area for litigation, with two main angles: (i) the tortious one of causing psychological injury in the form of stress; and (ii) the contractual one of acting in such a way as to breach the duty of mutual trust and confidence.

9.10.1.4   Psychological injuries: the safety angle

In *Page* v *Smith* [1995] 2 WLR 644 the House of Lords held that, as a matter of general principle, physical and psychological injury are subject to the same test of foreseeability. The first major case to deal with stress in the workplace was *Walker* v *Northumberland County Council* [1995] ICR 702. Here, the employers knew the employee was under stress as he had already taken time off work for this, but they failed to take this into account in piling on even more work when he returned. The employers were held liable for the psychological injury that followed. In various cases this notion was then tested in cases which did not involve a 'second incident'.

In the joined cases of *Sutherland* v *Hatton* [2002] EWCA Civ 76, [2002] ICR 613 the Court of Appeal held that the ordinary principles of employer's liability applied to stress-at-work cases. The case went on appeal to the House of Lords under the name *Barber* v *Somerset County Council* [2004] UKHL 13, [2004] ICR 457 where their Lordships held that an employer's duty is to take positive thought for the safety of the workers *in the light of what the employer knows or ought to have known*. The key point that emerges from *Barber* is that this is a general *positive* duty to take some steps to be aware of pressures on employees, not one which only applies where the employer is aware of a vulnerable employee. This is not an absolute duty, however, and where the evidence does not support the view that the employer should have known about the stress etc, then no liability can follow.

The topic was examined again by the Court of Appeal in six more joined cases under the lead name of *Hartman* v *South Essex Mental Health and Community Care NHS Trust* [2005] EWCA Civ 6, [2005] IRLR 293. Scott Baker LJ cites with approval Hale LJ's (as she then was) guidelines drawn in *Hatton*. These guidelines survived the House of Lords' decision and include examining things such as: the nature and extent of the work done by the employee, signs from the employee of impending harm to health, the size and scope of the employer's operation, its resources and the interests of other employees in any redistribution of duties. It is not enough to merely set up a counselling service and hope the problem goes away; the employer's duty is to act on the knowledge available: *Intel Corporation (UK) Ltd* v *Daw* [2007] EWCA Civ 70, [2007] IRLR 355. This is even more so when the employee is returning to work after physical or psychological injury: an employer should ideally have in place an adequate return-to-work programme.

9.10.1.5 Psychological injuries: harassment

The Protection from Harassment Act 1997 was devised to deal with the problem of stalkers, but in *Majrowski* v *Guy's and St Thomas's NHS Trust* [2006] UKHL 34 the Court of Appeal and then the House of Lords (on different reasoning) held that

(a) an employer could be vicariously liable for an employee's breach of statutory duty provided the legislation does not expressly or impliedly exclude such liability; and

(b) the 1997 Act had no such exclusion and therefore applied to employment situations, e.g., in the case of bullying by work colleagues.

This decision takes us beyond the bounds of negligence as described above because, once harassment has been found, the next test is whether the employer is vicariously liable on the facts (now subject to a wider and less employer-friendly test of 'work connexion') and, if this is found, the Act creates strict liability (so that foreseeability is irrelevant). Harassment is undefined in the 1997 Act, but it has to be a course of conduct not just a single incident and will include causing the victim alarm or distress through speech as well as conduct (s. 8(3)). However, as the Court of Appeal commented in *Conn* v *Council of City of Sunderland* [2007] EWCA Civ 1492 the conduct must cross the boundary from that which is unattractive or even unreasonable into something oppressive and unacceptable.

Section 3(2) states that 'On such a claim, damages may be awarded for (among other things) any anxiety caused by the harassment and any financial loss resulting from the harassment'. Note that the use of the word 'anxiety' sets a much lower standard than proving 'personal injury' and that the limitation period under the Act is six years instead of the personal injury three-year period.

9.10.1.6 Psychological injuries: mutual trust

Running alongside the *safety* argument has been a debate about whether an employer's actions (which might produce psychological injury) might constitute a breach of the implied term of mutual trust and confidence. Once the case of *Malik* had extended the duty to matters such as how an employer's conduct affects an employee's reputation (see above at **9.10.1.1**), the opportunity to argue an extension of the duty of mutual trust to conduct which causes psychological harm became ever-present. The limits of *Malik* are being well and truly tested.

The first major test arose in *Johnson* v *Unisys Ltd* [2001] UKHL 13, [2001] ICR 480 where the Court of Appeal [1999] ICR 809 and then the House of Lords revisited the area in the context of a dismissed employee who claimed that his summary dismissal (based on allegations made against him) represented a breach of the term of trust and confidence leading to severe psychiatric illness and financial damages. Their Lordships held that, though *Addis* v *Gramophone Co. Ltd* might be reviewed in modern circumstances, here the position was clear: there was no need to develop the common law to overlap this remedy. Further, whereas *Malik* may be applicable to breaches of contract arising *during* the employment relationship, it was not relevant to the manner of the *termination*.

This apparently simple distinction has complications: what happens where an employer commits a breach of mutual trust (say, in terms of false allegations or bad faith disciplinary measures) and the employee is eventually dismissed or resigns? Is the breach one occurring 'during' the contract and so actionable as a common law claim under *Malik*, or one related to termination and so *not* actionable under *Johnson?*

In *Gogay* v *Hertfordshire County Council* [2000] IRLR 703, the Court of Appeal upheld an employee's claim for damages for psychological injury arising from the employer's breach of mutual trust and *Johnson* was distinguished on the grounds that that case involved a dismissal and here there was only a suspension; the significance of the suspension being that the employment relationship was still continuing.

Again, in *King* v *University Court of the University of St Andrews* [2002] IRLR 252, the Court of Session (Outer House) distinguished *Johnson* and held that it did not apply while an employer was carrying out investigative procedures which might not necessarily culminate in dismissal. During that time an employee was entitled to rely on the implied duty of trust and confidence as subsisting so that the failure by the employer to allow the employee the opportunity to reply to the charges made and cross-examine witnesses amounted to an actionable breach of confidence.

Inevitably, cases arose where a dismissal did result and the *Johnson* v *Unisys* distinction had to be tested. In the joined cases of *Eastwood* v *Magnox Electric plc* and *McCabe* v *Cornwall County Council* [2004] UKHL 35, [2004] 3 WLR 322 the House of Lords pronounced on this position. Their Lordships decided that a common law claim for psychological injury arising from a breach of the duty of mutual trust will only arise where the cause of action has accrued *before* dismissal. Unfortunately (as their Lordships recognised) the distinction between discipline and dismissal can become very fudged and, if dismissal does result, we shall see that injury to feelings, etc. is not something which an employment tribunal can award as part of unfair dismissal compensation either: see **10.13.4.5** below. This is not helpful.

9.10.1.7 Employers' damages

It should be noted that employers are also entitled to sue for damages where the employee has not served proper notice according to the contract (the contract is the only real issue here as the ERA 1996, s. 86 minimum for employees is fixed at one week). Employers may also counterclaim in any contractual claim brought by an employee (but not under an ERA 1996, Part II claim).

The amount of the employer's damages in these circumstances will be limited to the sum needed to find a replacement. A general clause which allows employers to deduct a sum of money from any final payment owed to an employee (e.g., outstanding pay) when the employee leaves without giving notice is not a genuine pre-estimate of loss and so likely to be classed as a penalty clause: *Giraud* v *Smith* [2000] IRLR 763. Such 'recovery' clauses can be drafted so as to amount to genuine estimations, though: see *Neil* v *Strathclyde Regional Council* [1984] IRLR 14, on recovering the costs of a training scheme. If another employer has induced the employee to break his or her contract that employer will also be liable. But these are not usually real, practical issues. If employers need to do something in these circumstances they will either seek an injunction to hold employees to their notice period ('garden leave' injunctions), or seek to enforce a restraint of trade clause (see **Chapter 8**).

9.10.2 Deductions from employees' damages

Nothing in life, so they say, is free. The employee may well have a good claim for wrongful dismissal, but deductions can be made from any award. First, the employee cannot avoid tax liabilities so the award will generally be made net of tax and National Insurance. This applies to all cases where the damages are under £30,000.

If the award exceeds £30,000 complications set in. The basic rule is that the courts must decide on the loss and then add to this figure ('gross up') an amount representing the tax which will eventually have to be paid by the employee. This grossed up figure represents the damages awarded against the employer, and the employee can then sort out the tax position with the Inland Revenue. Thus, if a court calculates that the damages come to £60,000 it may have to award £80,000 so that the employee will actually get £60,000 after the taxman has made a request the employee cannot refuse (see *Shove* v *Downs Surgical Supplies Ltd* [1984] IRLR 17).

There are different methods used for grossing up. The two main methods depend in part on the level of detailed information available to the court/employment tribunal. The *Shove* approach is the more accurate. It involves the following steps:

1. Take the value of gross salary and benefits;
2. Calculate taxable value of 1 above;
3. Calculate tax and NI payable after deduction of allowances;
4. Deduct tax and NI from gross salary and benefits;
5. Multiply this net figure of annual loss by period of damages/compensation;
6. Make any deductions for mitigation;
7. Make deductions for accelerated receipt;
8. Deduct £30,000;
9. Gross up taxable slice and add back the £30,000.

In all cases, damages may be reduced because of the 'duty' to mitigate any loss. This means that the victim of any breach must minimise the loss, not act unreasonably to increase the loss, and account for any benefits received. The burden of proving failure to mitigate lies with the employer.

Deductions from damages

Usually deducted	Not usually deducted	Debatable
Payment in other work (including fringe benefits, commission, shares, etc.).		*Failure to make use of appeals procedure. The most recent EAT authority (Lock v Connell Estate Agents [1994] IRLR 444) disapproves of such a deduction being made.*
Any payment in lieu received.	*Payment in lieu, where the basis of the claim is a debt action: Abrahams v Performing Rights Society [1995] IRLR 486—below.*	*Money from temporary or short-term employment. The chain of causation may not be broken where employee finds new work and then that employment fails.*

Sum representing failure to take reasonable steps to find new employment (i.e. failure to mitigate).	*No deduction for failure to mitigate where ex-employee has failed to make profits in new (self-employed) enterprise.*	*Offer of re-employment by employer. Always debatable, but must certainly be made or repeated* **after** *dismissal: Shindler v Northern Raincoat [1960] 1 WLR 1038.*
Jobseekers' allowance, to the extent that this constitutes a net gain: Westwood v Secretary of State for Employment [1985] ICR 209.	*Private pension payments: Hopkins v Norcross [1994] ICR 11, CA—possible with caveat that contract may disallow this.*	*Compensatory award for unfair dismissal: O'Laoire v Jackel International Ltd [1990] ICR 197.*
Income support to the extent that this constitutes a net gain.	*Statutory redundancy payment and the Basic Award element of Compensation for unfair dismissal.*	*Failure to make a claim for social security benefits: Secretary of State for Employment v Stewart [1996] IRLR 334.*
Tax, NI, and pension contributions.	Insurance moneys or charitable payments other than by employer.	Sick pay.
Accelerated receipt (usually only in cases of very long-term notice periods or remainders of fixed-term contracts), of 5–10 per cent deduction.		*Ex gratia* payments by the employer. These are certainly deductible if clearly intended to compensate employee for dismissal.

Note: Deductions in unfair dismissal cases are treated differently (see **10.13.4** below).

9.10.3 Action for debt

In *Abrahams* v *Performing Rights Society* [1995] IRLR 486 the Court of Appeal added a new gloss to this area. Here, in March 1992, the parties had failed to reach agreement concerning the extension of the employee's fixed-term contract. Instead, the employee agreed to continue working *'under the terms of his existing contract'* for two years until March 1994. That fixed-term contract had contained a clause allowing for two years' notice or payment in lieu to be given.

After only six months of the new contract the employer dismissed the employee summarily. Following considerable debate as to the exact meaning of the phrase 'under the terms of his existing contract', it was held that the employee was still entitled to two years' notice or payment in lieu (a trifling sum of £232,292). In a case full of twists and turns, the central question then became whether, on what appeared to be a straightforward wrongful dismissal, the employee had to mitigate his loss on the principles described above.

In an uncommon reversal of arguments, the *employer* contended that this was indeed a wrongful dismissal and so subject to mitigation. The employee argued that where, as in this case, the contract of employment expressly provides that the employment may be terminated by the employer on payment of a sum in lieu of notice, any summary dismissal is a *lawful* termination, not a breach of contract, and the amount unpaid constitutes a debt (which is not subject to mitigation). The court agreed with the employee:

(a) the provision in the contract for payment in lieu gave rise to a contractual entitlement and therefore created a debt; and, *obiter*,

(b) even if the notice provision were to be regarded as liquidated damages, no duty to mitigate would apply.

Amongst the many practical implications to this case we would note the following:

(a) most senior employee contracts (and many others) incorporate a payment in lieu provision, so the ramifications of this case are extensive;

(b) many of these contracts use this clause so as to take advantage of the reasoning in *Rex Stewart Jeffries Parker Ginsberg Ltd* v *Parker* and avoid any technical breach of contract (see above at **9.9**);

(c) employers and their solicitors must therefore balance the potential sums due *as a debt* against the need for restraint of trade protection when drafting the contract.

The decision in *Abrahams* has had a mixed reception. In *Gregory* v *Wallace* [1998] IRLR 387, *Hutchings* v *Coinsee Ltd* [1998] IRLR 190 and *Cerberus Software* v *Rowley* [2001] IRLR 160 the Court of Appeal has confirmed the basic principle in *Abrahams* that a payment in lieu clause can create a debt rather than a contractual claim but placed emphasis on the wording of the clause itself. If the clause reserves to the employer the *right* to decide whether to make the payment or not it is more likely that any non-payment can only be recovered in a claim for damages rather than debt (and so be subject to mitigation).

9.10.4 Where there is no dismissal

We have so far fixed on wrongful dismissal. It may be that the employee is not dismissed and yet suffers loss. Such was the case in *Rigby* v *Ferodo* [1988] ICR 29 (discussed in **Chapter 5**), where the employees, faced with a pay cut in breach of contract, remained in employment and sued for damages representing their lost wages.

The employee may likewise always sue for any other form of breach of contract. A difficulty arises here, however. *Rigby* v *Ferodo* was an easy case because the quantum was the lost wages. If the employee is suing for a breach relating to an unlawful order, e.g., to move to another site or undertake different responsibilities, damages will be more difficult to quantify. This problem has not really been addressed by the courts.

Again, a claim under ERA 1996, Part II, Protection of Wages, should be noted here as a possibility (see **Chapter 4** at **4.4** above).

9.10.5 Limited-term contracts

We repeat in this context that damages for breach of a limited-term contract will be for the remainder of the term *unless* the contract contains a notice provision, in which case damages will be for that notice period.

Clearly, if the remainder of the term is the relevant period the employee will be claiming a large sum in many cases. Here tax implications will come into their own. However, some heed must be taken of the fact that instead of earning a £25,000 salary each year for the next, say, three years the employee will be getting this money in one fell swoop. The courts therefore take account of this *accelerated receipt* and reduce the award to reflect this. A rule of thumb deduction has been 5 per cent but recent judicial comments have indicated a willingness to equate this with the personal injury figure of 2 per cent.

9.10.6 Equitable remedies

These discretionary remedies do not have a strong foothold in employment contracts, especially if they amount to a request for an injunction for specific performance.

9.10.6.1 Declarations

An employee (or employer) may seek a declaration by the court as to the contractual position and rights of the parties. There must be a genuine grievance to pursue—the courts are not prone to giving lecture courses. A declaration is not a decision, it is an opinion. It cannot require the parties to undertake a particular act—though it would seem generally inadvisable to ignore it.

9.10.6.2 Injunctions

The courts are not keen to turn service into servitude and will therefore be loath to come to any decision which smacks of specific performance of the contract. Damages will usually suffice here as a remedy so, *unless damages are inadequate,* injunctions will not be granted. The concern of *employers* seeking injunctive relief regarding the maintenance of confidentiality, 'garden leave' clauses and restraint of trade was dealt with in **Chapter 8** (at **8.12**). Those points will not be repeated here.

An *employee* may seek an injunction in three main circumstances:

(a) to prevent a dismissal occurring which will be in breach of contractually enforceable rules of procedure;

(b) to prevent a dismissal taking place at all;

(c) to get the employee's job back.

It is unlikely that an injunction will be granted for the last point: *Marsh* v *National Autistic Society* [1993] ICR 453. Injunctions preventing dismissals in any circumstances are again a rare event. However, injunctions to hold the dismissal until procedures have been adhered to have become more common over the years. Thus, although a dismissed employee will not be able to obtain an order for specific performance to *regain* employment, it is feasible that a court would grant an interim injunction requiring the dismissal not to take effect *unless and until* the employer had complied with the contractual terms (e.g., disciplinary procedures).

The decisions are not consistent in this area but it seems that injunctions may be granted (remember it is a discretionary remedy) where:

(a) the dismissal is in breach of a mandatory contractual procedure (usually relating to disciplinary action; but this may also extend to things such as redundancy selection procedures: *Anderson* v *Pringle of Scotland Ltd* [1998] IRLR 64). Injunctions can be granted to restrain dismissals which do not comply with set contractual procedures: *Dietmann* v *Brent London Borough Council* [1988] ICR 842;

(b) trust and confidence has been maintained between the parties, i.e., the parties are still content to continue working together (judged on rational, not purely subjective, grounds: *Powell* v *Brent London Borough Council* [1988] ICR 176), or at least the contract is still 'workable'.

Injunctions come in two forms: interim (pending a full hearing of the issues) and final (granted at the conclusion of the full action). In most cases a prohibitory interim injunction will be granted or refused on the *American Cyanamid* principles (from *American Cyanamid Co.* v *Ethicon Ltd* [1975] AC 396—see **Chapter 8**).

9.10.6.3 Part 24, Civil procedure rules

One of the problems in this area is that if an employee fails to obtain an interim injunction preventing dismissal this will effectively decide the issue, because by the time the full action comes to trial the issue will be dead and buried except for damages.

Thus we noted in **Chapter 5** the case of *Jones* v *Gwent County Council* [1992] IRLR 521, where a novel and interesting approach to these problems was taken when RSC Ords 14A, r. 1 was used to prevent a letter of dismissal being effective. RSC Ords. 14 and 14A have now been amalgamated into CPR, Part 24. This part covers applications by claimants or defendants for summary judgment and allows a court to determine any question of law or construction of any document at any stage in the proceedings (there must be no dispute of fact) where the question is suitable for determination *without a full trial* and that determination will decide the claim.

In *Jones* a catalogue of ineptly handled disciplinary hearings took place until Jones eventually received a letter of dismissal. Jones sought an injunction to restrain the Council from dismissing her pursuant to the letter until full trial. Chadwick J held that, for the purposes of Ord. 14A, the status of the purported dismissal letter could be determined as easily in the current hearing as at full trial. That being so, the letter of dismissal was not a valid and effective dismissal because it did not comply with the disciplinary procedures set out in the contract. Further, it was held that under Ord. 14A the presence or absence of mutual trust *was irrelevant.* A permanent injunction was therefore issued restraining the Council from dismissing Jones *pursuant to its dismissal letter* and an interlocutory injunction was granted restraining the Council from dismissing unless proper grounds existed after carrying out the correct procedure.

Part 24, CPR could thus prove to be a very effective weapon for employees where the dispute is only about the meaning of documents, e.g., in cases of threatened demotion or dismissal which hinge on the wording of the contract. The number of cases making use of this device is steadily increasing; although use of RSC Ord. 14A in *Abrahams* v *Performing Rights Society* was the subject of some critical comment from Hutchinson LJ. Whether Part 24, CPR could be applied to confidentiality or restraint of trade cases is debatable. If there is no dispute as to fact so that 'reasonableness' is purely a point of law, there seems no reason why this should not be the case.

9.10.6.4 Judicial review

Judicial review is not relevant to employment law except in very limited circumstances. These were defined in *McLaren* v *Home Office* [1990] ICR 824 as being (i) that the decision was made by a public body; or (ii) where an employee or employer is entitled to refer disputes on the employment relationship to a disciplinary or other body established by statute.

9.11 Outline of tax considerations

This section makes no attempt to describe in detail the various schemes employed by companies to deal with taxation matters, merely to note some key points to be considered when termination is effected.

9.11.1 Normal rule

Monies paid on the termination of a contract will be subject to tax in the same way that wages are where there is a contractual obligation to make that payment and this still applies even when:

(a) the payment is expressed as being discretionary; and

(b) the contract is silent on the point but such payments constitute normal practice.

This will apply equally to express terms allowing for payment in lieu of notice (*EMI Group Electronics Ltd* v *Caldicott (Inspector of Taxes)* [1999] IRLR 630) and will apply to other benefits such as the retention of company cars. Where the contract (or practice) does not allow payment in lieu of notice employers may still, theoretically, deduct tax; but most will pay gross as the first £30,000 is not taxable in the employee's hands under ss. 401–405, Income Tax (Earnings and Pensions) Act 2003. The Revenue has issued guidance notes on tax and pay *in lieu* of notice: see www.inlandrevenue.gov.uk/bulletins/tb63.pdf

9.11.2 Compensation for loss of office

Ex gratia payments (e.g., 'golden handshakes') will not be subject to the general rule provided they do not relate to services rendered and are not a contractual right. In such cases the first £30,000 is not taxable.

As *any prior agreement* may be subject to tax, various schemes have been devised to help reduce the chance of tax being charged where there is no contractual obligation but termination terms are being negotiated. Such tactics involve complicated assessments of liabilities for relevant tax years.

9.11.3 Damages for wrongful dismissal

The basic principles in this area were set out in *British Transport Commission* v *Gourley* [1955] 3 All ER 796. The employee should be placed in the same position as if the contract had been performed properly. The *Gourley* principle means that deductions must be made from any award for tax, as described in **9.10.2** above.

9.11.4 Statutory payments

Such payments are taxable, but in general are treated as exempt from tax up to £30,000.

(a) The basic award in unfair dismissal (see **Chapter 10**) is payable as a gross figure.

(b) The compensatory award in unfair dismissal is already calculated on a net pay figure (but see **10.15.1** below) so no further adjustment is necessary.

(c) The additional award in unfair dismissal is payable as a gross figure.

(d) Statutory redundancy pay (see **Chapter 11**) is payable gross.

(e) Contractual redundancy pay, strictly, should be treated as a contractual right and subject to tax. However, the Inland Revenue have issued a Statement of Practice on this (SP1/94) to the effect that if the scheme is a genuine redundancy payment no tax will be taken. The amount will still go towards the calculation of the £30,000 exemption (this point is explained further in **10.15.1** below).

9.12 Summary

- A contract of employment may be terminated in a number of ways, most commonly dismissal and resignation.
- The common law is only concerned with the contractual aspects of termination so its focus is on whether or not adequate notice was given to terminate the contract.

- A dismissal made without adequate notice is a wrongful dismissal and the employee will be able to recover damages to the amount of notice that should have been given.

- Just because a dismissal has been without notice does not mean it is wrongful. The employer may be able to justify this by referring to a serious breach of contract by the employee which brought about the dismissal.

- The employer is permitted to rely on evidence of the employee's breach even if this was not known at the time of dismissal.

- A resignation brought about by the employee's acceptance of the employer's repudiatory breach allows the employee to claim wrongful repudiation of the contract. Damages are treated in the same way as wrongful dismissal claims.

- Although the parties are free to determine what notice is due on termination from either side, there are statutory minimum periods of notice which alter according to length of service.

- These periods of notice (and other terms for that matter) must not be discriminatory. As regards any term which is service-related there may be problems with age discrimination.

- The assessment of damages is subject to the normal contractual rules so that issues of actual loss, mitigation and taxation all come into play. Damages are generally not awarded for injured feelings, but stress claims may be tagged on to other contractual damages.

Unfair dismissal

10.1 Introduction and overview

10.1.1 Jurisdiction

This chapter is concerned with the most important (or at least the most notorious) of the statutory rights: the right to claim unfair dismissal. The sole arena for deciding these claims is the employment tribunal; unfair dismissal actions *cannot* be heard in the ordinary courts. The bulk of employment tribunals' workload is made up of unfair dismissal cases. Many are settled before going to a tribunal; most of the cases heard are decided in favour of the employer. Appeal lies to the Employment Appeal Tribunal (EAT) on 'a question of law' (a term which has been given an increasingly narrow ambit by the EAT and the Court of Appeal).

10.1.2 Relationships with wrongful dismissal

Right at the start the differences between *wrongful dismissal* actions and *unfair dismissal* actions should be noted. We have seen that wrongful dismissal is concerned with awarding damages for breach of contract. Unfair dismissal rights centre on the *reason for* the dismissal and *the manner* in which the dismissal was handled. It is quite possible to have the following combinations:

(a) a dismissal which is unfair but which is not wrongful;

(b) a dismissal which is wrongful but which is not unfair;

(c) a dismissal which is both unfair and wrongful;

(d) a dismissal which is neither unfair nor wrongful.

10.1.3 Overview of unfair dismissal actions

- Only employees, not independent contractors, have the right to claim unfair dismissal: s. 94 ERA 1996. The right extends to those employed in casual or part-time work and to those who have limited-term contracts, but some employees are excluded from the right (e.g., those working outside Great Britain).

- In most cases an employee must have been employed for one year to qualify for the right, though there is an ever-growing list of exceptions as set out in **10.8.8** below.

- There is no upper or lower age for claiming unfair dismissal, though compulsory retirements are still possible provided certain procedures are followed.

- To claim the right an employee must have been dismissed. The term 'dismissal' can include a termination of the contract arising from a resignation—known in this context as a 'constructive dismissal'. A constructive dismissal only arises where the employer has seriously breached or repudiated the contract and this has been accepted by the employee in resigning. If challenged, it is for the employee to show a 'dismissal' occurred.

- There are six potentially fair *reasons* for dismissal set out in s. 98(2) ERA 1996. They are: capability, conduct, retirement, redundancy, statutory illegality, and 'some other substantial reason'. If the employer cannot show one of these reasons the dismissal is unfair.

- Even if the dismissal is for a fair *reason*, this will not make it a fair dismissal: there is a second limb. Where the fair reason is conduct, capability, redundancy, statutory illegality or 'some other substantial reason', s. 98(4) ERA 1996 *fairness* is judged by examining whether the employer acted reasonably or unreasonably in treating the reason as sufficient to justify dismissing the employee. This breaks down into two key tests: (i) whether a fair procedure was used; and (ii) whether the decision to dismiss fell within the 'range of reasonable responses open to a reasonable employer'. As we shall see, however, 'retirement' dismissals are treated as a special case and are subject to slightly different rules for determining 'fairness' under s. 98ZG ERA 1996.

- The extent to which a company adheres to its procedures (and how these follow the ACAS Code and Guidelines) is extremely important in judging questions of fairness.

- A dismissal will be automatically unfair in certain circumstances (set out at **10.8.8** below). Examples include dismissal for reason of pregnancy and dismissals because the employee made a legitimate public interest disclosure.

- If a finding of unfair dismissal is made the tribunal should consider whether to direct that the employee should be reinstated in their job, but this is hardly ever ordered so the main remedy is compensation. Tribunals award compensation under two main headings:

  — The Basic Award (a sum of money calculated on a fixed formula relating to age and years of service). The maximum sum that can be awarded (for 2007–08) is £9,900. This figure is updated every February.

  — The Compensatory Award. This is assessed on the basis of what the tribunal considers just and equitable and it is sub-divided into: (i) loss from date of dismissal to the tribunal hearing; and (ii) future loss. The maximum Compensatory Award that can be awarded is £63,000. This figure is also updated every February. Some dismissals, e.g., relating to public interest disclosures, are not subject to the statutory maximum.

- Deductions may be made from these awards e.g., for contributory fault, even resulting in a finding of unfair dismissal leading to no compensation.

10.1.4 Practice note

As we mentioned in the Preface, at the time of writing there are certain statutory procedures in place regarding dismissals and resignations. These overly-complicated rules will be replaced in April 2009 with what appears to be a return to a much simpler system whereby the company must follow its own contractual procedures, which in turn must be in line with the ACAS Code on Discipline and Dismissal. The Code issued by ACAS (and backed-up by more detailed Guidelines) will not be binding but an employer who departs from this may find any compensation payable will be increased and an employee who is at fault (e.g., by not making proper use of any grievance procedures) may find their compensation reduced. Consequently, we have not dealt with the statutory procedures in this edition but will say a few words below on the ACAS Code.

10.2 Preventive measures

Most employers these days are aware of the importance of being able to justify dismissal decisions and of the need to follow correct procedures. But many dismissals (especially in small companies) can result from hasty management decisions; and it is not uncommon for employers to sit on problems (e.g., an employee's incompetence) and then expect to be able to dismiss without any warning having been given to the employee, without any consultation, and immediately. Another common practice is to dismiss for the event *following* the big one, i.e., the employer misses or dodges the opportunity to dismiss for the misconduct which would have been easy to defend but, almost as a knee-jerk reaction, dismisses for an event that is not justifiable.

You may not have control over any of this because usually the parties will come to you with a *fait accompli* rather than in advance for advice. However, if you can advise your client prior to dismissal there are some general industrial relations and personnel points to note. The reasons why these pieces of advice are given here will become clear later when we look at how employment tribunals judge the fairness of dismissals.

There are two main practical categories in which the employer will wish to dismiss:

(a) *Maintaining standards.*

Employers regard it as important to maintain standards of acceptable behaviour on the part of employees, relating for example to quality of workmanship, rate of output, punctuality, attendance, and working relationships with other staff. Employees who fail to meet these standards will (or at least should) generally be warned about their shortcomings but dismissal is the final sanction that can be used.

(b) *Relationship impossible to maintain.*

The employee's actions here will include dishonesty (especially in a position of trust), sexual misconduct and harassment of other staff, and assault.

Quite often both strands are present in a single case so that the position can become muddied and the employer may need advice on analysing the reason for any dismissal. For instance, senior management may centre on the maintenance of standards whilst supervisors focus on the effect of misconduct on fellow workers. When evidence is given as to why dismissal occurred it is clearly better if everyone is in general agreement, and this is better sorted out *before the dismissal.*

Before any dismissal employers should also be advised to examine other available courses of action and to:

(a) make proper use of their disciplinary procedures (which should comply with the ACAS Code);

(b) consider the effect on remaining employees in terms of future loyalty and performance (arising from leniency or excessive severity);

(c) consider the effect of any decision on supervisors, e.g., undermining their authority;

(d) consider the effect on any relationship with trade unions;

(e) consider all the alternatives if business reorganisation or redundancy is the reason for dismissal.

If dismissal is inevitable, try to control the manner of the dismissal. Your checklist should include:

(a) consider the terms of the contract;

(b) make sure that all the evidence is available and clear;

(c) make sure that the employer genuinely believes that dismissal is a reasonable course of action;

(d) make sure that all the relevant procedures have been complied with;

(e) make sure that any hearing is properly conducted;

(f) make sure that dismissal is consistent with previous practice within the company.

10.3 Qualifying for the right

Although ERA 1996, s. 94 states that every employee has the right not to be unfairly dismissed, there are certain conditions to be met. We noted these qualification aspects in **Chapter 5**. So, if we assume that your employee-client has asked you for advice following a dismissal, you need to ascertain, to begin with:

(a) that your client was in fact an employee; and

(b) that your client had one year's continuous employment (although there are many exceptions to this rule, see **10.8.8** below); and

(c) whether your client has fulfilled his or her part in any company dispute resolution procedures; and

(d) that your client is not prevented from claiming because of the application of international law; and

(e) that your client does not fall within a miscellaneous excluded category; and

(f) that your client is still within the three-month limitation period which begins at the effective date of termination (the EDT).

These points are expanded below.

10.3.1 Service

The length of time an employee has spent with his or her employer (the continuity of employment) has always been a vital factor in determining whether or not he or she qualifies for unfair dismissal rights. The general requirement is for one year's service. Thus, in most cases, an employee dismissed before the expiry of one year will have no claim. Further, employing a person on a fixed-term contract for just less than one year so as to avoid liability for unfair dismissal is not 'less favourable treatment' for the purposes of the Fixed-term Employees (Prevention of Less Favourable Treatment) Regulations

2002, SI 2002/2034—even when it is the government trying to avoid liability under its own regulations: *Department for Work and Pensions* v *Webley* [2004] EWCA Civ 1745, [2005] ICR 577.

10.3.1.1   The effective date of termination

The period of continuity ends at the effective date of termination (EDT) and the limitation period for bringing claims starts at this point. The EDT is not necessarily the date when an employee is told that he or she is dismissed: *it varies according to whether notice is given or not.* Any notice given begins to run on the day after notification. So the EDT is defined in ERA 1996, s. 97(1), as:

- the date the notice period expires, if the employee is given notice (whether or not all the notice is worked and whether or not the correct notice was given); or
- the date of dismissal, if the employee is summarily dismissed (i.e., dismissed without any form of notice); or
- the date of dismissal, if the employee is dismissed with payment in lieu; or
- the date a fixed-term contract expires without being renewed.

The distinction between the first and third points may seem to be one of semantics; sometimes this is true. But the basic difference is that in the first instance the employee is either given the choice of working out the notice, or the employer insists on some work, e.g., to tidy up existing jobs or to pass on operational information to other employees; payment in lieu, on the other hand, is of immediate and unchallengeable effect. The position can, however, be complicated further. The way the employer expresses (orally or in writing) the dismissal and making of the payment in lieu may also affect the EDT. If the employer makes it clear that he is dismissing the employee immediately but paying him his notice entitlement, the EDT is that date of notification (this is the usual pattern). However, if the employer gets carried away (or has no concept of the problems) and talks about dismissing with notice but giving a payment in lieu instead of asking for notice to be worked, the EDT is the date the notice would have expired (see *Adams* v *GKN Sankey Ltd* [1980] IRLR 416).

Employers frequently use the third option described above (pay in lieu) because, provided there is no contractual term guaranteeing payment in lieu, it may avoid the tax liability due for the notice period. These distinctions prove to be a common point of confusion and need to be treated very carefully. For instance, although the third option may have tax advantages if there is no contractual right to dismiss with payment in lieu this is a technical breach of contract which will render any restraint of trade clause ineffective (as we saw at **8.9**).

10.3.1.2   Appeals

If an employee is dismissed he or she may well appeal against that decision using the company's disciplinary/grievance procedure. The question then arises: if the dismissal is confirmed on appeal, is the employee's date of dismissal the original date of the decision or the confirmation of that decision at the culmination of the appeals procedure? In most cases, unless there is express contractual provision to the contrary, the *original date* will count: *West Midlands Co-operative Society Ltd* v *Tipton* [1986] ICR 192. Thus any summary dismissal runs from that date and any notice given runs from that date too. If, however, the employee is suspended *pending a decision to dismiss,* the time can only run from the actual decision to dismiss. The employee's case becomes even easier to argue where that suspension was on full pay: *Drage* v *Governors of Greenford High School* [2000] IRLR 314.

10.3.1.3 Varying the EDT

It is not open to the parties to agree an EDT which is different from the normal method of calculation: *Fitzgerald* v *University of Kent at Canterbury* [2004] EWCA Civ 143, [2004] ICR 737. The effective date of termination is a statutory construct which depends on what has actually taken place and not on what the parties agreed. Note, however, that the parties may agree to vary the notice *period,* e.g., where the employee has been given notice but wishes to leave earlier. A genuine variation such as this will mean that the EDT moves as well (see *Palfrey* v *Transco* [2004] IRLR 916, EAT, with disastrous consequences for the employee's unfair dismissal claim being out of time).

10.3.1.4 Extending the EDT

Under ERA 1996, s. 97(2), the EDT may be deemed extended in certain circumstances by adding on to it the s. 86 statutory minimum period of notice (see **9.7.1.1** above).

EXAMPLE

An employee is dismissed summarily after 51 weeks' service. Strictly, she does not have the requisite one year's (52 weeks) service to claim unfair dismissal. However, s. 97(2) allows the employee the fiction of adding on the s. 86 notice that should have been given (here, one week) in calculating the EDT. Thus the employee gains the one year's qualification and can claim unfair dismissal. This device lessens the opportunities for unscrupulous employers to engage in brinkmanship tactics.

Note, however, that only the s. 86 notice can be used this way. The contractual notice (which may be longer) is irrelevant. The statutory extension also applies where the employee has waived his right to notice or has received payment in lieu of notice because such matters relate only to the employee's contract and do not affect his statutory rights: *Secretary of State for Employment* v *Staffordshire County Council* [1989] ICR 664. This method of extending the EDT also applies to constructive dismissal claims (see below at **10.6**). Note, however, that if the summary dismissal was contractually justified (e.g., because the dismissal was for gross misconduct or other serious breach by the employee) then this device cannot be applied.

As well as ensuring statutory rights in borderline situations the same technique can be used to calculate years of service for compensation purposes; so a dismissal close to four years' service would normally count as three years (because only whole years are considered), but the use of the s. 86 notice might take the qualification over the line into four years' service. This might affect the quantum of an employee's entitlement to, say, redundancy pay.

10.3.1.5 Exceptions to the service qualification

Some unfair dismissals do not require a one-year qualification period. These are set out in ERA 1996, s. 108 and TULRCA 1992, s. 154. Most of these types of dismissal are also deemed 'automatically unfair', so we have detailed these reasons in a table under that heading at **10.8.8** below.

10.3.2 Hours worked and minimum age

Under ERA 1996, s. 210(4) an employee does not have to work for any set number of hours per week in order to qualify for statutory rights such as unfair dismissal, redundancy or maternity leave. There is also no minimum age for claiming unfair dismissal.

10.3.3   Retirement age

The rule whereby an employee lost all rights to claim unfair dismissal at age 65 has been removed: see sch. 8, para. 24 Employment Equality (Age) Regulations 2006, SI 2006/1031. However, some companies have a 'normal retirement age' for employees. In most cases this is set below 65, though not always (if companies have no such requirement the default retirement age is presently 65). Subject to what we say below at **10.3.3.2**, where employees reach 65 or have a 'normal retirement age' then any dismissal *for retirement* at that age is potentially fair. This begs the question: how do you determine whether there is a 'normal retirement age'?

10.3.3.1   Determining 'normal retirement age'

This is a technical term and does not just mean the date employees generally or commonly retire. It has been the subject of much case law. In *Waite* v *GCHQ* [1983] ICR 653, the House of Lords held that the normal retirement age was *prima facie* to be determined by what the contract said even if some employees happened to be kept on past the stated age of, say, 60. However, if the employees' reasonable expectations are that they will work past this age (e.g., because nearly everyone does so) there is probably no normal retirement age and the default of 65 comes into play. One of the key factors here is that one is not looking for a normal retirement age for the company as a whole but the age which applies to the *group of employees* to which the employee in question belongs. For instance, there may be different ages for clerical staff and manual workers. Even employees sharing the same job title have been found to be in different 'positions' under closer examination—and one person can constitute a group here: *Wall* v *British Compressed Air Society* [2003] EWCA Civ 1762.

The test was developed further in *Brooks* v *Telecommunications plc* [1991] IRLR 4, where the EAT held that one should determine a normal retirement age by:

(a) identifying the undertaking in which the employee is employed (in case this is a multi-site company);

(b) identifying which employees hold the *particular position* also held by the employee in question; and

(c) establishing the normal retirement age *for that group* of employees.

To this, the Court of Appeal has set out ten common sense guidelines for determining normal retirement age. These start with the rebuttable presumption that the contract provides the answer before subjecting this to a reasonable expectations test by looking at company practice: *Barclays Bank plc* v *O'Brien* [1994] IRLR 580.

Although the Employment Equality (Age) Regulations 2006, SI 2006/1031 allow for companies to utilise a normal retirement age below 65, such policies are potentially discriminatory unless objectively justifiable, so most employers are moving their retirement age to 65. This may involve renegotiating the employment contract.

10.3.3.2   The legality of the default retirement age

The default retirement age of 65 is permitted under reg. 30. However, as we noted in **Chapter 6**, the legality of that default age has been challenged in *R (on the application of Incorporated Trustee of the National Council for Ageing (Age Concern England)* v. *Secretary of State for Business, Enterprise and Regulatory Reform* [2007] EWHC 3090 (Admin), [2008] 1 CMLR 425 (a case known simply as *Heyday*). At the time of writing Advocate General Mazak has just issued his opinion that the default age can 'in principle be justified under

Article 6(1) of Directive 2000/78 if that rule is objectively and reasonably justified in the context of national law by a legitimate aim relating to employment policy and the labour market and it is not apparent that the means put in place to achieve that aim of public interest are inappropriate and unnecessary for the purpose'. So, until we have the judgment of the ECJ it looks as though the UK's default retirement age is secure. All this should be determined finally in early 2009.

10.3.4 Working outside Great Britain

Some employees spend some or all of their time working abroad. Because the ERA 1996 says nothing about territorial range, jurisdiction over such contracts is now determined by the rules of international law such as the Brussels Convention on Jurisdiction and Enforcement of Judgments in Civil and Commercial Matters and the Rome Convention on the Law Applicable to Contractual Obligations (transposed respectively into our law via the Civil Jurisdiction and Judgments Act 1982 and the Contracts (Applicable Law) Act 1990). These focus on where the employee's work has some connexion with the UK. The test is essentially: during the whole of the contract's duration, where does the employee habitually carry out his work? If his habitual place of work cannot be determined, the applicable law is that in which the place of business through which he was engaged is situated unless the circumstances show that the contract is more closely connected with the law of another country.

In addition, the Posting of Workers Directive (96/71/EC) deals with the position where a person is posted temporarily abroad for a limited period (either from the UK or to the UK) and was implemented in the UK via the ERA 1999. Article 6 of the Directive provides: 'In order to enforce the right to the terms and conditions of employment guaranteed in Article 3, judicial proceedings may be instituted in the Member State in whose territory the worker is or was posted, without prejudice, where applicable, to the right, under existing international conventions on jurisdiction, to institute proceedings in another state.' In the joined cases of *Serco Ltd* v *Lawson; Botham* v *Ministry of Defence; and Croft* v *Veta Ltd* [2006] UKHL 3, [2006] IRLR 289 the House of Lords attempted to give guidance as to when an employee fell within the jurisdiction of the tribunals for unfair dismissal purposes. Their Lordships held that the idea of 'employment in Great Britain', developed by the Court of Appeal, was the general yardstick. The terms of the contract and prior conduct would be factors to consider, but the common sense approach was to look at the employee's base. It would therefore be unusual for an employee based abroad to fall within the scope of unfair dismissal legislation but, if the employee was posted abroad (e.g., a foreign correspondent) or the territory in question was effectively a 'British enclave' (an armed forces base: *Botham's case;* or remote outpost such as Ascension Island: *Lawson's case*), such expatriate employees could gain protection. This is because the connexion between the employment relationship and the UK was a strong one.

10.3.5 Contracting out

The general position is that it is not possible to contract out of statutory rights except where there is an ACAS conciliation or a compromise agreement under ERA 1996, s. 203 (see **10.12** below).

10.3.6 Limited-term contracts

We noted in **9.4.2** that, in the past, clauses commonly appeared in limited-term contracts which permitted the contracting-out (or waiver) of the employee's statutory rights to claim unfair dismissal or redundancy payments on expiry and non-renewal of the term. However, under: (i) ss. 18(1) and 44 and ERA 1999, sch. 9 a limited-term contract entered into on or after 25 October 1999 can no longer exclude rights relating to unfair dismissal; and (ii) under EA 2002, s. 45 and sch. 2, para. 3(13)-(17) and the Fixed-Term Employees (Prevention of Less Favourable Treatment) Regulations 2002, SI 2002/2034 [para. 5], the same applies to redundancy payments rights where the dismissal occurs on or after 1 October 2002. However, any waiver/contracting-out clauses entered into before these respective dates will remain valid until the term expires so you may still (just) encounter valid waiver clauses in the case of lengthy fixed-term contracts. One limitation on this is that such waivers cannot be included in any renewal or extension of the limited term.

You may also encounter the position where there has been a succession of limited terms. The non-waiver provisions above apply to these but there is a further point: where the *renewal* of a fixed-term takes the total of successive terms over four years (discounting any employment before 10 July 2002) employment is deemed to be permanent as from the renewal date or the date on which four years was attained.

10.3.7 Excluded categories

There are a number of miscellaneous categories. The most common ones are:

(a) the police force. This includes all those who have the powers or privileges of a constable;

(b) share fishermen, i.e., masters and crews of fishing vessels who take a share in the profits of the catch;

(c) employees working under illegal contracts.

10.3.7.1 Employees working under illegal contracts

This category deserves special comment. As with the ordinary law of contract, a contract of employment which is illegal will be unenforceable. No rights, under common law or statute, will therefore flow from a dismissal. The most obvious example is a contract designed to evade tax liabilities: *Napier* v *National Business Agency Ltd* [1951] 2 All ER 264 (agreement to classify wages as expenses). In some cases the illegal part of the contract may be severed, leaving the rest to stand. For example, an unlawful restraint of trade clause will not affect the validity of the remainder of the contract and discriminatory clauses can be ignored or modified.

If the employee is innocent of the fact of illegality it seems that he or she may still claim unfair dismissal rights. The test is subjective and relates to ignorance of the relevant facts, not ignorance of the law. Likewise, if the employee gains no advantage from the illegality (e.g., participates in a VAT evasion) it is likely that the right to claim unfair dismissal is not damaged: *Hewcastle Catering Ltd* v *Ahmed and Elkamah* [1991] IRLR 473. And a short-term illegality may have the effect only of breaking the employee's continuity of employment, which can start again after the duration of the illegality.

10.3.8 Limitation period

In general, the employee must present any claim within the three-month limitation period which begins at the EDT: ERA 1996, s. 111(2). The period begins on the EDT itself and 'month' means calendar month, so one must find the EDT, take the date of the day before the EDT and project this forward three months. Thus a dismissal on 3 October must be presented *on or before 2* January of the following year (3 January is too late). This topic is dealt with more extensively in **Chapter 13**.

10.4 Burden of proof

Before turning to the detail of what is meant by fairness and unfairness, it is important to note that there are three stages in an unfair dismissal action and the burden of proof at each stage is different. Thus:

(a) the *employee* (if challenged) must prove there was a dismissal. This may be an issue where the employee has resigned but claims constructive dismissal;

(b) the *employer* must show that the dismissal was for one of the six accepted *fair reasons;*

(c) the burden of proving the *fairness* of the dismissal is neutral.

We will now examine what is meant by 'dismissal', 'fair reason', and 'fairness'.

10.5 The meaning of 'dismissal'

We noted in **Chapter 9** that the term 'dismissal' is a technical term which can occasionally confuse, and one which can certainly trap the unwary. Employees may therefore find themselves 'dismissed' (as legally defined) in the following circumstances:

(a) where the employee is 'given the sack';

(b) where the employer uses language which amounts to dismissal;

(c) where the employer intimates a future dismissal;

(d) where the employer says 'resign or be sacked';

(e) where the employer repudiates the contract and the employee resigns;

(f) where a limited-term contract is not renewed;

(g) on retirement.

Points (a) to (f) were discussed in detail in **Chapter 9** at **9.6** and **9.8** and we will consider retirement in more depth below.

10.6 Constructive dismissal

10.6.1 A resignation which is deemed a dismissal

We saw in Chapter 9 that when an employee resigns this may still constitute a dismissal for common law purposes (termed a 'wrongful repudiation'). The position is the same as regards *statutory rights* and is governed by ERA 1996, s. 95(1)(c). This states that a resignation will amount to a dismissal if 'the employee terminates the contract under which he is employed (with or without notice) in circumstances in which he is entitled to terminate it without notice by reason of the employer's conduct'.

In this statutory context this is known as 'constructive dismissal'. But the definition leaves a problem: what sort of conduct by the employer *entitles* the employee to resign and claim unfair dismissal?

10.6.2   The Western Excavating test

The issue of 'entitlement' was determined by the Court of Appeal in the key case of *Western (ECC) Ltd* v *Sharp* [1978] QB 761. Lord Denning MR held that one must use a contractual analysis so an employee is entitled to resign and claim unfair dismissal only if:

(a) the employer's actions are a significant breach of contract (an employer who is merely acting unreasonably is not necessarily in breach of contract, but we shall see that the two can overlap substantially);

(b) the resignation is obviously related to the employer's conduct; and

(c) the employee responds quickly.

10.6.3   Are all breaches repudiatory?

The short answer to this question is 'no': *Western Excavating* v *Sharp* established that a *serious* breach is required. Moreover, in *Hilton* v *Shiner* [2001] IRLR 727, the EAT confirmed and applied previous *dicta* to the effect that the employer's conduct must have been without reasonable and proper cause. For instance, instigating disciplinary action against an employee would not *per se* be a breach of mutual trust and confidence if there appeared good grounds for doing so. A gloss was added to this by the EAT in *Morrow* v *Safeway Stores* [2002] IRLR 9 that, once a breach of mutual trust has been found, this implied term is so fundamental to the workings of the contract that its breach automatically constitutes a repudiation—a tribunal cannot conclude that there was such a breach but, on the facts, hold that it was not serious. Like many EAT decisions, if one starts trying to apply this to real situations these two judgments do not sit together comfortably. It is suggested that the solution seems to be that a tribunal must make a clear finding of serious breach/no breach, incorporating the *Hilton* v *Shiner* aspect and, if there is a breach, must make a finding of constructive dismissal accordingly.

So, in general terms, the *Western (ECC) Ltd* v *Sharp* analysis still holds good. The test was held to be a contractual one because, to repeat the key statutory phrase, the conduct must be so serious as to 'entitle [the employee] to terminate [the contract] without notice by reason of the employer's conduct'. But over the years the boundary between 'serious breach' and 'unreasonableness' has been tested often and the latest variation on using a pure contractual analysis has now appeared in the form of the EAT decision in *Abbey National plc* v *Fairbrother* [2007] IRLR 320. This case, as we shall see, applies a different test to determine whether there has been a dismissal when there is a resignation based on the inadequate operation of a grievance procedure. First, however, we should look at the general situation.

10.6.4   Type of conduct required to bring a claim

10.6.4.1   Classic examples

A good example of the general application of a contractual analysis of 'dismissal' occurred in *Cawley* v *South Wales Electricity Board* [1985] IRLR 89. The employer utilised the disciplinary procedure (technically within the contractual bounds) to demote an employee by many grades. The EAT decided nevertheless that this was an excessive use of the contractual power and found a breach of contract. In reality, many cases have to turn on a judgment call. The line between merely unreasonable conduct (which is not a constructive dismissal) and seriously unreasonable conduct (which will be) has to be a question of fact: *Brown* v *Merchant* [1998] IRLR 682. Another variation of this can occur when salespeople have their areas or range of products changed under company reorganisations. If the contract defines area, commission, etc. any change by the employer will at least technically constitute a breach. But even if the contract is unclear on these matters (yes, it does occur) one would expect the courts to find an implied term to the effect that the company should at least come to some agreement concerning the impact on commission: *Star Newspapers Ltd* v *Jordan* (1993, unreported, EAT 709/91). Wider still, in *Woods* v *WM Service (Peterborough) Ltd* [1981] ICR 666, it was stated that employers will not, without reasonable and proper cause, conduct themselves in a manner calculated or likely to destroy or seriously damage the relationship of confidence and trust between employer and employee. Examples of constructive dismissal actions other than failure to conduct grievance procedures properly are:

(a) harassment (including harassment by other employees) and any discrimination that is statutorily barred (e.g., sex or race);

(b) victimisation: *Gardner* v *Beresford* [1978] IRLR 63;

(c) unilaterally changing the employee's job content or status: *Coleman* v *Baldwin* [1977] IRLR 342;

(d) humiliating employees in front of others: *Isle of Wight Tourist Board* v *Coombes* [1976] IRLR 413;

(e) Unwarranted demotion or disciplinary sanctions: *Cawley* v *SWEB* (above); or improper use of disciplinary sanctions such as issuing a final warning for a minor offence, as happened in *Stanley Cole (Wainfleet) Ltd* v *Sheridan* [2003] ICR 297;

(f) falsely accusing an employee of misconduct or incapability: *Robinson* v *Crompton Parkinson Ltd* [1978] IRLR 61;

(g) unilateral variation in contract terms, e.g., a change in hours or pay: *Woods* v *WM Service (Peterborough) Ltd* (above);

(h) deliberately withholding pay: *Cantor Fitzgerald International* v *Callaghan* [1999] IRLR 234;

(i) demanding that the employee undertakes a substantial transfer of location (certainly if without reasonable notice);

(j) suspension without pay where the contract does not allow for this—and even with pay if prolonged;

(k) failure to support a manager in the light of well-known operational difficulties;

(l) failure to provide a working environment that is reasonably suitable for the performance of contractual duties;

(m) Failure to investigate properly the possibility of finding alternative work for an employee who is suffering from work-related stress or failure to make reasonable adjustments to working conditions in the case of an employee suffering from a disability: *Nottinghamshire County Council* v *Meikle* [2004] EWCA Civ 859, [2005] ICR 1.

These are just examples and one would need to investigate the alleged breach very carefully. For instance, as we noted extensively in **Chapter 5**, an employee is expected to be adaptable in the operation of the contract. Therefore, what appears to be a unilateral variation of the contract may prove to be no such thing in law. Equally, the breach must be *serious* and much will depend upon the particular facts and the particular contract—though points such as harassment and victimisation will be easier to argue.

10.6.4.2   The 'last straw'

It is usually one breach that is in issue, but the idea of a 'last straw' can also apply so that a history of incidents can be drawn together: see *Lewis* v *Motorworld Garages Ltd* [1986] ICR 157. There does not necessarily have to be temporal proximity between the events, but the larger the gap the weaker the case becomes. The 'last straw' does not have to be a breach itself; it is the overall picture that counts. Nevertheless, the 'last straw' must contribute to the alleged continuing breach of mutual trust: *Omilaju* v *Waltham Forest LBC* [2004] EWCA Civ 1493, [2005] ICR 481. Further, in both *Fairbrother* and *Claridge* (above) it was noted that the application of the 'range of reasonable responses' test to the question of 'dismissal' does not apply to 'final straw' cases where the final straw is the handling of the grievance itself (confirming *GAB Robins* v *Triggs* [2007] 3 All ER 590).

10.6.4.3   Additional reasons for leaving

The mere fact that an employee has other, additional, reasons for leaving (e.g., to go to a different job) does not mean that the effective cause of the resignation has ceased to be the employer's breach. Neither does a delay of a few weeks in order to find such work damn the employee's case automatically.

10.6.4.4   Anticipatory breach

A constructive dismissal can arise by way of anticipatory breach but where an employer tells the employee that he will impose changes to the contract and will do this by giving proper notice to terminate and then re-engage on the new terms, this is not an anticipatory breach or a constructive dismissal: *Kerry Foods* v *Lynch* [2005] IRLR 681 (EAT).

10.6.4.5   Construction of the contract

Particular care should be taken where the only issue is the *construction of the contract* itself. Authorities (occasionally used in employment cases) have indicated that the employer's conduct has to show that he clearly intends not to be bound by the contract before a breach will occur. This is an uncertain and little-used area: see *Brigden* v *Lancashire County Council* [1987] IRLR 58.

10.6.4.6   Who breached first?

We saw in Chapter 9 that an employer may use any evidence, whenever discovered, to show an employee was in breach of contract. As you will see below the rules on unfair dismissal require the employer to show what was in his mind at the moment of dismissal, so subsequently discovered information is not strictly admissible. However, because constructive dismissal actions are a cross between common law and statute an employer can bring evidence to show that the employee had breached the contract before the potential dismissal event even if the employer did not know this at the time he himself was repudiating the contract: *RDF Media Group plc* v *Clements* [2007] EWHC 2892 (QB), [2008] IRLR 207. Here, an employer's adverse published comments on an employee (who was about to join a competitor) might have been repudiatory had not the employer subsequently discovered that the employee had already leaked confidential information in breach of contract.

10.6.5   Resignations following faulty grievance procedures

The case of *Abbey National plc* v *Fairbrother* [2007] IRLR 320 posed the question: what happens if the employee has a grievance, utilises the grievance procedure, is dissatisfied with the outcome and the way it was handled and then resigns? Until *Fairbrother* the answer was that the tribunal would use the contractual analysis as described and judge (as it would with a common law wrongful repudiation) whether the procedural failure demonstrated a serious breach based on the implied term of mutual trust and confidence.

In *Fairbrother* Lady Smith spotted a problem with this established analysis: if the employee had simply been disciplined and dismissed for some alleged breach (what we shall refer to throughout this chapter as an 'overt' dismissal to distinguish it from a constructive dismissal claim) then the question of whether there had been a dismissal would only be a question of fact to be established and the reasonableness of the employer's conduct would only come into play when deciding on 'fairness'. A key part of that test (as we shall see at **10.9.5**) is whether the employer's actions fell within a range of reasonable responses open to a reasonable employer (which is nowhere near as strict a test as a purely contract one as it allows for quite a bit of discretion on the employer's part in how things are conducted).

However, in a constructive dismissal claim it is for the employee to prove the fact of 'dismissal' and, where a constructive dismissal follows on from a resignation based on the allegation of a failure in the operation of a grievance procedure, a tribunal has to somehow decide whether that failure is a serious breach of contract. As a contractual test, this does not involve asking whether these actions fall within any band of reasonable responses: either there is a breach or there is not. A range of reasonable responses test, however, would allow for some failures (falling within a scale) to be tolerated.

The EAT in *Fairbrother* felt that two quite different tests were being applied to similar situations and the analysis was different only because of the way the dismissal came about—overtly or constructively. This, it was thought, should not be allowed.

The EAT therefore applied a 'range of reasonable responses' test to the question of whether the resignation amounted in law to a dismissal. This looks fairly innocuous but it very much changes the balance in favour of the employer. For example, assume the employee perceives that the employer's conduct is repudiatory. She lodges a grievance. The employer handles the grievance procedure poorly and decides there is no ground for the grievance. The employee resigns and claims constructive dismissal, claiming a breach of the implied term of mutual trust and confidence in the handling of the procedure (and so a serious breach of contract). Until now, the tribunal would make a decision on a contractual basis—and (a key point) it is *their* interpretation of 'serious breach' that matters.

Fairbrother demands, however, that the tribunal must investigate the handling of the grievance as part of the constructive dismissal claim and, if it decides it was handled badly but that the employer's actions fall within the 'range of reasonable responses open to a reasonable employer' it should hold that there was no repudiation by the employer and dismiss the claim at that stage. 'Only', says Lady Smith, 'if the [grievance procedure] has been conducted in a manner which no reasonable employer would have conducted it can it be said that the employer did not have reasonable and proper cause for his conduct.' Thus a properly held grievance procedure can negate any previous repudiatory conduct on the part of the employer. As the editors of IRLR state: this reasoning 'is troubling' as it changes the emphasis from a contract-based objective question (was there a repudiatory breach?) to a question of perversity of the employer's actions—and, in doing so, favours employers. It particularly favours employers because it is a well-established rule in unfair dismissal actions that tribunals cannot substitute their own views of reasonableness for those of the employer: they can only find the employer's conduct is faulty where it falls outside the band of reasonable responses (whereas in a pure contractual analysis the tribunal is free to decide its own standard of 'serious breach').

Many employment lawyers wondered whether this analysis would stand up, but it was affirmed by the President of the EAT in *Claridge* v *Daler Rowney* [2008] IRLR 672: 'Once a tribunal concedes to itself that there may be more than one view as to whether the [employer's] conduct is sufficiently unreasonable, that undermines its conclusion that the employment relationship has been sufficiently damaged.'

In truth, this whole debate is really a re-opening of the issues we thought were settled in *Western Excavating* all those years ago: in a constructive dismissal case, what is the boundary between repudiatory breach and unreasonable conduct? These latest cases have moved us back again (at least where faulty grievance procedures are concerned) towards a test of unreasonableness.

10.6.6   Apparent resignations

Problems can arise with apparent resignations which turn out to be nothing of the sort, e.g., resignations in the heat of the moment. As we saw in **Chapter 9**, employees are allowed some leeway with heated outbursts. If the words spoken are ambiguous there is the preliminary point as to whether they constitute a resignation at all. If the words are unambiguous the employer is entitled to take these at their face value and the employee must live with the consequences. This approach has been confirmed in *Hogan* v *ACP Heavy Fabrications Ltd* (1994, unreported, EAT 340/92) where the EAT held that there is no obligation on the employer formally to accept the employee's resignation where the employee has responded to a clear breach by the employer. The EAT indicated that an employer *would have to accept the resignation* if the employee simply resigned without giving proper notice; which only adds to the confusion because it means an employer effectively has to judge its own actions. However, an employee is allowed to retract within a reasonable time if the words were spoken in anger or the intellectual capability of the employee is in question: *Kwik-Fit (GB) Ltd* v *Lineham* [1992] ICR 183. An employer who refuses to allow a reasonable retraction will have *dismissed* the employee from the point.

Inviting employees to resign is often seen by employers as an honourable way of avoiding dismissing them so that, in future job applications, the employees will not have the stigma of 'dismissal' on their record. However, such invitations may in themselves constitute a breach of mutual trust and confidence if, say, in the context of a non-disciplinary hearing an employee is advised to consider this course of action (see *Billington* v *Michael Hunter and Sons* (unreported, UKEAT/578/03/DM); nor does the tag 'without prejudice' aid the case, as this may not always prevent such discussions or letters being used in litigation: *BNP Paribas* v *Mezzotero* [2004] IRLR 508, where the EAT held communications were only privileged under the 'without prejudice' rule where they were made in a situation where there was a genuine attempt to settle an extant dispute.

10.6.7   Consequences of showing a constructive dismissal

Proving a constructive dismissal means nothing in itself. There is no statutory remedy for being constructively dismissed (though there may be a wrongful repudiation claim at common law). All that a constructive dismissal proves is that the employee was dismissed. This can be seen in **Figure 10.1** below. As you will see later in this chapter, once an employee has established a constructive dismissal the question of the fairness of that dismissal has to be decided in the normal way.

EXAMPLE

Suppose Aquitaine Ltd employs Eleanor on terms that include a mobility clause. Aquitaine asks Eleanor to move to a newly acquired site close by. Eleanor is unhappy and raises various objections. Aquitaine does its best to meet these objections but Eleanor is quite uncooperative and refuses to move. In desperation, Aquitaine issues an instruction to Eleanor to move on a stated date, having met all the practical difficulties. Eleanor still refuses, resigns, and claims unfair dismissal.

If the mobility clause is not as watertight as the company had hoped Eleanor may succeed in persuading the employment tribunal that there was a constructive dismissal, but, as you will see when we look at 'fairness', it is unlikely that the tribunal will find that it was an unfair (constructive) dismissal. Whether this action amounts to indirect discrimination is another matter.

10.6.8 What should the employee do when faced with a serious breach?

We have not yet dealt with the question of how swiftly the employee must act in the face of the breach. All the case law since *Western Excavating* has stressed that, if the breach is supposedly repudiatory, the employee must act quickly and resign within a reasonable time in response to that breach. If the employee did not act quickly enough he or she was said to have *affirmed* the breach and lost the right to claim constructive dismissal.

The case law shows us that a delay of a few days, even a month, will not usually be fatal provided the employee has objected to the conduct. If the employee then resigns in the face of the breach he or she is said to have *accepted the repudiation*.

We have summarised the requirements for a constructive dismissal action in the diagram below (**Figure 10.1**). We should stress that **Figure 10.1** does not tell the full story because once a constructive dismissal has been proven the tribunal must then consider whether that deemed dismissal was fair or unfair in the circumstances. So please note the bottom-right box: *it is possible to have a constructive dismissal which is still fair.*

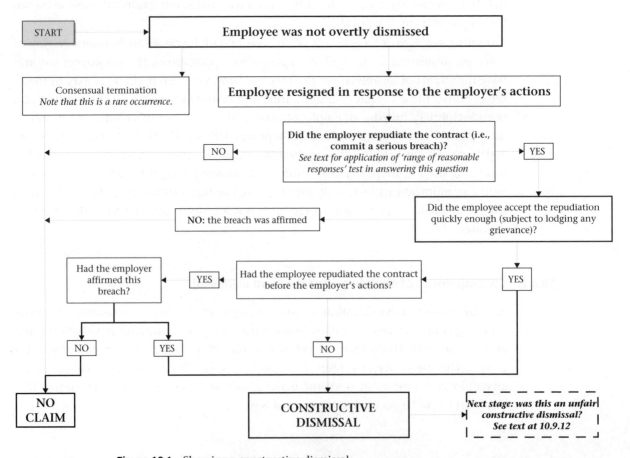

Figure 10.1 Showing a constructive dismissal.

10.7 Standard of proof

We noted above in **10.4** where the burden of proof lay for each stage of an unfair dismissal claim. The question raised in this section relates specifically to the issues of 'fair reason' which we are about to discuss in **10.8**. If the employer says that he or she dismissed the employee for incompetence, is it enough that the employer simply *believed* the employee was incompetent, or does that belief have to be tested against some wider, objective analysis? In other words: to what standard of proof is the employer to be put? The short answer is that the employer only needs to have an honest belief in the reason he puts forward.

10.7.1 What is an honest belief?

The principal case is the House of Lords' decision in *Devis (W) & Sons Ltd* v *Atkins* [1977] AC 931. This established that the employer must *honestly believe at the time of the dismissal* that the facts disclosed a fair reason to dismiss. Provided there is an honest belief it does not matter that the employer was mistaken. Thus, if an employer honestly believes that the employee has committed theft and dismisses for that reason (misconduct), it is irrelevant at this stage whether the employee did or did not commit the theft.

Most employees will not believe your advice when they are told this. They will argue that the employer has no right to dismiss them unless the offence can be proven. They will be wrong. In an unfair dismissal claim, positive proof of the offence is not required.

Practically speaking, of course, in order for the employer to show this honest belief he or she will have to show that the evidence was at least *capable* of generating the conclusion. Waking up one morning and 'honestly believing' an employee is incompetent is clearly not enough. Thus, although the employer does not have to *prove* the incompetence, the decision to dismiss must flow from an *honest belief based on reasonable grounds*. Indeed, in some cases the employer does have to show that the reason for dismissal exists and mistake is no defence, e.g., redundancy dismissals and dismissals on grounds of statutory requirements.

10.7.2 Timing of the belief

As the test is one of honest belief it follows that the employer can only rely on evidence known to him at the date of dismissal. Any evidence which comes to light after the dismissal relating to the employee's conduct *during* the relationship cannot be relied upon as it could not have been known to the employer at the point of dismissal. So, if an employer dismisses for theft (honestly believing the employee was guilty) this will constitute a fair reason. The tribunal will then have to decide whether it was fairly handled. If, subsequent to the dismissal, the employer discovers new facts which show that the employee had committed other acts of misconduct these facts are irrelevant in judging the fairness or unfairness of the dismissal—they were not in the employer's mind at the moment of dismissal. Note the contrast here with the common law position where the employer *is entitled* to rely on evidence not known to him at the time of dismissal: *Boston Deep Sea Fishing and Ice Co.* v *Ansell* (1888) 39 ChD 339 (see **Chapter 9** at **9.7.3.3**).

'Honest belief' is not always a restricting influence: in *St Anne's Board Mill* v *Brien* [1973] ICR 444 the employees were dismissed because, after proper investigations, the employer believed they were unreasonably refusing to obey a lawful order. The employees had refused to work with a colleague because they said he was dangerous and had caused the injury of another employee. The employer believed otherwise. Some time after the dismissal it was shown that the employees were correct. But this did not matter. The employer had acted fairly on the evidence reasonably available at the time of dismissal.

The case of *West Midlands Co-operative Society Ltd* v *Tipton* [1986] ICR 192, added an interesting angle to this. The employees here were dismissed and then were refused the right to an internal appeal under the disciplinary procedure, as granted in the contract. Part of their case was that the employer had acted unfairly in not allowing them to appeal. But any appeal must logically come after a dismissal and so, strictly, is irrelevant under *Devis* v *Atkins*. The House of Lords resolved this by treating the matter of appeals as part of the *continuing process of the dismissal.* Not necessarily logical, but good common sense.

Lastly, it should be noted that although subsequently discovered events are generally irrelevant to the fairness of the dismissal, they *can* be taken into account in the following situations:

(a) where the evidence relates *directly* to the reason for the dismissal and helps to substantiate that reason;

(b) in assessing the level of compensation (see **10.13.3** below);

(c) where the event occurs during the employee's notice period, e.g., the employee dismissed on grounds of ill-health recovers before the expiry of the notice or the redundancy situation is rectified. The employer is expected to react to this change: *Williamson v Alcan (UK) Ltd* [1978] ICR 104.

This reasoning means that the 'reason' has to be assessed both in relation to the point at which notice is given and the termination itself. A fair redundancy selection, for instance, might become unfair if the circumstances of the business change in this period: see *Stacey* v *Babcock Power Ltd* [1986] ICR 221, *Alboni* v *Ind Coope Retail Ltd* [1998] IRLR 131 and *West Kent College* v *Richardson* [1999] ICR 511.

In *Devis* v *Atkins* the main concern of the House of Lords was to outlaw the use of *fresh reasons* by an employer to justify a dismissal. That point is still sacrosanct. Thus the order of analysis is:

(a) What was the reason for the dismissal?

(b) Was that reason a fair reason under ERA 1996, s. 98?

(c) Did the employer handle the dismissal fairly in treating that reason as a sufficient reason for dismissal?

10.8 Potentially fair reasons

As can be seen in (b) and (c) above, assessing fairness involves a two-stage process.

It cannot be over-emphasised that these stages are *separate* and will be considered in sequence by the employment tribunal. Employers frequently misunderstand the process and suppose that an outstandingly good reason (e.g., strong evidence of theft) somehow makes up for a poor handling of the situation (e.g., not giving the employee a chance to explain). Nothing can be further from the truth. If the handling is unfair the dismissal will most likely be unfair, no matter how good the reason.

Thus, proving that the dismissal was for one of the fair reasons set out below does not mean that the employer has won. This is just the first stage. If the employer *cannot* show a fair reason, however, the employee will win at this stage and, as will be seen in

10.8.8, some reasons may be classed as *automatically unfair* irrespective of how they were handled.

10.8.1   The reason or principal reason

Under ERA 1996, s. 98 the burden of proof lies with the employer to show a defence under one of the headings detailed below as the *reason or principal reason* for dismissal.

In the text below we will first note some basic rules on assessing 'reasons', then we will give the basic requirements of each potentially fair reason and then turn to the fairness of their operation in **10.9**. The six fair reasons for dismissal are:

(a) capability (s. 98(2)(a));

(b) conduct (s. 98(2)(b));

(c) retirement (s. 98(ba));

(d) redundancy (s. 98(2)(c));

(e) statutory illegality (s. 98(2)(d));

(f) some other substantial reason (s. 98(1)(b));

10.8.1.1   Multiple reasons

The employer may have more than one reason for the dismissal; the notion of a 'principal reason' does not mean 'a single reason'. But the section does prevent an employer relying on a 'shotgun approach' of detailing every unsatisfactory aspect of the employee's work in the hope that one will hit the target: *Smith* v *Glasgow City District Council* [1987] ICR 796. The weakness with multiple reasons (certainly those which are interdependent) is that as the structure of reasons becomes more complicated the questions of proof become more difficult to establish clearly. The most common overlaps arise:

(a) when the employer cites different incidents to justify the dismissal, e.g., various forms of misconduct; and

(b) between misconduct and incapability, e.g., a history of intermittent absences could be a case of incapability (e.g., health) or misconduct.

An exception to this overlap occurs where the reason is 'retirement'. That either stands or falls as a reason on its own.

10.8.1.2   The label given by the employer

Tribunals do not have to accept an employer's stated reason. The reason can be rejected as a fraud or as a mistake. A discovered fraud—for example, dismissing an employee because of trade union activities but citing incapability—will lead to a finding of unfair dismissal at this stage. But where there is simply a genuine mistake of labelling on the employer's part at the time of dismissal the tribunal may have more sympathy if the facts relied upon by the employer as constituting the reason for the dismissal were clear to the employee at the time of termination: *Abernethy* v *Mott, Hay and Anderson* [1974] ICR 323. The key element, therefore, is that if the employer consistently relies on the same *facts* to justify the dismissal a change of *legal reasons* may not be fatal. It will nevertheless be a dangerous course of action to dismiss for one stated reason and then plead another in the tribunal.

Where employers have sought to soften the blow of dismissal by labelling it as a 're-dundancy' when no redundancy actually exists they run the risk of being trapped by that stated reason. The same applies where the reason given is retirement.

10.8.1.3   ERA 1996, s. 92

Section 92 allows an employee to demand from the employer written reasons for the dismissal. There must be a specific request and the employer must reply within 14 days of that request. Any unreasonable refusal or lies by the employer may lead to the employer having to pay the employee two weeks' pay (whether dismissed unfairly or not). The employer's statement is admissible in any proceedings. Except for women dismissed while pregnant or on maternity leave, qualification for this right requires one year's service. There is, however, no upper age limit.

10.8.1.4   Disagreement as to reasons

As well as the obvious case where an employer gives a reason (say, misconduct) and the employee denies this, there may be cases where the employee puts forward another reason—what he or she says is the *real* reason—for the dismissal. For instance, the employer may cite misconduct and the employee may claim the real reason was that he disclosed evidence about the employer's nefarious activities to the police. If the employee is right then the employer has not shown a fair reason and, in this example, the employee will gain much more compensation (see **10.8.8.3** on public interest disclosures). In such instances, if a tribunal finds that the employer was wrong it does not automatically mean the employee was right. That claim must still be investigated, with the employee producing 'some evidence' not just mere assertion: *Kuzel* v *Roche Products Ltd* [2008] EWCA Civ 380, [2008] ICR 799.

10.8.1.5   Pressure of industrial action

The ERA 1996, s. 107, states that, in assessing the reason for dismissal, the employment tribunal must ignore pressure placed on the employer to dismiss arising from threats etc. of industrial action made by third parties, e.g., other employees or trade unions. Expressions of disgruntlement about the employee from third parties do not fall within this section. But if fellow employees say that they will go on strike unless an employee becomes a member of a union, that is the area covered by s. 107.

10.8.2   Capability as a fair reason

Section 98(3) of ERA 1996 defines capability as 'capability assessed by reference to skill, aptitude, health or any other physical or mental quality'. This breaks down into three sub-headings:

(a) *Qualifications.*

Cases in this area are rare. Section 98(3)(b) states that qualifications means 'any degree, diploma or other academic, technical or professional qualification relevant to the position which [the employee] held'. What amounts to qualification (as opposed to a licence or permit, for instance) has been given a narrow interpretation in *Blue Star Ship Management Ltd* v *Williams* [1978] ICR 770. The qualification must be connected substantially to the employee's job.

(b) *Incompetence.*

Employees are incompetent when they cannot perform their duties as required under the terms of the contract. It is rare for one-off incidents of incompetence to justify a dismissal, though not impossible; where, for example, bad workmanship causes the employer a massive loss. Examples of incompetence include: slow completion rates; making misjudgments or mistakes; lack of adaptability; inability to work with colleagues; and inability to deal with clients.

(c) *Ill-health.*

If an employee's absence from work (either on prolonged absence or on an intermittent but frequent basis) means that he or she is unable to do the job, an employer is entitled to rely on this as the reason for dismissal. Unjustified absence (e.g., being caught painting the house while drawing company sick pay on the pretext of back pain) will probably count as *conduct* (see **10.8.3** below). Employers who categorise ill-health absence as *capability,* on the other hand, are not necessarily doubting that the reason is perfectly genuine: the employee may simply be incapable of attending often enough to comply with the contract.

It is often thought that if the employer's actions caused the illness or injury the employer cannot then dismiss for reasons of incapability. This view is incorrect, but the more troublesome question is whether employers owe some extra duty to sick employees if they are responsible for the illness. Various EAT judgments have given some or no sympathy to this view. The Court of Appeal's view in *McAdie* v *Royal Bank of Scotland* [2007] EWCA Civ 806, [2007] IRLR 895 was to endorse the findings of the latest EAT decision and hold that an employer can dismiss in such cases but should be seen to 'go the extra mile' in handling any dismissal.

10.8.3 Conduct as a fair reason

The difference between conduct and capability is often that the employee can improve conduct but capability can imply something about the employee's innate ability that cannot be changed (in the same way that the authors might improve their attendance record at an athletics club but will never run a mile in under four minutes). Some issues, such as excessive absence or incompetence, may fall under both heads and the choice of one over the other may rest on how far the employee is believed to be at fault—doing one's best, albeit one's incompetent best, is better argued as capability for instance.

The heading therefore covers a diverse range of activities, such as:

(a) disobedience to lawful orders;

(b) gross insubordination;

(c) abusive language;

(d) theft;

(e) fraud;

(f) taking bribes;

(g) drunkenness at work;

(h) possessing a personality which amounted to a disabling and negative approach to the job and destroyed the trust and confidence between employer and employee;

(i) disclosing confidential information;

(j) gaining unauthorised access to computer files;

(k) assault;

(l) intermittent absenteeism;

(m) persistent lateness;

(n) taking unauthorised and prolonged leave; and even

(o) conduct occurring outside the employment relationship which has a direct bearing on the contract of employment.

There is no requirement that the misconduct must have been gross: the culmination of a series of incidents over which warnings have been issued will also fit the bill.

10.8.4 Retirement as a fair reason

The *compulsory* retirement of an employee is a potentially fair reason for dismissal (s. 98(ba) ERA 1996). Unlike the other fair reasons, however, for this reason to be acceptable certain procedures have to be followed—otherwise the retirement will *not* be taken as the reason (or a reason) for dismissal. Regulation 30 of the 2006 Regs states that whether or not the reason for a dismissal is a retirement shall be determined in accordance with the conditions set out in ss. 98ZA–98ZF ERA 1996 (inserted by sch. 8, para. 3 of the 2006 Regs). In the sections below we consider the effects of different retirement ages.

10.8.4.1 Retiring at 65 or above

The 'default' age for retirement has been set at 65 so any dismissal for retirement will be for a fair reason, if:

- as set out in s. 98ZB(1) and (2), there is no 'normal retirement age' in the company for that group of employees and the employee retires at or after 65; or
- as set out in s.98ZD(1) and (2), the 'normal retirement age' is 65 or higher and the employee retires at or after that age,

provided in both instances that the procedures laid out in sch. 6, para. 2 of the 2006 Regs are followed (see below for details). It is also worth noting in this context that employees may also have claims for unlawful discrimination running alongside or instead of unfair dismissal claims where the reason for dismissal relates to age. This means that any normal retirement age less than 65 has to pass the non-discrimination test.

10.8.4.2 Retiring earlier than 65

Where the employee's 'normal retirement age' is below 65 and the employee retires at or after that retirement age, this will also be a fair reason for dismissal (see s. 98ZE(1)). Again, the sch. 6 procedures must have been followed and the 'normal retirement age' must not be discriminatory (s. 98ZE(2)).

10.8.4.3 Schedule 6, para. 2 procedures

These are straightforward and require the employer:

- to inform the employee in writing of the date on which he intends the employee to retire and of the employee's right to make a request to continue working past the retirement age. This must be done not more than one year and not less than six months before the proposed retirement date; and
- to consider that request at a meeting where the employee may be accompanied by a fellow worker (if it is not reasonably practicable to hold a meeting an employer must still consider representations made by the employee); and
- to consider any appeal made by the employee.

The word 'consider' should be noted. It does not mean 'negotiate' and does not even require the employer to provide reasons for refusal.

10.8.4.4 Terms and other sources of information

Under para. 2(2), the duty to notify applies regardless of any term in the employee's contract of employment indicating when his retirement is expected to take place, any other notification of, or information about, the employee's date of retirement given to him by the employer at any time, and any other information about the employee's right to make a request given to him by the employer at any time.

10.8.4.5   Schedule 6, para. 4

If the employer fails to notify the employee six months in advance of the proposed retirement as per sch. 6, para. 2, he will still have an ongoing duty to do so, 'until the fourteenth day before the operative termination'. This looks like a peculiar provision but its importance can be seen in the next section.

10.8.4.6   Section 98ZF ERA 1996

Imagine that a tribunal is faced with a retirement dismissal where the para. 2 procedures have not been followed. At first sight this cannot therefore be a fair reason for dismissal. However, if:

- the dismissal is at or after 65 and there is no retirement age; or
- the dismissal is at or after the normal retirement age when that age is higher than 65; or
- the dismissal is at or after the (non-discriminatory) normal retirement age but that is set below 65,

then—

- the tribunal must take into account the matters listed in s. 98ZF to determine whether what has happened may still amount to a fair reason for dismissal.

The s. 98ZF matters are:

- Whether or not the employer has notified the employee in accordance with sch. 6, para. 4;
- if the employer has so notified the employee, how long before the notified retirement date the notification was given;
- whether or not the employer has followed, or sought to hold a meeting with the employee in accordance with sch. 6, para. 7.

10.8.4.7   Failure to follow procedures

If the employer fails to comply with either sch. 6 or s. 98ZF procedures he is prevented from using 'retirement' as a fair reason and the dismissal is automatically unfair. Further, a finding that a dismissal was not actually for 'retirement' may also give rise to a claim for age discrimination.

10.8.4.8   What may prevent a retirement being a fair reason?

Retirement will *not* be a fair reason for dismissal where:

(a) The sch. 6 procedures have not been followed.

(b) The sch. 6 procedures *have* been followed but the contract terminated before the intended date of retirement.

(c) Where there is a normal retirement age lower than 65 and it is found to be unlawful discrimination within the 2006 Regs.

(d) There is no 'normal retirement age' and the dismissal occurs before 65 (s. 98ZA).

(e) There is a 'normal retirement age' (whether above or below 65) but the employee was dismissed before that age (s. 98ZC).

Of course, with (b), (d) and (e) dismissals there may be other fair reasons why an employee is dismissed e.g., conduct.

10.8.4.9 Breach of procedures: a separate cause of action

Under sch. 6 para. 11 an employee may complain to a tribunal that the employer has failed to comply with para. 2 procedures. If the tribunal decides there was a breach of para. 2 it shall award up to eight weeks' pay (the meaning of 'a week's pay' is discussed at **10.13** below).

10.8.5 Redundancy as a fair reason

To make someone redundant is to *dismiss them* for reasons of redundancy. Redundancy has its own particular rules which are dealt with in **Chapter 11**, but one may have a fair or unfair dismissal for reasons of redundancy. The meaning of 'redundancy' is given in ERA 1996, s. 139(1) and (6). This provides a highly technical definition. In general terms s. 139 states that a redundancy occurs in three situations:

(a) where there is a cessation of the business;

(b) where there is a closure of the employee's particular workplace;

(c) where there is a cessation or diminution in the requirements for employees to do work of a particular kind (i.e., there is a surplus of labour for that particular type of job).

Tribunals will rarely second-guess an employer's decision to declare a redundancy.

10.8.6 Statutory illegality as a fair reason

In rare cases it may become legally impossible to continue to employ the employee, e.g., on the expiry of a work permit, or where a teacher has been declared unsuitable by the Department for Children, Schools and Families. The ERA 1996, s. 98(2)(d), states that such occurrences provide a fair reason for dismissal where the employee 'could not continue to work in the position which he held without contravention (either on his part or on that of his employer) of a duty or restriction imposed by or under an enactment' (thus statutory instruments are included in the definition). It is for the employer to show that any continued employment would have contravened the statute etc.

It is also now a criminal offence under s. 8 of the Asylum and Immigration Act 1996 to employ a person who does not have permission to work in the UK.

10.8.7 Some other substantial reason as a fair reason

Under ERA 1996, s. 98(1)(b), the employer can show 'some other substantial reason of a kind such as to justify the dismissal of an employee holding the position which the employee held'. This sounds like some sort of major catch-all category. It is. The words are not read *eiusdem generis* with the other fair reasons. The most common forum in which this reason is argued, however, is that of a business reorganisation falling short of redundancy, e.g., where the workload remains the same but certain employees are deemed unsuitable for the new requirements of the business or will simply not put up with the changes to their terms or status and resign.

The line between dismissal for reasons of business reorganisations and dismissal by reason of redundancy can be a fine one. However, the key point is whether the statutory definition of redundancy is fulfilled or not: put simply, did the requirement for employees to do their particular work cease or diminish? If all that has happened is that there is a reorganisation of the way existing work is performed then the fact that an employee is replaced by someone with different skills or doing a slightly different job does not mean there is a redundancy. For instance, in *Shawkat v Nottingham City Hospital NHS Trust (No. 2)* [2001] EWCA Civ 954, [2001] IRLR 555, the Court of Appeal held that when the hospital merged two departments so that a thoracic surgeon was required to also take on cardiac work (and refused to do so and was dismissed) there was no redundancy as there was no diminution in the employer's need for employees to carry out thoracic surgery.

Other examples of 'some other substantial reason' have been:

(a) a refusal to accept the imposition of a restraint of trade clause. This is a good example of 'some other substantial reason' in action as the Court of Appeal stressed in *Willow Oak Developments Ltd* v *Silverwood* [2006] EWCA Civ 660, [2006] IRLR 607 that even if the clause is unreasonable in itself this does not matter in establishing that there is a *reason* for dismissing. The reasonableness of the clause might go to determine whether the employer acted fairly but does not affect the existence of the reason unless the employer has acted whimsically or capriciously or the reason is inadmissible because of discrimination;

(b) a refusal to accept a change in terms relating to hours, or pay or job content;

(c) discovering that the employee had originally concealed medical problems from the employer;

(d) where heavy pressure to dismiss was brought to bear on the employer by a valued customer (though it is advisable to have a term in the contract allowing for such dismissals) and the employer still needs to look at the extent of any injustice to the employee;

(e) a mistaken belief that continuing to employ the employee would be in breach of a statute: *Klusova* v *London Borough of Hounslow* [2007] EWCA Civ 1127, [2008] ICR 396;

(f) reasonably believing (mistakenly as it turned out) that an employee had resigned;

(g) termination of employment as chief executive as an automatic consequence, under the express terms of the contract, of the termination of a directorship: *Cobley* v *Forward Technology Industries plc* [2003] EWCA Civ 646, [2003] ICR 1050.

This area is full of unpredictability. The temptation is to over-use it because it provides what has been described as an 'employer's charter'. This label is probably accurate in relation to business reorganisations, but the examples cited above should not be treated as precedents. Sometimes it is useful to plead it on behalf of the employer 'in the alternative': see **Chapter 13**.

10.8.8   Automatically unfair reasons

Certain reasons for dismissal are deemed automatically unfair. This means that, once the tribunal finds that the reason for the dismissal was one of these reasons they *must* make a determination that the dismissal was unfair. As with ordinary unfair dismissal claims the burden of proof is on the employer to establish the reason for the dismissal but, if the employee does not have one year's service, the Court of Appeal has held that it is for the employee to prove the dismissal was for an automatically unfair reason: *Smith* v *Hayle Town Council* [1978] ICR 996. Once a finding of automatically unfair dismissal has been made, some reasons carry with them what is termed a **Minimum Basic Award** and this is explained at **10.13.2** below (the relevant points in the table below are: 1, in limited cases, 5, 7, 8 and 9).

10.8.8.1 Summary of unfair dismissal qualification rights

We noted above that, for most dismissals, an employee must have one year's service to qualify for unfair dismissal rights. There are exceptions, and most of these exceptions are also deemed automatically unfair dismissals. The table below illustrates this.

	Reason for dismissal	Service qualification	Automatically unfair?
1	Dismissals relating to a transfer of an undertaking.	*One year*	*Yes, but the employee may lose this protection in defined circumstances: see* **Chapter 12**
2	'Retirement dismissals' where the appropriate procedures have not been followed.	*One year*	Yes
3	Dismissal where the worker exercised or sought to exercise, the right to be accompanied (or accompanied another worker) at a disciplinary hearing or a retirement meeting.	None	Yes
4	Dismissals falling within ERA 1996, s. 99 (leave for family reasons), e.g. those relating to pregnancy, childbirth, maternity, maternity leave, parental leave or to an employee taking time off to care for certain dependants (described in s. 57A).	None	Yes
5	Dismissals relating to health and safety matters which fall within ERA 1996, s.100.	None	Yes
6	Dismissals of certain shop and betting workers who refuse to work on Sundays, as set out in ERA 1996, s. 101.	None	Yes
7	Dismissals relating to the enforcement of the Working Time Regulations, as set out in ERA 1996, s. 101A.	None	Yes
8	Dismissals of occupational pension scheme trustees within the ambit of ERA 1996, s. 102.	None	Yes
9	Dismissals of certain employee representatives falling within ERA 1996, s. 103.	None	Yes
10	Dismissals under the Public Interest Disclosure Act 1998, as set out in ERA 1996, s. 103A: the so-called 'whistle-blower provisions' (see below at **10.8.8.3**).	None	Yes
11	Dismissals relating to the assertion of statutory rights as set out in ERA 1996, s. 104 (including employees dismissed for reasons connected with flexible working arrangements under SIs 2002/3207 and 2002/3236): see below at **10.8.8.2**.	None	Yes
12	Dismissals in relation to national minimum wage claims falling within ERA 1996, s. 104A.	None	Yes
13	Dismissals relating to the claiming of tax credits under the Tax Credits Act 1999, as set out in ERA 1996, s. 104B	None	Yes
14	Dismissal of part-time workers under ERA 1996, s. 108(i) who have, or have sought to, exercise rights set out in reg. 7, paras 1 and 3 of the Part-time Workers (Prevention of Less Favourable Treatment) Regulations 2000, SI 2000/1551.	None	Yes

15	Dismissals where the principal reason is that the employee has exercised, or sought to exercise, certain rights relating to limited-term contracts. For details, see reg. 6(3) of the Fixed-Term Employees (Prevention of Less Favourable Treatment) Regulations 2002, SI 2002/2034.	None	Yes
16	Dismissal relating to the performance of jury service, under ERA 1996, s. 98B(1), as amended by ERA 2004, s. 40(3).	None	*Yes, but the employee may lose this protection in defined circumstances set out in s. 98B(2)*
17	Dismissals for a conviction which is 'spent' under the Rehabilitation of Offenders Act 1974: s. 4(3)(b) unless the employee falls within a category excluded from the provisions of the Act.	*One year*	Yes
18	Dismissal for trade union activities and membership as defined in TULRCA 1992 s. 152 (as amended by sch. 2, ERA 1999). *Note that taking industrial action is not counted as a 'trade union activity'.*	None	Yes
19	Dismissal (in defined circumstances) for taking part in official industrial action—known as 'protected industrial action' under TULRCA 1992, s. 238A	None	Yes
20	Dismissal of employees for a defined reason connected with the recognition or de-recognition of a trade union: TULRCA 1992, sch. A1, paras 161 and 164.	None	Yes
21	Dismissals relating to the Transnational Information and Consultation of Employees Regulations 1999.	None	Yes
22	Dismissal in connexion with reg. 30 of the Information and Consultation of Employees Regulations 2004, SI 2004/3426.	None	*Yes, though with exceptions regarding disclosure of confidential information*
23	Dismissal in connexion with the establishment of a European Public Limited-Liability company under reg. 42 of the European Public Limited Liability Company Regulations 2004, SI 2004/2326.	None	*Yes, though with exceptions regarding disclosure of confidential information*
24	Dismissals arising out of suspension on medical grounds as defined in ERA 1996, s. 64(2) *(note, this is a narrow category related to employees who work with dangerous substances and is not the same as a dismissal because of illness).*	*One month*	*No*

Where an employee is *selected for redundancy* and the reason for that selection is one of the automatically unfair reasons noted above then that selection is automatically unfair and normal qualifying periods do not apply (see TULRCA 1992, s. 153 and ERA 1996, s. 105). **However, the automatic unfairness provisions do not apply to selection for redundancy where points 1 or 3 in the table above apply.**

A selection for redundancy for reasons of trade union membership, activities or recognition issues will fall within the automatically unfair provisions: TULRCA 1992, s. 153 and sch. A1 para. 162.

If the reason for dismissal is discriminatory an action may be brought for that discrimination (see **Chapter 6**) rather than being tied to an unfair dismissal action. In either case there are no qualification periods and a dismissal for, say, reasons of sex discrimination, will be automatically unfair (though not so with disability discrimination). However, where a tribunal finds a dismissal to be both unfair and discriminatory it will set-off the awards to avoid double recovery. Given that compensation for discrimination is not subject to any upper limit (whereas unfair dismissal claims are—see **10.13** below), a distinct discrimination claim should always be considered if there is evidence to support this.

Two points covered in the table above require further explanation

10.8.8.2   Asserting statutory rights

Under ERA 1996, s. 104, if the employee complains to the employer that certain statutory rights have been infringed then any dismissal by the employer in response to this is automatically unfair. Thus retaliatory action by the employer now carries with it specific penalties. It does not matter that the employee's claim was wrong, nor that it was not correctly labelled, as long as it was made in good faith. The first case in this area (*Mennell v Newell & Wright (Transport Contractors) Ltd* [1996] ICR 607) reinforced the interpretation of the 'good faith' test as being of the 'pure heart but empty head' variety. The Court of Appeal stated that:

(a) the employee must have made an allegation to his employer that a statutory right was being infringed;

(b) the allegation need not be specific, provided it has been made reasonably clear to the employer what right was claimed to have been infringed;

(c) it does not matter whether the statutory right has actually been infringed, nor need the allegation be correct as to the employee's entitlement to the right, provided the claim is made in good faith;

(d) the onus will lie on the employee to establish that he was dismissed for his assertion of a statutory right.

The term 'reasonably clear' has been given a liberal interpretation by the EAT: the employee is not required to spell out the infringement.

The 'relevant statutory rights' are set out in s. 104(4) of ERA 1996. They include:

(a) any right conferred by the Act for which the remedy for its infringement is by way of a complaint or reference to an employment tribunal' (e.g., minimum notice, right to receive a written statement, health and safety dismissals)— the list is extensive;

(b) rights concerning the protection of wages under ERA 1996, Part II;

(c) rights conferred under TULRCA 1992 concerning union activities.

A twist has now been added to the concept of 'asserting' a right. Item 8 in the table above relates to dismissals for refusal to comply with a requirement (e.g., overtime) which would itself contravene the Working Time Regulations. It is clear from *McLean* v *Rainbow Homeloans Ltd* [2007] IRLR 14 (EAT) that such a refusal is not 'asserting' a statutory right but is a separate head of 'automatic unfairness' and so not subject to the rules just described in (a) to (d) above. All that is required, say the EAT, is that the employer has refused to accede to a requirement which would have breached the Regulations and the dismissal is because of that refusal.

10.8.8.3 Public Interest Disclosure Act 1998

We noted the main provisions of this Act in **Chapter 7** (at **7.3.5**). The purpose of the Act is to permit employees to make certain disclosures about the activities of their employers without suffering any penalty for having done so. This is achieved through the insertion into ERA 1996 of two new sections: s. 47B and s. 103A.

Section 47B(1) of ERA 1996 (as inserted by PIDA 1998, s. 2) states that: 'A worker has the right not to be subjected to any **detriment** by any act, or any deliberate failure to act, by his employer done on the ground that the worker has made a protected disclosure.'

Section 103A (as inserted by PIDA 1998, s. 5) states: 'An employee who is **dismissed** shall be regarded for the purposes of this Part as unfairly dismissed *if the reason (or, if more than one, the principal reason) for the dismissal is that the employee made a protected disclosure.*' The employee only has to act in 'good faith' when making the allegations in order to come under the umbrella of 'protected disclosure' and the burden of showing bad faith is on the employer. However, this is not a licence for employees' flights of fantasy: there must be a clear causative link between the detriment/dismissal and the disclosure before protection is given (see *London Borough of Harrow* v *Knight* [2003] IRLR 140). A detriment may occur even after the employee has left the organisation, e.g., with the refusal to provide references: *Woodward* v *Abbey National plc* [2006] EWCA Civ 822, [2006] IRLR 677.

There are different compensation rules depending on whether the employee suffered a detriment or a dismissal. Where the claim is for detriment s. 49(1)(b) calls for an assessment of loss akin to discrimination claims so that there is no statutory limit on the amount and damages for injury to feelings may be included. In the case of a dismissal there is also no statutory limit on compensation but injury to feelings is not included. This leaves the problem of assessing compensation when a 'detriment' turns into 'dismissal' (e.g., the employee cannot take the detriment any longer and resigns). Here, detriment losses are taken up to the point of termination, dismissal losses from that point: *Melia* v *Magna Kansei Ltd* [2005] EWCA Civ 1547, [2006] ICR 410.

10.8.9 Automatically fair reasons

The basic premise of ERA 1996, s. 98 is that although the reason may be *fair* this does not mean that the dismissal is fair; this has yet to be decided. However, in the case of dismissal involving national security the tribunal may never get to debate the issue of fairness: see ERA 1996, s.10.

Some confusion has been added to this area by the EAT in *B* v *BAA plc* [2005] All ER (D) 321 (May) which held that the tribunal must still investigate the reasonableness of such dismissals to see whether alternative courses of action could have been taken (e.g., redeployment). This is a very surprising decision and we will have to see if it stands future tests.

10.9 Fairness

The question of 'fairness' is a judgment call and depends very much on the facts. Nevertheless, we can detail some general points that tribunals will look at for each 'fair reason'. In **Figure 10.2** we can see the pathway that tribunals trace in analysing an unfair dismissal case.

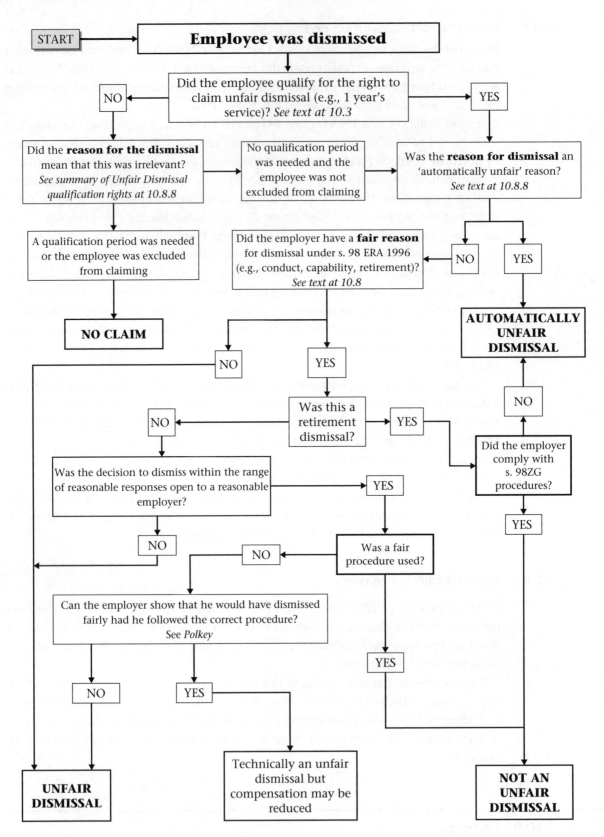

Figure 10.2   Determining fairness.

Figure 10.2 is concerned only with the way 'fairness' is determined. It does not deal with the financial consequences of any particular finding; that is left until later in this chapter at **10.13**.

You can see **in Figure 10.2** that once the employee qualifies to bring the claim and shows dismissal (even though the employer has established a fair reason), the question of whether that reason was handled fairly is the determining matter.

What is meant by 'fairness' tends to be something of a mixture of fact and law. The 'fact' part relates to investigating the way in which the employer relied on the cited fair reason; the 'law' relates to general guiding principles that have been established over the years. The best way to describe fairness, therefore, is by recounting some general principles used by tribunals and then relating them to the particular fair reasons.

10.9.1 General principles of fairness

The ERA 1996, s. 98(4) states:

the determination of the question whether the dismissal is fair or unfair (having regard to the reason shown by the employer)—

(a) depends on whether in the circumstances (including the size and administrative resources of the employer's undertaking) the employer acted reasonably or unreasonably in treating it as a sufficient reason for dismissing the employee, and

(b) Shall be determined in accordance with equity and the substantial merits of the case.

Leaving aside 'retirement' dismissals for the moment, the s. 98(4) test may be broken down into *two* pervasive questions:

(a) Did the employer utilise a *fair procedure?*

(b) Did the employer's decision to dismiss fall within the *range of reasonable responses* open to a reasonable employer?

The burden of proof regarding *fairness,* it will be remembered, is *neutral.* But all this really means is that the employer does not bear the burden when the facts are doubtful or in dispute. The reality is that, since the employer made the decision and generally has the greater access to information, the tribunal effectively expects the employer to show *why* the decision was made and *how* it was reasonable.

The impact of the Human Rights Act 1998 on unfair dismissal was considered by the Court of Appeal in *X* v *Y* [2004] EWCA Civ 662. Although no breach of human rights was found in this case (which centred on art. 8 ECHR—'privacy') Mummery LJ set out some suggestions on dealing with human rights points, especially as regards actions taken against private employers. The statement must be *obiter* but it is nevertheless extremely useful. His Lordship suggested the following framework of questions at [64]:

(1) Do the circumstances of the dismissal fall within the ambit of one or more of the articles of the Convention? If they do not, the Convention right is not engaged and need not be considered.

(2) If they do, does the state have a positive obligation to secure enjoyment of the relevant Convention right between private persons? If it does not, the Convention right is unlikely to affect the outcome of an unfair dismissal claim against a private employer.

(3) If it does, is the interference with the employee's Convention right by dismissal justified? If it is, proceed to (5) below.

(4) If it is not, was there a permissible reason for the dismissal under the ERA, which does not involve unjustified interference with a Convention right? If there was not, the dismissal will be unfair for the absence of a permissible reason to justify it.

(5) If there was, is the dismissal fair, tested by the provisions of s. 98 of the ERA, reading and giving effect to them under s3 of the HRA so as to be compatible with the Convention right?

In *McGowan* v *Scottish Water* [2005] IRLR 167 the EAT in Scotland dealt with art. 8 again, this time regarding covert surveillance of an employee's home: the employee was thought to be falsifying timesheets on call-out times. Although recognising that such surveillance 'raised at least a strong presumption that the right to have one's private life respected is being invaded' no breach was found as the action was held to be proportionate to the case.

10.9.2 The first general aspect of fairness: fair procedure

It has always been a key feature of employment law that an employer must operate a fair procedure when dismissing an employee. An employer contemplating a dismissal must therefore be aware of the significance of:

- the ACAS Code and Guidelines; and
- the employer's own contractual procedures

and we will deal with each of these in turn.

10.9.3 Fair procedure: procedural matters

10.9.3.1 The ACAS Code and Guidelines

Under TULRCA 1992, s. 199 ACAS may issue codes of behaviour. A new statutory Code is to be issued to accompany the enactment of the proposed Employment Act. The Code is not legally binding. However, though a failure to follow any part of this Code does not, in itself, make a person or organisation liable to proceedings, employment tribunals will take the Code into account when considering relevant cases. Perhaps even more importantly, a tribunal will be able to increase or decrease any award of compensation by up to 25 per cent where an employer or employee unreasonably fails to follow the Code. Similarly, arbitrators appointed by ACAS (see **10.12.2** below) to determine relevant cases under the ACAS Arbitration Scheme will take the Code into account. In addition to this ACAS will also issue more detailed guidelines on handling disciplinary and grievance matters.

The Code represents a common sense approach to industrial relations matters and generally recommends the use of informal action to resolve matters followed by formal action (such as a first warning, second, and final warning). It sets out procedures designed to help the employee correct the behaviour. The full Code can be accessed through www.acas.org.uk.

At the time of writing we only have a draft available but ACAS guidelines go back a substantial number of years so this basic outline is unlikely to change in the final version. Here are some highlights:

On disciplinary procedures:

- deal with issues promptly and consistently;
- establish the facts before taking action;
- make sure the employee is informed clearly of the allegations;
- allow the employee to be accompanied and to state their case;
- make sure that the disciplinary action is appropriate to the misconduct or incapability;
- provide employees with an opportunity to appeal.

On grievances:

- the employee should clearly inform the line manager of the nature of the grievance;
- the employee should be allowed to bring a companion to any hearing;
- the action taken should be appropriate to the grievance;
- an appeal System should be in place.

10.9.3.2 Contractual procedures

Tribunals are also interested in the employer's own contractual procedures and whether these have been adhered to. The more elaborate these are the more complications set in when the employer finds he cannot comply with them. The risks are obvious. Thus, in one case the authors once dealt with, a Cornish company had, as its final appeal, the involvement of the parent-company chairman. He was in Switzerland and did not speak English. When this procedure was tested it was found wanting and came under severe criticism.

Company disciplinary codes often spell out what is meant by 'gross misconduct' or 'gross breach of duty'. If these clauses pretend to give *exhaustive* definitions they lose the possibility of flexibility in the face of the unexpected and employers may be caught by their own wording. Some provisions should also be made in the contract for determining when a warning becomes 'stale', e.g., three or six months for an oral warning, six months for a written warning, and 12 months for a final warning. No tribunal will allow reference to be made to a warning given five years previously as proof of compliance with the disciplinary code (though these earlier incidents might be referred to in the hearing as evidence of the employment history).

If the employer wishes to impose suspension without pay as a penalty this must be spelt out in the contract; otherwise it will be a breach which may, in itself, lead to claims for contractual damages, or even constructive dismissal.

10.9.3.3 Failure to operate the contractual procedures properly

The question is simple: what happens if an employer fails to operate a dismissal procedure properly but, had he done what he was meant to do, it is very likely that the dismissal would have been fair? Should a tribunal find that the failure in procedure 'made no difference' to the outcome and so decide the dismissal was not unfair, or should it call it an unfair dismissal but reduce any compensation (possibly to zero). Throughout the 1980s the 'it makes no difference' test ruled so tribunals could engage in a 'what if?' exercise and conclude that the employee was doomed anyway. Then the House of Lords laid this to rest in *Polkey* v *A.E. Dayton Service Ltd* [1987] AC 344, deciding that this all-or-nothing test was too simplistic. Instead, the test should be: make a finding of unfair dismissal but assess the chances of whether the employee *might* have been dismissed had the procedure been followed - or by looking at future employment prospects within the company generally (e.g., the likelihood of a redundancy occurring soon)—and reduce the compensation accordingly. Under the Employment Act 2002, s. 98A ERA 1996 a statutory form of the 'it makes no difference' test was created and became the governing test—but the new Employment Act will re-instate the *Polkey* test as from April 2009.

This in turn means that the case law which flowed from *Polkey* is relevant again. In *Duffy* v *Yeomans & Partners Ltd* [1995] ICR 1 and again in *Lord Mayor and Citizens of the City of Westminster* v *Cabaj* [1996] ICR 960 the Court of Appeal held that there is no proposition of law that *any* failure in procedure leads inevitably to a finding of unfair dismissal. The *Polkey* test is not that blunt a weapon. Instead, one should: (i) ask whether the consequences of the breach in procedure effectively denied the employee 'due process' by impeding his ability to defend his position; and (ii) why did the employer not follow his own procedures? Thus minor breaches may well be passed over but a failure which affected the general fairness of the procedures would be damning.

10.9.3.4 Relevance of appeals' procedures

In *West Midlands Co-operative Society* v *Tipton* (see above at **10.7.2** above) the House of Lords held that the appeals' procedure was an integral part of deciding the question of fair procedure. Indeed, a properly conducted appeal can remedy some procedural deficiencies in the original hearing.

10.9.3.5 A fair hearing

In misconduct dismissals especially, but also with incapability and 'some other substantial reason', the employee should have a chance to state a case. In *Clark* v *Civil Aviation Authority* [1991] IRLR 412, the EAT stated that a hearing should adopt the following pattern:

(a) Explain the purpose of the meeting.

(b) Identify those present.

(c) If appropriate, arrange representation.

(d) Inform the employee of the allegations.

(e) Indicate the evidence—in writing or by calling witnesses.

(f) Allow the employee to ask questions (though there is no legal obligation to allow the employee to cross-examine witnesses: *Santamera* v *Express Cargo Forwarding* [2003] IRLR 273). In some cases fellow employees might be reluctant to be seen acting as informants. In *Linfood Cash & Carry Ltd* v *Thomson* [1989] ICR 518 the EAT established guidelines for dealing with instances where the employees might be in fear of being named.

(g) Allow the employee to call witnesses.

(h) Listen to the arguments raised.

To this we would add that the hearing needs to be seen to be fair, so that staff who were involved in earlier stages which generated this hearing should not also act as judge and jury. In particular, an appeal should not (wherever possible) be heard by the same panel which decided to dismiss.

10.9.3.6 Right to be accompanied

Under ERA 1999, s. 10 a *worker* (defined in s. 13) is entitled to be accompanied at a disciplinary or grievance hearing by a single companion where the hearing 'could result in . . . the administration of a formal warning . . .'. The label attached to any disciplinary hearing ('informal' or 'formal') is irrelevant; the right is triggered where the warning will become part of the employee's disciplinary record: *London Underground Ltd* v *Ferenc-Batchelor* [2003] IRLR 252. It is not that common these days for an employer to issue oral informal warnings and keep no record at all, so this decision widens the right substantially.

However, a meeting called to investigate an issue is not a disciplinary hearing (*Skiggs* v *South West Trains Ltd* [2005] IRLR 462) and only if it becomes apparent during the meeting that disciplinary action may occur does the s. 10 right kick in—at which point the meeting should be terminated and a fresh one started later. The person accompanying the worker must be either a trade union official or another of the employer's workers. If the employer fails to comply with this the worker may present a complaint to an employment tribunal under s. 11, the maximum compensation being two weeks' pay. Under s. 12, a worker dismissed as a consequence of seeking to exercise these rights or for making a complaint to an employment tribunal will be regarded as automatically unfairly dismissed.

10.9.4   Second general aspect of fairness: range of reasonable responses

In this part the tribunal sets what has happened against the actions of the 'reasonable employer' (a figure drawn from the extensive experience of employment tribunal panels). This part of the assessment is derived from *British Leyland (UK) Ltd* v *Swift* [1981] IRLR 91 (and *Iceland Frozen Foods* v *Jones* [1983] ICR 17). The question posed will be: is it possible that a reasonable employer, faced with these facts, would have dismissed? For instance, let us imagine that an employee has committed theft; the employer has investigated the matter thoroughly and has to decide whether to dismiss. The range of options open to the employer could include:

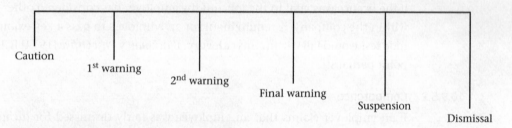

Caution
1st warning
2nd warning
Final warning
Suspension
Dismissal

Figure 10.3 Range of reasonable responses.

Some employers may not have dismissed in these circumstances; they may have gone to a final warning instead: but if the decision to dismiss falls within *the band of reasonableness* then this will show fairness. The theft example would satisfy this test, even though with a long-serving employee *some* employers might stop short of dismissal (for example, because of the employee's disciplinary record: see *Strouthos* v *London Underground* [2004] EWCA 402, [2004] IRLR 636). With questions of frequent lateness, absenteeism, incapability, or refusal to obey an order the debate opens out a little. However, what the tribunal should not do is to substitute its own standard of reasonableness—the test is whether the employer acted as a reasonable employer, having regard to the size and administrative resources available. Thus, the employer's beliefs that the grounds for dismissal justified the action have to be weighed against the tribunal's *perception* of reasonable practice based on its experience of industrial practice. The decision to dismiss may be one the employer would always follow, but the key question is whether the rest of industry would be so like-minded.

Where an employee has already been subject to various stages of the disciplinary process it is not too difficult to justify the final decision to dismiss. Most problems will arise when stages are bypassed or, in the case of gross misconduct, omitted. There the tribunal has to be clear that a reasonable employer could have dismissed in the circumstances. After some debate at the end of the century the Court of Appeal confirmed the range test in *Foley* v *Post Office; HSBC (Formerly Midland Bank)* v *Madden* [2000] IRLR 827: the role of employment tribunals is not to impose their own standards of reasonableness, but to test the employer's actions against those of a reasonable employer.

In *Sainsburys Supermarkets Ltd* v *Hill* [2002] EWCA Civ 1588; [2003] ICR 111, the 'range of reasonable responses' test was held to apply equally to the procedures used as to the penalty being imposed (the dismissal). And, as we have seen at **10.5** above this test is also relevant to notion of 'dismissal' in a constructive dismissal claim based on the inadequate operation of a grievance procedure.

10.9.5   Capability and qualifications: fairness

Where an underlying reason could have been classed as conduct *or* capability, we noted in **10.8.3** above that *conduct* may be more appropriate where the employee is easily able to improve with a little effort; *capability* is more appropriate if it is accepted by the employer that the employee either is or has become incapable of meeting the requirements (perhaps because the job has changed). With *conduct* the emphasis on handling the dismissal fairly is one of giving a chance for improvement; with *capability,* on compassionate treatment over such things as investigating alternative and more suitable work.

10.9.5.1   Qualifications

We noted above that the qualification must be connected substantially to the employee's job. So, if an employee loses his or her driving licence this will merit dismissal only if the licence was vital to the job and the employer has considered other alternative jobs within the company. A requirement for an employee to pass a key examination or aptitude test would fall within this category: *Blackman* v *Post Office* [1974] ICR 151 (a salutary point perhaps!).

10.9.5.2   Competence

If an employer claims that an employee was fairly dismissed for incapability the employment tribunal will expect clear evidence, not just some vague subjective assessment that the employee 'couldn't cut it'. As a basic checklist, therefore, the following matters should be considered:

(a) How good is the evidence of incompetence? Is it objectively proven, e.g., after a proper investigation?

(b) Was there a proper appraisal system in operation, or at least some formal way in which the employee could know of the defective performance?

(c) Were warnings given? In particular, was it made clear what would be the consequences for failure to improve?

(d) Were the warnings/objectives impossible to meet? For instance, an instruction that unless the company obtains a market share of 80 per cent by the end of the year the employee–manager will be dismissed may or may not be pure fantasy.

(e) Were any opportunities for training or retraining given?

(f) What form of supervision was operative?

(g) Were alternatives considered?

(h) What consideration was taken of the employee's status, length of service and past performance?

(i) Have incompetent employees been dismissed in similar circumstances in the past?

The relevance of some of these factors will depend upon the size of the company. For instance, a small, backstreet engineering company will not have the facility to look at many (if any) alternative jobs.

With incompetence dismissals emphasis has to be placed here on giving an opportunity to the employee to improve and listening to the employee's opinion, e.g., are the demands impossible to fulfil? Equally, if the employee challenges the employer's assessment it would be advisable to allow the employee (if feasible) the chance to demonstrate his or her case: *Morgan* v *Electrolux* [1991] IRLR 89. In that case the employee was found to have overbooked piece-work. In explaining her activities she asked to demonstrate her work speed. This request was refused. The Court of Appeal held that the employers had not acted reasonably in denying her this opportunity.

As with gross misconduct, there may also be gross incompetence which will justify dismissal without previous warnings, but greater care needs to be taken with incompetence. Indeed, if a single incident is that important it often involves an overlap between incompetence and misconduct, e.g., *Alidair Ltd* v *Taylor* [1978] ICR 445, where a pilot 'bounced' the company jet.

10.9.5.3   Ill-health

Dismissals on the grounds of ill-health have always been treated more cautiously by employment tribunals than any other potentially fair reason. Two forms of absence for ill-health may arise: intermittent absences and those lasting for prolonged periods. In the latter case it may be that the contract is frustrated (though for reasons noted in **Chapter 9** at **9.5.1** reliance on this should be avoided). General guidelines on dealing with sickness dismissals have been proffered in a number of cases, e.g., *Spencer* v *Paragon Wallpapers Ltd* [1977] ICR 301 and *East Lindsey District Council* v *Daubney* [1977] ICR 566. From these cases we can draw up a list of actions expected of the employer.

When dealing with long-term absence there is a duty on the employer to ascertain the true position, to discuss the future with the employee (and possibly his or her doctor), and to look for alternative work. When dealing with intermittent absences the employer needs to make the employee aware of the standard required, giving the employee time to meet this and perhaps attempting to resolve the issue via medical investigations and analysing the possibility of alternative work. Thus, the employer should:

(a) investigate the nature of the illness;

(b) investigate the likely length of absence;

(c) assess the impact on the business (i.e., does that employee hold a key position?). The more important the employee is to the business the more the absence cannot be tolerated for any great length of time. It is therefore perhaps ironic that the more valued employee might have to be dismissed sooner than the lesser employee in order to find a replacement. Temporary replacements provide an answer, but not realistically in key positions, for few recruits would be found on this basis;

(d) assess the impact the absence will have on other employees, i.e., the increase in *their* workload or the effect on their pay if part of a team working on commission or bonuses;

(e) take account of available medical evidence. This will often mean that the employer will have to obtain appropriate medical reports;

(f) take notice of the employee's length of service and any contractual sick pay scheme;

(g) consider alternative work;

(h) consult the employee over the issues noted above (warning an employee to get better is somewhat futile, but an employer may have to indicate at some time that the position cannot go on forever).

There are three points that need some elaboration:

(a) *Obtaining proper evidence.*

The aspect of discussion and consultation is useful not only to keep the employee informed of developments, but also to ascertain exactly what the position is at any time. Dismissing shortly before the employee is set to return does not, for instance, exemplify good management. Equally, if the employer needs medical evidence in order to make a decision the employee's assistance is needed; more so under the provisions of the Access to Medical Reports Act 1988 and the Data Protection Act 1998 (see **Chapter 7**). In all cases tribunals must decide (i) as a matter of fact, what level of consultation was necessary or desirable; and (ii) whether the process employed was adequate in the circumstances. A failure to seek medical advice damages the employer's argument of fairness. The employee's own GP, or possibly a specialist, is the obvious source to provide independent medical assessments (especially if there is a conflict of medical opinion). However, unless there is an express contractual power to request the employee to undergo a medical examination the employer cannot force the employee to do so. Any such *demand* would constitute a repudiatory breach: *Bliss* v *South East Thames Regional Health Authority* [1987] ICR 700 (request for a psychological examination). But if the employee does refuse to cooperate the employer is entitled to make a decision on the facts available.

(b) *Intermittent absences.*

These pose a different kind of problem. The employer's tolerance of such situations does not have to be *infinite*. Warnings following consultation may be more appropriate here because of both the disruptive effect of short-term but frequent absence and also the possibility that there is a question of misconduct as well as or instead of incapability. Medical evidence may prove useful here too, though if an employee has been diagnosed as suffering from, say, back trouble which flares up periodically this evidence does not actually resolve the problem.

(c) *Relationship with contractual sick pay scheme.*

Most companies operate a sick pay scheme (as noted at **5.2.3.1** above) and a frequently asked question is: can an employer dismiss someone who is still on sick leave? The usual advice is, yes, but with great caution. If the employee commits an act of gross misconduct during the sick leave or fails to cooperate with the reasonable requests of the employer whilst on sick leave that will justify dismissal for misconduct: *Briscoe* v *Lubrizol Ltd* [2002] EWCA Civ 508, [2002] IRLR 607; likewise if the employer has to make people redundant, being ill is no safeguard against selection: *Hill* v *General Accident Fire & Life Assurance Corporation plc* [1998] IRLR 641.

But the real problem comes where the employer wishes to dismiss *because* of the employee's absence owing to illness. Tribunals have long accepted that an employer may have to dismiss someone, despite the presence of a clause which seems to 'guarantee' an employee a period of sick leave, if genuine business needs drive them that way e.g., in the case of a key employee. The question is then whether the dismissal is handled fairly.

At **5.2.3.1** we noted that a conflict has developed (as it often does in employment) between the form of analysis used by the ordinary courts and that used by employment tribunals in dealing with dismissals of employees who are on contractual sick leave. We saw that a recent run of cases has, by reliance on express or implied terms, concluded that an employee can only be dismissed *for cause* (e.g., redundancy) whilst on sick leave, especially if the dismissal would adversely affect any health insurance entitlements. The ordinary courts are concerned only with the contractual analysis. Thus, in *Hill* v *General Accident*, Lord Hamilton (in the court of Session, Outer House—the equivalent to the High Court) stated that: 'Where provision is, as here, made in the contract for payment of salary or other benefit during sickness, the employer cannot, solely with a view to relieving himself of the obligation to make such payment, by dismissal bring that sick employee's contract to an end.' An implied term is created to this effect that can only be ousted by clear express wording.

What of the position as regards unfair dismissal? There is no case directly covering whether the presence of private health insurance, for instance, prevents the employer from dismissing fairly on ill-health grounds, but in a related area such a limitation has been placed: *First West Yorkshire Ltd* v *Haigh* [2008] IRLR 182. Here, the EAT held that an employer had not acted within the range of reasonable responses when dismissing a long-term sick employee without considering how he might qualify for 'early medical retirement' under their pension scheme (coupled here with a finding that the employer had chosen the dismissal route for purely financial reasons and also because the employer had failed to obtain proper medical evidence as to how long the illness would last).

10.9.5.4   Overlap with disability discrimination

In **Chapter 6** we noted the main provisions of the Disability Discrimination legislation in relation to recruitment, terms, promotion opportunities, etc. The legislation also has relevance as regards any dismissal based on a person's disability. The term 'dismissal' when applied to disability discrimination is likely to include the non-renewal of limited-term contracts and constructive dismissal, although there is no definition given in the Act.

Thus a disabled person who has been dismissed has two main statutory claims:

(a) a discrimination action under DDA 1995 (as amended); and

(b) an unfair dismissal action under ERA 1996.

There can be considerable overlap in the substantive analysis of these claims. There is nothing in DDA 1995 to prevent an employee from also claiming unfair dismissal under ERA 1996 either exclusively or in the alternative and a finding of unfair dismissal will not mean that the statutory cap in unfair dismissal action (currently £63,000) will, by a side wind, limit the open-ended compensation possible under a discrimination claim: see *Beart* v *HM Prison Service* [2005] EWCA Civ 467, [2005] ICR 1206.

However, the dismissal of a 'disabled person' is not automatically unfair. Neither does DDA 1995 specifically alter the general provisions of s. 98 of ERA 1996. Equally, if an employee falls within the provisions of DDA 1995 it is highly unlikely that it will be sufficient for an employer merely to show that the disabled employee was incapable under

s. 98(2)(a) in order to defend an unfair dismissal claim. Effectively, where a 'disabled person' is dismissed or subjected to any other detriment then, in any unfair dismissal action defended on the grounds of capability, the tribunal will have to take into account the requirements laid out in DDA 1995 as evidence of good practice and, as seen in the House of Lords' disability discrimination case of *Archibald* v *Fife Council* [2004] UKHL 32, [2004] IRLR 651 this may mean making extensive arrangements for transferring jobs, etc as part of the duty to make 'reasonable adjustments'. This does not mean that an employer cannot take into account absences which are disability-related; it simply means that where the sickness is tied in with a disability the employer has to be able to justify any actions as regards the disability as part of defending the unfair dismissal claim: *Royal Liverpool Children's NHS Trust* v *Dunsby* [2006] IRLR 351.

The safest advice for all employers must therefore be that an employer must have in mind, when dealing with an employee who is ill or who has absences from work (or who might be made redundant), the requirements of DDA 1995.

There are advantages to pursuing a claim directly under DDA 1995, e.g., no age limit; no qualifying period of employment; the specific inclusion of 'injury to feelings' as a head of compensation; and no limit on the amount of compensation that may be awarded. However, to succeed in a claim under DDA 1995 the employee must have been the subject of direct discrimination, disability-related discrimination, harassment or victimisation. This might be difficult to establish in any given case. An unfair dismissal claim, although initially less attractive, might still prove to be the better course of action.

It is possible for there to be an unfair dismissal under s. 98 of ERA 1996 but for a disability discrimination claim to fail where the employee may not be able to establish all elements for the latter claim (e.g., the employer's actions were justified) but in assessing the overall reasonableness of the employer's actions in an unfair dismissal claim they are found wanting. The converse is less likely.

10.9.6 Misconduct: fairness

In the text below we consider the special requirements affecting conduct dismissals. The forms of misconduct can be legion. However, standard methods of dealing with misconduct dismissals emerge from the cases. The employer needs to show:

(a) an honest belief that the employee was guilty of the offence;

(b) that there were reasonable grounds for holding that belief; and

(c) that these came from a reasonable investigation of the incident(s).

This is not an immutable checklist and, given that the burden of proof as to fairness is neutral, minor failures under these principles will not inevitably damn an employer's case: *Boys' and Girls' Welfare Society* v *McDonald* [1996] IRLR 129.

These principles were first clearly stated in relation to dishonesty dismissals in *British Home Stores* v *Burchell* [1980] ICR 303, and have been approved on wider grounds since then. They are therefore often referred to as the '*Burchell* principles'. They demonstrate that *conclusive proof is not necessary.* So the employer is required to formulate an opinion and then to decide whether, on that evidence, a dismissal is justified. The tribunal will then examine the basis for the belief and then go on to determine whether a reasonable employer would have dismissed in those circumstances.

There is no requirement to find some form of *mens rea* in the employee's actions. The test is simpler than this: did the employee commit the act complained of? For example, say an employee has assaulted another employee. The employee claims that the other employee provoked him by teasing him about his inability to carry out a temporary task. The employee also says that he cannot remember hitting the other person; that he 'blacked out'. Provided the dismissal is dealt with fairly (see below) the employer is not expected to launch into criminal law in order to establish the state of the employee's mind. Equally, an employer does not have to cogitate on whether there is a line to be drawn between intent and commission where the employee has been discovered, about to commit an act, e.g., a theft: *British Railways Board* v *Jackson* [1994] IRLR 235.

A general checklist for misconduct dismissals would therefore be:

(a) The employer must adhere to the spirit of the *Burchell* principles, or the evidence must be so obvious (or there is a confession) that it fulfils the same function.

(b) The employer must adhere to the company's procedures (which should fit with the ACAS Code).

(c) The employer must have conducted a proper hearing.

(d) The employer should review the status of previous warnings.

(e) The employer should note the employee's disciplinary record.

(f) The employer should take note of the employee's length of service.

(g) The employer's policy of dealing with misconduct should show consistency.

(h) Alternatives to dismissal should be considered.

(i) The relevance of criminal proceedings, or acquittals or convictions should be considered.

Some of these matters, such as the conduct of a fair hearing, have been noted above. One or two deserve further elaboration. A misconduct dismissal does not have to be for gross misconduct. A series of lesser incidents might bring about a fair dismissal if proper procedures have been followed. Gross misconduct will more easily justify moving straight to dismissal, without going through warnings, but otherwise all forms of misconduct fall under the same general guidelines.

There is an obvious question here: what is 'gross' misconduct? Many contracts define what is regarded as gross misconduct. If they are so tightly drawn that they provide an exhaustive list it will be difficult to add to this. But most contracts merely give the primary examples. These would include: dishonesty (usually whatever the amount and whatever the form), fighting at work and assault, disclosure of confidential information, setting up in a competing business (at least as regards senior employees), and gross insubordination. The list will vary from industry to industry though. Thus, 'fighting' might take various forms. A snowball fight in a foundry, where pieces of metal, etc. may be on the floor, could prove dangerous and an employee could fairly be dismissed for participating. Equally, an offence may be serious without being gross misconduct, e.g., where an employee incompetently fails to deal with invoices and so loses the company money. He or she may have committed a serious offence but, if the amount is small, this will hardly be gross negligence. In the end, the definition of 'gross misconduct' is relevant only:

(a) to show why the employer bypassed the warnings stage and went straight to dismissal;

(b) in relation to *wrongful dismissal*, to show why summary dismissal was chosen.

10.9.6.1   The employee's disciplinary and service history

The point of emphasis here is that in each case the employer is dealing with an individual, therefore that individual's history in the company is a major component of any decision to dismiss. This is especially true where the dismissal relates to conduct which is not gross misconduct.

As a rule of thumb, employers will treat long-serving employees with a little more leniency because of the loyalty factor. Thus, although this does not afford complete protection, a reasonable employer will at least take service into account in deciding whether to dismiss or impose some lesser penalty. But if the employment record shows a history of disciplinary problems, this can equally damn the employee and if warnings for other matters are still operative this will have a major influence on the decision to dismiss. Normally one would expect an employer to issue the next-level warning. If some stages are to be omitted the employer will need to justify this.

In some cases an employee may have a history of warnings but these may have expired (most warnings are given a limitation period of three months, six months etc depending on their level). Employers frequently ask whether they can take such expired warnings into account. The traditional answer has always been 'No' but the Court of Appeal has decided that though taking into account expired warnings may not generally be good industrial practice there is nothing in the language of ERA 1996, s.98(4) to prohibit this if the employer can show it was reasonable to do so: *Airbus UK Ltd* v *Webb* [2008] EWCA Civ 49, [2008] ICR 561.

10.9.6.2   Consistency of treatment

There are two matters here. There should be consistency in dealing with employees involved in the same incident, e.g., a fight. But, wider than this, there should be some consistency across the years in dealing with types of offence. This may apply even when the management personnel has changed over the years: *Proctor* v *British Gypsum Ltd* [1991] IRLR 7. Here the EAT stated three points on consistency of treatment:

(a) An otherwise fair dismissal might be classified as unfair in the light of inconsistency of treatment.

(b) Though ERA 1996, s. 98 demands consideration of the *individual's* case, comparisons may be valid if they reveal a pattern that it is understood in the company that such conduct will be overlooked, that the comparisons reveal that the reason given for dismissal is not genuine, or that the cases are analogous.

(c) Changes in circumstances, e.g., an increase in theft, might well justify changes in policy (though some form of prior notification would be necessary). In such cases, acting severely as a deterrent to others may be acceptable.

The Court of Appeal issued further guidance on 'consistency' in *Paul* v *East Surrey District Health Authority* [1995] IRLR 305. Whilst not overturning any of the above, there is a recognition that similar incidents are not that common across the years when examined carefully and employers do have some flexibility. Thus, an employer may take account of mitigating personal circumstances (or aggravating circumstances), how contrite the employee is, and the levels of seriousness of the offences involved. Points (a) and (b) above also received specific approval. Nevertheless, the quite common cry of the employer that 'We will make an example of this one' is therefore prone to attack.

Linked with this is the problematic area of suspected theft when the employer can pinpoint a group of employees but cannot identify the guilty individual or individuals specifically. Should the employer dismiss one, some, all or none? The cases reveal that, provided the employer's investigations are reasonable and all other factors have been taken into account, dismissing *all* of the group will be a fair method of dealing with the problem: *Monie* v *Coral Racing Ltd* [1981] ICR 109. The employer must be convinced on 'solid and sensible grounds' that one or more *of that group* has committed the act. The employer does not, however, *have* to dismiss all the members of the group (this is where the other factors may be relevant, e.g., past disciplinary record). This principle has been extended to other situations where it is impossible directly to apportion blame to a group, e.g., for faulty workmanship.

10.9.6.3   The relevance of criminal proceedings

Employers are not required to await the outcome of criminal proceedings before deciding on dismissal. Equally, employers cannot dismiss simply because an employee has been charged with an offence. First, the mere fact of being charged is irrelevant and, secondly, the offence will ultimately have to have some bearing on the employment relationship to justify the dismissal: *Singh* v *London Country Bus Services Ltd* [1976] IRLR 176.

This means that employers will have to conduct their own investigations before any decision to dismiss is likely to be fair: *Lovie Ltd* v *Anderson* [1999] IRLR 164. All this is quite awkward in practice because the employee (unless confessing) is hardly liable to prove cooperative! Indeed, the Court of Session in Scotland and the English EAT have disagreed over the appropriateness of employer investigations. Perhaps the key point is that the employer, on the evidence available, has to be sure that dismissal is the right course; any doubts may mean having to wait.

A conviction does not absolve the employer from some investigation of the matter, but this relates more to matters such as mitigation; an employer is certainly entitled to treat a conviction as proof of guilt: *P* v *Nottinghamshire County Council* [1992] ICR 706. But neither will an eventual acquittal turn an existing properly conducted dismissal into an unfair dismissal. Further, if the employer does await the outcome of the trial a dismissal following acquittal may still be fair because the standards of proof are different and other matters may have come out at the trial. Employers who state that *they will be bound* by the outcome of the trial are in a difficult position: any subsequent dismissal will most likely be unfair.

10.9.6.4   Concluding points on misconduct

Because the forms of misconduct are so various, all that can be given here are the general guidelines. These will hold true in each case, but the considerations for absentee dismissals, dismissals for fraud, fighting, disobedience, and so on will each have their variations in terms of appropriate forms of procedure and investigation. Most importantly, the employer must be able to demonstrate, as regards whichever type of misconduct is pertinent, that the decision to dismiss that particular employee for that particular offence was warranted.

One further point worth emphasising arises where the employee is dismissed for misconduct in refusing to obey an order from the employer. Most employees believe that if the order was unlawful (i.e., in breach of the contract) they cannot be dismissed fairly for refusing to obey it. In many cases the lawfulness of the order will indeed affect the fairness of any dismissal, but it is only a factor in the equation. If the employer has, for instance, given ample warning of any change being implemented, consulted sufficiently and acted reasonably any resulting dismissal in the face of the employee 'sticking to the contract' may not be unfair.

10.9.7   Retirement: fairness

The fairness of retirement dismissals is not subject to the general principles described above.

For a retirement to be a fair *reason* for dismissal under s. 98(2)(ba), the employer must comply with the points set out in ss. 98ZA–ZF ERA 1996 and sch. 6 of the Employment Equality (Age) Regulations 2006, SI 2006/1031 (see **10.3.3**). But that still leaves the question whether that fair reason was handled fairly. To answer that question we need to look at an additional set of procedures. These are contained in s. 98ZG ERA 1996.

Section 98ZG states that the dismissal will be *automatically fair* provided the employer has:

- given proper notification to the employee of her right to request to continue to work beyond the retirement date, in accordance with sch. 6, para. 2 of the 2006 Regs or, failing that, given proper notification prior to the fourteenth day before dismissal in accordance with sch. 6, para. 4;

- considered that request under paras 6 and 7;

- considered any appeal against a decision not to allow the employee to continue working, in accordance with the rules set out in para. 8.

If the employer fails to comply with any of these points, the dismissal is *automatically unfair*. However, it is also possible (somewhat bizarrely) that, where the NRA or age requirements have been respected but there is a fault in the application of the duty to inform, the tribunal still has a discretion under s.98ZG ERA 1996 to consider whether the dismissal is fair where the employer has complied with the continuing duty to inform the employee up to two weeks before the intended retirement date

10.9.8   Redundancy: fairness

With a redundancy dismissal the tribunal will be concerned to discover whether the redundancy was implemented fairly. It is rare for a tribunal to question the need for redundancy; that is a business decision for the employer to make (unless there is bad faith): *James W. Cook & Co. (Wivenhoe) Ltd* v *Tipper* [1990] ICR 716. Instead, the area most rife for debate is that of *selection* for redundancy. Thus if selections for redundancy are badly handled and the selection criteria are not objectively justifiable, there may be an unfair dismissal for reason of redundancy (a full discussion of these points occurs in **Chapter 11** generally, and specifically at **11.5**). Indeed, certain dismissals for redundancy will be automatically unfair.

The burden of proving that any of the above reasons apply lies with the employee. Thus the fact that trade unionists are selected does not in itself breach any provisions: the selections have to be *because* the employees were trade unionists, or had asserted a statutory right, etc.

In ordinary cases the employer may still have acted unfairly. Thus an employer must also:

(a) ensure that the selection criteria were objectively justifiable and applied fairly;

(b) undertake proper individual and/or collective consultation; and

(c) ascertain whether suitable alternative employment is available.

Hence the selection process and the procedure for decision-making and implementation will be called into question in deciding fairness.

Selection for redundancy because of a person's disability is not automatically unfair but will have to be justified, and that justification must be both material to the circumstances of the particular case and substantial.

10.9.9   Statutory illegality: fairness

We have already noted that it is for the employer to show as a fact that any continued employment would have contravened the statutory rule in question in order to claim this as a fair reason for dismissal. As with other 'fair reasons', the citing of an enactment does not absolve the employer from showing that the dismissal was handled fairly. The problem of the illegality, for instance, might only have a short life-span and so might easily be corrected, or the illegality might affect only part of the employee's duties so that alternative work or a change in duties could be looked at. In other words, if the situation can be remedied the employer would be unwise to dismiss before checking this.

10.9.10 Some other substantial reason: fairness

10.9.10.1 A catch-all category?

In the text below we consider the special requirements affecting 'some other substantial reason' dismissals. The tag of 'catch-all' does indeed apply to this area, dragging along with it all the lack of definition inherent in the phrase. Thus if the dismissal does not fall within any of the other four fair reasons it *might* come within this heading. Equally, many employers will plead this catch-all in the alternative, e.g., if the dismissal was not for redundancy it was for 'some other substantial reason etc.' such as a business reorganisation; or if the employer was mistaken about the effect of a statutory rule and dismissed for statutory illegality, the honest belief might be pleaded as 'some other substantial reason'.

The most common form of 'some other substantial reason' is that of business reorganisations. We noted in **Chapter 5** that where an employer effects a change to the employee's terms and conditions a range of alternative consequences is possible at common law, e.g.:

(a) the change may be lawful via the express or implied terms of the contract;

(b) the employee might simply accept the change (reluctantly or otherwise);

(c) the employee might object and seek an injunction or damages;

(d) the employee might refuse to accept the change and be dismissed, in which case there may be a claim for wrongful dismissal;

(e) the employee might resign and claim wrongful repudiation.

To this we have added, in the earlier stages of this chapter, that:

(f) the employee might refuse to accept the change and be dismissed, in which case there may be a claim for unfair dismissal; or

(g) the employee might resign and claim constructive unfair dismissal.

Whichever way the unfair dismissal claim comes about, the employer can argue that the fair reason was 'some other substantial reason' under ERA 1996, s. 98. How will this be analysed by the employment tribunal?

10.9.10.2 Business reorganisations

Employers frequently wish to reorganise parts of a business in order to increase efficiency. Often this will simply involve a change in working patterns or methods, and, as seen in *Cresswell* v *Board of Inland Revenue* [1984] ICR 508 in **Chapter 5**, this may not involve any variation of the employment contract at all. An employee who refuses to cooperate and who resigns in the face of such changes will have no claim for wrongful repudiation at common law or for unfair dismissal because there will have been no dismissal. If the employee refuses to cooperate and is dismissed there may be a claim for wrongful or unfair dismissal; but from the unfair dismissal perspective the fair reason could be incapability or misconduct (and fairness would be decided accordingly).

If the change does constitute a breach of contract the employer may still argue that the dismissal was not unfair because of the business reorganisation. The tribunal is not allowed to second-guess the employer's business decision, so the employer can establish the 'fair reason' quite easily, e.g., insisting on the insertion of restraint of trade clauses because of recent problems with ex-employees joining competitors: *RS Components* v *Irwin* [1973] ICR 353. The test was once quite stringent: was there a 'pressing business need' for the change? However, greater leniency is now evident so that all that is needed is a 'sound business reason' (see *Hollister* v *National Farmers' Union* [1979] ICR 542), or even merely that the change was beneficial to the operation of the company. A mere assertion that there is a business reason is not enough, but employers are only expected to show the factual *evidence* as the basis for making their business decision.

The question of fairness still has to be decided, however. As with any unfair dismissal claim, the manner in which the employer handled the dismissal is still important. The tribunal is therefore seeking to find out whether the reorganisation was effected in a reasonable way. One of the difficulties that crops up here is that just because the employer is acting reasonably in seeking to implement the change it does not automatically follow that the employee is acting unreasonably in refusing to accept it. All manner of reasons may be relevant, e.g., family commitments or travel arrangements and, again, one must also consider the question of indirect discrimination arising from any reorganisation (see, for instance, *London Underground Ltd* v *Edwards (No. 2)*, at 5.5.2.3 above).

The tribunal will therefore need to look at:

(a) whether the employer consulted with the employee and any employee representatives;

(b) whether the employer considered alternative courses of action;

(c) whether the terms were those which a reasonable employer would offer;

(d) what is the balance of advantages and disadvantages to both parties;

(e) whether the majority of employees have accepted the change.

No one factor is given greater weight than another and the whole context of the reorganisation needs to be examined: *St John of God (Care Services) Ltd* v *Brooks* [1992] IRLR 546. Again, however, one needs to be aware of the possible impact of DDA 1995. For instance, employers must now look at making reasonable adjustments to working arrangements and physical features of premises in relation to disabled employees. These adjustments include such matters as altering working hours, modifying equipment, and assigning a different place of work. Thus, these matters must be taken into account in effecting a business reorganisation otherwise there is a likelihood that the change in terms etc. will be seen as unreasonable.

10.9.11   Constructive dismissal and fairness

It is a common assumption that a constructive dismissal is automatically unfair. This view is wrong. All that a finding of constructive dismissal does is to show that the employee (despite having resigned) was in fact *dismissed*.

The question of fairness is a separate matter. Constructive dismissal asks whether the employer's conduct was repudiatory. It is a contractual test and, as with any other dismissal, the employer's breach of the contract is not what the idea of 'fairness' centres on. *Thus there may be fair or unfair constructive dismissals.* If you look back at **Figure 10.1** you will see that it only dealt with the analysis of whether or not there had been a constructive dismissal; it said nothing about fairness. It only told half the story because, once a constructive dismissal has been found the tribunal's attention then shifts to the analysis in **Figure 10.2**—as with any other unfair dismissal action.

Having said all this, in many cases it will be quite unusual for an employment tribunal to be convinced that a constructive dismissal was nevertheless fair in all the circumstances. For instance, in *Cawley* v *South Wales Electricity Board* [1985] IRLR 89, an employee had been seen (by a member of the public) urinating out of the back of a SWEB van as it travelled down a main street. Apparently the employee had bladder trouble and the whole incident arose out of a practical joke being played by his workmates. The employee was at first dismissed but on appeal this was turned into a heavy demotion. He complained that, although the demotion was allowed for in the contract, its implementation was an abuse of power. He resigned and claimed that he was (unfairly) constructively dismissed. The tribunal found constructive dismissal and never really directed its mind to the question of fairness. However, on appeal the two points were found to be so closely intertwined that the general points had been covered. So it will be with most misconduct constructive dismissals.

The major exception to all this arises with constructive dismissals based on business reorganisations. Here the two questions of serious breach and fairness are quite distinct. Let us say, for example, that an employer decides unilaterally to change the terms of the contract for good economic reasons. The employees object. The employer insists, and eventually your employee–client resigns and claims unfair (constructive) dismissal. There is probably very little difficulty in showing a serious breach of contract by the employer here (though one cannot be sure of this without considering such factors as implied terms and employee adaptability: see **Chapter 5** at **5.5.3**). But, assuming that a serious breach can be shown, there is a constructive dismissal. We are also assuming that the employee qualifies to bring a claim for unfair dismissal in the first place and has complied with the relevant statutory grievance procedures, otherwise all we are left with is a common law claim for wrongful repudiation.

Now, the next question is: was this dismissal unfair? The employer may claim business reorganisation as 'some other substantial reason' and this is not the most difficult hurdle to overcome. Thus it is quite likely that, although the change was a repudiation of the contract, and although the employee was contractually entitled to refuse to accept the alteration, any resulting dismissal may well not be unfair.

Your employee–client may well have difficulty accepting this point (along with some of the others noted above). Your employer–client may be equally surprised.

You can analyse a constructive (unfair) dismissal claim from either of two angles:

- you can use **Figure 10.1** to determine whether the resignation will count as a dismissal at all and then go on to examine whether, if it is a constructive dismissal, that dismissal was fair or unfair; or

- you can start with **Figure 10.2** and determine whether the employee qualifies for claiming unfair dismissal (because, if he does not all the rest is irrelevant), then go back to the analysis in **Figure 10.1** to consider whether the resignation is a constructive dismissal and return to **Figure 10.2** to look at fairness.

There is no one answer to which method to use but it is probably better to follow the first route because even if your client will not qualify to claim unfair dismissal he or she may still be able to bring a wrongful repudiation action (the test for wrongful repudiation and constructive dismissal being practically identical).

10.10 Industrial action

Under ERA 1996, s. 16 and sch. 5, the relevant provisions in TULRCA 1992, i.e., ss. 238–239, were amended and a new section (s. 238A) inserted. The dismissal of an employee *because* he or she is taking part in *official* (otherwise called 'protected') industrial action will be *automatically unfair* if:

(a) the dismissal takes place within the period of 12 weeks beginning with the day the employee started to take industrial action; or

(b) it takes place after the end of that period and the employee had stopped taking industrial action before the end of that period; or

(c) it takes place after the period, and though the employee had not stopped industrial action, the employer had not taken defined procedural steps (defined in s. 238A(6)) to resolve the dispute.

10.10.1 What is industrial action?

Industrial action may take many forms, including a strike, a work-to-rule, a go-slow, or an overtime ban. The question of what is and what is not industrial action in any particular set of circumstances is *a question of fact* for the employment tribunal. The action does not need to be in breach of contract: *Power Packing Casemakers Ltd* v *Faust* [1983] ICR 292. In this case the employees refused to work non-contractual overtime (so there could hardly be a breach) as part of wage bargaining tactics. What was present in *Faust,* however (and is generally required), is some pressure, some disruption of the employer's business for industrial relations reasons, e.g., pay demands. Rendering only partial performance of a contract as part of an industrial action campaign (i.e., 'we will do x but not y', when x and y are part of the contract) is still industrial action and the employee may lose some or even all of his pay, despite the partial performance.

Although there is no statutory definition of 'industrial action', 'strike' is defined in ERA 1996, s. 235(5) as '(a) the cessation of work by a body of employed persons acting in combination, or (b) a concerted refusal, or a refusal under a common understanding, of any number of employed persons to continue to work for an employer in consequence of a dispute . . .'. This must be done to compel the employer to accept the employees' view on bargaining positions or for showing sympathy with other workers. This definition has, however, been limited to determining continuity of employment; so essentially the definition of strike is also a question of fact.

10.10.2 What is 'taking part'?

This has proved to be a problem area as regards employees who are on holiday or sick when the action occurs, or who feel unable to go into work because they are afraid to cross picket lines.

It is vital to know who is 'taking part' because the employer must be careful (at least with official action once the protected period seen in **10.10** has passed) to treat all those taking part, at the moment that one participant is dismissed, in the same way. Thus an employer does not want later to discover that an employee was not dismissed along with others taking part in an official action, because this would mean that the employees who were dismissed would once again be able to claim unfair dismissal. The employer's ignorance is no defence and the employee's motives are also irrelevant: *Coates & Venables* v *Modern Methods & Materials Ltd* [1982] ICR 763. Again, participation is a question of fact.

The employer therefore has to be sure, before dismissing anyone, *which* employees are taking part. For to dismiss the relevant employees *but miss one* will be a fatal error; and to dismiss someone who *is not taking part* will mean that that individual will have a good claim for unfair dismissal. The burden lies on the employer. As regards those employees who are absent from the company (e.g., those on sick leave), the employer needs to ascertain by reasonable investigation whether they are *associated* with the action: *Hindle Gears Ltd* v *McGinty* [1985] ICR 111. But if an employee originally took part in the industrial action and returned to work before any dismissals occurred, he or she is not participating at the relevant time.

10.10.3 Rules vary according to the type of action

Industrial action can be classed in a number of ways depending on whether a trade union has sanctioned the action. Thus, if a trade union supports the action it is referred to as *'official action'* and the employee gains certain protection from this tag. If a trade union does not support the action this is called *'unofficial action'* and the industrial action is not protected. Industrial action will be unofficial *unless:*

(a) the employee is a union member and the action has been authorised or endorsed by the union; or

(b) although the employee is not a union member, some of those taking part are and the action has been authorised or endorsed by the union (see TULRCA 1992, s. 237).

An employee who is dismissed whilst taking part in *unofficial action* has no right to complain of unfair dismissal even if others are not dismissed: TULRCA 1992, s. 237 (but note s. 238A: there is a day's grace allowed if the action was official and then was repudiated by the union).

Where none of the participants is a union member the action is sometimes called *'not unofficial action'*. This means that it is not protected action within s. 238A, but is covered by s. 238 which, broadly, allows the employee to claim unfair dismissal if all those taking part were not treated the same by the employer.

10.11 Action short of dismissal

Before we turn to the remedies for unfair dismissal we should note that, in certain cases where an employee has action taken against him short of dismissal he will gain rights to obtain a declaration against the employer or compensation. The aim here is that where an employee has sought to enforce rights under the contract and is then subjected to a detriment by the employer as a result of this but is not dismissed, he should have some right of recourse against the employer. We will not cover all the detailed provisions here, but, in outline, the grounds contained in Part V, ERA 1996 (ss. 44–49) are:

(a) cases where the employer has carried out activities in connexion with health and safety matters (s. 44);

(b) cases where the employee has refused to work on Sundays (s. 45);

(c) cases involving the working time regulations (s. 45A);

(d) cases concerning the actions of trustee of occupational pension schemes (s. 46);

(e) cases concerning employees acting as employee representatives under TULRCA 1992 (s. 47);

(f) cases where employees have sought to enforce rights relating to trade union activities or membership (TULRCA 1992, s. 146 as amended);

(g) cases involving employees who have sought time off in certain defined circumstances (s. 47A);

(h) cases where employees have made protected disclosures (s. 47B);

(i) cases where employees have sought leave for family and domestic reasons (s. 47C);

(j) cases involving employees seeking to enforce tax credits rights (s. 47D); and

(k) cases involving applications for flexible working (s. 47E).

The remedies for such actions are set out in ERA 1996, s. 49. Awards may be made that include a sum for injury to feelings (akin to discrimination claims and using the *Vento* guidelines applied in such cases—see **Chapter 6**): *Virgo Fidelis Senior School* v *Boyle* [2004] IRLR 268 (a case of disciplinary action being taken by the school against a teacher following a protected disclosure).

10.12 Other methods of dispute resolution

10.12.1 Settlements and conciliation

Many cases are settled before the hearing. Any settlement concluded through an ACAS officer, reached orally or in writing, is binding on the parties. An ACAS officer is always given the employee's ET 1 (the equivalent to a statement of claim) and the employer's ET 3 (the defence). The officer will then seek to conclude a settlement between the parties.

A settlement can be reached at any stage in the proceedings. Settlements through ACAS are usually put down in writing on a form known as a COT 3.

For years this was the only way to ensure that a settlement was binding on the parties. However, under ERA 1996, s. 203(2)(f) and (3) the parties may now reach their own binding compromise agreement. In outline:

(a) the agreement must be in writing;

(b) it must relate to the particular complaint;

(c) the employee must have received advice from a relevant independent adviser; and

(d) the employee's adviser must be insured or have indemnity provided for members of a profession or professional body.

The issue of settlements and the considerations involved are dealt with more fully in **Chapter 13**.

10.12.2 ACAS arbitration scheme

In May 2001, a voluntary arbitration scheme was introduced under the auspices of ACAS as an alternative to going to an employment tribunal for dealing with simple unfair dismissal disputes. It was designed to relieve some of the workload of tribunals. The scheme is limited in its form and only applies to cases of alleged unfair dismissal or claims under flexible working legislation. Even then, ACAS also strongly recommends that questions of EC Law are left to employment tribunals. Both parties must agree, in writing, to go to arbitration and this agreement contains certain waivers, e.g., a very limited right of appeal against the arbitrator's decision. The ACAS arbitrator may conduct proceedings anywhere (e.g., at the workplace), those proceedings are held in private, no oath is administered, the arbitrator will take a strong inquisitorial role, and the matter will be decided on general grounds of fairness, not the rules developed under unfair dismissal case law (e.g., the range of reasonable responses test).

A full description of the scheme can be found at www.acas.org.uk. The Arbitration Act 1996 does not apply to this scheme.

10.13   General principles of compensation

10.13.1   What remedies are available?

10.13.1.1   Reinstatement

Reinstatement means to be put back in the same job with compensation for loss between dismissal and reinstatement. If reinstatement is requested by the employee the employer can refuse to reinstate only where it is reasonable to do so, e.g., where the mutual trust and confidence has been shattered. The employee is not obliged to request reinstatement, nor is the tribunal bound by any request. Indeed, the employee can have a change of mind at any time. However, tactically some employees request reinstatement (although they do not really want it) because a refusal *may* increase the amount of compensation. This tactic can also backfire.

An unreasonable refusal by the employer to reinstate where it would have been practicable to do so may lead to an *additional award* being given in addition to the *basic award* and the *compensatory award* (see below). Though reinstatement is the primary remedy (as emphasised in *Polkey* v *A. E. Dayton Services Ltd* [1987] AC 344), it has traditionally occurred in fewer than 2 per cent of cases.

10.13.1.2   Re-engagement

This consists of returning the employee to a similar job or to a job with an associated employer. Re-engagement is subject to the same tests as reinstatement.

10.13.1.3   Compensation

The two main elements are the basic award and compensatory award. They are assessed on quite different grounds which are discussed in detail below. The figures which form the basis for calculating these awards are now changed annually according to the Retail Price Index changes for September of each year (see ERA 1999, s. 34) and brought into effect in the following February. The principles for assessing compensation are set out in ERA 1996, ss. 118–126 (as amended).
The figures given here, therefore, are only valid for dismissals occurring before 1 February 2009. When the figures for 2009–10 become available we will put these on the Online Resource Centre.

10.13.1.4   Interim Relief

Under ERA 1996, s. 128, employees who have been dismissed may apply for 'interim relief' in a limited number of cases. The claim must be presented before the end of the period of seven days immediately following the EDT. Where the tribunal finds that it is likely that on final determination the tribunal will find that the reason for dismissal falls within:

- s. 100(1)(a) or (b) ERA 1996—health and safety-related dismissal;
- s. 101A(d)—working time-related dismissal;
- s. 102(1)—occupational pension scheme trustee-related dismissal;
- s. 103—employee representative-related dismissal;
- s. 103A—protected disclosure-related dismissal; or
- para. 161(2) sch. A1, TULRCA 1992—trade union membership and activities-related dismissal,

it may order continuance of the contract or, ultimately, award compensation. Interim relief actions are not common.

10.13.2   Assessing the basic award

This is calculated on length of service. It is a fixed formula. When a client asks how much he or she will get or have to pay in an unfair dismissal case, this is the one figure that provides some level of certainty. The formulation is set out in ERA 1996, s. 119(2). It is almost identical to the redundancy entitlement.

CALCULATION:	[AGE factor] × [SERVICE] × [WEEK'S PAY]
AGE:	For any service where the employee was 41 or over the factor is 1.5
	For any service between the ages of 22 and 41 the factor is 1
	For any service below the age of 22 the factor is 0.5
SERVICE:	Subject to a maximum of 20 years
WEEK'S PAY:	Subject to a maximum of £330 per week

The maximum basic award is therefore £9,900 i.e., 1.5 × 20 × 330.

The method of calculating this can be seen in the following examples.

EXAMPLE 1

An employee is aged 56 at the time of dismissal and has 10 years' service with the company (only complete years can count). He earns £350 per week. To calculate the basic award you must take the length of service as at the EDT and count back from the employee's present age to see how many years of service fall into each age bracket. This tells you that here all the years of service fall within the age bracket of 'over 41'. Therefore the factor for each of these years will be 1.5. As the employee earns more than the maximum 'week's pay' he is limited to the £330. Thus 1.5 × 10 years × £330 gives a figure of £4,950 (i.e., 15 × £330).

EXAMPLE 2

Where the employee's years of service straddle two of the age brackets the computation becomes more difficult. If we take the same employee but change his age to 46 the method of calculation becomes: (1.5 × 5 years) plus (1 × 5 years) × £330 giving a figure of £4,125 (i.e., 12.5 × £330). This is because five years of his service fall within the age bracket of '41 or over' and are given a multiple of 1.5, but the remainder fall within the age bracket '22–41' and are only given a multiple of 1.

The Department for Business, Enterprise & Regulatory Reform (BERR) issues a 'ready reckoner' for calculating these figures (called a PL808). **Figure 10.4**, derived from the PL808, shows the calculations for unfair dismissal. We have taken 16 as the start date as this is the 'school-leaving age'.

Service (years)	1	2	3	4	5	6	7	8	9	10	11	12	13	14	15	16	17	18	19	20
Age (years)																				
17	½																			
18	½	1																		
19	½	1	1½																	
20	½	1	1½	2																
21	½	1	2	2½	3															
22	½	1	1½	2½	2½	3														
23	1	1½	2	2½	3	3½	4													
24	1	2	2½	3	3½	4	4½	5												
25	1	2	3	3½	4	4½	5	5½	6											
26	1	2	3	4	4½	5	5½	6	6½	7										
27	1	2	3	4	5	5½	6	6½	7	7½	8									
28	1	2	3	4	5	6	6½	7	7½	8	8½	9								
29	1	2	3	4	5	6	7	7½	8	8½	9	9½	10							
30	1	2	3	4	5	6	7	8	8½	9	9½	10	10½	11						
31	1	2	3	4	5	6	7	8	9	9½	10	10½	11	11½	12					
32	1	2	3	4	5	6	7	8	9	10	10½	11	11½	12	12½	13				
33	1	2	3	4	5	6	7	8	9	10	11	11½	12	12½	13	13½	14			
34	1	2	3	4	5	6	7	8	9	10	11	12	12½	13	13½	14	14½	15		
35	1	2	3	4	5	6	7	8	9	10	11	12	13	13½	14	14½	15	15½	16	
36	1	2	3	4	5	6	7	8	9	10	11	12	13	14	14½	15	15½	16	16½	17
37	1	2	3	4	5	6	7	8	9	10	11	12	13	14	15	15½	16	16½	17	17½
38	1	2	3	4	5	6	7	8	9	10	11	12	13	14	15	16	16½	17	17½	18
39	1	2	3	4	5	6	7	8	9	10	11	12	13	14	15	16	17	17½	18	18½
40	1	2	3	4	5	6	7	8	9	10	11	12	13	14	15	16	17	18	18½	19
41	1	2	3	4	5	6	7	8	9	10	11	12	13	14	15	16	17	18	19	19½
42	1½	2½	3½	4½	5½	6½	7½	8½	9½	10½	11½	12½	13½	14½	15½	16½	17½	18½	19½	20½
43	1½	3	4	5	6	7	8	9	10	11	12	13	14	15	16	17	18	19	20	21
44	1½	3	4½	5½	6½	7½	8½	9½	10½	11½	12½	13½	14½	15½	16½	17½	18½	19½	20½	21½
45	1½	3	4½	6	7	8	9	10	11	12	13	14	15	16	17	18	19	20	21	22
46	1½	3	4½	6	7½	8½	9½	10½	11½	12½	13½	14½	15½	16½	17½	18½	19½	20½	21½	22½
47	1½	3	4½	6	7½	9	10	11	12	13	14	15	16	17	18	19	20	21	22	23
48	1½	3	4½	6	7½	9	10½	11½	12½	13½	14½	15½	16½	17½	18½	19½	20½	21½	22½	23½
49	1½	3	4½	6	7½	9	10½	12	13	14	15	16	17	18	19	20	21	22	23	24
50	1½	3	4½	6	7½	9	10½	12	13½	14½	15½	16½	17½	18½	19½	20½	21½	22½	23½	24½
51	1½	3	4½	6	7½	9	10½	12	13½	15	16	17	18	19	20	21	22	23	24	25
52	1½	3	4½	6	7½	9	10½	12	13½	15	16½	17½	18½	19½	20½	21½	22½	23½	24½	25½
53	1½	3	4½	6	7½	9	10½	12	13½	15	16½	18	19	20	21	22	23	24	25	26
54	1½	3	4½	6	7½	9	10½	12	13½	15	16½	18	19½	20½	21½	22½	23½	24½	25½	26½
55	1½	3	4½	6	7½	9	10½	12	13½	15	16½	18	19½	21	22	23	24	25	26	27
56	1½	3	4½	6	7½	9	10½	12	13½	15	16½	18	19½	21	22½	23½	24½	25½	26½	27½
57	1½	3	4½	6	7½	9	10½	12	13½	15	16½	18	19½	21	22½	24	25	26	27	28
58	1½	3	4½	6	7½	9	10½	12	13½	15	16½	18	19½	21	22½	24	25½	26½	27½	28½
59	1½	3	4½	6	7½	9	10½	12	13½	15	16½	18	19½	21	22½	24	25½	27	28	29
60	1½	3	4½	6	7½	9	10½	12	13½	15	16½	18	19½	21	22½	24	25½	27	28½	29½
61 and above	1½	3	4½	6	7½	9	10½	12	13½	15	16½	18	19½	21	22½	24	25½	27	28½	30

Figure 10.4   Calculating the Basic Award [adapted from PL808 (rev 6)].

Note: *If the employee earns less than £330 per week it is that lower figure that will be used in the calculation,* subject to the National Minimum Wage rate as described in **4.2.3** above: *Pagetti v Cobb* [2002] Emp LR 651.

10.13.2.1   Minimum Basic Award

Under ERA 1996, s. 120(1) a minimum Basic Award of £4,400 will be made where the reason for dismissal is one specified in ERA 1996, ss. 100(1)(a) and (b), 101A(d), 102(1) and 103 (see 10.13.1.4 on which types of dismissals these sections refer to).

10.13.2.2 Minimum Basic Award and certain redundancy cases

In some cases (detailed in ERA 1996, ss. 138 and 141) an employee may be made re-dundant but be offered re-engagement immediately or soon after dismissal. There are detailed rules as to whether a refusal by the employee to be re-engaged destroys his right to claim redundancy pay. Section 121 ERA 1996 sets out an employee's rights to a mini-mum basic award in such instances.

10.13.2.3 Reductions in the Basic Award

The situations where a tribunal may reduce the basic award are listed in **10.13.6** below and are dealt with in ERA 1996, s. 122.

10.13.3 Assessing the compensatory award

The method of calculation is set out in ERA 1996, s. 123. Compensation is based on what is 'just and equitable in all the circumstances having regard to the loss sustained by the complainant in consequence of the dismissal' and the tribunal must be satisfied that there was a causal link between the dismissal and the loss suffered: *Simrad Ltd* v *Scott* [1997] IRLR 147. It is calculated on *nett* payments.

The maximum Compensatory Award is £63,000 (see ERA 1996, s. 124).

Tribunals have long used one leading case as the basis for calculating the Compensa-tory Award: *Norton Tool Co. Ltd* v *Tewson* [1973] 1 All ER 183.

We have noted above that discrimination claims (e.g., sex or race) are not subject to any 'capping' of compensation. Section 37, ERA 1999, lists the following reasons for an unfair dismissal as also not being subject to any cap:

- a dismissal falling under the 'whistleblower' provisions of the Public Interest Dis-closure Act 1998 and ERA 1996, s. 103A;
- a dismissal falling under ERA 1996, ss. 100 and 105(3) (automatically unfair dis-missal where the reason relates to health and safety).

A selection for redundancy based on these reasons will also be automatically unfair and not subject to capping.

10.13.4 The Norton Tool principles

Under the principles enunciated in *Norton Tool,* certain general principles for calculating loss have been laid down. These include the following headings:

10.13.4.1 Immediate loss of wages

This heading deals with loss dating from the EDT to the date of hearing. This normally is an easy calculation. If notice or payment in lieu of notice has been given, the em-ployee's loss will date from the expiry of that period worked or the period covered by the payment. The corollary to this is that, if notice has not been given, loss flows from the date of dismissal (in effect compensating the employee for not receiving a notice payment).

The following special cases should be noted:

- Section 123(4) ERA 1996 states that, in assessing loss, 'the tribunal shall apply the same rule concerning the duty of a person to mitigate his loss as applies to damages recoverable at common law . . .'. Thus, if the employee obtains a new job at a lower rate of pay before the tribunal hearing the amount received will be deducted from this heading of loss. Equally, if the employee does not do all that is expected to mitigate loss, a sum will be deducted.

- There must be proof of loss. If an employee is unfit to work in the period following dismissal there is an argument that there was no loss of earnings during that time. In *Dignity Funerals Ltd* v *Bruce* [2005] IRLR 189, the Court of Session (Inner House) accepted this idea but held that if the dismissal was a cause of the inability to work (in this case psychiatric illness) then an award, in full or in part, was still due (and see *Burlo* v *Langley* below).

- Where the employee obtains a new job which pays better than the old one the EAT settled (after long debate) in *Whelan* v *Richardson* [1998] IRLR 114 for a method of taking account the payment but not penalising the employee further, if the payment exceeded the loss for this period, by continuing to deduct the excess from the award of compensation.

- Certain social security payments have to be accounted for. If the employee receives benefits between the EDT and the hearing, including incapacity benefit (*Morgans* v *Alpha Plus Security Ltd* [2005] IRLR 234, EAT) but excluding income support and housing benefits, these sums are treated in a special way. The tribunal must formally identify the loss for the period between dismissal and hearing (after deductions have been made) in its judgment. That sum (known as the 'prescribed element') is then withheld until the Department for Work and Pensions has determined how much it wishes to reclaim under the Employment Protection (Recoupment of Jobseeker's Allowance and Income Support) Regulations 1996, SI 1996/2349. Once the recoupment figure is known the excess (if any) is paid to the employee.

10.13.4.2 Immediate loss and the notice period

Here we ask: what happens where the employee has not been given some or all of his due notice and has found a new job during that time? Is the notice period (or at least the statutory minimum) to be regarded as sacrosanct (e.g., as a debt) and so not subject to mitigation, or should this period be treated like any other claim in damages and any sum received set off against the notice due? *Norton Tool* suggested that it was good industrial practice not to apply the rules of mitigation to the notice period, or at least to what is now the s. 86 minimum notice entitlement. So, you would be forgiven for thinking that this problem should have been sorted out, but it has not: there has been over 30 years of debate. Two Court of Appeal decisions now lead the way, but not all the avenues have yet to be explored. The first is *Babcock FATA Ltd* v *Addison* [1987] ICR 805. This held that an employee who had received a payment in lieu of notice could not claim that sum again as part of any unfair dismissal compensation—there was no loss for that period to compensate. The second decision is *Burlo* v *Langley* [2006] EWCA Civ 1778, [2007] ICR 390. This case decided that if an employee is dismissed without notice or payment in lieu of notice but was sick during the period notice would have run then her loss was the sick pay she should have received and not her full wages for that period. Thus the amount attributed to that notice period in any unfair dismissal compensation should be limited to that payment she would have received had she worked through her notice. This all makes sense but it has the downside that unscrupulous employers may well simply not pay notice and take the chance of the employee mitigating his or her loss—they have nothing to lose here (except as regards any restraint of trade points: see **8.4** above).

10.13.4.3   Future loss of wages

This involves a degree of industrial guess-work. The tribunal will need to establish how long the applicant is likely to be unemployed, what are the employee's attributes, skills, the market for such skills, and whether he or she might have been dismissed for redundancy anyway in the near future. The tribunal will therefore seek to make an award relating to the employee *as an individual,* so that similarly-aged employees dismissed at the same time might still receive different compensations. The award is discretionary.

If the employee has already found another job which is better paid there will probably be no loss under this heading; if less well paid, the tribunal will have to judge when (if at all) the equivalent payment will be reached. These general statements are subject to the points made above in *Whelan* v *Richardson,* and also to those made by the Court of Appeal in *Dench* v *Flynn & Partners* [1998] IRLR 653. Here, an employee had been dismissed, had lodged a claim for unfair dismissal and then taken up new permanent employment; but within two months of starting had then terminated that employment. The question was whether, once the employee took up the (eventually aborted) permanent position, that marked the end of the period for which she could claim compensation from her original employer.

The Court of Appeal said that the question for the tribunal is whether the unfair dismissal can be regarded as a continuing course of loss when the employee is subsequently dismissed by her new employer with no right to compensation after a month or two in her new employment. They held that it could be: tribunals must assess what is a just and equitable compensation; in doing so, they must determine *why* the new employment did not last. If there was good reason why it did not last (e.g., where the new job might only last for the probation period—and did), its presence does not in itself break the chain of causation between dismissal and loss.

Cases such as *Leonard* v *Strathclyde Buses Ltd* [1998] IRLR 693 have made it clear that the test for causation should be one of applying common sense—what are the natural and direct consequences of the dismissal?—rather than intricate legal arguments on remoteness. Nevertheless, the reasonableness of the dismissed employee's actions subsequent to dismissal will come under scrutiny. Thus, for instance, what should be the position where an employee's response to dismissal is to set up in business (which will have a major lead-in period before profits can be made) or decides to go to university to increase his or her marketability? Should the immediate financial loss which results from these decisions still be attributable to the employer's actions? The latter example was seen in *Khanum* v *IBC Vehicles Ltd* (2000, unreported) where an obviously progressive employer dismissed Khanum for attending an open day at a university. She had great difficulty in finding another job—there was evidence she had been black- listed—and, after ten months, enrolled on a university degree course. It was accepted in evidence that, given the job market, this was a reasonable course of action and the chain of causation remained unbroken (unlike the earlier case of *Simrad Ltd* v *Scott* [1997] IRLR 147 where a decision to retrain was a matter of choice rather than need).

10.13.4.4   Loss of fringe benefits

These can be included: for example, company cars or accommodation or even the difference in value between shares sold back to the company by the employee on termination (at the then market value) and the new market value of those shares at the date of the hearing.

10.13.4.5   The manner of dismissal

In *Johnson* v *Unysis Ltd* [2001] UKHL 13, [2001] ICR 480 the House of Lords rejected a claim in contract for damages for injury to feeling arising *from the manner of dismissal.*

In doing so, Lord Hoffmann contemplated (unfortunately, out loud) whether, instead, an employment tribunal might be able to compensate for injury to feelings in an unfair dismissal action. This was news to employment lawyers but sparked a raft of cases where this was pleaded. In turn this led to the House of Lords (including Lord Hoffmann) holding that Lord Hoffmann's words were *obiter*: *Dunnachie* v *Kingston upon Hull City Council* [2004] UKHL 36, [2004] 3 WLR 310. Further, the natural meaning of the word 'loss' in s. 123 ERA 1996 did not admit damages for injury to feelings or psychiatric injury as part of unfair dismissal compensation.

We should note three things here:

- first, that compensation in discrimination actions can include an award for injury to feelings;
- secondly, that an award for injury to feelings can be made in relation to an action short of dismissal (see *Virgo Fidelis Senior School* v *Boyle* above);
- thirdly, that damages can be awarded for injury to feelings where the **cause of action accrues before dismissal** (see the joined cases of *Eastwood* v *Magnox Electric plc* and *McCabe* v *Cornwall County Council* [2004] UKHL 35, [2004] 3 WLR 322 above at **9.10.1.6**—which consisted of the same House of Lords' panel as in *Dunnachie*).

10.13.4.6 Loss of statutory employment protection rights

When an employee starts a new job he or she will generally have to work for one year before any unfair dismissal rights accrue. This heading provides some compensation for that loss, although the figure is nominal (usually about £250). Tribunals may also award compensation for loss of ERA 1996, s. 86 statutory notice rights (usually assessed at half the employee's statutory entitlement, e.g., four weeks for eight years' service).

10.13.4.7 Loss of pension rights

The losses under this heading can be very high. Odd then, you may think, that the exact principles for determining loss have never really been worked out. One document which seeks to provide help here is *Compensation for loss of pension rights—Employment Tribunals (2003)*, produced by a committee of Employment Tribunal Chairmen and the Government Actuary. This sets out two alternative methods of calculating loss: (i) the simplified approach (essentially the sum of the contributions an employer would have made but for the dismissal); and (ii) substantial loss approach (which involves the use of actuarial tables). This is what is said on the two approaches:

Section 4.11. *The simplified approach* ... involves three stages (a) in the case of a final salary scheme, the loss of the enhancement to the pension already accrued because of the increase of salary which would have occurred had the applicant not been dismissed, (b) in all cases, the loss of rights accruing up to the hearing and (c) the loss of future pension rights. These last two elements are calculated on the assumption that the contribution made by the employer to the fund during the period will equate to the value of the pension (attributable to the employer) that would have accrued. In the case of a final salary scheme, it may be necessary to make an adjustment to the employer's contribution as discussed in section 6.5. No such adjustment is necessary in the case of a money purchase scheme because the scheme is personal to the employee.

4.12. *The substantial loss approach,* by contrast, uses actuarial tables comparable to the Ogden Tables to assess the current capitalized value of the pension rights which would have accrued up to retirement. There may be cases where the Tribunal decides that a person will return to a job at a comparable salary, but will never get a comparable pension ... . In such cases the substantial loss approach may be needed even where the future loss of earnings is for such a short period. But it must be remembered that loss of pension rights is the loss of a fringe benefit and may be compensated by an increase in salary in new employment.

The EAT has now bravely waded in to this quagmire in *Greenhoff* v *Barnsley Metropolitan Borough Council* [2006] ICR 1514. The steps recommended (in this sequence) involve a tribunal:

(a) identifying all possible benefits that the employee could obtain under the pension scheme;

(b) setting out the terms of the pension relevant to each possible benefit;

(c) considering in respect of each such possible benefit first the advantages and disadvantages of applying what we have described as 'the simplified approach' or 'the substantial loss approach' and also any other approach that might be considered appropriate by the Tribunal or by the parties;

(d) explaining why they have adopted a particular approach and rejected any other possible approach; and

(e) setting out their conclusions and explaining the compensation they have arrived at in respect of each head of claim so that the parties and this Appeal Tribunal can then ascertain if they had made an error.

An employee who draws a pension early following a dismissal does not have to offset this money against any unfair dismissal compensation: *Knapton* v *ECC Card Clothing Ltd* [2006] ICR 1084 (EAT)

10.13.5 Increased compensation

A tribunal may **increase** an award by no more than 25 per cent where the employer fails to comply with an ACAS statutory code and that failure was unreasonable. As we have noted above, ACAS will be issuing a statutory code to cover discipline, dismissal and grievance practices. Although there are two other codes in existence (relating to trade union activities), it is this dismissal etc code that interests us here.

Clause 3 of the Employment Bill proposes the insertion of a new s. 207A to TULRA 1992 to achieve this. It is worth noting that cl. 1 of the Bill states that this section 'applies to proceedings before an employment tribunal relating to a claim by an employee under any of the jurisdictions listed in Schedule A2'. This schedule lists claims such as unfair dismissal and redundancy but also includes claims relating to equal pay, discrimination, the national minimum wage and other more technical areas of employment law. So, an employee bringing a claim for discrimination who demonstrates that the employer has failed to follow, say, a proper grievance procedure, may be entitled to an uplift in any compensation.

More particularly here, this is where an employer who has ignored proper procedures in dismissing an employee will find that the tribunal has a discretion to increase the compensation payable.

We should also repeat at this stage the point made back at **3.5.3** that another, different, adjustment may be made: ERA 1996, s. 124A (inserted by EA 2002, s. 39) states that, where an award of compensation for unfair dismissal falls to be increased under s. 38 EA 2002 (failure to give statement of employment particulars), the adjustment shall be in the amount awarded under ERA 1996, s. 118(1)(b) (the compensatory award) and shall be applied immediately before any reduction under s. 123(6) or (7) (contributory fault on the part of the employee).

10.13.6   Deductions from the overall award

Deductions may be made from both the basic award and compensatory award figures. These deductions are generally at the discretion of the tribunal. In the summary chart below you will see that there are a number of reasons why deductions can be made. One deserves special mention, namely deductions concerning the statutory dispute resolution procedures.

The new s. 207A TURCA 1992 described immediately above also allows for a tribunal to **reduce** any award of compensation by no more than 25 per cent where an ACAS Code applies and the employee has failed unreasonably to comply with that code (e.g., did not take full advantage of the grievance procedures). Section 124A ERA 1996 states that, where an award of compensation for unfair dismissal falls to be reduced the adjustment shall be in the amount awarded under ERA 1996 s. 118(1)(b) (the compensatory award) and shall be applied immediately before any reduction under s. 123(6) or (7) (contributory fault on the part of the employee).

10.13.6.1   The Polkey reduction

We saw in **10.9.3.3** above that, where a tribunal finds that a dismissal was unfair it may still reduce the award payable by any amount if it is convinced that, had the employer followed the correct procedures it was likely that the dismissal would have been fair. So, if the tribunal thinks it was only a matter of time before the employee would have been dismissed (usually for a different and fair reason) or there was only a minor defect in the procedures used and had this been corrected the employee would have been dismissed fairly it will make a finding of unfair dismissal but only award compensation to reflect this 'lost time' or minor defect.

Because this is an exercise in speculation the tribunal will require evidence to work on (e.g., of future risk to that person's job or to the industry as a whole) but the fact that there are uncertainties does not mean a tribunal should avoid the question: *Scope* v *Thornett* [2006] EWCA Civ 1600, [2007] ICR 236.

That just leaves us one question here: at what point are the deductions made? The general position is set out in the chart at **10.13.6.3**. Any *Polkey* reductions are taken from the **Compensatory Award**.

We should also note some key points as regards *Polkey*:

- Does the *Polkey* reduction apply only to 'procedural' defects? The answer is 'no', though practically this will have to be the source for most such arguments: see, for instance *Lambe* v *186k Ltd* [2004] EWCA Civ 104, [2005] ICR 307.

- Compensation should still be awarded if the evidence shows the employer *would not* have dismissed, even if he *could* in fact fairly have dismissed (see the Court of Appeal decision in *Trico-Folberth Ltd* v *Devonshire* [1989] ICR 747).

- Some processes adopted by the employer can be *so* unfair or so fundamentally flawed that it is impossible to formulate the hypothetical question of what percentage chance the employee had of still being dismissed even if the correct procedure had been followed: *Davidson* v *Industrial & Marine Engineering Services Ltd* (EAT) (unreported, EATS/0071/03) 24 March 2004 (on redundancy procedures).

10.13.6.2   Types of deduction made

DEDUCTIONS FROM THE BASIC AWARD	DEDUCTIONS FROM THE COMPENSATORY AWARD
(i) Any amount for an unreasonable refusal on the employee's part to be reinstated.	(i) Recoupment of benefits including some part of sickness and invalidity benefits.
(ii) Any amount for conduct before dismissal whenever discovered. There need be no causal link with the dismissal.	(ii) Mitigation, as with ordinary contractual principles.
(iii) Any amount for contributory fault.	(iii) Any contractual redundancy payments which are in excess of the statutory scheme.
(iv) Any statutory redundancy payments already made, but only if the dismissal is for redundancy.	(iv) Any *ex gratia* payments.
	(v) Any contributory fault.
	(vi) No more than 25 per cent of the award (under s. 207A TULRCA 1992).
	(vii) An amount representing the likelihood that the employee would have been dismissed sometime in the future anyway (e.g., for redundancy)—the *Polkey reduction*.

The basic award is not reduced for a failure to mitigate loss, even where the employee has not actually suffered any financial loss (e.g., on getting a new and better paid job immediately). Also, it should be noted that, even where the tribunal has made a finding of contributory fault on the part of the employee and reduced the compensatory award by a discretionary percentage, it still has a discretion whether to reduce the basic award as well, and may (because the two awards rest on different principles) legitimately decline to do so: *Optikinetics Ltd* v *Whooley* [1999] ICR 984.

Where an employer has reached a settlement on compensation with the employee, or has made an *ex gratia* payment, it is advisable that the ambit of either payment is made clear. If the payment or settlement is not expressed to cover the basic award as well as the compensatory award, there is a danger that the employee will still be entitled to the full basic award (see *Chelsea Football Club and Athletic Co. Ltd* v *Heath* [1981] ICR 323).

10.13.6.4   Order of making deductions

The basic award calculation is relatively straightforward, even when deductions are involved. With compensatory award calculations, however, tribunals have to estimate the employee's actual loss and attempt to award a 'just and equitable sum' on the facts. The exercise of discretion thus brings with it obvious problems. What is not so obvious at first glance is the importance of deciding in which order to make any deductions.

The order in which one applies percentage reductions (e.g., for contributory fault or failure to mitigate) may mean that vastly different figures are reached depending upon that order. For instance, say an employee is earning £20,000 net per annum and is dismissed. The tribunal finds an element of contributory fault to the extent that the employee was 50 per cent to blame for the dismissal. The employee has mitigated his loss by immediately finding a new job but it only pays £10,000 net. Ignoring Basic Award etc, what is the loss? If you apply the percentage reduction first, you get: (i) 50 per cent of £20,000 = £10,000; then (ii) deduct the £10,000 earned, as mitigation—leaving you with no loss. But if you deduct the mitigation amount first (£20,000 less £10,000), this leaves £10,000; apply the 50 per cent reduction and you have £5,000 per annum loss.

The cases in this area have been all over the place because the tribunals and courts have been in disagreement as to what elements go to calculating *the actual loss suffered as a result of the dismissal* and what factors go to *reducing loss,* e.g., if an employer makes an *ex gratia* payment to the dismissed employee, does that reduce the actual loss suffered or should you calculate loss and then take away the *ex gratia* payment made? As with the simple example above, the answer can make a big difference.

The conflict in the case law has thankfully now been simplified by a line of cases starting with the decision of the Court of Session in *Heggie* v *Uniroyal Englebert Tyres Ltd* [1999] IRLR 802. These cases, together with all the comments on deductions in the text above give us the list below for determining the order for making deductions. We start with the general rule that any percentage reductions should be made after straightforward cash deductions have been implemented and that the last thing to apply is the statutory cap on compensation (presently £63,000). The only exception to this rule is where the dismissal was for redundancy and the employer has already paid a contractual redundancy payment that is greater than the statutory maximum (presently £9,900) — this is a 'cash' payment but ranks as the second last item. So, the order is:

- deduct any payment already made (e.g., *ex gratia* or *payment in lieu)* other than a contractual redundancy payment;
- make deductions relating to mitigation or for failure to mitigate;
- make any *Polkey* reduction;
- adjust in favour of either party up to 25% for failure to follow the ACAS Code;
- make any reduction for contributory fault;
- deduct any contractual redundancy payment to the extent that it exceeds the Basic Award;
- apply the statutory cap.

A word of warning based on experience: tribunals in different regions often apply their own methods of calculating the order of deductions.

10.13.7   The Additional Award

Where a tribunal has ordered reinstatement or re-engagement (generally referred to here as re-employment) and the employer has not complied with this the tribunal must make an additional award, unless the tribunal is satisfied that it was not practicable to comply with the order. Where the employer has unreasonably refused to re-employ the employee an Additional Award of 26–52 weeks' pay on top of the Basic and Compensatory Awards can be ordered by the employment tribunal (ERA 1996, s. 117(3)(b) as amended by ERA 1999, s. 33(2)).

10.14   The overlap between unfair dismissal and wrongful dismissal

We noted at the start of this chapter that it is quite possible to have the following combinations:

(a) a dismissal which is unfair but which is not wrongful;

(b) a dismissal which is wrongful but which is not unfair;

(c) a dismissal which is both unfair and wrongful;

(d) a dismissal which is neither unfair nor wrongful.

This overlap often causes confusion to those new to the area. The following points are therefore repeated by way of guidance.

10.14.1 Jurisdiction overlap

Employment tribunals have sole jurisdiction to deal with statutory rights such as unfair dismissal and redundancy pay claims. However, in cases such as wrongful dismissal and wrongful repudiation an applicant may choose whether to pursue these claims in the ordinary courts or in an employment tribunal under ETA 1996, s. 3. Employees may pursue actions for wrongful dismissal etc. in a tribunal even though they are not claiming unfair dismissal or redundancy payments.

In the ordinary courts there is no limit to a claim for breach of contract. By contrast, any claim for contractual damages in a tribunal is limited to a maximum of £25,000 (this amount has not changed in years)—even where there are a number of claims involved. The limitation period for such claims is the same as for unfair dismissal (three months from the EDT). Further, tribunals are still restrained from deciding upon contractual points *during* the currency of the employment relationship (e.g., whether an employee's contract has a mobility clause) as well as all matters such as personal injury claims and restraint of trade disputes.

10.14.2 The substantive overlap

Wrongful dismissal and wrongful repudiation claims are concerned only with whether the employee received adequate notice according to the contract and ERA 1996, s. 86 statutory minima (plus the fringe benefits relating to that notice and minus any deductions). Unfair dismissal claims are concerned with the *reason why* and the *manner in which* an employee was dismissed. Whether or not an employee was dismissed with adequate notice is irrelevant to an unfair dismissal claim. Thus:

EXAMPLE 1

An employee has worked for a company for ten years. He is dismissed without notice for absenteeism.

(a) He might have a claim for wrongful dismissal in the ordinary courts or in an employment tribunal if his employer cannot justify the summary dismissal. Justification depends upon whether or not the employee's actions constituted a repudiation of contract which the employer was accepting by dismissing him.

(b) He might (at the same time) have a claim for unfair dismissal in an employment tribunal, *whether or not he was wrongfully dismissed.*

(c) He has no claim for redundancy pay as there is no redundancy situation here.

EXAMPLE 2

An employee (of ten years' service) is dismissed owing to a surplus of labour because the company's sales have been hit by a recession.

(a) He might have a claim for wrongful dismissal if he does not receive adequate notice (here, at least ten weeks).

(b) He appears to have a claim for redundancy pay. Likely as not the employer will simply pay the statutory (and perhaps contractual) amount due. There would be no need to go to a tribunal on this aspect.

(c) He may still have a claim for unfair dismissal on the grounds that:
  (i) the redundancy was conducted unfairly (e.g., selection procedure); or
  (ii) there was no redundancy situation—it was a sham; or
  (iii) the employer correctly claims there was a business reorganisation and not a redundancy situation.

EXAMPLE 3

An employee is told that major changes will be made to her terms and conditions of employment (e.g., pay levels). She refuses to accept these and resigns.

(a) She may have a claim for wrongful repudiation in the ordinary courts or in an employment tribunal. She will claim that she has accepted the employer's repudiation of the contract by resigning. Her claim will be for her notice period.

(b) She may have a claim for unfair dismissal, but first she will have to prove she was constructively dismissed and comply with the statutory grievance procedures.

(c) She may have a claim for redundancy pay, in that she might prove she was constructively dismissed but the employer shows that this was for reasons of redundancy and was fair in all the circumstances.

(d) In addition she may also have a claim based on discrimination (direct or indirect).

10.14.3   The financial overlap

It has long been established that an employee should not benefit from 'double recovery'. Thus any payments, or awards, made for the notice period should be accounted for when assessing loss from date of dismissal to date of hearing. With the introduction of limited contractual jurisdiction for employment tribunals it has been much easier to assess the relevant loss (including therefore both wrongful and unfair dismissal awards) in one fell swoop. In assessing unfair dismissal claims tribunals:

(a) first assess the loss relating to the basic award;

(b) then assess the compensatory award, which in turn is split into the two elements of:

  (i) loss between the EDT and the date of hearing—the prescribed element; and

  (ii) future loss.

As seen above, the tribunal's assessment of the 'prescribed element' takes into account the notice period (and whether it was given or not). Under the principle preventing 'double recovery' the employee will not obtain compensation covering the period from dismissal to hearing *and* be awarded notice entitlement if the notice has already been paid or served out: only the actual loss is compensated. A problem can arise, however, where the tribunal awards compensation (say, £70,000), which includes a figure representing unpaid notice entitlement (say, £10,000), and then, the £70,000 has to be reduced to the statutory maximum of £63,000. Effectively, the employee has been deprived of his or her notice as this has been swallowed up in the capping exercise. One way round this is for the tribunal to first award damages for the wrongful dismissal under its contractual jurisdiction and then turn to the compensatory award. True, in this example it will still be capped, but the difference in the actual amount awarded is marked. There seems nothing in principle to prevent this.

In the unlikely event that an employee has succeeded in a separate county court action for wrongful dismissal claim *before* having the tribunal hearing, the tribunal can still make the normal award but will not give compensation for loss covered by the notice period.

Note: The basic award remains unaffected by all this. That is due to the employee irrespective of any wrongful dismissal claim or proper notice payment because it is equivalent to a redundancy pay claim.

10.15 Calculating the compensation

10.15.1 Tax implications

The possibility of being awarded £63,000 compensation brings with it a need to examine whether tax might be payable on the award. There are two elements to be borne in mind.

- The first is that tribunals have traditionally assessed the compensatory award on the basis of net pay (though this is not strictly a requirement) because that figure represents the actual loss an employee suffers. This equates with how wrongful dismissal damages are assessed (see *British Transport Commission* v *Gourley* [1956] AC 185, HL). In most cases, therefore, there will be no further tax implications on any award made because problems only arise where £30,000 or more is awarded.

- The second element arises where the £30,000 threshold is exceeded. Here, the compensatory award may count as employment income under s. 62 and Chapter 3 of Part 6, Income Tax (Earnings and Pensions) Act 2003 and so be subject to tax. Section 401(1) states that: 'This Chapter applies to payments and other benefits which are received directly or indirectly in consideration or in consequence of, or otherwise in connexion with: (a) the termination of a person's employment . . . '. Section 403(1) states that: 'The amount of a payment or benefit to which this Chapter applies counts as employment income of the employee or former employee for the relevant tax year if and to the extent that it exceeds the £30,000 threshold.'

The effect of all this is that, on any tribunal award or compromise agreement of £30,000 or greater, the employee will receive a tax demand on the amount over £30,000. Therefore, for the employee to gain the actual amount assessed by the tribunal, some 'grossing up' (as described at **9.10.2**) is necessary so that the employee will have the correct amount net after payment of tax (i.e., in order for the employee to actually receive, after all tax is paid, say £35,000, the tribunal may have to award £40,000).

This begs the further question: can tribunals award more than the £63,000 cap as a grossed up figure so that, when tax is later paid under s. 401, an employee will have actually received the £63,000? On the wording of ERA 1996, s. 124 (inserted by ss. 33 and 37 ERA 1999) this appears unlikely as it says 'The amount . . . of the compensatory award . . . shall not exceed [£63,000]'.

It should also be noted that payments made for wrongful dismissal, payments in lieu of notice, the Basic Award, the Compensatory Award, *ex gratia* payments, and statutory or contractual redundancy payments will all have their own rules as to tax, but they all go to the calculation of the £30,000 trigger point. Liability for National Insurance Contributions follows tax liability.

The assessment point for tax will be the tax year in which *payment is received*. This may matter where the dismissal and hearing do not fall within the same tax year and the employee is unemployed at the time of hearing.

EXAMPLE

An employee who is awarded £70,000 (by a combination of the awards/damages noted above) will have this reduced to £63,000 by the capping restriction. Any tax due would then be calculated on the £63,000 figure. No grossing up would be available because the tribunal has reached its limit. Thus, instead of the £70,000 (or even the £63,000) which the employee has been awarded, there will be a subsequent tax bill on the excess of the award over £30,000. For instance, the employee would at some future date receive a bill from the Inland Revenue assessed on, say, 40 per cent of the excess (here 40% × £33,000 = £ 13,200). This obviously means that out of the original tribunal assessment of £70,000 the employee only ends up with £49,800 (£63,000–13,200) in his pocket.

10.15.2 The calculation

Although we have summarised this chapter at **10.16** below, we have not set any self-test questions. Instead, we have set out below an example of how an unfair dismissal claim can be assessed in terms of the technically complex area of compensation. So, on the basis of all that we have discussed above we may now consider a fairly simple worked example. In this case, John Collins, aged 40, was employed at Hall & Lee Ltd for the past ten years. He was dismissed on the grounds of frequent absenteeism. His appeal within the disciplinary procedure failed. He earned £400 per week gross. He was given ten weeks' pay in lieu of notice and has remained unemployed since his dismissal some 20 weeks ago (the present date being the date of the hearing). You represent the company and, on the facts, you had previously advised reaching a settlement. The company had offered £3,500; you could not persuade them to go higher and their offer was rejected. You will argue that the dismissal was not unfair but, on the facts, you are not optimistic. Thus, you also intend to argue that the applicant contributed to his dismissal owing, amongst other things, to his aggressive attitude at the disciplinary hearing. You have already advised that the company are likely to lose because Hall & Lee did not adhere strictly to their own procedures and really dismissed Collins in order to set an example for the workforce. Further, you have grave doubts over some of the company's witnesses. You have calculated that the compensation figure is likely to top £7,000.

The employment tribunal has now made a finding of unfair dismissal. All your fears were realised, except that you think you may have convinced the tribunal that Collins contributed to his dismissal. You are hoping for a 50 per cent reduction.

The tribunal must now assess the level of compensation due. Fortunately for you and the tribunal (and the authors), there is no loss of pension calculation to be made here. The 'recoupment of benefits' figure is calculated at £1,000 for our purposes.

We must consider three basic steps and then make a final calculation. These steps are laid out in **Figures 10.5 to 10.8**.

N.B.: In all these tables the figures apply to dismissals occurring before 1 February 2009.

Steps to be taken	Amount	Notes on making the calculation
Step 1: Calculate the employee's *gross* weekly pay (including the value of fringe benefits)	£400	*This is equivalent to approx. £20,800 per annum.*
Step 2: Impose a ceiling of the maximum weekly wage allowed in calculating the Basic Award	£330	*This is equivalent to approx. £17,000 per annum and is well below the national average wage.* *No real calculation is therefore necessary where the Claimant is earning more than £16,000 per annum.* *If the claimant is earning less than £17,000, then the actual figure will be taken, e.g. £10,000 per annum equals approx. £192 per week.*
Step 3: Make an initial calculation of the basic award *(The claimant has 10 complete years of service)*	£330 × 10 = £3,300	*The maximum figure is £9,900 (see **10.13.2** above)*
Step 4: Make any necessary deductions	£3,300 *less* £825 = £2,475	*Deductions may be made by the tribunal for the reasons set out in **10.13.6** above* *Here a sum of £825 has been deducted for contributory fault (representing a finding of 25% contribution)*
Step 5: The Basic Award	£2,475	*This figure will be carried forward to the final calculation in Figure 10.8 below*

Figure 10.5 Method of calculating the Basic Award.

Steps to be taken	Amount	Notes on making the calculation
Step 1: Calculate the employee's weekly pay (including the value of fringe benefits)	£308	*This time the net figure must be taken after deducting tax and National Insurance.* *The £330 'weekly pay' ceiling does not apply here even if the net wages figure exceeds it*
Step 2: Calculate loss from the date of dismissal to the date of hearing	£308 x 20 = £6,160	*This assumes a 20 week gap between dismissal and hearing as stated in the instructions. The actual gap may of course be greater or smaller, depending on the complexities of preparing the case and tribunal hearing date pressures.*
Step 3: Calculate the sum received (if any) in relation to earnings for this period or notice/payment in lieu of notice received	£308 x 10 = £3,080	*We are told that the claimant received 10 weeks pay in lieu as per the minimum statutory entitlement (s. 86 ERA 1996). This will have to be accounted for.* *The sum here is the net payment, but note that some employers pay the gross salary—in which case it would be that gross sum which would be deducted.*
Step 4: Deduct the sum calculated in step 3 from the loss calculated in step 2.	£6,160 *less* £3,080 = £3,080	
Step 5: Make any necessary further deductions	£3,080 *less* £770 = £2,310	*Deductions may be made by the tribunal for a number of reasons (see **10.13.6** above)* *Here a sum of £770 has been deducted for contributory fault (representing a finding of 25% contribution)*
Step 6: The prescribed element (begin the loss between dismissal and hearing after appropriate adjustments)	£2,310	*This sum will not be paid over to the employee immediately. The employer must wait for notification of deductible social security benefits and only then pay over the remainder.* **This figure will be carried forward to the final calculation in Figure 10.8 below**

Figure 10.6 Method of calculating the Prescribed Element in the Compensatory Award.

Steps to be taken	Amount	Notes on making the calculation
Step 1: Assess loss from date of hearing to some future point	£308 x 15 = £4,620 **plus** £400 = £5,020	*The tribunal will refer to the* Norton Tool *v* Tewson *Principles (see above at* **10.13.3***). A Key part of this calculation is the fact that the tribunal must assess for how long the Claimant will remain unemployed or suffer other loss (e.g., if in employment but at lower wage). Here we have taken an estimate of 15 weeks at the net weekly sum. We have then added a figure for the remaining heads under* **Norton Tool**
Step 2: Make any necessary further deductions	£3,020 less £1,255 £3,765	*Deductions may be made by the tribunal for a number of reasons (see* **10.13.6** *above).* *Here a sum of £1,255 has been deducted for contributory fault (representing a finding of 25% contribution).* **Note:** *As with the 'Prescribed Element' we have taken the position here that the tribunal is satisfied the Claimant has not received any payments which mitigates loss, nor has there been any failure to find suitable work.*
Step 3: The calculation of other/ future loss	£3,765	*This figure will be carried forward to the final calculation in Figure 10.8 below*

Figure 10.7   Method of calculating Other/Future Loss in the Compensatory Award.

To obtain the final figure payable to the employee we need to make the following calculations given in **Figure 10.8**. Note that in these calculations we have not made any *Polkey* reductions because the evidence given in **10.15.2** above was that the employee was dismissed as an example to others so dismissal was not inevitable and no procedures could have corrected this.

Note the net Basic Award calculation (found in **figure 10.5** above)	£2,475	
Calculate any 'Additional Award' (see **10.13.7**)		*n/a here*
Take the 'Prescribed Element' (see **Figure 10.6** above).		£2,310
Take the Net Compensatory Award for other/future loss **(see Figure 10.7** above)		£3,765
Add together all parts of the Compensatory Award to obtain what is called the 'Monetary Award'	£2,250 + £3,675 = £6,075	
Add the Basic Award to the Monetary Award to obtain the total award but note that the prescribed element will not be paid until the recoupment figure has been calculated.	£6,075 + £2,475 = £8,550	
This figure of £8,550 is the amount for which the employer is liable.		£8,550
Deduct the recoupment figure	£1,000	(£1,000)
FINAL FIGURE **This is the sum the employee will actually receive**		£7,550

Figure 10.8   Making the final calculation.

10.16 Summary

As this chapter is central to any study of employment law and, for that reason, is quite lengthy and complex, we provided an overview of unfair dismissal actions at the beginning (see **10.1.3**). The reader is referred to that section. **This summary provides additional points better left until you have read the chapter.**

- In most cases an employee must qualify for the right to claim unfair dismissal by being employed for at least one year. We have seen that there are numerous exceptions to this rule, most of which tie in with 'automatically unfair' dismissals.

- The non-renewal of limited-term contracts does not naturally trigger thoughts of unfair dismissal but we have seen that this area can cause particular problems for employers.

- Although the list is quite short, some employees are expressly excluded from bringing a claim, e.g., those who work outside Great Britain.

- Employees cannot opt-out (or be persuaded to opt-out) of their unfair dismissal rights.

- Unfair dismissal actions depend first on establishing a 'dismissal'. A constructive dismissal is not a cause of action in itself. If a constructive dismissal is proven the tribunal must still decide whether the dismissal was fair in all the circumstances.

- If the employer has shown a fair reason the burden of proof is neutral as to whether this reason was handled fairly. However, most of the evidence tends to be in the employer's possession and, in a tribunal action, it is the employer who usually goes first. The legal burden may not be on the employer, but the reality is that the employer has to demonstrate: (i) that the employer utilised a fair procedure; and (ii) that the decision to dismiss fell within the range of reasonable responses open to a reasonable employer.

- Many, if not most, successful unfair dismissal claims centre on the employer's failure in conducting a fair procedure.

- Compulsory retirement dismissals are treated differently from the other fair reasons inasmuch as they have their own prescribed procedures both for determining the existence of a fair reason and the question of fairness.

- Some reasons for dismissal are classed as automatically unfair; the list is extensive.

- If a tribunal finds that an employee has been unfairly dismissed it may order re-instatement or re-engagement, but this rarely occurs so the most commonly used remedy is that of compensation. Whereas the Basic Award depends entirely upon a fixed formula relating to length of service (subject to deductions), the Compensatory Award focuses on what has been lost up to the date of the hearing and what is the likely projected loss. The touchstone is a 'just and equitable amount'. This, too, is subject to deductions.

Redundancy

11.1 Introduction

This chapter examines the meaning of redundancy, the obligations of the employer, and the circumstances in which the law may give a redundant employee some redress. Rights to a redundancy payment first arose in 1965 and are now found in ERA 1996.

First and foremost, it needs to be stressed that *redundancy is merely a particular reason for dismissal*. Clients—both employers and employees—often miss that obvious point and use 'make redundant' instead of 'dismiss' in the belief it sounds less harsh. Indeed, the really trendy now use a range of euphemisms from 'downsizing' to allowing jobs to 'fall away', many of them obscuring the key legal issue of whether or not the employer dismissed the employee. Lawyers need to be more precise. So we shall refer to 'dismissal for redundancy'.

Why, then, is dismissal for redundancy any different from dismissal for anything else? The answer is that the dismissed employee may have any of four claims against the former employer, three of which are peculiar to this reason for dismissal:

(a) a complaint of wrongful dismissal. This is the one possible claim that is the same as for any other dismissal;

(b) a claim for a statutory redundancy payment;

(c) a complaint of unfair dismissal. Redundancy is one of the potentially fair reasons for dismissal;

(d) a claim for a higher level of severance payment based on some alleged contractual entitlement.

We shall return to those four possible claims in **11.5**. Meanwhile, though, we need to ask two important preliminary questions in *every* individual case:

(a) *Has there been a dismissal?*

This is dealt with in **11.2** below. The definition of dismissal for the purpose of entitlement to a redundancy payment is slightly broader than for the other purposes.

(b) *Was that dismissal for redundancy?*

This is dealt with in **11.3** below. The essence of redundancy is that the employee's job must have disappeared, possibly along with the jobs of other employees.

After looking at those preliminary questions we shall consider in **11.4** a list of steps an employer needs to work through in handling a redundancy fairly, a list drawn mostly from decided cases on unfair dismissal. That will bring us back to the employee's point of view in **11.5**.

The chapter will therefore be set out in the following four sections:

(a) The definition of dismissal.

(b) The definition of redundancy.

(c) Duties of the employer in carrying out a redundancy.

(d) Remedies for the redundant employee.

There is one final introductory comment to make. In general this book deals only with individual employment law: the law involving the employer and the employee. It does not attempt to cover collective employment law involving employers and trade unions, or other employee representatives. In the present chapter some blurring of that rule is necessary. For instance, if an employer failed to comply with a duty to consult employee representatives about which employees were selected for dismissal, that may appear to have little to do with the individual employees. However, the solicitor representing one of them will want to argue that proper consultation might have led to a different method of selection and to the dismissal of someone else instead of the client. Possibilities like that mean that we must mention in outline some of these collective matters at various points in the text. Those advising clients who need to know more may find the ACAS advisory booklet useful, obtainable from its website at www.acas.org.uk.

11.2   The definition of dismissal

As we have seen, redundancy is a particular *reason* for dismissal. It is not something alternative to dismissal. So whether a particular set of circumstances constitutes a dismissal has to be measured against the tests that we considered in **Chapters 9** and **10**. In **Chapter 9** we noted that at common law a contract can end in various ways: resignation by the employee, dismissal by the employer, operation of law, and termination by mutual consent. As with unfair dismissal, dismissal is defined for purposes of redundancy payments more broadly than that. Indeed, the two definitions in ERA 1996, s. 95 and s. 136 are almost the same, and we shall concentrate here on specific points relating only to redundancy payments. In both matters, doubt can arise whether particular events do actually constitute a dismissal.

11.2.1   Uncertain dismissals

In practice the most common circumstance in which doubt arises as to whether there has been a dismissal is the giving by an employer of advance warning of redundancy. As we shall see shortly, employers are required to consult employees before issuing formal notices and such advance warnings are common. Sometimes the distinction between a warning and notice is a fine one.

The basic rule is that for a dismissal to be effective it must enable a precise date of termination to be ascertained: *Morton Sundour Fabrics Limited* v *Shaw* (1967) 2 ITR 84.

In *ICL* v *Kennedy* [1981] IRLR 28, the employer announced on 12 October 1979 that a factory was to be closed by the end of September 1980. K resigned so that her employment ended on 2 November 1979 and, *inter alia*, claimed that she was under notice of dismissal. The EAT held there was no dismissal. A general statement about closure did not permit precise ascertainment in October 1979 of *when* the particular employee would be dismissed.

11.2.2 Constructive dismissals

As we noted in **Chapter 10**, an employee is entitled to resign without notice if the employer has committed a serious or 'fundamental' breach of the contract of employment. Such a resignation is called a constructive dismissal, and under s. 95(1)(c) of ERA 1996 it qualifies as a dismissal for purposes of unfair dismissal law. By s. 136(1)(c) of ERA 1996 it similarly qualifies for purposes of entitlement to a redundancy payment. The statutory language is almost identical and the cases set out in **Chapter 10** therefore also apply here.

A constructive dismissal for redundancy might arise in circumstances like these. The production director in a company retires and is not to be replaced, at least for the time being. His secretary is told to go to work for the production manager. She refuses on the grounds it is a more junior post and resigns. If the secretary's contract was specifically as secretary to the production director, this is probably a constructive dismissal for redundancy. There will be no constructive dismissal for redundancy or anything else if her contract required her to perform whatever secretarial duties the employer requires. In that case she has been given an instruction within the terms of the contract.

11.2.3 Dismissals for redundancy payment purposes

There are three sets of circumstances set out in ERA 1996 which might not obviously seem to constitute a dismissal by the employer but which nevertheless qualify as such for purposes of entitlement to a redundancy payment:

    (a) rejection of an alternative job during or after a trial period;

    (b) anticipation of the employer's notice;

    (c) resignation because of lay-off or short-time.

Case (c) rarely occurs. An employee who has been kept on short-time for a defined period may resign and serve notice on the employer that the resignation is a dismissal under s. 148 of ERA 1996. Cases (a) and (b) occur more often, however, and require further attention.

11.2.3.1 Trial periods for alternative jobs

An employer can escape the obligation to make a redundancy payment by offering a different job as an alternative to dismissal. The employee must be given a trial period in the new job—see **11.4.7** below. Rejection of the alternative job during the trial period is treated as a dismissal, but entitlement to a redundancy payment will depend on the reasons for rejection—see **11.4.7.1**.

11.2.3.2 Anticipation of the employer's notice

It often happens that the employer gives the employee notice of dismissal for redundancy and, during the notice period, the employee manages to find another job which it is necessary to start as soon as possible. Can the employee leave early and still claim a redundancy payment?

Such a resignation is regarded as a dismissal for redundancy and a redundancy payment is due provided the requirements of s. 136(3) of ERA 1996 have been met:

    (a) The employee must be under actual notice of dismissal and not merely have received some vague or preliminary warning.

    (b) The employee must give written notice of resignation. It must be submitted to the employer close enough to the original termination date that the outstanding period is less than the employee's contractual notice.

(c) The employer must not have served on the employee a counter-notice requiring the employee to remain in employment until the original termination date. If that is done, entitlement to a redundancy payment depends on an assessment by the employment tribunal of whether it would be just and equitable to award all or part of it in the light of the employer's reasons. See ERA 1996, s. 142.

There is a way of avoiding these requirements, established in *CPS Recruitment* v *Bowen* [1982] IRLR 54. B resigned in advance of the obligatory period, but it was held that the circumstances constituted a *consensual variation* of the date of termination set by the employer. That was sufficient to qualify as a dismissal by the employer, and a redundancy payment was due.

11.2.4 Volunteers for redundancy

An employer wishing to reduce the size of the workforce will often invite employees to volunteer to leave, perhaps offering some enhanced severance payment as an inducement, and/or giving the opportunity to those approaching retirement age to retire early with some augmentation of pension.

The question arises whether such circumstances constitute a dismissal for any purpose. There is no general answer: everything depends on the facts. Sometimes the termination of employment will be by mutual consent and there will be no dismissal by the employer: *Birch* v *University of Liverpool* [1985] ICR 470. Most *early retirements* are likely to be of this kind. In other cases, however, the employee may merely have intended to enquire what the severance payment might be, and in the absence of any clear mutual consent any termination is likely to be a dismissal.

11.3 The definition of redundancy

The essence of a dismissal for redundancy is that the employer requires fewer people. Redundancy can be contrasted with capability, conduct or the other reasons contemplated in s. 98(1) and (2) of ERA 1996, in that those other reasons imply some criticism of the employee, whose job then needs to be filled by someone else. Redundancy involves no criticism and no need to replace. Employees dismissed for redundancy may have been brilliant performers at their job; they lose their jobs solely because the employer is affected by circumstances often (if inelegantly) described as a redundancy situation.

11.3.1 The statutory definition

The statutory definition of redundancy is contained in s. 139(1) of ERA 1996:

> 139.—(1) For the purposes of this Act an employee who is dismissed shall be taken to be dismissed by reason of redundancy if the dismissal is wholly or mainly attributable to—
>
> (a) the fact that his employer has ceased or intends to cease—
>
>   (i) to carry on the business for the purposes of which the employee was employed by him, or
>
>   (ii) to carry on that business in the place where the employee was so employed, or
>
> (b) the fact that the requirements of that business—
>
>   (i) for employees to carry out work of a particular kind, or

(ii) for employees to carry out work of a particular kind in the place where the employee
was employed by the employer,

have ceased or diminished or are expected to cease or diminish.

That definition is a good example of a statutory provision that is at first sight unintelligible and yet which uses precise words that practitioners will need to borrow when drafting documents. It will be found to envisage four possible sets of circumstances, each of which we shall consider further below:

- The employer is shutting down the business entirely. (The business disappears.)
- The employer is shutting down the business in the place where the employee works. (The place of work disappears.)
- The employer eliminates the work the employee does, either generally or in the particular place of work. (The job disappears in its entirety.)
- The number of people doing that job is to be reduced but not eliminated. (Fewer people are required in the job.)

Before we proceed any further, it is worth spotting two key omissions from the definition in s. 139(1):

(a) Nothing is said about the reasons why the employer's requirement ceases or diminishes. Indeed, s. 139(6) reinforces that point and states that the reduction may be permanent or temporary and for whatever reason. So a reduction in the workforce because of a loss of orders and a reduction because of a wish to increase profits are both covered: *Cook* v *Tipper* [1990] ICR 716.

(b) There is no suggestion of any objective test of the needs of the business. An employment tribunal will not normally go behind the employer's assessment of what the requirement was, at least in relation to examining whether the definition of redundancy is satisfied. (The question of whether the employer acted reasonably is another matter: see **11.4.1** below.)

11.3.2 The business disappears

If the employer ceases business, there is rarely in practice any dispute that the ending of employees' employment was by reason of redundancy. The only complication arises when the employer ceases business but someone else takes over. In many such cases there is no dismissal and no redundancy because employment is automatically taken over by the new owner—see **Chapter 12**.

11.3.3 The business survives but the job disappears

The other three cases—paragraphs (a)(i) and (b)(i) and (ii) in the statutory definition—are not quite so straightforward. At one time, there was much argument about the correct construction of the statutory language. With luck, the uncertainty has been removed by the decision of the House of Lords in a Northern Irish case, *Murray* v *Foyle Meats Ltd* [1999] ICR 827. Before returning to that case it may help to explain the problem.

As a solicitor in practice you will find that private clients often misunderstand completely the legal notion of redundancy. They complain that the employer has described their dismissal as for redundancy but it cannot be so: their work remains to be done and it is in fact being shared out among other former colleagues. A friend-of-a-friend has told them that it is always jobs and not people who are redundant; on that reasoning their job clearly remains in existence. You will need to take the client back to the statutory language and explain that it is the *requirement of the business* for employees that matters. So the friend-of-a-friend is making a meaningless distinction. Yet you may still find that the statutory language causes problems.

Sometimes the uncertainty relates to the *work of a particular kind* that the employee was employed to do. In *Cowen v Haden* [1983] ICR 1, for example, Mr Cowen had been employed as a divisional contracts surveyor, having previously been a regional surveyor, until a heart attack made it difficult for him to travel and he was promoted to a more static job. He argued that the work he actually did was as a surveyor and that, when the employers decided to eliminate the particular job of divisional contracts surveyor, they should not simply have dismissed C as the holder of that post but rather should have made a selection from all surveyors. In the jargon that has since become widely used, the employee interpreted his work in that case by reference to a *function test*; the employer had used a *contract test*. The Court of Appeal held that it was the terms of the contract that mattered and the case became authority for the contract test.

In other cases an analogous question arises in a different form and relates to the place where the employee was employed. Lots of employees nowadays have some sort of mobility clause in their contracts, entitling the employer to move them, perhaps in defined circumstances or with defined notice, to other sites. If there is a surplus of employees at one site but not at another, it becomes important whether the place of work is to be defined by the terms of the contract including the mobility clause (a *contract test* again) or by reference to what actually happens and where the employee in fact works (the *factual* or *geographical* test)?

The preference of the authorities for the contract test in both cases was never popular with the employment tribunals, where lay members sometimes resented having to ignore practical reality in favour of outdated scraps of paper. Indeed some remarkably imaginative reasoning can be found in certain decisions.

In *Safeway Stores plc v Burrell* [1997] ICR 523, the EAT adopted a radical new approach which supposedly reverted to the language of the statute and resolved the conflict between the two tests. Mr Burrell was employed as petrol station manager at a supermarket. There was to be a major reorganisation of the management structure and B was invited to apply for a more junior job as petrol filling station controller. His duties as controller would be less than those set out in his contract as manager, but substantially the same as the work he actually performed. The two lay members of the employment tribunal applied the function test and concluded B was not redundant; the chairman felt bound by the *Cowen v Haden* authority to find that he was indeed redundant. The EAT held that both the contract test and the function test were predicated on a misreading of the statute and suggested that the correct approach was similar to the sequence of questions we set out at the start of the chapter:

(a) Was the employee dismissed?

(b) If so, had the requirements of the employer's business for employees to carry out work of a particular kind ceased or diminished, or were they expected to cease or diminish?

(c) If so, was the dismissal of the employee caused wholly or mainly by the state of affairs identified at (b)?

A little later, the Court of Appeal, dealing with the issue of the place of work, took the opportunity of also going back to the statutory language in preference to either test in *High Table* v *Horst* [1998] ICR 409. The employees in that case were waitresses employed by an agency under a contract which provided for mobility, but they had in fact worked throughout their employment at one particular canteen. The Court of Appeal rejected the employers' contention that there was no 'redundancy situation' because of the mobility clause. They did so on the basis of a pragmatic consideration of all the factual circumstances, and related that to the statutory language in a way that depended more on the geographical test than the strict terms of the contract.

The saga was not yet over. In *Church* v *West Lancashire NHS Trust* [1998] ICR 423, a different division of the EAT, including the President, cast doubt on some aspects of the *Safeway* decision. Furthermore the *Cowen* v *Haden* decision had never been overruled by any court with the authority to do so.

That is the background against which the House of Lords decided *Murray* v *Foyle Meats Ltd* [1999] ICR 827. Murray was employed in a slaughterhouse and was described like everyone else as a 'meat plant operative'. In fact he worked exclusively in the slaughter hall. The employer decided to reduce the number of 'killing lines' from two to one and to reduce the number of staff accordingly. The industrial tribunal (Northern Ireland has not changed the name) had to address the question we have been discussing, applied in this case to the equivalent Northern Irish statutory wording: should they regard the work as that specified in the contract (the contract test) or should they consider what Murray actually did (the function test)? The tribunal and the Northern Ireland Court of Appeal both found that dismissal was for redundancy and the applicants appealed against that decision.

Their Lordships rejected the appeal. They described the statutory language as 'simplicity itself' and regarded both the contract test and the function test as 'missing the point'. They expressly approved the reasoning of the EAT in *Safeway Stores* that we summarised earlier. First a tribunal must ask whether there exists in a particular case one of the sets of economic circumstances described in s. 139 of ERA 1996, and secondly they must ask whether the dismissal was *attributable* to those circumstances. This pragmatic approach based on the statutory language must now be regarded as authoritative, but many practitioners have not found it easy to accept that 30-plus years of authorities are quite so instantly made obsolete. Furthermore, the new approach seems to make the statutory words *work of a particular kind* superfluous and there just may be some scope for further consideration in due course.

The *Murray* decision is so dismissive of most of the earlier cases that it is probably now unwise to rely on any of them. Indeed many reflect history and not the current state of the law. Early cases about redundancy were brought under the Redundancy Payments Act 1965, now consolidated into ERA 1996, and it suited the employee to argue that dismissal was for redundancy so as to claim a redundancy payment. It was the employer who argued otherwise. The arrival of unfair dismissal in 1972 meant that the tables were turned. Now the employer often argues redundancy as a potentially fair reason for dismissal, and it is the employee who resists that, suggesting that there was no valid reason for dismissal within ERA 1996, s. 98.

In *Shawkat* v *Nottingham City Hospital Trust (No. 2)* [2001] EWCA Civ 954, [2001] IRLR 555, the Court of Appeal used the *Murray* principle to rule that the question whether a business reorganisation did or not amount to a redundancy was a question of fact for the employment tribunal to decide.

11.4   Duties of the employer in carrying out a redundancy

A succession of statutes, beginning with the Redundancy Payments Act 1965, and a vast body of case law has now created an extensive list of duties for the employer to fulfil when reducing the size of the workforce. Failure to follow the steps the law expects may make resulting dismissals unfair. We shall therefore now proceed to examine the topic from the employer's standpoint. A solicitor advising a company how to handle a redundancy will need to cover the nine interlinking steps in **Figure 11.1**:

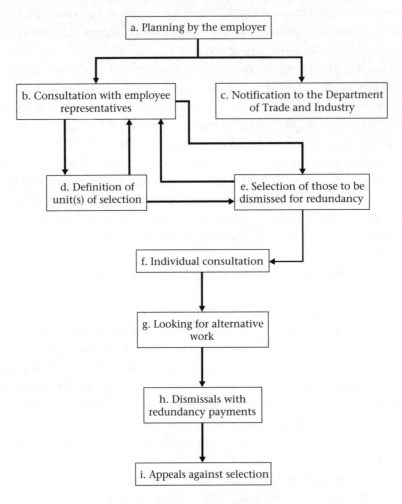

Figure 11.1   Scheme for handling a redundancy.

As the steps are drawn mostly from decided cases about unfair dismissal, this is also a useful checklist for a solicitor advising *either* party about such a complaint. Although the steps are set out in sequence, they interrelate closely and the list must also be viewed as a whole.

Although some of the steps may sound like common sense, some such organised approach by the employer is essential to avoid missing something important. The employment tribunals seem recently to have exposed dismissals for redundancy to particularly close scrutiny. Perhaps it is out of concern that, because employers tend to select for retention the best workers and to dismiss the poorest performers, an unscrupulous employer can use a redundancy to lose those who contribute least but are not so bad as ever to have been warned under a disciplinary procedure. A systematic approach is good evidence that the employer is behaving compassionately and fairly. In practice employers are most often found at fault in tribunal hearings about unfair dismissal in connexion with steps (e), (f) and (g).

11.4.1 Planning the redundancy

The employer's wish to reduce numbers employed normally reflects some kind of business planning and employers often reach fairly clear decisions about what they wish to do. We shall see shortly that an essential part of the proper handling of a redundancy is consultation of employees and possibly also their representatives—see **11.4.2** and **11.4.6** below. It is therefore important that the solicitor contributes to the planning process while redundancies remain a *proposal* and before a firm *decision* to dismiss has been made.

11.4.1.1 The needs of the business

The employer needs to identify clearly why the redundancy is necessary at all. In due course the reason may have to be disclosed to employee representatives and the Department for Business, Enterprise and Regulatory Reform (DBERR, formerly DTI). The form HR 1 which can be used for notification to the Department suggests the following reasons: the employer may find that more than one is appropriate, or that other reasons beyond those on the list are involved:

(a) lower demand for products or services;

(b) completion of all or part of contract;

(c) transfer of work to another site or employer;

(d) introduction of new technology/plant/machinery;

(e) changes in work methods or organisation;

The reason or reasons for the redundancy may dictate in whole or in part the way the employer then has to handle it. In particular, the selection of those to be dismissed will depend very much on the business plan, and especially on the question of what activities (and therefore what jobs) are to remain in the new, smaller organisation.

11.4.1.2 A programme of action

After being guided through all the steps in handling the redundancy, the employer will need to draw up a detailed programme setting out target dates for the various steps we are now considering. There are minimum periods for the collective consultation described in the next section and time will be required for other steps in the sequence.

11.4.1.3 Examining alternatives to redundancy

Except where the employer manages to achieve the required reduction in a workforce by volunteers, redundancy always involves the dismissal of people through no fault of their own and with likely consequent hardship in many cases. The tribunals expect employers to recognise the human cost of redundancy and to regard dismissal as a last resort in reducing costs. Other options should be explored, such as the reduction of overtime, or ceasing sub-contract work.

The point is reflected in a leading case on the handling of redundancies by an employer: *Williams v Compair Maxam* [1982] ICR 156. In the course of its decision the EAT set out five principles to be followed by the employer—see later at **11.4.5.2** for the full list. The first reads as follows.

1. The employer will seek to give as much warning as possible of impending redundancies so as to enable the union and employees who may be affected to take early steps to inform themselves of the relevant facts, consider possible alternative solutions and, if necessary, find alternative employment in the undertaking or elsewhere.

As with so many of these duties on the employer, the important point for the tribunal is not whether the employer has actually adopted any of these alternatives to dismissal, but rather that there is evidence that they were considered seriously. The employer must seek to reach agreement with the employee representatives about ways of avoiding or minimising dismissals for redundancy—see **11.4.2** below.

11.4.1.4   Fixing the number of dismissals

As we have seen, the statutory definition of redundancy speaks of the employer's *requirement* for people to do work. The implication is important. It is not some objectively determined requirement of the business but the *employer's* requirement, and in practice the tribunals almost always accept that it is the employer's responsibility to decide how many people the business needs.

Sometimes it is tempting to challenge the 'need for' redundancy on behalf of the dismissed employee on the basis that the employer could perfectly well have kept the employee in employment. This may be worth trying if the employer has failed to consider alternatives, or if it appears that the so-called redundancy is in truth a cover for dismissal for some other reason. Experience suggests it will rarely do much for the dismissed employee to argue in effect that the employer should have run the business in some other way. The employment tribunals will not 'second-guess' the employer and speculate what they might have done in the employer's shoes. See, for example, *Watling v Richardson* [1978] ICR 1048.

11.4.2   Consultation

11.4.2.1   The duty to consult employee representatives

Whenever 20 or more people are to be dismissed for redundancy, the employer is required to consult employee representatives. This is part of collective employment law and beyond the scope of the book, but any failure by the employer to consult collectively as the law requires may tend to make individual dismissals unfair and this topic cannot be ignored.

The duty appears in TULRCA 1992, s. 188. A solicitor advising a private client may find the following points of help in deciding whether it is worth exploring further. Anyone wanting to know more about this topic should refer to one of the standard works on collective issues or on redundancy.

(a) The statutory duty to consult arises if 20 or more dismissals are proposed. Minimum periods (of 30 or 90 days) are specified depending on the number involved.

(b) Where the employer normally negotiates terms and conditions of employment with a trade union, consultation must be with union representatives. In those circumstances the tribunals will probably expect the employer to discuss all redundancies with the union, even where less than 20 are involved. In cases of 20 or more where there is no union recognition, representatives must be elected.

(c) Amongst the matters about which the employer will need to consult are means of avoiding dismissals altogether, reducing the numbers to be dismissed and mitigating the consequences and also the proposed method of selection—see **11.4.4** and **11.4.5** below.

(d) 'Consultation' is defined by the statute as an attempt to reach agreement with the representatives.

(e) A claim that the employer has failed to consult as required may be presented to the employment tribunal by the trade union or other employee representatives, or (subject to some restrictions) by any of the employees who have been dismissed as redundant.

(f) This collective consultation about proposed redundancy is quite separate from the individual consultation about selection for dismissal—see **11.4.6** below. Neither replaces the other.

(g) It is now dangerous to rely on some of the older cases that suggest that individual notices of dismissal may be issued during the period of consultation, so that notice and consultation periods run concurrently, provided consultation is not made a sham. The current view, as in *Middlesbrough Borough Council* v *TGWU* [2002] IRLR 332, is that it undermines consultation if the employer names those to be dismissed or issues notices for dismissal while the topics at (c) above are supposedly still under active discussion. The ECJ has gone farther still, ruling that the Directive requires consultation to take place *before* the issue of individual notices—*Junk* v *Kühnel* (C-188/03) [2005] IRLR 310. Recent decisions in the UK have followed *Junk*—e.g., *Leicestershire County Council* v *Unison* [2005] IRLR 920. See also *UK Coal Mining Ltd* v *National Union of Mineworkers (Northumberland Area)* [2008] ICR 163.

(h) Agreements resulting from collective consultation must be regarded with care, like any other collective agreement, as they may not be legally enforceable. In *Kaur* v *MG Rover Group Ltd* [2004] EWCA Civ 1507, [2005] ICR 625, the Court of Appeal held that an agreement providing that there was to be no compulsory redundancy was not apt to be incorporated into individual contracts of employment.

11.4.2.2   Remedy for failure to consult

If a claim has been presented to the employment tribunal that the employer has not consulted as required and the claim is established, the tribunal has a mandatory duty under TULRCA 1992, s. 189(2) to make a declaration to that effect. It has a discretion to make a protective award. This is effectively an order to the employer to keep the redundant employees in employment, or at least to pay their wages, for a defined protected period.

The maximum possible protective award is 90 days, which can be a significant extra cost for the employer. There may however be an even greater consequence. A serious procedural failing like inadequate collective consultation (especially if of sufficient culpability as to have caused the employment tribunal to have exercised its discretion to make a protective award) may well lead to a finding of unfair dismissal since the decision of the House of Lords in *Polkey* v *A. E. Dayton Services* [1988] ICR 142—see **11.4.6**, below. An award of compensation is not automatic but could well follow if it can be shown that better consultation might have changed the final result.

Where a solicitor acting for a private client suspects that collective consultation was required but has been inadequate or absent, it is always worth investigating whether anyone has made a claim about that failing. If so, a copy of the decision should be obtained, or, if the other case remains to be decided, an application should be made to the employment tribunal to delay listing of the individual claim until after the collective claim has been decided.

If no claim has been presented, an attempt should be made to find out why not: for example, a trade union may have consented to a curtailment of the consultation process in order to obtain some other benefit (like notice to be paid in lieu in order to escape tax) for its members and any criticism of the employer in such circumstances could be counterproductive.

11.4.3 Notification to the DBERR, the Government Department

An employer proposing to dismiss as redundant between 20 and 99 employees must notify the DBERR 30 days before the first dismissal takes effect. If 100 or more employees are to be dismissed the period is 90 days. The precise details are set out in TULRCA 1992, s. 193.

Although the statute speaks of notifying the Secretary of State, in practice the duty is easily met by completing the standard form HR 1, obtainable from the Department. A copy of the form must also be given to employee representatives.

The form HR 1 is reproduced on pages 349 and 350.

11.4.4 Definition of the unit of selection

We noticed in **11.3** above that the definition in s. 139(1) of ERA 1996 allowed four kinds of redundancy:

(a) the business disappears;

(b) the place of work disappears;

(c) the job disappears in its entirety;

(d) fewer people are required in the job.

Case (d) is different from the other three: not everyone doing the particular job is to be dismissed, but only one or more out of several. Which employees will the employer choose to dismiss and which to retain? This is the very important question of selection, to which we shall return shortly in **11.4.5**.

First, though, there is an important preliminary point: what exactly is 'the job' in which fewer people are required? If that sounds like a non-issue, it is certainly not in practice. For example, many modern methods of production demand considerable versatility from a workforce. So a particular person may operate this machine today, that machine tomorrow and have been doing something else entirely yesterday. To say that the redundancy affects work on one machine in particular reduces selection to a game of musical chairs in which the music stops whenever the employer happens to make the selection. The group from which a selection is made is known as the 'unit of selection'.

This issue is not at all easy for the employer. If the unit of selection is defined too narrowly, employees who are selected will complain that a wider group should have been considered, in which case they themselves might well have kept their jobs. If the unit of selection is drawn too broadly, there will be some employees who argue that the work they were doing remains wholly unaffected by the redundancy, so that their dismissal was not really for redundancy at all. In some circumstances different people could pursue the two arguments about the same selection.

Until recently, it seemed that the second group might well have a good argument. In *Church* v *West Lancashire NHS Trust* [1998] ICR 423, Mr Church was employed in computer services. The hospital trust, like a good many employers nowadays, wanted completely to reorganise that department. Every available job was 'up for grabs' and C, like

Department of Trade and Industry   Trade Union and Labour Relations (Consolidation) Act 1992

Advance notification of redundancies

0390/1

What you are required to do

As an employer, you are required by law to notify a **proposal to make redundant 20 or more employees within a 90 day period.**

- If 20 to 99 redundancies may occur at one establishment, *you must notify us at least 30 days before the first dismissal.*
- If 100 or more redundancies may occur at one establishment, *you must notify us at least 90 days before the first dismissal.*
- The date on which we receive your completed form is *the date of notification.*

How to complete this form

- Use a separate form for each establishment where 20 or more redundancies may occur within a 90 day period.
- Write your answers in CAPITALS, as this will make it easier for us to read.
- Where tick boxes appear, please tick those that apply.
- If there is not enough space for your answers, please use a separate sheet of paper and attach it to this form.
- Please return the completed form to:
  Department of Trade and Industry
  Redundancy Payments Office
  Hagley House
  83-85 Hagley Road
  Birmingham B16 8QG
- You must send a copy of this notification to the representatives of the employees being consulted.
- If the circumstances outlined in this form change, please notify us immediately.

Data Protection Act 1998

We will store the information you give us in a computer system, which will help us deal with it more efficiently.

- We may give it to selected government agencies and Training and Enterprise Councils/Local Enterprise Companies and Careers Services, who may offer to help you deal with proposed redundancies.
- We will *not* give it to any other agencies or organisations without first obtaining your consent.

Further Information

- A more detailed explanation of this subject can be found in our booklet PL833 "Redundancy consultation and notification".
- You can get booklet PL833 from any Jobcentre

1   Employer's Details

Name

Address

Post Code

Telephone number

2   Employer's Contact

Name

Address *(If different to that given at 1)*

Post Code

Telephone number *(If different to that given at 1)*

3   Establishment where redundancies proposed

Address given at **1** ☐

Address given at **2** ☐

Address different to that given at **1** or **2** ☐ ▶ *please give address below*

Post Code

Nature of main business

over ▶

4 Reasons for redundancies

Please tick one or more boxes to show the main reason(s) for the proposed redundancies:

- lower demand for products or services ☐ **A**
- completion of all or part of contract ☐ **B**
- transfer of work to another site or employer ☐ **C**
- introduction of new technology/plant/machinery ☐ **D**
- changes in work methods or organisation ☐ **E**
- another reason ▶ *please give brief details below* ☐ **F**

5 Staff numbers/redundancies at this establishment

Occupational group	Number of employees	Number of possible redundancies
Manual		
Clerical		
Professional		
Managerial/technical		
Other		
Totals		
Number of long-term trainees included in above who may be made redundant		
Number of long-term trainees under 20 years of age included in above who may be made redundant		

6 Closure of establishment

Do you propose to close the establishment?

Yes ☐
No ☐

7 Timing of redundancies

Date of first proposed redundancy ☐☐☐
Date of last proposed redundancy ☐☐☐

8 Method of selection for redundancy

Please give brief details of how you will choose the employees to be made redundant

9 Consultation

Are any of the groups employees, who may be made redundant, represented by a recognised trade union?

Yes ☐ ▶ *please list these trade unions below*
No ☐

Have you consulted any of the trade unions listed above?

Yes ☐ ▶ *Date consultation started* ☐☐☐
No ☐

Have you consulted elected representatives of the employees?

Yes ☐ ▶ *Date consultation started* ☐☐☐
No ☐

Declaration

I certify that the information given on this form is, so far as I know, correct and complete.

Signed
Date ☐☐☐
Position held

For our use

other employees, was assessed for his suitability. He was unsuccessful, but his own job remained in existence. Could he be said to be dismissed for redundancy when he had in fact been dismissed to make way for someone else, and it was another person's job that had disappeared? In *Safeway Stores plc* v *Burrell* [1997] ICR 523, the EAT had held that such a *bumped redundancy* (as the jargon has it) was indeed a redundancy. In *Church* the EAT noted that that part of the *Safeway* decision was *obiter*, went back to the statutory language and held that *bumping* was not redundancy.

Now we have to review both the *Safeway* and *Church* decisions by the EAT in the light of the House of Lords decision in *Murray* v *Foyle Meats Ltd* [1999] ICR 827 (see **11.3.3** above), which specifically approved the reasoning of the EAT in *Safeway*. Their Lordships held that a tribunal must first ask whether there exists in a particular case one of the sets of economic circumstances described in s. 139 of ERA 1996, and secondly whether the dismissal was attributable to those circumstances. Under that pragmatic approach, which takes an overall view of the employer's requirements, it seems inevitable that *Church* would now be decided differently. Bumping may now fall within the definition of redundancy.

Those cases guide the employment tribunal in the view it should take if the employer *chooses* to adopt an approach of bumping. There is no clear rule of law that tells the employer how to define a unit of selection. Provided regard is had to the principles in *Safeway*, the employer is usually free to define the job in whichever way best suits the business. Sometimes, though, the choice is limited. In the example we considered of the versatile machine operators, it is almost inevitable that the unit of selection must include all machine operators.

Cases where the employer will need to take particular care in defining the unit of selection include the following:

- where there is some versatility or flexibility amongst employees affected by the redundancy (as above);

- where people with similar skills or doing a similar job are employed in several departments or functions: should the employer take each such group separately or together?

- where people doing similar but not identical work are employed on different grades or their equivalent, reflecting different degrees of skill: is it appropriate to divide the function into several units or to take it all together, and (if the latter) how does the employer ensure a result giving the right balance of 'chiefs and Indians'?

In all these instances, the important point is that the employer should have considered the choice of the unit of selection with some care and be able to justify the result logically to an employment tribunal. There are no general rules of law as to which answer should be given. So the solicitor acting for a dismissed employee will usually achieve more by showing that the employer failed to address the point than by arguing that a particular choice lay outside the band of reasonableness.

So far this question of the unit of selection has been examined only in relation to the fourth kind of redundancy, that where the job is not to be eliminated but numbers are just to be reduced. Perhaps it is already obvious that the point is in fact of somewhat wider application. When in case (c) we speak of the job as *disappearing*, exactly the same consideration needs to be given to what may be the job. It is not good enough for the employer to treat a particular employee as redundant on the basis that that individual's job has disappeared if one of the examples described above raises doubt about the definition of that job. Similarly in case (b), an employee who is required to be mobile between several places of work may be unfairly selected for redundancy if that is done solely on the basis of his or her happening to be working at a particular site that is being closed on the day the selection is carried out—see **11.3.3** above.

This issue of the choice of the unit of selection is one that ought to be included in collective consultation about the redundancy. Sometimes, even where employee representatives are unwilling to agree with the employer a method of selection for dismissal from within the unit, it is still possible for the two sides to reach agreement about the definition of the unit. The employer will need to consider properly any suggestions put forward by employee representatives: hence the arrows in both directions in **Figure 11.1**.

11.4.5   Selection

We now need to turn to the aspect of the employer's handling of the redundancy which is perhaps more likely than any other to lead to a claim in the employment tribunal of unfair dismissal—the selection of which employee or employees in the unit are to be dismissed and which retained. More tribunal applications are concerned with alleged unfair selection than with any other aspect, and the parties probably have radically different outlooks.

Employees and trade unions often prefer the employer to select for dismissal on the basis of length of service alone, arguing that this is impartial, well understood by those affected and consequently generally accepted as fair. The practice of 'last-in-first-out' is widely referred to by its initials: LIFO.

The employer probably has quite a different view. If the workforce is being drastically reduced, it is extremely important to the employer that the business retains those key skills that are essential to its survival. Some process of evaluating employees' skills and suitability is therefore required.

At one stage there was widespread public belief that LIFO was the normal way to select for redundancy, and it is possible to detect something close to a legal presumption to that effect in some early cases: *International Paint v Cameron* [1979] ICR 429. By 1987, however, LIFO had been described as outdated: *Suflex v Thomas* [1987] IRLR 435. Meanwhile some form of evaluation of employees had become common, and in 1982 the EAT laid down some important guidelines about the way it should be done: *Williams v Compair Maxam* [1982] ICR 156. Those guidelines still make *Compair Maxam* the leading case on selection, but various others have followed since.

We need to consider two main kinds of case—those where some method of selection has been established on a previous occasion, and those where, because no such precedent exists, a method has to be designed from scratch.

11.4.5.1   Use of established criteria, customary or agreed

Until 1994 there was an important rule that the selection of an individual employee for dismissal on the ground of redundancy would be *automatically unfair* if it was in breach of a customary arrangement or agreed procedure. There was an exception if special reasons could be shown to justify departure from the customary arrangement or agreed procedure, but the cases gave a very narrow interpretation to those terms.

The rule caused employers great difficulty. There were many cases where an agreement had been reached during an earlier redundancy, for example, providing for selection by LIFO. Now that numbers were already much reduced, it was impossible for the employer to continue to operate LIFO without risking the loss of employees with skills vital to the survival of the business. The Draconian effect of a rule providing automatically unfair dismissal made it difficult to know how to cope with this practical problem.

The Deregulation and Contracting Out Act 1994 repealed the rule of *automatically* unfair dismissal. It does not give employers a free hand to ignore all past practice or to break existing agreements. Any such action by the employer is now assessed alongside any other consideration of reasonable behaviour under ERA 1996, s. 98(4).

It should not of course be assumed that all past practices are necessarily bad or in need of changing. Many employers who recognise trade unions have reached an agreement on a method of selection for redundancy that can be operated whenever the need arises and is regarded as satisfactory by all concerned.

11.4.5.2   Design of a method of selection

We now need to consider what should happen if there is no satisfactory past practice to rely on. How should the employer select who is to go and who to stay?

There is no single right answer to the question. Nowadays, though, the most common solution by far is to choose a set of criteria and to mark each employee under each of them, to add up the resulting scores, and to select for dismissal those whose total is lowest. We shall look further at this method shortly. It is not the only possibility, however.

Occasionally employers are still content to select on the basis of LIFO despite all its shortcomings although this has become less straightforward since the Employment Equality (Age) Regulations 2006—see **6.12** above. Younger employees are likely to have shorter service than older employees and consequently to be disadvantaged. The employer must justify the selection as a proportionate means of achieving a legitimate aim.

Sometimes the decision rests on a single criterion. For example, if a company has a European sales force of two, one of whom speaks French and the other French and German, it is probable that the second will need to stay and the first to be dismissed, irrespective of their relative sales abilities. The only alternative choice would limit the sales territory available to the company.

Occasionally, the needs of the business can be set out in a sequence of decreasing priorities, so that they can be applied as a series of criteria. So, for example, if the redundancy arises from a decision to reduce the scope of operations in the business, discontinuing one or more activities in order to concentrate on others, the employer may decide first to choose for dismissal those with no experience at all of the continuing activities. Other criteria may then follow to choose a second and third group.

More often, the various factors all have some part to play and it is better to apply them simultaneously. This brings us back to the score-sheet approach we have already mentioned as the most common, certainly amongst large employers. An example of a score-sheet, or 'matrix' as it is often described, is shown at **Figure 11.2**. It is quite common to attach different weighting factors to the different criteria and to have some predetermined tie-break arrangement to distinguish those with equal totals. The tie-break may well be length of service.

Because the matrix approach is so common, much of the guidance to be drawn from the cases is actually expressed in those terms. Indeed the leading case on methods of selection—*Williams* v *Compair Maxam* [1982] ICR 156—is based on that approach. We have already encountered the first of five principles set out by the EAT in that decision. It is now necessary to set out the remainder.

(1. The employer will take steps in collaboration with any trade union to avoid dismissals altogether.)

2. The employer will consult the union as to the best means by which the desired management result can be achieved fairly and with as little hardship to the employees as possible. In particular, the employer will seek to agree with the union

EXEMPLARY MANAGEMENT LIMITED
ASSESSMENT FOR REDUNDANCY SELECTION – JANUARY 2009

Employee's Name ....   Department ....   Clock No ....

Job ....   Date of start ....   Date of birth ....

	D 1 point	C 2 points	B 3 points	A 4 points	Factor	Score
1 Length of service as at 31 December 2006	Less than 2 years	2 years but less than 5	5 years but less than 10	10 years or more	X2	
2 Attendance record a) Days absent during 2005–06	More than 20	20 or less but more than 10	10 or less but more than 5	5 or less	X1	
b) Number of absences	11 or more	6–10	3–5	0–2	X1	
3 Quantity of work	Requires supervision to achieve acceptable level.	Average worker for the grade, normally achieves expectations without frequent supervision.	Always achieves targets and often exceeds them.	An exceptionally good worker, consistently exceeding targets by a substantial amount	X3	
4 Quality of work	Correction of errors is often necessary; work needs to be checked.	Occasionally makes errors requiring correction, but quality usually acceptable.	Seldom makes errors. Usually reliable.	Almost never makes mistakes. Consistently reliable.	X3	
5 Versatility	Limited to skills of own job.	Can carry out tasks closely related to usual job.	Can undertake a broad range of work within department or discipline.	Capable of a wide range of work within the discipline and outside it.	X4	
6 Adaptability	Tends to resist change	Adapts to change slowly	Generally accepts change and adapts well to new ideas	Shows a positive attitude to change and adapts on own initiative.	X3	

Total

Assessment performed by ....   Date............

Approved by ....   Date............

Checked by HR Department ....   Date............

Figure 11.2   An example of a redundancy selection matrix.

the criteria to be applied in selecting the employees to be made redundant. When a selection has been made, the employer will consider with the union whether the selection has been made in accordance with those criteria.

3. Whether or not an agreement as to the criteria to be adopted has been agreed with the union, the employer will seek to establish criteria for selection which so far as possible do not depend solely upon the opinion of the person making the selection but can be objectively checked against such things as attendance record, efficiency at the job, experience, or length of service.

4. The employer will seek to ensure that the selection is made fairly in accordance with these criteria and will consider any representations the union may make as to such selection.

5. The employer will seek to see whether instead of dismissing an employee he could offer him alternative employment.

Since those five principles were first set out in 1982 there has been some criticism of the EAT for adopting the approach in that and several other cases of setting out guidelines for future reference as if they were a statute or a code of practice. Nevertheless, the principles have never been overturned and remain valid. Indeed subsequent cases have tended to enlarge them. We can therefore set out some advice for employers in designing a matrix:

(a) Discuss it with trade unions or employee representatives and 'seek to agree . . . criteria': *Williams* v *Compair Maxam*.

(b) Include some factors on the list that are capable of objective measurement and are not solely subjective opinion: *Williams* v *Compair Maxam*. Subjective judgments can be given a greater objectivity if two or more people are involved.

(c) Ensure that enough guidance is given to those doing the marking that they clearly understand what they are to do: *Rolls Royce Motors* v *Dewhurst* [1985] ICR 869. In practice, however, a competent manager or supervisor is unlikely to experience much difficulty if the categories are clearly defined.

(d) Be careful of vague factors like attitude which appear to give excessive scope for personal prejudice, but do not necessarily exclude them if relevant: *Graham* v *ABF* [1986] IRLR 90.

(e) It is best to include length of service as a factor, although there is no definite authority that its omission is wrong. Using it merely as a tie-break is probably not enough: *Westland Helicopters* v *Nott* (1989, unreported, EAT/342/88). See the remarks at **11.4.5.2** above, however, about the risk of age discrimination. The matrix at **Figure 11.2** gives the maximum mark for length of service to those who have been employed for 10 years or more, a common practice before the rules on age discrimination. Some may now prefer to remove any preference based on service longer than five years, so as clearly not to offend the regulations, but many consider that in this context longer service represents a proportionate means of achieving the legitimate aim of rewarding loyalty, as approved in principle (for a different purpose) in *MacCulloch* v *Imperial Chemical Industries plc* EAT 0119/08.

(f) Avoid any selection criterion which is directly or indirectly discriminatory on grounds of sex, race or the other prohibited heads, or trade union membership or activities. See **Chapter 6** about sex and race etc; **11.4.5.3** below about trade union membership.

(g) Exercise particular care when a factor such as rate of work, quality of output or attendance record may be influenced by the employee's disability: see **6.11** above about disability discrimination.

(h) Ensure that the assessments are made accurately and fairly according to the criteria: *Williams* v *Compair Maxam*. Although this sounds like common sense, simple errors often occur in practice, e.g., misreading a sickness record or making a mistake of arithmetic.

(i) Give some thought to whether employees selected for dismissal will be permitted to see the marks scored by other employees in the unit of selection—during individual consultation, on appeal, only during employment tribunal proceedings (see **13.8.3** below), or never. This is a difficult issue: most employers do not wish to risk demotivating those who, unbeknown to themselves, were 'near misses' for selection.

The example of a matrix in **Figure 11.2** attempts to reflect that advice. In an example at the end of the chapter we shall look at one that does not. While tribunals are unwilling to fault an employer's method of selection simply on the basis that they might have done differently—see, for example, *British Aerospace plc* v *Green* [1995] ICR 1006—many established methods are very susceptible to challenge, especially on the grounds of disability discrimination.

11.4.5.3 Selection related to trade union membership or activities

Under s. 153 of TULRCA 1992, a selection for redundancy is automatically unfair if the reason for it is the employee's trade union membership or activities.

Selection based on trade union membership or activities does not have to be deliberate. An evaluation influenced by trade union activity, perhaps because a shop steward was unable to achieve as high an output as some others because of the amount of time spent on trade union business, may well be caught by this rule.

11.4.6 Individual consultation

After the process of selection, the employer will have decided who is to stay and who to go but the employees concerned do not yet know. The next step is to inform them.

The law makes it very clear that this step involves much more than merely conveying information. Redundant employees have the right to be consulted individually about their redundancy before notice of dismissal is given. The leading case on this individual consultation is the House of Lords' decision in *Polkey* v *A. E. Dayton Services* [1988] ICR 142. It is important and well worth reading. As this requirement forms part of the concept of reasonableness in unfair dismissal it has been possible to argue that consultation is inappropriate or superfluous in particular cases, although the circumstances in which the tribunals have been prepared to accept such an argument have become fewer as a consultative approach to employment relations generally has become more established. In *Mugford* v *Midland Bank* [1997] ICR 399, for example, it was suggested that the employer would have to show that consultation would have been an utterly futile exercise.

What is the employer actually obliged to do? This question is not precisely answered by the *Polkey* decision, although *Rowell* v *Hubbard Group Services* [1995] IRLR 195 gives useful guidance on the need for consultation to be proper and genuine. The authors offer the following as an indication of the approach of the tribunals:

(a) Do not rush the process. Encourage the employee to be accompanied by a colleague. Recognise that the employee may be in a state of some shock from the announcement, and allow time for a response.

(b) Explain to the individual why the particular job is affected by redundancy at all.

(c) Explain why this particular employee is at risk of selection for redundancy, but do nothing at this stage that could be interpreted as giving notice of dismissal. If an assessment matrix has been used, show it to the employee and explain the marks given. In *Alexander* v *Bridgen Enterprises Ltd* [2006] IRLR 422 the EAT held that the employer's failure to provide such particular information made dismissal unfair. While such disclosure is not mandatory in every case, the employee must have sufficient information to understand selection and to challenge it—*Davies* v *Farnborough College of Technology* [2008] IRLR 14.

(d) Give the employee and/or the representative a few days to express any views about (b) or (c) and consider them properly and genuinely. In particular, examine any representation which suggests that the assessment may have been performed incorrectly.

(e) Discuss whether there is any possibility of alternative work—see **11.4.7** below—or any other alternative solution.

(f) Do not finalise the redundancy list or issue any notices of dismissal until the process of individual consultation has been completed. Alterations may be required.

(g) Hold a second interview to confirm the selection if no alternative solution has been found. Issue notice of dismissal only at this stage.

The processes of collective consultation with employee representatives and individual consultation are not alternative processes. However extensive the first, the second is necessary too: see *Rolls Royce Motors* v *Price* [1993] IRLR 203. The required scope of individual consultation may well be reduced in practice by collective consultation, especially if the trade union or other employee representatives have agreed some aspects of the redundancy. See *Mugford* v *Midland Bank plc* [1997] ICR 399. In cases where there has been no collective consultation, individual consultation needs to be especially thorough and to include at least some elements of the topics considered at **11.4.2.1** above.

Solicitors advising smaller employers may well find that these requirements are not well understood. There are still employers without previous experience of handling a redundancy who believe that the whole process can be completed effortlessly in a couple of hours. Thus, whilst selection of individuals may be the most common issue in tribunal applications concerning large companies, lack of consultation is very common amongst smaller ones.

11.4.7   Alternative work

The employer will next want to consider the possibility of alternative work for a redundant employee. Curiously this step arises for two quite different reasons. First, the employer, by making an offer of suitable alternative work, may escape the liability of making a redundancy payment if the employee unreasonably refuses it: ERA 1996, s. 141. Secondly, and quite unconnected with that express statutory provision, there is the general requirement on the employer as part of acting reasonably to seek alternative solutions to whatever problem caused the redundancy, including looking for alternative work for the employee who might otherwise be dismissed. Without that step dismissal may be unfair. We shall look at both aspects in turn.

11.4.7.1   Alternative work as an alternative to a redundancy payment

The rule in s. 141 of ERA 1996 permits two possible kinds of offer by the employer as a means of avoiding a redundancy payment: an offer of employment which is identical to the old job in all respects, and an offer of some different job which is suitable for the employee. The first is unusual in practice and generally arises only if the employer, having dismissed the employee, then finds that the dismissal was a mistake and that the business now has a continuing requirement for that employee after all. In either case, though, the entitlement to a redundancy payment is lost only if the employee unreasonably refuses the offer. In the more common case of a different job, the two elements of a *suitable* job and an *unreasonable* refusal must be considered separately.

The question whether the offer is of suitable employment is primarily a matter of objective fact for the tribunal to assess: *Cambridge and District Co-op* v *Ruse* [1993] IRLR 156. All aspects of the job can be taken into account, including, for example, the level of skill involved and not only the pay and conditions: *Standard Telephones and Cables* v *Yates* [1981] IRLR 21.

The question whether the employee has refused the offer unreasonably often requires consideration of broadly the same matters, but viewed this time from the subjective standpoint of the individual employee: *Carron* v *Robertson* (1967) 2 ITR 484. It is not necessary to imagine the viewpoint of a notional reasonable employee nor to take account of the views of other people who may have been made the same offer: *Everest's Executors* v *Cox* [1980] ICR 415 and *Fowler (John) (Don Foundry)* v *Parkin* [1975] IRLR 89. Thus, for example, if the employer closes one factory and offers alternative jobs at another a few miles away, some employees who have farther to travel to work in consequence may be found to have refused reasonably, whilst others living close to the new jobs may have refused unreasonably.

It is not entirely clear from the cases how far reasons for a reasonable refusal have to be related to the job. The better view seems to be that there must be some connexion. Refusal for a wholly extraneous reason like the wish to take another job would almost certainly be unreasonable.

11.4.7.2 The timing of such an offer

For an offer of alternative work to be effective in denying an employee a redundancy payment the new job must start no later than four weeks after the ending of the old job: ERA 1996, s. 141(1). The offer must be made before the old job ends.

In every case where the employee accepts different, alternative work the first four weeks of performing the new job are to form a trial period, unless the parties expressly agree a longer period for purposes of retraining. At any time during that period or at the end of it, the employee can reject the new job and elect to be treated as dismissed for the purposes of receiving a redundancy payment: ERA 1996, s. 138.

11.4.7.3 Alternative work as part of reasonableness

The cases such as *Williams* v *Compair Maxam* [1982] ICR 156—and in particular the first of the five principles we set out at **11.4.1.3**—as well as the codes of practice make it clear that the employer should always try to avoid dismissals for redundancy if possible. In almost every case that requirement will oblige the employer to take the trouble to look on behalf of every redundant employee for possibilities of continuing employment in the same company or in 'associated' companies, i.e., other companies within the same group of companies: *Vokes* v *Bear* [1974] ICR 1.

In some groups of companies where there are many plants scattered over a wide area, the requirement in *Vokes* v *Bear* is demanding. More recent cases such as *Quinton Hazell* v *Earl* [1976] ICR 296, make it clear that the duty of the employer is to take reasonable steps to look, but not to conduct an exhaustive search. The employer is not permitted to eliminate some possibilities because of an assumption that the employee will not be interested, perhaps because the alternative job is of a lower status: *Avonmouth Construction Co.* v *Shipway* [1979] IRLR 14. The employee should be given the chance to decide, and this is one of the purposes of the individual consultation we considered at **11.4.6** above (see also *Huddersfield Parcels* v *Sykes* [1981] IRLR 115).

11.4.7.4   'Bumping'

Sometimes a redundant employee A is capable of doing other jobs in an organisation and would like to take B's job thereby displacing B who is dismissed instead, a process often referred to as *bumping* (discussed at **11.4.4** above). Maybe B is of much shorter service. The general rule is that the employer is not required to accede to A's wish. Most employers refuse to do so, reflecting the view of the EAT in *Elliott Turbomachinery* v *Bates* [1981] ICR 218 that bumping, a term they described as 'singularly inelegant and esoteric,' was a recipe for industrial unrest amounting to chaotic proportions if applied wholesalely and indiscriminately. (Note that, since the House of Lords decision in *Murray* v *Foyle Meats Ltd* [1999] ICR 827 mentioned at **11.4.4**, employers can no longer safely resist bumping by arguing that B's dismissal falls outside the definition of redundancy.) However, A may sometimes be able to present the same case in a different way, by arguing that A and B are doing such similar jobs that they should have been considered together and the unit of selection was in fact too narrowly defined (again see **11.4.4**). If A proposes bumping during individual consultation the employer is at least under some duty to consider the proposal seriously—*Lionel Leventhal Ltd* v *North* EAT/0265/04.

11.4.8   Redundancy payments

The original reason for a separate legal category of dismissal for redundancy was that it qualified the employee for a redundancy payment, subject to certain rules. So the next duty for the employer is to see what redundancy payment is due to each of the dismissed employees. There are two matters to consider: statutory redundancy payments and contractual severance terms. In addition, of course, there is an entitlement to notice or pay in lieu. The position sometimes appears complicated by the way contractual payments are expressed, so as to include both a statutory payment and pay in lieu of notice. It is, however, convenient for us to look at each in turn.

11.4.8.1   Statutory redundancy payments

In essence the statutory scheme of payments is very simple. As the calculation of the amount (unlike possible entitlement) is scarcely ever in issue, we shall do no more than to sketch the rules in outline. Under ERA 1996, s. 162, the redundant employee is entitled to a number of weeks' pay, depending on both age and service. There is no entitlement whatever below two years' service.

The definition of 'service' is the same as for other statutory purposes: see ERA 1996, ss. 210–219 and also **5.4**—s. 211(2). If a redundancy payment was made at some earlier point in the employee's service, continuity of service runs only from that date—see s. 214.

A week's pay is similarly the same as for other statutory purposes: the normal pay for the normal hours if pay does not fluctuate; the average of the previous 12 weeks if it does; and subject in all cases to the statutory maximum of £330, apparently now also subject to the national minimum wage—see **10.13.2.** above. See ERA 1996, ss. 220–229 for the detailed rules.

The Government booklet on redundancy payments contains a convenient ready-reckoner on the entitlement in weeks for all possible combinations of age and service.

The calculation is almost the same as for a basic award of compensation for unfair dismissal as set out in **Figure 10.12** above:

CALCULATION: [AGE factor] × [SERVICE] × [WEEK'S PAY]

AGE: For any service where the employee was 41 or over the factor is 1.5

For any service between the ages of 22 and 41 the factor is 1

For any service below the age of 22 the factor is 0.5

SERVICE: Subject to a maximum of 20 years

WEEK'S PAY: Subject to a maximum of £330 per week

The maximum statutory redundancy payment is therefore £9,900, i.e., 1.5 × 20 × 330. (These are the figures from 1 February 2008.)

Disqualifications of those under 18 or over 65 were removed by the Employment Equality (Age) Regulations 2006. The Government defends the continuation of the different multipliers for different age bands as justified by the greater difficulty older workers continue to face in finding other employment after redundancy.

If the employee was dismissed with less than the minimum statutory notice appropriate to length of service and thereby failed to meet the minimum of two years' service, or just missed the anniversary of starting so as to obtain one more year's service, it is possible to read forward the date of termination of employment accordingly.

11.4.8.2   Contractual severance payments

There are many employers, especially large companies and those that were or still are publicly owned, which have set up their own schemes of redundancy or severance payments (sometimes known by some other name) in excess of the statutory scale. We have used the term 'severance payment' in this book to distinguish such contractual payments from statutory redundancy payments, but that terminology is not standard and it should not be assumed to apply elsewhere. There is a risk that such schemes (which often provide benefits related to age, length of service or both) may offend the rules on age discrimination. Employers will in general need to justify such schemes as a proportionate means of achieving a legitimate aim under Employment Equality (Age) Regulations 2006, reg. 3 (1) (b), but there is an express exemption in reg. 33 for schemes based on the statutory scheme. A scheme is based on the statutory scheme if it either ignores the statutory maximum week's pay, or it multiplies years of service under the statutory scheme by some factor. In *MacCulloch* v *Imperial Chemical Industries plc* [2008] IRLR 846 and *Loxley* v *BAE Systems Land Systems (Munitions and Ordnance) Ltd* [2008] IRLR 853 the EAT had to examine schemes that were not within the reg. 33 exemption. In both cases the employment tribunal had found that age-related differences in severance terms were justified. The EAT, especially in *MacCulloch*, stressed that tribunals must consider properly both parts of the statutory rule—that the differences relate to a legitimate aim, and that they are a proportionate means of achieving it. The claimants' appeals succeeded because the tribunal reasoning was inadequate, but the EAT accepted that the reward of loyalty through service-related payments was a legitimate aim, as also was greater protection for older workers who would probably find it more difficult to obtain another job after redundancy.

An important question, when employees are then dismissed for redundancy, is whether the better scheme has become a contractual entitlement or not. The tests are no different in this matter from any other examination of contractual status discussed in **Chapter 3**. A scheme that was mentioned in the staff handbook in a section dealing with benefits and rights in *Keeley* v *Fosroc International Ltd* [2006] EWCA Civ 1277, [2006] IRLR 961 was held to be apt for incorporation in the contract of employment, even if its detail was only set out elsewhere. Particular attention will be paid to the circumstances in which the scheme was first introduced and the apparent beliefs of the parties at the time: see, for example, *Lee* v *GEC Plessey Telecommunications* [1993] IRLR 383.

Many employers, aware of the danger of establishing a contractual entitlement that might be a financial embarrassment on a future occasion, take care to explain that better terms are specific to a particular redundancy.

It should not be assumed that any superior set of terms automatically becomes a contractual entitlement because used once or more in the past: it will be necessary to produce some evidence to turn mere practice into a contractual term. The question of whether mere past practice has been turned into a contractual entitlement depends on a detailed examination of all the surrounding circumstances as listed in *Albion Automotive Ltd* v *Walker* [2002] EWCA Civ 946.

11.4.8.3   Cancellation of contractual arrangements

Most of the cases that have reached the courts have concerned employers who have established (intentionally or not) some contractual scheme of enhanced severance payments and who have then wanted to abandon it. A company of some 500 employees and a severance payment scheme that yields an average of £20,000 per employee has a potential liability of £10 million. This is likely to exceed the total value of the business if it is put up for sale, and the consequence of such schemes is often serious for the future of the business concerned.

In such circumstances some employers have sought to bring such schemes to an end and to replace them with something poorer, or even with nothing at all except the statutory scheme. The mechanism for doing so is the same as for introducing any other change in the terms of employment as discussed in **Chapter 5**. Employees or their representatives may agree to the abandonment of the severance scheme, but this is obviously rather unlikely when the employer has no significant inducement to offer. More likely the employer will have to terminate the employment of all the employees on the existing terms of employment and then offer re-engagement on terms that are identical in all respects except for the loss of the severance scheme: see **5.4.4.5**.

Such a mass ending of employees' contracts of employment is, of course, a dismissal and the people concerned will be able to bring complaints of unfair dismissal. The employment tribunal will still have jurisdiction to hear those complaints even though the employees may have accepted the new jobs under protest: see *Hogg* v *Dover College* [1990] ICR 39. The employer will classify the dismissals as for a substantial reason, and the question whether the employer acted reasonably in so dismissing the employees will enable the employment tribunal to examine the importance of ending the severance payment scheme.

The employer will need to consult employee representatives about this mass dismissal under the provisions discussed at **11.4.2** above. This is not because the employees are truly redundant under the definition we have been considering throughout the chapter; clearly they are not. It is because there is a special definition of redundancy for the purposes of collective consultation, introduced to comply with the European Directive on multiple dismissals. Collective consultation is required about all dismissals not related to the individual employee. The employer may therefore find that the very act of seeking to end generous severance payments is argued by employees to constitute a redundancy, and to give rise to an entitlement to the payments! However it is unlikely that any scheme of contractual severance payments will in fact depend on such a definition.

11.4.9   Appeals

Most employers who operate some formal mechanism for selecting employees for dismissal for redundancy then provide an opportunity for those selected to appeal against that decision. This is usually separate from and subsequent to the individual consultation we considered at **11.4.6**. There has been no clear authority requiring such a stage: indeed, in *Robinson* v *Ulster Carpet Mills* [1991] IRLR 348, the Northern Ireland Court of Appeal expressly found that it was not necessary.

While the statutory dismissal procedures have been in force, it has generally been considered that the employer must provide some opportunity to appeal, and we assume that the expectation will survive despite the repeal of the statutory procedures. Certainly, where some appeal opportunity is provided, it must comply with the rules of natural justice. In particular the person hearing it must not be in a position of bias by having been involved in the decision to dismiss. So employers need to ensure that selection is made low enough in a management hierarchy to leave someone more senior to hear the appeal.

11.5   Remedies for the redundant employee

So far, this chapter has looked at redundancy from the point of view of giving advice to the employer before dismissals have taken place. Now it is necessary to look at the other side of that coin and to consider the redress available to an employee who has been dismissed. The principles apply equally, of course, whether the solicitor acts for the dismissed employee or for the ex-employer. As we noted at the start of the chapter, any redress at all depends on establishing that there has been a dismissal, but there are then four possibilities that we shall need to consider in turn:

(a) A complaint of wrongful dismissal, i.e., a claim for notice or pay in lieu of notice.

(b) A claim for a statutory redundancy payment.

(c) A complaint of unfair dismissal, seeking reinstatement, re-engagement or compensation.

(d) A claim for a contractual severance payment.

11.5.1   Wrongful dismissal

The same rules about the employee's right to notice apply to a dismissal for redundancy as to any other dismissal. If the employee appears not to have been given due notice or pay in lieu, you should refer to **9.10**.

There is just one special point that is probably peculiar to dismissal for redundancy. Some severance payment schemes provide a total sum including pay in lieu, a statutory redundancy payment and an additional payment, without any specific identification of the amount of the component parts. At one stage there was a tax benefit to be gained from this device but the loop-hole has now been blocked. Nevertheless the approach remains in some severance payment schemes and it is worth checking that an individual client who seems not to have received pay in lieu of notice is not in fact covered by a scheme of this kind.

In one Scottish case, *Anderson* v *Pringle of Scotland Ltd* [1998] IRLR 64, the Court of Session held that selection on the basis of LIFO had become an incorporated term of the contract and they granted interdict (equivalent to an injunction) restraining the employer from selecting for redundancy on any other basis. Use of the injunction effectively to require specific performance of a contract of personal service is of course contrary to conventional principles of equity, and the case is exceptional.

11.5.2 Statutory redundancy payments

We have already considered the method of calculating a statutory redundancy payment at **11.4.8.1** above.

An employee with more than two years' service is entitled to a statutory redundancy payment and can present a claim of non-payment or insufficient payment to the employment tribunal. In practice most employers are aware of the need to pay redundancy payments and such cases are nowadays rare, except where there is a dispute as to whether the dismissal was for redundancy.

A typical case where redundancy may be in dispute as the reason for dismissal is provided by the example of constructive dismissal for redundancy we considered at **11.2.2** above. The employer gives the employee (the production director's secretary) an instruction to change job (to be secretary to someone else), regarding it as a lawful instruction within the existing contract. The employee regards the proposed job as of lesser status and outside the terms of the contract, refuses to move, and resigns in protest. The employee's entitlement to a redundancy payment will depend upon the true construction of the contract, and that may be a matter for the employment tribunal.

11.5.3 Unfair dismissal

Of the four possible remedies, the one most often adopted is a claim to the employment tribunal of unfair dismissal. We have seen in **Chapter 10** that there are four potentially fair reasons for dismissal (plus the catch-all fifth of 'some other substantial reason') and that redundancy is one of them. Under ERA 1996, s. 98(4), the employer must act reasonably in dismissing for the stated reason. The advice to employers we have been considering in **11.4** above is distilled from cases of alleged unfair dismissal, and therefore reflects the tribunals' view of what constitutes reasonableness when the reason is redundancy. So a solicitor acting for either party will need to establish the facts and then to match them against the nine stages in **Figure 11.1**.

Before we return to that sequence there are two preliminary questions worth asking:

- Was the dismissal truly for redundancy?
- Is the dismissal automatically unfair?

11.5.3.1 Was the dismissal truly for redundancy?

The dismissed employee may have received a dismissal letter which refers to a redundancy, but the solicitor acting for the dismissed employee doubts whether that is really an accurate description. It is worth examining the facts against the definition of redundancy we considered at **11.3** above.

Sometimes an employer will describe as a redundancy the dismissal of an employee, perhaps quite a senior person, who is not considered to have been performing very well but whom the employer does not wish to retain while going through the disciplinary procedure. The redundancy in such circumstances may be rather obviously false: perhaps steps are already being taken to recruit a replacement, thereby demonstrating that the employer's requirement for people to do work of that kind has neither ceased nor diminished. Since the burden of proof as regards the *reason* for dismissal rests with the employer (unlike the burden of proof as regards *reasonableness* which is neutral), the employer who has wrongly described a dismissal in this way will find it difficult to satisfy that burden and the dismissal will be unfair.

The employee may well be unclear whether dismissal in the context of a business reorganisation is for redundancy or not. We have already discussed the topic in relation to dismissal for some other substantial reason at **10.8.7** above. As we noted at **11.3.3**, the question whether there is a redundancy depends on application of the statutory definition as required by *Murray* v *Foyle Meats Ltd* [1999] ICR 827, and that is a matter of fact for the employment tribunal to decide: *Shawkat* v *Nottingham City Hospital NHS Trust (No. 2)* [2001] EWCA Civ 954, [2001] IRLR 555.

11.5.3.2 Is the dismissal automatically unfair?

As was noted at **11.4.5.3** above, an employment tribunal is *bound* to find a selection for redundancy unfair under TULRCA 1992, s. 153 if it was based intentionally or otherwise on trade union membership or activities. This finding is mandatory and does not depend on any question of reasonableness under ERA 1996, s. 98(4). The solicitor representing the employee has only to show that the reason for dismissal was redundancy, that other similar employees were not dismissed and that the reason for selection of this employee reflected trade union membership or activities, whether the employer discriminated deliberately or not. This right covers trade union representatives, safety representatives, and those functioning as employee representatives for the purposes of consultation about the redundancy.

Recent cases suggest that this kind of challenge to a selection for redundancy may be becoming increasingly common. Employees selected for dismissal often have a difficult task in challenging the method of selection adopted by the employer and dicta in *British Aerospace plc* v *Green* [1995] ICR 1006 imply that the task will become no easier. It is suggested in that case that it is sufficient for the employer to show a good system of selection and that it was fairly administered, and that ordinarily there is no need for the employer to justify all the assessments on which the selection for redundancy was based. Against that background, challenge under s. 153 becomes an attractively safe mechanism for attacking the employer's selection. Perhaps, though, as we mentioned at **11.4.5.2**, there are now more other opportunities than there were before the Disability Discrimination Act 1995 came into force.

There is no parallel provision of automatic unfairness if the selection can be shown to be discriminatory on grounds of race, sex, disability, or age but the effect is similar. Such a complaint could, of course, be brought either under the relevant anti-discrimination statute or under unfair dismissal law, or indeed under both. If discrimination is involved, compensation is potentially unlimited. If an employee is disabled and has been selected for dismissal as a result of assessment according to a matrix like that described at **11.4.5.2**, it is often possible to show that one or more of the marks obtained may adversely have been affected by the disability.

11.5.3.3 Unreasonableness

Unless the employee's case can be brought within the special rule we have just described, and if the stated reason of dismissal for redundancy seems genuine, we must return to the issue of reasonableness under s. 98(4) of ERA 1996. Each of the nine stages of the employer's checklist (except perhaps notification and redundancy payments) is worth examining for possible objections. The most likely stages for finding material failings may well be:

- selection (perhaps unit of selection);
- individual consultation;
- failure to look for alternative work.

The employment tribunal will examine those three key aspects of the employer's handling of the redundancy, whether or not they are expressly pleaded in the claim to the tribunal: see *Langston v Cranfield University* [1998] IRLR 172.

11.5.3.4   Remedies for unfair dismissal for redundancy

We noted in **Chapter 10** that the remedies for a successful claim of unfair dismissal were to be considered in sequence by the employment tribunal: reinstatement, re-engagement (if the employee so wished), and compensation. That rule applies in exactly the same way to a dismissal for redundancy as to any other reason.

In practice, except for cases like those at **11.5.3.2** above, orders for reinstatement are very uncommon where the reason for dismissal is redundancy. The employer would need to find someone else to dismiss if ordered to reinstate the employee, although occasionally re-engagement in a different job or at a different place of work may be feasible. The more common remedy where there has been a finding of unfair dismissal on grounds of redundancy is compensation.

11.5.3.5   Compensation in redundancy cases

In principle the rules applying to other unfair dismissals also apply to compensation where dismissal was for redundancy but has been found unfair. However, the following points occur:

(a) A statutory redundancy payment and a basic award of compensation for unfair dismissal are normally exactly the same figure. By s. 122(4) of ERA 1996 the redundancy payment is offset against the basic award. This will normally exactly extinguish it entirely, except where the basic award has already been reduced for some other reason. The scope of this rule is unclear, since deduction by reason of the employee's contributory conduct is expressly excluded where the reason for dismissal is redundancy: s. 122(3).

(b) Any redundancy payment in excess of the basic award is to be offset against the compensatory award: ERA 1996, s. 123(7). This rule includes any contractual or *ex gratia* severance payment but not pay in lieu of notice: *Rushton v Harcros Timber* [1993] ICR 230. However, this offset, like other calculations affecting a compensatory award, is performed before application of the statutory maximum, so that the employer paying a substantial non-statutory severance payment may still have to pay the maximum compensatory award in addition if the employee's loss is considerable: *McCarthy v BICC* [1985] IRLR 94.

(c) There is provision in s. 123(3) of ERA 1996, apparently very little used, that in assessing the appropriate amount of a compensatory award the employment tribunal can include the excess of any redundancy payment (or, as we have been calling it, a severance payment) above the statutory payment if the employee had a potential entitlement to such a payment, or even an expectation of it. This last element of an expectation being sufficient makes the lack of use of the rule surprising. It appears to permit an employee whose dismissal for redundancy is found to be unfair to enforce against the employer a voluntary severance scheme even where that scheme has no contractual basis, provided the employee had some expectation, presumably reasonably founded, of being paid.

(d) The important decision of the House of Lords in *Polkey* v *A. E. Dayton Services* [1988] ICR 142, which we have already mentioned in connexion with individual consultation, also resolved a long-running argument about the effect of a finding that some procedural failing in fact made no difference to a final decision to dismiss. *Polkey* v *Dayton* determined that a procedural failing that truly made no difference to the result should be reflected in the amount of compensation awarded. Since then the tribunals have very often adopted an approach of trying to assess the chances, usually on the basis of a percentage probability (rather than the horse-racing equivalent of odds), that a correct approach might have led to a different result. This is particularly relevant to a dismissal for redundancy. If the dismissed employee was one of a unit of selection of three of whom one was to be dismissed for redundancy, and it is found that the method of selection was unfair, then it can be said that there was a 33 per cent chance the same result would have ensued if a correct method had been followed (unless of course there is evidence that the three were not in fact equally at risk). So, having assessed compensation on the basis of actual gross loss, the tribunal then reduces it by one-third to take account of that probability. Further guidance was given by the EAT in *Cox* v *London Borough of Camden* [1996] IRLR 389, and this case now sets out the correct sequence of calculations. In *Software 2000* v *Andrews* [2007] ICR 825 the employment tribunal had found that the method of selection was not unfair, but that it had been applied improperly. The EAT held that it was not enough to say simply that the claimant would or would not have been dismissed if the method had been applied properly; the tribunal should have assessed the possibility.

(e) Sometimes where the employer has failed properly to consult the individual it is found under the *Polkey* reasoning that consultation would have made no difference to the result. In such cases, compensation is normally limited to wages for a period that the tribunal estimates proper consultation might have lasted—usually about two weeks as in *Mining Supplies (Longwall) Ltd* v *Baker* [1988] ICR 676. Where it can be shown that the lack of consultation had a greater effect, compensation may be greater, as in *Elkouil* v *Coney Island Ltd* [2002] IRLR 174, where the employee was disadvantaged in looking for another job because the employer concealed the likelihood of redundancy for 10 weeks.

11.5.3.6   Civil action to recover a contractual severance payment

We have already noted when considering the matter from the employer's standpoint that there may be a contractual scheme of redundancy or severance payments higher than the statutory scheme. We also noted that employers (especially successor employers following a change of ownership) sometimes try to avoid meeting contractual duties, especially if the business is now less profitable than when the contractual scheme was first introduced.

Employees seeking to enforce a contractual entitlement to a superior severance payment can do so in the employment tribunals as we noted at **5.8** above, but only up to the maximum amount of £25,000. Larger amounts will still have to be sought in the county court or High Court.

As we mentioned at item (c) in the list at **11.5.3.5**, it may be possible for an employee who can show unfair dismissal as well as redundancy to include the *expectation* of a superior severance payment as a head of compensation, even where the entitlement was not strictly contractual.

11.6 Summary

- Redundancy is a reason for dismissal and not an alternative to dismissal.
- There is a precise statutory definition of redundancy in terms of the requirement of a business for people to do certain work.
- The cases lay down a series of steps that employers are expected to take with some care in handling a redundancy. Experience suggests that employers most often fail on three of them.
- First it is essential to consult—to consult representatives if 20 or more people are being dismissed and to consult the individual in every case. Consultation must be genuine or 'meaningful'—i.e., it must not be a sham and the outcome must not be predetermined.
- Secondly, selection of those to be dismissed must be done carefully and in some organised way.
- Thirdly, the employer must seek alternatives to dismissal, including looking for alternative work.
- The redundant employee is entitled to a redundancy payment, calculated according to a statutory scheme that takes account of age, length of service, and weekly pay.

11.7 Self-test questions

1. Which of the following examples involves a dismissal for redundancy and why?

    (a) The employer's business makes and packs foodstuffs for several supermarket and other outlets. One of the largest customers moves its contract elsewhere and the employer declares a redundancy of a quarter of the production workers.

    (b) The circumstances are the same as (a) except that there is no loss of a contract. The employer has decided to reduce costs in order to boost profits and that the factory is currently over-staffed. About a quarter of the workers will lose their jobs. The trade union objects strongly that there is no reduction in work and therefore no redundancy: such chasing of excessive profits is immoral.

    (c) The production supervisor has not been performing well. The managing director tells him that the post is being eliminated and he is redundant. The supervisor then learns that a production director is being appointed, with substantially the same duties but a bit more responsibility, including a seat on the local board of management.

(d) The site in Bristol is being closed and the work is being transferred to another factory in Clevedon, about 13 miles away. The employer says there is no redundancy because work is available for everyone in Clevedon.

(e) In the context of the reduction in numbers at (a) one of the quality control inspectors is to lose her job. She objects. She has never been involved in any of the work under the contract that is being cancelled; the work she does remains exactly as before and she cannot therefore be redundant.

2. Mr Vijay Patel comes to your office while you are out to talk about his recent dismissal for redundancy by St Werburgh's Electrical Apparatus Testing Shop Limited. Your secretary has arranged for him to come to see you tomorrow and meanwhile he has left for you to study beforehand a copy of his assessment form—**Figure 11.3**. You will note he scored 31 points; he was obviously close to retention as a colleague who scored 33 kept his job. Try to compile a list of all the possible grounds to argue unfair dismissal so that you can explore the evidence tomorrow.

ST WERBURGH'S ELECTRICAL APPARATUS TESTING SHOP LIMITED
ASSESSMENT FOR REDUNDANCY SELECTION – JANUARY 2009

Employee's Name   V PATEL   Department   Nai Nine   Clock No   789

Job   Storekeeper   Date of start   7.7.86   Date of birth   31.1.49

	Poor 1 point	Satisfactory 2 points	Good 3 points	Excellent 4 points	Factor	Score
1. Absenteeism	16 days plus ✗	6 – 15 days	2 – 5 days	0 – 1 days	X4	4
2. Output of work	Fails to meet targets ✗	Meets targets if constantly supervised ✗	Output above average	Always meets or exceeds targets; actively works to increase productivity	X3	6
3. Initiative and judgment	Judgment suspect; needs help in organising	Organises work fairly well and judgment usually sound ✗	Uses initiative when required. Uses common sense to advantage	A lot of initiative; a good organiser.	X4	8
4. Attitude	Unco-operative	Prefers the status quo but will change if forced to ✗	Keen to try new ideas and responds well to requests for change	Exceptionally co-operative with any request	X6	12
5. Potential	Will not progress further ✗	Limited promotability; more likely to remain in present job	Will be promotable with greater experience and/or training	Could undertake more senior job now	X5	5
					Total	31

Total   31

Assessed by   J. Morris   Steve Foreman   Date   12. 12. 07

Figure 11.3   Redundancy selection matrix for self-test question 2.

Takeovers and transfers of undertakings

12.1 Introduction

In this chapter we examine the consequences for employees and their contracts of employment when the ownership of a business changes. It is convenient to add the implications for employment of an employer's insolvency or death.

Why, it might be asked, is there a problem at all? If employer B buys employer A's business as a going concern, does the sale not include the employees as well as the premises, plant, equipment, and work-in-progress?

One answer might be that slavery was abolished in this country rather a long time ago. The common law rule of privity of contract requires that every contract, of employment or anything else, is a private relationship between two contracting parties, neither of whom has any unilateral right to assign its rights or obligations to anyone else: *Dunlop* v *Selfridge* [1915] AC 847. Applying that common law rule to the example above, we find that on ceasing the business that is being sold, A will no longer have anything for the employees previously involved in it to do. So they must all be dismissed, and the reason is redundancy within the definition we considered in **11.3**. If B wishes to recruit some or all of A's former employees, it will be necessary to enter into new contracts with them as with A's former customers and suppliers. There will be no continuity of service.

Rather obviously, a rule under which any change in the ownership of a business results in the wholesale redundancy of all those employed by it is incompatible with modern legal principles of employment protection that we have been considering in this book. So there are various statutory rules to give some continuity of employment and to reverse the common law rule in five broad categories of change of ownership. Simple continuity is provided by ERA 1996, s. 218, but there are other matters we shall need to consider:

(a) The employer is a limited company and the ownership of shares in that company changes through some takeover or sale of shares. We shall look at this further in **12.2**.

(b) One legally constituted employer transfers a business activity to another such employer. This kind of change brings in a European Directive as well as the Transfer of Undertakings (Protection of Employment) Regulations 2006 (TUPE). We shall look further at the regulations in **12.3**, and at the Directive in **12.4**. In **12.5** we shall examine which transfers the regulations cover, and in **12.6** the practical effects when they apply.

(c) There is a transfer between associated companies: see **12.7**.

(d) The employer becomes insolvent and a business activity is available for acquisition from the receiver, liquidator or administrator. The various possible kinds of insolvency will be examined briefly in **12.8**.

(e) The employer dies: see **12.9**.

12.2 Share transfers

We need to remind ourselves of the principle of company law that regards a limited company (both plc and Ltd) as a legal person. The company can sue and be sued in its own name, it can own property, and it can enter into contracts. All of those external activities are unaffected by changes in the shareholders' identities or ownership of shares.

Thus, since employees of a limited company look to the company as the legal employer and are not directly interested in what individuals or corporate persons own the shares of the company, it follows that a change in share ownership has no consequence for the position of the employees. Their rights and obligations relate to the legal person that employs them, and that has not changed. This principle applies equally to a small-scale sale of a few shares in a personal shareholding as to a change in the controlling interest, majority shareholding or even wholly-owned status of a limited company.

This principle is of great importance. In the United Kingdom (as contrasted with some of the rest of Europe) most changes in ownership of a business are in fact executed by a transfer of shares. The legal entity that employs employees therefore does not change, and neither do any of the conditions of employment. The courts have shown themselves unwilling to 'pierce the corporate veil' but they are quite prepared to examine critically something described as a share transfer to see whether it is truly only that or also a transfer that falls with TUPE 2006—see for example *The Print Factory (London) 1991 Ltd* v *Millan* [2007] EWCA Civ 322, [2007] ICR 1331.

Since the next kind of change in ownership that we shall have to deal with is much more complicated, it is always worth checking before embarking on any detailed consideration of the application of TUPE 2006 to a particular case that it is not in fact merely a share transfer. Clients often ask questions about TUPE 2006 which on closer examination prove to be about share sales where those regulations have no impact.

12.3 The Transfer of Undertakings (Protection of Employment) Regulations 2006

Before we proceed to look in more detail at the operation of the regulations, it is useful to summarise their effect.

Where there is a *relevant transfer*:

(a) employment is *automatically transferred* (unless the employee objects) with full continuity of service;

(b) the transferred employment is on the *same conditions*—including trade union recognition but excluding pensions;

(c) any dismissal because of the transfer is *automatically unfair* (unless in narrowly defined circumstances);

(d) employee Representatives of both transferor and transferee must be *consulted*.

Those five elements, beginning with the definition of a 'relevant transfer', need to be examined in turn. First, it may help to give an example. Suppose an engineering company makes and sells both agricultural equipment and garden machinery. Its business is organised in two separate divisions for the two sets of products, with the first rather larger and more profitable than the second. It receives an offer for the garden machinery business from another garden machinery manufacturer which believes it could run the division more profitably, perhaps by some economies of scale through combining some parts with its existing business. If the sale goes ahead, TUPE 2006 operate to protect the continuity of employment of the employees in the garden machinery division with unchanged conditions of employment. If the two activities were organised as subsidiary companies rather than as divisions of one company, then a sale of the shares involves no change in the legal identity of the employer and continuity of employment is preserved in any event.

We shall see shortly that a second kind of relevant transfer is a *service provision change*. A good example might be a decision of the same engineering company to cease staffing its security gates with its own gatekeepers and to subcontract security to a specialist company. The difference between this and the first example is that the garden machinery business was an enterprise run (whether successfully or not) for profit; the security operation is an identifiable service to the factory but the first engineering company would never have viewed it as a business enterprise in its own right. Nevertheless, the effect of TUPE 2006 is to preserve the continuity of employment of the gatekeepers.

Some people find it easier to follow such a sequence if it is set out in the form of a diagram, and we hope that **Figure 12.1** may help. It may be useful to keep it in mind for the remainder of this part of the chapter.

The TUPE 2006 Regulations took effect on 6 April 2006. In this book we aim to concentrate on the law as it is now, but we shall find in this subject that an understanding of the current position requires some appreciation of the history. The key stages are these.

- The Acquired Rights Directive 77/187/EEC was the first European attempt to protect the rights of employees when a business changes hands.

- After some delay, TUPE 1981 implemented the 1977 Directive in the UK, but with many restrictions, like the exclusion of the transfer of any undertaking not run as a commercial venture.

- Various decisions under the Directive in the ECJ widened its scope beyond anything most people had expected in 1977. Among its decisions the ECJ found that TUPE 1981 inadequately implemented the 1977 Directive.

- TUPE 1981 were consequently amended in 1993; among other significant changes was the removal of the exclusion for activities not run as a commercial venture.

- Important decisions continued to be made, both in the ECJ under the Directive and in the domestic courts under TUPE 1981, and their scope was widened further.

- The 1977 Directive was amended in 1998. In 2001 it was repealed, to be replaced by Directive 2001/23/EC.

- The UK failed to implement the 1998 amendments separately, but incorporated them and the changes under the 2001 Directive in a new set of regulations, TUPE 2006, which now adopt some of the rules from decided cases in the ECJ and in the UK courts.

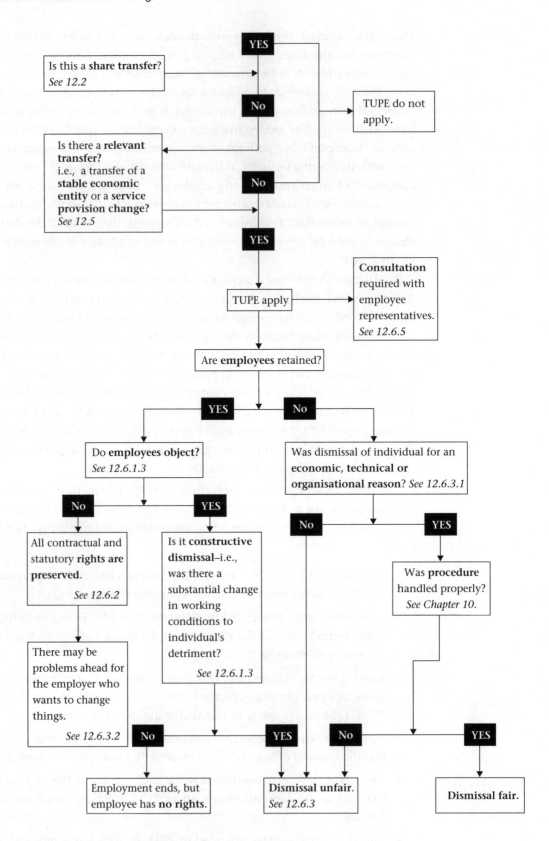

Figure 12.1 Effect of the Regulations.

A recurring theme throughout that history has been the way in which the courts in the UK have been influenced in their interpretation of the statutory instruments by the European Directive and by decisions of the ECJ under the Directive. We need to pause to consider that process.

12.4 The Acquired Rights Directives (77/187/EEC and 2001/23/EC)

Most readers reaching this point in their legal training will already be familiar with the basic principles of the law of the European Union. Indeed you may well remember that many of the leading cases you had to remember were about the Acquired Rights Directive. For the rest, or any whose memory is getting a little rusty, a quick reminder may help.

A European Directive is an instruction from the Council of the EU (after completion of the appropriate procedures) addressed to the Member States and requiring them to legislate within a defined time-scale so as to achieve specified results. Thus the original Acquired Rights Directive was adopted by the Council on 14 February 1977 and required legislation in the Member States within two years of that date. Like most Directives it set general objectives and not precise rules. It contained only ten articles and had the simple aim of preserving continuity of employment when a business changes hands. This simplicity creates some difficulty in Member States like the UK that are accustomed to very precisely drawn statutes, especially since (for reasons we shall consider very shortly) the terms of the Directive may come to be construed in the British courts. To be on the safe side, governments of Member States sometimes 'copy out' parts of a Directive so as to ensure that their own statute complies with the Directive but does not go beyond its terms. The problem arises when such 'Eurojargon' is itself incomprehensible. 'Economic, technical and organisational reasons' are a good example: see **12.6.3** below.

As we noted, a Directive is addressed to the Member States. Of itself it does not establish rights that can be enforced by one person in a Member State (e.g., an employee) against another (e.g., an employer). As the jargon has it, there is no *horizontal direct effect*. A Treaty obligation like art. 141 that we considered in **Chapter 6** is different: it has horizontal direct effect. A Directive has *vertical* direct effect, i.e., it can be enforced by an individual against the state, and this includes the case where the state (or an 'emanation of the state') is the employer. It may also give the individual rights against the state if the state has failed to implement the Directive, according to the rule first set out in *Francovich* v *Italian Republic* [1995] ICR 722. See **1.6** above for further explanation of all of this, but it is not of much relevance to the Acquired Rights Directive. Of much greater relevance here are the circumstances in which a Directive may have *indirect* effect in this country. There are two aspects to consider.

(a) *Purposive construction*

It is now well established that, if a British court is required to construe a British statute or statutory instrument like TUPE 2006 that is intended to implement a European Directive, it must do so in such a way as will as far as possible give effect to the terms of the Directive. One of the leading cases in this rule of *purposive construction* is *Litster* v *Forth Dry Dock* [1989] ICR 341 that we shall return to at **12.6.1** below.

(b) *References for preliminary ruling*

Under art. 234 of the Treaty of Rome any court in a Member State may refer to the ECJ any question of interpretation of a Directive that is relevant to a case it is handling. Often this arises where a purposive construction is being given to a domestic statute or equivalent. The procedure, known as a reference for a *preliminary ruling*, has been used by the full range of courts from employment tribunals to the House of Lords. The courts of the other Member States also use it and, although the ECJ does not operate any strict rule of binding precedents, decisions relating to other states frequently establish interpretations that then have to be followed here. This explains why the authorities cited below, for example, are such a mixture of British and foreign cases.

Few would disagree that the scope of the Directive has been broadened by decisions of the ECJ beyond anything that was in the mind of those drafting it in 1977. In *Schmidt v Spar- und Leihkasse der Früheren Ämter Bordesholm, Kiel und Cronshagen* (Case C-392/92) [1995] ICR 237, it was held to protect the job of a single office cleaner when a bank 'privatised' its cleaning operations. The British courts have then been required to give a purposive construction to TUPE 2006 so as to reflect all these ECJ decisions.

There is one other aspect of the interaction of European and UK law that we need to mention. Under the European Communities Act 1972 a Secretary of State may use delegated legislation in the form of statutory instruments to introduce measures required to comply with a European Directive; primary legislation is not essential. But the power is limited to measures *necessary* to meet the Directive; there can be no 'gold-plating' with anything additional. However, the Government plainly wanted to take the opportunity, when replacing TUPE 1981, to do rather more than that. So there is a separate provision in ERA 1999, s. 38, giving the Secretary of State power to make regulations additional to the requirements of the Acquired Rights Directive.

The result is that TUPE 2006 contain some more extensive changes, and, for example, almost certainly exceed the requirements of the Directive in relation to the sub-contracting of business services. At the same time the Government's stated aim was to reduce the uncertainties of TUPE 1981, although many practitioners are sceptical whether that aim has been realised. The new regulations incorporate many decisions under TUPE 1981 and the original 1977 Directive, so that we need to consider some of the old cases, especially as there are few cases yet under TUPE 2006.

12.5 Relevant transfers

Having looked at the source of TUPE 1981 in a European Directive, we must now return to the five key elements we noted earlier. The various consequences we set out at **12.3** above follow if (but only if) the events that occurred fall within the definition of a 'relevant transfer' in reg. 3 of TUPE 2006.

Under the current rule (but not under TUPE 1981), there are two, alternative aspects of the definition:

(a) there is a transfer of some business activity from *one legal person*, the transferor, to *another*, the transferee, and that which is transferred is an *economic entity* which *retains its identity*; or

(b) there is a *service provision change*.

We shall need to look at both possibilities. Unfortunately the complicating feature in our consideration is that the addition of the very broadly defined (b) as an alternative to (a) is new in 2006 and does not exist in the same form in the Directive. Many of the leading cases from the ECJ and from the courts in the UK on the meaning of (a) are about events that, in the UK, would now fall within (b) and possibly would no longer be contentious, but they still establish relevant principles about the meaning of (a).

Despite the appearance of a back-to-front explanation, it may be best to dispose of the rather broad coverage of (b) before looking at the tighter rules surrounding (a).

12.5.1 A service provision change

It so happened in the early years of TUPE 1981 that many employers, both in the public and private sectors, were considering the improvement of overall business efficiency by subcontracting various activities ancillary to their main businesses. Many employers, for example, found that operation of their staff canteens was costly, and that they could make significant savings by subcontracting the canteen to a specialist company with the expertise, resources, and economy of scale to run it as a profitable enterprise. In the UK the original provision of TUPE 1981 excluding from their scope activities not in the nature of a commercial venture meant that such a subcontracting of the canteen was not a relevant transfer. So employees did not receive the protection of the regulations. But in *Rask and Christensen* v *ISS Kantineservice* [1993] IRLR 133, the ECJ held that contracting-out of the Philips works canteen fell within the scope of the Directive, even though the subcontractor was paid a flat fee by Philips and had no opportunity to run the canteen as a normal commercial venture.

Following that decision and the 1993 amendments removing the 'not in the nature of a commercial venture' exception, the UK courts accepted that such 'privatisations' could fall within the scope of TUPE 1981. However, application of the rules still gave rise to uncertainties (as we shall see shortly when discussing point(a) about the definition of an economic entity and what is involved in retention of its identity: **12.5.4**). For example, one case raised the suggestion that an entity lost its identity, partly because the subcontractor took on none of the original employer's employees—a circular argument and a logical nonsense. In addition there was some conflict in the cases as to whether the transfer of a subcontract from one contractor to another, or its transfer back to the original employer fell within TUPE 1981. (We have not cited these authorities as they are mainly now only of historical interest.) Principals and subcontractors were left in some doubt whether TUPE 1981 applied in given circumstances and tenders often contained contingency provisions or indemnities that made normal business relations difficult.

That is the background against which TUPE 2006 now aim to remove all uncertainty by providing in reg. 3(1)(b) a straightforward rule that every service provision change (SPC) qualifies as a relevant transfer, irrespective of whether it consists of a transfer:

(i)   of activities from client to contractor;

(ii)   from one contractor to a subsequent contractor; or

(iii) transfer or transfer back of activities from contractor to client.

There is no express definition of 'activities' or of 'service provision' but it seems that almost all provisions of services can be covered, including commonly subcontracted activities like catering, cleaning, and security. Additional possibilities exist in some fields of employment: one case involved a firm of delivery drivers for motor cars.

Three exceptions are provided in the regulations. The first exception is to require that before every SPC there is an organised grouping of employees in Great Britain whose principal purpose is the work for the client. An example might be the following. Suppose that some aspect of the cleaning of an office is carried out by a cleaning company with a team of people that goes around a number of workplaces with specialist equipment. If the occupier of the office decides to change contractor, there is no grouping of employees whose principal purpose is that work and therefore no SPC. It would be different if the contractor employed people to work exclusively at that office. It is not immediately obvious that an 'organised grouping' includes a single person, as in *Schmidt*, mentioned at **12.4** above. However, the courts would be bound to follow that authority and we know of one employment tribunal decision in which a single public relations consultant was held to fall within the definition.

The second exception is to exclude activities concerned with a single specific event or task of short-term duration. It seems that the definition requires *both* something single and specific *and* for it to be of short-term duration.

The last exception excludes as a possible SPC the supply of goods. This is a welcome clarification. The constant enlargement of the scope of 'relevant transfer' in relation to the provision of services, especially in decisions of the ECJ, had seemed to raise the possibility of arguing, for example, that the switch by a major manufacturing company of the supply of some component from one supplier to another could be a relevant transfer, especially if the contract was on such a large scale that there was an identifiable group of people engaged exclusively on that work. That possibility is now closed, certainly under UK law.

12.5.2 Transfer from transferor to transferee

If the circumstances we are examining are not a SPC, we need to look at case (a). We have already reminded ourselves in **12.2** that company law operates to provide continuity of employment where a business changes hands through a change in share ownership and that there is no need for any special statutory protection. Regulation 3(1)(a) defines a relevant transfer in terms of the transfer of the business from one legal person to another, and this means that share transfers are in fact completely excluded from the scope of TUPE 1981.

12.5.3 An undertaking or business

The definition in reg. 3(1) of the scope of a relevant transfer provides that it applies to an undertaking or business or to part of an undertaking or business. It must be situated immediately before the transfer in the UK, and there must be a transfer of an economic entity which retains its identity. This formula, which reflects Directive 2001/23/EC, is much broader than that under TUPE 1981 and at least the English version of the earlier Directive. It adopts wording which derives from cases under the old legislation, and it is useful to explain briefly how this has evolved.

Under TUPE 1981 a relevant transfer was defined in terms of the transfer of an undertaking, and that was defined as including a trade or business. Although the terms appeared in the English version of the Directive, the ECJ pointed out in *Schmidt* v *Spar- und Leihkasse der Früheren Ämter Bordesholm, Kiel und Cronshagen* (Case C-392/92) [1995] ICR 237 that there were significant differences in the terminology of the different languages of the Directive. Most used a term better translated as 'economic entity' than 'business'.

Following that decision, the courts in the UK generally interpreted TUPE 1981 as if the term 'economic entity' appeared there, so that the change in terminology in TUPE 2006 has limited practical consequence and we can still rely on many of the older cases.

12.5.4   Continuity of the economic entity

Once an economic entity has been identified either before or after the possible transfer, the next question is whether it retains its identity. This issue requires consideration of the two key questions identified by ECJ in the leading case of *Spijkers* v *Gebroeders Benedik Abattoir CV* [1986] 2 CMLR 296: first, can we identify a stable economic entity before and after the transfer; and, secondly, has it retained its identity as a result of the transfer? In that case the transferor's business of running a slaughterhouse had ceased entirely. After a break in time the transferee took over all the employees except Mr Spijkers, but none of the customers. Advocate-General Sir Gordon Slynn recommended 'a realistic and robust view' that involved considering all the facts. In the particular case the ECJ held that there had indeed been a transfer within the Directive despite the break and the lack of transfer of goodwill. The new slaughterhouse business was sufficiently similar to the old one to say that there was a stable economic entity that had retained its identity. No one factor alone is decisive. It is necessary to look at everything—the function, assets, and employees before the possible transfer and the function, assets and employees afterwards.

Although the *Spijkers* decision pre-dates both TUPE 2006 and the underlying Directive, we suggest that it remains good authority for interpretation of the statutory language in reg. 3, especially as that language can be traced back to the *Spijkers* decision. That is not to say that there have not been conflicting decisions since. Some later cases, both domestic and in the ECJ, especially *Süzen* v *Zehnacker Gebäudereinigung GmbH Krankenhausservice* [1997] ICR 662, seem to involve a step back from the very broad interpretation in *Spijkers*. From time to time the courts have attempted to clarify the confusion by setting out new lists of factors to consider when comparing the economic entity before and after the possible transfer. Often such lists help very little, especially when they are interpreted as implying that one factor should be given greater weight than another. For example, there is no requirement that any property should pass from transferor to transferee; that is merely one of many items on the *Spijkers* list. The Court of Appeal usefully confirmed in *RCO Support Services Ltd* v *UNISON* [2002] EWCA Civ 464, [2002] ICR 751 that the authority remains *Spijkers* and that as no one factor alone is decisive it is necessary to look at the total answer to the underlying two key questions.

TUPE 2006, reg. 4 (1) confirms that relevant transfers include public and private undertakings, whether or not they are operating for gain. This incorporates the decision of the ECJ in a Dutch case, *Dr Sophie Redmond Stichting* v *Bartol* [1992] IRLR 366. The ECJ found that the Directive applied to employees of a charitable drug-rehabilitation foundation who lost their jobs when local authority funding was withdrawn. It is confirmed in reg. 3(6)(a) that a transfer may be effected in two or more transactions, but we shall see from *North Wales Training and Enterprise Council Ltd* v *Astley* [2006] UKHL 29, [2006] ICR 992 in **12.6.1.1** that this does not mean the transfer is gradual: it must always be possible to ascertain a time when it happens.

12.5.5   Some uncertainty

Prior to the replacement of TUPE 1981 by TUPE 2006, practitioners sometimes found it very difficult to say with any certainty whether a given set of circumstances fell within the definition of a relevant transfer or not. There were some conflicting decisions, especially from the ECJ. The Government has expressed the hope that the new rules lessen the uncertainty. In some regards that will undoubtedly happen: in relation to a SPC, technical arguments about economic entities maintaining their identity are now irrelevant. However it would be wrong to imply that all the uncertainty had been removed.

In a case that would now fall within the SPC category in the UK, the ECJ reached a surprising decision in *Süzen v Zehnacker Gebäudereinigung GmbH Krankenhausservice* [1997] ICR 662. Mrs Süzen was dismissed by a school cleaning contractor after the cleaning contract was reallocated from another contractor. The ECJ applied the *Spijkers* tests and found it impossible to identify a stable economic entity that had retained its identity. The second contractor took over from the first no significant assets and no major part of the relevant workforce. There was no relevant transfer. The trouble now was that employers appeared to be able to circumvent TUPE under this view of the rule from *Süzen* by ensuring that the transferee took over none of the transferor's employees. It was a circular argument and a logical nonsense.

In subsequent cases the ECJ seems not to have followed Süzen, but its approach is not entirely consistent. Slightly unhelpfully the ECJ put some emphasis in its decision in *Abler v Sodexho MM Catering GmbH* (Case C-340/01) [2004] ICR 168—that reallocation of a hospital catering contract constituted a transfer within the Directive—on the reasoning that the new caterer took over a lot of catering equipment. The reasoning deviates from the general thrust of cases unless it is seen in the light of the requirement explained above to consider all the surrounding circumstances, in which case it does not indicate that a different conclusion would be drawn simply from the absence of any handing over of equipment.

An interesting example of a case where the ECJ found there was no transfer within the meaning of the Directive occurred in *Ledernes Hovedorganisation v Dansk Arbejdsgiverforening* [1996] ICR 333 (*Rygaard's* case). Here the supposed economic entity being transferred consisted of a part of the work under one specific building contract, transferred with a view to its completion. It was held that the item transferred, consisting of two apprentices and one employee together with some materials, lacked the stability to constitute an economic entity. The Directive did not apply.

The extent of uncertainty must not be exaggerated. In most cases in practice it is reasonably clear whether the circumstances constitute a relevant transfer or not. The problems occur inevitably at the margins. Occasionally large sums of money may hang on the question whether the transferor's employees have continuity of employment and you will find in practice that the application of TUPE 2006 has become a matter of great interest in large firms of solicitors both to the employment department and to those concerned with mergers and acquisitions. Many commercial contracts for the sale of businesses now contain indemnity clauses in relation to the effect of TUPE 2006 and you will be concerned with trying to assess the risk to your client.

One possible difficulty is a long delay between the date of a transfer and the date its status under the regulations comes to be considered. If the matter in dispute concerns employees' rights when their employment is terminated, for example, the question whether they have continuity of employment may not be addressed for many years after a transfer took place. So there may still be cases for some years to come where the relevant law is TUPE 1981, which applied at the time of the transfer.

12.6 The consequences

We have already noted that if a transfer of a business falls within the statutory definition of a relevant transfer there are four consequences, that we now need to examine in detail.

12.6.1 Automatic continuity of employment

Wherever there is a relevant transfer, TUPE 2006, reg. 4 provides that the transferor's responsibilities under contracts of employment pass automatically to the transferee. The rule is expressed as applying to all those employed *immediately before* the transfer *assigned to* the organised grouping transferred and unless *the employee objects*. Each of those elements emphasised requires further examination.

12.6.1.1 'Immediately before'

Not surprisingly, the expression has been exposed to some scrutiny in the cases and an argument as to how short a time constituted employment immediately before a transfer was finally resolved in *Secretary of State for Employment* v *Spence* [1986] ICR 651. The Court of Appeal held in that case that it was to be taken quite literally. A gap of even an hour or two was sufficient to break continuity.

An important qualification of that rule was introduced by the House of Lords in *Litster* v *Forth Dry Dock* [1989] ICR 341, however. In that case, the use of a purposive interpretation led to the imaginary insertion of additional words into TUPE 1981. The words now appear in TUPE 2006 in reg. 4(3) so as to include both those employed immediately before the relevant transfer and also those who would have been so employed if they had not been unfairly dismissed in the circumstances described by reg. 7(1), which we shall consider at **12.6.3** below. See also **12.6.2.4** for an important question left unanswered by *Litster*.

It was noted at **12.5.4** above, that a relevant transfer did not have to occur in a single transaction but could result from a series of events. In *Celtec Ltd* v *Astley* (C-478/03) [2005] IRLR 647 the precise date of the transfer became important in relation to former employees of the Department of Employment seconded to privatised Training and Enterprise Councils in 1990. After some dispute whether a transfer could happen gradually or whether it must always be possible to ascertain a single date, the House of Lords referred the matter to the ECJ who decided that 'the date of transfer' in art. 3(1) of the Directive is always a particular point in time when responsibility as employer moves from the transferor to transferee. In the particular case, when it returned to the House of Lords as *North Wales Training and Enterprise Council Ltd* v *Astley* [2006] UKHL 29, [2006] ICR 992, the employees were allowed the full continuity of service they claimed.

12.6.1.2 Which employees are transferred?

In some cases it is obvious what it is that constitutes the economic entity transferred. In other cases it is not so clear, and there may be people who work both in the part of the transferor's business that is transferred to the transferee and in the part that the transferor retains. For example, in the two-division agricultural equipment and garden machinery company that we described earlier in the chapter, there may be departments such as buying or finance that support both divisions. It is important to know whether such employees are transferred or not.

The answer is now found in reg. 4(1). The employees transferred are those *assigned to* the economic entity. The formula is that set by the ECJ in *Botzen* v *Rotterdamsche Droogdok Maatschappij* [1985] ECR 519. It is essentially a matter of the employee's function rather than of the terms of the contract. Thus a mobility clause in the contract that is not in fact operated is irrelevant: *Securicor Guarding Ltd* v *Fraser Security Services Ltd* [1996] IRLR 552.

The application of the test of assignment to the part of the undertaking transferred does not require the employee to work *exclusively* for that part: *Buchanan-Smith* v *Schleicher & Co. International Ltd* [1996] ICR 547. It is a matter of fact for the employment tribunal to decide, as in *CPL Distribution Ltd* v *Todd* [2002] EWCA Civ 1481, [2003] IRLR 28. Similarly, where a transfer involves two or more transferees, it is for the employment tribunal to decide which employees go to which using the same test of *assignment*: *Kimberley Group Housing Ltd* v *Hambley* [2008] ICR 1030. It was not good enough in that case for the employment tribunal to have split liability between two transferees on a *pro rata* basis.

12.6.1.3   The employee's objection

Until 1993 the transfer of employment of the employee from transferor to transferee was entirely *automatic*. In effect none of the three parties involved had any choice in the matter. Now the employee is given a statutory right to object, but in a strange form. Under reg. 4(7) it is provided that an objection to being transferred has the effect of ending the contract but that it is not for any purpose to be regarded as a dismissal. An objection must consist of an actual refusal to be transferred, and not merely an expression of concern or unwillingness: *Hay* v *George Hanson (Building Contractors) Ltd* [1996] ICR 427.

Regulation 4(9) preserves the employee's right to resign and to claim constructive dismissal if some substantial change is made in working conditions which is to the employee's material detriment. Thus in *University of Oxford* v *(1) Humphreys and (2) Associated Examining Board* [2000] IRLR 183 the employee successfully claimed damages for wrongful constructive dismissal against the transferor when his terms of employment were altered to his detriment. The same rules apply here as under domestic unfair dismissal law—see **10.6** above. In *Rossiter* v *Pendragon plc* [2002] EWCA Civ 745, [2002] ICR 1063, the Court of Appeal overturned an earlier EAT decision that the rules were different. The transferee employer's revision of a commission scheme was not a breach of a salesman's contract, entitling him to resign, and, in any event, he had affirmed the contract by working under it for 16 months. It is provided in reg. 4(11) that all these rules are without prejudice to the right of an employee to resign and claim constructive dismissal in the event of a repudiatory breach by the employer apart from TUPE 2006.

12.6.2   Maintenance of terms and conditions of employment

All employees whose continuity of employment is preserved on a relevant transfer take with them their existing terms and conditions of employment, entirely unchanged except for one matter we shall consider at **12.6.2.3** below.

12.6.2.1   Individual and collective matters

In this country contractual relationships between employer and employee are considered to be individual, even where employees are treated as a group for some purposes. The European origin of TUPE 2006 means that this rule extends to some collective matters as well as individual terms. So all collective agreements are maintained, and this includes trade union recognition.

12.6.2.2   New recruits

The continuity of terms and conditions applies to those transferred at the time of the transfer. Those subsequently recruited into employment cannot claim the same terms: *Landsorganisation i Danmark* v *Ny Mølle Kro* [1989] ICR 33.

12.6.2.3   Pensions as an exception

TUPE 2006, reg. 10 excludes from the automatic transfer of terms and conditions almost anything to do with occupational pension schemes. The exclusion is restricted to provisions concerned with old age, invalidity or survivors' benefits, a clarification apparently designed to ensure that superior redundancy payment schemes linked to early retirement were not included and to bring British law into compliance with the decision of the ECJ in *Katsikas* v *Konstantinidis* [1993] IRLR 179. In *Beckmann* v *Dynamco Whicheloe Macfarlane Ltd* (Case C-164/00) [2002] IRLR 578, the ECJ held that even a pension paid early under an early retirement arrangement in a redundancy was not covered by the exception, as it was not an old-age benefit.

Since 6 April 2005 the Transfer of Employment (Pension Protection) Regulations 2005, implementing provisions under the Pensions Act 2004, have covered the protection of pensions following a relevant transfer. Employees who were members of an occupational pension scheme before the transfer are entitled to have a scheme provided by the transferee, but there is no obligation on the transferee to match the transferor's scheme. The transferee is free to choose the type of pension scheme (defined benefit, money purchase, and so on), provided that it meets a statutory standard under the Pension Schemes Act 1993. An earlier suggestion that the transferee's scheme should provide benefits that are of overall equivalent value to those of the pre-transfer scheme was abandoned. (The detail of the statutory standard is outside our scope, but in many cases it will require the transferee to continue the transferor's 'relevant contributions' to a pension fund, up to a limit of 6 per cent of basic pay.) Many employees who enjoyed good defined benefit schemes prior to a transfer will find the new rules give little additional protection. Under TUPE 2006, reg. 10(4), employees transferred are not permitted to bring claims against the transferor for breach of contract or constructive unfair dismissal based on loss of pension rights.

12.6.2.4   Maintenance of terms and the possibility of variation

TUPE 2006, reg. 4(2) preserves the employee's contract of employment so that the terms of employment with the transferee after the transfer or for a reason connected with it are exactly the same (except for pensions) as those with the transferor beforehand.

Let us return to the earlier example in **12.3** above. The engineering company wanted to sell the garden machinery business because it was not sufficiently profitable. The transferee wanted to buy it because it hoped to make it more profitable. The difference in profitability will not be achieved by magic. The new owner will need to cut costs by integrating the undertaking transferred into the existing garden machinery business. Employees will need to be interchangeable between old and new businesses, but this may well be unrealistic if conditions of employment are sufficiently different as to cause resentment between the two groups of employees. Very often one group will have a better condition under one head and a poorer condition under another. The employer may well be able to obtain the agreement of individuals or their trade union to some programme of harmonisation. The question is whether that is permitted under TUPE 2006 and we shall return to it at **12.6.4** below.

It is not only benefits to the employee that may be in issue. In *Crédit Suisse First Boston (Europe) Ltd* v *Lister* [1999] ICR 794, the Court of Appeal had to consider a case in which the transferee had given employees additional benefits in return for a post-termination restraint. The transferee now tried to enforce the latter. The Court held that the change in terms and conditions was by reason of the transfer, and therefore void under reg. 4.

12.6.3   **Automatically unfair dismissal**

By reg. 7 of TUPE 2006, any dismissal of an employee by transferor or transferee *because* of the transfer or for a reason connected with it is automatically unfair, unless it can be shown to be for an 'economic, technical or organisational reason entailing changes in the workforce'. This is a strict rule. If it applies and the case does not fall within the exception, dismissal is always *automatically unfair*. If the exception applies, this is deemed to be a fair reason under s. 98(2) of ERA 1996 (either redundancy or some other substantial reason) and the tribunal will proceed to consider whether the employer acted reasonably. The requirement for qualifying service of one year applies as for other complaints of unfair dismissal: see **Chapter 10**.

In *Morris* v *John Grose Group Ltd* [1998] ICR 655 the EAT was required to consider a dismissal by receivers *before* any transfer had been arranged. They rejected the contention that the equivalent of reg. 7 presupposed the existence of a particular transfer and held that it still applied if dismissal was because of a transfer still to be arranged.

12.6.3.1 Economic, technical, and organisational reasons

The words 'economic, technical or organisational' ('eto') are taken literally from the Directive and it is not immediately clear what they are intended to mean in the law of this country. Each of them must also involve changes in the workforce. Some Government guidance given earlier on the application of TUPE 1981 to privatisations in the public sector gave three examples:

(a) An *economic* reason might arise where demand for the employer's output has fallen to such an extent that profitability could not be sustained unless staff were dismissed.

(b) A *technical* reason might arise where the transferee wishes to use new technology and the transferor's employees do not have the necessary skills.

(c) An *organisational* reason might arise where the transferee operates at a different location from the transferor and it is not practical to relocate the staff.

For the exception to have any effect it must be shown that the 'eto' reason entailing changes in the workforce was indeed the actual reason for dismissal in a particular case. In *Berriman* v *Delabole Slate* [1985] ICR 546, the transferee sought to standardise conditions of employment for newly transferred and existing employees and Berriman resigned, claiming constructive dismissal. The Court of Appeal held that the actual reason for dismissal was not one entailing changes in the workforce. See also *Crawford* v *Swinton Insurance* [1990] ICR 85.

We noted in **Chapter 10** that under the general law of unfair dismissal the tests of fairness and of a constructive dismissal were different so that not every constructive dismissal is unfair. We must ask whether the same can be true here, given the different definition of constructive dismissal we considered at **12.6.1.3** above. Can the employer who has altered terms of employment to the employee's detriment then claim an 'eto' reason for doing so? In theory it has to be possible, but the *Berriman* decision suggests it is so unlikely that we have not allowed for it in the algorithm at **Figure 12.1**.

In many actual examples there is a conflict between two very practical sets of considerations. The transferor wants to dispose of the undertaking because it is not sufficiently profitable. The transferee sees a prospect of making it profitable by combining it with an existing business and achieving some economies of scale, in other words by employing fewer people in the combined business.

To put too strict a test on the employer would discourage transfers and improved efficiency in business; to put too easy a test would undermine the whole purpose of TUPE 2006 and the Directive. The compromise the tribunals seem to have evolved puts a fairly broad interpretation on an 'eto' *reason* but then investigates quite thoroughly whether the employer behaved *reasonably*. This happened in *Meikle* v *McPhail* [1983] IRLR 351, where the business was a public house and its small size was held to be a relevant factor in determining reasonableness in dismissing a barmaid.

The Court of Appeal has examined the scope of economic reasons within the 'eto' exception. In *Warner* v *Adnet Ltd* [1998] ICR 1056 they confirmed that 'eto' cases form an exception to the general rule of automatic unfairness and that consequently reg. 7(1) and reg. 7(2) are not mutually exclusive. The dismissal of an accountant in that case was for redundancy, and was held to be fair (despite a lack of consultation) because of the urgency of the transferor's financial problems. In *Hynd* v *Armstrong* [2007] CSIH 16, [2007] IRLR 338 the claimant had been a solicitor in the transferor's firm who dismissed him before the transfer because he was surplus to the requirements of the transferee. It was held that it was not within the 'eto' exception for the transferor to anticipate the transferee's future business requirements in this way: transferor and transferee could each use it only in relation to their own future conduct of the business. The Court of Session contrasted the position in *Warner* where the transferor's dismissal of the claimant for redundancy was required in any event, quite apart from the transfer.

12.6.4 Variation of contractual terms

We must now return to try to answer the question we left unanswered in **12.6.2.4**. When, following a relevant transfer, can the employer change terms of employment for transferred employees? There is express provision in TUPE 2006, reg. 4(4) and (5) that appears designed to try to provide an answer. This is a new provision not found in TUPE 1981. A variation of the employee's contract is void in either of two circumstances; if:

(a) the reason is the transfer itself; or

(b) the reason is connected with the transfer and it is not an 'eto' reason entailing changes in the workforce.

However, the employer and employee are permitted to agree a variation:

(a) if the reason is connected with the transfer and it is an 'eto' reason entailing changes in the workforce; or

(b) the reason is unconnected with the transfer.

This formula seems strange. It is not immediately clear why it is permitted to vary a contract for an 'eto' reason entailing changes in the workforce if the reason is merely connected with the transfer, but not if it is the transfer itself. That may be a fine distinction in many cases. Furthermore the formula does not seem to provide much clarity regarding the unresolved issue from the old rules under TUPE 1981. The leading authority is the House of Lords decision in the joined cases of *British Fuels Ltd* v *Baxendale*; *Wilson* v *St Helens Borough Council* [1998] IRLR 706.

Mr Wilson and some others were employed by Lancashire County Council at a children's home. The council gave notice that they would cease to run the home and St Helens Council agreed to take it over, but on condition that it would not be a charge on their resources. As a result of negotiations between the transferor and a trade union, it was agreed that some staff would be redeployed to other jobs and others (including W) would be dismissed for redundancy by the transferor and re-engaged by the transferee on different terms and conditions. Subsequently, W argued that TUPE 1981 operated to preserve continuity of employment on identical terms and complained of unlawful deductions from wages by the transferee. The EAT found in his favour on the basis that the reason for the variation was the transfer of the undertaking. It therefore offended reg. 5 (equivalent to new reg. 4) despite the passage of time. That decision suggested that employers would have considerable difficulty in rationalising conditions of employment in circumstances such as were set out above.

The Court of Appeal noted that W had been dismissed by the transferor and that the employment tribunal had expressly found that the dismissal was not automatically unfair. It was not merely because of the transfer, but for an 'eto' reason entailing changes in the workforce. His argument of continuity of employment therefore failed, because it depended on the rule in *Litster* (see **12.6.1.1** above), which only applied to those automatically unfairly dismissed before the transfer.

Mr Meade had been employed as a plant operator by National Fuel Distributors Ltd who had then merged with another company in circumstances that constituted a relevant transfer to form British Fuels Ltd. M was dismissed by the transferor, given a redundancy payment and was re-engaged by the transferee on less favourable terms. Here there was no evidence to bring M's dismissal within the 'eto' exception. The evidence suggested it was *because of* the transfer. The Court of Appeal found that he could therefore claim the benefit of the rule in *Litster* which gave continuity of employment with the transferee on unchanged conditions of employment. Mr Baxendale's case raised similar issues although the employment tribunal found that he had not been dismissed at all, at the relevant time.

The Court of Appeal decision brought out into the open a difficult question that had remained unresolved since the decision in *Litster* v *Forth Dry Dock* [1989] ICR 341. Where an employee is dismissed shortly before a transfer by the transferor, does reg. 8 (similar to new reg. 7) operate to give the employee a remedy against the transferor for unfair dismissal, or does the rule in *Litster* make the dismissal a nullity, so that automatic transfer of employment occurs, and any remedy is then against the transferee?

The House of Lords gave a clear answer to the unresolved question. Reviewing the history of ECJ decisions, they rule that the equivalent of new reg. 7 gives a right to compensation but does not provide for a dismissal to be nullified. They analyse in some detail the speeches of the Law Lords in *Litster* and hold that they should be construed as deeming the contract of employment to be kept alive only for the purpose of enforcing rights for breach of it or enforcing statutory rights dependent on it. A dismissal that offends reg. 7 is *unfair* but nevertheless *legally effective*.

Although the House of Lords has very helpfully given a clear answer to the question whether a pre-transfer dismissal is at risk of being nullified, they have not disposed so finally of the question we posed at **12.6.2.4**: when can the employer safely change terms and conditions after a relevant transfer?

The question was of course raised by the cases of each of the three applicants in *British Fuels* but it became irrelevant in relation to *Wilson* and *Meade* because of the decision on the first point that their dismissals were not a nullity and in relation to *Baxendale* because of a finding of fact by the employment tribunal that he had accepted a variation of conditions. Comments on the issue of when conditions can lawfully be varied were therefore *obiter*. Lord Slynn of Hadley (with whom the other Law Lords agreed) rejected the argument that the automatic preservation of rights and duties under reg. 4 (new numbering) was restricted to the time of the transfer. A purported variation would still be invalid if *due to the transfer and for no other reason even if it came later*. He accepted that there must come a time when the link with the transfer could be said to be broken, but said that, if the appeal turned on that point, he would refer it to the ECJ under art. 234. He did not venture any further guidance on it.

In practice the question remains a very real one in circumstances such as we discussed earlier. In most examples, the transferor wants to dispose of some business undertaking because it is not sufficiently profitable. The transferee is prepared to take it over in order to put into effect some rationalisation plan that will improve efficiency. The rationalisation does not necessarily involve dismissing anyone. It sometimes will, but it may also involve harmonisation of conditions of employment, especially if the transferee wants to amalgamate the transferred undertaking with an existing enterprise. The solicitor will be asked when it is safe to take such steps. After *British Fuels* it seems that the answer has to be a pragmatic one based on common sense. If the variation is *due to* the transfer and for *no other reason* it is invalid according to Lord Slynn's dictum. If it is for an 'eto' reason involving changes in the workforce, it is possible to read across the language of reg. 7 into reg. 4 (new numbering) and the variation will not be due solely to the transfer. We can now recognise Lord Slynn's dictum as lying behind the formula we encountered in reg. 4(4), (whose rationale was not immediately clear). There is no exception within that formula for harmonisation of the conditions of transferred employees with those of the transferee's existing workforce, despite the likely importance of that process to a transferee who wants to maintain good employee relations. However, the more time has passed since the transfer, the more difficult it will be for a claimant to show that the variation was due solely to the transfer. That was the approach adopted by the EAT in *Solectron Scotland Ltd* v *Roper* [2004] IRLR 4 which traces the authority for it right back to the ECJ decision in *Foreningen af Arbejdsledere i Danmark* v *Daddy's Dance Hall A/S* (324/86) [1988] IRLR 315.

It would be futile to pretend that the difficulty of providing clear advice in these cases has been removed. Sometimes the willingness of the ECJ to answer preliminary questions referred to it in ways that seem to try to face in opposite directions at once is particularly frustrating to practitioners, and shows less appreciation than Lord Slynn of the need for employers to know where they stand in advance of acquiring near-insolvent businesses. In *Boor* v *Ministre de la Fonction publique et de la Réforme administrative* (C-425/02), [2005] IRLR 61 the ECJ was asked whether the Acquired Rights Directive precluded the Luxembourg Ministry of National Education from reducing the pay of an employee transferred from a private not-for-profit organisation, because she was now placed on a public sector contract governed by national pay scales under national law. The ECJ held that Directive 77/187 did not preclude such a reduction, provided the competent authorities took account of the purpose of the Directive, and in particular the employee's length of service if pay depended on it. However if there was a substantial reduction in the employee's remuneration, that fell within art. 4(2) of the Directive, entitling the employee to resign and claim constructive dismissal. No British solicitor specialising in mergers and acquisitions is likely to get much help in advising clients from that case.

12.6.5 Joint and several liability

It is possible under art. 3.1 of both the 1977 and 2001 Directives for member states to legislate that transferor and transferee share joint and several liability for obligations to employees. There is no such provision in TUPE 2006, where reg. 4(2) provides simply that all rights, powers, duties and liabilities pass from transferor to transferee on the transfer. Indeed in *Bernadone* v *Pall Mall Services Group* [2000] IRLR 487, the Court of Appeal held that the rule even extended to liability (and consequently an insurance indemnity) in respect of a personal injury, because it was 'in connexion with' the contract of employment.

In *Allan* v *Stirling District Council* [1995] ICR 1082 employees sought to enforce rights against the transferor on the basis of the Directive. The Scottish Court of Session overruled the EAT and held that the power given to member states by the Directive was permissive and not mandatory, and could not therefore contradict the clear provision of reg. 4(2). Once the transfer has taken place, the transferor no longer has any rights or duties under the employees' contracts of employment.

12.6.6 Consultation of employee representatives

The employers—both transferor and transferee—are required to consult employee representatives about the forthcoming transfer. This duty is not unlike the requirement to consult representatives about proposed dismissals for redundancy (see **11.4.2.1** above) but no minimum time periods are defined. The main practical problem is that commercial negotiations often need to remain confidential, and it is consequently almost impossible for either employer to inform anyone until the deal has reached a point at which consultation is unlikely to change the result. If no trade union is recognised, the employer must arrange for employee representatives to be elected and failure to do so can lead to an award of compensation to individuals—*Howard* v *Millrise Ltd* [2005] ICR 435.

12.6.7 Employee liability information

There is a new provision in TUPE 2006, reg. 11 requiring the transferor to notify the transferee in writing or in some other readily accessible form of certain key information about each employee assigned to the economic entity transferred (and therefore covered by the transfer):

(a) the identity and age of each employee;

(b) particulars of employment as in the written statement issued to the employee;

(c) information about any disciplinary procedure or grievance procedure involving the employee during the previous two years;

(d) information about any court or tribunal claim brought by the employee during the previous two years or likely to be brought; and

(e) information about any relevant collective agreements.

12.7 Transfer between associated employers

Within large groups of companies, reorganisations of company structure are common, and in some cases frequent. There may be tax advantages or some administrative benefit in shifting responsibilities from a parent company to a subsidiary or vice versa, or between subsidiaries. Sometimes the company is organised into divisions or different establishments of the same limited company. There is no legal significance at all in a shift of administrative responsibility within one limited company; but technically any transfer of employees from one limited company to another is probably covered by TUPE 2006, even if the companies are associated.

Few employers properly comply in such circumstances with the TUPE 2006 requirements, although it is probably only the duty to consult recognised trade unions that has any practical significance. Most regard it as purely administrative. Even so, there is a duty on them to inform employees of any change in the identity of the employer within one month of its happening: ERA 1996, s. 4.

Whenever any employee's employment moves from one company to another associated company, continuity of employment is preserved: ERA 1996, s. 218(6). This rule applies irrespective of the circumstances. So an employee of one company in a group who happens to get a job in another group company will have continuity of employment preserved, even if the move resulted from an advertisement on the open market and was not in the usual sense a transfer initiated by the group.

12.8 Insolvency

One of the circumstances where the ownership of a business certainly undergoes some change is when the employer becomes insolvent. Insolvency is, of course, a very complex aspect of company law and we shall not attempt to deal with it in any detail here. We are concerned only with the position of the employees when an insolvency occurs, and there are two questions we shall want to answer:

(a) Does the employment of the employees come to an end on insolvency, or is it possible for them to continue to be employed—and, if so, by whom and on what conditions?

(b) What rights have the employees against the assets of an insolvent business for arrears of pay, outstanding holiday pay and other debts owing to them, especially in comparison with other creditors?

Before we proceed to address those questions it is convenient to put them in context by describing the various kinds of insolvency that now exist.

12.8.1 Kinds of insolvency

There are four main kinds of insolvency that we shall need to consider in outline:

12.8.1.1 Bankruptcy
This applies only to individual traders and to partnerships. It is less important for our purposes than the kinds of insolvency affecting companies.

12.8.1.2 Administration
This is the newest of the procedures, having been introduced in the Insolvency Act 1986. The intention is to provide a temporary means by which companies in difficulty but capable of being rescued can indeed be saved. The issue of an administration order requires a reference to the court leading to the appointment of an administrator, who has extensive powers to run the business and is deemed to act as an agent of the company.

12.8.1.3 Receivership
A receiver is appointed to receive the income of a company, to realise its assets and to meet its debts in a statutorily defined sequence of priorities. There are various ways that the receiver can be appointed, some leading to a receiver who is deemed to be an officer of the court and some as an agent of the company. In practice it is now very rare to find anyone other than an *administrative receiver*, a category introduced by the Insolvency Act 1986 and given the power to continue to run the business. An administrative receiver is not the same as an administrator, the first being an open-ended appointment and the second normally requiring a conclusion within three months.

12.8.1.4 Liquidation or winding up

This is the final ending of the existence of the company and may be set in train by court order (compulsory winding up) or through a voluntary winding up if the directors believe the company can pay its debts.

12.8.2 The effect on contracts of employment

If the employer is an individual or a partnership that becomes bankrupt, the employment comes to an end.

The reason why the basis of appointment of the administrator, receiver or liquidator (the 'specialist') is important is that appointment by the court leads, under a long-standing rule, to the automatic termination of employment of the employees: *Reid* v *Explosives Co. Ltd* (1887) 19 QBD 264 and *Golding and Howard* v *Fire Auto and Marine Insurance (in liquidation)* (1968) 4 ITR 372. The reason for dismissal is redundancy; but the employee's right to a redundancy payment will depend on having the necessary two years' service, and the ability to obtain it will depend on the matters we discuss in **12.8.3** below.

In all other cases the specialist's appointment as agent of the company has no effect on the employees' contracts of employment: *Re Foster Clark's Indenture Trusts* [1966] 2 All ER 403.

The Insolvency Act 1986 expressly provides that an administrative receiver is personally liable in relation to any contract of employment 'adopted' in connexion with performing his functions. Adoption cannot occur within 14 days of the administrative receiver's appointment but is otherwise not defined. Until recently it had been unclear whether some specific act of adoption was required or whether mere continuance beyond 14 days was sufficient. As there was some authority for the second possibility, administrative receivers usually issued a disclaimer to prevent adoption. However, in *Powdrill* v *Watson* [1995] ICR 1100, the House of Lords held that adoption is a matter of fact if employees are continued in employment for more than 14 days. A full or partial disclaimer was ineffective.

Very often the specialist dismisses some at least of the employees in an effort to reduce the outgoings of the business. This is normally a redundancy. Employees have the same rights to notice and to statutory redundancy payments that we discussed in earlier chapters. Although it is usually the rule that legal proceedings cannot be brought against an insolvent company without the leave of the court, it appears that this does not prevent a dismissed employee from complaining to the employment tribunal, except in connexion with a compulsory liquidation. For example, the employee may wish to complain of unfair selection for redundancy—see **Chapter 11.**

Although one of the specialist's main objectives is to get the insolvent company into such a state that it can be sold as a going concern, it is dangerous to dismiss employees solely for this purpose because of the effect of TUPE 2006: *Litster* v *Forth Dry Dock* [1989] ICR 341.

12.8.3 Rights of employees to outstanding debts

When the employer becomes insolvent, various creditors may be competing for the assets. The rights of the employees can be considered in two parts:

(a) rights against the assets of the insolvent employer; and

(b) rights to claim from the National Insurance Fund.

12.8.3.1   Rights of employees against assets of the insolvent employer

In any insolvency there is a strict order of priority in which the specialist must seek to meet the claims of outstanding creditors. In outline the sequence is as follows:

(a) the costs of realising the assets;

(b) other costs and remuneration of the specialist;

(c) claims from holders of fixed charges;

(d) preferential claims;

(e) claims from holders of floating charges;

(f) unsecured claims.

Each item in that list must be met in full before the next item is considered at all. If there is insufficient in the assets to meet the whole of an item it must be met in proportion to the amount that is available. So, for example, if there is enough on liquidation to meet the first three items but then only half the amount required for preferential claims, they will be satisfied only as to half their full amount and holders of floating charges and unsecured creditors will receive nothing at all.

Under sch. 6 of the Insolvency Act 1986, certain debts due to employees count as preferential debts for the purposes of that sequence:

(a) remuneration (defined to include wages and salary and various other items) in respect of the period of up to four months prior to the appointment of the receiver or liquidator, subject to the statutory maximum of £800;

(b) accrued holiday pay.

Any claim from an employee in addition to those amounts can still be pursued, but will rank as an unsecured claim and will be amongst the lowest priorities.

12.8.3.2   Rights against the National Insurance Fund

Very often the assets of an insolvent employer are insufficient to meet the debts due to preferential creditors, including employees. Even where that is not the problem, the process of liquidation is often so slow as to leave some employees in financial difficulty because of the absence of immediate income.

Some help is provided by s. 182 of ERA 1996, which provides some limited immediate payment to the employee from the National Insurance Fund, which then stands in the employee's shoes in seeking redress from the insolvent employer. Insolvency is defined for this purpose as meaning bankruptcy or any of the corporate states of insolvency defined at **12.8.1** above, but not merely that the employer cannot meet debts. This provision meets the requirements of European Directive 80/987/EEC.

Payments available from the National Insurance Fund are in all cases limited to the statutory maximum week's pay of £330 which we have encountered elsewhere, and are as follows:

(a) arrears of pay for up to eight weeks;

(b) minimum statutory notice as in s. 86 of ERA 1996;

(c) holiday pay for up to six weeks;

(d) a basic award for unfair dismissal;

(e) statutory redundancy pay: ERA 1996, s. 166;

(f) certain unpaid pensions contributions—those due from the employer and those employee's contributions already deducted but not paid over by the employer;

(g) statutory maternity pay.

12.9 Death of the employer

The rights of the employee when the employer dies are set out in s. 206 of ERA 1996. The rights of personal representatives of a deceased employee are covered in s. 207.

The death of an employer obviously changes the status of the employee only if the employer was acting as a sole individual. If the employer was a partnership, the usual rule of survivorship provides that the remaining partners become the new employer; if the employer traded as a limited company, the death of a major shareholder does not affect the continuing existence of the company.

The essence of the statutory rules is that rights enjoyed by the employee against the employer can be maintained against the personal representatives. This includes employment tribunal proceedings, subject only to the rule that in a case of unfair dismissal, reinstatement or re-engagement cannot be ordered against personal representatives.

If the death of the employer results in the ending of the employment, that is to be treated as a dismissal for redundancy: ERA 1996, s. 136(5). This will usually apply to domestic servants and the like. However, if the employment is a business the personal representatives are more likely to want to keep it going to maximise its resale value, and there is continuity of employment in such cases. The liability of the personal representatives to make a redundancy payment can be avoided if the employee unreasonably refuses an offer of suitable continuing employment. However, the employment will not be continued by default: there needs to be some agreement between the employee and the personal representatives to continue: *Ranger* v *Brown* [1978] ICR 608.

12.10 Summary

Although this chapter deals with several kinds of change in the ownership of a business, the main topic is the Transfer of Undertakings (Protection of Employment) Regulations 2006 (TUPE 2006).

We noted at **12.3** an outline of the effect of TUPE 2006:

- where there is a *relevant transfer*—the transfer of an *economic entity* that *maintains its identity* or a *service provision change*;
- employment is *automatically transferred* (unless the employee objects) with full continuity of service;
- the transferred employment is on the *same conditions*, including trade union recognition, but excluding pensions;
- any dismissal because of the transfer is *automatically unfair* unless for an *economic, technical or organisational reason entailing changes in the workforce*; and
- employee representatives of both transferor and transferee must be *consulted*.

Some expansion of that summary will be found in **Figure 12.1**, which appears at section **12.3**.

12.11 Self-test questions

1.   Is there any single test you can apply when a business (or part of one) changes hands to decide whether there has been a relevant transfer within the meaning of TUPE 2006?

2.   A client comes to you wanting to discuss his proposed purchase for a very favourable price of an unprofitable part of an existing business, in the hope of amalgamating it with his current business and making it profitable through economies of scale. Your detailed enquiries indicate quite clearly that the purchase will be a relevant transfer within the meaning of TUPE 2006. What key employment law consequences would you bring to the client's notice as a result of that conclusion?

Employment tribunal procedure

13.1 Introduction

The feature that links most of the rights of employees set out in this book is that the remedy for infringement is a complaint to the employment tribunal. There are, of course, a few items where this is not the case—mostly matters involving alleged breach of contract, including wrongful dismissal. The procedure there is to be found in any standard work on civil procedure and the key points have been noted in **Chapters 5** and **9**, but the employment tribunals are unique to employment law and we need in this chapter to describe their operation and procedure.

New rules of procedure in the tribunals came into effect in October 2004. It would be comforting to report that the new arrangements have settled in nicely and that we now have a clear idea of how the 2004 rules operate. Comforting but not true. In *Richardson v U Mole Ltd* [2005] IRLR 668 the President of the EAT was moved to remark that the sooner the 2004 rules were looked at again the better. The problem seems to be that in some respects the 2004 rules are very strict, and allow tribunals much less discretion than the previous 2001 version. There is a suggestion in the *Richardson* case that some tribunal chairmen have been construing the rules strictly to the letter in order to draw attention to shortcomings they see as existing in the current rules, and that a more flexible approach should be adopted in the interests of justice. For the time being there remains some uncertainty, and also some variation among different regions and different individual tribunal chairmen. We have presented this chapter on the basis that the new rules operate as written, but we shall indicate where it seems that some variation may occur.

For our purposes the claimant presenting a claim to the tribunal is always the employee (or, in appropriate cases, the applicant for a job, the 'worker', or the ex-employee) and the employer is the respondent. Except for the rare case mentioned at **6.8** above, there are no circumstances in which an employer can make a claim to the employment tribunal. Employers have other remedies: dismissal or very occasionally civil litigation, perhaps, for example, in order to seek an injunction restraining an ex-employee from disclosing trade secrets. If the ex-employee brings a claim for breach of contract in a tribunal, the employer may counterclaim, but the employer cannot initiate proceedings.

There are a few jurisdictions in which an employee can bring proceedings in the employment tribunal against a trade union or a trade union against the employer, but the number of such cases in practice is so small that we shall ignore both possibilities.

The solicitor is most likely to become involved on behalf of either side once something has already gone wrong in the employment relationship. As in any other branch of the law, litigation is the last resort and clients should be advised not to ignore obvious and less formal solutions. We have always regarded it as good practice to suggest that the employee could complain personally to the boss or use the trade union to pursue a grievance. As we have noted throughout this book, the more formal rule that has required many claimants since 2004 to use the statutory grievance procedure before presenting their claim to the tribunal is due to be abolished in April 2009. Although from that date tribunal offices will no longer be able to refuse claims where the procedure should have been used but the claimant has failed to do so, the proposed new ACAS code of practice about discipline and grievances seems likely to suggest that voluntary procedures must be used before starting tribunal proceedings. So a claimant who has unreasonably failed to exhaust voluntary solutions may still suffer some disadvantage in the tribunal (see **13.4.5** below). Similarly, as we saw in **Chapter 10**, a claimant who successfully complains of unfair dismissal will find compensation reduced if there is no good explanation for not having used the employer's appeal procedure. Both sides, though, will need to take care to ensure that discussions held 'without prejudice' do not adversely affect them if tribunal proceedings follow. The 'without prejudice' rule only applies once a dispute can be said to exist and in any case does not protect from disclosure any remark that involves unlawful discrimination—*BNP Paribas* v *Mezzotero* [2004] IRLR 508.

If those informal steps fail, an application to the tribunal becomes inevitable and we shall set out the procedure to be followed in the remainder of the chapter, which takes the following form:

(a) The constitution and workload of the employment tribunals.

(b) Bringing a claim.

(c) Presentation of the claim on time.

(d) Acceptance of the claim.

(e) The response.

(f) Acceptance of the response and default hearings.

(g) Case management.

(h) Pre-hearing reviews.

(i) Conciliation and the role of ACAS.

(j) The hearing.

(k) The tribunal decision.

(l) Costs and preparation time orders.

(m) The remedies available to the tribunal.

(n) Challenge of an employment tribunal decision.

(o) A summary of main jurisdictions, time limits, and awards.

In trying to understand how the procedures work it will be helpful to use four imaginary examples, three of them complaints of unfair dismissal: Anastasia was dismissed for redundancy and Basil for alleged dishonesty; Catherine claims constructive unfair dismissal; Dmitri complains of disability discrimination. The detailed facts will emerge as we introduce and develop the cases.

13.2 Constitution and workload of the employment tribunals

13.2.1 History

The current workload of the employment tribunals is broad, but their origin is surprisingly narrow. From humble beginnings in 1964 their workload has burgeoned.

As we explained at the start of the book, the employment tribunals were known as industrial tribunals until 31 July 1998. The Employment Rights (Dispute Resolution) Act (ERDRA) 1998, s. 1, provides that from 1 August 1998, every reference to an industrial tribunal in earlier statutes and elsewhere should be deemed to be a reference to an employment tribunal. We have followed that rule throughout this book, even when referring to decisions in old cases.

Since 1 October 2004 the operation of the employment tribunals has been governed by the Employment Tribunals (Constitution and Rules of Procedure) Regulations 2004 (the ET Regs 2004), which contain in sch. 1 the Employment Tribunal Rules of Procedure (ET Rules 2004). We shall not concern ourselves with the special rules for certain specific jurisdictions that are contained in sch. 2 to 6. Those familiar with the previous regulations and rules from 2001 will notice many differences, not least that the new provisions apply to the whole of Great Britain, whereas there were previously separate sets for England and Wales and for Scotland.

13.2.2 The composition of the tribunals

Under the Tribunals, Courts and Enforcement Act 2007 (TCE 2007), the employment tribunal system is a distinct part of the unified tribunal system administered by the Tribunals Service of the Ministry of Justice. Its judicial side is headed by the President.

The system in England and Wales is organised into 21 offices, 14 of which have the status of regions. Under TCE 2007 the former tribunal chairmen have been known since December 2007 as employment judges. Each region is headed by a regional employment judge, and there are also several full-time employment judges and a number of part-time employment judges who can be called on to help when the workload is heavy. By reg. 8 of the ET Regs 2004 an employment judge must be a barrister or solicitor of seven years' standing. The part-time employment judges in fact consist of some practising lawyers and some retired, former full-time employment judges.

When the tribunal sits it must be chaired by the President or another employment judge, who normally is accompanied by one person from each of two lists (or 'panels') of people representative of employers' organisations and of employed people's organisations. In interlocutory matters and uncontested cases the employment judge sits alone. There has been increasing use of the provision under ETA 1996, s. 4(2) as amended by ERDRA 1998, s. 3, whereby employment judges sit alone in other matters and that is now normal practice in relation to protection of wages and breach of contract questions. It is possible for employment judges to sit alone if parties consent in other matters including unfair dismissal. They sometimes sit with one other member, usually where the third member has become indisposed or is forced to withdraw for some reason.

13.2.3 Procedure at the tribunals

The employment tribunals were originally intended to provide a means of resolving employment disputes that was informal, speedy, and cheap. To an extent they still do, but the informality is more apparent to lawyers who compare them with the courts than to the general public who often find them daunting. Under ET Regs 2004, reg. 3, their overriding objective is to deal with cases justly.

Perhaps the most noticeable change in tribunal procedure under ET Regs 2004 is the increased emphasis on case management by the tribunals. In many ways it mirrors the Woolf reforms in the courts. The practical difference is not as great as might have been expected because even the old rules gave tribunals a wide power to determine their own procedure and many employment judges adopted Woolf-type practices. In the early days of the tribunals' operation the issues in a case were often not really identified until a hearing, but nowadays almost every case is well prepared and the issues are fully identified well before any hearing. The problem for practitioners has been that individual employment judges have different preferences, and it has been difficult to know how cases will be handled in an unfamiliar region. Such tight procedural management is often very unpopular with clients, both claimants and employers, who prefer an informal style in which they feel they can have their say. Sometimes they feel that cases are won or lost on legal technicalities rather than the merits.

As in the courts, terminology is changed to make it less arcane, and, for example, interlocutory proceedings now become interim hearings. A claim (previously an originating application) is presented by the claimant (applicant), usually using form ET 1 (IT 1) and the respondent (no change) replies in a response, form ET 3 (notice of appearance, IT 3).

Under reg. 13 of ET Regs 2004 the President has the power to make practice directions. We expected that the power would be used very soon after the new rules came into effect on 1 October 2004 so as to start to standardise practice across the country, especially in matters like the use of witness statements where practice has varied considerably—see **13.8.10** below. In fact nothing has been issued. We understand that the President prefers to write informally to regional employment judges commending examples of good practice rather than to be prescriptive by issuing practice directions. Thus far, this 'softly softly' approach has left in place many regional variations.

We shall note the most important aspects of the tribunals' procedure as we work through the progress of a case in the following sections.

13.2.4 Jurisdictions

Although, as we have noted, there is a wide range of jurisdictions for the employment tribunals, the largest part of their workload is concentrated on relatively few issues. As we go to press detailed statistics for employment tribunal applications during the year 2007-8 have not been published. A report from the unified Tribunals Service records receipt of 189,348 applications, compared with 143,474 in 2006-7. There appears to have been some change in the basis of measurement as the annual report of the Employment Tribunal Service for 2006-7 shows 132,557 applications received, which contained 238,546 complaints. Those figures also showed an increase on the previous year. In the absence of more recent information we show in **Table 13.1** the subject matter of those complaints in 2006-7.

Table 13.1 **Workload of the employment tribunals in 2006–7**

Unfair dismissal	44,491	19%
Redundancy pay	7,692	3.%
Deductions from wages	34,857	15%
Discrimination: race, sex, equal pay, disability, part-time etc.	85,810	36%
Breach of contract	27,298	11%
Working Time Regulations	21,127	9%
All other jurisdictions, i.e., miscellaneous employment rights, and trade union issues	17,271	7%
Total	238,546	100%

Source: Employment Tribunal Service Statistics, 2006–7—www.employmenttribunals.gov.uk.

13.2.5 Appeals

An appeal from a decision of the employment tribunal lies on a point of law only to the EAT, and thereafter in the usual way to the Court of Appeal and the House of Lords. We shall consider briefly the mechanism for appealing to the EAT in **13.15.2** below.

13.2.6 Scotland

The substantive statute law that we have been considering throughout this book applies equally to Scotland as to England and Wales. There are, of course, a few differences as to the common law.

Although, as we noted at **13.2.1** above, ET Regs 2004 apply equally to Scotland as to England and Wales, the Scottish structure of employment tribunals is separate, with its own Central Office in Glasgow and its own President. Appeals lie to a Scottish division of the EAT, then to the Court of Session and finally to the House of Lords. In a statement arising out of *Davidson* v *City Electrical Factors Ltd* [1998] ICR 443, however, the President of EAT has explained that there is one EAT and not two, so that a judgment of EAT wherever it sits has an equal effect in law in Scotland and in England and Wales. We should refer to 'the EAT sitting in Scotland' and not to a 'Scottish EAT'.

Practitioners may occasionally find themselves called upon by clients in England and Wales to deal with cases in Scotland. For example, a company with its only premises in the south of England that dismisses a service engineer who used his home in Edinburgh as a base for work in that area will find an employment tribunal claim sent to a Scottish tribunal (see **13.3** for the reasons why). We expect that the few remaining differences in practice in Scotland will become less significant under the common rules of procedure, but practitioners straying north of the border must expect any reference they make to documents, costs or staying proceedings to be corrected to 'productions', 'expenses', and 'sisting' proceedings.

13.3 Bringing a claim

The means of bringing an action in the employment tribunal is to present a claim to the appropriate local office of the tribunals, determined by reference to the postcode of the place of work or former place of work. Very clear guidance for claimants can be found at the employment tribunal website www.employmenttribunals.gov.uk, which is worth visiting. It includes the standard form ET 1, use of which is now mandatory under r. 1(3). The first nine pages of the current version (omitting three final blank pages for additional information to be supplied) are reproduced below by kind permission of the Employment Tribunal Service, who advise readers to check that it is still the latest version.

The form contains sections specific to particular kinds of claim. It is designed to be user-friendly and straightforward, and we shall comment only on a few aspects.

13.3.1 How much information is required?

There is a list in r. 1 (4) of ET Rules 2004 of the matters that have to be covered in a claim and provision is made for all of them in the mandatory form ET 1. As we shall see shortly at **13.3.4** there seems at present to be some conflict between some at least of the employment tribunal judges who have operated r. 1(4) strictly and the EAT which has favoured much greater flexibility, perhaps reflecting in part the previous approach as in *Burns International* v *Butt* [1983] ICR 547 which seemed to ignore the more limited rule at the time and to regard the only statutory requirement as being that an application was in writing. We do not expect that degree of flexibility to survive, but the conflict is not yet resolved.

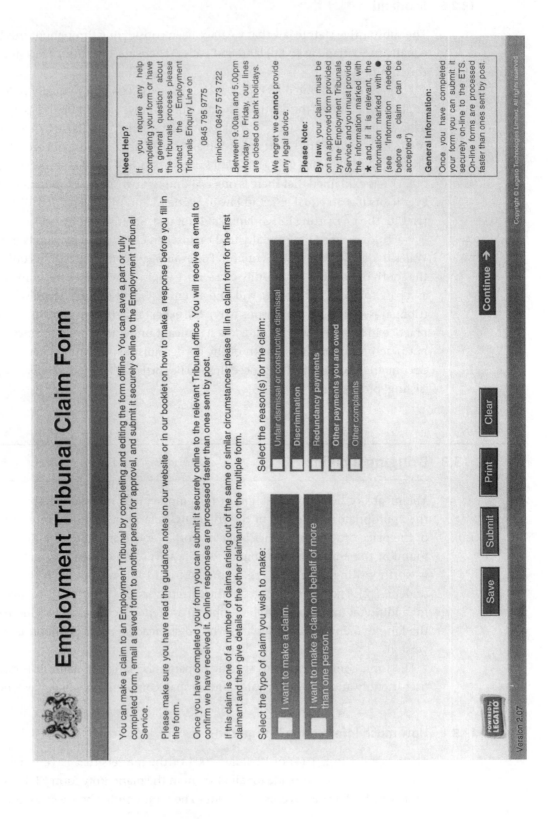

Employment Tribunal Claim Form

You can make a claim to an Employment Tribunal by completing and editing the form offline. You can save a part or fully completed form, email a saved form to another person for approval, and submit it securely online to the Employment Tribunal Service.

Please make sure you have read the guidance notes on our website or in our booklet on how to make a response before you fill in the form.

Once you have completed your form you can submit it securely online to the relevant Tribunal office. You will receive an email to confirm we have received it. Online responses are processed faster than ones sent by post.

If this claim is one of a number of claims arising out of the same or similar circumstances please fill in a claim form for the first claimant and then give details of the other claimants on the multiple form.

Select the type of claim you wish to make:

☐ I want to make a claim.

☐ I want to make a claim on behalf of more than one person.

Select the reason(s) for the claim:

☐ Unfair dismissal or constructive dismissal

☐ Discrimination

☐ Redundancy payments

☐ Other payments you are owed

☐ Other complaints

Need Help?
If you require any help completing your form or have a general question about the tribunals process please contact the Employment Tribunals Enquiry Line on

0845 795 9775

minicom 08457 573 722

Between 9.00am and 5.00pm Monday to Friday, our lines are closed on bank holidays.

We regret we **cannot** provide any legal advice.

Please Note:

By law, your claim must be on an approved form provided by the Employment Tribunals Service, and you must provide the information marked with ★ and, if it is relevant, the information marked with ● (see "Information needed before a claim can be accepted")

General Information:
Once you have completed your form you can submit it securely on-line to the ETS. On-line forms are processed faster than ones sent by post.

Save   Submit   Print   Clear   Continue →

POWERED BY LEGATIO

Version 2.07

⌐1 Your details

■ 1.1 Title: Mr   Mrs   Miss   Ms   Other   ■

1.2* First name (or names):

1.3* Surname or family name:

1.4 Date of birth (date/month/year):   Are you: male?   female?

1.5* Address: Number or Name

Street

    +   Town/City

County

Postcode

■ 1.6 Phone number **(where we can contact**   ■
you during normal working hours):

1.7 How would you prefer us to   E-mail   Post   Fax
communicate with you?
(Please tick only one box)

  E-mail address:

                              @

  Fax number:

2   Respondent's details

■ 2.1* Give the name of your employer   ■
or the organisation you are claiming
against.

2.2* Address: Number or Name

Street

Town/City

    +   County

Postcode

Phone number:

■ 2.3 If you worked at an address   ■
different from the one you have
given at 2.2, please give the
full address and postcode.

  Postcode

  Phone number:

2.4● If your complaint is against more than one respondent please give the names, addresses and
postcodes of additional respondents.

■   ■

3 Action before making a claim

3.1* Are you, or were you, an employee of the respondent? Yes No
If 'Yes', please now go straight to section 3.3.

3.2 Are you, or were you, a worker providing services to the respondent? Yes No
If 'Yes', please now go straight to section 4.
If 'No', please now go straight to section 6.

3.3 Is your claim, or part of it, about a dismissal by the respondent? Yes No
If 'No', please now go straight to section 3.5.
If your claim is about constructive dismissal, i.e. you resigned because of something
your employer did or failed to do which made you feel you could no longer continue to
work for them, tick the box here and the 'Yes' box in section 3.4.

3.4 Is your claim about anything else, in addition to the dismissal? Yes No
If 'No', please now go straight to section 4.
If 'Yes', please answer questions 3.5 to 3.7 about the
non-dismissal aspects of your claim.

3.5 Have you put your complaint(s) in writing to the respondent?

Yes Please give the date you put it to them in writing.

No

If 'No', please now go straight to section 3.7.

3.6 Did you allow at least 28 days between the date you put your Yes No
complaint in writing to the respondent and the date you sent us this claim?
If 'Yes', please now go straight to section 4.

3.7 Please explain why you did not put your complaint in writing to the respondent or,
if you did, why you did not allow at least 28 days before sending us your claim.
(In most cases, it is a legal requirement to take these procedural steps. Your claim
will not be accepted unless you give a valid reason why you did not have to meet
the requirement in your case. If you are not sure, you may want to get legal advice.)

⌐4   Employment details

4.1   Please give the following information if possible.

When did your employment start?

When did or will it end?

Is your employment continuing?   Yes   No

4.2   Please say what job you do or did.

4.3   How many hours do or did you work each week?   hours each week

4.4   How much are or were you paid?

Pay before tax   £   .00   Hourly

                                                                    Weekly
Normal take-home pay (including   £   .00   Monthly
overtime,commission, bonuses and so on)
                                                                    Yearly

4.5   If your employment has ended, did you work
        (or were you paid for) a period of notice?   Yes   No

If 'Yes', how many weeks or months did   weeks   months
you work or were you paid for?

5   Unfair dismissal or constructive dismissal

Please fill in this section only if you believe you have been unfairly or constructively dismissed.

5.1 ● If you were dismissed by your employer, you should explain why you think your dismissal
        was unfair. If you resigned because of something your employer did or failed to do which
        made you feel you could no longer continue to work for them (constructive dismissal)
        you should explain what happened.

5 Unfair dismissal or constructive dismissal continued

5.1 continued

5.2 Were you in your employer's pension scheme? Yes No

5.3 If you received any other benefits from your employer, please give details.

5.4 Since leaving your employment have you got another job? Yes No
    If 'No', please now go straight to section 5.7.

5.5 Please say when you started (or will start) work.

5.6 Please say how much you are now earning (or will earn). £   .00 each

5.7 Please tick the box to say what you want if your case is successful:

    a To get your old job back and compensation (reinstatement)

    b To get another job with the same employer and compensation (re-engagement)

    c Compensation only

6   Discrimination

Please fill in this section only if you believe you have been discriminated against.

6.1 ● Please tick the box or boxes to indicate what discrimination (including victimisation) you are complaining about:

Sex (including equal pay)   Race

Disability   Religion or belief

Sexual orientation

6.2 ● Please describe the incidents which you believe amounted to discrimination, the dates of these incidents and the people involved.

7 Redundancy payments

Please fill in this section only if you believe you are owed a redundancy payment.

7.1 Please explain why you believe you are entitled to this payment and set out the steps you have taken to get it.

8 Other payments you are owed

Please fill in this section only if you believe you are owed other payments.

8.1 Please tick the box or boxes to indicate that money is owed to you for:

unpaid wages?

holiday pay?

notice pay?

other unpaid amounts?

8.2 How much are you claiming? £ .00

Is this: before tax? after tax?

8.3 Please explain why you believe you are entitled to this payment. If you have specified an amount, please set out how you have worked this out.

9   Other complaints

Please fill in this section only if you believe you have a complaint that is not covered elsewhere.

9.1 Please explain what you are complaining about and why.
Please include any relevant dates.

10 Other information

10.1 Please do not send a covering letter with this form.
You should add any extra information you want us to know here.

11 Disability

11.1 Please tick this box if you consider yourself to have a disability   Yes   No
If 'Yes', please say what this disability is and tell us what assistance, if any, you will
need as your claim progresses through the system.

12 Your representative

Please fill in this section only if you have appointed a representative. If you do fill this section in, we will in future only send correspondence to your representative and not to you.

12.1 Representative's name:

12.2 Name of the representative's
organisation:

12.3 Address: Number or Name

Street

+   Town/City

County

Postcode

12.4 Phone number:

12.5 Reference:

12.6 How would you prefer us to   Post   Fax   E-mail
communicate with them? (Please tick only one box)
Fax number:

E-mail address:

@

13 Multiple cases

13.1 To your knowledge, is your claim one of a number of claims   Yes   No
arising from the same or similar circumstances?

Please sign and date here

Signature: Date:

Data Protection Act 1998. We will send a copy of this form to the respondent(s) and Acas. We will put some of the
information you give us on this form onto a computer. This helps us to monitor progress and produce statistics.
Information provided on this form is passed to the Department of Trade and Industry to assist research into the use
and effectiveness of Employment Tribunals.

Express provision is now made for multiple claims against the same employer. Names and addresses must be given for each claimant.

13.3.2 Representation (box 12)

At item 12 the claimant is asked to name a representative if one exists. The ET Rules 2004 do not specify who may appear in the employment tribunals, but in practice representatives include counsel and solicitors, representatives of trade unions, employers' associations, and Citizens' Advice Bureaux and various personnel consultancies. Contingency-based fees are common.

As legal aid is not available in the tribunals and costs have rarely been awarded (see **13.13** below), many claimants choose to appear in person, being reluctant to incur the cost of instructing lawyers. Employers sometimes do so too. It will be found in practice that employment judges have always aimed to meet the objective of ET Regs 2004, reg 3(2) (a) to ensure that the parties are on an equal footing and try to compensate for any disadvantage suffered by an unrepresented party, especially a claimant. The procedural rules are applied less strictly than to any professional representative. However, in *Mensah* v *East Hertfordshire NHS Trust* [1998] IRLR 531, the Court of Appeal (unlike the EAT) refused to allow a claimant to reopen a ground of complaint merely because the employment tribunal had allegedly not been astute in ensuring that she covered during the hearing all matters contained in the claim form.

13.3.3 The remedy being sought (box 5.7)

At item 5.7 on the form ET 1 the claimant is asked to state in relation to claims of unfair dismissal what remedy is being sought: reinstatement, re-engagement or compensation. It is perhaps strange that such a question should be asked at this early stage, and indeed the form makes clear that the claimant is not bound by the answer given here but may ask for something else at the end of tribunal proceedings.

There is, of course, a tactical advantage to the claimant in asking for reinstatement or re-engagement, even if not having any real wish to go back to work for the same employer. As we noted in **Chapter 10**, the amounts of compensation awarded if the employer has failed to carry out an order for reinstatement or re-engagement are substantially increased. So such a request at this stage may assist in the negotiation of an out-of-tribunal settlement—see **13.10** below.

13.3.4 Particulars of the claim

Each of the main sections of form ET 1 contains a box for details of the claim—box 5.1, 6.2, 7.1, 8.3, or 9.1, depending on the subject of the claim. The question then arises of how much detail is required.

Until the 2004 rules came into effect the answer to such a question represented one of the most noticeable aspects of greater informality in the tribunals compared with the rules in the courts that you will have learned in civil procedure. It was merely necessary to identify the category or categories of claim that the claimant was making and to include sufficient detail that the respondent could not complain of being taken by surprise, but the practice, for example, of including every element in a contract that was essential to its legal enforceability and therefore to the jurisdiction of the court was unknown in the tribunals. The list in r. 1(4) of ET Rules 2004 now sets out much more and includes at item (e) 'details of the claim'. There is some anecdotal evidence of rejection by employment judges of forms ET 1 that contain insufficient information.

However, in *Grimmer* v *KLM Cityhopper* UK [2005] IRLR 596 the EAT held that, as the claimant had given details that enabled it to be discerned that she was claiming a right where the employment tribunal had jurisdiction, neither the tribunal secretary nor a chairman should deny her access by interpreting *details of the claim* as if it read *sufficient particulars*. More information could always be sought later. This very flexible approach by the EAT seems to cut across the apparent aim of the 2004 rules of streamlining the operation of the tribunals and leaves practitioners in an unsatisfactory state of uncertainty. Yet, while claimants in person may be treated leniently as in *Grimmer*, it would be dangerous for any lawyer to expect the same latitude and a professional standard should be met. The balance between too much and too little detail is difficult to describe in the abstract and an example may help.

EXAMPLE 1

Consider the following draft prepared by Anastasia herself for box 5.1 on her ET 1 when her claim is solely of unfair dismissal:

I was called into my manager's office in the afternoon of Friday, 28 November and was told that I was being dismissed as redundant. I was told to collect my personal belongings at once and to leave the premises before the end of the afternoon. I do not accept that I was fairly selected. There was no individual consultation before notice was given to me. At the time of my dismissal there were sub-contractors working in the design office in jobs that I could easily have filled. My employment ended on 5 December.

This is a good statement, brief and devoid of legal jargon. It succinctly sets out the essential facts of the case and clearly identifies the items that the claimant is putting in issue. By implication at least it therefore also identifies those that are not being challenged. The items put in issue are three:

(a) unfair selection;

(b) lack of individual consultation;

(c) failure to look for alternative work.

The statement does not challenge matters such as the following:

(a) that the dismissal was not truly for redundancy (although, as we noted at **10.8.1** above, the burden of proof of a reason for dismissal always rests with the employer and the tribunal may always require the employer to prove it);

(b) that the claimant's selection was automatically unfair by being based on trade union activities;

(c) that Anastasia's selection involved any discrimination on grounds of race, sex, or disability, all of these being arguments that if successful could lead to unlimited compensation.

A solicitor representing a claimant like Anastasia will not normally be permitted to raise such arguments at the hearing without warning. The respondent will be unprepared to defend them and will object. If the arguments are allowed at all, the hearing may then be adjourned until another day. Whilst costs are not normally awarded in the employment tribunals, extra costs resulting from such an adjournment may well have to be borne by the party responsible for it.

Note that while the statement clearly defines the issues for an eventual tribunal hearing, it does not attempt to identify in advance all the arguments that may be used at an eventual hearing. One reason used to be that it was tactically advantageous to deny the respondent's witnesses the chance to prepare for cross-examination. Thus, for example, if Anastasia's selection depended on use of the type of matrix we encountered in **Chapter 11**, her solicitor would wish to cross-examine the manager who completed it about some of the entries—whether records were properly researched, whether a reason for poor attendance was investigated and so on. The argument was that the respondent could not complain about lack of notice of such questions in the ET 1 or elsewhere without scoring an own-goal; the answers should have been in the manager's mind when making the selection. Current practice in the tribunals, especially the exchange in advance of witness statements that we shall mention shortly, now makes it more difficult to surprise a witness with such questions; in any event the effect is lessened if Anastasia never raised them during any appeal against dismissal. A more important reason nowadays for not setting out the arguments at this early stage is that it is difficult to produce an exhaustive list while preparation of the case is incomplete, and it is better not to be so precise now than to keep needing to add to a list as the case progresses. Nevertheless it is useful for a solicitor representing Anastasia to start now giving some thought to when and how to identify specific points of which the respondent needs warning—such as an argument that another, named employee was treated differently a year or two ago.

It is usually a good idea to avoid statements that leave the reader unclear what exactly it is you are talking about. References to 'certain shortcomings', for example, merely invite the other side to apply for additional information (see **13.8.3** below) about precisely what shortcomings you mean. In the above example it is possible to argue that the reference to sub-contractors is unclear in this way, and that might be a criticism. In practice, though, the employer is probably well aware of exactly who is meant, as there are unlikely to be many people fitting the description.

Anastasia's ET 1 was drafted by the claimant and written in the first person. Often solicitors will find that they are not consulted until the ET 1 has already been presented, and not every claimant is as precise as this, so that you may have to decide later whether to seek leave to amend an inadequate ET 1. In other cases you may be asked to draft the ET 1 yourself, in which case you will probably do it in the third person. As with most other forms of legal drafting, there is no single right or wrong way to complete employment tribunal documents and different practitioners have different preferences, especially in relation to how much detail to include at an early stage and how much to keep until the hearing. Nevertheless, we can summarise points that emerge from the example like this:

(a) Be as succinct as possible. As a rule of thumb, it should not usually be necessary to expand beyond the space provided at item 5.1 on the ET 1, although an increasing number of representatives now do so. (Beware that any expansion beyond the blank additional pages of the ET 1 may be regarded as not meeting the requirement to use only that form.)

(b) Ensure that nothing so important is omitted as to entitle the other side to complain of being taken by surprise.

(c) Do not disclose unnecessarily facts that would more effectively be used with some surprise value in cross-examination.

(d) Avoid loose ends which almost invite the other side to apply for additional information. For example, the passive voice 'The claimant was told' invites the question, 'Who told her?'. Unless the answer is obvious or well-known to the other side, it is better to use the active voice from the outset: 'The manager told the claimant.'

13.4 Presentation of the claim on time

It is important that the claim is presented on time. 'Presentation' consists of delivering the originating application to the tribunal office, by hand, through the post, by fax or using the internet. In the case of the post it is the time of arrival and not the time of posting that counts. We shall return to issues concerning the internet at **13.4.3** below.

If we look at the first six groups of jurisdictions of the tribunals set out in **Table 13.1**, which together account for more than 90 per cent of the workload, we find that each has its own rule and we need to look at them in turn.

13.4.1 The various time limits

13.4.1.1 Unfair dismissal

A claim can be presented on or after the date notice is given, even if that is before the employment terminates. It must be presented to the tribunal office within *three months* beginning with the effective date of termination, or such further period as the tribunal considers reasonable if presentation within three months was *not reasonably practicable*: ERA 1996, s. 111(2).

13.4.1.2 A claim for a redundancy payment

A claim must be made within *six months* beginning with the relevant date, or within a further six months if the tribunal considers it *just and equitable*. A 'claim' in this context is widely defined: it includes a demand directly of the employer, a claim in the tribunal for a redundancy payment or a complaint to the tribunal of unfair dismissal: ERA 1996, s. 164.

13.4.1.3 Protection of wages

A claim about a deduction from wages must be presented within *three months* beginning with the most recent date of payment of wages from which the unlawful deduction was allegedly made, or such further period as the tribunal considers reasonable if satisfied that it was *not reasonably practicable* for the claim to be presented within the three months: ERA 1996, s. 23.

13.4.1.4 Racial discrimination

A claim must be presented to the tribunal within *three months* of the allegedly discriminatory act, or such further period as the tribunal considers *just and equitable*: RRA 1976, s. 68(1) and (6). If the discrimination was continuous over a period, time runs from the most recent occurrence: *Barclays Bank* v *Kapur* [1991] ICR 208.

13.4.1.5 Sex discrimination

A claim must be presented to the tribunal within *three months* of the allegedly discriminatory act, or such further period as the tribunal considers *just and equitable*, an exactly similar rule to that relating to racial discrimination: SDA 1975, s. 76. The *Barclays Bank* rule about repeated discrimination applies here too. If discrimination occurs through the employer's refusal of a request by the employee, time starts to run again *every* time the employer reconsiders the request and refuses again: *Cast* v *Croydon College* [1998] ICR 500.

That rule relates to proceedings brought under the SDA 1975. There is *no time limit* in relation to proceedings brought directly under the European Treaty or a European Directive, but the ECJ normally regards such procedural matters as appropriate for determination by the Member States.

A particular problem has arisen in relation to the time limit within which claims must be brought when decisions of the ECJ or domestic courts in effect create new rights, e.g., the right to equality in pensions schemes following *Barber* v *Guardian Royal Exchange Assurance Group* [1990] ICR 616 (see **6.4.3** above). The approach seems to be one of regarding time as running from the point when the claimant ought to have been aware that a right existed (see *Biggs* v *Somerset County Council* [1996] ICR 364, and **13.4.4** below).

13.4.1.6 Discrimination on grounds of religion, belief, sexual orientation or age

These newer heads of discrimination all adopt the same rules about presentation as RRA 1976 and SDA 1975.

13.4.1.7 Disability discrimination

The DDA 1995, sch. 3 sets the same rules as RRA 1976 and SDA 1975, of a claim within *three months* beginning when the act complained of took place, and allows extension if the tribunal considers it *just and equitable*.

13.4.1.8 Discrimination against part-time and fixed-term workers

The same rule of a claim within *three months* (or, in this case, *six months* if concerning a member of the armed forces) and extension if the tribunal considers it *just and equitable* exists under these regulations as for the other categories of discrimination.

13.4.1.9 Equal pay

A claim may be presented at any time during the continuation of employment. As regards arrears, see **6.8** above. A claim must be presented within *six months* of the termination of the employment. There is *no extension* of this period: Equal Pay Act 1970, s. 2.

13.4.1.10 Breach of contract

The rule here is the same as for unfair dismissal. See **13.6.3** below for the time limit regarding any counterclaim by the employer.

13.4.1.11 Claims under the Working Time Regulations 1998

Under reg. 30(2) a claim must be presented within *three months* (or *six months* for the armed forces) of the alleged start of infringement, with a possibility of extension if it was *not reasonably practicable* to present before the end of that period.

13.4.2 Presentation within time and the possibility of extension

As we noted at the start of this section, the rule about presentation in time is important. The reason is that it has been held to be a rule about *jurisdiction* and not merely *procedure*: see *Rogers* v *Bodfari (Transport) Ltd* [1973] ICR 325 and *Dedman* v *British Building and Engineering Supplies Ltd* [1974] ICR 53. If it were procedural, the tribunal could refuse to let a respondent employer use the time limit as a defence if it felt that the lateness was wholly or partly the respondent's fault or that the respondent's conduct had ignored the time limit. As the rule is jurisdictional there is no such flexibility and it must be applied strictly. Nevertheless, the effective date of termination in an unfair dismissal application is a matter of fact, not law, and an agreement about that was binding on the parties in *Lambert* v *Croydon College* [1999] ICR 409.

There are two aspects to the operation of the time limit and we shall consider each in turn:

(a) whether the claim was presented in time; and, if not,

(b) whether time should be extended in the circumstances.

Where a time limit is expressed as beginning on a particular date, it has been held to mean precisely that: see *University of Cambridge* v *Murray* [1993] ICR 460 for confirmation. Thus, if the employee was dismissed on 3 April and wishes to complain of unfair dismissal, a claim must be presented at the tribunal on or before 2 July. Presentation on 3 July is one day after the end of the three-month period *beginning on* 3 April, and a claim received then would be out of time. It is calendar months that count, notwithstanding variations in their length. So, for example, periods of three months beginning with an effective date of termination between 29 November and 1 December will all end on 28 February (in a non-leap year). The rule about statutory periods of time starting *on* a date is different from that under ET Regs 2004, reg. 15, which provides that any period defined under ET Rules 2004 or in a tribunal decision *excludes* the start date.

The rules about the application of time limits when a claim is presented by post were reviewed in *Consignia plc* v *Sealy* [2002] EWCA Civ 878, [2002] ICR 1193. It is now to be assumed as in Civil Procedure Rule 6.7 that first-class post arrives on the second day after it is posted, excluding Sundays, bank holidays, Christmas Day, and Good Friday. So a claim due to be received on a Saturday or Sunday will be in time if it is posted first class no later than the previous Thursday, even if the tribunal office does not open it until the Monday or it is unexpectedly delayed even longer. For this reason the tribunals retain the envelopes in which claims arrive.

If you have visited the Employment Tribunal Service (ETS) website www.employment-tribunals.gov.uk you will have seen that claimants are encouraged to present claims by e-mail. Solicitors should be warned that electronic methods allow for very accurate fixing of the time of presentation. In *Beasley* v *National Grid Electricity Transmissions* EAT 0626/06 the EAT approved an employment judge's rejection of a claim presented 88 seconds too late.

In *Tyne and Wear Autistic Society* v *Smith* [2005] ICR 663, the form ET 1 was completed on-line and was sent by e-mail to the 'host' used by ETS, but for some internal reason was not passed on to ETS itself. The EAT accepted that the claim could be presented electronically but it must reach the website and be accepted there; in *Smith's* case the claimant had done all that was required and the claim was in time. By contrast, in an unreported case, *Mossman* v *Bray Management Ltd* EAT/0477/04, the EAT held in December 2004 that a claim had not been presented in time when the claimant failed to notice that a claim had not been acknowledged as received. This seems a harsher decision than in *Initial Electronic Security Systems Ltd* v *Avdic* [2005] IRLR 671 where the EAT held that an e-mail claim could be expected to arrive within 30 to 60 minutes of transmission, and that the claimant was in time when she sent her ET 1 eight hours before the time-limit expired, albeit unsuccessfully.

The detailed time limits we considered at **13.4.1** contained two broad definitions of an exception:

(a) the 'just and equitable' rule in relation to redundancy payments and all the various heads of discrimination; and

(b) the 'not reasonably practicable' rule in relation to unfair dismissal, the protection of wages, breach of contract and claims under WT Regs 1998.

Those two rules are of very different severity and we shall consider each in turn.

13.4.3   The 'just and equitable' rule

In relation to claims for redundancy payments and claims of discrimination, the relevant time limit can be extended if the tribunal considers it *just and equitable* to do so.

The discretion allowed to the tribunal by this formula is very broad: *Hutchinson* v *Westward Television* [1977] ICR 279. Furthermore, there can be circumstances in which the extension may be lengthy, so that cases considerably out-of-time can still be heard. In *Southwark London Borough Council* v *Afolabi* [2003] EWCA Civ 15, [2003] ICR 800, the claimant was allowed to present a claim of racial discrimination almost nine years late because the facts only came to light when he inspected his personal file. In *Chohan* v *Derby Law Centre* [2004] IRLR 685 the EAT accepted a late claim under this rule where delay was due to bad advice the claimant had received from her legal adviser. Respondents need to be warned that some flexibility may be allowed in claims of disability discrimination. In *Department of Constitutional Affairs* v *Jones*_[2007] EWCA Civ 894, [2008] IRLR 128 the claimant's late presentation of a claim under DDA 1995 (related to a depressive illness) resulted in large part from his reluctance to admit to himself or anyone else that he was disabled, and the Court of Appeal approved the exercise of discretion to allow him to present a claim late, while indicating that discretion was not to be exercised without limit.

13.4.4   The 'not reasonably practicable' rule

By contrast with the rule in those three jurisdictions, the rule in relation to claims of unfair dismissal, of unlawful deductions from wages under ERA 1996, Part II, or of breach of contract or WT Regs 1998 is much stricter. An extension of time is permitted only if:

(a) it was not reasonably practicable to present in time; and

(b) the length of the extension is reasonable.

The meaning of 'not reasonably practicable' has been exposed to much scrutiny in the cases over a long period of time. An early example was *Dedman* v *British Building* [1974] ICR 53, in which Lord Denning MR held that when a claimant, through no fault of his own, was ignorant of the time limit for presentation, that was enough to make it not reasonably practicable for him to meet it. Fault therefore became an important criterion. If the claimant's lateness was not his fault he might well get through; if he or his advisers were in some way at fault that would usually be fatal.

The authorities were reviewed by the EAT in *Trevelyans (Birmingham)* v *Norton* [1991] ICR 488. Wood J suggested that as time passed it would become more difficult than it was in 1974 to persuade employment tribunals that claimants did not know of the time limit. While it sets out some important principles that are still relevant, that case can no longer be regarded as authoritative in relation to an old rule that bad advice (or negligent failure to present the claim) by a solicitor or other adviser was not enough to make it not reasonably practicable. The old rule was that the claimant had a remedy against the solicitor in such a case, but not against the employer. Recent authorities regard that as an unjustified windfall for the employer and take the opposite view—see

Virdi v *Commissioner of Police of the Metropolis* [2007] IRLR 24 for a recent example that reviews the relevant authorities.

The rule had earlier been reviewed by the Court of Appeal in *London Underground Ltd* v *Noel* [1999] IRLR 621. In that case an offer of alternative employment had been accepted by the claimant who therefore did not present a claim of unfair dismissal within the three-month period. The employer subsequently withdrew the offer. The Court of Appeal held that it would nevertheless have been reasonably practicable for her to have presented the claim within the period. The case seems to impose a rather stricter test than that adopted by the same Court only three months before in *Schultz* v *Esso Petroleum Co. Ltd* [1999] IRLR 488. In that case the claimant suffered from depression during the latter part of the three-month period but had been fit and capable of presenting a claim in the first part. It was held that attention had to be focused on the latter part of the period, and that the claimant had established that presentation within the period was not reasonably practicable. Similar leniency may not be extended to a claimant's solicitor. In *Agrico Ltd* v *Ireland* EAT/0024/05, a solicitor's secretary fell ill on the last day of the three-month period and the claim was consequently faxed one day late. The EAT held that it was reasonably practicable for it to have been presented in time; a competent solicitor must have systems in place to comply with time-limits.

The second half of the statutory discretion is also important. If it is established that presentation within the statutory period is not reasonably practicable, the period should be extended only by as much as is *reasonable*. The claimant must act without delay once presentation becomes reasonably practicable: *James W. Cook (Wivenhoe)* v *Tipper* [1990] IRLR 386. So, for example, a claimant who claims ignorance of the time limit must act as quickly as possible on learning of it.

A particularly difficult category of case for exercise of either statutory discretion occurs where a decision of the ECJ or one of the higher courts in this country effectively establishes a new jurisdiction. So, for example, until the decision of the House of Lords in *R* v *Secretary of State for Employment, ex parte Equal Opportunities Commission* [1994] ICR 317, it was generally believed that most part-time employees did not have the right to present a claim of unfair dismissal. In *Biggs* v *Somerset County Council* [1996] ICR 364 an employee who was dismissed in August 1976 argued that her complaint of unfair dismissal was in time because, as a part-time teacher working 14 hours per week, her right to claim only ran from the date of the House of Lords decision on 1 June 1994 and her claim was presented within three months of that date. Her claim was brought under art. 141 of the EC Treaty, and therefore did not need to wait for UK legislation about part-time workers. The Court of Appeal held that time ran from her dismissal in 1976 and the 'not reasonably practicable' rule could not be stretched to the extent she suggested. A different result occurred with the 'just and equitable' rule: *Director of Public Prosecutions* v *Marshall* [1998] ICR 518.

13.4.5   Interrelation with the statutory grievance procedure

We noted at the start of this book that the statutory grievance procedures (SGPs) together with the statutory dismissal and disciplinary procedures (D&DPs) are all due to be abolished in April 2009, and we have deliberately not covered them. That leaves a slight gap as we do not know as we go to press exactly what will replace them. There are two important connexions of the SGP in particular with presentation of an ET 1. First, if the complaint has recently been about something where the SGP should have been used, an ET 1 has not been accepted if the claimant has not used it. As we noted at the start of the chapter, it appears at present that such a strict rule will not apply from April 2009, but the claimant's action in going to a tribunal without making use of voluntary means of resolving disputes may nevertheless be in breach of the ACAS code of practice, which the tribunals are required to take into account. Furthermore, under the Employment Bill currently before Parliament claimants who have not used voluntary means will find their compensation reduced by up to 25 per cent. Secondly, where the complaint to the tribunal is about anything other than dismissal (but not other than constructive dismissal) it has been possible to extend the time limit for presentation by three months while the SGP is completed, or an appeal under D&DP. It was held in *Ashcroft* v *Haberdashers' Aske's Boys' School* [2008] ICR 613, for example, that these rules overtook the previous position, so that some authorities were no longer relevant—especially *Palmer* v *Southend-on-Sea Borough Council* [1984] ICR 372, where the Court of Appeal held that a pending appeal should not delay presentation of a claim and did not make presentation not reasonably practicable. Until some other rule is put into place, those advising claimants would do well to assume that the rule from *Palmer* will now apply again.

13.5   Acceptance by the tribunal office of the claim

Under rr. 2 and 3 of ET Rules 2004 a new step is added to the tribunal procedure. Hitherto, receipt of the claim (then known as the originating application) involved the tribunal office merely in the administrative tasks of stamping it with the date, giving it a reference number and a code indicating the nature of the complaint, and notifying the employer accordingly. Now the office is given a duty to examine the content of the claim and to consider whether it can be accepted.

Any administrative decision within the tribunal office not to accept a claim must be referred to a chairman who makes the final decision. The grounds for refusing to accept are set out in r. 3:

(a) the claim is not made on the prescribed form (from 6 April 2005);

(b) it does not include the relevant information;

(c) the tribunal has no jurisdiction to consider it; or

(d) (until now) the claim is not in accordance with rules about pursuit of statutory grievances.

If rejection is on ground (a), the claimant is told the reason and sent a copy of the form. Although employers have sometimes complained that it is too easy for disgruntled employees to bring cases to the tribunal that stand no prospect of success, this provision allows tribunals to reject claims only because of formal failings and not because they lack merit. As we noted at **13.3.4**, some tribunal chairmen have been interpreting the requirements of r. 1(4) regarding (b) above with great strictness, and have refused to accept claims that do not contain the required information. The EAT has criticised excessive strictness and in *Richardson* v *U Mole Ltd* [2005] IRLR 668, for example, accepted a claim that did not expressly state that the claimant had been an employee of the respondent, although it was clear from the context. The tribunals do not seem to be given any discretion under ET Rules 2004, and the slightly strange EAT suggestion is that they should exercise the power to review decisions in the interests of justice. See also **13.15.1**.

13.6 The response

If the claim is accepted, the tribunal office stamps it with the date, gives it a reference number, and sends a copy with a covering letter ET 2 to the employer named on the form together with a blank response form ET 3 and an explanatory booklet. Use of the form ET 3, like that of ET 1 as discussed earlier, is now mandatory. With permission from the Employment Tribunal Service we have reproduced a copy of the form below.

The response must be presented to the tribunal office within 28 days of the date the copy of the claim was sent to the employer—r. 4(1). The employer may apply for an extension of time to present a response but must do so within the 28-day period and give an explanation—r. 4(4). This seems the best way of dealing with an ET 1 which gives inadequate information for a proper response – as approved by the EAT in *Amey Services Ltd* v *Cardigan* [2008] IRLR 279. Unlike earlier versions of the rules, there is no discretion allowed to the tribunals to validate late responses where no such application has been made, except following a default judgment, as we shall see at **13.7.2**. Nevertheless in *Moroak* v *Cromie* [2005] ICR 1226 the EAT allowed an ET 3 that was submitted by fax 44 minutes late after the respondent's representative's computer broke down. The EAT did so on the basis that a tribunal has power under r. 34 to review all judgments and decisions, and held that refusal to accept a response was included. A less flexible approach was perhaps demonstrated in *Bone* v *Fabcon Projects Ltd* [2006] ICR 1421. The evidence was that the employers had not received the usual ET 2 notification, and, after contact from ACAS, wrote to the tribunal office to say so. The office then sent a duplicate and accepted the employers' response presented later than 28 days from the sending of the original but within 28 days of the sending of the duplicate. The EAT held that there was no provision for resending in such circumstances, that the ET 3 was therefore late, and that the case should have proceeded to a default judgment. Employers have sometimes failed to recognise the importance or urgency of tribunal communications and in some large companies internal post often seems to take a long time to get papers to the right individual. Papers sometimes sit waiting for the right person to return from holiday. Solicitors instructed to act for client employers when only a very short time is left to draft a response will wish to emphasise to the client the importance of acting more speedily next time.

13.6.1 The use of form ET 3

Completion of form ET 3 is as straightforward as that of ET 1. There are, however, a few points worthy of note:

At box 1.1 it is necessary to enter the employer's name and at 1.2 the address. The name and address to which the notices have been sent will be those the claimant has given on the ET 1 and may be incorrect. Claimants sometimes give a trading name that has no standing to defend litigation. This is the opportunity to make any corrections. Solicitors will find that some large companies reorganise themselves remarkably often, and it may take some effort to get proper instructions about the identity of the employer, ending with 'Limited' or 'plc,' but it is better to do the investigation now than to suffer the indignity at a tribunal hearing of being unable to identify your client properly.

In cases where the claim depends on a dismissal, the respondent must answer at box 2.3 whether dismissal is admitted. The practical significance of the answer to this question is that if the claimant claims to have been dismissed and the employer denies it, the

Employment Tribunal Response Form

You can make a response to an Employment Tribunal by completing and editing the form offline. You can save a part or fully completed form, email a saved form to another person for approval, and submit it securely online to the Employment Tribunal Service.

Please make sure you have read the guidance notes on our website or in our booklet on how to make a response before you fill in the form.

Once you have completed your form you can submit it securely online to the relevant Tribunal office. You will receive an email to confirm we have received it. Online responses are processed faster than ones sent by post.

Select the type of claim you wish to make:

☑ I want to respond to a claim.

In order to proceed you must enter the case number and names of the parties printed on the form and letter we sent you:

Case Number

Names of Parties   ∨

Save   Submit   Print   Clear   Continue →

Version 2.07

Need Help?

If you require any help completing your form or have a general question about the tribunals process please contact the Employment Tribunals Enquiry Line on

0845 795 9775

minicom 08457 573 722

Between 9.00am and 5.00pm Monday to Friday, our lines are closed on bank holidays.

We regret we **cannot** provide any legal advice.

Please Note:

By law, your claim must be on an approved form provided by the Employment Tribunals Service, and you must provide the information marked with ● and, if it is relevant, the information marked with ✱ (see "Information needed before a claim can be accepted")

General Information:

Once you have completed your form you can submit it securely on-line to the ETS. On-line forms are processed faster than ones sent by post.

Case number:

1 Name of respondent company or organisation

1.1* Name of your organisation:

Contact name:

1.2* Address

+

Number or Name
Address Line 1
Address Line 2
Address Line 3
Postcode

1.3 Phone number:

1.4 How would you prefer us to   E-mail   Post   Fax
communicate with you? (Please tick only one box)
    E-mail address:
    Fax number:

1.5 What does this organisation mainly make or do?

1.6 How many people does this organisation employ in Great Britain?

1.7 Does this organisation have more than one site in Great Britain?   Yes   No

1.8 If 'Yes', how many people are employed at the place where the claimant worked?

2 Action before a claim

2.1 Is, or was, the claimant an employee?   Yes   No
If 'Yes', please now go straight to section 2.3.

2.2 Is, or was, the claimant a worker providing services to you?   Yes   No
If 'Yes', please now go straight to section 3.
If 'No', please now go straight to section 5.

2.3 If the claim, or part of it, is about a dismissal,   Yes   No
do you agree that the claimant was dismissed?
If 'Yes', please now go straight to section 2.6.

2.4 If the claim includes something **other than** dismissal,   Yes   No
does it relate to an action you took on
grounds of the claimant's conduct or capability?
If 'Yes', please now go straight to section 2.6.

2.5 Has the substance of this claim been raised by the claimant   Yes   No
in writing under a grievance procedure?

2.6 If 'Yes', please explain below what stage you have reached in the dismissal and disciplinary
procedure or grievance procedure (whichever is applicable).
If 'No' and the claimant says they have raised a grievance with you in writing, please say
whether you received it and explain why you did not accept this as a grievance.

3   Employment details

3.1   Are the dates of employment given by the claimant correct?   Yes   No
       If 'Yes', please now go straight to section 3.3.

3.2   If 'No', please give dates and say why you disagree with the dates given by the claimant.

            When their employment started

            When their employment ended or will end

            Is their employment continuing?   Yes   No

       I disagree with the dates for the following reasons.

3.3   Is the claimant's description of their job or job title correct?   Yes   No
       If 'Yes', please now go straight to section 3.5.

3.4   If 'No', please give the details you believe to be correct below.

3.5   Is the information given by the claimant correct about being   Yes   No
       paid for, or working, a period of notice?
       If 'Yes', please now go straight to section 3.7.

3.6   If 'No', please give the details you believe to be correct below. If you gave them no notice or
       didn't pay them instead of letting them work their notice, please explain what happened and why.

3.7   Are the claimant's hours of work correct?   Yes   No
       If 'Yes', please now go straight to section 3.9.

3.8   If 'No', please enter the details you believe to be correct.   hours each week

3.9   Are the earnings details given by the claimant correct?   Yes   No
       If 'Yes', please now go straight to section 4.

3.10 If 'No', please give the details you believe to be correct below.

            Pay before tax   £   each

            Normal take-home pay (including overtime, £   each
            commission, bonuses and so on)

4 Unfair dismissal or constructive dismissal

4.1 Are the details about pension and other benefits given by the claimant correct? **If 'Yes', please now go straight to section 5.**   Yes   No

4.2 If 'No', please give the details you believe to be correct below.

5 Response

5.1✳ Do you resist the claim? **If 'No', please now go straight to section 6.**   Yes   No

5.2● If 'Yes', please set out in full the grounds on which you resist the claim.

6 Other information

6.1 Please do not send a covering letter with this form. You should add any extra information you want us to know here.

7 Your representative If you have a representative, please fill in the following.

7.1 Representative's name:

7.2 Name of the representative's organisation:

7.3 Address   Number or Name
                  Address Line 1
              +   Address Line 2
                  Address Line 3
                  Postcode

7.4 Phone number:

7.5 Reference:

7.6 How would you prefer us to   E-mail   Post   Fax
     communicate with them?
     (Please tick only one box)
     E-mail address:

     Fax number:

Please sign and date here

Signature: Date:

Data Protection Act 1998. We will send a copy of this form to the claimant and Acas. We will put some of the information you give us on this form onto a computer. This helps us to monitor progress and produce statistics. Information provided on this form is passed to the Department of Trade and Industry to assist research into the use and effectiveness of Employment Tribunals.

claimant will have to prove dismissal and will have to open the case at the hearing: see **13.11.3** below. If the employer admits dismissal, the employer begins in order to prove the reason for dismissal. The employer will usually wish to deny dismissal if:

(a) challenging a claim of constructive dismissal;

(b) the employee resigned voluntarily or there was a termination by mutual consent;

(c) the contract ended through frustration;

(d) the claimant is regarded by the employer as still employed.

At box 5.1 the employer must answer whether the claim is resisted. Under ET Rules 2004 it appears that any case where the employer's response fails to indicate resistance will proceed to a default hearing.

The next box, 5.2, is the one where the employer is required to set out the grounds of resistance and this requires rather more consideration.

13.6.2   Grounds of resistance—box 5.2

The general remarks at the end of **13.3.4** about completion of a claim apply equally to the response, and especially to the descriptive part. Parties are not expected to meet High Court standards, but, especially where lawyers are acting for the employer, tribunals will expect the points at issue to be identified clearly. This still leaves considerable scope for individual practitioners to follow their own preferences.

We shall discuss technique by reference to our first three examples: Anastasia whose ET 1 we thought at **13.3.4** was well drafted, and two others, Basil and Catherine, where the ET 1 is badly drafted. Basil's is too long; Catherine's is too brief.

13.6.2.1   An ET 3 for Anastasia

Consider the following as a response to the ET 1 we have already examined at **13.3.4**:

The Respondent company suffered a severe loss of business as a result of the cancellation of a large order by a major customer in September 2008 and was forced with much regret to reduce the size of its workforce by approximately 10 per cent.

The Applicant's dismissal on 5 December was for redundancy. It was essential if the company was to remain in business and was not unfair.

This response is inadequate. While some practitioners prefer to leave as many of their options open as possible, brevity to this extreme is disliked by the tribunals. It deals with the *reason* for dismissal, perhaps in more detail than is necessary, but makes no attempt to show that the employer *acted reasonably* in dismissing for that reason. The tribunal would probably react by asking for additional information (see **13.8.3** below) of *how* it is alleged the employer acted reasonably. This may include questions that the employer might have preferred to leave to be answered at the hearing.

It is therefore better to prepare a fuller response which deals with those matters in the way the employer chooses. The ET 3 should show that the employer knew how to handle a redundancy reasonably and aimed to do so, especially in relation to the matters put in issue by the ET 1. Consider the following second attempt:

On 17 November 2007 the Respondent company announced a redundancy of 20 people because of the cancellation of an important order and started consultation with the recognised trade unions. The unions declined to agree a method of selecting who was to be dismissed, but urged the Respondent to select speedily and to allow those selected to leave as soon as possible immediately after interview on 28 November so as to maximise the value to them of severance payments by avoiding tax.

The Claimant was employed as a design engineer and the Respondent decided to reduce the number so employed from eight to seven. All eight were marked for their length of service, attendance record, quality and quantity of work, and their versatility. The Claimant scored the lowest total mark and was therefore selected for dismissal.

She was called to an interview on 28 November. She declined the offer of being accompanied by another employee. The reason for the redundancy and the selection method were explained to her. She was told she was at risk of redundancy and did not need to attend at work during a consultation period. She had the right to appeal against selection, and to remain in employment while the appeal was heard. She did not appeal, or raise any other questions and, in the absence of any alternative, her dismissal was confirmed on 5 December.

At the time of the claimant's dismissal, two sub-contract design engineers were working in the design office. They were engaged in the final stages of a specific project which was expected to last only two more weeks and which in fact ended at the Christmas holiday. The claimant would have required training to undertake that work and it could not have been completed in the available time.

In all the circumstances the claimant's dismissal for redundancy was not unfair.

This is much better. Unlike a High Court defence it does not follow exactly the same sequence as the ET 1 it is answering and admit or deny each element one by one. Indeed, it appears to tell a remarkably different story. Yet it demonstrates that the employer was aware of some at least of the legal requirements of handling redundancy reasonably and attempted to satisfy them. It states clearly the employer's point of view about the key contentions we spotted in the ET 1 but does not waste time asserting things that are not in issue in any event. Nor does it gratuitously expose the weaknesses the solicitor has uncovered in the respondents' case. We shall see later that it will probably prompt Anastasia's solicitor to ask for inspection of documents, but, apart from that, the case is now ready for hearing.

It is a good test of a well-drafted ET 1 and ET 3 that, taken together, they clearly establish the points at issue.

13.6.2.2 An ET 3 for Basil

Basil was dismissed for theft of company products. The employer understood the requirements of *British Home Stores* v *Burchell* [1980] ICR 303, and aimed to comply with them.

Basil, by contrast, has never heard of *BHS* v *Burchell* and is simply aggrieved that he has lost his livelihood in circumstances where the police say there is insufficient evidence to press criminal charges. He submits an ET 1 claiming unfair dismissal. His entry in box 5.2, completed in a spidery handwriting, runs on beyond box 5.1 on to two more sheets. The following is a considerable précis:

He stresses his long and hitherto unblemished record of employment with this company and earlier employers going back thirty years. He was a willing and cooperative worker and the quality of his workmanship has never been questioned. The evidence against him is scanty. In any event, dismissal is an excessive penalty for petty pilfering. Minor theft and other corrupt practices are widespread in the workplace and he threatens to reveal misconduct by senior people. No disciplinary action has been taken against anyone else. Perhaps he was set up.

Dealing with long and rambling claims like this is often difficult. Basil's statement is so wide-ranging that it is impossible to discern his real complaint. He does not expressly deny theft, but it would be unfair to assume that such an omission by an unrepresented claimant was deliberate. One device is to ask for additional information, specifying precisely what are the grounds for complaining of unfair dismissal, perhaps even seeking leave to delay completion of the ET 3 until it is supplied. In other cases it is better tactically to ignore irrelevant grouses. The claimant may well have been upset by the dismissal and have included in the ET 1 various things written in the heat of the moment that will not in fact be pursued.

Basil's case is probably more of the second kind than the first. The employer will probably want to refute the allegations of widespread dishonesty, more for the record than for this case. (If Basil did not mention such allegations at disciplinary interviews or any appeal hearing, the usual rule that fairness is to be judged by reference to the employer's knowledge *at the time of dismissal* will mean that he gains little by raising them for the first time here.) If there is a serious prospect of accusations being made at the hearing that could take the employer by surprise, it may be necessary to ask later for information: see **13.8.1** below.

Applying the above reasoning, Basil's employer's solicitor may decide to produce an ET 3 which denies general dishonesty in the workplace but otherwise concentrates entirely on showing that the employer tried to comply with the *BHS* v *Burchell* tests and followed a correct procedure:

The Respondent company manufactures small domestic electrical appliances. Because of its susceptibility to petty theft, random security checks are undertaken from time to time.

On 5 November such a random search found the Claimant leaving the works with a machine, in its sales carton, in his bag. He was suspended on full pay while his departmental manager obtained written statements from the security officer and others involved and checked computerised stock records. The statements were sent to the Claimant.

The Claimant was called to a disciplinary interview on 12 November which he attended with his shop steward. His manager invited his comments. He said he did not know the item was in his bag and could not explain how it got there.

During an adjournment the manager and a colleague considered the Claimant's explanation and decided they did not believe it. On resumption the manager told the Claimant they concluded he was trying to steal the machine and he was summarily dismissed.

The Claimant exercised his right of appeal but was unsuccessful.

It is not admitted that dishonesty is widespread or tolerated in the works as alleged or at all.

13.6.2.3   An ET 3 for Catherine

The third of our examples concerns an ET 1 which, by contrast with Basil's, is extremely brief and really gives the employer little indication of Catherine's complaint. Her ET 1 reads like this:

Box 3.5
No.
Box 3.7
Because I have complained informally so many times without anything being done that I needed to react firmly at the time described at 5.1 below.
Box 5.1
Since Mike Jones became my manager two years ago he keeps picking on me for all the unpleasant jobs that the other girls do not want to do. Obviously he does not like me and prefers the younger, prettier ones. I have complained about this treatment on several occasions but nothing is ever done. On 6 November he told me to change jobs. This was the last straw and I resigned.

The employer cannot proceed to the tribunal hearing with a claim as vague as this. At some stage it will be necessary to establish answers to three questions:

(a) What exactly is Mike Jones supposed to have done?

(b) When, how, and to whom were the complaints made?

(c) Is the implied complaint of sex discrimination going to be pursued? (Under old versions of the ET 1 form the category of claim was less clear than now and complaints like this could sometimes be pursued. The new form is clearer and in theory Catherine should not be allowed to pursue such a claim if section 6 of the ET 1 is left blank; the tribunals are not always so strict.)

The mechanism for dealing with such vagueness is through a request for additional information: see **13.8.3** below.

Meanwhile, it is a question of tactics whether or not the employer prefers to delay completion of the ET 3 until that information is supplied. It is of course the claimant's responsibility to show that she was dismissed, and not the employer's to show that she was not. In view of that burden, a blanket denial by the employer may seem to be enough:

It is not admitted that any act or omission by the Respondent employer entitled the Claimant to resign without notice as alleged or at all.

Note the addition of 'as alleged or at all'. This is a standard device in any drafting, and avoids a trap called the *pregnant negative*. If the employee alleges in the ET 1 that something was done to her by a named person on a Friday afternoon in the office, and the ET 3 denies it in precisely the same terms, someone reading the statement may conclude that the event did indeed take place, but the claimant has made some minor error of detail, perhaps with the date, or time or place.

At one stage, when tribunal proceedings were much more informal and hearings more exploratory, such a brief response would probably have been accepted. Now, with the emphasis on case management and clarification of issues in advance of hearing, a tribunal office might well not accept it (see **13.7** below) and insist on more information. In any event an employer who knows the background to Catherine's complaint would probably wish to demonstrate a coherent and reasonable approach to her and think it tactically better to produce a fuller version:

The Claimant was employed as a machine operator and it was a term of her employment that she could be moved at any time from one machine to another and from one shift to another. Whilst the departmental manager usually tries to accommodate the personal preferences of the operators in terms of allocation to machines, this is not always possible and the terms of the contract sometimes have to be adhered to.

During October the Claimant repeatedly declined requests to move to a particular stapling machine. The manager realised that this refusal was causing ill-feeling amongst other operators and told the Claimant she would have to move. He offered to try to resolve any particular difficulties the Claimant might have in complying with such a request but she raised none and persisted in her refusal. The Respondent has a well-used grievance procedure which requires any grievance to be sent in writing to the human resources department but the Claimant has never registered any complaint under it.

On 6 November the manager therefore instructed the Claimant to move.

The said instruction was within the terms of the Claimant's contract of employment. Neither that instruction nor any other act or omission by the Respondent entitled the Claimant to resign without notice.

If, which is not admitted, the said instruction constituted a dismissal, it was for the substantial reason of needing to share out unpopular work and was not unfair.

The final paragraph of that revised version may be important. As we emphasised in **Chapter 10**, a constructive dismissal is not necessarily unfair. Sometimes, in cases of alleged constructive dismissal, it is therefore necessary to plead '*in the alternative*' so that the defence about fairness is in place lest the issue of whether there was a dismissal is lost. Occasionally, if the employer omits to do this, the tribunal office will write asking whether it is wished to do so.

13.6.3   Breach of contract counterclaim by the employer

As we noted in **Chapter 5**, the provision that has now become ETA 1996, s. 3 was brought into effect by the Employment Tribunals Extension of Jurisdiction (England and Wales) Order 1994. Employees can now bring a claim of breach of contract *in the employment tribunal*, rather than only in the courts as previously.

The novel feature of the breach of contract jurisdiction is that the employer is permitted to make a counterclaim against the employee, but only if the employee's claim alleges breach of contract, and not (for example) if the ET 1 is about unfair dismissal alone. Counterclaims are covered by ET Rules 2004 in r. 7, which requires very little except that the counterclaim should be in writing and permits the President to make a practice direction about counterclaims. The requirement as to timing seems not to have been changed from the 1994 Regulations, so that it must be presented by the employer to the tribunal office within six weeks of the date that the employer *received* the copy of the claim. (Those familiar with the old rules will recognise this timing from receipt of the copy of the claim; generally under ET Rules 2004 timing is from the date the copy is *sent*.) The counterclaim cannot relate to the topics listed at **5.8**, which remain actionable in the courts alone, especially:

(a) intellectual property;

(b) restrictive covenants.

13.7   Acceptance and non-acceptance of the response

We have already noted at **13.5** a new provision under ET Rules 2004 for the tribunal to accept the claimant's claim. There is an equivalent provision in r. 5 for the tribunal to accept the respondent's response.

13.7.1   The acceptance procedure

The procedure for acceptance of the response is parallel to that for acceptance of the claim, and there are three grounds for the tribunal office to decline to accept:

(a) the response is not on the prescribed form;

(b) it does not include all the required information; or

(c) it was not presented within the time limit.

As with acceptance of the claim, acceptance of the response does not depend on the merits of the case. If it is rejected on ground (a) above, the employer is told the reason and sent a copy of the appropriate form. Note the point made at **13.6** above about acceptance of late responses.

13.7.2   Default judgments

Under ET Rules 2004, r. 8 any claim where a response has not been presented within time or where a response has not been accepted may be referred to an employment judge for a default judgment, which may deal with liability alone or liability and remedy. The employer (who technically has not even become a respondent) will not be heard. The judgment will be reached without a hearing on the basis of information available to the tribunal, which presumably means the information contained in the ET 1, although it is also possible under r. 10 for the tribunal itself to ask the claimant for additional information.

The only opportunity for the employer subject to a default judgment to be heard about the case is by applying for a review of the default judgment under r. 33. The application must be in writing and be presented within 14 days of the date the default judgment was sent to the parties. It must include a response to the claim, an application of an extension of time to present it and an explanation of why it was not presented within time.

The discretion allowed to the tribunals under ET Rules 2004 to review default judgments seems very limited, but the EAT has used the overriding objective of reg. 3 as the basis to interpret it more broadly. See, for example, *Pendragon plc* v *Copus* EAT 0317/05, where Burton J held that discretion could still be exercised according to principles from a case under the pre-2004 rules concerning late responses. This has surprised some, because the old rules were plainly much more lenient to employers, to an extent indeed that many regarded as unfair compared with the strict rules governing claimants' presentation of the ET 1 on time.

An aspect of the rule regarding default judgments that does not seem to be covered in ET Rules 2004 is the interrelationship with employers' counterclaims. As the time limit for an employer to present a counterclaim is just over two weeks longer than the time to present a response to the claim, it seems to be possible for a claim to have entered the default judgment procedure in the absence of a response, but for a valid counterclaim still to be raised. These circumstances do not yet seem to have arisen in any reported case.

13.8 Case management

We have already noted in the imaginary cases we have been considering that the ET 1 and the ET 3 do not always adequately define the issues that need to be explored at a hearing to decide a case. Often the parties need to communicate with one another, or in default of agreement the tribunal must ensure that a case is properly prepared. In rr. 10–13 of ET Rules 2004 under the title 'Case Management' we find grouped together a number of powers given to employment judges to make orders for the efficient handling of cases. Although some of the terminology is new, most of these powers are based on earlier rules. A list of orders is set out in r. 10(2), but it expressly states that the items listed are examples and the full range envisaged by s. 10(1) could therefore be even more extensive. Orders can be made on consideration of the papers or at a case management discussion. The list of possible orders is comprehensive and includes the manner in which proceedings are to be conducted including setting time limits, linking together of cases and separation of issues in a case. Particular matters that we need to consider further are these:

(a) case management discussions;

(b) provision of additional information;

(c) witness orders ('attendance of any person to give evidence');

(d) disclosure of documents;

(e) supply of written answers to questions;

(f) dealing with part of the proceedings separately;

(g) pre-hearing reviews;

(h) leave to amend claim or response;

(i) witness statements; and

(j) penalties for non-compliance.

In many regions such as Southampton some simpler categories of cases bypass this procedure entirely. Straightforward claims of unlawful deduction from wages or breach of contract, for example, are put into a 'fast-track' system whereby they are simply listed for hearing and some regions set aside time on a fixed day each week to deal with a large number of such cases.

13.8.1 Cooperation between the parties

Before we start to look at the list from the standpoint of orders made by the tribunal it is worth repeating that in practice these steps often start, especially if the parties are legally represented, with an exchange between parties or representatives.

We have already observed, for example, that Catherine's ET 1 was so lacking in detail that the respondent employer was having difficulty in filling in the ET 3. The respondent requires more information, and we shall see shortly in **13.8.3** and **13.8.6** how the tribunal can be asked to order its disclosure. However, the employment judge will expect, especially if the parties are represented, that, before the respondent seeks an order, the claimant will have been asked to comply voluntarily. The employment judge will want to know what was in the request and in the reply to it, and any order may cross-refer to the request.

13.8.2 Case management discussions

A case management discussion (CMD) is a hearing to consider making any of the orders we have been discussing or any other orders about the handling of a case. Such hearings used to be known as hearings for directions, prior to the express provision for them in ET Rules 2004, r. 17(1). They may be instigated by the tribunal or they may be requested by the parties, provided the requirements of r. 11 concerning all applications for orders are satisfied.

(a) An application for any order must be made at least 10 days before the hearing at which it is to be considered.

(b) It must be in writing, be sent to the tribunal office and include the reference number and the reasons for the request.

(c) An application for a CMD must identify what orders will be sought at it.

(d) An application for an order must explain how it will assist the tribunal in dealing with proceedings efficiently and fairly.

(e) Legal representatives must notify other parties of any application for an order (except a witness order) with the reasons for it and notify them of their right to object within seven days.

A CMD is held by an employment judge alone, it may be in private and it cannot determine the rights of a case. That last rule has not prevented employment judges in some regions from expressing an opinion about the merits of a case with a view to encouraging settlement, not necessarily having regard to all the complexities of that matter described in **13.10.3**. There is provision in r. 15(1) for a CMD to be held using electronic communications and this rule permits continuation of the recent practice whereby they are usually in the form of conference telephone calls.

At one stage CMDs were held only exceptionally, reflecting the cost to the parties of attending a hearing in person at the tribunal office and the time requirement for the employment judge. There was even a worry in some regions that the use of telephone conferences offended the requirement to hold hearings in public, but that was resolved and they are now used extensively in all cases of any complexity.

As an example of the usefulness of a CMD it is time to introduce our fourth claimant. Dmitri is a salesman in a furniture shop who has applied several times for promotion to supervisor but has been unsuccessful. He alleges in the ET 1 that his departmental manager told him that he was rejected because of his high level of sickness absence since he developed a serious intestinal disorder, and he claims discrimination on grounds of disability contrary to DDA 1995. The ET 3 says that Dmitri was turned down on his merits and denies that the manager ever made such a statement; it also denies that Dmitri is a disabled person within the meaning of DDA 1995. In cases like this it is very common for the tribunal to take the initiative in calling a CMD at which the employment judge will check that the employer continues to deny that Dmitri is disabled and a timetable will then be set to deal with that issue. Dmitri's solicitor will be instructed to serve the necessary medical evidence on the employer by a defined date and the employer will be given a deadline to respond, conceding disability or not. (Tribunals are urged by ET Regs 2004, reg. 15(4) to set calendar dates rather than time limits where possible.) The employer may be warned about an order for costs if a challenge to Dmitri's status is regarded as unreasonable. The tribunal may then decide to hear the question of Dmitri's disabled status and the merits of the discrimination case as separate issues and will require the parties to estimate the time needed for both hearings in the case. Dates will be set for hearings, for agreeing documents and for exchange of witness statements (see later) and the employment judge will ask whether there are any other orders required by the parties. The tribunal will then be very reluctant to change any of these agreed arrangements unless one party can show an extremely good reason for doing so.

It will be seen from the example that solicitors taking part in a CMD need to be well-prepared. Employment judges usually expect to end a CMD by fixing a date for a hearing, which requires the solicitor to have established the availability of witnesses, and that in turn requires the solicitor to know enough about the case to have decided which witnesses need to give evidence. Sometimes such case management seems to add to the costs of cases that may well not in the end proceed to a hearing.

13.8.3 The provision of additional information

The tribunal will order a party to provide further information if the ET 1 or ET 3 does not give the other side sufficient to prepare for the hearing. Hitherto 'further and better particulars' (as the information used to be known) necessarily involved some kind of development of something already contained in either ET 1 or ET 3; the new name seems likely to allow much broader requests to be made, and the older fine distinctions no longer matter.

In our examples there is plainly a need for the employer to request additional information in Catherine's case. This is done either in the body of a letter or more formally. In either case the request itself will look something like this:

REQUEST FOR ADDITIONAL INFORMATION
ABOUT THE CLAIM

Under Item 5.1

Of 'I resigned' describing precisely with dates and the names of persons involved each and every act or omission by the Respondent employer which allegedly entitled the Claimant to resign her employment without notice.

Of 'I have complained about this treatment on several occasions' specifying the subject matter of the complaints, when and to whom they were made, whether orally or in writing, and what was the result in each case.

We have deliberately not requested any additional information to establish whether Catherine is in fact pursuing the implied claim of sex discrimination. The likelihood is that the discrepancy between the implication at box 5.2 on the ET 1 and the blank in box 6 may be sufficient to prompt an employment judge to call a CMD at which it will be explored. If she says she wishes to pursue the point her representative may in effect be invited to apply to amend the ET 1 accordingly—see **13.8.9** below. If she does not do so, she will not be permitted to raise it without warning at a hearing. So there is no benefit to the respondent in seeking information about it.

We noted above that one of the objectives of making such a request direct of the other party is to prepare the ground to ask for an order if the other party does not comply voluntarily. Such a request can be made during any CMD or as a written application to the tribunal office that complies with the requirements of r. 11 set out at **13.8.2**.

13.8.4 Witness orders

The employment tribunal can issue witness orders against witnesses, usually those who are not willing to attend a hearing voluntarily. The difference between this order and the other orders we are considering is that this is not issued against the other party but directly to the witness. The party applying for the order is not required by r. 11 to notify the other party. Thus the employer may find that witness orders have been issued to several members of staff on the claimant's application and without the employer having any opportunity to express a view.

Basil's case provides two examples of the kind of instance where this rule may be used.

Basil has alleged that dishonesty is widespread in the workplace. If he wishes to proceed with this contention, he may well want to call as witnesses other employees who would not wish to attend voluntarily. A witness order forces them to attend, to give evidence, and (if the order so provides) to bring documents with them.

The employer may also find it necessary to apply for a witness order. Perhaps a shop steward of the trade union would admit that dishonesty is not widespread or would give evidence against Basil's conduct during the disciplinary procedure. The shop steward might well feel it was wrong to give evidence voluntarily against a union member, but would respond favourably if a witness order was issued.

An application to set aside a witness order must be made by the individual to whom it is issued. In practice, however, there is no problem if an employer coordinates applications from an excessive number of staff called to give evidence.

13.8.5 Disclosure of documents

As in the county court, each party in the employment tribunal is entitled to know what documents the other party has in its possession that are relevant to the case and, subject to very limited safeguards, to inspect them. In practice parties almost always comply by supplying the other with photocopies. If disclosure is not given voluntarily, it can be ordered by the tribunal. This rule often causes practical problems: employers frequently regard documents as confidential and resist disclosure, while the tribunals take a different view.

For example, Anastasia was selected for dismissal for redundancy because her score on an assessment was less than that of seven colleagues. She will naturally want to see how the other seven were marked. The employer, on the other hand, will regard the other forms as confidential to the seven individuals and will resist disclosure. This disagreement has been explored in the cases.

Under the old rules, the tribunals could order disclosure only of documents that actually existed and a party could not be required to produce documents or statistics specially: *Carrington* v *Helix Lighting* [1990] IRLR 6. Under ET Rules 2004, that distinction is less important as the tribunal can now order disclosure of documents *or information*, and we shall see at **13.8.6** that they can also order a party to answer questions.

The rule is to be used for documents that can be identified and not for 'fishing': *Clwyd County Council* v *Leverton* [1985] IRLR 197. Thus it is for the parties to make specific requests and usually disclosure depends on the initiative of the party wanting to see a document. There is an increasing tendency, however, especially in some regions, towards the practice in the courts of requiring parties to disclose to each other all relevant documents in their power, possession or control. In *Scott* v *Commissioners of Inland Revenue* [2004] EWCA Civ 400, [2004] IRLR 713 the employer was criticised for not disclosing a revised retirement policy that had an effect on the claimant's expected future working life before retirement and therefore on compensation.

There is no immunity for confidential documents, although sometimes the tribunal will inspect them before ordering disclosure: *Science Research Council* v *Nassé* [1979] ICR 921. If the names of other people in documents are not necessary, they can be obliterated: *Oxford* v *DHSS* [1977] ICR 884. Documents may be anonymised or redacted to protect the confidence of informants if the principles set out in *Linfood Cash & Carry Ltd* v *Thomson* [1989] ICR 518 are observed, although the principles can be applied with some flexibility when necessary, as in *Ramsay* v *Walkers Snack Foods Ltd* [2004] IRLR 754. The employer was not required to disclose the identity of witnesses in *Asda Stores Ltd* v *Thompson* [2002] IRLR 245, where dismissals resulted from the alleged use of hard drugs. Whilst documents passing between a client and the lawyer in connexion with litigation are *privileged* and cannot be included in an order for inspection, this rule is restricted in the tribunals to lawyers and does not apply to other representatives: *New Victoria Hospital* v *Ryan* [1993] ICR 201.

Anastasia's care raises an issue about disclosure of documents that is common in cases of dismissal for redundancy: can she insist on seeing the assessment forms for the others in her unit of selection? She will argue that such information is essential to the preparation of her case, while the employer may feel that disclosure breaks the confidence owed to the other employees. In *British Aerospace plc* v *Green* [1995] ICR 1006 the employer sought to avoid disclosure of other forms. The Court of Appeal declined to support the employment judge's order for disclosure of the forms. The tribunal was concerned only with the question of whether an assessment system was properly applied, and should not scrutinise its workings officiously; disclosure of the forms of those retained in employment was unnecessary for this purpose. Despite that authority, many tribunals seem in practice to have found reasons to distinguish *Green* and have continued to order disclosure. Thus, for example, in *John Brown Engineering Ltd* v *Brown* [1997] IRLR 90, the EAT in Scotland supported an employment tribunal finding that withholding other employees' marks rendered the appeal procedure 'a sham'. If disclosure is required for an internal appeal, it is difficult to see how it could be refused for tribunal proceedings.

A middle course that the tribunals sometimes adopt is to order disclosure of forms with names and other personal details obliterated. Obviously Anastasia is bound to respect the confidentiality of any documents she receives and will expose herself to action if she discloses them outside the tribunal case.

13.8.6   Supply of written answers to questions

The tribunal may order either party to answer questions posed by the tribunal. In practice, the tribunal may require the applicant to produce a schedule of losses (which quantifies the claim) but most other questions are prepared and posed by the other party. Quite often the dividing line between questions and additional information becomes blurred, and requests are made that fall somewhere between the two.

In some kinds of case it is useful to be able to serve questions that could not possibly be described as additional to ET 1 or ET 3. A solicitor acting for Dmitri may well want to exploit this provision, perhaps asking for statistical information about numbers of disabled and non-disabled people who have been promoted. As we noted at **6.6.1** above, the employer cannot be forced to reply to the statutory questionnaire in a discrimination case. However, if Dmitri asks some of the same questions under this provision, the tribunal can require the employer to answer. There are also occasions when the rule can be used to agree non-contentious matters of fact between the parties, thus reducing the evidence that needs to be given at the eventual tribunal hearing and possibly saving a lot of time. Solicitors will generally resist answering questions that really amount to cross-examination in advance.

13.8.7   Dealing with part of the proceedings separately

We have already encountered this possibility in the context of the CMD we discussed for our fourth imaginary example at **13.8.2** above. Dmitri claims to be a disabled person within the meaning of DDA 1995, and the employer challenges that claim. The issue whether he falls within the statutory definition is clearly a matter of some importance; if he does not, the whole of the remainder of his claim fails and there is no point in the parties' wasting time preparing for a hearing about the merits or of course in the tribunal's holding such a hearing. So that point is decided first as a separate matter, and (although the term does not appear in ET Rules 2004) this is usually called a preliminary hearing.

Preliminary hearings have often taken place about issues of jurisdiction, such as whether a claim was presented in time or whether a claimant has sufficient service to make a particular claim. Under ET Rules 2004 we may find that some of those issues are considered by the tribunal when deciding whether to accept a claim, and the only hearing would then be on an application to review a decision not to accept.

A preliminary hearing is a full hearing of the tribunal, but it can often be heard by an employment judge sitting alone, especially since the widening of that power by ERDRA 1998, s. 3. The EAT held in *Sutcliffe* v *Big C's Marine* [1998] ICR 913 that employment judges should not sit alone if contentious issues of fact are involved, apparently overruling their earlier decision to the contrary in *Tsangacos* v *Amalgamated Chemicals Ltd* [1997] ICR 154.

13.8.8   Pre-hearing reviews

One of the case management orders available to a tribunal is an order to hold a pre-hearing review (PHR). There are special provisions about PHRs in ET Rules 2004, rr. 18–19 and we shall consider them separately at **13.9** below.

13.8.9   Leave to amend a claim or response

Among the case management orders listed at ET Rules 2004, r. 10(2) is (q) the giving of leave to amend a claim or response. At a time when tribunals were more informal, such amendments were unimportant; new arguments were often raised at a hearing. Now, it would be inconsistent with the modern style of case management for parties to be taken by surprise, and it is necessary to apply to amend a claim or response if in the course of preparation for a hearing you find that the original version inadequately covers the case you wish to make. This often happens if the client drafted a claim or response and sent it in to the tribunal before you were instructed.

Sometimes it can be difficult to know whether the omission is important enough to matter, or whether it puts you at a tactical disadvantage to seek leave, or even looks incompetent to your client unless done carefully. Catherine's case is a good example where amendment is undoubtedly necessary, as we noted at **13.8.3**. If she is serious about her allegation of sex discrimination, section 6 of her ET 1 must be completed. The employer will want if possible to resist the broadening of her claim in this way. So we must ask what grounds there are to object, and how the tribunal decides the matter.

The authority on this matter is *Selkent Bus Co. Ltd* v *Moore* [1996] ICR 836 and the tribunal will not allow an amendment that has the effect of circumventing the usual rules about time limits. So, if a claimant completes an ET 1 about one jurisdiction and is then out of time to present a claim about something different, the tribunal will not allow an amendment to the first so as to bring in the second by the back door. It is different if the first is so expressed as to include the second, so that the second claim is in fact merely a tidying-up of the legal process. Catherine's case is of this latter kind: the reference in the ET 1 that we examined at **13.6.2.3** contains sufficient to put the respondent on notice that there is an element of sex discrimination in her allegation and leave to amend the ET 1 will not be refused. In *Ali* v *Office of National Statistics* [2004] EWCA Civ 1363, [2005] IRLR 201, the Court of Appeal reviewed all the relevant authorities and held there was no material difference between the test of whether allowing an amendment was *just and equitable* and the test of a *balance of injustice and hardship* suggested in *Selkent*. In *Lehman Brothers Ltd* v *Smith* EAT/0486/05 it was held that the tribunal must always look at the balance of prejudice and hardship, so that the question whether a new claim is out of time is not determinative; an amendment was allowed in that case.

13.8.10   Written witness statements

There is an express reference in the list at r. 10(2)(s) to an order for the preparation or exchange of a witness statement. In some tribunal regions it is now almost invariable practice with all cases except those put into the 'fast-track' (see **13.8** above) to issue an order requiring agreement between the parties about a bundle of documents for the hearing and the exchange of witness statements. Occasionally the parties are ordered to prepare a schedule of agreed facts or events in the case. Dates are set for all these steps to be completed.

Recent practice has varied considerably among regions and we had expected that a practice direction issued by the President under ET Regs 2004, reg. 13 might introduce some standardisation. No practice direction has been issued and we do not expect that the letter to regional employment judges commending good practice will remove the differences. So solicitors must for the time being read such orders carefully. In the Leeds and Bedford regions, for example, the order has often required a bundle to be agreed four weeks after presentation of the ET 3 and witness statements to be exchanged two weeks later. In Bristol and Birmingham the bundle must be agreed 14 days before the hearing and witness statements must be exchanged seven days before hearing. In Cardiff no such orders are usually made at all.

We shall return to both bundles of documents and written witness statements when we discuss preparation for the hearing in **13.11** below.

13.8.11   Penalties for non-compliance with an order

The penalties for failing to comply with any of these orders are laid down in ET Rules 2004, r. 13 and there are three possibilities open to a tribunal.

(a) Costs may be awarded.

(b) After notice is given to the defaulting party, the whole or part of the claim or response may be struck out, but this can only be done at a hearing or PHR.

(c) If the order itself provides that failure to comply will lead to striking out, then the claim or response can be struck out on the date of non-compliance without further ado.

In practice striking out for failure to comply with an order has been very rare indeed and costs have usually been considered the appropriate penalty. Unusually, in *Blockbuster Entertainment Ltd* v *James* [2006] EWCA Civ 684, [2006] IRLR 630, the employment tribunal struck out a claim where it found that the claimant showed 'wilful and deliberate disobedience' of an order for disclosure for documents and failed also to comply with other orders. The Court of Appeal regarded the power to strike out as a draconic power, not to be readily exercised, and only to be used when it was a proportionate response—which it was not in this case.

13.9   Pre-hearing reviews

The provisions regarding the holding of a PHR are now to be found in ET Rules 2004, r. 18. The idea is to discourage parties from pursuing hopeless cases.

Either party can apply for a PHR, or the tribunal can take the initiative itself. In practice very few claimants apply. The tribunals have in the past seldom instigated PHRs themselves and in many regions have been reluctant to grant respondents' applications. Recently they have been used more extensively. In Bristol, for example, where PHRs are often held as telephone conferences, the tribunal has indicated it will hold them as a normal course in claims of unfair dismissal involving the rule in *British Home Stores* v *Burchell* [1980] ICR 303, where the facts seem largely agreed. So Basil's case would probably proceed to a PHR if his employment was in that region.

Under r. 18, a PHR is an interim hearing and is to be conducted by an employment judge alone, unless one party makes a written request ten days beforehand for a hearing by a full tribunal or the employment judge decides that substantive issues of fact have to be decided and that a full tribunal is desirable. A PHR is to be held in public but it can use electronic communications. So the employment judge must conduct any telephone conference from a room to which the public has access.

The purpose of a PHR is to carry out a preliminary consideration of the case. Under the old rules of procedure this was confined to the ET 1, the ET 3 and written representations and/or oral argument, with a view to identifying contentions that stood no reasonable prospect of success and warning the appropriate party accordingly. The provision under ET Rules 2004 is less narrow and allows the employment judge or tribunal to look at evidence and to reach a broader set of conclusions:

(a) to determine interim or preliminary matters;

(b) to perform any of the functions of a CMD;

(c) to require a party to pay a deposit as a condition of proceeding with a contention that has little reasonable prospect of success; and/or

(d) after giving due notice, to strike out all or part of a claim or response which is scandalous, vexatious or has no reasonable prospect of success, or has been conducted scandalously, unreasonably or vexatiously, or which has not been actively pursued (see r. 18(7)).

The deposit that the employment judge or tribunal can order is up to £500, subject to enquiry about the party's ability to pay, and it has to be paid within 21 days of the date the decision is sent to the parties in writing. If the deposit is not paid, the claim, response or part concerned is struck out. Most such orders are made against the claimant and it is unusual for the deposit to be paid, so that the claim is struck out, but if the deposit is paid and the case proceeds to a hearing where that contention fails, the party concerned may lose the deposit as a contribution to costs.

If a PHR considers the possibility of requiring a deposit, whether or not such an order is made, no employment judge or member of the tribunal who heard the PHR may then sit at the full hearing of the case.

The most radical of the above provisions is (d), the right to strike out various categories of case, including those with no reasonable prospect of success. We see no evidence that employment judges are now any less reluctant than before to strike out any but the very obviously hopeless cases.

13.10 Conciliation and the role of ACAS

13.10.1 How ACAS becomes involved

Under all the jurisdictions of the employment tribunals we have been considering in this chapter there is a standard procedure under ETA 1996, s. 18 that a copy of every claim to the tribunal is sent by the tribunal office to ACAS. It is the job of the ACAS conciliation officer to seek to reach an agreement between the parties to settle the complaint without its being determined by the employment tribunal. Conciliation was extended to cover claims to redundancy payments as well as all the other jurisdictions by ERDRA 1998, s. 11.

The conciliation officer makes contact as a matter of course with both parties, usually telephoning professional representatives and arranging to meet unrepresented parties. This initiative avoids either party creating the appearance of lack of confidence in their case. The role of the conciliation officer is to try to promote a settlement and not to adjudicate on the merits of the case. In practice this is often too fine a distinction to draw and some debate on the merits takes place.

A new element is introduced into the conciliation process by ET Rules 2004, r. 22. Except for claims that include any complaint of discrimination or claim of equal pay (even if among other jurisdictions), there is a fixed period for conciliation, during which no full hearing is permitted to take place, although a CMD or PHR may take place and dates can be fixed. Claims concerning breach of contract or deductions from wages and claims for a statutory redundancy payment are subject (unless an employment judge directs otherwise) to the *short conciliation period of seven weeks* beginning with the date the copy of the ET 1 is sent to the respondent. The other categories of claim we have been considering in this chapter (unfair dismissal and claims under the Working Time Regulations 1998) and claims from the first group where an employment judge so directs are subject to the *standard conciliation period of 13 weeks*, beginning on the same date, with the possibility of extension by two weeks if everyone agrees.

It had widely been assumed that the description of the conciliation period as 'fixed' meant only that a full tribunal hearing could not happen during that period, and that ACAS conciliators would still make themselves available if required after it was over. That has proved to be wrong. Involvement after the end of the fixed period requires the express authorisation of an ACAS manager, which is not easily obtained. So, if agreement is difficult to reach, it may then become necessary to switch to a compromise agreement—see below.

The ACAS officers use a number of standard forms, often referred to by their initials. Form COT 1 is the office record for ACAS, but the others may be seen by the parties.

COT 2 is the form used to record reinstatement or re-engagement of the claimant.

COT 3 is used to record terms of a settlement, usually involving some payment of money, but sometimes other matters like the provision of a reference (either in addition to money or instead of it) or confidentiality as to the terms.

COT 4 is used to record a withdrawal by the claimant.

As soon as the conciliation officer reaches some settlement of the claim, the tribunal office is notified and the case is held in abeyance pending receipt of the appropriate form, signed as necessary by one or both of the parties.

13.10.2   Binding settlements

Most of the statutory rights we have been considering in this book are subject to the rule that the parties cannot contract out of them. For example, the right to complain of unfair dismissal is protected by s. 203 of ERA 1996. Exceptions, where they exist at all, are closely defined.

Because of the breadth of that rule, even an agreement between the parties to settle terms of dismissal will not preclude a later change of mind by the ex-employee who can then start tribunal proceedings. There are two exceptions, where settlements are binding. The first is in relation to agreements reached with the involvement of ACAS. However, ACAS has become unwilling to act merely as a 'rubber stamp' in giving its formal blessing to agreements already concluded between the parties and declines to prepare a COT 3 settlement in relation to negotiations it has not led, partly because of worries about the resulting workload and partly because to do so might exceed its statutory powers. This has caused practical problems where both sides have wanted a COT 3 settlement and ACAS has felt unable to help.

The second exception is contained in ERA 1996, s. 203(2)(f), which provides that a 'compromise agreement' is binding if reached with the advice of the applicant's *relevant independent adviser*. The adviser concerned must be covered by insurance, and the agreement itself must be in a form that complies with each of the requirements of s. 203(3). Under amendments introduced by ERDRA 1998 into s. 203(3A) and (3B), advisers covered by this rule include not only lawyers (as hitherto) but also trade union officials and workers in advice centres, except in relation to their own employees. There is sometimes a problem under either method when such representatives purport to have the authority to settle on their members' behalf, but have not properly obtained it—see *Gloystarne & Co. Ltd* v *Martin* [2001] IRLR 15.

13.10.3 Considerations for the parties about whether to settle

The decision whether to fight a case in the employment tribunal or to seek to settle before the hearing may be a complex one for both parties.

In the simplest cases the matter is merely one of the amount of money involved. Suppose, for example, that the claim is of unfair dismissal, and both sides are considering the possibility of settlement through the involvement of ACAS.

The claimant may consider that the likely award of compensation from the tribunal if the claim is successful may be £5,000, but that the chances of success are only 50:50. Maybe, therefore, a definite promise of £2,500 is as good as taking a chance on £5,000. However, the costs of contesting the case in the tribunal may be £1,000 more than has already been incurred. This suggests that settlement at anything in excess of £1,500 may be worthwhile.

The employer's estimate of the likely award may be lower (perhaps £4,000) and the estimate of the chances of losing rather higher (say three to one). So applying the odds of one-in-four to the likely award suggests a settlement of £1,000. The employer may also be likely to incur additional costs by contesting the case, perhaps £1,000. So the employer will be attracted by the prospect of settling at anything below £2,000.

The conciliation officer has a relatively easy task in such a case. Where the parties eventually come together in the range between £1,500 and £2,000 will obviously reflect their respective skills as negotiators.

Cases in real life are rarely quite so simple. Both parties have a much more complicated agenda and will look to their solicitors for advice. The issues involved in such a decision may be significantly different from those in most civil litigation, and the solicitor may wish to encourage the client to try to analyse some of the factors involved. **Table 13.2** below provides a model for use in complaints of unfair dismissal; cases like Dmitri's where it is necessary to preserve a continuing relationship between the parties raise even more complex issues.

13.10.3.1 Other issues

In assisting clients to analyse issues like those listed above, solicitors will wish to discourage reliance on irrelevant reasoning:

(a) Claimants such as Basil (**13.6.2.2**) sometimes want to go ahead to clear their names, especially against implications of dishonesty. Such logic displays a widespread but erroneous view of the role of the tribunals. The solicitor will have to try to explain the principles of *British Home Stores* v *Burchell* [1980] ICR 303. However, it is difficult for claimants to understand that tribunals are concerned only to assess the *reasonableness* of the employer's belief and not its objective proof to a criminal standard.

(b) Both parties often see the issue for the tribunal as one of principle and are keen to get their own back on the other side. It needs to be explained that this too is not the role of the tribunals. As time passes, however, both sides probably become more pragmatic and less concerned about the supposed principles.

Table 13.2 **Issues for both sides in deciding whether to settle a tribunal claim**

Issues for the claimant	*Issues for the employer*
How much will be awarded if I win?	How much is at stake if we lose, including any special or additional awards or orders for reinstatement or re-engagement?
What are my chances of winning?	What are the chances of losing?
What are the legal costs of continuing the fight?	What are the legal costs of fighting?
What are the costs or disadvantages of losing a day or more in the hearing, especially in a new job?	What is the cost in management time?
What is the effect of the Recoupment Regulations (see **13.14.1**)?	
How much might the other side offer?	How much will the claimant accept?
Will the publicity of a tribunal hearing, probably reported in the local press, adversely affect my chances of future employment or my security in my present job?	Will publicity be damaging in the local labour market, with customers or with the boss at group headquarters?
Can I and any witnesses face the personal strain of a tribunal hearing?	Might fighting the case require us to call witnesses we would rather not use, e.g., the fellow-employee who originally brought dishonesty to our notice or to disclose confidential documents?
Has the employer more to lose than I have by going to the tribunal?	What precedents are set by being seen to have settled out of court for any future cases where employees will expect like treatment? Will the manager who originally made the decision to dismiss feel that his or her authority has been compromised?
	Shall we lose the opportunity of training supervisors in the importance of following procedures by avoiding a tribunal hearing? Does settlement compromise the integrity of our disciplinary procedure or damage the motivation of other employees?
Is my former employer likely to be offended by my refusal to settle in a way that may prejudice any future reference? (Victimisation is in theory forbidden but is difficult to prove.)	

13.10.4 Drafting a settlement

A compromise agreement must meet the requirements of ERA 1996, s. 232(3) as to its format. In particular it must be in writing, identify the adviser, and state that the conditions regulating compromise agreements have been satisfied. A model can be found in books of precedents.

A solicitor preparing such an agreement or the wording for a COT 3 must give some thought to the question of what it should cover. In relation to a dismissal, for example, an employer will want any payment to settle all claims (whether or not yet made) for unfair dismissal, wrongful dismissal, discrimination of any kind, and any contractual or similar claim that may be outstanding on the termination of employment. Employees, on the other hand, will wish to ensure that any such broad definition does not preclude them from enforcing their future pension rights or from litigation about some future industrial disease or personal injury. Many solicitors acting for employees and also ACAS conciliation officers ask for these matters to be excluded expressly. The courts have tended to construe compromise agreements strictly against the party (usually the employer) seeking to rely on them, and the express exclusion of claims of a different nature or which have not yet arisen is probably unnecessary. In *University of East London* v *Hinton* [2005] EWCA Civ 532, [2005] ICR 1260 the Court of Appeal held that a specific type of claim (in that case one of public interest disclosure under ERA 1996, s. 47B) was only compromised if particularly specified.

It is unlikely, whatever words are used, that a settlement will preclude a party from pursuing an action which was not known about and could not be known about at the date of the agreement. See, for example, the House of Lords decision in *Bank of Credit and Commerce International* v *Ali* [2001] ICR 337. Former employees were permitted to pursue a claim for damages for disadvantage on the labour market caused by widespread publicity about corruption and dishonesty at the bank, despite accepting terms 'in full and final settlement'. When signing the agreement neither party could realistically have supposed that such a claim was a possibility. Claims unknown to the claimant at the time of signing a compromise agreement can only be compromised by 'extremely clear words'—*Royal National Orthopaedic Hospital Trust* v *Howard* [2002] IRLR 849. Thus in *Hilton UK Hotels* v *McNaughton* EAT/0059/04 an equal pay claim about pension rights of part-time workers could still be pursued; that case also suggests that such extremely clear words are unlikely to occur very often. In practice the wording used in compromise agreements has been given more searching scrutiny than that on forms COT 3.

13.10.5   The arbitration alternative

In May 2001, there was brought into force a scheme of arbitration in unfair dismissal applications provided for under s. 7 of ERDRA 1998 as an alternative to tribunal proceedings. See ACAS Arbitration Scheme (England and Wales) Order 2001, SI 2001/1185. It was mentioned at **10.12.2** above. The parties may agree, through the ACAS conciliation officer, to submit a dispute about unfair dismissal to binding arbitration, which ACAS will then arrange but not itself conduct. The scheme took a long while to develop because of worries that the denial of a fair trial, albeit by agreement, might breach the HRA 1998, and the result is consequently somewhat cumbersome. It has been very little used.

13.10.6   Withdrawal

Claimants can withdraw their claims at any time, and frequently do so, whether on their own initiative or as a result of the involvement of ACAS. It is in theory possible for the respondent to claim costs, but this almost never happens, and costs have rarely been awarded: see **13.11.2** below. In *Ako* v *Rothschild Asset Management Ltd* [2002] EWCA Civ 236, [2002] ICR 899, the Court of Appeal advises a tribunal to ask an applicant about the circumstances of withdrawal, as a cause of action estoppel will arise if the application was dismissed judicially on the applicant's withdrawal, but not if it was merely discontinued. Now, under ET Rules 2004, r. 25 dismissal of the claim no longer follows automatically on the claimant's withdrawal, but requires an application from the respondent. However, the tribunal has no discretion to set aside a withdrawal if the claimant has a subsequent change of mind—*Khan* v *Heywood & Middleton Primary Care Trust* [2006] EWCA Civ 1087, [2006] IRLR 793.

Care should be taken in relation to complaints of breach of contract. In *Patel* v *RCMS Ltd* [1999] IRLR 161, the EAT held that the employer's counterclaim survived the employee's withdrawal. Obviously a settlement providing for mutual withdrawal would have been a safer option for the applicant than unilateral action.

13.11 The hearing

If the efforts of ACAS prove unsuccessful the claim now proceeds to a hearing in the employment tribunal. If the ET 1 and ET 3 are reasonably well drafted and the case management procedures have been used properly, it should by this stage be fairly clear what the issues for the tribunal are going to be.

For example, in Anastasia's case (**13.3.4**), a key issue is whether the assessment that led to her selection for redundancy was fairly and properly carried out. The employer will presumably call as a witness the person or people who performed it; Anastasia herself, and possibly other witnesses, will want to challenge its fairness, partly by their own evidence and partly by challenging the employer's evidence. Both sides may wish to produce documents to support their contentions.

We now need to examine how that all happens in practice. We shall do so by reference to the main hearing (denoted hearing by ET Rules 2004, r. 26) of the merits of a claim, but we have already noted at **13.8.7** that the tribunal can order under r. 10(2) that part of the proceedings should be dealt with separately. Each part, like any CMD or PHR, then qualities as a hearing under r. 14(1) and the following remarks apply to each part.

13.11.1 Preparations

By the ET Rules 2004, r. 14(4), the tribunal office is required to give the parties 14 days' notice of a hearing except a CMD, unless the parties agree to shorter notice. Many dates of hearing are fixed in the course of a CMD, so that the parties have already agreed their availability, but some are notified by post or e-mail. If the parties have not been consulted about a date, the tribunal office is normally very amenable to granting one postponement, although some regions have been known to require detailed justification for such a request. The request is more likely to be granted if the party making it has consulted the other parties and is able to write as soon as possible after the notification, proposing an alternative date or dates. The tribunal offices are much less willing to grant late requests, and will require detailed justification for any request to postpone an agreed date, including evidence of the illness or other non-availability of a witness. No postponement will usually be granted, for example, if a witness has booked a holiday *after* the tribunal date was fixed.

Increasingly notices of hearing include the employment judge's estimate of the likely length of hearing and it is for the parties to say so if they disagree for any reason. Many employment judges are already limiting cross-examination and speeches to ensure that cases are completed in the time allocated.

Hearings are normally public and the press are admitted. Under r. 16(1) of ET Rules 2004 hearings may be in private in tightly defined and exceptional circumstances. Under r. 50 hearings may be subject to restricted reporting orders where allegations of sexual misconduct are involved. In *X v Commissioner of Police of the Metropolis* [2003] ICR 1031 the EAT held that this provision should be used to ensure applicants were not deterred from bringing such cases, a protection required by art. 6 of the European Equal Treatment Directive 76/207/EEC.

We noted when discussing the operation of a CMD at **13.8.2** above that it was important for a solicitor acting for either party to have given careful thought at a very early stage to the presentation of the client's case at an eventual tribunal hearing. So as we come now to consider how it should be done, we hope you are not looking at this part of the chapter for the first time once the hearing is fixed.

Appearing for a client at a tribunal hearing is all about *persuasion*. You have to persuade the employment judge or a tribunal of three, none of whom has any personal interest in the outcome, to adopt your client's version of the facts and your interpretation of the law rather than your opponent's. You have three tools available to you: the documents, the evidence of witnesses, and the authorities. Without compromising your personal integrity you have to decide how to use each of them most effectively in support of your case.

13.11.2 Documents

We have already discussed at **13.8.10** the orders that tribunals often issue for parties to agree a joint bundle of documents. There is an increasing tendency for the order to limit the permitted size of the bundle, perhaps to a total of 40 pages in a tribunal scheduled for hearing in a single day, and 90 pages for a two-day hearing, with any extra pages requiring express permission from the tribunal. Where requested, with reasons, such permission is not usually refused, but of course good reasons must be supplied. This does not usually cause a problem where both parties are represented, as representatives are willing to compromise, but sometimes it happens that unrepresented claimants make unreasonable demands. In such a case you will wish to write formally proposing fewer documents so that it is clear to the tribunal where the fault lies in failing to comply with their order. The tribunals are less strict than the courts in operating the 'best evidence' rule, and photocopies of documents are usually sufficient, but it is a wise precaution to take originals to the hearing in case any issue of authenticity arises.

Sometimes certain documents are obviously required. Thus in Basil's case the employer's disciplinary procedure, any rules stipulating what conduct may lead to summary dismissal and the notes of disciplinary meetings will probably be required by both parties. Irrelevant material should be left out—both because the tribunals dislike needlessly large bundles and because the persuasive power of anything good is reduced if it is buried in a lot of paper. So if, for example, the procedure and rules are contained in an employee handbook, it is a good idea to take a copy of the handbook to the hearing in case anyone wants to see the whole, but only the relevant parts should go into the bundle.

Contemporaneous documents have much greater persuasive power than anything written up after the event. So working documents concerned with Anastasia's selection may be very helpful in showing how carefully the employer approached the task. Any manuscript notes taken by either side during the crucial meeting with the departmental manager in Dmitri's case will far outweigh typed notes prepared subsequently.

Documents should be assembled in a folder, in chronological order, with an index at the front and with the pages (rather than the documents) numbered in sequence. It will be found that this makes reference during the hearing as simple as possible.

13.11.3 The order of proceeding and burden of proof

Under ET Rules 2004, r. 14(4) it is provided that either party may send in to the tribunal written representations as an alternative to attending in person. They must be lodged at the tribunal office at least seven days before the hearing. In practice this is a very unsatisfactory alternative and should be used with great reluctance.

Apart from that possibility, the parties turn up on the day appointed to give their own evidence, to cross-examine witnesses for the other side, and to address the tribunal. Although the tribunal is given wide powers under the rules to determine its own procedure, that power is in practice much circumscribed by custom and by cases such as *Aberdeen Steak Houses* v *Ibrahim* [1988] ICR 550, which sets out some general principles.

In practice the order of proceeding is standardised. Generally speaking it is for the party on whom the burden of proof rests to start the proceedings. Thus, in relation to deductions from wages, discrimination, and equal pay it is for the *claimant* to start by making out a case. In dismissal cases (unfair dismissal and claims for redundancy payments), it is for the *claimant* to go first if it is necessary to prove dismissal, i.e. if the employer denies dismissal. If the employer admits dismissal, the *employer* goes first to prove the reason for dismissal. This rule is of long standing (*Gill v Harold Sheepbridge* [1974] ICR 294) and pre-dates the present statutory provision about burden of proof.

13.11.4 Opening statement

In the past the party opening proceedings often made an opening statement, as in the county court. Occasionally employment judges still permit that to happen and it can be helpful in identifying the real issues in a case. Increasingly, though, and especially where witness statements and the bundle are handed in to the tribunal in advance, employment judges regard opening statements as superfluous and prefer to get on with the evidence. Solicitors may sometimes be permitted to draw the attention of the tribunal to key parts of the bundle before the evidence starts.

13.11.5 Evidence-in-chief

The two sides will need to decide what facts they need to prove in order to establish their cases and to decide what witnesses need to be called. As in the courts, this evidence given on behalf of the party calling the witness is called evidence-in-chief.

13.11.5.1 The rules of evidence

The rules of evidence followed in the employment tribunals are based on those in the county courts, but are less rigid. The rule against hearsay is not strictly followed, and evidence is often permitted that would be forbidden in the courts. Indeed, the definition of hearsay is complicated by the slightly special nature of the issues the tribunals often need to investigate. If a manager decided to dismiss a claimant because of a report made to him by a subordinate about the claimant's behaviour, the content of the report may sometimes be direct evidence of the manager's reasoning in deciding to dismiss, rather than hearsay evidence of the claimant's behaviour.

During evidence-in-chief, the solicitor should follow the normal rule of not asking leading questions, except when presenting background evidence about non-contentious aspects of the case. Even then it is courteous to ask the tribunal's permission before leading a witness.

13.11.5.2 Written witness statements

At one stage the tribunals required all evidence to be given through oral examination. The employment judge was required to write down the salient points and, if the case went to appeal, could be required by EAT to produce a transcript of the notes. From 1991 onwards the tribunals in several regions experimented with systems of written witness statements as a means of saving time at the hearing. Most regions now impose some such requirement but there is considerable variation.

It must be stressed that the saving of time is of tribunal hearing time and not in preparation. A solicitor preparing written statements of witnesses' evidence needs to be meticulous in achieving complete accuracy. If a proof of evidence for the use of counsel contains a minor inaccuracy (e.g., the colour of a car), it will be corrected during examination-in-chief. If a witness statement contains such an inaccuracy, it will cast doubt on the reliability of more important elements. So the additional work in preparing such statements is in fact considerable. Each statement should end with a statement of truth signed by the witness.

Most regions order witness statements to be exchanged between the parties who may be required to arrive early and to hand in copies of the bundle and of the witness statements so that members of the tribunal can read them before the start of the hearing. The tribunal may then require witnesses to read the statements aloud under oath or, increasingly, they take the statements as read and move straight on to cross-examination. Representatives are sometimes not permitted to ask additional questions by way of examination-in-chief without leave of the tribunal, although such leave is usually given in relation to points raised by the other side's statements. Such procedures do not add much to informality in the tribunals.

The variation in procedure causes problems for solicitors and other representatives. The style of a witness statement prepared for reading aloud may be rather different from one prepared for the tribunal to read for itself. It is always a good idea to try to find out local practice before appearing before any tribunal for the first time.

13.11.6 Cross-examination

The art of cross-examination cannot be learned from a book but only by practice. The rules are the same as in the courts and it is important that key elements in your case are 'put to' the witnesses of the other side so that they have a chance to refute them. With an unrepresented claimant the tribunal will sometimes permit recall of the witness for the purpose, as the claimant may not have understood the requirement, but solicitors may not be given that flexibility.

13.11.7 Questions from the tribunal and re-examination

The final stage of evidence from each witness is for the party calling that witness to tidy up loose ends resulting from cross-examination. This gives the representative the chance to give the full story of any matter raised during cross-examination in a way that tells only half a story. For example, if Basil's solicitor puts to one of the respondent's witnesses during cross-examination some unexpected version of the facts which appears to clear Basil of blame, the respondent's solicitor may try to draw the sting from the new argument by obtaining in re-examination (without asking a leading question) confirmation that the argument was never made by Basil in his disciplinary or appeal hearings. It is not permitted to raise completely new material at this late stage. While the tribunal may permit an unrepresented claimant to do so, and then give the other side a chance of further cross-examination, a solicitor will not normally be allowed to make this mistake.

At some stage the employment judge and members of the tribunal will wish to ask questions of the witness. Practice varies considerably. Some employment judges interrupt continuously during evidence-in-chief; others wait until the end. The lay-members are not usually given their chance until the end. There is no uniform practice as to whether re-examination or questions from the tribunal come first.

13.11.8 Closing addresses

When all the evidence has been presented, the two parties or their representatives each have the chance to address the tribunal. This gives them the opportunity both to review the evidence and to refer to any statute and to relevant authorities. Recent practice in the tribunals has been to discourage excessive dependence on the authorities and to concentrate on the statutory provisions. It is therefore unwise to encumber a closing address with references to the very well-known cases like *British Home Stores* v *Burchell* or *Williams* v *Compair Maxam*. The tribunals dislike being treated like imbeciles! It is also unnecessary to waste time on authorities where a decision really rests entirely on the facts. Some employment judges limit the time allowed. Skeleton arguments are not normally submitted in writing, but their use has become more common than it was. Even if a skeleton argument is not prepared it is worth trying to give a closing address a clear structure, especially if you wish to present alternative lines of reasoning that need to be considered in a particular sequence. It is also important to ensure that you cover all the factual matters from the evidence that are essential to your case.

It is usual for the party that went first at the beginning of the hearing also to have the last word by giving the second closing address. This practice is not invariable, however, and some employment judges prefer to reverse it, especially in Scotland.

13.12 The tribunal decision

We have been used to calling the final result of a tribunal hearing the decision, but that term is not used in ET Rules 2004. Instead in r. 28(1) we find definitions of judgments and orders. The first represents a final determination of the whole or part of a claim and may include an award of compensation, a declaration or a recommendation, while the second is an interim decision, most often resulting from a CMD or PHR.

Under r. 28, the tribunal may issue its judgment or order orally at the end of the hearing (almost always after an adjournment to consider it), or it may reserve its decision and issue the judgment or order in writing later. Judgments must always be recorded in writing, and reasons must be given, but there is no longer any requirement for the reasons for an oral judgment to be recorded in writing unless one party so requests either at the hearing or within 14 days, or the EAT so orders. There is no obligation on the tribunal to give reasons for an order unless a request for reasons is made at the hearing.

A judgment may simply be on the merits of the case, so that the tribunal announces whether it finds for the claimant or dismisses the case, or (if it finds for the claimant) it may go on to announce a remedy. A subsequent hearing is sometimes arranged as to remedy, leaving the parties time meanwhile to try to negotiate a settlement.

The tribunal may reach a unanimous decision, or it can decide by a majority. Employment judges usually work hard to try to achieve unanimity. Where a tribunal is reduced to an employment judge and one other, the judge has a second, casting vote. Despite a growing tendency for decisions to be announced at the end of a hearing, the Court of Appeal has suggested that a reserved decision is to be preferred if the lay members form a majority and the employment judge preparing the decision is in the minority—*Anglian Home Improvements Ltd* v *Kelly* [2004] EWCA Civ 901, [2005] ICR 242.

Where reasons are given, the rule until now has been that they must contain enough detail to allow the parties to see how the decision was reached, but need not necessarily address each and every contention advanced at a hearing: *Meek* v *City of Birmingham District Council* [1987] IRLR 250. We cannot be certain that the authority survives the change in procedural rules.

The tribunal may correct clerical errors in a decision but is otherwise *functus officio* having given its decision and may not change it.

13.13   Costs and preparation time orders

13.13.1   The new rules in 2004

There is now a new regime about the award of costs in the employment tribunals and much has been written elsewhere about the changes. Part comes from the new s. 13 and s. 13A inserted into ETA 1996 by EA 2002 (with effect from July 2004) and part from ET Rules 2004 (with effect from October 2004). Recent experience suggests a long-running battle between the legislators (who see costs as a good way of discouraging hopeless cases and thereby reducing the massively increased public expenditure on the employment tribunal service) and most employment judges, especially those who support widespread access to justice, who have been reluctant in practice to award costs unless parties behave outrageously. So everything hinges on the question whether the new rules are applied more often in practice than their predecessors. We therefore propose to restrict ourselves to a fairly brief section on this topic.

13.13.2   The meaning of costs and preparation time

Costs are defined in r. 38(3) to mean fees, charges, disbursements or expenses incurred in relation to tribunal proceedings and a tribunal may make a costs order only in favour of a party which is legally represented. A costs order can be made up to £10,000 without detailed assessment under the Civil Procedure Rules, more with such assessment.

A preparation time order can be made in favour of a party which is not legally represented, but not in addition to a costs order in favour of the same party in the same case. Preparation time is time spent by the party or its employees or advisers in preparation for a hearing but not at the hearing itself—r. 42(3). A preparation time order has to be calculated by multiplying the number of hours actually spent by £26, subject to a maximum of £10,000.

13.13.3   When costs are awarded

Despite other changes to the rules, there has been no major change in the general provision as to when costs (or equally, a preparation time order) may be awarded. Costs *must* now be awarded against an employer if postponement or adjournment of a hearing was because the employer failed without a special reason to provide evidence about availability of the job in a case of unfair dismissal where the claimant sought reinstatement or re-engagement. Costs *may* (much as before) be awarded against a party or representative who has acted vexatiously, abusively, disruptively or otherwise unreasonably or if the bringing or conducting of proceedings has been misconceived—r. 40(3) for costs and r. 44(3) for preparation time. See *Salinas* v *Bear Stearns International Holdings Inc* [2005] ICR 1117 for an example where the EAT approved a tribunal award of costs under a similar rule. The employment tribunal had been mindful of the basis of its discretion, but the claimant had based his complaint of sex discrimination on events that the tribunal found did not happen and there was no discriminatory element to any of them. Costs were awarded subject to detailed assessment as in the county court.

A new provision allows for the award of wasted costs *against a representative* and not the party in the event of any improper, unreasonable, or negligent act or omission by the representative. It remains to be seen whether the new rules make any difference to the practice.

13.13.4   Applying for costs

Under ET Rules 2004, r. 38(7) or r. 42(5) respectively, an application for costs or a preparation time order can be made during proceedings, at the end of a hearing or in writing to the tribunal office within 28 days from the issue of the judgment.

Past experience suggests that the highest chance of success in an application arises when the tribunal has held a PHR and the other side has been ordered to pay a deposit, has paid it and has then lost the case on the grounds predicted. It doesn't happen often but it is a pleasant dream.

More often the threat of an application for costs on the ground that the other side has been pursuing the case unreasonably has been much more significant in practice, especially where you are having difficulty in getting the other side to negotiate seriously about a settlement.

In the courts, where the possibility exists of paying money into court, this procedure involves the writing of a formal letter threatening an application for costs if the offer is rejected, as in *Calderbank* v *Calderbank* [1976] Fam 93. In *Kopel* v *Safeway Stores plc* [2003] IRLR 753, the EAT suggested that this procedure cannot be copied in the tribunals where there is no system of paying money into the tribunal, but in fact a similar procedure to the *Calderbank* letter is sometimes operated.

In *Beynon* v *Scadden* [1999] IRLR 700, the claimants' trade union, Unison, supported them in a complaint of a breach of the consultation requirements under TUPE (see **12.6.6** above). The case was in fact hopeless because the transfer of the business was achieved by a share transfer and was not covered by TUPE. The employment tribunal had found as a fact that the reason Unison pursued the case was the collateral purpose of achieving recognition. That finding was enough for the EAT to support an award of costs, based on vexatious conduct by the claimants or their representatives. In *Kovacs* v *Queen Mary & Westfield College* [2002] EWCA 352, [2002] ICR 919, the Court of Appeal approved the reasoning in *Beynon* and held that an award of costs did not require the tribunal to assess a party's ability to pay, something that is now permitted by r. 41(2) and r. 45(3) but is not mandatory.

13.14   The remedies for the tribunal

We have already considered the appropriate remedies relevant to the various jurisdictions in earlier chapters, but several points remain to be made here.

13.14.1   Recoupment of benefits

Under the Employment Protection (Recoupment of Jobseeker's Allowance and Income Support) Regulations 1996, the full amount of a monetary award of compensation may not be payable to a claimant who succeeds in a claim of unfair dismissal. The tribunal is required to assess the approximate amount of jobseeker's allowance and income support benefit the claimant has received between the date of dismissal and the date of hearing. This figure is called the 'prescribed element'.

The compensatory award is assessed without regard to any benefits the claimant may have received during that period. Only the excess of the compensatory award over the prescribed element is payable immediately to the claimant at the end of the hearing. The Department of Social Security then sends the employer a demand in respect of benefits actually paid to the claimant, an amount that may not exceed the prescribed element. The employer pays that amount to the DSS, and any surplus remaining to the claimant.

Since the Recoupment Regulations apply to tribunal awards and not to conciliated settlements, it is an inducement to both sides to settle and to avoid their effect.

13.14.2 Payment of interest

Under the Employment Tribunals (Interest) Order 1990, interest is payable on tribunal awards still outstanding on a date 42 days after a decision is issued to the parties. The rate of interest is as laid down for other similar purposes in relation to court awards and varies from time to time.

13.14.3 Remedy hearings

In October 1999 there was a very large increase from £12,000 to £50,000 in the maximum amount of the compensatory award that can be made in cases of unfair dismissal, now raised further to £63,000. We speculated that the increase might result in a more rigorous approach from the tribunals to the assessment of compensation, but there does not seem to have been any significant change. Although a few cases result in very large awards, the average amount actually awarded in 2006–7 was £7,974, and the median was £3,800. The tribunals often require a claimant to prepare at an early stage of preparation a schedule of loss. Calculation at the hearing is speeded up because the relevant facts have already been ascertained.

In discrimination cases unlimited compensation has been available since 1993. In *Buxton* v *Equinox Design Ltd* [1999] ICR 269 (which we encountered at **6.11.5** above), the EAT stressed the need for proper management by the tribunal of the assessment of compensation in a disability discrimination case. It was not good enough to assess future unemployment on the basis of 'guestimate'; some medical evidence was required about the claimant's employability, given his multiple sclerosis.

A tribunal decision about remedy has usually required additional evidence beyond that used at the hearing on the merits of the case. Is reinstatement or re-engagement feasible? If not, and the tribunal moves on to the assessment of compensation, what was the state of the employment market locally and how much did the claimant do to mitigate loss? Now, as a stricter approach starts to be taken, even more evidence may be required in some cases. For example, if the employer loses in Basil's case, the evidence called about the alleged theft at the hearing on the merits will have concentrated on the reasonableness of the employer's belief. In assessing contributory fault, the issue is one of fact: did Basil steal or not? That may require different witnesses whom neither side needed to call at the first hearing.

The availability of a much higher limit may also give rise to some new heads of compensation. In *Sheriff* v *Klyne Tugs (Lowestoft) Ltd* [1999] IRLR 481, the Court of Appeal held that compensation for psychiatric damage as well as injury to feelings fell within the jurisdiction of an employment tribunal in a case concerning racial discrimination.

13.14.4 The effect of tax

At **10.15** above we dealt with the general principles of taxation of compensation awarded by the tribunals in cases of unfair dismissal. It is still relatively unusual for these rules to apply in practice: most awards are well below £30,000 and therefore are not taxable in the applicant's hands. Reference should be made to the earlier chapter if there is a need to consider 'grossing up' to compensate for the effect of tax.

13.15 Challenge of a tribunal decision

There are two ways a tribunal judgment or decision can be challenged after it is given: it can be reviewed by the tribunal, or an appeal can be taken to the EAT.

13.15.1 Application for review

The power for a tribunal to review a decision is contained in r. 34 of the ET Rules 2004. The application must be made in writing within 14 days of the issue of a decision. The application must be on one or more of the following grounds:

(a) an administrative error has occurred;

(b) a party did not receive notice of proceedings;

(c) the decision was made in the absence of a party;

(d) new evidence, not reasonably foreseeable, has come to light;

(e) the interests of justice require a review.

Until the ET Rules 2004 came into force this power was very restricted. It was the appropriate way to correct minor slips discovered shortly after a hearing—*British Midland Airways* v *Lewis* [1978] ICR 782—but any challenge to the reasoning that led to a tribunal decision had to form an appeal to the EAT—*Trimle* v *Supertravel* [1982] ICR 440.

Some employment tribunals have operated under the ET Rules 2004 as if the same restricted power to review still operated, as we saw in some of the cases we discussed **13.7.2** concerning completion and presentation of claim ET 1 and response ET 3. As we noted there, a broader approach is now being adopted by the EAT. In *Sodexho Ltd* v *Gibbons* [2005] ICR 1647 the EAT interpreted the power to review in the *interests of justice* in the light of the overriding objective. This has the effect of mitigating some of the strict requirements of the ET Rules 2004, including those about ET 1 and ET 3. In that case the tribunal had rightly reviewed a strike-out judgment after it emerged that the claimant's solicitors had not received the notice requiring him to pay a deposit, because he had given the wrong postcode for their office in his claim. In *Onwuka* v *Spherion Technology UK Ltd* [2005] ICR 567 the EAT allowed a review to amend a claim to add an additional respondent.

Whilst other applications for review can be considered and refused without a hearing, an application for review of a default judgment must always be considered at a public hearing—r. 33. See **13.7.2** above for the rules regarding information that must be included in applications for this special kind of review.

13.15.2 Appeal to EAT

If the decision of an employment tribunal contains an error of law, an appeal lies to the EAT. Under a Practice Direction issued by the EAT in May 2008, all notices of appeal in the appropriate form must be accompanied by the claim form ET 1, the response ET 3, and the employment tribunal judgment, decision or order appealed against, with written reasons or an explanation of why any of that list is not included. Appeals have to be entered within 42 days of the date the employment tribunal sent an order or decision to the parties, or within 42 days of the date written reasons for a judgment were sent to the parties. Employment tribunal judgments are usually sent to the parties with an accompanying leaflet explaining how standard forms can be obtained from the EAT at Victoria Embankment in London.

The full rules about appeals to the EAT are outside the scope of this book. Suffice it to say that full compliance is essential. The President has recently stated that many appellants are not complying with the Practice Direction concerning inclusion of the claim and response and that the EAT intends to operate the rule from *Kanapathiar* v *London Borough of Harrow* [2003] IRLR 571, under which an appeal lodged without the correct papers is not considered to be lodged at all. A further appeal which complies may then be out of time.

Parties often express a wish to appeal on the basis that they do not like the judgment of the employment tribunal and wish for a second opinion. It has to be explained to them that this is not the function of the EAT, which will not interfere with a properly-reached judgment of the employment tribunal on the facts of the case. It is also almost always impossible to raise at the EAT new points of law that were not raised at the employment tribunal: *Jones* v *Governing Body of Burdett Coutts School* [1998] IRLR 521.

13.16   A summary chart of the main jurisdictions

Jurisdiction	Source	Service condition	Time limit for IT application	Extension of time	ACAS involvement	Maximum award*
Unfair dismissal	ERA 1996, s. 94	1 year	3 months from EDT	'not reasonably practicable'	Yes 13 weeks	£72,900 unless re-employment ordered
Redundancy payment	ERA 1996, s. 135	2 years	6 months from RD	'just and equitable'	Yes 13 weeks	£9,900
Deductions from wages	ERA 1996, Part II	Nil	3 months from payday	'not reasonably practicable'	Yes 7 weeks	Unlimited
Racial discrimination	RRA 1976	Nil	3 months from act complained of	'just and equitable'	Yes—no fixed period	Unlimited
Sex discrimination	SDA 1975	Nil	3 months from act complained of	'just and equitable'	Yes –no fixed period	Unlimited
Equal pay	Equal Pay Act 1970	Nil	6 months after termination	None	Yes–no fixed period	Unlimited
Disability discrimination	DDA 1995	Nil	3 months from act complained of	'just and equitable'	Yes–no fixed period	Unlimited
Breach of contract	ITA 1996, s. 3 and 1994 Order	Nil	3 months from EDT	'not reasonably practicable'	Yes 7 weeks	£25,000
Working time	WT Regs 1998	Nil	3 months from infringement	'not reasonably practicable'	Yes 13 weeks	No general limit

* These are the figures from 1 February 2008 and will change from 1 February 2009.

SUGGESTED ANSWERS TO SELF-TEST QUESTIONS

Chapter 4

---

1. First let us look at the position under WTRegs 1998. It is only in relation to adolescent workers that employers are required to take account of time spent in other jobs. So, while your friend's daily rest over Friday night is less than 11 hours, he is an adult and the shopkeeper is not required to take account of time spent working in the bar. There is no breach of reg. 10. Similarly, as an adult worker, not an adolescent, he is not entitled to a rest break under reg. 12 until his working time exceeds six hours. The shop manager is wrong, however, to deny him paid holidays. Regulation 13 gives all workers a right to paid annual leave irrespective of hours of work and indeed we shall see later in **6.5.8** that it is unlawful discrimination to treat part-time workers less favourably than those on full time.

The position regarding NMW is not quite clear from the information you are given. If his rate of pay is stated either as £30 for the morning or as £6 per hour, he is paid more than the £4.77 appropriate for his age of 19, and the shop manager is within the regulations. If, however, there is anything, preferably in writing, to confirm his entitlement to time-and-a-half, the portion of his pay (£10 of the £30) that represents a premium for working at a particular time must be disregarded under reg. 31(1)(c)— see **4.2.2** above— and the remainder is less than the minimum of £4.77 he is entitled to receive.

2. Yes. The question is about jurisdiction and the case does not fall into any of the exceptions from s. 27(2) that we set out at **4.4.1** above. So the missing quarter (the difference between time-and-a-half and time-and-a-quarter) can certainly be presented as a deduction, thereby bringing the matter within ERA 1996, s. 23. The example is very similar in that sense to the case we discussed at **4.4.4** above.

The case will then raise some interesting and difficult contractual issues. When is acquiescence deemed to be consent to a variation? Has a contractual change taken effect? What is the precise evidence about the employees' question and the supervisor's reply? (For example it would be different from the report of evasiveness if the supervisor's story is of having said that the notified change would take effect, but that anyone dissatisfied could raise this as a grievance later.) Is there an argument, since each employee has the option of working overtime when requested or of declining, that each occasion of working overtime is a separate contract? All these matters will need to be considered, but, on the limited evidence we have, none of them seems to be a contention with no reasonable prospect of success, and their complexity does not detract from the answer about jurisdiction.

Chapter 6

1. After trying to answer this question, have a look at the analysis of the issues by the EAT at [2004] IRLR 348. The employment tribunal had found unlawful discrimination because women were given greater choice than men, but the EAT ruled that they had asked the wrong question. The correct question was whether on contemporary standards the required smartness for men could be achieved otherwise; if so (but by implication only if so) men had received less favourable treatment. The cases they cited seem generally to accept that some detailed differences of rule about dress or appearance between men and women are permitted if they reflect normally accepted contemporary standards. This case was remitted to a different employment tribunal.

2. Refer to **6.11.1.2** above and DDA 1995, s.1. The key elements are that the person must have:

    (a) a physical or mental impairment;

    (b) which has a substantial [adverse effect]; and

    (c) [a] long-term adverse effect;

    (d) on his ability to carry out normal day-to-day activities.

Chapters 7 and 8

This question requires an assessment of:

   (i) if any dismissal proved to be a wrongful dismissal would this invalidate the restraint—no matter how well-drafted it is—and (more arguably) the confidentiality duties, implied or express? (see **7.5.1** and **8.3**)

  (ii) the distinction between trade secrets/confidentiality and 'employee know-how', as developed through examining the supposed secrets identified in Setters' statement and the contract. (see **7.5.3**, **7.5.4** and **7.6.4**); and

 (iii) the drafting of the express term on confidentiality (if found relevant under the *Faccenda* tests) and the **quality** of the clauses regarding restraint of trade as it applies to the **individual employee** (see, in particular, **8.7**)

In a question such as this, you cannot be expected to have mastered all the intricacies of a new industry without a lot more information and without interviewing the client. It is therefore difficult to reach any firm decision here on whether a practice or a secret is really protectable. What you should be aware of, therefore, is how what details you would need to acquire and how they fit in to the general pattern of the law.

The specific question: if *Phoenix Guitars Ltd* go ahead and dismiss Setters, will they still be able to enforce the confidentiality and restraint of trade clauses against him?

On the evidence from Mr Burek it may well be that Mr Setters is going to leave anyway. If this is so, there is the practical point of giving the employer as much time as possible to obtain a replacement (and dismissing Setters immediately will not do this). There is also the practical/legal point that, in dismissing Setters, the company jeopardises the confidentiality and restraint clauses which they say are so important to them. You therefore need to consider the following points:

(a) Effect of any dismissal

We have seen that, if the dismissal is wrongful this will constitute a breach of contract so that the restraints (and arguably the confidentiality clause) will be invalid in any case: *General Billposting* v *Atkinson*. Your client needs to be aware of this. For you to be able to make a decision on whether any dismissal would be wrongful you will need to read **Chapter 9**. However, we can say here that the basic question is whether *Phoenix* can dismiss without notice in the face of the gross misconduct on Setter's part. If *Phoenix* dismiss with proper notice they cannot have committed a wrongful dismissal. One might also note:

(i) the irrelevance of any unfair dismissal claim;

(ii) the possible impact of the *Rock Refrigeration* analysis, especially as developed through *Campbell* v *Frisbee* and

(iii) the relevance of the *Rex Stewart* case—that even where the employer makes a payment in lieu of notice this may still bring *General Billposting* into play.

Further information would also be required on the apparent 'throwaway' line in section 3 of Mr Burek's statement that Setters has already been in negotiation with a rival company. If Setters is already in breach of contract (see *Laughton* v *Bapp*) there is the possibility that, whatever the state of the express terms on confidentiality and restraint, the springboard doctrine might apply (see **7.3.4**). However, this is dangerous ground and should not be relied upon alone.

(b) Confidentiality

First, consider the relevance of the implied term of good faith. If the information Setter's possesses can be classed as a trade secret then it automatically receives protection under the continuing implied term. The express wording of the contract (good or bad) will not be needed. So, which of the 'secrets' identified in the contract might be classed as trade secrets, or at least as highly-confidential? How convinced are you that any of these could be defended in court?

This requires a discussion of the effects of *Faccenda Chicken* and should involve some discussion of the later cases (such as *Lansing Linde*) which have developed the meaning of 'trade secrets' as opposed to confidential information. You should also be aware of the major battle-ground of distinguishing between trade secrets (or 'confidential information' generally) and the employee's know-how. Recent cases, such as *FSS Travel* v *Johnson* show just how difficult it may be for an employer to demonstrate clearly *what* secrets require protection and why they are distinguishable from the employee's know-how. In particular, you need to try to apply your understanding of 'trade secrets', 'know-how', etc directly to the matters identified in the contract and in Burek's statement at para. 2(c). The *Series 5* case demonstrates that the burden is on the employer to clearly identify the material which it is claimed amounts to a trade secret (rather than merely state it so).

If the information is not a trade secret it may not be protectable at all. If protection is going to be given it must be based on the effectiveness of the express confidentiality clause (clause 8). *Faccenda* would have us believe that an express confidentiality term is of no use anyway, so this could be a major stumbling-block. But even if the clause is valid, its wording is loose. It has no 'lifespan' built into it and one might question whether the confidential information may have a shorter lifespan than the unlimited period given in clause 8 (given Mr Burek's own assessment). Clause 8 may not be defendable on its wording anyway.

(c) Restraint of trade

It should be noted that:

- You need to find a 'legitimate interest' and be aware of the presumption that any restraint will be void unless reasonable.

- It may be difficult to base any restraint argument on confidentiality as:

  (i)   this could only apply to trade secrets, and we have decided this issue one way or the other already;

  (ii) the restraint clause (9) seems to have inappropriate time scales in it as regards confidentiality, given the evidence;

  (iii) the efficacy of the restraints therefore depends on the question of customer contacts/reputation as Setters also has (limited) access to some of these people.

- You should have identified the types of clauses involved (non-dealing in 9.1, non-solicitation in 9.2 and non-poaching in 9.3—*there is no non-competition clause so the company cannot prevent Setters working for their rivals as such*) and their relevance to the case in hand.

- You should consider the reasonableness of clause 9 based on 'time, geography and market setting'. For instance:

  (i)   the clauses have very long 'relation back' periods, which would be difficult to defend in terms of establishing reasonableness;

  (ii) the non-poaching clause (9.3) is badly drafted as it does not define the employees affected in terms of seniority. It is unlikely to be enforceable.

One might also consider the practical issue as to the procedures involved. Enforcement will have to be through an application for injunctive relief. This demands an understanding of the requirements of *American Cyanamid*. These principles apply both to applications regarding the protection of confidential information and restraint of trade: *Johnson and Bloy* v *Wolstenholme Rink and Fallon*.

Chapter 11

1.   The key quotation from ERA 1996 that must be applied to all these examples is that redundancy means that the requirement of the employer's business for people to do work of a particular kind ceases or diminishes—either generally or at a particular place.

(a) This case is a straightforward example of a reduction in the employer's requirement for people to do work of a particular kind. It is a classic redundancy.

(b) The practical consequences of the employer's decision here are exactly the same as in (a). The statutory test of redundancy is a reduction in the employer's requirement, and the reason behind that reduction is immaterial. This case is as much a redundancy as (a). Whether dismissals are unfair may be another matter, although tribunals generally avoid 'second-guessing' the employer's decision about how many people are required by a business.

(c) This does not sound like a redundancy. An unsatisfactory employee is being replaced by someone else the employer likes better. There is no indication of any reduction in any requirement for people to do work of a particular kind. We cannot give a definitive view without hearing the employer's argument, which may be that the jobs of supervisor and director are genuinely different, so that there is a reduction in the requirement for supervisors. That sounds a difficult case for the employer to make sound convincing!

(d) The statutory definition allows for the possibility that the reduction in the employer's requirement is at a particular place. So this too is a redundancy. The employer's denial may make defence of any claims of unfair dismissal difficult: if the reason for dismissal is not redundancy, which else of the permitted fair reasons can apply? If, on the other hand, the employer admits redundancy there is the possibility of arguing that the Bristol employees, or some of them, unreasonably refused an offer of suitable alternative employment in Clevedon and are not due any redundancy payment—see **11.4.7.1**.

(e) It is difficult not to sympathise with the an employee in a position like this, but her argument rests on a much narrower view of the employer's requirement than the tribunals adopt. On a broader view the employer's requirement for people to do work like hers has diminished and she is therefore redundant. There may be scope for her to argue about the basis of her selection.

2. Some possible points to explore could include the following:

(1) Was there a customary arrangement or agreed procedure (e.g., LIFO) that has been broken by this method of selection? That no longer leads to automatic unfairness but is still a relevant question.

(2) Mr Patel may be from an ethnic minority. If his selection depends on racial discrimination (even if inadvertant, perhaps because his English is limited), it may be unlawful by the Race Relations Act 1976 as well as unfair by unfair dismissal law.

(3) Mr Patel has scored particularly badly at lines 1 and 2, which could well be exactly the factors affected by some disability. Make a note to investigate whether he is disabled.

(4) The unit of selection may be wrong or unreasonable.

(5) The form may be defective in giving no recognition at all to service, despite the rules on age discrimination

(6) The form has been marked by only one person: is the result too subjective? Worse still, is there any evidence of personal antagonism from the assessor towards VP?

(7) What steps were taken to check consistency if others in the unit of selection were marked by someone else?

(8) There is a remarkable precision implied by the range of weighting factors. Can it be justified?

(9) Line 1 should accord with some factual record. Is it accurate?

(10) There is no definition of the period considered for line 1. Was a fixed period taken, is it reasonable and has it been applied consistently?

(11) There is no stated scope for examination of reasons behind line 1. Was VP's absence for any extenuating reason and, if unlikely to recur, should some allowance have been made?

(12) What rule was applied where someone's absence fell between two definitions in line **1**, e.g., 5 days as a result of being sent home in the middle of a working day? Was it applied consistently?

(13) Establish whether SWEAT-Shop operates any regular appraisal of employees and, if so, obtain recent appraisals of VP with a view to exploring any marked discrepancy between the appraisal and lines 2 to 5 of the assessment, which may measure the same qualities.

(14) In line 2 the definition of 'poor' which VP scored implies some unsatisfactory behaviour. Has he ever been warned?

(15) Why is there an alteration here? Has someone adjusted the marking to give a predetermined result?

(16) In line 3, the definitions are quite ill-defined. Why has VP been given 2 points rather than 3 when the difference is so vague? What more would have been required of him to get the higher mark?

(17) In line 4, 'attitude' is always a vague and highly subjective quality. Yet it is here given the highest weighting of all. What evidence can SWEAT-Shop adduce to show that VP's low mark is factually justified?

(18) Why is line 5 included at all? If VP's job remains to be done, why penalise him for being likely to stick at it?

(19) The score is added up wrongly. It should be 32. Is such carelessness indicative of a cavalier attitude to the whole process? (Do not suppose this is fanciful: it derives from the authors' experience.)

Chapter 12

1. Helpfully or not, the correct answer is Yes and No! Yes, in that the key test is the two-stage question from *Spijkers* that we introduced at **12.5.3.1**: can we identify a *stable economic entity that retains its identity* before and after the transfer? No, in that the decision in that case and all the others that have developed from it since emphasise that the answer depends on all aspects—function, assets (which includes premises, plant and machinery, goodwill, work-in-progress, stocks and so on), employees, etc.— and that no one factor is ever decisive.

2. There are at least five important points to make.

(a) The client will automatically acquire with the transferred undertaking all its current employees—unless any object, which is unlikely to happen.

(b) Their transfer will be on their existing terms and conditions of employment, which may present the client with a significant practical problem if his existing staff are materially different.

(c) Dismissal of anyone because of the transfer is automatically unfair. If the client's wish to achieve economies of scale means reducing the number employed, he can only avoid that automatic result by ensuring that any dismissals fall within the statutory exception of being for an economic, technical, or organisational reason entailing changes in the workforce. It will then be necessary to proceed as for a redundancy—see **Chapter 11**.

(d) The client must consult representatives of his existing employees about the proposed transfer and supply the transferor with information sufficient to enable the transferor to consult employees there too.

(e) The client should ensure that those negotiating the purchase on his behalf are aware of these employment matters so that necessary indemnities can be included in the terms of sale.

INDEX

C

AS FILM STUDIES

THE ESSENTIAL INTRODUCTION

Sarah Casey Benyahia, Freddie Gaffney and John White

Routledge
Taylor & Francis Group

LONDON AND NEW YORK

First published 2006
by Routledge
2 Park Square, Milton Park, Abingdon, Oxon OX14 4RN

Simultaneously published in the USA and Canada
by Routledge
270 Madison Ave, New York, NY 10016

Routledge is an imprint of the Taylor & Francis Group, an informa business

© 2006 Sarah Casey Benyahia, Freddie Gaffney and John White

Typeset in Novarese and Bell Gothic by Keystroke, Jacaranda Lodge, Wolverhampton
Printed and bound in Great Britain by CPI Bath Press, Bath

British Library Cataloguing in Publication Data
A catalogue record for this book is available from the British Library

Library of Congress Cataloging in Publication Data
A catalog record for this book has been requested

ISBN10: 0–415–39310–8 (hbk)
ISBN10: 0–415–39311–6 (pbk)

ISBN13: 978–0–415–39310–2 (hbk)
ISBN13: 978–0–415–39311–9 (pbk)

▼ CONTENTS

▼ FIGURE ACKNOWLEDGEMENTS

▼ PREFACE

It wasn't that long ago that the examining team for WJEC (Welsh Joint Education Committee) AS (then simply A Level) Film Studies could all sit around a small kitchen table, and that to study film was seen as a 'soft option', often associated with a solitary enthusiast teacher. Now however Film Studies is offered in a rapidly increasing number of centres, is supported by a large examining team, and is rightly perceived to be a challenging, exciting, and life enhancing choice for thousands of candidates who take this subject each year.

This book was conceived to offer advice and guidance to both student and teacher alike, and closely follows the most up-to-date specification from WJEC (which comes into use in September 2006). Crammed full of film facts with easy explanations of terminology, case studies, activities, and sample exam questions, it is intended that it be used to support each unit of the course, and extend learning beyond the baseline for succeeding at AS Level, into concepts, techniques, and films that stretch and stimulate the mind.

It has not been written as a 'crammer', nor to establish an orthodoxy or 'canon' of films that are deemed worthy of study. Indeed the writers hope rather that it will act as a springboard for the reader in building the confidence to apply the concepts contained within it to their own choice of film, with no sense that *American Pie* or *Layer Cake* are any less use to the study of film or have less to offer than *Casablanca* or *Brief Encounter*.

Furthermore, the book reflects an underpinning feature of the WJEC specification, that gives priority to the students' point of entry as a place to build from rather than on to, thereby valuing any initial filmic knowledge they bring as the best place to start from. It aims to foster an approach to film that will enable the study of any film as a valuable artefact, and thereby encourage personal response, active research, the practical application of learning, and greater diversity in study, allowing interests and enthusiasm a place in education.

We would like to express our thanks to Katrina Chandler (Development Editor, Routledge), Julene Knox (Picture Researcher) and Rosemary Morlin (Copy Editor) for their help in the preparation of this book. Thanks are also due to those colleagues and family members who provided invaluable support and understanding throughout; and to the staff and students of the Media and Film Departments at Colchester Sixth Form College and Cambridge Regional College for their helpful contributions.

We hope you enjoy the selections we have made, the activities we have designed, and the explanations we have offered, and that we can usefully keep you company on your journey into the world of film.

▼ INTRODUCTION

What is Film Studies? What does it mean to study films?

This introductory chapter:

- puts forward the idea that studying films will involve you in something over and above simply enjoying going to the cinema – what that 'something' is should begin to become clearer as you work your way through this book;
- suggests studying films will involve you in taking a more analytical approach to your whole experience of cinema;
- highlights how important it is for you to be prepared to entertain new ideas about something that is perhaps already an important part of your life;
- offers an initial introduction to some of the activities you will need to be prepared to undertake if you are studying films;
- suggests the sort of questions you might need to consider asking yourselves about films;
- introduces a range of different writing skills required of Film Studies students.

NOTEBOX

This chapter will be directly relevant to the module FS1 – Film: Making Meaning 1 in that it starts to introduce possible ways of approaching films. In particular it is directly relevant to what the examiners describe as 'spectator study', which is about how each of us watches and makes sense of films. More importantly though, this section should act as a general introduction to the whole idea of Film Studies allowing you to gain an overview of the subject and the sorts of things that are going to be asked of you before you begin work on the more specific syllabus requirements.

GOING TO THE CINEMA

Going to the cinema has been a pleasurable pastime enjoyed throughout the world for around 100 years. With a fast expanding DVD market it seems people are increasingly enjoying watching films at home, but even so the spectacle offered by the cinema experience continues to be appreciated as something distinctively different.

ACTIVITY . . .

1 How often do you go to the cinema? If possible, discuss this in groups. What seems to be the average? Who goes the most and how often is this?

2 Now, a perhaps more difficult question. Why do you go to the cinema? Try to decide on a list that covers as many reasons as possible for you personally. If you can, discuss your ideas with others. Are there similarities or differences in the reasons given?

3 If you are in a class with others, in small groups try to decide on a collective list that covers as many reasons as possible.

NOTEBOX . . .

We all enjoy watching films, whether in the cinema or on TV. Cinema attendance, after many years of decline, is increasing each year and a new generation of film-goers is appreciating the pleasures of the 'big screen', a pleasure which even a 30-inch TV set cannot provide.

(Nelmes 2003: 1)

(Note the double use of the word 'pleasure(s)' here, emphasizing the key factor determining why we watch film and also why we chose to try to study it in more depth.)

CAN'T WE JUST ENJOY FILMS?

Amongst some people who attend the cinema and/or watch DVDs on a regular basis there is a certain resistance to the idea of 'studying films'. For people taking this approach, watching films at the cinema is seen as an especially intense form of entertainment that offers the chance of escapist fantasies that will only be undermined or devalued in some way by analysis. After-the-event discussion of the emotional experience offered by one film compared to another is encouraged and indeed is an important part of the whole experience as far as these enthusiasts are concerned. The physical attributes (whether of strength or beauty or some other feature) of one star are readily compared with similar attributes in other stars. The thrills provided in one film are assessed against the thrills provided in another. Discussion and debate over

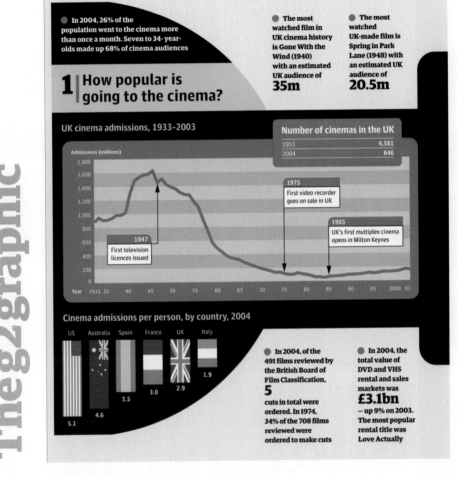

Each week, the Guardian's Leo Hickman and award-winning information design agency Grundy Northedge collaborate on a unique in-depth graphic providing an instant briefing on one of the issues of the week

The UK film industry

Friday sees the release of what will almost certainly be the biggest 'British' film of the year – Harry Potter and the Goblet of Fire. But what exactly qualifies a film as British? And is the industry worth the amount of subsidy it gets?

● In 2004, 26% of the population went to the cinema more than once a month. Seven to 34- year- olds made up 68% of cinema audiences

● The most watched film in UK cinema history is Gone With the Wind (1940) with an estimated UK audience of **35m**

● The most watched UK-made film is Spring in Park Lane (1948) with an estimated UK audience of **20.5m**

1 │ How popular is going to the cinema?

UK cinema admissions, 1933-2003

Admissions (millions)

1,800
1,600
1,400
1,200
1,000
800
600
400
200
0

Year 1933 35 40 45 50 55 60 65 70 75 80 85 90 95 2000 03

Number of cinemas in the UK

1951	4,581
2004	646

1975 First video recorder goes on sale in UK

1985 UK's first multiplex cinema opens in Milton Keynes

1947 First television licences issued

Cinema admissions per person, by country, 2004

US 5.1
Australia 4.6
Spain 3.5
France 3.0
UK 2.9
Italy 1.9

● In 2004, of the 491 films reviewed by the British Board of Film Classification, **5** cuts in total were ordered. In 1974, 34% of the 708 films reviewed were ordered to make cuts

● In 2004, the total value of DVD and VHS rental and sales markets was **£3.1bn** – up 9% on 2003. The most popular rental title was Love Actually

Theg2graphic

Figure i The UK Film Industry
Source: Graphic by Grundy Northedge from *The Guardian*, 14 November 2005 © Guardian Newspapers Limited 2005. Reproduced with permission

	Film	Country of origin	Box office gross (£m)	No. of opening cinemas	Opening weekend gross (£m)	Distributor
1	Shrek 2	USA	48.10	512	16.22	UIP
2	Harry Potter and the Prisoner of Azkaban	UK/USA	46.08	535	23.88	Warner Bros
3	Bridget Jones: The Edge of Reason	UK/USA	36.00	504	10.44	UIP
4	The Incredibles	USA	32.27	494	9.75	Buena Vista
5	Spider-Man 2	USA	26.72	504	8.77	Sony Pictures
6	The Day After Tomorrow	USA	25.21	429	7.32	Twentieth Century Fox
7	Shark Tale	USA	22.82	504	7.55	UIP
8	Troy	UK/USA/Mal	18.00	504	6.02	Warner Bros
9	I, Robot	USA	17.98	447	4.75	Twentieth Century Fox
10	Scooby-Doo Too	USA	16.49	489	3.55	Warner Bros
11	Van Helsing	USA	15.15	458	5.43	UIP
12	Lemony Snicket's A Series of Unfortunate Events	USA	13.26	452	2.21	UIP
13	Starsky & Hutch	USA	12.60	81	0.41	Buena Vista
14	The Last Samurai	USA/Jap/NZ	11.90	430	2.72	Warner Bros
15	The Bourne Supremacy	USA/Ger	11.56	418	2.72	UIP
16	The Passion of the Christ	USA	11.08	46	0.23	Icon
17	School of Rock	USA/Ger	10.50	376	2.74	UIP
18	The Village	USA	10.31	433	2.95	Buena Vista
19	Lost in Translation	USA/Jap	10.06	96	0.80	Momentum
20	Dodge Ball: A True Underdog Story	USA	10.03	315	2.20	Twentieth Century Fox

Figure ii *The Top 20 Films at the UK Box Office, 2004*
Source: UK Film Council Statistical Yearbook 2004. Reproduced with permission of the UK Film Council

the relative merits of one star over another, or one film over another, is endlessly recycled. However, engagement in an academic way with film is seen as detrimental to the experience itself.

Hopefully, as a film student you will continue to enjoy these sorts of discussions with your friends since it will form an important foundation to your studies, but you will also be prepared to try out new methods of approach that will often involve being more analytical in your viewing.

ACTIVITY . . .

- On average how often do you watch films at home: once a week, twice a week, or more?
- Do you watch on your own generally, or with others? And, if with others, is this family or friends?
- Do you usually view films you have recorded from TV, rental DVDs, pay-to-view films, or film channel films?
- Do you discuss the films you have watched with other people? If so, try to compile a list of the sorts of things you talk about.

ACTIVITY . . .

1   Write a short 250-word review of a film you saw recently for a film magazine or newspaper of your choice. Name the magazine and try to write in an appropriate style. Write a further 100 words describing who you were seeing as your target audience and how you were trying to write the piece.
2   If you are able to, in groups exchange reviews and read those written by other people.
3   Decide on the best one in each group to be read out to the whole class. List the features of the chosen article that as a group you believe made it the best.
4   After the chosen articles have been read, try to compare the lists of key factors for these articles that each group has arrived at. Has each group used the same sorts of criteria or are there significant differences?

No problem

There is no problem with adopting an attitude towards films that sees them as pure entertainment or escapist fantasy since pleasure is clearly an important part of the whole experience of cinema. Indeed, this is a part of the experience we will be seeking to emphasize and explore in some depth.

PLEASURE Films clearly give us pleasure in a range of ways, otherwise we would not watch them, and yet studying academic subjects is somehow often seen to be at odds with the idea of pleasure. However, since pleasure is the thing that beyond all else stimulates our initial interest in films we should not dismiss it out of hand. In fact, the idea of exactly how films provide us with pleasure will be a key approach to film for us.

The way in which film gives pleasure is most apparent when we consider not just audiences in general but our own personal response to films and yet it is so often neglected by those of us who wish to study film. Maybe this is because the concept of pleasure does not seem to sit well in relation to the idea of study. Or perhaps this neglect of the pleasure principle is to do with a difficulty in deciding how to study such a seemingly vague notion.

However we view all of this, the concept is clearly important not only in relation to narrative structure but also in relation to the way in which human beings seem to be able to respond to the sheer aesthetic joy of colour, movement, light, shape and size and in particular changing colour, movement, light, shape and size.

The best way to think about the ways in which films create pleasure for an audience is to analyse our own enjoyment of films. Pleasure could be provided by (among other things) an exciting or romantic narrative, the escapism of identifying with characters unlike ourselves or by the visual pleasure provided by the big screen. Film Studies academics have spent a long time trying to explain the different pleasures experienced by film spectators, particularly the enjoyment of aspects of film which do not immediately seem pleasurable such as watching horror films.

ACTIVITY . . .

At this early stage in your studies, how would you describe the pleasures film gives you? Try to list the variety of possible pleasures and compare your list with others.

FILM STUDIES AS A SUBJECT

Using films as pure escapist entertainment is one possible approach to films, but as Film Studies students we are going to be concerned with considering a much greater range of ways of understanding and experiencing film. This will involve recognizing the complexity of our interaction with film and acknowledging that there is no simple way of approaching film. Hopefully you are now beginning to gain some idea as to what Film Studies is and, perhaps, some inkling of what studying film is going to involve.

Before you read the rest of this section, put the heading 'Film Studies' at the top of a sheet of paper and take a few minutes to list all the things you would expect to be doing whilst studying film. Remember to take into account the sorts of things you have been asked to do so far. If possible compare your list with others.

You may have heard other people joke that Film Studies is just about sitting around and watching films. Happily, it has to be admitted, there is a certain element of truth to this since it is clearly impossible to study a film without first watching it closely, just as it is impossible to analyse critically a novel without first reading it carefully. However, there is rather more to Film Studies than this description suggests.

Questions we might ask ourselves

Early in our investigation of possible ways of approaching films it would be useful to ask ourselves exactly what activities we should expect to undertake in order to explore films in a way that will offer more than immediate, easy entertainment.

So, what does it mean to study a film? Dictionary definitions of 'study' often involve the idea of 'devoting time and thought'. So we could suggest studying film would involve spending time thinking about it; but how would we do this and what would we think about? What exactly are we supposed to be thinking about as we are watching a film at the cinema or a DVD or video at home?

Initial uncertainties might raise questions such as:

■ Are there particular ways of thinking about film that we should be adopting?
■ What should we be looking for as we watch these films?
■ How will we know if we have found anything worth commenting upon?

And then, if we do find something we think is interesting how should we comment?

■ Is there a particular sort of language, or range of critical terms, that we should be using?
■ Or is this really nothing more than jargon and should jargon be avoided?

And, perhaps most interestingly, what is meant when people talk about 'reading' films?

■ In what sense is the activity of watching films akin to reading?

'Reading' films

Reading is often defined as interpreting symbols in relation to intended meanings. So, in the straightforward everyday sense of 'reading', the symbols 'c', 'a' and 't' can be combined in that sequence to suggest a certain type of animal that exists in our common, shared experience of the everyday world. The concept of 'reading' implies a shared language that is common to the writer and the reader and that enables messages to be transferred, or communicated. It also implies a shared world in some sense and a shared understanding of that world. Thinking about this we might wonder:

- What symbols might we need to interpret when 'reading' films?
- How will we know the intended meanings?
- Do we naturally go through this process as we watch films, or is this a special activity we are going to have to learn in the same way that we learnt to read books in our early years?
- Is it true to say that films depend upon the existence of a shared language common to both the makers of films and their audiences?

ACTIVITY

How would you define this shared language that is common to both filmmakers and the audiences for their films? In writing we obviously have words, sentences and paragraphs but what do we have in film that might in some way correspond to these elements? If possible, discuss your thoughts with others.

(Do not worry if your thoughts are rather vague and uncertain at the moment: the key thing is simply to start to think about the idea of film as a language that we might be said to be reading as we watch.)

WHAT ARE FILMS?

For the moment we will go no further in trying to answer these questions to do with the concept of 'reading', but let's bear them in mind as we try to set out from a slightly different starting point. Let us begin by asking ourselves the apparently straightforward question: what are films? To start we might suggest that they are stories recorded on film by a camera to be shown in cinemas via projectors (although even this is becoming increasingly problematic as both the form implied by 'film' and the outlets available for 'film' are becoming increasingly diverse as new technologies multiply).

Stories

We could argue that stories, cameras and cinemas are likely to be some of the key elements in our investigation. In which case we would need to question the nature of stories:

■ What subject areas do the stories typically cover?
■ Are there particular subject areas in which film has shown special interest over the years?
■ How are the stories constructed? Are there typical elements, often or always to be found?

1 Go through each of these questions and answer them quickly in note form.
2 Discuss your ideas in small groups if possible and report back to the whole class. Try to add other people's ideas to your initial notes as the discussions develop.

Cameras

Let's look now at the issue of cameras.

■ What are these cameras like and how are they used?
■ Has the technology of cameras changed over time and how has this affected films and the filmmaking process?
■ What is the relationship between the director, the camera and the actors in the making of films?
■ What is the relationship between cameras, the real world and the fictional world of stories?

1 Go through each of these questions and answer then quickly in note form.
2 Discuss your ideas in small groups if possible and report back to the whole class. Again, add to your own notes as the discussions develop.

(Once more, do not worry at this stage if you are rather vague and uncertain about how to answer some of these questions; the key thing is simply that you should begin to think carefully about the nature of films.)

Cinemas, or the 'viewing experience'

Let's now consider more closely the whole notion of cinemas: the strange idea of entering a darkened auditorium with a group of strangers to sit and watch projected images on a large screen. (Although, to emphasize the point once again, we need to be aware that this viewing experience seems to be changing with people increasingly turning to DVDs.)

- What are cinemas exactly and what are the key elements to a cinema? To what extent have these always been the same?
- Who goes to cinemas and why do people go to them? Has the sort of people who go to cinemas changed over time?
- What is the experience of being in the cinema like and how has all this changed over time?
- How is the film and the experience of watching it altered when we watch at home? Is the experience (and therefore the film?) changed when we watch at home with others? And what if the 'others' are parents or alternatively friends of our own age? Does that alter the experience?

ACTIVITY

1 Go through each of these questions and answer then quickly in note form.
2 Discuss your ideas in small groups if possible and report back to the whole class. Add to your own notes.

NOTEBOX

Try to keep your notes for Film Studies together in one place and organized in such a way that you can find specific topic areas as and when required. Above all, try to find a few minutes after each session to go back over the notes you have made and the ideas that have come up. This will remind you of the key ideas and will help to ensure you have really taken them on board. So much to do with studying is really simply about organization; and above all, about organizing your time effectively.

Questions, questions, questions

As we ask these questions about film in relation to stories, cameras and cinemas more questions might quite naturally spring to mind.

- Aren't films shown on television, video, DVD and the Internet now as well as in cinemas?

- And aren't they shown not just on terrestrial television but via satellite, cable and pay-per-view?
- And so, how would watching films via these different media change or affect the experience?
- And, are films all stories? What about filmed documentaries, are they part of our study?
- And, where is the boundary between a fictional story and a factual documentary?

In some ways this is moving into the realm of philosophical questions because we are going to be forced to ask, what fact and fiction are, what it means for something to be true to life and, indeed what truth is and how we recognize it. Soon the questions will begin to come thick and fast.

- Why are films made? There must be a whole host of reasons, but what are they?
- Who makes them? We always hear about the stars and the directors, but who else is involved?
- How are films made and what exactly does the process involve?
- To what extent is it a creative process? To what extent is it an industrial process? To what extent is it a commercial process?
- Why do we talk about different types of film, like sci-fi, horror, film noir, thriller, melodrama, or western?
- What about these cameras: who operates them and who decides what to shoot and when?
- And then how do they decide the order in which to put the shots together, what bits of film to use and what not to use?
- What is the role of actors? They seem to be accorded quite a degree of importance. What exactly is a star? How do you move from being an actor to being a star?
- For that matter, what exactly is a director? What does he do? Or, what does she do? I wonder if there have been many women directors? How many female directors do you know?
- And, who runs the production companies that make films and the chains of cinemas that show films?
- And, what about the marketing and the advertising, who is responsible for that? We are constantly being subjected to it but who decides the level of publicity and advertising?

INDUSTRIAL PROCESS An industrial process is one that is involved in the manufacture of goods that are being made for sale.

COMMERCIAL PROCESS A commercial process is one that is focused upon achieving a financial return, in other words making a profit.

You should notice how both of these terms emphasize the idea of films as being at the heart of a series of processes. These processes can be followed through for individual films and this will give us a greater understanding of the exact nature of films and their place within our society.

The more we consider the nature of films, the more it sounds like there is a whole massive industry of multinational proportions behind what definitely seems to amount to a massive commercial enterprise.

■ How does it operate both within individual countries and globally?
■ Has it always been as big as it would seem to be today?
■ Is it set to get bigger still or is it in decline in the face of new technologies?

NOTEBOX

Questions

If there is one key to understanding the approach taken throughout this book this is it. As a Film Studies student (indeed as a student of any sort) you must be continually asking yourself questions and seeking answers. It sounds easy and only too obvious but adopting a questioning attitude demands real effort, commitment and above all, thought. If you can get this questioning and thinking approach right then everything else will fall into place.

HISTORY, SOCIAL CONTEXT AND POLITICS

We are beginning to get somewhere. We have a whole series of questions, the answers to which would seem to form some part of finding out about film and the way it operates within the present context, and the way it has operated within a historical context. We also have the feeling that the more questions we ask the more we find, with all of them taking us further into the subject and each of them seeming to demand some part of our attention. In fact, we begin to get a sense of the wide-ranging nature of the studies we are about to undertake.

■ Already we begin to realize that films do not exist outside of a society and certain social relations.
■ Already we begin to see that since we are dealing with an industry we are going to have to at least be aware of business and economic considerations.
■ Already we begin to see films as products of particular societies at particular moments in their historical development.

But at the same time we are wondering about the contributions of directors and actors, and perhaps camera operators (or cinematographers, if we know the word). Clearly close investigation of individual films is going to be necessary, but at the same time it is already looking as if we are not going to be able to 'read' films in isolation but rather that we are going to have to see them to some extent at least within social, historical, cultural and perhaps even political contexts.

HOLLYWOOD AND ALTERNATIVE CINEMAS

Most of the films we will be looking at in this book would probably be seen as representing the dominant Hollywood mainstream, while others might be seen as constituting art-house or alternative offerings. Most of the films we deal with will be American or British but we will also be considering one or two films from other countries. So, we are going to need to be aware from the beginning of our studies that there have been different film movements in history and that there are different national cinemas around the world, and also that each of these film movements and national cinemas could be seen in some sense to be operating against the backdrop of a dominant Western cinema known as Hollywood. Sometimes there will be a strong sense of alternative cinemas being anti-Hollywood, but at other times the most powerful impulse will seem to be towards cross-fertilization between different cinemas (or approaches to filmmaking) and the Hollywood 'norm' or 'standard'.

CONCLUSION

Studying film requires us:

■ to 'read' individual films carefully and thoughtfully;
■ to recognize that films are made and viewed in particular ways that can be studied;
■ to be aware of the need to adopt a questioning attitude.

FURTHER READING

Dyer, R. (1998) 'Introduction to Film Studies', in J. Hill and P. Church-Gibson (eds) *The Oxford Guide to Film Studies*, Oxford: Oxford University Press.

Monaco, J. (2000) 'Preface to 2nd edition' in J. Monaco *How to Read a Film: Movies, Media, Multimedia*, 3rd edn, New York and Oxford: Oxford University Press.

Nelmes, J. (2003) 'Introduction' in J. Nelmes *An Introduction to Film Studies*, 3rd edn, London: Routledge.

Phillips, P. (2000) *Understanding Film Texts: Meaning and Experience*, London: BFI (Chapter 1).

PART 1
MAKING MEANING 1 (FS1)

Although each chapter here will have a slightly different focus in relation to the demands of AS Film Studies, taken as a whole this part of the book should work as direct preparation for the WJEC coursework module FS1 – Film: Making Meaning.

▼ 1 FILM FORM

What is film construction? What does it mean to say a film has been 'put together'?

This chapter:

- outlines the four key areas of film 'language' denoted as mise en scène, cinematography, editing and sound;
- considers ways of analysing film construction techniques.

NOTEBOX

This chapter will be directly relevant to your study of film form in FS1 – Film: Making Meaning 1 for the WJEC's AS Level in Film Studies and will form vital underpinning knowledge for that part of your coursework described as 'Written Analysis 2'. It will also help put in place vital underpinning foundations for all that you do in FS3 – Messages and Values: British and Irish Cinema. In addition the section on the film *Orphans* could form a useful introduction to that film as part of your study of British cinema.

FILMS MENTIONED

If you are working your way through the whole or parts of this chapter you will find it useful to have watched *Seven* (Fincher, 1995) and helpful to have access to scenes, clips and single shots from at least some of the following films:

- *Lock, Stock and Two Smoking Barrels* (Ritchie, 1998)
- *Lord of the Rings: the Fellowship of the Ring* (Jackson, 2001)
- *Whale Rider* (Caro, 2002)
- *A Hard Day's Night* (Lester, 1964)
- *Mildred Pierce* (Curtiz, 1945)
- *The Crying Game* (Jordan, 1992)
- *East is East* (O'Donnell, 1999)
- *Psycho* (Hitchcock, 1960)

- *On the Waterfront* (Kazan, 1954)
- *La Haine* (Kassowitz, 1995)
- *Raging Bull* (Scorsese, 1980)
- *Schindler's List* (Spielberg, 1997)
- *The Searchers* (Ford, 1956)
- *My Beautiful Laundrette* (Frears, 1985)
- *Visions of Light* (Glassman, McCarthy and Samuels, 1992)
- *Reservoir Dogs* (Tarantino, 1991)
- *Bloody Sunday* (Greengrass, 2002)
- *The Blair Witch Project* (Myrick/Sanchez, 1999)
- *Donnie Darko* (Kelly, 2001)
- *Jackie Brown* (Tarantino, 1997)
- *Russian Ark* (Sokurov, 2002)
- *The Killing Fields* (1984)
- *Orphans* (Mullan, 1999)

What does it mean to say films are 'put together'?

What people mean when they use this phrase is that each of the films we see in the cinema is built by using a few basic elements of film construction. As a filmmaker you always need a setting or a location in which to film and a cast of actors who will be dressed in certain ways and be expected to use certain props while delivering certain (usually) predetermined lines. You will also need a camera or cameras to film the action, and then some means of chopping up the resulting footage you have taken and putting it back together again in the order you decide suits the story you are trying to tell. Settings, actors, costumes, props, a script and the derived footage to be edited: out of these basic elements you will 'put together' your film. Out of convention but also in order to evoke certain responses from your audience you might also add a music soundtrack.

Any successful approach to the study of film will depend upon coming to terms with the idea that films are constructs that have been 'put together' by filmmakers from a series of common component parts that we can identify and name. To create a film, filmmakers work with each of these individual parts; and so in studying any film we can take it apart in an effort to see how and (most importantly) why the various bits might have been used in the particular way they have.

MISE EN SCÈNE: SETTING

Mise en scène is a French term that refers to a series of elements of film construction that can be seen within the frame of the individual shot; perhaps the most obvious and all encompassing of these is setting.

Consider the opening to any film you have seen recently. What was the setting and why do you think it had been chosen? Was it appropriate to the film and if so, in what ways?

If, as in the opening to *Lock, Stock and Two Smoking Barrels* (Ritchie, 1998), we find ourselves in an urban landscape of markets, small shops and lock-ups that is full of East End 'wide-boys' we know where we are in film terms and begin to have an idea of what to expect. If, as in the opening to *Lord of the Rings: the Fellowship of the Ring* (Jackson, 2001), we find ourselves in a fantastical other world of grey volcanic mountains, expansive plains and vast 'war games-style' armies we know we ought to prepare ourselves for a different experience.

The settings given to us during the openings to some films may leave us with more questions and not place us within a particular world with quite the same certainty. *Whale Rider* (Caro, 2002), for instance, cuts between two very distinct settings within the first few minutes: there is the relatively straightforward naturalism of the hospital maternity ward, but there is also the fantasy-style, other worldly, underwater space. Nevertheless, these settings have been carefully and appropriately chosen to set us up for what we should expect from the film.

KEY TERM

MISE EN SCÈNE This is a term that is borrowed from the theatre and really refers to staging, or 'putting on stage'. It sometimes helps to think of the elements that you can see in the staging of a play: a particular location will be suggested on the stage, characters will be dressed in particular ways, particular objects will be carried by characters or will be prominently placed on the stage, and the actors will be directed to move or perform in particular ways. These theatrical elements are the sub-section parts of the cinematic term; and this effectively reminds us of the way in which the theatre is a key element of film's cultural and artistic origins.

Lighting (including the use of areas of darkness or shadow) will also be part of any theatre performance and is often also classified as part of a film's mise en scène since its effects can clearly be seen 'within the frame'. However, this aspect of film construction also links into cinematography (or the use of the camera). (Even those of us who have only taken holiday snaps will know the extent to which the correct lighting determines the success or failure of any photographic effort.)

And this way in which lighting in effect straddles both mise en scène and cinematography helps to alert us to something very useful: the demarcations we are dealing with here are essentially no more than a convenient device for helping

us to gain an overall understanding of the range of techniques available to filmmakers for the creation of meaning.

In a somewhat similar way, sound effects (to say nothing of the words themselves) will also be an important part of the total effect created on the audience in a theatre, but here with respect to film we are dealing with these elements under the heading of 'sound'.

MISE EN SCÈNE: PERFORMANCE AND MOVEMENT

As with setting, the performance and movement of the actors (also part of mise en scène) can operate in similar ways to suggest possibilities for how we might understand given characters and relationships between characters. Characters sitting with their backs to each other present a certain sense of relationship, while characters moving towards each other and embracing clearly present a different sense of relationship. This much is obvious, but within the performance and movement between any two characters there is, of course, a limitless range of possible permutations.

PERFORMANCE AND MOVEMENT This refers to the acting that is taking place but the phrase also helps to define a little more clearly what it is we should be looking for: there is a performance going on and essentially it revolves around movement. These movements can range from the miniscule to the expansive, and can involve the whole body or the smallest parts of the body. Everything is included from slow movements of the eye to sudden running and jumping, and each can be 'read' in some way (or several possible ways).

Body language

We need to be alert to the subtleties of such interactions, bearing in mind that each movement and gesture will have been decided upon in order to convey some meaning. Interactive movements involving two or more characters will have been carefully choreographed with attention to the details of body language that is designed to communicate a sense of character and/or character relationships to us, the audience. Once again, as with all aspects of film construction, choices will have been made for particular reasons by those involved in the creative process and we need to ask ourselves why those particular choices might have been made. Often the reason becomes clear upon simple reflection. When in A Hard Day's Night (Lester, 1964) (see FS3 British and Irish Cinema – the Swinging Sixties) the Beatles find their way out through a fire escape and free themselves from the various entrapping room spaces in which they have previously found themselves the resulting change in their movements is clear; they cavort wildly through the open, outside space, running, jumping and extending limbs in all directions. (And, lest we should miss the point being made through performance, Richard Lester uses fast motion to bring further attention to the sudden change.) The idea behind the exaggerated change of movement is obvious. They have found a momentary escape from a confined existence, but it can be easily missed if we neglect the active thinking interaction with the screen images that is vital for Film Studies.

The range of body codes

Actors are able to generate audience response to their performance in a whole range of subtle ways. A range of ten body codes has been identified:

- direct bodily contact;
- the proximity of one character to another (or proxemics);
- the orientation of one to another i.e. the extent to which characters stand with their bodies turned towards or away from each other;
- general appearance e.g. tall and thin, or short and fat;
- head movements e.g. nodding or shaking of the head;
- facial expressions;
- gestures (or kinesics);
- body posture;
- eye movement or contact;
- aspects of speech, such as pitch, stress, tone, volume, accent, speech errors (all of which are termed paralinguistic codes).

(Argyle quoted in Hinde 1972 and Fiske 1982)

You do not need to memorize these ten body codes, nor do you need to use any of the jargon associated with this list such as 'proxemics' and 'kinesics'. It is useful, however, to have a series of areas such as eye movement, body posture, facial expressions, and so on to look out for as you are watching the performance of any particular actor.

Performance and movement in *Seven*

It is only when you look closely at actual examples of screen acting that you begin to realize the ways in which all these elements can be employed. There are, of course, countless examples that would serve to display a range of these elements of performance; but to take one example consider *Seven* (Fincher, 1995). In this film there is a scene in which Morgan Freeman and Brad Pitt (playing two detectives who do not get on well) are together in the confined space of an office that Pitt's character is about to take over from Freeman's older character who is leaving the force. While they are cramped together in what is a small space made all the more uncomfortable by the fact that they do not really like each other (note the use of setting for a specific reason again) they receive a phone call from Pitt's wife.

ACTIVITY . . .

- If possible, watch this scene several times; and as you do consider:
  - the different ways in which the actors' bodies are orientated in relation to each other;
  - the body postures adopted by both;
  - the facial expressions used by the actors;
  - any changes in speech patterns they employ;
  - the timing required for the delivery of the lines.

- Note your thoughts on each of these points before discussing your ideas with a few other people.

By way of contrast, in the same film you could consider the lines delivered in the grey, box-like space of the police interview room by the man from the brothel who has just been forced to commit the 'lust' murder. This is delivered in close-up but notice how the body posture remains important (and how the use of clothing in the shape of the white towel works to frame our attention on his face). Each movement of the facial muscles is intimately linked to movements of the eyes and to the carefully timed rising and falling voice pattern used to deliver the lines themselves.

ACTIVITY . . .

Watch this second scene several times now; and as you do so consider the ways in which each of Arygle's suggested ten body codes are being employed by the actor.

ACTIVITY . . .

Choose one of the two scenes from *Seven* mentioned above and write a 600-word analysis of the way in which the acting performance is used to convey meanings to the audience and/or to generate particular emotional responses in the audience.

You should work hard here to achieve as microscopic attention to detail as possible. Michael Caine has said film acting is all to do with the eyes: prolonged looks or minute glances towards or away from some object or person can convey (obviously with the assistance of the camera) so much meaning. Again, we have a connection with the theatre but also a difference: through the use of the camera, film is able to give the spectator a privileged close-up perspective on characters

continued

and events that is not available to either the theatre director or the theatre audience to use. Through the choice of particular shots film is able to emphasize minute details of body language.

Again, what we find is that the demarcations we are setting up in order to help to give us a basis for film analysis are in practice false: we are attempting to deal with performance and movement as a distinct area of film construction but in reality it is intimately connected to camerawork, shot choice and composition, and the editing (or ordering) of shots.

To further illustrate the point being made above, watch the scene in *Seven* in which in the face of opposition from Freeman's character, Pitt as Mills asks the police chief to be allowed to take over the whole case himself. Both his language and his gestures are brash and expansive but this air of confidence is reinforced by the use of low angle camera shots. Then, by contrast, when next morning Mills is given his own case involving the murder of a district attorney we are given an image of someone who is nervous and uncertain of his abilities. This is shown through Pitt's performance especially the way in which he folds his arm across the top of his head to reveal an almost childlike vulnerability. But notice that this gesture is highlighted for us by the use of a close-up and our interpretation is further aided by the use of point of view sound as Pitt's character enters the building that is used to give a sense of the isolation and pressure he is feeling. It is Pitt's performance that gives us an understanding of his character as someone who displays confidence but is in reality much more fragile and vulnerable, but it is his performance in conjunction with the use of camerawork, sound and editing (the juxtaposition of these two contrasting scenes) that is really at work here.

ACTIVITY ...

1   Find two examples of your own that seem to you to show effective acting; one of a single character on her own in front of the camera and the second of two actors working together.
2   Bring your examples to show to other members of the class. Screen your clips for a small group and talk them through your chosen performances pointing out how various effects are being achieved. (Make sure you also try to consider ways in which the camera and the editing process could be said to be working with the actors to achieve particular effects.)
3   Working in the same groups choose one example from those that were screened showing two actors working together and attempt to recreate this scene with two members of the group taking on the required roles.
4   If possible, use a camera to record the scene using the same shots as in the original. Edit your film and then play the scene back to compare your version

with the original. (In order to do this you might need to storyboard the scene in an effort to get it as close to the original as possible. You should find that the planning that is inevitably involved in the storyboarding process will save time in the long run and enable you to be more accurate in what you are trying to achieve. You might even like to have one group storyboarding and another trying to complete the task without going through this stage in order to enable you to compare and discuss the results.)

MISE EN SCÈNE: COSTUME AND PROPS

Allied to the performance and movement of the actors, and still within the overall area of mise en scène, are considerations by the filmmakers regarding costume to be worn and props to be placed within a setting or used by a particular character. So, for instance, again taking *Seven* as an example, notice the way in which the two detectives Mills and Somerset are dressed differently right from the start of this film. What do the differences in costume tell us about the two men? (You might also be interested in the way in which in the same film the 'baddie', John Doe (Kevin Spacey), is sometimes shown as being dressed in a similar way to Somerset – that is in a dark hat and long cloak-like coat. Why has this been done? Does it suggest something about these two characters, and if so, what?)

In order to consider the differences between Mills and Somerset, you could look at the scenes in which we are shown the two cops dressing to get ready to go to work. If you do this, notice that it is not simply a question of the types of costume or props being employed but also the nature of the way in which the two actors perform the actions of putting on particular items or laying out particular items to be used. When we are shown Somerset getting dressed by methodically laying out items of clothing and picking up a series of again carefully laid out objects to put in his pockets we immediately know something of his personality and character.

So, in trying to consider props we again notice that our convenient demarcations between elements of film construction do not really hold up when we begin to analyse any given film clip. It is the relationship between objects in the scenes discussed above and the performances of the actors (highlighted and brought to our attention by editing and camerawork, notice) that creates meaning.

KEY TERM

COSTUME AND PROPS This refers to items of clothing being worn by characters and objects seen within any given setting. At its simplest, costume clearly acts as a type of uniform, linking a character to a particular group and often to a rank or position within that group. But costume can also 'announce' a character, giving an insight into what this person is supposed to be like, for instance shy or flamboyant. At their simplest, props work to give an authentic sense of place, but can also be used in more complex ways to suggest important characteristics of particular individuals or even key themes for the whole film.

Dress code and character

It has often been pointed out that, when Joan Crawford taking the title role in *Mildred Pierce* (Curtiz, 1945) changes her clothes from stereotypical suburban housewife attire centring on an apron to power-dressing businesswoman-style suits, an important indication of her personal transformation of character is being presented to us. A similar alteration to character (although with vastly different outcomes) occurs in *The Crying Game* (Jordan, 1992) (this film could be considered further under FS3 British and Irish Cinema – Passions and Repressions/Social and Political Conflict) in which the IRA operative, Jude (Miranda Richardson), adjusts her persona markedly from the first half of the film to the second and signals this change by a distinctive change of dress. In other words, costume has always been important in helping to create meaning for the viewer. In *East is East* (O'Donnell, 1999) (see FS3 British Cinema – Comedy) our awareness of Nazir's change of lifestyle and assertion of his sexuality is reinforced for us by his new-found dress sense when he moves to Manchester.

Figure 1.1 *Jude (Miranda Richardson) in The Crying Game*
Source: C4 / RGA

In fact, the example involving the film *Mildred Pierce* given above has been used far too often according to some film examiners and usually with little real understanding of the film. So, important point: make sure you try to come up with your own examples for as many of the general ideas being given here as possible.

Take away with you the general points that are being made in any film textbooks and then make sure you try to apply the ideas to films you know. In this way you will gain a much better understanding of the concept itself and have at your disposal an example that is fresh and exciting instead of stale and overused.

Props and character

As regards props, consider the way in which books are used in relation to Mills and Somerset. Where Somerset studies the original texts in the calm academic environment of a library in order to try to understand the killer, Mills tries to read student guides to the texts but finds even these to be hard work. Or, consider the way that whenever he cannot sleep Somerset throws a flick-knife at a dartboard. What does that suggest about his character because it certainly seems to add some sort of complication to our understanding of him as the orderly, emotionally controlled, academically minded cop?

In a similar way, as Norman Bates leads Marion Crane into his parlour behind the reception area of the Bates Motel in *Psycho* (Hitchcock, 1960) we cannot avoid noticing the stuffed birds. There is the predatory owl in mid-swoop and then the ominously sharp beaked shadow of a crow, a harbinger of death. Nor should we miss in this scene the paintings of classical nudes on the walls: the female body displayed in all its naked vulnerability before the essentially male gaze. For the purposes of Film Studies we have to be intensely aware of all of this in an analytical fashion that is going to enable us to decide exactly how meaning is being created for us as members of the audience.

Props as symbols

In this way props or costume items can take on considerable significance for the whole film; they can in effect become symbols for some key idea or concept. In *On the Waterfront* (Kazan, 1954) when the first person willing to speak out against the corruption in the docks is murdered, his jacket is symbolically passed on to the next person willing to do the same and ultimately to the hero, Terry (Marlon Brando). In effect, what is seen within the film as the mantle of truth and justice is being passed from one to another. Similarly, in *East is East*, Sanjid's parka, standing perhaps for an attempt by the character to shield himself from the pain of the world around him, has the hood accidentally but highly symbolically ripped off towards the end of the film. In *La Haine* (Kassowitz, 1995) (this film could be considered further under FS5 Studies in World Cinema – Single Study Films) the key prop of the gun is symbolically handed over to Hubert by Vinz towards the end of the film in acknowledgment of the fact that he has learnt something important both about himself and about the reality of gunplay. Once again, the prop takes on a role and significance within the film over and above its mere presence as a material object.

CINEMATOGRAPHY: COLOUR

One of the key points to recognise as a Film Studies student is the way in which as spectators of film our reading (or interpretation) of one strand of film construction such as performance and movement, or costume and props, can be influenced or reinforced by the filmmaker's use of further elements of visual language. The cinematographer's choice (made in conjunction with others) of lighting and colour, for example, can clearly affect the 'look' of the film as a whole but can also influence our understanding of individual scenes.

KEY TERM

COLOUR This can be used in highly artificial ways for particular expressive purposes as in the make-up employed by the changed Jude in *The Crying Game*, for instance, (where it would seem to perhaps suggest the danger of a femme fatale) or it can be employed in an effort to achieve naturalism by re-creating the colours of the real world.

Black and white

The fundamental choice of colour or black and white may often be an economic decision but it may also be a more creative one: consider the use of black and white in *Raging Bull* (Scorsese, 1980) which looks back to boxing in the postwar period, or *Schindler's List* (Spielberg, 1993) in which the story is set amidst the horrors of the Holocaust.

When watching *Seven* there are many scenes where you almost have to remind yourself that this is a colour film; greys and 'washed out' colours almost totally predominate in order to give a sense of this bleak, murky urban landscape. In the case of *La Haine* which looks at confrontations between the police and young people in and around Paris in the mid-1990s, a very deliberate creative choice has been made to screen this film

in black and white. The question we must ask ourselves is why this might have been done. How might this have been considered appropriate or 'correct' for the film? There will be a range of possible answers but the key point is that we must ourselves ask the question.

NOTEBOX

Spielberg's brilliant decision to film *Schindler's List* in black and white is a key ingredient in the movie's aesthetic success.... The lack of colour allows Spielberg to be explicit without becoming tastelessly graphic.

Spielberg's black and white also achieves a number of other coherent aesthetic objectives. It echoes newsreels and documentaries of the Holocaust made at the time, thus establishing historical context and a feeling of authenticity.
    Alan A. Stone, 'Spielberg's Success', *Boston Review* (www.bostonreview.net)

ACTIVITY

1   If possible, look at relevant extracts from some of these films and decide why you believe black and white might have been used on each occasion. As usual, if possible, it would be good to try to compare your ideas with those of others.
2   Choose a film you know that seems to use colour in an interesting way and pick an extract that seems to demonstrate an especially good example of the way in which colour works in this film.
3   Think about how you feel colour is contributing to creating meaning and generating audience response in your film extract. If possible discuss your ideas with others.

Colour

Most obviously colour as with bright lighting simply gives pleasure to the audience. Film literally can bring light and colour into our lives. Particular colours or tints can also be used to suggest (often through their association with the colours of the natural world) warmth or coldness, or particular seasons, or emotions. They can also be used symbolically, as for example in the use of red to suggest blood and danger, or passion and lust. One way to make this clear would be to consider the way in which colour is used in *Seven*. Look at the scenes in the brothel, the interview room and the library. Decide the dominant colours in each and ask yourself why each has been chosen.

CINEMATOGRAPHY: LIGHTING

In terms of the lighting for a film the fundamental choice is obviously whether to use natural lighting or not (i.e. whether to film outside or in the studio), but in reality even natural lighting will usually be supplemented by lights set up by the film crew. The use of relatively bright lighting sources (high key lighting) as used in perhaps romantic comedies suggests a certain atmosphere or attitude to life that is distinctly different from that set up by the relatively dark lighting (low key lighting) used in film noir, or a neo-noir like *Seven*. Similarly, hard light that is created by a narrow, intense beam of light and gives sharp-edged objects and shadows sets up a distinctly different mood than the soft lighting that is created by a broad, more diffuse beam that gives soft-edged objects and shadows.

Possible sources of light

Lights can be placed anywhere around, above or below the object being photographed. Consider a face lit from the front (front lighting), compared with a face lit from behind (back lighting), or from the side (side lighting), or from above (overhead lighting), or from below. Each will obviously create a different image and within the context of the particular film suggest something about the character being lit in this way. Overhead lighting for example can be used to cast heavy shadows, conceal the eyes and create an image of a face that is mysterious, sinister, perhaps conveying danger (a classic example of this would be some of the shots of John Wayne's character, Ethan Edwards, in *The Searchers* (Ford, 1956) with the shadow of the brim of his hat putting his eyes in deep shadow). Or, sometimes the left or right half of a character's face may be lit while the other half remains in shadow, perhaps again suggesting a person with darker and lighter aspects to their character. This is the case when we encounter the Daniel Day-Lewis character, Johnny, with the other members of his British National Party gang beneath the railway line in *My Beautiful Laundrette* (Frears, 1985).

ACTIVITY

- Working on your own or with one or two others, find a range of shots that light faces in interesting and perhaps distinctive ways.
- Try to decide how you think the lights must have been arranged to create the shots you have found. You might like to experiment with lighting arrangements to see if you can re-create the type of shots you have been considering. (Your equipment does not need to be sophisticated: simple torches will suffice to give some sense of the possibilities for casting shadows on the face.)

Lighting from below challenges the viewer by reversing all our usual expectations for lighting, which derive from the positioning of the sun overhead; we are used to facial shadows falling in a certain way and when this norm is disrupted we are disorientated finding that with which we are confronted to be strange and otherworldly. As with colour, lighting can be used in highly contrived, artificial ways to achieve particular purposes or in naturalistic ways in order to achieve in some sense a replication of the real world.

ACTIVITY ...

If possible, discuss with other people the ways in which you believe lighting has been used for particular purposes in any films you have seen recently. Try to talk as accurately as possible about specific scenes in specific films.

LIGHTING This refers to the various ways in which the light whether in the studio or on location is controlled and manipulated in order to achieve the 'look' desired for a particular shot or scene.

KEY TERM

ACTIVITY ...

- Choose one film that you know well that seems to you to use lighting in an interesting way and pick an extract that seems to demonstrate an especially good example of the way in which lighting works in this film.
- If possible, show your chosen extracts to others and explain in as much detail as possible how you feel lighting is contributing to creating meaning and generating audience response in your film extract.

(In order to make a good job of this you will need to practise your delivery. You are not aiming to give an in-depth talk but you should still attempt to be as professional as possible.)

Conventional lighting norms

Most often in the filming of a commercial film a combination of lighting positions will be used around the main subject. This will conventionally involve a key light (usually on an arc 45 degrees either side of the camera), a fill light (giving softer lighting from the opposite side of the camera to the key light) and a back light (making the subject stand out from the background). But these are only general positions; more lights can be added or lights can be taken away. The angle at which any light is positioned in relation to either camera or subject can (obviously) be varied, and there is a choice of hard or soft lighting that is available for each lighting position. All of which begins to make it clear why the work of cinematographers has often been referred to as 'painting with light'. (This is a key phrase in the highly recommended film *Visions of Light* (Glassman, McCarthy and Samuels, 1992) which looks back at key cinematographers in Hollywood.)

NOTEBOX

As with every other aspect of film construction so far discussed, we again notice not only how extensive the range of choices available to filmmakers is but also how critical these choices are to the creation of a particular meaning, or range of potential meanings, for the spectator.

ACTIVITY

1   Watch the scene in *Seven* where the detectives, Mills and Somerset, go down into the brothel to investigate the 'lust' murder. If possible, discuss in detail with others the ways in which light and colour have been used in this sequence.
2   Write a short piece (400–500 words) explaining the meanings you see as being created for the audience and the responses likely to be generated by the use of light and colour in this short sequence.

ACTIVITY

1   If you have time, watch *Visions of Light*, stopping, rewinding and watching again any effects of cinematography that you find particularly interesting.
2   List interesting films (with dates), along with the cinematographers and directors who worked on them. What were the features of these films that made you see them as interesting in some way?
3   If possible, discuss the choices of interesting films you have made with other people who have looked at *Visions of Light*. When these other people watched the film did they identify the same clips, or different ones, as being especially interesting? Were you able to express clearly the reasons for each of your choices?

(The word 'interesting' has been used several times above. It is a vague word and usually you should expect to try to use language in as precise a way as possible. Try never to describe a film as simple 'good', or 'enjoyable', or even 'interesting', but instead always attempt to suggest why you found it to be any of these things. As always, 'why' is our key word: by referring to details of film construction you should try to identify exactly what it is about any film that makes it 'interesting' (or 'good' or 'enjoyable'). The usefulness of such a vague word as 'interesting' here is that it leaves it open for you to come up with your own ideas.)

CINEMATOGRAPHY: CAMERAWORK

All of the elements of construction so far considered can influence the way in which we 'read' the visuals being presented to us; but, in addition, the filmmaker also has within her control the manipulation of our physical point of view through camerawork. The filmmakers can put us into positions that are comfortable or uncomfortable, dominant or weak, simply by deciding on the positioning and movement of the camera.

If you have seen the well-known scene in *Reservoir Dogs* (Tarantino, 1991) in which the police officer has his ear sliced off, you may have noticed the way in which the camera as it were 'looks away' at the actual moment of the cutting almost as if the whole thing is too uncomfortable or painful to watch. If you have seen the interrogation scene in *La Haine* in which two police officers racially abuse and beat two of the central characters you may have noticed how, in contrast to *Reservoir Dogs*, a static camera is used, refusing us any respite from viewing what is going on. In this film the filmmakers deny us the potential relief of looking away and yet by refusing this possibility they in fact only highlight how much we would like to turn our heads. The point is that choices that are made about the use of the camera are often made in order to create particular effects on the audience.

KEY TERM

CAMERAWORK This clearly and quite simply refers to the work done with the camera in the making of a film. However, the possibilities open to the cinematographer are anything but simple. Fundamentally, the camera can be positioned at any distance from the subject being filmed and at any angle to that subject. It can be turned left or right to follow a subject within a horizontal plane, or tilted up or down to follow the same subject in a vertical plane. It can also be moved at any speed towards, away from or around the subject, and this movement can be as smooth or as shaky as the filmmakers decide. In addition, lenses can be used to give the appearance of movement towards or away from the subject at any speed, or to make the image of the subject either sharper or more indistinct, or even to alter the appearance of the subject in the style of a fairground 'hall of mirrors'.

The only limitation on the fluidity and mobility of the camerawork in any film is the availability of the necessary technology to enable the desired effect to be achieved; and, in general terms, camera and lens technology has developed throughout film history in such a way as to permit increasingly complex camerawork. So, for instance, new lightweight cameras (and sound recording gear) in the 1950s made it easier to take the equipment out on location.

However, what you will find if you get the chance to watch some clips from old silent films is that even from very early in film history cinematographers were devising imaginative ways of getting moving shots with these rather large, heavy wooden cameras. So, yes, available technology must to some extent impose limitations upon what can be achieved, but often it is the creativity with which available technology is used that is of most interest.

(Please note: this is not to say simple camerawork is not possible, nor to suggest that simple camerawork cannot be at least as effective as complex permutations of distances, angles, movements and lens usage. Recall the example from *La Haine* given above.)

Distance and angle of shot

By varying the distance between the camera and the subject, the cinematographer can employ anything from an extreme long shot (ELS) (often used to establish the setting and then also known as an establishing shot), to an extreme close-up (ECU) closing in on just part of the face. In between there are possibilities for a long shot (LS) giving a full-length character shot, a medium shot (MS) giving half a standing character, and a close-up (CU) giving a head and shoulders shot (and obviously all sorts of further slight variations within this range of possibilities).

By varying the angle of shot the cinematographer can place the spectator in the position of looking down on or looking up at a character; alternatively, we can be positioned at eye level with a character in shot. If the editing suggests the camera is taking up the point of view of a particular character (a point of view shot, or POV) then again the angle can be used to create a particular impression of the character's situation. So, a low angle POV shot might suggest a character was being overpowered by whatever was towering over her.

Establishing shots

Usually you will find that each scene in a fictional narrative film uses an establishing shot; that is a shot that gives the setting in which the scene is to take place and enables the viewer to establish the spatial relationships between characters involved in the scene. But, although this is what might be known as the Hollywood standard and was certainly the expected norm throughout the period of Classical Hollywood, the practice of using an establishing shot has not always been followed by filmmakers. By omitting an establishing shot the viewer is put in the position of struggling to make sense of the relationship between the characters shown. We are effectively dis-orientated and this will be part of what the filmmakers are attempting to achieve; as well as perhaps defying the expected filmic norm and thereby challenging any presumption that there are certain correct (and therefore, certain incorrect) ways of making films.

1　Choose a sequence from a film you know that seems to use camerawork in a significant way.

2　In small groups show your chosen sequences to each other and explain in as much detail as possible how you feel camerawork is being used to contribute to creating meaning and generating audience response in your chosen extracts.

(In doing this you should expect to refer to distances and angles of shot, and you might like to use diagrams (perhaps as handouts or on an overhead projector) to illustrate your points. As an alternative, you might like to use members of the group to take roles within your chosen film clip enabling you to move amongst them in order to demonstrate your understanding of how the camera has been used to film the sequence.)

Camera movement

The variations in terms of permutations of distance from subject and angle of shot are obviously endless; but in addition the cinematographer can also move the camera while taking the shot. This could involve panning to left or right to take in more of a scene or bring into view additional objects, or tilting up or down to create a similar effect. But it could also involve moving the whole camera along on a track (a tracking shot), or simply on wheels (a dolly shot), or even on a crane (a crane shot). And by using the lens on the camera the cinematographer can create further adjustments to the type of shot we see. She could zoom in to give more detail or out to take in more of the setting; or might adjust the lens to bring some objects more sharply into focus while leaving others blurred; or could employ deep focus to have objects from foreground to background all in acceptable focus. All sorts of combinations are obviously possible, so for example the camera could pan while tracking forward and rising up on a crane. Finally, shots could also be hand-held and therefore deliberately somewhat shaky.

If you watch *Bloody Sunday* (Greengrass, 2002) (see FS3 British Cinema – Social and Political Conflict) one of the first things that will strike you will probably be the distinctive use that is being made of the camera. We are familiar with shaky handheld camera effects from films like *The Blair Witch Project* (Myrick/Sanchez, 1999) and tend to associate it with low budget films. But what both of these films demonstrate is that these sorts of uses of the camera can be employed to create very particular atmospheres and involve the audience in the experience in very striking ways.

In both of these cases, you will probably be immediately aware that something different from what you are used to is being done with the camera. This highlights the fact that because we tend to be familiar with mainstream Hollywood films we do have certain expectations about how the camera will be used. Changes from the norm will be potentially challenging to us.

The extent of the range of camera possibilities

The important point, of course, is that if the cinematographer and director as a team are 'on top of their game' then each permutation of possibilities will be carefully chosen in an effort to achieve a particular desired effect whether in the creation of meaning or the generation of audience response. Consider the elaborate camera movement forming the opening to *Donnie Darko* (Kelly, 2001) in which the camera seems to track past half-lit undergrowth before moving towards the central character lying in the road and circling him. There is then a cut to what at first looks as if it might be a point of view shot panning across the early morning skyline before the character stands and emerges suddenly into the foreground of the shot, half turns towards the camera and seems to smile, almost laugh to himself. Why has this opening camera movement been chosen? How does it work to introduce the film and the central character, and in what ways is it appropriate for the film and the character? How does it contribute towards ensuring the opening engages our attention? Or, what about the opening to *Jackie Brown* (Tarantino, 1997), what sorts of camera movement are being used here? If you get a chance to look at this you will see the way in which the opening tracking shot has been complicated by having the central character standing on a moving walkway somewhat confusing our sense of movement. You will also see how a low camera angle has been used in places to perhaps give a sense of a strong individual. Consider all of this for yourself and ask the same three questions as for *Donnie Darko* above:

- Why has this opening camera movement been chosen and, how does it work to introduce the film and the central character?
- In what ways is it appropriate for the film and the character?
- How does it contribute towards ensuring the opening engages our attention?

There is much more that could be said about camerawork and many more terms that could be used, but the essential point to recognize is the range of possibilities that are open to the director/cinematographer. And also of course that every choice of position, movement, or lens will be made with the aim of creating some sort of impression on the spectator and generating some meaning. Film exists only in relation to those who are watching it. (This is a key point, perhaps the key point: do think about it carefully.)

NOTEBOX

> Be reassured that knowing all of the technical terms here is not what Film Studies is really essentially all about. The important thing is to respond thoughtfully to the way in which the camera is being used to create potential meanings for you as a reader. Try to work out what the filmmakers are attempting to get you to feel and think about. These are the important things. Asking yourself why this or that technique has been used, this is the crux of the matter. Knowing the technical terms simply allows you to describe in a succinct, shorthand fashion the effect within the film that you are attempting to focus upon.

1   If possible, watch the opening to *Donnie Darko*, *Jackie Brown* and one other film of your choice.
2   Try to find time to discuss these scenes with other people, noting any particular aspects of camerawork you find interesting. Do not be afraid to play and replay these scenes as many times as necessary in order to try to see exactly how the camera is being used. You need to attempt to detach yourself from the narrative so that you are mentally in the position of watching over the shoulder of the cinematographer as the scene is being filmed.

NOTEBOX . . .

The skill mentioned above of being able to detach yourself from the film and imagine you are on location with the crew as they are filming is immensely useful for Film Studies. Essentially it involves the attempt to try to imagine just how the shots you are being given as a viewer of the film have been achieved.

EDITING

After the film has been shot in the camera it still of course has to be edited, and what you will have found whilst discussing camerawork is that it is actually almost impossible to talk about either of these two elements of film construction in isolation. Editing gives narrative shape and coherence to the array of shot sequences recorded by the camera(s). This part of the process involves hours of film that may have been taken being cut to what is as a matter of convention deemed to be an appropriate exhibition length: sometimes 90 minutes, usually around 120 minutes, and occasionally 150–80 minutes. As with much else connected with narrative film, these lengths seem to owe most to the traditional time spans allocated for theatre drama, and apart from that there seems little reason for the choice of time span.

ACTIVITY . . .

■   Choose a sequence of film you know that seems to use editing in a significant way to create particular meanings for the audience.
■   In small groups show your chosen sequences to each other and explain how you feel editing is being used to contribute towards creating meaning and generating audience response.

To use a long take, or a montage of shots

Editing has been seen by some to be a key defining feature of film. For some theorists the long take involving filming a lengthy sequence of events without cuts has been seen to be the essence of filmmaking allowing the spectator to follow a whole scene as a privileged 'presence'. (This idea was taken to its logical extreme in a film called *Russian Ark* (Sokurov, 2002) which was essentially one highly choreographed long take.) For others who have come up with theories about the best way to make films, cutting a variety of shots together in a montage that challenges the spectator to make meaning from perceived connections between the shots has been seen as the key to film-making. In practice most filmmakers recognizing that both cinematography and editing are useful tools of their trade have used a combination of these two possible extremes.

Case Study: *The Killing Fields* (1984)

(Director: Roland Joffe. Screenwriter: Bruce Robinson. Editor: Jim Clark. Cinematographer: Chris Menges. Music: Mike Oldfield. Cast: Sam Waterston (Sydney Schanberg), Dr Haing Ngor (Dith Pran), and John Malkovich (Al Rockoff).)

Camerawork and editing

There is an interesting scene in this film around the point where Pol Pot's rebel communist forces are entering the outskirts of Phnom Pen. The journalist, Sydney Schanberg, whose story we are following finds himself in a Coca-Cola warehouse and the 'camera-eye' (from a privileged viewer's position) becomes involved in trying to make sense of the situation. Initially it calmly surveys the scene taking in the irony of the expulsion of American influence from this country occurring in the midst of so much bottled essence of American Dream. As soon as the first explosion takes place, however, perhaps significantly shattering the fragile glass bottles, the camerawork becomes increasingly frantic and the editing from shot to shot much quicker. Thus the sudden confusion of the situation is reinforced and the spectator finds herself having to work at an increased pace to take in all the images being thrown in front of her. Images of Coca-Cola dispenser-machines and lorries (first of all relatively intact even if broken but later being blown up) continually intrude inter-cut with shots of child soldiers, lost or abandoned toddlers screaming, and cattle in their death throes. East and West are continually juxtaposed, the West in the shape of high-tech weapons and Coca-Cola and the East in the shape of a low-tech Cambodian bullock-cart way of life. Coca-Cola is the symbol, perhaps, of Western capitalism, the American way of life, multinational globalization of trade, and American imperialism. We note the American soldier's introduction of himself as 'Made in the USA' as well as the way he enters at speed, in a jeep, sounding the horn. However, more powerfully than anything else because of the editing the spectator notices the presence of children in this

---

extract: this is an indictment of war, and of what war does to ordinary people and to children and the innocence of children. These children have guns instead of toys: see the carefully composed shot of the child-soldier firing above a dead child and the final shot of the child crying with his hands over his ears. Through the juxtaposition of a series of shots, additional meaning is produced (although the exact nature of that meaning is highly dependent upon the work being done in terms of interpretation by the viewer).

(Although this look at *The Killing Fields* has been sub-titled 'camerawork and editing' you will have noticed that the reality is that we cannot divorce these elements of film construction from mise en scène (setting, performance and movement, costume and props) and we certainly cannot divorce all of this from the way in which film continually works to create meaning for us.)

Editing tools and 'tricks'

Editors can use straight cuts so that we are instantaneously transported from one shot to another. Or they can use 'fades' where the shot fades out to a blank screen (and fades in to the next shot from a blank screen), or 'dissolves' where through superimposition one shot dissolves into another; or a range of other less used transitions. They can aim to maintain continuity through using cause and effect, ensuring each shot has a 'cause' in the previous shot and an 'effect' in the following shot. Or they can construct a discontinuous sequence that disorientates viewers and makes them 'work' to make sense of the series of images with which they are confronted. At all times the juxta-position of shots will be vital to the creation of meaning with one shot in some way 'commenting on' or adjusting the potential meaning of the previous shot.

Editing and time

It is via editing that film is able to transport the spectator through space and time, allowing a flashback to a previous temporal and spatial dimension (and even flash forward to the future) to take place or permitting movement (cross-cutting) between parallel actions taking place contemporaneously. In *La Haine* the filmmakers need to show the boredom of everyday life for young unemployed people living in the working-class satellite towns around Paris: a single static shot of our three central characters sitting equidistant from each other in a bleak, waste area is held for some time and then a flash-forward edit is used to a shot of the same three characters in the same space but occupying slightly different positions within the frame. It is the combination of holding the initial shot for longer than we might normally expect and then using a distinctive editing cut that ensures the required meaning is conveyed clearly and effectively to the viewer.

SOUND

What we have considered so far in this chapter are those aspects of film construction dealing with the visual aspects of filmmaking, but there is of course a further obvious dimension to film, that of sound. This might be said to operate today on three levels; that is via dialogue, sound effects and musical accompaniment.

ACTIVITY ...

- Find a scene in a film that you know where a range of types of sound seem to you to be used particularly effectively.
- In small groups screen your chosen scenes and explain why you think the filmmakers have chosen to use sound in these ways at this point in their film. In particular try to explain how you think the particular uses of sound found in your film extract contribute to meaning and enhance audience response.

The uses to which sound can be put range from merely enhancing a sense of realism to helping to suggest quite subtle aspects of character or theme. In a sequence from *Seven* mentioned earlier, the younger detective, Mills, is allocated his own murder case to work on after displaying great confidence in the police chief's office (low angle camera shots, for example, adding to a sense of his personal assurance in this scene). However, when he arrives at the scene of the murder and walks in, we follow him and the sound we are given is what might be described as 'point of view' sound, the indistinct, half-audible voices of those around him. It is this distinctive use of sound (added to several other aspects of film construction such as performance and editing) that gives the viewer the idea that Mills is in fact not as confident as his 'performance' in the police chief's office might have suggested.

NOTEBOX ...

> **Silent cinema**   The period stretching from the start of cinema in the mid-1890s to about 1930 has come to be known as silent cinema; although, in fact, it was no such thing with live musical accompaniment being the order of the day from early on. In creative terms this music, provided by anything from a single piano to a larger array of instruments, added meaning by, for example, enhancing dramatic or romantic moments, and in practical terms it drowned out any accompanying mechanical noises from the projector.

Sound: dialogue

Clearly dialogue (which may include a narrator's voiceover) is now an important part of film and vital to our perception and understanding of the narrative. It makes a critical

contribution to the way in which we gauge who the characters are, what they are like, what they have done, what they are going to do and what their relationship might be to others in the film. But dialogue is also often critical in alerting us to any wider ideas or themes that might be dealt with by the film. So, in the extract considered above from *The Killing Fields*, although it was minimal, dialogue contributed to our awareness of the importance for the filmmakers of the theme of American imperialism and globalization of trade, with the American officer using the very distinctive phrase 'made in the USA' to describe himself. In *La Haine* the word 'killer' comes back time and again, particularly as a way of describing the punch-line to a story, and in the light of the film's ending this usage takes on a special resonance.

Sound: sound effects

In addition to dialogue there are also sound effects. These can be used simply to enhance a realistic sense of place as in the use of traffic noise for a city street setting. However, they may move beyond this and work to engage heightened audience response and expectation as in the sound of the kitchen knife being drawn from its holder in the opening to *Scream* (Craven, 1996). Or, to return to our traffic noise, look at *Seven* to see how the noise of the city as this oppressive, intrusive presence is always there in the background. In *La Haine* you will find that the sound of the metro train running on its tracks which might be seen simply to add to a sense of realism is in fact also used at the start of the final sequence to echo what is perhaps the key recurring sound effect in the film, that of a clock ticking.

Sound: background music

There is also the possibility of using background music that does not arise realistically out of the imagined world on screen to give a sense of mood or atmosphere. If you ever have people suggesting film is a naturalistic medium you could alert them to this sort of use of music in film. (Where are the violins, is it just me who is not hearing them!) And, it is important to remember of course that silence, the absence of sound, can be used just as effectively (sometimes more effectively) to create audience engagement.

ACTIVITY...

- Find a scene in a film that you know where silence seems to be used particularly effectively.
- In small groups screen your chosen scenes and explain why you think the filmmakers have chosen to use silence at this point in their film and how you think it contributes to meaning and enhances audience response.

FILM FORM: OVERVIEW

Filmmakers use a vast array of strategies for communicating ideas and/or emotions. These revolve around the use of various settings, the presentation of character, the application of a range of camera techniques, the editing of shots into particular scenes and sequences, and the use of sound. Each of these strategies is used to influence our perception of events as shown and deliberately suggest ways of making sense of any film. Awareness of the techniques being used and careful consideration of the effects that might be achieved by the application of these techniques is perhaps the fundamental skill required by anyone wishing to study film since it enables us to either accept or reject the suggested meanings that seem to be on offer.

ACTIVITY

1   Watch the whole of any film mentioned earlier in this chapter; and then, with a group of others if possible, choose one sequence of no more than seven minutes to analyse in detail.
2   Spend time as a group discussing how your chosen sequence works in terms of its use of mise en scène, cinematography, editing and sound.
3   Individually write a commentary (1,000–1,200 words) discussing the ways in which one or two of these areas of film construction work to create meaning and generate audience response in your chosen sequence. Give your piece of writing a title in the form of a question:

How do mise en scène and/or cinematography and/or sound and/or editing work to create meaning and generate audience response in the (name or timing of scene) scene in (name of film)?

Case Study: *Orphans* (1999)

(Director: Peter Mullan. Producer: Frances Higson. Scriptwriter: Peter Mullan. Cast: Michael (Douglas Henshall); Thomas (Gary Lewis); John (Stephen Cole); Sheila (Rosemarie Stevenson); Tanga (Frank Gallagher).)

This film is a focus film for the section on Scottish cinema in the WJEC exam on British and Irish cinema. The opening sequence offers an interesting contrast in camera movement and carefully directed understated performances from the actors.

In the initial shot we are shown a series of objects before a hand comes in from the right to pick up a pair of scissors. In film terminology this is an example of props being used for particular effects. What is our reaction to each of these items and how does starting like this make the spectator feel? Is the response different on a first viewing compared with subsequent viewings, and if so how? There are a lot of items here. Make sure you identify each of them and consider their significance.

It is only after this series of shots that there is a cut to a shot of the room in which these objects are to be found and we gain some impression of the four main characters. How do we view these characters in relation to the previous panning shot of the objects? In other words, how does this cut work? What response does it gain from the audience? Again, does our understanding change or develop on subsequent viewings, and if so in what way(s)? How do we initially respond to each of the main characters and what is it about them that makes us respond in this way? Notice at this point the role that casting might be said to play in the process of creating meaning and how important dress, appearance, body language and the smallest of movements can be in creating understanding.

How does camera movement contribute to creating meaning at this stage? How would you describe the camera movement and how does it make the audience feel? What is the effect on the audience of the central prop in the room and how is the camera movement appropriate for a scene involving this sort of prop? How do we feel as the scissors are passed round? How does each character use the scissors and what does this tell us about each? At each point notice the responses of the other actors as well as the particular character with the scissors. In what order are the scissors passed around and why?

When the haircutting is over how do we respond to Sheila's request to kiss her mother and the way in which Michael and John lift Sheila? How do we feel as an audience at this point? (Remember that we could feel several emotions at any one point in a film and that it is even possible that these emotions could be contradictory.) How are the ways in which each of the characters performs the kissing individualized? What about the things each character has to say during this time round the coffin? How are the lines both in terms of content and delivery appropriate for each character? What other sounds apart from the characters talking are used in this scene, and why?

When we move to the next shots of the box, how do we feel as an audience, and why do we feel this? Then, when we cut to the four siblings again, how are they arranged in relation to each other and in what ways might this be significant? How would you describe the camera movement at this point and in what way could it be considered as appropriate and contributing meaning to the scene? How does sound now begin to work? How would you describe the following elaborate camera movement and why has it been chosen? How do the colours change at this point and why has the change been chosen by the filmmakers? How do the colours used at this point contrast with the earlier shots around the coffin? In what ways are the mother's words and the setting given to this flashback scene appropriate? What other sounds can you hear in the scene and why have they been chosen?

Using the notes you have made in response to these questions write an analysis of the ways in which film language creates meaning in the opening sequence of *Orphans* (1,000–1,500 words).

CONCLUSION

- A film is constructed from the mise en scène, cinematography, editing and sound.
- The possible combinations of these elements available to filmmakers are endless.
- In analysing film we can dissect these chosen uses to understand how meaning is created in film.

FURTHER READING

Bordwell, D. and Thompson, K. (2000) *Film Art: An Introduction*, New York: McGraw Hill (Chapters 5, 6, 7 and 8).

Lacey, N. (2005) *Introduction to Film*, Basingstoke and New York: Palgrave Macmillan (Chapter 1).

Nelmes, Jill (ed.) (2003) *An Introduction to Film Studies*, London: Routledge (Chapter 4).

Phillips, W.H. (2005) *Film: An Introduction*, 3rd edn, Boston: Bedford/St Martin's (Chapters 1, 2, 3 and 4).

Roberts, G. and Wallis, H. (2001) *Introducing Film*, London: Arnold (Chapters 1, 2 and 3).

USEFUL WEBSITES

www.bfi.org.uk

www.filmeducation.org

▼ 2 NARRATIVE

Aren't all films just stories? What is narrative structure?

This chapter:

- explains the terms 'narrative' and 'narrative structure';
- examines the role of the narrator;
- explores the importance of stories in our everyday life;
- outlines the expected or common features of stories;
- considers ways in which we as viewers read film.

NOTEBOX

This chapter will be directly relevant to the section on film form in FS1 – Film: Making Meaning 1 of the WJEC's AS in Film Studies and will help to form part of the necessary underpinning knowledge for one of the two required pieces of analytical coursework.

FILMS MENTIONED

If you are working your way through the whole or parts of this chapter you will find it useful to have watched *Seven* (Fincher, 1995) and perhaps *Run Lola Run* (Tykwer, 1999), and helpful to have access to scenes, clips and single shots from at least some of the following films:

- *Pulp Fiction* (Tarantino, 1994)
- *Lock, Stock and Two Smoking Barrels* (Ritchie, 1998)
- *Lord of the Rings: the Fellowship of the Ring* (Jackson, 2001)
- *Four Weddings and a Funeral* (Newell, 1994)
- *Casablanca* (Curtiz, 1942)
- *High Noon* (Zinnemann, 1952)
- *Billy Elliot* (Daldry, 2000)

- *La Haine* (Kassowitz, 1995)
- *Ratcatcher* (Ramsey, 1999)
- *The Matrix* (Wachowski, 1999)
- *Donnie Darko* (Kelly, 2001)
- *Strike* (Eisenstein, 1924)
- *Moulin Rouge* (Luhrmann, 2001).

ACTIVITY . . .

1   Summarise in 100–200 words the story of any film you have seen recently. Make sure you mention each of the central characters succinctly and that you give a clear sense of the beginning, middle and end of the story.
2   Exchange your synopsis with someone else, if possible, and read each other's. Discuss the two pieces of work looking for differences and similarities of approach. Which one strikes you on a first impression as telling the story more effectively? What are the features of this piece of writing that seem to make it an effective re-telling of the film's storyline? Does it follow a logical order? Is it using shorter, sharper sentences conveying information in a simple, straightforward way?

(The skill of being able to re-tell the central narrative for a film in just a few hundred words will be necessary when you take on your third piece of coursework, completing the storyboard or screenplay for a short scene within an imagined film.)

NARRATIVE

Usually, although not always (we could consider documentaries, for example) our concern in studying film will be with works of fiction, narratives with characters and a setting that are told to us in some way and claim in some way to represent the world to us. Given that this is the case we are going to need to consider the fundamental nature of narratives, or stories, and the role and use to which they are put within human society.

To begin with, it might be worth noting that narrative seems to be integral to human experience of the world. We constantly use stories (and it seems we have always done so) to make sense of and to create meaning out of our otherwise chaotic experiences. In telling stories we give order and shape to a series of events.

- In pairs tell each other the story of your life. (Before you do this you will need to plan it a little: write down the things you want to tell the other person and put them into an order you think is suitable and effective. You should only tell your stories to each other when you are absolutely sure you have shaped them as you want to.)
- Remember things like the need to immediately engage the interest of the person to whom you are telling your story, the importance of retaining that person's attention and the need to put things into an order that will enable the listener to make sense of what has happened to you during your life. (Notice as well that you have only been asked to tell the other person things you want to let them know.)
- One final condition: there is a time limit of ten minutes on the length of your story. (Notice there seems to be some unwritten rule about the length of films you watch in the cinema: they almost always seem to run from 90 to 120 minutes. Why is this? What factors could have determined this length?)

Narrative structure

Narratives can be seen as particular arrangements of events within a structure. This structure may be the simplest one of relating events in chronological order, or it might be more complex. It could, for instance, involve the use of parallel episodes that form a deliberate contrast to each other, or the repetition of events seen from different perspectives, or the integration of symbolic events or images used in order to create significance.

PARALLEL EDITING This refers to moving back and forth between two or more narrative lines of action supposedly occurring at the same time.

KEY TERM

If there is no apparent relation between the events in a film, it is without plot (that is there is no sense of a controlling order having been imposed on events) and it may be that what is being represented to us is the chaotic nature of human experience, or a lack of meaning in the universe. (Or perhaps we are dealing with a surrealist who aims to delve into the unconscious or the subconscious.) But such lack of structure is extremely rare, and not something that will be found in mainstream cinema. The very nature of storytelling is essentially that of giving order to events.

Even if the structure is extremely complex involving unexpected time-shifts and demanding that the viewer should keep elements of the story on hold until the bigger picture becomes clearer (think of Tarantino's *Pulp Fiction* (1994), for example, if you know it), order and shape will eventually be found. Indeed, the sense of achievement that

THE WRITER'S JOURNEY MODEL

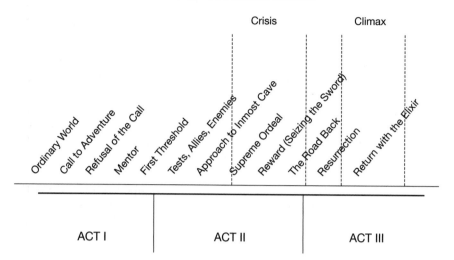

Figure 2.1 *The Writer's Journey Model*
Source: Provided courtesy of Michael Wiese Productions,
www.mwp.com

comes from eventually recognizing and understanding the shape and form of the narrative is one of the pleasures offered by film. Through narrative we are reassured that any events that may happen are not random, and that the world we face is not a place of chaos but one of order.

NOTEBOX

> How did you structure your story when you told it to your partner? How did you choose the order in which to relate events? Which events did you choose to include and why? Which events did you leave out and why? What effect did the time limit have on your choices?
>
> However you chose to do this, you will have been making choices in order to give structure i.e. shape and significance to the random, chaotic ongoing stream of events that have actually been the reality of your life.

The role of the narrator

Narration requires a narrator, someone (or more than one person) who tells the story. If you watch the opening to two films as different as *Lord of the Rings: the Fellowship of the Ring* (Jackson, 2001) and *Lock, Stock and Two Smoking Barrels* (Ritchie, 1998) you will find both use the device of having a formal narrator's voice. However, often the narrator's role is in effect fulfilled by the filmmakers who position themselves outside the story and decide what to include, what not to include and the order in which to place events. It is they who are narrating the story for us, but we will usually be barely aware of the filmmakers' presence as narrator.

If, as with *Fellowship of the Ring* and *Lock, Stock and Two Smoking Barrels*, the device of a narrator as a character or presence within the film itself is used, it may be more obvious that the narrator has a particular perspective on events. If such a narrator is also a character within the story it will be clear that this person will see things from a certain perspective and will have their own relationship to events and characters. If an internal narrator is positioned outside of the main story and appears to be telling us what happened in an apparently objective way he may be reliable or he may be unreliable. The key point is that as readers of films we always need to ask ourselves who the narrator might be, what he can know and cannot know about events within the narrative, and what his or her perspectives might be on any narrative event. For example, consider again the ending to *Seven*. Why have the filmmakers decided to use Somerset's voiceover narration at this point?

ACTIVITY

- Try to find a contemporary film of your own choice that uses a narrator. What is her/his relationship to events shown in the story and how reliable a narrator should we take her/him to be? Are we expected to unquestioningly adopt her/his perspective on events, and if so should we be happy to do so?
- How difficult is it to adopt a perspective outside of this narrator's viewpoint? If it is difficult, what makes it hard to achieve?
- Explain your film's use of a narrator (or narrators) to other people in a group, but only after you are absolutely clear as to your answers to the questions above. Do people who know the film agree with your analysis? If not, what did they disagree with you about?

PLOT STRUCTURE

The story is the basic chronological order of events: the plot is the rearranged, highly selected chain of events in the film that has been given its own internal logic. By using narrative's ability to move backwards and forwards through time and space and rearranging the elements of simple stories, let's say 'Little Red Riding Hood' or 'Cinderella', we can create individual plot arrangements of the basic story events.

For example, we could start our story of Cinderella at the ball or our story of Little Red Riding Hood at the point at which she is about to be eaten and then in both cases use flashback sequences to tell the story. In fact, we could start our narrative at any point within the chronology of the story that we chose. But what will always happen in a mainstream cinema narrative is that the plot will consist of a cause-and-effect flow of actions. You should be able to take any film and see how the sequence of events has been rearranged into a particular cause-and-effect chain.

Case Study: *Four Weddings and a Funeral* (1994)

(Director: Mike Newell. Scriptwriter: Richard Curtis. Cast: Charles (Hugh Grant); Carrie (Andie MacDowell); Tom (James Fleet); Gareth (Simon Callow); Matthew (John Hannah); Fiona (Kristin Scott Thomas); David (David Bower); Scarlett (Charlotte Coleman).)

This film would seem to be at least to some extent an exception to the rule in that it is almost a series of set-piece scenes. Can you think of any other films that might in some ways be said to not have a structure of cause and effect?

But is this film really an exception? Within each set-piece scene the events that take place always follow a cause and effect sequence. And there is in fact a sense of linkage between the individual episodes:

■ Bernard and Lydia get together as a couple at the first wedding and as a result constitute the occasion of the second wedding;
■ we meet Carrie and her fiancé, Hamish, at this second wedding thus leading naturally into the third wedding;
■ Gareth has a heart attack and dies at Carrie's wedding moving us logically by cause and effect to the funeral of the title;
■ and from this gathering of the friends the necessity to marry pronounced by Gareth, the increased calm of Henrietta, and Tom's telling Charles that he had never hoped for a blinding flash, all lead naturally to the final wedding.

ACTIVITY . . .

1   Choose your own film and draw a diagrammatic representation of the ways in which cause and effect work within a single scene of your choice and within the structure of the whole film.
2   Explain your diagrams to a small group of other students who have undertaken the same exercise.

Characters

When approaching a film we should also consider carefully each of the main characters. Usually they will provide the filmmakers with a means of exploring various aspects of the human experience. Often they display particular commonly recognised traits of human nature, or complex inner conflicts of values and emotions. Often there will be contrasting, or parallel characters, who are used to highlight the oppositional possibilities open to human beings; love and hate, compassion and brutality, vengeance and forgiveness, etc. Sometimes characters are dramatized as unique individuals, and at other times they are presented as symbolic representations of what are seen as particular types of character (perhaps a Christ-like character, perhaps a Satanic character, perhaps something on that broad spectrum in between). Certainly characters and the relationships between characters will be a key element of any film's approach to storytelling.

ACTIVITY . . .

- Define the natures of the characters in any film you have seen recently. List what you saw as being the key features of each character.
- Did you see them as being well rounded three-dimensional characters that you felt really could have existed or as being rather flat, one-dimensional and ultimately unbelievable?

NOTEBOX . . .

Flat and rounded characters are terms used by the novelist, E.M. Forster, when discussing literature in *Aspects of the Novel*. Rounded characters, it is suggested, have psychological depth, the complexity of real people. Often they are seen as being in some sense 'better' than flat characters that are underdeveloped or seem only to represent one aspect of human nature.

Stories in everyday life

Throughout our lives (or at least, from the time we are able to use language) we are surrounded by stories: fairy tales, nursery rhymes, myths and legends, novels, histories, biographies, biblical narratives, plays, TV soaps, comic books, newspaper articles, songs, even conversation and, perhaps, dreams. Every day in almost every everyday situation in which we find ourselves it seems storytelling plays a part. Eavesdrop on a few conversations and you will continually hear phrases that signal a story is being told: 'So, I said to her . . .', or 'I remember when . . .', or 'When we got there . . .' and so on and so forth.

ACTIVITY . . .

- List the types of story with which you have come into contact so far today and expect to come into contact with later today. (Think carefully about this and you should find that stories are a much more integral part of your everyday experience than you might have at first realized.)

continued

- Compare your list with that of at least one other person, if possible. See if anyone has thought of sorts of stories missed by other people in the group. Try to arrive at as exhaustive a list as possible.

ACTIVITY ...

- What story do you remember above all others from your childhood? Write the story down keeping as close as possible to the original that you were told.
- Think about the story: what was it about it that made it memorable to you? Who told you the story? Do you remember where? Were these factors important in you remembering the story?
- Exchange memories with other people and see if their experiences are in any way similar to yours.
- If you were to analyse the story what would you say were its key aspects? Does it, for example, build tension, use suspense or surprise, involve colourful characters, or employ a repetition of events?

Storytelling expectations

All the evidence would suggest that the use of narrative is one of the fundamental ways in which we make sense of the world; stories could be said to bring order and structure to our otherwise chaotic experiences. As a result, as viewers who are already familiar with the storytelling conventions of narrative structure, we approach film with definite expectations. We expect to see a range of characters, or character types, involved in a series of structured events that occur in certain places and at certain moments in time. There are likely to be problems and conflicts, and these are likely to be finally resolved in some way after having reached some climactic moment of confrontation.

NARRATIVE This term is really quite simply used as another term for 'story'. But it can also be seen (perhaps more correctly) as a more technical term relating to attempts to theorize the principles by which stories are structured. Some theorists, for example, have suggested that all stories have 'deep-seated' underpinning common narrative structures.

The expectations we bring to a film's narrative are derived from our general experience of life, but also, just as importantly, from our previous experience of film and other narrative forms (we know, for instance, that both when friends tell us about something that has happened to them and when we watch films there is usually a clear sense of a beginning, middle and end to the story). Within this prior experience, our knowledge of genres (or different types of film and storytelling) will be responsible for the creation of a major component of audience expectation. So, if we are talking about storytelling forms in general we will know that fairy tales, for example, tend to follow certain conventions while novels follow slightly different 'rules'. And, if we are talking about types of film we will know that the conventions attaching to horror might in certain ways be different from those associated with sci-fi films. Within each genre there is a slightly different set of rules of narrative construction at work, a slightly different language of narrative structure that is known to both the filmmaker and the audience. The filmmaker may follow these rules, or (and this is a major part of the pleasure of narrative for the audience) they may subvert our expectations, creating surprise for the viewer.

EXPECTATIONS The set of ideas each of us brings with us when we watch any film. These may be expectations to do with story structure, character development, or themes we anticipate will be dealt with; and they will be based upon our previous experience of these things.

KEY TERM

GENRE This term has at least a double usage here. It can be used to denote different general types of storytelling extending across a range of different media such as fairy tales, plays and TV soaps; so, simply different types of storytelling. But it can also be used to refer to the classification of films into types such as horror, romantic comedy, thriller or science fiction.

KEY TERM

ACTIVITY . . .

- Think about a film you saw recently and jot down the outline of the plot structure (that is what happened in the order in which it happened in the film) perhaps in the form of a flow chart using arrows to show how one thing followed another.
- Try to decide what expectations you had when you went to see the film and whether the opening confirmed or challenged these expectations. Then, work your way through the narrative and decide at which points your expectations were fulfilled as you had expected and at which points you were surprised by what happened next.
- How did your expectations change and develop as the film progressed and what caused these changes?

Do all stories have the same basic structure?

Theorists interested in narrative structure have suggested that all films (indeed all stories) are structurally the same:

- we are introduced to a hero/heroine and shown the world in which they live;
- the normality of this world is disrupted;
- the hero/heroine sets out to restore order.

In basic terms we deal with a scenario of good versus evil, and a world in which order is set against chaos. Certainly experience would tend to suggest all stories are founded upon the idea of a conflict between two or more central characters or groups of characters.

ACTIVITY . . .

- Is it true in your experience that all stories seem to work around a central conflict and involve the basic features mentioned above?
- Discuss these ideas in small groups, considering a selection of films from different genres if possible. Do these general ideas hold true in all cases?
- What were, or who were, the representatives of good and evil in the narratives you discussed? Where could you see ideas about chaos and order at work? Was there always a point at which you could see the 'normality' of the given world being disrupted in some way?

Syd Field

But it is not just theorists looking at stories in general who have suggested there are deep-seated structures at work. Syd Field[1] advising on screenwriting said good scripts comprised three clear acts. The first gave the set-up showing where the action was taking place, introducing who was involved and suggesting in broad terms what was going to happen. At the end of the first act there was a crucial point at which the direction of the whole of the rest of the film was set up. According to Field this was followed by a second act with a key note of confrontation as the main character faced a series of obstacles to completing the central dramatic need of the film. At the end of this act there should be a further crucial point, he said, at which the central character would seem to have their goal in sight but would be faced with one final problem. And then in act three all the plots and sub-plots would be resolved.

ACTIVITY . . .

- Take any film of your choice and try to apply Field's outline for a good script to it. Does it fit? Can you identify the two key plot points at the end of acts

The simple story

Even a simple sentence, such as 'The cat sat on the mat', amounts to an observation
of a subject within a particular environment and as such could well form the exposition
(or opening) to a story. The tranquil ordinariness of normality has been set up and
as such is ripe for disruption. If we add to this first sentence a second, perhaps, 'A
mouse passed slowly before the cat', we have developed the situation and (because
of the nature of the relationship between cats and mice) introduced a complication to
the basic situation. Continuing with a third sentence, 'The cat pounced and pounced
again, while the mouse dodged this way and that', we are building towards a potential
climax that might come with 'The cat brought down its paw on the mouse's tail, held
him fast and bared its teeth'. Our reader because of her knowledge of narrative structure will now be waiting for the resolution phase and perhaps a twist in the tale: 'The
mouse smiled. The cat looked confused. The mouse pointed behind the cat. A large
dog bounded into the room. The cat ran. The mouse continued slowly on its way'.

ACTIVITY . . .

- Try to come up with your own short story comprising no more than 10–12
  short sentences. The first sentence should set out a basic situation. The
  second should develop this a little and perhaps introduce some sort of
  complication. You should then move towards a climax before adding an
  ending that resolves the problem in your imagined world in some way.
- Alternatively, pass a sheet of paper around a small group of students and ask
  each person to write one sentence of a story. The first person sets out a basic
  scenario; the second introduces a further character or adds a complication,
  and so on. Aim to finish the story in 10–12 sentences and nobody is allowed
  to write more than one sentence at a time. Only read out the whole story at
  the end.

The use of time in stories

When we watch a film, we have to hold in mind at least three different time frames.
There is story duration (the time frame in which we conceive of the story taking place),
plot duration (the time frame within which we conceive of ourselves being told the

story), and screen duration (the amount of time we are actually sitting in front of the screen). The story is the simple chronology of narrative events. The plot is the arrangement of these events within the film.

CHRONOLOGY The ordering of a series of events in time sequence. This is the simplest way of setting out a story and is important in films such as *Bloody Sunday* (Greengrass, 2002) (see FS3 British Cinema – Social and Political Conflict), involving the shooting of people taking part in a civil rights demonstration in Northern Ireland in 1972, where the development of events in sequence over a set period of time is a vital part of the whole creative enterprise.

In the classic romantic wartime drama *Casablanca* (Curtiz, 1942), through the use of flashback the story is able to cover a period of a year or more since Rick (Humphrey Bogart) met Ilsa (Ingrid Bergman) during the German occupation of Paris, but the plot takes place during just three days and nights as they meet again in Casablanca, and all of this occurs over a screen duration of just 98 minutes. Here flashback as well as the way in which stories leave out anything that is not essential to the progression of the narrative allows the compression of time to occur. Details given within the dialogue, such as Rick's involvement in prewar conflicts in Spain and Ethiopia, although they have no visual presence within the film enable us to extend story time still further into our characters' pasts. In the western *High Noon* (Zinnemann, 1952) in which we follow Gary Cooper's character, the sheriff, awaiting the arrival in town of the 'baddies' the screen duration of 85 minutes is the same as the plot duration since we experience his waiting minute by minute.

In *Billy Elliot* (Daldry, 2000) (this film could be considered further under FS3 British and Irish Cinema – Passions and Repressions) we essentially follow our central character over a period of about a year around the time of the miners' strike of March 1984 to March 1985. However, the story depends upon us being made strongly aware of the death of Billy's mother two years previously and includes a final scene some years later showing his ultimate success as a dancer. In *Orphans* (Mullan, 1999) (see FS3 British Cinema – Scottish Cinema) set in a contemporary period in Glasgow, in a film that is 98 minutes long we follow the stories of three brothers and their sister over the evening, night and morning before their mother's funeral. There is a clear pattern to the narrative structure with the four starting off together gathered around the coffin, dividing off into pairs and then further splitting off as individuals before coming back together by the end of the film. In the French film *La Haine* (Kassovitz, 1995) (this film could be considered further under FS5 Studies in World Cinema – Single Study Films) we essentially follow the intertwined stories of three friends living in the working-class suburbs of Paris over a single day. The film opens the morning after a night in which groups of young people have been involved in violent confrontation with the police, and it follows the three friends through the day and night and into the early hours of the next morning.

Please note: there is absolutely no reason why you should have heard of any of the films mentioned in the two paragraphs above (although you might know of one or two of these films, at least by name), or in any other paragraph in this book. Gradually we hope you will widen your interest in films to encompass more and more different sorts, whether they are older movies, films from different countries, or films from genres you have not previously spent time watching.

The key thing with regard to the above examples is that you pick up the principles they are being used to explain and that you then try to apply these principles to films that you know.

- List the story length, plot duration and screen time for any two films you have seen recently (they could of course be films you have used before for other exercises).
- Explain the narrative structure in as succinct a way as possible for both films. Use the explanations given above for structures of *Orphans* and *La Haine* as models for your work.
- Can you think of any films you know or have heard of where screen time is the same as plot duration?

The use of imagined space within stories

In spatial terms watching a film involves us in exploring at least two spatial dimensions. There is screen space visible within the frame, but there is also off-screen space that we are asked to imagine or remember from earlier. In effect we are asked to contain a whole imagined world within our minds. So, in *La Haine* we have some imagined spatial sense of the housing estate on which the three friends live and some sense of this as existing at a certain train journeying distance from the heart of Paris, and in *Billy Elliot* we have a strong sense of the mining community in which our central character lives. Similarly in *Orphans* there is a spatial sense of all of the events taking place within an imagined Glaswegian cityscape. *Casablanca* may have been filmed entirely in the Warner Brothers' studio in California, but as the opening image of the map of Europe and North Africa urges we are expected to inhabit for the duration of the film the imagined spaces of Casablanca and Paris.

Time and space travel

Time and space could be said to operate as the two key dimensions for film narrative structure. The film's storyline moves us through time and through space, from one place to another and one moment to another, in order for us to follow a particular sequence of events that are set out in a specific sequence to tell the story.

This is at heart the 'magic' of storytelling and narrative film: we can be in Casablanca and then in Paris, in 1942 and then in 1940. However, do notice that this 'time travel' is not fundamentally based on the ability of the storyteller or filmmaker, the producer of the tale, to recreate other worlds and other times, but rather on the innate human ability to imaginatively occupy spaces outside of the here and now. The 'reader' of the film in other words is crucial to the successful realization of the imagined story.

ACTIVITY . . .

1   Watch any of the films mentioned here alongside a film of your own choice that you believe has an interesting narrative structure. As you are watching, make brief notes about where and when each scene takes place.
2   After you have watched each film decide what you would describe as being the beginning, middle and end to the film; in other words, its very basic narrative structure.
3   Without consulting with others try to draw a plan or diagram giving the pattern, shape or structure of the narrative.
4   For the films mentioned above in the text, if possible find somebody else who has watched the same film and compare your diagrams. Look for similarities and differences. Try to decide who has come up with the best outline plan and be very clear about why you think it captures the narrative structure most effectively.
5   For the film of your own choice, explain the narrative structure in detail to somebody else using your diagram for that film to help.

(Important: there is absolutely no need to complete all of the tasks suggested in this book. This one for example, will take time to do well and you might well not have the time. Activities are simply suggestions for things to do that will help you to ensure you understand the ideas being put forward.)

Cause and effect

As we are watching, we expect each element within the narrative to be seen to have both cause(s) and effect(s); we expect events to be motivated in some way, to have been caused by something we have seen in the film and to have some discernible outcome. Without this, all we would have would be a random series of unconnected scenes leading from nowhere to nowhere. By its very definition a story has an ordered series of events that leads to a conclusion.

CAUSE AND EFFECT This refers to the way in which mainstream films are moved forward by one scene or event having been caused by an earlier one and in turn giving rise to an effect which is seen in a subsequent scene or event. What this means is that everything we see has been motivated by something we have seen earlier and in turn motivates something we see further on in the film.

Resolution

To a large extent because of our experience of mainstream film, we expect issues that have been set up within the film to be resolved in some clear-cut way so that we know what finally happens. And, in most films this does happen, especially since this resolution of the issues at stake is often a means of confirming social norms and accepted consensual values. So, perhaps, in *Casablanca* for example it is the necessity of personal sacrifice in time of war and the placing of collective social aims over and above individual wishes that is asserted.

In *Orphans* it is the bringing of the brothers and their sister together as a united family around the graves of their parents in the final scene and what might be interpreted as their collective realization of the need to move on that gives some sort of answer to issues faced by the characters in the film. But, it could be argued that through the film (and specifically through the experiences of the central characters) we too have in some sense faced and gained a perspective on the important human concerns they have faced. In *Billy Elliot* a large part of the feel-good factor gained from the ending comes as a result of us feeling that Billy's goal of becoming a dancer has been achieved. But there is also satisfaction being gained from the sense of 'family' unity achieved as a result of seeing his father, brother and best friend in the audience.

However, filmmakers can use our expectation that things will be sorted out by the end as a means of leaving us with uncertainty and ambiguity rather than answers. To some extent matters are resolved at the end of *Seven*, for example, but we are also surely left with a whole series of questions about both of our central characters and certainly the issues raised by the film are left (necessarily) unresolved. In fact we could go further and suggest the ending actually resolves matters in favour of evil in this film, with John Doe's (Kevin Spacey) plans being fulfilled to the letter. This is very unusual, certainly for a mainstream Hollywood film, and is worth considering in some depth if you have seen the film.

At the end of *La Haine* we are given the basic outcome of the day's events for our three central characters, but the wider issues raised by the film are clearly unresolved. We have been given a whole set of possible reasons for the state of society and a further set of potential outcomes that might result from this, but nothing within this wider social context has been resolved. At the end of *Seven* we can create our own possible future scenarios for Mills and Somerset: at the end of *La Haine* we can create our own possible future scenarios for a whole society. Both sets of filmmakers have in one way or another refused to totally close down the possibilities and left room for reader interpretation. Some spectators might feel themselves deprived of the comforting sense of satisfaction that a story with all the loose ends tied up may offer: others may be excited by the challenge offered by such final disconcerting uncertainty.

KEY TERM

RESOLUTION The final phase of a narrative film that quite simply resolves all the storylines that have been set running. Films may of course leave some matters unresolved.

ACTIVITY . . .

- Take any scene within a film of your choice and work out a list of the effects and consequences that arise from that scene.
- Look back in the narrative and try to list the events that have caused your chosen scene to take place.

KEY TERM

EXPOSITION This is the opening to a film, which can often be *in medioreum* 'in the middle of things'. It sets up expectations and possibilities, and introduces key characters, locations and ideas.

Goal-oriented plots

In goal-oriented plots a character takes steps through the narrative to achieve a certain well-defined end. Such plots commonly revolve around searches, quests and journeys. *Billy Elliot*, for example, has already been referred to as having a goal-oriented plot: we essentially follow Billy's journey. Or plots can, as with detective stories, centre on the investigation (or search for information). *Seven* for instance works to resolve the mystery revolving around not only who the 'seven deadly sins killer' might be but also what his motivation might be.

ACTIVITY . . .

Can you think of any films you have seen that do not have clear goals, or objectives, set out? Is it the case that this is a feature of all narrative films?

Films that focus strongly upon the psychological state of a central character can internalize this search or investigation so that what we have is this character's inner struggle for meaning or some understanding of the self. This might be said to be true in relation to all three central characters in *La Haine* and at least two of the brothers, Michael and John, in *Orphans*. The ending, as we have said, may represent a closed resolution of the problem(s) faced by the main character(s), or it may be left more open to interpretation.

NARRATIVE STRUCTURE AND THE VIEWER

The narrative is, of course, also taking the viewer on a journey. Patterns of development within the plot will engage the viewer in the creation of expectations, which may be immediately fulfilled, delayed in their fulfilment, or cheated. That is, the filmmaker engages in gratification, suspense and surprise. The interesting thing is that each of these storytelling strategies is found to be pleasurable for the viewer.

Furthermore, however the storyline is structured it seems that because of our under-pinning knowledge of narrative (whether inherent in some way to human beings or culturally learnt) we as the viewer have no choice but to actively engage in attempting to make logical narrative sense of what is unfolding before us. We are complicit in a vital way with the creative storytelling act; we willingly engage in the process, giving of ourselves both emotionally and intellectually.

ACTIVITY ...

- Watch *Ratcatcher* (Ramsey, 1999) (see FS3 British Cinema – Scottish Cinema), if you have the time. Perhaps this is a film that could be seen in relation to a central character's journey or search.
- How would you define the goal being sought by James in such an inter-pretation? Would the ending suggest James reached his goal, and if so, in what way(s)?
- Decide on your interpretation or understanding of the ending and then discuss your ideas with others. Did everyone have the same interpretation?
- After discussion did you agree on one interpretation or did people still hold on to their individual understandings?

(Similar activities could be undertaken using a range of other films. *The Matrix* (Wachowski, 1999) and *Donnie Darko* (Kelly, 2001), for example, would be possibilities.)

The position of the reader

The view of events offered to us as we watch a film may be unrestricted, that is we may be permitted a godlike overview enabling us to know more than any single character or even all of the characters; or our view on things may be restricted, that is we may only be able to see events from one character's perspective. In *Orphans* we occupy a privileged position being able to see what is happening to each sibling as they pursue their own individual narrative trajectories, but at the key climactic moment as John sets out with the shotgun to avenge his brother's stabbing it is vital that information is withheld from us in order to achieve the required shock effect. As this example suggests there is, of course, a whole range of possible ways films might use restricted and unrestricted narrative. Sometimes a single story incident may appear twice or more in the plot. Sometimes multiple narrators may describe the same event (in the famous Orsen Welles' film, *Citizen Kane* (1941), different narrators give their individual interpretations of Kane's personality and driving motivations).

ACTIVITY

Draw up flow charts for *Seven* and any other film you have watched recently marking out at which points in the plot the viewer's perspective on events has been restricted and at which points unrestricted, that is to say at which moments our knowledge is in line with that of the central characters and at which moments we are privileged to know more than them.

As readers it is useful to continually ask ourselves if we know more than, less than, or as much as any given character. We may have greater knowledge than a character (this tends to lead to suspense – we anticipate events happening that the character cannot know about and wonder when these things will happen or whether our character will find out what we know before the anticipated event occurs), or we may have less knowledge than the character or be confined to that character's perceptual subjectivity (this tends to lead to surprise – we don't anticipate events but experience them in as unexpected a fashion as our central character). The director, Alfred Hitchcock explained this in classic terms by using the idea of two people at a table having a conversation with a bomb in a bag beneath the table. If we as the audience knew more than the characters and were aware of the presence of the bomb, suspense would be at work because we would be on edge wondering if it was going to explode. However, if we didn't know about the bomb and it went off we would experience the filmmaker's use of surprise.

We may also usefully ask ourselves as we are watching a film exactly how well we know any given character's thoughts, feelings and perception of the world. How sure can we be that we 'know' our chosen character? How confident can we be in their assessment of any given situation? Most films consider there is an objective narration (a position of detached, balanced judgement) to which we return from more subjective episodes; but some alternative approaches may see such objectivity as unattainable or at least severely problematic. There was much debate amongst the filmmakers over the way *Seven* should end. The ending that we have maintains Somerset's status as the reliable voice of reason and his concluding words as a narrator (despite the fact that a narrator has not been used throughout the rest of the film) are justified because of this position of balanced judgement that he has occupied throughout the film. But you might want to look at the alternative endings that were mooted and discuss this point further.

When you begin to consider these sorts of issues and look at the range of possible positions for the reader you begin to gain some awareness of the complexity of the reading process that is being undertaken as we watch a film. We are continually being expected to take up new perspectives, engage in new understandings, and shift our position in relation to new information.

Hollywood narratives

Hollywood narrative tends to focus on the psychological causes for actions or events that take place, for the decisions or choices that are made, and for individual character traits that are revealed. Often the narrative is driven by some form of desire, with the central character wanting to achieve some end; and there is usually a counter-force preventing him or her from achieving that end, perhaps a character that embodies an oppositional outlook or goal. So, in *Seven* we are continually being asked to understand events in terms of the psychology of our three central characters, the young rookie cop who believes in attempting to act as a force for good, the cynical older cop who believes nothing will ever change, and the insane psychopathic killer. (This sort of approach is very different from a narrative such as that used by the famous Soviet director Sergei Eisenstein for *Strike* (1924) (see FS5 World Cinema – German and Soviet Cinema of the 1920s) where events are seen to be caused not by individuals but to come about as the result of massive social forces embodied in whole groups (or classes) such as workers and factory owners. However, films that do not see events as motivated by the psychological make-up of characters are rare.)

1   Consider these ideas in relation to a contemporary Hollywood film of your own choice. What are the psychological causes for each of the central characters' actions? What are the psychological causes for each central characters' key decisions or choices? What ends does each central character wish to achieve at various points in the narrative and what are the counter-forces working to prevent them from achieving these ends?
2   Explain your ideas briefly to a small group of other students if possible, perhaps using diagrams to illustrate your ideas.

In general, within Hollywood films of the 1930s, 1940s and 1950s there is a strong sense of closure with no loose ends being left unresolved, the moral message is clear and good triumphs over evil. However, it is also true to say that endings can rarely be entirely tied down and often space is left for the reader to in part at least construct their own conclusion. At the end of *Casablanca* the German 'baddie' has been shot and the question of who gets the girl has been resolved for us, but what happens next to the characters we have followed throughout the film is to some extent unknown and open to conjecture.

Seven may have been made more than 50 years after Casablanca but fundamentally it works in the same way. We may be left somewhat uncertain about the future for Mills and Somerset, but the story involving the seven killings has come to a definite close. Our initial questions about why these events were taking place have been answered. The difference, perhaps, is that far from being defeated, evil might even be said to have triumphed.

Chris Vogler

Chris Vogler[2] claims any story involving a hero undertaking a journey involves several stages:

- the hero's ordinary world is established and he is given a challenge or quest;
- the hero meets someone who gives him advice or he obtains something that will help in the quest;
- moving into the special world the hero faces tests/enemies, finds allies and learns the rules of this world;
- the hero faces his greatest ordeal, almost fails, achieves his goal, but still faces the return journey;
- the hero returns to the ordinary world as a changed person.

The importance of the reader or viewer

Finally, it is important to realize that as spectators in the cinema we are not inactive: narrative depends upon an interaction between the text and the reader. Throughout the process it seems we are continually examining what has just happened and on the basis of our comprehension of that event within the context of the chain of events that have so far unfolded we ask questions about what is likely (based on our previous experience of similar narratives) to happen next. Although of course the notion of 'asking questions' is not quite correct since all of this seems to happen in a psychological flash.

Tzvetan Todorov

Todorov[3] sees narrative as following a common pattern of movement from a stable equilibrium to disruption of the equilibrium to a re-ordered equilibrium (achieved by action being taken against the force causing the disruption). You should be able to apply this template to the whole film and perhaps also individual scenes (do remember though that the initial balance may be suggested very briefly).

- Choose a film and in a group work together to apply Todorov's narrative theory. (Obviously it will have to be a film that you all know well.) Alternatively, take a film that we have already considered as a case study.
- When you have done this try to do the same with Vogler's perhaps slightly more complicated suggested structure.

(This is a simplified version of Vogler's ideas, if you have time research his ideas in more detail. In particular find out the names of the seven key characters (or archetypes) he claims are always present and see if you can apply these definitions to characters in your chosen film.)

- Watch *Run Lola Run* (Tykwer, 1999) making careful notes about the storyline, including characters and their relationships to each other.
- If possible, discuss with others what you would describe as being the beginning, middle and end to this film; and then try to construct a flow chart showing the film's narrative structure.
- How would you describe your relationship with this film and with the central character? Were you interested in what happened next and in what happened to Lola and Manni? Why? Discuss your ideas in groups.
- Why do you think Tykwer constructed his narrative in the way that he did? Was the construction aiding him in conveying certain meanings? Discuss your ideas in groups.

Narrative pleasure

One of the key functions of narrative is to deliver certain gratifications to us as an audience; films if they are to be successful in box-office terms must give pleasure to the audience in very particular, very predictable ways. We are 'pleasured' by knowing Todorov's pattern and seeing it unfold before us. We receive gratification from seeing our expectations confirmed but also from existing within the tension of wondering whether our expectations will be fulfilled or undercut. And perhaps we are most intensely 'pleasured' by finding the surprise of a new and unexpected twist that we are now able to add to our 'back-catalogue' of expectations. Another theorist, Barthes[4] proposed that narrative worked through enigmas or the setting up of mysteries for the reader to solve. Again, the idea is that this is a process by which pleasure is provided for the reader.

Narrative dependence on oppositions

Taking a further possible approach, the work of Lévi-Strauss[5] is often taken as suggesting that narrative structure depends upon binary oppositions. This concept is essentially based around thematic concerns found in the text and suggests that for every theme you locate in the narrative its opposite will also be at work. So, if the notion of predator is attached to the scene with Marion and Norman in the parlour in *Psycho* then the idea of prey will also be relevant. Do be careful, however, about linking a single idea too strongly to one character. For example, if Norman is associated with darkness and the night then Marion will simply be linked to light and the day. Although in this case we might suggest this could be argued quite strongly, often the truth of a scene like this is more to do with the good and bad in both characters (and perhaps ultimately in all of us).

In *Seven* Mills and Somerset are clearly set up as binary opposites: the older, cynical, world-weary cop near to retirement and the young, enthusiastic rookie who wants to make a difference to the world. Interestingly though, this is far too simplified an analysis; for instance it begins to emerge that they may be much closer to each other in their attitudes than such a binary opposition might at first suggest.

STORIES AND SOCIETY

The stories (legends, myths and sagas, for example) that are told in different cultures have often been seen as a means of coping with a society's experience of the world; from this perspective stories are seen as a way of making sense of a whole community's experience. Stories have also been viewed as the place where the collective memory

or experience of the society is held and by means of which that collective memory and experience of the world is passed on to successive generations. Could film function in these ways? Could films be said to offer a society a way of negotiating its way through or making sense of contemporary experience and perhaps a means of passing on that negotiated understanding to the wider community or next generation? How important might Hollywood prove to be in enabling American society to come to terms with the trauma of 9/11? How important was it in enabling that society to deal with the fractures within society that opened up around the Vietnam experience?

ACTIVITY . . .

What is your view on this? Had you for instance ever thought of film as perhaps performing through its created stories some sort of ritual function for society as a whole? Discuss your response with others.

(It may well be that you have never thought of film in these terms. If so, that is absolutely fine. What is being offered all the time here are potentially new ways of considering film. You should give each of them your careful consideration and then hold on to the basic idea so that you can try to see if it might fit any new films you come across.)

ACTIVITY . . .

1   Analyse a sequence of no more than ten minutes from *Run Lola Run* or any other film in terms of its narrative structure.
2   Make notes on your chosen sequence and then if possible discuss your ideas with somebody else, or several others, who are looking at the same film.
3   Write an analysis (1,000–1,500 words) of the ways in which narrative structure works to create meaning and generate audience response in your chosen sequence.

Case Study: *Moulin Rouge* **(2001)**

(Director: Baz Luhrmann. Screenwriters: Luhrmann and Craig Pearce. Producers: Luhrmann, Fred Baron and Martin Brown. Director of Photography: Donald McAlpine. Director of Music: Marius DeVries. Cast: Nicole Kidman (Satine), Ewan McGregor (Christian), John Leguizamo (Toulouse-Lautrec), Jim Broadbent (Harold Zidler), Richard Roxburgh (the Duke).)

If we watch the first ten minutes of this film certain key elements of the narrative will already have been set up for us and we will have a set of narrative expectations about the rest of the film. This case study provides a framework for a narrative analysis which can be applied to any film of your choice.

The first prerequisite of any story is that it should grab our attention from the outset:

- How does *Moulin Rouge* seek to do this even before we have been introduced to any characters?
- What devices are used by the filmmakers to make the opening different from anything we have seen before?

And yet, at the same time because of the musical refrains that are chosen certain themes are already being suggested to us: what would these be?

- Is the hero clearly introduced? How do we feel about our hero? Have we, for instance, already started to identify with him? Do we have a clear sense of what he is like? What makes us fairly certain he is going to be the hero of the film? What possible complications or obstacles are already being set up for the hero?
- Which other characters are introduced in the opening sequence? What information do we find out about them?
- What information are we given about the world in which the film is set? Has the opening managed to create an imagined world in your mind? How has this been achieved? Can you apply the idea of equilibrium to this setting? What conflicts might cause a disruption to this world? Do we already feel we have some idea of what we think might happen?
- Have we been able to follow a clear cause and effect pattern between events in the opening? Has each event been clearly motivated so that we can understand why it has occurred?
- What questions are raised by the opening? How do you think these will be resolved by the end of the film? Are there mysteries or uncertainties about which we are keen to know more?
- Have goals been given or possible objectives suggested for the hero? Do we have any idea what he might find out about during the course of the film? Are there indications as to what his likely journey, search or quest might be?

Write an analysis of the ways in which the various aspects of narrative work to create meaning and generate audience response in the opening to *Moulin Rouge* (1,000–1,500 words).

Figure 2.2 *Moulin Rouge*
Source: Twentieth Century Fox/The Kobal Collection

CONCLUSION

One way of approaching films is to see them as stories. Essentially this involves analysing the various ways in which as stories or narratives they utilize certain common recurring features of storytelling or narrative structure.

FURTHER READING

Armstrong, R. (2005) *Understanding Realism*, London: BFI (Chapter 2).

Hayward, S. (2005) *Cinema Studies: the Key Concepts*, London and New York: Routledge.

Lacey, N. (2005) *Introduction to Film*, Basingstoke and New York: Palgrave Macmillan (Chapter 2).

Nelmes, J. (ed.) (2003) *An Introduction to Film Studies*, London: Routledge (Chapter 4).

Phillips, P. (2000) *Understanding Film Texts: Meaning and Experience*. London: BFI (Chapter 2).

Phillips, W.H. (2005) *Film: An Introduction*, 3rd edn, Boston: Bedford/St Martin's (Chapter 7).

Roberts, G. and Wallis, H. (2001) *Introducing Film*, London: Arnold (Chapter 4).

USEFUL WEBSITES

www.bfi.org.uk

www.filmeducation.org

NOTES TO CHAPTER 2

1 Syd Field, author of a key screenwriting text, *Screenplay*, who has worked as a consultant for Twentieth Century Fox, Disney, Universal and Tri Star Pictures.

2 Chris Vogler, author of another key screenwriting text, *The Writer's Journey: Mythic Structure for Writers*, who has also worked for Disney and Twentieth Century Fox.

3 Tzvetan Todorov, a Bulgarian literary theorist interested in the structural principles underlying narrative.

4 Roland Barthes, a French cultural critic who through a varied series of approaches consistently rejected the idea that any sign simply worked as a representation of reality.

5 Claude Lévi-Strauss, a key exponent of structuralism, seeing apparently separate elements as only understandable when placed within the context of a system of relationships.

▼ 3 GENRE

What is genre and why is it such an important term
in Film Studies?

This chapter deals with:

- defining the concept of genre;
- genre as a means of giving pleasure;
- acknowledging genres as dynamic and subject to change over time;
- recognizing the possibility of seeing genre as a form of film language;
- looking for similar thematic concerns across genres;
- recognizing the use made of genre as a marketing strategy;
- introducing the genre of film noir;
- suggesting possible approaches to *Seven*.

NOTEBOX

This chapter will be directly relevant to the section on film form in FS1 – Film: Making Meaning 1 for the WJEC's AS in Film Studies and could be used to form part of the underpinning knowledge for one of the two required pieces of analytical coursework.

FILMS MENTIONED

If you are working your way through the whole or parts of this chapter you will find it useful to have watched the whole of *Seven* (Fincher, 1995) and at least the opening to *Scream* (Craven, 1995). You will also find it helpful to have access to scenes, clips and single shots from at least some of the following films:

- *Psycho* (Hitchcock, 1960)
- *East is East* (O'Donnell, 1999)
- *Runaway Bride* (Marshall, 1999)
- *From Dusk Till Dawn* (Rodriguez, 1995)

- *The Ballad of Little Jo* (Greenwald, 1993)
- *Notting Hill* (Michell, 1999)
- *Nosferatu* (Murnau, 1922)
- *Blade Runner* (Scott, 1982)
- *Total Recall* (Verhoeven, 1990)
- *Independence Day* (Emmerich, 1993)
- *The Full Monty* (Cattaneo, 1997)
- *Collateral* (Mann, 2004)
- *The Big Combo* (Lewis, 1955)
- *Sin City* (Tarantino, 2005)

GENRE: THE CONCEPT

Most often narrative films are classified by both the producers of films and audiences according to the concept of genre; that is they are seen in terms of categories such as sci-fi, or musical, or western, or horror, or even sub-genres such as spaghetti western or 'slasher' movie. However, this way of classifying film is not usually analysed or examined in any way by most of us but is simply taken for granted.

If, however, we were to consider the issue we might recognize that each genre has its own iconography, that is to say characteristic props, costumes, settings and character types that act as visual signifiers alerting us to the appropriate category within which we can expect to pigeon-hole any particular film. There will also be musical signifiers (characteristic features of the soundtrack) and verbal signifiers (characteristic dialogue features), that is to say in general terms sound signifiers, indicating the genre being used by the filmmakers.

KEY TERM

ICONOGRAPHY As explained above, this simply refers to characteristic features of a genre, the things you expect to see and sounds you expect to hear that taken together collectively tell you the type of film, or genre, you are watching.

Again, as with all other film terms, knowing the name and what it means may be useful but it is not essential; it is recognizing the characteristic features that are signalling to you that this is a specific genre and being able to identify them at work within particular scenes within particular films that are important.

Case Study: *Scream* (1995)

(Director: Wes Craven. Screenwriter: Kevin Williamson. Cinematography: Mark Irwin. Music: Marco Beltrami. Cast: Drew Barrymore (Casey Becker), Neve Campbell (Sidney Prescott), Skeet Ulrich (Billy Loomis), Courtney Cox (Gale Weathers), Rose McGowan (Tatum Riley), David Arquette (Dwight 'Dewey' Riley).)

Watch the opening to this film. It should quite quickly become apparent what is being referred to here as the opening since it almost operates as a 'stand alone' short film in its own right concluding with a dramatic camera movement that propels us towards an equally dramatic image of a body hanging from a tree.

Assuming you were unaware of the film's genre when it first started, how quickly would you become certain of the genre? What main genre heading would you classify this as belonging to, and would there be sub-categories, or sub-genres, within this major classification that you would see this film as fitting into?

What would be the factors that would alert you to genre from an early stage? Do you initially become aware of an overall category, and then later sub-categories? If so, at what point do these two things become clear and what are the elements within the make-up of the film that make these categorizations apparent?

In practice, of course, an audience in a cinema, or people who had bought or rented the video or DVD, would already have a good idea of what they were about to watch. What factors prior to coming to view the film would mean the spectator was pre-warned about genre and had in fact probably made a conscious choice to watch the film on this basis? (The list of ideas you arrive at here will make it clear just how much use both audiences and the producers of films make of the concept of genre before the actual moment of viewing. Posters, trailers, critical reviews and the director's previous work, for example, should all be on your list.)

Work your way through the whole sequence, listing as many elements as possible that are used by the filmmakers to make the genre clear to us. One of the keys to completing as comprehensive a list as possible is to remember the work done earlier on film form. Use the headings, mise en scène, cinematography, editing and sound and note ideas beneath each for ways in which these elements of film construction are being used to signal the genre to us. You should also find factors relating to narrative such as character types, character relationships and plot structure that help in indicating genre.

Examples under each heading would include:

- the setting of the isolated house in the country;
- the use of knives as props in the kitchen;
- the change in Casey's (Drew Barrymore's) movements as she begins to realize the situation;
- the way in which a tracking shot is used within the house to follow Casey;
- the single shot of the raised knife;
- the change in pace of the editing towards the climax of the scene;
- the sound of the knife being replaced in its holder in the kitchen;
- sudden violent uses of language within the dialogue;
- the use of the attractive, blond girl home alone.

You should be able to add many more ideas to this list (especially if you are a fan of this type of film). You will notice, for instance, that colour, lighting and music are not even mentioned here. Particularly if you are a fan of the genre, you might like to spend some time picking out the references that are made to other horror films not only in the dialogue but also in the ways the film is constructed.

Make sure you watch the sequence several times and that you find time to compare your list with those made by other people. When you have done this you will in effect have completed a genre analysis of the opening to this film.

Research a list of films that are generally seen as having followed in the wake of *Scream*. (If you are a fan of the genre you will probably be able to come up with a very respectable list without doing any research.) You might like to discuss a sequence from one of these films applying the same approach as suggested above for *Scream*. *Scary Movie* (Wayans, 2000) would be an interesting choice for this exercise because of the ways in which it references *Scream*.

Figure 3.1 *The opening sequence of Scream*
Source: Dimension Films / RGA

Subverting audience expectations

As an audience we always need to be alert to the fact that our genre expectations may be subverted or undercut in some way by filmmakers who are well aware of the things audiences normally expect to find in films from any particular genre. So, for example, prior to *Scream* we would have expected the actor playing what is apparently the central female role to survive beyond the opening scene; and watching in 1995 we would have been shocked by the way in which our comfortable certainty was torn from us. Although you will also notice that once we have seen this particular shock tactic used, it becomes part of the array of horror genre possibilities to which we are alert as we watch our next horror movie (see *Scream* 2, for example). In fact it becomes part of the genre, something we look out for in subsequent films. In this way genre, and more importantly genre expectations, change and develop as filmmakers play with the norms of their chosen genre. (If we are enthusiastic enough to know some old horror films, we might even recall that it was Hitchcock who had his heroine killed off in a similarly challenging way in the middle of *Psycho* (1960), and armed with this knowledge we might not be quite so shocked by the opening to *Scream*.)

In a similar way but in a very different genre, *East is East* (O'Donnell, 1999) (see FS3 British Cinema – Comedy) is commonly seen as a comedy and yet if we approach it with too simplistic a notion of what a comedy can be, then it will confront us with some particularly challenging dramatic moments. This is a comedy that examines physical abuse within the home and is prepared to take on the potentially tragic aspects of a fundamentally loving inter-cultural relationship. It challenges our notions of what a comedy can be, or should be.

ACTIVITY

- Choose any film you have seen recently and decide how you would describe it in genre terms (it might be a film that you see as related in genre terms to *Scream*). List the visual signifiers and sound signifiers that you believe confirm your categorization.
- Try to find time to compare your ideas with those of other people. Pay particular attention to similarities and differences between your ideas and those of anyone who has considered a film from the same genre as you.

Genre as a film language

The rules and conventions of genre constitute a type of language, or code, by which filmmakers construct film whilst at the same time also operating as a language, or code, by which the audiences read film. However, these rules and conventions are subject to change over time as social outlooks alter or filmmakers develop the genre. So, the horror 'rules' were changed by Drew Barrymore's character being killed off within the opening sequence to *Scream*, and this has now became part of the set of horror genre possibilities.

Gaining pleasure from the expected and the unexpected

Making choices within the conventional expectations of the audience for a particular genre will give that audience a certain comforting pleasure; we feel we know where we are and that we have been given what we have come to see. However, making choices outside the conventional paradigms, or sets of possibilities, available within any given genre will create a surprise for the audience, which can be at least as pleasurable as fulfilling expectations.

KEY TERM

PARADIGM The term used to describe the range of choices available at any given moment of film construction. This covers a huge area, everything from which actor from the paradigm of possible actors should be chosen to play a given role, to which hat (from the paradigm ranging from no hat to top hat to deerstalker) a character should wear at any given point in a film.

It is a useful term for us for one reason only and that is it reminds us that at all times choices are being made in the construction of films and it is our job to try and decide why those choices might have been made.

The use of a black sheriff in *Blazing Saddles* (Brooks, 1974) or the use of a whaling harpoon as weapon of choice in *Terror in a Texas Town* (Lewis, 1958), challenges our expectations of the western but also in the process excites us as a result of the novelty of the take on genre conventions that is being offered to us. One of our central notions of what romantic comedies are all about is severely challenged by the idea that Maggie Carpenter (Julia Roberts) in *Runaway Bride* (Marshall, 1999) should fight shy of marriage rather than going all out to obtain it. As with the mask in *Scream* (inspired by the iconic painting of the same name by Munch) and a scene such as that in the garage in the same film the effort is always to find new iconographic effects for the genre.

ACTIVITY

- Imagine that you were to change the actors playing the lead roles in any film you have seen recently. What might have been the most bizarrely inappropriate possible choices? Discuss your ideas with others if possible.
- Take a genre you know well and decide what events you can imagine happening that would most upset your expectations for that genre. Again, discuss and compare your ideas with other people.

FROM THE DIRECTOR OF PRETTY WOMAN

JULIAROBERTS RICHARDGERE
RUNAWAYBRIDE

"A splendid romantic comedy"
– The Daily Mirror

Figure 3.2 *Publicity poster for Runaway Bride*
Source: Paramount Pictures / Touchstone Pictures / RGA

In horror films the viewer knows a series of killings is likely to be carried out but the hoped-for novelty of how, when and where remain to be discovered. Similarly, as we journey with Mills and Somerset and the killer towards the final scene in *Seven*, as viewers of psychological thrillers we know there is going to be some disturbing final twist. We know we are inhabiting the lull before the final storm and in one sense we await to have our expectations fulfilled, but our hope is that this will occur in an unexpected way that we have not previously experienced. In *Runaway Bride* we have been startled by the opening concept of a woman who is fearful of marriage, but if we know the genre well we will probably hold on to the hope that the resolution will be a bringing together of the key characters in a heterosexual romance.

ACTIVITY ...

- Can you think of any films you have seen where your normal genre expectations have been challenged in some way, or where the usual formula has been given some powerful new twist?
- List your ideas and discuss them with other people, taking careful note of their ideas as well as your own.

Hybrid genres

The fun audiences derive from having their expectations fulfilled on the one hand and on the other subverted has been intensified in recent years by the way in which filmmakers have been happy to mix genres in order to create hybrid, or crossed, genres. In *Scream* there is a clear mix throughout the film of 'teenpic' with the 'slasher' movie; a mix which really creates something new, a 'teen horror'.

KEY TERM

TEENPIC A film featuring teenagers as the central characters and aimed at teenage audiences. The stories focus on the sorts of problems and difficulties faced by young people of this age.

KEY TERM

SLASHER MOVIE A type of horror film in which the story revolves around psychotic males with plans to murder a group of young people. This sub-genre was at its height in the 1970s and early 1980s with films such as *The Texas Chain Saw Massacre* (Hooper, 1974), *Halloween* (Carpenter, 1978), *Friday the 13th* (Cunningham, 1980) and *Nightmare on Elm Street* (Craven, 1984).

(There is often a disturbingly strong focus on the brutal murders of teenage girls, but there is also usually a 'final girl' who heroically wins out at the end and has been seen as an empowering female character.)

To some extent this mixing of genres has always taken place: noir films from the 1940s and 1950s were always thrillers and often also detective films. And in *Seven*, dealt with as a noir film in a case study at the end of this chapter, you will recognize elements throughout that might well lead you to classify this too as a detective film or a thriller.

In a modern film like *From Dusk Till Dawn* (Rodriguez, 1995) however something genuinely different occurs; rather than there being a hybrid mix throughout there is a sudden moment when the film moves from being a road movie and becomes a vampire/zombie film. This is a much more dangerous strategy for filmmakers since it breaks the unspoken pact between producers and audience under which the filmmakers have agreed to make a certain type of film that the spectators have agreed to watch. The break is so abrupt that it risks alienating the audience rather than delighting them.

VAMPIRE MOVIE A horror sub-genre that owes a lot to Bram Stoker's novel *Dracula* (1897) and again tends to feature male characters preying upon female victims, on this occasion by sucking their blood.

KEY TERM

ZOMBIE FILM A horror sub-genre in which the dead (the zombies) come back to life and attack the living. See *Night of the Living Dead* (Romero, 1968) and *Shaun of the Dead* (Wright, 2004) to compare older and more recent treatments of the genre.

KEY TERM

Genre and binary analysis

From the point of view of genre analysis, as an alternative to looking for telltale iconography that reveals film type it is also possible to list oppositions found within a film. Different genres are often concerned with different sets of oppositions, and as a result have different thematic concerns. These are known as binary oppositions (a term mentioned previously in the chapter on narrative).

- In romantic comedies there is often a sense of a difficult opposition between the two central romantic figures that needs some how to be bridged if they are to be brought together. Often the woman may desire marriage while the man fights shy of such commitment.
- Westerns often focus to some extent on the tension between the untamed natural world to be found in the 'wild' West and 'civilized' city-based society in the East. (See Maggie Greenwald's *The Ballad of Little Jo* (1993) for a feminist perspective on this genre.)

- Film noir has classically often been concerned with the antagonism between a seductive (but deadly) female and a male character at the mercy of these alluring charms.
- Horror often focuses upon the opposed extreme possibilities of human nature with women as the embodiment of trusting innocence and vulnerability and a male figure as the personification of violent predatory desire: in short we inhabit a world that contains both good and most frighteningly, evil.

For each of these genres it would be possible to trace the existence of a host of other related oppositions. In a romantic comedy like *Notting Hill* (Michell, 1999) (this film could be considered further under FS3 British and Irish Cinema – Comedy) it is not just the sense that our two characters come from different social worlds but also that they represent in a sense England and America and that these countries somehow stand for oppositions between perhaps an intellectual literary culture and a rather shallow popular culture founded upon fame and wedded to financial accumulation as a barometer of success. And, since *Nosferatu* (Murnau, 1922) (this film could be considered further under FS5 Studies in World Cinema – German and Soviet Cinema of the 1920s) in film terms, and beyond that back into gothic novels and ultimately folk tales, the horror genre has explored the relationship of our comfortable, everyday experience of society to the hidden danger of the dark outsider lurking just beyond the pale; or, in an even more potent variation, the relationship of the community to the hidden monster lurking unnoticed within society.

ACTIVITY . . .

- Consider any film you have seen recently from a particular genre and decide how you would view it thematically in terms of binary oppositions.
- Taking two strongly opposed characters within a film and listing their characteristics can sometimes help to make the central oppositions within the whole film clear.
- Think of other films you know in the same genre. Are the ideas you have come up with for your film generally used as oppositions within the genre?

The recurrence of themes and interests across genres

We might also explore the ways in which different genres find different ways of negotiating, managing, or dealing with the same fundamental social issues. The city, for example, which is a focus of noir films also often appears in science fiction films where it is frequently a place of dehumanized brutality and isolation not so different from the labyrinthine place of entrapment found in noir films (see for example *Blade Runner* (Scott, 1982) and *Total Recall* (Verhoeven, 1990)). In sci-fi it is usually very clear that it is human society which has brought things to this situation. It is not, as with horror, that there is some inexplicable evil at the heart of man but that governments or huge corporations have mechanized, de-personalized and regimented the human experience of life. The city in *Seven* is the dark, foreboding place of rain found in *Blade Runner*, but interestingly it is also the place of horror where evil lurks in human form as well as being the nightmare world of noir films. As we explore genres in more depth what is often most startling is the extent of the overlapping interests that emerge.

Romantic comedies deal humorously with misunderstandings between the sexes that get in the way of the achievement of harmonious heterosexual marriage. They focus on women who desire the state of matrimony and men who to begin with are none too sure it is what they want. But the re-assertion of the role, value and importance of marriage (at a time, we might note, when more couples have been choosing not to get married) is not confined to romantic comedies. There is, for instance, a sub-plot that runs throughout the American 'feel-good' alien invasion sci-fi film *Independence Day* (Emmerich, 1993) that is entirely devoted to re-asserting romantic love and the institution of marriage. This strand of the film comes to a climax worthy of the most romantic of romantic comedies when as one couple get married the second couple who were parted before the film began hold hands and we see the wedding ring that has been loyally worn by the man throughout the time of their separation. Similarly, at the end of a comedy such as *The Full Monty* (Cattaneo, 1997) (see FS3 British Cinema – Comedy) that does not have a dominant romantic focus, one of the clear implications is the re-establishment of romantic links between each of the two central couples. The partners in each relationship have been estranged from each other for different reasons but the use of camerawork and editing visually reunites them for us in an emotionally gratifying way in the final scene.

The value of this sort of approach to genre is that by looking at films in this way we will be able to identify particular themes that are of central concern to a range of films that do not initially appear to be linked by an analysis based upon simple iconography.

ACTIVITY...

- Can you think of any two films (or more) you have seen from different genres where the same thematic concerns or interests have been apparent?
- Take time to jot down any ideas you might have on this before discussing the issue with other people. Take careful note of their ideas as well as your own.

Genre as a means of bringing order

There is a sense in which genre is like narrative in giving a certain shape and order to events. Each genre can be seen as a set of rules that allow the shaping of the disorder of life into some sort of controllable order. Within film genres the insoluble problems and contradictions of life can be, if not resolved, at least shaped into manageable, understandable forms. By the end of *Collateral* (Mann, 2004) the psychopathic killer in our midst has been tamed by the ordinary guy who through the experience has somehow been elevated to the status of hero.

You should expect to develop further this sort of approach to genre during the second year of the Film Studies A-level but it is worth giving it some initial thought at this stage.

Genre as a marketing strategy

Finally, it should also be noted that genre conveniently operates as a marketing and production strategy, enabling the audience to establish the type of product on offer and therefore to purchase its favoured flavour of film. So, when you enter a DVD rental outlet or a shop selling DVDs, the posters and the DVD boxes themselves will usually announce fairly specifically the genre of the products on offer.

At the same time in production terms clearly marked out genres enable the economic organization of materials and workers to take place, as seen for example in the production of a whole string of gangster films in the 1930s by Warner Brothers or a whole string of British comedies by 'the makers of *Four Weddings and a Funeral*'. Re-making the same film with some difference enables sets, locations, costumes and other elements of film fabric to be re-used and helps to set up easily reproducible working patterns in which little time is lost in preparation because the cast and crew have essentially done it all before.

FILM NOIR

General features

Film noir was a term initially used by French critics (literally 'dark' or 'black film') to describe Hollywood films of the 1940s and early 1950s characterized by cynicism and pessimism and set within an oppressive urban world of crime and corruption. The 'heroes' are usually disillusioned men who face an uncertain future alone. Friendship is difficult and only possible at a certain distance. Love is most usually perverted in some way, and innocence cannot survive.

In style the films are dark, stark and bleak with sets dominated by shadows of various depth and threat, and frames that often contain black or fog-bound or smoky spaces that threaten to engulf not only the characters but the film itself and the society it presents for our attention (as a classic example see the ending to *The Big Combo* (Lewis, 1955) with the blinking, uncertain light offering only a faint possibility of hope for the future).

Influence of German Expressionism

The trend towards this type of film in the period is seen as having been influenced by the influx of immigrant filmmakers from central Europe and disillusionment caused by the Second World War. It has also been suggested it was economically driven by the cutbacks in sets and lighting made during the war and more feasibly the desire to produce low budget films with good percentage profit margins.

Certainly there is a strong sense in which these films both in terms of cinematic style and bleak thematic content echo German Expressionist film of the 1920s, a movement that can also be seen as having been influenced by the traumatic experience of world war.

Reflecting the period

Films of this sort from Hollywood in the 1940s and 1950s then tended to be cheap B-movies about life on the streets that investigate the darker side of human nature. This is an area of life, it could be argued, that mainstream Hollywood films have tended to ignore other than in some unrealistic romanticized fashion. The central character in noir films is caught in a nightmare experience, and is often trapped by a seductively alluring woman. Is this the continuation of wartime trauma in a domestic situation? Was there a sense of the world as a doomed place during this period? Is this, in some films at least, anything to do with the Cold War fear of communism? Is this the nightmare of filmmakers caught up in the McCarthyite era when anyone with socialist sympathies was liable to be ostracized? Psychoanalytically, is this a representation of the male fear of the emerging 'new woman'? Or, is this simply an economically driven transposing of popular pulp fiction to the screen motivated by the realization that if pulp fiction sold there would also be a market for pulp film? Technically, faster films, portable cameras and button microphones made it increasingly possible at this time to film on the streets and at night (see, for example, the bank heist and chase sequence in *Gun Crazy* (Lewis, 1949)).

ACTIVITY

1. Watch the opening to *The Big Combo* and one modern neo-noir of your choice, perhaps *Sin City* (Tarantino, 2005). Make notes on the ways in which these films announce their genre to us.
2. As always, do try to discuss your ideas with others, if possible.

More recent examples

There was a revival of this style in the 1980s and early 1990s in films such as *Blade Runner* (Scott, 1982), *Jagged Edge* (Marquand, 1985), *Blue Velvet* (Lynch, 1986), *The Usual Suspects* (Singer, 1995) and *Seven*. Perhaps it would be worth considering what social and political factors could be reflected in this renewal of interest in the darker side of humanity (if indeed this is not simply something that is always there in storytelling and is just expressed in slightly different ways in different periods).

ACTIVITY . . .

If you have seen the whole of *Sin City* how does it fit into this picture? Should it be seen correctly as the latest addition to the noir genre? And if so, how does it, while still being recognizable as part of the noir strand of genre filmmaking, reflect the contemporary period in which it was made?

Approaching noir films

For films in the classic noir or neo-noir mode it is always worth considering:

- the psychological exploration of the darker side of humankind that takes place;
- the social exploration of the darker side of society that takes place;
- the urban realism that often sees modern life as a labyrinthine hell;
- the use of light and shadow as representations of good and evil/danger;
- the use of sparse sets that could be seen to represent the bleak psychological world in some way;
- the use of psychological and actual violence, often within relationships and particularly within the sexual dimension of male–female relationships.

Case Study: *Seven* (1995)

(Director: David Fincher. Screenwriter: Andrew Kevin Walker. Cinematographer: Darius Khondji. Music: Howard Shore. Cast: Brad Pitt (David Mills); Morgan Freeman (William Somerset); Gwyneth Paltrow (Tracey Mills); Kevin Spacey (John Doe).)

ACTIVITY . . .

- Watch the opening sequence built around the credits noting as many images and sounds as possible.

ACTIVITY . . .

- Record your impressions making sure to try to decide what this opening makes you think the film will be about, justifying your ideas by reference to the images and sounds encountered.
- Discuss your ideas with a group of others, if possible. To what extent did you agree with each other's assessments?

The relationship between two central characters

In *Seven* we have the classic detective genre combination of the older, hard-bitten professional and the younger, less cynical prodigy. This is a combination often used in other genres of course such as the western. What it allows for is the classic confrontation and need for reconciliation between old age embodying experience of life and youth embodying enthusiasm for life. Of course, what we also have at work here is a potential father–son relationship and the working out of the tensions and joys to be found in that relationship. (Furthermore we also have the now often favoured Hollywood combination of lead actors: black and white.)

ACTIVITY . . .

- Can you think of other black–white pairings of this sort?
- How do these relationships work? Is race an issue in these relationships? Isn't it always an issue simply by being there on screen before us?
- Why do you think these combinations are used?
- Discuss your ideas with others if possible.

Use of film noir genre

What is very clear from the continual murky gloom and rain of the city to the dark central thematic idea of the seven deadly sins is this film's noir heritage. Outside we are frequently positioned in such a way as to be surrounded by bleak, grey city buildings that tower over us, or we see things from behind fences that seem to cage and enclose. Inside we find ourselves in dark corridors and box-like rooms, and always the intrusive sounds of the city remain inescapable. The city is this terrifying place where Tracey, the Ophelia-like embodiment of innocence, shudders at the thought of bringing up a young child and where even the perverse logic of the serial killing John Doe contains a horrifying element of truth. Notice the way in which even the calm, ordered, learned and apparently highly civilized Somerset has this midnight habit of throwing a switchblade at a dartboard. For

Somerset, if Mills is his younger self with a belief that with others he can contribute towards bringing about change for the better, then Doe is almost his alter ego, an other self whose thinking as a result of his own world weary cynicism he is able to only too fully understand.

Dark themes and outlook

Anything that is good cannot live in this world of darkness and so the fate of Tracey and her unborn baby, as with Ophelia in *Hamlet*, is entirely to be expected. Notice how we do not see her death and even when John Doe talks about it, the details are left to our imagination. See as well the way in which it is not simply the death of Tracey that is at stake here but the death of hope and faith in humanity and confidence in the future (see what happens ultimately to Mills).

The evening meal scene in which we initially come to identify with Tracey also serves to set up her relationship with Mills as the ideal high school romance. They are in their 'young love' relationship in many ways the embodiment of 'the American Dream' and of course this is what is also therefore destroyed in the resolution phase.

The woman here is not the femme fatale of classic postwar film noirs but much more like the embodiment of innocence that has often had to sacrifice itself to save others in horror movies, only this time the sacrifice is pointless and fails to defeat evil. It is perhaps in this dimension of the film, as much as in the central often commented upon triangular relationship between the male characters, that the way in which this film reflects a late twentieth-century perspective can be seen most clearly.

ACTIVITY...

- Which parts of this film did you find most shocking? Why? Write down your ideas.
- Compare your thoughts with those of other people, if possible. Were there any similarities or interesting differences in your ideas?

Analysis of a scene

The brothel scene in which the detectives investigate the 'lust' murder would serve as an excellent example of this film's style. We descend from the dark, chaotic streets above following the detectives down into the red hell-like depths of the brothel. We are confused by the noise, which makes it difficult to pick out what is being said, and by the editing that works to further disorientate us as we struggle to get our bearings. The overall feeling is one of being enclosed in claustrophobic tunnel-like spaces, which is not relieved when we come into the dark boxed space of the room in which the murder took place. Here we are placed in such a position as to be unable to make out exactly what has happened. In other words we are left with further uncertainty and confusion. Only gradually in the interview session that follows are we permitted to piece together bit by horrifying bit the gruesome details of the murder. Shots such as that of the close-up of the male visitor to the brothel who has been forced to carry out the murder compel us to confront the full extent of the horror. The blank grey background and the white blanket framing his face only serve to make doubly sure that we concentrate on the actor's facial performance; and isn't it a powerful cameo performance?

ACTIVITY . . .

Watch these two successive scenes and discuss with others the ways in which elements of film construction work to create a specific impact on the audience.

The Christian context

Sin is the concept of human faults that offend a God who embodies all good. These faults, or evil, bring with them a sense of guilt for any being with a conscience (and guilt of course carries connotations of the need for punishment). According to Christian teaching, the seven Deadly sins are anger, lust, gluttony, sloth, pride, envy and avarice.

ACTIVITY . . .

Construct a flow chart showing the narrative structure of this film in terms of these seven sins showing how they relate to different elements of the plot.

The existence of sin in the wor ld brings with it the need for a Redeemer or Saviour, in Christian terms Christ, who is seen as having died for our sins, making himself a sacrifice that we might be forgiven. Without this sort of basic knowledge of the Christian religion it is difficult to fully appreciate *Seven*, but with it you begin to see the way in which John Doe could be seen to believe himself to be some sort of Messianic figure, perhaps even a divine agent sacrificing himself in order to provide a message/lesson for humanity.

- After you have watched the whole film, return to the opening sequence.
- How has your reading of this section of the film changed?
- What images and sounds seem significant now in ways that they did not to begin with?

1   Analyse a sequence of no more than ten minutes from a film of your own choice in terms of its genre and narrative structure.
2   Make notes on your chosen sequence and then if possible discuss your ideas with somebody else, or several others, who are looking at or know well the same film.
3   Write an analysis (1,000–1,500 words) of the ways in which genre and narrative structure work to create meaning and generate audience response in your chosen sequence. Give your piece a title in the form of a question:

How do genre and narrative structure work to create meaning and generate audience response in the (name or timing of scene) scene in (name of film)?

CONCLUSION

- Genres have distinctive individual characteristics that enable us to distinguish one from another in a general functional way.
- Genres can be understood as being utilized by filmmakers, spectators and the film industry in a variety of ways.
- Often the boundaries between genres will be blurred and similar interests/concerns will be detectable across genres.

FURTHER READING

Abrams, N., Bell, I. and Udris, J. (2001) *Studying Film*, Arnold: London (Chapter 10).

Altman, R. (1999) *Film/genre*, London: BFI.

Armstrong, R. (2005) *Understanding Realism*, London: BFI (Chapter 3).

Cameron, I. (1992) *The Movie Book of Film Noir*, London: Studio Vista.

Hayward, S. (2005) *Cinema Studies: the Key Concepts*, London and New York: Routledge.

Lacey, N. (2005) *Introduction to Film*, Basingstoke and New York: Palgrave Macmillan (Chapter 2).

Neale, S. (2000) *Genre and Hollywood,* London and New York: Routledge.

Phillips, W.H. (2005) *Film: An Introduction,* 3rd edn, Boston: Bedford/St Martin's (Chapter 6).

Scorsese, M. (1999) *A Personal Journey Through American Movies,* London: Faber.

USEFUL WEBSITES

www.bfi.org.uk

www.filmeducation.org

www.filmsite.org

en.wikipedia.org

▼ 4 OVERVIEW

How should we approach a film we have not seen before?

This chapter deals with:

- essential questions to ask yourself when studying a new film;
- the importance of adopting a proactive, questioning attitude;
- possible model approaches to interrogating films.

NOTEBOX

In terms of preparing for the WJEC's AS in Film Studies, this chapter should help you to draw together ideas from the opening chapters and consolidate a sensibly organized approach to the viewing of films. Most directly this chapter will be of relevance to the work you will be doing under FS1 – Film: Making Meaning and FS3 – Messages and Values: British and Irish Cinema for the AS (and FS5 – Studies in World Cinema for the second year of A Level study).

FILMS MENTIONED

If you are working your way through the whole or parts of this chapter you will find it helpful to have access to scenes, clips and single shots from at least some of the following films:

- *My Beautiful Laundrette* (Frears, 1985)
- *My Son the Fanatic* (Prasad, 1997)
- *Independence Day* (Emmerich, 1993)
- *La Haine* (Kassowitz, 1995)
- *Sin City* (Tarantino, 2005)

QUESTIONS

By now you should have noticed just how much emphasis is being placed in this book on the need to adopt a continually questioning approach towards film. In order to analyse a film text, it is being suggested we need to be prepared to ask ourselves a whole range of key questions. This chapter will try to give a brief overview of what those central questions should be.

The fundamental basis to this approach is that we should always confront ourselves with the question of why the filmmakers have chosen to use certain sounds or images at particular points in their film. Remembering that there are a whole array of possible choices and combinations of choices before the filmmakers (with regards to setting, costume, props, performance, camerawork, sound and editing) we must question why particular clearly identifiable choices have been made.

Posing questions for ourselves as we watch films is at the heart of film analysis. In order to study film effectively we need to have questions like the following in mind throughout the viewing experience:

1   Messages and values

- What are the main subject areas of interest in this film and what are the main themes and ideas being addressed? Could it be said that there are certain key messages and values that underpin the film?

- Answering these sorts of questions demands the ability to be able to stand back from the narrative and attempt to see the film from an objective distance but we can make it seem to be much more difficult than it actually is. For example, if the film is made within a predominantly white society but focuses on an ethnic minority, as with something like *My Beautiful Laundrette* (Frears, 1985) or *My Son the Fanatic* (Prasad, 1997) (this film could be considered further under FS3 British and Irish Cinema – Single Study Films), then the film will inevitably be dealing with issues of race in some form or other. And, if you have a Hollywood film that is called *Thelma and Louise* (Scott, 1991) there is a good chance that in some form or other it might have something to say about the female experience in modern Western society. Or, if you have a film entitled *Independence Day* (Emmerich, 1993) it is very likely to be addressing the American understanding of the United States as a freedom-loving democracy.

- Of course, you need to go further than this and ask in some detail exactly how men and women, or different races, cultures and creeds are represented in any particular film. Do they comply with stereotypical role models, or defy the conventional and challenge social norms in some way? Or, how exactly are ideas of democracy and freedom being represented and with what relationship to the politics of the real world?

MESSAGES AND VALUES Films can be seen in some sense to embody certain messages that they are working to communicate to the audience. They can also be seen to be attempting to advance certain values while questioning others.

 KEY TERM

La Haine (Kassowitz, 1995) has been attacked as a film that has a message that is anti-police: whether this is true or not would depend upon how we interpreted characters and scenes within the film and how we understood the filmmakers to be using film construction techniques to emphasize and elevate certain perspectives above others.

2   Genre

- Is this film typical of any particular genre (sci-fi, horror, action, comedy, musical, road movie, etc.) or sub-genre (dystopia, alien invasion, 'slasher', vampire, zombie, etc.)? In what ways is it typical and in what ways is it not typical (atypical)?
- Could this film be said to use several genres, and if so which ones and why have they been combined in this way? Does it demonstrate the current trend towards hybrid genres?
- More importantly, how does the chosen genre relate to views and perspectives in society in general? How does it reflect the period in which it has been made? How does a noir film like Sin City (Tarantino, 2005), for example, adapt its particular chosen genre and in doing so reflect contemporary society?

3   Narrative

- How is the story being told: is a narrator used, and if so, why? Does he or she have a marginal or important role in the story itself? What effect does using a narrator or not, have on the perspective given to the viewer?
- How effective is the opening, and what makes it so? How effective is the ending, and what makes it so?
- Are there clear moments of complication and climax within the film? Could you plot as if on a graph the rising tensions and climaxes of the story?
- Could you usefully complete a diagram, or diagrams, representing the relationships between characters within the story?
- Are conventional aspects of storytelling such as the confrontation between good and evil, or the use of a journey as a narrative device being employed?
- And most importantly what are the meanings being created for us by the particular narrative structure and devices being employed?

4   Mise en scène

- What would be your evaluation of the performances of the actors? Are the characters created complex or simple to understand? Is their motivation clear? Are they rounded and complex, or flat and stereotypical?
- What is the social status of each character and how dominant are they? Does their use of language reflect their character? What tone or attitude does each adopt? What ideas or feelings are being expressed?
- What can you tell about the character from the body language and delivery of lines? How long does each person speak and what does this tell us (in

different circumstances it could convey different things of course – a silent foreboding Clint Eastwood in a spaghetti western is very different from someone who is being marginalized by the force of events taking place such as the rookie policeman forced to witness a racist attack by fellow officers in the interrogation room in *La Haine*)?

■ What is the significance of costume in particular scenes? Does it help to convey character and/or oppositions? Does it operate to mark out particular groups? Is it simply used to suggest period and place? Are the costumes wonderfully authentic but actually used to little effect in terms of conveying meaning to the audience?

■ Are there any significant uses of props? Are there any props used in such a way as to become recurring images? Do the props remind us of themes or ideas in the film, or tell us something about character?

■ How is the setting or location used? Is it used to create a sense of realism? Is it used to create mood? Is it used to create a sense of certain states of mind or feelings? Is it used to stand for, or symbolically represent, other things?

5 Cinematography

■ Are there any scenes or single shots in which you think the camerawork has been particularly effective? If so, how and why do you believe it to be successful?

■ What significance do particular shots or camera movements have in terms of creating meaning for us? (Referring to particular shots and scenes to illustrate meaning in this way will be a key skill.)

■ What is the significance of the lighting in particular scenes? Are some scenes particularly light or dark? If so, why? How is shadow being used? Is it being used in particular ways in relation to particular characters?

6 Sound

■ Do any extracts from the dialogue seem to be especially important? In what ways might these lines be seen to be significant? Why have particular words or phrases been chosen? If it is a Hollywood script the dialogue will have been honed to the bare minimum in all probability which only means each utterance is even more certain to have been chosen for a specific reason.

■ Are sound effects used simply to create a sense of place, or do they in some way contribute towards meaning over and above this?

■ What is the significance of the music chosen for particular scenes? How does it work to contribute to the creation of meaning? Is it diegetic or non-diegetic (see page 100), and what difference does this make?

7 Editing

■ Is the pace of the editing in particular scenes giving us images that are flashing quickly before us, or images that we are able to survey in a leisurely way? Why has this style been chosen?

■ How do the shots, as they are structured into sequences via editing, work to create meaning? Is the way in which one shot follows another used in such a way as to allow one to comment in some way on the other?

- Which images are stressed? Why? Are there repetitions of certain visual images, or parallels between individual shots or sequences?

PROACTIVE READING

With so much to look out for this must mean that our reading of films has to be intensely active and analytical; at no time should we sit before the screen in classic 'couch potato' mode. Naturally there is an extent to which we may simply wish to enjoy the cinema experience on first encountering any film. However, even during a first viewing we should remain alert otherwise potentially we end up at the position apparently reached by a majority in Hitler's Germany of accepting the implied message behind watching shots of Jews inter-cut with shots of rats scurrying across the screen. Passivity before the media in any form allows that medium to be used not as a site of democratic discussion but as an agent of indoctrination. Josef Goebbels apparently said of *Jew Suss* (Harlen, 1940) in which the central character, an 'evil Jew', rapes Aryan women that it was: 'Highly recommended for its artistic value, and to serve the politics of the state recommended for young people.'

NOTEBOX

> The main approach to be adopted is always to move from the specific to the general. Observe the details of film construction closely and then think carefully about why the particulars of form and style have been chosen. If you cannot find enough to say about a particular scene it means you are not observing the fine details of film construction closely enough. Try to, as it were, 'zoom in' closer, slow down your viewing, go back over a scene time and again as you work to understand what is happening under each area of film construction.

A PRACTICAL APPROACH

Obviously investigating a film in this way means that there are big questions raised that can never be answered in any final sense. Is *La Haine* anti-police? The presence of the police within so many controversial scenes within the film means it must be seen to raise the question of the role of the police in relation to the issue of race within contemporary French society, but whether this makes it anti-police is another question.

The point to be aware of is that we will never get to the stage of even noticing the existence of these bigger issues within the film unless we devote ourselves to a detailed questioning of the text. It is in the asking of the little 'why' questions (why is there that little moment in *La Haine* where Sayid and Hubert get Vinz to speak for them when they enter the expensive block of flats in central Paris?) that we stumble along our way towards some awareness of the larger issues that could be at stake. (Quite simply, Sayid is of ethnic Arab descent and Hubert is black, while Vinz, although a Jew, is at least white. It is a minute incident that we can easily miss but if we slow our viewing down so that we notice it, it becomes a telling comment.)

Before you can begin to answer some of the questions posed by a film like *La Haine* you may need to have watched the film several times and have taken some notes along the way. If you are studying in a formal way you will need to sit for some time with a DVD (or video) stopping and starting it, rewinding and re-running it, and all the time adding to your notes.

On a practical note, you might find it useful first time around to leave sizeable spaces between individual ideas that you note down. These gaps can then be filled in with further ideas during subsequent viewings. Ideally, you should also aim to write down timings next to notes in order to make it easier to find significant sections at a later date.

Your notes should be made up of references to settings, characters, props (and perhaps their symbolic significance), the soundtrack, themes and ideas that the film seems to be addressing, clues about the director's approach, ideas on the acting approaches being taken, and possibly significant extracts from the script; in other words, all of the areas detailed briefly above and a little more fully in previous chapters. A series of viewings should allow your reading to become steadily less narrative-driven and increasingly technically and thematically analytical.

ACTIVITY

1   Choose your own film to analyse, preferably one you have at home and therefore can easily access. As you are watching this film for the first time note any interesting elements of film construction, but at the same time try to put down ideas you might have about when and where this film is set.
2   After you have watched the film write 200–300 words assessing how important you think it might be to understand the historical context in order to gain a full appreciation of this film.

ACTIVITY

1   Re-watch the opening to this film several times and make detailed notes about film construction.
2   Spend time discussing with others if possible how this opening sequence works in terms of creating meanings for the audience and generating responses.

continued

3   Write a commentary (500–600 words) discussing the ways in which meanings
     are created and responses generated in this sequence.

CONCLUSION

Approaching a new film requires that we:

- already know the sort of questions that need to be asked of any film;
- apply those questions in a probing, analytical way.

▼ 5 PRACTICAL APPLICATION OF LEARNING

In this chapter we look at:

■ how learning from other areas of the course can be applied to a piece of practical work (storyboarding, screenwriting, or production);
■ how to develop ideas in a cinematic way;
■ practical techniques of constructing storyboards, screenplays, and filmed extracts.

Studying film offers a wealth of learning about technique, styles, approaches, methods, and devices which of itself is a fantastic way of understanding more about how films make meaning, and what filmmakers have to do in order to get their meanings across to audiences. A great way to make further sense of this learning is to use it to make a filmed sequence, a short film, or even a feature, and in doing so apply the learning that has been gained in other areas of the course.

The Practical Application of Learning (PAL) allows this earlier learning to be applied to a choice of practical projects in order to convey meaning to a specific, defined, audience, and in doing so demonstrate constructional and technical ability. Whilst it is an opportunity to apply previous learning, it is also the opportunity to develop new learning in the practical arena, and practise skills that are used in all areas of the film industry to make films.

NOTEBOX

PAL: film form

A number of macro and micro aspects can be applied directly to the construction of a practical piece of work:

Narrative – a structuring device, both across a whole film and across a single scene or sequence. The ordering of information within a practical piece of work is of vital significance to how a spectator will make meaning from it.

Genre – the use of signifying devices within a practical piece of work that are recognizable as belonging to a group of films. Use of codes and conventions will help structure a work and ensure the spectator views it in terms of other similar films.

Cinematography, editing, mise en scène, performance, and sound – these aspects are all directly manipulated either by technicians or by the director in order to maximize the opportunity to ensure an audience is exposed to an intended meaning. These are elements that are absolutely in the control of a filmmaker: there should be nothing in a shot, scene, sequence, or film, that is there accidentally, as all these ingredients should have been within the filmmakers' control.

In the PAL there are three options for the creation of practical work, each in equal value to another, and each developing and demanding particular skill bases:

- Screenplay: the opportunity to script a key sequence from an imagined film, where activity is the key and where dialogue is kept to a minimum. What is important here is that the story is treated *cinematically*, in that it is clear that this is a story for the screen and not just a play or novel that happens to be in screenplay form.
- Storyboard (photographed or drawn): the opportunity to sketch out how a movie sequence would look as it moves from shot to shot. Whilst drawing or photographic skills are not being judged here (so stick men and less than representative photos are accepted), framing is absolutely vital. Using lens-based media to produce a storyboard clearly allows the maker to get a better understanding of how things actually look within a frame, and how they relate to other frames. The individual frames are important, but the transitions between frames – and the interplay between frames are equally important.
- Video production: the opportunity to put together a short (1–2 minute) sequence and filmically apply both macro and micro learning. If this is made by a group, then each group member must take responsibility for a particular micro component relevant to their role. It is accepted that there will be varying quality between productions (some may be shooting on a domestic VHS camera whilst others may be using Digi-Beta and a Steadicam rig), but it is the approach to the role and the achievement despite any limitations that are significant here.

Accompanying each of these three options are two pieces of written work that give the practical production work a context, and offer a reflection on intentions and on the finished work. The 'cinematic ideas' is the first piece of work that goes towards the project and sets out to outline intended approaches and devices, along with a brief (100-word maximum) summary of the imagined film from which the sequence comes.

At the other end of the process, after the production work is completed, comes the 'evaluation' where the filmmaker evaluates the success of the production work in making meaning.

These practical skills developed in the PAL are the building blocks of filmmaking, and as such are the essential tools for making meaning. Each contributes to the production line that is filmmaking – script, storyboard, film – and all stem from the most important fundamental: the idea.

The idea

The idea is the key starting point for any practical work and as such it is worth spending some time working through an idea to make it as good as it can get.

An idea initially develops into an outline for a story, and as such may well begin to grow characters. At this stage it is important to keep control of the idea to stop it spiralling off into unstructured developments. This can be done very easily by applying a simple set of questions:

1   What is the situation? This opens the story and may well be disrupted.
2   Whose situation is it? This defines the lead character (or protagonist).
3   What is the central quest? This relates to the main body of the story and is often defined by a lead character trying to restore what has been disrupted. This is where most conflict and drama arises in a story and is often described simply as the 'conflict'.
4   Who stands in the way of success? This defines another principal character who will be in opposition to the lead character (and is often referred to as the 'antagonist').
5   How does the quest end? Often this will be where the antagonist is defeated, and the protagonist's situation is restored. This is often called the resolution.

Once the story idea is fleshed out, it is then important to check whether or not it is actually a filmic idea.

If it is set in one room with two characters talking to each other for 90 minutes then it may be better placed on the stage.

If it involves considerable internal monologue (the characters' thoughts rather than their actions or conversations) then it may well make a better novel or short story.

Filmic ideas are ones that involve action – not necessarily fights and car chases, but rather activity – characters *doing* things on screen. Activity is visual, and this is most important in film stories. Activity tells an audience not only about the events, but about the characters performing those events. A character who dashes off a perfect love letter is defined by the activity in the same way as the character who spends the scene crossing lines out, screwing up paper and throwing it to the floor, and sitting with pen in mouth looking skyward. Similarly the character of a bank robber is defined by their actions – the hooded figure that bludgeons a customer to the floor to make a point is different from the suited robber who passes a note calmly to a bank clerk and walks away with the money without the customers even realising a robbery is taking place.

CINEMATIC IDEAS

This piece of paperwork is extremely important not only in explaining the meanings you are trying to develop and the learning you are applying in one of the three practical activities, but also in getting your thoughts in order to undertake the practical activity. As such it is possibly the most important assessed element. It is always advisable to head this with an appropriate title for the film: 'Galaxy Wars' does far more to locate a film in its genre and narrative form than 'Imaginary Film', and shows that the creator has genuinely thought about the nature of the film, and is making the effort to engage with the task.

The cinematic ideas should begin with a very brief (no more than 100 words) summary of the imagined film from which the sequence comes that is to be scripted, story-boarded, or filmed. This should be a straightforward telling of the story, and not the cliff-hanger type synopsis found on the back of a DVD or video box. It should identify the principal characters and should outline the situation, conflict and resolution of the story. This is the context for the sequence selected for creating, and so should allow the marker the opportunity to place the sequence in relation to the rest of the imagined film.

Following this contextualizing summary, the focus switches from the overview to the specific, from the film in general to the chosen sequence in particular. It is worth noting at the start where the sequence comes in the overall order of the film, and then identify the micro and macro elements involved in its production.

NOTEBOX

For groups carrying out a video project it should be noted that each group member's cinematic ideas should be different: it should be *their* summary of the film (not a combined group summary) and the macro and micro elements should relate to *each* member's chosen focus and role (so, for example, the camera operator may well look at cinematography and/or mise en scène).

If the film has been identified as a genre film then it would be sensible to highlight how genre-specific macro and micro elements will appear and shape the sequence.

Similarly, if the film is adopting a particular style (documentary realism for example) then the sequence should reflect this, particularly in the micro elements as these will be more identifiable in the sequence.

It is worth writing a number of drafts of the cinematic ideas in order to *craft* the words to maximize the potential for success. This also serves to encourage a way of thinking about the sequence and the film as a whole that sees it not as fixed as soon as the first idea hits the page, but as fluid and continually developing. Drafting the cinematic ideas allows each idea to be questioned, challenged, and weighed against the others in the piece, resulting in only the strongest, most focused remaining in place.

NOTEBOX

Example cinematic ideas – *The Crossing*

This is a crime thriller set in a modern Eastern European republic. A British diplomat's visiting teenage son, Mike Harrington witnesses a horrific 'hit' on an American businessman. Scheduled to testify against the gangsters, the embassy is bombed and Mike's family killed. Emerging from the wreckage with American journalist Patty Flyte, both are pursued by secret police, MI6, the CIA and gangsters. Betrayed by friends, unsure who to trust, they are shot at, imprisoned, chased, and nearly drowned, before reaching the border with a 'friendly' neighbouring country where they meet and destroy the crime boss (Mike's diplomat father) to make the crossing.

(99 words)

The sequence comes approximately five minutes into the film after the initial set-up of locations, characters and relationships usual in such genre films. It begins with Mike walking across a brightly lit grand square, noticeably filled with military personnel and checkpoints to indicate that it is a military state and dangerous. Initially the shots are framed in ELS and LS to establish the location and orientate the viewer, but also to depict Mike as insignificant within the scale of the scene. Occasionally the camera shot will cut to a hand-held shot from a high angle to suggest that someone is watching the events from a building. Lens flare may be used to imply 'realism'.

As Mike reaches a café in the centre of the square and buys an ice-cream we first see the American businessman sitting at a table in the rearground, high-lighted by a shaft of sunlight, and dressed in a lighter suit than anyone else nearby to make him stand out in the crowd. At this point the high angle ELS zooms in on the scene to frame the man, de-focusing and then re-focusing to suggest the POV is from someone who is using a lens (perhaps a rifle sight?). As the gangster's car screeches onto the square, the shots from here change to become MS, CU, and BCU, except for the final shot which reverts to ELS to show the carnage.

The editing of this sequence will be conventional in terms of the genre, with longer timed shots fitting the ELS and LS, and shorter timed shots fitting the MS, CU, and ECU. There will be a rhythm to the timing, and this will build gradually with shots becoming progressively shorter as the events get nastier. The shots of the American businessman getting shot will be rendered in slow-motion – usual in this genre. The final ELS shot of the scene will be one of the longest to allow the spectator to take in the enormity of what Mike has witnessed.

The sound will be naturalistic, and relatively quiet with a city atmosphere at the beginning. When the gangsters arrive, however, it will become loud to contrast, and the diegetic classical music playing on the café radio will become a non-diegetic theme that will play over the violence, again as a genre reference (like in *Carlito's Way*) and to counterpoint the scene.

(396 words – total 495 words)

You should notice that the above example (*The Crossing*) is divided between story and techniques, and that the first paragraph (the summary) not only offers the situation, characters, quest and resolution (all in 99 words), but also sets a clear context for the sequence that is mapped out in the succeeding paragraphs. These paragraphs reference both macro (genre and narrative) and micro aspects in relation to particular points in the sequence. It is worth relating chosen aspects to specific points as this makes it clearer for the reader to imagine how they will work, but also demonstrates that the techniques employed have been thought through and located in the sequence, and so have clear relevance. The micro aspects considered include cinematography (lighting and camera), mise en scène (location and dress), sound (both diegetic and non-diegetic), and editing (pace, duration, rhythm).

KEY TERM

DIEGETIC SOUND Diegetic sound is the sound that is heard in the fictional world, the sound that the characters in that world can hear. Most diegetic sound is not recorded 'on location' but is fabricated and 'dubbed' on to the film by sound designers and 'foley artists' (people who generate sound effects such as cutting into a cabbage to make the sound of someone being guillotined).

KEY TERM

NON-DIEGETIC SOUND This is the sound that is outside the fictional world, and that characters in the fictional world cannot hear. This would include overlays of soundtrack music and any voice-over narration.

CONTRAPUNTAL SOUND This is a great technique where the sound is not directly related to the image, but when placed together an additional meaning (or depth of meaning) is created. Thus the sound of a boxing match playing on a television in shot becomes more significant when the person watching the match walks into another room and begins beating an elderly person in there. The sound carried across from the television to the room where the beating is taking place is in counterpoint to the image of the abuse, yet serves to make a bigger statement about violence in general. It may be that a mix of contrapuntal sound and the diegetic sound of the beating may heighten this statement further.

ACTIVITY...

- Look at a sequence of activity from a film that is familiar to you. What genre codes and conventions are built into it? How are they conveyed? How is the sequence structured? What does this structure do in terms of storytelling?
- Under the micro headings of cinematography, editing, mise en scène, performance, and sound, list the significant features of this sequence. Do you notice that one heading has more features listed? Why do you think this is?
- Write out the cinematic ideas for the sequence you have looked at. Avoid re-telling the story. What macro aspects can you highlight? Which particular micro aspects are important?

THE SCREENPLAY

Screenplay writing is a lengthy and complex process, with a feature film taking anything from six weeks to six months of intensive work to produce a decent first draft, and up to two years to get to a stage where the script could go into production. Importantly, it is the screenplay that sets all other activities in motion, from storyboarding, through casting, through production, distribution, and exhibition, to a spectator telling someone what a great (or lousy) film they saw last night.

Feature screenplays are largely broken down into 'acts' (units of action in which the story is following a particular path). The most common structures for screenplays revolve around either a three-act structure (beginning/establishing, middle/developing, end/concluding) or a five-act structure (set up, development, recognition, crisis, resolution), with each act broken up into sequences, which in turn are made up of scenes (small units of action, usually located in one place). Each scene, no matter how small can also be further broken down into set-up, development, and conclusion.

Screenplays are inhabited by three-dimensional characters who have past histories, have ambitions, have problems, and have relationships. These characters have internal aspects (beliefs, hopes, fears, dreams, opinions, etc.) that are shown through their external actions: the hardened ruthless criminal who stops to pick up and return a child's dropped teddy bear; the cop whose hand shakes when he points his gun at a suspect; the doctor who unlocks the desk draw at the end of the day, pours a large whiskey, and stares at it without drinking. Internal characteristics, that are the essence of novel writing, are of no use to the screenwriter unless they can be externalized, unless they can become an action, a look, a gesture, or expression, which conveys this internal aspect.

Whilst dialogue is a key feature of screenplay writing and of characterization, it is an aspect that is often over-relied on to 'tell' the story. Good screenplays do not tell the story. They 'show' the story through the actions and interactions of the characters populating them, and in doing so reveal more by relying on the audience to 'fill the blanks'.

There are many forms to a screenplay but the most fall into a standard, industry-wide layout that indicates a professional approach:

---

12. EXT. LARGE EASTERN EUROPEAN SQUARE. DAY.   12.

The square is busy with people on their lunch hours, exiting the imposing embassy buildings, meeting friends, talking on mobiles, clutching their lunch bags, sitting at café tables, and rushing, forcing a sandwich down as they hurry through. SOLDIERS and POLICE in ones and twos also cross the square, but with more purpose. At either end of the row of embassies sits a sandbagged barricaded checkpoint through which a steady trickle of vehicles and pedestrians pass.

MIKE HARRINGTON jumps the last three steps of the British Embassy, and nearly lands on COLONEL INCHALYKA, a heavy-set, hardened-faced, giant, who pats him gently away with his huge hands, tutting a caution.

MIKE HARRINGTON

(*apologetic*)

Less speed! Sorry Colonel!

The colonel smiles briefly as he continues up the marble steps into the embassy. A brief flash from an upper-story window catches his eye and holds him momentarily. Shrugging it off he continues.

Mike waits on the pavement as an Army APC rumbles past, crushing a Coke can with a BANG. Mike sees this, licks his lips, and crosses onto the Square, towards the café.

The first thing you should notice is that scenes are numbered consecutively through the screenplay, starting from scene 1. Sometimes if the writer intends the camera to follow the character from one location to another in a continuous movement then a sequence of scenes may be numbered 1a, 1b, etc. You will also notice that there are no specific camera instructions included in the script: camera decisions are not made by screenwriters – they are made by directors and directors of photography who interpret the 'master scene script'. A good screenwriter will be able to write action to suggest a particular shot, which a good director or director of photography will be able to visualize from the description. In the PAL however, it is accepted that there may be a desire to indicate camera shots and angles, and delivering a 'shooting script' will not disadvantage you.

ACTIVITY . . .

- In the screenplay extract above what camera shots do you think the writer had in mind? How would you sequence the shots for the section involving Colonel Inchalyka? How would you sequence the shots for the section where the army APC is passing?
- In a group make up individual shot listings (LS, MS, CU, etc.) for the screenplay extract. Sequence the shots so that they 'flow'. Consider the timing of each shot, and the duration of the sequence as a whole.
- Compare sequences. Are there any individual shots that are the same (or roughly the same)? Are there any combinations of shots that are the same? Are the shot durations similar? Are the sequence durations similar? Can you account for any similarities?

The scene number is at the beginning of a line of essential information, called the 'slug line', which is always written in upper-case. Here, scene number is followed by the designation of INT (Interior) or EXT (Exterior), the location, and whether day or night (sometimes this may be more specific, but realistically this is simply an indication of what lighting set-up will be needed, and this falls easily into these two categories). It is important that slug line conventions are adhered to as these enable the production crew to do their jobs easily.

Following the slug line comes the 'action descriptor'. This usually consists of a few lines to 'set the scene', but in an activity scene such as the one above it may extend to several paragraphs or even a whole scene. Within this character names are capitalized for their first appearance, but are in lower-case after that. Background characters remain in lower-case unless they are significant to the scene (such as the soldiers and the police). When characters are introduced for the first time they are usually accompanied by a brief physical description. This is only repeated subsequently when there has been a dramatic change (when Mike Harrington later emerges from the ruins of the bombed embassy for example).

The action descriptor should try to capture not only the look of the scene (in terms of mise en scène, lighting, and general mood), but the sound also, and specific sounds that are important are also capitalized as a clue for the sound crew to ensure they are included (the Coke can popping with a BANG is an example of this).

Screenwriters should always be wary of writing something that cannot be physically expressed – a thought for example. In the extract above Mike looks at the Coke can exploding, licks his lips, and then moves towards the café. From this the audience can infer his thirst. Other than inferring this, the only other way to tell the audience he is thirsty would be for Mike to have a conversation with someone about it (*with someone* as opposed to with himself, which is really the worst kind of exposition).

Dialogue is always separated from action description by a double space and is always indented (set in from the margins at each end) to ensure it is seen as dialogue and not description. The speaker's name is always centred and capitalized, and may have an indication of the tone of the speech centred underneath, bracketed and in italics. Speech itself should always be short – listen to a conversation in progress and you will discover that it is full of interruptions, digressions, unfinished sentences, pauses, etc.

You should see from the screenplay extract that dialogue may be kept fairly limited in an activity sequence, since it is the action that will carry the scene and the information. Already the audience has a sense of who Colonel Inchalyka is, and what he is like, purely from his reaction to a teenager nearly colliding with him. His internal aspects are revealed through his external actions, and more specifically this is in an incident that is relatively inconsequential to the story or plot of the film. Colonel Inchalyka is introduced here in a sequence whose sole purpose is to introduce him and indicate that he is known to Mike Harrington (and hence probably significant to the later development of the plot). Without the need to introduce this character, and without the need to introduce a relationship, the sequence of Mike jumping down the steps of the embassy could be cut.

ACTIVITY . . .

- Consider how Colonel Inchalyka was introduced in the screenplay extract. What do you learn about him, both physically and in terms of character? Does his physical appearance influence the view of his character?
- At what other points in the scene could Colonel Inchalyka have been introduced? Choose one and re-write the sequence. What difference has it made to the meaning(s) produced by the sequence? Has it changed what is learnt about the colonel? Has it changed the relationship between the colonel and Mike?

THE STORYBOARD

The purpose of the storyboard is to photograph or draw out each and every shot of a film with a list of key information written underneath, so that a director can see how the finished film will look before a single frame is shot. This allows him or her to calculate the technical requirements of a shoot, and gives an opportunity for the director to revise sequences that seemed like a good approach when thinking the story through, but seem less possible or less appropriate with pictures in place.

The storyboard is made up from a set of 'standard' shot sizes each with an accompanying abbreviation:

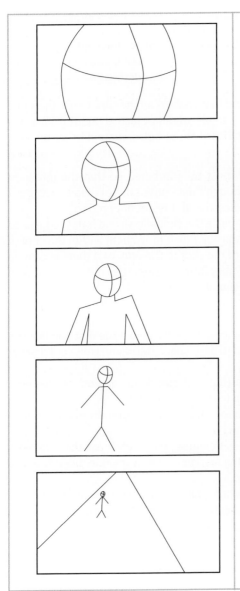

ECU *or* BCU: *extreme or big close up*
So close that only part of the subject is in view (eyes, mouth, etc.).

CU: *close up*
Close enough to see detail on a subject without losing a sense of the subject as a whole (chest to top of head).

MS: *mid shot*
Describes a position somewhere between LS and CU (waist to top of head).

LS: *long shot*
Usually describing a subject where you can see all of it in shot (head to toe if it is a person).

ELS: *extreme long shot*
Describing a subject that is placed well within its setting. In the case of a person could be a little beyond LS and out to infinity (most of the opening of *Lawrence of Arabia* is in ELS).

Between these shot descriptors are a range of other shots (such as MLS and MCU) which help to describe the photographed or drawn images, and which help the production crew make sense of the requirements for a shoot. Other abbreviations and terms that are likely to be found on a storyboard include:

H/A	High angle	Track/dolly	Move camera on wheeled platform
L/A	Low angle	Crab	Sideways move
POV	Point of view	Pull focus	Change what is focused on
2-shot	Two people in shot	Fade	Shot fades in/out
OTS	Over the shoulder	Dissolve	Shot fades out as another fades in underneath

This terminology offers an industry shorthand that enables all the crew to use the same document to relate their part of the process to an overall objective. Apart from a picture and the camera descriptions, the storyboard should also contain other relevant information such as:

Shot number Each shot in the storyboard must be numbered so that the intended sequence of shots can be followed. Although this is only a minor detail it can have serious consequences for shooting and editing if it is not adhered to.

Action A brief description of what is happening in the shot allows one frame to be used for the whole shot, even though there may be much movement within the shot. If it is radically different from beginning of the shot to the end, or if there is camera movement that results in radically different framing, then the shot may be drawn across a number of storyboard frames (numbered a, b, c, etc.).

Camera This should not only indicate shot size and angle but should also give a clear sense of what is being framed.

Dialogue Single lines may be written but for longer speeches just the first and last few words covered by the shot are included to save space (Morgan: 'Hell no, I'd never . . . no sir, never!')

Sound FX This indicates specific sounds that will stand out against the general soundscape; ones that the makers wish to draw attention to.

Sound atmos The overall background 'atmosphere' of a fictionalized location is important in capturing the nature of the place.

Sound music This relates largely to non-diegetic music; the soundtrack that has been placed on the film to create an emotional response. It may include diegetic music if it transforms into non-diegetic sound.

Shot duration This is a vital piece of information as it gives the storyboard rhythm and indicates that the filmmakers have considered the shot-to-shot relationships and the overall relationship of individual shots to the timing of the film as a whole. It is important not only to be able to calculate how long an action may take, but also how long it should take on screen.

- Look at a one-minute-long film extract that you are familiar with. Using the list above analyse the way the extract has been constructed.
- What do you notice about the way in which shot size and angle varies?
- What do you notice about the way each shot deals with movement within the frame?
- Generally what framing is used for dialogue?
- How are sound FX, atmos, and music related? What does the combination achieve?
- Is there a rhythm to the extract? Do you notice anything about the timings? Do they relate to the shot sizes? What does the rhythm do for the extract?

On pages 108 and 109 you will see two storyboarded extracts from *The Crossing*, one photographed and one drawn. It should become clear how the pictures and text support each other and how they aid the construction of meaning.

VIDEO PRODUCTION

Essentially the making of a video sequence can be divided into three distinct areas: pre-production (planning), production (shooting) and post-production (editing). Both scripting and storyboarding come into the pre-production stage, and so can be seen as primary functions that have to occur before any other pre-production stage can happen.

Pre-production

Even a short sequence can take an enormous amount of planning, and the time involved in organizing a shoot should not be underestimated. Other than scripting and storyboarding the essential tasks in pre-production are casting, location scouting, budgeting, scheduling, and rehearsing. If each one is carefully managed, then it is likely that the shoot will go relatively smoothly. If one area is ignored, then it can easily impede or even prove disastrous for a shoot.

- Casting: the difficulties of finding any actors yet alone talented ones are well understood, but there are some things that can be done to mitigate against circumstance. First it is important to get the right person for the right role – no point in casting a 17-year-old as the aging father of a 15-year-old – and the right 'look' can cover many casting problems. If possible look to performing arts groups, or local amateur dramatics companies, as they will have had some acting experience, though not necessarily for the cinematic medium. Try to ensure there is real choice in casting and that it is not done merely as an exercise in first come first served.

Shot no. 9

Action: There is slight movement behind the open window. Sunlight catches something inside and a reflection flashes briefly out.

Camera: L/A LS window

Dialogue: N/A

Sound FX: N/A

Sound atmos: City square

Sound music: N/A

Shot duration: (2 seconds)

Shot no. 10

Action: The flash catches Colonel Inchalyka's eyes and he looks up to the window.

Camera: MS (side) Colonel Inchalyka on embassy steps

Dialogue: N/A

Sound FX: N/A

Sound atmos: City square

Sound music: N/A

Shot duration: (2 seconds)

Shot no. 11

Action: Colonel Inchalyka scans the building from where the flash came. Seeing nothing he hesitates, then shrugs it off.

Camera: H/A ECU Colonel Inchalyka's eyes scan the building's windows.

Dialogue: N/A

Sound FX: N/A

Sound atmos: City square

Shot duration: (3 seconds)

Figure 5.1 *Three storyboard video shots*
Source: Freddie Gaffney

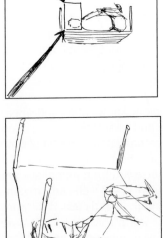

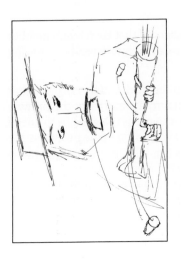

Shot no.: 22

Action: A gangster stands on a table spraying the square with bullets.

Camera: MCU (front) gangster firing from left to right, shells ejecting sideways. SLO-MO

Dialogue: N/A

Sound FX: LOUD machine-gun fire

Sound atmos: Panicked city square

Sound music: Low orchestral (under)

Shot duration: (6 seconds)

Shot No.: 23

Action: The American businessman shelters behind an overturned table as the machine-gun fire rattles around him

Camera: MS (side) American businessman sits huddled against the underside of an overturned table.

Dialogue: N/A

Sound FX: Machine-gun fire

Sound atmos: Panicked city square

Sound music: Low orchestral (under)

Shot no.: 24

Action: The American businessman shelters nervously behind a table, desperately looking for a way out of the carnage.

Camera: H/A LS ZOOM, PAN WITH, DE-FOCUS, and RE-FOCUS to CU back of American businessman's head, looking rapidly around. CUT TO BLACK.

Dialogue: N/A

Sound FX: Distant machine-gun fire ending with loud retort of single rifle shot

Sound atmos: Distant panicked city square

Sound music: Rising orchestral (under)

Shot duration: (6 seconds)

Figure 5.2 *Three storyboard sketch shots*
Source: Freddie Gaffney

- Location scouting: many productions are marred by using the wrong, or inappropriate locations, and again, with some foresight and preparation this should never be a problem. Discussions with the screenwriter at an early stage can head off script decisions that are almost certain to prove a location nightmare – outside a spaceship in mid-flight; a Transylvanian castle; inside the cabin of a commercial jet airliner, etc. However, with a little effort one location can become another: a local church can become the Vatican with some Italian signage, some Latin hymns added in, and a couple of extras speaking Italian in the background. Locations that are secured should be confirmed with time and date, preferably in writing, and preferably at least a week in advance of shooting.
- Budgeting: this is not an essential component of this task, but it is worth remembering that in group productions money is often the source of argument, so it may be worth establishing a budget from the start, and establishing who is going to contribute what to it. If the budget starts to run away from the production, then it is important that this is brought to everyone's attention as soon as possible.
- Scheduling: a well scheduled shoot is one where everyone knows when and where they are supposed to be, how long they will be there, and what they are supposed to be doing. It is wise to ensure that a schedule over-estimates the amount of time it takes to travel to a location, and the amount of time the shoot itself will take – people will thank you if they finish early, but curse you for running late. On average a production should be able to shoot between 12–18 well crafted, considered shots per eight-hour day on location, and usually slightly less if they are in the studio or have significant lighting set-ups. It is worth spending some time preparing 'call-sheets' for cast and crew, detailing daily arrangements and contact information.
- Rehearsing: the area least likely to be considered is possibly one of the most important. Rehearsals are not only a way of working the script through with actors, but they are also a way of ensuring a production team gets into the rhythm of working with each other.

Production

Production is unquestionably a team effort, and it is essential that each team member has a defined role and area of responsibility. A small crew is likely to have the following production roles:

- Director: responsible for the overall construction of the work and for ensuring that both actors and crew perform to their best. The dual role means that the primary responsibility of getting the actors to deliver a performance is matched by the need to direct the crew to ensure that this performance is captured in the best possible manner. The director is likely to choose performance as a focus area, but may also look to mise en scène in structuring the 'look' of a finished sequence.
- Cinematographer or director of photography: is responsible for capturing the image to film (or more likely tape), and will be focused on camera and lighting (though again may focus on mise en scène). The skill here is in manipulating camera controls and lighting techniques to create (and enhance) the director's vision.

- Art director: directly responsible for set dressing, set design, props and costume, and as such entirely focused on mise en scène.
- Sound recordist: responsible both for location sound and for providing sound intended for post-production. On set it is likely that the job will simply involve recording the purest sound possible, and being cautious of outside noise: planes flying overhead, traffic, neighbours arguing, etc..

There are some basic shooting rules that it is wise to adhere to even if they are not fully understood at this level, in order to produce material that is usable and most importantly editable. With a minimum structure in place shooting becomes a less stressful process, and the results are dramatically improved. However ignoring the simple rules of production leads to material that simply will not cut together, and well planned shoots, with all the accompanying effort, being ruined.

NOTEBOX

Basic shooting rules

1. Always use a tripod to support the camera, unless you have a specific reason for wanting the shaky look that hand-held will give you. This can be dynamic in certain situations (chase sequences for example) but often it simply makes a production seem lazy or amateurish.
2. If something is wrong in shot, call 'Cut' and re-take the shot. If you accept a shot that has problems, then that will be the shot that creates problems for you in post-production.
3. Always adhere to the 30° rule. This states that to avoid 'jump cuts' (where the camera appears to lurch towards a subject or the subject appears to 'jump' position between shots) any shots that are intended to be joined with each other in editing should be shot from camera positions that have at least 30° between them.
4. Avoid cutting whilst in mid-camera movement – let the shot come to a 'rest' position as this will benefit the editing.
5. Let the camera run for five seconds prior to calling 'Action' and after calling 'Cut'. This not only serves the editing, but it also gives some 'moments' where the actors' bodies and expressions are relaxed – these are often valuable.

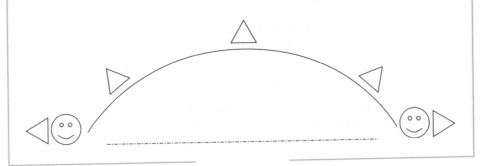

6   Always adhere to the 180° rule. This rule is often complex to understand and even more complex to implement. The 'line of action' is an imaginary line – usually between two people, but it can run through one person – that the camera must stay one side of. The camera can travel anywhere on a 180° axis as long as it does not 'cross the line'; as soon as it does that then all spatial continuity is lost and editing becomes an exercise in confusion.

Post-production

Modern post-production is invariably carried out on a non-linear computer system (most commonly Avid, Final Cut, Pinnacle and Premiere) which ingests digitized material (and on some systems analogue material), and facilitates not only basic assembly editing, but the addition of effects, sound editing, and the use of corrective tools such as grading. It is likely that a single editor will work through the shot material to produce a final cut of the sequence, and may be working from a storyboard, or more actively with a director.

The editor's role is one that should be governed by process in order for him or her to maximize creativity. This process involves digitizing material and importing it into the chosen editing programme; adding clips to a timeline to construct the sequence; trimming clips to tighten the sequence; laying audio tracks; laying any necessary video and audio effects; correcting any shot-to-shot problems (such as colour correction); creating title and credit sequences; and finally dubbing the finished product off to disc or tape.

Editors have a range of creative options open to them that determine the nature of the finished piece. Like all options these should be used sparingly to enhance the sequence and only when appropriate.

NOTEBOX

Basic options in editing

Dissolve: an image fades out as another fades in, making a connection between the two (girlfriend fades out as mother fades in).

Fade: often to black but can be to any colour. The duration of screen time given over to the fade and the end colour can suggest particular meanings.

Graphic match: two shots can be connected through shapes within the frame (a clock matched to a car wheel).

Match on action: two shots can be connected by the replication of an action across each (character begins putting drink down in seedy Soho bar, and cuts to drink reaching bar counter of Caribbean beach bar).

Montage: placing one image next to another creates meaning (person's face with apple pie = hungry, person's face with coffin = sadness).

EVALUATION

The area of a PAL that is often weakest is the evaluation, and like the cinematic ideas section it too can benefit from careful development, editing, and drafting. The evaluation should consider both process and product, and should show a clear awareness of the audience and their reaction(s) to the finished work, and should do this in approximately 500 words.

It is often worthwhile stating who the intended audience was for the sequence, as this then allows some element of testing (letting a representative of that audience – family member, friend, teacher – see the finished piece and express their responses to it) and then some reflection on their responses. This in turn can lead to a consideration of intended meanings and their production, which then focuses the piece on process and techniques. A personal response to the work can make a suitable conclusion to the evaluation.

ACTIVITY . . .

- Show your finished screenplay/storyboard/film to a group of people who are representative of your target audience. Try (if appropriate) to get a wide range of ages, genders, and social groupings. Get them to discuss the work as a group, and shape the discussion with reference to the macro and micro focus of the piece.
- Revise the work in the light of their comments.
- Design a questionnaire to test the revised work on an audience. Focus the questions on issues raised in the previous discussion.
- Show the revised work to the same group, and get them to complete the questionnaire.
- Use the questionnaire results to inform any final revision of the work.
- Look at the finished work yourself and fill in one of your own questionnaires. How do your results compare with those offered by your audience?

Example evaluation – screenplay *The Crossing*

I wrote my screenplay for an audience of 18–25 year olds as they are in the appropriate age group for thrillers and the content of the film is likely to mean that it will secure an 18 certificate from the BBFC. I titled it *The Crossing* as this has several meanings including referencing the border crossing, double crossing, and the rite-of-passage crossing for the central character. I based this character on an amalgamation of several of my friends in an attempt to reach my target audience better.

The script was given to a selection of my target audience and they gave me some very positive responses. Thankfully they were all surprised that Mike's father turned out not only to be alive but to be the crime boss. Most said they were shocked by this and by his attempts to kill his own son, and I was happy that my intended meaning had been understood. What surprised me however, was that the majority of people believed Colonel Inchalyka was the bad guy – when I worked hard to signpost his honesty and integrity. Maybe I was too subtle, or maybe my audience has a genre-based response to such characters that means they are automatically suspicious of them. Perhaps I should have made Colonel Inchalyka a woman instead?

The oldest in my target audience felt that Mike appeared too grown up for his age and dealt with all the terrible situations he found himself in too well. I am not sure that this is the case and none of the other audience members commented on this.

To help me write the screenplay I looked at several books, and found the Film Education booklet on screenwriting very useful in terms of working through the idea and structuring the script. Making the characters seem real without letting them speak too much was difficult and I kept having to invent ways of showing, not telling. The gunfight sequence was fun to do and I decided to use the techniques I have seen in other films such as the work of John Woo and Sam Peckinpah.

I wrote three drafts of the screenplay, showing each to my teacher (who is outside my target age group) and to a friend who is in my target audience. My teacher was able to offer some good advice, but my friend seemed to think each version was OK, and I didn't find much of use in his comments. Overall I am very happy with the finished piece and I feel I have learnt a lot about the nature of storytelling and the structure of screenplays. I have also learnt that I can apply learning from academic areas of the course to the practical areas, and this has increased my enjoyment of both. I'm looking forward to writing the rest of *The Crossing*, especially in the light of what is on the menu for my A2 studies.

(487 words)

FURTHER READING

Scriptwriting

Gaffney, F. (2006) *Screenwriting*, London: Auteur.

Hicks, N. (1996) *Screenwriting 101*, Oxford: Wiese.

Storyboarding

Begleiter, M. (2001) *From Word to Image: Storyboarding and the Filmmaking Process*, Oxford: Wiese.

Fraioli, J. (2000) *Storyboarding 101*, Oxford: Wiese.

Production

Jones, C. and Jolliffe, G. (1996) *The Guerrilla Film Maker's Handbook*, London: Cassell.

Katz, S. (1991) *Film Directing Shot by Shot*, Oxford: Wiese.

USEFUL WEBSITES

http://www.cyberfilmschool.com (cyber film school: Pro-end DV filmmaking site)

http://www.filmundergound.com (film underground: DV filmmaking site)

http://www.script-o-rama.com (Drew's scriptorama: script and screenwriting site)

http://www.themakingof.com (the making of Hollywood's hit movies)

http://w3.tvi.cc.nm.us/~jvelez/MMS170/storyboard (storyboarding: history, purpose, and techniques)

PART 2
PRODUCERS AND AUDIENCES – HOLLYWOOD AND BRITISH CINEMA (FS2)

▼ 6 FILMS AS PRODUCTS

This chapter will:

- encourage you to see films as products of a global industry dominated by Hollywood;
- outline the stages that make up film production, or the actual making of the film;
- outline the stages in the commercial process that come after the film has been made, essentially distribution, marketing and exhibition;
- encourage you to try to follow through the process behind bringing one of your own favourite films to the screen.

NOTEBOX

This section will be particularly relevant to FS2 – Producers and Audiences: Hollywood and British Cinema for the WJEC's AS in Film Studies. This part of the AS course tries to get you to understand how in addition to being viewers of films, or spectators, people who watch films could also be seen as consumers. And, in relation to this approach, how films themselves could be discussed in terms of being products made in particular ways and designed to be consumed in particular ways.

THE GLOBAL AND LOCAL DIMENSIONS

The film industry reaches right around the globe. In terms of the making of films, they can be shot on location, or in film studios, all over the world. In terms of showing films, although they may initially be shown in one country or another, with the right marketing and distribution back-up they can quite quickly be seen by audiences around the world.

In studying film, you should be intensely aware of this increasingly important global dimension to film; globalization is a process that in recent years has affected films and the film industry as much as any other commercial enterprise. However, you should also be alert to the fact that this global aspect to the industry is actually expressed and experienced locally. As a result we are able to give due consideration to the film industry as a worldwide phenomenon simply by paying careful attention to the presence of film within our everyday lives.

The magazines and newspapers we read, the TV we watch, the conversations we have with friends, the streets we walk and the shops we visit, to say nothing of the DVDs we buy and the cinemas we attend, will all announce the presence of the film industry as a worldwide commercial fact.

ACTIVITY...

1   Compile a list of local cinemas within say five to six miles of either your college or your home. How long has each cinema been open? Can you find out brief details for the development of each cinema? Do any local cinemas have a particularly long history? How many screens are available at each cinema?

2   What sorts of films are shown at these local cinema(s)? If there are several cinemas, do they tend to specialize in any way? Is their programme dominated by mainstream Hollywood films? Do they show what might be called 'art-house' films at any time? If so, when are they screened and how often?

3   Find out the cost of tickets. If there are several cinemas, is there much difference between prices? If so, can you see any reasons why this might be? Are there special discount times or discount deals at particular cinemas?

4   Where are the cinemas situated and why are they sited in these places? Are they in town or out of town, and why? Are they easily accessible by road? Are there any bus and/or rail stations nearby? Is car parking easily available?

5   Do they advertise their presence and what they are currently showing in local newspapers and/or on local radio? Do they offer press screenings of new films before they are shown to the public?

6   If you can, try to arrange a visit to a local multiplex (and/or smaller cinema) and interview the manager. Try to find out:

   - how the cinema decides which films it will be showing and for how long;
   - what percentage of films shown would be classified as American;
   - whether they have any deals with particular distributors or studios;
   - how they decide which advertisements and trailers to show;
   - what percentage of their takings come from the box-office;
   - what percentage of their takings come from other sources particularly food and drink.

(Perhaps you can come up with a further list of questions to ask before your visit.)

HOLLYWOOD

Alongside the type of film analysis we have undertaken with a variety films in Part 1, as film students we need to remember that the films we see at the cinema and the DVDs we watch at home are the products of this massive ongoing industrial process. In the case of most of the films we have so far considered, we have been dealing with products of Hollywood, that suburb of Los Angeles in California that has been home to the big American film studios since the early days of silent films so that the place name has itself become a shorthand term for the American industry as a whole.

KEY TERM

HOLLYWOOD As early as the 1910s the US film industry began to shift its base from the East Coast to what was essentially a place in the Californian desert, a rural area on the edge of Los Angeles. The name 'Hollywood' has, of course, become a term signifying something much more than simply a place in California.

ACTIVITY

1   Consider why Hollywood might have become the American centre for industrial filmmaking. What advantages might it have offered the business initially, and later as it developed as a filmmaking centre?
2   Discuss your ideas with others, if possible.
3   Try to find time to undertake a little research to see if any of your ideas hold up to scrutiny. Basically you are trying to find out where the industry started in America and how it came to be located in Hollywood.

(The history of all of this is in a sense by the by. What is crucial is that you begin to think about film in business terms – why would a film industry interested in churning out as many film products as possible in as short a space of time as possible and for the greatest profit possible move to Hollywood? Begin to think in these terms and you will be well on the way to understanding this part of the Film Studies A level.)

STUDIOS

Most famously Hollywood has been built around studios, well-financed big-name companies in the business of making films and in the business of making money from films. *Casablanca* (1942), for example, the 'classic' wartime romantic drama set in what was seen as an exotic North African location, was made by Warner Brothers, one of the major companies operating during that phase of film history spanning the 1930s, 1940s and into the 1950s known as the studio system. Perhaps the most famous 'classic' text from the same period, *Citizen Kane* (1941), was made by another studio known as RKO, Radio-Keith-Orpheum.

120 PRODUCERS AND AUDIENCES: HOLLYWOOD AND BRITAIN (FS2)

Casablanca (1942) was filmed and then released just as the United States was entering the Second World War and was made by Warner Brothers in an effort to encourage the country to take up the struggle against Hitler's Germany. It featured two famous stars from the period, Humphrey Bogart and Ingrid Bergman.

Citizen Kane (1941), directed by and starring Orson Welles, is one of those films that nearly always features near the top of '100 best movies ever' lists that you tend to find at regular intervals in film magazines.

The first of these studios, Warner Brothers, will be familiar to most people since it is still very much one of the major 'players' in the industry. However, you may well not have heard of the second name because RKO went out of business in 1955. It was the only one of the major studios from the period to go out of business in the face of the huge competition offered to the industry by the advent of TV. So to some extent studios come and go, although most seem to manage to be taken over or become involved in mergers rather than actually go out of business. (We will consider the studios based in Hollywood in a little more detail in a later chapter that looks specifically at 'Old and New Hollywood'.)

Warner Brothers was formed as a production company in 1923 under Harry, Albert, Sam and Jack Warner. In 1927 the company introduced synchronized sound for the film *The Jazz Singer* and revolutionized the industry. They quickly took over a chain of theatres and also another production company, First National. In 1989 Warners merged with Time Inc. which then merged with Turner Broadcasting in 1996 and then with AOL in 2000 to become one of the largest media entertainment conglomerates. (See how the history of this company is built upon mergers, and also the effort to take advantage of new technologies to obtain a commercial advantage over rivals whenever possible.)

RKO (Radio-Keith-Orpheum) was formed in 1928 through a merger between RCA (Radio Corporation of America) and the Keith, Albee and Orpheum cinema chains. In 1931 the company bought Pathé's studios and distribution outlets. At this time sound was just coming in and RCA for obvious reasons felt it had useful experience in this field. By 1955 the company had been wound down and most of its assets sold off. (See how the way this company starts at a time of change for the film industry demonstrates the more usual process of mergers and takeovers.)

1: GONE WITH THE WIND
Estimated Attendance: 35 million

2: The SOUND OF MUSIC
Estimated Attendance: 30 million

3: SNOW WHITE AND THE SEVEN DWARFS
Estimated Attendance: 28 million

4: STAR WARS
Estimated Attendance: 20.76 million

5: SPRING IN PARK LANE
Estimated Attendance: 20.5 million

6: The BEST YEARS OF OUR LIVES
Estimated Attendance: 20.4 million

7: The JUNGLE BOOK
Estimated Attendance: 19.8 million

8: TITANIC
Estimated Attendance: 18.91 million

9: The WICKED LADY
Estimated Attendance: 18.4 million

10: The SEVENTH VEIL
Estimated Attendance: 17.9 million

11: HARRY POTTER AND THE PHILOSOPHER'S STONE
Estimated Attendance: 17.56 million

12: GREASE
Estimated Attendance: 17.2 million

13: SOUTH PACIFIC
Estimated Attendance: 16.5 million

14: JAWS
Estimated Attendance: 16.2 million

15: JURASSIC PARK
Estimated Attendance: 16.17 million

16: The LORD OF THE RINGS THE FELLOWSHIP OF THE RING
Estimated Attendance: 15.98 million

17: The COURTNEYS OF CURZON STREET
Estimated Attendance: 15.9 million

18: THUNDERBALL
Estimated Attendance: 15.6 million

19: The LORD OF THE RINGS THE RETURN OF THE KING
Estimated Attendance: 15.22 million

20: The BELLS OF ST. MARY'S
Estimated Attendance: 15.2 million

21: The TEN COMMANDMENTS
Estimated Attendance: 15 million

22: The LORD OF THE RINGS THE TWO TOWERS
Estimated Attendance: 14.4 million

23: The FULL MONTY
Estimated Attendance: 14.19 million

24: HARRY POTTER AND THE CHAMBER OF SECRETS
Estimated Attendance: 14.18 million

25: MARY POPPINS
Estimated Attendance: 14 million

26: The THIRD MAN
Estimated Attendance: 14 million

27: GOLDFINGER
Estimated Attendance: 13.9 million

28: STAR WARS EPISODE I THE PHANTOM MENACE
Estimated Attendance: 13.59 million

29: The BLUE LAMP
Estimated Attendance: 13.3 million

30: BEN-HUR
Estimated Attendance: 13.2 million

31: E.T. THE EXTRA-TERRESTRIAL
Estimated Attendance: 13.13 million

32: The GREATEST SHOW ON EARTH
Estimated Attendance: 13 million

33: The BRIDGE ON THE RIVER KWAI
Estimated Attendance: 12.6 million

34: The SPY WHO LOVED ME
Estimated Attendance: 12.46 million

35: The GREAT CARUSO
Estimated Attendance: 12.4 million

36: DOCTOR IN THE HOUSE
Estimated Attendance: 12.2 million

37: TOY STORY 2
Estimated Attendance: 12.18 million

38: RANDOM HARVEST
Estimated Attendance: 12 million

39: The TOWERING INFERNO
Estimated Attendance: 11.78 million

40: FANNY BY GASLIGHT
Estimated Attendance: 11.7 million

41: The JOLSON STORY
Estimated Attendance: 11.6 million

42: PICCADILLY INCIDENT
Estimated Attendance: 11.5 million

43: The GUNS OF NAVARONE
Estimated Attendance: 11.4 million

44: DOCTOR ZHIVAGO
Estimated Attendance: 11.2 million

45: The STING
Estimated Attendance: 11.08 million

46: The GODFATHER
Estimated Attendance: 11 million

47: INDEPENDENCE DAY
Estimated Attendance: 10.79 million

48: CARRY ON NURSE
Estimated Attendance: 10.4 million

49: I LIVE IN GROSVENOR SQUARE
Estimated Attendance: 10.3 million

50: MRS. MINIVER
Estimated Attendance: 10.2 million

51: SUPERMAN
Estimated Attendance: 10.19 million

52: BRIDGET JONES'S DIARY
Estimated Attendance: 10.15 million

53: MONSTERS, INC.
Estimated Attendance: 9.93 million

54: A CLOCKWORK ORANGE
Estimated Attendance: 9.9 million

55: CROCODILE DUNDEE
Estimated Attendance: 9.8 million

56: FINDING NEMO
Estimated Attendance: 9.79 million

57: MEN IN BLACK
Estimated Attendance: 9.73 million

58: FOR WHOM THE BELL TOLLS
Estimated Attendance: 9.7 million

59: ONE FLEW OVER THE CUCKOO'S NEST
Estimated Attendance: 9.65 million

60: HIGH SOCIETY
Estimated Attendance: 9.6 million

61: MOONRAKER
Estimated Attendance: 9.41 million

62: I'M ALL RIGHT JACK
Estimated Attendance: 9.4 million

63: 49TH PARALLEL
Estimated Attendance: 9.3 million

64: LOST HORIZON
Estimated Attendance: 9.2 million

65: STAR WARS EPISODE II ATTACK OF THE CLONES
Estimated Attendance: 9.16 million

66: ONE HUNDRED AND ONE DALMATIANS
Estimated Attendance: 9.1 million

67: The EMPIRE STRIKES BACK
Estimated Attendance: 9.09 million

68: SATURDAY NIGHT FEVER
Estimated Attendance: 9.02 million

69: LIVE AND LET DIE
Estimated Attendance: 9 million

70: The GREAT DICTATOR
Estimated Attendance: 9 million

71: The BIG COUNTRY
Estimated Attendance: 9 million

72: BAMBI
Estimated Attendance: 9 million

73: REBECCA
Estimated Attendance: 8.9 million

74: OLIVER!
Estimated Attendance: 8.9 million

75: FOUR WEDDINGS AND A FUNERAL
Estimated Attendance: 8.81 million

76: GHOST
Estimated Attendance: 8.78 million

77: LOVE ACTUALLY
Estimated Attendance: 8.76 million

78: REACH FOR THE SKY
Estimated Attendance: 8.7 million

79: MY FAIR LADY
Estimated Attendance: 8.6 million

80: DIE ANOTHER DAY
Estimated Attendance: 8.58 million

81: CLOSE ENCOUNTERS OF THE THIRD KIND
Estimated Attendance: 8.54 million

82: The CITADEL
Estimated Attendance: 8.5 million

83: PINOCCHIO
Estimated Attendance: 8.5 million

84: A BUG'S LIFE
Estimated Attendance: 8.41 million

85: LAWRENCE OF ARABIA
Estimated Attendance: 8.4 million

86: The DAM BUSTERS
Estimated Attendance: 8.4 million

87: RETURN OF THE JEDI
Estimated Attendance: 8.35 million

88: MR. DEEDS GOES TO TOWN
Estimated Attendance: 8.3 million

89: SWISS FAMILY ROBINSON
Estimated Attendance: 8.3 million

90: YOU ONLY LIVE TWICE
Estimated Attendance: 8.3 million

91: The EXORCIST
Estimated Attendance: 8.3 million

92: The KING AND I
Estimated Attendance: 8.2 million

93: CHICKEN RUN
Estimated Attendance: 8.12 million

94: The LION KING
Estimated Attendance: 8.08 million

95: NOTTING HILL
Estimated Attendance: 8.05 million

96: The MATRIX RELOADED
Estimated Attendance: 7.96 million

97: The PRIVATE LIFE OF HENRY VIII
Estimated Attendance: 7.9 million

98: CINDERELLA
Estimated Attendance: 7.9 million

99: GLADIATOR
Estimated Attendance: 7.8 million

100: The MAGNIFICENT SEVEN
Estimated Attendance: 7.7 million

Figure 6.1 *The Ultimate Film Chart*
Source: Reproduced by permission of BFI National Library

1   Research the development of TV in both the United States and Britain. It might be more interesting to try to complete this task with someone else rather than on your own.

   ■   What are the key dates for the development of TV as a commercial enterprise?
   ■   How rapidly did TV sets make their way into the home in both countries?
   ■   When did satellite and cable first appear, and again how rapidly did this new technology and the accompanying increase in available channels make its way into the home?
   ■   In what ways could TV be seen as a competitor to film and the cinema, and in what ways could it be seen as a useful parallel medium that could be used by the film industry in commercially advantageous ways?

2   Discuss your research findings with other people who have undertaken the same work. Take particular note of any ideas they have come up with that you missed.

The Internet clearly represents a wonderful resource for this sort of work, but two pieces of advice:

■   first, do not neglect relevant books that you might perhaps find in the media studies section within a library;
■   and second, undertaking Internet searches does not absolve you from the responsibility of reading carefully what you find and extracting thoughtfully the particular information you require.

TELEVISION This might perhaps at first seem a strange choice of key term when considering cinema and film. However, TV is clearly in the business of screening staged film dramas and from this perspective is in immediate competition with cinema. On the other hand, since TV has provided a ready-made screen in every home since the 1960s the potential of a further space in which to show film products also becomes apparent. And when we reach the era of first video and then DVD, these products depend entirely for their success or otherwise upon people having access to screens within as wide a variety of places as possible.

KEY TERM

FILMS AS COMMERCIAL PRODUCTS

If you pick up a DVD copy of *Citizen Kane* today you will see that it is marketed by Universal and so, despite the fact that the company originally responsible for making it no longer exists, as a commercial product it continues to this day to be a valuable commodity capable of making money for whoever owns it. If you have more recent films at home and look carefully at the packaging you will be able to see a logo or a series of logos proclaiming the company or companies responsible for distributing these products. For example, pick up a copy of *Collateral* (Mann, 2004) and you will see it has been brought to you by a company called Paramount, which as with Warners will in all likelihood be a familiar name to you.

ACTIVITY

1   Research the development of VHS and DVD in both the United States and Britain. Again, it might be more interesting to try to complete this task with someone else rather than on your own.

   ■   What are the key dates for the development of these two formats as commercial enterprises?
   ■   How rapidly did video recorders and DVD players make their way into the home in both countries?
   ■   In what ways have these two technological developments been important for organizations involved in marketing old films like *Casablanca* and *Citizen Kane*?

2   After you have considered this on your own and perhaps with someone you have been working with, try to discuss your ideas with other people comparing the ideas you have come up with.

KEY TERM

VHS Video Home System, Matsushita's video tape format which became the home norm for recording after overcoming its commercial rival, Sony's Betamax system, in the 1980s.

KEY TERM

DVD Digital Versatile Disc, the system that has now almost replaced VHS video. Discs can hold much more information than video tapes (providing the possibility for all sorts of 'extras' to be included alongside the main film) and offer a higher quality image.

ADAPTABILITY OF THE FILM INDUSTRY

Perhaps the key to understanding the success of Hollywood over the past 100 years is to recognize the way in which it has always demonstrated an incredible ability to adapt to changing business circumstances. At heart the mainstream American film industry has recognized that what it is offering the public is a product and that its success depends upon adapting that product to a constantly changing market. Hollywood has continually managed to find ways to embrace new technologies such as those mentioned above.

On the Waterfront (Kazan, 1954), an early film starring Marlon Brando, was made during a period when the American industry was facing perhaps its major challenge. It needed to re-organize itself in the face of competition from the then stunning new technology of TV. Studios were beginning to use independent producers; they would finance a one-off project for one of these producers and then distribute the resulting films. This meant they no longer had the ongoing, week in, week out expense of staffing and running studio production facilities. The package of business arrangements (cast and crew to be signed up and paid for a given period, clearance for filming at various locations to be obtained, studio space to be booked for filming on set, editing facilities to be lined up, etc.) necessary to complete the On the Waterfront project was organized by independent producer, Sam Spiegel, who then released the finished product through Columbia. It was a relatively low budget film being made for just $800,000 on a tight 35-day shooting schedule but made $9.5 million at the box office when first released.

NOTEBOX

> Keep looking for parallels between anything you find out about Hollywood in the past and Hollywood today. On the Waterfront amounts to a low budget, high profit product: today massive studios like Twentieth Century Fox set up small in-house low budget filmmaking companies like Fox Searchlight precisely because in percentage terms films that are (relatively) cheap to make can produce high percentage profits. (In simple terms, making $2 million profit on a $100 million outlay is one thing but making $2 million on a $20 million outlay is a much better percentage return and thus a better business proposition.)

In the face of continued competition from TV and changing leisure patterns, the industry continued to lose ground during the 1960s and 1970s, but in general Hollywood continued to maintain its recognition of film as a commercial product. In the mid-1970s during a time of continuing difficulties for the industry Star Wars (Lucas, 1977) took more than $46 million during its first week. This was achieved by coming up with a strong initial concept, marketing the film imaginatively and making a big play of releasing the film at the same time to more cinemas than was usual at the time. The film became the first to gross more than $400 million at the US box office and effectively changed marketing practices and release strategies for the industry.

Figure 6.2 *Star Wars*
Source: British Film Institute

The main thing to take on board is the fact that despite difficult times, in general Hollywood has been able to continually re-invent itself by seeing film as a commercial product that has to respond to a changing marketplace and take advantage of new opportunities offered by new technologies. At each moment in its history when the industry has faced the need to re-organize in the face of new competition the effort has always been to re-organize in as effective a way as possible in order to continue to make money.

ACTIVITY

1   Research a few of the films mentioned in this chapter so far. Who were the main stars in each film? See what you can find out about the main star from each film. Who directed each film? Again, see what you can find out about these people.
2   Write a short 100–200 word biography on the star you find most interesting and another on the director you have found most interesting.

Change over time

As a student of film it is important to know a little about the history of Hollywood:

- to be aware of early 'silent' cinema and the change to 'talkies' around 1930;
- to be able to identify differences and similarities between the studio system of the 1930s and 1940s and contemporary Hollywood filmmaking;
- to understand something of how the studio system broke up in the 1950s before re-inventing itself during the 1970s with films like *Jaws* (Spielberg, 1975) and *Star Wars*.

To emphasize the point once more, the continuity link through all this time and the factor that it is most important to recognize from the outset is that film has always been seen by Hollywood as a commercial product to be made in as cost-effective a way as possible and to be sold for the greatest profit achievable.

Casablanca, Sin City and baked beans

So, when we enter our local DVD shop and take from the shelf the film marked *Casablanca* or the film marked *Collateral* or *Sin City* it is not in some senses any different from entering a supermarket and picking up a can of our favourite baked beans. We will look at the labelling, paying particular attention to the maker's name and noting what the pictures on the box suggest about the item we are considering purchasing. We will decide if this is the product we want, buy it, take it home, open the package and prepare ourselves to enjoy what the advertising and marketing has told us to expect. Films in their DVD and VHS formats are packaged using visual images and wording in as effective a way as possible to tell us exactly the sort of thing we are buying; or perhaps sometimes we might think in order to trick us into purchasing something that does not turn out to be half as good as the packaging suggested, or as the trailers and other adverts suggested.

ACTIVITY . . .

1. Look at your DVD collection when you get home and choose one or two with what you believe to be interesting, eye-catching packaging.
2. Analyse the ways in which the covers are 'working' to attract attention and convey messages about the product to potential purchasers.

   - What words or names are being used and why? How prominent are they and why? What colouring is used? What typeface is employed? Why?
   - How about the image, why has it been chosen? Break the image down into component parts, if possible: how does each work to create meaning for us?

3. If possible take the DVD cover about which you feel you have the most to say to a meeting with other students studying film with you. Explain your understanding of your chosen DVD cover to them and compare your ideas with the ideas they have about the covers they have brought for discussion.

Films and the cinema

But of course films do not just come as DVDs. Films are usually first seen as new releases screened in cinemas (although you can get made-for-TV films, and also films that go straight to video or DVD rather than having a theatrical release). Indeed the ultimate financial success of any film is usually determined by its level of success in the cinema. And here we are not just talking about final box-office takings for the year of release: it is usually true to say that by the end of the opening weekend analysts working for the studio concerned already have a pretty strong indicator as to the film's eventual level of financial success, or failure. Films shown in the cinema are sold to us via still images and wording in ways that are reminiscent of DVD covers through the use of posters. In addition to this, when we attend the cinema trailers work hard to attempt to persuade us to return in the future to see further films.

ACTIVITY . . .

1   Choose a film poster you have seen recently and examine the way in which it has been put together. Is it effective or not? In what ways is it effective? In what ways do you think it is not effective? How do layout, wording and images chosen attempt to make the poster effective?
2   Write 600 words explaining how you feel layout, wording and images work to attempt to sell this particular film.

ACTIVITY . . .

■   What has been the most effective trailer you have seen recently at the cinema?
■   What made it effective? Was it something to do with the voiceover? Or the visual images selected? Or the style of the filmmaking? Or the challenging nature of the ideas that seemed to be examined by the film?
■   Do you think it would have been equally attractive to other cinemagoers, or is there a reason it was particularly interesting to you?

Films and TV

Films are also available for us to watch on TV of course and as such have been for around 50 years, but only comparatively recently has this space become so important for film sales. With the proliferation of channels brought about by the appearance of cable and satellite TV, a massive new 'window' for the exhibition of film has been opened up for the industry. Previously there were only a relatively few terrestrial channels.

1   Research preview trailers on any pay-to-view channel. Analyse the ways in which these previews are 'working' to attract attention and convey messages about the product to potential purchasers.

- What words or names are being used visually and why? How prominent are they and why? What colouring is used? What typeface is employed?
- Do the previews use a voiceover? If so, how has the voiceover been constructed? What elements of the film are being emphasized in the voiceover script and why? Is there a particular tone of voice employed?
- How about the images, why have they been chosen? Break the images down into component sections, if possible. How does each work to create meaning and generate responses from us?

2   If possible, take a recorded copy of the preview trailers you have looked at to a meeting with other people studying film with you. Explain your understanding of your chosen previews to them and compare your ideas with the ideas they have about the previews they have brought for discussion.

Economics and the film industry

For now, the main thing to take on board is that a commercial film is the product of an industrial production process involving the use of a variety of technologies and human labour. The inter-related roles of industrial relations, markets, business agendas and issues of profit and loss accounting, for example, are all therefore of relevance to an understanding of how we as an audience come to be presented with the films we are studying. Perhaps you were not expecting to have to deal with these sorts of areas in studying film but you have to appreciate this is a multi-million pound industry.

1   Organize yourselves into groups and either nominate one photographer in each group or agree to take turns in this role.
2   Go to your nearest town or city and take shots of as many film-related images that you can see in the streets as possible.
3   Before you go out on location, list specific places you know in the town/city where you might find images related to film (cinemas, bookshops, shops selling DVDs, DVD rental outlets, billboards, etc.).
4   Create a montage of images to be displayed in the classroom or on your school/college website if possible with the aim of showing just how inescapable a part of everybody's life film has become in recent years.

(If you wish to take shots inside any premises, make sure you explain what you are doing and ask permission before pressing the shutter.)

FILMMAKING: THE PROCESS

There are then, as we have seen, a whole series of ways in which we as consumers of film come into quite immediate contact with the industry in our everyday life. What will most likely be outside our direct experience, though, will be the various stages involved in the making of commercial films.

There are three phases to the actual production, or making, of a film:

- preparation, or pre-production – the initial idea is developed and written as a script, and funds are obtained;
- shooting, or production – images and sounds are physically recorded and put on film (or digitally recorded);
- assembly, or post-production – the images and sounds are edited and put together in their final form.

Obviously each of these stages can be carried out on a very small scale, within a school or college for example, and if you have taken part in the process you will be aware of how well you have to be organized and how carefully you have to plan each of these stages. But if we are looking at the commercial film industry, beyond the actual making of the film, there will also be issues of distribution and marketing to be considered, because once it has been made, the film has to find an audience and be placed in an accessible form for that audience. It has to be decided where and when the film is going to be exhibited.

- In what countries is it to be shown?
- Should there be a single global release date?
- Should some countries receive the film before others?
- In which cinema chains is it to be shown in particular countries?
- Initially how many cinemas should it be released to in each country?
- How should this initial release be built upon in order to maximize the potential audience? How quickly is it to move on to DVD release?
- How long should it be before it is shown on satellite, cable and terrestrial TV?

In other words, what are the marketing and distribution strategies that should be followed for this particular product (bearing in mind that potentially each film might need to employ strategies individually tailored to the particular nature of the product)?

KEY TERM

MARKETING This refers to the total package of strategies used to try to promote and sell a film. Large distribution companies in charge of marketing will employ researchers to investigate the market for any particular film and enable them to keep abreast of shifting trends in consumer practices. They will also use focus groups (or members of the public) from the supposed target market to view and comment upon the film at various stages with the idea of altering the script if necessary. Such early showings of the film behind closed doors are known as test screenings.

All of this will occur before those elements more usually associated with marketing, the screening of cinema trailers, the launching of a press campaign and the instigation of a poster campaign, come into play. Although, of course, the planning for each of these strands involving the development of a clear timetable for each stage of the marketing process will be under way even as the film is being shot.

To some extent if you have a big budget blockbuster these decisions are easy; you swamp every other opposition product if you can through a saturation release that hits as many screens as possible from day one. But if you do not have a big budget then a carefully planned release strategy can make your film initially create good 'word of mouth' through a limited opening release pattern and then build on this as what the business calls 'want to see' is created. In fact, of course, even if you are producing a very low budget small-scale film you will still be thinking in terms of some audience or other. It may be you are only producing it for yourself and your friends to view, or perhaps as a home movie for your immediate family, or as a short to be put out on the college website, but still you will be aiming to engage the interest of your prospective audience. You will want to create something that means something for them and generates some sort of envisaged response from them. Ideally, what the producers of commercial films are looking for is a film with 'legs', that is one that is going to keep on running thereby making money at the box office over an extended period.

RELEASE PATTERN This is the part of the marketing strategy that determines the number of prints of the film that are to be initially put out to cinemas, which cinemas are to receive the film to begin with, and then how that initial release of the film is to be expanded and built upon.

A film might be given a 'general release' right across the country or it might have a 'select release' to a few cinemas in a few cities where the audience is felt to be right for this particular film. A 'saturation release' would indicate that the effort has been to put the film out immediately to as many cinemas as possible.

A film is usually released first of all within its country of origin before moving out to other countries in a developmental fashion, although it is now possible for a big Hollywood film to have a single global release date.

Whatever pattern is adopted, the key thing to recognize is the way in which market analysts will have worked together to try to decide upon the strategy that will be best suited to maximizing box-office returns on their product.

So, a film (any film) can always be seen as going through:

- a production phase;
- a distribution phase;
- an exhibition phase.

Distribution

This involves making sure a release pattern is put into place that will enable the product to reach the widest and largest audience possible. Of course, film distributors may be small firms specializing in certain types of film or multinational corporations with global networks of offices, and the products they deal with and markets they focus upon will vary enormously. However, essentially, the distributor:

- acquires the rights to the film;
- decides the number of prints to be made and released to exhibitors;
- negotiates a release date for the prints;
- arranges delivery of prints to cinemas;
- provides trailers and publicity material for exhibitors;
- puts together a package of advertising and publicity to promote the film;
- negotiates related promotional and/or merchandising deals.

Marketing

This can be seen as three distinct areas: advertising, publicity, and promotional deals worked out with other companies. Within an overall marketing budget, possibilities within each of these areas will be considered in terms of the likely return on ticket sales weighed against cost. The big plus in favour of publicity is that it is essentially free, although there might be some associated costs such as expenses for one of the film's stars who is going to be interviewed on a TV show. Advertising, on the other hand, has to be paid for: so, if as a marketing executive for a particular film you succeed in getting a review on the film pages of a newspaper next to an advert for your film, the first of these things will be free whereas the second will have to be paid for.

Advertising

A range of media will be considered – newspapers, magazines, TV, radio, etc. – with a clear agenda to hit a specific target audience. The poster campaign is often the primary medium for advertising a film comprising the central image that will also feature heavily in the publicity campaign. Some films will have teaser posters before the release date, a main poster to coincide with the release date, and later a third poster with comments from critics. You will also have noticed how posters for any film often vary according to where they are 'placed'. For example a poster designed to catch your eye as you are walking, cycling or driving will be different from one in a magazine where you are expected to have more time to take in information.

POSTER CAMPAIGN A marketing strategy involving the use of a prominently displayed series of posters to promote a film. Each poster will be carefully put together to present what is seen to be a desirable image to be associated with the film and will be strategically placed in the press and positioned on hoardings in such a way as to attempt to catch the eye of the film's target audience. The aim will be to present the public with a clearly defined notion of exactly what is special or particular about this film. This is sometimes referred to as the film's 'unique selling point', or USP.

ACTIVITY . . .

1   Find your own examples of posters for one film that have been designed for a range of placements.
2   How do they differ? How are they constructed to fit their likely audience? Explore layout, text and visual images in detail in relation to each other but most importantly in relation to the chosen outlet position.
3   Write a short essay (600 words) exploring the differences.

Publicity

Since they are essentially free, reviews, articles, interviews, photographs used in any of the media have a special importance for the success of a marketing campaign. Press kits are sent out comprising authorized stills, cast and crew credits, production notes, and biographies of cast/director/producer. There will be efforts to get key personnel especially stars involved with any new film on to as many TV and radio outlets as possible. Again, be aware of your own experience: you know only too well that when you start seeing a particular favourite star of yours on TV, on one programme after another, it always coincides with the release of their latest film (or the latest instalment of their autobiography). A trailer is also usually put out several weeks before the release in order to raise awareness of the product, as you will be aware from your own cinema visits.

TRAILERS A short advert for a film put together by the distributors. It will usually be comprised of extracts from the film in question with an added voiceover designed to sell the film. A shorter version of the trailer sometime before the film is due out is known as a 'teaser'.

1   Take a high profile Hollywood film of your choice that is about to be released, and by looking carefully through the *Radio Times* or any other magazines or Internet sites with programme schedules, try to see whether the marketing team have been successful in gaining time and space to promote their company's new product.
2   Draw up a list of programmes with dates and times that are reviewing the film, interviewing 'the talent' involved in the project, and/or showing extracts from the film.

KEY TERM

'THE TALENT' This is a film industry term for the main creative players involved in the production of any particular film. It is often used to refer to the director, the producer, the screenwriter and the lead actors as a group of key personnel, but may include others such as an art director, director of cinematography and musical director.

Promotions

Special concessionary deals might be offered to sectors of the public believed most likely to be interested in the film being promoted; competitions connected to the film might be set up in magazines or newspapers, or on food packaging likely to be picked up by the target audience; and merchandise related to the film in some way might be given away or offered at special rates. In each case the effort will be to raise awareness of the forthcoming film amongst potential consumers within the profiled target audience.

1   Without researching the ways in which this film was actually marketed, choose a newly released film and decide what you would see as being the likely target audience for this film. Describe what you would see as the profile of this audience.
2   What concessionary deals might appeal to this audience in relation to this film?
3   What competitions might help to promote this film to this target audience?
4   How would you use merchandising to promote this film, again with your chosen target audience in mind?
5   Discuss your ideas with others, putting forward your ideas and explaining the reasoning behind each idea.

Exhibition

Cinema exhibition has always tended to be controlled by a relatively small number of companies. And often the major studios responsible for making films will have considerable stakes in some of these companies that are responsible for showing their products. If small independent exhibitors want to screen less well-known films, they need to know their local film-going market well, since they will be working without the back-up of the major marketing campaigns that accompany big studio productions.

But as was previously suggested, exhibition no longer refers simply to showing films in the cinema. We can now see films on terrestrial TV, satellite and cable TV (including specialist pay-to-view channels), on video or DVD using high quality home cinema set-ups, and now via the Internet and even mobile phones.

ACTIVITY

1   Research the ways in which the Internet is now used in relation to film.
2   Find as many different sites as possible. These may be critical magazines, fan-based sites, industry-organized sites or educational sites.
3   Allocate one website per person to be explored in some depth.
4   Each person should prepare a short one-page A4 handout on their website for everyone else describing the main features and in particular setting out what its role and purpose within the film process might be said to be.

ACTIVITY

1   How many films are to be shown on terrestrial TV next week? How many hours of terrestrial TV scheduling do these films take up? How much does the terrestrial TV licence cost?
2   How many specialist film channels are available on satellite and cable TV? How many hours per day are films shown on these channels? How much does it cost to subscribe to these channels?
3   How many pay-to-view channels are now available to subscribers? How many hours per day are films shown on these channels? How much does it cost to purchase each film on these channels?
    (You will obviously need to use either the *Radio Times* or some other magazine showing programme schedules to complete this exercise. And you might like to work in groups to complete the task more efficiently.)

FILM PRODUCTION, DISTRIBUTION AND EXHIBITION

Take any two films of your choice and try to trace their development through from their initial inception as embryonic ideas to their box-office success (or failure). Use the

Internet to help you with your research, but be pragmatic about your choice of films; look to see how much information seems to be available before you make your final choice. The only limitation on your choice is that one film must be from Hollywood and the other must be British. For each film you might try to answer the following questions but do not treat these as anything more than guidelines. You will not be able to find the answer to each of these questions and you might well have ideas of your own for additional relevant information to include under each phase of the industrial/commercial process.

1   What happened during pre-production?

- Whose idea was the film? Did the idea start with the writer, or were writers brought in to develop a preconceived idea?
- Where did the idea come from? Was it an original idea, or was it perhaps a book first, or TV series, or comic strip, or from some other source?
- Who wrote the original script? Did other people become involved in the writing as the project progressed?
- How easy was it to arrange the financial backing to make the film? Who were the financial backers?
- How well known was the production company? What was its track record?
- Who was the producer? How did he or she become involved?
- Who was the director? How did he or she become involved?

2   What happened during the production phase?

- Was it an easy 'shoot'? If there were difficulties what were they? Were there tensions between any of the key creative personnel, often known as 'the talent'?
- Was any part of the film shot on location? If so, where?
- Was any part shot in a studio? If so, which studio, where?
- Were there any difficulties with casting, or with acquiring the stars/actors the producer wanted?
- Was it shot within budget? Was it ever in danger of going over budget? What was that budget? Can you find a breakdown for the budget?
- Were there any changes to the script during production? How many changes or re-writes? Did the same scriptwriter(s) stay 'on board' all the time, or were some replaced?
- List as many people as possible making contributions to the production.
- If possible highlight some of their individual contributions.

3   What happened during the distribution phase?
- Who were the distributors? How well known was the company? What was their track record as distributors?
- How did the filmmakers decide where to release the film and when? What was the eventual release pattern?
- What deals were made for distribution abroad? How easily were these deals secured?
- Did they at any stage change their plans for the release pattern, and if so why?

- What was the marketing and advertising strategy for the film? Was there a première, and if so where?
- What outlets were used for advertising? Was TV used, for example?
- Were there any merchandising tie-ins?
- Was any additional publicity gained, and if so, how?

4   What happened during the exhibition phase?

- When was the film first released; also where and on how many screens?
- Was there a particular strategy attached to increasing the number of prints available?
- Were there any difficulties with the censors? How did the censors classify the film?
- Were there any other special restrictions placed on the exhibition of the film?
- What was the reaction of the critics to the film? Was it considered a critical success? Has it been re-assessed since then?
- Did the film create any particular media debate, or create news headlines?
- How much money did the film take in its first year? Was it considered a commercial/financial success?
- Did it have 'legs', that is did it continue to run in the cinema for some time?

To make the point once more, there may well be questions here to which you cannot find the answer for your chosen film and there may be important points you would like to include that are not covered in the questions as set out. Remember all of this is only here to offer guidelines and possibilities; it is for you to work on tracing the development of your own chosen product from concept to the screen.

OVERVIEW

The production of film followed by the distribution of film and then the exhibition of film is then the general process, but of course there have been and continue to be changes over the years since cinema began at the end of the nineteenth century and there have been and continue to be differences between the systems adopted from one country to another. Hollywood's greatest period of fame and cultural importance was arguably during the 1930s and 1940s in that period we have called the studio system but has also been known as 'the Golden Age of Hollywood' or 'Classical Hollywood' and is now sometimes known simply as 'Old Hollywood'. But even in this one American site of industrial-style film development there were differences before and after this period and even changes during this period (including differences in approach from one studio to another). In all likelihood you will have noticed during your research considerable differences between the processes bringing your two chosen films to the screen. These differences may have been a product of the different strategies of different studios, the different cultural backgrounds of Hollywood and Britain, and perhaps most obviously as a result of differences in budget.

1   To what extent are Hollywood films simply 'products' made to make a profit?

2   How important is marketing in influencing people to watch Hollywood films both at the cinema and on DVD?

3   How are posters and poster-style advertisements in newspapers and magazines used to create audiences for films?

CONCLUSION

In order to study film it is important:

■   to maintain a thoughtful and perceptive awareness of the fact that films exist as part of a film industry;
■   to realize that there is a complex commercial process to be gone through before a film reaches the screen;
■   to see films on one level at least as being sold to consumers and knowingly bought by those consumers as commercial products.

FURTHER READING

Abrams, N., Bell, I. and Udris, J. (2001) *Studying Film*, London: Arnold (Chapter 2).

Corrigan, T. and White, P. (2004) *The Film Experience: An Introduction*, Boston: Bedford/ St Martin's (Chapter 1).

Gomery D. (1988) 'Hollywood as industry' in Hill, J. and P. Church Gibson (eds) *The Oxford Guide to Film Studies*, Oxford and New York: Oxford University Press.

Kawin, B.F. (1992) *How Movies Work*, Los Angeles and London: University of California Press (Part 3).

Kochberg, S. (2003) 'Cinema as institution' in Nelmes, J. (ed.) *An Introduction to Film Studies*, London: Routledge.

Lacey, N. (2005) *Introduction to Film*, Basingstoke: Palgrave Macmillan (Chapter 3).

Miller, F. (1994) *MGM Posters: The Golden Years*, Atlanta: Turner Publishing.

Nourmand, T. and Marsh, G. (eds) (2005) *Film Posters of the 90s: The Essential Movies of the Decade*, London: Aurum Press.

(There is a range of poster books that are fairly easily available and are similar to the two above.)

USEFUL WEBSITES

www.hollywoodreporter.com

www.filmfestivals.com

www.variety.com

▼ 7 AUDIENCES AS FANS AND CONSUMERS

This chapter will deal with:

- ways in which audiences can be seen to have a role within the filmmaking process as both fans and consumers of films;
- ways in which audiences as both fans and consumers can put pressure on the film industry to produce the products they want to see;
- ways in which the film industry is able to exert pressure to try to create fans and encourage consumption.

NOTEBOX

This chapter will be particularly relevant to FS2 – Producers and Audiences: Hollywood and British Cinema for the WJEC AS level in Film Studies. Obviously this will involve exploration of the roles of both groups mentioned here, producers and audiences, and if you have read and worked on the previous chapter you will already have started to do this. When we consider the role of the producers, or makers of films, it may turn out to be more complex than we anticipate but it does at least seem relatively clear-cut initially in a way that is not perhaps the case when we come to consider the role of audiences. (Considered in conjunction with work on 'Fandom' in the companion to this book, A2 Film Studies: The Essential Introduction, this will also be relevant to the final exam at the end of the full A Level, FS6 – Critical Studies.)

THE EARLY CINEMA EXPERIENCE

As the initially perhaps rather strange nature of film came to be accepted during the early 1900s, so too the practice of going to watch films as a form of entertainment came to be accepted socially and thought of as a normal, everyday experience. But, it is as well to recognize early on in your studies of the film industry that the experience of going to the cinema is, in fact, a socially engineered practice that is to be found only in societies where the culture has embraced not only film technology but also the idea of film as a commercial proposition. In order to make money from films, the early exhibitors of film had to attract the public to a venue where they could be charged for watching the products on offer. In doing so they were beginning to engineer a situation in which the public could be encouraged to become consumers of film products on a regular basis.

The commercial development of the idea of cinema

Early cinemas were primitive affairs – perhaps a former shop that had been cleared and filled with chairs or a fairground tent erected in one town after another. But by as early as the 1910s and 1920s in some places in America, the concept had been developed to the stage where cinemas were such grand places that they were known as 'picture palaces'. These venues to all intents and purposes were like 'palaces' with rich curtains, thick carpets, intricate plasterwork, magnificent entrance halls, expensive chandelier lighting, sweeping flights of stairs and uniformed ushers whose job was to treat patrons with the respect due to their betters. It is often said that multiplex cinemas were such an important innovation for the film industry in Britain in the mid-1980s because they recognized the need to give the public not only a choice of films but also an appealing social experience. Yet the importance of the 'total experience', the recognition that what was being sold was not just the film itself, was appreciated just as strongly by the exhibitors who invested money in building the 'picture palaces' in the early years of cinema. They were part of a large group of entrepreneurial businessmen in the United States who recognized early on the commercial possibilities for film.

The popularity of the cinema experience

Of course, the presence of a large domestic market looking for cheap entertainment helped to make the possibilities clear to the business community. In particular, it has been suggested that with large immigrant communities in the United States lacking a good command of English, silent cinema was an especially appropriate form of entertainment that was always likely to become instantly popular. By 1930, Americans were making 80 million visits a week to cinemas across the country – a figure that equated to 65 per cent of the population going once a week. This percentage dropped off a little during the economic depression of the 1930s but still held steady at around 60 per cent.

In terms of sheer numbers, the cinema was at the height of its popularity immediately after the Second World War, with 90 million visits a week being made to cinemas in America and more than 30 million a week in Britain. Today, despite increases in attendance over the past ten to 15 years, those figures are down to 27 million a week in the US and just over 3 million a week in Britain.

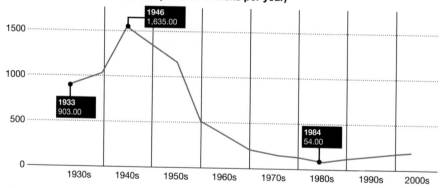

Figure 7.1 *Timeline of cinema attendance*
Source: www.bbc.co.uk

1   Try to find older members of your family or family friends who are willing to be interviewed about their cinema-going experiences. Draw up a series of questions before you sit down to interview them, but do not feel restricted to these areas if you find the discussion developing in unexpected but interesting directions. Think carefully about ways that might ensure you obtain a useful interview: can you find a time and place where both you and the person you are interviewing will feel comfortable and relaxed, for example. Interviewing parents and grandparents (or people of equivalent ages) would be particularly useful because setting their views alongside your own would give you some insight into the experience of three generations.

2   Obvious questions would include:

■   where and when they first went to the cinema;
■   how regularly they went to the cinema when they were in their teens and early 20s;
■   which films they particularly remember seeing and why;
■   how popular cinema-going seemed to be amongst their friends during this period;
■   why they think people went to the cinema at that time;
■   what cinemas were like then and how they would compare to today's cinemas.

3   Try to put the ideas and perspectives you obtain from the interviews into the form of a comparative table showing how the different people you interviewed have responded to the same sort of questions.

4 Discuss the responses you have obtained with other people who have undertaken the same exercise. Bring your final table of responses with you in order to help you to look for similarities and differences between the results of your interviews and those conducted by other people.

The nature of the cinema experience

And yet, at the same time, in a way how strange is the idea of going to the cinema? We choose to venture into a dimly lit, soon-to-be-darkened auditorium with a group of strangers and sit before a large screen in order to share with these people we have never met a lightshow display of 'magically' created images of the real world or maybe of distinctly unreal imaginary worlds.

On the other hand, maybe this is not so strange; the gathering together of communities to listen to specialist members of the group given the job of telling stories has always, it would seem, been a feature of human society. In the years prior to film projection, magic lantern shows (which involved storytelling and the projection of images on to a screen) would be taken from town to town. And audiences were used to gathering to watch live performances on stage in these years whether it was 'high brow' plays in up-market theatres or 'low brow' vaudeville acts (comedians, singers, dancers, acrobats and the like) in music halls.

ACTIVITY

- Why should communities always have gathered together in this way? What do the individuals concerned gain from the experience? What does the society or community gain from allowing the activity to take place?
- Why have storytelling and performance always seemed to be important during such gatherings? What do audiences gain from listening to stories and from watching performance?
- Discuss your answers to these questions with others, if possible.

ACTIVITY

- Think about your own cinema-going patterns. Do you ever go on your own? Do you tend to go with the same people to the same sorts of films? How does the experience differ depending on whether you are on your own or with particular friends? How do you decide what you are going to go to see and who you are going to go with? Do you simply go to watch the film at a set time or do you combine this with some other activity (or activities) such as shopping or eating out?

ACTIVITY

CHANGING PATTERNS OF CONSUMPTION

All of the above, of course, neglects to take account of one factor of which you will be well aware from your own experience: films are no longer solely or even mainly consumed in the cinema. Young people in particular increasingly watch films on small screens using various models of DVD player.

This trend towards home consumption really began in the 1960s when studios began to realize they could use television to show films long after they had passed their sell-by-date for cinema exhibition. By the following decade home video systems began to be cheap enough and lightweight enough to be marketable on a commercial scale and rental outlets began to supply feature films to this expanding market. By the late 1980s satellite technology was beginning to be used to broadcast to domestic receivers, and specialist film channels began to offer feature films some time in advance of their video release. What we are now witnessing in the High Street is the rapid disappearance of videos as they are pushed from the shelves by a deluge of DVDs. These are easier and cheaper for distribution companies to produce than videos and therefore provide good profit margins, but they are also easier and cheaper for the public to copy. Hence, there are growing concerns in the industry about the illegal copying of DVDs.

ACTIVITY

- how often they go to the cinema;
- how often they watch films on terrestrial TV;
- how often they watch films on satellite or cable channels;
- how often this is a pay-to-view channel;
- how often they watch films on DVDs;
- where they do this and on what types of DVD player.

2 If possible, display the resulting information in the form of a graph, one which will help anyone coming to the material for the first time. (In the exam covering this part of the course you might have to interpret information set out in graphs and/or tables, and you are certainly likely to come across information laid out in this form in textbooks or articles relating to film consumption.)

THE ROLE OF THE AUDIENCE IN THE FILMMAKING PROCESS

So, in general terms what exactly is the role of film audiences within the film industry? At its simplest, the role of producers is obviously to create product, in this case films, and following this line of thought the role of the audience is to turn up and watch the films; but more importantly from an industry perspective the audience has to be prepared to pay money for the product on offer. In order for this to happen the audience clearly has to see the product as being worth the price being asked. If they are unsure of this and marketing is unable to convince them, then the whole business of filmmaking on a commercial scale is no longer viable.

The power of the audience within the film concept-to-screen process becomes clearer if we bear in mind from the start that the industry could churn out as many films as they wished but unless the punters materialize in the cinema the products on offer will never come to represent a commercial proposition. Hollywood spends millions of dollars trying to persuade audiences to queue up at the box office and no multinational corporation is going to do that unless it feels the returns are likely to make that marketing outlay a sound investment. Clearly audiences coming to a film in their droves or staying away in equal numbers can either make or break a film as a commercial proposition.

ACTIVITY

1 Draw a diagram to show the relationship between audiences and the film industry. It can take any form you choose but you should aim to include as many factors as possible that contribute to the relationship. You might choose to put the film as product at the centre of the diagram and then try

continued

to show how producers and audiences relate to this central focus as well as to each other. Above all you should be looking to show how the producers can work to attempt to influence audiences to buy their product (see the previous chapter) and how audiences can exert pressure on producers to come up with the sorts of products they wish to see available. (Amongst your ideas here you might like to consider how the Internet has altered the possibilities for audiences.)

2   If possible, show your diagram to other people and in turn consider their efforts to complete the same task. Note similarities and differences in the diagrammatic forms chosen but above all look for points of agreement and disagreement over the strategies employed by both groups. (Using diagrams is often a good way to think your way through (or think your way towards understanding) these sorts of complex relationships. Incidentally, they can also be useful as a revision tool since diagrammatic/pictorial representations can often be more easily recalled than simple lists of ideas.)

The pleasures of cinema

There is also a very real sense in which those of us studying film need to enjoy the experience of the cinema ourselves, or we will never be able to understand its power and position in our culture. The primary effect of a film on an audience has to be recognized as being that it 'pleasures' the members of that audience in some way so that they are enticed to spend time watching it (and the primary prerequisite for being a Film Studies student is that we find that films give us pleasure). However, there is also a very real sense in which if we are unable to detach ourselves and analyse what is happening to ourselves and others as we watch, that is how particular effects are being made on the audience, then we are in danger of being controlled (and perhaps even manipulated in dangerous ways) by what is undeniably a pleasurable experience.

KEY TERM

VIEWING PLEASURE There is the simple human pleasure of looking, or scopophilia (seen by Freud as one of the infantile sexual drives) and voyeurism, the act of watching others without their knowledge, both of which have been explored in film theory in relation to the act of watching films in a darkened room. But there are also pleasures derived from aspects of the film viewing experience such as being able to solve mysteries, to follow a causal chain of events, to identify with strong characters, to recognize narrative patterns or genre features seen before, to be surprised or even shocked by images or portrayed events, to be able to experience fear in safety and so on.

1   In groups undertake a survey of up to 20 people trying to find out what it is they find pleasurable about films. First of all you need to compile a list of questions for the survey. The first might most usefully be: do you find films pleasurable? From here you can then ask a further series of questions to attempt to pinpoint what it is that is found to be pleasurable. You will need to decide (and agree) on these questions as a group. It might be useful to have a final more open question that allows the respondent to put forward any of their own ideas for what is pleasurable in films that have not been covered in your questionnaire.

2   When you have completed the survey analyse your results and present your findings briefly to the rest of the class accompanied by an A4 sheet summarizing your key points.

3   As a class try to compile an agreed rank order list showing those aspects of film that are found to be the most pleasurable.

1   Why do you watch the type of films you do? Is it that you like particular genres or types of storytelling? Is it that you follow the work of a particular star or director? Do you choose to watch different films at different times for different reasons, sometimes wanting material that is going to make you think and at other times wanting relaxing entertainment for example?

2   Do you ever watch anything other than fictional narrative film? Why do you think more documentaries seem to have been made for the cinema in recent years than used to be the case?

3   If you have seen the film, what did you think of the use of animation in *Kill Bill, Part 1* (Tarantino, 2003)? Did you enjoy it? Was it successful, in your view? What other films have you seen that use animation in a similar way?

4   While you are thinking about Tarantino, if you have seen it what did you make of *From Dusk Till Dawn* (Rodriguez, 1995) in which he played the role of the psychotic desperado Richard Gecko? In particular how did you react at the moment of this film's transformation into a vampire movie? List any other films you have seen that use different genres or combine genres in this way or in similar ways.

5   Discuss the ideas you have come up with on these points with others if possible, taking especially careful note of where their ideas might differ from yours.

Box-office takings and breaking even

When evaluating the relationship between audiences and the industry it does have to be said that in the long run there are so many money-spinning possibilities attached to a big budget Hollywood product along with such levels of marketing expertise and funding that even a box office flop, say *Waterworld* (Costner, 1995), is likely to eventually turn in a profit however slender. There will be box-office takings from around the world; distribution rights can be sold in countries around the world; satellite, cable and terrestrial TV channels around the world will all pay to show the film at some stage; and the DVD will go on selling and being re-packaged and re-sold at appropriate moments. So, *Waterworld* that cost a reported $175 million to make took only $88 million at the US box office and was heralded as an expensive flop and yet managed to make a further $166 million abroad. Box office takings are clearly important and the relative success or failure of a big budget Hollywood film in terms of profits will become clear over the first weekend of a film's release. But there are a series of further commercial possibilities beyond immediate box-office takings that attach to any major film and enable studios to recoup their outlay.

ACTIVITY ...

1   Research the takings made by any recent film that has been considered to be a relative box-office flop. Try to find out the costs of production and marketing and then weigh these against money taken. Draw up a list of possible further revenue sources that are either still in the future for this film or about which you have been unable to find any data.
2   Present your information in brief (no more than half a side of A4 paper). Exchange copies of your findings with other people if possible.

Facts in focus

■   *Shrek 2* was the biggest film of the year, earning over £48 million.

■   Three UK films made it into the top ten – *Harry Potter and the Prisoner of Azkaban*, *Bridget Jones: The Edge of Reason* and *Troy*.

■   The USA was involved in every production in the top 20 films at the UK box office, partnering the UK on three films.

■   The top 20 UK films grossed £176.3 million at the UK box office, over 20% of the total, a 45% increase on the last year's figure.

Figure 7.2 *Facts in focus*
Source: Chapter 2 of the UK Film Council Statistical Yearbook, 2004. Reproduced with permission of the UK Film Council

Films as entertainment for audiences

Of course, unless the creative personnel involved in making a film ('the talent' as they are referred to within the industry) are prepared to simply make the films they like for their own satisfaction and with no view to showing their efforts they must always have some sense of audience in mind during the production process. If the director, the actors, the cinematographer and others want people to see their efforts, they must create something that is in some way a commercial product; the bottom line is that it has to sell. Their perspective may be somewhat different from the pure business perspective on audiences found amongst studio executives which is solely focused upon whether people can be persuaded to pay money to watch a particular film, but it at least has to take account of this perspective.

As a form of entertainment competing with all the other forms of entertainment on offer, film must inevitably pay attention to its intended audience. The whole notion of entertainment implies an awareness of an audience that is to be entertained. The film industry does all it can to provide audiences with the stories they like framed within the genres they like. The producers of film make every effort to provide audiences with intrigue, spectacle, tension, suspense, surprise, shock, gratification and pleasure. Test screenings before an invited audience from the general public can even result in scenes being re-shot or endings to films being changed. Cinema chains invest huge sums in providing high quality exhibition facilities for audiences in order to accommodate further the desires of the audience. As a business, film must take careful account of the paying public since these are the people who will either agree to consume the product on offer or not. All of this, of course, suggests once again that audiences are powerful players within the filmmaking process.

ACTIVITY

1   Find the official websites of any two major Hollywood studios and analyse and compare the layout of the sites. You should aim to explain how you see each element of the two sites as operating in relation to potential audiences. How do the visual images chosen, the written words and the sounds used work to grab the attention of the visitor to the site and perhaps attempt to turn her into a consumer?
2   Write 600 words comparing and contrasting the two sites. Explain ways in which they use similar techniques and any ways in which the two sites seem to take different approaches.

Films as dangerous influences on audiences

An alternative view of audiences has often seen them as weak-willed, and easily manipulated or even corrupted by films. All types of mass media from dangerous new musical forms to children's television have been seen as having the power to bring about anti-social behaviour, especially amongst the working class and the young. As a result it has always been deemed necessary to try to control the content of films (and the media in general) in order to control the potential audience response.

As early as 1922 an industry-based organization, the Motion Picture Producers and Distributors of America (re-named the Motion Picture Association of America in 1945), was set up by the Hollywood studios in effect to agree a level of self-censorship that would obviate the need for any government interference. Most famously under Will Hays during the 1930s, when it became known as the Hays Office and adopted the Hays Code, this organization imposed strict censorship particularly over sexual morality. The code stipulated the maximum length of on-screen kisses, for example, and limited bed-scene possibilities by saying at least one partner had to have at least one foot on the floor at all times.

Moral campaigners (at the time of the Hays Code it was the Catholic Legion of Decency) have repeatedly seen the media as being run by those who wish to challenge traditional morality. Some theorists have used psychological explanations to suggest there is a direct cause and effect relationship between violence on film (or in the media generally) and acts of violence in society; watching too much violence makes people violent goes this line of argument.

ACTIVITY

1   Find a film from the past (pre-2000) that has been opposed by groups and/ or individuals on the basis that it was likely to have some adverse effect on society (and perhaps in particular the young). For example, if you were interested in the early 1970s, films you could use would include A Clockwork Orange (Kubrick, 1971), Straw Dogs (Peckinpah, 1971) and The Exorcist (Friedkin, 1973). However, you have the whole history of film from which to choose, so try not to feel limited to a particular period: one of the recurring features of films is the way in which they constantly address taboo subjects (perhaps indeed this is some part of the role of storytelling within any society during any historical period).

2   Research your chosen film and if possible make a short (3–5 minute) presentation to others showing your findings. Try to use handouts and visual aids to show your audience exactly what was being said about this film at the time of its release. You might like to undertake this exercise in pairs or small groups.

Moral panics

At frequent intervals every society seems to become worried that some group within the community (often it seems, the young) is being corrupted in some way by some arm of the media. At this stage what have become known as moral panics break out, ironically within the media itself, as those who in some way see themselves as guardians of traditional values feel that social attitudes they believe in are under threat.

Stories proliferate in newspapers and magazines, and on TV and radio, about the latest trend that is offering a threat to society. There was, for example, a panic in the 1980s in Britain around films released on to VHS that came to be known as 'video nasties'. Often these moral panics have focused on the idea of the supposed way in which vulnerable sectors of the public are being either de-sensitized to violence or are losing sexual inhibitions that have long been in place.

ACTIVITY . . .

1   Conduct your own research using newspaper websites to see if you can find any articles on films currently causing controversy (or alternatively films from the recent past that have been viewed as in some way dangerous in their potential effects on audiences).
2   Download an article that deals with one such film at some length and analyse the argument being used. What is the attitude of the article towards the film in question? What are the main points put forward in the article? What evidence is used to support key ideas? Are any 'experts' quoted and if so what is their perspective on the relationship between films and audiences?
3   Do you personally find the line taken by the author to be convincing? Try to outline your main reasons for finding it either convincing or unconvincing.

CENSORSHIP AND CLASSIFICATION

The British Board of Film Classification is a non-governmental body funded by the industry through fees charged to those submitting films, videos and DVDs for classification. The main role of the BBFC, which used to be known as the British Board of Film Censors, is to classify films into a range of categories in order to prevent young people seeing material not thought to be suitable for them. The following categories are used:

U – 'Universal': films suitable for everyone.
PG – 'Parental Guidance': films anyone can see but with a warning that they might contain material thought unsuitable for children.
12A: films containing material suitable for those who are 12 years old or over but only for children under this age who are accompanied by a responsible adult.
15: films containing material suitable only for those who are 15 years old or over.
18: films containing material suitable only for those who are 18 years old or over.

There are a few other categories used alongside the ones above for videos:

Uc – video releases thought particularly suitable for pre-school children.
12 – releases containing material suitable only for those who are 12 years old or over.
R18 – releases that can only be sold in licensed sex shops (or shown in specially licensed cinemas).

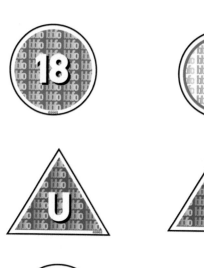

Figure 7.3 *The British Board of Film Classification logos. Trademark and copyright protected*
Source: BBFC. Reproduced with permission

1 Do you think this is a useful classification system? Do you agree with the categories or are there any you think should be changed? In your experience is it effective?

2 Why do we have a classification system? Does it help audiences, and if so in what way? Could it be said to help those involved in making, distributing and exhibiting films, and if so in what way? Does it help those who are selling videos and DVDs?

3 What system of classification is used in the United States? List the categories used there. In what ways is this different from and in what ways similar to the British system?

4 Try to find out what other categories have been used in the past in Britain (and obviously what they meant). Why has the way in which films are classified changed over the years? How many factors can you think of that might contribute to this?

FAN POWER

It is often said that the critical factor for any film is whether or not it manages to obtain good 'word-of-mouth'; essentially whether or not those people who initially go to see the film come out singing its praises and telling their friends to go. But, of course, in addition to good 'word-of-mouth' a film can also receive bad 'word-of-mouth' and probably even worse is indifferent 'word-of-mouth'; at least bad 'word-of-mouth' means the film has roused some sort of impassioned response. What is interesting about 'word-of-mouth' is the increasing speed and intensity with which it can now be delivered by fans. Websites, e-mail, mobile phones and text messaging now mean that verdicts on any new release can be communicated instantly and with increased potency.

Furthermore with new technologies at their disposal fans are much more able to interact and maintain an ongoing fan base for particular types of film product whether that is with a genre, director, or star focus or taking some other perspective as a starting point. Fan clubs and conventions have traditionally been maintained via newsletters and paper-based fanzines, but now e-mail newsletters and website fanzines magnify and intensify the possibilities. Fans have always been able to create slow-burning cult classics out of films that have initially flopped at the box office but perhaps there is now greater opportunity for this sort of activity.

ACTIVITY

Use an Internet search to locate two or three fanzine-style websites dedicated to different films, stars or directors. Analyse the language used, the attitude of contributors and the nature of the sites themselves. In particular look to see if there are any recognizable common features to be found in each of your examples.

INDUSTRY POWER

But if fan power is potentially on the increase as a result of new technologies, then as a result of these same new technologies and a movement towards business global-ization the power of the film industry to exert control over the public is also growing. As a result of mergers and takeovers media companies are increasingly coming together in single stables or conglomerates of media interests.

Through working under the same umbrella organization these media companies are able to support each other in a reinforcing symbiotic exchange. A single multinational could have subsidiary companies:

- making, financing and distributing films;
- reviewing films in newspapers, or on TV/radio stations;
- publishing film scripts and distributing film soundtracks;
- screening films via cinema chains or satellite TV.

With this sort of interconnected involvement in the film industry the power of such a global enterprise becomes clear.

Media ownership, it seems, is quite simply becoming increasingly concentrated in a handful of laterally and vertically integrated multimedia conglomerates. And these companies are powerful; you only have to look at the engaging quality of their official websites to see just how they might be able to use their resources to influence the film-going/DVD-buying public.

- In 1989 Time Incorporated purchased Warner Communications to form Time Warner. In 1996 Time Warner merged with Turner Broadcasting forming the world's largest media conglomerate. In 2000 Time Warner merged with America On-Line to form the $350 billion corporation AOL-Time-Warner. This company has interests in cable television, film and television production and distribution, book and magazine publishing, the music industry, and now the Internet. All this is in addition to owning Warner Brothers film studio, New Line Cinema and being one of the largest cinema owners in the world.
- Rupert Murdoch's News Corporation combines film and television production with distribution at Twentieth Century Fox, has invested in lower budget filmmaking at Fox Searchlight and runs Fox network television. It also has worldwide cable and satellite television interests including ownership of BSkyB in Britain and Star TV in the potentially huge Asian market. In addition this conglomerate has book publishing interests and controls a portfolio of newspapers that includes the *Sun* and *The Times* in Britain.
- In 1993 Viacom bought Paramount. This conglomerate is now involved in both film and television production and distribution, owns cable channels like MTV, VH1 and Nickelodeon, controls television stations, has interests in book publishing and runs the Blockbuster video rental chain. In association with another company, Vivendi, they own a chain of cinemas worldwide.

ACTIVITY . . .

1   Use an Internet search engine to find the websites of AOL-Time-Warner, News Corporation, Viacom and/or other big players such as Disney or Sony.
2   Find out as much as you can about the media interests of these organizations paying particular attention to areas that you feel could be related to film (noticing how it has already been suggested above that in fact many areas could be relevant in some way or other).
3   Compile diagrams in your own chosen style to show the inter-related business interests of each of these multinational conglomerates in as much detail as possible.

GLOBALIZATION

These multimedia multinationals would be prime examples of the much discussed move towards 'global capitalism', or globalization. Each of them is able to utilize resources from around the world, most importantly perhaps cheap labour, during the making of media products. So, for instance, you might find that Hollywood films are being made on location in places where union regulations protecting wage levels are not as tight as in some Western countries.

Having made best use of global resources to keep down costs, these multinationals are then able to access global markets when selling the resulting products. So, there is a demand for Hollywood films right around the world that maximizes profit on a global scale rather than simply within North America. The commercial extent and financial power of these corporations enables them to contribute towards setting the agenda for the worldwide development of capitalism. So, if trade discussions are under way between countries, governments will be lobbied by these huge companies to try to make sure the resulting trade deals are advantageous to their future development.

One way of understanding what is happening here would be to suggest that it is the emergence of a whole series of new technologies (satellite TV, the Internet, mobile phones, etc.) that has led to this increasing media globalization and the formation of what has been dubbed 'the global village'. This concept of a 'global village' amounts to the suggestion that as a result of new technologies the world has effectively shrunk to the size of a village; the vast distance between places has in effect disappeared since it now only takes an instant to flash an e-mail from one side of the globe to the other.

> **GLOBALIZATION** A perceived economic trend towards the whole world becoming a single market so that major multinational corporations are increasingly able to control trade on a global scale.
>
> **KEY TERM**

ACTIVITY . . .

1   If possible, discuss the ideas of 'global capitalism' and 'the global village' with a group of other people.
2   Before you begin the discussion jot down your own thoughts on these ideas and try to work out your own personal perspective on each. Do you for example believe that there is definitely a trend towards 'global capitalism' or 'globalization' taking place in the world? Do you think the concept of the 'global village' is a useful way of looking at one aspect of the change that is taking place?

'Windows' and 'synergy'

Two key terms now for this area of Film Studies are 'windows' and 'synergy'. A film can now be viewed not only in the cinema but in a variety of ways, that is, via a series of 'windows'. We can attend the traditional cinema or a multiplex to watch a film; we can rent it on DVD (or maybe video); we can buy it as a DVD (or video); we can view it at home via satellite or cable pay-to-view channels or dedicated film channels, or if we miss these opportunities we can catch it a little later on terrestrial TV. Furthermore, each of these 'windows' needs increasingly to be seen within the context of the global market discussed above rather than simply the domestic market.

KEY TERM

WINDOWS A term used to suggest the variety of places that films can now be viewed.

KEY TERM

SYNERGY The multiplied business energy that is created by multinational multimedia ownership. By owning newspapers, magazines, book publishing and music companies, TV and radio stations, satellite/cable TV companies, alongside their involvement in cinema production, distribution and exhibition these massive corporations might be able to:

- publicize and advertise their films via their own print, sound and visual media arms;
- put out associated books and music, again from within their own organization;
- show their films via their own various TV and cinema outlets.

Increasingly, media corporations are now in effect able to give publicity to, advertise and promote films made by their film production arm via their own newspapers, magazines, radio stations, TV stations, satellite or cable channels, or over the Internet. Increasingly, important financial spin-offs from films are contained 'in-house' as it were: film-related books can be published by a company that is part of the media corporation's stable of companies; TV or satellite rights can be sold to a company within the same group; soundtrack CDs can be put out by another company within the group. In these sorts of ways the business energy of any single company is magnified, even multiplied. Thus 'synergy' is created.

Less than 20 per cent of total film revenue now comes from the domestic box office. So, although a good first weekend is crucial in giving a film that vital initial impetus, there is now a whole array of ways of subsequently recouping the financial outlay involved in making films.

EXAMPLE EXAM QUESTIONS

1   What role does the Internet now play in enabling people to develop their interest in films?

2   In what ways do factors such as who we watch films with and where we watch them influence our viewing experience and our response to film material?

3   How has the experience of watching films changed in recent years and how do you think it might develop in the future?

CONCLUSION

In order to study film it is important:

■   to maintain a thoughtful and perceptive awareness of the fact that the film industry attempts to put the public under considerable pressure to buy their products;
■   to realize that as fans and consumers the public may be able in turn to exert considerable influence over the film industry.

FURTHER READING

Abrams, N., Bell, I. and Udris, J. (2001) *Studying Film*, London: Arnold (Chapter 3).

Corrigan, T. and White, P. (2004) *The Film Experience: An Introduction*, Boston: Bedford/St Martin's (Chapter 1).

Gledhill, C. and Williams L. (eds) (2000) *Reinventing Film Studies*, London: Arnold.

Kochberg S. 'Cinema as institution' (2003) in J. Nelmes (ed.) *An Introduction to Film Studies*, London: Routledge.

Lacey, N. (2005) *Introduction to Film*, Basingstoke: Palgrave Macmillan (Chapter 3).

USEFUL WEBSITES

www.bbfc.co.uk (the British Board of Film Classification)

www.bfi.org.uk

www.disney.co.uk or disney.go.com

www.newscorp.com

www.sony.net

www.timewarner.com

(Websites such as the last four above give a powerful sense of the global reach of such corporations and an immediate visual impression of the range of interlocking media owned by each of them.)

www.cjr.org (up-to-date information on who owns what in the media entertainments industry)

▼ 8 STARS – WHAT ARE THEY AND WHY DO WE HAVE THEM?

This chapter deals with:

■ viewing stars as commodities or products of the film industry;
■ understanding stars as having commercial value;
■ seeing stars as embodying certain social or cultural values and ideological perspectives.

NOTEBOX

This section will be directly relevant to FS2 – Producers and Audiences for the WJEC AS level in Film Studies. (It will also be of relevance to the second year of the A level where you have the possibility of researching the work of a single star leaving his or her distinctive mark on a body of film. In addition, considered in conjunction with the section on performance and movement in Part I of this book and viewed in relation to the option on Performance Studies, this chapter will also be relevant to the final exam at the end of the full A level, FS6 – Critical Studies).

YOUR EXPERIENCE OF STARS

When studying film it is always best to begin by considering carefully your own experience. Therefore, when starting to look at the idea of stars and their role within films and the wider film industry this is the place to open your investigations. Try some initial questions:

■ Who are your favourite stars? Whose latest film do you really look forward to seeing?
■ Why? What is it about their work that you really like? Is it something about the sorts of characters that these people play that really engages your interest? Is it

something to do with the subject matter their films deal with, or the attitudes they put forward through their characters?

■ Have the stars you like most changed over the years? Are there stars whose films you used to be interested in but no longer are? Have you recently taken an interest in the work of stars that never used to interest you? Why have these changes occurred?

STARS: THE CONCEPT

In the early days of Hollywood the studio bosses who ran the film industry were not too keen on the idea of 'stars'. And since you are now so aware of the fact that films are not so much an art form as a business (or at least, as much a business as an art form) you will immediately see why: quite simply, anonymous actors are not able to command large salaries, and it is only when you become famous and have a public waiting to see your next film that you are able to ask for more money to play the part. The first star known to her fans by her name is usually said to have been Florence Lawrence. Before 1910 she was simply known as 'the Biograph Girl' because she was seen in so many of that company's films (in 1909 for instance she performed in 81 short films!) but when she moved to the studio that was to become Universal she was named in the credits for the first time. She made the first ever personal appearance of a film star at St Louis in March 1910 and other studios followed suit with actors and actresses making a variety of media appearances.

The moment you turn actors into stars you implicitly acknowledge that they are a commercial asset to your business and that their presence is capable of attracting more paying punters than might otherwise come to see your film. At this point you potentially have to start paying at least the going rate and maybe an inflated rate to obtain the leading man and/or woman you want for your film. Studios recognized the chance to boost the ratings of their films by creating stars but they were also being driven by the public demand to know the names of these actors they kept seeing (and enjoying) in successive films. This points to the importance of actors in the filmmaking process but also, of course, to the importance (even from the earliest days of cinema) of fans – the passionate consumers of the industry's products.

ACTIVITY

1   Find a poster for a film that uses a star of your choice as its central visual image. Analyse both the visual image itself and the overall layout of the poster in relation to the star.

2   How does the title of the film combined with any words used to describe the film relate to the public perception of the star in question? Does it seem to be the sort of film in which most people would expect to see this star? How does the title and/or other words used reinforce (or contradict) the notions people might have of this particular star?

3   How does the visual image given of the star work to create meaning and generate responses from us? Consider the posture or positioning of the body: is he or she standing, sitting or lying down? Why has this positioning been chosen? What does it suggest? How are other aspects of body language and facial expression, including eyes and mouth, working to create potential meanings? What about costume, hairstyle and any objects placed nearby or being held by the star? Do not forget to consider the camera angle being used, particular colours being employed (or maybe it is in black and white), and lighting. Remember each of these elements of construction will have been carefully chosen. Do they work to reinforce (or again, possibly contradict) certain ideas normally embodied in this star's image?

4   When you are sure about all of these things in your own mind, explain your understanding of the poster and the image of the star that is being conveyed to other people. Ask them if they would agree, or perhaps disagree at certain points, with your analysis and discuss the ideas that come up.

Around 100 years after actors' contributions began to be acknowledged via film credits the industry seems to have taken to the concept of stars with some enthusiasm since the cash paid to them is now often the largest component part of any top Hollywood film's budget. Furthermore, it is not unusual for big name stars to receive the script from the studio even before a director has been appointed to the film project and then to be asked if there is a director with whom he (and it still is predominantly 'he' rather than 'she') would like to work. This suggests that getting the right star name attached to a project is often seen as more important than obtaining the services of a particular director.

NOTEBOX

Tom Cruise was paid a reported $75 million for *Mission Impossible* II (2000), $25 million plus a percentage of the profits for *The Last Samurai* (2003) and a straight 20 per cent of the profits for *War of the Worlds* (2005).

Stars and studios

The relationship between stars and the studios has never been an easy one: studios, aware as always of the financial bottom line, have not been keen to agree to increasing star salaries unless they have been forced to do so in order to protect the market share for their product. On the other hand studios were quick to realize that stars could help to sell their product: Charlie Chaplin, for instance, may have been an artist in front of the camera and a perfectionist as a director behind the camera but to the studio

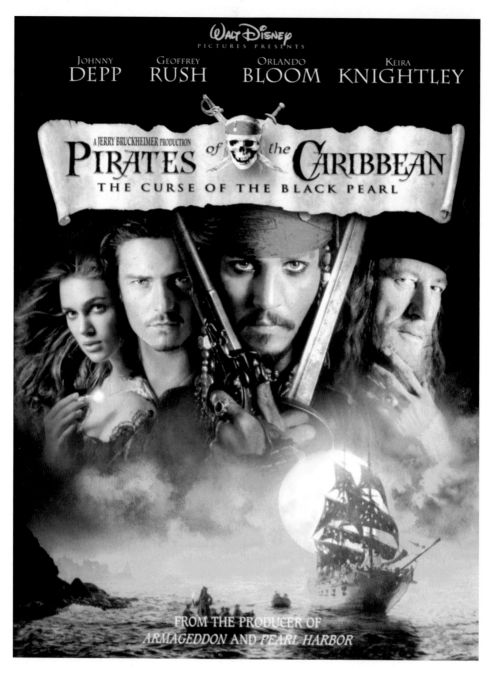

Figure 8.1 Publicity poster for *Pirates of the Caribbean*
Source: Walt Disney / RGA

	Name	Movies	100+	Total Box Office
1	Tom Cruise	30	14	$2,917,132,893
2	Tom Hanks	35	14	$3,106,560,663
3	Eddie Murphy	30	11	$2,916,743,946
4	Harrison Ford	33	11	$3,255,071,666
5	Mel Gibson	35	11	$2,316,662,303
6	Samuel L. Jackson	66	11	$3,813,765,044
7	Jim Carrey	23	10	$2,021,169,088
8	Julia Roberts	31	10	$2,113,978,693
9	Morgan Freeman	41	10	$2,229,310,831
10	Will Smith	16	9	$1,827,463,970
11	John Ratzenberger	21	9	$2,256,208,920
12	Cameron Diaz	23	9	$1,857,922,767
13	James Earl Jones	42	9	$2,852,303,700
14	Robin Williams	45	9	$2,365,747,226
15	Robbie Coltrane	21	8	$1,812,419,083
16	Jim Cummings	27	8	$2,268,304,071
17	Arnold Schwarzenegger	27	8	$1,863,338,881
18	Sven-Ole Thorsen	30	8	$1,668,532,827
19	Dustin Hoffman	31	8	$1,867,154,906
20	Philip Baker Hall	33	8	$1,693,433,950

Figure 8.2 *The top 20 box office stars who have starred in movies that made more than $100 million*
Source: The Numbers www.the-numbers.com. Reproduced with permission

employing him he was first and foremost a guarantee of financial success. There is film of Chaplin, who was from London, returning to the city and being mobbed by literally thousands of people – such was his popularity. And it is that popularity that is the key to the issue of stars because it equates to power, the power to make money by guaranteeing the financial success of commercial films.

In the 1930s and 1940s under the studio system stars were held under the control of the studios by the use of tight contracts: each star had to take the projects offered or risk having their careers sidelined by the big film bosses running the studios. Stars were loaned out from one studio to another for the making of one-off films in exchange deals and their public image was carefully manufactured and then controlled by studio image makers. Some did, of course, try to take more control over their careers: it was, for instance, Chaplin who with two other mega-stars from the period, Mary Pickford and Douglas Fairbanks, and the first Hollywood star director, D.W. Griffiths, moved to create their own production company, United Artists, as early as 1919, in order to distribute their own films and escape studio interference in the creative process.

The power may now have shifted in favour of the stars (and very importantly, their agents) compared with the situation during the studio system but the struggle between studios and stars has always been there as part of the equation of filmmaking. While studios have basically always wanted stars to reproduce the same winning formula that has proved successful in previous films, the stars themselves have often wanted to try to take on the challenge of playing different sorts of parts.

KEY TERM

AGENTS Not only actors but also directors, screenwriters, producers, cinematographers and others involved in commercial filmmaking have agents. The system under which these people would have been kept on full-time contracts to the studios came to an end during the 1950s, and from this point agents became especially important within the industry as they had the power to continually re-negotiate one-off film deals for those on their books.

The role of agents representing top stars is particularly powerful. If as a studio you believe it is the stars who really sell films you will be prepared to pay a large percentage of your budget to secure the services of the star you believe will best embody the image required for your film.

ACTIVITY . . .

1 List your favourite six stars and for each one describe, in no more than two sentences, what it is about them that you like. See if you can find out how much each of them was said to have been paid for their last film. What percentage of the budget for the whole film did this amount to?
2 Exchange your lists with others. See if there are any stars that appear on several people's lists. If so, how are they described? Are the same star qualities attributed to them by everyone in the group who has nominated them? Are these facets of their image the features that make them generally popular with fans?

3   Are there any actors put forward by one person that other people in the group would not describe as stars? If so, why? Discuss what it is that particular actors might lack that means that, in your opinion, they would not qualify as stars.

4   Compile a collective list grouping the stars according to whether they are male or female, black or white? Which group within each of these two splits contains the most names? Discuss why this might be?

(Your most useful starting point for this activity will probably be the Internet Movie Database (www.uk.imbd.com) a superb resource for this area of Film Studies.)

ACTIVITY . . .

1   Working with others, if possible, undertake a little research into the history of black actors in Hollywood. Your starting point will be to discuss how you are going to divide up the workload amongst members of the group.

    a   Who was the first black actor who could really be described as a star in your opinion? What can you find out about him (or her)?

    b   What sorts of roles did black actors have in early American cinema before 1920? What about under the studio system through into the 1950s?

    c   Why did the status of black performers in Hollywood begin to change a little during the 1960s? What is the overall name given to the black political movement of the period in the US and what can you find out about it?

    d   Which actors would you describe as the major black stars in Hollywood today? Can you find any short quotes (no more than two sentences) that seem to you to sum-up their star image?

2   Prepare an illustrated wall display (or perhaps a web page) to display your findings.

Stars as cultural products and media creations

In essence a star is a media-constructed image: Brad Pitt the actor, for example, has become something more than that which he started out in the film industry. He has become a multimedia presence within Western, or perhaps that should be within a now global culture. A star is created from a range of activities: the succession of roles taken up in films is of course critical, but there is also advertising, promotional work and media coverage to be considered as part of the process involved in the construction of a star. A star is not a person but a complex representation: in effect a cultural product. As spectators of his films, we know the performances of Brad Pitt, the actor. As fans we also know Brad Pitt as a star who appears in our newspapers, in our film magazines, on our DVD extras and occasionally on our TV screens. But neither as simple viewers of the films nor as fans do we know Brad Pitt, the human being or the man.

ACTIVITY . . .

1   Take one contemporary Hollywood star and research the roles they have played throughout their career. Is there any sense of continuity between the roles? Do the types of characters played have any similarities? Has the way in which the actor has played these roles involved the use of similar character traits? Are there any particularly significant roles that have created this actor's star image? What would you say is physically distinctive about the way in which this actor is shown in their films? Is there anything distinctive about the delivery of lines, or about the body language employed from film to film?
2   Collect as much information as possible about your chosen star from current newspapers, magazines, fanzines, industry-based websites, fan-based websites and books over a period of a month.
3   Examine your material carefully to see how the media has worked over this period to construct the star's image. What are the key features of the media image of your chosen star? How are words and photographs used in the articles to construct this image? How important to their image as a star are their physical attributes (physique, bodily proportions, facial features, etc.)? How important in the construction of their star image are the attitudes and approaches to life attributed to them? How important are events in their personal life?

Stars as commercial products

So stars rather than being individuals might be seen as 'media constructs' with a specific role to play within the film industry. But if we consider stars to be controlled by big business organizations then we might also see them as commodities being produced to create profits as a result of consumers buying the image they embody. From this perspective it is not Brad Pitt the person that we need to understand if we are to gain insight into the role and place of stars within the film industry but 'Brad Pitt' the constructed media image. In financial terms, a star represents to the studio a certain capital outlay upon which a return is expected.

William Bradley Pitt, the only person to twice be voted the 'sexiest man alive' by *People* magazine in the United States, has spent plenty of time in the media spotlight. One of the stars of *Troy* (2004) and *Ocean's Twelve* (2004), he has been romantically attached to Gwyneth Paltrow, Geena Davis and Juliette Lewis amongst others, as well as having been married to Jennifer Aniston for four years. He was first in *Company* magazine's '100 sexiest men' in 2004, sixth in VH1's '100 Hottest Hotties', fiftieth in *Première* magazine's 'greatest movie stars of all time' and thirty-second in a similar poll in *Empire* magazine. For his first feature film in 1988 he was paid $1,500 a week for a seven week shoot: for *Mr and Mrs Smith* in 2005 he received a reported $20 million.

In keeping with this financial perspective stars are marketed in ways that deliberately emphasize particular facets of their constructed image in order to sell films. At the same time this market image also operates as a labelling mechanism denoting a particular type of star-related product to be found within the range of such brands available. So, if we go into a DVD rental outlet or walk past a cinema and see a certain star's name on a product on the shelf or on a poster outside the cinema door we will know what to expect if we choose to take this film home or go in to watch the movie. In this respect stars can be seen to work as one further means of organizing the film-related marketplace. Bruce Willis on a poster or DVD cover guarantees something different from Brad Pitt who in turn guarantees something different from Tom Cruise or from Jude Law.

Stars and lifestyle choices

This process of using stars to market and sell not only their films but perhaps certain associated life choices has intensified in recent years with the intensification of new technologies and the creation of a multimedia entertainments industry. But essentially the process itself is no different from the way in which film stars of the 1940s (and before) were also used to sell cigarettes, cosmetics or other lifestyle choices through and alongside their films.

- Do stars influence the way in which ordinary people live their lives? Look back at all the material you have collected on stars through work you have done for this chapter so far. How might any of this material suggest stars could be influencing, or attempting to influence, the lives of people watching them or reading about them? What sorts of choices could the images portrayed of these stars encourage people to make about their own lives?
- Consider your own ideas on this carefully before discussing your thoughts with other people.

Today film stars might be said to have to compete with a much wider range of celebrity figures, from television and sport in particular, to gain coverage in the newspapers and magazines devoted to the lives and loves of stars. On the other hand, the proliferation of television channels and the arrival of the Internet means there are now many more spaces waiting to be filled with images, and details about the lives, of stars.

Interestingly, although stars are now said to have more power and influence within the industry than they did in the past, because of their dependence upon the media and the use to which their image is put to sell goods, they could be argued to be just as tied into promoting the capitalist ideology, or worldview, as they have ever been.

IDEOLOGY A person's or a society's set of beliefs and values, or overall way of looking at the world. The Western world in general is said to be built upon a belief in capitalism, or the idea that what is best for society, or what brings the greatest benefits to a society, is for business to be given free rein to operate without restrictions in an open, competitive market.

Stars and the nature of their power

What is being suggested here is that the only 'power' stars have is the power to make money both for themselves and for other people. Out of a range of potentially commercially viable projects they may be able to determine which gets 'green-lit' but they do not have carte blanche to get any film they please with any messages and values they like up and running. Their power, such as it is, depends upon a status that is derived directly from their place within the media entertainments industry; if they lose (or choose to begin to abandon) the Midas touch that has enabled them to become one of the chosen few A-list stars then their options for their next film project immediately diminish. The size and site of the 'soap-box' available to them from which they may occasionally back what they see as 'worthy' causes is a precise reflection of their value as a commercial asset.

ACTIVITY . . .

Do you agree with the above point of view completely, partially or not at all? Discuss your thoughts on this with others, if possible. Try to decide how you see the power of stars. How much power do they have within the film industry and how far does it extend? Do you know of any examples of stars who have been able to exert a serious influence on any of the film projects in which they have been involved?

(This is a difficult issue. You are being asked to think about something you may well not have previously considered. We tend to simply take for granted the nature of the world around us, but the questions being raised here hopefully require you to go beyond this. You are being asked to question the whole basis of the way things are within the Hollywood-dominated film industry.

At this stage, you are not expected to necessarily come up with any final conclusions. You are simply being asked to consider the questions being raised seriously for yourself and to listen carefully and thoughtfully to the responses of others.)

'GREEN-LIT' This is a jargon term used within the film industry for obtaining the 'go-ahead' for a film project to move from being a concept to actually starting production.

ACTIVITY . . .

1 Research the work of two recent stars, such as Sean Penn or Tim Robbins, who have been politically outspoken and radical in their views.
2 List the films they have worked on, outlining for each the storyline and any messages you believe the audience is supposed to take away.
3 How have your chosen stars been presented/ treated by the film industry and the media? What projects or political issues have they been involved in outside filmmaking, and how have these things been presented in the media?
4 For each of them define what you see as being their political stance (200 words).
5 Name two or three films for each in which you believe you can best see their political stance embodied. Try to identify particularly strong scenes as evidence.
6 Show one of your chosen scenes to the class and explain the thinking behind your choice of star and film clip.

Stars as embodying social values

Each star has a specific relationship to film audiences; they are known by audiences for the types of characters they portray and for the attitudes and values their characters seem to embody. (They might also be said to have a further more intense relationship to those individuals within these audiences who choose to become fans.) Within their roles in films each star might be said to carry certain meanings, to endorse or reject certain lifestyle choices.

And, since audiences often consume stars for the meanings they represent in their films (but also in their lives as displayed in the wider media) this can be a powerful way of ensuring the public buys into a certain range of perceptions and outlooks. Essentially what is suggested here is that film, like all other media, has the power to influence the ways in which we live our lives: one of the ways in which we can be brought to understand and see things in certain ways is through the influence of stars.

NOTEBOX

'Audiences often consume stars for the meanings they represent.' Watch out for phrases like this in any text you read: phrases that sound like they should mean something but are initially perhaps quite difficult to understand. Such phrases need to be considered carefully: they may be jargon and as such poor writing; they might be gobbledegook that actually when you analyse it means very little; or they might actually contain a useful idea that you just need to consider a little more in order to fully understand.

Any books you read may contain (indeed, should contain) sentences that demand a little more thought and effort on the part of the reader than usual. The question might be how much time and effort you are prepared to put in.

(Notice how this particular phrase sees the people watching films as essentially 'consuming' something and stars in films as essentially embodying 'meanings'. These are two key ideas for this chapter.)

Gender, race and stardom

Female stars from Marilyn Monroe to Jennifer Aniston are often presented on and off screen in such a way as to re-confirm male ideas of the sexual woman. Sometimes, however, in the roles they play in films they might be seen to threaten or challenge male notions of sexuality and dominance. Men may like to look at women in films (and elsewhere) in certain ways but they might in reality be rather threatened by the sexual power exuded by the very personifications they desire to see.

ACTIVITY

1   Research the work of any contemporary female star. What sorts of roles does she play? Is she strong, powerful and independent, or weak, manipulated and at the mercy of others? What are the main themes and ideas to be found in her films?
2   Define what you see as being her main type of role (200 words).

Where would black stars fit into this pattern? Certainly both female and black actors occupy only a limited number of spots within the A-list of stars. Does this simply reflect a social reality? Or, does it re-confirm (and work to perpetuate) the values of a male-dominated essentially racist society? And, if it does, is this part of the role and function of the star system? Obviously we can consider such issues for ourselves in relation to any stars we care to examine. The key point is that it is important for us not to simply accept such a phenomenon as 'stars and stardom' but rather to question and explore the basis on which it comes into being and continues to be of importance for cinema.

Figure 8.3 *Publicity shot of Gwyneth Paltrow Source: © Theo Kingman_ Idols. Courtesy of www. idols.co.uk*

Stars and ideology

Stars exist within a film industry that is owned and controlled by certain extremely powerful vested interests. As a result is it inevitable that stars have to adopt attitudes and assumptions that support the current status quo? Or can they in some way challenge current attitudes and ways of looking at the world while continuing to be allowed to operate within the industry? Can the process of reinforcing (and/or subverting) attitudes be seen at work both in the filmmaking process and within the resulting films themselves? Is it inevitable given the powerful position within society occupied by the major film studios especially when they form part of some multi-national conglomerate that most films and most stars will reinforce attitudes approved by those studios?

ACTIVITY

- How do you feel about each of these issues?
- Organize a debate in which one side suggests (with the support of examples) that film works to reinforce accepted norms and values and the other side argues (again with the support of examples) that films work to challenge and perhaps undermine existing norms and values.

EXAMPLE EXAM QUESTIONS

1   To what extent are star images controlled by the film industry?

2   To what extent are fans now able to determine the success or failure of individual stars?

3   What are some of the ways in which fans and the film industry work together to create a star's image?

CONCLUSION

In order to study film it is important:

- to maintain a thoughtful and perceptive awareness of the fact that stars can be seen as an integral commercial aspect of the film industry;
- to see stars on one level at least as capable of embodying social and cultural perspectives in their roles and performances.

FURTHER READING

Abrams, N., Bell, I. and Udris, J. (2001) *Studying Film*, London: Arnold (Chapter 11).

Butler, J.G. (1998) 'The star system and Hollywood' in J. Hill and P. Church (eds) *The Oxford Guide to Film Studies*, Oxford and New York: Oxford University Press.

Dyer, R. (1986) *Heavenly Bodies: Film Stars and Society*, London: Macmillan.

Finler, J.W. (2003) *The Hollywood Story*. London and New York: Wallflower.

Gledhill, C. (ed.) (1991) *Stardom: The Industry of Desire*, London and New York: Routledge.

Hayward, S. (2005) *Cinema Studies: The Key Concepts*, London and New York: Routledge.

Lacey, N. (2005) *Introduction to Film*, Basingstoke: Palgrave Macmillan (Chapter 3).

McDonald, P. (1998) 'Reconceptualising stardom' in R. Dyer *Stars*, London: BFI.

Roberts, G. and Wallis, H. (2001) *Introducing Film*, London: Arnold (Chapter 8).

USEFUL WEBSITES

www.entertainmentlink.co.uk

www.film.guardian.co.uk

www.imdb.com

▼ 9 HOLLYWOOD BACK IN THE DAY AND HOLLYWOOD TODAY – OLD HOLLYWOOD AND NEW HOLLYWOOD

This chapter deals with:

■ production under Old Hollywood and New Hollywood;
■ distribution under Old Hollywood and New Hollywood;
■ exhibition under Old Hollywood and New Hollywood;
■ continuity between Old Hollywood and New Hollywood;
■ a wider historical perspective on Hollywood.

NOTEBOX

This chapter will be directly relevant to FS2 – Producers and Audiences for the WJEC AS Level in Film Studies. (Considered in conjunction with work on Fandom and Hollywood and indigenous film production in the A2 book on Film Studies in this series this chapter will also be relevant to the final exam at the end of the full A Level, FS6 – Critical Studies.)

OLD HOLLYWOOD–NEW HOLLYWOOD: A SIMPLIFICATION

As has already been made quite clear, films go through production, distribution and exhibition phases; they have to be made, brought to the attention of the public and then shown. However, the relative importance of each of these three areas for Hollywood has been subject to change over time. Under the studio system a few major companies tried as much as possible to make, distribute and show their own films, thereby effectively exerting direct control over all three stages of the process. But this system, also known as Old Hollywood, began to break up in the 1950s as the film business began to evolve different industrial strategies to try to meet new challenges, particularly those offered by the advent of TV as a competitive medium and the movement of people out of town into newly developed suburbs and away from the old established cinemas. Old Hollywood came to be replaced by New Hollywood with the major studios not so involved in making their own films, but increasingly interested in financing independent productions and then controlling their distribution.

Of course, this is an oversimplification. The studio system of the 1930s, 1940s and early 1950s was never static but was instead constantly changing, or evolving, whether in response to economic factors such as the Depression of the 1930s or external influences such as the Second World War. Within the general industrial framework known as the Studio System individual studios were also attempting different commercial strategies at different times. In the same way, so-called New Hollywood has followed a similar pattern, constantly adjusting to meet new challenges and take advantage of new commercial opportunities over the past 50 years.

NOTEBOX

Beware of 'oversimplification' and the advocacy of any one line of thought in a textbook or any other piece of writing. Be prepared to think for yourself. In doing so you will sometimes be wrong and need to be prepared to admit the fact but this is much preferable to simply accepting anything you are told. Be prepared to try to find out more about any subject area so that you are in a position to judge whether to accept what you have been told, wholly, partially or not at all.

Old Hollywood's unit-producer system

During the early years of the Studio System a few top executives such as Jack Warner and Darryl Zanuck at Warner Brothers would oversee all film production, effectively keeping a tight personal control over everything that was going on in 'their' studio. But in some studios this strong top-down management was later modified into a 'unit-producer system' where a crew worked together under one producer to complete six to eight films a year. These teams of workers, employed directly by the studio, would sometimes specialize in a particular genre: examples often given include Arthur Freed's unit at MGM which specialized in musicals, Val Lawton's horror unit at RKO and Jerry Wald's unit at Warners specializing in noir melodramas. (If you have not yet found time to watch *Mildred Pierce* (Curtiz, 1945) see if you can find time to do so since this will provide you with an excellent example of noir-melodrama.) This was clearly an economically sound way of working since everybody in the team would become a specialist on a particular type of film and therefore able to set up equipment efficiently and effectively. Those responsible for setting up the lighting, for example, could become noir melodrama, musical or horror specialists and as a result able to create the desired genre lighting effects with the minimum of direction, thereby saving time and most importantly money.

1   Research any studio of your choice that was in business during the 1930s and 1940s.
2   Try to sum up in note form the key developments in its evolution during this period using no more than one side of A4 paper.
3   Find other people who have researched other studios and exchange copies of your notes for copies of theirs in order to try to compile a package giving details of several studios from this period.
4   Find a film that you think shows the work of your chosen studio during this period particularly well and, if possible, show an extract to other people studying film. As you do so explain the making of the film identifying important personnel who worked on it and explaining their roles, and also pointing out where, how and when it was filmed.

New Hollywood's package unit system

By contrast, in contemporary Hollywood there is what is known as a 'package-unit' system at work: studio space is rented and personnel hired for the duration of the one project. Individual producers now have to put together a one-off package of finance, personnel, equipment and studio time for each film being made. The studios no longer have to be concerned with keeping busy what was effectively a factory full of workers permanently on their payroll; instead arrangements can be made to film each one-off production wherever is most convenient around the world, perhaps in places where union laws might be less stringent and rates of pay considerably lower. The main Hollywood companies were driven over to this system in an effort to cut expenditure in the 1950s in order to survive in the face of the decline of cinema-going as a leisure activity.

You might like to try to look into the changes in leisure patterns and indeed home lifestyle that evolved in the US after the Second World War. In what ways is it usually suggested that life changed for the majority of Americans at this time? Try to list as many features as possible of the new way of life that emerged post-1945.

ACTORS, DIRECTORS AND AGENTS

Actors and directors have always been key personnel in the industry, but under Old Hollywood structures they were very much subservient to studio producers and executives. They were told to work on one project and then when that was finished they were assigned by their studio bosses to a new project: contracted to the studios they were quite simply at the beck-and-call of those studios. Stars sometimes tried to resist being typecast or undertaking a project that they did not feel was right for them in some other way, but in doing so they risked being sidelined by the studio which effectively had the power to make or break their career.

Nowadays both directors and stars have agents cutting deals for them and they (and their agents) have become relatively much more powerful within the business especially since they are no longer held under exclusive contracts to one particular studio as they were in the past. It could be argued that since the 1970s, agencies have perhaps become the real power brokers in Hollywood controlling stables of stars, directors, screenwriters, cinematographers, producers and other filmmaking personnel and striking deals for clients in return for a percentage of earnings. A possible analogy would be with British football where there has been increasing concern in recent years that agents have become the most powerful behind-the-scenes people in the game: every footballer is signed to an agent and it is the agent who negotiates a player's contract with a club.

PRODUCERS

Finding themselves under the financial pressures outlined above in the 1950s, the studios were prepared to support the emergence of independent producers who offered them greater business flexibility enabling them to pick and choose projects. The studios could back a particular production with these independent producers without any need to bankroll a workforce that stretched from stars to catering staff on a long-term basis. But this change also opened up the possibility of top creative personnel like stars and directors being able to negotiate freelance deals.

Under the Studio System producers exerted overall management control at any one time across a range of film projects that might be at various stages of completion. They would bring together a team of workers to complete each project under the supporting umbrella of the studio. With the end of the Studio System, producers retained their importance with regard to each one-off film project since they remained the lynchpin executive needed to bring together the total package.

The place of cheaper products within a big budget industry

The big players in the industry have of course always been interested in cheap-to-produce films that were likely to offer good percentage profits. In the era of Old Hollywood companies such as Columbia and Universal invested in cheap B-movies (as opposed to expensive A-movies) from early in the 1930s. As the Depression hit America some cinemas began trying to attract hard-up customers by offering two feature films instead of one creating a demand for these cheap supporting films. By the mid-1930s up to half of the output at Warners, Fox and RKO were also taken up with these films.

At the same time about 10 per cent of studio output in the 1930s and 1940s was made up of 'series pictures' such as those made by Warners using the 'Dead End Kids' or MGM's 'Andy Hardy' series starring Mickey Rooney.

NOTEBOX

Incidentally, it is often suggested that the market for films under Old Hollywood was much more homogenized, that is that there was a single market to be catered for rather than a series of smaller market segments with differing demands. But 'series pictures' such as these show that the segmented nature of the market was recognized at the time with teenage audiences in particular, for example, being targeted by the 'Dead End Kids' films.

- See what you can find out about the 'Dead End Kids' series (or another series from the 1930s and 1940s of your own choice). How many films were made in the series? How popular were they?
- If you have the time, try to watch *Angels With Dirty Faces* (Curtiz, 1938) to see how the popular concept of the 'Dead End Kids' could be integrated into a bigger budget film.

In more recent times there may not be B-movies but there are similar products such as made-for-TV movies. At the same time big studios have more recently recognized (especially on the back of the success of films coming out of the Sundance Film Festival for independent American films, perhaps) the potential profitability of low cost films and have as a result set up arms-length low-budget companies such as Fox Searchlight at Twentieth Century Fox.

ACTIVITY . . .

1   What is the Sundance Festival? How long has it been going? What well-known films have first been shown there? How has it changed over the time it has been running?
2   What other film festivals do you know of? Create a list of festivals with an indication of the time of year each takes place. Also where possible try to explain briefly what the key focus is for each festival according to the organizers. Share information with others and try to come up with a class list.
3   Try to agree on a ratings list for the festivals perhaps from 1 to 3 showing whether the festival is 'very important', 'quite important' or 'less important'. What factors make this a difficult exercise?
4   Produce a chart listing the festivals in some way and illustrated as you see fit (perhaps for publication on a college website).

PRODUCTION: AN OVERVIEW

Although the film industry has clearly changed in many ways since the 1930s and 1940s you could argue it is the similarities that are most striking. For example, the teenage market was recognized from quite early on, as was the place within the industry of cheap, quickly made films alongside those demanding larger budgets.

1   Draw up two lists alongside each other, one showing the key features of
     contemporary Hollywood with examples (e.g. star directors such as Spielberg
     and Scorsese) and the other highlighting parallel features of Hollywood
     during the studio system (e.g. star directors such as Ford and Hawks).
2   Get together with other people if possible and compare the lists you have
     managed to compile. Use each other's ideas to add to your own lists.

Similarly, although it is true that the status and power of stars has changed, a further
constant factor within the business has been the way in which stars have always been
used to promote and sell the film product. One of the major types of film on offer during
the Studio System era was the feature film marketed and made as a 'star vehicle' to
show off the qualities that made the particular star attractive to his or her target
audience. In this environment, stars signed to particular studios were seen as a hugely
valuable resource. Nowadays, as we have said, stars receive massive salaries compared
with their counterparts under the Old Hollywood structures but in fact this only reflects
their continued importance in marketing and securing box-office returns: they are being
used by the industry we could argue in very similar ways to the 1930s and 1940s. (On
the other hand, it is true to say that stars are now often additionally important in
securing finance for a project: if as a producer you can get a top star signed up to a
project, the other parts of the package are likely to begin to fall into place.)

One possible approach to any question that asks how Old Hollywood is different
from New Hollywood is for you to recognize the differences between the two
periods but at the same time to work to point out that it could be suggested that
it is actually the similarities that are most striking.

Related to the role of stars there is also of course the way in which the 'star–genre'
formula has been utilized in both Old and New Hollywood. At Warners, during the
Classical Hollywood period for instance, it could be argued that the presence of James
Cagney and Edward G. Robinson meant a cycle of crime dramas and gangster films
were likely to be inevitable products of this studio. The genre approach and linking
of particular stars to particular genres has continued to be used by New Hollywood
since it still seems to continue to work as an effective marketing strategy: in effect the
'star–genre' relationship means a known, tried and tested product is being guaranteed
to the customer. The British actor, Hugh Grant may have succeeded in creating
something of a career for himself in Hollywood but it is on Hollywood's terms. Grant
guarantees the re-production in film after film of a certain 'loveable young man,
requiring mothering', a romantic comedy character that the industry finds particularly
useful in attracting an audience (and therefore profit) for a certain genre of film.

- List your favourite Hollywood film actors and beside each note the genre (or genres) most usually attached to each.
- Make a note of any roles in which this actor has stepped outside his or her normal character portrayal and genre framework.
- Consider whether these films that show the actor outside of his or her normal range were successful or not at the box office. If they were relatively unsuccessful reflect on whether you think the change in expected role for this actor could have had anything to do with the lack of success.
- Because of their increased power within the industry, do contemporary stars have more opportunities to move outside a small potentially typecasting range of parts than the stars of Old Hollywood? If possible, discuss this with a small group of other people studying film.

DISTRIBUTION IN OLD HOLLYWOOD AND NEW HOLLYWOOD

Despite having their production 'factories' located in sunny California (the sun of course meant that you could film outside for longer each day and for more days in a year), during the studio era all the major studios had New York offices that were the site of ultimate power. It was from here that finance, marketing and sales were controlled. The industry during this period was entirely market-driven and commercially motivated: today at this fundamental level nothing is any different. It is still within production, finance and distribution that the major studios hold most power and in many cases we are still talking about the same companies that dominated the 1930s and 1940s: Paramount, Warner Brothers, Columbia, Universal, Disney and Twentieth Century Fox. The control of advertising and promotion networks guarantees a market for the products of these major corporations; and it is the distributor who dictates the terms of any deals agreed with both producers and exhibition outlets.

- Over a period of several weeks collect data on the top ten films in the US and Britain (available in several weekend newspapers and film magazines).
- Note the distributors of each film, taking particular note of which names occur most frequently. But also look to see how much their films are taking because one successful blockbuster could take more than the accumulated total made by several other films with less financial backing.

Remember to be aware of the key strategic position occupied by the distributor. The producers of films can in theory make any films they want and as many films as they wish; however, if they cannot get the films out to the public, that is they cannot distribute them, then their films will never be seen. Exhibitors can in theory show any films they like in their cinemas; however, in practice they can only screen films the distributors are willing to let them have. Therefore, in effect, if you have control over distribution then you have control over the whole film industry.

In the studio era, in addition to A-movies and B-movies, studios also occasionally put out more expensive 'prestige pictures', such as MGM's *The Wizard of Oz* (1939), released in selected first-run cinemas. Today high cost, potentially lucrative 'special attractions' such as Twentieth Century Fox's *Titanic* (Cameron, 1997) might be said to fulfil the same function; but now immediate saturation of the marketplace, flooding the film into as many cinemas as possible from the first weekend, would be the opening strategy. In both eras the films make a statement about the power of the studios involved. Despite the costs involved, it is still calculated in both cases that the film will make money, although it has to be said that Twentieth Century Fox studio boss, Bill Mechanic, is on record as saying *Titanic* was definitely not meant to cost as much as it did with the director, James Cameron, apparently continually going over budget.

The recognition of films as viable commercial propositions

In America a key factor in the film industry's commercial success has been the way in which it has received backing from both the banks and the government. Wall Street bankers became especially important in backing the industry during the Depression of the 1930s while the government basically condoned the control over the industry operated by just a few powerful companies (by 1939 the Big Five controlled about 2,600 cinemas, only about 15 per cent of the total but 80 per cent of the metropolitan first-run cinemas). And although the studios were forced by court intervention to back away from vertical integration in the 1950s this in fact only worked to strengthen their economic position within the changing circumstances of the period. They were able to reduce costs while reinforcing their control over distribution, the most important sector within the film business.

Today the US government continues to show it is fully aware of the worldwide importance of its film industry and negotiates to secure global trade deals that are as favourable as possible to Hollywood. The central international body regulating world trade, the General Agreement on Tariffs and Trade (GATT) which was replaced by the World Trade Organization in 1995, has since shortly after the Second World War worked towards 'the liberalization of world trade'. In practice this has meant opening up as many areas as possible within the global market to products from the rich industrialized countries of the West. In relation to the film industry, the US has consistently argued that other countries should not be able to operate trade policies designed to defend their film industries against American competition. In Europe, France and Italy in particular have tried to limit the market for Hollywood products in their countries. In Britain at any one time more than 90 per cent of screens are showing American films.

1   In groups choose one national newspaper each and for the next week photocopy any articles you can find that are in any way related to the film industry.
2   Spend time comparing the articles you have come up with. How many articles have you managed to find in each paper? Do some papers seem to give more coverage to film-related issues than others? Do they all cover the same issues?
3   Were there any articles in the business sections of papers? Remember, these could be about a parent company or multinational corporation that has involvement in a wide range of media with film production, distribution and/or exhibition only being a one part of their operations. Were there any articles that discussed world trade agreements?
4   Have any members of the group chosen articles that other people would not at first have thought were related to the film industry?

Reading an upmarket newspaper is probably one of the best ways to keep abreast of changes happening in the film industry. (It will also help you to improve your use of language, discovering new ways of structuring sentences and widening your vocabulary.) Start off by simply trying to find a couple of articles a week that seem interesting and perhaps in some way relevant to your studies.

Awareness of the importance of marketing

Marketing might be said to be an increasingly important part of the industry with budgets for this part of the operation in some cases almost matching production costs (although in truth the importance of selling the product often as an escapist fantasy has always been recognized by Hollywood). For the studios, marketing (as covered in the first chapter of this part) essentially involves:

■   securing free publicity in the editorial sections of the media whenever possible;
■   devising eye-catching paid-for advertising;

- obtaining tie-ins with other consumer products that will result in symbiotic promotional pay-offs for both products;
- clinching merchandising deals that will create additional income but also further work to keep film product as a whole in the public eye.

Clear summer, Christmas and spring holiday blockbuster seasons have now emerged; and films are perhaps being reviewed by critics with increased seriousness as art as well as entertainment.

However, as suggested above, do keep in mind that this is nothing new for the industry. Gimmicky publicity stunts, merchandising, and magazines devoted to the stars and their films were also features of the studio system; the pressure to see film as an art form as well as entertainment goes back to the silent era; and gossip-driven interest in the lives, loves and lies of stars has been a constant feature of the media.

Figure 9.1 *Vintage movie magazines*
Source: © IPC+ Syndication

1   Go through the *Radio Times* or a similar magazine showing next week's TV
     schedules and make a note of the film review shows available according
     to channel, day and time.
2   Record as many of these programmes as possible and watch them with a
     group of fellow students if possible.
3   How do the shows compare? Do they review the same films? Do they handle
     their reviews in similar or different ways? Are there features that make each
     show distinctively different? How serious-minded would you say each show
     is aiming to be?
4   Does each show seem to be targeted at a particular audience? Can you find
     out each show's ratings? Which is the most popular? From your viewing why
     would you think this is the case?

Willingness to integrate independents into the system

The major Hollywood studios have always it seems been willing to integrate independent companies into the industry. In a sense in doing so, they have only been
responding to business pressures so that, for example, as the studio system began to
break up they were increasingly willing to use independent companies often almost
as arm's length production units. This attitude could be seen as further evidence of
the sensible business pragmatism displayed by the studios for the most part since the
earliest days.

There were several factors moving the industry towards using independent companies
for film production during the 1940s and 1950s.

■   With cinema attendance rising there was increased demand for top feature films
     during the Second World War and this meant studios were prepared to distribute
     independent films to help meet this demand. Production facilities and financing
     as well as distribution expertise would be provided by the studio for these films.
     An example of this trend would be Frank Capra's *Meet John Doe* (1940) which was
     made with Warners.
■   At the same time an increased number of people within the industry also began
     to work as 'hyphenates' that is they fulfilled two major roles on any single film. This
     accorded them increased status and power within the industry: examples would
     be producer-director Mitchell Leisen and writer-director Preston Sturges at
     Paramount.
■   Also the Screen Actors Guild (recognized by the studios in 1938), the Screen
     Directors Guild (1939) and the Screen Writers Guild (1941) emerged as collective
     organizations prepared to challenge total studio control. In this changing atmos-
     phere top 'talent' such as Howard Hawks, for example, began to work on a freelance
     basis.

In a sense this trend has continued so that independent filmmakers like Spike Lee have established their own production companies. However, it still remains the case that these production companies depend for distribution on the majors: Paramount, Warner Brothers (Time-Warner-AOL), Universal Pictures (Matsushita), Twentieth Century Fox (News Corporation), Disney, and Columbia Pictures (Sony), so that ultimate control of the industry remains with these organizations.

Often successful independents which go on to distribute their own films end up being taken over by one of the big names. New Line, for example, was quite successful in the early 1990s but was taken over by Turner Broadcasting which became part of Time Warner in 1996. Miramax, another successful independent from the period was taken over by Disney in 1994.

Importance of the overseas market

It is also the case that from its inception as an industry the American film business recognized the importance of the overseas market. The domestic market was large enough to sustain the industry independently and yet there was still a willingness to consider in particular possibilities offered by the European market. By the late 1930s Hollywood derived more than 30 per cent of its revenue from overseas markets with 45 per cent of this coming from Britain and a further 30 per cent from continental Europe. Today, although other areas of the world especially Japan have become increasingly important within the US overseas market, the essential fact remains the same in that a huge onus is put on securing global sales with blockbusters regularly grossing more abroad than in the US.

Willingness to adapt to new technologies

When radio in the home posed an alternative to cinema for family entertainment in the late 1920s, the industry quickly adopted sound. When television posed a similar threat in the 1950s the industry quickly adopted colour, widescreen and other new technologies in an effort to beat off the new rival. Clearly TV sets used small screens and were initially only available in black and white so adopting colour and widescreen were obvious ways of marking out the cinema experience as something special.

In its battle against TV, the industry was certainly not entirely successful with the decline in cinema attendance through the 1950s and 1960s mirroring the uptake of TV sets in the home. But it still remains the case that overall the cinema industry has always been responsive to potentially alternative new technologies intruding into their marketplace.

Although initially perceiving new technologies as a threat, the industry, especially in recent years, has been quick to make use of them for their own ends. Hollywood has capitalized on new markets in the home and at the multiplex, utilizing cable and satellite film channels to get TV viewers to pay for films they watch at home. (It is worth stopping to consider carefully the extent of the use the film industry now makes of TV, which was initially seen as such a threat.)

The industry made similar use first of videos and then DVDs. By 1986 video sales surpassed box-office takings in the US, and by the 1990s the rentals and sales market was worth more than $10 billion; and yet seemingly this did not detract from cinema-going with 20 million a week visiting multiplexes in the US by the early 1990s.

The theatrical release is still the key commercial moment for any film in the sense that success or failure here determines the profitability of any deals that are going to be secured for the release of the product into other 'windows': you can obviously charge cable and satellite suppliers, terrestrial television companies and overseas distributors more for the rights to a film that has been a success on its initial release. But the key factor is that there is now an array of further marketing opportunities for any film over and beyond its cinema release.

ACTIVITY . . .

1 The balance between box-office takings and income from DVD rentals and sales can obviously change each year. From research (perhaps on the Internet, where the UK Film Council website would be a good starting point) can you find out the current situation? Can you find out the trend over recent years?

2 How does the number of cinema tickets sold in a year compare to number of DVDs rented and sold?

3 What happens when you include illegal DVD sales? How accurate are 'guesstimates' in this area?

Control of exhibition outlets

Eight companies dominated the 1930s and 1940s: five corporations (Paramount, Loew's (later MGM), Fox Film (later Twentieth Century Fox), Warner Brothers, and Radio-Keith-Orpheum (RKO)) who each ran a studio, undertook marketing and distribution, and owned a chain of cinemas, and three smaller companies (Universal, Columbia, and United Artists) owning no cinemas but co-operating with the 'Big Five' to control the industry. Films went to cinemas owned by the 'Big Five' for first-runs (Paramount owned over 1,000 cinemas during the 1940s) and only then to independent cinemas. These independents often had to accept 'block booking' of a corporation's output and 'blind buying'. This system was known as vertical integration, namely the main studios operated within each of the three main areas within the industry – production, distribution and exhibition.

'BLOCK BOOKING' This means you have to agree to take all of the films produced by a studio in a year including the lesser films in order to get the major productions.

KEY TERM

'BLIND BUYING' This means you have to take the films on offer without having a chance to first view them to see if you want them or not.

VERTICAL INTEGRATION The way in which studios in the 1930s and 1940s integrated the whole process from making to screening films under their control.

Although this oligopoly situation was broken in the 1950s, following a 1948 court ruling against Paramount which found that such extensive control of the industry was illegal, the industry giants seem to have re-established similar if not stronger control today. Despite being forced to divest themselves of cinemas in the 1950s the majors had interests in 14 per cent of US and Canadian screens by the late 1980s with four cinema circuits controlling almost 30 per cent of exhibition outlets in the US and the top 12 cinema circuits controlled 45 per cent of cinemas. Paramount, Universal and Warners have significant UK exhibition interests in that out of about 200 exhibition companies, six (Odeon, Virgin, Warner Village, ABC, UCI and National Amusements/Showcase) take 80 per cent of box-office revenues.

OLIGOPOLY A term used to describe the situation in which a small group of companies exerts powerful, almost exclusive, control over the business being done within any particular industry.

(Please note: this is not the same as a monopoly which is where just one company dominates a whole industry.)

Target audiences

It could be argued that target audiences have changed since the Studio System days with major companies such as AMC (American Multi-Cinema) in the US aiming to locate their multiplexes in 'middle-class areas inhabited by college-educated families'. Perhaps audiences were much more predominantly working class in the 1930s and 1940s.

It could also be argued that the market is now much more strongly divided into segments with a range of screens catering to a range of tastes. And yet, genre and star categorizations of product always meant the Hollywood product was in fact carefully differentiated for specifically targeted market segments. So, perhaps the audience was not really that much more homogeneous in the Classical Hollywood period.

Domination of the major studios over distribution means they effectively continue to control exhibition since no exhibitor is going to jeopardize retaining a major source of income. In addition, of course, the Hollywood product has the advantage of massive financial resources for marketing and production.

Cinemas and multiplexes

The multiplex has perhaps made the cinema experience somewhat different from that of the 1930s and 1940s, although, even then, the effort was often to sell the total experience of the evening out rather than simply the film. Just consider, as suggested earlier, the picture palaces of the 1930s and 1940s. These were huge cavernous spaces, palace-like in their dimensions and in their décor. Compare this with the homes that most of the punters were coming from. Remember also that the clients would be waited on by uniformed ushers and usherettes and then you will realize that the idea of selling 'the whole experience' is nothing new in the cinema business. All of which is not to say that the multiplex has not played a major role in reviving cinema fortunes in the UK: the year before the opening of the first multiplex in Milton Keynes in 1985 attendance was down to 52 million admissions per year, but by 1996 that was up to more than 123 million.

Conclusion: difference or continuity?

The simple fact is that the major studios continue to dominate the film industry with takeovers and mergers within the wider media entertainments industry ('horizontal integration') only serving to further reinforce this control. It could be argued in the 1960s and 1970s there was some loss of control for the major Hollywood studios but it could also be argued that since the mid-1980s the major studios have regained the sort of overall level of control over production, distribution and exhibition that they enjoyed in the 1930s and 1940s.

The major difference is that now the income of these studios is no longer so dependent upon immediate box-office takings. Cinema exhibition is important and initial success here means guaranteed profits in every succeeding sales window associated with the film. However, powerful marketing, global distribution and the ability to sell essentially the same product again and again in a variety of 'windows' around the world means losses can generally be avoided on even the biggest box-office 'flop'.

Exam questions and the historical perspective

When you take the AS-Level exam on the film industry and its workings entitled 'Producers and Audiences' you could well be faced with a question that essentially asks how the US has managed to dominate the global film market for so long. One way of dealing with this would be to adopt a historical approach. This does not mean regurgitating a series of dates: it simply means being aware that the film industry has developed and changed over the course of more than 100 years but more particularly that it has in terms of emphasizing the central importance of returning profits shown great continuity of purpose, flexibly adapting itself to economic and political contingencies as and when necessary.

- The early pioneers in film production were based in Europe with early filmmaking notably going on in Britain, France and Germany. However, you could justifiably argue the early commercial pioneers were found in the US and perhaps particularly in Hollywood. These people introduced quick production systems, distribution outlets, and chains of purpose-built cinemas ('nickelodeons'). Crucially they also had the natural advantage of a large ready-made domestic market being available. And this early economic advantage taken by American entrepreneurs was further reinforced when the First World War devastated the European economy and the US took the opportunity to begin widespread distribution in this new market.
- The Golden Age of Hollywood in the 1930s and 1940s was in many ways built around a continually developing studio system. This was a factory-style system for the production of films that no European country was able to match (apart perhaps from Germany during the 1920s). The 'Big Five' (and the 'Little Three') studios:

    - developed 'vertical integration', controlling production, distribution and exhibition of films;
    - continued mass production throughout the Second World War while Europe was again otherwise occupied;
    - and flooded Europe with their back catalogue of products after the war at the precise moment when cinema audiences were peaking.

- When a court ruling against Paramount in 1948 effectively ended vertical integration, the major studios made a strategic business decision to hold on to the distribution arms of their businesses. What they recognized was that if you controlled distribution you also controlled production and exhibition. In the new economic environment for film caused by the advent of TV, risk was offloaded by using independent production companies for one-off projects. Financial security was safeguarded by takeovers that saw the studios becoming subsidiary companies within umbrella corporations owning a wide-ranging portfolio of quite disparate companies.
- During the 1980s video was belatedly recognized as a co-functioning medium (something that could be used to support and magnify the impact of film) and was integrated into the film business as the studios began to realize that the way forward was to position film as the central focus of a multimedia business. Multinational multimedia corporations eventually came to dominate the industry (e.g. Time-Warner-AOL and News Corporation), effectively re-introducing vertical integration in a magnified form. Smaller supposedly independent filmmakers are now often in fact owned by multinationals, e.g. Miramax (Disney) and New Line (Time-Warner). What the industry utilizes now is a special form of business energy known as synergy.
- The American presence around the world as an imperial power, particularly after the Second World War, has given additional access to global markets (e.g. Germany

and Japan). At the same time American companies have become multinational companies in a process that has gone on alongside the globalization of American-English as a first international business language, further assisting market penetration. Finally the level of financial resources available to these massive corporations also of course crucially means that they are able to absorb greater levels of risk than smaller companies and therefore have inevitably achieved business longevity.

EXAMPLE EXAM QUESTIONS

1   What are some of the differences and/or similarities between Hollywood film production now compared with the 1930s and 1940s?

2   What part has Hollywood had to play in any recent increases in cinema box office takings in Britain?

CONCLUSION

In order to study film it is important:

■   to have some awareness of the historical development of the film industry in Hollywood;
■   to be able to compare Old Hollywood with New Hollywood, that is former processes used in Hollywood with more contemporary processes.

The key to understanding Hollywood as a whole is:

■   to realize that filmmaking in Hollywood has always been seen as a commercial process;
■   to recognize that for every part of the commercial process today there is likely to have been some similar element in the past.

FURTHER READING

Abrams, N., Bell, I. and Udris, J. (2001) *Studying Film*, London: Arnold (Chapters 1 and 4).

Balio, T. (1996) 'Adjusting to the new global economy: Hollywood in the 1990s' in A. Moran *Film Policy*, London: Routledge.

Balio, T. (1998) 'A major presence in all the world's important markets: the globalization of Hollywood in the 1990s' in S. Neale and S. Murray (eds) Contemporary Hollywood Cinema, London: Routledge.

Belton, J. (1996a) 'Technology and innovation' in G. Nowell-Smith (ed.) *The Oxford History of World Cinema*. Oxford and New York: Oxford University Press.

Belton, J. (1996b) 'New technologies' in G. Nowell-Smith (ed.) *The Oxford History of World Cinema*, Oxford and New York: Oxford University Press.

Finler, J.W. (2003) *The Hollywood Story*, London and New York: Wallflower.

Gomery, D. (1996a) 'Transformation of the Hollywood system' in G. Nowell-Smith (ed.) *The Oxford History of World Cinema*, Oxford and New York: Oxford University Press.

Gomery, D. (1996b) 'The new Hollywood' in G. Nowell-Smith (ed.) *The Oxford History of World Cinema*, Oxford and New York: Oxford University Press.

Gomery, D. (1998) 'Hollywood corporate business practice and periodizing contemporary film history' in S. Neale and S. Murray (eds) *Contemporary Hollywood Cinema*, London: Routledge.

King, G. (2005a) *American Independent Cinema*, London and New York: I.B.Tauris (Chapter 1).

King, G. (2005b) *New Hollywood Cinema: An Introduction*, London and New York: I.B. Tauris.

Lacey, N. (2005) *Introduction to Film*, Basingstoke: Palgrave Macmillan (Chapter 3).

Maltby, R. (1998) 'Nobody knows everything: post-classical historiographies and consolidated entertainment' in S. Neale and S. Murray (eds) *Contemporary Hollywood Cinema*, London: Routledge.

Moran, A. (1996) 'Terms for a reader: film, Hollywood, national cinema, cultural identity and film policy' in A. Moran *Film Policy*, London: Routledge.

Parkinson, D. (1995) *History of Film*, London and New York: Thames and Hudson (Chapters 4 and 6).

Schatz, T. (1996) 'Hollywood the triumph of the studio system' in G. Nowell-Smith (ed.) *The Oxford History of World Cinema*, Oxford and New York: Oxford University Press.

Smith, M. (1998) 'Theses on the philosophy of Hollywood history' in S. Neale and S. Murray (eds) *Contemporary Hollywood Cinema*. London: Routledge.

USEFUL WEBSITE

www.ukfilmcouncil.org.uk

▼ 10 IS THE BRITISH FILM INDUSTRY IN ANY WAY DISTINCTIVE AND DIFFERENT? HOW DOES IT COPE WITH HAVING TO SURVIVE IN THE SHADOW OF HOLLYWOOD?

In this chapter we look at:

- what is distinctive and different about the British film industry;
- what the government and the Film Council are doing to support the British film industry;
- what the current state of the industry is in relation to the world market, and what the future looks like for the British film industry.

The British film industry controls a powerful medium that tells British stories, and shapes how the British see themselves, how the world sees them, and how they see the world. It offers reflections on, and explorations of British life (and the lives of other nations from a British perspective), and adds to a sense and construction of a national identity.

British film serves many diverse cultural purposes, engaging British society with issues that impact on their lives and the lives of those with whom they may not have direct contact, but they nevertheless share common ground within that society. It reflects the make up of society, offering representations of self and others, and thus plays an important role in defining social debate, and relationships between groups within society. In reflecting society it has an equally important role in enriching the viewer, by exposing the range of cultural experiences available within their own society. In recent years British film has become confident in expanding its range to include a wider cross-section of ethnic groupings, gender groupings, and cultural groupings and as such is promoting the diversity of regional identities and from this diversity is offering a more representative and inclusive national identity.

Three billion people (approximately half of the world's population) have seen a James Bond film. James Bond is, of course a British brand, with films made by British technicians and artists, starring British actors, shot (more often than not) in British studios, and produced by a British company.

The same British studios, production companies, artists, actors and technicians were behind the worldwide successes of films such as *The Full Monty* (TCF/Redwave 1997, Director: Peter Cattaneo), *Gosford Park* (Entertainment/Capitol/Film Council/Sandcastle 5/Chicagofilms/Medusa 2001, Director: Robert Altman), and *Love Actually* (Universal/Working Title/DNA 2003, Director: Richard Curtis), with millions more enjoying these British films across the surface of the globe.

A DISTINCTIVE AND DIFFERENT CINEMA

In her paper 'Government and the Value of Culture', Tessa Jowell, Minister for Culture and the Arts, made no mention of film as a significant medium of culture, and in doing so indicated that she does not perceive film as being in the same kind of cultural arena as other art forms (theatre for example). Perhaps this is due to British cinema being a victim of its own success, with increasing numbers of indigenous films being produced and cinema-going reaching record levels (or at least levels not seen since the 1940s). UK cinema admissions are currently on an upward trend seeing them increasing on average between 8 per cent and 12 per cent each year for the past four years. With in excess of 180 million tickets sold (a figure that was inconceivable 20 years ago), much of the credit should go to the cinemas themselves as they have inwardly invested significant proportions of their profits to improve the cinema-going experience. If government sees a successful, thriving economy generated by British film then it is likely to be blinded to its artistic and cultural significance, concentrating instead on other cultural arenas that do not see such high audiences, nor levels of economic success.

What the government does not see from admissions figures is that approximately 80 per cent of UK box office comes out of mainstream films distributed by American distributors and that in comparison with other EU countries Britain is exposed to a limited range of films, with American product squeezing out indigenous exhibition.

Other than the product that a British film delivers (in artistic terms of story), which is often centred around British 'themes' and values, the 'little Englander', or the Englishman abroad, and may well be classed as a 'heritage film', it is the structure of the industry here that makes it distinctive and different, and which is both a boon and problem to its success.

In America the film industry has realized (a long time ago) that it is in international distribution where the serious money is to be earned (up to 80 per cent of a film's profit can come through this source), and so they invest heavily in this end of the market.

Retaining the distribution rights to their films also means that these films continue to offer potential profits for many years into the future, thus ensuring a continuity of cash flow. Additional profit can be re-invested in the creation of product, and as such distribution successfully 'pulls' production.

The British market however has evolved from a historic position of being production led, with entrepreneurial producers determinedly 'pushing' their films through to completion and distribution. This distribution is almost invariably through an American company, and in order to complete the film the producer may have agreed a dis-advantageous pre-sale of the distribution rights (cinema, DVD/video, pay per view, satellite TV, terrestrial broadcasting, alternative platforms, etc.), meaning that any money made is not likely to be reinvested in British production, being instead diverted overseas.

The British film industry has been compared to a 'cottage industry' when seen in relation to the industrialized American model, and this, coupled with its inability to deliver a production line of products and in doing so mitigate risk by having a large enough slate of films to ensure failures do not have such a devastating effect, appears as a disincentive to potential investors. Integrated support from the broadcasting industry is deceptive as it appears to play a significant role, yet the BBC spends approxi-mately 1 per cent of its revenue on filmmaking, while the other broadcasters (with the notable exception of Channel 4) spend even less per year.

This cottage industry is also reflected in production where many companies are established to produce just one film, and may well disappear after its completion (whether successful or not) resulting in an industry that is continually reinventing itself, and never establishing the fixed financial structures, systems, and infrastructures that can be utilized and exploited continually into the future. With 95 per cent of production companies in Britain employing fewer than ten people, it is no surprise that they are unable to compete with American, or indeed other, national cinemas. Forty-three domestic British films were produced in Britain in 2003 and 27 in 2004 (there were only two made in 1982 however), whereas by comparison Bollywood's output is approaching 1,000 per year. With limited distribution, these British films did not fare well at the box office either in Britain or internationally, with the most successful production of 2004 in terms of box office receipts being *Shaun of the Dead* (Big Talk/Studio Canal/WT2/Working Title 2004, Director: Edgar Wright), the comedy zombie movie spoof. Worldwide demand for film has exceeded all records, with growing audiences and growing diversity of exhibition platforms to meet that demand. The British film industry however has not been in a position to successfully and vigorously respond to this demand and (since in 1984 it was celebrating its ability to produce 20 features) currently appears to be sinking back to a position it was in over 20 years ago.

This is in clear contrast to the American model where the film industry has diversified to strengthen and develop links with other media and other delivery platforms, and in doing so have created vast media empires, conglomerates that maximize the profit from a single film through owning and controlling the rights to every element in it. Thus even a weak film will eventually come into profit without damaging the parent company.

Figure 10.1 *The Constant Gardener – a British co-production*
Source: Focus Features / The Kobal Collection / Buitendijk, Jaap

However, it did produce such cinematic gems as *Enduring Love* (Film Four/Film Council/Pathé/Free Range/Inside Track/Ridgeway 2004, Director: Roger Michell) and *Bullet Boy* (BBC/Film Council/Shine 2004, Director: Saul Dibb) in the same year, both of which exceeded their box office expectations considerably. Each was connected solidly with contemporary city life and each reflected the landscape and architecture of London as a vibrant, diverse, multicultural melting-pot, updating the stereotype and rewriting London and indeed Britain once more. Both presented a London that was known and real to the British audience, and, as such, this may have prefaced their respective successes.

ACTIVITY

Discussion point

If Britain cannot compete on the world stage, and retiring to a 'cottage industry' style of production is not moving the film industry forward, what approach should British film take? Consider developments in production, distribution, and exhibition.

> What measures could the British government take to ensure 'distinctive and different' is compatible with financially successful?

SURVIVING IN THE SHADOWS

The picture is not all negative however. The amount of international awards that British filmmakers have won (particularly in the last 20 years) is notable and is significantly out of proportion to the size of the British film industry on the world stage. As Alan Parker noted in his 2002 presentation to the UK film industry entitled 'Building a Sustainable UK Film Industry':

> First. We have outstanding creative skills. We've got superb writers, directors and actors – not to mention the creators of hugely valuable intellectual properties like Harry Potter. Richard Curtis, for instance, has written British films which have grossed over a billion dollars at the world box office.

> Second. We have outstanding studios and facilities companies, world-class costumiers, camera companies and digital post-production houses – studios and facilities which have been a magnet for inward investment, principally from the US.

> Third. We still have – just about – the finest technicians and craftspeople anywhere – although their numbers are diminishing at a worrying rate.

> I could also add a fourth: we have the English language – not just the same language of American movies, but that of the Internet.

In fact, in terms of the rest of the world, the British film industry is in good shape and is seen as one of the most dynamic in the world. With the global market for film estimated at $63bn in 2002 – and the American industry taking an 80 per cent share of this global market – the British film industry's took 5 per cent, a figure that may superficially seem low when compared with the 80 per cent American share, but when compared with the rest of the world it means that Britain has 25 per cent of the non-American share, a healthy figure by any standards. Britain is now in fact the world's third largest film market against revenue (after America and Japan).

The British government has been fundamental in creating the conditions for this success, and one particular piece of tax law – the Section 42 tax break (which offers producers about 10 per cent of their budget back in the form of a tax break, and which makes Britain a very attractive place in which to shoot a film) has proved incredibly useful in attracting filmmakers to British shores in the face of stiff competition from Eastern Europe, South Africa, Canada, and New Zealand, and has promoted Britain as a destination that is high on the priority lists of many of the world's filmmakers.

Distribution is changing with the Film Council taking determined measures to develop and support indigenous distribution companies that can compete on the world stage. Distribution is currently controlled by America through a number of powerful distribution companies, who prefer their own and other American product above British releases, creating the situation where British films find it hard to reach their audiences. The American-owned Buena Vista, which distributes Disney and Miramax films, has the largest share of the British distribution market, with another American company UIP following hot on its heels. With players of this size and strength dividing up the market between them it is perhaps surprising that running a reasonably close third is an independent British owned company Entertainment, who have brought a remarkable slate of successful films on to the market and have had considerable commercial success.

The Film Council is also looking at ways of improving the balance in ownership of Britain's cinemas, and is already piloting a number of schemes designed to offer support to the great number of independent cinemas that dot the country. The landscape has changed for the major players also in recent years with cinema chains being acquired by venture capitalists who see them as reliable investments.

The Odeon and UCI chains were bought by a venture capitalist group, Terra Firma, in August 2004, and the Warner Village chain was purchased and re-branded by Vue (another venture capitalist group) in May 2003. The American Blackstone Group bought both Cine UK and the UGC chains at the end of 2004, which means that in terms of British exhibition, the American production conglomerates now own very little. With the advent of digital acquisition, distribution, and exhibition in cinemas, which is being advocated and supported by the Film Council, it is possible that controlling interests in British cinemas could return to British industrial control for the first time in over 50 years.

ACTIVITY

- Look at the strengths outlined by Alan Parker (above). Which do you feel is the most important to maintain? What other strengths would you add to this list?
- The market for exhibition is changing rapidly. Find out who owns your local cinemas. Are they independent or part of a chain? What are the practical differences? List the advantages and disadvantages of each – which one comes off best?
- Visit the Film Council website and look at the papers there on digital futures. In a group, discuss the potential that digital distribution and exhibition offers the British Film Industry. Do you think it will impact on broadcasting? What overall effect do you think it will have on the British film industry?
- How well do you think the British film industry is surviving in the shadow of Hollywood? What can it do to ensure this survival continues?

USEFUL WEBSITES

http://www.filmcouncil.org

http://www.skillset.org/film

▼ 11 NEW TECHNOLOGIES AND THE FILM INDUSTRY

This chapter deals with:

- the historically ongoing and continually developing relationship between film and new technologies;
- ways in which new technologies have affected the consumers' experience of film;
- what opportunities new technologies have offered the producers of films;
- an overview of the relationship between new technologies and the cinema experience.

NOTEBOX...

This chapter will be directly relevant to FS2 – Producers and Audiences for the WJEC's AS Level in Film Studies. (Considered in conjunction with work on 'The dominance of Hollywood' and 'Fandom' in the A2 companion book on Film Studies, this will also be relevant to the final exam at the end of the full A Level, 'FS6 – Critical Studies'.)

ACTIVITY...

- Undertake a survey amongst as many people as possible to investigate their use of modern film-related technologies. Try to bracket your responses into groups according to age and sex. You should put together your own carefully thought out questionnaire but aim to find out the answers to the following sorts of questions:

  - How many have access to satellite or cable TV and how many subscribe to the film channels? How many satellite or cable TV films do they watch in a week? How many pay-to-view films do they watch in a week?

continued

- How many have a DVD player? How extensive is their DVD film collection? How many DVD films do they watch on average in a week?
- How many use the Internet to download films? How many use the Internet to read film reviews or other film-related material?
- How many have digital cameras? How many have or have used a film editing software package?

(Remember to modify these questions and add to them as you see fit: this is an important part of the exercise since it is asking you to think for yourself and that is the key skill above all others that you should be aiming to cultivate.)

- Display the results of your survey using a series of graphs of whatever type you believe best show the information.
- Write a short report (600–800 words) explaining what your survey shows about modern-day usage of film-related technologies.

Facts in focus

- 153 million VHS videos and DVDs were rented, while 234 million VHS videos and DVDs were sold.

- DVD sales increased 35% on 2003.

- The total value of the rental and sales market in 2004 was £3.1 billion, up 9% on 2003.

- The top rental title on VHS and DVD was *Love Actually*. The most popular purchase on VHS was *Finding Nemo*, and on DVD it was *The Lord of the Rings: The Return of the King*.

- 9.48 million DVD players and 3.7 million video cassette recorders were sold in 2004.

- Over 60% of households now own a DVD player compared to only 45% in 2003.

Figure 11.1 Facts in focus
Source: Chapter 10 of the UK Film Council Statistical Yearbook, 2004. Reproduced with permission of the UK Film Council

FILM AND TECHNOLOGY

Behind any discussion regarding exactly how we are going to define the 'film' in Film Studies, there must be the question of technology: without the necessary technology film is impossible to make and impossible to watch, it is a form of expression that is intimately related to technology. Mainstream films are so closely connected to an industrial process that it is perhaps difficult for some people to consider film as a form of artistic expression. Everything we have been investigating in this part of this book would be leading us to see film as a commercial product rather than anything else. Indeed, one of the most interesting aspects of Film Studies is the way in which we are driven to see film texts as both creative works and profit-driven enterprises.

As a student of 'film' at least part of your studies must involve the need to consider in some detail the relationship of the film industry to new and changing technologies. In the process we should remember above all that this is not a new relationship but one that goes back to the early days of cinema. Cinema itself was clearly a stunning new technology in the late 1890s and early 1900s: when the Lumière brothers, for example, set up their first screenings of 'actualities' in a basement in Paris in 1895, people were fascinated by the representations of life in moving images offered by this new technology.

ACTIVITY . . .

- Take a recent Hollywood film that you have on DVD and watch a few scenes you know reasonably well with the TV adjusted to show black and white images.
- How does this change the experience? Does it feel strange? Can you imagine a world with only black and white television, where the only place you could see colour images would be at the cinema? Ask any older people you might know if they can remember this period before 1970 in Britain.

ACTIVITY . . .

- Find a copy of a short silent film from the early period of filmmaking. It will probably come with a musical soundtrack which may well not have been originally written to accompany the film. Turn this down and, if possible, find someone who is a skilled musician (and hopefully is also studying film) to provide a live accompaniment to the film.
- Watch the film in this way with a group of other people. As you are doing so, try to imagine the experience of early cinema audiences. Make sure you find time to discuss the experience afterwards.

The key thing to notice as you undertake research into the relationship between film and new technologies is the way in which these new technologies are rarely adopted immediately they become available. Every new technology involves a (usually large) set-up cost for the industry. Therefore, if the new technology is to be adopted, either sizeable profits have to be seen as virtually guaranteed or the industry has to feel itself to be under such threat from an outside force that adopting the new technology is seen as the only way to maintain cinema's current share of the leisure market. Colour and widescreen technologies, for example, were available well before the 1950s but were not widely adopted until the advent of TV meant that cinema audiences were in steep decline and some additional attraction was seen as needed to woo the public back to the darkened auditorium experience. The first colour film is often said to be *Becky Sharp* (Mamoulien, 1935) but there were colour processes being used as early as the silent period, using labour-intensive hand painting of individual prints for example. However, why would you spend money on expensive colour possibilities if the public was continuing to pay good money to come to a black and white experience and there was no competitive edge to be gained by the change to a new technology?

ACTIVITY . . .

- Watch extracts from *Man With a Movie Camera* (Vertov, 1929) (see FS5 World Cinema – Soviet and German Cinema of the 1920s) and then discuss with others what this film has to say about filmmaking and cinema-going in the early 1900s.
- In this film you will see centre stage being given over to the film camera itself. You will also see the cameraman and the editor at work, and have several glimpses of audiences in a cinema auditorium. The film was made in Russia under very particular circumstances and by filmmakers interested in the avant garde possibilities of the medium but nevertheless it does give some insight into how film technology was viewed and used in the period.

FILM AND CHANGES IN TECHNOLOGY

The film industry has always used new technologies relating to the making and showing of films (although crucially, as already mentioned, this has not always occurred as soon as the technologies have become available). A brief list of crucial technological moments in the history of cinema would include:

- the projection of moving images to create the original silent films in makeshift cinemas in the late 1890s;
- commercially unsuccessful attempts to introduce colour processes and synchronized sound within a few years of the first screenings in the early 1900s;
- the financially successful introduction of sound (the 'talkies') in the late 1920s/early 1930s which led to massive changes in the industry;
- the widespread adoption of colour and widescreen in the 1950s in an effort to combat the competition from television caused by the mass production of TV sets, changing leisure patterns, and the movement of much of the population out to newly built suburbs after the war;
- the gimmicky ultimately unsuccessful efforts to offer the public three-dimensional film in the same period again in an effort to offer the public something different from television;
- the increasing use of television from the 1960s as a medium for showing films with the accompanying realization that in this way old films could effectively be recycled or re-sold;

- the advent of VHS rental and recording from the 1970s opening up the possibility of again re-selling old films but also effectively re-releasing relatively new films to a new 'window' after a period at the cinema;
- the introduction of satellite and cable channels from the 1980s which again offered a further 'window' for both old and relatively recent films (main package channels, premium subscription channels and pay-to-view channels of course effectively further sub-divided this 'window');
- the increased marketing of the 'home cinema concept' from the 1990s so that with technology allowing larger screens and surround sound something approaching an analogous experience becomes possible;
- the limited use of IMAX and other large screen formats from the 1990s which because they would cost the industry so much to introduce on a wide scale have never so far been used to offer anything more than the occasional theme park-style experience;
- the move to DVD technology from the late 1990s which with the use of 'extras' and an enhanced experience encouraged consumers to replace their old video film library with the latest disc format;
- the increased use of the Internet from the late 1990s, for marketing initially but also increasingly for downloading films;
- the advent from around 2000 of digital filmmaking and digital projection facilities in cinemas.

Each of these moments of technological change for the industry is essentially concerned with the viewing experience but it is also true of course that there has been a parallel series of technological changes in the making of films. For example, when sound is successfully integrated into film then the cameras have to become silent in order that their mechanical noises are not picked up and obviously sound technology has to develop quickly in order to enable voices to be picked up clearly; in fact a whole new field of production and creativity opens up. And perhaps we have currently reached a similar turning point because the big question now is what impact new digital possibilities for filmmaking and exhibition are going to have on the industry.

ACTIVITY . . .

- Working with others if possible, research the current development of digital filmmaking and projection. Find out only in very broad terms how the new technology works but make sure you obtain some estimates as to how costs compare with old methods.
- Try to form a clear picture of the advantages of the new digital technology but also an idea of obstacles in the way of introducing full-scale change.

(The key factor to bear in mind is the cost of replacing/discarding old cameras, editing equipment and projection facilities that are currently in use.)

- If possible work with others to try to research the early years of the film industry. Clearly you are expected to focus on Hollywood and Britain, but do not neglect to look at the rest of Europe and do make some effort to find out about film in other countries from around the world. It would be a useful practical approach to allocate various areas of research to different people. Try to find out about the earliest screenings in as many countries as possible.
- If you are working with others, present your information to the whole group giving them a short one-page handout at the end summing up your main points. Try to illustrate your points by showing visuals from books or short film clips, if possible.

New technologies and the consumer

New technologies might be said to offer consumers:

- an improved overall qualitative experience as a result of better sound and/or image reproduction;
- a heightened emotional experience as a result of a stronger sense of empathy with characters who in some sense seem more real;
- enhanced spectacle perhaps through the sheer overpowering size of the screen or the impact on the senses of a surrounding wall of sound;
- improved ease of access, or ease of use, for instance through enabling people to own their own film collections in various formats;
- new, easier and intensified ways of using film to pleasure themselves, for example IMAX would seem to offer an intense 'fairground ride' for the senses;
- an enhanced intellectual experience through the provision of increased knowledge or understanding, for instance through the use of commentaries by directors on DVDs;
- the chance to use new, ever cheaper and more compact devices to make films for themselves.

- Try to add to the above list, if possible by discussing the idea of new technologies and the consumer with others. You might even want to cross ideas off the list given here if you do not agree with them (for example, the second point seems at least worth debating carefully).
- Apply each of these ideas to the various new technologies so far mentioned in this chapter. What will each new technology offer the consumer? You should consider sound, colour, widescreen, surround sound, TV, VHS, satellite and cable, DVD including 'extras', home cinema, the Internet and any other technologies you think are important.

New technologies and the film industry

New technologies offer the industry:

■ the possibility of an improved opportunity to create profits (the costs or required expenditure involved in bringing in the new technology will be carefully balanced against the projected additional income before any new technology is introduced);

■ a way to protect current market share in the face of new potential competitors (in this case the costs will be set against the potential loss of income arising if the new technology is not adopted);

■ the chance to re-package and re-sell old products especially cult and 'classic' movies thereby establishing a new audience base, or even fan base, for an old product (notice that this is even true of an older technological change like the move to sound);

■ an opportunity to place products for sale in new 'windows' thereby lengthening the commercial life of each film (a film can now be sold to consumers via the cinema, satellite and cable TV, DVD, and terrestrial TV);

■ the chance to encourage multiple purchases of essentially the same product (so any one consumer might pay to see a film in the cinema, then later pay to watch the same film on pay-to-view, before later still buying her own copy on DVD);

■ a means of still managing to make a profit or break even on films that initially perform poorly or below expectations at the box office (such products can be re-packaged, re-marketed and re-sold through a succession of 'windows');

■ overall, enhanced production, distribution and exhibition possibilities.

Facts in focus

■ 2,237 films were shown on terrestrial channels in 2004, down 4% on 2003. This is an average of just over six films per day. Of these 509 (23%) were UK films, and 60 (2.7%) were foreign language films.

■ An average of 2.3 million people watched each film on peak time TV (down from 2.8 million in 2003), compared to median audiences for the top 50 films at the cinema of 1.9 million.

■ The top film on terrestrial television was *Shrek* on BBC1, with 9.5 million viewers.

■ Multi-channel television accounted for over 26% of the UK television audience in 2004, up from 24% in 2003.

Figure 11.2 Facts in focus
Source: Chapter 11 of the UK Film Council Statistical Yearbook, 2004. Reproduced with permission of the UK Film Council

- Try to add to the above list, if possible by discussing the idea of new technologies and the film industry with others.
- Then see how many of the ideas from your list can be applied to each of the various new technologies so far mentioned in this chapter. What has each new technology offered the industry? Why has the industry (and essentially we are talking about Hollywood here) decided to introduce each new technology at its particular chosen historical moment? You should consider sound, colour, widescreen, surround sound, terrestrial TV, VHS, satellite and cable TV, DVD, home cinema, the Internet and any other technologies you think are important.
- This may involve considerable research. Try to work in groups with each person taking one area to work on. Then, present your findings to the rest of the group supplying everyone with a one-page handout summarizing your research.

New technologies and the cinema experience

It could be argued that new technologies have always added to, rather than detracted from, the cinema experience. The size and/or quality of the spectacle have been enhanced by each new development adding to the unique nature of the cinematic 'event' (even the advent of TV in a sense only highlights the difference and in particular the spectacle of the cinema experience).

The experience of the cinema itself cannot be easily replicated or replaced but the alternative experiences of pay-TV, or home cinema, have their own attractions particularly in terms of flexibility of viewing. The advent of TV and changed leisure patterns ended the social dominance of the cinema as a source of entertainment and information (remember this was once the only place you could see visual images of news events). The cinema experience has made something of a comeback although attendance is never going to match the heights attained in 1946 in both the US and Britain.

As with studying the content of the films themselves, what we find is that the industry and its technological base always have to be seen within social, economic, political and historical contexts. Towards the end of the Second World War and just after, cinema attendance peaked, as without the presence of TV sets in the home, people sought news images and perhaps some sort of collective, community-enhancing escape. The nature of cinema attendance at this moment was determined by the nature of the historical moment, and this is always the case. Our job is to try to understand how changes and developments within the film industry might be connected to the contexts of the period in which they take place.

- Find out how levels of cinema attendance in the US and Britain have changed from 1940 to today. Try to find a graph showing these changes or plot your own graph from the figures you have obtained.
- Compare your graph to those completed by other people. Hopefully they will be at least roughly similar. If not, discuss any differences. Are there differences in the figures used, if so why? (Or has anyone made a mistake in the plotting!)
- Discuss in as much detail as possible how the various ups and downs, peaks and plateaus of the graph might reflect technological change.

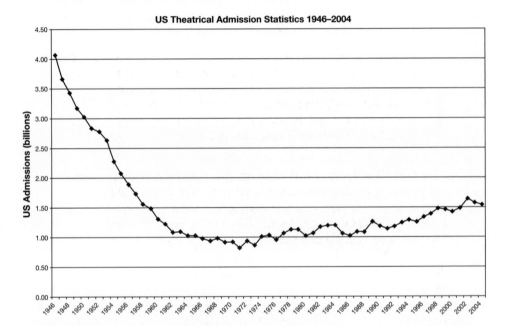

Figure 11.3 *US theatrical admission statistics 1946–2004 Source: Reproduced with permission of Motion Picture Association of America Worldwide Research*

New technologies: an afterthought

We have given some initial consideration to the importance of new technologies to the film industry but we may be able to take those thoughts a little further. Some theoretical approaches that claim to give an insight into understanding society would see the development of new technologies as fundamental in determining the shape of society. Technological determinism not only assumes progress is inevitable but also suggests it is technological development that essentially shapes society.

TECHNOLOGICAL DETERMINISM The assumption that technological progress is inevitable and determines the shape and nature of social change.

Supporters of the Internet suggest that this form of communication marks a new era of democratization and freedom of choice empowering ordinary people to produce and receive information and entertainment from all over the world. Others, such as some Marxist critics, might suggest that this development, by isolating consumers from face-to-face human interaction, enables them to be more tightly controlled and manipulated. Other critics note the increased access to pornography and extreme right-wing propaganda available on the Internet, or point to an increasing gap between information-rich populations and information-poor populations (less than one in a thousand black South Africans, for example, own a phone).

ACTIVITY

- How do you see the Internet? Is it a positive or negative development?
- Draw up a list of ways in which it could be considered to be (a) positive and (b) negative.
- In groups compare your ideas with each other.
- What does all of this have to do with Film Studies? Discuss this in your groups and then as a whole class.

ACTIVITY

Undertake further research if necessary, and then write an essay (1,000–1,500 words) on the continually evolving relationship between the film industry and new technologies. You should aim to consider the introduction of sound, colour and widescreen to cinemas as well as more recent technologies.

CONCLUSION

New technologies:

- have always been of vital importance to the film industry;
- have only ever been adopted when the industry has been sure of their commercial importance.

FURTHER READING

Abrams, N., Bell, I. and Udris, J. (2001) *Studying Film*, London: Arnold (Chapter 5).

Allen, M. (1998) 'From Bwana Devil to Batman Forever: technology in contemporary Hollywood cinema' in S. Neale and Smith, M. (eds) *Contemporary Hollywood Cinema*, London: Routledge.

Lacey, N. (2005) *Introduction to Film*, Basingstoke: Palgrave Macmillan (Chapter 3).

McKernan, B. (2005) *Digital Cinema: The Revolution in Cinematography, Postproduction and Distribution*, New York: McGraw-Hill.

Neale, S. (1998) 'Widescreen composition in the age of television' in S. Neale and M. Smith (eds) *Contemporary Hollywood Cinema*, London: Routledge.

Sergi, G. (1998) 'A cry in the dark: the role of post-classical film sound' in S. Neale and M. Smith (eds) *Contemporary Hollywood Cinema*, London: Routledge.

Webster, C. (2003) 'Film and technology' in J. Nelmes (ed.) *An Introduction to Film Studies*, London: Routledge.

PART 3
MESSAGES AND VALUES –
BRITISH AND IRISH CINEMA
(FS3)

▼ 12 INTRODUCTION: WHAT IS THE RELATIONSHIP BETWEEN FILMS AND THE EVERYDAY WORLD?

In this section we look at:

■ how messages and values are expressed in film;
■ how meaning is made by spectators in response to specific films;
■ how films offer representations of their subjects, and how these representations are interpreted;
■ how filmmakers can 'position' an audience to respond to representations, messages, and values.

Films offer filmmakers the opportunity to express their own messages and values, and reflect the messages and values of the societies they inhabit. Similarly audiences watch films and understand the messages and values on screen through the filter of their own values and beliefs.

KEY TERM

MESSAGES Messages are deliberately placed communications in a film that are intended to be read, or de-coded by an audience, and which should then affect the spectator's individual understanding of the film. A message may be explicitly expressed (perhaps by having a character spell it out) or may be implicitly expressed and in need of interpretation (in *Get Carter* (MGM/Mike Klinger 1971, Director: Mike Hodges) for instance, the women in the film are all victims, and receive summary punishment at the hands of men – is this a 'hidden' message from the director?).

Explicit messages are normally straightforward with little opportunity for misinterpretation. Implicit messages are more complex and their understanding is reliant not only on how they have been 'coded' into the film, but also on the spectator's own experiences and belief system.

VALUES Values are an expression of what an individual or a society considers important, in terms of social behaviour, laws, attitudes, beliefs, etc. Values are of course both changeable and relative to each other and situations where they are applied.

Systems or sets of values can be expressed as an *ideology* (a belief system), which, again, can be an individual ideology or an ideology defined by a society.

It is perfectly possible for an individual to hold their own set of values within a broader set of values belonging to a society. Thus someone could accept the broad values of a democracy whilst being a tyrant in their own home.

Unit FS3 explores the messages and values within British cinema and to do this effective skills need to be developed in:

- being able to identify and understand explicit or implicit messages and values both from a contemporary perspective and by considering how an audience at a particular time would have perceived these messages and values;
- being able to contextualize films in terms of when they were made, in what production context, and for what specific audience(s);
- being able to analyse films critically and extract relevant information, and able to understand that the information is not fixed, but is seen by one person from one perspective: it is vital to develop an understanding that meaning is negotiated from a film by a spectator who brings with them filters and barriers through which information has to first pass;
- being able to reflect critically on a personal response to a film's messages and values, and understand that this response is constructed not only by the film, but also by the experiences, temperament, mood, and inclination of the viewer;
- understanding that there are many 'correct' responses to messages and values in a film, and that these may not be shared between individual viewers;
- understanding that filmmakers will try to position an audience into a narrow range of responses (a 'preferred reading') in order to control the construction of meaning.

These skills take time to develop and develop in people at different rates. It is important to note that there are no 'wrong' responses to messages and values expressed by a film, merely differences of opinion. What is important is the skill of expressing this opinion and of finding the best language to support an argument. Learning from Units FS1 and FS2 can readily be brought in to the study of this unit to aid the development of informed opinions and their expression.

REPRESENTATION Representation is the re-presentation or interpretation of an image, an action, a conversation, etc. As it re-presents the original from the perspective of the person (screenwriter, director, cinematographer, etc.) constructing the representation, it can never accurately capture the original, but will instead offer a partial view, coloured by messages and values.

- Collect together some photographs of yourself. Give them to a friend who has no knowledge of the circumstances in which they were taken, and ask them to look carefully at each photograph, then write down what they understand is happening. At the same time, write down what you recall of the events captured by the photograph.
- Compare notes. How accurate is your friend's view of what is happening in each photo? Have they missed things out that you see as obvious? Have you included information from memory of the actual event that is not possible to extract from the photographic representation of the event?
- Try conducting the same experiment with someone who knows you little. Do they construct the same view of the events in the photos as your friend? If not, why do you think they are different?

Messages and values are represented in a single film, and are built on and challenged or reinforced by the messages and values represented in other films within the same or similar groupings (such as 'Swinging Britain', and 'Passions and repressions'). Aspects of everyday life are represented in film, and may conform to an understanding of how these aspects usually appear, or may challenge this understanding. What is important is that representations are not simply accepted as being the way things are, but are considered either as symptoms of a society's attitudes and values, and/or as deliberate constructs designed to achieve a desired outcome, and positioning the spectator into accepting the messages and values being expressed.

The relationship between films and the everyday world is one in which representations are constructed and messages and values are placed within the film to be extracted, explored, considered, and compared with the representations our own 'real life' experience offers us. It is at this point that meaning is developed, or negotiated from a film, and it is in this context of a meeting point between the real and the unreal that concepts of pleasure and of beliefs are introduced.

In order to explore messages and values in this unit, students are asked to undertake a comparative study in representation (class, gender, race, sexuality, national or regional identity, social or political institutions, etc.) and in the social and historical context in which particular films were produced. The study will be contained within one of these areas:

MESSAGES AND VALUES – BRITISH AND IRISH CINEMA (FS3)

- The 1940s – the war and its aftermath
- Swinging Britain 1963–1973
- Passions and repressions
- Social and political conflict
- Scottish cinema
- Comedy

To complement this study a close study of a single film's messages and values is also required, focusing on close textual study and/or study of the film's social and historical production context.

Without understanding how meaning is produced and messages and values are conveyed (either through the study of a single film or through the study of a group of films) then film remains separated from the everyday world, a world that provides points of reference, experience, and a context for the film to be placed against, and which itself may be explained a little as it helps explain a film. Messages and values are at the heart of film, and are at the heart of societies from which they come, and so with a pre-existing relationship, placing both film and the wider world at the centre of study would seem to be the only logical approach to making sense of both.

▼ 13 THE 1940s: THE WAR AND ITS AFTERMATH

In this chapter we look at:

- the content and contexts of the focus films;
- the key issues which underpin the study of the films of this period;
- the wider historical and production context of filmmaking in this period.

Focus films:	*In Which We Serve* (Rank/Two Cities 1942, Director: Noel Coward/David Lean)
	Passport to Pimlico (Ealing 1949, Director: Henry Cornelius)
Suggested comparison films:	*Millions Like Us* (GFD/Gainsborough 1943, Director: Frank Launder/ Sidney Gilliat)
	The Way to the Stars (Two Cities 1945, Director: Anthony Asquith)

This topic area focuses not only on the films made by British filmmakers and British studios during the Second World War (controlled and shaped by the British government through the Ministry of Information), but also on those films made in the immediate postwar period (up to the end of the 1940s) which reflected on the wartime experience and on 'the peace'. This exciting and vibrant period of British filmmaking reflects a number of issues that can be studied in terms of messages and values including:

- national identity – how the diversity of the British as a nation is portrayed as a unifying strength;
- class, rank, and gender representation – how groups within society are depicted during and after the war;

- social and political institutions – how the war is seen to affect family life, and how the authorities (from bank managers to senior government and military figures) are seen to react;
- propaganda and the historical context – films made to strengthen a nation under attack, and films made by the victors in the aftermath (and among the ruins) of war;
- production context – the films of this period in relation to a broader context of British film (both fiction and non-fiction), and the context of key filmmakers/studios.

IN WHICH WE SERVE – SUMMARY

In Which We Serve was co-written, produced, and directed by the theatrical genius Noel Coward, and a young filmmaker David Lean. The film was commissioned as a propaganda piece at a time when the tide of war had not yet turned in Britain's favour, but when there were signs of hope emerging. Britain was waging an unparalleled war at sea with many thousands of Royal Navy and Merchant Navy seamen being lost in the Atlantic convoys, the Baltic convoys, and in the Mediterranean, as island Britain

Figure 13.1 *In Which We Serve*
Source: British Film Institute

received goods from the West to support the war effort, and sent goods to the East to bolster a 'second front'.

Based on the experiences of Lord Louis Mountbatten (later Earl Mountbatten of Burma) whose ship HMS *Kelly* was sunk under him, *In Which We Serve*'s lead character Captain Kinross was played by the co-director Noel Coward. The Ministry of Information was not keen on seeing Noel Coward take this role due to his reputation both as darling of an elite 'café society' but also due to his having played upper-class characters in light comedy on stage and thus being perceived as 'wrong' to represent a heroic fighting man (particularly a character based on a member of the royal family).

The film tells the story of a Royal Navy destroyer (HMS *Torrin*) and of her crew, told in flashback after the ship is torpedoed and sunk, and the survivors suffer perilous conditions on a life raft. It begins and ends with documentary-like footage of ships being built, launched, and fitted out, and of ships' companies assembling and working. This footage is thrown into sharp relief by the image of the survivors struggling in the aftermath of HMS *Torrin*'s sinking during the Battle for Crete and the succeeding flashbacks from crew-members who reflect diversity of age and class. The flashbacks allow the spectator to engage with both civilian and military life as the sailors are knitted together under Captain Kinross, as they are shown returning on leave to the 'home front', as three Christmas scenes are juxtaposed, as the impact of their war on their families and loved ones is depicted, and as the events of battle are given screen time.

Not only does the film deal with the crew's reaction to the harsh reality of war, but it allows the spectator to gain a new perspective on these fighting men in revealing their home lives, family relationships, and friendships, and how they deal with the difficulties that war wages on these aspects. The Ministry of Information were uncertain of the depiction of Chief Petty Officer Hardy's (Bernard Miles) wife and mother-in-law being killed in an air raid (an everyday event for many servicemen, but one that could affect morale if portrayed on film), but his reaction and determination to continue the 'good' fight convinced them of the value of this scene. It was scenes such as these that marked this film out as more than just a propaganda piece.

PASSPORT TO PIMLICO – SUMMARY

Passport to Pimlico was made by Ealing Studios, who, after their wartime effort of producing morale-boosting comedy with films like *The Foreman Went to France* (1941, Director: Alberto Cavalcanti) and stirring propaganda pieces such as *Went the Day Well?* (1943, Director: Alberto Cavalcanti), had already turned their attention to the postwar period with films such as *Hue and Cry* (1946, Director: Charles Crichton). The end of the Second World War heralded a period of great political and social change with returning servicemen and those who had served on the home front determined to rebuild Britain as a 'land fit for heroes'.

A postwar Labour government was voted into power with a landslide majority and began a programme of social change that established many of the institutions underpinning today's society, such as the National Health Service, and the Welfare

State. However, on the ground the privations of war continued, with vast tracts of cities such as London laid waste by Nazi bombing remaining as bomb sites. Rationing (where 'luxury' items such as fuel, chocolate, silks, and even bananas could only be purchased by saving up ration coupons) was still in place, and the black market (the illegal trade in goods – largely rationed goods, but often simply stolen or 'liberated' from bomb sites) was affecting all levels of society.

Henry Cornelius uses this melting pot of social directions as the backdrop for his story of a small part of central London (Pimlico – bordered by Victoria railway station to the north and the Thames to the south) where an accidental discovery of ancient treasure on a bomb site leads to it declaring itself independent from Britain and part of the ancient kingdom of Burgundy. The innocence and expectation of this act is soon forgotten as opportunists and bureaucrats bring a harsh economic and political reality to the Burgundians in Pimlico.

When greengrocer Arthur Pemberton (Stanley Holloway) has his dreams of turning a local bomb site into a lido (an open-air swimming pool and leisure complex) for the people of Pimlico rejected by local council planners (they want to sell the site), his

Figure 13.2 *Scene from Passport to Pimlico*
Source: British Film Institute

peacetime world suddenly reflects the recent wartime one when an unexploded bomb on the site detonates to reveal (amongst the riches of uncovered buried treasure) a parchment decreeing the land around Miramount Place, Pimlico as belonging to the Duke of Burgundy. Innocent, middle-class Pemberton sees this simply as a means to bypass the council and get the lido built, but it soon becomes apparent that with Pimlico as a separate state the rule of British law is no longer relevant. Initially this is to the advantage of the people there who, in a spirit of unrestricted free enterprise, can buy what they like, can drink when they like, and can do what they like, but this advantage is short lived as suddenly and rapidly hordes of 'barrow boys' and 'spivs' descend on their peaceful area to sell 'off the ration' and illegal goods, both to locals and to queues of Londoners descending upon them.

A wartime unity of spirit is evoked as the locals have to face not only this immediate enemy but also one embodied by Whitehall, a British government determined to crush a tiny independent state that asserts its rights and stands up for its community values. It is interesting to see how Cornelius separates state and people: penned in and blockaded (water cut off and no food allowed across the border), the children of Pimlico are 'evacuated' and return to the border to throw food parcels across to their families – an act of kindness that is soon taken up by the ordinary British people.

Figure 13.3 *Scene from Passport to Pimlico*
Source: British Film Institute

The film's key message is encapsulated in its ending, where the British (and Burgundian) spirit of 'fair play', of community, and of cooperation is highlighted in a compromise as Pimlico rejoins the United Kingdom. The bureaucrats are defeated, and the people of Pimlico get their lido. The damage inflicted by the free-market (the criminals undercutting local prices with their illegal trade), the privations of independence (a worse rationing than that inflicted by the British ration card system), and the breakdown of social structures (families torn apart, law and order crumbling) are replaced by the lesser of evils (government-organized national rationing and restrictions) and the triumph of communal values over individual benefit.

NATIONAL IDENTITY

The significance of film as a tool for promoting a unified image of the United Kingdom was not lost on the wartime British government who (after an initial panic that meant the closure of cinemas in fear of mass casualties through bombing) took control of filmmaking through a newly created Ministry of Information (which had the power to veto a film or any aspect of a film from script, through budget, to actors, and editing decisions), placing regulations on production that ranged across both fiction and documentary.

National identity was an essential ingredient of British wartime productions and to a lesser extent those made in the immediate postwar period, and some underpinning principles defining this identity were described in a memorandum from the first Minister for Information, Lord Macmillan, as independent spirit, caring for the underdog, and resilience or 'backbone'. He also emphasized that the unifying strengths of British institutions such as policing by consent, and parliamentary democracy should be consistently contrasted with Nazi institutions such as the Führer and the Gestapo (the Nazi secret police).

Lord Macmillan saw that for a people engaged in 'total war', the British public would need to be reminded of what they were fighting for, and of what the unifying aspects of society were, across social, regional, and national borders. Under the direction of the Ministry of Information filmmakers began to construct a clear national identity that identified British strengths, linking them not only in opposition to the current enemy, but also to past victories. Historical epics such as *Henry V* (Rank/Two Cities 1944, Director: Laurence Olivier), *Lady Hamilton* (Alexander Korda Films 1941, Director: Alexander Korda), and *The Young Mr Pitt* (TCF 1942, Director: Carol Reed), depicted British heroes (King Henry V, Vice-Admiral Lord Nelson, and Prime Minister William Pitt) all facing – and facing down – foreign enemies and the threat of European invaders. Each revises history to highlight the contemporary position of Britain's fight against the Nazis and each adds to the image of 'plucky little Britain' uniting in the face of a common enemy.

It was the Ministry of Information's view that filmmakers should join the war effort in creating a national cinema that would be part of the overall war effort, producing shorts and features, documentaries and dramas for a variety of uses and a variety of audiences.

Some British films of the period that are directly aimed at specific audiences beyond the 'home' audience include:

A *Canterbury Tale* (Rank/The Archers 1944; Directors: Michael Powell and Emeric Pressburger) – released on the eve of the D-Day landings, this film has an American GI (soldier) as one of its central characters, who spends most of the film either literally or symbolically drawing parallels between Britain and America. It was directed at an American market prior to the invasion of Europe, an invasion that was predicted to (and did) cost many American lives.

Listen to Britain (The Crown Film Unit 1941; Director: Humphrey Jennings) – a documentary short depicting 'snapshots' of Britain at work, at play, and at war. Two versions were produced, one with an additional 'preface' which was targeted at the Canadian allies who were supplying Britain with a tremendous amount of goods and raw materials towards the war effort.

San Demetrio, London (Ealing 1943; Director: Charles Frend) – based on the true story of a merchant ship carrying American oil across the Atlantic, torpedoed, abandoned, and recovered by her crew: aimed at the American market to highlight the importance of their continued support.

The Goose Steps Out (Ealing, 1942; Directors: Will Hay and Basil Dearden) – a star vehicle for the popular comedian Will Hay, full of comedic impersonations of leading figures in (and stereotypes of) the Nazi leadership. Whilst the principal audience would have been the home market, films such as these were brought to the attention of 'the enemy' as tools of propaganda.

Each of these films offers specific messages and representations of values to targeted audiences for a definite and considered purpose.

Think about other films of this period that you have become aware of:

- What messages and values do they offer?
- How are these depicted on screen?
- What character types are employed and in what roles?
- Is there more than one audience for these films?

Through images of the British at war, at the various fighting fronts and on the home front, an impression of a British subject, loyal to the Crown, fearless in the face of the enemy, strong, determined, and above all (and in contrast to the enemy) fair, just, and with right on their side, was created. Idealized characters with their idealized actions (in some cases stereotypical characters and stereotypical actions) were placed in opposition either to 'the enemy' in films such as *Went the Day Well?* (Ealing 1942; Director: Alberto Cavalcanti) and *Next of Kin* (Ealing 1942; Director: Thorold Dickinson) or those who sought to undermine the British 'way of life' in films such as *Cottage to Let* (Gainsborough 1941; Director: Anthony Asquith) and *Waterloo Road* (GFD/Gainsborough 1944; Director: Sidney Gilliat). Some filmmakers (notably Michael Powell and Humphrey Jennings) at times subverted this image to comment on British society, but this was contained within an overall commonality of view that promoted a single, united representation.

The characters created in this period did not necessarily reflect real individuals at the time, but rather those that could be held up as role models of the time. It was important not only to show those in the Armed Forces and government agencies as heroic in carrying out their duty to Britain, but also to show those on the 'home front' (the miners, the dockers, the factory workers, the firemen, the Land Army, the postmistress, etc.) as equal in heroism: holding society together and retaining everything good about Britain until the troops came home. At a time (particularly in the early years of the war, and again in the aftermath) when there was so much uncertainty, fear, doubt, and anguish, the continuation of familiar actions and behaviours despite the horrendous conditions of 'total war' became a touchstone of hope against adversity.

ACTIVITY

Look at the films you have studied and list some of the principal British characters in a grid like the one below. Try and get a mix of different ages, classes, ranks, and genders. Score each on a scale of 1–10 in each column (1 being weak in the quality and 10 being strong in the quality). Then do the same with the principal 'enemy' characters.

Character name	Loyal to Crown	Fearless	Strong	Determined	Fair	Just	Right	Total score

What do the scores tell you?

Do you notice anything significant about class, rank, or gender?

Where are the key differences between British and 'enemy' characters?

Are there any other columns you think should be added, or should replace those above?

In *In Which We Serve* the filmmakers show the seamen both at war and at home. Are the characteristics listed above shown differently in relation to the fighting and the home fronts?

CLASS, RANK, AND GENDER REPRESENTATION

Individual acts of heroism were celebrated more often in postwar films that sought to reinforce a British identity that filmmakers were concerned would disappear in the social and economic changes occurring as Britain rebuilt itself. During the war, collective heroism was promoted, where 'everyday heroes' came together from the farms and factories, from the pubs and pulpits, from the council house and the country house, to do their duty and to defeat a common enemy. The ship's stoker was depicted as having equal importance to the ship's captain, the air raid warden as significant a hero as the fighter pilot. Class, rank, and gender representations that dominated British film of the 1930s were quickly revised to ensure depictions of unity: a coming together of the British peoples which in itself is identified as part of the British character – unity in the face of adversity.

Thus, whilst the 1950s offered war films populated by individual (or small teams of) heroes in films such as *Reach for the Sky* (Rank/Pinnacle 1956, Director: Lewis Gilbert) *The Cruel Sea* (Ealing 1953, Director: Charles Frend), *The Wooden Horse* (British Lion/Wessex/London Films 1950, Director: Jack Lee), and *Carve Her Name With Pride* (Rank/Keyboard 1958, Director: Lewis Gilbert), films made during the war concentrated on collective actions such as that of the firemen during the blitz in *The Bells Go Down* (Ealing 1943, Director: Basil Dearden) and the documentary *Fires Were Started* (Crown Film Unit 1943, Director: Humphrey Jennings), or of an 'average' working family who have to deal with war work, and loss in *Millions Like Us* (GFD/Gainsborough 1943, Directors: Frank Launder and Sidney Gilliat).

It is unsurprising that issues of class, rank, and gender seem to pour out of virtually every British film made in this period, since these aspects were all undergoing significant change as the war progressed. The defeat of the British Expeditionary Force and the evacuation of the survivors at Dunkirk lost not only significant material reserves, but also many of the most experienced officers and non-commissioned officers the British armed forces had. As they were rebuilt post-Dunkirk (particularly the Army which had suffered significant loss, and the Royal Air Force which needed to boost its pilot training to make up for the significant losses it was suffering) the armed forces saw changes in leadership that saw many more ordinary middle-class (and even working-class) men becoming officers – something that was once reserved for the British ruling classes. As the war progressed, merit and deeds became a determinant for climbing through the ranks, and this was reflected in a growing number of films of the time, with *The Life and Death of Colonel Blimp* (GFD/The Archers 1943, Directors: Michael Powell and Emeric Pressburger) perhaps showing this most clearly as the aging, upper-class Colonel Blimp is out-performed by Lieutenant 'Spud' Wilson, a young lower middle-class, middle-ranking officer (admittedly this is with a suggestion that the young officer's ruthless nature is akin to the Nazis). *Went The Day Well?* (Ealing 1943, Director: Alberto Cavalcanti) offers a range of class and gender representations, from the Cockney evacuee who alerts British forces to the presence of the Nazi infiltrators, through the working- and middle-class land girls, to the lady of the manor. Despite offering heroic roles to those traditionally denied them, rank remains to the fore, with hierarchies (be they military or village) seen to structure society, though with challenges that reflect the changing nature of Britain at war.

With men being conscripted into the armed forces, with fighting in North Africa and the Far East, and with servicemen stationed from Iceland to India, the social make up of Britain during the war began to change. Women took on traditionally male jobs such as farming through the Women's Land Army, armaments and other factory work, and roles in the armed forces such as drivers and translators. By the middle of the war nearly 90 per cent of all single women (over 18 and under 40 years old), and 80 per cent of married women with 'grown up' children (over 14) were working, with a radical increase in typically male occupations such as heavy engineering. The arrival of retreating allied fighters (Poles, Czechs, French, etc.) on the streets of British cities, towns and villages, and the subsequent arrival of the Americans during the war and millions of American troops stationed in Britain, exposed those left to fight on the 'home front' to peoples, attitudes, and values that made them reflect on their own positions. The constant presence of imminent death (either of a loved one fighting on one of the fronts, or of those at home through bombing) also changed attitudes towards status and social position (a luxury city house was as likely to be bombed as a slum, a bank as likely as an orphanage) and barriers that had survived the First World War were now breaking down.

The resolute nature of women at war was highlighted in a number of films that often placed women in traditional male roles. In *Went The Day Well?* women (from the lady of the manor to the working-class city land girl) are forced to take up arms alongside the men to defend their village (and the country) from the infiltrating Nazi force, and even the aging, petite postmistress reluctantly takes the life of a Nazi soldier, in an axe-murder scene that must have horrified yet unified the wartime audience. Similarly in *Two Thousand Women* (GFD/Gainsborough 1944, Director: Frank Launder) a range of British national characters and characteristics are displayed as interred British women (civilian women who stayed in Europe, who were left behind by retreating British forces, or who were captured in territories overrun by the Nazis) suffer the consequences of helping Allied bombers finding their targets, and are shipped off to a Nazi concentration camp. Class barriers do not prevent the women working together to defeat their common enemy.

Accordingly the principal characters of British wartime films changed. Gainsborough introduced strong female characters in their costume dramas such as *Madonna of the Seven Moons* (GFD/Gainsborough 1944, Director: Arthur Crabtree), *They Were Sisters* (GFD/ Gainsborough 1945, Director: Arthur Crabtree) and *The Wicked Lady* (GFD/ Gainsborough 1945, Director: Leslie Arliss). There was moral contrast offered by the fact that most of these films had strong women who were aggressive in their pursuit of independence, but who suffered and were destroyed by their desires, placed alongside (or in opposition to) equally strong women who looked for compromise and partnership, women who usually prospered. Perhaps this was a message to women who had found independence during the war that whilst situations would not revert to prewar male dominance, certain freedoms and levels of independence may need to be sacrificed (for the good of the nation) when the men return from the fighting.

Similarly as the end of the war came in sight, diverse films began to look forward to what a new, postwar Britain may look like. Documentaries such as A *Diary for Timothy*

(Basil Wright/Crown Film Unit 1945, Director: Humphrey Jennings) offered predictions of a postwar society where class did not matter and where equality was the foremost principle, of a meritocracy where it was not status of birth that mattered, but of what one could offer the nation that determined futures. The earlier feature *They Came to a City* (Ealing 1944, Director: Basil Dearden) reflects this view as assorted individuals find themselves outside the gates of a mysterious city and have to decide what kind of future world they want to live in. An immediately postwar feature, and the first 'Ealing comedy' *Hue and Cry* (Ealing 1946, Director: Charles Crichton) delivers a clear view of what this postwar world would be like as thousands of London's East End boys (ragamuffins, wild, working-class) work together to prevent criminals (who are using the boys' favourite comic to pass information) from succeeding in their crimes, and round them up in a climactic scene set against a backdrop of London's destroyed docklands. This film depicts a world wherein even the lowest contribute to the rebuilding of a moralistic nation, where children of every class join together to defeat a common enemy, and where cooperation and common purpose (the very things celebrated in the war films) lead to victory.

SOCIAL AND POLITICAL INSTITUTIONS

It was not in the interest of Britain at war to have its social and political institutions directly questioned during the war, and the Ministry of Information ensured that Parliament and the Ministry for War were never criticized or seen in a negative light. Indeed the Crown Film Unit was quickly established (by effectively 'nationalizing' John Grierson's GPO Film Unit) as the likelihood of war became a certainty, so that morale-boosting documentaries about government and military activities could be produced to assist the war effort.

However, part of Britain's national identity was rooted in the gentle mimicry and direct mockery of the music hall tradition, and whilst public favourite George Formby continued to make his traditional musical fare of feel-good 'working-class lad makes it good' stories, in films such as *Let George Do It* (Ealing/Basil Dearden 1940, Director: Marcel Varnel), and stage knockabout comics, the Crazy Gang, tried to unsuccessfully translate their acts on to film, others used their comedy to parody Britain's institutions (and still show them to be preferable to those of the Nazis). Comedian Will Hay defeated the enemy through comic ineptitude in *The Black Sheep of Whitehall* (Ealing 1941, Director: Basil Dearden) in which he plays the role of an incompetent teacher who is mistaken for a government economics expert, saving the real expert from Nazi spies who want to kidnap him. This role was reprised in *The Goose Steps Out* (Ealing 1942, Director: Basil Dearden) where the incompetent teacher is sent into Nazi Germany to replace his Nazi double and steal a secret weapon. In both films the Nazis are easily defeated by an incompetent, whilst the British institutions and authorities are portrayed as comically inept, yet the gentle criticism of 'Britishness' offers a message that is also testament to its critical strength – even if inept, British institutions are still strong and effective enough to defeat the Nazi system.

Humphrey Jennings did much to capture the social institutions of Britain in his prewar work and his wartime documentaries. In *Spare Time* (Crown Film Unit 1939, Director:

Humphrey Jennings), which was released on the eve of war, much of what could be viewed as great about Britain's institutions was woven into a patchwork of the activities that Britons engaged in outside of their working hours, from north to south, east to west. There is an eerie calm about the film when viewed with the knowledge that within a year of its release Britain, and those depicted, would be involved in 'total war', and scenes of choirs, amateur dramatics, pigeon racing, dancing, and an almost surreal kazoo marching band highlight both institutions that would be changed irrevocably by war, and simultaneously representations of institutions that in their very 'Britishness' were worth fighting for.

Whilst direct criticism of political (and more significantly military) institutions was suppressed by the Ministry of Information, some filmmakers were able to build indirect criticism into their films. Michael Powell and Emeric Pressburger were such film-makers, and (possibly due to the patriotic perception of their wartime work) offered clear criticism of Britain's institutions both obliquely through their image systems and more directly through the script of A *Canterbury Tale*. Here the authorities (both civil and military) that stand on the eve of the invasion of Europe and who are central to the defeat of Nazism are portrayed as impotent in the face of the actions of the 'glue-man' (who throws glue in women's hair). In a world of wartime chaos there is a warmth in the homely attempts to maintain the world as known (the blacksmith in a traditional forge talking to the soldier who uses the mass produced tools of war; the shop names marked out on the bomb-site rubble of historic Canterbury's Rose Lane), and yet something strangely cold in the emptiness of the magistrates' court (and in Culpepper, the magistrate), and in the vast cathedral service for the soon-to-depart British soldiers. The sheep herded past as the soldiers enter the cathedral gate may have been missed by the Ministry of Information, but offer a clear critique of the way government and military viewed the servicemen. Perhaps the most obvious criticism of institutions came in the form of Humphrey Jennings' *The Silent Village* (Ministry of Information, 1943) where the Nazi atrocity in the Czech village of Lidice was transposed to a mining village in Wales. Here it is not particularly British institutions that are being exposed, but the cold logicality behind any institution that leads to atrocity.

A clearer critique of social and political institutions came in the postwar period both in films dealing directly with a fighting war, and those set in more peaceful locations. *The Dam Busters* (Allied British Picture Company 1954, Director: Michael Anderson) is essentially a celebratory biography of the inventor Barnes-Wallace and his endeavours to successfully create a 'bouncing' bomb that could be used to destroy the Ruhr Valley dams in Germany's industrial heartland. Central to this story is the reluctance and obstruction of various government ministries (including the Ministry of Armaments and the Ministry of War) in advancing the project, and the inventor's determination for the project to succeed despite such institutional indifference. Such a criticism of the two central ministries directing the war effort would not have been possible during the conflict, nor would the obvious criticism of the intellectual abilities of those directing and representing the ministries (both civilian and military) who are portrayed as largely upper-middle-class incompetents.

Similarly Ealing's wartime mocking of institutions became sharper in the immediate postwar period with *Passport to Pimlico*, and with a film that looked back to the wartime period, *Whiskey Galore!* (Ealing 1948, Director: Alexander MacKendrick). A wartime cargo of whiskey bound for North America is wrecked off a small Hebridean island, and the islanders unite against the (English) army officer and the customs officers sent to retrieve the salvaged bottles, in a sharp critique of the inflexibility and inherent weakness of institutions when faced with a united population.

PROPAGANDA AND THE HISTORICAL CONTEXT

Early in the war many of Britain's film studio complexes were requisitioned by the government for use in the war effort. Some became food stores or munitions stores due to the rural nature of their locations (most of the stages at Pinewood were converted to such use) and others were used for secret operations. The studios that continued making films were put to the practical use of making propaganda by the Ministry of Information. Documentaries and features were commissioned to boost morale, to encourage Britain's allies or sympathizers to continue or increase their support, and to signal strength to the enemy.

In the build-up to war and in its early stages British cinema focused on promoting cautionary tales over spies and 'fifth columnists'. *The Lady Vanishes* (Gaumont British/ Gainsborough 1938, Director: Alfred Hitchcock) offers a clear sense of more to come as two ubiquitous Englishmen abroad, Charters and Caldicott (rushing home to England for a test match), and a group of other English passengers aboard a train crossing a fictional central European country, are confronted by the country's secret police (whose accents and uniforms shred any attempt to thinly disguise their Nazi models). Charters and Caldicott (who were of course victorious, yet sporting, in the subsequent battles with the secret police) reappear in *Night Train to Munich* (TCF 1940, Director: Carol Reed) where they reprise their roles in saving a Czech inventor from being captured by the Gestapo, and again through being good sports and being determined they outwit the enemy. British values were being espoused, and a clear message sent to foreign powers.

This message was amplified and re-contextualized at another time of instability and European terror, in a retelling and updating of the story *The Scarlet Pimpernel*. Repackaged as *Pimpernel Smith* (British National 1941, Director: Leslie Howard) the actor/director reprises his role in the earlier peacetime costume drama *The Scarlet Pimpernel* (London Films 1934, Director: Harold Young), and plays a professor of archaeology who crosses into Nazi-occupied Europe to rescue refugees. The Nazis are shown as lacking in character, morality and humour, with the scene in which the Gestapo chief, General von Graum investigates the British sense of humour (concluding that it is a myth) demonstrating succinctly these flaws and highlighting them against the British strength of character, fair play and humour. The message of historical strength and the historical values of courage and cunning were not buried deeply in this film and would have sent a clear message to the enemy, paralleling an earlier British (fictitious) hero and triumph with a future one.

British documentaries of the period were clearly designed as pieces of propaganda that were often used to mitigate British defeats and highlight even the smallest of British victories. Apart from the morale boosting function of such works, and their role in making appeals to allied or sympathetic nations to support Britain's war effort, they often had a more direct propaganda role. The Ministry of Information commissioned *Trois Chansons de Resistance* (*Three Songs of Resistance*, Ministry of Information 1943, Director: Alberto Cavalcanti) to be dropped into occupied Europe to communicate with resistance groups. Resistance groups in occupied countries would use British films for propaganda, either by ensuring they were 'discovered' by the enemy (who would then watch them and be demoralized) or in the case of the Danish resistance movement by forcibly taking over a cinema and making the audience watch films such as *Hoch der Lambeth Valk* (*Swinging the Lambeth Walk*, Ministry of Information 1941, Director: attributed to Charles Ridley) in which marching Nazi troops and even Hitler himself are edited to 'dance' to the popular song 'The Lambeth Walk'.

Whilst the fighting front was highlighted in films such as the tense submarine drama *We Dive At Dawn* (GFD/Gainsborough 1943, Director: Anthony Asquith) which promoted a determined, valiant, and united message, in the latter part of the war when victory seemed possible if not likely, British filmmakers began to focus their attention on 'winning the peace'. *Went the Day Well?* begins in a postwar period, reflecting back on wartime events and their consequences. *A Canterbury Tale* shot prior to D-Day, has its characters looking ahead to peacetime, as they slowly recover the elements of their lives lost to them during the war, and *A Diary for Timothy* considers what the future will hold for a child born in the closing months of war, and in doing so offers a new set of values for Britain to consider as it headed towards victory. Similarly the messages and values of *The Way to the Stars* (Two Cities 1945, Director: Anthony Asquith) are those of the postwar period as guests at a small hotel near a wartime airfield reflect on victory and loss, on the past and on the future, on the price of war and on the price of peace.

In the immediate aftermath of the war, filmmakers (and most probably audiences) were reluctant to engage directly with recollection of armed conflict itself, and the focus became one of reflection on these events' postwar impact, the rebuilding of Britain, and the need to offer a new generation images and stories of British heroes. *The Wooden Horse* (British Lion/Wessex/London Films 1950, Director: Jack Lee) was one of the first features to herald a change of approach in response to the war, offering a suspense-filled prisoner-of-war drama and a new set of messages and values suited to the postwar period of prosperity. The film was notably shot in a reconstructed POW camp in Germany, and featured many actors who had served in (and in some cases had been POWs during) the war.

PRODUCTION CONTEXT

The advent of war meant that filmmakers were under significant restriction and suffered shortages of materials, technicians, artists, and most of all money with which to make their films. Movement was restricted, not only due to fuel rationing but also due to whole areas being sealed off for military use. With the fall of Dunkirk British forces retreated to their island nation and this caused further restrictions on filmmakers who realized that many of the locations once available to them for shooting would now have to be replicated in Britain, and Britain was rapidly becoming a crowded place. Indeed, in 1943 and 1944 when Powell and Pressburger were shooting A *Canterbury Tale* in east Kent, it was difficult for them to get within six miles of the coast and they had to have special passes for many of the village locations where they were filming as they were near airfields or troop marshalling yards which were classed as restricted areas for 'essential' personnel only.

Many of the skilled technicians and artists were conscripted into the armed forces, and many of the studio facilities were either requisitioned by the government for military or civil defence purposes (Pinewood had its sound stages camouflaged so that it could be used as a food storage facility for London) though some such as Denham Studios (host to Rank, Two Cities, and London Films among others) was allowed back into production as the war progressed and the Ministry of Information made a case for the value of filmmaking to the war effort. It was here that *Brief Encounter* (Eagle-Lion 1945, Director: David Lean) was shot.

Both Emeric Pressburger, and Alberto Cavalcanti were detained as enemy aliens on returning from trips abroad, narrowly escaping internment (where foreign nationals were rounded up and placed in detention camps for fear they may be enemy agents), and numerous travel restrictions were placed on other foreign nationals who were working in the film industry in Britain.

Against this background many remarkable films were made with the assistance of the Ministry of Information and the Ministry for War, and Powell and Pressburger benefited considerably from this assistance. *One of Our Aircraft is Missing* (British National 1941, Directors: Michael Powell, Emeric Pressburger) utilized the offer both of footage of RAF bombers and the use of an RAF bomber itself to create the story of a downed bomber crew escaping through Nazi occupied Holland. It was filmed in the restricted areas around airfields in the fenland of Norfolk and this again was facilitated by the Ministry for War. Similarly, the Ministry of Information were persuaded to release the funding to make *Forty-ninth Parallel* (GFD/Ortus 1941, Director: Michael Powell) on location in Canada. The story is of five survivors of a Nazi U-boat destroyed off the coast of Canada and their attempts to cross to the neutral territory of America (the Americans had not entered the war at this point). On the way they meet the peoples of Canada – the French, the German, the British, and the Canadian – and their brutish interactions soon clarify what their Nazi values are as the filmmakers spell out an explicit message to both the allied audiences and to the Americans who were remaining neutral in the face of mounting evidence of Nazi intentions and Nazi atrocities.

Documentary filmmakers who flew with the RAF and were shipped out with the Royal Navy and the Merchant Navy, were given priority in the battles of the North African Desert Campaign, and were assigned to the Normandy beaches for the D-Day invasion of Europe, following the Allied troops through to the conclusion of the war and victory. Some of this material was used in newsreels (news programming shown in cinemas as part of a programme of films), some released as documentaries, and much simply shot and stored, a record of the time of war (much of this now is archived by the Imperial War Museum in London). Filmmakers were given scarce resources because of the power of the medium in conveying messages and values. There is some irony then that this period of filmmaking ended with filmmakers returning to Europe and to one of the subjects of the early films of the period, spying and secret agents. *Odette* (Herbert Wilcox 1950, Director: Herbert Wilcox) was a biopic of the special operations executive agent Odette Sansom who fought with the French resistance and was executed by the Gestapo, and was shot on the locations in which the events took place. The collective heroes were being replaced by individualized heroes as the restrictions of wartime filmmaking were being replaced by the freedoms of a victorious peace. Audiences were changing, and the messages and values expressed by films reflecting on the period were changing too to express new ideas and shape new opinions.

EXAMPLE EXAM QUESTIONS

1   What cinematic elements convey specific characteristics of Britain in the films you have studied?

2   What particularly British values do the central characters exhibit in the films you have studied?

3   Has the war impacted differently on the male and female characters, and how is any difference displayed?

4   The key message of films of this period is one of unity. How is this message expressed in the films you have studied?

5   Is class of any significance in the study of films from this period?

6   How have the filmmakers used sound and image to present the messages and values of their films?

FURTHER READING

Barnouw, Erik (1993) *Documentary: A History of the Non-Fiction Film*, Oxford: Oxford University Press.

Chapman, James (1998) *The British at War*, London: I.B. Taurus.

Drazin, Charles (1998) *The Finest Years: British Cinema of the 1940s*, London: André Deutsch.

Murphy, Robert (1997) *The British Cinema Book*, London: BFI.

Murphy, Robert (2000) *British Cinema and the Second World War*, London: BFI.

Richards, Jeffrey (1997) *Films and British National Identity*, Manchester: Manchester University Press.

Warren, Patricia (1995) *British Film Studios*, London: Batsford.

USEFUL WEBSITES

http://www.channel4.com/culture/microsites/J/ (the site for the Channel Four programme *Humphrey Jennings – The man who listened to Britain*) http://www.britishpathe.com (the Pathé newsreel archive)

http://www.britishpictures.com (a resource offering essays, articles, reviews, and title-specific information)

http://www.britmovies.co.uk (valuable for synopses, cast lists, etc.)

http://www.iwmcollections.org.uk (the Imperial War Museum online collection)

http://www.powell-pressburger.org (a well designed fan-operated site)

▼ 14 SWINGING BRITAIN: 1963–1973

This chapter will look at

- the content and contexts of the focus films;
- why this period was such a pivotal moment for the British film industry;
- the context of messages and values underpinning a study of this period.

Focus films:	*Darling* (Anglo-Amalgamated/Vic/Appia 1965, Director: John Schlesinger)
	Performance (Warner/Goodtimes 1970, Director: Nicolas Roeg/ Donald Cammell)
Suggested comparison films:	*Billy Liar* (Vic Films 1963, Director: John Schlesinger)
	The Knack (and How to Get It) (Woodfall 1965, Director: Richard Lester)
	Get Carter (MGM/Mike Klinger 1971, Director: Mike Hodges)

It is not necessarily the dates that define this topic area, but rather the dramatic changes in filmmaking (both stylistically and in terms of subject) that occurred across this period. Roughly bounded by the transition from the films of the British New Wave (approximately 1963) and a decade later (1973) where the British film industry is seen as freefalling into decline, this topic area deals with the 'new' filmmaking that reflected the 'swinging' Britain of the 1960s. As such it offers opportunity not only to study the focus films and others from the period, but the lively and relevant social and historical background against which (and from which) these films were produced. Broader issues of changing representations are central to this study and should be considered in relation to the developments across the period of time.

SWINGING BRITAIN This term relates to changes in a whole range of attitudes, behaviours, and moralities where Britain finally shook off the bleak, postwar way of living, where caution, practicality, repression, and obedience were the norms. The term 'swinging' comes from a form of music that was more relaxed and open in its style. The 'swinging sixties' really began in 1963 with the emergence of the Beatles and the Mersey music scene, and its London counterpart. With full employment, young people had a greater disposable income, and music and fashion came to dominate the culture. Confident in peace and prosperity, this 'swinging' approach developed across social boundaries, and an 'anything goes' attitude was popularized.

This pivotal moment of British cinema can be used as a platform to study a range of issues in terms of messages and values including:

- London versus the regions – 'swinging' capital city, with the rest of the country depicted through the dirt of realism;
- National/regional identity – how areas are marked out as 'different' and, in some cases, how the country is unified under a 'new' identity;
- Class, sexuality, and gender representation – how changing attitudes towards class are depicted, how the eroding of class barriers is represented, and how, with the 'sexual revolution' in full swing, a new-found liberation is reflected in film;
- Social and political institutions, and the rise of youth – the relationships of individuals to family and more formalized institutions, and how youth takes centre stage in this decade of rebellion and redefined boundaries through music, fashion, and lifestyle choices;
- production context – the films of this period in relation to a broader context of British film, the tightening grip of television, and within the context of key filmmakers.

DARLING – SUMMARY

Director John Schlesinger had established his 'swinging sixties' credentials two years earlier with his successful *Billy Liar*, the story of a repressed working-class young man from Manchester who longs for the excitement of a modern world offered in the lure of London, but who retreats into fantasy rather than stride into his own future. The actress Julie Christie goes to London at the end of the film, and Schlesinger uses her again as the lead, Diana Scott, in *Darling*, in which she presents the same confident sense of self, and the same desire for freedom as she depicted in her earlier role.

Here in *Darling*, however, Schlesinger places Diana in the shallow, fashionable London of the wealthy and powerful that serves as a stark contrast to the industrial northern back streets, and dated funeral parlour of his previous work. Whilst the story addresses issues that at the time were still considered by many as taboo (such as sex, pregnancy, abortion, homosexuality, and infidelity), and offers fashionable 'swinging' attitudes, *Darling* is much more attached to an earlier, traditional style of filmmaking than many others made around this time, and particularly lacks reference to the music scene of the time (which, with the Beatles, the Rolling Stones, and many others, was changing the face of music worldwide).

NOTEBOX

Changing the law

Darling seemed to portray many activities as the 'norm', as acceptable even though they were actually illegal. Subsequent changes in the law happened throughout the late 1960s:

- ■ 1967   Abortion Act ending decades of illegal 'back street' abortions;
- ■ 1967   Sexual Offences Act decriminalizing homosexual acts between consenting adults in private;
- ■ 1969   Divorce Reform Act making it easier for couples to divorce.

The film begins when the young model Diana meets and starts a relationship with Robert Gold (Dirk Bogarde) a television arts programme director in London. Leaving their partners (and more significantly for the audience of the day, Robert abandons his children) to move in together, they soon become part of the trendy arts/media crowd in 'swinging' London, where Diana begins mixing with men who can progress her career and who can lead her to the lifestyle she wants. It is this self-serving determination to become rich and famous that marks Diana Scott out as a different kind of lead female character, one who contrasts with the strong women of the 1940s war films, but perhaps

Figure 14.1 *Darling*
Source: British Film Institute

has more in common with Margaret Lockwood's Lady Skelton in *The Wicked Lady* (GFD/Gainsborough, 1945 Director: Leslie Arliss).

Robert introduces her to public relations executive Miles Brand (Laurence Harvey) with whom she has sex in order to get a part in a thriller film. Miles leads her into a higher social realm of the international 'jet-set' where she is met by a different set of attitudes, behaviour, and morals, all of which she embraces with enthusiasm and a 'carefree' look. Discovering she is pregnant she casually has an abortion, quickly falling further into a world of outlandish parties, cross-dressing, sexual freedom, decadence, and ultimately, emptiness.

Returning to London, Robert leaves her, calling her a whore. Miles then casts her in a major advertising campaign as 'The Happiness Girl', taking her to Italy for a location shoot. Here she meets an Italian widower, Prince Cesare, and tries to fill her empty life by dabbling in Catholicism. Cesare asks her to marry him, but refusing she returns to London, where disillusionment leads her to accept his offer. As a Princess, Diana has achieved the riches and fame she set out for, yet still remains unhappy and empty.

Left alone by her aged husband, she retreats to London and back into the arms of Robert who persuades her (easily) into his bed. Her thoughts of re-establishing a stable and meaningful relationship are cruelly crushed when Robert reveals that he slept with her for revenge and then he packs her off back to Rome. At London Airport the press hound the Princess della Romita as she returns to the empty prison of her loveless marriage and the life she has created.

From the opening credits Schlesinger is offering a clear message and commentary on the emerging 'swinging sixties' and the consequences for those whose immorality (or perhaps amorality) leads rather than guides them.

ACTIVITY...

- Look at the opening sequences in *Darling* where Diana Scott is introduced. What values do you think she displays?
- Consider Diana's relationships with men. Particularly look at her relationships with Robert, Miles, and Cesare. Does power rest in a traditional way with men in these relationships, with Diana, or with each at different times? What message do you think is being conveyed here?
- Why do you think John Schlesinger portrays Diana in the way he does?
- Which of the men in the film do you think represents the values of the time? In which specific scenes or sequences are these values conveyed?
- Create a 'relationship map' for Diana, charting her journey from partner to partner. Indicate on it her level of happiness by numbering each relationship on a scale of one to ten, with one being saddest and ten being happiest. What do you notice about her relationships?
- Robert says to Diana 'Your idea of fidelity (being faithful) is not having more than one man in bed at the same time'. Do you think Robert represents a

continued

different set of morals to Diana? Are there any particular scenes or sequences where their differences are heightened?

- What messages are conveyed by Miles and Robert? Do you think they are of the same class, or do you think they differ in some way? What tells you this?
- Adultery, casual sex, and abortion are all dealt with in a matter-of-fact manner. What does this tell you about the values of the time?
- Age and class dominate the representations in this film – what do you think John Schlesinger is trying to say about each, and about their relationship to each other? Is there something corrupting about the older figures in the film, or is it the drive of youth in Diana that corrupts?

PERFORMANCE – SUMMARY

Performance is often cited as the directorial debut of Nicolas Roeg, but it is worth noting that this was actually a collaborative effort with writer Donald Cammell, and also worth noting that Roeg is also credited as director of photography. It was released at the end of a decade that had seen the optimism of the early 1960s disappear amidst the harsher realities of organized crime, drug abuse, and the end of a period of economic boom in the UK, and the steady spiral of violence of the Vietnam war crushing idealism on the world stage.

Warner Brothers who financed the film kept it back from audiences for three years due to their disbelief at the excess they had funded. Heavily edited in this period to damp down concerns over drug use, and violence, it is often seen as the film that put a 'full stop' on the 1960s, and is certainly one that stands on the dividing line between 1960s commercialism and the more self-indulgent cinema of the 1970s.

Case Study: *Nicholas Roeg* (1928–)

Beginning his career with MGM British at the age of 18 as an apprentice editor, Roeg developed his career as a cinematographer from the mid-1950s, working as second-unit cameraman on *Lawrence of Arabia* (Columbia/Horizon, 1962 Director: David Lean). After co-directing and acting as director of photography on *Performance* (1970) he consolidated his reputation with *Walkabout* (Max L. Raab/ Si Litvinoff, 1970), and *Don't Look Now* (BL/Casey/Eldorado, 1973). His trademarks of confusion, boredom, and frank sexual scenes continued through the 1970s and 1980s with *The Man Who Fell to Earth* (British Lion, 1976) and *Bad Timing* (Rank/RPC, 1980), though his most successful film to date has been his adaptation of Roald Dahl's *The Witches* (Warner/Lorimar, 1990).

Performance is a complex film in which actor James Fox plays Chas Devlin, a nightmarishly violent small-time enforcer for a London gangster (Harry Flowers played by Johnny Shannon), whose 'skill' and talent for violence and intimidation has earned him a reputation as a 'performer'.

The first third of the film is relatively simple to follow as it stumbles through a fairly realistic depiction of the late 1960s London's criminal underworld, where in a particularly vicious attack on betting shop owner Joey Maddox (Anthony Valentine) Chas is witnessed killing him, implicating his boss and making him an accessory to murder. Harry Flowers has one option; Chas must be eliminated.

On the run, Chas decides to stay in London and rents a room in a Notting Hill flat from aging, failing rock star Turner (played by Mick Jagger, whose career with the Rolling

Figure 14.2 *Performance*
Source: British Film Institute

Stones was in turmoil at this point amid sordid sex and drug scandals, and a high profile 'drugs bust'). Here he contacts Tony Farrell (Kenneth Colley) to get a fake passport made up so he can escape the country.

Turner lives in a world of sexual depravity and heavy drug use with two girlfriends, Pherber (Anita Pallenberg) and Lucy (Michèle Breton), and is a complete opposite to Chas. Recognizing something of his younger self in Chas, Turner decides to expose him to the delights of sex and drugs and rock 'n' roll, offering him his girlfriends, and progressively stronger drugs.

It is here that the film takes a major stylistic turn, as the structure of the film itself replicates the slow disintegration of Chas's personality by using a jumble of editing styles and visual effects, jump cutting, shifting and confusing point of view, and blurring the line between reality and (drug-fuelled) hallucination. The directors introduce an increasingly frequent use of mirrors from this point onwards to illustrate not only the psychological state, but the suggestion that the two men are mirrors of each other.

In the house Chas's personality slowly breaks down and he begins to assume Turner's identity, cross-dressing, being fed magic mushrooms, having sex with Turner's girlfriends, and discussing eastern poetry and 'paradise'. Turner, however, slowly drops the hippy 'flower-child' personality and becomes increasingly aggressive, and out of control.

The film ends with Tony double-crossing Chas, and Harry Flowers' men arriving to take him away. Before leaving, Chas goes up to Turner's bedroom and shoots him in the head (an ultimate 'trip'), and is then taken away to Harry Flowers and certain death.

The explicit sexual nature of the film and the brutal violence set a new yardstick for British cinema, and presented the BBFC with the first of many similar problems it would face in the 1970s where the mix of sex and violence created suggestions of a link between the two (even sexualizing violence).

ACTIVITY...

- Donald Cammell and Nicolas Roeg deliberately contrasted the working-class London underworld with a middle-class arts/music background. What do you think they achieve in doing this? What does the 'collision' of values expressed in the film, say about the society of the time?
- Chas Devlin is undoubtedly a villain. Are there moments when you become sympathetic to his character? Grid the film horizontally into scenes (scene one at the left) and then map your level of sympathy with him onto this (zero at the bottom meaning no sympathy and ten at the top meaning very sympathetic). Compare the graph line produced with your peers. What do you notice from this? Is the audience 'positioned' into a view on Chas, or does each individual react differently to the messages and values on screen?

- How are the women used by Chas and Turner in this film? Does this change across the film? What difference is there between the women? What values do these representations express?
- Compare this film with one from earlier in the decade. Is there a different message emerging from each? What does this tell you about the changing values of society across the period?
- In a group, choose to discuss either the male or female values expressed in the film and make a list of positives and negatives. Compare lists. Is there significant difference in the balance between positives and negatives across the genders? Do the positives outweigh the negatives, or vice versa? What messages are established about men and/or women in this film?
- The blurring of traditional divides (between male and female, working class and middle class, criminals and 'civilians, etc.) is central to this film. Choose a particular area of representation and list five examples of where it is blurred. What do you think the directors were trying to achieve in doing this?
- List the differing styles, techniques and filmic references that the directors have used in this film. Chart them on a time line, alongside key points in the story. Is there a relationship between the structure and style of the film and its story? How do they help convey messages?
- The film is set against the backdrop of London – the 'swinging capital' of the world. Do you think the messages and values would have been different had it been set elsewhere (Liverpool or Newcastle for example)? If so, in what way, and why? Take a sequence from the film and transpose it to another location. What would you change to make it 'fit' the new location? How are the messages and values altered?

LONDON VERSUS THE REGIONS

Whilst *Billy Liar* is set in Bradford much of its bleak realism is countered by Billy Fisher's dreams of heading south to London, where everything is more dynamic, more exciting, more 1960s. Similarly with the Beatles' first film *A Hard Day's Night* (UA/Proscenium, 1964 Director: Richard Lester) the scenes in the north of England are stark and almost belong to a preceding decade in contrast to the lively excitement of 'swinging' London, where even Ringo's departure to the Thames foreshore and the war-damaged docklands leads to adventure. London is very much depicted as offering a sense of 'something happening', of the 'new', and of the 'now' that the locations outside the city did not offer.

Regional-based filmmaking continued as it had started with the 'kitchen-sink' dramas of the British New Wave through films such as *A Taste of Honey* (British Lion/Bryanstone/Woodfall, 1961 Director: Tony Richardson), *The Loneliness of the Long Distance Runner* (British Lion/Bryanstone/Woodfall, 1962 Director: Tony Richardson, and *This Sporting Life* (Rank/Independent Artists, 1963 Director: Lindsay Anderson).

BRITISH NEW WAVE A movement of well-educated, leftist filmmakers largely from a northern England, working-class background, that used 'realism' to construct stories of working-class lives ('kitchen-sink dramas'). Originally working on short films and documentaries as part of their 'free cinema' concept they graduated to feature film production establishing a north of England production base to compete with what they saw as a London-focused and London-centred industry. They included filmmakers Lindsay Anderson, Karel Reisz, and Tony Richardson.

From 1963 onwards however, both films and filmmakers began to gravitate towards London, the centre of music and fashion. This of course changed the films that these filmmakers made, and the representations of the regions they offered when viewed from the vibrant, exciting, rebuilding, metropolis. Tony Richardson stayed with his regional roots, but transposed them historically, directing *Tom Jones* (UA/Woodfall, 1963), a costumed romp through eighteenth-century society, whilst Karel Reisz and Lindsay Anderson moved from realism towards surrealism in *Morgan, a Suitable Case for Treatment* (British Lion/Quintra 1966, Director: Karel Reisz), and *If . . .* (Paramount/Memorial 1968, Director: Lindsay Anderson). In *Morgan, a Suitable Case for Treatment*, Reisz has transposed his northern, Communist hero to London, and in *If . . .* Anderson removes all sense of location by placing the action in an anonymous public school.

Both *Georgy Girl* (Columbia/Everglades, 1966 Director: Silvio Narizzano) and Richard Lester's *The Knack (and How to Get It)* told the stories of northern working-class girls (Lynn Redgrave and Rita Tushingham respectively) coming to London to seek their fortunes and getting caught up in the 'swinging London' scene of 'cool' fashion, sexual liberation, and disappearing class boundaries. All this (of course) against the backdrop of a very recognizable London with its grand buildings (in the case of *Georgy Girl*) and its bomb sites and suburban terraces (in *The Knack*).

It is a point worth making that as the period moved towards its close, London became associated with decadence and a collapsing society, as illustrated by *Performance*. It is interesting that among the last of the period's significant films should be one that has its hero leave London to return to his roots in the North-East of England, perhaps symbolically demonstrating that the 'swinging sixties' were coming to a close. *Get Carter* has Michael Caine's Jack Carter leave the London underworld with its 'classy' apartments, drugs, and 'model-like' girlfriends, to return to his Newcastle home town to avenge his brother's death. Here he finds grimy bed and breakfast lodgings, visits a smoke filled 'traditional' pub, searches through crumbling rundown terraces, and interacts with hardened women. Indeed the 'locals' are shot in a way to emphasize their 'otherness' to Jack Carter's softened London manner (the camera even highlighting one with six fingers on one hand).

This difference is embedded not only in the location, but in the style of construction. In the early part of the film, as Jack Carter leaves London, the style reflects much of its contemporaries in using hand-held camera, jump cuts, unusual framing, canted angles, etc. Once in Newcastle a realist style is adopted which sharpens the contrast between the two cities. Indeed there is almost a sense of a return to the British New Wave style of filmmaking here, where there is seemingly less structuring, and more use of the city's real backdrop to work against.

Whilst the distinction between London and the regions is still there as it was at the start of the period, by the end of the 'swinging sixties' the realism of the north seems more attractive than the distorted fantasy of London.

ACTIVITY . . .

- Take one of the films you have studied and transpose its locations (a regional location becomes London; London becomes a regional location). How does this affect the messages and values expressed? Is there anything else you would need to change to ensure that the story still works?
- What messages and values are expressed by London at the start of the period? Can you find examples of how this is expressed in a film you have studied? Does London represent different messages and values at the end of the period? Can you again find examples of how this is expressed in a film you have studied?
- In a group, discuss how style differs between films (or sequences) set in London and those set elsewhere in the country. Is there a difference between the styles used to depict town and country outside of London? Is central London (the tourist spots for example) shot differently from other parts of London? What does a differing style for a particular location do to help convey messages and values?
- Is there a difference between the London of *Darling* and the London of *Performance*? How is each depicted, and to what effect?

NATIONAL/REGIONAL IDENTITY

Whilst there was a clear focus on London and on the difference between the metropolis and the regions, what were simultaneously emerging were new regional identities, which in turn developed a new national identity. People from the north were depicted as 'flocking' to London, yet they were not overawed by the city, but instead brought an edge of realism with them, and a healthy dose of cynicism.

This is symbolized well in *A Hard Day's Night* where the Beatles constantly criticize, challenge and undermine the old figures of authority, including the police, 'elders and betters', the upper class, and bowler-hatted 'city gents'. This mocking of an old national identity (forged largely during the war years) is one that Richard Lester continued in *The Knack (and How to Get It)* where he captures local people in a documentary realist fashion, adding a commentary of their 'thoughts', all of which are critical of the attitudes and behaviour of the young people in the film. It is with additional irony that he has the central character, Colin (Michael Crawford), repeat and echo these same views as he fights his repression and his desires to have 'the knack' that housemate Tolen (Ray Brooks) has with women.

Suddenly in the 'swinging sixties' national identity was not about defocusing on differences but was about celebrating differences within a unifying context of freedom. Thus, Nancy Jones' (Rita Tushingham) broad Lancastrian accent is not out of place against the southern sounds of Tolen and Colin, as it is made insignificant against their shared ability (to varying degrees) to celebrate their freedom through action (such as in the sequence of bringing the bed home from the scrap yard).

Furthering the national identity was the sense of England in general (and London in particular) as the centre of the fashion world. Throughout the films of this period, there is a unifying representation of a fashion-conscious, youthful nation, eager to spur ahead into a future shaped by (as Prime Minister Harold Wilson termed) the 'white heat of technology'. The nation is seen as new, as 'cool', as witty, and as forward thinking, not held back by out-dated notions of class, caste, religion, gender or rank.

Music also defined this new national identity from the Beatles' films through the Dave Clark Five's *Catch Us If You Can* (Anglo Amalgamated/Bruton, 1965 Director: John Boorman), to Mick Jagger's acting in *Performance*. Indeed, not only were there films where pop artists performed, but the soundtrack scene also changed away from orchestral numbers to tracks that could be (or already had been) released as singles. This encouraged the potential for music to grow beyond a regional unifier to a national unifier, and, when coupled to the new trend for music shows on television, this became a powerful force in defining a new national identity that was forward looking, not anchored into its past.

Nowhere do all these ingredients combine more powerfully than in Lindsay Anderson's *If . . .*, where the setting is a bastion of national identity, the public school. Here we meet an individual, Mick Travis (Malcolm McDowell) who makes a stand for freedom and against the old authorities. His music and fashion inspired youthful sense of what could be, is suppressed not only by the authorities (in the shape of the school teachers, heads of houses, and the headmaster) but also by those of his peers who choose to collaborate with them. His protest spirals into anarchy and an armed (but fashionable) rebellion where the authority figures come under sustained attack from the rooftops after he sets the school hall ablaze during the Founders' Day ceremony. Mick Travis was the youthful herald of the new national identity, where respect had to be earned through action, not through historic 'right'.

ACTIVITY . . .

■ Create two columns, one marked 'old national identity' and the other marked 'new national identity'. From the films you have studied note down the defining features of the national identity that existed at the start of the

MESSAGES AND VALUES – BRITISH AND IRISH CINEMA (FS3)

'swinging sixties' and those of the national identity that emerged during the period. Are they completely separated from each other or are there some features that appear on both lists? Why do you think this is?

■ How important do you feel regional representations are? Is it right that they become lessened in the face of aspects of national identity?

■ Look at the principal characters from the films you have studied. Does their regional background affect the messages and values they promote? If so, in what ways?

■ From a film you have studied, note down where all the characters appear to be from (this can be place specific, or as loose as 'southern England'). Is there a significant pattern to their backgrounds? Does it vary between principal and background characters?

■ Are there any other categories you can think of that would help to define an emerging national identity in this period? Which films can evidence these? Do these categories offer any further insight into the films' messages and values?

CLASS, SEXUALITY, AND GENDER REPRESENTATION

From Darling's social climbing Diana Scott, through Morgan, a Suitable Case for Treatment's 'class traitor' Morgan Delt (David Warner), to If . . .'s public schoolboy Mick Travis, class is directly addressed in many of the films of the 'swinging sixties'. Indeed it is the very challenging of class boundaries that may well have helped the period 'swing', by encouraging a wider social intermingling, and exposure to a broader perspective.

Some filmmakers, such as Ken Loach, chose to approach issues of class (and indeed sexuality and gender) more directly still through films such as Poor Cow (Anglo Amalgamated/Vic/Fenchurch, 1967 Director: Ken Loach). Here, in a contrastingly un-swinging part of London, Loach introduces Joy (Carol White) the young mother who lives a life of squalor, confined by her position in society, and by her petty criminal husband. Joy is almost a mirror image of Darling's Diana Scott, and uses her physical attributes and some of the same techniques as Diana to further her aims, but to significantly less effect (largely because of the difference in starting point).

Joy is also an echo of one of the many women that appear in Alfie (Paramount/Sheldrake, 1966 Director: Lewis Gilbert). Here, working-class chauffeur, Alfie, seduces women from a variety of classes and backgrounds, offering commentaries on each one, and high-lighting their class differences. This, of course, is all offered in a sense of irony, with Alfie representing the 'old' establishment views, which a young, modern, 'swinging' audience would not share. It is interesting that as Alfie climbs the social ladder, meeting modern women, he becomes less confident in 'handling' them – the breaking of traditional class barriers and of traditional gender roles confuses his sense of who he is.

Whilst a traditional sense of masculinity carries across the films of the 1940s and 1950s, the 'swinging sixties' not only sees a shift of focus towards representations of women, but also of non-traditional men, or men adopting non-traditional roles/attitudes (such as Chas Devlin in *Performance*), and clearly the suggestion is that there is a process of evolution in terms of attitudes occurring in this period. This change is illustrated well by an obscure film from the middle of the period, *Work is a Four-Letter Word* (Universal/Cavalcade, 1968 Director: Peter Hall). This futuristic fantasy looks to a time of full employment and an entrenched social hierarchy, where the only unemployed man, Valentine Brose (David Warner) is forced to take a job as a power station attendant much to the delight of his girlfriend Betty Dorrick (Cilla Black – who also sings the title song). Here he grows magic mushrooms that eventually (due to an explosion) 'liberate' the whole town from class and gender restraints.

The nudity and sexual scenes of Lindsay Anderson's *If* . . . set the ground for the explicit sexual scenes in *Performance*, for the telephone sex of *Get Carter*, and the violent rapes in *A Clockwork Orange* (Warner/Polaris, 1971 Director: Stanley Kubrick), and *Straw Dogs* (Talent Associates/Amberbroco, 1971 Director: Sam Peckinpah). Here both sex and sexuality came onto the agenda explicitly and were explored in a variety of ways. It is interesting that, despite the moral freedoms granted by the 'swinging sixties', sexually active women were generally punished for their actions (from being trapped in a loveless marriage in *Darling*, to being murdered in *Get Carter*). Whilst attitudes seemed to have changed radically in this period, it appears that they had not shifted that far – the groundwork was done here that set the path for today's society.

ACTIVITY . . .

- What differences can you see in terms of class representation, gender representation, and the representation of sexuality across films you have studied spanning this period?
- Talk to parents and grandparents (and others in older generations) about what their understanding of class, gender roles, and sexuality were in the 1963–1973 period. Do they recall seeing any of the films you have studied at the time? If so, do they recall their reactions to them? Do they recall if they influenced their attitudes or behaviour?
- Take the characters from one of the films you have studied and swap their class and/or genders. How does the swap affect the film's messages and values. Is there anything that now needs to be done to the film's story to allow it to work?
- Consider your own class/gender/sexuality. Does this affect the way you perceive the films you have studied? If so, in what way? Discuss this with your peers. Consider whether you each have individual responses to these issues of representation or whether the filmmakers have positioned you into a preferred response.

MESSAGES AND VALUES – BRITISH AND IRISH CINEMA (FS3)

- What would you need to do to one of the films you have studied to take its representations back to the preceding decade? What would you need to do if you were remaking the film for today's audience? Consider both story and stylistic devices.

SOCIAL AND POLITICAL INSTITUTIONS AND THE RISE OF YOUTH

Representations of young people were being established by the British New Wave in the 1950s, though these were largely contextualized by their family relationships, the communities they lived in, and the organizations they worked for (including some mention of trade unions and political parties). The figure of the autonomous youth did not fully emerge until the films of swinging Britain, and in the early period there was little to distinguish them from their adult forebearers.

Quickly however, through films such as A Hard Day's Night, The Knack (and How to Get It), and Work is a Four-Letter Word, the 'swinging', fashion conscious, music loving, trendy, and most importantly independent young person arrived on screen. Little in the way of family relationships were displayed other than those consciously entered into (marriage etc.), and work seemed to play very little part in the lives of these young people, so this contextualizing institution was also removed from them. Political and generally of the left, these youths would discuss political concepts but often with a cynical or ironic sense of 'truth' or understanding, that gave such discussions a throw-away quality. This is well illustrated in The Knack (and How to Get It) where the discussion comes rattling along at speed, and where there is little time to sense whether the characters are actually meaning what they say.

Case Study: *Richard Lester* (1932–)

Born in Philadelphia, USA, Richard Lester began his career in American television, arriving in Britain in 1956 where he worked with Spike Milligan and Peter Sellers on the television comedy 'A Show Called Fred' (BBC, 1956). This in turn led to working with them again on a short film *The Running, Jumping and Standing Still Film* (1959), which acted as a very effective calling card for his first features A Hard Day's Night (1964), Help! (UA/Walter Shenson/Suba Films, 1965), and The Knack (and How to Get It) (1965).

This early success was developed through the successful *Musketeer* series of films in the 1970s and 1980s, but his style of filmmaking dropped out of fashion and his career faltered from the 1980s onwards.

Richard Lester encapsulates the image of swinging Britain better than any other director of the time. In using odd, surreal humour accompanied by a broad use of cinematic devices, he was able to capture the moment in all its excitement, experimentation and triviality. His insolent use of film technique mirrored his subject's insolence in the face of tradition and authority, and so form and content merged perfectly, if only for a short while.

The political landscape of the period is one of consensus politics with power swapping between Harold Wilson's Labour government and Edward Heath's Conservatives. As the period progressed the prosperity that was present at the start of swinging Britain was in a steady decline, with rising concern over unemployment, membership of the Common Market (now the European Union), immigration, and the decline in traditional heavy industries (coal, steel, shipbuilding, etc.). This changing landscape is reflected in the films of the period, as the exuberance of the early films gives way to decadence and political reflection in the later ones.

ACTIVITY

- Discuss with members of older generations what it was like to be young in the period of swinging Britain. Try to discover what their relationships with family and community were like. What do they remember of the politics of the time? Do they recall their attitude towards tradition and authority?
- What messages and values do the youths convey in the films you have studied? Are they different to those conveyed by older characters? If so, in what way?
- What macro (narrative, genre, etc.) and micro techniques do the filmmakers of swinging Britain use to bring social and political issues to the fore?
- If you were to re-make one of the films you have studied for a modern audience, what social and political values would you want to convey? What changes to the film's story/structure would you need to make for it to succeed?
- How are figures of authority depicted in the films you have studied? What messages and values are being promoted in this depiction?

PRODUCTION CONTEXT

The development of television in Britain throughout the 1950s encouraged not only new approaches to filmmaking that filtered through in the 1960s, but also the development of a training ground for filmmakers to hone their craft and to practise their skills. Both BBC and the later arrival ITV had regional production centres, which allowed the regions (such as Manchester) to develop and retain local talent (which differed from the film industry which centred on London). Television gave a solid production base for the 1960s boom in film production to build from, and provided a body of skilled labour to meet the creative demands.

The strength of the British New Wave filmmakers in the early 1960s attracted the interest of the Hollywood studios who were looking to outsource much of their production so that they could downsize their operations (and operational costs) in their extensive studios in Hollywood. The money that companies like Warners and MGM brought with them was a very welcome boost to the British film industry which was used to filmmaking on a minimal budget, and the majority of the films of swinging Britain are co-productions with Hollywood companies.

Towards the end of the 1960s however, the Hollywood studios were in severe financial crisis back in America, and the decision was made for them to axe British co-production, and axe their offices in the UK. The withdrawal of such significant amounts of funding was a considerable shock to the British industry, and it immediately meant that the less commercial films (like *Work is a Four-Letter Word*, and perhaps even films like *Performance*) could not now be made as they would not be commercially viable. This led to an immediate crash as the industry struggled into the 1970s with the final committed American funds drying up. By 1973 the industry was on its knees. Cinemas were being converted into bingo halls, and the era of swinging Britain was truly and unquestionably over.

Case Study: *Anglo-Amalgamated*

Anglo-Amalgamated was set up in 1945 at studios in Merton Park, London, by Nat Cohen and Stuart Levy to make low-budget thrillers (B-movies). They produced Michael Powell's *Peeping Tom* (1960), a number of horror films including Roger Corman's *The Masque of the Red Death* (1964) and *The Tomb of Ligeia* (1964), and all the Carry On Films up until 1966. In the early 1960s they began working with some of the most important filmmakers of the period including John Schlesinger, Tony Richardson, John Boorman, and Ken Loach.

Losing significant financial advantage as the Hollywood studios pulled out of British production at the end of the 1960s, this small, but shrewd studio fell into financial difficulties, and in 1969 was bought out by ABPC/EMI.

EXAMPLE EXAM QUESTIONS

1   How are issues of liberation explored in the films you have studied?

2   What for you are the most striking messages and values of the period as conveyed in the films you have studied?

continued

3   Do the films you have studied have anything to say about class in this period?

4   The films of swinging Britain are essentially about freedom. Discuss how the films you have studied engage with the issue of freedom.

5   Is there any benefit to understanding messages and values in the films of swinging Britain in exploring the attitudes of young people in the films you have studied?

6   What can you discover about issues of identity from looking at the depiction of male and/or female characters in the films you have studied?

7   What particular images/use of sound capture best the messages and values of swinging Britain in the films you have studied?

FURTHER READING

MacCabe, Colin (1998) *Performance*, London: BFI Film Classics.

Murphy, Robert (1992) *Sixties British Cinema*, London: BFI.

Walker, Alexander (1974) *Hollywood England: the British Film Industry in the Sixties*, London: Michael Joseph.

Savage, Jon (1993) 'Snapshots of the sixties', *Sight and Sound*, 3(5): 14–18. (The 1960s may haunt us – but what did happen exactly when pop music and swinging London took to celluloid in films ranging from *A Hard Day's Night* to *Performance?* Savage discusses the lasting influence of 1960s pop culture in relation to *A Hard Day's Night*, *Blow-Up* and *Performance*.)

USEFUL WEBSITES

http://www.britishpictures.com (a resource offering essays, articles, reviews, and title specific information)

http://www.britmovies.co.uk (valuable for synopses, cast lists, etc.)

▼ 15 PASSIONS AND REPRESSIONS

In this chapter we look at:

- the representation of gender, sexuality and the family;
- the social and institutional context of *Beautiful Thing*;
- definitions of realism;
- narrative structure;
- the 'coming of age' film;
- New Queer Cinema;
- how messages and values are constructed in the focus film.

NOTEBOX

Focus film:	*Beautiful Thing* (Hettie Macdonald, 1998)
Suggested comparative film:	*My Summer of Love* (Pavel Pawlikovski, 2004)

This topic is one of the widest ranging of those offered. It is not limited to a specific period or genre. Passions and repressions as an area of study initially sounds rather abstract and difficult to define:

- We can be passionate about a great variety of things – people, places, sport, art, food, wine, etc.
- A passion can be a positive force or a destructive one – hatred can be defined as a passion.
- How would you define the term passion? Is there anything that you are passionate about?
- Looking again at the first point above, which films have you seen recently which take passion as a central subject?

Because of the range of passions experienced by human beings, films belonging to different genres, in different styles and appealing to different audiences can be studied in this topic area.

THEME In analysing the subject matter of films and the way that they construct messages and values, we need to distinguish between the story and the themes. The plot is the action or story of the film; when someone asks you what a film is about, this is usually what you would relate to them. The themes of a film are what the plot makes you think about, the way that the film comments on wider issues. For example the story of *Bridget Jones's Diary* is: a 'thirty-something' single woman falls in love with the wrong man before realizing that Mark Darcy is her true love. The theme of the film is: the changing position of women in society – now that women are independent in terms of career and financial power how does this affect their traditional roles in society and their relationships with men?

ACTIVITY . . .

Think of a film you have seen recently. Write a sentence which describes the main plot and then one which refers to the themes.

Here are some suggestions of films with passion as a central theme:

Billy Elliot (Stephen Daldry, 1999)
Billy's passion for dance is a way of expressing his difference from his family and community.

Bend it like Beckham (Gurinder Chadha, 2002)
Jesminder's desire to play football is her way of defining herself to her family.

ACTIVITY . . .

Now add two films of your own, including a short sentence explaining the central plot of the film.

In both of these examples the passion which is explored – dancing, football – is driven by the need of the central character to express who they are and how they are different from the expectations placed on them. Another way of putting this is to say that Billy's dancing is part of his identity as a young man, which in turn signifies his character as an adult.

IDENTITY The concept of identity refers to the way that different groups (family, friends, schools, government, etc.) in society see us and the way in which we see ourselves. These two views are likely to be different, even conflicting. The factors affecting our identity include gender, race, religion, class, sexuality and nationality which are interlinked and have become more and more complicated. Some people may wish to identify themselves as gay; for others to do so may suggest discrimination or prejudice.

The growth in identity politics such as gay rights and feminism has indicated a move away from political parties to single-issue politics in society.

Central to all the films mentioned above is the conflict created between the central character's need to follow their passion and the different forces which oppose it. As you know from the work on narrative, conflict is often central to a film's plot creating oppositions between characters which are worked through and – usually – resolved at the end.

ACTIVITY...

Select one of the films which you have chosen as having passion as a central theme and make notes on the following:

- What is the central passion explored in the film? Is it a passion for a person, a place, an art form, etc.?
- Is the reason for the passion explained?
- Are there any characters who try to prevent the central character from following their passion? If so who?
- What motivates these characters? Why do they want to prevent the pursuit of this passion? (Their reasons may be to do with religion, gender, age, race, class, etc.)
- How are the conflicts resolved at the end of the film? Are they?

This battle between the different characters in the film creates the narrative conflict.

Example: *Bend it like Beckham*

- The central passion is for football – although there are sub-plots about friendship and a love story.
- The passion for football is a way for Jesminder to express her identity as an independent young woman; football is used as a metaphor for Jesminder's desire to move away from the traditional culture of her parents.

- The characters who try to prevent Jesminder playing football are her parents and extended family.
- These characters are motivated by their views on religion and gender; as a British Asian girl Jesminder is expected to conform by becoming a wife and mother.
- The conflicts are resolved at the end when the parents realize how important football is to Jesminder or – to continue the use of football as a metaphor – they realize that they have to let their daughter live her own life rather than conform to other people's expectations. It is an upbeat and optimistic ending.

The conflicts evident in the above films (and probably in the ones you have chosen) and the obstacles which face the hero are some of the ways in which the messages and values of the films are constructed. For example the story of *Billy Elliot* (a working-class boy from a 'macho' community who wants to be a ballet dancer) suggests that traditional expectations about class and gender can be detrimental to individuals and society. This could be read as the messages and values of the film.

Conflicts are also the basis for the theme of repression in this topic area. By preventing Jesminder from playing football and Billy from dancing, the parents in these films repress their children and refuse to recognize their true identity.

KEY TERM

REPRESSION Repression is the process of being kept down by force (not always physical); it refers to the way that a person's right to freedom of expression whether politically, socially or culturally can be denied.

In psychoanalysis the term 'repression' has a different meaning. Freud defines repression as a defence mechanism. It is the way that individuals protect themselves from harmful but attractive desires (often sexual). According to Freud such desires can never be completely repressed but return, in the form of dreams for example.

FOCUS FILM: *BEAUTIFUL THING*

Beautiful Thing is the focus film chosen for this topic and the following section will suggest a process for analysing the film. It is important to remember that you will need to think about *Beautiful Thing* in comparison to your other chosen film for this topic rather than on its own.

The analysis of *Beautiful Thing* can be constructed in two sections:

1 An analysis of the film itself:

- film language and film style;
- narrative and genre;
- representation of gender/sexuality, place and class.

2 The wider contexts which shape the film:

- British film industry (institutions);
- social/cultural/historical contexts of the themes explored in the film and the time the film was made (gay rights and legislation);
- New Queer Cinema.

It is important to integrate these approaches to analyse the way that the film uses a range of techniques – film language, soundtrack, representations, narrative structure, etc. – to construct messages and values. It is also important to consider the wider contexts which influenced the making of the film – limitations of budget, the need to find an audience, etc.

Both sections above develop skills and knowledge from other parts of the specification: Section 1 refers to FS1 and Section 2 to FS2, as well as introducing new approaches to the study of films. This development of links between the different parts of the specification is very important and you should get used to developing your ideas about films by linking together areas from different parts of the specification.

Beautiful Thing is the story of Jamie, a schoolboy living on the Thamesmead estate in London, and follows his life during one summer as he realizes he is in love with his friend Ste. It is a low budget (£1.5m) British film and it premièred at the London Lesbian and Gay Film Festival in 1996. It was funded by Channel Four (before it set up FilmFour as a film production arm) and took less than £0.5m at the UK box office. It is a category 'A' British film as defined by the British Film Institute. This means that it was produced in Britain with British money. The cast and crew are mainly British and the story reflects British subject matter. *Beautiful Thing* received positive reviews and was also released in the US where it took $1.5m at the box office.

- Do the above points about production and exhibition create expectations about the film?
- What do you think the film will look like?
- Do you expect it to be a comedy? A drama?
- What are these expectations based on? Is it to do with your ideas about British (rather than Hollywood) films?

ACTIVITY . . .

How would you research information about a film's budget and box office, cast and crew?

Find the entries for *My Summer of Love* on the following websites:

www.imdb.com
www.screenonline.org.uk
www.launchingfilms.com

Answer the following questions:

- What is the film about?

continued

- Which production companies produced the film?
- Was any public money used to finance the film? If so give details.
- What was the budget for the film?
- Who directed the film? What other films have they directed?
- Who wrote the screenplay?

Using the same websites, look up *Beautiful Thing* to research the writer of the film, Jonathan Harvey:

- Is it an adapted or an original screenplay?
- What else has Jonathan Harvey written (film, TV, theatre)? Can you see any similarities in themes and style with *Beautiful Thing*?

Before continuing with the analysis you will need to watch *Beautiful Thing*. The first time you watch it you should make a note of the following:

- the names and a brief description of the main characters;
- the main settings used;
- any themes of passion and repression in the film.

As your work on the film develops, you will need to watch particular sequences – and probably the whole film – again to prepare for your exam.

ANALYSIS OF THE OPENING OF THE FILM

The opening of a film is often a useful sequence to study because of the way it introduces key themes, setting and characters, and these can suggest the messages and values of the film.

Watch the pre-credit and credit sequence of *Beautiful Thing* which finishes with Jamie turning off the TV (3 minutes 40 seconds), and make notes on the following:

Film language

- Describe the type of shots used:

    - are they medium/long/close-ups, etc.?
    - are any extreme angles used?
    - are the shots long takes or average length?

- Describe the setting used:

    - what do the settings tell us about the characters?
    - is it a positive representation of place?

- Describe the music on the soundtrack:

    - is it upbeat, melancholy, pop or classical?

- what are the lyrics and what mood does the music create?
- is it the type of music you expect to hear as a soundtrack to this setting?

Throughout the film, songs by the Mamas and Papas (whose lead singer, Mama Cass, is idolized by Jamie's neighbour, Leah) are used as a soundtrack to montage sequences. Watch these sequences to construct an analysis of the way that the music contributes to the meanings created in the film.

In *My Summer of Love*, very different music is used to represent class and character; after watching the entire film suggest particular scenes from the film where this is evident and which could be used in contrast to *Beautiful Thing*.

Narrative and genre

- Are there any clues to the narrative and genre of the film?
    - Consider character, setting, plot (so far).

Institutions

- From looking at this extract, how would you define the film as British?
- At this point in the film does it seem similar to any other British films (or TV series)?

REALISM Realism is a visual style which is particularly associated with British cinema such as the British New Wave of the 1960s. It is an attempt to show the world as it really is and tends to concentrate on social and political issues and how these affect working-class characters. A realist style has its own codes and conventions (particular style of acting, lighting, dialogue, setting, plots, etc.) which the audience recognizes as realist.

Some British realist films for further research:

Saturday Night and Sunday Morning (Director: Karel Reisz, 1960)
Brassed Off (Director: Mark Herman, 1996)
Sweet Sixteen (Director: Ken Loach, 2002)
Last Resort (Director: Pavel Pawlikowski, 2000)

KEY TERM

Summary analysis of the opening sequence of *Beautiful Thing*

Points to note in the opening sequence:

The opening of the film is structured around the journey of Jamie, the central character, after he leaves the school football match early and runs home. This journey allows the audience to understand something about character and place; it is a multi-cultural area with black, Asian and white characters introduced. There is humour in the relationships between the characters but already some tension is evident. As Jamie travels from the football pitch to home, the main setting of the Thamesmead estate is introduced and this is predominantly concrete spaces without any greenery. This type of setting – a council estate in a big city – is typical of a realist style in British cinema but *Beautiful Thing* does not just use a conventional realist style. The use of music and the appearance of a rainbow over the estate challenge the usual representations of working-class settings as repressive and a place the characters want to escape from. The use of the rainbow is an interesting point to use to debate a realist style – is it conceivable that there was a rainbow at the moment of filming and therefore this is an example of a realist style, or do you think the film maker is using the rainbow for expressive purposes?

The film language in this sequence is typical of the rest of the film – continuity editing with a predominance of medium shots or close-ups with static camera. There is also the use of hand-held camera which is a technique associated with realism and documentary, and Jamie's journey through the city is told through overhead (bird's eye view) shots. These shots, in combination with the music, tell the audience about Jamie's optimistic and independent spirit, which in turn suggests that this will be an uplifting film.

ACTIVITY

Comparative analysis: *My Summer of Love*

Once you have completed your analysis of the opening sequence of *Beautiful Thing*, watch the opening sequence of *My Summer of Love*. What comparisons can you make between the two films? Use the headings above as a starting point for your comparative analysis. The different representations of England – the city and the country – are particularly noticeable.

BEAUTIFUL THING AND NARRATIVE STRUCTURE

The plot of *Beautiful Thing* revolves around the desires and passions of the main character Jamie and the supporting characters in the film.

Figure 15.1 Scene from *Beautiful Thing*
Source: C4 / RGA

Figure 15.2 Scene from *My Summer of Love*
Source: UK Film Council / BBC / The Kobal Collection

Narrative and character in *Beautiful Thing*:

■ Make a list of the main characters in the film and describe their passions and desires.

For example Sandra (Jamie's mum) wants to:

■ manage her own pub;
■ leave the Thamesmead estate;
■ be a good mother (is worried that she's not);
■ have a better standard of living.

■ Once you've completed your lists consider the following:

■ Are the desires fulfilled by the end of the film?
■ Does the fulfilment of the desires suggest anything about the messages and values of the film? (For example, are the characters' choices seen as positive or negative in the film?)

MESSAGES AND VALUES: RESOLUTION IN *BEAUTIFUL THING*

The endings of films can function in different ways; in mainstream films we expect an ending to tidy up the plot of the film, to give us the answers to the questions raised in the story. Will the central couple finally get together? Who was the killer? Will the team of underdogs win the championship, and so on? These endings can be very satisfying to an audience, like the solution to a puzzle. Other endings can be more ambiguous, leaving the audience to wonder what will happen next to the characters. These types of endings are more commonly found in non-mainstream cinema or art cinema and have been referred to as 'open' endings.

KEY TERM

NON-MAINSTREAM/ALTERNATIVE/ART CINEMA Although these terms all have slightly different meanings they are often used interchangeably to refer to films which are produced outside of the major film studios – usually Hollywood. They refer to films which in terms of narrative structure (often open rather than closed endings), subject matter, film language, budget, etc. are different from mainstream film. In some cases filmmakers choose to work in this way as they oppose the style and messages and values of Hollywood cinema; in others filmmakers who start in this area move on to big budget films. These areas will be studied in more detail at A2.

A variation on this type of ending is found in contemporary genres such as horror and action films where the ending is left unresolved to allow for a sequel. As you can see, the kind of ending a film has is linked to the genre, narrative and institutional context. When watching different types of films we expect different types of endings; if we don't find out what happened at the end of a thriller we may feel cheated but a drama may work better with certain strands of the narrative left open – it may be too unrealistic to tie up all the loose ends. Such endings can be linked to the style of realism.

Points for discussion:

- What type of ending do you think is more realistic, an open or closed ending? Why?
- Should films be realistic? Can genre films ever reflect reality?

NARRATIVE THEORY AND RESOLUTION When Film Studies was first developing as an academic subject in the 1960s and 1970s there was a suspicion amongst academics about popular, usually, genre films. Influenced by Marxist views of popular culture many theorists argued that genre films spoon-fed their audiences rather than letting the audience think for themselves. An example of this was the way that endings, or resolutions, of popular films explained everything, while other types of films and filmmakers, European, 'art' cinema, etc., often left the audience with unanswered questions.

Why does it matter whether the audience is given the answers in a film or questions are left open? Some theorists argued that what happens in the cinema (where most people watched films at this time) has an influence on audience behaviour in the 'real world'; if people get used to being told what to think they will not question society and their place in it. In other words, Hollywood was seen as part of a system which kept the masses in their place – poor, hard-working and unquestioning. These ideas are similar to the hypodermic theory in Media Studies – that the audience is injected with messages from popular culture and is unable to question them.

- Do you think there is still a division between popular/mainstream and art cinema? Consider:

  - Do these different types of films have different audiences?
  - Are some types of films considered 'better' than others? If so in what way? By whom?

- Would you define either *Beautiful Thing* or *My Summer of Love* as art cinema?

ANALYSIS OF THE FINAL SEQUENCE OF *BEAUTIFUL THING*

In the context of the discussion of realism and different types of endings, the final sequence of *Beautiful Thing* provides many points for analysis. The way that the different desires of each character and the conflict between them are treated in an ending is also indicative of the point of view of the filmmaker and the messages and values of the film. However this view can also be challenged by the audience who may not agree with the message.

Watch the closing sequence of *Beautiful Thing* (1 hour 21 minutes to the final credits, 3 minutes) and make notes on the following:

Film language

- Describe the type of shots used.

    - How are the shots and use of camera different from the opening sequence?
    - What does the use of camera in this sequence suggest about the emotions of the characters?
    - Do you think that the type of shots and editing used in a film can affect the audience response?

- Describe the mise en scène in this sequence.

    - How are elements of the mise en scène used in the opening referred to in the final sequence?

- Soundtrack.

    - The final sequence of the film continues the use of the Mamas and Papas' songs heard throughout the film. How do the lyrics reflect the themes of the film?

Narrative structure

- Conflicts and oppositions.

    - Which conflicts in the narrative are resolved in this sequence?
    - Which characters are ignored in the final sequence? Why is this?

- Resolution.

    - Is this an open or closed ending? (Are the problems set up in the narrative resolved at the end, or are we left to wonder what will happen next?) Is it a mixture of both?
    - Would you describe this as a realistic ending? Consider the following:

        - Can you imagine this happening in real life – if not, why not?
        - What would be a realistic ending for this film? Why do you think the film-makers chose the conclusion they did?
        - Does the ending work in terms of the narrative, themes and style of the film? (Is it a logical ending?)

Messages and values

With reference to your previous analysis of film language and narrative consider the point of view of the film. What position do the filmmakers take on the central passion of the film; the relationship between Jamie and Ste? How is this evident in the resolution of the film? What does this suggest about the values of the film?

These ideas will be developed in the discussion of representation in *Beautiful Thing*.

Comparative analysis: *My Summer of Love*

Compare the ending of *Beautiful Thing* to *My Summer of Love*. Are they different in terms of how much of the narrative is resolved? How are the messages and values of the film evident in the way the film is resolved?

How does the discussion of realism affect your understanding of this ending?

Is it a happy ending?

Messages and values: representation of gender and sexuality

In analysing the messages and values in *Beautiful Thing* the representation of gender and sexuality are central and need to be discussed together.

WHY DOES REPRESENTATION MATTER?

The concept of representation reveals that media texts are constructions; they re-present the world to the audience. Any media text, including film, is mediation, an interpretation of the world, produced for a variety of artistic, economic and social reasons.

Representations rely on the shared recognition of ideas, groups and places. However there can certainly be disagreement in the interpretation of representations – whether, for example, they are read as negative, positive, inaccurate or partial images – and it is the analysis of how and why these representations are constructed and received that is important.

One of the reasons that representations are important is that they may influence the way people think about a particular group etc.:

> [How] social groups are treated in cultural representation is part and parcel of how they are treated in life, that poverty, harassment, self-hate and discrimination (in housing, jobs, educational opportunity and so on) are shored up and instituted by representation.
>
> (Dyer 1993).

Figure 15.3 Scene from *Beautiful Thing*
Source: C4 / RGA

Figure 15.4 Scene from *My Summer of Love*
Source: UK Film Council / BBC / The Kobal Collection

- Are 'negative' representations responsible for the prejudicial treatment of a particular group (perhaps defined by sexuality, class, gender, race, etc.)?
- Can 'negative' representations be challenged by 'positive' ones, which will in turn change people's attitudes and behaviour?
- If representations do affect the way that we think about particular groups, what does that suggest about the film (and wider media) audience?

One of the notable aspects of *Beautiful Thing* is the representation of young gay men. In considering the nature of this representation you should keep in mind the above debates and also consider the social and political context of being a gay male (or female) in the late twentieth century. The following chronology provides one kind of context but you should also consider wider issues of representation across society such as news stories, TV drama, soap operas, sitcoms and other films.

Social and political contexts

NOTEBOX

Selected chronology of gay rights and legislation

1957: the Wolfenden Committee publishes its report recommending the decriminalization of consensual homosexual acts between adult men (lesbianism has never been illegal).

1967: ten years after it was recommended, the Sexual Offences Act was passed in the United Kingdom allowing sex between two consenting men over the age of 21.

1969: Stonewall riots: when police raided a gay bar – the Stonewall Inn – in New York the customers resisted arrest, leading to a series of violent riots which spread across the city. The Stonewall riots were a catalyst for the gay rights movement in the US and beyond. The Gay Liberation Front was set up in response to these events.

1970: first US gay pride parade held in New York City.

1981: in the US the Moral Majority starts an anti-gay campaign. Norway becomes the first country in the world to enact a law to prevent discrimination against homosexuals.

1988: Section 28 passed in the UK. The aim of this legislation was to stop local authorities 'promoting' homosexual relationships. In practice this meant that council funding for books, plays, films, support groups, etc., which presented gay relationships as natural was banned.

1990: OutRage! formed in the UK.

1997: UK extends immigration rights to same-sex couples.

1998: in the US Matthew Shepard was murdered. His life story is the subject of the film *Boys Don't Cry*.

2000: Section 28 repealed in Scotland. Age of consent for homosexual sex made equal to that for heterosexual sex (16) in the United Kingdom.

2003: Section 28 repealed in the rest of the UK.

2004: same-sex marriage: in the United States, Massachusetts legalizes same-sex marriage. Eleven US states ban the practice after public referendums. The UK government passes a civil partnership law but same-sex marriage remains illegal. Pressure groups such as Stonewall continue to campaign for equal rights in this area.

2005: Governor of California, Arnold Schwarzenegger, announces he will veto proposals to allow same-sex marriages, blocking the bill which was passed by the state government. The first civil partnerships take place in the UK.

Links for further research: www.stonewall.org.uk, www.outrage.nabumedia.com

Does the knowledge of the political and social context of gay rights affect the meaning of the representations in *Beautiful Thing* and *My Summer of Love*? Could you interpret them as a political statement? Are the representations positive or negative – or is this a problematic idea in itself?

NOTEBOX

Cultural context: film movement – New Queer Cinema

The production and distribution of *Beautiful Thing* was possible due to a more open attitude in society to gay issues but also because of the influence of an earlier movement in US cinema.

New Queer Cinema is the term given to a group of films which emerged in the US in the early 1990s. The films were examples of independent cinema and were first shown at film festivals – particularly the Sundance Film Festival founded by Robert Redford – from where many gained crossover distribution to a wider audience. These films had in common a central character who was on the margins of society – an outsider – usually due to their sexuality but issues such as race, gender, class and physical disability were also referred to. While there had been films which featured gay characters and storylines before, New Queer Cinema was different in that it rejected the idea of positive representations which would be acceptable to the heterosexual, mainstream audience and instead deliberately attempted to shock and anger that audience. In a similar approach, the term 'queer' which had previously been used as a term of abuse was appropriated by some organizations and individuals and used as positive form of identification.

Some examples of New Queer Cinema (US):

Poison (Todd Haynes, 1991)
Go Fish (Rose Troche, 1994)
The Living End (Gregg Araki, 1993)

UK:

Looking for Langston (Isaac Julien, 1988)
Young Soul Rebels (Isaac Julien, 1991)

Figure 15.5 *Scene from Beautiful Thing*
Source: C4 / RGA

Analysis of key sequence: representation of gender and the 'coming of age' film

The third sequence for analysis is when Ste stays the night at Jamie's flat after a row with his family, and they have a discussion in Jamie's bedroom (22 minutes–24 minutes).

This sequence is important because it develops the themes of gender expectations and sexuality as well as showing the increased closeness between Jamie and Ste. It is a quiet, intimate scene with none of the noise and clutter of the rest of the film.

KEY TERM

GENDER AND SEX Gender and sex are often used interchangeably but there are important differences:

Sex refers to the biological differences between men and women. Sex is fixed and does not change over time; it is the same across countries and across cultures, while gender is often different.

Gender refers to the social differences between men and women, girls and boys. These are the expectations that society has about men and women's roles and responsibilities. These gender expectations will change over time and will be different in different countries and amongst different cultures.

KEY TERM

GENDER IDENTITY The study of representations of gender is important partly because gender is a political issue: Feminism is a social movement that questions gender inequalities and tries to change them, hoping to achieve gender equality, particularly in relation to work and pay. Part of the campaign for equal opportunities relied on pointing out the way that gender expectations prevent equality – and affect men as well as women.

After watching the sequence make notes on the following:

- Describe the mise en scène of the sequence. What does it tell us about the two boys and their characters? (Remember that mise en scène includes composition and figure placement.)
- What signifiers of gender are used (visual and through dialogue) in the sequence? Are these conventionally seen as masculine or feminine?
- Describe the use of shots and editing in the sequence. How does this style of film language contribute to the atmosphere of the sequence?
- There are three other sequences in the film which take place in the bedroom – two between Jamie and Ste and one between Jamie and his mother after they've had a row. Look at these scenes again:

  - What is the function of each of the sequences in the overall structure of the film? (Consider how plot and character are developed in each sequence.)
  - How are the themes of the film developed across the three sequences?
  - From looking at these sequences, what do you think is the filmmaker's view of Jamie and Ste's relationship? What evidence do you have for this?

Representation

The representation of gender is only one of a range of representations which can be studied in *Beautiful Thing* and should be developed to include an analysis of Sandra. Other important areas to look at include the representation of the *family*, of *place* and of *class*.

■ What key sequences would you choose to illustrate these three areas from the film?
■ In *My Summer of Love* the central protagonists are female – how do they conform to or subvert (go against) gender expectations?
■ Can you see any similarities between Mona and Jamie?

The conversation between Jamie and Ste about their responses to the world around them is typical of a type of narrative which has been defined as the 'coming of age' film and it is interesting to place *Beautiful Thing* in this context (one which has been more often associated with Hollywood cinema). The 'coming of age' film is often a sub-genre of the teen movie, although there are examples across a range of genres. It isn't a discrete genre but there are some recognizable codes and conventions:

Conventions of the 'coming of age' film

■ The coming of age is a period of transition from 'childhood' to 'adulthood' which is characterized by the need to make decisions about the future – to do with family, friends, education, work, sexuality, etc.
■ The time scale for taking these important decisions is often a short period – such as a summer.
■ 'Coming of age' films tend to rely on dialogue and emotion rather than physical action.
■ The actual age of the central character can vary, but tends to be around mid-teen.
■ The story is often told in flashback by the central character who is now older and wiser.
■ The central character is usually male.

Discussion points

■ What 'coming of age' films have you seen? Include British and US films.
■ Who do you think is the audience for these films? Why do you think they have remained so popular?
■ Would you define *Beautiful Thing* and *My Summer of Love* as 'coming of age' films? Do the conventions apply to both films?

SUGGESTIONS FOR FURTHER WORK

Alternative comparative films:

My Beautiful Laundrette (Stephen Frears, 1985)
The Crying Game (Neil Jordan, 1992)
Young Soul Rebels (Isaac Julien, 1991)
Wilde (Brian Gilbert, 1997)
Get Real (Simon Shore, 1998)
Scandal (Michael Caton-Jones, 1989)
Wish You Were Here (David Leland, 1987)

In constructing an analysis of your chosen films, consider:

- What are the main themes of the film?
- What conflicts are evident in the narrative? Which are resolved?
- What type of film language is used?
- Which representations are the most important in the film and why?
- How are the messages and values linked to the representations?
- What information can you find out about the political and/or social context of the film?

To provide evidence for your analysis of the film, you need to choose key sequences which illustrate your points. These should be chosen to reflect the themes and the film language.

EXAMPLE EXAM QUESTIONS

Make reference to at least two films, one of which must be a *focus* film.

1   Is the social world in which the characters live represented as a significant influence on key characters' passions or repressions?

2   How are the emotions and experiences of the characters in the films you have studied communicated through sound and image?

MESSAGES AND VALUES – BRITISH AND IRISH CINEMA (FS3)

▼ 16 SOCIAL AND POLITICAL CONFLICT

In this chapter we look at:

- representations of the state and state power (specifically the government and the army);
- representations of the 'enemies' of the state (who defines who they are?);
- forms of opposition to authority (such as demonstrations, protests) and how these are dealt with (questions of justice);
- national identity: inclusion and exclusion, who is defined as British and who isn't and by whom;
- conflict at the community/family level; particularly generational and religious conflict;
- the social and political contexts of the events of *Bloody Sunday*.

Focus film:	*Bloody Sunday* (Paul Greengrass, 2002)
Suggested comparative film:	*In the Name of the Father* (Jim Sheridan,1994)

As with the previous topic 'passions and repressions', the 'social and political conflict' topic is centred on the idea of oppositions in story and plot. To begin with it is important therefore to define what is meant by the term 'social and political conflict'. There is likely to be some overlap with the themes in 'passions and repressions'. However, that topic emphasizes personal expressions of desire and identity while this area is more explicitly concerned with organized groups in political and social contexts. The different areas of conflict at family, community, national and state level are likely to be interlinked.

British cinema and class

Representations of class and class conflict have been a central theme in British cinema history. Definitions of British cinema as a national cinema often include a preoccupation with class, particularly in the realist films of the 1960s and the costume dramas of the late 1980s and 1990s.

Listed below are some recent British films with social and political conflict as a central theme:

Gosford Park (Robert Altman, 2002)

Gosford Park is set in the 1930s in an English country house. It deals with the lives of a group of aristocrats, who have gathered for the weekend, and the servants who look after them and the house. The central conflict is one of *class division* between those 'above and below stairs' but there are also the hierarchies within the different groups; the housekeeper is of a higher status than the cook, etc.

My son the fanatic (Prasad, 1997)

(This is currently a close study film for this unit and could be studied as an extension of this topic area.)

This film deals with several social conflicts and is a good example of the way these conflicts intertwine. The central character is Parvez, an immigrant who lives in Bradford and has integrated into British society. Farid, his son is a student who rejects the values of Western society and becomes a Muslim fundamentalist. The conflicts include those between the different generations and between religions. The film also raises questions of national identity – who is defined as British and who is not.

The representation of these conflicts is one of the ways that the messages and values of the films are constructed by the filmmaker and interpreted by the audience. Which other British films can you add which deal with conflict? Which different conflicts are represented?

ACTIVITY

Discussion point

- Which social and political conflicts do you think are particularly relevant to contemporary British society? You might consider race, religion, laws. Try to give examples for each.
- Do you think British films should represent these issues?
- Does Hollywood cinema represent contemporary conflicts?

Both the chosen films in this topic area deal with the politics of Northern Ireland and particularly the conflict between Irish Republicans and the British government. This is a complex area with a long history – and a still changing present with peace negotiations – but it is important to have some understanding of the wider contexts of the events depicted.

FOCUS FILM: *BLOODY SUNDAY*

ACTIVITY

Read the following summaries of the two films:

Bloody Sunday

On 30 January 1972, 13 civilians were shot dead by the British army while taking part in a civil rights march against internment in the Bogside area of Derry (also known as Londonderry).

In the Name of the Father

In the early 1970s, four Irishmen and women were wrongly convicted by a British court of the bombing of a pub in Guildford, in which civilians died, and of being members of the IRA.

As a start to researching this area find out the following (remember there may be conflicting points of view evident in some of the answers):

■ What is meant by the term 'civil rights'? What examples of other civil rights movements are there in history?
■ What is internment and how was it used in Northern Ireland?
■ Why was the British army in Northern Ireland in the 1970s?
■ Why is Derry also referred to as Londonderry? Which groups refer to it by which name?
■ What do the initials IRA stand for? What is their main political aim?

For further information about the situation in Ireland and its history see: www.bbc.co.uk/history/war/troubles/origins.

Having read the summaries and completed some research into Irish politics make a list of what you think will be the main conflicts dealt with in the two films.

NOTEBOX

Civil rights movements

Sharpeville and Amritsar

In the emotional final speech of *Bloody Sunday* the central character, Ivan Cooper, refers to the bloody Sunday shootings as 'our Sharpeville, our Amritsar'.

The Amritsar massacre was a defining part of the struggle for Indian independence from British rule and took place on 13 April, 1919, a Sikh festival. Mass protests against the Rowlatt Act, a series of repressive measures passed by the British, started peacefully but soon became violent. In Amritsar, where leaders of the Indian Independence movement had been arrested, the British army declared 'No gatherings of persons or processions of any sort will be allowed. All gatherings will be fired on'. When thousands of unarmed people protested in the centre of Amritsar the order was given to fire without warning and at least 400 people were killed and 1,200 injured.

In the town of Sharpeville in 1960, 69 black South Africans were killed and 180 injured by the South African police force during a protest against the 'pass laws'. Introduced in 1923 the pass laws were part of the apartheid system (rule by the minority whites over the black majority) of racial control and prevented black South Africans from leaving their 'homelands' to move to the cities. The Sharpeville Massacre as it became known caused international condemnation of both the event itself and the wider context of the apartheid system of government in South Africa.

POLITICAL AND INSTITUTIONAL CONTEXTS

Bloody Sunday is a British and Irish co-production with funding from a range of sources including private and public money; this is a common institutional context for British films. The dominant partner is Granada Film, part of the commercial TV production and distribution company which is the primary producer for ITV; it also distributes programmes internationally. Shortly after the release of *Bloody Sunday*, Granada Film was closed as an independent film company and merged with Granada's comedy and drama department when Granada decided to concentrate on TV rather than film production. This means that the BBC is now the only British broadcaster with a separate film production arm. One of the other producers – Hell's Kitchen Films is an Irish company set up in 1992 by Jim Sheridan, the director of *In the Name of the Father*. In addition to money from commercial organizations, public funding through lottery money was also received from the Film Council.

Bloody Sunday was first broadcast on ITV as part of the thirtieth anniversary commemoration of the march, it also coincided with the findings of the Saville Report, an independent enquiry which was set up in 1998. *Bloody Sunday* was a very controversial film and was criticized for bias towards the marchers and against the army. Another film about these events, *Sunday* (Jimmy McGovern), was shown on Channel 4 at the same time; both films were followed by studio discussions about how accurate the portrayal of events was and wider debates about the future of the conflict.

Bloody Sunday also received a limited cinema release in Britain, the US (where it was shown on two screens) and across Europe. It was premièred at a London cinema on the same night that it was shown on television and this meant that it was ineligible

Figure 16.1 Scene from *Bloody Sunday*
Source British Film Institute

for an Oscar nomination. The film did receive two prestigious awards; Best Film at the Berlin Film Festival and the Audience Award at Sundance. The lead actor, James Nesbitt, had previously been associated with comedy roles and his performance as the MP Ivan Cooper was seen as a successful breakthrough into 'serious' acting.

NOTEBOX

British cinema and television

The relationship between film and TV in Britain is very close in a variety of ways:

- drama on TV and in film often use a similar realist aesthetic;
- film and TV programmes often deal with similar social issues to do with life in Britain today;
- TV series are used as the basis for cinema spin-offs ('The League of Gentleman', 'Kevin and Perry Go Large', etc.)
- TV companies fund filmmaking;
- TV is an important form of exhibition for British films.

Yasmin (2004) another possible focus film for this unit, had a cinema release in France but was only shown at the London Film Festival in this country with its main exhibition platform being Channel 4.

Figure 16.2 *In the Name of the Father*
Source Universal / The Kobal Collection / Jonathan Hessian

In the Name of the Father is a similarly controversial film. It was one of a group of Irish films made in the 1990s which dealt with the wider contexts of the fight for Irish independence. These films include: *The Crying Game* (Neil Jordan, 1992), *Nothing Personal* (Thaddeus O'Sullivan, 1995), *Michael Collins* (Neil Jordan, 1996), *Some Mother's Son* (Terry George, 1996). The directors of these films have become internationally known and work in Hollywood as well as Ireland; Terry George, the writer of *In the Name of the Father*, directed *Hotel Rwanda* in 2004.

ACTIVITY

Research the institutional context of *In the Name of the Father*:

List the different production companies involved in the making of the film:

- Are there any similarities with the funding of *Bloody Sunday*?
- What nationality are the different companies?
- Would you define *In the Name of the Father* as an Irish film, a British film, or an American film? Give evidence for your answer.

Before continuing with the analysis you will need to watch *Bloody Sunday* and *In the Name of the Father*. The first time you watch them you should make a note of the following:

- the names and a brief description of the main characters;
- the main settings used;
- any conflicts between individuals, groups, countries, etc., in the film.

FILM LANGUAGE: THE DOCUDRAMA

Bloody Sunday is based on real, and contentious, events. Rather than create a fictionalized account, the filmmakers used the technique of docudrama: a hybrid form which mixes the film language style of documentary and drama.

NOTEBOX

> ### History of the docudrama
>
> Docudrama is a relatively recent form. One of the first examples was *Cathy Come Home* (Ken Loach, 1966) a film made for television with the specific aim of highlighting the problem of homelessness in Britain. Docudrama is currently a very popular television genre with examples such as *Out of Control* (Dominic Savage, 2002), an improvised film about young offenders and *The Navigators* (Ken Loach, 2001) about the privatization of the British rail network. Both of these received limited cinema release. One of the most influential figures in this area is Jimmy McGovern whose work is explicitly political; *Hillsborough* (1997), *Dockers* (1999), *Sunday* (2002).

Docudrama is a controversial form precisely because of its technique of dramatizing real events. Some documentary makers are particularly critical of the form, seeing it as a corruption of the traditional documentary representation of real events. At first documentary and drama may seem to be opposing forms: the documentary is a non-fiction form based on real events and uses techniques such as interviews and a voice-over to impart information about the real world. Drama is a fictional form which uses techniques such as acting, editing, lighting, etc. to make the audience forget they are watching a film and provide a form of escapism. In fact it can be very difficult to define the difference between drama, docudrama and documentary – although we tend to know it when we see it. Read the following summaries of two films. Which form do you think they belong to?

Film 1

A single mother who is accused of child neglect, battles social services to be allowed to keep her existing children and her unborn child.

Film 2

Two friends have an accident while mountaineering in Peru. To save his own life, one of the men cuts the rope which is holding his friend, knowing that this will result in his friend's death. In fact the friend survives and although very badly injured he struggles back to base camp where the two men are reunited.

Both of these stories could be told in any of the forms suggested, although the first is *Ladybird, Ladybird* (Ken Loach, 1993), a fiction film, while the second is the documentary *Touching the Void* (Kevin Macdonald, 2003). Further complications arise when we take into account the fact that *Ladybird, Ladybird* was based on real events and uses non-actors while *Touching the Void* uses reconstructions in which real people are played by actors.

Another reason that definitions in this area are so complicated is that documentary is not one single style but a range of styles. Three popular styles of documentary are the classic or expository, the performative and the observational. While there are over-laps in these styles they do have recognizable codes and conventions. The first uses traditional techniques of interviews and voice-over which explains the events to the viewer. Performative is a recent form where the documentary maker becomes part of the film, appearing on screen and giving their reaction to events; Michael Moore (*Bowling for Columbine*, 2002) and Morgan Spurlock (*Super Size Me*, 2004) are performative documentary makers. Observational documentary is in some ways very different from these two forms as there is no voice-over or interviews and the filmmaker is never seen or heard. This form is sometimes referred to as 'fly on the wall' and this suggests that its aim is to see everything as it happens, to let events unfold naturally without any disruption or intervention from the filmmaker. To achieve this, observational documentaries use a specific film language which includes hand-held camera and long takes. It is this style which is most commonly found in docudrama. The influence of this style can be seen in popular TV genres such as reality TV and docusoap, hybrid forms which also challenge traditional definitions of documentary. Some recent examples of observational documentaries include: *Être et Avoir* (France, Nicholas Philbert, 2002) and *Dark Days* (US, Marc Singer, 2000).

ACTIVITY

Discussion point

Do you think it is ever possible for a documentary accurately to reflect reality?
Does the process of filming and editing fundamentally alter the event being recorded?
Can a documentary ever be objective?

If you continue Film Studies at A2 you can continue the work on documentary at FS6 which is the synoptic module drawing together a range of areas studied on the course.

KEY TERM

FREE CINEMA, DIRECT CINEMA, CINÉMA VÉRITÉ (TRUTH) These three documentary movements of the 1950s and 1960s, from Britain, the US and France respectively, are all examples of the development of observational documentary styles. These movements were interested in finding new ways of telling stories in film, thus creating a new film language as well as presenting new subject matter.

Some examples of films from these movements:

Mama Don't Allow (UK, Richardson and Reisz, 1956), about working-class youth culture, particularly jazz and dancing.

Every Day Except Christmas (UK, Anderson, 1957),which follows people who work at Billingsgate Fish Market in London.

The filmmakers involved in Free Cinema went on to make some of the most influential social realist fiction films in the 1960s.

High School (US, Fred Wiseman, 1969), follows the lives of American High School students.

Don't Look Back (US, Chris Hedegus and D. A. Pennebaker, 1965), a record of the singer Bob Dylan's tour of Britain.

One important characteristic that the documentary and drama forms do have in common is the reliance on storytelling, the shaping of events into a coherent structure.

REAL EVENTS AND NARRATIVE STRUCTURE

Although *Bloody Sunday* is based on real events, the filmmakers have to construct a watchable, interesting story from these events in the same way that the makers of fiction-based films do. As with any fiction film, *Bloody Sunday* uses narrative devices such as identification with a hero, oppositions and conflict between groups and the build-up of tension to construct the story.

Bloody Sunday uses a chronological narrative structure with the events taking place on one day; this means that there is a close link between story and plot.

- How are the story events organized in *In the Name of the Father*?
- Why do you think this particular organization is used? Does it affect the way the audience reacts to Gerry Conlan?

Another example of narrative techniques used in drama and documentary is exposition. Exposition refers to the 'facts' of the story, whether in fiction or non-fiction. It is the explanation of plot, character and setting and is there to aid the audience's under-standing. In the opening of *Bloody Sunday* Ivan Cooper's speech to the press is a form of exposition.

MESSAGES AND VALUES: IDENTIFICATION AND REPRESENTATION IN *BLOODY SUNDAY*

There are several areas of representation which are central to analysing the messages and values of the film. These representations are constructed through the use of:

■ identification with character;
■ film language and film style.

The main groups of people represented are:

■ the civil rights marchers;
■ the British army (the Parachute Regiment).

Other areas of representation would include:

■ the IRA;
■ the people of Derry who don't march;
■ the city of Derry itself.

Identification in film

What is meant by the term identification? Identification is a crucial component in film – and all storytelling forms – as it is the way that a spectator is able to place themselves 'in' the film, to understand what motivates the different characters. It also allows the filmmaker to control our response and to help us become engaged with the film; if we don't care about the characters it is hard to remain interested. We don't just identify with the 'good' characters in a film. Part of the excitement of watching a thriller can come from our identification with the villain, and it is common to shift our identification from character to character during a film.

To identify with a character we need to 'see what they see' and this can be achieved through a combination of aspects of film construction:

■ Time on screen: if a character hardly appears in a film it is difficult to understand their motivation; the hero of a film tends to appear in the majority of the scenes.
■ Actions and motivations: understanding what the character is feeling and why they act in the way that they do – this is a function of the narrative.
■ Dialogue: how does the way the character speaks and what they say reveal their personality?
■ The use of point of view shots literally place us in the position of the character – to 'see what they see', but this on its own will not create identification without the previous techniques.

In *Bloody Sunday* the use of identification is a vital tool in communicating the messages and values of the film – specifically who the filmmaker believes to be responsible for the events of Bloody Sunday. Using the above points, analyse the following two sequences from the film to consider the use of identification.

Sequence analysis: identification and representation

The manipulation of audience identification is part of the way that the representations in the film are created. Looking at the following sequence, analyse the way that identification is created with Ivan Cooper and how this affects the representation of the civil rights marchers – and the British army.

Analysis of extract: 10.45 minutes–14.31 minutes

This extract is part of the build-up to the march and follows Ivan Cooper, the local MP as he tries to encourage people to join the march. Watch the extract carefully and make notes on the following:

- Which character has the most screen time in this sequence? Is this typical of the film as a whole?
- At the start of the sequence we see Ivan with his parents – what does this tell us about his character? Why do you think this scene was included?
- Make a note of Ivan's dialogue – who does he speak to? What tone of voice does he use? What does he say?
- How does the sequence help you understand Ivan's motivation – his reasons for organizing the march?
- The casting of James Nesbitt, a familiar, and handsome, face, is very important. What effect do you think this casting has on the way the audience reacts to the character?

NOTEBOX

Sunday Bloody Sunday and The Magnificent Seven

When Ivan Cooper walks past the cinema we can clearly see the two films which are showing:

Sunday Bloody Sunday (Schlesinger, 1972) was a drama which had just been released; its storyline about a romantic triangle has no connection to the events of Bloody Sunday. The use of the title therefore, seems to be a comment on the events we watch unfolding. Of course it is only the audience who can see the link between the title of the film showing at the local cinema and what is about to happen in Derry; Ivan is oblivious. This gap between what the audience knows and what the character knows suggests that identification isn't always created through just 'seeing what the character sees'.

The Magnificent Seven (Sturges, 1960) has a much clearer link in terms of plot in which seven gunmen defend a Mexican village from bandits. However the film had actually been released twelve years before *Bloody Sunday*.

Once you have completed your notes write them up into a character study of Ivan. What does this suggest about the representation of the marchers and the point of view of the filmmakers?

- The British army is also represented in this scene. Analyse the representation of the soldiers through reference to screen time, dialogue, motivation and interaction with other characters.

Whenever you analyse a sequence from a film you need to include reference to the film language:

- Describe the use of camera, the editing, and the soundtrack. Are different groups in the sequence filmed in different ways? Is the use of film language linked to the representation of those groups?
- What techniques from documentary forms are evident in this sequence?

Figure 16.3 *Scene from Bloody Sunday*
Source British Film Institute

MESSAGES AND VALUES – BRITISH AND IRISH CINEMA (FS3)

Summary analysis

The sequence is structured around the immediate build-up to the march and clearly sets up the conflicting points of views of Ivan Cooper and the Parachute Regiment. It is also an important plot point in the film as it sets up motivation for the killings on the part of the army and the innocence, perhaps naiveté, of Ivan Cooper. In order to communicate these points to the audience, the filmmaker has used different types of film language to represent the different groups as well as creating contrasts through the editing.

The sequence starts with Ivan talking to his parents. They are filmed in their kitchen, which is a realist mise en scène; the tone of the scene is warm and humorous. Ivan's mother still speaks to him as if he were a young boy and he jokes to her in an affectionate way. (The humorous dialogue concerns religion. Later in the sequence Ivan makes a joke about being a Protestant, and this is perhaps done to indicate that Ivan is not motivated by religious extremism which might make him less appealing to an audience.) Ivan reassures his mother that the march will be 'just a Sunday afternoon stroll', a comment which the audience, with their knowledge about the events to come, interprets ironically. This scene was filmed in one take and this technique is continued as Ivan goes into the street; the camera is hand-held and shaky and the shot lasts for about 40 seconds. These are techniques borrowed from observational documentary and are used to give the scene authenticity. The realism is also enhanced by the breaking of some of the 'rules' of filmmaking: characters have their backs to the camera; they move in and out of frame; people mumble and talk over each other. As Ivan walks along the street the film language emphasizes his determination and purposefulness; he is always on the move, always busy. He seems to know many of his constituents by name and is warm and funny in his dealing with them. From this scene of movement and long shots of the street setting, the film cuts to the Parachute Regiment, also preparing for the march. Now the film language is far more static; the group is shot in close up and it is hard to differentiate between them; they are represented as a mass rather than individuals with particular characteristics. This style creates the image of an isolated group which is not part of the community of Derry. The dialogue is crucial in providing an explanation for what happens on the march; the soldiers refer to the marchers as 'hooligans' and there is an order for the soldiers to show 'maximum aggression and make lots of arrests' before the march has even begun.

This sequence is typical of the organization of events in the rest of the film as it cuts between Ivan Cooper and the marchers and the British army, using film language and dialogue to emphasize the differences between the two. This is a successful way of creating identification with one side of the conflict against another.

A useful comparison with this scene is the one which comes very near the end of the film and echoes the earlier sequence.

Analysis of extract: 1 hour 22 minutes–1 hour 26 minutes

This sequence takes place in the hospital after the march and shows Ivan Cooper trying to find out the extent of the tragedy.

Watch the sequence and make notes on the following:

■ What similarities are there between the two sequences?
■ How is the character of Ivan represented differently in this sequence?
■ How does our identification with Ivan affect our reaction to this sequence?

What you will have noticed is the way that the structure of the two sequences is very similar, cutting from scenes of Ivan and the marchers to the soldiers.

■ What effect does the cutting between the two groups have on the representation of each?

These two sequences, one from the beginning, the other from near the end of the film, chart the development of Ivan's character. A third sequence to study to develop your analysis of representation and identification is the final sequence, when Ivan is addressing a press conference and a list of the dead is read out.

ACTIVITY

Using the approaches outlined above write a detailed analysis of this sequence which discusses the:

■ representation of Ivan and the civil rights marchers;
■ representation of the British army.

and

■ how the construction of audience identification with character affects audience reaction to the events.

As a comparative sequence to this one you could look at the opening sequence which also involves a press conference. This mirroring of the opening in the ending is a fairly common narrative device and gives a sense of completion and balance to the story. This idea is linked to the concept of resolution discussed in the previous topic. Do you think there are other issues to consider about resolution when the story is based on real events?

■ Choose two other sequences from the film which seem to 'mirror' each other in the way described above. Why has the film been structured in this way? How does it help communicate the messages of the film?

COMPARATIVE ANALYSIS: *IN THE NAME OF THE FATHER*

Representation and identification in *In the Name of the Father*

Watch the opening sequence of In the Name of the Father and make notes on the following:

- Which different characters are introduced and what do we find out about them?
- Describe the relationship between Gerry Conlon and his father.
- How is the city of Belfast represented in this sequence?

A range of conflicts are introduced in this sequence between people, groups and places, for example, the conflict between Irish and British life:

The Irish are represented as traditional, family centred and religious with a sense of community. The British are viewed with suspicion by Gerry's parents as they are seen as having rejected the values which are important to them; such as family, 'there's no family life there', and religion. Another way of expressing this would be to say that the Irish are associated with tradition, the British with modernity. This of course is one of the reasons that Gerry wants to go to London.

For each of the other conflicts introduced write a similar list of characteristics.

Representations of the British and Irish

In *Bloody Sunday*, the political conflict between the Irish civil rights marchers and the British state is central to the film's narrative. In this film, Britain is represented by the army; the creation of identification means that we care more about the marchers than the army. In *In the Name of the Father* there are two central conflicts; one between the Guildford Four and the British state, the other between Gerry and his father.

ACTIVITY . . .

You are going to prepare a presentation to other members of your group on the two main conflicts in In the Name of the Father. For this you will need to:

- select one or two sequences which illustrate the conflict between the Guildford Four and the British;
- and one or two which illustrate the conflict between Gerry and his father.

(The total running time should be between 8–10 minutes.)

For each of your examples write an analysis for presentation which explains:

- how the audience identifies with one side of the conflict over another;
- what effect this has on the political message of the film;
- how the use of film language is linked to the audience reaction (plot, character, dialogue, camera, etc.).

continued

It is also important to consider whether there are any other ways of looking at the conflicts. For example, do all the British and Irish characters fit into each side easily?

SUGGESTIONS FOR FURTHER WORK

Alternative comparative films:

The Crying Game (Neil Jordan, 1992) and *Angel* (Neil Jordan, 1982) both deal with the conflicts arising from the struggle for Irish independence.

The Navigators (Ken Loach, 2000): this docudrama uses the privatization of the railways and the policies of New Labour to examine a range of social and political conflicts.

Yasmin (Beaufoy, 2004) and *Dirty Pretty Things* (Frears, 2002) look at the social conflicts which develop in a multiracial society, focusing on questions of national identity.

In this World (Winterbottom, 2003) and *Last Resort* (Pawlikovski, 2000) both use realist techniques to examine the lives of refugees and the conflicts arising from fears of 'invasion'.

To construct an analysis of the representations of conflict in your chosen film, you need to choose key sequences which illustrate your points. These should be chosen to reflect the themes and the film language.

EXAMPLE EXAM QUESTIONS

1   How do the filmmakers use sound and image to create the violence of conflict in the films you have studied?

2   Discuss some of the ways in which the filmmaker represents social and/or political conflicts in the films you have studied.

This chapter will look at:

- the content and contexts of the focus films;
- what is distinct and different about Scottish cinema;
- a range of textual and contextual issues surrounding Scottish cinema.

Focus films:	*Local Hero* (Enigma/Goldcrest 1983, Director: Bill Forsyth)
	Orphans (Downtown/Channel 4 1999, Director: Peter Mullan)
Suggested comparison films:	*Another Time, Another Place* Cinegate/Umbrella/Rediffusion/ Channel 4/Scottish Arts Council 1983, Director: Michael Radford)
	Small Faces (Guild/BBC/Glasgow Film Fund/Skyline 1995, Director: Gillies MacKinnon)
	Morvern Callar (Momentum/Alliance Atlantis/BBC/Company 2002, Director: Lynne Ramsay)

This topic area looks at films made in Scotland or about Scotland, from Bill Forsyth's *That Sinking Feeling* (Glasgow Youth Theatre/LakeFilms/Minor Miracle Film Co-op 1979) to the present day, and encompasses the opportunity to study particular genres of Scottish film, and to explore broader representational issues that underpin the films in this period, such as the filmic construction of Scotland, social issues, the rural and the urban, and the concept of a constructed 'Scottishness'. This distinct and exciting national cinema existing within a broader context of British (as opposed to English) cinema directly engages with a number of diverse issues that can be studied in terms of *Messages and Values* including:

■ Scottish genres – comedy, crime, and the pastoral: how Scottish film positions itself to an audience;
■ national identity – how defining Scotland and 'Scottishness' underpins much of the work in this period;
■ class, regional identity, sexuality, and gender representation – how groups within Scottish society are depicted and how this representation evolves;
■ social and political institutions – how Scotland and the Scots shape their society and react to outside agents;
■ production context – the films of this period in relation to a broader context of Scottish film (both fiction and non-fiction), of funding schemes, and the context of key filmmakers.

LOCAL HERO – SUMMARY

Local Hero was written and directed by Bill Forsyth, who by 1983 had already won acclaim both with his preceding low budget works *That Sinking Feeling* (1979) and *Gregory's Girl* (Lake/NFFC/STV, 1981), and with his work as a producer for BBC Scotland. The film had the backing of Lord (David) Puttnam's Goldcrest Productions (then one of the most significant players on the British scene), giving Forsyth the opportunity not only to ramp up production values on his previous films, but also to engage Hollywood legend Burt Lancaster to play the head of an American oil company.

The film was made at a time of deepening social unrest in Britain (and Scotland in particular) as the right-wing agenda of Margaret Thatcher's government saw rising unemployment and the destruction of traditional industries including the mines, shipyards, and fishing that had been central to Scottish life for several generations. Oil, which had been seen as Scotland's saviour on its discovery had not produced the benefits predicted for Scotland, and, in a historically socialist Scotland, there was a growing suspicion of foreign capitalists in general, and more specifically oil companies.

The film tells the story of Mac (Peter Riegert), who works as a junior manager at Knox Oil (an American company) who is sent to a small Scottish coastal town with the mission of buying it up so Knox Oil can tear it down to build a refinery on the site. However, once Mac arrives in Ferness he begins to see the virtues of the town: the simplicity and pace of life there and its contrast to his corporate life back in Houston, Texas. Although the majority of the locals are keen to sell up to Knox Oil and move away from what they see as a barren, dying way of life, Mac becomes increasingly fond of the town, wanting to settle there and forget the business world and his career. All is not simple however, and when Ben (Fulton Mackay) a villager with his own agenda, threatens to delay or even negate the sale, it looks like both the villagers and corporate America will join together to crush him, with Mac forced to take sides in the fight. The building tensions and in-fighting are dissolved when Happer, the head of Knox Oil (Burt

Figure 17.1 *Local Hero*
Source British Film Institute

Lancaster) arrives in presidential style by helicopter, and recognizes the innate beauty and value of Ferness, resolving to build an observatory in the town rather than an oil refinery (he is a keen stargazer and there has been a running theme of Mac reporting back to him regularly on the night sky). The locals return to their lives, Happer returns to his business, and Mac leaves for Houston and his empty corporate life, with his glossy but empty apartment where, in remembering Ferness, he is forced to admit his own emptiness.

The film however is not as clear cut as it may seem, as the representations are illusions, with the idyllic Scottish landscape being cut through by an RAF fighter on a training flight (a political issue of the time), Mac not having any Scottish ancestry despite having been sent to Ferness because of a presumed Scottish ancestry, and the happy simple population seeing their own lives as desolate and in decay. Forsyth plays with both representations and the very concept of representation.

ACTIVITY . . .

- Look at the sequence in *Local Hero* where Mac arrives in Ferness. What values are being expressed both by him and by the townspeople?

continued

- There is a distinct 'look' to the film that shapes audience response. What message(s) do you feel that Bill Forsyth was trying to express with this style?
- How does the director convey the changing beliefs of Mac? Are there specific moments where decisions are made?
- Mac is deliberately positioned as an outsider: discuss with peers what effect this positioning would have on an audience in terms of messages and values. Do you think his being American and representing a big corporation is a tool for delivering a message? Make Mac Scottish and have him working for a Scottish oil company – does this change the messages and values of the film in any way?
- Write out a timeline for Mac's journey and mark on it the points where he makes decisions that reflect his changing character. Do these change points coincide with any key story moments? If so, how do they combine and what message or value is expressed?
- When Gordon Urquhart informs Victor that the local population is going to be rich he adds 'We won't have anywhere to call home, but we'll be stinkin' rich.' and Victor later tells Mac 'It's their place, Mac. They have a right to make of it what they can. Besides, you can't eat scenery!' What messages and values about the local population do these lines express? Are there any other key lines that develop these views?
- Investigate the political and economic contexts of the time. How well do you feel *Local Hero* represents its time?
- Who is the local hero and just how local is he? Do you think Forsyth was being ironic with his title?

ORPHANS – SUMMARY

Orphans was the directorial debut of Peter Mullan, a jobbing actor who appears in many of Scotland's best films in this period, and who used his acting fees to support him whilst he wrote scripts. Beginning with shorts, Mullan took *Orphans* to the Cannes Film Festival alongside his starring role in Ken Loach's *My Name is Joe* (Parallax/Road Movies 1998), for which he won Best Actor. Mullan subsequently went on to direct *The Magdalene Sisters* (Momentum/Scottish Screen/Film Council/IrishFilm/PFP/Temple 2002).

The film was released towards the end of the first term of a Labour government, and at a time when the promised changes were beginning to be seen in Scotland, but were also beginning to show that they were not all that they were believed to be. Unemployment was falling, and the hearts of the principal cities were being restored and rebuilt, yet alcohol abuse and violent crime were both rising. The fabric of Scotland was being repaired, but the needs of the Scottish people to re-define themselves for new, and modern times had not been addressed. Whilst other filmmakers were concentrating either on an ultra modern Scotland of gloss and superficiality, or were retreating to the safe territory of 'kilt movies', Mullan met the spirit of the time head on.

Figure 17.2 *Orphans*
Source British Film Institute

The central characters are the Catholic Flynn family, three brothers and their wheelchair-bound sister, who are orphaned as adults and face individual struggles across the night before their mother's funeral. Kissing their mother in her coffin, they retreat to a Glasgow pub, where Thomas (Gary Lewis) sings an embarrassingly emotional lament, and Michael (Douglas Henshall) is stabbed when he defends his brother from the reactions of someone in the pub. Youngest brother John (Stephen McCole) gets his brother away, leaving sister Sheila (Rosemarie Stevenson) in the hands of the unreliable and distraught Thomas. Thomas keeps his vow to his mother to keep watch over her coffin, but in doing so abandons his sister (to the mercy of a bizarre family of Good Samaritans). Michael meanwhile puts a positive spin on his stabbing and decides to wait until morning before seeking treatment as he can then falsely make an industrial injury claim, but in doing so risks bleeding to death. John is determined to seek revenge for the attack on his brother and with the help of a borderline psychotic cousin spends most of the film trying to obtain a gun.

The film's central value (that of 'the family') is constantly challenged throughout, and yet at the end it is this value that reunites and restores the grieving siblings. It also has at its heart the issue of masculinity in a post-industrial world, and Mullan uses the Glasgow landscape and even the harsh Glasgow weather to highlight the primal responses of the brothers as they find varying approaches to dealing with their grief and with their central problem (as men) of expressing it. The role of the disabled sister is one that equally serves to highlight the male emotional disability and Mullan often uses her responses to illustrate the weakness and ill-thought-through responses of the brothers. It is here that Mullan exposes the real damage inflicted by social change and inequality, in a raw and often brutal onslaught of cinematic expression.

ACTIVITY

- Peter Mullan deliberately chooses to place his events against a background of Catholicism. How does this background 'flavour' the messages and values expressed in the film?
- The Flynn family bonds drive both the story and define the relationships within the film. What do you learn about Scottish family life from them? How is this representation of family different from or similar to other films you have studied?
- Peter Mullan uses a wide range of both macro and micro techniques and filmic references in telling his story. List the differing styles and techniques (and any wider filmic references) and note where they appear in the film. How do they help express values? What additional messages do they send?
- If Sheila had been the one looking to take revenge for her brother's stabbing, how would it have affected the messages and values expressed? List five things you learn from this film about gender representation.
- Discuss the male values expressed in the film and make a list of both positive and negative. Do the positives outweigh the negatives, or vice versa?

What message does this convey about men and maleness at this particular time?

- The film is set against the backdrop of Glasgow. Visit the Scottish Tourist Board website and look at the images of Glasgow offered there. How does Mullan's Glasgow compare? What do you think his careful choice of setting is saying about Glasgow, and more broadly about Scotland? What does the setting say about the characters and the events portrayed?

SCOTTISH GENRES

Since Bill Forsyth almost single-handedly re-launched Scottish film on the wider world in the early 1980s, the industry has produced a variety of features (and significantly more shorts) that have begun to define particularly Scottish genres of filmmaking, and in doing so have defined the audience for Scottish film.

Throughout Scotland's film history the 'kilt movie' dealing with 'great' historic moments from Scotland's past (both factual and fictional) has played a central role in depicting representations of Scotland, and in embedding a distinct image of both place and people. Often this representation came not from an indigenous people but from an external view: largely American through diverse films such as *Mary of Scotland* (RKO 1935, Director: John Ford) and *Braveheart* (TCF/Icon/Ladd 1995, Director: Mel Gibson), and English through films such as *Bonnie Prince Charlie* (British Lion/London Films 1948, Director: Anthony Kimmins), and *Mary Queen of Scots* (Universal/ Hal B. Wallis 1971, Director: Charles Jarrott). These films romanticized Scotland, depicting it as a land of rebels and heroes, as bleak and raw, and as fixed in time. It is therefore interesting that there has been little by way of tartanry from Scottish filmmakers themselves in this more recent period and that in the light of new representations offered by Scottish cinema the external view of historical Scotland has also changed, focusing more on the Celtic, and (again romanticized) indigenous people, victims of oppressive rulers (both Scottish and English) and of inter-clan division.

This is intrinsically linked with the 'pastoral' Scottish genre of rural or coastal communities with a cinematic focus on the landscape and on both the 'homespun' nature of communities and the desire to escape from a life that is as restrictive as it is idyllic. *Local Hero* fits neatly into the pastoral, as does *As An Eilean* (*From The Island*, Peculia Films/SFP 1993, Director: Mike Alexander) a Gaelic language film which offers a view of life on an island off the Scottish mainland where the concerns and foibles of island life are explored. Both films offer a mix of character types: the 'simple' inhabitants whose craft is that of survival, the educational elite (often those who have been away and have returned), and the mysterious outsider who has moved into the area, and both use the magnificent scenic backdrop to illustrate and reflect their stories.

TARTANRY, KAILYARDISM, AND CLYDESIDEISM There are three types of representation that rise above all others in Scottish film and suggest not only some regional variance within Scotland, but also a sense of internal conflict between the past and present, the rural and the urban.

Tartanry encompasses a range of representations that see the Scots in traditional dress: either as the noble heroic Highland rebel, the laird or educated intellectual, or as the drunken, bagpipe-playing comedy act, and is one that focuses on the tartan as the key to Scottish identity (for better or worse).

Kailyardism emphasizes the small town or largely rural aspects of Scotland, depicting those who live in these areas as 'simple folk' of the land. This is usually accompanied by empowering them with folk wisdom and a 'natural' understanding of people (more often than not of either city types or the English), and with a strong sense of community that often involves intrigue.

Clydesideism perhaps reflects a more modern view of Scotland and is based around the working-class, industrialized people and areas, again offering a strong sense of community, but with a clearer sense of unromantic realism. With the demise of heavy industry in Scotland, Clydesideism is developing a sense of historic rather than current representation on the one hand, and on the other is evolving to reflect a disaffected working class, and declining communities.

In contrast to the pastoral, recent Scottish cinema has concentrated on the urban as a palette for a number of filmic representations, particularly those dealing with social issues. Most playfully was the use of the urban to define and characterize the heroin users in *Trainspotting* (Polygram/Channel 4/Figment/Noel Gay 1996, Director: Danny Boyle), where they are masters of their urban kingdoms (even though their urban kingdoms are declining as rapidly as they are). The working-class landscape, housing estates, betting shops, pubs, and the grey tenements of its predecessors are re-imaged as an under-class landscape stripped bare by the hunger of addictions and disconnected through years of hardship and neglect. This is then placed in stark contrast with the magnificence of the Highland landscape that dwarfs the four principal characters when they decide to leave the city and take a walk in the hills. Here they are markedly out of place and, whilst Tommy adopts a traditional viewpoint when he asks 'Doesn't it make you proud to be Scottish?', Renton's rebuke which defines all that is wrong with being Scottish further emphasizes the changing face of urban Scotland. This is echoed in *Orphans*, where the urban landscape similarly defines the characters and separates them both from a traditional pastoral setting and from Clydesideism, with the material decay of the city reflecting their moral and emotional crises.

A dominant genre of Scottish cinema is that which deals with significant social issues, be they drug problems, unemployment, or loan sharks, and a key exponent of this type of film has been Ken Loach who brought his brand of English social-realism to Scotland with screenwriter Bill Jesse's *Riff-Raff* (BFI/ Parallax, 1990) which whilst set largely outside Scotland focused on a Scottish building site worker (played by Robert Carlyle).

This was then followed by several other forays into Scotland for films such as *Carla's Song* (Polygram/Channel 4/GFF/Parallax/Road Movies, 1996), and *Sweet Sixteen* (Icon/Scottish Screen/BBC/ARD/Road Movies, 2002), the latter of which was shot in Greenock and was subtitled for the English-speaking audience. All three reflect the harsh reality of poverty and social breakdown, and represent a body of films that continue to represent aspects of Scottishness.

Connected to this genre is an associated genre that focuses purely on one key social problem, crime. The crime genre has been one that came to the fore in Scottish television drama in the late 1970s/early 1980s through the work of writers and directors such as Peter McDougal and John MacKenzie and was spectacularly launched on Scottish cinema by two key films: *Shallow Grave* (Rank/Figment/Channel 4/GFF 1994, Director: Danny Boyle) and *Small Faces* (Guild/BBC/GFF/Skyline 1995, Director: Gillies MacKinnon). The former deals with the criminal repercussions of a decision to dump the body of a deceased flatmate in order to keep the suitcase full of money he kept with him, whilst the latter deals more directly with the more traditional and recognizable crimes of Scotland's city gang warfare. The urban setting is central to these films and forms the backdrop for *The Debt Collector* (Film 4/GFF/Dragon, 1999, Director: Anthony Neilson) which sees Billy Connolly asserting his Glaswegian credentials as a hard man (refining his television role in Peter McDougal's 1993 *Down Among the Big Boys*) in a story which echoes the biography of real-life gangster Jimmy Boyle.

The black comedy which emerges in *Orphans*, *Shallow Grave*, and *Trainspotting* allies them all to the final significant (and perhaps oldest) Scottish film genre, comedy. Scottish film has a long history of comedy running though it, and in turn has used comedy to define Scottishness. Scots are perceived as having a peculiar, dry, witty humour which betrays a certain educated air and an inherent understanding of psychology (it is interesting that within Scotland itself there is a perception of regional variations to humour that roughly correspond with west coast Clydesideism, east coast Tartanry, and highland/island Kailyardism). *Local Hero* is a prime example of the 'gentle' Scottish comedy which, along with Bill Forsyth's earlier hit *Gregory's Girl* (Lake/NFFC/STV 1980) has defined much of the output in this genre, linking back to such 'classic' comedy as *Whiskey Galore!* (Ealing 1948, Director: Alexander MacKendrick), and encompassing many similar themes. Forsyth's work spawned a sub-genre of Scottish comedy which could be described as Forsythian through such films as *Restless Natives* (Thorn EMI/Oxford Film Company 1985, Director: Michael Hoffman), *The Girl in the Picture* (Rank/NFFC/Antonine 1985, Director: Cary Parker), and *Heavenly Pursuits* (Island Films/Skreba/Film Four 1986, Director: Charles Gormley), which relies on gentle, quirky and sometimes absurd narratives or characters and visual 'gags'.

ACTIVITY . . .

- Create two columns, one headed *Local Hero*, and the other headed *Orphans*. Under these headings list the scenes or sequences that associate these films with particular genres, and identify the key genre that each film belongs to.

continued

- In the Scottish genre films you have studied, can you arrive at a definition of the key features of that genre? Do the features evolve with time?
- Take one of the films you have studied and change the genre (for instance change *Local Hero* from comedy to social drama). What does this do to the story? Are there any key changes you have to make to ensure the story still works? Can you still use the same characters and locations? What would you have to significantly change to ensure the genre change 'works'?
- Look at the definitions of Tartanry, Kailyardism, and Clydesideism. Pick one of these and apply it to one of your focus films. How much evidence of these are in the films? Is the evidence found in the setting, the mise en scène, the script, or the characters?
- Select a genre. In a group, discuss what representations of Scotland and Scottishness are offered in this genre. What messages and values are promoted by this genre that are absent or down-played in other genres?

NATIONAL IDENTITY

At the same time that Bill Forsyth was building a raft of light comedies on which his version of Scottish national identity was being forged (and since they were international successes, this was a version of contemporary Scotland that was broadly accepted as representational) another filmmaker was making a film that would firmly position Scotland and Scottish film as 'other' to England and English film. *Hero* (Channel 4/Maya Films 1982, Director: Barney Platt-Mills) was the first Scottish film to be made in the Gaelic language and, whilst it was not the success it was expected to be, it set the idea in motion that not only could Scotland be defined within the English language, but it could be defined in its own tongue. Indeed shortly afterwards, funding became available through the Gaelic Film Fund to make Gaelic films (or films that were in more than one language) and to subtitle them for international distribution (including to England).

A resurgence of concern over national identity was growing through the 1980s and 1990s as was the demand for a Scottish Parliament, and with its birth came renewed efforts to support filmmaking that reflected a Scottish national identity (in all its forms). Whilst filmmaking had been receiving support for some years in Scotland, the focus had been on trying to produce films generic enough to succeed in international markets, yet the concerns over the dilution of Scottish identity saw this focus change to encourage filmmakers to explore Scottishness, in all its forms, including the un-diluted accents found in both *Trainspotting* and more so in *Sweet Sixteen*. Not only was Scotland speaking its own cinematic language, it was also doing it in its own accents.

Whilst for some considerable time this Scottishness had been defined in film not by what it was, but as 'other' to Englishness (often resulting in Tartanry or Kailyardism), as the period progressed, and progresses, a clearer, twenty-first century Scottish national identity is emerging with a representative set of messages and values. Lynne Ramsay's 2002 success *Morvern Callar* is illustrative of an emerging and changing national identity in its darkly comic tale of Morvern Callar (Samantha Morton), a 21-year-old small town supermarket checkout girl from western Scotland, who wakes on Christmas morning to find her writer boyfriend has committed suicide. In a moment of opportunism she decides to conceal his death, and pass off his unpublished novel as her own. Selling it, Morvern escapes the life that the small port town offers, taking her best friend Lanna (Kathleen McDermott) with her to Ibiza to live a life of clubbing and partying. This grim, minimalist fairy tale offers a post-Thatcherite view of Scotland and of the values of the young, presented in a way that makes it hard to disapprove of Morvern's actions. The symbolism is not lost: in one of Scotland's declared 'greats' of Scottish cinema is a woman – something that was unlikely to have been possible in preceding generations of filmmaking – who is making films about the redefining of Scottish identity.

ACTIVITY . . .

- Make a list of those features you see as essentially Scottish. Compare this list with how often they appear in a film you have studied. Revise this list in the light of what your viewing reveals, and then compare it with a second film you have studied. What does this tell you about representations of Scottishness?
- Is it important for a small country, part of the United Kingdom, to have its own distinctive cinema? If so, why? How do you think this affects its perception internationally?
- Look at the principal characters from a film you have studied. Is there anything distinctively Scottish about their attitudes, values, and behaviour?
- Consider Tartanry, Kailyardism, and Clydesideism in terms of what they tell us about a national cinema. Are there any other categories you would like to add to this list that helps define national characteristics in film from the films you have watched? If so, what messages and values do these additional categories convey?

CLASS, REGIONAL IDENTITY, SEXUALITY, AND GENDER REPRESENTATION

Whilst Scotland is one country, it is a country that is radically different from lowland to highland, from east to west, from urban to rural, and its films reflect this difference, often through taking characters from one environment and placing them in another (as in *Local Hero*, *Restless Natives*, and *Trainspotting*). This strong sense of regional identity within Scotland often replaces the divisions of class found in English film, with a hierarchy which to all extents and purposes is structured around Clydeside, Tartan, and Kailyard. Indeed these divisions can sharply mark out a community and individuals within it, as in Michael Radford's *Another Time, Another Place*. Here in the Highlands of the Second World War, Janie (Phyllis Logan) an isolated crofter's wife begins a doomed affair with Luigi (Giovanni Mauriello) an Italian prisoner of war assigned to help on her husband's farm. Not only is she breaking the sexual codes of her society, but she is also breaking with her regional identity and in doing so not only faces the wrath of her husband but also of the community she lives in. The regional identity is highlighted beautifully by the national identities that meet in the two principal characters, and at the same time this film serves to address issues of sexuality and gender representation. Can a crofter's wife, a Kailyard, be seen as a sexual being, and can a woman of this time be shown to take command of her own destiny?

Whilst masculinity is at the heart of films such as *Orphans*, *Trainspotting*, *Small Faces*, and *The Big Man* (Palace/Miramax/BSB/British STV Film Enterprises 1990, Director: David Leland), exploring what men are in a post-industrial landscape, the changing roles and perceptions of women have been central to the films of this period, and to constructing representations of Scottishness. Masculinity is often contextualized and commented on by the female roles, with contemporary men weakened by a changing society and adrift without a traditional role to fulfil. Danny Boyle depicts heroin-use as an almost male preserve in *Trainspotting* where the users are not victims of the drug, but of their own inability to forge a new role in communities that have been destroyed by the greed and disregard of the 1980s and 1990s. The women in this film support these men up to the point when they realize the inertia and inability of the men to adapt to the times that the women have already adapted to, and then cut them loose. This lack of evolution underpins the male roles in *Orphans* resulting in the inability to act, the inability to seek help, the inability to think rationally, and the inability to deal with their emotions, whereas Sheila's actions on screen evidence quite the reverse, delivering her both power and emotional strength.

In *Local Hero*, Bill Forsyth sets up a number of stereotypical characters and situations that initially confirm a range of traditional Scottish representations. However, as the film progresses, it becomes clear that Forsyth is satirizing the traditional representations and the only reasons they are established in this way is to challenge the stereotypes and to re-engage the audience with issues of representation and the debate around Scottish representation. Not only does he mock traditional 'maleness' but he also mocks the middle class who, in their belief of superiority, maintain and promote outdated representations.

ACTIVITY . . .

- Produce a grid with the titles of films you have studied on the horizontal axis and the names of a range of principal characters on the vertical axis. Try to get a mix of genders, classes, and ages. In each box place either a 'C' (for Clydeside), a 'T' (for Tartan), a 'K' (for Kailyard), or an 'O' (for Other).
- Does a pattern emerge within a film, and is there a pattern across a range of films?
- Are there significant gender differences?

- Does age play a factor in how a character is represented?
- Compare your results with the results for the same activity carried out on older Scottish films. What do you notice?
- Do you feel that any difference in pattern reflects changes in society?
- Discuss your results with others who have completed the same activity. What values do you think are being expressed by the filmmakers in relation to class, regional identity, sexuality, and gender representation?
- What messages do you believe the filmmakers want to convey to their audience(s) about these issues?
- Do you feel that these individual and specific representations combine to affect national identity?
- How do you feel these representations work in relation to each other when combined either into family or community?

SOCIAL AND POLITICAL INSTITUTIONS

Whereas earlier periods of Scottish cinema either wholeheartedly supported social and political institutions (particularly the prewar documentary movement, of Stirlingshire-born John Grierson), or gently mocked them (as in *Whiskey Galore!*), the films of this new Scottish cinema take a fresh look at them, confronting, and in some, demolishing the established status quo.

Small Faces looks squarely at the often romanticized nature of gangs, and in doing so not only criticizes the working-class societies that have allowed them to flourish to the point of institutionalizing them, but also the underpinning religious sectarianism that fuels them. In 1960s Govanhill, a decaying Glasgow housing estate, the territory is divided up between the Glens, and the Tongs, led respectively by Charlie Sloan (Garry Sweeney), a sinister, would-be sophisticate, and Malky (Kevin McKidd) who is described by his peers as 'mental'. The three teenage McLean brothers who live on the borderline are drawn into gang warfare when Alan (Joseph McFadden) gets involved with Charlie Sloan's ex-girlfriend, and Lex (Iain Robertson), the youngest of the three, accidentally shoots Malky in the face with an airgun. As the 'decent' people of the estate stand by and watch, the 'institutional' violence grows, climaxing in Bobby McLean (Steven Duffy) being viciously murdered in a reprisal attack. Gang culture was (and to some extent, is) a part of everyday Scottish life for some members of society, and yet it was over-looked in film (though television had dealt with the issue of sectarian violence nearly fifteen years earlier). Whilst viewers are offered representations of the gangs at the start of the film that encourage understanding, sympathy, and even empathy, Gillies MacKinnon quickly reveals the disorder, dishonesty, and disregard that operates within such groups, and in doing so heightens the responsibility of society in letting such people take control of areas.

> **Case Study: Bill Forsyth**
>
> Glaswegian Bill Forsyth (1946–) began his career in cinema when as a teenager he applied for an assistant's job with the Thames and Clyde Film Production Company, and was successful because he could lift the heavy equipment there. He continued working with this and other small companies, working on documentaries and corporate films for private companies and government offices, and all the time learning the craft.
>
> At the age of 32, tired of being denied funding for proposed feature film projects, Forsyth scraped together some money, and secured the assistance of actors from the Glasgow Youth Theatre, in order to make his first feature *That Sinking Feeling* (1979) which tells the comic story of a group of impoverished young men who hatch a plan to rob a warehouse full of sinks.
>
> The success of this first feature led Forsyth to find funding for his second film *Gregory's Girl* (1981), and from this to develop a career as a BBC producer. His third feature *Local Hero* (1983) consolidated a career that would take him to Hollywood where his career would almost end in the box-office-driven demands of commerciality.
>
> Returning to Scotland some fifteen years later, Bill Forsyth returned to one of his successes, making the sequel *Gregory's Two Girls*.

The political landscape had changed dramatically in Scotland since Bill Forsyth's first films, with not only the establishment of a Scottish Parliament, but also with the disappearance of the Conservative Party at constituency level in the 1997 General Election, but the anger at the destruction wrought on Scotland, both industrially and socially, in the Thatcherite years still dominates the films of this period. It can be detected in *That Sinking Feeling* when Ronnie (Robert Buchanan) argues drunkenly with the statue of a British war hero, concluding with his demanding 'So why don't I have a job?', and is certainly more evident in *Trainspotting* when Renton makes his 'state of the nation' speech after Tommy extols the virtues of the Scottish landscape, saying:

> It's shite being Scottish. We're the lowest of the low; the scum of the fuckin' earth. The most wretched, miserable, servile, pathetic trash that ever shat in civilization. Some people hate the English, I don't . . . [we] can't even find a decent culture to be colonized by.

This raw anger, directed at England as colonists, reflects a broader discontent with the way that a British Parliament had paid for (English) tax cuts with Scottish oil, had closed the Scottish collieries, and had allowed the Scottish shipbuilding industry to disappear into history as it bought cheaper built ships from around the world. The resulting unemployment paved the way for an epidemic of drug abuse, which has left Scotland with a lost generation.

This is graphically portrayed in Ken Loach's *Sweet Sixteen* where Greenock teenager Liam (Martin Compston) waits for his drug-addict mother Jean (Michelle Coulter) to be released from prison just in time for his sixteenth birthday, and plans to buy a caravan on the edge of the Clyde as a new home for them. Liam (in a ruthless capitalist approach) decides to fund the purchase by stealing Jean's drug-dealing boyfriend's stash of heroin, and selling it himself. Unfortunately this brings him to the attention of a local crime lord who invites him to join his business, and soon Liam, who was trying to escape the deprivation of drug culture finds himself at the heart of it. This boy (for he is no more than a boy) should be going to school, should be heading into work, should be making a valuable contribution to society, but instead he has a parental role model who is a junkie convict, and a broader community that rejects him out of hand.

The politics of this period of filmmaking is not played out on the grand scale, but is built into the representations of community, of family, and of individuals, and comes as a response to the distance (both literal and political) of government from the problems faced by the Scottish people on a daily basis.

ACTIVITY...

- Discuss the relationships between locals and outsiders in the films you have studied. Do you think that there are political messages being conveyed about Scotland in the way these two groups interact? If so, what are they?
- What macro (narrative, genre, etc.) techniques do Scottish filmmakers use to bring social and political issues to the fore? Do these techniques work or do they date quickly? What techniques would you use to address these issues if you were re-making these films today?
- Scottish humour is used to prick the balloon-like vanity of many social and political institutions. How effective is it in highlighting problems? Does it de-value the issue by contextualizing it through humour? How else could it be done?
- Discuss the social and political values that Scottish films express in this period. What future are the filmmakers offering? What do they show as so wrong with the past/present?

PRODUCTION CONTEXT

The arrival of television money (initially through Channel 4, and then through BBC Films, Scottish Television, and the Comataidh Telebhisein Gaidhlig (CTG) the Gaelic Television Committee) kick-started regional filmmaking in Scotland in the early 1980s. Up until this point Scottish film had been reliant on English filmmakers finding their way north of the border, American filmmakers seeking an 'authentic' backdrop for their stories, and the occasional funding opportunity afforded to home grown talent.

This platform was built on aggressively with the development of Scottish Screen, the Highlands and Islands Film Commission, the Glasgow Film Office, and Edinburgh Film Focus, government funded agencies whose role was to encourage, develop, support and sustain home grown filmmaking, and to entice filmmakers from outside Scotland

to make films there. Realizing the huge task set for them, these agencies looked to create funding schemes that would offer opportunities for new talent to see their visions realised, and to nurture filmmakers at the start of their careers.

Feature film production received considerable financial support through Scottish Screen's Scottish Film Production Fund, through the Glasgow Film Fund, and the Scottish Arts Council's National Lottery Fund (with *Orphans* collecting funding from all three sources). The production of short films (which are often used as 'calling cards' to secure feature film funding, and hence 'seed' the industry) is supported through four schemes: Tartan Shorts, Prime Cuts, New Found Land, and Gear Ghearr which is a scheme targeted specifically at encouraging Gaelic language filmmaking.

NOTEBOX

Figment Films

Figment Films was established in 1991 by Glasgow brothers Andrew and Kevin MacDonald, grandsons of the screenwriter/director Emeric Pressburger. Together with writer Dr John Hodge (who was a Registrar in Edinburgh's Eastern General Hospital) they secured funding from the Scottish Film Production Fund, the Glasgow Film Fund, and most importantly, Channel 4 to produce the black comedy *Shallow Grave* (Rank/Figment/Channel 4/GFF 1994, Director: Danny Boyle). Once they had secured the services of director Danny Boyle they made a film that launched the careers of Christopher Ecclestone and Ewan McGregor, secured a number of awards, and brought contemporary Scottish cinema back to the attention of a world audience. Together with Danny Boyle the brothers went on to make box office successes of *Trainspotting* (1995), *Twin Town* (Polygram/Figment/Agenda/Aimimage 1996, Director: Kevin Allen), *A Life Less Ordinary* (Polygram/Figment 1996), and *The Beach* (TCF/Figment 2000).

There is no question that Scottish film production is in a period of growth with a number of plans being submitted for Scottish National Film Studios including a complex at Aberuthven in Perthshire.

EXAMPLE EXAM QUESTIONS

1   How are issues of Scottish identity addressed in the films you have studied?

2   What values expressed in the films you have studied could be described as specifically Scottish, and how are they conveyed?

3   How does Scottish film use the landscape to convey messages and values?

4   Scottish film is about the reaction of an indigenous population to outside influences. Discuss this statement in relation to the films you have studied.

5   Is there any benefit to understanding messages and values in Scottish films in exploring the use of stereotypes?

6   Men and women are used differently in Scottish films. What are some of the ways in which they are used, and what does this convey?

7   What can you discover about issues of identity from looking at the depiction of community in Scottish film?

8   How have the filmmakers used sound and image to present the messages and values of their films?

FURTHER READING

Bruce, David (1996) *Scotland the Movie*, Edinburgh: Polygon/SFC.

Dick, Eddie (ed.) (1990) *From Limelight to Satellite: A Scottish Film Book*, London: BFI/SFC.

Forsyth Hardy, *Scotland in Film* (Edinburgh University Press, 1990)

Hill, John (1999) *British Cinema in the 1980s*, Oxford: Clarendon Press.

McArthur, Colin (1982) *Scotch Reels: Scotland in Cinema and Television*, London: BFI.

Pendreigh, Brian (2002) *The Pocket Scottish Movie Book*, Edinburgh: Mainstream.

Petrie, Duncan (2000) *Screening Scotland*, London: BFI.

Smith, Murray (2002) *Trainspotting*, London: BFI.

USEFUL WEBSITES

http://www.baftascotland.co.uk (BAFTA (Scotland))

http://www.britishpictures.com (a resource offering essays, articles, reviews, and title-specific information)

http://www.britmovies.co.uk (valuable for synopses, cast lists, etc.)

http://www.edinfilm.com (Edinburgh Film Focus – strategic agency for film in Edinburgh)

http://www.glasgowfilm.org.uk (Glasgow Film Office – strategic agency for film in Glasgow)

http://www.scotfilm.com (the Scottish Highlands and Islands Film Commission)

http://www.scottishscreen.com (Scotland's leading film body (and film archive))

http://www.visitscotland.com (the Scottish Tourist Board site)

▼ 18 COMEDY

This chapter deals with:

- the nature of comedy as a genre;
- representational ways of seeing the world to be found in comedies;
- possible approaches to recent British comedies;
- possible approaches to postwar British comedies.

NOTEBOX

This chapter will be directly relevant to your work on FS3 – Messages and Values: British and Irish Cinema for the WJEC's AS Level in Film Studies, particularly if you are studying comedy films but also in offering further ways of approaching films in general. (More indirectly, because of the way in which it examines films in terms of messages and values, this chapter will be helpful if you study later FS5 – Studies in World Cinema.)

FILMS MENTIONED

As you work your way through this chapter you need to watch at least some of the following films in full and at least short sequences from the others:

- *East is East* (O'Donnell, 1994)
- *The Full Monty* (Cattaneo, 1997)
- *Passport to Pimlico* (Cornelius, 1949)
- *The Lavender Hill Mob* (Crichton, 1951)
- *Genevieve* (Cornelius, 1953)

WJEC focus films: *East is East* (O'Donnell, 1994) and *The Ladykillers* (Mackendrick, 1955)

- Ask yourself the question, what is comedy and what are comedies? Brainstorm your own ideas about the nature of comedy and comedy films. These films would seem to present the world to us in a particular way that enables us to recognize them as falling within a specific category, but how exactly do you see them as doing this? What is it about the nature of the subject matter and the way in which that subject matter is presented to us that marks them out as comedies?
- Sum-up in 200 words the way in which you would define comedy and the nature of comedy films.
- If possible, read the definitions that several other people have come up with, and identify any similarities and differences.
- If you are working with a whole class, try to agree on a single collective definition, perhaps limiting it to no more than 150 words.

DEFINING COMEDY

In the theatre, 'comedy' originally simply referred to a play that was not a tragedy and did not necessarily imply the fundamental association with humour that the word tends to carry today. Aristotle saw it as referring to a play dealing with ordinary characters in ordinary situations in an amusing way. The term has strong associations with drama and the theatre but in common usage today the term has largely been taken over by cinema, television and radio.

Think of comedies you know, whether films or on TV. Do they deal with ordinary people in ordinary situations in an amusing way? Is this a good definition of the comedies you can think of? Does it fit all the comedies you can think of?

How many different sorts of television and/or cinema comedy can you list? For each type, try to give an example. Romantic comedies would be an obvious example, but how many others can you think of?

The Greek word 'komos', from which we derive the word 'comedy', does refer to merry-making and in this tradition these plays did have some association with fertility rites, a convention with which 'romantic comedies' are obviously in tune. You may be familiar with the convention found in Shakespeare's plays that comedies should end with differences being resolved in a happy marriage.

However, comedy has also been used in a perhaps more serious way to satirize authority and ridicule social codes or human behaviours. The form often depends upon intricate plots and the use of surprise but can also employ exaggerated imitation, clowning, buffoonery, slapstick and knockabout farce.

Think about comedies you know. Do any of them involve:

- bringing together young couples in love, and perhaps ending in marriage?
- ridiculing, or in a more gentle way poking fun at, certain sorts of behaviour or people in positions of authority?
- the use of complicated plots and unexpected events?
- exaggerated imitations, clowning or slapstick style humour?

KEY TERM

SATIRE The use of ridicule, irony or sarcasm to expose vice or stupidity; the lampooning of self-important individuals.

(Obviously now you are going to need to make sure you know what 'ridicule', 'irony' and 'lampooning' mean. We are sure you know what 'sarcasm' means.)

FILM AND WAYS OF SEEING THE WORLD

Comedy films, in line with all other types of film, attempt to re-present what we might call the 'out-there' world or the world as it exists, in a very particular way that presents to the audience a specific way of seeing that world. Therefore, in reading comedy films just as with other genres, we should consider the ways in which such concepts as gender, class, race, sexuality, national identity, regional identity, cultural identity and religious identity are being addressed. With one eye on the so-called 'war on terror' and our experience of living with its consequences, we might also note that during any period of potential political intolerance it is especially vital to champion the importance of comedy as a means of exploring these sorts of serious issues involving divisions between people.

Race

In considering representations of race and racial identity in films we need to decide how we would define the concept of 'race' and how we might consider racial identity to be acquired. We could then assess:

- whether any given film was defining 'race' in a similar way, or in a different way;
- whether the film under consideration was showing racial identity as being acquired in any particular way;
- whether it was seeing the concepts of race and racial identity as being fixed, or as varying between places and over time;
- whether particular races were being given roles within the narrative while others were being excluded;
- whether particular alliances between races were being shown;
- whether racial stereotypes were being employed;
- whether race was being shown as a means of oppression;
- whether the racial difference of 'outsiders' was accepted within the film's narrative or not.

Fundamentally, the concept of race is a means of categorizing people according to supposed biological characteristics such as skin colour or hair texture. This angle of approach will be an especially important aspect of our analysis when considering a film such as *East is East* (O'Donnell, 1999) which deals with the experience of a British Pakistani family living in Salford in 1970.

ACTIVITY . . .

- Go through the above list with a small group of other people if possible. Consider each idea carefully and see whether any further possible questions occur to you.
- Try to feed back your ideas to the whole class if time allows and discuss any areas of difference or uncertainty.

Gender

In considering the representation of gender identities we need first to ask how we might define the idea of 'gender': what is it and how is it acquired? In particular we need to define the term 'gender' as distinct from 'sex' and 'sexuality'. Basically, a person's sex is denoted by their genital make-up or the biology of their body; a person's sexuality is defined by their sexual feelings and behaviour; and a person's gender is that male or female construction of self given to a person by the society and culture they inhabit. In considering gender in any given film we need to investigate:

- whether men and women are represented in particular identifiable ways;
- whether the film makes an assumption that gender is fixed, as opposed to recognizing that gender as a social construct might vary across time and between cultures;
- whether the dominant descriptions of femininity and masculinity presented to the audience are simply those that fit the standards of a patriarchal society, or a society built upon fundamentalist religious beliefs;
- whether men are shown as active and women as passive;
- whether men dominate the narrative while women tend to be marginalized.

This will be an especially important approach when considering a film such as *The Full Monty* (Cattaneo, 1997) in which the disruption of traditional gender roles forms the very heart of both the comedy and the narrative.

ACTIVITY . . .

- Go through the above list with a small group of other people if possible. Consider each idea carefully and see whether any further possible areas for investigation occur to you.
- Try to feed back your ideas to the whole class and discuss any areas of difference or uncertainty.

Sexuality

In considering representations of sexuality we might begin by looking to see:

- whether sexual identity is seen to be fixed from birth or acquired via socialization;
- whether sexual identity is seen as being certain or something more fluid and ambiguous;
- whether there are clear representations of heterosexual behaviour, homosexual behaviour, and/or bisexual behaviour;
- whether sexual stereotypes are being employed, and if so from where they might derive (whether for instance this is again a case of a patriarchal society displaying its machismo beliefs or fundamentalist religious attitudes);
- whether any particular sexual behaviours or feelings are being presented in a negative or positive light;
- whether there is any awareness of how sexual norms and expectations may have changed over time.

This approach might be helpful in relation to both *East is East* and *The Full Monty*.

Class

In considering class representations, which is basically the idea that a society can be seen in terms of a hierarchy of stratifications with those in higher classes having more power, wealth and status than those in lower classes, we could investigate a film to see:

- whether class is seen as fixed from birth, or is used as a flexible concept;
- whether there are clear representations of working-class, middle-class and upper-class values;
- whether these are stereotypes, or more complex representations;
- whether these major class definitions are shown as subject to further sub-division;
- whether a hierarchical class structure is questioned, or simply accepted by the text.

It would be interesting to see how you felt about these sorts of questions in relation to *The Full Monty* and *East is East*; but such questions might offer an even more fruitful approach in relation to the post-Second World War comedies considered here later.

ACTIVITY . . .

Go through the questions posed here for sexuality and class with other people, and as before see if you can add to the lists.

'Britishness'

Similar approaches should be taken to issues of nation and national identity, and culture and cultural identity, paying particular attention to the issue of what might be said to constitute 'Britishness' and how this concept is presented in any given film. Again, this area will be particularly useful in relation to *East is East* where the issue of 'Britishness' and cultural difference is at the heart of both the comedy and what could be called the tragedy of the film. However, it is also especially relevant to the postwar comedies where in the absence of the multiculturalism of *East is East* the notion of national identity will be paramount. Often films attempt to suggest that a cohesive national identity exists within a country. Our interest is first of all in the exact nature of that representation of national identity and second in what relationship that representation might have to the social and historical reality.

> **NATIONAL IDENTITY** A sense of national identity seems to depend upon some shared stock of images, ideas, norms and values, stories and traditions. Nations might be described as imagined communities or communities that exist in the individual (and the collective?) imagination within the physical borders of a nation-state. This affects the way we see both ourselves and others classified

KEY TERM

as existing outside the 'in-group'. Yet, national identity does not exist in some singular, uncontested form. Rather it is a site of struggle constantly undergoing a process of re-affirmation or re-definition.

KEY TERM

CULTURAL IDENTITY This can refer to personal identity chosen for yourself or an identity ascribed to you by others. You might choose to describe your-self as 'British Pakistani' showing your identification with what you feel to be an intertwined cultural background, while others might identify you as 'Asian'. However, notice this will in fact only be part of your cultural identity, the racial/national identity part. Your cultural identity will also be formed from your categorization within other cultural spheres such as class, gender and age. So, for example, the key foci of your cultural identity might be young, male, middle-class, Christian, British Pakistani.

NOTEBOX

The really important point is that, whilst paying particularly close attention to the details of the films themselves and thinking about ideas of comedy, it is also vital for you to be questioning what you are seeing in relation to the nature of the world around you, or the nature of the society from within which the film is made.

Case Study: *The Full Monty* **(1997)**

(Director: Peter Cattaneo. Screenwriter: Simon Beaufoy. Cinematographer: John de Borman. Music: Anne Dudley. Cast: Robert Carlyle (Gaz); Mark Addy (Dave); Tom Wilkinson (Gerald); Lesley Sharp (Jean); Steve Huison (Lomper); Emily Woof (Mandy).)

ACTIVITY

■ After having watched the film once decide how you think this film represents issues of class, gender and sexuality. Make notes and discuss your ideas with others if possible.

Male gender roles

Within the social norms of British society men are traditionally expected to fulfil certain roles and embody certain values. They should be physically and emotionally strong, sexually virile and determinedly heterosexual. Above all their role is to work and provide financial security for the family. But in this film:

■   Dave is fat, out of condition and unable to perform in bed;
■   Gaz is emotionally vulnerable and struggles to show his love for Nathan;
■   Gerald lacks the courage to tell his wife he has lost his job;
■   Horse is worried about the size of his penis;
■   Lomper and Guy turn out to be gay;
■   most importantly they are all unemployed ('on the scrapheap' as Gaz calls it).

ACTIVITY....

Consider the scene early in the film in which Gaz, Dave and Nathan are walking down the steps towards a woman and then past the working men's club with the poster advertising the forthcoming show by male strippers. In groups, discuss as many aspects as possible of this scene that deal with issues of gender and/or sexuality.

Female gender roles

In contrast to the men, both Dave's wife, Jean, and Gaz's former wife, Mandy, are in work (with Jean being the main breadwinner in her home and Mandy twice offering her former partner, Gaz, a job). In addition it is Gerald's wife, Linda, who reveals real strength of character when she finally finds out about her husband being unemployed. Previously, Gerald has portrayed her as a stereo-typical spendthrift housewife roaming the High Street intent on spending the male breadwinner's hard-earned money but in fact at the moment of crisis she reveals a strength and dignity that her husband has been unable to manage to that stage. Finally, notice that not only are these women taking over the work roles of men but they are also seen symbolically invading male spaces such as the working men's club and even the men's toilet.

Messages and values

In traditional terms then, the men are seen as having been emasculated by this society. (How is the scene in the job centre, for instance, deliberately structured to emphasize the male loss of power?) But what the film also shows is the men struggling to re-define their roles in a new society, and indeed succeeding in doing so:

- Gaz improves his relationship with Nathan (and it is perhaps suggested by the ending, also with Mandy);
- Dave successfully rekindles his sexual relationship with Jean it seems;
- Gerald secures a new job but also develops an enhanced sense of loyalty to his former mates;
- Lomper and Guy are accepted within the male group despite their homosexuality.

ACTIVITY . . .

Consider the scene in which Gaz takes Nathan to school. How is this filmed in order to give a sense of the difficulties being experienced in the father-son relationship? In particular, you should look at aspects of performance including the delivery of specific lines, and the deliberately symbolic structure employed in the composition of specific shots.

ACTIVITY . . .

Are there any other messages and/or values that you feel are important to mention in relation to this film? Brainstorm your own ideas and then discuss these with other people if possible.

The Full Monty as a comedy

In adopting an approach such as that above it is important not to neglect the fact that this film is a comedy. So, in addition to investigating the ways in which male and female roles are being represented we do also need to explore the use of comedy.

ACTIVITY . . .

- Working with one or two others if possible, divide the comedy in this film into as many different categories as possible and give at least one example of each. You might like to refer back to the opening section to this chapter where the nature of comedy was considered.

■ For each example used see if you can identify a more serious under-pinning issue that is being touched upon.

Figure 18.1 *The Full Monty*
Source: *C4 / RGA*

Case Study: *East is East* (1999)

(Director: Damien O'Donnell. Screenwriter: Ayub Khan-Din. Cinematographer: Brian Tufano. Cast: Om Puri (George); Linda Bassett (Ella); Jordan Routledge (Sajid); Archie Panjabi (Meenah); Emil Marwn (Maneer); Chris Bisson (Saleem); Jimi Mistry (Tariq); Raji James (Abdul); Ian Aspinall (Nazir).)

Genre

There are plenty of serious issues in *The Full Monty* but the comedy remains to the forefront. There is also a strong feel-good factor attached to the final scene that perhaps could be accused of glossing over the reality of working-class hardship and suffering under Thatcherism. But with this film there are moments when you have to doubt whether it can truly be classified as a comedy and should not more correctly be described as a drama.

ACTIVITY . . .

Try to identify and list for yourself points in the film at which the sense of this as a comedy almost seems to be lost.

Characters and narrative structure

In any film such as this where there are a fair number of central characters it is important to make sure you have a clear grasp on the nature and role of each within the narrative. Notice that there are elements of straightforward comedy attached to each character. For example, it is important that we should not simply see George as some sort of ogre as we have to understand why Ella loves him, and so there are those endearing moments such as the buying of the dentist's chair for his wife.

ACTIVITY . . .

- Use a single diagram to represent the relationship between the central characters.
- Beneath each character note one or two comic scenes within which they play a central role and sum up their character in one sentence.
- Keeping words of explanation to a minimum, construct a flow diagram showing the development of the film's narrative.
- Compare your diagrams with other people's if possible, and discuss both similarities and differences.

Historical context

The context of the period in which this is set is clearly important. The Khans are an Anglo-Pakistani family living in Salford in 1970. War between India and Pakistan is about to break out over East Pakistan, shortly to become Bangladesh, and in Britain racist attitudes against immigrants are being encouraged by right-wing political groups and given a central focus by the Conservative MP, Enoch Powell.

Representation

After watching the film, consider the representation of the following areas:

- race relations/relationships;
- cultural tensions/expectations;
- social values and norms;
- religion;
- national identity.

ACTIVITY . . .

- Briefly note your thoughts on each of these areas, referring to actual shots or sequences within the film to illustrate your ideas.
- Compare your ideas with those of other people if possible. In particular you should find yourself discussing ideas relating to:

  - patriarchy and domestic violence;
  - difficulties faced by first-generation immigrants;
  - difficulties faced by second-generation immigrants.

As a comedy

Comedies traditionally have happy endings: there are ways in which this ending might be said to conform to this pattern but the dénouement certainly remains challenging. Maybe we need to consider other possible comedy types for this film: dark comedy, black comedy or tragi-comedy. These are terms that often describe comedies of this ilk: perhaps dark comedy would be most suitable.

ACTIVITY . . .

- Working with one or two others if possible, divide the comedy in this film into as many different categories as possible and give at least one example of each.
- For each example you use, see if you can identify a more serious underpinning issue that is being touched upon.
- Does this underlying seriousness make the term 'dark comedy' appropriate?

Re-watch the opening to the film and discuss with others ways in which this might be a particularly appropriate exposition phase. How could the events of the opening be considered in some way symbolic of the whole film?

Try either or both of these essays:

1   By referring to no more than two sequences, one in *East is East* and another in *The Full Monty* show how messages and values relating to family issues are central to both films. Remember that within your answer it is important to refer to ways in which meaning is created through the use of cinematography, mise en scène, editing and sound, and perhaps also through narrative structure and genre.
2   By a close analysis of either the opening or the ending of either of these films explore key messages and values to be found in your chosen film. Again, remember that within your answer it is important to refer to ways in which meaning is created through the use of cinematography, mise en scène, editing and sound, and perhaps also through narrative structure and genre.

POSTWAR COMEDIES

The Second World War brought about considerable social change in Britain with the old established class structure beginning to show signs of disintegration. In 'We are the masters now' Anthony Howard claims (French and Sissons 1986), 'The war had eroded practically every traditional social barrier in Britain.' But the Prime Minister, Clement Atlee, was calling on people to display in peace the (supposed) unity shown in war and to be prepared to continue to endure hardships: 'We have come through difficult years and we are going to face difficult years and to get through them we will require no less effort, no less unselfishness and no less work than was needed to bring us through the war' (Johnson 1994).

There was social change taking place with, for example, the founding of the National Health Service but at the same time the war had been costly and British industry was increasingly inefficient. Rationing actually increased after the war with, for example, bread and potatoes being rationed for the first time and clothing and furniture rationing staying in place until the end of 1949 (see the opening to *Passport to Pimlico*). People were disgruntled with officialdom: demobilization, for instance, proceeded too slowly for some with almost twice as many people still being in the armed forces in 1948 as there were in 1939. There was a winter fuel crisis during the extremely cold winter of 1947 with power output being below prewar levels so that electricity cuts had to be made. At the same time all over the former British Empire, in India, Burma, Ceylon, Malaya and Kenya for instance, independence movements were springing up and further questioning Britain's status as a world power. It is against this sort of background that comedies from this period have to be read.

Case Study: *Genevieve* (1953)

(Director: Henry Cornelius. Screenwriter: William Rose. Cinematographer: Christopher Challis. Composer: Larry Adler. Cast: John Gregson (Alan), Dinah Sheridan (Wendy), Kenneth More (Ambrose), Kay Kendall (Rosalind).)

England: a green and pleasant land?

If you are looking at some older British films, *Genevieve* would be an interesting comedy to consider. This film seems to portray England as a green and pleasant land where the worst that could happen is that your vintage or veteran car might break down on the annual London to Brighton run. There appear to be no serious issues or social criticism beneath the light superficial fun of the film's surface. Politically the suggestion emanating from such comedies could well be said to be that everything in England is fine and we are lucky to live in such a place. If this is the case, notice that this in itself is actually still political in the sense that it supports the status quo and suggests there is no need for change. From this perspective the film works to pacify the audience into believing all is well in 1950s Britain.

However, what if we were to see the whole comfortable middle-class perspective of peace and prosperity for all that is displayed in so many films from this period as being exaggerated to the point of ridicule here? If you have already seen *Passport to Pimlico* (dealt with below and in Chapter 13) does the fact that the same person directed both of these films complicate our interpretation of *Genevieve*? Could *Genevieve* be deliberately parodying, even satirizing, Establishment notions of England and the British national identity?

Britishness

If we take the first view of the film suggested then this is a gentle comedy which could be described as summing up a particular sort of 'Britishness': a cosy couple, Alan and Wendy, race against their friends, Ambrose and Rosalind, through the South-East heartland of England on the London to Brighton vintage car rally. From this perspective, this is an escapist fantasy taking the audience into a world where nothing bad ever happens, or can ever intrude; an upper middle-class film

---

made for the consumption of the working class within the dominant British cinematic tradition. Notice the language use ('sport', 'old man', 'darling', 'don't be such a stinker', 'she must be blotto'); the food and drink (sherry, and olives in the sandwiches); and the clothes of our central characters. But the question remains as to whether we might not see this as a more interesting tongue-in-cheek, even satirical, take on 'Britishness' and the Little Englander mentality. Certainly it raises just as many issues to do with national identity as *East is East*.

ACTIVITY

After you have watched the film discuss with others how you think it should be read. Try to put forward evidence from the film for your position. Could it be equally valid to read it in either of the ways suggested here?

EALING COMEDIES

If you undertake any background reading on films from the Ealing Studio you will notice how their comedies are often described as classically British. In fact, they could be seen as setting up a working-class notion of 'Britishness' that is essentially distinct from the more usual middle-class filmic notion of what it means to be British. The principal characters in, for example, both *Passport To Pimlico* (Cornelius, 1949) and *The Lavender Hill Mob* (Crichton, 1951), are all outsiders: they are not members of 'the Establishment' with social power and standing as Alan and Ambrose are in *Genevieve*, and their struggle is clearly portrayed as a struggle against that established order. The director of Ealing Studios during the period, Michael Balcon, described the attitude of those working there towards filmmaking in this way: 'The bloodless revolution of 1945 had taken place, but I think our first desire was to get rid of as many wartime restrictions as possible and get going . . . There was a mild anarchy in the air' (Balcon 1969).

Representations of the working class

Characters in these films are often alienated from the established order and spend their time rebelling against the constrictions imposed upon their lives by 'the Establishment'. These films are, in short, characterized by a strong sense of rebellion, what Balcon calls 'mild anarchy'. In this way it might be possible to suggest these films are in tune with the mood of the age: there were a rash of strikes in late 1944, and in 1945 Attlee's Labour Party won a landslide general election victory launching plans for a welfare state and widespread nationalization (Balcon's 'bloodless revolution').

In *Passport to Pimlico* ordinary working-class people are shown to have a defiant resilience and tenacity, while those in positions of power and authority are exposed as autocratic, bureaucratic and repressive, and driven by concerns of monetary gain. See too how (as with the bank manager in *Passport to Pimlico* and the bank employee, Mr Holland, in *The Lavender Hill Mob*) society is shown as attempting to suppress individuality. One character ironically comments on Mr Holland that he has no imagination and his only virtue is his honesty. Is this the way most employees/workers are viewed? Isn't this a traditional view of the working class that is in this film exposed as false?

Working-class revolt

Passport to Pimlico shows working-class people taking charge of their lives in revolutionary ways: see how they tear up their ration books and identity cards, the symbols of uniformity, conformity and centralized control over the individual. (The range of goods covered by rationing actually increased in Britain after the war and continued in some cases into the 1950s.) The central characters continually define themselves as 'English', but their idea of Englishness centres upon a form of defiant working-class self-sufficiency and a determination not to bow beneath the yoke of officialdom being imposed from above. To emphasize the point once more, what is certain here and what is glossed over by popular descriptions of Ealing comedies is that the Englishness given expression in these films is often strongly working class: it is not the upper middle-class, public school-based Englishness (Britishness?) that is more usually found in British cinema of the 1940s and 1950s.

ACTIVITY

- How would you define the difference between the two terms, 'Britishness' and 'Englishness'? How is each used and in what sorts of circumstances is one used in preferences over the other?
- When you are clear in your own mind about these two concepts, exchange thoughts with other people, if possible.

ACTIVITY

Try either or both of these essay titles:

1 In your opinion how serious are the postwar comedies you have studied? Remember to refer to at least two films and to use detailed examples to support your points.
2 In what ways would you say the postwar comedies you have studied could be considered to be similar and in what ways are they different? Remember to refer to at least two films and to use detailed examples to support your points.

1 How is comedy used to represent serious situations and issues in the films you have studied?

2 How useful have you found it to know something about the period in which the comedies you have studied were made?

3 To what extent in your experience do comedy films tend to rely on stereotypes?

4 What have been the chief comedy features of the films you have watched and how useful have these features been in helping to convey messages and values?

5 What have the films you have studied had to say about the concept of 'Britishness'?

CONCLUSION

- Comedy is a very old form of creative human expression that uses a range of identifiable techniques.
- Essentially the world is being represented, or re-presented, to us via comedy films in the same way as in other films.
- What we see is not the world but a highly constructed interpretation of it; and we have to be aware of the ways in which concepts such as class, race, gender, sexuality and national identity are just as relevant to comedy films as to other types of film.
- It is also useful to try to see these representations within the context of the historical moment that the film is made.

FURTHER READING

Ashby, J. and Higson, A. (eds) (2000) *British Cinema, Past and Present*, London: Routledge.

Balcon, M. (1969) *Michael Balcon Presents: A Lifetime in Films*, London: Hutchinson (p.157).

Barr, C. (1998) *Ealing Studios*, Moffat: Cameron and Hollis.

Caughie, J. and Rockett, K. (1996) *The Companion to British and Irish Cinema*, London: BFI.

French, P. and Sissons, M. (eds) (1986) *Age of Austerity*, Oxford: Oxford University Press (p.18).

Johnson, P. (ed.) (1994) *Twentieth Century Britain: Economic, Social and Cultural Change*, Harlow: Longman (p. 300).

King, G. (2002) *Film Comedy*, London: Wallflower Press (Introduction).

Richards, J. (1997) *Films and British National Identity: From Dickens to Dad's Army*, Manchester and New York: Manchester University Press.

Sargeant, A. (2005) *British Cinema: A Critical History*, London: BFI.

Street, S. (1999) *British National Cinema*, London: Routledge.

▼ GLOSSARY

Agents Not only actors but also directors, screenwriters, producers, cinematographers and others involved in commercial filmmaking have agents. The system under which these people would have been kept on full-time contracts to the studios came to an end during the 1950s, and from this point agents became especially important within the industry as they had the power to continually re-negotiate one-off film deals for those on their books.

The role of agents representing top stars is particularly powerful. If as a studio you believe it is the stars who really sell films you will be prepared to pay a large percentage of your budget to secure the services of the star you believe will best embody the image required for your film.

'Blind buying' This means you have to take the films on offer without having a chance to first view them to see if you want them or not.

'Block booking' This means you have to agree to take all of the films produced by a studio in a year including the lesser films in order to get the major productions.

British New Wave A movement of well-educated, leftist filmmakers largely from a northern England, working-class background, that used 'realism' to construct stories of working-class lives ('kitchen-sink dramas'). Originally working on short films and documentaries as part of their 'free cinema' concept they graduated to feature film production establishing a north of England production base to compete with what they saw as a London-focused and London-centred industry. They included filmmakers Lindsay Anderson, Karel Reisz, and Tony Richardson.

Camerawork This clearly and quite simply refers to the work done with the camera in the making of a film. However, the possibilities open to the cinematographer are anything but simple. Fundamentally, the camera can be positioned at any distance from the subject being filmed and at any angle to that subject. It can be turned left or right to follow a subject within a horizontal plane, or tilted up or down to follow the same subject in a vertical plane. It can also be moved at any speed towards, away from or around the subject, and this movement can be as smooth or as shaky as the filmmakers decide. In addition, lenses can be used to give the appearance of movement towards or away from the subject at any speed, or to make the image of the subject either sharper or more indistinct, or even to alter the appearance of the subject in the style of a fairground 'hall of mirrors'.

The only limitation on the fluidity and mobility of the camerawork in any film is the availability of the necessary technology to enable the desired effect to be achieved; and, in general terms, camera and lens technology has developed throughout film history in such a way as to permit increasingly complex camerawork. So, for instance, new lightweight cameras (and sound recording gear) in the 1950s made it easier to take the equipment out on location.

However, what you will find if you get the chance to watch some clips from old silent films is that even from very early in film history cinematographers were devising imaginative ways of getting moving shots with these rather large, heavy wooden cameras. So, yes, available technology must to some extent impose limitations upon what can be achieved, but often it is the creativity with which available technology is used that is of most interest.

Cause and effect This refers to the way in which mainstream films are moved forward by one scene or event having been caused by an earlier one and in turn giving rise to an effect which is seen in a subsequent scene or event. What this means is that everything we see has been motivated by something we have seen earlier and in turn motivates something we see further on in the film.

Chronology The ordering of a series of events in time sequence. This is the simplest way of setting out a story and is important in films such as *Bloody Sunday* (Greengrass, 2002) (see FS3 British Cinema – Social and Political Conflict), involving the shooting of people taking part in a civil rights demonstration in Northern Ireland in 1972, where the development of events in sequence over a set period of time is a vital part of the whole creative enterprise.

Clydesideism This perhaps reflects a more modern view of Scotland and is based around the working-class, industrialized people and areas, again offering a strong sense of community, but with a clearer sense of unromantic realism. With the demise of heavy industry in Scotland, Clydesideism is developing a sense of historic rather than current representation on the one hand, and on the other is evolving to reflect a disaffected working class, and declining communities.

Colour This can be used in highly artificial ways for particular expressive purposes as in the make-up employed by the changed Jude in *The Crying Game*, for instance, (where it would seem to perhaps suggest the danger of a femme fatale) or it can be employed in an effort to achieve naturalism by re-creating the colours of the real world.

Commercial process A commercial process is one that is focused upon achieving a financial return, in other words making a profit.

Contrapuntal sound This is a great technique where the sound is not directly related to the image, but when placed together an additional meaning (or depth of meaning) is created. Thus the sound of a boxing match playing on a television in shot becomes more significant when the person watching the match walks into another room and begins beating an elderly person in there. The sound carried across from the television to the room where the beating is taking place is in counterpoint to the image of the abuse, yet serves to make a bigger statement about violence in general. It may be that a mix of contrapuntal sound and the diegetic sound of the beating may heighten this statement further.

Costume and props This refers to items of clothing being worn by characters and objects seen within any given setting. At its simplest, costume clearly acts as a type of uniform, linking a character to a particular group and often to a rank or position within that group. But costume can also 'announce' a character, giving an insight into what this person is supposed to be like, for instance shy or flamboyant. At their simplest, props work to give an authentic sense of place, but can also be used in more complex ways to suggest important characteristics of particular individuals or even key themes for the whole film.

Cultural identity This can refer to personal identity chosen for yourself or an identity ascribed to you by others. You might choose to describe yourself as 'British Pakistani' showing your identification with what you feel to be an intertwined cultural background, while others might identify you as 'Asian'. However, notice this will in fact only be part of your cultural identity, the racial/national identity part. Your cultural identity will also be formed from your categorization within other cultural spheres such as class, gender and age. So, for example, the key foci of your cultural identity might be young, male, middle-class, Christian, British Pakistani.

Diegetic sound Diegetic sound is the sound that is heard in the fictional world, the sound that the characters in that world can hear. Most diegetic sound is not recorded 'on location' but is fabricated and 'dubbed' on to the film by sound designers and 'foley artists' (people who generate sound effects such as cutting into a cabbage to make the sound of someone being guillotined).

DVD Digital Versatile Disc, the system that has now almost replaced VHS video. Discs can hold much more information than video tapes (providing the possibility for all sorts of 'extras' to be included alongside the main film) and offer a higher quality image.

Expectations The set of ideas each of us brings with us when we watch any film. These may be expectations to do with story structure, character development, or themes we anticipate will be dealt with; and they will be based upon our previous experience of these things.

Exposition This is the opening to a film, which can often be *in medioreum* 'in the middle of things'. It sets up expectations and possibilities, and introduces key characters, locations and ideas.

Free cinema, direct cinema, cinéma vérité (truth) These three documentary movements of the 1950s and 1960s, from Britain, the US and France respectively, are all examples of the development of observational documentary styles. These movements were interested in finding new ways of telling stories in film, thus creating a new film language as well as presenting new subject matter.

Gender and sex Gender and sex are often used interchangeably but there are important differences:

Sex refers to the biological differences between men and women. Sex is fixed and does not change over time; it is the same across countries and across cultures, while gender is often different.

Gender refers to the social differences between men and women, girls and boys. These are the expectations that society has about men and women's roles and responsibilities. These gender expectations will change over time and will be different in different countries and amongst different cultures.

Gender identity The study of representations of gender is important partly because gender is a political issue: Feminism is a social movement that questions gender inequalities and tries to change them, hoping to achieve gender equality, particularly in relation to work and pay. Part of the campaign for equal opportunities relied on pointing out the way that gender expectations prevent equality – and affect men as well as women.

Genre This term has at least a double usage here. It can be used to denote different general types of storytelling extending across a range of different media such as fairy tales, plays and TV soaps; so, simply different types of storytelling. But it can also be used to refer to the classification of films into types such as horror, romantic comedy, thriller or science fiction.

Globalization A perceived economic trend towards the whole world becoming a single market so that major multinational corporations are increasingly able to control trade on a global scale.

'Green-lit' This is a jargon term used within the film industry for obtaining the 'go-ahead' for a film project to move from being a concept to actually starting production.

Hollywood As early as the 1910s the US film industry began to shift its base from the East Coast to what was essentially a place in the Californian desert, a rural area on the edge of Los Angeles. The name 'Hollywood' has, of course, become a term signifying something much more than simply a place in California.

Iconography This simply refers to characteristic features of a genre, the things you expect to see and sounds you expect to hear that taken together collectively tell you the type of film, or genre, you are watching.

As with all other film terms, knowing the name and what it means may be useful but it is not essential; it is recognizing the characteristic features that are signalling to you that this is a specific genre and being able to identify them at work within particular scenes within particular films that are important.

Identity The concept of identity refers to the way that different groups (family, friends, schools, government, etc.) in society see us and the way in which we see ourselves. These two views are likely to be different, even conflicting. The factors affecting our identity include gender, race, religion, class, sexuality and nationality which are interlinked and have become more and more complicated. Some people may wish to identify themselves as gay; for others to do so may suggest discrimination or prejudice.

The growth in identity politics such as gay rights and feminism has indicated a move away from political parties to single-issue politics in society.

Ideology A person's or a society's set of beliefs and values, or overall way of looking at the world. The Western world in general is said to be built upon a belief in capitalism, or the idea that what is best for society, or what brings the greatest benefits to a society, is for business to be given free rein to operate without restrictions in an open, competitive market.

Industrial process An industrial process is one that is involved in the manufacture of goods that are being made for sale.

Kailyardism This emphasizes the small town or largely rural aspects of Scotland, depicting those who live in these areas as 'simple folk' of the land. This is usually accompanied by empowering them with folk wisdom and a 'natural' understanding of people (more often than not of either city types or the English), and with a strong sense of community that often involves intrigue.

Lighting This refers to the various ways in which the light whether in the studio or on location is controlled and manipulated in order to achieve the 'look' desired for a particular shot or scene.

Marketing This refers to the total package of strategies used to try to promote and sell a film. Large distribution companies in charge of marketing will employ researchers to investigate the market for any particular film and enable them to keep abreast of shifting trends in consumer practices. They will also use focus groups (or members of the public) from the supposed target market to view and comment upon the film at various stages with the idea of altering the script if necessary. Such early showings of the film behind closed doors are known as test screenings.

All of this will occur before those elements more usually associated with marketing, the screening of cinema trailers, the launching of a press campaign and the instigation of a poster campaign, come into play. Although, of course, the planning for each of these strands involving the development of a clear timetable for each stage of the marketing process will be under way even as the film is being shot.

Messages Messages are deliberately placed communications in a film that are intended to be read, or de-coded by an audience, and which should then affect the spectator's individual understanding of the film. A message may be explicitly expressed (perhaps by having a character spell it out) or may be implicitly expressed and in need of interpretation (in *Get Carter* (MGM/Mike Klinger 1971, Director: Mike Hodges) for instance, the women in the film are all victims, and receive summary punishment at the hands of men – is this a 'hidden' message from the director?).

Explicit messages are normally straightforward with little opportunity for mis-interpretation. Implicit messages are more complex and their understanding is reliant not only on how they have been 'coded' into the film, but also on the spectator's own experiences and belief system.

Messages and values Films can be seen in some sense to embody certain messages that they are working to communicate to the audience. They can also be seen to be attempting to advance certain values while questioning others.

La Haine (Kassowitz, 1995) has been attacked as a film that has a message that is anti-police: whether this is true or not would depend upon how we interpreted characters and scenes within the film and how we understood the filmmakers to be using film construction techniques to emphasize and elevate certain perspectives above others.

Mise en scène This is a term that is borrowed from the theatre and really refers to staging, or 'putting on stage'. It sometimes helps to think of the elements that you can see in the staging of a play: a particular location will be suggested on the stage, characters will be dressed in particular ways, particular objects will be carried by characters or will be prominently placed on the stage, and the actors will be directed to move or perform in particular ways. These theatrical elements are the sub-section parts of the cinematic term; and this effectively reminds us of the way in which the theatre is a key element of film's cultural and artistic origins.

Narrative This term is really quite simply used as another term for 'story'. But it can also be seen (perhaps more correctly) as a more technical term relating to attempts to theorize the principles by which stories are structured. Some theorists, for example, have suggested that all stories have 'deep-seated' underpinning common narrative structures.

Narrative theory and resolution When Film Studies was first developing as an academic subject in the 1960s and 1970s there was a suspicion amongst academics about popular, usually, genre films. Influenced by Marxist views of popular culture many theorists argued that genre films spoon-fed their audiences rather than letting the audience think for themselves. An example of this was the way that endings, or resolutions, of popular films explained everything, while other types of films and film makers, European, 'art' cinema, etc., often left the audience with unanswered questions.

Why does it matter whether the audience is given the answers in a film or questions are left open? Some theorists argued that what happens in the cinema (where most people watched films at this time) has an influence on audience behaviour in the 'real world'; if people get used to being told what to think they will not question society and their place in it. In other words, Hollywood was seen as part of a system which kept the masses in their place – poor, hard working and unquestioning. These ideas are similar to the hypodermic theory in Media Studies – that the audience is injected with messages from popular culture and is unable to question them.

National identity A sense of national identity seems to depend upon some shared stock of images, ideas, norms and values, stories and traditions. Nations might be described as imagined communities or communities that exist in the individual (and the collective?) imagination within the physical borders of a nation-state. This affects the way we see both ourselves and others classified as existing outside the 'in-group'. Yet, national identity does not exist in some singular, uncontested form. Rather it is a site of struggle constantly undergoing a process of re-affirmation or re-definition.

Non-diegetic sound This is the sound that is outside the fictional world, and that characters in the fictional world cannot hear. This would include overlays of soundtrack music and any voice-over narration.

Non-mainstream/alternative/art cinema Although these terms all have slightly different meanings they are often used interchangeably to refer to films which are produced outside of the major film studios – usually Hollywood. They refer to films which in terms of narrative structure (often open rather than closed endings), subject matter, film language, budget, etc. are different from mainstream film. In some cases filmmakers choose to work in this way as they oppose the style and messages and values of Hollywood cinema; in others filmmakers who start in this area move on to big budget films. These areas will be studied in more detail at A2.

Oligopoly Term used to describe the situation in which a small group of companies exerts powerful almost exclusive control over the business being done within any particular industry.

Paradigm The term used to describe the range of choices available at any given moment of film construction. This covers a huge area, everything from which actor from the paradigm of possible actors should be chosen to play a given role, to which hat (from the paradigm ranging from no hat to top hat to deerstalker) a character should wear at any given point in a film.

It is a useful term for us for one reason only and that is it reminds us that at all times choices are being made in the construction of films and it is our job to try to decide why those choices might have been made.

Parallel editing This refers to moving back and forth between two or more narrative lines of action supposedly occurring at the same time.

Performance and movement This refers to the acting that is taking place but the phrase also helps to define a little more clearly what it is we should be looking for: there is a performance going on and essentially it revolves around movement. These movements can range from the miniscule to the expansive, and can involve the whole body or the smallest parts of the body. Everything is included from slow movements of the eye to sudden running and jumping, and each can be 'read' in some way (or several possible ways).

Pleasure Films clearly give us pleasure in a range of ways, otherwise we would not watch them, and yet studying academic subjects is somehow often seen to be at odds with the idea of pleasure. However, since pleasure is the thing that beyond all else stimulates our initial interest in films we should not dismiss it out of hand. In fact, the idea of exactly how films provide us with pleasure will be a key approach to film for us.

The way in which film gives pleasure is most apparent when we consider not just audiences in general but our own personal response to films and yet it is so often neglected by those of us who wish to study film. Maybe this is because the concept of pleasure does not seem to sit well in relation to the idea of study. Or perhaps this neglect of the pleasure principle is to do with a difficulty in deciding how to study such a seemingly vague notion.

However we view all of this, the concept is clearly important not only in relation to narrative structure but also in relation to the way in which human beings seem to be able to respond to the sheer aesthetic joy of colour, movement, light, shape and size and in particular changing colour, movement, light, shape and size.

The best way to think about the ways in which films create pleasure for an audience is to analyse our own enjoyment of films. Pleasure could be provided by (among other things) an exciting or romantic narrative, the escapism of identifying with characters unlike ourselves or by the visual pleasure provided by the big screen. Film Studies academics have spent a long time trying to explain the different pleasures experienced by film spectators, particularly the enjoyment of aspects of film which do not immediately seem pleasurable such as watching horror films.

Poster campaign A marketing strategy involving the use of a prominently displayed series of posters to promote a film. Each poster will be carefully put together to present what is seen to be a desirable image to be associated with the film and will be strategically placed in the press and positioned on hoardings in such a way as to attempt to catch the eye of the film's target audience. The aim will be to present the public with a clearly defined notion of exactly what is special or particular about this film. This is sometimes referred to as the film's 'unique selling point', or USP.

Reading This is a fundamentally important term in our whole approach to Film Studies. 'Reading' immediately suggests a depth of investigation and an intensity of focus that 'watching films' simply does not convey.

Realism Realism is a visual style which is particularly associated with British cinema such as the British New Wave of the 1960s. It is an attempt to show the world as it really is and tends to concentrate on social and political issues and how these affect working-class characters. A realist style has its own codes and conventions (particular style of acting, lighting, dialogue, setting, plots, etc.) which the audience recognizes as realist.

Release pattern This is the part of the marketing strategy that determines the number of prints of the film that are to be initially put out to cinemas, which cinemas are to receive the film to begin with, and then how that initial release of the film is to be expanded and built upon.

A film might be given a 'general release' right across the country or it might have a 'select release' to a few cinemas in a few cities where the audience is felt to be right for this particular film. A 'saturation release' would indicate that the effort has been to put the film out immediately to as many cinemas as possible.

A film is usually released first of all within its country of origin before moving out to other countries in a developmental fashion, although it is now possible for a big Hollywood film to have a single global release date.

Whatever pattern is adopted, the key thing to recognize is the way in which market analysts will have worked together to try to decide upon the strategy that will be best suited to maximizing box-office returns on their product.

Representation Representation is the re-presentation or interpretation of an image, an action, a conversation, etc. As it re-presents the original from the perspective of the person (screenwriter, director, cinematographer, etc.) constructing the representation, it can never accurately capture the original, but will instead offer a partial view, coloured by messages and values.

Repression Repression is the process of being kept down by force (not always physical); it refers to the way that a person's right to freedom of expression whether politically, socially or culturally can be denied.

In psychoanalysis the term 'repression' has a different meaning. Freud defines repression as a defence mechanism. It is the way that individuals protect themselves from harmful but attractive desires (often sexual). According to Freud such desires can never be completely repressed but return, in the form of dreams for example.

Resolution The final phase of a narrative film that quite simply resolves all the storylines that have been set running. Films may of course leave some matters unresolved.

Satire The use of ridicule, irony or sarcasm to expose vice or stupidity; the lampooning of self-important individuals.

Slasher movie A type of horror film in which the story revolves around psychotic males with plans to murder a group of young people. This sub-genre was at its height in the 1970s and early 1980s with films such as *The Texas Chain Saw Massacre* (Hooper, 1974), *Halloween* (Carpenter, 1978), *Friday the 13th* (Cunningham, 1980) and *Nightmare on Elm Street* (Craven, 1984).

Swinging Britain This term relates to changes in a whole range of attitudes, behaviours, and moralities where Britain finally shook off the bleak, postwar way of living, where caution, practicality, repression, and obedience were the norms. The term 'swinging' comes from a form of music that was more relaxed and open in its style. The 'swinging sixties' really began in 1963 with the emergence of the Beatles and the Mersey music scene, and its London counterpart. With full employment, young people had a greater disposable income, and music and fashion came to dominate the culture. Confident in peace and prosperity, this 'swinging' approach developed across social boundaries, and an 'anything goes' attitude was popularized.

Synergy The multiplied business energy that is created by multinational multimedia ownership. By owning newspapers, magazines, book publishing and music companies, TV and radio stations, satellite/cable TV companies, alongside their involvement in cinema production, distribution and exhibition these massive corporations might be able to:

- publicize and advertise their films via their own print, sound and visual media arms;
- put out associated books and music, again from within their own organization;
- show their films via their own various TV and cinema outlets.

Tartanry This encompasses a range of representations that see the Scots in traditional dress: either as the noble heroic Highland rebel, the laird or educated intellectual, or as the drunken, bagpipe-playing comedy act, and is one that focuses on the tartan as the key to Scottish identity (for better or worse).

Tartanry, Kailyardism, and Clydesideism There are three types of representation that rise above all others in Scottish film and suggest not only some regional variance within Scotland, but also a sense of internal conflict between the past and present, the rural and the urban.

Technological determinism The assumption that technological progress is inevitable and determines the shape and nature of social change.

Teenpic A film featuring teenagers as the central characters and aimed at teenage audiences. The stories focus on the sorts of problems and difficulties faced by young people of this age.

Television This might perhaps at first seem a strange choice of key term when considering cinema and film. However, TV is clearly in the business of screening staged film dramas and from this perspective is in immediate competition with cinema. On the other hand, since TV has provided a ready-made screen in every home since the 1960s the potential of a further space in which to show film products also becomes apparent. And when we reach the era of first video and then DVD, these products depend entirely for their success or otherwise upon people having access to screens within as wide a variety of places as possible.

Theme In analysing the subject matter of films and the way that they construct messages and values, we need to distinguish between the story and the themes. The plot is the action or story of the film; when someone asks you what a film is about, this is usually what you would relate to them. The themes of a film are what the plot makes you think about, the way that the film comments on wider issues. For example the story of *Bridget Jones's Diary* is: a 'thirty-something' single woman falls in love with the wrong man before realizing that Mark Darcy is her true love. The theme of the film is: the changing position of women in society – now that women are independent in terms of career and financial power how does this affect their traditional roles in society and their relationships with men?

'The talent' This is a film industry term for the main creative players involved in the production of any particular film. It is often used to refer to the director, the producer, the screenwriter and the lead actors as a group of key personnel, but may include others such as an art director, director of cinematography and musical director.

Trailers A short advert for a film put together by the distributors. It will usually be comprised of extracts from the film in question with an added voice-over designed to sell the film. A shorter version of the trailer sometime before the film is due out is known as a 'teaser'.

Values Values are an expression of what an individual or a society considers important, in terms of social behaviour, laws, attitudes, beliefs, etc. Values are of course both changeable and relative to each other and situations where they are applied.

Systems or sets of values can be expressed as an *ideology* (a belief system), which, again, can be an individual ideology or an ideology defined by a society.

It is perfectly possible for an individual to hold their own set of values within a broader set of values belonging to a society. Thus someone could accept the broad values of a democracy whilst being a tyrant in their own home.

Vampire movie A horror sub-genre that owes a lot to Bram Stoker's novel *Dracula* (1897) and tends to feature male characters preying upon female victims, on this occasion by sucking their blood.

Vertical integration The way in which studios in the 1930s and 1940s integrated the whole process from making to screening films under their control.

VHS Video Home System, Matsushita's video tape format which became the home norm for recording after overcoming its commercial rival, Sony's Betamax system, in the 1980s.

Viewing pleasure There is the simple human pleasure of looking, or scopophilia (seen by Freud as one of the infantile sexual drives) and voyeurism, the act of watching others without their knowledge, both of which have been explored in film theory in relation to the act of watching films in a darkened room. But there are also pleasures derived from aspects of the film viewing experience such as being able to solve mysteries, to follow a causal chain of events, to identify with strong characters, to recognize narrative patterns or genre features seen before, to be surprised or even shocked by images or portrayed events, to be able to experience fear in safety and so on.

Windows A term used to suggest the variety of places that films can now be viewed.

Zombie film A horror sub-genre in which the dead (the zombies) come back to life and attack the living. See *Night of the Living Dead* (Romero, 1968) and *Shaun of the Dead* (Wright, 2004) to compare older and more recent treatments of the genre.

▼ WEB RESOURCES

www.baftascotland.co.uk	BAFTA (Scotland)
www.bbc.co.uk	British Broadcasting Corporation
www.bbfc.co.uk	The British Board of Film Classification
www.bfi.org.uk	British Film Institute
www.bostonreview.net	Boston Review
www.britishpictures.com	a resource offering essays, articles, reviews, and title specific information,
www.britmovies.co.uk	valuable for synopses, cast lists, etc.
www.britishpictures.com	a resource offering essays, articles, reviews, and title specific information
www.cjr.org	Columbia Journalism Review (up-to-date information on who owns what in the media entertainments industry)
www.cyberfilmschool.com	Cyber Film School: Pro-end DV filmmaking site
www.disney.co.uk or disney.go.com	Disney online
www.edinfilm.com	Edinburgh Film Focus – strategic agency for film in Edinburgh
www.en.wikipedia.org	Wikipedia: the free online encyclopedia.
http://www.filmcouncil.org	Film Council
www.filmeducation.org	Film Education
www.filmfestivals.com	Filmfestivals
www.filmsite.org	Filmsite
www.filmundergound.com	Film Underground: DV filmmaking site
www.glasgowfilm.org.uk	Glasgow Film Office – strategic agency for film in Glasgow

www.film.guardian.co.uk	The Guardian online – film
www.hollywoodreporter.com	the Hollywood Reporter – online entertainment news
www.imdb.com	the Internet Movie Database
www.newscorp.com	News Corporation
www.script-o-rama.com	Drew's Scriptorama: script and screenwriting site
www.scotfilm.com	The Scottish Highlands and Islands Film Commission
www.scottishscreen.com	Scotland's leading film body (and film archive)
www.sony.net	Sony
www.skillset.org/film	Skillset
www.stonewall.org.uk	Stonewall
www.timewarner.com	Time Warner
www.themakingof.com	the making of Hollywood's hit movies
www.ukfilmcouncil.org.uk	UK Film Council
www.variety.com	Variety
www.visitscotland.com	the Scottish Tourist Board site
www.w3.tvi.cc.nm.us/~jvelez/MMS170/ storyboard	storyboarding: history, purpose, and techniques

▼ BIBLIOGRAPHY

Abrams, N., Bell, I. and Udris, J. (2001) *Studying Film*, London: Arnold.

Altman, R. (1999) *Film/genre*, London: BFI.

Armstrong, R. (2005) *Understanding Realism*, BFI.

Ashby, J. and Higson, A. (eds) (2000) *British Cinema, Past and Present*, London: Routledge.

Barr, C. (1998) *Ealing Studios*. Moffat: Cameron and Hollis.

Barnouw, E. (1993) *Documentary: A History of the Non-Fiction Film*, Oxford University Press.

Begleiter, M. (2001) *From Word to Image: Storyboarding and the Filmmaking Process*, Oxford: Wiese.

Bordwell, D. and Thompson, K. (2000) *Film Art: An Introduction*, New York: McGraw Hill.

Bruce, D. (1996) *Scotland the Movie*, Polygon/SFC.

Cameron, I. (1992) *The Movie Book of Film Noir*, London: Studio Vista.

Caughie, J. and Rockett, K. (1996) *The Companion to British and Irish Cinema*. London: BFI.

Chapman, J. (1998) *The British at War*, London: I.B. Taurus.

Corrigan, T. and White, P. (2004) *The Film Experience: An Introduction*, Boston: Bedford/St Martin's.

Dick, E. (1990) *From Limelight to Satellite: A Scottish Film Book*, London: BFI/SFC.

Drazin, C. (1998) *The Finest Years: British Cinema of the 1940s*, London: André Deutsche.

Dyer, R. (1986) *Heavenly Bodies: Film Stars and Society*, Basingstoke: Macmillan.

Dyer, R. (1993) *The Matter of Images*, London: Routledge.

Dyer, R. (1998) *Stars*, London: BFI.

Finler, J.W. (2003) *The Hollywood Story*, London: Wallflower.

Fiske, J. (1982) *Introduction to Communication Studies*, London: Routledge.

Fraioli, J. (2000) *Storyboarding 101*, Oxford: Wiese.

Gaffney, F (2006) *Screenwriting*, London: Auteur.

Gledhill, C. (ed.) (1991) *Stardom: The Industry of Desire*, London: Routledge.

Gledhill, C. and Williams L. (eds) (2000) *Reinventing Film Studies*, London: Arnold.

Hardy, F. (1990) *Scotland in Film*, Edinburgh: Edinburgh University Press.

Hayward, S. (2005) *Cinema Studies: the Key Concepts*, London: Routledge.

Hicks, N. (1996) *Screenwriting* 101, Oxford: Wiese.

Hill, J. (1999) *British Cinema in the* 1980s, Oxford: Clarendon Press.

Hill, R. and Church-Gibson, P. (1998) *The Oxford Guide to Film Studies*, Oxford: Oxford University Press (1998).

Hinde, R. (ed.) (1972) *Non-Verbal Communication*, Cambridge: Cambridge University Press.

Jones, C. and Jolliffe, G. (1996) *The Guerrilla Film Maker's Handbook*, London: Cassell.

Katz, S. (1991) *Film Directing Shot by Shot*, Oxford: Wiese.

Kawin, B.F. (1992) *How Movies Work*, Berkeley: University of California Press.

King, G. (2002) *Film Comedy*, London: Wallflower Press.

King, G. (2005a) *American Independent Cinema*, London: I.B.Tauris.

King, G. (2005b) *New Hollywood Cinema: An Introduction*, London: I.B.Tauris.

Lacey, N. (2005) *Introduction to Film*. Basingstoke: Palgrave Macmillan.

McArthur, C. (1982) *Scotch Reels: Scotland in Cinema and Television*, London: BFI.

MacCabe, C. (1999) *Performance*, London: BFI Film Classics.

McKernan, B. (2005) *Digital Cinema: The Revolution in Cinematography, Postproduction and Distribution*, New York: McGraw-Hill.

Miller, F. (1994) MGM *Posters: The Golden Years*, New York: Turner Publishing.

Monaco, J. (2000) *How to Read a Film: Movies, Media, Multimedia*, 3rd edn, Oxford: Oxford University Press.

Moran, A. (1996) *Film Policy*, London: Routledge.

Murphy, R. (1992) *Sixties British Cinema*, London: BFI.

Murphy, R. (1997) *The British Cinema Book*, London: BFI.

Murphy, R. (2000) *British Cinema and the Second World War*, London: BFI.

Neale, S. (2000) *Genre and Hollywood*, London: Routledge.

Neale, S. and Murray, S. (1998) *Contemporary Hollywood Cinema*, London: Routledge.

Nelmes, J. (2003) *An Introduction to Film Studies*, 3rd edn, London: Routledge.

Nourmand, T. and Marsh, G. (eds) (2005) *Film Posters of the 90s: The Essential Movies of the Decade*, London: Aurum Press.

Nowell-Smith, G. (1996) *The Oxford History of World Cinema*, Oxford: Oxford University Press.

Parkinson, D. (1995) *History of Film*, London: Thames and Hudson.

Pendreigh, B. (2002) *The Pocket Scottish Movie Book*, Mainstream.

Petrie, D. (2000) *Screening Scotland*, London: BFI.

Phillips, P. (2000) *Understanding Film Texts: Meaning and Experience*, London: BFI.

Phillips, W.H. (2005) *Film: An Introduction*, 3rd edn, Boston: St Martin's.

Richards, J. (1997) *Films and British National Identity: From Dickens to Dad's Army*, Manchester: Manchester University Press.

Roberts, G. and Wallis, H. (2001) *Introducing Film*, London: Arnold.

Sargeant, A. (2005) *British Cinema: A Critical History*, London: BFI.

Scorsese, M. (1999) *A Personal Journey Through American Movies*, London: Faber.

Smith, M. (2002) *Trainspotting*, London: BFI.

Street, S. (1999) *British National Cinema*, London: Routledge.

Walker, A. (1974) *Hollywood England: the British Film Industry in the Sixties*, London: Michael Joseph.

Warren, P. (1995) *British Film Studios*, London: Batsford.

▼ INDEX

Note: page numbers in *italics* denote references to illustrations

Related titles from Routledge

A2 Film Studies: The Essential Introduction

Sarah Casey Benyahia, Freddie Gaffney, John White

Building on the groundwork laid by the AS Film Studies syllabus, A2 *Film Studies: The Essential Introduction* introduces students to the diversity of cinematic styles and to different film cultures as well as positioning film within wider political, cultural and artistic debates. The book is designed to support students through the transition from a focus on textual analysis to the consideration of the wider contexts that inform any study of film.

Individual chapters cover the following key areas:

- The Small Scale Research Project
- Practical Application of Learning
- Studies in World Cinema
- The Film Text and Spectator
- Producers and Audiences – Issues and Debates
- Messages and Values – Critical Approaches

Specially designed to be user-friendly, A2 *Film Studies: The Essential Introduction* includes:

- Activities
- Sample exam questions
- Further reading
- Glossary of key terms and resources
- Case studies

A2 *Film Studies: The Essential Introduction* is a great way for film students to continue their studies at A Level.

ISBN10: 0–415–39957–2 (hbk)
ISBN10: 0–415–39956–4 (pbk)

ISBN13: 978-0-415-39957-9 (hbk)
ISBN13: 978-0-415-39956-2 (pbk)

Available at all good bookshops
For ordering and further information please visit:
www.routledge.com